NOTABLE BLACK
AMERICAN MEN

2
NOTABLE BLACK AMERICAN MEN

Jessie Carney Smith, Editor

THOMSON

GALE

Detroit • New York • San Francisco • New Haven, Conn. • Waterville, Maine • London

Notable Black American Men, Book II

Jessie Carney Smith, Editor

Project Editor
Dana Barnes

Image Research and Acquisitions
Leitha Etheridge-Sims

Rights Acquisition and Management
Jacqueline Key, Susan J. Rudolph, Tim Sisler

Imaging
Lezlie Light, Michael Logusz

Indexing Services
Lynne Maday

Product Design
Christopher Miller, Jennifer Wahi-Bradley

Manufacturing
Rita Wimberley

Composition
Evi Seoud

LIBRARY OF CONGRESS CATALOGING-IN-PUBLICATION DATA

Notable Black American men. Book II / Jessie Carney Smith, editor.
    p. cm.
    Includes bibliographical references and indexes.
    ISBN-13: 978-0-7876-6493-0
    ISBN-10: 0-7876-6493-6 (hardcover: alk. paper)
    1. African American men—Biography—Dictionaries. I. Smith, Jessie Carney.
    E185.86.N682 2007
    920.71089'96073—dc22
    [B]
                                                   2006021193

Printed in the United States of America
10 9 8 7 6 5 4 3 2 1

Contents

Introduction

The success of Book I in the Gale series, *Notable Black American Men*, is an incentive to continue the work of offering convenient and accurate information about black American men of outstanding achievement. Although all such men who helped to shape a race and a nation by their deeds never will be fully recognized, Book II in this series extends the effort to remember more of them. To the five hundred entrants in the first volume is added another three hundred, but scholars have only begun to present the numerous men whose work deserves to be highlighted. Such luminaries as Frederick Douglass, Martin Luther King Jr., and Colin Powell have taken their rightful places in publications. To these men of recognized stature many others have been added—some obscure, but no less important. Although no ranking is implied, the men selected for *Notable Black American Men, Book II*, who now join their predecessors, have a commendable record of achievement. All too often full recognition of the greatness of the work of outstanding black American men is impaired by the scarcity, inaccuracy, and inconsistency of records, thus preventing future generations from knowing the full contributions and value of these men to history. Nonetheless, the legacy of the men has stood the tests and changes of time, and I hope further investigation may find new sources to round out the information presented here.

The three hundred additional entrants to *Notable Black American Men, Book II* confirm the words of John Hope Franklin: "[T]he history of a nation is to be found not only in victorious battles or in the lives of notable personages but also in the lives of the most humbly born, the most consistently despised, and the most miserably improvident" (*Race and History: Selected Essays, 1938-1988*, Louisiana State University Press, 1989). Many black male notables have disappeared from view, an understandable circumstance when you consider that the entire black race historically has been subject to the derision and cruelty of others who lacked understanding of people different from themselves, who were intolerant, and who stubbornly resisted change. However, despite these acts of injustice across the centuries against people of color, black men have lived, flourished, and left visible marks—whether recognized or not—wherever they have dwelled. As Franklin says about one of his favorite subjects James Boon, a prosperous, black businessman in

North Carolina in the 1800s, "It is difficult to believe that a man of his vitality and business initiatives could have continued to live without intruding his name into the records of the community."

The *Notable Black American Men* series is a convenient compilation of men from a long-despised race, men whom Susan L. Taylor calls "our wisdom warriors" ("In the Spirit," *Essence*, September 2005). At first, they are men who refused to remain silent about slavery; later, they are men who would not hold their peace when racial barriers remained high. There are warriors on all fronts who have made and who continually make permanent imprints in all arenas. For example, no one can deny the excellence of architect J. Max Bond, chief surgeon Benjamin Carson, scholar and educator William H. Crogman, basketball coach Clarence E. "Big House" Gaines, actor Samuel L. Jackson, portrait painter Simmie Knox, organization leader Michael L. Lomax, and religious activist Paul M. Washington. They are, in the words of Susan Taylor, "our sages" and "our griots" whose work makes the black American race less despised while simultaneously making the race more recognized, understood, accepted, and appreciated.

Perhaps contemporary achievers will read about themselves, examine their accomplishments, and be proud. Perhaps those who have yet to achieve—particularly present-day youth—will read about these warriors and be influenced to make a positive difference during their own lifetime. Perhaps some readers will find a mentor among these men, dead or alive, who will guide them to achieve. And perhaps some will examine the work of these men as a whole and understand that they have done so much, often with so little, yet have influenced and/or improved the lives of so many.

As our writers prepared their entries, they understood the difficulty before them to locate records of men who lived during the 1700s, 1800s, and 1900s. Moreover, writers of contemporary figures discovered a pitfall. Many contemporary black male notables had neglected to publicize their remarkable achievements for public consumption, thus leaving a void. Researchers know the importance of accurate birth dates and places and the role that personal interviews play to refine details of a biographical work. Because such information as this and more has seemingly fallen into obscurity for some of the entrants of *Notable Black American Men, Book II*, I urge other scholars, researchers, and readers to close this knowledge gap as they find answers which up to this point have been elusive. Especially do I urge notable black men to see that the complete story of their lives—until now—is told.

I am resolved to continue the work of unearthing the histories of the many men whose stories are yet to be told. Some were omitted in this volume due to space limitation. Others were omitted because at present there is a dearth of records to tell the story of their lives as they ought to be told. A young African American woman who is quoted in Benjamin Quarles' *Black Abolitionists* (London, Oxford Press, 1969) captures in verse my feelings about many who remain in the background of black American culture: "Their works shall live when other deeds/ Which ask a nation's fame./ Have sunk beneath Time's whelming wave/ Unhonored and unnamed."

The Selection Process

The original list of 2,500 names developed for *Notable Black American Men, Book I* was expanded to fill in gaps where names were missing. Added is a representative number of men who recently have emerged as outstanding figures; the names of other new entrants were suggested by scholars. Thus, the project team selected from some 3,000 names a gamut of obscure, semi-known, and popular black American males. In addition, lest we omit some obvious choices, we examined such standard references as *Biographical Directory of Afro-American and African Musicians, Contemporary Black Biography, Dictionary of American Negro Biography, Who's Who among African Americans*, and *Who's Who in Colored America*. The editor retained the right to screen the final list and to approve the final selections. Nominees for the book met one or more of the following criteria:

- a pioneer in a particular area, such as the first black man elected to public office in a city or state, or first black man to edit a newspaper; or

- an important entrepreneur, such as a manufacturer of cosmetics for blacks, the founder of a publishing firm, or founder of a bank; or

- a leading businessman, such as the president of an advertising firm, the owner of an automobile dealership, the head of a construction company, the vice-president of a major bank; or

- a literary or creative figure of stature, such as an outstanding poet, well-known writer, author of works on a unique theme, important artist, outstanding sculptor; or

- a leader for social or human justice, such as an abolitionist, freedom fighter, outstanding participant in the civil rights movement; or

- a major governmental or organizational official, such as president of the United Negro College Fund, president of the National Bar Association; or

- a creative figure in the performing arts, such as the first black American man to perform at the Metropolitan Opera, outstanding popular singer, actor, composer; or

- a noted orator, elocutionist, or public speaker (particularly for the nineteenth and twentieth centuries); or

- a distinguished educator, such as the first black American president of a major college or university, president or founder of an historically black college or university, first black American man to receive a college degree in a particular subject; or

- a noted scholar, such as a scientist, mathematician, historian, or sociologist; or

- a leader, pioneer, or contributor in other fields, particularly new and emerging fields, who meet the basic criteria suggested above for selection as an outstanding black American man.

To ensure accuracy of the essays, when possible the subjects were asked to review the work, to expand the coverage, and to correct factual errors arising from published sources. In other instances when reference sources gave conflicting information, the writers were asked to address the differences as best they could.

Contributions Acknowledged

Aiding in the preparation of this work are writers from many academic institutions across the nation as well as from a variety of professions. I appreciate the contributions that make this a scholarly work which will add significantly to the pool of literature on black American biography and biography, in general. At times scholars made great sacrifices as they put aside other important activities to spur on the completion of *Notable Black American Men, Book II*. For those in my workplace, the John Hope and Aurelia E. Franklin Library at Fisk University, I ponder how to show my appreciation for the mammoth tasks they performed. This team of researchers checked the format of references, searched for materials in other libraries, retrieved material via Interlibrary Loan, photocopied texts, suggested additional names and/or interests; some of them also wrote entries for Book II. These persons to whom I owe a debt of gratitude include Shannon Mathis (my assistant), Antoya Bethel, Cheryl Jones Hamberg, Beth Madison Howse, Vanessa Smith, and Janet Walsh. Before retiring from his post at the Franklin Library, Robert L. Johns, my scholar-friend of many years, was a source of encouragement and a provider of numerous biographies he found as he searched daily the World Wide Web.

To my editor, Dana Barnes, I say that the work has been a labor of pure pleasure. Moreover, our work together has produced a document of which both of us can be very proud. Thank you. Thanks also to Leitha Etheridge-Sims, Lezlie Light, and Tim Sisler for their excellent work on the images included here.

As has been the case with all of my writing projects, I acknowledge with deep appreciation my family, friends, and colleagues—both those who understood that, for a while, the book took precedence over practically everything else, and those who failed to understand but kept a good relationship with me anyway. Publications such as *Notable Black American Men, Book II* are vital to my continued research and the production of works to guide researchers, educators, and young people, in particular, to learn as much as possible about black American biography.

Jessie Carney Smith

Entrants

Advisory Board

Thomas C. Battle

Director, Moorland-Spingarn Research Center, Howard University

Vivian Davidson Hewitt

Retired librarian and consultant, New York, New York

Helen R. Houston

Professor of English, Tennessee State University

Reavis L. Mitchell

Chair, Division of Social Science, Fisk University

Linda T. Wynn

Tennessee Historical Commission/Fisk University

Contributors

Regina T. Akers, *District Heights, Maryland*

Glenda M. Alvin, *Tennessee State University*

Nkechi G. Amadife, *Kentucky State University*

Virginia D. Bailey, *Abilene Christian University*

Brandy Baker, *Baltimore, Maryland*

Gabriella Beckles, *Baltimore, Maryland*

Kathleen E. Bethel, *Northwestern University*

Rosa Bobia, *Kennesaw State University*

Lean'tin L. Bracks, *Fisk University*

Orella Ramsey Brazile, *Southern University at Shreveport*

Carol Brennan, *Grosse Pointe Park, Michigan*

John H. Britton, Jr., *Meharry Medical College*

Sharon D. Brooks, *University of Maryland Eastern Shore*

Prudence White Bryant, *Alabama Agricultural and Mechanical University*

Linda M. Carter, *Halethorpe, Maryland*

Mario A. Charles, *College of New Rochelle*

Felicia A. Chenier, *Baltimore, Maryland*

Arlene Clift-Pellow, *North Carolina Central University*

Crystal A. deGregory, *Vanderbilt University*

Rebecca Dixon, *Tennessee State University*

Anne K. Driscoll, *University of Maryland Eastern Shore*

De Witt S. Dykes, Jr., *Oakland University*

Elizabeth Sandidge Evans, *Hampton University*

Marie Garrett, *University of Tennessee*

Cheryl Jones Hamberg, *Fisk University*

Gloria Hamilton, *University of Chicago*

Dana Hammond, *Baltimore, Maryland*

Helen R. Houston, *Tennessee State University*

Denise Jarrett, *Baltimore, Maryland*

Edwin T. Johnson, *Baltimore, Maryland*

Kevin C. Kretschmer, *Des Moines, Iowa*

Lovenia A. Leapart, *Upper Marlboro, Maryland*

Connie Mack, *Alabama Agricultural and Mechanical University*

Mark L. McCallon, *Abilene Christian University*

Sharon McGee, *Kentucky State University*

Kevin McGruder, *New York, New York*

Mattie McHollin, *Fisk University*

LaVerne Laney McLaughlin, *Albany State University*

Ronald Elbert Mickens, *Atlanta, Georgia*

Fletcher F. Moon, *Tennessee State University*

Oral Moses, *Kennesaw State University*

Baiyina W. Muhammad, *Morgan State University*

Clarissa Myrick-Harris, *Atlanta, Georgia*

Debra Newman Ham, *Morgan State University*

Shelhea C. Owens, *Baltimore, Maryland*

Jewell B. Parham, *Nashville, Tennessee*

Annie Malessia Payton, *Mississippi Valley State University*

Patricia A. Pearson, *Kentucky State University*

Lois A. Peterson, *University of Illinois*

Annette Petrusso, *Austin, Texas*

Janette Prescod, *University of Tennessee*

Beverly E. Richards, *Baltimore, Maryland*

Brenna Sanchez, *Los Angeles, California*

Theodosia T. Shields, *University of Maryland Eastern Shore*

Frederick D. Smith, *Nashville, Tennessee*

Jessie Carney Smith, *Fisk University*

Sheila A. Stuckey, *Kentucky State University*

Althea Tait, *Baltimore, Maryland*

Darius Thieme, *Fisk University*

Clarence Toomer, *Alabama Agricultural and Mechanical University*

Janet Walsh, *Antioch, Tennessee*

Irvin Weathersby, Jr., *Baltimore, Maryland*

Teri B. Weil, *University of Maryland Eastern Shore*

Linda T. Wynn, *Tennessee Historical Commission/Fisk University*

Acknowledgments

Abernathy, Ralph David, photograph. AP Images./ **Alexander, Archie Alphonso**, photograph. AP Images./ **Anderson, Michael P.**, photograph. AP Images./ **Baquet, Dean P.**, photograph. Vince Bucci/Getty Images./ **Bennett, Lerone**, photograph. (c) Steve Liss/Time Life Pictures/Getty Images./ **Bolden, Buddy**, photograph by Frank Driggs Collection Getty Images./ **Bond, J. Max**, photograph. (c) Mario Tama/Getty Images./ **Boston, Ralph**, photograph. AP Images./ **Branton, Wiley A.**, photograph. AP Images./ **Brooks, Vincent K.**, photograph. (c) Carlo Allegri/Getty Images./ **Brown, Henry "Box"**, photograph. (c) Bettmann/CORBIS./ **Brown, James "Buster"**, photograph. (c) Julie Lemberger/CORBIS./ **Brown, Lee**, photograph by Tim Johnson. AP Images./ **Burleigh, Harry T.**, photograph. Jerry Cooke/Pix Inc/Time Life Pictures/Getty Images./ **Butts, Calvin O.**, photograph. Scott Eelis/Getty Images./ **Carey, Archibald, Jr.**, photograph. (c) Francis Miller/Time Life Pictures/Getty Images./ **Carson, Benjamin**, photograph. (c) Richard T. Nowitz/Photo Researchers, Inc. Reproduced by permission./ **Carter, Lisle C.**, photograph. AP Images./ **Carter, Stephen L.**, photograph by Woodfin Camp & Associates. Reproduced by permission./ **Cassell, Albert I.**, photograph. AP Images./ **Combs, Sean**, photograph. AP Images./ **Cook, Will Marion**, photograph. (c) Frank Driggs Collection/Getty Images./ **Crouch, Andrae**, photograph. AP Images./ **Dash, Darien**, photograph by Hosea Johnson. AP Images./ **Davenport, Willie**, photograph. AP Images./ **Days, Drew Saunders**, photograph. AP Images./ **DeLarge, Robert**, "First Colored Senator and Representatives, 41st and 42nd Congress," lithograph by Currier and Ives. The Library of Congress./ **DePriest, James**, photograph. AP Images./ **Dwight, Edward**, photograph. AP Images./ **Dymally, Mervyn M.**, photograph. AP Images./ **Dyson, Michael Eric**, photograph by Richard Ellis. Getty Images./ **Farr, Mel**, photograph. AP Images./ **Fletcher, Arthur A.**, photograph. AP Images./ **Ford, Harold, Jr.**, photograph by Mark Humphrey. AP Images./ **Ford, Harold, Sr.**, photograph. AP Images./ **Fuller, Charles**, photograph. AP Images./ **Gaines, Clarence E.**, photograph. AP Images./ **Gaines, Ernest**, photograph by Alex Brandon. AP Images./ **Giles, Roscoe C.**, photograph. Charles E. Steinheimer/Time Life Pictures/Getty Images./ **Gomes, Peter**, photograph. Jerry Bauer. Reproduced by permission./ **Gomillion, Charles G.**, photograph. Don Cravens/Time Life Pictures/Getty Images./ **Gordone, Charles**, photograph. AP Images./ **Gourdine, Meredith C.**, photograph. AP Images./ **Gregory, Frederick D.**, photograph. U.S. National Aeronautics and Space Administration (NASA)./ **Gumbel, Greg**, photograph. AP Images./ **Harris, Bernard A.**, photograph. AP Images./ **Harris, E. Lynn**, photograph by Martin Christopher. Reproduced by permission of E. Lynn Harris./ **Harris, Wesley L.**, photograph. AP Images./ **Hatcher, Andrew T.**, photograph. AP Images./ **Healy, Michael**, photograph. (c) The Mariners Museum/CORBIS./ **Hendrix, Jimi**, photograph. AP Images./ **Henry, Aaron**, photograph. AP Images./ **Henson, Josiah**, photograph. Kean Collection/Getty Images./ **Herndon, Angelo**, photograph. (c) Bettmann/Corbis./ **Hines, Gregory**, photograph. AP Images./ **Hooker, John Lee**, photograph. (c) Neal Preston/Corbis./ **Jackson, Jesse L., Jr.**, photograph. AP Images./ **Jackson, Reggie**, photograph by Ray Stubblebine. AP Images./ **Jackson, Samuel L.**, photograph. Pascal Le Segretain/Getty Images./ **Johnson, Charles**, photograph. John Storey/Time Life Pictures/Getty Images./ **Jones, Bobby**, photograph. Bryan Bedder/Getty Images./ **Jones, Edward P.**, photograph. AP Images./ **Joyner, Tom**, photograph. Bevil Knapp/Time Life Pictures/Getty Images./ **Julian, Hubert**, photograph. (c) Bettmann/CORBIS./ **King, Preston**, photograph by Todd Stone. AP Images./ **Knox,**

Simmie, photograph. (c) Ron Sachs/Corbis./ **Lawson, James M., Jr.**, photograph. AP Images./ **Lewis, Theophilus**, photograph. AP Images./ **Long, Eddie L.**, photograph. (c) Jason Reed/AFP/Getty Images./ **Loury, Glen C.**, photograph. (c) Jacques M. Chenet/CORBIS./ **Mac, Bernie**, photograph. Courtesy of Bernie Mac./ **Marable, Manning**, photograph. Mario Tama/Getty Images./ **Marsalis, Branford**, photograph by Kwaku Alston. Courtesy of Wilkins Management. Reproduced by permission./ **Mathis, Johnny**, photograph. (c) Reuters/Corbis./ **McGruder, Robert G.**, photograph. Reproduced by permission of Robert G. McGruder./ **Menard, John Willis**, photograph by Mathew Brady. *Harper's Weekly*, January 23, 1869./ **Michaux, Solomon Lightfoot**, photograph. AP Images./ **Mitchell, Arthur W.**, photograph. (c) Bettmann/Corbis./ **Moon, Henry Lee**, photograph. AP Images./ **Moron, Alonzo G.**, photograph. AP Images./ **Myers, Walter Dean**, photograph by David Godlis. Reproduced by permission of Walter Dean Myers./ **Nabrit, Samuel**, photograph. AP Images./ **Obama, Barack**, photograph. AP Images./ **Paige, Rod**, photograph. AP Images./ **Parker, Barrington D.**, photograph. AP Images./ **Parsons, James Benton**, photograph. AP Images./ **Parsons, Richard**, photograph by Stephen J. Carrera. AP Images./ **Phillips, Channing E.**, photograph. AP Images./ **Pryor, Richard**, photograph. AP Images./ **Raines, Franklin**, photograph. AP Images./ **Rainey, Joseph**, "First Colored Senator and Representatives, 41st and 42nd Congress," lithograph by Currier and Ives. The Library of Congress./ **Reason, J. Paul**, photograph. AP Images./ **Redding, Louis L.**, photograph by NAACP. AP Images./ **Richardson, Scovel**, photograph. AP Images./ **Sharpton, Al**, photograph by Bebeto Matthews. AP Images./ **Shores, Arthur Davis**, photograph. (c) BettmanCORBIS./ **Singleton, Benjamin**, photograph. Kansas State Historical Society. Reproduced by permission./ **Slater, Rodney**, photograph by Doug Mills. AP Images./ **Smiley, Tavis**, photograph. Frederick M. Brown/Getty Images./ **Smith, Tubby**, photograph. University of Kentucky. Reproduced by permission./ **Smith, Will**, photograph by Claudette Barius. The Kobal Collection. Reproduced by permission./ **Stanton, Robert G.**, photograph. (c) ReutersCorbis./ **Swygert, H. Patrick**, photograph by Reggie Pearlman. AP Images./ **Travis, Dempsey J.**, photograph. AP Images./ **Turner, Benjamin S.**, "First Colored Senator and Representatives, 41st and 42nd Congress," lithograph by Currier and Ives. The Library of Congress./ **Tyson, Neil de Grasse**, photograph. Chris Hondros/Getty Images./ **Vivian, C.T.**, photograph. (c) Flip Schulke/CORBIS./ **Walker, George**, photograph by Mike Derer. AP Images./ **Walker, Wyatt T.**, photograph. Howard Sochurek/Time Life Pictures/Getty Images./ **Walls, Josiah**, photograph. Fisk University Library. Reproduced by permission./ **Walton, Lester A.**, photograph. AP Images./ **Washington, Paul M.**, photograph. Sal Dimarco Jr/Time Life Pictures/Getty Images./ **Watts, J.C.**, photograph. (c) Wally McNamee/CORBIS./ **Wharton, Clifton R.**, photograph. AP Images./ **Wilkens, Lenny**, photograph. AP Images./ **Williams, Peter, Sr.**, photograph. (c) New-York Historical Society/ReutersCorbis./ **Wilson, William Julius**, photograph. Reproduced by permission./ **Winans, BeBe**, photograph by Dana Tynan. AP Images./ **Wolf, George C.**, photograph by Richard Drew. AP Images./ **Yerby, Frank**, photograph. Library of Congress.

Ralph David Abernathy
1926–1990

Minister, civil rights activist

Ralph David Abernathy was born on March 11, 1926, the tenth child of twelve children born to William L. Abernathy and Louivery Valentine Bell in Linden, Alabama. Shortly after his grandmother delivered him she told her daughter that he was a strange child and predicted that he would be known throughout the world. From the age of twelve he was called David, and indeed it is the name on his birth certificate, which has never been officially changed. His sister Manerva, however, was very impressed by one of her college professors whose name was Ralph David, and started calling her little brother by that name.

David Abernathy grew up on his father's five-hundred-acre Linden farm. His father had married well; he was given a milk cow and a calf as a wedding gift. He immediately started buying land, a few acres at a time, until he acquired the whole five hundred acres. The Abernathys lived in the large, long bungalow with six rooms that the father William built. Prosperous yet frugal, the family set aside money for church and education. In fact, David remembered his father donating up to $1,000 toward education during a Sunday morning plea from the Linden Academy principal.

Abernathy's high school was interrupted by military service: when he turned eighteen he was immediately drafted. After serving in the segregated U.S. Army, during which time his father died, Abernathy returned home and earned a GED certificate. In 1945, using his GI benefits, he enrolled at Alabama State College in Montgomery, a school committed to higher education for blacks.

In his sophomore year, as student council president, Abernathy directly faced his first case of injustice. A campus controversy arose over two separate menus being prepared for faculty and students. The problem gave Abernathy his first opportunity to lead a demonstration in protest against discriminatory practices. After several conversations with the dining hall supervisor, Abernathy encouraged a strike of the entire student body, boycotting

Ralph David Abernathy

the dining hall and refusing to eat anything until the food they were served improved. All students enthusiastically supported the idea and agreed to begin in two days. Two mornings later the faculty marched in to eat their usual meal of eggs, bacon, and cereal; the supervisor fixed hundreds of pieces of toast for the students but no one showed up to eat them. The boycott was effective in bringing about an improvement in student meals.

Alabama State College may have seemed sleepy and docile to outsiders, but black professors such as J. E. Pierce, who taught political science, made students understand how important the ballot was to their future and how courageous they would have to be to ensure black suffrage. Emma Payne Howard, director of extracurricular activities, stressed the need for racial progress and made

Chronology

1926	Born in Linden, Alabama on March 11
1944	Drafted into the U.S. Army in an all-black unit
1945	Discharged from the Army; enrolls at Alabama State College in Montgomery
1948	Announces decision to enter the ministry
1948	Becomes pastor of Montgomery's black First Baptist Church
1950	Earns B.A. from Alabama State University
1952	Marries Juanita Odessa Jones
1955	Begins work with Martin Luther King Jr.
1956	Joins in 381-day bus boycott in Montgomery, Alabama
1963	Participates in march on Washington, D. C. on August 28
1968	Witnesses assassination of King in Memphis, Tennessee
1969	Mounts campaign for the hospital employees in Charleston, South Carolina
1970	Travels to Europe and South America promoting peace and human rights
1982	Lobbies Congress for the extension of the Voting Rights Act of 1965
1990	Dies of heart failure in Atlanta, Georgia on April 17

students understand that a religious vocation can be compatible with a social conscience. In 1950 Abernathy graduated with honors from Alabama State College with an undergraduate degree in mathematics, and he was accepted at Atlanta University to work on a master's degree in sociology.

Call to the Ministry

During his college days Abernathy was devoutly religious. In fact, he was superintendent of the student Sunday school, and people anticipated he would enter the ministry. In April 1948, at age twenty-two, Abernathy announced his call to preach. Immediately churches filled to capacity with students from school and family members all eager to hear him. During this time he led a protest regarding the need for improved living conditions in the dormitories.

In the fall of 1950 when Abernathy enrolled in Atlanta University, he visited Ebenezer Baptist Church and heard Martin Luther King Jr. give a sermon. After the service he went over to shake King's hand and in that moment both men recognized a kindred spirit in the other. Also while at Alabama State College, Abernathy met Juanita Odessa Jones, the woman who became his wife.

At age twenty-six, Abernathy became the seventh pastor of the historic First Baptist Church of Montgomery, Alabama. He was married in this church and while serving at this church the couple's first child was born and died.

Abernathy became pastor at First Baptist during a propitious time. A new generation of black men and women were coming along, people who were less patient and

less afraid of making trouble. Born and reared in an environment where a black man was not free to use public facilities, drink from water fountains, or sit anywhere he wanted to on a bus, Abernathy knew this younger generation had not lived with racial discrimination quite as long and many had traveled beyond its limitations. These young people knew life could be different and were half-inclined to believe that the promised changes were really going to come soon. Instead of preaching about submission and the virtues of patient suffering, Abernathy preached about courage and justice and the necessity of gaining equality. He warned people of struggles to come and explained to them that they would be fighting for their own dignity as creatures of God and for the dignity for their children and grandchildren.

Joins the Civil Rights Movement

In 1955 Reverend Martin Luther King Jr. and his wife, Coretta Scott King, moved to Montgomery where King became pastor of the Dexter Avenue Baptist Church. Abernathy and King began working together. Though they both had heavy pastoral responsibilities, they tried to meet for dinner every day to talk and make plans. During these conversations the civil rights movement took shape. In December of the same year they suddenly found themselves at the center of the Rosa Parks controversy. The men formulated plans to turn Montgomery into a model of social justice and racial harmony. Using the principles of passive resistance promoted by Mahatma Gandhi and Henry David Thoreau, Abernathy and King decided that the implementation would be completely nonviolent.

On December 1, 1955, Rosa Parks refused to give up her seat on a Montgomery city bus and thus set events in motion that led to the Montgomery bus boycott. Hers was not the first refusal to obey a bus driver's orders, for two black women had already been arrested earlier in the year for doing so. One of them, a fifteen-year-old student, had been dragged from the bus and charged with assault and battery as well as failure to comply with laws governing public transportation. What made the arrest and media coverage of Rosa Parks so significant was Parks' own appearance and demeanor. She was soft-spoken and courteous, a slight woman who worked as a seamstress at a large department store. She had an air of gentility about her that usually evoked respect from whites and blacks alike. No one imagined that she could end up in jail, but that is precisely what happened. Word quickly spread of Parks' arrest. Jo Ann Robinson, who had been instrumental in assisting the other two women who were arrested, was already preparing to hand out leaflets for the boycott. Abernathy joined in handing out leaflets to the black community.

On Friday evening at a quickly planned citywide meeting the black community agreed to support a boycott. On the following Monday morning empty buses drove their routes. The boycott was working. On Monday evening Abernathy and King were further surprised to find that their planned meeting had attracted thousands, all cheering to the strength and power of their unity. The boycott's success made them realize they needed to organize to be more effective and to include supportive non-blacks as well. That evening the Montgomery Improvement Association (MIA) was formed.

In January 1956 King's home was bombed and in December of that year Abernathy's home was bombed. On that same night in December someone also bombed his church. In the midst of this agitation, Abernathy and King and their wives had been working to form a region-wide organization that would extend the influence of the Montgomery Improvement Association. After these bombings King went to New Orleans in order to form a new group, which was called the Southern Christian Leadership Conference (SCLC). Through their leadership in this organization, Abernathy and King became known as the "civil rights twins." Abernathy was respected and honored as one of the two vanguards of the civil rights era.

As a black Baptist preacher, Abernathy believed in a new social gospel that many thought was both radical and worldly. He had visions in which black Americans would win their freedom and exercise all the rights and privileges of that freedom. As a leader, he was willing to take life-threatening risks to achieve unimagined victories for black Americans. His sermons were not scholarly discourses written in lofty language. Rather, they were delivered in simple language full of folk sayings and anecdotes reminiscent of his rural upbringings.

After King's assassination in 1968, Abernathy assumed the leadership position of the organization they had both formed together, SCLC. He was elected president without reservation. In the spring of 1968 he led the Poor People's Campaign which brought thousands of poor people to Washington, D.C., and focused the nation's attention on the ugly reality of hunger and poverty. He worked to improve the living wage and working conditions to thousands of hospital workers in the nation. In 1977 he resigned his position as president of SCLC due to lack of financial stability of the organization.

Abernathy received more than three hundred honors, including the Man of the Year Award from the Atlanta Urban League, the Unheralded Hero of Human Rights from the YMCA, the Peace Medallion of the German Democratic Baptist Churches, and the Martin Luther King Jr. Award from the Southern Christian Leadership Conference. He was also the recipient of twenty-seven honorary doctorate degrees.

In January 1970 he traveled to Europe and South America. In Scandinavia he talked of his own vision of eventual oneness of all poor and dark-skinned people of the world. One month after returning from Europe he flew to Panama and Brazil. In Brazil he called for an international movement to eradicate racism, poverty, and war. In 1971 he traveled to Moscow State University in the Soviet Union to promote, world peace and understanding and to promote nonviolence.

In 1989, after more than thirty years in the struggle in the civil rights movement, Abernathy wrote his autobiography, *And The Walls Came Tumbling Down*. He had two reasons for writing this book: to describe life under the Jim Crow laws and to describe the civil rights movement.

Abernathy's leadership in the movement, along with that of Martin Luther King Jr., ranks him at the top of a list of those who led boycotts and marches through many hostile segregated U.S. cities, Montgomery, Selma, and Birmingham, Alabama; Albany, Georgia, and Chicago, to gain equal justice for African Americans during and following the civil rights era. On April 17, 1990, Ralph David Abernathy died while being treated for a heart attack. He and his wife had four children: Juandalyn Ralpheda, Donzaleigh Avis, Ralph David III, and Kwame Luthuli.

REFERENCES

Books

Abernathy, Donzaleigh. *Partners to History: Martin Luther King Jr., Ralph David Abernathy, and the Civil Rights Movement*. New York: Crown Publishers, 2003.

Periodicals

Bennett, Tom. "Ralph David Abernathy 1926-1990" *Atlanta Journal and Constitution*, 18 April 1990.

Waite, Lori. "Ralph Abernathy Continues the Struggle for King's Dream." *Atlanta Tribune* (February 1989).

Oral Moses

Abraham
c. 1790–?

Slave, linguist

Abraham was a full-blooded African slave who escaped and adapted himself to the customs and language of the Muskogee Seminole Indians living in Florida. As was their custom toward runaway slaves, the Seminoles' welcomed Abraham. Over time, Abraham's relationship with the Seminole Indians evolved such that they regarded him as both a brother and ally. Eventually he became chief of Peliklakaha, one of four major Seminole Negro communities under the tribal authority of prin-

Chronology

late 1790s	Born in Georgia or Florida
1814	Joins British military forces to fight U.S. Army
1816	Survives explosion at Fort Negro
1826	Becomes principal interpreter for Seminole Chief Micanopy and accompanies an official delegation to Washington, D.C.; gains freedom from Chief Micanopy as a reward for services rendered
1830	Takes part in the negotiations of the Indian Removal Act
1832	Enters negotiations with Colonel James Gadsden concerning the relocation of the Seminoles; is sent with six other leaders to examine the territory designated for the Creek Indians west of the Mississippi
1836	Initiates a peace agreement with General Edmund P. Gaines following the Indians' seizing of a U.S. military installation, Camp Izard
1837	Meets with U.S. Major General Thomas Jesup at Fort Dade to discuss peace negotiations; reaches an agreement regarding relocation of Seminole Indians and Seminole Negroes
1838	Moves west of the Mississippi with Seminole Indians and other Seminole Negroes
1850	Accompanies Wild Cat and Gopher John to Mexico to avoid continued U.S. government harassment
1858	Returns to Oklahoma following Wild Cat's death

cipal Chief Micanopy (sometimes spelled Mickenopah). Peliklakaha became the most influential of the Negro communities located in Seminole Indian territory because Abraham lived in it and because Chief Micanopy preferred living there much of the time rather than at his official residence in Okihumpky.

Little is known about Abraham's birth, boyhood, and family life. Some historians say he was born in Georgia in the late 1790s; others contend that he was born in Florida sometime during this same period. Before escaping from his master, Abraham lived and worked as a slave for a Spanish doctor in Pensacola, Florida. It is apparent that Abraham came in contact with teachings of the Christian religion, which was not unusual for slaves living on a plantation. His speech was spiced with religious expressions, earning him the nickname "the Prophet."

Little is known about Abraham's family. Jeff Guinn, in *Our Land Before We Die: The Proud Story of the Seminole Negro,* records an excerpt from a letter U.S. Army General Thomas Sidney Jesup wrote to the commissioner of Indian Affairs: "I have promised Abraham the freedom of his family if he be faithful to us." On another occasion, Abraham delayed attending a meeting scheduled to negotiate Indian and American affairs because he needed to care for his family, but information about his family was not preserved.

In 1814 when the British military came to Florida to fight the U.S. Army over territory in the region, Major Edward Nicolls announced that all blacks living in Florida who joined England in its war against America would be rewarded with free land in the West Indies. Moreover, they would not be returned to former masters. Abraham was numbered among the 3,000 Indians and 400 blacks who joined the British forces. Immediately he and the other new recruits were armed and trained for military maneuvers. As part of his duty as a British soldier, Abraham helped to build a new fort about 150 miles east of Pensacola, near the mouth of the Apalachicola River. The believed-to-be indestructible three-walled fort, eventually called Negro Fort, was manned by escaped slaves, Abraham among them, and Seminole Indians. A black man served as its commander when Major Nicolls was called back to England. In 1816, Abraham miraculously survived being killed when the U.S. Army Marines and 500 Creek Indian mercenaries blew up Negro Fort following the orders of General Andrew Jackson. U.S. Navy ships bombarded the fort with a red hot cannonball heated in the furnace of the ship. The cannonball landed on hundreds of barrels of gunpowder, igniting Negro Fort into a burning inferno. The attack resulted in 270 dead and 64 wounded. Only three men escaped without injury.

Abraham as Interpreter and Negotiator

Abraham became significant when he was appointed the official spokesman for Chief Micanopy and when he served as interpreter between the Seminole Indians of Florida and the U.S. Army. His experience as a slave afforded him the ability to understand the thinking and actions of white men, an attribute which made him a keen negotiator, a masterful military strategist, and a fierce warrior. It is likely that Abraham spoke several languages, probably English, Spanish, the two primary Seminole languages—Hitchiti and Muskogee—and his own language, a Creole similar to Gullah. The interpreter's native language was likely a mixture of these and the African tongues he spoke. Abraham was so gifted with languages that government agents and military personnel with whom he negotiated expressed mixed feelings about him. On the one hand, they acknowledged his undeniable intelligence; on the other hand, they complained about Abraham and other black Seminole interpreters like him, such as Cudjo and John Horse. The agents and military men recognized, and rightly so, that the black interpreters dictated policy as they translated language between factions. According to an article by Dana Peck, General Jesup described Abraham as "a good soldier and an intrepid leader. He is a chief, and the most cunning and intelligent negro we have here." Another military officer said, "The negro Abraham is obviously a great man . . . . His countenance is one of great cunning and penetration. He always smiles, and his words flow like oil. His conversation is soft and low, but very distinct, with a most genteel emphasis."

Despite his genteel mannerism, Abraham was as fierce a negotiator for both the Seminole Indians and Seminole Negroes as he was a warrior. For example, he was a staunch opponent of the 1832 Treaty of Payne's Landing, a decree which stated that all Indians in Florida would move west of the Mississippi River to Indian Territory (in what later became Oklahoma) assigned to them by the U.S. government. Abraham fought this relocation treaty vehemently for at least two reasons. First, his loyalty to the Muskogee Seminoles made him want to protect them from being driven from their homesteads and land. Second, according to the treaty, Seminole Negroes would be returned to their white owners and/or sold back into slavery. Initially, Abraham, like other runaway slaves, was not willing to accept the Payne's Landing Treaty. The Seminole Negroes stood a double chance of losing their freedom. If the Seminole Indians agreed to relocate, the Seminole Negroes would be separated from them. All ties between the two groups would be severed by the Anglo Americans as the Seminole Indians boarded ships headed west from Tampa Bay. Or if the Seminole Negroes made the trip to Indian Territory, the Creek Indians, longtime enemies and excessively brutal slave owners, would capture and enslave the Seminole Negroes or sell them back into slavery. After intense bargaining, Abraham and the Seminole chiefs reached an agreement with U.S. Army General Jesup. During negotiations, Abraham would not compromise the welfare of the Seminole Negroes any more than he would compromise the Seminole Indians. According to Guinn, following the talks, General Jesup would write in a letter, "We have, at no former period in our history, had to contend with so formidable an enemy."

Broken Peace Agreement

Abraham used his diplomatic skills and the assistance of several Seminole chiefs to construct a peace agreement. The treaty promised that the Seminole Negroes could migrate to Indian Territory with the Seminole Indians and that both, as quoted by Guinn, "shall be secure in their lives and property." Among other promises, the peace agreement stated that the American government would pay a fair price for the horses and cattle the Seminole Indians and Negroes would leave behind, provide rations for one year, and provide seed for planting crops. In return, the Anglo Americans would have the Florida territory to themselves.

When the details of the treaty were publicized, General Jesup faced the ire of southerners from Georgia, South Carolina, Alabama, and Florida. The plantation owners wanted their escaped slaves returned to them. They demanded the return of the slaves and the slave children and grandchildren of the runaways. Angry planters converged upon Fort Dade demanding their human property. The southerners' demands caused Jesup to relent. This decision put Abraham in a precarious position because it was he who urged the Seminole chiefs to agree to the relocation plan.

The subject of moving to Indian Territory generated much conflict and threatened to cost Abraham his life. At this time, close to a thousand Seminole Indians and Seminole Negroes were encamped around Fort Dade preparing to move west. Several Seminole chiefs were in this number as well. When slavers began to harass the Seminole Negroes, the Seminole Indians became irritated and began to distrust Jesup. Some sensed something was amiss and fled into the swamps. Some Seminole Negroes in the camp, however, were seized and returned to white masters or sold.

Osceola, the great warrior chief who never agreed to the Payne's Landing Treaty, came to the camp under cover of night and rescued almost all of the Seminole chiefs, Indians, and Negroes. Abraham was not among those rescued. At this point, his life was in danger. If he left camp, General Jesup could charge him with treason. Moreover, he would not be safe among the Seminole Indians and Negroes since some would blame him for Jesup's not honoring the treaty. Still others might feel Abraham had tricked them. Too, Abraham was reluctant to leave camp because he had witnessed Chief Osceola's rage when he fatally shot Chief Charley Emathla because Emathla decided to move his tribe west of the Mississippi. Osceola's influence among the Seminoles was as great as his rage against moving to Indian Territory, and Abraham was no longer viewed as a brother or ally. In the end, Abraham stayed in protective custody of the U.S. Army until he migrated west with several hundred Seminoles. There, in what later became Oklahoma, he lived, except for a brief time spent in Mexico, and continued to be engaged in the affairs of his people. Abraham—runaway slave, interpreter, warrior, freedom fighter, diplomat, Seminole chief—faced the challenges of his day with resolve and a tenacity to promote the wellbeing of his people. He is buried in Bruntertown Cemetery in Oklahoma.

REFERENCES

Books

Guinn, Jeff. *Our Land Before We Die: The Proud Story of the Seminole Negro.* New York: Jeremy P. Tarcher/Putnam, 2002.

Lancaster, Jane F. *Removal Aftershock: The Seminoles' Struggles to Survive in the West, 1836–1866.* Knoxville: University of Tennessee Press, 1994.

Porter, Kenneth W. *The Black Seminole Indians: History of a Freedom-Seeking People.* Eds. Alcione M. Amos and Thomas P. Senter. Gainesville: University Press of Florida, 1996.

Online

Bird, J. B. "Trail Narrative." http://www.johnhorse.com/trail/05/conclusion.htm (Accessed 10 February 2006).

"Black Seminoles." http://www.encyclopedia.thefreedictionary.com/Black+Seminoles (Accessed 2 February 2006).

Chu, Chun W. "The Black Seminoles' Long March to Freedom." http://www.ccny.cuny.edu/library/News/seminoles2.html (Accessed 20 February 2006).

Peck, Dana. "Original Seminoles." http://www.fsu.edu/~fstime/FS-Times/Volume6/sep00web/13sep00.html (Accessed 21 February 2006).

West, Jean. "Seminoles and Slaves: Florida's Freedom Seekers." http://www.slaveryinamerica.org/history/hs_es_seminole.htm (Accessed 24 February 2006).

Jewell B. Parham

Chronology	
c. 1810	Born near Richmond, Virginia
1831	Moves to Missouri
1863	Becomes a fugitive slave
1865	Freed by state law
1876	Immortalized in bronze in the Lincoln Freedmen Memorial
1879	Dies in St. Louis, Missouri on December 8
1885	Biography, *The Story of Archer Alexander: From Slavery to Freedom, March 30, 1863*, is published in Boston

Archer Alexander
c. 1810–1879

Slave

Archer Alexander was the model for the slave depicted in the Lincoln Freedmen Memorial in Lincoln Park, Washington, D.C. Thought to be the last slave captured in Missouri under the terms of the Fugitive Slave Act, Alexander was working at the time for William Greenleaf Eliot, a minister in the Unitarian Church and grandfather of poet T. S. Eliot. Reverend Eliot was a staunch abolitionist who put up his own money to secure Alexander's freedom. He later wrote Alexander's life story and published the biography in 1885 with the title *The Story of Archer Alexander: From Slavery to Freedom, March 30, 1863*.

Alexander was born around 1810 outside Richmond, Virginia. His mother, Chloe, and father, Aleck, were the property of a Presbyterian minister named Delaney, and they worked on the Delaney plantation, Kalorama. Around 1831, after the elder Delaney died, his son, Thomas Delaney, took Alexander to Missouri. Slavery was permitted there, but it was a controversial subject that divided Missouri residents and had also been the subject of a significant congressional debate a decade earlier.

Tom Delaney hired Alexander out for a time to a St. Louis brickyard called Letcher & Bobbs, before moving to a farm in St. Charles County. There Alexander married a slave woman named Louisa, with whom he had ten children. In the early 1840s, Delaney decided to move to Louisiana, where his wife's family was from, and he sold Alexander to Louisa's owner, a man named Hollman. Alexander spent the next twenty or so years as a trusted manager of the Hollman farm.

Alerts Union Army to Confederate Sabotage

When the Civil War broke out in 1861, Missouri became a battleground for pro- and anti-slavery factions. Many residents supported the Confederate cause and wanted to keep their slaves, but Union troops moved quickly to prevent Missouri from seceding along with the rebel Southern states. Tensions were high, and in February of 1863 a pro-slavery group cut the wooden timbers below a bridge that was expecting to bear the weight of a trainload of Union soldiers in the next day or two. Hollman was part of this group, and when Alexander learned of the sabotage, he walked five miles in the middle of the night to tell someone he knew was sympathetic to the Union cause. That man alerted others, and the bridge was repaired in time.

Hollman's fellow Confederate supporters suspected Alexander as the informant, and plans were made to question him. Realizing he would likely be killed, Alexander fled Hollman's farm, leaving behind his wife and family. He met up with a group of runaway slaves, but all were captured by slave hunters and taken to a tavern for the night. The bounty hunters locked them in an upstairs room and then spent the night drinking. Alexander managed a solo escape from the second-floor window when the guard dog below was distracted. He made his way to St. Louis, where he asked a sympathetic butcher to help him find a job. The butcher, a Dutch immigrant, put him in touch with William Greenleaf Eliot.

Eliot and his family lived in a well-appointed house that had been built by a Missouri governor some years before. He hired Alexander to take care of the farm, though Alexander admitted that he was a runaway slave. Eliot, a Unitarian minister and founder of Washington University in St. Louis, was morally opposed to slavery. He asked the local marshal for help, and, according to the biography, obtained a certificate that read: "The colored man named Archer Alexander, supposed to be the slave of a rebel master, is hereby permitted to remain in the service of W. G. Eliot until legal right to his services shall be established by such party, if any, as may claim them. Not to exceed thirty days unless extended."

Hides in Illinois

Eliot sent word, anonymously, to Hollman and offered to pay the full market price for Alexander. Hollman managed to learn his slave's whereabouts, and at the end of the thirty-day period Alexander was forcibly taken from the property—and viciously beaten in front of Eliot's young children—by slave hunters. Technically, because martial law had been declared in Missouri, captured runaway slaves were supposed to be handed over to Union Army troops for protection. Eliot found out where Alexander was being held and used his connections to have him brought back to his property. After another unsuccessful attempt to negotiate a purchase with Hollman, Eliot sent Alexander to safety in Alton, Illinois, which was not a slave state, to work on a friend's farm.

President Abraham Lincoln's Emancipation Proclamation was issued in September 1862 and went into effect on the first day of 1863, but it only freed slaves in Confederate states that were still in rebellion. Slaves in border states which had not seceded, such as Missouri, were not immediately affected by the decree. But Missouri's lawmakers enacted a gradual emancipation law in June 1863, and Alexander was able to return to Eliot's farm. "We had all by this time become so attached to him, and felt so great respect for his manly, patient character, that we would have spared neither cost nor pains to secure his freedom beyond all possible contingency," wrote Eliot in his biography of Alexander. "He settled down quietly to his work, earning his wages well, and taking care of every thing on the four-acre lot as if it were all his own."

Alexander managed to contact his wife Louisa, and she escaped with their teenaged daughter to Eliot's farm. All became free in January 1865, when slavery was formally abolished in Missouri at the state convention. One of their sons—named Thomas in honor of the younger Delaney who had brought Alexander to Missouri—was one of the war's casualties, having joined one of the newly formed Union regiments for blacks. In the early 1870s, an image of Alexander was sent to Thomas Ball, the sculptor commissioned by a group of freed slaves who had collected funds to erect a monument to Lincoln, who was assassinated in 1865. "Emancipation" depicts an African American man kneeling before the president, with his arms outstretched as if he is breaking the chains that bind him. Sometimes called the Lincoln Freedmen's Memorial, the monument was dedicated by Frederick Douglass at an 1876 ceremony.

Alexander was not at that ceremony, but did see photographs of the monument before his death in 1879. Six years after his death, Eliot's biography of him was published in Boston. "It is the record of a humble life, but one which was conformed, up to the full measure of ability, to the law of the gospel," the reverend concluded. "I have felt as proud of the long-continued friendship and confidence of Archer Alexander as of any one I have known."

REFERENCES

Books

Eliot, William G. *The Story of Archer Alexander: From Slavery to Freedom, March 30, 1863.* Boston: Cupples, Upham, and Company, 1885.

Meyer, Jeffrey F. *Myths in Stone: Religious Dimensions of Washington, D.C.* Berkeley, Calif.: University of California Press, 2001.

Online

"Archer Alexander—Freedoms Memorial." Ebony Society of Philatelic Events and Reflections (ESPER). http://esperstamps.org/aa3.htm (Accessed 28 December 2005).

Carol Brennan

Archie Alphonso Alexander
1888–1958

Engineer, governor

After the dean of the engineering school at the State University of Iowa told him that he had never heard of a Negro engineer and tried to persuade him to find another career choice, Archie Alexander became more determined than ever to pursue his professional goal. Although denied employment with white architectural firms early in his career, Alexander remain steadfast and later became a successful engineer and builder of large-scale construction projects, such as highways, bridges, viaducts, and municipal power and sewage plants. He established his own engineering company, several times entering in interracial partnerships—an unusual venture of that time—and became a wealthy man. He was also a politician and worked for civil rights causes.

Early Interest in Higher Education

Born in Ottuma, Iowa, on May 14, 1888, and one of eight children, Archie Alphonso Alexander was the son of Price Alexander, a janitor and coachman, and Mary Hamilton Alexander. The town of 14,000 residents was predominantly white with only 500 blacks; it included the poor who were both black and white. As young Archie played with his siblings in a creek behind their home, he was especially interested in building dams. When Archie was only eleven years old, the family relocated to a small farm on the outskirts of Des Moines. Price Alexander was hired as head custodian at the Des Moines National Bank, then a prestigious post for a black man. Young Archie

Archie Alphonso Alexander

Chronology

1888	Born in Ottuma, Iowa on May 14
1912	Receives B.S. degree, State University of Iowa
1914	Establishes A. A. Alexander Inc. engineering firm
1917	Forms Alexander & Higbee, Inc.
1925	Receives degree in civil engineering, State University of Iowa
1926	Receives Harmon Award
1927	Constructs heating station at University of Iowa
1929	Forms Alexander & Repass Company; receives contract for sewage treatment plant
1934	Receives NAACP's Spingarn Medal
1935	Designs and builds Union Pacific Railroad Bridge
1940s	Builds Tuskegee Airmen's training site; designs and builds Tidal Basic Bridge and Sewall, Washington, D.C.
1954	Becomes governor of the Virgin Islands
1955	Designs Frederick Douglass Memorial Estate Apartments
1958	Dies in Des Moines on January 4

studied at Oak Park Grammar School and in 1905 graduated from Oak Park High School. In the view of local residents, the son of a janitor, whether black or white, was expected to end his education at that level; thus Archie's determination to attend college was surprising. Nevertheless, Archie Alexander continued his studies for one year at the now-defunct Highland Park College and then the Cummins Art School, both in Des Moines.

Committed to Engineering

In 1908 Alexander entered the College of Engineering at the State University of Iowa (subsequently the University of Iowa) to further his ambition to become an engineer. The only black in the university's engineering program, he was advised by various teachers that because of his race the field would be twice as tough for him. He could not hope to succeed and he should select another major, they said. Their efforts to dissuade Alexander became efforts to persuade him—in his view—and Alexander worked hard in part-time jobs and in his courses to reach his goal. A versatile young man, Alexander joined the university's football team, becoming its first black member. He also became a star tackle and won the nickname "Alexander the Great." He joined the black fraternity, Kappa Alpha Psi.

Alexander graduated in 1912 with a B.S. degree, the school's first black engineering graduate. He continued

his studies, first in bridge design at the University of London (1921) and at the State University of Iowa, where he obtained a degree in civil engineering in 1925. In 1947 Howard University in Washington, D.C., awarded him an honorary doctorate in engineering. After receiving his first degree, Alexander found the business world unready to acknowledge his expertise. Perhaps his engineering professors' gloomy warnings were valid. Local engineering firms refused to hire him; consequently, to earn a living Alexander became a laborer for a steel shop at Marsh Engineering, earning twenty-five cents an hour. Two years later he was in charge of bridge construction in Iowa and Minnesota and earned seventy dollars a week. He resigned that year (1914) and founded his own company, A. A. Alexander Inc. Mindful of the need to expand his modest business beyond a few minority clientele and scarcely any other bidders, in 1917 he partnered with white contractor George F. Higbee, with whom he had worked at Marsh Engineering. The new company, Alexander & Higbee, Inc., specialized in projects with potential for serving the company well: bridge construction, road construction, and sewer systems.

An injury from a construction accident took Higbee's life in 1925; thus, from 1925 to 1929, Alexander ran his company alone. He received his largest contract to date in 1927, when he was asked to build a $1.2 million central heating and generating station for his alma mater, the University of Iowa, a system apparently still in use as of the early 2000s. During this period, Alexander built mostly projects in which he specialized, bridges and viaducts, but some apartment buildings and sewage systems as well. On occasions he faced racial prejudice and hostility, yet the record of his work for that period gives only a positive report on his ability to achieve despite such potential obstacles. Alexander took on a second white (junior) partner in 1929, Maurice A. Repass, who had been his football teammate in college and was an engineering graduate as well. They were a good mix and their fortune grew considerably. Alexander & Repass affiliated with Glen C. Herrick, prominent local white contractor and road builder, who had been contracted to build a canal system in Nebraska. For bridge work connected with his project, Herrick hired Alexander & Repass and later on financed a number of projects for the new company. Their largest project was in 1935, when Alexander & Repass designed and began to build the Union Pacific Railroad Bridge across the North Platte River in Nebraska.

Constructs Famous Airfield

Alexander & Repass was now positioned to bid on projects across the country. As the federal government expanded the areas of its contracts due to World War II, the company was successful in its bid to construct an airfield at the U.S. Army base located in Chewhaw, Alabama. This airbase achieved widespread acclaim, particularly in later years, as the training site for the 99th Pursuit Squadron Air Base and Pilot Training School of the famous Tuskegee Airmen, the highly decorated, all-black flying squad in the then-segregated U.S. Amy Air Corps.

So lucrative was their business by that time that Alexander & Repass opened a second office in Washington, D.C. The second office was necessary for the company had received additional contracts from the federal government for publicly visible projects in the D.C. area. Among these projects were the granite and limestone Tidal Basin Bridge and Seawall, built at a cost of $1 million and employing 160 workers. The firm also built the K Street elevated highway and underpass that runs from Key Bridge to 27th Street, N.W. Along the Potomac River it built the $3.5 million Whitehurst Freeway, diverting traffic around Georgetown. Another project was the overpass that took Riggs Road under the Baltimore & Ohio Railroad tracks. Other projects included the Frederick Douglass Memorial Estate Apartments in the Anacostia section of Washington, D.C., that Alexander designed and his company built in 1955. Alexander's role as designer of other projects is undocumented.

A lifelong Republican, Alexander was politically active. He was assistant chairman of the Iowa Republican State Committee in 1932 and again in 1940. He supported Dwight D. Eisenhower and his bid for the presidency. For his work with the Republican Party, Alexander was appointed governor of the Virgin Islands in April 1954. He was far less successful as governor than he was as an engineer, and his blatant contempt for the residents often alienated the easy-going islanders and the legislature to the extent that they were unsupportive. His personality was offensive, and he was accused of cronyism and one who sought only to promote his growing business interests in the Caribbean and South America. His declining health and questionable performance led to his resignation in August 1955, sixteen months after his appointment.

His stature in Des Moines and in Washington, D.C. was enhanced, however, by his work in civil and race relations activities. Alexander was president of the Des Moines NAACP in 1944. He also was president of the local Interracial Commission from 1940 to 1941. He was a trustee at Tuskegee Institute (subsequently Tuskegee University) and at Howard University. In 1934 he was a member of the investigative team that, at the request of the Haitian president, looked into the economic development possibilities for Haiti. Alexander chaired the Polk County (Iowa) draft board and presided over the local Negro Community Center. His organizational activities included national polemarch (president) of his fraternity, Kappa Alpha Psi, and board member of the Colored YMCA. Among his recognitions were the Harmon Award (1926) for outstanding achievement in black business and the Spingarn Medal from the NAACP (1934) for becoming the second most successful black American entrepreneur.

Alexander has been described as aggressive, blunt, outspoken, dogmatic, paternalistic, and a hard and difficult taskmaster. He was an attractive man with blue-grey eyes and an imposing, commanding personality. When traveling in connection with his work, Alexander often stayed in white hotels throughout the country, his race not an identifiable factor.

There are claims that Alexander's unsuccessful performance in the Virgin Islands led to his death from a heart attack at home in Des Moines on January 4, 1958. His wife, Audra A. Lindzy, whom he married in 1913, survived him. Archie Alphonso Jr., their only child, had died in his early years. The University of Iowa, Tuskegee Institute, and Howard University were among beneficiaries of his will, but upon the death of his wife. The schools each received $105,000 in 1975, to support engineering scholarships.

Archie Alphonso Alexander had been a successful engineer who defied the predictions of his college teachers that he could not survive in the field in which he pioneered. Although he was unsuccessful as governor of the Virgin Islands, he was prominent in local Republican politics and in civil rights and interracial activities.

REFERENCES

Books

Bullock, Ralph W. *In Spite of Handicaps*. New York: Association Press, 1927.

Lufkin, Jack. "Archibald Alphonse Alexander (1888–1958)." In *African American Architects: A Biographical Dictionary 1865-1945*, edited by Dreck Spurlock Wilson. New York: Routledge, 2004.

Nichols, J. L., and William H. Crogman. *Progress of a Race*. Naperville, Ill.: J. L. Nichols & Co., 1925, 329-30.

Robinson, Wilhelmina S. *Historical Negro Biographies*. New York: Publishers Company, under the Auspices of the Association for the Study of Negro Life and History, 1967, 154-55.

Wynes, Charles E. "Archie Alphonso Alexander." In *American National Biography*, edited by John A. Garraty and Mark C. Carnes. New York: Oxford University Press, 1999.

Periodicals

"Bridge-Building Team." *Ebony* 4 (September 1949): 59-60.

Jessie Carney Smith

Chronology

1864	Born in Helena, Arkansas on January 6
1879	Graduates high school
1880	Enrolls at Oberlin College in Ohio
1883	Enters West Point Military Academy
1887	Graduates from West Point Academy; reports to Fort Robinson, Nebraska
1888	Transfers to Fort Washakie, Wyoming
1891	Serves as training instructor in North Carolina
1893	Passes examination for first lieutenant at Fort Leavenworth, Kansas
1894	Serves as professor of military science and tactics at Wilberforce University in Ohio
1894	Dies in Springfield, Ohio of a heart attack on March 26

John Hanks Alexander
1864–1894

Army officer, educator

John Hanks Alexander was the second black graduate of the United States Military Academy at West Point following Henry O. Flipper and preceding Charles Young, the third graduate. He was the first black officer to hold a regular command post in the U.S. Army. In 1894 he received military orders to serve as professor of military science and tactics at Wilberforce University, a black institution in Ohio offering military training programs for blacks.

Born January 6, 1864, John Hanks Alexander was the fourth of seven children born in Helena, Arkansas, to former slave parents, James Milo Alexander and Fannie Miller Alexander. James Milo Alexander, who died in 1871, was a dry-goods merchant and owned property in Helena. He served as the first black justice of the peace in Arkansas and later served in the state legislature from Phillips County. Believing education was the key to success, John Hanks Alexander, along with his siblings, graduated from high school and three attended Oberlin College in Ohio.

Attends Oberlin and West Point

After graduating first in his high school class in 1879, Alexander moved to Carrollton, Mississippi, where he accepted a teaching position for six months. In the fall of 1880, he enrolled at Oberlin College in Ohio, where he did well academically. Upon hearing about a competitive examination for admission to West Point Military Academy, Alexander decided to apply. He, along with William Waite, the son of Chief Justice Morrison Waite, became contenders. Alexander, who was appointed alternate, made the highest score on the academic part of the examination and Waite, appointed delegate, scored better on his physical. Friends raised money so that Alexander could attend regardless of his rank as alternate. However, as luck would have it, Waite failed his entrance examination; Alexander passed his and was admitted to West Point in May 1883. He then left Oberlin to become the second black cadet to attend the academy.

At West Point Alexander continued to excel academically. He was noted for his skills in mathematics and languages and was also a skilled pugilist. Although he experienced white ostracism at the academy, according to Patricia W. Romero in *I Too Am America*, one professor described Alexander as "having character and behavior to admire and respect." Four years later, he graduated thirty-second in a class of sixty-four. His class initially had one hundred thirty-two members; however, over a period of four years, members of the class were cut because they were "unable to keep up," wrote Romero. Alexander may have ranked higher if he had not received a number of demerits for minor infractions. For example, twice he was reprimanded for skating on the frozen Hudson River. One of his former classmates, C.D. Rhodes, second lieutenant sixth U.S. Calvary and professor of military science and tactics, stated in his condolences upon the death of Alexander that on the day of graduation, Alexander was applauded by the audience longer than any other graduate. Perhaps this statement is a testament to his character and begs to question the demerits he received.

During the graduation ceremony Alexander was commissioned a second lieutenant and on September 30, 1887, he reported to the Ninth U.S. Calvary Regiment, nicknamed by the Kiowa Indians the Buffalo Soldiers, at

Fort Robinson, Nebraska. The Ninth Calvary, an all-black regiment, was commanded by white officers. Alexander became the only black officer to serve in a command position. Over the next seven years he was assigned to Fort Washakie, Wyoming, and Fort Duchesne, Utah. At these frontier posts, where he served with distinction, his responsibilities included garrison duties, operating a post commissary, escorting prisoners to Omaha, supervising the building and maintaining a post sawmill and telegraph line, and serving at court martial proceedings. Also during these seven years he had a temporary-duty assignment training an all-black infantry unit in Raleigh, North Carolina. During his off-duty hours he read military biographies, kept a diary of his daily military activities, and wrote letters to his family. In October 1893, Alexander qualified for first lieutenant at Fort Leavenworth, Kansas, after passing a rigorous physical and military examination.

Begins Teaching Career

As early as 1887 Booker T. Washington expressed an interest in Alexander's serving as an instructor of military science at Tuskegee Institute in Alabama. According to military regulations, an officer serving in this capacity had to have previously served three years with a regiment. Such regulations precluded Alexander from serving in this capacity because he had recently graduated from West Point, not to mention that the state of Alabama already had its prescribed number of black college-assigned officers. Between 1892 and 1894 the president of Wilberforce University in Ohio requested the services of Alexander as a professor of military science and tactics. Although Alexander met the qualifications for the position, he was told that the State of Ohio already had its quota of assigned officers. Though he may have felt discouraged by this second rejection, his circumstances were about to improve. The U.S. Congress unexpectedly increased the number of officers for academic tour duty. Upon learning of the change, the Reverend S. T. Mitchell, president of Wilberforce, once again requested Alexander's services. On January 6, 1894, Alexander was assigned to Wilberforce University to serve as professor of military science and tactics. Unfortunately, on March 26, 1894 he died of a heart attack or apoplexy, the result of excessive cigarette smoking, in Springfield, Ohio. He is buried in Xenia, Ohio.

On August 15, 1918, the War Department issued General Orders 294 in honor of John Hanks Alexander. This order designated that a military installation in Newport News, Virginia, be named Camp Alexander in his honor because of his ability, attainments, energy, and outstanding military performance.

REFERENCES

Books

Logan, Rayford W., and Michael R. Winston. *Dictionary of American Negro Biography.* New York: Norton, 1982.

Romero, Patricia W. *I Too Am America: Documents from 1619 to the Present.* Cornwells Heights, Pa.: The Association for the Study of Afro-American Life and History, 1976.

Schubert, Irene, and Frank N. Schubert. *On the Trail of the Buffalo Soldier II: New andRevised Biographies of African Americans in the U.S. Army, 1866-1917.* Lanham, Md.: Scarecrow Press, 2004.

Online

"The African-American Experience in Ohio: Cadet John H. Alexander." Ohio Historical Society. http://dbs. ohiohistory.org/africanam/page.cfm?ID=14436 (Accessed 11 March 2005).

"The African-American Experience in Ohio: Lieut. John H. Alexander." Ohio Historical Society. http://dbs. ohiohistory.org/africanam/page.cfm ?ID=18021 (Accessed 10 March 2005).

"The Black Officers: John Hanks Alexander." Dr. John Productions. http://www.abuffalosoldier.com/ hanks.htm (Accessed 15 December 2004).

Gatewood, Willard B., Jr. "John Hanks Alexander of Arkansas: Second Black Graduate of West Point." Arkansas Historical Quarterly. http://www.cals.lib.ar. us/butlercenter/eoa/entries/Alexander.pdf (Accessed 10 March 2005).

Collections

Alexander's papers are in the Henry E. Huntington Library, San Marino, California.

Patricia A. Pearson

Macon Bolling Allen
1816–1894

Lawyer, judge

Macon Bolling Allen was the first recorded licensed African American lawyer in the United States. He was a self-taught lawyer who gained his knowledge and legal skills by serving as an apprentice and law clerk to practicing white lawyers in the pre-Civil War era. Negro professionals received their training by apprenticeship;

however, they could not depend upon the practice of law for a living. They had to work at other crafts. Allen was also known as a businessman but the nature of the business is not known.

Very little is known about Allen's early years other than the fact that he was named A. Macon Bolling when he was born a free Negro in Indiana in 1816, the same year Indiana was admitted as the nineteenth state to join the Union. He was actually a mulatto (a first generation offspring of a Negro and a white). However, mulatto was listed as a race on early census forms. Allen learned how to read and write as he grew up, and his first job in Indiana was that of a schoolteacher.

Faces Challenges in New England

In his late twenties, Allen moved to Portland, Maine, where he changed his name from A. Macon Bolling to Macon Bolling Allen. It is not known why Allen moved to there, but Maine's stance on slavery could have been a deciding factor. Maine joined the Union in 1820 as a free state (one in which slavery is illegal). Allen was an anti-slavery advocate and Maine's enthusiasm for national reform in the 1830s and 1840s was widely known. Anti-slavery was a popular cause in Maine. In fact, Harriet Beecher Stowe, then of Brunswick, Maine, wrote the novel, *Uncle Tom's Cabin* in 1851, which evoked strong anti-slavery feelings and is cited as one of the causes of the Civil War.

Allen became a friend of the local anti-slavery leader, General Samuel Fessenden, who established a law firm and took on Allen as an apprentice. In 1844, Fessenden introduced Allen to the Portland District Court while it was in session and proposed that Allen be permitted to practice as a lawyer. According to Maine law at that time, anyone of good moral character could be admitted to the bar. Allen was rejected, though, because he was not a citizen. Allen then applied to be admitted by examination. He passed, was recommended, and admitted. On July 3, 1844, Allen was declared a citizen of the State of Maine with good moral character. After paying twenty dollars to the Treasury of Maine, he was granted a license to practice law as an attorney. However, Allen had very little opportunity to practice law in Maine because there were very few blacks to hire him and others were not eager to have a black represent them in a legal matter.

Opens Law Practice

In 1845, Allen moved to Boston, Massachusetts, where he was required to take another examination. While in Boston, he met and married his wife Hannah. Very little is known about her except that she was born around 1838 and is listed in the census records as a mulatto and a housekeeper. The records state that her parents' birthplace was South Carolina. Allen fathered five sons. John was born in 1852, and the 1880 United States Federal Census listed him as a single mulatto male with

Chronology	
1816	Born in Indiana
1840	Moves to Portland, Maine
1844	Changes his name to Macon Bolling Allen
1844	Passes the bar in Maine on July 3
1845	Moves to Boston, Massachusetts, and is admitted to the bar on May 3
1846	Writes letter to *The Liberator*
1848	Becomes justice of the peace for Middlesex County
1868	Moves to Charleston, South Carolina
1872	Becomes a partner in William J. Whipper and Robert Brown
1873	Elected judge of the Inferior Court of Charleston in February
1874	Elected to the office of judge probate for Charleston County
1894	Dies in Washington, D.C. on October 10

the occupation of schoolteacher. Edward, born in 1856, was also listed as a single mulatto male schoolteacher, as was Charles, born in 1861. Arthur was only twelve at the time of the 1880 census. Records are sketchy about Macon B. Allen Jr., the youngest child, other than the fact that he was a schoolteacher in Beaufort, South Carolina, according to the 1880 census.

After passing two bar examinations, one in the State of Maine and the other in the State of Massachusetts, Allen passed a rigid examination to become a justice of the peace for Middlesex County, Massachusetts. This examination was tough for anyone but for a black to pass was unheard of in the Commonwealth of Massachusetts. A justice of the peace played an important role in the early development of the States. Officers of the justice of the peace heard civil cases that involved small sums of money, but their powers varied in different states. In some instances, the justice of the peace had powers to perform marriage services. Becoming a justice of the peace was commendable for a black professional. Allen is believed to be the first black to hold a judiciary position.

On May 5, 1845, Allen was admitted to the practice of law in the State of Massachusetts and in Suffolk County. With Robert Morris Jr., Allen opened the first black law practice in the United States. Allen gained the attention of William Lloyd Garrison and the black abolitionists in Boston. Garrison was a journalist and reformer who became famous for his denunciation of slavery. Garrison began publishing *The Liberator* in 1831 in Boston. In 1832, Garrison formed the society for the immediate abolition of slavery. Both were used as vehicles to arouse public reaction to slavery.

In May 1846, Allen attended an anti-slavery convention in Boston. Petitions were circulated to obtain signatures of convention participants of people who opposed the federal government in the Mexican War (1846–1848), which had just started. Northerners believed that the war was a plot to obtain land for the expansion of slavery. Allen did not sign the petition. He reasoned that he had just taken an oath to defend the Constitution and the laws of the land. It was announced that he had refused to sign, and no additional explanation was given to the other convention participants.

Allen later wrote a letter, dated June 1, 1846, to *The Liberator*, to set the record straight regarding his reasons for not signing the petition. Allen stated that he was under oath to support the laws of the country. He sympathized deeply with blacks in bondage, and he was willing to do all he could for their cause. The letter ends with his asking his friends not to be prejudiced against him, assuring them it had no justification.

Yields to Politics

In 1868, Allen moved to Charleston, South Carolina, where he became active in politics as a Republican. Allen became a partner in the law firm of William J. Whipper and Robert Brown Elliot, located at 91 Broad Street, the first black law firm in the United States. In 1872, Allen ran for secretary of state on a Republican ticket that had split from the national Republican Party. During this same year, he also made an unsuccessful bid for the judgeship in the New Inferior Court.

In 1873, Allen was nominated to the office of Judge of the Inferior Court of Charleston, South Carolina, to replace George Lee who had died in office. Among the contenders for the position was his former law firm partner, William J. Whipper. The Inferior Court had exclusive jurisdiction over all criminal cases, except capital offenses, that came from courts of the trial justices.

In 1874, Allen purchased a house on Montaque Street in Charleston and Charleston became his permanent home. A few years later, he was elected to serve as a judge. In 1876, Allen was elected to the Office of Judge Probate for Charleston County. Allen served as a probate court judge until 1878.

Some time after Reconstruction, Allen moved to Washington, D.C., where he was employed as an attorney for the Land and Improvement Association. On October 10, 1894, in Washington, D.C., after fifty years of legal service, Allen died. He was seventy-eight years of age. The National Bar Association elected to honor him for fifty years of service. The records indicated that his widow and son Arthur survived him. He was memorialized at the Saint Mark's Protestant Episcopal Church in Charleston, South Carolina, and interred in the Friendly Union Cemetery.

Macon B. Allen left a legacy to be remembered. A Bar Association (New York), Civil Rights Clinic (Boston), and other organizations are named in his honor.

REFERENCES

Books

Foner, Eric. *Freedom's Lawmakers: A Directory of Black Officeholders during Reconstruction.* New York: Oxford University Press, 1983.

Logan, Rayford W., and Michael R. Winston. *Dictionary of American Negro Biography.* New York: Norton, 1982.

Low, W. Augustus, and Virgil A. Clift. *Encyclopedia of Black America.* New York: McGraw-Hill, 1981.

Ploski, Harry A., and Roscoe C. Brown. *The Negro Almanac.* New York: Bellwether Publishing Company, 1967.

Smith, J. Clay Jr. *Emancipation: The Making of the Black Lawyers 1844-1944.* Philadelphia: University of Pennsylvania Press, 1993.

Periodicals

Brown, Charles. "The Genesis of the Negro Lawyer in New England." *The Negro History Bulletin* 148 (April 1959): 147-52.

Contee, Clarence G. "Macon B. Allen: First Black in the Legal Profession." *The Crisis* 83 (February 1976): 67-69.

Houston, Charles. "The Need for Negro Lawyers." *The Journal of Negro Education* 4 (January 1935): 49-52.

"Letters to Antislavery Workers and Agencies." Part 5. *The Journal of Negro History* 10 (July 1925): 444-68.

Taylor, A. A. "Opposition to the Reconstruction." *The Journal of Negro History* 9 (October 1924): 463.

Online

Historical Timeline of American Indians, African Americans and People of Color in Maine. http://www.pressherald.Mainetoday.com (Accessed 11 January 2005).

"Macon B. Allen." 1880 United States Census. http://www.ancestry.com (Accessed 20 January 2005).

Macon B. Allen Manuscript Document. http://www. galleryofhistory.com/archive (Accessed 11 January 2005).

"Making Bricks Without Straw: The NAACP Legal Defense and the Development of Civil Rights Law in Alabama, 1940-1980." www.law.ua.edu./lawreview (Accessed 6 January 2005).

Orella Ramsey Brazile

Michael P. Anderson
1959–2003

Astronaut

Michael P. Anderson was one of seven astronauts on the space shuttle *Columbia*, which disintegrated over Texas 16 minutes before its scheduled landing on February 1, 2003. Anderson was the sole African American on the mission, which also included the first Israeli astronaut, Col. Ilan Ramon, and the first Indian-born female in space, Dr. Kaplana Chawla. His childhood dream of becoming an astronaut led to a distinguished career in the U.S. Air Force, which culminated in his becoming the first African American in space in 1998. There were no survivors from the *Columbia* explosion, which was caused by a faulty heat tile on the bottom of the shuttle. NASA immediate halted further space shuttle missions after the event.

Michael Phillip Anderson was born December 25, 1959, in Plattsburgh, New York to Barbara and Bobbie Anderson. He grew up in Spokane, Washington, which is mainly a military and government town and is 92 percent white, 2 percent African American. At age four he announced his intention to become an astronaut. He built countless model planes and rockets and hung them with invisible wire from his bedroom ceiling. He was so dedicated to his dream of flying that he wore goggles while mowing the lawn to prevent eye damage that would keep him from joining the Air Force. His family members saw his future early on. "We knew even then that if he was going to be anything, he was going to be a pilot," an aunt told the *Washington Post*.

"I was interested in everything...from the sciences to music to writing to literature," Anderson said in an interview located at Space.com. "But as I got older...I found that science was something that really caught my attention." Even in high school Anderson knew, he said, that he would have to attend college and study science if he wanted to be a pilot, let alone an astronaut. So he joined the ROTC program, which later provided him a partial scholarship to college.

Anderson graduated from the University of Washington with a bachelor's degree in physics and astronomy. He joined the U.S. Air Force as a second lieutenant specializing in communications and computers. He completed a year of technical training at Keesler Air Force Base in Mississippi and was assigned to a base in Texas. In 1990, he earned a master's degree in physics from Creighton University. "He didn't come from wealth, or the best schools," a former science instructor in Spokane told the *Washington Post*, "but he had an insatiable desire for knowledge."

Like his father before him, Anderson joined the Air Force. Bobbie Anderson joined the Air Force to escape

Michael P. Anderson

poverty in rural Mississippi. He served in Vietnam and lived with his wife and four children at bases in New York, Ohio, and Arizona before getting stationed near Spokane. He was never a pilot; he was a mechanic who serviced jets. Michael Anderson was selected to attend United States Air Force undergraduate pilot training in 1986. He was an Air Force pilot for twelve years, logging more than three thousand hours. He spent much of the 1980s stationed at Offutt Air Force Base in Nebraska and flew one of the military's airborne command posts during the waning days of the Cold War. In the 1990s, he was an instructor pilot and tactics officer. He qualified for a NASA flight crew assignment in 1994.

Becomes First African American in Space

Columbia was Lt. Col. Anderson's second space launch. The first took place in 1998, aboard the space shuttle *Endeavor*, and made him the first African American in space. He and his crew were assigned the task of moving more than nine thousand pounds of scientific equipment, hardware, and water from the space shuttle *Endeavor* to the Russian space station *Mir*. He was not afraid to admit he was nervous. Anderson recalled getting sweaty palms before he pushed the button to dock to the *Mir*. "I'd done it a million times in the simulator," he said in a previous interview, according to the *Washington Post*, "but when it was real, it was a different moment entirely." Anderson's wife, Sandy, knew how important it was to Anderson to be the first African American astronaut in space. "He said he wanted to do it again," she told *Ebony*. "He wanted to be the first man to go to Mars." Since Anderson first went into space, Leland Melvin and Alvin Drew have joined the ranks of African American astronauts.

As the payload commander onboard the *Columbia* in 2003, Anderson was responsible for overseeing more than eighty scientific experiments during the sixteen-day mission. One experiment used a bioreactor to grow cells of prostate cancer which, as he noted in an interview with National Public Radio conducted onboard the *Columbia*, is prevalent among African American males. "We're exceeding almost all of our expectations, and we're getting some really good science," he said in the radio interview.

Ironically, as much as Anderson loved flying in space, he was apprehensive about the launches. "When you launch in a rocket, you're not really flying that rocket," he said in an interview with Space.com. "You're really taking an explosion and you're trying to control it. I understand the serious nature behind a rocket launch. There are a million things that can go wrong." He went on to add that exhaustive training and planning are required for handling those situations, but that the benefits of the science they do in space "are well worth the risk."

Perishes in International Tragedy

The *Columbia* exploded as it reentered the earth's atmosphere on February 1, 2003, just forty miles from the landing strip. Blame was placed on a heat-resistant tile that had fallen off the shuttle during liftoff. The *Columbia* disaster triggered a global outpouring of grief. After the tragedy, Anderson was honored at memorial services in various places, including Houston, Chicago, Detroit, and Atlanta. He was buried at Arlington National Cemetery. The State Transportation Commission voted unanimously to rename part of Washington's Route 904,

near where he grew up, in his honor. The library at the Chicago Military Academy at Bronzeville also now bears his name.

President George W. Bush and other dignitaries traveled to Houston to attend a ceremony at NASA's Johnson Space Center to commemorate the seven astronauts. Bush hailed them as explorers of great daring and purpose. At a more personal event, approximately three thousand people filled the interdenominational church Anderson attended, Grace Community Church in Houston. The church held a memorial ceremony for Anderson and his crewmate and fellow parishioner, Col. Rick D. Husband. Friends, family members, and coworkers recalled memories of the two men, who were both described as deeply religious and family-oriented. Anderson was a regular at Grace's weekly prayer breakfasts for fathers. Friends and family remembered Anderson as "kind, caring, quiet….he was never boastful and was always smiling and positive," according to *Ebony* Anderson also worked with the Bronze Eagles, a Houston-based African American flying club that introduces aviation to inner-city youth.

Anderson's wife, Sandy, and the couple's two daughters were among the group of Anderson's large, extended family who watched in horror as the *Columbia* tragedy unfolded. When she first heard radio contact with the shuttle had been lost, Sandy Anderson hoped it was a temporary glitch. She avoided the press for some time after the tragedy. When she spoke to a reporter from *Ebony*, she said she was always aware that her husband's job was dangerous. She also stated that she supported his dream and that she would never have asked him to switch to a safer profession. "I wouldn't change anything even knowing what I know," she said. "I wouldn't talk him out of it because that was his calling. You never think it's really going to happen to you, but at the same time, he loved what he was doing. I have to honor that." His daughters had different feelings, she added, and "wish they could turn the clock back."

"We are going to be O.K.," Sandy Anderson told the *New York Times*. According to the *Times*, Anderson told his minister before *Columbia* launched, "If this thing doesn't come out right, don't worry about me, I'm just going higher." When he died, Anderson was one of only seven African American astronauts actively serving in NASA's Astronaut Corps.

REFERENCES

Periodicals

"Church Two Astronauts Attended Remembers Their Faith." *New York Times*, 6 February 2003.

Dwyer, Timothy. "Celebrating an Explorer's Life; Astronaut's Passion Recalled at Funeral." *Washington Post*, 11 March 2003.

Gilbert, Marsha. "The Private Grief of a Public Tragedy: Astronaut Michael P. Anderson's Family Copes with Their Loss." *Ebony*, 58 (May 2003): 84-90.

LeDuff, Charlie. "Gathering to Mourn the Hero Few Knew They Had Produced." *New York Times*, 3 February 2003.

Sanchez, Rene. "'It Was Always His Strong Desire to Fly'; Youthful Dreams Propelled the Son of an Airman to Lifelong Flights of Fancy." *Washington Post*, 4 February 2003.

Wilson, Stephanie D. "Astronaut Michael P. Anderson Reached New Heights." *New Crisis*, 110 (March/April 2003): 12.

Online

"Anderson: Bright Future for Black Astronauts." CNN.com. http://www.cnn.com/2003/US/02/01/ shuttle.astronaut.sister/ (Accessed 8 March 2006).

"Astronaut Biography: Michael Anderson." Space.com. http://www.space.com/missionlaunches/bio_mike_ anderson.html (Accessed 8 March 2006).

"Michael P. Anderson (Lieutenant Colonel, US AF)." Lyndon B. Johnson Space Center. http://www.jsc. nasa.gov/Bios/htmlbios/anderson.html (Accessed 8 March 2006).

Brenna Sanchez

Vinton Randolph Anderson
1927–

Bishop

Bishop Vinton Randolph Anderson has made the United States his home since 1947 when he migrated from Bermuda, a small island in the Caribbean, where he was born in Somerset, on July 11, 1927. Anderson is a religious stalwart, who was involved in the social, educational, and economical well being of the African American communities he served. In 1972 Anderson was nominated as the 92nd bishop of the African Methodist Episcopal (AME) Church in Dallas, Texas. He retired at the 47th General Conference at Indianapolis in February 2004. Anderson's main goal as a member of the clergy was to foster reconciliation, which he described as harmonious race relations irrespective of the diversity in the society.

Anderson's parents were Bermudans, but there are no recorded details about their livelihood. His parents could afford to send him to private elementary and high schools on the island where he performed well. Anderson came to

Chronology	
1927	Born in Somerset, Bermuda on July 11
1951	Ordained itinerant deacon
1952	Ordained itinerant elder; marries Vivienne L. Anderson
1972	Elected 92nd bishop of the African Methodist Episcopal Church
1972-76	Presiding bishop for the 9th Episcopal District
1976-84	Presiding bishop for the 3rd Episcopal District
1984-88	Elected as a member of the Office of Ecumenical Relations and Development, and chair of the Bicentennial Celebration
1988-96	Presiding bishop for the 5th Episcopal District
1991	Receives Religion Award, American Black Achievement Awards
1992	Receives Daniel A. Payne Award for Ecumenical Leadership by AME Church
1993	Receives Scroll of Merit Award by National Medical Association
1996-2004	Presiding bishop for the 2nd Episcopal District
2004	Retires at the 47th General Conference at Indianapolis

the United States when he was twenty years old and entered the Wilberforce University in Ohio, which is affiliated with the AME Church and is the oldest historically black private college in the United States. He received a B.A. with honors from Wilberforce. Anderson strengthened his religious knowledge as he gained his master's of divinity from Payne Theological Seminary in Ohio in 1952. He also received an M.A. in philosophy from Kansas University. Anderson continued postgraduate studies at Yale University Divinity School. In addition, Anderson gained honorary doctoral degrees from Paul Quina College, Wilberforce University, Paine Theological Seminary, Temple Bible College, Morris Brown College, Interdenominational Theological Center (ITC), and Eden Theological Seminary.

In preparation for his pastoral duties, Anderson was ordained an itinerant deacon in 1951 and then an itinerant elder in 1952. As early as 1952, Anderson became a pastor at the St. Mark's AME Church in Topeka, Kansas, where he remained until 1953. He then moved to Parsons, Kansas, where he was in charge of the Brown Chapel AME Church from 1953 to 1955. Anderson continued his religious mission in Kansas as he served St. Luke AME Church in Lawrence from 1955 to 1959. His final duties in Kansas were performed at the St. Paul AME Church in Wichita from 1959 to 1964. Anderson then moved to St. Paul AME Church in St. Louis, Missouri where he served from 1964 to 1972.

Becomes Presiding Bishop

Anderson's good work in the ministry was recognized. After twenty years of serving as a pastor in Kansas and Missouri, he was elected the 92nd bishop of the AME Church in 1972. As presiding bishop he served the AME Church in five Episcopal districts. First, he served in the 9th district in Alabama from 1972 to 1976 before moving on to the 3rd district that encompasses Ohio, West Virginia, and West Pennsylvania where he served from 1976 to 1984. Anderson was absent from serving in the districts as he took on another role until 1988 when he returned to the 5th district which included fourteen states west of the Mississippi River. He also served in the 2nd district based in Washington D.C. from 1996 until his resignation in 2004. Anderson then served as presiding bishop for the 15th Episcopal District in South Africa in a church named for him—Cathedral of Vinton Anderson AME.

In the United Methodist Church, Anderson was a member of the General Commission of Christian Unity and Interreligious Concerns from 1984 to 1988. He became the first vice president for the World Methodist Council for the North American region. He was also a member of the executive committee and a delegate to the World Methodist Council and Conference beginning in 1961. His involvement in religious affairs was not limited to the Methodist Church, however; he was a member of the governing board of the National Council of Churches from 1984 to 1989. As a member of the National Council of Churches, he then became the vice chairperson of the Faith and Order Commission and a member of peace pilgrimage of ecumenical leaders that went to the Middle East in 1990. Additionally, he was active in the Congress of National Black Churches (CNBC) where he was vice president, and he was also the vice president of the Consultation on Church Union along with chair for the Worship Commission between 1973 and 1988. From 1984 to 1988, Anderson was involved in the Office of Ecumenical Relations and Development where he served as chair of the Bicentennial Celebration.

Internationally, Anderson was involved in the World Council of Churches that had over 560 million members and represented 322 denominations. He was elected president in 1991, and he served for seven years. He also moderated the U.S. conference, board of directors from 1987 to 1991 and, earlier, the liaison committee of Historical Black Churches in 1972. In addition, he was a member of the Site Visit Team to New Zealand and Australia for its program to combat racism in 1972.

Anderson is a renowned international figure. He has preached and lectured all over the world. His travels took him to the Caribbean, South and West Africa, South America, Canada, Taiwan, and Australia. He is well known for his sermons at the Mar Thomas Convention in India in February 1993. At this convention, Anderson preached a series of sermons to the 150,000 people who attended the convention. In 1976, Anderson was a member of a team of church leaders of Africa and African descent visiting nationalist China, and he also toured the Middle East, Europe, the South Pacific, Singapore, Chile, and Russia. In 1994, Anderson returned to Africa with a delegation of twenty-four church leaders on a solidarity journey to the Republic of South Africa and the kingdom of Swaziland. In 1995, Anderson led a delegation from the Washington Annual Conference (WAC) to the home of the Lubicon Cree Nation in Canada. He has also preached and lectured in all regions of the United States.

Becomes Involved in Community

During Anderson's twelve years in St. Louis, Missouri, he was known for his practical ways in ministering to the people of the community. His pastorate was inspired by a strong commitment to community development. Anderson wholeheartedly believed in social and educational welfare. To fulfill the needs of the people, Anderson developed an adult education program, created a summer youth program, promoted the first African American owned supermarket in St. Louis, developed 162 units of low-income housing in St. Louis County, and chaired Vanguard Bond and Mortgage Company—a company run by community funds. He was, of course, involved in the civil rights movement, advocating for social advancement of African Americans.

Despite his numerous religious involvements, Anderson found time for many community organizations. He was a member of the national census advisory committee on the black population for the 1990 census. Interested in ecology, he joined the Joint Appeal by Religion and Science for the Environment. Anderson was concerned about the whole man, and this led to his involvement in the national Commission on the School/Community Role in Improving Adolescent Health. He also had influence in education as he was a member of the Wilberforce University Board of Trustees, and he was the former chairperson of Payne Theological Seminary Board of Directors. His civil rights involvements included life membership in the NAACP, and he was a member of the St. Louis NAACP, labor industry committee. He also chaired the Urban League of Wichita, Kansas. Anderson was a life member of the Alpha Phi Alpha fraternity.

Anderson is celebrated globally as a writer and scholar. He wrote and edited many books, articles, and other publications. He wrote the script and delivered the Episcopal address for the 44th session of the General Conference of the African Methodist Episcopal Church. His most renowned work is *My Soul Shouts: The Spiritual Wisdom of Bishop Anderson*. Anderson was also instrumental in the development of the bicentennial edition of the AMEC hymnal and the first book of worship.

Receives High Honors

Many organizations have honored Anderson. He was recognized by the Historic Calendar in 1993. He received the Scroll of Merit Award from the National Medical

Association (1993), and the Daniel A. Payne Award for Ecumenical Leadership by AME Church (1992). Additionally, he received the American Black Achievement Awards (1991), and he was a distinguished alumni honoree of the National Association for Equal Opportunity in Higher Education (1988). A citation was published for Anderson in *Ebony* magazine, which gave him a religious award in 1988. His name appears in *Profiles in Black* under the heading, "100 Living Black Unsung Heroes," by Core (1976). He is listed in *Who's Who in America*, *Who's Who Among Black Americans*, *Who's Who in Religion*, and *Who's Who in the Caribbean*. Anderson made regular appearances in the media, but his two most memorable moments were on *Face the Nation* and *Tony Brown's Journal*.

Vivienne Louise Cholmondeley became Anderson's wife in 1952, and they produced four sons—Vinton Jr., Jeffrey, Carlton, and Kenneth. Anderson also has three grandchildren: Natina Louise, Carlton Jr., and Jordan Isaiah Anderson.

REFERENCES

Books

Phelps, Shirelle, ed. *Who's Who Among African Americans.* Detroit, Mich.: Gale Research, 1996.

Denise Jarrett

Chronology	
1863	Born in Haywood, in Chatham County, North Carolina, on June 11
1881?	Co-founds the North Carolina Negro Teachers Association
1884	Receives B.A. from St. Augustine's Normal and Collegiate Institute
1884-90	Heads the Grammar School Department at Livingstone College in Salisbury, North Carolina
1888-90	Serves dual role as business manager and head of Livingstone's grammar school
1889	Marries Oleona Pegram
1890	Edits the journal *The Southland*; becomes principal of Depot Street School
1891	Helps to settle Columbian Heights
1892	Moves to Columbian Heights; establishes Slater Industrial Academy
1904-13	Serves as full-time secretary of education for the African American Episcopal Zion Church; remains nominal head of Slater
1913	Returns to presidency of Slater (later Winston-Salem Teachers College)
1934	Resigns the presidency of Winston-Salem Teachers College and is named president emeritus; dies on June 28

Simon Green Atkins
1863–1934

Educator, college president

Simon Green Atkins distinguished himself in his home state of North Carolina as a teacher and advocate of teacher-training programs for African Americans. Doubtless his success was known beyond the state's boundaries, for he founded a small school that he developed into Winston-Salem Teachers College, a four-year institution, and oversaw its transition from private to state control. His abiding interest in teacher-training also led him to become a founder of the North Carolina Negro Teachers Association—an organization that served his race well, especially during racial imparity.

The oldest child of farmers and former slaves Allen and Eliza Atkins, Simon Green Atkins was born on June 11, 1863, in the village of Haywood, in Chatham County, North Carolina, between Sanford and Raleigh. His town flourished during the period just after the Revolutionary War, but by the late 1800s the railroad and the neighboring town of Moncure had overshadowed it. At one time the area was considered as a location for the state capital as well as the state university. As a child, Atkins worked on a farm with his parents.

Atkins studied in the town school under pioneer black educators who came from St. Augustine's Normal and Collegiate Institute (later St. Augustine's College in Raleigh). One of these was Anna Julia Cooper, later prominent for her work as an activist, scholar, feminist, and school administrator in Washington, D.C. This cadre of educators went out into remote communities to teach rural blacks. Atkins also taught at the town school for a while before his college years, and in 1880 he enrolled in St. Augustine's. He spent summers teaching in the rural schools of Chatham and Moore counties. After he graduated with distinction in 1884, renowned educator and orator Joseph Charles Price, president of Livingstone College, an African Methodist Episcopal Zion church-supported institution in Salisbury, North Carolina, invited Atkins to join his faculty. Atkins agreed and became grammar school department head. He spent six years at Livingstone (1884-90) and spent the last two years of his tenure there in the dual role as educator and treasurer of the college. During summer months he conducted institutes for black teachers in various counties.

The town educators of Winston (before its merger in 1913 with Salem to become Winston-Salem) lured Atkins to the post as principal of the Depot Street School, where he remained from 1890 to 1895. This was the state's largest public school for African Americans. His work with the North Carolina Negro Teachers' Association (NCNTA), which he helped to organize about 1881, had stimulated his interest in teacher-training schools for blacks. He directed this group as it established the foundation for a standard black teachers' college in the state. Soon after he began his duties at Depot Street, he intensified his efforts to build such a school for African Americans and sought assistance from the Winston Board of Trade, Chamber of Commerce, and local white residents. By then, the state had begun plans to fund an agricultural college for its African American residents; hearing this, Atkins sought funds to locate the new college in Winston. Local support for this move was good, as the black community donated $2,000, R. J. Reynolds of tobacco fame contributed $500, and Atkins obtained fifty acres of land along with the backing of the Chamber of Commerce. Although Atkins lobbied the state legislature in Raleigh on behalf of this plan, Winston and its residents lost out to nearby Greensboro, where citizens offered fourteen acres of land and $11,000.

Sets Foundation for Teacher College and Hospital

The town of Winston had become an industrial center. The black population lived in crowded conditions in rented facilities—conditions that Atkins found unhealthy. He also became an advocate of black home-ownership in the section of town known as Columbian Heights, which he helped to settle. After moving there in 1892, Atkins continued to work at Depot Street School. On September 28, 1892, Slater Industrial Academy was incorporated as a private entity with a board of trustees. To support the school he received funds from local businessmen as well as the Slater Fund established by New England textile mogul and philanthropist John F. Slater. Although Atkins became founding principal and president in 1892, classes at Slater school began in September 1893 with one teacher and twenty-five students who were housed in the one-room schoolhouse. Atkins resigned his post at Depot School in 1895 and concentrated on developing Slater. The school caught the state's attention, and in that year the state established a normal school for training teachers that was connected to Slater. The new entity was chartered in 1899 and incorporated as Slater Industrial and State Normal School of Winston-Salem, North Carolina. Atkins had more ideas for the school and in 1899 began efforts to establish a hospital and nurse training department. These efforts resulted in the Slater Hospital, the city's first such facility for blacks. The hospital had the support of tobacco mogul R. J. Reynolds and other white and black town residents. With matching funds from Reynolds and those that Atkins raised, Slater Hospital and Nurse Training Department formally opened at the school's commencement exercises on May 14, 1902.

In 1905 the state purchased Slater Industrial/Normal and the Board of Education took over the title as well as full control of the school; it became a part of North Carolina's public education system. State control meant that their work would advance, and they would be reorganized as a standard two-year normal school. At that time, all black normal schools were essentially high schools with teacher-training courses included in the curriculum. Over the years, the school grew in enrollment, faculty size, facilities, and in finances. The General Education Board and the Rosenwald Foundation provided support as well, to be used for a dormitory, schoolroom, and library equipment. The school graduated its first class in the standard two-year normal program in 1920—the first offered entirely above high school level. High school work was discontinued in 1923.

Atkins was on leave from the presidency of Slater from 1904 to 1913. When he returned, he continued to oversee its continuous growth. He had been sought out to head other black colleges as well. In 1896, for example, he was asked to head A&T College when its founding president retired. In 1916, he was offered the presidency of Livingstone College but chose to remain at the school he had founded. In 1925 the General Assembly issued the institution a new charter, as Winston-Salem Teachers College, and it began to offer a full four-year program leading to the bachelor of science degree, with a specific mission to train teachers, supervisors, and principals. It became the first black institution in the nation to grant degrees for teaching in the elementary grades. In 1963, the name was changed to Winston-Salem State College, and in 1969, the institution became Winston-Salem State University. In 1972, it became one of the sixteen constituent institutions of the University of North Carolina, subject to the control of the Board of Governors.

Atkins was a devoted member of the African Methodist Episcopal Zion (AMEZ) Church. His love for his church led him to leave the presidency of Slater from 1904 to 1913. He remained the school's nominal head until his official return in 1913. His work as secretary of education for the church for sixteen years and secretary of the church extension for four years involved extensive travel throughout the United States; he also represented the church at two international ecumenical conferences in London (1901 and 1921) and one in Toronto (1911). In a speech given before the 1901 conference, Atkins made clear the importance of industrial education. Quoted in Newbold's *Five North Carolina Negro Educators*, he said, "We want to educate the people for service rather than for success. We are not opposed to industrial education; we believe in it. We believe that the Negro's industrial opportunity in... [the United States] is very great, and he ought to be prepared for it." He also appealed to those at the conference, to Methodists in the United States, and "friends of suffering and struggling humanity everywhere, to antagonize the idea that the Negro is to be prepared only for a field hand. Let him be made a man, and everything else will take care of itself," he added.

Atkins extended his work into many arenas. While at Livingstone College he became editor of *The Southland*, a monthly magazine that Joseph C. Price founded; the first number appeared in February 1890. He was president and secretary of the NCNTA, with his last presidency ending in 1927. In the 1880s Atkins and Charles H. Hunter edited the organization's publication, *The Progressive Educator*. Before his term ended in 1927, he gave a presidential speech before the National Association of Teachers in Colored Schools, held at State College (later South Carolina State University) in Orangeburg. Among other educators of the 1880s whose work he praised in his speech, excerpted in Newbold's work, Atkins cited Joseph C. Price, whom he called "the greatest Negro apostle of higher education" and Booker T. Washington, whom he recognized as "the greatest Negro apostle of industrialism." Both were "benefactors of their race as well as patriots and friends of humanity," he said.

Atkins was recognized in the state and beyond. In 1926, North Carolina sent an exhibit to the Sesquicentennial held in Philadelphia. He was represented in the exhibit as one of the seven leading black educators who had done the most to advance the education of blacks over the preceding twenty-five years. Howard University in Washington, D.C. awarded him the doctor of laws degree in 1926. In addition to his work as educator, Atkins was a member of the American Academy of Social and Political Science, the American Statistical Association, and the American Negro Academy. In civic affairs he was instrumental in the founding of Forsyth Savings and Trust Company, Winston's first black bank initiated in 1905-06 and chartered in 1907. He was a member of the local YMCA and assisted in the sale of Liberty Bonds during World War I. For nine years he was a member of the Advisory Committee of the North Carolina Division of Negro Work, which was a part of the North Carolina State Board of Charities and Public Welfare. As a member of the North Carolina Interracial Commission, according to Simona Atkins Allen's biography of her grandfather, he wrote to T. J. Woofter Jr. of Vanderbilt University that the U.S. Supreme Court's decision in favor of integration on common carriers was "the result of our Interracial Commission in this State." Continuing in that letter, he said, "Negroes did not consider it any major achievement per se to ride the same bus with whites, but they were concerned about having an equal opportunity for better conditions in all phases of life."

Newbold's *Five North Carolina Negro Educators* described Atkins as "humble and unassuming" with irreproachable character. He was called "singularly modest and self-effacing" but spoke his mind when he found it appropriate. He was "honest, industrious, humble and yet aggressive and conservative." He knew that he had a mission to perform. Atkins was firm in his views on race. In his undated letter to Reverend Julius D. Dreher of Roanoke College in Salem, Virginia, cited in Newbold's work, he wrote, "It is not the 'Jim Crow' car that troubles me; it is the spirit of public sentiment which demands the 'Jim Crow' car." As cited further in Newbold's work, to his students he often gave his favorite motto: "self support, self respect, and self defense."

On September 3, 1889 Atkins married Oleona Pegram (1867-1936), who taught at Scotia Women's College (later Barber Scotia College) in Concord, North Carolina, and at the Slater school. She joined her husband in founding the institution at Winston-Salem and aided in its growth and development. Simon and Oleona Atkins had nine children—six sons (Russell Crowe; Harvey Bryan; Leland, who died early; Clarence Auter; Francis Loguen; and Jasper Alston) and three daughters (Miriam Atkins Hamblin; Olie Atkins Carpenter; and Eliza Atkins Gleason). Apparently Atkins' health was failing by the early 1930s. In 1934, he had an undisclosed but acute illness and resigned from his post at Winston-Salem. He was highly touted at the commencement exercises that year and elected president emeritus but was unable to attend the services. At that same meeting, the trustees elevated his son Francis L. Atkins, who had served as teacher, registrar, and dean at the school, to succeed his father as president beginning in 1934. After retirement, Atkins' health improved some, but he suffered a relapse and died in Winston-Salem on June 28, 1934, when he was seventy-one years old. He was buried in the local Evergreen Cemetery.

On June 11, 2005, the 142nd anniversary of his birth, the Chatham County Historical Association unveiled an historic marker near the school where Atkins received his early education. It was dedicated to Atkins in recognition of his achievements as educator and advocate of teacher training, college founder, and religious leader. The Depot Street School site has been named a state historical site. Simon G. Atkins Academic and Technology High School, which opened in 2005 as a part of the Winston-Salem/Forsyth County Schools, also carries his name and continues the tradition of excellence provided by the original Atkins High School which was dedicated on April 2, 1931 and later served as a middle school.

REFERENCES

Books

Atkins, S. G. "Should the Negro Be Given an Education Different from that Given to the Whites?" *Twentieth Century Negro Literature*. Ed. D. W. Culp. Naperville, Ill.: J. L. Nichols & Co., 1902.

Caldwell, Arthur Bunyan. *History of the American Negro*. North Carolina Edition. Vol. IV. Atlanta: A. B. Caldwell Publishing Co., 1921.

Gainor, Samuel M. "Simon Green Atkins." In *Dictionary of North Carolina Biography*. Vol. 1. Ed. William S. Powell. Chapel Hill: University of North Carolina Press, 1979.

Newbold, N. C. *Five North Carolina Negro Educators.* Chapel Hill: University of North Carolina Press, 1939.

Pamphlets

Allen, Simona Atkins. "Simon Green Atkins." Winston-Salem: Printed by the Winston-Salem/Forsyth County Schools, July 2005.

"Dedication Program for Simon G. Atkins Academic & Technology High School, Winston-Salem, North Carolina, Monday, October 24, 2005, 9:30 a.m. and Sunday, October 30, 2005, 3:00 p.m." Winston-Salem/Forsyth County Board of Education, 2005.

Online

"Dr. Simon G. Atkins." Presidents and Chancellors Gallery. http://www/wssu.edu/WSSU/About/Administration/Information%20Resources.C.G.%2o)Kelly%20Libr (Accessed 13 January 2006).

"Historical Marker Dedicated to Dr. Simon Green Atkins, Saturday, June 11." Chatham County Historical Association. http://www/chathamhistory.org/atkinsarchive.html (Accessed 8 February 2006).

Interviews

Allen, Simona Atkins. Telephone interviews with Jessie Carney Smith, February 21 and 27, 2006.

Collections

The papers of Simon Green Atkins are in the archives of the C. G. O'Kelly Library at Winston-Salem State University and in the Atkins Family Papers, in the family's possession.

Jessie Carney Smith

Alexander T. Augusta
1825–1890

Surgeon, physician, educator

Determined to become a medical doctor, Alexander T. Augusta moved to various cities in search of employment to support his dream, finally graduating from medical school in Toronto. He distinguished himself in all of his appointments. He was the first black commissioned and the highest black officer in the segregated U.S. Army, serving with the U.S. Colored Troops. He headed the old Freedmen's Hospital at Camp Barker,

---

Chronology

1825	Born in Norfolk, Virginia on March 8
1847	Marries Mary O. Burgoin
1856	Receives Bachelor of Medicine degree from University of Toronto
1863	Commissioned major in the U.S. Colored Troops, 7th U.S. Colored Infantry, U.S. Army; heads Freedmen's Hospital, becoming first black to head a hospital
1865	Assigned to Department of the South; brevetted a lieutenant colonel, U.S. Volunteers, the first black to hold that rank
1866	Musters out of army; opens private practice in Washington, D.C.
1868	Becomes first black teacher at any medical school in the United States
1871	Receives honorary M.A. degree from Howard University
1877	Reenters private practice
1890	Dies in Washington, D.C. on December 21
1896	Receives honorary degree of Medicinal Doctor from Howard University

---

where he was the first black in the country to direct a hospital. One of the original faculty members of the nearly all-white Howard University Medical Department, Alexander Augusta became the first African American faculty member of any medical school.

Alexander Thomas Augusta was born free in Norfolk, Virginia, on March 8, 1825. Although by Virginia law blacks were forbidden to read, Daniel Payne, later a bishop in the African Methodist Episcopal Church, taught Alexander the little reading that he knew early on. The young Augusta served as an apprentice with a local barber, where his reading was developed further, and then he moved to Baltimore where he worked as a journeyman barber. At the same time he studied medicine under private tutors. He relocated to Philadelphia, where he hoped to study medicine formally at the University of Pennsylvania's medical school. His inadequate preparation led the school to refuse Augusta admission. Then William Gibson, a professor in the school, took an interest in him and arranged to have the young man study in his office. Augusta's interest in formal medical study never waned.

Early Work in Toronto City Hospital

Augusta returned to Baltimore and on January 12, 1847, married Mary O. Burgoin, a woman of Huguenot descent, and the couple left for California. He worked in hopes of earning enough money to support his medical training but returned to Philadelphia three years later. A medical degree remained uppermost in his mind. Still later he moved to Canada, and in 1850 he was accepted into the Medical College of the University of Toronto. Six years later (1856), he received a B.M. degree from the university. The city took an immediate interest in him and acknowledged his expertise by placing him in charge of Toronto City Hospital and later in charge of an industrial school. In the meantime, Augusta set up private practice in Toronto. Sometime before 1860 he went to the West Indies and in 1861 returned to Baltimore and made a brief return to Toronto. Meanwhile, Augusta had become interested in the Union forces, the army's volunteer medical service, and in October 1862 he sought a post in that service.

When he was given a medical commission and appointed surgeon of the U.S. Colored Troops, U.S. Army, on April 14, 1863, Augusta had the rank of major. He was the first of eight black physicians commissioned and the highest ranking black officer in the segregated U.S. Army. Augusta was sent to the 7th U.S. Colored Infantry and joined them in garrison at Camp Stanton, near Bryantown, Maryland. White officers, who were also surgeons, complained because they were subordinate to a black officer, causing him to be transferred to what became known as Freedmen's Hospital, at the site of Camp Barker near Washington, D.C. There he became the first black to head any hospital in the United States. (This location was a different site from the Freedmen's Hospital of later times.)

Racism in the U.S. Army

During the Civil War, thousands of escaped slaves settled in Washington, D.C., and lived in overcrowded, filthy quarters. Disease was rampant. Although the federal government built new hospitals and enlarged others, sick freedmen were treated at Camp Barker in the fall of 1863, where Alexander was in charge. The War Department continued to direct the hospital until 1865, when it came under the auspices of the newly created Freedmen's Bureau. Later on, the Freedmen's Hospital was established on a permanent basis and erected on the campus of Howard University. Alexander remained at Freedmen's from autumn 1863 to spring 1864. In that time he examined black recruits at Benedict and Baltimore, Maryland. Yet racism followed him. For example, the army paymaster initially paid him at the same rate that was provided for enlisted men after their clothing deduction: $7 a month. However, Senator Henry Wilson of Massachusetts heard Augusta's complaint, wrote to the secretary of war about the matter, and two days later the paymaster general was ordered to compensate the surgeon according to his rank.

In 1865 and 1866, Augusta was assigned to the Department of the South. For his meritorious service, in March 1865 he was promoted to lieutenant colonel in the U.S. Volunteers, becoming the first black to hold that rank. While on a lengthy tour of duty, he headed a hospital in Savannah, Georgia. Many black casualties of the Civil War resulted from the hesitancy of the U.S. Army to arm these soldiers in the first place. The excessive casualty rate of the colored troops was also due to the lack of med-

ical care that they received. White surgeons resisted serving with black troops and were reluctant to treat ailing black soldiers. Of the eight black physicians who were appointed surgeons in the army, seven were attached to hospitals in the Washington, D.C. area. These included Charles B. Purvis and John Rapier. John V. De Grasse had only a brief stint with the 35th U.S. Colored Infantry, as assistant surgeon. In *The History of the Negro in Medicine*, Herbert M. Morais writes: "Of this small band of doctors in blue, the most illustrious was Alexander T. Augusta." Augusta mustered out of service on October 13, 1866, and returned to Washington, D.C., where he opened private practice.

Augusta's prominence in the field of medicine was acknowledged in 1868, when the newly organized Medical Department at Howard University elected him demonstrator of anatomy, making him the first black to be offered a teaching position at any medical school in the United States. In what was called the Panic of 1893, a time of severe financial difficulties at the medical school, the medical faculty faced the dilemma of resigning or having their salaries cut in half. Some resigned, but Augusta, Purvis, and Gideon Stimson Palmer remained. Augusta continued on the faculty until September 14, 1877, holding a succession of professorships in anatomy while serving on the staff of Freedmen's Hospital. The school reorganized and wanted to move Augusta from the head of the Anatomy Department to chair of Materia Medica. Augusta declined the new appointment and was terminated. He reentered private practice in 1877.

Honors Come Slowly

On June 9, 1879, Augusta and Purvis were proposed for membership in the Medical Society of the District of Columbia, an affiliate of the American Medical Association. On June 23, Dr. A. W. Tucker's name was added to the list. All of the men were rejected. On February 8, 1870, Senator Charles Sumner of Massachusetts introduced a bill in the U.S. Senate to repeal the charter of the Medical Society of the District of Columbia because it worked against black practitioners and was guilty of discriminatory practices. The bill was unsuccessful, and the fight continued. Blacks, however, on January 15, 1870, formed their own National Medical Society of the District of Columbia and accepted whites into membership. The fight to integrate the local white medical society continued for many years; eventually the local society revised its regulations and allowed consultations with black physicians.

Howard University recognized its star medical school faculty on June 27, 1871, when it awarded honorary M.A. degrees to Augusta, Purvis, and Robert Reyburn. Augusta also received an honorary degree of Medicinal Doctor on June 30, 1896. In honor of the noted surgeon and educator, in 1913 doctors Simeon L. Carson, B. Price Hurst, Peter M. Murray, and E. A. Robinson formed the

Alexander T. Augusta Medical Reading Club; it grew to a maximum of twelve but ceased to exist around 1940 due to the deaths of several members.

Augusta, a quiet, slender, and handsome man, died at his home, 1319 L Street, NW, Washington, D.C., on December 21, 1890. After the funeral at St. John's Episcopal Church at Lafayette Square, held on December 24, his body was buried in Arlington National Cemetery. Augusta is remembered as a pioneer black surgeon, medical school professor, and practicing physician who persevered against odds early on and obtained a medical school degree and broke racial barriers in the military, in hospital administration, and in medical education.

REFERENCES

Books

Green, Constance McLaughlin. "Alexander Thomas Augusta." In *Dictionary of American Negro Biography.* Ed. Rayford W. Logan and Michael R. Winston. New York: Norton, 1982.

Logan, Rayford W. *Howard University: The First Hundred Years, 1867-1967.* New York: New York University Press; issued under the auspices of Howard University, 1969.

Morais, Herbert M. *The History of the Negro in Medicine.* International Library of Negro Life and History. New York: Publishers Company, Inc., issued under the auspices of the Association for the Study of Negro Life and History, 1967.

Periodicals

Cobb, W. Montague. "Alexander Thomas Augusta." *Journal of the National Medical Association* 44 (July 1952): 327-29.

Jessie Carney Smith

Houston A. Baker, Jr.
1943–

Literary critic, editor, poet, educator

During the last quarter of the twentieth century, Houston A. Baker Jr. gained national and international prominence as a literary critic and scholar. Decades after the publication of his first book in 1972, Baker continues to play pivotal roles in the advancement of African American literature and culture as critic, editor, poet, and university professor.

Baker was born on March 22, 1943 in Louisville, Kentucky; he was the second of three sons born to Houston Alfred Baker Sr., a hospital administrator and businessman, and his wife, Viola Elizabeth Smith Baker, an English teacher. In *Turning South Again* (2001), the renown critic writes that his father emphasized the importance of culture during his son's formative years; they were exposed to classical music, theater, and books. The Baker children received a dime for every book they read and a quarter for each written book report. Houston A. Baker Jr. was not the first member of his family to earn advanced degrees. His father earned a graduate degree in hospital administration from Northwestern University as well as an MBA from the University of Pennsylvania's Wharton School of Business (1938), and his mother earned an MA from Indiana University.

After graduating from the predominantly white male high school in Louisville, Baker attended Howard University where he earned a BA in English literature (magna cum laude, Phi Beta Kappa) in 1965. One year later, Baker received an MA from the University of California at Los Angeles (UCLA). He then completed a year of doctoral studies at the University of Edinburgh in Scotland (1967-68) before he returned to UCLA where he was awarded a PhD in 1968.

Distinguished Career as Educator

His distinguished career as an educator began at Howard University, his undergraduate alma mater, where Baker was an instructor in English during the summer of 1966. Then from 1968 to 1969, he was an instructor in

Chronology	
1943	Born in Louisville, Kentucky on March 22
1965	Receives B.S. (magna cum laude, Phi Beta Kappa) from Howard University
1966	Completes M.A. at the University of California at Los Angeles; teaches at Howard University during the summer
1967	Begins one year of doctoral work at the University of Edinburgh, Edinburgh, Scotland
1968	Earns Ph.D. at the University of California at Los Angeles; accepts a teaching position at Yale University
1970	Joins the faculty of the University of Virginia
1971	Edits his first book, *Black Literature in America*
1972	Publishes his first book of literary criticism, *Long Black Song: Essays in Black American Literature and Culture*
1974	Holds dual appointments at the University of Pennsylvania as the director of the Afro-American Studies Program as well as a professor of English
1976-78	Serves as a delegate for the United States Delegation of Five to the First Conference on Literature and National Consciousness (Moscow)
1979	Publishes his first book of poetry, *No Matter Where You Travel, You Still Be Black*
1988	Receives his first honorary doctorate (Berea College)
1992	Becomes the first African American president of the Modern Language Association
1999	Joins faculty of Duke University where he is the Susan Fox and George D. Beisher Professor of English and African and African American Studies
2000	Assumes editorship of *American Literature*

English at Yale University. The next year, Baker was appointed for a four-year term as assistant professor in English at Yale, but he left in 1970 in order to accept the positions of associate professor and member of the Center for Advanced Studies at the University of Virginia (1970-73) and then professor of English (1973-74). During the early 1970s, Baker, an expert in British Victorian literature, began to focus on African American literature and culture. Consequently when he joined the University of Pennsylvania faculty as a professor of English in 1974, he was appointed as the first director of the University's Afro-American Studies Program, a position he held until 1977. During his tenure at the University of Pennsylvania, Baker was a member of the Graduate Group in Comparative Literature and Literary Theory (1979-82 and 1988), the Albert M. Greenfield Professor of Human Relations (1982), and the director for the Center for the Study of Black Literature and Culture (1982). Since 1999, Baker has taught at Duke University where he is the Susan Fox and George D. Beisher Professor of English and African and African American Studies.

A National Phi Beta Kappa Visiting Scholar (1975-76), Baker has held visiting professorships at such institutions as Cornell University (1977 and 1988), Tougaloo College (1980), Haverford College (1983-85), Colgate University (1991), the University of Vermont (1992), and New York University (1994). He has lectured at more than sixty institutions of higher learning, including George Mason University, Cornell University, Purdue University, Yale University, Fisk University, Brown University, Morgan State University, Morehouse College, Stanford University, Princeton University, and Howard University. Baker has conducted seminars and lectured in such foreign locales as Moscow (1976-78), Nigeria (1990), Belgium (1991), and Ottawa (1994).

Exceptional Service to Academe

Baker's influence extends beyond university classrooms and lecture halls. In 1992, he served as president of the Modern Language Association (MLA); Baker was the first African American elected to head the influential organization of more than 30,000 members that was founded in 1883. Baker is editor of *American Literature,* the journal founded at Duke University in 1929 that is considered as the preeminent periodical in American literary studies. His inaugural issue (June, 2000) was entitled "Unsettling Blackness." In the Preface, Baker asserts that after the Integrationist, Black Aesthetic, and Reconstructionist/High Vernacular analyses of the last twenty-five years of the twentieth century, "Unsettling Blackness" heralds a "fourth critical position— . . .[one that] reads modernism, progressivism, architecture, avant-gardism, montage, hybridity, anxiety of influence, and continental theory through African American texts and authors thought by some of us-in an earlier day . . . —to be merely black."

Scholarly and Creative Achievements

Although Baker's work with the MLA and *American Literature* are remarkable achievements, he is best known as a prolific literary critic. He has written more than 90 articles, essays, and reviews, as well as authored or edited more than 20 books. In books such as *Long Black Song* (1972), *Afro-American Poetics* (1988), *Workings of the Spirit* (1991), *Critical Memory* (2001), and *Turning South Again* (2001), Baker analyzes the works of writers such as James Baldwin, Imamu Baraka, Countee Cullen, W. E. B. Du Bois, Frederick Douglass, Ralph Ellison, Frances E. W. Harper, Pauline Hopkins, Zora

Neale Hurston, Harriet Jacobs, Toni Morrison, Jean Toomer, Booker T. Washington, and Richard Wright. Baker is also a poet, and his volumes of poetry include *No Matter Where You Travel, You Still Be Black* (1979), *Spirit Run* (1982), *Blues Journeys Home* (1985), and *Passing Over* (2000).

Awards

Among Baker's many honors are Competitive Scholarship, Howard University (1961-65); Kappa Delta Phi, Howard University (1965); John Hay Whitney Foundation Fellow (1965-66); NDEA Fellow, UCA (1965-68); Alfred Longueil Poetry Award, UCA (1966); Legion of Honor, Chapel of the Four Chaplains, Philadelphia Community Service Award (1981); Christian R. and Mary F. Lindback Foundation Award for Distinguished Teaching, University of Pennsylvania (1984); Alumni Award for Distinguished Achievement in Literature and the Humanities, Howard University (1985); Outstanding Alumnus Award of Howard University, Alumni Club of Greater Philadelphia (1985); Distinguished Writer of the Year, Middle-Atlantic Writers Association (1986); Creative Scholarship Award, College Language Association for *Afro-American Poetics* (1988); and Pennsylvania Governor's Award for Excellence in the Humanities (1990). He is the recipient of fellowships such as the John Simon Guggenheim (1978-79); National Humanities Center (1982-83); Rockefeller Research Fellowship Program for Minority Group Scholars (1982-83); and Council of the Humanities (Princeton), Whitney J. Oates Short-term Fellow (1991-92). Baker's honorary doctorates include Berea College (1988),Williams College (1989), Beaver College (1990), Ursinus College (1990), State University of New York at Albany (1991), Knox College (1992), Marymount Manhattan College (1993), and the University of Louisville (1994). An additional honor was bestowed upon Baker when a special issue of *Chung Wai,* was devoted to the "Work of Houston A. Baker Jr." (November, 1993).

Houston Baker is married to Charlotte-Pierce Baker, a professor of Women's Studies and English at Duke University and whose publications include *Surviving the Silence: Black Women's Stories of Rape*(1998), and two works co-written with her husband: *Renewal* (1977), a volume of African American poetry; and "Patches: Quilts and Community in Alice Walker's 'Everyday Use,'" an article that was published in the *Southern Review* (Summer 1985). The couple has one son, Mark Frederick Baker, who during his undergraduate years at the University of Pennsylvania founded the African American Arts Alliance, an organization that promotes Black cultural awareness via African American theater.

For three decades, Houston A. Baker Jr. has reigned as one of the most prolific and eloquent voices in African American arts and letters. Thus expectations are high for his continued, significant contributions to African American literature and culture.

REFERENCES

Books

Awkward, Michael. "Houston A. Baker Jr." In *Oxford Companion to African-American Literature*. Eds. William L. Andrews, Frances Smith Foster, and Trudier Harris. New York: Oxford University Press, 1997.

Jeffords, Susan. "Houston A. Baker Jr." In *Dictionary of Literary Biography, Vol. 67: Modern American Critics Since 1955*. Ed. Gregory S. Jay. Detroit, Mich.: Gale, 1988.

Periodicals

Berube, Michael. "Hybridity in the Center: An Interview with Houston A. Baker Jr." *African American Review* 26 (Winter 1992): 547-64.

Online

Eakin, Emily. "Black Captive in a White Culture?" "http://www.racematters.org/blackcaptivewhiteculture.htm (Accessed 25 January 2005).

"Houston A. Baker, Jr." *Contemporary Black Biography* 6 (1994). Reproduced in *Biography Resource Center*. Farmington Hills, Mich.: Thomson Gale, 2005. http://galenet.galegroup.com/servlet/BioRC (Accessed 17 February 2005).

Linda M. Carter

Edward M. Bannister
c. 1826–1901

Artist, painter, photographer

Edward Mitchell Bannister is widely thought to be the only prominent African American artist of the late nineteenth century to develop his talents without the benefit of European exposure. But during his lifetime his work was excluded from major museum collections, and it received neither public nor critical comment. Bannister's work was rediscovered in the late twentieth century.

Bannister was born between 1826 and 1828 in St. Andrews, a tiny seaport on the Atlantic Ocean at the mouth of the St. Croix River in New Brunswick, Canada. His father, who may have been a native of Barbados, West Indies, died early in Bannister's life. The racial

Chronology

c. 1826	Born in St. Andrews, New Brunswick, Canada
1848-50	Works on ships around New Brunswick; moves to Boston
1850	Listed as hairdresser in Boston census
1854	Receives first painting commission
1857	Marries Christiana Carteaux on June 10
1858	Declares profession as artist and portrait painter
1859-60	Lives in the home of Lewis Hayden, a stop on the Underground Railroad and gathering place for abolitionist leaders
1862	Studies photography in New York
1869	Moves to Providence, Rhode Island; becomes recognized in artistic community and gains several patrons
1876	Wins first prize at Philadelphia Centennial Exposition
1878	Forms what would later become the Providence Art Club
1879	Becomes a regular contributor to Boston Art Club exhibitions; exhibits painting at National Academy of Design, New York
1890	Teaches weekly art classes to children of wealthy Rhode Island families
1891	Exhibits thirty-three paintings at Providence Art Club, to much acclaim
1899	Returns to Boston
1901	Dies in Boston on January 9

identity of Bannister's mother, Hannah Alexander Bannister, is not known. Throughout his life, Bannister credited her with fostering his earliest artistic interests. After his mother's death in 1844, Bannister and his younger brother William were sent to live and work on the nearby farm of Harris Hatch, a prominent and wealthy white lawyer from Boston. As was customary for young men in St. Andrews, Bannister then worked on ships along the coast of New Brunswick during the late 1840s.

Pursues Painting and Abolitionism in Boston

Bannister and his brother moved to Boston before 1850. Bannister's decision to move was pivotal; the city was a national center for both white and black abolitionist activity in the United States, and its African American community represented the third-largest population of free blacks in the northeast. Additionally, the city was known as a center for intellectual and artistic achievement. That said, African Americans in Boston were still relegated to separate neighborhoods, churches, public transport, and segregated in many public institutions. Pro- and anti-slavery tensions created an often dangerous racial climate.

Unable to find an apprenticeship with an established artist, Bannister held a variety of menial jobs before becoming a hairdresser. Denied the academic tutelage, studio apprenticeships, and foreign travel that were the training stages for white American artists, Bannister developed independently. He learned from visits to Boston museums and by fraternizing with other young artists. Few of Bannister's paintings from the 1850s and 1860s have survived, so an assessment of his early period in Boston is difficult. It is known, however, that for his first ten years in Boston, he advertised himself as a portrait painter.

Bannister must have seen and been influenced by the landscape paintings of William Morris Hunt who had studied in Europe, had been inspired by the Barbizon School, and held numerous public exhibitions in Boston during the 1860s. American landscape painters of the time were increasingly aware of the simple rustic motifs and pictorial poetry of French Barbizon paintings by Jean-Baptiste Corot, Jean-Francois Millet, and Charles Francois Daubigny in the mid-nineteenth century. Bannister was no exception; his landscapes make up the largest portion of his body of work.

In Boston, Bannister fell in with a group of African Americans who were active in the fight against slavery. These abolitionists were the same people that were most supportive of Bannister's painting, giving him financial support and artistic recognition. He was friends with fellow artist William H. Simpson and lawyer George L. Ruffin, sang with the Crispus Attucks Choir, and joined the African American Histrionic Club, which performed dramatic selections around Boston and satirical farces at political meetings. He lived for two years (1859-60) in the home of Lewis Hayden, a black activist. Hayden's house was a stop on the Underground Railroad. Bannister also was recording secretary for the abolitionist group Colored Citizens of Boston and, later, the Union Progressive Association (UPA). It was with the UPA that Bannister participated in the most historic event for African Americans of that era. He was present with the organization when President Abraham Lincoln released the Emancipation Proclamation freeing the slaves on January 1, 1863.

Begins Earning Commissions and Reviews

In 1853, Bannister found work with Madame Christiana Carteaux, a successful black businesswoman who owned a string of beauty salons in Boston and Providence, Rhode Island. Carteaux was a Narragansett Indian who was born in North Kingston, Rhode Island. In 1854, Bannister received his first commission for an oil painting, from a prominent African American doctor in Boston. "The Ship Outward Bound" was the first of Bannister's many seascapes, inspired, no doubt, by countless hours spent sketching along the Rhode Island coast and at Boston's harbor. Bannister married Carteaux on June 10, 1857. In 1858, with her financial support, he began painting full time. She also gave Bannister excellent critical guidance. Sometime around 1862, Bannister spent a year studying photography in New York City. For several years, he listed his profession as photographer, and likely shot portraits to earn extra money.

Around 1863, Bannister began to make headway in the white artist community and was finally able to study formally. He was the only African American artist in the evening drawing classes of Dr. William Rimmer. By 1864, Bannister was able to acquire space in the Studio Building, where he worked alongside other Boston artists. In 1866, his name began appearing in Boston art reviews.

Christiana's family and business ties in Rhode Island likely led to the couple's move to Providence by October 1869. Increasing racial tensions in Boston may have also been a factor. Providence and nearby Newport were thriving arts communities, replete with a host of wealthy, supportive patrons. Within five years of the couple's moving there, one of Bannister's paintings, "Under the Oaks," was accepted in the Philadelphia Centennial Exposition of 1876, and was selected for the first-prize bronze medal. The judges, after discovering that Bannister was African American, became indignant and wanted to reconsider the award. Bannister's white competitors, however, supported Bannister and he was awarded the medal.

Enjoys Success in Providence

Bannister's reputation grew in Rhode Island, and he received numerous commissions. He produced many landscapes, most of which depict quiet, bucolic scenes rendered in somber tones and thick impasto. Bannister's landscapes of the 1870s were painted with less detail and with heavier impasto. They evoke a tranquil mood that became one of the hallmarks of Bannister's style. Landscapes of the 1880s and 1890s employed a lighter impasto and loosely applied, broken color that suggest impressionist influences. Picturesque motifs including cottages, castles, cattle, dawns, sunsets, and small bodies of water were featured frequently in Bannister's works; he portrayed nature as a calm and submissive force. Interestingly, Bannister's paintings reflect no social or racial themes, and the small figures seen frequently in his landscapes appear to be white. Although the majority of Bannister's paintings are landscapes, he also painted portraits, figure studies, religious scenes, seascapes, and still lifes.

By 1878, Bannister was a founding board member for the Rhode Island School of Design. He also helped form what was to become the Providence Art Club in order to bring together artists, art lovers, and patrons. Bannister exhibited in the club's annual spring and fall shows. He became a regular contributor to Boston Art Club exhibitions, and showed his work at New York's National Academy of Design. He enjoyed the support of many local patrons, including prominent white businessmen, and began teaching weekly art classes to the children of wealthy Rhode Island families. Regular summer trips on his sloop yacht, *Fanchon*, influenced Bannister's later, dramatic seascapes.

In 1891, Bannister mounted the largest exhibition of his works, thirty-three paintings, at the Providence Art

Club. The show was a retrospective, as it included works from as far back as 1869. After the show, Bannister's output seems to have diminished. The quality of his work from this period remained high, but either lack of exhibition opportunities or age slowed him down. In the late 1880s, the Providence Art Club had begun to display works featuring racist images, which were still acceptable to many white art lovers. This, too, may have inhibited Bannister from creating more work.

Rediscovered in Twentieth Century

Bannister died on January 9, 1901, while attending a prayer meeting at his church. Shortly after his death, the Providence Art Club mounted a memorial exhibition of 101 of Bannister's paintings owned by Providence collectors. Christiana Bannister died, penniless, two years after her husband's death. The couple had no children, and there was no one left in the family to promote interest in Bannister's work.

Some of Bannister's paintings have appeared in museum exhibitions, in particular the Rhode Island School of Design (1966, 1986) and the Newport Art Museum (1991). But Bannister's work was long overlooked by scholars and curators because his paintings looked murky when reproduced in photos. However, Bannister's papers piqued the interest of a contemporary Providence Art Club member, and New York's Kenkelaba House Museum received funds to research and create a Bannister exhibition in 1989. Some of his works are housed in the collection of African American universities, and more than 100 of his paintings and works on paper are held by the National Museum of American Art in Washington, D.C. But the whereabouts of many of his works is unknown.

Bannister's grave in North Burial Ground, Providence, is marked by a rough granite boulder ten feet high bearing a carving of a palette with the artist's name and a pipe.

REFERENCES

Books

Holland, Juanita Marie. *Edward Mitchell Bannister.* New York: Whitney Museum of Art, 1992.

Periodicals

Kinzer, Stephen. "A Struggle to Be Seen." *New York Times*, 22 February 2001.

Online

"About Edward Mitchell Bannister." http://www.ric.edu/bannister/BannisterBio.html (Accessed 23 March 2005).

Brenna Sanchez

Dean P. Baquet
1956–

Journalist, newspaper editor

Dean P. Baquet moved up in rank in journalism from part-time reporter for an afternoon newspaper in New Orleans to a prized post with a major newspaper. He took the helm of the *Los Angeles Times* in October 2005, becoming the first African American journalist to lead a top newspaper in the United States. In the interim, however, he had made a name for himself with two other well-known newspapers, the *Chicago Tribune* and the *New York Times*.

Born in New Orleans in 1956, Dean P. Baquet was the fourth of five brothers who were raised in one of that city's working class neighborhoods. He had a part-time job early in life, cleaning his parents' Creole restaurant called Eddie's. The family lived in the back part of the building that housed their restaurant. At first the father worked as a mail carrier, but he gave up that job to open his own business. Dean Baquet took his first trip out of New Orleans when he left to study English at Columbia University; he became so homesick that he returned to New Orleans and, after his sophomore year, held an internship post for the city's afternoon newspaper, the *States-Item*. Soon Baquet fell in love with his job. Rather than complete his studies at Columbia, Baquet took a full-time job as reporter, promising Columbia that he would transfer to Tulane University in New Orleans. He soon gave up formal training.

Baquet's assignment with the *States-Item*, which the *Times Picayune* subsumed later on, was to cover news items related to the police force, the courts, and city hall. Later, he began what would become a triumphant career—investigative reporting. Baquet watched his older brother die after years of heavy drinking and smoking. Baquet believes that his writing about people he knew in New Orleans when he began his career contributed to his brother's death. Also, corruption stories he wrote upset a local black political group to the extent that it boycotted his father's restaurant. Writing about people and places where he lived was difficult for Baquet; he had trouble separating the good guys from the bad, writing about them fairly, and then seeing them face-to-face the next day.

After seven years with the New Orleans press, Baquet moved to the *Chicago Tribune* in 1984, where he later became associate metropolitan editor for investigations. As chief investigative reporter, in 1988 Baquet led a team of three reporters that documented corruption in the Chicago City Council. According to an article on *LAObserved*, the team wrote stories on "the self-interest and waste that plagued Chicago's City Council," and for that

Dean P. Baquet

Chronology	
1956	Born in New Orleans, Louisiana
1984	Becomes associate metropolitan editor for the *Chicago Tribune*
1988	Shares Pulitzer Prize with teammate
1990	Becomes investigative reporter for the *New York Times*
1995	Becomes national editor for the *New York Times*
2000	Moves to *Los Angeles Times* as managing editor
2005	Becomes first African American editor of a major newspaper, the *Los Angeles Times*

Becomes First Black to Head a Major Newspaper

Baquet was given the number two spot at the *Los Angeles Times*—that of managing editor. Over a five-year period, he and Carroll made major changes, replacing fourteen editors on the paper's masthead. The Orange County bureau was significantly scaled back because, as Baquet told the *New Yorker*, "it was marketing; it wasn't journalism." Company officials pressed Carroll and Baquet to republish stories from other papers that the Tribune Company owned; they resisted, asserting that, if decisions on articles that they published were written elsewhere, they would become a second-tier paper. By then, the Tribune Company had also acquired the family-owned *Times*. Baquet worked with Carroll to restore the broadsheet and help it receive thirteen Pulitzer prizes. One was a Pulitzer gold medal for public service, having published a series on the Martin Luther King Jr./Drew Medical Center, uncovering dangerous conditions for patients at the center. The series singled out the hospital's management team, which was African American. African American community leaders in Los Angeles denounced the prize.

Such honors that the paper received continued to challenge Baquet, up to and through his appointment in October 2005 as editor of the *Los Angeles Times*. Baquet knew that he had to satisfy profit demands and enhance the paper as well. "I'd like the paper to have more of a sense of California," he told Rachel Smolkin for *AJR*. "We have as strong a sense of place here as any paper in America." Located in the center of Hollywood, where books and movies are inspired, it follows, according to Baquet, that the paper should do the right thing and have California represented more fully within its pages. This innovation called for improvements in the coverage of the entertainment industry, greater coverage of metropolitan Los Angeles, and daily stories of interest. While more resources were needed to support his vision, he said, "You identify some of the writers who can wander around and . . . come up with stories that surprise people, and you let them loose and get out of their hair." As much as he wants to find new readers, Baquet is opposed to committing a "youth spinoff" and to endorsing the new

project Baquet and Ann Marie Lipinski shared a Pulitzer Prize in 1988.

Leading newspapers continued to take notice of Baquet's work in investigative reporting. He left the *Chicago Tribune* in 1990 and became an investigative reporter for the *New York Times*. He despised his job the first year but liked it later on. He told the *New Yorker* that he had no aspiration to become an editor. Baquet began his work with the *New York Times* as deputy metro editor. He concentrated on investigations in New York and in Washington, D.C. During this time, he and another reporter were finalists for the Pulitzer Prize for the series of stories that they wrote about poor care that patients received in New York City's hospitals. In 1995, Baquet was named national editor. Although he had succeeded at the paper and had a promising career there (there are claims that he might have later headed the *New York Times*), John S. Carroll, editor of the *Los Angeles Times*, lured Baquet away. Shortly after joining that paper in 2000, Carroll persuaded Baquet to move his wife Dylan and their ten-year-old son to Los Angeles. But his persuasion was apparently not difficult, for Baquet believed that he could make a greater contribution in journalism by working in Los Angeles than in New York. As well, his vision was "to make the West Coast *Times* edgier and more focused on investigative work," he told Rachel Smolkin for *AJR*.

mantra of giving young readers the information that they want rather than what editors view as significant.

Carroll and Baquet demonstrated mutual trust and respect for each other's opinions, whether or not their opinions differed. They were journalists whose divergent styles and backgrounds were a cool contrast that meshed well. However, they failed to improve the corporate relationship and to remove the cloud that hung over the paper. In 2003, when Carroll and the *Tribune* office disagreed over mandatory newsroom cuts, Baquet considered leaving the paper. In spring 2005, the Tribune Company wanted Carroll to cut the staff again; Carroll saw the move as an "annual thing." He had seen newsroom cuts and layoffs, attrition, buyouts—altogether a loss of nearly two hundred employees. Such cuts were among the disagreements between Carroll and the company that resulted in Carroll's decision to leave and Baquet's threat to follow. But Baquet was concerned that he and Carroll could have been responsible for the fractious relationship with the Tribune Company. After Carroll announced his retirement to his staff in October 2005, Baquet assured workers of his continuing interest in the paper's future. "I'm taking over one of the best newspapers in America at the top of its game in a city I care about, succeeding somebody who's a close friend," he told *AJR*. He knew that all newspapers are now under great budget pressure, but he said that he "wouldn't be doing this if [he] didn't think [he] could still make the paper better." Baquet liked the paper's hard-hitting stories and those that were beautifully written. His dream was for the *Times* to become the country's best newspaper. He made one immediate organizational change: the editorial and opinion papers would now report to the publisher rather than the editor.

As Carroll bowed out, Orville Schell, dean of the graduate school at the University of California, Berkeley, told Robertson and Smolkin that Baquet was challenged to maintain the *Los Angeles Times* "true to the distinguished journalistic traditions he and Carroll share." He called Baquet "a very good editor" who would "have his hands full to keep the *L.A. Times* a great paper as well as a paper that makes a lot of money, or makes enough money."

Baquet expressed his intention to become a better leader in the newsroom, where budget cuts had an impact on size of staff and where communication has been lax. In April 2001, while still with the *New York Times*, he told a panel for the American Society of Newspaper Editors (ASNE), cited by Cicely K. Dyson, that newsroom staffs should "be honest and open. Let them [the newspaper editors] know when you disagree with the budget and other cuts." While all panelists expressed concern for the lack of communication with their writers, Baquet's advice was that "Senior editors don't talk to reporters any more. . . . They should sit in on meetings and let their colleagues know they care." He was concerned that editors may ignore ideas that reporters find exciting when they should take time to listen to the enthusiasm that the reporter has for a story.

Baquet's closest friend in New York, Martin Gottlieb, the *New York Times*'s associate managing editor, told the *New Yorker* that Baquet "has enormous empathy for people"; he attributed this to Baquet's having a close-knit family. Baquet has been spotlighted in his role as new editor of the *Los Angeles Times*. A man filled with energy, enthusiasm, a whirlwind of ideas, and an intense passion for his craft, he is poised to raise the paper to new levels of success.

REFERENCES

Periodicals

Auletta, Ken. "Faule Line." *New Yorker* (10 October 2005): 51-61.

Online

"Baquet Era Begins." *LAObserved*. http://www.laobserved.com/archive/2005/07/baquet_era_begi.html (Accessed 28 October 2005).

Dyson, Cicely K. "In Your Journalism Career, Who Has Been An inspiration?" asne reporter 2. http://www.asne.org/2001reporter/wednesday/barrier4.html (Accessed 28 October 2005.)

E & P Staff. "Auletta Details *LATimes/Tribune* Rift in Major Article." *Editor & Publisher*. http://www.editorandpublisher.com/eandp/news/article_display.jsp?vnu_content_id=100. (Accessed 28 October 2005).

Smolkin, Rachel. "Nothing but Fans." *AJR*. http://www.ajr.org/Article.asp?id=3912 (Accessed 28 October 2005).

Jessie Carney Smith

John Pembroke Barton
1845–?

Minister, evangelist

In order to foster a greater sense of community John Pembroke Barton organized church groups and other organizations to support ideas and promote positive change. As an active member of the Baptist church, he organized the first District Sunday School and the first State Sunday School Convention. After being ordained as a minister, he organized the first Woman's Missionary State Convention in Alabama. Barton's insight and planning laid the foundation for these key institutions in the

Chronology

1845	Born in Franklin County, Alabama on November 27
1861	Leaves slave home
1863	Learns from R. F. Dyer, surgeon in 104th Il. Infantry
1872-79	Clerks for Baptist Association
1874	Organizes first colored District Sunday School in U.S. at Tuscumbia, Alabama
1875	Marries Ruth Ann Jacobs
1877	Ordained as a minister
1886	Organizes first Woman's Missionary State Convention in Alabama
1892	Graduates from Theological Department, Talladega College
1894	Organizes first U.S. State Sunday School Convention at Union Springs, Alabama
1900	Receives divinity degree from Guadalupe College, Seguin, Texas; completes course in therapeutics at Weltner Institute, Nevada, Missouri

African American community. Guided by his interest in therapeutic healing Barton amassed a comfortable fortune. He was able to provide care to as many as ten thousand persons.

Born on November 27, 1845 in Franklin County, Alabama, John Pembroke Barton spent his early years in slavery. With the outbreak of the Civil War, Barton ran off from his master and traveled the Union line. In 1863 he received instruction from Dr. R. F. Dyer, a surgeon in the 104th Illinois Infantry. After the Civil War came to a close in 1866, Barton purchased a home in Johnsonville, Tennessee, but later he returned to his birthplace in Alabama to farm. He was baptized in 1871 in the Little Zion Baptist Church by Reverend W. E. Northeross of Tuscumbia, Alabama. Finally in 1872 he settled down and became a clerk for the Baptist Association. On February 9, 1875, Barton married Ruth Ann Jacobs.

As clerk for the Baptist Association, Barton became a key person in organizing and developing various groups. He organized the first African American District Sunday School in the United States. It was held in Tuscumbia, Alabama in 1874. Barton also organized the first Woman's Missionary State Convention in Alabama. Recognizing the need of the community Barton bought land in Tuscumbia and established the first African American city school. He taught at the school for four years and then entered Ministerial Institute in Montgomery, Alabama. As Barton's commitment to his work grew, so did his spiritual development. In 1877 Barton completed his studies at the Ministerial Institute and was ordained as a minister. From 1879 to 1886, he served as the minister for Mt. Canaan Baptist Church. He continued his studies at Talladega College and graduated from the theological department in 1892, receiving his divinity degree in 1900 from Guadalope College in Seguin, Texas.

Barton's style was easy and impressive, and his leadership abilities were further supported in his roles as chairman of the Board of Visitors of the Colored Deaf and Dumb Asylum of Alabama and as president of the Alabama State Convention. He was known as an energetic leader and was well liked. Although he resigned as pastor in 1900, his lectures and speeches inspired many people. His work led to the organization of eight churches and five houses of worship. Barton became a very well-known evangelist. He baptized more than 3,000 persons, and united over 2,500 couples in marriage. With the success of the District Sunday Schools, Barton organized in 1874 the first U.S. Sunday School Convention in Union Springs, Alabama. Barton was also involved in the National Baptist Southern Convention and was president of the Alabama Colored Baptist State Convention from 1893 to 1899.

Barton was known for his love of science and as a ready and generous helper. He was also interested in the process of physical and spiritual healing. He took courses in therapeutics at Weltner Institute in Nevada, Missouri, and completed his studies on March 20, 1900. Barton became a practitioner in suggestive therapeutics. He provided treatment to persons at home, in their offices, or by mail, and amassed a comfortable fortune in the process. Mailings and announcements regarding Barton's therapeutic treatments consisted of pamphlets such as *Barton's Road to Health and Prosperity*. His clientele numbered well over ten thousand.

REFERENCES

Books

Boothe, Charles Octavius. *The Cyclopedia of the Colored Baptists of Alabama: Their Leaders and Their Work*. Birmingham: Alabama Publishing Co., 1985, pp. 117-18.

Who's Who of the Colored Race. Vol. 1. Chicago: Who's Who in Colored America Publishing, 1915, p. 21.

Lean'tin L. Bracks

Robert Benjamin
1855–1900

Journalist, newspaper editor, educator, lecturer

One of the nation's most productive newspaper editors and outspoken journalists, Robert Benjamin worked in twelve states before settling in California, where he became best known as editor of the *San Francisco Sentinel*. Whether teaching school, practicing law, or working on the newspaper, Benjamin was as concerned with imparting information as he was with protecting the rights of his race and, with fearless expression, exposing the racial injustices that blacks suffered in the South. As a result of his lectures throughout the South, he was well known as a speaker.

Information on Robert Charles O'Hara Benjamin's family, early childhood, and death is scarce, and those details that are published often are undocumented and undated. Generally known as R.O.C. Benjamin, he was probably born on the island of St. Kitts, the British West Indies on March 31, 1855, and as local laws required, he began school while a young child. When he was eleven years old, he was sent to England to study with a private tutor to prepare for college. While still young, he enrolled in Trinity College, at Oxford University. His biographical statement in *The Afro-American Press and Its Editors* reports that he graduated, yet his entry in *Men of Mark*, which Arnold H. Taylor claims that Benjamin actually wrote, says that he spent three years there and left before receiving his degree.

Benjamin loved to travel, and he took a two-year tour of Sumatra, Java, and other islands in the East Indies. Soon after his return to England, he took a passenger vessel to America and arrived on April 13, 1869. By then, he was only fourteen years old. His love for the sea continued, and ten days later he shipped out as a cabin boy on the Lepanto; for six months Benjamin traveled to Venezuela, Curaçao, Demerara, and the West Indies. He returned to New York City in the fall of 1869 and worked in various jobs until 1877.

Becomes Newspaper Agent and Editor

In New York, Benjamin became active in public affairs and associated with such luminaries as black abolitionist Henry Highland Garnet. Another contact, Joe Howard Jr., who edited the *New York Star*, hired Benjamin as soliciting agent and office assistant. A few months later he became acquainted with the *Progressive American*'s editor J. F. Freeman, who helped to further Benjamin's career by hiring him as city editor. Realizing

the importance of citizenship, in 1875 Benjamin became a naturalized U.S. citizen.

In the political arena, Benjamin became involved in Rutherford B. Hayes' bid for the U.S. presidency. When Hayes entered competition against Samuel J. Tilden on the Democratic side, Benjamin helped by organizing political clubs in various wards and also stumped for the party, giving speeches in Hempstead, Long Island, and elsewhere in the state. His reward for helping Hayes to win came in the form of a job as letter carrier in the New York post office, but he grew weary of the work and left it after nine months.

Benjamin moved to Kentucky and taught school in several counties. He had developed an interest in law as well, and while teaching in Hodgensville, Larne County, Kentucky, he borrowed law books from a former congressman and read law after the school day ended. Each week he recited lessons to county attorney Dave Smith, who later became a state senator. Next, he moved to Decatur, Alabama, where he became a public school principal while continuing to read law.

Benjamin went to Brinkley, Arkansas, and elsewhere, all the while teaching school and saving enough money to support his trip to Memphis, Tennessee. There he presented himself before local lawyer Josiah Patterson. He was admitted to the Tennessee bar in January 1880.

Benjamin practiced law in twelve different states and at the same time maintained his interest in journalism, the field in which he appears to have sealed his place in black and American history. He owned and edited the *Colored Citizen* in Pittsburgh and the *Chronicle* in Evansville, Indiana. According to Arnold Taylor for the *Dictionary of American Negro Biography*, the *Chronicle* "championed ably the cause of Negroes." Benjamin relocated to Birmingham in 1886 where he became editor of the *Negro America*—an outspoken black newspaper established in September 1886. As editor, he attacked the city's hiring practices that excluded blacks from positions as firefighters, police officers, and so on, and called for a balance of power that the black vote could bring. He called local law a farce and denounced the increasing number of lynchings of blacks in Alabama. He wrote that blacks wanted only their constitutional rights and civil privileges. Whites became so incensed over Benjamin's constant agitation against these injustices and for disturbing public peace that they forced him out of Birmingham in the summer of 1887. At some point, Benjamin was also the corresponding editor for the Nashville *Free Lance*, published in Nashville, Tennessee, and wrote under a pen name, Cicero.

Clearly he had first-hand knowledge of racial conditions in the South, for he had worked there and had seen conditions for himself. Armed with this knowledge, Benjamin also wrote about such matters in various pamphlets. He moved to California sometime before 1888, where he practiced law for whites as well as blacks, continued his lectures, and strengthened his ties to journalism. He became an editor for the Los Angeles *Observer*. He worked also for the Los Angeles *Daily Sun*, becoming the only local black editor for a white newspaper. But by 1890, Benjamin edited the San Francisco *Sentinel*, which brought him wide recognition.

Puts Race First, Friends Next

Benjamin's motto was: "My race first, and my friends next." This statement became the motto for the *Sentinel*. Benjamin used the *Sentinel* to denounce racial problems in the South, such as lynchings, the railroad companies and their mistreatment of blacks, and other troubles. The *Sentinel* took the West Coast by storm and had no difficulty becoming nationally recognized. It was a lively paper, taking its place among the best black newspapers in the country. His work as editor and writer caused readers to take notice. While other black journalists of that period might have been more widely known, apparently Benjamin's work was as good as theirs. I. Garland Penn wrote in the *Afro-American Press and Its Editors* that Benjamin was "fearless in his editorial expression," and he gave opinions on current issues "in a courageous manner."

Whether Benjamin entered the ministry is omitted from accounts of his life; however, his twelve-page work *The Zion Methodist*, published in 1893, indicates that the work was prepared by Rev. R. C. O. Benjamin. Beyond his work as journalist and newspaper editor, Benjamin wrote two works of fiction: *The Boy Doctor* and *The Adventures of Obediah Kuff*. His book of poetry, *Poetic Gems*, was published in 1883, and his work *Don't: A Book for Girls* appeared in 1891. Three other books were published as well; they were *The Life of Toussaint L'Ouverture . . . with a Historical Survey of Santo Domingo* in 1888; *Southern Outrages: A Statistical Record of Lawless Doings*, in 1894; and *Benjamin's Pocket History of the American Negro: A Story of Thirty-One Years from 1863 to 1894*, in 1894. His essays include: "The Boy Doctor," "History of the British West Indies," "Future of the American Negro," "The Southland," and "Africa, the Hope of the Negro." It is unclear whether or not his essays were published; or, if so, where and how they appeared. Benjamin's address on "The Negro Problem and Its Solution" before an African Methodist Episcopal Zion Church in Portland, Oregon was published in 1891.

Benjamin's *Southern Outrages* was a compilation of lynching reports and a record of abuses suffered by blacks. On several occasions Benjamin had been assaulted by southern whites, spurring him to produce this work. His interest in promoting black culture led to his *Pocket History of the American Negro*, in which he praised black progress and noted the contributions of blacks in the arts, education, literature, religion, and inventions, noting that, since 1863, blacks had received over two hundred patents.

Beyond his work as writer, editor, and lecturer, in California Benjamin became active in church and community activities. He was elected presiding elder of the California Conference of the African Methodist Episcopal Church; his jurisdictions included California, Oregon, Nevada, and Washington. He was general financial agent and superintendent of the Connection's Sabbath School on the West Coast. He declined President Benjamin Harrison's offer to serve as consul to Aux Cayes, Haiti, on the grounds that he wanted to remain head of the *Sentinel*.

Benjamin was fluent in French and Spanish. A popular lecturer in the South, he also took his message to major cities in Canada, where large, white audiences attended. His legacy is seen in his work as editor of the San Francisco *Sentinel*. He is remembered as a strong advocate of the race and for the fearless way he made his views known.

In *The Afro-American Press and Its Editors*, Arnold H. Taylor cited an article in the *Seattle Republican* for October 19, 1900, which noted that Benjamin was murdered. He had been shot years earlier by southern Democrats, who protested his work in voter registration for blacks in Kentucky when he served as editor of the *Lexington Democrat*. No further details concerning his life or death are known.

REFERENCES

Books

Penn, I. Garland. *The Afro-American Press and Its Editors* (1891; repr.) Salem, N.H.: Ayer Company, 1988.

Simmons, William J. *Men of Mark: Eminent, Progressive and Rising*. Cleveland, Ohio: Geo. M. Rewell & Co., 1887.

Suggs, Henry Lewis, ed. *The Black Press in the South: 1865-1979*. Westport, Conn.: Greenwood Press, 1983.

Taylor, Arnold H. "R[obert] C[harles] O['hara] Benjamin." In *Dictionary of American Negro Biography*. Ed. Rayford W. Logan and Michael R. Winston. New York: Norton, 1982.

Jessie Carney Smith

Lerone Bennett
1928–

Journalist, historian, writer

In a distinguished career that has spanned more than five decades, journalist and historian Lerone Bennett Jr. has eloquently and steadfastly documented African American life. Bennett, the author of a dozen books and the executive editor of *Ebony* magazine, is revered as a modern-day

Lerone Bennett

griot whose writings have educated scholars and the reading public about the black presence in the United States.

Bennett was born on October 17, 1928 in Clarksdale, Mississippi to Lerone Bennett, a chauffeur, and his wife, Alma Reed Bennett, a restaurant cook. The Bennett family moved to Jackson, Mississippi, where the future journalist and historian became interested in writing and history while attending the city's public schools. In "Black America's Popular Historian," Bennett comments that he fell in love with "the word" before his tenth birthday and that he realized that it was a weapon that could save his life as well as the lives of other African Americans. In the same article, Bennett admits that he "hung around" Jackson's two African American newspapers: *The Jackson Advocate* and the *Mississippi Enterprise*. Bennett's first newspaper editorial was published when he was eleven years old, and in high school, he edited his school's newspaper and yearbook. Bennett credits his high school history teacher, Mrs. M. D. Manning, with developing his interest in history; her dramatic teaching style made historical figures exciting as she encouraged her students to realize that history is more than names and dates and to become vicariously involved in historical events.

Bennett was also influenced by several male public school teachers and Jackson State College administrators. In Golphin's article, "A Distinguished Gentleman," Bennett remembers, "This was a terrible time with almost total violence against and oppression of black people, and these men tried to act like men, and walk and talk like men at a time when it was dangerous to be a black man." When Bennett realized that his role models had graduated from Morehouse College, the private liberal arts institution for African American men, he decided to enroll there. After graduating from high school in 1945, Bennett matriculated at Morehouse where Martin Luther King Jr. was also enrolled, and Benjamin E. Mays, esteemed educator, scholar, clergyman, civic leader, and orator, was president. According to Bennett, Mays' influence was omnipresent at Morehouse as the college transformed boys into men. Each Tuesday in chapel, Mays' talks with the collegians covered manhood, the struggle for their rights, excellence, manners, dignity, integrity, and books. Bennett further comments in "A Distinguished Gentleman, "Everybody who had the rare opportunity to listen to [Mays] and study with him in that campus environment was changed. He had one of the most profound influences on Martin Luther King Jr." While at Morehouse, Bennett edited the college's newspaper.

Exceptional Career as Journalist

Bennett graduated from Morehouse in 1949. That same year, he pursued graduate study at Atlanta University and began his career as a journalist. Bennett was a reporter (1949-52) and later city editor (1952-53) of the *Atlanta Daily World* newspaper. During this period, Bennett served in the United States Army (1951-52) and was promoted to the rank of first sergeant. He began his association with Johnson Publishing Company when he assumed the position of city editor of *Jet* magazine (1953) before becoming associate editor (1954-57), senior editor (1958-87), and executive editor (1987-) of *Ebony*, where his articles have consistently ranked as the magazine's best writing. Although Bennett served as a visiting professor of history at Northwestern University (1968-69) as well as a senior fellow at the Institute of the Black World (1969) and has lectured at colleges and universities nationwide, tenure at an institution of higher learning was not his goal. Nor was Bennett interested in writing for white magazines and newspapers; in fact, he rejected job offers from mainstream publications. Bennett, early in his life, realized that he wanted to write for a mass audience of African Americans; writing articles for *Ebony* and writing books afforded him that opportunity. Bennett planned to retire as *Ebony*'s executive editor in 2003, the year he celebrated his seventy-fifth birthday; however, John H. Johnson, publisher, chairman and founder; and Linda Johnson Rice, president and CEO, encouraged Bennett to remain at *Ebony*.

Publications Defining the Black Experience

Decades earlier, Bennett's reputation as a prominent social historian was established with the publication of his first book, *Before the Mayflower: A History of the Negro in America* (1963). The book began as a series of articles that were published in *Ebony* in 1962. *Before the Mayflower* was selected by *QBR: The Black Book Review* in 1999 as one of one hundred essential African American books, and it was revised in 2003 as the "New Millennium Edition" with three new chapters. His second book, *What Manner of Man: A Biography of Martin Luther King Jr.* (1964) is one of the first biographies of the civil rights leader and consequently one of few King biographies published during his lifetime. Bennett's third book, *The Negro Mood* (1964), discusses the failures of white liberals and integration while *Confrontation: Black and White* (1965), Bennett's fourth book, analyzes the social problems affecting African Americans in the 1960s. Bennett's fifth book, *Black Power, U.S.A.: The Human Side of Reconstruction, 1867-1877* (1967) focuses on African Americans and politics during a pivotal nineteenth-century decade. *Pioneers in Protest* (1968), Bennett's sixth book, discusses the contributions of twenty-two individuals, most of whom are African American and male, who dared to assert their rights. Bennett's seventh book, *The Challenge of Blackness* (1970), has been described as an important work from the Black Power era. Bennett's next book, *Ebony Pictorial History of Black America* (1971) is a four-volume collaboration with his *Ebony* co-editors. *The Shaping of Black America* (1975) is considered the companion piece to *Before the Mayflower*. Bennett's tenth book, *Wade in the Water* (1979) highlights important events in African American history while his eleventh book is *Succeeding Against the Odds* (1989), John H. Johnson's autobiography with assistance from Bennett. In his most controversial work, *Forced into Glory: Abraham Lincoln's White Dream* (2000), Bennett opines that Lincoln's objective was to keep as many blacks in bondage until he could gain support for gradual emancipation and deportation of African Americans. Bennett has been hailed as a pioneer in the "writing of popular black history" and as one of Mississippi's most successful black writers of the twentieth century. He is also the author of short stories and poems that have appeared in a variety of anthologies.

Memberships and Awards

Bennett is a member of the Black Academy of Arts and Letters; Phi Beta Kappa; Kappa Alpha Psi; Sigma Delta Chi; and the Presidential Commission, created in 2001, of the National Museum of African American history as part of the Smithsonian. He is a former member of President Clinton's Committee on the Arts and Humanities. Bennett holds memberships on the board of directors of the Institute of Black World and the Chicago Public Library, and the board of trustees of the Martin Luther King Memorial Center, Chicago Historical Society, Morehouse College, and Columbia College. He was a delegate to the Sixth Pan-African Congress, Tanzania (1974) and the Second World Festival of Black and African Art in Nigeria (1977). In addition, Bennett has served as an advisor/consultant to the National Advisory Commission on Civil Disorders.

Bennett is the recipient of numerous honors and awards. His contributions as a journalist and historian have been acknowledged by his alma mater on two occasions; Bennett was awarded an honorary doctorate (1965) from Morehouse, and, on the fiftieth anniversary of his graduation, Bennett delivered the commencement address (1999). At that time, he was presented with Morehouse's Candle in the Dark Award for exemplifying the Morehouse tradition and for continuing to serve as an African American role model. Bennett has also received honorary degrees from such institutions as Wilberforce University (1977), Marquette University (1979), Dillard University (1980), Lincoln College (1980), University of Illinois (1980), Morgan State University (1981), Voorhees College (1981), Morris Brown College (1985), South Carolina University (1986), Boston University (1987), Rust College (1987), Lincoln University (1988), Tuskegee University (1989), Winston-Salem State University (1989), and Fisk University (2002). Among Bennett's additional honors are the Capital Press Club's Book of the Year Award (1963); Society of Midland Authors' Patron Saints Award (1964); Literature Award, American Academy of Arts and Letters (1978); Lifetime Achievement Award, National Association of Black Journalists (1981); United Negro College Fund's Humanitarian of the Year Award (1991); Salute to Greatness Award of the Martin

Luther King Jr. Center for Nonviolent Social Change Inc. (1996); Trumpet Award, Turner Broadcasting System (1998); American Book Awards' Lifetime Achievement Award (2002); and the Carter G. Woodson Lifetime Achievement Award, Association for the Study of African American Life and History (2003).

Bennett married Gloria Sylvester on July 21, 1956. They are the parents of Alma, twins Constance and Courtney, and Lerone III. Although Lerone Bennett is the biological father of four children, his legacy may extend to generations of African American journalists and historians who consider Bennett as their literary progenitor.

REFERENCES

Books

"Lerone Bennett Jr." In *Black Writers: A Selection of Sketches from Contemporary Authors*. 2nd ed. Ed. Sharon Malinowski. Detroit, Mich.: Gale Research, 1994.

Periodicals

Dawkins, Wayne. "Black America's Popular Historian." *Black Issues Book Review* 6 (Jan./Feb. 2004): 12-13.

Online

Golphin, Vincent F. A. "A Distinguished Gentleman." http://www.abouttimemag.com/nov00stoty.html (Accessed 25 January 2005).

"Lerone Bennett Jr." *Contemporary Black Biography*. Vol. 5. 1993. Reproduced in *Biography Resource Center*. Farmington Hills, MI: Thomson Gale, 2005. http://galenet.galegroup.com/servlet/BioRC (Accessed 23 February 2005).

"Lerone Bennett Jr." *Contemporary Southern Writers*, 1999. Reproduced in *Biography Resource Center*. Farmington Hills, MI: Thomson Gale, 2005. http://galenet.galegroup.com/servlet/BioRC (Accessed 23 February 2005).

Linda M. Carter

Leonidas H. Berry
1902–1995

Physician, lecturer

In a remarkable and innovative medical career spanning over forty years, Leonidas H. Berry became a world-renown physician who dedicated his life to the pursuit of

---

Chronology

1902	Born in Woodsdale, North Carolina on July 2
1924	Receives B.S. from Wilberforce University
1925	Receives second B.S. from University of Chicago
1929	Earns M.D. from Rush Medical College of the University of Chicago
1930	Interns at Freedmen's Hospital, Washington, D.C.
1933	Earns M.S. degree in pathology from the Graduate School of Medicine at the University of Illinois; begins interdisciplinary career in gastroenterology at Provident Hospital
1936	Joins Cook County Hospital as the first African American attending staff physician in fifty years; begins career as first African American gastroscopist; invents the first direct-vision instrument, the gastroscopy scope, to remove diseased stomach tissue
1946	Joins the staff of Michael Reese Hospital
1947	Becomes the first medical director of the AME Health Commission and serves for thirty years
1951	Implements the Berry Plan to provide medical counseling for black narcotics users
1954	Begins presentations at World Congresses
1966	Travels to Africa on behalf of the National Medical Association; lectures in medical schools and hospitals in Kenya, Uganda, Nigeria, Liberia, and Senegal; lectures on and demonstrates treatment of stomach diseases in Japan, Korea, Hong Kong, Philippines, and Hawaii
1970	Organizes the Flying Black Medics to provide medical, dental, dietary, and social services to poor blacks in Cairo, Illinois
1974	Authors fifteen of thirty-five chapters of *Gastrointestinal Pan-endoscopy: esophagoscopy, gastroscopy, bulbar and postbulbar duodenoscopy, procto-sigmoidoscopy, colonoscopy, and peritoneoscopy*, a technical, instructional work
1986	Publishes autobiography, *I Wouldn't Take Nothin' for My Journey*
1995	Dies in Chicago, Illinois on December 4

---

racial, physical, and economic parity for African Americans in Chicago through medicine, teaching, writing, lecturing, and community service. Berry was a pioneer in gastroscopy and gastroenterology. His expertise in the study of the human stomach was acclaimed worldwide beginning in the 1930s due to his ability as a physician and his pioneering success in the use of the endoscope. Berry produced several books, video recordings, and motion pictures to illustrate the study of the stomach and other organs affected by digestive disorders. In his fight against racial discrimination, Berry made unprecedented achievements in hospitals, medical societies, and medical associations around the world. He lectured worldwide as an individual and as a representative of several medical associations and societies. Contrary to theories that resonated throughout the medical community, when evaluating illnesses, Berry placed more emphasis on physical and economic causes than on race.

Berry's family history and lifestyle shaped his career path and provided him with the initial determination necessary to become an outstanding physician and person.

Berry's great-grandparents had been slaves. His paternal grandfather, also enslaved, lived in St. Mary's County, Maryland when he escaped slavery in 1863 by carrying a horse saddle over his shoulder as a decoy to get past slave hunters. When he had traveled sufficiently northward, he changed his name to John Berry and joined the military to fight in the Civil War. John Berry was one of the few African American soldiers who applied for pension payments after his military service. Berry's paternal and maternal grandparents became self-sufficient farmers, owning more than 368 acres. His parents, Llewellyn L. Berry and Beulah Ann Harris, met at Kittrell College and graduated in 1898. After graduation, Llewellyn served as a minister in the pastorate of the African Methodist Episcopal (AME) Church for over thirty-two years and as secretary and treasurer of the department of home and foreign missions of the AME Church for twenty-three years. Beulah taught school for seven years after graduation. They were married in 1900 and the first of their six children, Leonidas H. Berry, was born on July 2, 1902 in Woodsdale, North Carolina.

Throughout his life, Berry's family was committed to community service with the AME Church as the anchor. The importance of education was instilled in the Berry family. Berry's father earned a doctor of divinity degree. All of the Berry children except one attended college and four were college students at the same time.

Berry grew up in Norfolk, Virginia where he graduated from Booker T. Washington High School and then attended Wilberforce University in Ohio. He was a member of the Wilberforce University Choir. He was also on the football team and participated in debates. Berry graduated with a B.S. in 1924 and then went on to attend the University of Chicago where he earned a second B.S. in 1925. Berry entered Rush Medical College of the University of Chicago in 1925. All students were required to engage in a medical school clinical clerkship for a three-month observation period. However, in 1927, such opportunities were not available to black students. In his autobiography, *I Wouldn't Take Nothin' for My Journey*, Berry describes how such instances can be turned into assets. For example, Berry completed his clinical clerkship at a small, private, black-run hospital where he lived, worked, and observed for his last two years of school. The additional clinical experience he received as a result of his college's discrimination policies against blacks benefited him. He earned his M.D. in 1929 and completed a one-year internship at Freedmen's Hospital in Washington, D.C. in 1930. Berry then went on to the Graduate School of Medicine at the University of Illinois, where he earned an M.S. degree in pathology in 1933. His master's thesis, "Tuberculosis and Race: Due to Adverse Economic and Social Conditions Not Race," challenged several theories that supported susceptibility of blacks to certain diseases. Between 1931 and 1934, Berry was a full-time University of Chicago fellow in internal medicine and digestive diseases at Cook County, Provident, and Billings hospitals.

He joined the U. S. Army Medical Reserves in 1931 as a first lieutenant and served until 1941. He was promoted to captain of the Medical Corp, Illinois Militia in 1942, and retired as a major in 1947.

Professional Achievements

Berry began his progressive, interdisciplinary career in gastroenterology at Provident Hospital in 1933 as a junior attending physician. He was the first African American specialist in the field and the first to be certified by the subspecialty board of gastroenterology. In 1934, Rudolph Schindler, a German gastroenterologist, introduced the modern, flexible gastroscope to the United States and trained Berry in using it. Two years later, Berry was a pioneer in its use and one of the first twelve Americans to use the instrument. Provident Hospital advanced him to the position of associate attending physician in 1938. Berry remained in that capacity for five years. Beginning in 1943 he took on more administrative responsibility at Provident, assuming the division chairmanship of digestive diseases. From 1943 to 1946, he assumed the role of vice chairman for the department of medicine, and he became department chairman in 1946. He held the position for two years. Between 1942 and 1951, Berry also served as chairman of the Provident Hospital Advisory Board Selective Service System.

In 1946, Berry became the first African American attending staff physician of Cook County Hospital in fifty years, as Dan Williams had served from 1896 until 1946. At the same time, he became the first African American professor at the Cook County Graduate School of Medicine, where he taught gastroenterology and gastroscopy. He developed and conducted a special course from March 18 through March 30, 1963, in the technique of gastroscopy and endoscopic pathology of the stomach. Berry also joined Community Hospital in Evanston, Illinois in 1946 as a consulting gastroenterologist and remained there until 1963. He became the first African American in 1946 to join the medical staff of Michael Reese Hospital. Initially, he was hired as a courtesy staff physician of the department of medicine at Michael Reese and remained in that position for seventeen years. After many special appeals to the hospital board and constant battles against racial bias, he was advanced from a limited courtesy appointment to the attending physicians' staff in 1963. In 1952, Berry became a clinical assistant professor of medicine at the University of Illinois where he served for five years. Berry was also called upon to serve as a consulting gastroenterologist and member of the governing board of the Women and Children's Hospital in Chicago in 1956. In 1974, he became a special deputy (in a part-time capacity) with the Cook County Hospital's governing commission, which supervised the operation of public hospital facilities in the Chicago area. The following year, after twenty-five years of service, Berry retired from Cook County Hospital as chief of endoscopy services and senior attending physician.

Berry combined his innovative medical career with outstanding community service. In 1931, Berry's father had published *A Century of Missions of the AME Church*, and Berry contributed a short chapter, "Opportunity of African Methodism in Medical Missions: A Prospectus." From that point forward, Berry's work addressed the physical and social welfare of humankind. Berry sought cures for disease by conducting research; as the medical director of the Correctional Health Commission of the AME Church, he addressed many people's needs. Then too he held dozens of other leadership positions in professional associations and societies.

Berry studied endoscopy under the German doctor Rudolph Schindler, who promoted the modern endoscope, a fiber-optic gastro-camera for viewing the digestive tract. Berry became one of the first Americans to use the instrument. He created the Eder-Berry biopsy gastroscope in 1936, the first direct-vision, suction instrument used to obtain stomach tissue samples for microscopic examination. The benefit of using this instrument is the minimal invasion necessary for obtaining the tissue sample. Berry taught hundreds of students and trained hundreds of physicians how to use the device. In 1941, Berry completed a first of its kind study of the stomachs of skid row alcoholics. Contrary to popular theories, Berry's study found that the livers, not the stomachs, were diseased as a result of alcohol. Berry read his research paper before the American Medical Association as the keynote speaker. Berry undertook another study in 1944 wherein he examined the possible areas and ways in which the AME Church might participate in the health field, as it had for the past one hundred years in the social services. Berry assumed the position of medical director of the Correctional Health Commission of the AME Church in 1946 and served in that capacity for thirty years.

In 1950, Berry set up the Council for Biomedical Careers, which funded health care conferences and career counseling sessions on such subjects as medicine, dentistry, nursing, pharmacy, medical technology, and how to use local and federal government facilities, public and private schools, and churches to encourage young black men to enter the health field. Berry also became president of the Cook County Physicians Association in 1950, at which time he led an interracial, interfaith, citywide movement for rehabilitating young drug addicts. Then-governor Adlai Stevenson set up an advisory committee to the Department of Public Health on narcotic programs to study the problem and made Berry a member. Berry proposed establishing four medical counseling clinics with the help of the state government to provide aid for drug addicts. Through an act of special legislation, the Illinois General Assembly appropriated $90,000 to set-up the Berry Plan. Berry set up medical clinics in Provident, Cook County, and Northwestern hospitals, and the Cook County Jail. The program was unique because it addressed the psychological and physical needs of the addicts and took a medical, rather than criminal, approach to treatment. The Berry Plan was operational

from 1951 through 1958. Berry completed his internship at Freedmen's Hospital and became a founding member of the Association of Former Interns and Residents of Freedmen's Hospital. In 1952, he coordinated the first annual scientific assembly of the alumni. When the new Freedmen's Hospital was built, the group erected a plaque in the main lobby that gives the history of the hospital and of the relationship of the original Freedmen's Hospital to the new facility. In 1964, Berry received the William A. Warfield Award as president of the former interns.

World Travel

Through his publications, lectures, and worldwide presentations, Berry strove to expand human knowledge and awareness. He contributed 84 articles to national and international journals and societies and wrote six books. He was the first black physician to join and lecture before several medical associations and societies, some of which were the National Gastroenterological Association, the American Gastroscopic Society, the American College of Gastroenterology, American Association for the Advancement of Science, Society for Experimental Biology and Medicine, and the American Medical Association. In addition, Berry participated in several world congress conferences, including the 1954 and 1981 World Congresses in Paris; the 1960 Pan American Congress in Santiago, Chili; and the 1966 World Congress in Tokyo. A conversation with Governor G. Mennen Williams in 1966 resulted in Berry's visit to five African countries for lectures and demonstrations on gastroenterology and gastroscopy. At the time, Williams, who was assistant secretary of state for African Affairs, arranged for Berry to take the trip under the auspices of the Department of State. Berry, who was president of the National Medical Association at the time, covered over 20,000 miles when he visited Kenya, Uganda, Nigeria, Liberia, and Senegal in July 1966. Berry also visited their governing offices and villages and informed them of the work of the AME Church in the United States. In the fall of 1966, Berry went to Asia. He visited nine medical schools and hospitals in Japan, Korea, Hong Kong, Philippines, and Hawaii, giving lectures and demonstrations on stomach diseases.

The Flying Black Medics

In the fall of 1969, Berry attended a task force conference on health in Cairo, Illinois, because of news of almost nonexistent health care provisions for black and poor people. In February 1970, Berry coordinated a group of medics, known as the Flying Black Medics, who chartered two airplanes at Berry's expense and flew to Cairo to address medical needs of the residents. They set up three medical clinics in the basement of the Wards Chapel AME Church giving free health care, supplies, and examinations.

Regarding his cancer research project, which ended in 1975, Berry concluded that preventive care is the newest technique to use for early diagnosis of cancer. Berry received the Rudolph Schindler Award from the American Society of Gastrointestinal Endoscopy. In 1978, Berry coordinated a forum and fellowship assembly on "Problems of Medical Care at the Cook County Hospital" that was sponsored by the AME Ministerial Alliance and Members of the Interdenominational Church Community.

Berry was frequently recognized for his medical accomplishments and his contributions to the national and international community. In 1963 he was appointed by President Lyndon Baines Johnson to a twelve-man National Advisory council of Regional Medical Programs against heart disease, cancer and stroke. As president of the National Medical Association, he received an invitation to the White House stag dinner with the president, cabinet, and other dignitaries. Berry was also the recipient of the Alumni Citation for Public Service in 1966 from the University of Chicago and the Alumni Professional Achievement Award in 1978. Berry was honored when his portrait was presented to Provident Hospital as a testimonial. Also, the DuSable Museum of African American History in Chicago exhibited photographs and memorabilia of Berry and his areas of expertise in 1987. The exhibit was entitled, "Dr. Berry: Medical Pioneer."

The triumph associated with the end of his career at Cook County Hospital was the publication of *Gastrointestinal Pan-endoscopy: esophagoscopy, gastroscopy, bulbar and postbulbar duodenoscopy, procto-sigmoidoscopy, colonoscopy, and peritoneoscopy* in 1974. This 650-page technical, instructional book contained 128 color photographs of ulcers, cancers, and other diseases of the digestive canal as seen through fiber-optic endoscopes. Berry designed and edited the book, and authored fifteen of the chapters. Contributors from ten countries and four continents wrote twenty additional chapters. The book is unique in two ways: it is a culmination of Berry's life work; and it covers endoscopy of the entire upper gastrointestinal canal to the colon with fiber-optic instruments, procto-sigmoidoscopy, and peritoneoscopy, all in one volume.

Berry published his autobiography, *I Wouldn't Take Nothin' for My Journey*, in 1986. He wrote the book, as he stated in it, "to put into perspective, not only the prejudices and obstacles against minorities, but to objectively and intelligently analyze and explain them and to illustrate how they can be overcome." Berry traces his family back to 1816, when Nace Jenifer was born a slave in St. Mary's County, the same year the AME Church was organized. Jenifer was a man of medicine in the tradition of the African doctor and a healer in St. Mary's County until he escaped from slavery and went to Canada. The title of the book came from a Negro spiritual that means life on this earth is only a journey of success and joy, despite overwhelming hardships. The reward comes from the journey and the spirit of survival. In 1986 Berry presented a copy of his autobiography and his personal papers to the National Library of Medicine, Washington, D.C. Berry died on December 4, 1995.

REFERENCES
Periodicals

"Berry Elected President at the 69th Annual Convention of the NMA, Predominately Negro Organization Organized in 1895." *The Bulletin of American Physicians*, 27 August 1964.

"Celebrating a Book Anniversary." *Ebony* (November 2000): 56.

"Dr. Leonidas H. Berry, AME Health Director, Heals: Flying Black Medics." *AME Christian Reader*, 12 May 1970.

"How Famous Physician Sees: Deprivation and Disease." *Sun Times* (17 July 1964): 15.

Moore, Jackie. "Dr. Leonidas Berry: 40 Years of Volunteer Service." *Chicago Defender*, 17 October 1977.

Saxon, Wolfgang. "Leonidas H. Berry Is Dead at 93: Medical Expert Helped Blacks. *New York Times*, 12 December 1995.

Snider, Arthur J. "How the Endoscope Has Averted Operations." *Chicago Daily News*, 31 August-1 September 1974.

Online

"African-American Contributions to Science and Industry." *Inventors Assistance League*. http://www. ial.org/multi-culturalcenter.htm (Accessed 18 March 2005).

Collections

The Leonidas H. Berry Papers (1907-1982) are located in the Modern Manuscripts Collection, History of Medicine Division, National Library of Medicine, Bethesda, Maryland.

Shelhea C. Owens

John T. Biggers
1924–2001

Muralist, artist, educator

The craft of mural painting owes itself immeasurably to the work of John Thomas Biggers. While his predecessors, such as Hale Woodruff, Aaron Douglas, and Charles White, have left indelible marks on the tradition,

Chronology

1924	Born in Gastonia, North Carolina on April 13
1937	Father dies from complications of diabetes
1940	Receives high school diploma from Lincoln Academy in King's Mountain, North Carolina
1941	Studies at Hampton Institute under Viktor Lowenfield
1943	Serves in the U.S. Navy as visual technician
1946	Returns to Hampton Institute; studies under Charles White
1948	Marries Hazel Hayes; receives B.A. in Art from Pennsylvania State University (January); receives M.A. in art education from Pennsylvania State University (September)
1949	Accepts positions as associate professor and department head of art at Texas Southern University
1954	Receives Doctorate of Education from Pennsylvania State University
1957	Earns United Nations Educational, Scientific, and Cultural Organization fellowship for six month study and travel in West Africa
1962	Publishes *Ananse: Web of Life*, a collection of drawings and writings from trip to Africa
1969	Travels to East Africa under a Danforth fellowship
1975	Mother Cora Fingers Biggers dies
1978	Co-authors *Black Art in Houston* with Carroll Simms
1995	"The Art of John Biggers: View from the Upper Room" opens at the Museum of Fine Art in Houston, Texas
2001	Dies in Houston, Texas on January 25

Biggers augmented the craft as a pioneering muralist and as an educator. At the age of twenty-five he co-founded the art department at Texas Southern University where he championed African and African American aesthetics and where he taught many young art students the techniques of mural painting at a time when few art departments focused on black art. As noted in an article by Frank H. Wardlaw, listed in *Black Leaders: Texans for Their Times*, in his own work Biggers viewed art "not primarily as an individual expression of talent but as a responsibility to reflect the spirit and style of the Negro people."

The impetus for genius is often difficult to determine. For Biggers, however, inspiration stemmed from his rich childhood in Gastonia, North Carolina. The youngest of seven children, John and his siblings all shared their father's gift of drawing. All of the Biggers children believed in hard work and had a passion for reading. When the children were not tending to the family farm, they were reading for at least two hours a day, a mandate strictly enforced by their parents. The strict parents sparked their children with creative energy. Evidence of this creativity lies in the fact that the children meticulously recreated their town of Gastonia out of clay under their house each year when John was a boy.

Paul Biggers, John's father, worked incessantly in spite of the fact that one of his legs was amputated as a result of a childhood accident. For the rest of his life, Paul Biggers refused a peg leg or prosthetic, walking with the support of a crutch. He never considered himself cripple, holding jobs as a carpenter, farmer, and shoemaker after he graduated high school. While working, he attended Livingston College in the summers, where he earned certificates to teach and preach. From then on he taught full-time at multiple schools and served as an itinerant preacher. Because he never accepted offerings for preaching, he also toiled for months at a time in the West Virginia coal mines to supplement his meager income. Although he died when John was thirteen, when speaking of his father, John acknowledged in an interview to Frank H. Wardlaw, "he was one of the most important influences in my life."

John's mother, Cora Fingers Biggers, was a Puritan, who demanded that her children adhere to its rigid morals. She supported her husband's theological endeavors while she tended the house. When her husband died, she worked as a domestic in other people's homes. John Biggers evoked the image of his mother as a hardworking domestic in his famous mural "The Contribution of Negro Women to American Life," completed in 1953.

At Highland Elementary School in Gastonia, Biggers was formally introduced to drawing by his second grade teacher who devoted a part of her daily instruction to drawing different species of birds. By the end of the year, deposited in his memory were the images of more than a hundred different species of birds, all of which he could draw.

While Biggers relished his gift as a young boy, he found few means of cultivating it when he entered high school in 1937. At Lincoln Academy in King's Mountain, North Carolina, the school in which both of his parents attended and the place where they met, he worked as a plumber in the boiler room and as a janitor in the carpentry shop. In the carpentry shop, he learned cabinetmaking and showed some artistic talent. Although he generally enjoyed his stay at Lincoln, had it not been for the school's president, Henry C. McDowell, the school's influence may have done him a grand disservice.

McDowell, a former missionary who had lived in Angola for twenty years, wanted to dispel negative images about Africa. Biggers gained a broader perspective about humanity, a perspective he would later refine on his own travels to Africa. McDowell also encouraged John to pursue a degree at Hampton Institute in Virginia, now Hampton University.

At Hampton, Biggers met his most influential teacher, Viktor Lowenfeld. An Austrian Jew who had transferred to Hampton from Harvard because he desired to work with Negro students, Lowenfeld created a desire for an art program at Hampton with a simple solicitation posted on a bulletin board for a non-credit art class offered at night. The 800 responses he received prompted the university to offer the class the following year. As a distinguished painter and teacher himself, Lowenfeld contributed to modern art education with his book *Creative and Mental Growth*. As noted by Olive Jensen Theisen, in her exhaustive work *The Murals of John Thomas Biggers: American Muralist, African American Artist*, Lowenfeld's approach to art "encouraged his students to explore the imagery of their own cultures. By placing value in the legends, art, and music of Africa, Lowenfeld opened the doors to a previously hidden treasure of symbols and culture which would become increasingly visible in John Biggers' works as he refined his artistic style."

After he served two and a half years in the U.S. Navy during World War II, Biggers continued his studies as a visual arts specialist, creating models of machinery and working under his ceramics teacher at Hampton, Joe Gillard, who was also serving in the navy. Because of their work together, Biggers saw no decline in his abilities once he returned to Hampton.

Upon his return to Hampton in 1945, Biggers worked with Charles White, a visiting artist-in-residence. While at Hampton, White created his "The Contribution of the Negro to Democracy," which portrays the struggles of heroic African American figures, including Harriet Tubman, Frederick Douglass, Sojourner Truth, Nat Turner, Lead Belly, and Marian Anderson. The relationship with White inspired some of the later works Biggers created.

During this period Biggers also met his future wife Hazel Hayes. But in 1946 Viktor Lowenfeld decided to leave Hampton for Pennsylvania State University; he encouraged Biggers to transfer with him. Faced with a dilemma, Biggers decided to leave Hazel to finish her studies at Hampton while he pursued his B.A., M.A., and Ed.D. in art education at Pennsylvania State University under Lowenfeld. In 1948, both his B.A. and M.A. degrees were conferred, and the two were married.

Pioneers Instruction in Mural Painting

In 1949 Biggers and his wife moved to Houston where he accepted a position to organize a department of art at Texas Southern University. Although this was a formidable challenge, Biggers reveled in the fact that he would be exposed to the influence of Diego Rivera, José Oroozco, and David Siquieros in a city rich with Mexican art. What he found, however, was a "wasteland". He further claimed that there was "no culture as far as visual arts and blacks were concerned" in the community of Houston, as noted in Elton Fax's *Black Artists of the New Generation*.

The administration's expectations of the new art department were equally disheartening. Others assumed the program would be a quasi-printing press, and he received innumerable solicitations for flyers and posters. He also received commissions to depict the heads of the faculty and administration, all of which he refused.

To embark upon the arduous task of creating an art department, Biggers enlisted one of his former classmates at Hampton, Joseph Mack, to teach alongside him that

first year. The following year, Carroll Simms, a native of Arkansas and a graduate of Cranbrook Art Academy in Bloomfield Hills, Michigan, joined the two, and together they sought to deliver art to the community in the form of a mural painting program, a program which was to become a defining element of the department.

In Houston, they found ready support from a few teachers who were teaching art in the public school system. These women, Willie Lee Thomas, Laura Sands, and Fannie Holman, were staunch supporters of the new department at Texas Southern University and shared Biggers's desire to promote art in the community.

The immediate effect of the mural painting program was the production of a host of murals painted by Biggers and Mack in public institutions around the city, in nursing homes, YMCAs, high schools, and libraries. Simms, a sculptor and ceramist, also brought art to the community in the forms of fountains, ceramic murals, and sculptures.

While Biggers's work received numerous awards during this period, notably from the Museum of Fine Arts in Houston and the Dallas Museum of Fine Arts, his chief achievement came indirectly through the work of his students. From his approach which "focused upon an appreciation of the black American's southern roots, his traditions, and his contributions to America's development from slavery to the 1960s," noted by Elton C. Fax in *Black Artists of the New Generation*, his teaching encouraged students to look to their heritage for inspiration, an approach which eventually buoyed many of them headlong into the black arts movement. As a credit to his teachings, along with that of his colleagues, housed on the campus of Texas Southern University are hundreds of examples of unrivaled student works: paintings, ceramics, sculptures, weavings, drawings, prints, and murals, some of which were to be profiled in the book, co-authored by Simms, *Black Art in Houston: The Texas Southern University Experience*. Of these student productions, Biggers was especially proud of the greatness achieved by his former pupils Kermit Oliver, Calvin Hubbard, Harry Vital, Leon Renfro, Harvey Johnson, and Trudell Mims Oliver.

Travels to Africa

In 1957 John and Hazel Biggers traveled to West Africa, visiting Ghana, Dahomey, Nigeria, and Togo under a United Nations Educational, Scientific, and Cultural Organization fellowship. The purpose of the six-month trip was to study and depict, according to Biggers as told to Alvia J. Wardlaw in *The Art of John Biggers: View from the Upper Room*, "what was intrinsically African." In his West African travels, Biggers also sought to convey the interconnectedness among Africans, particularly those who lived in the coastal communities, those who lived in the inner forest regions, and those who lived in the expanses of the open plateaus. The result of his study was the publication of *Ananse: The Web of Life in*

Africa, a collection of eighty-nine conte crayon drawings accompanied by writings detailing his discoveries. When asked by Frank H. Wardlaw about his trip, he remarked: "it was the greatest experience of my life."

In 1969, amidst the tumultuous, racially motivated violence of the 1960s, which had surfaced on the campus of Texas Southern University in 1966 with the death of a Houston policeman and the wounding of three students, John and Hazel Biggers escaped to Africa for another expedition courtesy of a grant from the Danforth Foundation. This time the couple traveled to East Africa, seeking revitalization from further self-discoveries like those they had experienced on their first trip to Africa. While they gained more invaluable images of African humanity, John Biggers returned to Houston suffering from tuberculosis. Upon his return, he battled a string of illnesses for the next four years. During this time Biggers produced only one drawing.

Biggers was fascinated with both African and African American images. His work asserts the importance and universality of African and African American humanity. His art affirms its subjects and provides a source of inspiration and purpose for his race and his African ancestors.

His first major work, "The Contribution of Negro Women to American Life," which was inspired by the works of Diego Rivera and by Charles White's mural, "The Contribution of the Negro to Democracy," was completed in 1953 as his doctoral dissertation at Pennsylvania State University. It affirms the important roles of African American matriarchs. The mural presents images of Harriet Tubman and Sojourner Truth protecting scores of children and leading them to freedom. The work was awarded the Purchase Prize at the National Negro Artist Expedition in Atlanta in 1953. The mural was later moved to the Blue Triangle YWCA in Houston, a building serving black women of all ages.

After his first trip to Africa, Biggers published *Ananse: The Web of Life in Africa*. This collection of drawings and writings depicts his experiences in West Africa and African life he saw there. Published in 1962, the book surfaced on the cusp of the civil rights movement and was appreciated in the circles that sought to replace Euro-centrism with an African-centered way of thinking. Thus, it was viewed as an essential companion to black consciousness for it was both instructive and inspiring. It was awarded the Dallas Museum Award: Best Texas Book Design in 1962.

Before the publication of *Black Art in Houston: The Texas Southern University Experience* in 1978, the administration's haphazard destruction of murals produced by his students almost prompted Biggers to resign. In his eyes, it was a blatant display of disrespect for his contributions to the university. Luckily, he and Carroll Simms, who co-authored the book, photographed many of those murals that were included in the book. Five

years after its publication, Biggers retired from his post at Texas Southern University.

After his retirement, Biggers received many life achievement awards. They include: the Creativity Award from the Texas Arts Alliance and Texas Commission on the Arts awarded in 1983; and the Achievement Award from the Metropolitan Arts Foundation and the Texas Artist of the Year from the Art League of Houston, both awarded in 1988. He also received an honorary doctorate of Humane Letters from Hampton University in 1990. A great tribute to his work, however, was the opening of "The Art of John Biggers: View from the Upper Room" at the Museum of Fine Art in Houston, curated by Alvia J. Wardlaw. Featuring more than 125 works, which spanned his complete fifty-year career, the show also included works he completed after his retirement. The traveling show was also exhibited at the North Carolina Museum of Art in Raleigh; the Wadsworth Atheneum in Hartford, Connecticut; the Hampton University Art Museum in Hampton, Virginia; and the Museum of Fine Arts in Boston, Massachusetts.

Working with his nephew, James Biggers, and professor Harvey Johnson, Biggers continued to paint murals throughout the 1990s. At Winston-Salem University in Virginia and at Hampton University from 1990 to 1992 he painted "House of the Turtle," "Tree House," "Origins," and "Ascensions." From 1997 to 1999, Biggers painted his final murals in Houston, "Salt Marsh" in 1998 and "Nubia: The Origins of Business and Commerce" in 1999. On January 25, 2001, after struggling with diabetes, John Biggers died in Houston, Texas.

REFERENCES

Books

Fax, Elton C. *Black Artists of the New Generation*. New York: Dodd, Mead, & Company, 1977.

Otfinoski, Steven. *African Americans in the Visual Arts*. New York: Facts On File, 2003.

Theisen, Olive Jensen. *The Murals of John Thomas Biggers: American Muralist, African American Artist*. Hampton, Va.: Hampton University Press, 1999.

Wardlaw, Alvia J., ed. *The Art of John Biggers: View from the Upper Room*. New York: Harry N. Abrams, 1995.

Wardlaw, Frank. H. "John Biggers: Artist." In *Black Leaders: Texans for Their Times*. Eds. Alwyn Barr and Robert A. Calvert. Austin, Tex.: Texas State Historical Association, 1981.

Collections

The work of John T. Biggers is in the collection of the Dallas Museum of Art; Atlanta University Museum; Hampton University Museum; Howard University;

Museum of Fine Arts, Houston; National Museum of American Art, Smithsonian Institution; Lubbock Museum; Texas Southern University; and numerous private collections.

Irvin Weathersby, Jr.

Adolpho A. Birch, Jr.
1932–

Lawyer, judge

Adolpho Augustus Birch Jr., a lawyer and jurist, became the first African American to hold several judicial posts in Nashville and the first to become a chief justice on the Tennessee Supreme Court. During his forty-three-year judicial career, Birch covered every level of the judicial branch of government in Nashville and the state of Tennessee.

Birch was born on September 22, 1932 in Washington, D.C., the second child of Mary Jefferson and Adolpho Augustus Birch Sr. His father was an Episcopal minister who migrated to the United States from British Honduras (now Belize) in 1894 seeking an education. His mother, before she married, taught school in Virginia. When Birch was only six years old, his mother died giving birth to a third child. After his mother's death, his authoritarian father reared the children alone. His father was a strict disciplinarian and instilled in his sons many values, including determination, endurance, responsibility, the importance of education, as well as the importance of maintaining their spirituality. An attendant of the church's Sunday school, Birch was also an acolyte and thereby assisted in the liturgical service. Birch was loved by the mothers of the church, who served as a source of inspiration and encouragement.

Birch attended Lucretia Mott Elementary School. While he learned the academic subjects, he also acquired the belief that he could be someone who mattered. The trick was to commit himself to all educational opportunities. Washington, like other places in the South and across the nation, operated under the separate-but-equal doctrine. Consequently, its educational system was racially segregated. After completing his elementary and middle school education, Birch entered Dunbar High School, an all-black secondary institution known across the nation for its excellent teachers and curriculum. It was among the few high schools for African Americans where many of its teachers held terminal degrees. While at Dunbar, Birch determined that he was only interested in one profession, the law.

Chronology	
1932	Born in Washington, D.C. on September 22
1956	Receives law degree from Howard University School of Law
1957	Passes the bar exam
1959	Admitted to practice before the United States District Court, Middle Tennessee
1963	Admitted to practice before the United States Court of Appeals
1963-66	Serves as assistant public defender
1966-69	Serves as assistant district attorney general
1969-78	Serves as general sessions judge
1978	Appointed criminal court judge
1980	Elected criminal court judge
1987	Appointed to the court of criminal appeals
1988-93	Serves on court of criminal appeals
1993	Appointed by governor to the Tennessee Supreme Court
1993-2006	Serves on the Tennessee Supreme Court
1996-97	Serves as chief justice of the Tennessee Supreme Court
2006	Retires from the Tennessee Supreme Court

Collegiate and Law School Years

After graduating from Dunbar High School in 1950, Birch entered Lincoln University in Pennsylvania. Later, he returned home and transferred to Howard University. While he attended Howard University, the university school of law and the National Association for the Advancement of Colored People (NAACP) were attempting to dismantle Jim Crow education. Charles Hamilton Houston and Thurgood Marshall initiated the strategy to end government-sanctioned legal racial segregation. Houston and Marshall recruited the best legal minds at Howard and from around the country to help end segregation. Two years before Birch graduated from the university, the Houston and Marshall team successfully argued the 1954 *Brown v. Board of Education of Topeka, Kansas* case before the United States Supreme Court. The court's unanimous *Brown* decision dismantled the separate-but-(un)equal doctrine established by the 1896 *Plessey v. Ferguson* decision.

A highlight of his academic career came when Birch was able to watch Marshall, James Nabrit, George E. C. Hayes, and others as they rehearsed for their argument before the U.S. Supreme Court in the *Brown v. Board of Education* case. Two years after the *Brown* decision, in 1956, Birch graduated from Howard University, where he earned both his undergraduate and law degrees at the same time.

Relocates to Nashville, Tennessee

Soon after earning his bachelor of arts and doctor of jurisprudence degrees, Birch was drafted; he joined the

U.S. Navy and served overseas. During his tour of duty, he studied for and passed the bar exam in 1957. After receiving an honorable discharge in 1958, Birch moved to Nashville, Tennessee, where he worked in the office of an African American attorney for office space and $12.50 per week. Later, he went into private practice with Robert E. Lillard, one of the first two African Americans to serve on the Nashville city council. The same year that Birch arrived in Nashville, leaders of and students in the African American community were in the process of preparing to bring an end to Nashville's era of racial segregation. In November and December of 1959, they began testing the city's exclusionary racial policy by holding sit-ins at lunch counters in local department stores. After several futile meetings with the department store owners, Nashville's civil rights leaders initiated their sit-in strategy the following year.

In February 1960, when Nashville college students began their sit-ins and law enforcement authorities arrested them, Birch was among the cadre of African American attorneys who represented the students. Like many in the civil rights movement, Birch understood that there was no ethical or legitimate foundation to sustain racism and segregation.

The 1960s witnessed Birch's rise in the legal and judicial professions. While still in private practice, in 1963 he served as assistant public defender. Three years later, he left private practice to serve as assistant district attorney general for Nashville and Davidson County, a position he held until 1969. Governor Buford Ellington appointed Birch, a Democrat, to the bench as a general sessions court judge in 1969, the first state judicial post held by an African American. Birch was twice reelected to the post, where he served until 1978. Then-Governor Leonard Ray Blanton appointed him to the bench of the criminal court. Birch received the endorsement of the Nashville Bar Association for his candidacy. He served in this position until 1987, when Governor Ned Ray McWherter elevated him to the court of criminal appeals. In 1988 and 1990, he was reelected to that court.

Becomes Chief Justice of the Tennessee Supreme Court

In December 1993 when Martha Craig Daugherty's seat on the Tennessee Supreme Court became vacant, Governor McWherter appointed Birch to the state's highest tribunal. With that appointment, Birch became the second African American (Justice George Brown of Memphis was the first) to sit on the Tennessee Supreme Court. In August of the following year, he was elected to the state's Supreme Court. After two years of serving on the bench of the Supreme Court, he was elected by his peers to serve as the court's chief justice, a position he held from May 1996 to July 1997. The following year he was reelected to a full-eight year term on the Supreme Court.

During his tenure on the various courts in both Nashville and the state of Tennessee, Birch received numerous accolades and awards. Birch is a Fellow of the Nashville and Tennessee Bar Associations and a past member of the Harry Phillips American Inn of Court. His commitments to other professional, civic, and community endeavors include: the conference of chief justices; state trial court of Davidson County, presiding judge; judicial conference criminal instruction committee, chair; National Bar Association, executive committee; the Napier-Looby Bar Association (formerly known as the J. C. Napier Bar Association), president; Meharry Medical College, adjunct faculty; Tennessee State University, adjunct faculty; Fisk University, adjunct faculty; Senior Citizens; Salvation Army; Kappa Alpha Psi, Nashville Alumni Chapter, polemarch; Golden Heritage Subscriber, NAACP; American Red Cross; Sigma Pi Phi Fraternity (the Boulé); standing committee, the Episcopal Church of Tennessee; and warden, St Anselm's Episcopal Church.

In 2002, the International Phi Alpha Delta Law fraternity gave him the Barbara Jordan Award, which is the fraternity's highest honor. The recipient of Howard University School of Law Distinguished Alumnus Award, in 2005 Judge Birch received the National Bar Association's William H. Hastie Award. That same year the Metropolitan Council of Nashville and Davidson County voted to name its new criminal and general sessions court building for the Tennessee Supreme Court justice.

In January 2006, Adolpho Augustus Birch Jr. announced his retirement, effective on August 31. With that announcement, he ended a forty-three-year judicial career. A member of the teaching faculty at the Nashville School of Law, Judge Birch stated in an interview with the *Nashville Tennessean* that his "service has proved to [him] that a well-lived life depends not upon what one obtains, but upon what one gives."

REFERENCES

Books

Darnell, Riley C.. *Tennessee Blue Book, 2001-2004*. Nashville: Tennessee Secretary of State, 2004.

Laska, Lewis. "A. A. Birch." In *Tennessee Encyclopedia of History and Culture*. Ed. Carroll Van West. Nashville: Rutledge Hill Press, 1998.

Lovett, Bobby L. *The Civil Rights Movement in Tennessee: A Narrative History*. Knoxville: University of Tennessee Press, 2005.

Morris, Akeia. "Adolpho A. Birch." In *A Wealth of Wisdom: Legendary African American Elders Speak*. Eds. Camille O. Crosby and Renee Poussaint. New York: Atria Books, 2004.

Periodicals

Paine, Anne. "African-American Was 'Trailblazer' on State's Court: Admirers Praise Adolpho Birch's 43-Year Career." *Nashville Tennessean*, 26 January 2006.

Linda T. Wynn

Horace W. Bivins
1862–1937

Soldier

Horace Waymon Bivins was born on May 8, 1862, on the eastern shore of Chesapeake Bay at Pungoteague, in Accomack County, Virginia. His parents, Severn S. and Elizabeth Bivins, were farmers. Bivins worked with his parents learning how to farm. At the age of fifteen, Bivins was placed in charge of an eight-horse farm located one mile from Keller Station, Virginia. But Bivins had bigger dreams that went beyond his father's farm. Bivins's father wanted to see the black race in his neighborhood have something that they could call their own. In 1862, he began to build the first church and schoolhouse for blacks to be built on Virginia's eastern shore. All was financed by Bivins himself. On the same day the church and schoolhouse were finished, the buildings were destroyed by fire.

Joins the Tenth Calvary

In June 1885, Horace Bivins enrolled at Hampton Institute in Virginia, where he studied and received his military training. He also studied at Wayland Seminary in Washington D.C. In 1887, Bivins enlisted in the U.S. Army in Washington D.C. He was sent to Jefferson Barracks, Missouri, and was assigned to Troup E, Tenth Calvary. Bivins joined the regiment at Fort Grant, Arizona Territory, in time to participate in the final phases of the Apache wars.

Bivins saw action in the Cuban campaign of 1898. He was commended for his bravery as operator of a Hotchkiss mountain gun in the battle for Santiago. For his outstanding performance, Bivins was promoted to squadron sergeant major in November 1900. In the summer of 1901, Bivins commanded a detachment at LaGranga, on Samar Island in the Philippines. In July, Bivins received an appointment as ordinance sergeant and left the Tenth Calvary to accept the new posts in December. He served at posts in Montana, California, Wyoming, New York, and Vermont, before he retired to a home he had established in Billings, Montana.

When World War I began, Bivins offered to organize some volunteers from his home town in Virginia. The

---

Chronology

1862	Born in Pungoteague, Accomack County, Virginia on May 8
1862	Father builds a church and schoolhouse at Pungoteague (first buildings for Negroes); buildings burn the same day they are completed
1885	Enters Hampton School to receive military training
1887	Enlists in the U.S. Army in Washington D.C.
1888	Joins troops at St. Grant Argon Territory
1889	Becomes gunner
1890	Promoted to rank of corporal
1892-94	Wins eight medals and badges at the department's competition
1899	Writes part and compiles *Under the Fire with the Tenth Cavalry*
1900	Promoted to squadron sergeant major
1901	Commands a detachment at LaGranga, on San Samar Island in the Philippines, leading patrols in the pursuit of insurrectionists
1901	Promoted to ordinance sergeant then leaves the Tenth Cavalry to accept new post
1937	Dies of unknown cause

---

government declined his offer, but they appointed Bivins a captain of Infantry. Bivins spent six months on active duty at Camp Dix in New Jersey in 1918; after his duty ended he returned to his Montana residence.

Bivins was a remarkable marksman, one of the best in the army. He won many medals in the military in different military competitions. In 1892 he placed sixth with the pistol in the combined departments of Dakota and Colorado. He placed second the following year in the same competition. In 1894, he won first place gold medals with both the revolver and carbine. Bivins represented the Department of Dakota in the 1894 army-wide carbine competition at Fort Sheridan, near Chicago, and won first place with an almost perfect score. Bivins still qualified as an expert marksman as late as 1910.

Writes about Military Life

Bivins's writings about his marksmanship developed into a short book called *Negro Troops in Cuba*. In this book he wrote about hardships that blacks faced in the army and experiences in Cuba. Bivins also writes about his offer to travel with Buffalo Bill Cody's Wild West Show, which he turned down to return to Hampton on furlough in December 1897. Bivins was in Hampton when the United States declared war on Spain in the spring of 1898.

On July 1, 1898, the same day on which men of Bivins's regiment successfully stormed San Juan Hill, Bivins was one of a three-man Hotchkiss crew. During the battles, two of the men were wounded, and Bivins had to operate the weapon alone in spite of heavy enemy fire and a slight head wound. His courage won him national fame. The semiofficial *Army and Navy Journal* chronicled his deeds, as did several black newspapers. Among these newspapers was the *Indianapolis Freeman* which called him "a character worthy of the emulation of every young man of the Negro race." W. E. B. Du Bois also took note of his career in an article in *The Crisis* in May 1930.

Shortly after Bivins returned from Cuba, he contributed to *Under the Fire with Tenth Calvary* (1899, reprint 1969) about the heroism of black regulars in Cuba. His thirty-page recollection of the Cuban campaign is one of several eyewitness accounts in the volume. He compiled the book with United States Land Office recorder Herschel Cashin and other black writers: Charles Alexander, and two Tenth Cavalry comrades, Chaplain William T. Anderson and surgeon Arthur M. Brown. The book provides important information about the black experience in the army. Bivins also documented his service in the military by writing a diary.

Bivins was married to Claudia Bivins, who became active in the Colored Women's Club of Montana. Bivins enjoyed a long life and died in 1937 at the age of seventy-five. A man of valor, courage, and enthusiasm, Bivins' determination and hard work brought him national fame as well as a sense of personal worth.

REFERENCES

Books

Cashin, Herschel V. *Under Fire with the Tenth U.S. Calvary*. Niwot, Colo.: University Press of Colorado, 1993.

Logan, Radford W., and Michael R. Winston, eds. *Dictionary of American Negro Biography*. New York: Norton, 1982.

Online

Buffalo Soldiers National Museum (2004). http://www. buffalosoldiermuseum.com/Buffalo_9th_10th_ Regiment.html(Accessed 2 February 2005).

LaVerne Laney McLaughlin

Robert Blackwell, Sr.
1937–

Consultant, entrepreneur, business executive

Robert Blackwell Sr. is the founder and chief executive officer of Blackwell Consulting Services, a Chicago-based company that is one of the top minority-

---

Chronology

1937	Born in Eastville, Virginia on July 28
1966	Joins International Business Machines, Inc. (IBM) as a systems engineer
1992	Retires from IBM to establish own company, Blackwell Consulting Services
2000	Becomes inductee of the Chicago Area Entrepreneurship Hall of Fame
2005	Teams with son's business, Electronic Knowledge Interchange, to form Chicago's largest minority-owned consulting firm

---

owned information-technology (IT) consulting firms in the Midwest. A longtime executive with International Business Machines Inc. (IBM), Blackwell struck out on his own in the early 1990s to take advantage of what he correctly forecast as a growing need for information-technology consulting work. He has noted in interviews that his success came somewhat by accident. "My father was a janitor," he is quoted as saying to *Crain's Chicago Business* writer Julie Johnsson. "People ask about careers, but I thought I needed a job. It was after I got to IBM and saw it that I became ambitious."

Born in 1937 in Eastville, Virginia, Blackwell grew up in Bryn Mawr, Pennsylvania, an affluent suburb of Philadelphia and home to the prestigious women's college of the same name. He earned a football scholarship to Wichita State University in Kansas, but an injury sidelined his athletic career. While nearing graduation and completion of a degree in psychology and English, Blackwell visited his math professor for some direction about his post-college plan. She suggested he apply to IBM, which had recently contacted her about recruits for their minority hiring program. Though he was a liberal arts major, the professor "told IBM, 'Hire him or never darken my door again for a recommendation. He can do this,'" Blackwell recalled in an interview with Michele Fitzpatrick for the *Chicago Tribune*. "She also is the professor who had taken me aside after I was goofing off in her Algebra class. She said she'd call my mother to report I was a disgrace if I didn't shape up. She set me straight. I had no tech training whatsoever, but I took the job."

Starts at IBM

Blackwell began his career at IBM in 1966 as a systems engineer at a time when the company was becoming a powerhouse in the nascent computer industry. He moved over to the sales force within a few years, and into a management position thereafter. Eventually, he became director of IBM's Greater Chicago Consulting Services Business, which was the company's Midwest information-technology services division. When he retired in 1992, his sector was bringing in some $300 million in business contracts for IBM. By then, Blackwell was in his mid-forties and was well aware of the opportunities arising in the information-technology field. "I thought that a small company could do it just as well as a big company," he explained to *Black Enterprise* writer Holly Aguirre. "I also thought that, as a small business, we could move quicker. There's no bureaucracy. And there is only one level of management."

Blackwell Consulting Services, L.L.C. was founded in July 1992, with Blackwell's son and namesake, Robert Jr., as a partner. It began winning impressive contracts with consulting work both in the Chicago area and elsewhere, but a difference in management styles forced father and son to part ways in 1995. "The happiest person in the world was his mother," Blackwell joked in the interview with Johnsson for *Crain's Chicago Business,* "because she was caught in between these two guys having almost what seemed to be sibling rivalries."

Blackwell's firm continued to prosper during the IT boom in the 1990s, and its client roster grew to include the city of Chicago, United States Naval Academy, and Illinois-based retail giant Sears, Roebuck & Co. As a manager, Blackwell was committed to building a diverse, fluid team at his company, as he told Fitzpatrick in the *Chicago Tribune*, and stressed that he hired from an international field of applicants. "You need some raw genius," he reflected, "some strong analytical skills, some project managers who are really task driven, somebody who is watching the whole forest instead of counting every tree, some persuasive people."

Building a Staff and Family-Run Business

By 2003, that staff roster at Blackwell's firm numbered some 240 employees, and the company was posting revenues of $30 million. It had offices in Cincinnati and Atlanta, among other cities, and did IT-consulting work for companies that by then included insurance giant Aon, Waste Management, Chicago Public Schools, and the Chicago Transit Authority. He has stressed that while municipal contract bids often include a requirement that a certain number of minority firms be included, in the end a strong results-oriented reputation has brought success to his firm. When asked to provide words of wisdom to a younger generation of IT entrepreneurs, he is quoted as saying to Aguirre in the *Black Enterprise* article, "You have to focus on doing a better job than your competition, not your race."

Blackwell's son prospered in the interim with his own IT consulting business, Electronic Knowledge Interchange, and in 2005 the two entities merged to become Chicago's largest minority-owned consulting firm. Each would continue to operate on his own, with Electronic Knowledge Interchange retaining its e-commerce focus for clients that include Bank One and the Chicago Board of Trade. The two divisions, which shared internal resources as well as a parent company called BCS, had a combined total of 400 employees and revenues projected in the $60 million range. Blackwell served as head of the BCS holding company and chief executive officer of the original Blackwell Consulting business, while his son served as vice-chair of BCS; Blackwell's daughter Pamela was also an executive with the family firm, and his other daughter, Leah, held a BCS board seat.

Blackwell is active in the New Jersey-based Association of Business Leaders and Entrepreneurs, a group comprised of leading African American executives, and is a trustee of the Illinois Institute of Technology. He was inducted into the Chicago Area Entrepreneurship Hall of Fame in 2000 and is an ardent patron of the arts, serving on the board of the ETA Creative Arts Foundation, a South-Side Chicago organization that promotes African American arts and culture, and the Joel Hall Dancers, another local group. He and his wife Marjilee are grandparents to six.

REFERENCES

Periodicals

Aguirre, Holly. "Secrets of His Success." *Black Enterprise* 33 (February 2003): 49.

Fitzpatrick, Michele. "Chicago Minority-Owned Consultancy Emphasizes Diversity in Technology Sector." *Chicago Tribune*, 17 August 2000.

Johnsson, Julie. "Blackwell Father-Son Partnership Tested Their Bond." *Crain's Chicago Business*, 7 April 2003.

——. "Father-Son Technology Consulting Team Reboots." *Crain's Chicago Business*, 24 January 2005.

Online

"Robert Blackwell: Biography." The HistoryMakers. http://www.thehistorymakers.com/biography/biography.asp?bioindex=665&category=businessMakers (Accessed 15 March 2005).

"Robert D. Blackwell, Sr., Chairman," Blackwell Consulting Services. http://www.bcsinc.com/about.aspx?p=1&c=bio (Accessed 15 March 2005).

Carol Brennan

Buddy Bolden
1877–1931

Jazz musician, bandleader

Buddy Bolden is known to jazz enthusiasts as the "Father of Jazz." He was the originator and leader of New Orleans' first jazz band, the first prominent New

Buddy Bolden

Chronology

1877	Born in New Orleans, Louisiana on September 6
1895	Leads his own band
1906	Begins to have headaches and show signs of erratic behavior
1907	Admitted to insane asylum in Jackson, Louisiana
1931	Dies in Jackson, Louisiana on November 4

Orleans jazz musician, the first to play blues for dancing, and the first King of Jazz. The stories about Bolden are legendary; some have claimed that when Bolden blew his horn it could be heard across the Mississippi River, and still others have asserted that the clarity and loudness of each note could be heard for ten or twelve miles in all directions when he blew his horn in the center of town at the park.

Charles Joseph "Buddy" Bolden was born in New Orleans, Louisiana on September 6, 1877, the son of a domestic. He had a sister who died of encephalitis when she was five years old. Two years later, his thirty-two-year-old father died of pneumonia. Much of Bolden's life story is shrouded in mystery because what survives about him comes via oral tradition. Contemporary black musicians, such as Jelly Roll Morton, Bunk Johnson, Kid Ory, Bud Scott, and Louis Armstrong, among others, have kept Bolden's memory alive with their recollections, stories, and anecdotes. Consequently, there are a number of discrepancies that surround relatively minor facts about his life, such as whether he graduated from high school, whether he had an occupation as a barber, whether he ever made a recording at the beginning of the twentieth century, and whether it was his mother or mother-in-law who was injured when he became violent during a mental breakdown.

Bolden is said to have been inspired by the music of a "holy roller" church and by gospel music heard in uptown African American Baptist churches. By 1895, he had organized the hot-jazz ensemble which became the standard for bands in New Orleans. The ensemble was comprised of six or seven men who played one or two cornets, the clarinet, the trombone, the double bass, the guitar, and drums. As a professional bandleader, Bolden and his group played in New Orleans dance halls, in Johnson Park, and in surrounding communities. In the 1890s bands in New Orleans were skilled enough to play tunes to the variety of dances that reflected the racial, cultural, and ethnic mixture of the city. Thus, music was played to accompany such dances as the waltz, polka, schottische, and mazurka. During the mid-1890s the two-step, a dance performed with ragtime tunes, also became popular.

Bolden's first horn did not come from a music store; rather, he found it in a New Orleans gutter. The broken instrument helped Bolden begin his musical career. Other than a neighbor's tutelage, Bolden had no formal training for playing the cornet.

Persons closest to Bolden say that he could read some music, but to what degree is unknown. In any event, he preferred to disregard written music and play by ear. What he lacked in formal training, he made up for in passion, style, and embellishments. Bolden's music inspired subsequent jazz greats such as King Oliver, Bunk Johnson, Kid Ory, Louis Armstrong, and Sidney Bechet. According to Donald M. Marquis, New Orleans jazz historian and author of *In Search of Buddy Bolden*, the early jazz player's greatest contribution was that he played blues and stomps for dancing and that he led a band ensemble that drew and engaged all the people of New Orleans regardless of class or race.

Bolden's improvisation as a cornetist issued in a new era of dance music. He played both traditional and popular melodies, turning them into his own creations by means of "paraphrasing and decorating them with personalized twists and turns rather than inventing new melodies over the fundamental harmonies," according to Don Heckman in *The Oxford Companion to Jazz*. Bolden's music was a departure from bands organized by John Robichaux, a black Creole violinist, and William Braun, both of whom organized bands composed of classically trained musicians. Bolden's band became so popular that these and other musical ensembles found themselves having to compete. In fact, Bolden eventually became Robichaux's fiercest rival. Thus, Robichaux's orchestra and other musical ensembles began to play like Bolden. Bolden became so popular that he organized several bands at one time. He would make appearances at half dozen or more engagements throughout the city on any given day or night. Bolden's signature musical selection was "Funky Butt," which was recorded as "Buddy Bolden's Blues" by Jelly Roll Morton. Other Bolden favorites include "Make Me a Pallet on the Floor," "B-Flat Society Blues," "Careless Love," "Tiger Rag," "Sugar Blues," "Oh, Didn't He Ramble," "Just a Little While to Stay," and "Lord, Lord, Lord, You've Sure Been Good to Me."

It is unfortunate that apparently there is no recording of the bandleader's music. A prevailing rumor is that Bolden recorded a cylinder in 1894, but scholars, researchers, and jazz enthusiasts have been unable to locate it. Though there is no known recording of Buddy Bolden's music, some approximations exist. Such contemporaries as Bunk Johnson and Jelly Roll Morton recorded some of Bolden's most popular tunes.

Bolden's Illness

Bolden's rise to popularity and fame came quickly. It appears that the extremely handsome man was being pulled so many different ways that he had little, if any, time to assess his situation. His good looks and talent made him especially attractive to women whom he allowed to complicate his life. Bolden played in the famed Storyville district of New Orleans but never in the brothels. In this district, the cornetist became a local celebrity. Bolden indulged in an excessive lifestyle. He became known as quite a womanizer, and he drank too much. Bolden was also flamboyant. In essence, he lacked ordinary restraint and lost his moral compass.

According to his contemporaries, Bolden began suffering from headaches in 1906, at the height of his career. Accounts about Bolden's illness suggest he began to demonstrate erratic behavior. In March 1906 Bolden believed someone had laced his medicine with poison. As his mother (at least one account says his mother-in-law) was attending him, Bolden attacked her with a water pitcher which left her with a superficial head wound. The police were summoned and Bolden was jailed for a short time. On September 9 of the same year, Bolden was arrested again and was charged with insanity. His third and final arrest occurred on March 13, 1907. Following this arrest, the judge signed papers that ordered the thirty-year-old Bolden to be committed to an insane asylum. On June 5, 1907, Bolden was transferred to the mental institution in Jackson, Louisiana where he spent the rest of his life.

Much speculation has surrounded the cause of Buddy Bolden's mental breakdown. Alcoholism, syphilitic dementia, migraine headaches, and an untreated ear infection have been offered as possible explanations.

According to Frederick J. Spencer in *Jazz and Death: Medical Profiles of Jazz Greats*, the diagnosis recorded by physicians at the asylum was "dementia praecox, paranoid type," commonly known as paranoid schizophrenia. Bolden was allowed to move about the asylum because he was not considered dangerous. He is known to have played his horn on occasion. As time progressed, however, Bolden's condition deteriorated. His mind was full of voices talking constantly, and he responded to them vocally and by vehemently waving his hands about the air. Following a stroke, Buddy Bolden died on November 4, 1931, having spent twenty-four years, nearly half of his life, in an institution for the insane.

REFERENCES

Books

Crow, Bill. *Jazz Anecdotes*. New York: Oxford University Press, 1990.

Hasse, John Edward, ed. *Jazz: The First Century.* New York: HarperCollins Publishers, Inc., 2000.

Heckman, Don. "The Saxophone in Jazz." In *The Oxford Companion to Jazz*. Ed. Bill Kirchner. New York: Oxford University Press, 2000.

Marquis, Donald M. *In Search of Buddy Bolden*. Baton Rouge: Louisiana State University Press, 1978.

Robinson, J. Bradford. "Buddy Bolden." In *The New Grove Dictionary of Jazz*. Ed. Barry Kernfield. New York: St. Martin's Press, 1996.

Spencer, Frederick J. *Jazz and Death: Medical Profiles of Jazz Greats*. Jackson: University of Mississippi Press, 2002.

Yanow, Scott. *The Trumpet Kings*. San Francisco: Backbeat Books, 2001.

Online

Radlauer, Dave. "Imagining Buddy Bolden (1877-1931)." Jazz Rhythm. http://www.jazzhot.bigstep.com/generic.html?pid=9 (Accessed 30 January 2006).

Jewell B. Parham

J. Max Bond
1935–

Architect, educator

An award-winning architect and designer of international acclaim, J. Max Bond has built a variety of structures; his range includes libraries in the States and abroad, cultural centers, university research facilities,

J. Max Bond

Chronology

1935	Born in Louisville, Kentucky on July 17
1958	Graduates from Harvard Graduate School of Design; awarded a Fulbright
1964	Works for Ghana National Construction Company
1965	Teaches at Ghana University of Science and Technology
1969	Collaborates with Don Ryder to form Bond Ryder and Associates
1970	Begins teaching at Columbia University
1985	Becomes dean and professor at City College of the City University of New York
1990	Merges with Davis, Brody and Associates to form Davis, Brody, Bond LLP Architects
1993	Becomes architect for Civil Rights Museum in Birmingham
1996	Becomes architect for the Audubon Research Center at Columbia University
1999	Completes Master Plan and Design for the National University of Science and Technology in Zimbabwe
2003	Completes plans for expansion of Harvard Club in midtown Manhattan
2004	Completes design of Munto Dance Theatre in Chicago
2005	Designs a memorial for World Trade Center area in New York City

office buildings, and museums. Although the plan was later discarded, he is the first African American to become a major player in redeveloping the trade center site, or the World Trade Center memorial, scheduled for erection at Ground Zero, the site of the terrorists attack in New York City on September 11, 2001.

Roots in an Educated Family

James Max Bond was born in Louisville, Kentucky, on July 17, 1935, the middle of three children. His father, J. Max Bond Sr., held doctoral degrees in sociology and economics from the University of Southern California, and his mother, Ruth Clement Bond, studied literature at Northwestern University. The Bonds valued education, and they wanted their son to become a doctor. When they lived in Louisville they arranged for him to work as a hospital emergency room orderly. "The first time I saw an operation, I virtually fainted," he told the *Washington Post*. After Bond Sr. served as a dean at Dillard University in New Orleans, the family moved to Tuskegee where he joined the faculty. From five to nine years of age, young Bond lived at Tuskegee where he was fascinated with the construction of a new residence hall on campus. The huge airplane hangar located near the campus impressed him as well. The hangar served a military base where the storied black pilots, the Tuskegee Airmen, trained.

Bond entered Harvard University where he studied architecture. One of his professors at Harvard told him that there were no famous and prominent black architects and that he should choose another profession. But Bond knew the reputation of several, including Hilyard Robinson and Paul Williams; in fact, he later worked with Williams. In 1955 Bond graduated magna cum laude from Harvard College, where he was inducted into Phi Beta Kappa. He continued to study at Harvard Graduate School of Design, graduating in 1958.

Bond spent a summer in Los Angeles where he worked with legendary African American architect Paul Williams. Afterwards he sought employment with architectural firms that were impressed with his credentials but unimpressed when they met and the firms' officials saw that he was black. Bond earned a Fulbright scholarship and worked in France for a year on projects for Le Corbusier (Charles-Edouard Jeanneret-Gris), the architect for the United Nations Building in New York and an urban designer, whom he actually never met. He studied Le Corbusier's designs as well as those of Auguste Perrett and others who had designed religious buildings. As the end of the year drew near, Bond wrote to five architectural firms in the United States and his credentials and experience again brought favorable response. Again when he came for interviews, somehow nothing was available or the firm claimed that there must have been some mistake.

Work in Ghana, New York, and Tunisia

Finally Bond was successful and worked for two firms in New York for a while, then, with his wife, he returned to Ghana. There he worked for the Ghana National Construction Corporation in 1964 and 1965. "Professionally, I grew up there," he told Jimmie Briggs for *Crisis* magazine. He thought about cultural issues and appreciated the modern culture that he saw in the villages and in the country. While there he built one of his largest projects and his favorite, the Bolgatanga Library in Northern Ghana. Later he built a broadcast station and the residence and offices of then-president Kwame Nkruma, for which he was jokingly referred to as "palace architect." From 1965 to 1967 Bond was an instructor in Ghana's University of Science and Technology.

Bond returned to New York and helped to establish the Architect's Renewal Committee of Harlem (ARCH) and was also its executive director in 1967 and 1968. ARCH was one of several early community design centers developed in the late 1960s and early 1970s. In 1969 Bond collaborated with black architect Don Ryder to form Bond Ryder and Associates; the firm was among the nation's largest and most successful black architectural firms. Among the projects that the firm undertook were the Martin Luther King Jr. Center for Social Change and Memorial in Atlanta, Georgia; the Schomburg Center for Research in Black Culture in Harlem; and the Studio Museum in Harlem. Bond's design for the King Center, where columns and a barrel-vaulted roof are used, reflects the influence of his travels in Tunisia. In 1960 he visited his parents in Tunisia when Bond Sr. was on a State Department assignment.

In addition to working as an architect, Bond began teaching. He served first as assistant professor and later as professor and chairman of the Graduate School of Architecture and Planning at Columbia University, during the years from 1970 to 1985. From 1985 to 1991, he was dean and professor of the School of Environmental Studies at the City College of the City University of New York.

Accomplishments of Davis, Brody, Bond LLP Architects

After Ryder left Bond Ryder and Associates in 1990, Bond merged with Davis, Brody, and Associates, a fifty-two-year-old company; the firm became known as Davis, Brody, Bond LLP Architects. Bond took with him nine of the employees of the previous company. In 1993 he was architect for the Civil Rights Museum in Birmingham and in 1996 the Audubon Research Center at Columbia University. In 1999 he completed the Master Plan and Design for the National University of Science and Technology in Zimbabwe. His design for an expansion of the Harvard Club in midtown Manhattan was unacceptable to traditionalists among the alumni, who wanted him to repeat the neo-Georgian style of the existing structure.

They ignored a club selection committee's approval of Bond's design for a modernistic glass building and challenged the project in court. Debate among club members was intense; in fact, the debate was believed to call Harvard's image into question. Bond and his supporters won, and the work was completed in 2003. His Munto Dance Theatre in Chicago was completed in 2004.

One of his firm's potentially most notable projects, for which it served as associate architects, was the World Trade Center Memorial that aimed to honor lives lost in the World Trade Center attacks in 1993 and 2001. Israeli-born Michael Arad and Peter Walker, a California-based landscape architect, collaborated on the design known as "Reflecting Absence"; Bond and his firm planned to ensure the construction. They proposed two pools of water over the footprint of the former towers. Bond's use of water with designs was seen surrounding King's crypt in the King Center. A wall surrounding the pools was to be inscribed with the names of all victims. Ramps leading underground would permit family members to view matter from the destruction site, while plantings and trees would be arranged in various places. Construction was scheduled to begin in 2006 but in 2005, after protest from prominent leaders, including builder Donald Trump, the plans were put aside.

Fighting Racism, a Bond Family Matter

From the time he was at Harvard until his work with the Harvard Club, Bond met racism repeatedly. Fighting racism, however, was something that the Bond family experienced as well. His cousin, Julian Bond, fought racism in a variety of ways, including his work as chairman of the NAACP. J. Max Bond knew that racism had gripped his father as well as his father's generation. After his father died in 1991, he reflected on the ills and evils of racism and became bitter. He never forgot the rejection that he experienced early on when he applied for jobs.

Community Service and Awards

In addition to his professional work, Bond has extended himself into the community and to professional organizations. Memberships include the New York City Planning Commission; board member of the Studio Museum of Harlem; the Municipal Arts Society; and the National Organization of Minority Architects. Widely honored for his achievements, Bond received the Award of Excellence from the Atlanta Urban Design Committee for his King Center project; the Harry B. Rutkins Memorial Award, AIA; the Whitney M. Young Jr. Citation Award, AIA; and the Architectural Achievement Award, Ernest D. David Scholarship Fund. He holds an honorary degree, Doctor of Humane Letters, from New Jersey Institute of Technology (1994). In 1995 he became a Fellow of the American Institute of Architects and in 1996 a Fellow of the American Academy of Arts and Sciences.

A genial, genteel man with white hair and an informal manner, Bond is married to Jean Davis Carey, a writer and a publicist for the Black Radical Congress, and they have two children, Carey Julian and Ruth Marian. For forty years Bond has been an architectural designer with primary concern in buildings of lasting importance. He is a man with vision. He is concerned with land use as well as human activity and interaction that should occur within a building. He was quoted in *Crisis* as saying: "I...hope my legacy would be a part of the effort to encourage more people of color to do what I do."

REFERENCES

Books

Who's Who among African Americans. 18th ed. Detroit, Mich.: Thomson Gale, 2005.

Periodicals

Briggs, Jimmie. "J. Max Bond, Building a 40-year Reputation in Design." *Crisis* 111 (September/October 2004): 43-44.

Duke, Lynn. "Blueprint of a Life: Architect J. Max Bond Jr. Has Had to Build Bridges to Reach Ground Zero." *Washington Post* (1 July 2004): C1, C4.

Online

Hudson, Frederick B. "An Architect Plans for Peaceful Plains." http://www/agoodblack man.com/hudson_ architects.html (Accessed 30 September 2004).

"J. Max Bond Jr., FAIA. University of Michigan. Taubman College of Architecture and Urban Planning. Visiting Faculty." http://www/tcaup.umich/ edu/facultystaff/visitingfaculty/bond.html (Accessed 30 September 2004).

Jessie Carney Smith

Simeon Booker
1918–

Journalist

Primarily a journalist who concentrates on race matters, Simeon Booker played a prominent role in documenting activities of the civil rights movement and the work of the Freedom Riders and their efforts to enforce federal legislation to integrate public transportation and interstate travel. In so doing, he lived at risk during the Freedom Rides, though not in fear, concluding that

Chronology	
1918	Born in Baltimore, Maryland on August 27
1942	Received B.A. from Virginia Union University
1950	Begins graduate study at Cleveland College; becomes Neiman Fellow at Harvard University
1950?	Becomes reporter for the *Cleveland Call & Post*
1952	Becomes first black full-time reporter for the *Washington Post*
1955	Named Washington Bureau Chief for Johnson Publishing Company and chief columnist for *Jet* magazine
1956	Elected president of Capitol Press Club
1959	Becomes syndicated radio commentator for Westinghouse Broadcasting Company
1982	Wins Fourth Estate Award from National Press Club
1984	Inducted into Hall of Fame, Washington chapter, Sigma Delta Chi
1993	Receives Career Achievement Award, Washington Association of Black Journalists
1998	Receives Master Communications Award, National Black Media Coalition

progress would never grow from fear. Like other journalists of that time, he disguised himself with his dress. He was present at all major civil rights demonstrations, including the first march on Washington and the Selma to Montgomery march. He became the *Washington Post*'s first full-time African American reporter and later one of the first two bureau chiefs for Johnson Publishing Company, with an assignment in Washington, D.C. His illustrious career enabled him to interview the country's powerbrokers. He is also a columnist for *Jet* magazine.

The second of four children, Simeon Saunders Booker Jr. was born in Baltimore, Maryland on August 27, 1918, to Simeon Saunders Booker Sr. and Roberta Waring Booker. When Simeon Jr. was five years old, the Booker family relocated to Youngstown, Ohio, where the elder Booker became executive secretary of a local branch of the YMCA. Thirty-five years later he retired and pastored Third Baptist Church in Youngstown. Apparently his father's service as a preacher impressed Simeon Jr., for later in life as he faced threatening situations while covering civil rights stories, he held a Bible in hand while posing as a preacher—an honorable tribute to his father.

Booker began his college education at Youngstown College but was insulted when he learned that the college distributed activity cards from the YMCA to white students and not to blacks. That led him to transfer to historically black Virginia Union University in Richmond, where he majored in English. To help support himself, he did publicity for the football and basketball teams. During summer vacations he returned to Youngstown and promoted the Negro Baseball League's games held there. In 1942, Booker graduated from Virginia Union with a bachelor of arts degree in English. Now with a keen interest in journalism, he joined the *Baltimore Afro-American* newspaper staff as a reporter. He returned to Ohio and about 1950 joined the *Cleveland Call & Post*. He wrote a series of articles on Cleveland's slum housing and received the Newspaper Guild Award, becoming the first black reporter to be so honored. Recognition for his fine journalistic skills continued, for later he won the Wilkie Award for another series that he wrote on schools in the ghetto. While with the *Cleveland Call & Post*, he organized a union and between 1945 and 1950 he also enrolled in graduate courses in radio, script writing, and journalism at Cleveland College.

On November 1, 1945, John H. Johnson founded *Ebony* magazine, which covered black news in the same way that *Life* magazine exclusively covered whites. Johnson's new magazine aimed to appeal to black readers as well as to mirror the civil rights struggle of blacks who sought to desegregate the railroads, busses, lunch counters, hotels, motels, public schools, and other public places. The magazine and its purpose appealed to Booker, who in 1946 wrote his first article for *Ebony*. He continued to witness and write about racial injustices in the community. Booker lived in a co-op owned by an interracial group of students; there he wrote stories of living conditions among the various groups, including African Americans, Chinese, and Jews. He expanded his focus on racial problems when he joined sociologist Herman Burrell of the Cleveland Urban League in a cross-country trip by automobile and wrote a series of articles for Johnson Publishing Company. Established first as Negro Digest Publishing Company, in 1949 founder John H. Johnson changed the name to Johnson Publishing Company. Booker's profiles included the first black cowboy in Wyoming, the first black American Mormons in Utah, and Schofield Barracks in Hawaii—the first racially integrated military site during World War II.

In 1950, Booker won the Nieman Fellowship for study at Harvard University, becoming only the second African American to receive the award since it was founded in 1938. Noted historian Arthur M. Schlesinger guided his research as Booker read widely on the history of African Americans. The fellowship ended in 1951 and Booker moved to Washington, D.C., where he expected to join the *Washington Post*. Since there was no position available to him then, he worked in a government library until 1952, when he became the *Post*'s first full-time African American reporter. Disappointed that he was hired as a general assignment reporter but was to write exclusively about African Americans, he left the paper in 1954 and moved to Johnson Publishing Company, where he thought that his articles on his race would be more meaningful. Booker was elevated to bureau chief for its several magazines in 1995 when the company expanded and was assigned to Washington, D.C. He and Allan Morrison, who was assigned to the New York office, became the publishing company's first bureau chiefs and

columnists for *Jet* magazine. When Johnson Publishing Company decided to open the Washington Bureau, officials faced immediate difficulty in penetrating the real estate market, for there were no black firms located in downtown Washington. This situation forced Booker and his assistant, E. Fannie Granton, to share space in a local law office. When the breakthrough finally came, the company became the first black-owned firm to rent space in a downtown Washington structure. Booker's training in broadcast journalism fit him well to serve as syndicated radio commentator for Westinghouse Broadcasting Company from 1959 to 1978.

Booker liked writing on civil rights issues, but he could also be as critical as he wished—much more so than he could have been at the *Post*. Soon Booker ventured into delicate ground, covering the 1955 trials pertaining to the murder of Emmett Till, a fourteen-year-old black youth whom two white men lynched in Mississippi for reportedly whistling at a white woman.

Joins the Freedom Riders

The modern civil rights movement escalated by May 1961, when African Americans grew impatient with conditions in the Deep South and its refusal to honor the U.S. Supreme Court's order to integrate bus stations and rail terminals serving interstate travelers. Those who tested the law were thrown out of the facilities, beaten, or jailed. As a result, the Congress on Racial Equality (CORE) organized a group known as Freedom Riders, who began their protest in Washington, D.C. by boarding buses en route to New Orleans. Simeon Booker, the only journalist involved in the protest, joined the racially mixed groups, who met mob violence all along the way. When the riders reached Annison, Alabama, mobs firebombed one bus and threatened the one that carried Booker. To escape the mob, he took a taxi to a local minister's house, called CORE's headquarters, and joined the nation in waiting for U.S. attorney general Robert Kennedy to take charge of the violent events. Booker wrote about the civil rights struggles of the era and his experience with the movement in his book *Black Man's America*. He noted the shift in racial conflict from courtroom to the rank-and-file black, and knew that every black, regardless of his economic or social status, could participate in street demonstrations. Of the black struggle, he wrote, "His century-plus freedom march resembled more of a hitchhike than a steady, onward march. But thrown onto the line were stragglers, grandmas, rabble-rousers, Harvard Ph.D.'s, racketeers, shoe-shine boys, doctors, widows_ all shouting, hollering, picketing, demonstrating and making a racket in so many cities and on so many issues . . . that even the civil rights generals lost control of the field troops."

Booker's work took him to Africa as well, where he traveled with President Richard M. Nixon in 1957, U.S. Attorney General Robert Kennedy in 1962, and with Vice President Hubert H. Humphrey in 1968.

Simeon Booker remained an untiring journalist with a fascination for race issues. He conducted one of the last televised interviews with civil rights martyr Martin Luther King Jr. In addition to his coverage of civil rights issues during the 1960s and early 1970s, he held numerous interviews with Washington's luminaries, including U.S. presidents and senators. His oral interviews with the nation's powerbrokers are housed in such collections as the John F. Kennedy Library, along with those of other people who were associated with Kennedy, and are described in the *American Journalism Historic Association's Occasional Papers No. 1, Oral Histories Relating to Journalism History* (2nd ed., 1999). In addition to his numerous articles, Booker is the author of *Black Man's America* (1964) and *Susie King Taylor, Civil War Nurse* (1960).

Booker is a member of the Capitol Press Club (elected president in 1956), the National Press Club, the Washington Speaker's Community, the Washington Press Club, and the Association of Black Journalists. Widely honored, his recognitions, in addition to those previously mentioned, include the Fourth Estate Award from the National Press Club, 1982; induction into the Hall of Fame, Washington chapter of Sigma Delta Chi, 1984; recipient, Career Achievement Award, Washington Association of Black Journalists, 1993; and Master Communications Award, National Black Media Coalition, 1998. Booker is a member of the Washington, D.C., Professional Chapter of the Society of Professional Journalists, and he is listed in its Pro SPJ Hall of Fame for 2004.

Booker is divorced from Thelma Cunningham; in 1973 he married Carol McCabe. He is the father of Theresa, Simeon Jr., and Theodore. His son James, known as Abdul Muhammad, died in 1992. In his post as columnist for *Jet* magazine (Booker writes *Ticker Tape USA*) and bureau chief for one of the nation's most prominent publishing companies, he continues to cover the noteworthy events in African American living history and culture.

REFERENCES

Books

The Ebony Success Library. Vol. 1. 1000 Successful Blacks. Nashville, Tenn.: The Southwestern Co., by arrangement with Johnson Publishing Company, 1973, p. 34.

Who's Who among African Americans. 18th ed. Detroit: Thomson Gale, 2005.

Periodicals

"Backstage." *Ebony* 56 (July 1991): 17.

"Simeon Booker, JPC Washington Bureau Chief, Honored by Black Media Group." *Jet* 95 (28 December 1998-4 January 1999): 46-47.

Jessie Carney Smith

Ralph Boston
1939–

Track and field athlete, sportscaster, business executive

Ralph Boston rose from a large family in small-town Mississippi during the era of segregation to become a world record holder and winner of Olympic gold, silver, and bronze medals in track and field. His talents and accomplishments extended beyond athletics into academic and corporate settings and led to continued success in these and other endeavors many years after the high points of his athletic career.

Ralph Harold Boston was born on May 9, 1939, in Laurel, Mississippi, the youngest of ten children born to Peter and Eulalia Boston. Peter Boston had worked as a railroad fireman on the Gulf, Mobile, and Ohio rail line, until losing his right eye in a hunting accident. As a result, he became a farmer, hauled junk, and did other odd jobs, while his wife was the homemaker and caregiver of their own large family and needy neighbors and strangers passing through their community.

One of Ralph's earliest memories was of riding with his father on a mule-drawn wagon from the Negro community to the section of Laurel where white people lived, and noticing the contrast in the quality of streets, housing, parks, and other facilities. Despite the segregated environment, Boston grew up in a warm and loving family and community. He learned the value of hard work as a young child, getting up early to go to the fields with his father before attending school, and considered his parents, brothers, and sisters as his first heroes and role models. Boston's older brother Peter was talented in several sports, which heightened Ralph's interest in athletics. Young Ralph learned to swim in a creek outside Laurel, and when the city provided the Oak Pool (for Negroes), he became a lifeguard at the facility.

Ralph Boston attended Oak Park High School in Laurel, where he began to develop his athletic talents in football, track, and other sports. He gave credit in later interviews to the dedicated teachers at his school, who also provided him with a solid academic foundation despite the separate and unequal educational resources and facilities.

Although Boston was a talented quarterback who led his team to the Negro state football championship, his high school track coach, Joseph Frye, realized early on that he had even greater potential in that sport. In both his junior and senior years, Boston was virtually a one-man track team, winning or placing in hurdling, throwing, sprinting, and jumping events as Oak Park continued its run of Negro high school track championships. He was also recognized beyond Mississippi when he set a

Ralph Boston

Chronology

1939	Born in Laurel, Mississippi on May 9
1956	Sets national high school record in hurdles
1960	Breaks world record and wins Olympic gold medal in long jump
1964	Wins Olympic silver medal in long jump
1968	Wins Olympic bronze medal in long jump
1975	Inducted into U.S. Track and Field Hall of Fame
1977	Inducted as first black athlete in Mississippi Sports Hall of Fame
1982	Becomes corporate executive
1985	Inducted into Olympic Hall of Fame
1996	Receives special recognition at Centennial Olympic Games in Atlanta
2001	Retires as corporate executive

national high school record in the 180-yard low hurdles event in 1956.

When he graduated from high school in 1957, Boston wanted the opportunity to compete with and against the best athletes, but the major institutions in his home state were closed to African Americans as students and athletes. Coach Frye recommended a historically black college/university (HBCU), Tennessee A&I State College (now Tennessee State University) in Nashville. Jackson State College, Alcorn State College, and other HBCUs in Mississippi did not have strong track programs, while Tennessee State was well-established, particularly in women's track where several female athletes had competed and won medals in national, international, and Olympic competition. Coach Frye knew some people at the school and also was aware that several people from Laurel were in Nashville who could provide Boston with some hometown connections.

As a result, Frye contacted Ray Kemp, the men's track coach, who accepted Boston without ever seeing him practice or compete. Boston arrived in Nashville during the fall of 1957, and after a short bout of homesickness, he settled into the life of a college student-athlete. By 1959 Boston was competing for Tennessee State with great success in the Midwestern Athletic Association, which included many of the larger southern HBCUs.

Breaks World and Olympic Long Jump Records

Boston made the adjustment from small-town Mississippi to college life in a fairly large southern city, and his horizons continued to expand along with his talent. In the summer of 1959, he was invited to compete in a major track meet at Madison Square Garden in New York City, and he flew in an airplane for the first time. He also realized his dream of competing against the best athletes in his sport, regardless of race. By this time, Boston was focused on his best event, the long jump, and he continued to improve his technique, distance, and ability to compete under pressure. He came in second in New York when one of his competitors set a new indoor world record. Boston was still approached about traveling to compete in the Middle East and in the summer of 1960 made the first of many international trips.

The 1960 Olympic Games were scheduled for Rome, Italy, and Boston was prepared to do well, provided he qualified for the United States Olympic team. He succeeded in doing so at the Olympic Trials in Palo Alto, California, then during a pre-Olympic competition in Pomona, California, Boston broke the world record in the long jump by leaping a distance of 26 feet, 11 and one quarter inches.

His effort eclipsed the long-standing record of African American and Olympic track legend Jesse Owens, set in 1935. As a result, Boston became a national celebrity literally overnight and the favorite to win the gold medal for the United States in Rome. He won the competition with a jump of 26 feet, seven and three-fourth inches, breaking the 1936 Olympic record of Owens. Boston dedicated his gold medal to his mother and the memory of his father, who had died on January 1, 1960.

Boston's victory in Rome was part of the outstanding collective accomplishment of African American athletes representing the United States, including Cassius Clay (later known as Muhammad Ali) in boxing, Oscar Robertson and Walter Bellamy in basketball, and Rafer Johnson in the decathlon. Tennessee State University (TSU) established a track and field record in 1960 that may never be surpassed by a single university in a single Olympiad. In addition to Boston, classmate Wilma Rudolph won three gold medals, and classmates Martha Hudson, Barbara Jones, and Lucinda Williams joined Rudolph to win gold for the United States in the 400 meter sprint relay race. Edward S. Temple, coach of the TSU Tigerbelles women's track team, was the coach for the U.S. women's track team.

As the best long jumper in the world, Boston received numerous honors and awards, including World Athlete of the Year in 1960 and North America Athlete of the Year in 1961. During that year he broke his own world record twice, with jumps of 27 feet, one half inch, and 27 feet, two inches. While maintaining a regimen of training, travel, and competition, in 1962 he also married the former Geneva Jackson Spencer, completed his B.S. degree in biochemistry at TSU, became the father of a son, Kenneth Todd Boston on November 9 of that year, and spent time as a medical research technician at Mount Sinai Hospital in Los Angeles until 1963. During that year Boston was also inducted into the Helms Hall of Fame in Los Angeles.

After returning to Nashville later that year, Boston served as an assistant track coach at TSU and prepared to return to the Olympics, which were scheduled for Tokyo, Japan in 1964. While he remained the number one long jumper overall, again breaking his world record twice in the same year, his main rival was Igor Ter-Ovanesyan of the Soviet Union. In Tokyo both Boston and Ter-Ovanesyan were outdistanced by Lynn Davies from Great Britain, and Boston took home the silver medal.

Boston broke his own world record one more time, with a jump of 27 feet, four and three-quarters inches in 1965, and he remained the top long jumper in the world and Pan American Games champion through 1967. During that year he also began playing golf and over time became quite accomplished in his new sport. In 1968 he moved to Knoxville, Tennessee, to become coordinator of minority affairs and special services at the University of Tennessee (UT), combining administrative responsibilities with preparations to return to the Olympics for a third time in Mexico City, Mexico.

Despite the controversies of the 1968 games, involving a boycott of the Olympics by several top African American athletes, Boston and others chose to participate. Some used the world stage of Mexico City to demonstrate solidarity with the 1960s Black Power movement, most notably the gloved "Black Power" salute by Olympic gold and bronze medalists Tommie Smith and John Carlos during the medal presentation after their event.

While their actions resulted in dismissal from the U.S. team and the Olympic Village, Boston and the other athletes refocused on the remaining competitions. In an amazing act of sportsmanship, Boston helped his chief rival in the long jump, African American teammate Bob Beamon. This set the stage for Beamon's incredible leap of 29 feet, two and one half inches, which shattered the existing world record by almost two feet.

Boston came in third and then held the unique distinction of winning the three different medals awarded (gold, silver, and bronze) in the same event in three consecutive Olympic Games. Another TSU Olympian, Wyomia Tyus, also made history in Mexico City when she won the gold medal again in the 100 meter sprint event. Four years earlier, she and Boston were teammates on the U.S. team in Tokyo, where she won her first gold. Added to Wilma Rudolph's victory in 1960, TSU set yet another record by winning the event for the United States in three successive Olympiads.

Boston decided to end his athletic career in track and field after Mexico City and return to his position at UT in Knoxville. Additional honors, awards, recognitions, travel, speaking engagements, and other public appearances continued to be part of his schedule, along with university responsibilities, including counseling students, advising the African American Student Liberation Force (AASLF) organization, and chairing the Tony Wilson Memorial Fund at UT. The fund was established after the untimely death of Wilson, a talented student-athlete and brother of singer, Nancy Wilson. Boston also conducted a behavioral study of UT African American students and developed publications for recruiting students to attend the university.

Boston's sports experience and knowledge contributed to his success as a sportscaster with Marvin Sugarman Productions, based in New York City, and later with ESPN, the cable television sports channel based in Bristol, Connecticut. Boston also served on the United States Olympic Committee from 1968 to 1972, and received the honors of being named the greatest long jumper of the century and induction into the Tennessee Sports Hall of Fame in 1970. His marriage ended in divorce in 1971. As a consultant to the U.S. Olympic Team for the 1972 Olympic Games in Munich, West Germany, Boston was in Munich when Palestinian terrorists killed eleven Israeli athletes, another event underscoring how world politics had changed the character of the Olympics since his first experience in 1960.

In 1973 Boston was recognized as honorary speaker for the Tennessee House of Representatives and inducted into the National Association of Intercollegiate Athletics (NAIA) Hall of Fame, followed by his 1975 induction into the U.S. Track and Field Hall of Fame. Although retired from active competition, Boston appeared on the ABC-TV "Superstars" program featuring celebrated athletes and was the winner in the senior division in 1976.

The year 1977 brought an award of great personal significance, as Boston became the first African American ever inducted into the Mississippi Sports Hall of Fame. Twenty years after graduating from all-black Oak Park High School in Laurel, he was recognized for his outstanding athletic achievements before and after the end of legal segregation in his home state. During the same year Boston also entered the business world, becoming a salesman for the Integon Insurance Company. The following year he was honored in his hometown when the City of Laurel dedicated the Ralph Boston Park, and in 1980 he was listed in *Who's Who Among Black Americans* for the first time.

Becomes Business Executive and Receives Additional Honors

In 1982 Boston became an account executive for the South Central Bell telephone company, based in their Knoxville office, thus ending his association with UT after thirteen years. During the 1982 World's Fair in the city, Boston was honored again when officials created a display, including his three Olympic medals, and the same year he was inducted into the Knoxville Sports Hall of Fame.

The following year Boston was named to the All-Time All-Star Indoor Track and Field Team, and in 1985 he received two more prestigious awards: he was inducted into the Olympic Hall of Fame and received the National Collegiate Athletic Association (NCAA) Silver Anniversary Award. In 1988 Boston left South Central Bell to become a general partner at WKXT-TV, the CBS affiliate station in Knoxville. His success was tempered with the death of his mother, Eulalia Boston, at age 94 on March 14, 1991.

Boston further diversified his corporate experience when he became director of customer relations for Ericsson Inc., the telecommunications company based in Atlanta, Georgia. As a result, he moved from Knoxville to Atlanta in 1992, yet continued his relationship with WKXT until 1996. In 1993 Tennessee State University named its annual homecoming event the Ralph Boston Golf Tournament, and a spring invitational track meet was also named for Boston and his TSU teammate John Moon, who went on to become head track coach at Seton Hall University in South Orange, New Jersey.

Receives Special Recognition during Atlanta Olympics

Being in Atlanta seemed fortuitous as well as convenient for Boston, as the city was the site of the 1996 Olympic Games. He participated in the Knoxville portion of the Olympic torch relay to Atlanta, and during the opening ceremonies he received the high honor of being one of the persons chosen to bring the Olympic flag into the new Olympic Stadium. Veteran NBC-TV sportscaster Dick Enberg referred to the "elegant Ralph Boston" in his commentary during the international broadcast of the Olympic Games.

Other connections to the 1960 Games were evident, as there was a tribute to Boston's fellow TSU classmate and Olympian, Wilma Rudolph, who had died in 1994. Another teammate, Muhammad Ali, was the final torchbearer lighting the cauldron to signify the start of the Centennial Olympic Games. Overall, the Atlanta Olympic Games were successful, but they were marred by the bombing in Centennial Olympic Park. An African American woman, Alice Hawthorne, and a Turkish cameraman, Melih Uzunyol, lost their lives, and 111 others were wounded. The person responsible, Eric Rudolph, was eventually brought to justice for his actions.

Boston and other Olympic veterans could not help but reflect back on the 1972 tragedy in Munich, but they continued to hold high the Olympic ideals of sportsmanship and international brotherhood as the games concluded. The following year, Boston moved to Peachtree City, an Atlanta suburb, and left Ericsson to become president and chief executive officer of ServiceMaster Services, a company based in Stone Mountain, Georgia.

After four years with ServiceMaster, Boston opted for full retirement to enjoy the fruits of his very successful life and multiple careers. Since 2001, he has divided his time between residences and family properties in Georgia, Mississippi, and Tennessee, and participated in charitable endeavors such as the Atlanta-based Trumpet Awards, created by his friend and TSU alumna Xernona Clayton and numerous professional and celebrity golf tournaments. At reunions and other gatherings Boston has documented his family history by recording interviews on videotape and also has spent time working on his autobiography.

In retirement, Boston curtailed many of the community involvements and board affiliations he held during his working years, including the President's Council on Physical Fitness and Sports, healthcare and hospital systems in Georgia and Tennessee, the Boys and Girls Club, and other organizations. He continued to speak and work with young people on a volunteer basis, motivating them to achieve the same balance in mind, body, and spirit that enabled him to achieve in his life.

REFERENCES

Books

Ashe, Arthur. *A Hard Road to Glory: The African American Athlete in Track and Field*. New York: Amistad Press, 1983.

Dawson, Dawn P., ed. *Great Athletes*. Pasadena, Calif.: Salem Press, 2002.

Lewis, Dwight, and Susan Thomas. *A Will to Win*. Mt. Juliet, Tenn.: Cumberland Press, 1983.

Matney, William C., ed. *Who's Who among Black Americans*. Lake Forest, Ill.: Educational Communications, Inc., 1985.

Wallechinsky, David. *The Complete Book of the Olympics*. Boston: Little, Brown, and Company, 1992.

Collections

The Special Collections of the Brown-Daniel Library, Tennessee State University, contain newspaper clippings, photographs, audio and videotapes, and other items related to the athletic and academic career of Ralph Boston.

Fletcher F. Moon

Midian O. Bousfield
1885–1948

Physician, business executive

The need for the recognition of African American health concerns along with a strong voice regarding education and the entrepreneurial spirit bolstered the groundbreaking contributions of Midian Othello Bousfield. Bousfield's successes as the Army Medical Corp's first African American colonel, the first African American member of Chicago's board of education, and president of Supreme Liberty Life Insurance changed attitudes regarding segregation in the North and the South. His successes, which follow a conservative approach for social change, were realized well before the civil rights movement of the 1960s.

Midian Othello Bousfield was born on August 22, 1885 to Willard Hayman and Cornelia Catherine Gilbert Bousfield. Willard Hayman was a barber and businessperson who set the stage for his son's interest in business. Education and activism as promoted by W. E. B. Du Bois's social agenda for the "talented tenth" inspired Bousfield; he graduated from the University of Kansas in 1907 with a bachelor's degree and 1909 with an M.D. from Northwestern University in Chicago. Bousfield exemplified the forward-thinking attitude of the time toward self-improvement and the advancement of the African American community. After serving as an intern at Howard University's Freedman's Hospital in 1910, Bousfield followed medical prospects that took him to Brazil in 1911. This venture did not work out as hoped, but before returning to Kansas City he spent time prospecting for gold. He practiced in Kansas City until 1914 before moving to Chicago with his new bride,

Chronology	
1885	Born in Tipton, Missouri on August 22
1907	Receives B.A. from State University of Kansas
1909	Receives M.D. from Northwestern University School of Medicine
1909-10	Completes internship at Freedmen's Hospital, Washington D.C.
1911	Prospects in Brazil
1914	Marries Maudelle Tanner Brown
1914-16	Becomes school health officer and school tuberculosis physician in Chicago, Illinois
1915-20	Serves as secretary of the Railway Men's Association
1921-25	Serves as incorporator, medical director, and vice-president of Liberty Life Insurance Company
1925-29	Serves as medical director and president of Liberty Life Insurance Company; president of Supreme Liberty Life Insurance Company
1934	Becomes director of Negro Health for Julius Rosenwald Fund
1939	Becomes first African American member of Chicago's board of education
1942	Becomes Medical Corp's first African American colonel, U.S. Army all-black hospital at Fort Huachuca, Arizona
1946	Assists in organizing Provident Medical Associates (funds education for aspiring African American specialists)
1948	Dies in Chicago on February 16

Maudelle Tanner Brown. Chicago would see both their careers and their family grow. The couple had one child.

Initially in Chicago, Bousfield spent time as secretary of the Railway Men's Association, an African American railroad union. He also served as school health officer and school tuberculosis physician. During the five years Bousfield served as secretary to the railroad union, membership soared from 250 to 10,000 and included African Americans from all over the country. In 1919 he gave up his railroad affiliation and became one of the original incorporators of the Liberty Life Insurance Company. Bousfield began this new business opportunity as medical director and vice president. After ten years, he became president and successfully completed a merger, forming the reorganized Supreme Liberty Life Insurance Company. He continued to serve as medical director and chairman of its executive committee.

As physician and businessman, Bousfield saw his interests become more focused. He saw a need to improve health care for the underserved African American population in the South and to improve the training opportunities and thus the quality of African American physicians. Bousfield championed these issues for the rest of his life. Understanding the need for a broad base of influence, Bousfield worked with Michael M. Davis, the medical director of the Chicago-based Julius Rosenwald Fund. He convinced Davis and others of the need and the opportunity for improving African American hospitals, increasing training for nurses and doctors, and providing more medical training opportunities for African American medical professionals. Bousfield's persuasiveness and straight talk made way for his appointment as director of Negro health for the Julius Rosenwald Fund in 1934. Bousfield developed programs that helped to improve care in African American hospitals and created positions for doctors in southern health agencies. He fulfilled these goals with strong support from the Rosenwald Fund until 1942. The commitment of this white organization and the determination of Bousfield resulted in decreasing the medical disparity created by segregation.

In concert with his work in the Rosenwald Fund, Bousfield became president of the all-African American National Medical Association, which placed him in the forefront as spokesman for African American medicine. He used the opportunity to become the first African American speaker at the American Public Health Association. His speech was published in the *American Journal of Public Health*. He bluntly stated in his speech that health officials "so complacently review, year after year, the unfavorable vital statistical reports of one-tenth of the population and make no special effort to correct them." He firmly attributed this lack of action to racist blinders. Because of these statements, a more sensitive approach was realized by health professionals. Never before had such a direct and clear perspective of neglected African American health care been presented to the association.

Seizes Opportunities to Serve

White leaders in Chicago did not overlook Bousfield's abilities as a leader, businessman, and physician. Opportunities to serve his community were offered and he embraced them. One such opportunity came in 1939, when he was appointed the first African American member of the Chicago board of education. This appointment had been sought by the African American community for twenty five years. It placed the Bousfield family firmly in the arena of African American education. Bousfield's wife, Maudelle Brown Bousfield, was the first African American dean in the Chicago schools in 1926 and assigned in 1928 as the first African American principal in Chicago.

In 1942, Bousfield was again called, but to a broader stage for service. He was selected to operate the U.S. Army's first and largest all-African American hospital at an Army Post in Fort Huachuca, Arizona. He enlisted, making the rank of lieutenant colonel, and retired as the Medical Corp's first African American colonel. His facility was so competent that many whites sought care at Fort Huachuca in preference to their own medical care facilities.

Midian Othello Bousfield died February 16, 1948 at his home in Chicago. Although Bousfield never joined the NAACP, he was a key leader for the Urban League. He remained close to the white power structure and used his influences to advocate for issues of importance. Just two years before his death, in 1946, Bousfield helped to organize the Provident Medical Association. This organization of prominent and progressive African American doctors in Chicago set about to support and fund medical specialists across the spectrum. Bousfield actively engaged in change for health care, insurance, and education, which made huge strides toward equality and opportunity for African American citizens. Because of Bousfield's efforts, the transition to integration in the health profession in the 1960s was more readily acceptable.

REFERENCES

Books

Beasley, E. H. "Midian Othello Bousfield." In *American National Biography*. Vol. 3. Eds. John A. Garraty and Mark C. Carnes. New York: Oxford University Press, 1999, pp. 259-60.

Murray, Florence, ed. *The Negro Handbook 1949*. New York: Macmillan, 1949, p. 347.

Who's Who of the Colored Race. Vol. 1. Chicago: Who's Who in Colored America Publishing, 1915, p. 31.

Yenser, Thomas, ed. *Who's Who in Colored America*. 6th ed. Brooklyn: Thomas Yenser Publisher, 1942, pp. 67-68.

Collections

Much of Bousfield's professional correspondence can be found in the Julius Rosenwald Fund papers in the Fisk University; John Hope and Aurelia Elizabeth Franklin Library (Special Collections) in Nashville, Tennessee; and the Peter Marshall Murray papers in the Moorland-Spingarn Research Collection at Howard University in Washington D. C.

Lean'tin L. Bracks

J. W. E. Bowen
1855–1933

Educator, minister, writer, lecturer

A multitalented scholar, J. W. E. Bowen helped to shape African American culture through his service as seminary administrator, minister, writer, and an indefatigable lecturer, and through his actions as a race man. He fought for full assimilation of African American ministers in leadership positions in the Methodist Episcopal Church, which finally led to the church's acceptance of black clergymen into the episcopacy. He co-founded two journals that addressed African American issues. Many of his views have been preserved in his various works.

He may have influenced more students to enter the ministry and attend Gammon Theological Seminary than anyone else on the faculty during his tenure. Bowen was also among such notable black leaders as W. E. B. Du Bois, William H. Crogman, Richard R. Wright Sr., and John Hope, who influenced thinking in the African American community of the late eighteenth and into the nineteenth centuries.

John Wesley Edward Bowen was born in New Orleans on December 3, 1855 (some sources say 1865) to former slaves Edward and Rose Simon Bowen. Edward Bowen had worked as a carpenter while living in Maryland but was forced into slavery after relocating to New Orleans. Determined to be free, he worked hard and purchased his own freedom and later on, in 1858, that of his wife and son John. He joined the Union army during the Civil War.

The ambitious, industrious, and intelligent Bowens wanted their son to be educated; recognizing his fine gifts and talents early on, they exposed him to the best education that they could manage. J. W. E. Bowen (as his name is often listed) studied at Union Normal School and then New Orleans University, a school founded by the Methodist Episcopal Church to provide education for freemen. (New Orleans University merged with Strait University on June 6, 1930, to become Dillard University.) In 1878 Bowen received an undergraduate degree (he was in the school's first graduating class), and in 1884 he was awarded a master's degree, both from New Orleans University. From there he moved to Nashville, and from 1878 to 1882 he taught ancient languages at Central Tennessee College, first known as Walden University.

In the autumn of 1882, he enrolled in the School of Theology at Boston University; while a student of theology, he served as pastor at Revere Street Methodist Episcopal Church in Boston. He graduated from Boston University in 1885 with the bachelor's degree in sacred theology. Bowen was honored at commencement, when he became one of two members of the graduating class in law, medicine, and liberal arts to deliver orations. He and a classmate represented the School of Theology. Soon after graduation, he held another pastorate, this time at St. John's Methodist Episcopal Church in Newark, New Jersey. Bowen continued graduate study in theology at Boston University, and in 1887 he was awarded the Ph.D., becoming the second African American to earn that degree in the United States.

Bowen left St. John's in 1888 and became pastor of Centennial Methodist Episcopal Church in Baltimore. While at Centennial, Bowen attracted over seven hundred people to a revival, all of whom claimed to have experienced a conversion at the gathering. Since Bowen enjoyed teaching as well, he continued to teach while attending to his ministry; thus, from 1888 to 1892 he was a professor of church history and systematic theology at Morgan College (now Morgan State University) in Balti-

Chronology

1855	Born in New Orleans, Louisiana on December 3
1878	Graduates from New Orleans University (now Dillard University)
1878-82	Teaches at Central Tennessee College in Nashville
1882	Enrolls in School of Theology at Boston University; pastors Revere Street Methodist Episcopal Church in Boston
1885	Receives bachelor's degree in Sacred Theology from Boston University; pastors St. John's Methodist Episcopal Church in Newark, New Jersey
1886	Marries Ariel Serena Hedges, who dies in 1904
1887	Receives Ph.D. from Boston University, the second African American to earn a Ph.D. in United States
1888	Becomes pastor of Centennial Methodist Episcopal Church in Baltimore
1888-92	Teaches church history and systematic theology at Morgan College in Baltimore
1889-93	Serves as member and examiner for the American Institute of Sacred Literature
1890-91	Serves as professor of Hebrew at Howard University, Washington, D.C.; pastors Asbury Methodist Episcopal Church in Washington, D.C.
1891	Represents Methodist Episcopal Church at conference on world Methodism, held in Washington, D.C.
1892	Serves as field secretary for the Missionary Board
1893-32	Teaches at Gammon Theological Seminary in Atlanta
1895	Leads three-day conference on Africa at Cotton States Exposition held in Atlanta
1896	Publishes proceedings of the conference on Africa
1896-1912	Serves as delegate to quadrennial general conference of the Methodist Episcopal church
1901	Represents Methodist Episcopal Church at conference on world Methodism, held in Washington, D.C.
1902	Co-edits proceedings on conference for young people, published as *The United Negro*
1906	Injured in Atlanta race riot; marries Irene Smallwood
1906-10	Serves as president of Gammon Theological Seminary while still teaching
1910-32	Serves as vice-president of Gammon Theological Seminary
1912	Protests racial discrimination in the church and publishes *An Appeal for Negro Bishops, but No Separation*
1932	Retires and becomes emeritus professor
1933	Dies in Atlanta on July 20

more. After becoming pastor of Asbury Methodist Episcopal Church in Washington, D.C., he taught at Howard University in Washington. In the 1890-91 academic year, he also taught Hebrew. In 1891 and again in 1901, Bowen was the Methodist Episcopal Church's representative at conferences on world Methodism held in Washington, D.C. He left his pastorate and served as field secretary for the Missionary Board from 1892 to 1893. His scholarship in the field of sacred theology led to his post as member and examiner for the American Institute of Sacred Literature, from 1889 to 1893. An eloquent speaker, he made his mark at annual conferences and conventions and before local congregations.

Gammon Theological Seminary, located in Atlanta, Georgia, attracted him to the position of professor of historical theology, which he accepted in 1893. The Methodist Episcopal Church had founded the school in 1883 for the purpose of preparing African Americans for the ministry. As was the case with many other colleges of that era established to educate African Americans, Gammon had a white faculty; Bowen became the school's first African American professor. The school honored him that year with an honorary doctor of divinity degree. During this period, Bowen was secretary of Gammon's Stewart missionary foundation; in that capacity, he also edited the *Steward Missionary Magazine*, the foundation's journal.

Heads Gammon Theological Seminary

As the Methodist Episcopal Church began to organize and strengthen its work in the South, it saw an immediate need to train black ministers to serve in their own churches. The Methodist Episcopal Church also organized conferences, some of which evolved into separate black conferences that brought more churches and more members into these meetings. As well, the Freedmen's Aid Society began to establish schools in the South and emphasized theological training in their academic programs. Thus, all of the black colleges founded before 1875 had a theological seminary or religious department. Among these schools were Clark University and its religious arm called the Theological School of Clark University, established in 1883. In 1888, the seminary became an autonomous Methodist Episcopal school called Gammon Theological Seminary and continued to recruit scholars to its faculty.

When Bowen went to Gammon, he filled the vacancy left by William Henry Crawford when he accepted the presidency of Allegheny College. Bowen brought rich and varied experiences that he had gained during his professional life as preacher and teacher. He remained at Gammon for thirty-nine years (1893-1932). During that period, he held other offices, the highest of which was president of the seminary from October 1906 to June 1910 and vice president from 1910 until he retired from that post. The administrative structure of the seminary changed in 1910, when it merged briefly with nearby Clark University and the merged institutions operated for only two years under one president. The school witnessed significant achievements under Bowen's leadership, among them an increase in enrollment. Although he stepped down from his additional post as head of the department of church history in 1926, he continued to serve the seminary by teaching various courses, including historical theology, and by spending two years as extension secretary. After he retired in 1932, he was given the rank of emeritus professor.

Gammon, which had been at its zenith during the 1920s and 1930s, when Bowen was there as a teacher, was one of the two African American seminaries in the United States that were nationally accredited. But several developments helped to destabilize the school. The Great Depression took its toll on the seminary's modest endowment, enrollment declined, and scholarly professors retired. The fledgling seminary received some financial support but continued to struggle. Funds for student scholarships and faculty salaries were lacking. In 1957, well after the Bowen years, Gammon's trustees approved in principle a proposal to join in a cooperative venture and became part of an Interdenominational Theological Center. After the charter was approved in 1958 and the new center opened, according to Grant Shockley in *Heritage & Hope*, Gammon was recognized as "one of the most singular experiments in theological education in North America."

Bowen respected Tuskegee Institute founder and president Booker T. Washington, who was a proponent of industrial education for African Americans. In fact, he praised Washington's address before the Cotton States Exposition held in Atlanta in October 1895, in which he gave his view on that subject. Just before the Washington address, on what was called "Negro Day," Bowen spoke on "An Appeal to the King." The exposition continued, and in December 1895 Bowen led an important three-day conference on Africa that he had organized and that was loosely connected to the exposition. He published the proceedings the next year under the title *Africa and the American Negro: Addresses and Proceedings of the Congress on Africa . . . in Connection with the Cotton States . . . Exposition, Dec, 13-15, 1895*. Sometime later, Bowen felt a need to distance himself from Washington and Washington's views on industrial education. Bowen advocated instead liberal arts education as a prerequisite for good preparation for leadership. Bowen became a man of protest as well, joining W. E. B. Du Bois in agitating for state legislation to desegregate railroad transportation. They crusaded for better educational provisions for black youth, calling on the legislature to develop a system of public high schools for them.

Agitates for Racial Parity in the Episcopacy

Apparently a man of enormous devotion to the Methodist Episcopal Church, from 1896 to 1912 Bowen served as delegate to its quadrennial general conference. He had become exceptionally distinguished—perhaps the most distinguished—among African American clergy. In an unsuccessful effort to promote him in the church, many delegates voted in favor of his rise to the episcopacy. He became disenchanted with the slow racial progress in the church, however, and in 1912 published *An Appeal for Negro Bishops, but No Separation*. It was not until the 1920s that the church elected its first African American bishops; unfortunately, however, Bowen was not among them. Instead, Robert Elijah Jones and

Matthew Wesley Chair were chosen. Despite the significance of Bowen's work and his widespread appeal, younger clergy were preferred.

Bowen sat on the Board of Control of the church's Epworth League, which gave him the privilege of organizing a national conference on the Christian education of African American youth. The Epworth League was organized in 1889, after several youth groups and societies of Methodist youth in parts of the denomination merged. Young black layman I. Garland Penn was elected assistant general secretary of the Epworth Leagues in 1896 and was charged with promoting the leagues in the black conferences. For Bowen, preparing for the national gathering was an easy task, for he had unusual skill for organizing and managing conferences. He joined educator, journalist, and religious workers as they edited and published in 1902 the conference proceedings under the title *The United Negro: . . . Addresses and Proceedings: The Negro Young People's Christian and Educational Congress, Held August 6-11, 1902.*

Bowen joined Jesse Max Barber in launching in January 1904 the literary journal *Voice of the Negro*; it targeted a national African American audience and clearly reached a fairly large part of the black middle class in Atlanta and throughout the South. Although the journal was less radical than many blacks hoped, it vigorously pursued public issues and race matters, particularly mob violence. By 1906, the journal had from twelve to fifteen thousand subscribers. Bowen also edited an important periodical called *The Negro*. Among his other publications is a volume of sermons and addresses, including "Plain Talks to the Colored People of America," "Appeal to the King," "The Comparative Status of the Negro at the Close of the War and To-day," "The Struggle for Supremacy Between Church and State in the Middle Ages," "The American and the African Negro," "University Addresses," "Discussions in Philosophy and Theory," and "The History of the Education of the Negro Race."

In his article "Did the American Negro Make, in the Nineteenth Century, Achievements Along the Lines of Wealth, Morality, Education, Etc., Commensurate with His Opportunities? If So, What Achievements Did He Make?" published in Culp's *Twentieth Century Negro Literature*, Bowen comments on the untold story of black America and freedom: "The story of the burdens and disadvantages of the Negro at the beginning of his days of freedom has not yet been committed to paper. It will require a black writer to perform this deed." Interestingly, he commented on black economic progress as well. In that same source he wrote: "Slavery did not teach him economy; on the contrary, it taught him profligacy, and, when he learned to economize, it was in spite of the system." Bowen notes that blacks did, in fact, achieve well in the nineteenth century. He concludes: "From every point of view, the growth of the Negro has more than kept pace with his opportunities."

Bowen belonged to the American Historical Association, the American Negro Academy, and the NAACP. His interest in race relations led him to endorse the Niagara Movement in September 1905. Led by Du Bois and William Monroe Trotter, a group of intellectuals and activists representing fourteen states met near Niagara Falls, New York, and organized the movement. The purpose of the new group was to press for immediate civil rights for black people. They would accept no compromise and clearly rejected the accommodationist policies that Booker T. Washington espoused. The Niagara Movement merged with the NAACP in 1909. Bowen also helped to found the Georgia Equal Rights League, whose objectives were similar to those of the Niagara Movement.

Provides Shelter during Atlanta Riot

By 1906, when Bowen became president of Gammon, Atlanta was involved in urban mob violence that became known as the Atlanta race riot. White mobs, ranging in size from several dozen to five thousand, attacked blacks, black-owned businesses, and property that blacks used, leaving twenty-five people dead and several hundred injured. Many blacks fled the city. The violence came after a staunch racist became a gubernatorial primary candidate; a crusade was launched against so-called vice in the black community, and yellow journalism practices of the local press reported an epidemic of rapes of white women. Bowen helped to protect blacks from the mobs, however, opening the seminary to blacks who needed shelter. Three days after the riot began, white police beat and then arrested him. Jesse Max Barber, Bowen's co-editor for the *Voice of the Negro*, left Atlanta—probably as much to escape harm to himself as to protect the journal—and took the journal to Chicago. There he continued to edit the publication, under the title *Voice*. Apparently Bowen had no further contact with the publication.

In 1886 Bowen married Newark, New Jersey-born Ariel Serena Hedges, the daughter of a Presbyterian minister, and an educator, missionary, performing artist, reformer, and club leader. She taught at Tuskegee Institute (now Tuskegee University) in Alabama, where Booker T. Washington was founder and president. After the Bowens moved to Atlanta, Ariel Bowman became professor of music at Clark University in 1895. She was also president of the Georgia Women's Christian Temperance Union (WCTU) No. 2, and was widely active in Christian and reform work. She wrote a number of works. Ariel and J. W. E. Bowen had four children: Irene, Juanita, John Wesley Edward Jr., and Portia Edmonia (who died in childhood). Son John Wesley Edward Bowen Jr. followed his father and became a prominent Methodist Episcopal minister. He also filled his father's vision for blacks in the Methodist Episcopal Church and was elected to the episcopacy in 1948. Ariel Bowen died in 1904 while visiting the World's Fair in St. Louis; two years later Bowen married Irene Smallwood, who taught in Calhoun School, then well known and located in Calhoun, Alabama. Their marriage lasted twenty-seven years.

Bowen died in Atlanta on July 20, 1933; he was the last of his graduating class from New Orleans University. His widow, a son, and two daughters survived him. The scholarly and intellectual Bowen was widely respected among Methodist circles as an educator and a seminary leader. In *Heritage & Hope*, Grant S. Shockley wrote that Bowen "was considered one of the most mature scholars of his race and one of its more trusted leaders." Bowen was among the outstanding black scholar-theologians who trained Gammon's students who themselves went on to become well known ministers, district superintendents, bishops, editors of religious publications, missionaries, church board executives, and college presidents. A recognized lecturer and public orator, Bowen served as a Chautauqua lecturer. He agitated against racial discrimination in transportation and education, and he called for full assimilation of black clergy in the segregated Methodist Episcopal Church, now known as the United Methodist Church.

REFERENCES

Books

Bardolph, Richard. "John Wesley Edward Bowen. In *Dictionary of American Negro Biography*. Eds. Rayford W. Logan and Michael R. Winston. New York: Norton, 1982.

Brawley, Benjamin. *Negro Builders and Heroes*. Chapel Hill: University of North Carolina Press, 1937.

Brawley, James P. *Two Centuries of Methodist Concern: Bondage, Freedom and Education of Black People*. New York: Vantage Press, 1974.

Culp, D. W., ed. *Twentieth Century Negro Literature: Or a Cyclopedia of Thought on the Vital Topics Relating to the American Negro*. Naperville, Ill.: J. L. Nichols & Co., 1902.

Luker, Ralph E. "John Wesley Edward Bowen." In *American National Biography*. Vol. 3. Eds. John A. Garraty and Mark C. Carnes. New York: Oxford University Press, 1999.

McCulloh, Gerald O. *Ministerial Education in the American Methodist Movement*. Nashville: United Board of Higher Education and Ministry, Division of Ordained Ministry, 1980.

Nichols, J. J., and William H. Crogman. *Progress of a Race, or the Remarkable Advancement of the American Negro*. Rev. and enl. ed. Naperville, Ill.: J. L. Nichols & Co., 1925.

Penn, I. Garland, and J. W. E. Bowen, eds. *The United Negro: His Problems and His Progress. Containing the Addresses and Proceedings the Negro Young People's Christian and Educational Congress, Held August 6-11, 1902*. Atlanta: D. E. Luther Publishing Co., 1902.

Shockley, Grant S., ed. *Heritage & Hope: The African American Presence in United Methodism*. Nashville: Abingdon Press, 1991.

Periodicals

Van Pelt, J. R. "John Wesley Edward Bowen." *Journal of Negro History*. 14 (April 1934): 217-21.

Collections

The papers of John Wesley Edward Bowen are in the archives of Gammon Theological Seminary located in the Woodruff Library at Atlanta University. Other papers are published in *The Booker T. Washington Papers*, edited by Louis Harland and others and published between 1972 and 1989. There are also unpublished materials in the Booker T. Washington papers located at the Library of Congress.

Jessie Carney Smith

Wiley A. Branton
1923–1988

Lawyer, civil rights activist

Wiley A. Branton was the mastermind behind the legal strategy that caused the Little Rock Nine to claim national attention in 1957 when nine African American students successfully integrated Central High School. These students and the adults who supported them faced great personal danger from whites who did not want to see the end of the South's rigidly segregated social system. Branton began working on school desegregation in Arkansas soon after the Supreme Court's *Brown vs. Board of Education* decision in 1954. An army veteran, Branton had just passed the Arkansas bar two years before *Brown*. *Washington Post* journalist Juan Williams wrote in 1988, that when asked about all the work and time that led to the Little Rock school desegregation victory, Branton replied, "I was just doing my job."

Branton was an indefatigable advocate for civil rights during his entire adult life and was liked and trusted by a broad spectrum of his contemporaries, black and white. In the same *Post* article Williams noted that when civil rights leaders needed someone to approach Martin Luther King Jr. about the harm to the civil rights movement that his sexual indiscretions caused and the negative publicity about King being aired by the Federal Bureau of Investigation, the leaders got together and selected Branton to talk to King. Branton was charged not only to speak to King about the matter but also to get

Wiley A. Branton

Chronology

1923	Born in Pine Bluff, Arkansas on December 13
1942	Enrolls at Arkansas Agricultural, Mechanical & Normal College; serves as full time manager of Branton's 98, his family's taxi business
1943	Joins the U. S. Army and trains in military intelligence; works as a bridge construction foreman in the South Pacific
1946	Honorably discharged from the army; returns to Arkansas and begins to actively fight for civil rights
1948	Marries Lucille McKee with whom he has five children; is charged and convicted of violating an Arkansas law for engaging in an NAACP voter registration drive; helps Silas N. Hunt integrate the University of Arkansas Law School; tries to enroll in the University of Arkansas business program but is unsuccessful
1950	Enrolls in University of Arkansas law school
1952	Through a special veterans preference program, passes the bar exam before graduation
1953	Becomes the third black person to graduate from the University of Arkansas Law School
1956	Defends the Little Rock nine and shares the national spotlight with NAACP Legal Defense Fund director Thurgood Marshall and the local NAACP branch president, journalist Daisy Bates
1960s	Serves as legal representative for the freedom riders in Mississippi
1962	Named executive director of the Southern Regional Council's voter education project based in Atlanta; registers almost 700,000 voters in eleven states during the three years of his tenure
1965	Moves to Washington, D.C. to become executive secretary of President Lyndon B. Johnson's Council on Equal Opportunity; later in the same year moves to the Department of Justice where he serves as a special consultant to the attorney general
1967	Serves as the executive director of the United Planning Organization in Washington, D.C., a poverty program
1969	Serves as AFL-CIO's director of Social Action for the Alliance for Labor Action
1971	Practices with the Washington, D.C. firm of Dolphin, Branton, Stafford & Webber
1978	Becomes dean of Howard University Law School in Washington, D.C.
1983	Serves in the Washington, D.C. office of Sidley & Austin law firm
1988	Dies in Washington, D.C., on December 15

him to agree to limits on his behavior. Branton was willing to go to King and discuss the controversy. King listened to him and agreed to curb his behavior. Many of Branton's friends and colleagues confirmed that Branton seemed to have an innate ability to deal courageously and tactfully with very different personalities in a variety of difficult and often dangerous situations.

Born on December 13, 1923, to a family of professionals in Pine Bluff, Arkansas, Branton was of African, Indian, and European descent. During the days of rigid segregation, he occasionally found himself in danger because he was mistaken for a white man. His father and grandfather ran a prosperous taxi service in Pine Bluff called Branton's 98. Wiley's mother, a Tuskegee Institute graduate, and maternal grandmother were both teachers. Wiley attended segregated institutions until he graduated from college—Missouri Street Elementary School, Merrill High School and Arkansas Agricultural, Mechanical & Normal College (AM&N; now University of Arkansas at Pine Bluff). Branton always believed that in spite of the segregation he faced, he received a good basic education. As a teen, he and his brothers worked with his father's taxi service, and while he was in college, he was the full time general manager of the business. Because of his active involvement in the taxi service as a young person, he believed that he would spend his career working

as a businessman. His undergraduate degree was in business administration.

In 1943, Branton joined the U. S. Army where he was trained in military intelligence and worked as a bridge construction foreman in the South Pacific. He did his work faithfully but was angered and humiliated by the segregation and mistreatment of African American troops. Branton came home determined to fight against racial injustice. One of the many experiences that played on his mind related to European prisoners of war. When he escorted Italian prisoners, they were allowed to eat at southern eateries while Branton, an American citizen and soldier, had to wait outside. This and many other demeaning occurrences only served to steel his determination to fight for the rights of all Americans. Along with so many other African American veterans, he was angered that black men could shed their blood but, for the most part, they could not cast their ballots. In 1946, Branton was honorably discharged from the armed services.

In 1948 Branton married Lucille McKee, who became his lifelong partner and occasional office manager. Together they had five children who enjoyed teasing their parents about their ongoing love affair and regaling listeners with stories about the comfortable home they shared. Married life did not keep Branton from engaging in civil rights initiatives. Soon after his marriage, for engaging in an NAACP voter registration drive, Branton was charged and convicted of violating an Arkansas law relating to using copies of ballots to teach people how to vote. This misdemeanor resulted in a $3000 fine that was soon paid for Branton with a collection of funds from members of Pine Bluff's African American community. A 2003 article by Judith Kilpatrick for the Arkansas Black Lawyers Association indicated that no one else has ever been convicted of breaking the same ballot law. In 1948 Branton also helped Silas N. Hunt integrate the University of Arkansas Law School. Branton tried to enroll in the University of Arkansas business program but was unsuccessful.

In 1950, Branton received a B.S. in business administration and subsequently enrolled in the University of Arkansas Law School. Through a special veterans preference program, Branton passed the bar examination in 1952 before he graduated. In 1953, Branton became the third black person to graduate from the University of Arkansas Law School and the fourth African American to attend. By the end of his career, Branton was a member of the bars of Arkansas, Georgia, the District of Columbia, and the Supreme Court of the United States. Later in his career, the Washington, D.C. Bar Association complimented Branton for expending his best efforts "on matters which are calculated to have the most positive effect upon the quality of life for his fellow human beings."

The Little Rock Nine

Branton practiced in Little Rock for ten years, from 1952 to 1962, and took on a variety of cases relating to labor, civil rights, and other mundane matters such as wills, deeds, and divorces. Yet, he actively sought to make a difference in the field of civil rights for all Americans. Soon after he began his practice the U.S. Supreme Court handed down the school desegregation decision. Branton actively sought the implementation of the *Brown* decision in Arkansas. Initially, it seemed that the Little Rock school board was quite progressive with a plan in place that would allow three hundred African American students into Central High School. However, school desegregation was such a volatile issue that—in response

to the violent displeasure of the segregationists—the board kept reducing the number. Finally the board decided that only twenty-five African American high school students would be admitted to Central. Of those twenty-five, only nine had parents who agreed to allow their children to undergo the ordeal of being the integration vanguard. The other parents refused to subject their offspring to the inevitable ordeal. The nine children who agreed to confront the racism gained national and international renown as the Little Rock Nine. Their courageous efforts have been repeatedly chronicled in articles, books, and television documentaries through the following decades.

NAACP lawyer Jack Greenberg explained in his 1994 memoir *Crusaders in the Courts* that at first Governor Orval Faubus seemed to be a moderate on racial issues. Later, though, he became wildly popular among many of his white constituents—as well as with segregationists and white supremacists throughout the South—when he rose up to oppose the Little Rock school board's desegregation decision. To the amazement of observers, he called out the Arkansas National Guard on September 2, 1957, just before school was scheduled to open. The guard's sole purpose was to prevent the African American students from enrolling at Central High. When the Little Rock school desegregation case began, Branton defended the Little Rock Nine and the desegregation plans in the court and remained as chief counsel in the case; he yielded much of the national spotlight to NAACP Legal Defense Fund director Thurgood Marshall, who became his lifelong friend. The nation's attention was galvanized when Governor Faubus took his unyielding stand with the segregationists against the nine youths who were attempting to integrate Central.

Artists, photojournalists, and television cameramen captured the hatred that rained down upon the nine young people. Hundreds of white adults spat at the youths and shouted obscenities and racial epithets as local police tried unsuccessfully to hold them back. Because Governor Faubus refused to comply with the federal mandate to desegregate, officials began to call on President Dwight Eisenhower to intervene. President Eisenhower nationalized the Arkansas National Guard, charging them to protect the Little Rock Nine, and ordered one thousand paratroopers of the 101st Airborne Division from Fort Campbell, Kentucky, to protect the students and restore order. Members of the Airborne Division met at local NAACP president Daisy Bates's house. It was there that the children assembled each school day to pray and fortify themselves for the day's battle. Some soldiers escorted the children to school, others surrounded the school, and still other servicemen escorted the students through the hallways. The servicemen guarded the students from September through most of November.

Litigating this case, Branton worked closely with other NAACP lawyers such as Marshall, Constance

Baker Motley, and Jack Greenberg as well as journalists Daisy Bates and her husband L. C. Bates. The segregationists' response to Branton and the others was brutal. The homes, possessions, and bodies of the civil rights workers were constantly in danger. Even in the face of cross burnings, rock throwing, bombs, and other types of intimidation, these lawyers fought and won several important U. S. Supreme Court decisions which disallowed the tactics that the Arkansas governor used to stop school desegregation, such as closing public schools or trying to turn public schools into private ones. Jack Greenberg in *Crusaders in the Courts* details Branton's pivotal role in Little Rock and the strategy the NAACP lawyers employed during the court battles. In his 1998 biography, *Thurgood Marshall: American Revolutionary*, Juan Williams states that, at first, Marshall was worried about Branton's ability to face tremendous pressure but later he said, "They had crosses burning on his lawn and everything, but he was a really tough guy." Together they learned that they should have taken less time to rejoice over the *Brown* decision and should have been designing strategies for implementation of desegregation.

Civil Rights and Voting Rights Campaigns

Branton was often able to act as mediator because he was able to cooperate with many civil rights leaders and lawyers without trying to focus the spotlight on himself. Central High was just one of the many skirmishes Branton had with white racists. During the 1960s Branton served as legal representative for some freedom riders in Mississippi. While a trial was in progress in Indianola in 1961, a white man came into the courtroom and sprayed insecticide on Branton and the defendants without the judge or court officials making any attempt to stop him. The man said that he was trying to free the court of vermin.

By 1962, Branton's role began to alter but was no less perilous. With the support of President John F. Kennedy, Attorney General Robert Kennedy, and a number of civil rights leaders, Branton was named executive director of the Southern Regional Council's Voter Education Project based in Atlanta, Georgia. In the nineteenth century, after the passage of the fifteenth amendment granting voting rights to all male citizens regardless of color, African Americans were able to elect people of color to many elective positions on local, state, and federal levels because African Americans vastly outnumbered whites in some parts of the South. To counter a perceived threat of African American domination, whites began to employ a variety of tactics to disenfranchise African Americans. These included poll taxes, grandfather clauses (if one's grandfather had not voted, then the citizen was ineligible to vote), various tests, white-only primaries, as well as outright intimidation and threats against African Americans who wanted to exercise the franchise. White segregationists resisted voting rights for African Americans as much as they resisted desegregation in general. They believed that if African Americans were armed with the ballot, white control of the black populace would come to an end. Consequently they opposed enfranchisement of African Americans in every way they could. Nevertheless, the Voter Education Project registered almost 700,000 voters in eleven states during the three years of Branton's tenure. His work on this project increased the momentum that led to the creation of the Voting Rights Act of 1965 and brought him to the attention of many federal officials.

Washington, D.C. and Howard University

Because of Branton's success with the Voter Education Project, in 1965 he was invited to come to Washington, D.C., to become executive secretary of President Lyndon B. Johnson's Council on Equal Opportunity. Later in the same year President Johnson shifted Branton to the Department of Justice to serve as a special consultant to the attorney general. Branton served until 1967 under both Nicholas Katzenbach and Ramsey Clark. While working for the federal government, he was able to continue his efforts to get African Americans registered to vote. Branton described his work in this way in the *Arkansas Gazette* of May 1, 1966: "Mostly I work with private organizations and individuals as a sort of liaison between the Justice Department and private groups and other government agencies in an effort to assist the implementation of the Voting Rights Act." Branton traveled all over the South explaining the Johnson administration's commitment to civil and voting rights. Branton also served as an overseer of proper voter registration procedures and acted to redress official complaints from those who felt they were being mistreated or defrauded in their efforts to register.

One of the goals of the civil rights movement was to relieve poverty, especially among minorities. From 1967 to 1969, Branton worked as the executive director of the United Planning Organization (UPO) in Washington, D.C. This poverty program helped D.C. communities design programs that would meet their own needs. UPO would review the program proposals to see if they were feasible and then could provide funding. In 1969 Walter Reuther, a prominent leader of the AFL-CIO, recruited Branton as director of Social Action for the Alliance for Labor Action. Branton assisted in supervising programs for the poor in the areas of jobs, housing, health care, and legal and social services. This position only lasted for two years, though. Upon Reuther's death in 1971, Branton rejoined the Washington-based law firm, Dolphin, Branton, Stafford & Weber, and was counsel to the Little Rock Arkansas firm of Walker, Kaplan and Mays.

In 1978 Branton became the dean of Howard University Law School in Washington, D.C., and served in that capacity until 1983. Howard Law School lawyers and instructors such as Charles Hamilton Houston, James Nabrit, William H. Hastic, and Thurgood Marshall were in the forefront of the legal battle against segregation and discrimination for many years. The success of the movement, however, ultimately presented a problem to the law school. During the decades of segregation, African Americans who wanted to study law had very few choices of law schools to which they could apply. Howard was considered by many to be the best law school available to them. After integration, white schools began competing with Howard and other historically black law schools for students with the most potential and highest test scores. Many Howard law students were not performing well on their bar exams because they lacked adequate writing skills. During his tenure as dean, Branton attempted to restore the law school to its "glory days," but he faced many daunting challenges from both the students and the administration. In 1983, Branton returned to private practice with the Washington, D.C. office of Sidley & Austin. Branton died on December 15, 1988.

During his illustrious career Branton received many honors and awards. Walter E. Fauntroy, D.C. delegate to the U.S. Congress, read into the Congressional Record on Thursday, February 9, 1989 a tribute to the life and work of Wiley A. Branton. In his posthumous salute to Branton, Fauntroy mentioned some of Branton's honors, including awards from the National Bar Association, the Civil Liberties Union, the Bar Association of the District of Columbia, the Lawyers Committee for Civil Rights under the Law, and the Martin Luther King Jr. Leadership Award from the District of Columbia Public Library just before he died in 1988. Congressman Fauntroy said that Branton had earned "respect, admiration and lasting friendship of all for his courageous, resolute dedication and unselfish efforts in forging new paths in our society. We shall miss him but we will never forget him."

REFERENCES

Books

Greenberg, Jack. *Crusaders in the Courts: How a Dedicated Band of Lawyers Fought for the Civil Rights Revolution*. New York: Basic Books, 1994.

Williams, Juan. *Thurgood Marshall: American Revolutionary*. New York: Random House, 1998.

Periodicals

Williams, Juan. "Little Known Wiley Branton." *Washington Post*, (19 December 1988): A13.

Online

Fauntroy, Hon. Walter E. "Wiley A. Branton, Civil Rights Leader, Attorney, Law School Dean." *Congressional Record* 9 February 1989. http://thomas.loc.gov/cgi-bin/query/z?r101:E09FE9-218 (Accessed 15 January 2006).

Kilpatrick, Judith. "Wiley Austin Branton: Arkansas Native Son. Arkansas Black Lawyers. www.

arkansasblacklawyers.net/branton.html (Accessed 15 January 2006).

Muse, Clifford L., Jr. "Wiley Austin Branton." *HUArchives Net: The Electronic Journal*, Howard University, November 1999. www.huarchivesnet.howard.edu (Accessed 15 January 2006).

Collections

The Wiley A. Branton Papers are in the Moorland-Spingarn Research Center, Howard University, Washington, D.C.

Debra Newman Ham

Edward M. Brawley
1851–1923

Religious leader, educator, college president

Edward McKnight Brawley was a religious leader and educator and one of the original founders of the National Baptist Convention. He championed the education of black ministers and the publication of their material. Brawley was the first black graduate of Bucknell University and the president of two Southern universities.

Brawley was born on March 18, 1851 in Charleston, South Carolina. He was the son of James M. and Ann L. Brawley, free blacks, and thus he was always free. At the age of four, Brawley was placed in a private school operated by an elderly woman, where he learned to read. The young Brawley continued his schooling there until after the uprising of John Brown at Harpers Ferry, which led to the closing of many schools in the South. In 1861, when he was about ten years old, his parents sent him to Philadelphia for further schooling. He attended the Institute for Colored Youth under Ebenezer Don Carlos Bassett until 1866. Following the Civil War and under the orders of his parents, Brawley returned to Charleston to learn a trade. He served three years as an apprenticed shoemaker and in 1869 returned to Philadelphia and worked as a journeyman at his trade.

While in Philadelphia, Brawley joined the Shiloh Baptist Church and worked in Shiloh's Sunday school. During this period, he decided to become a minister, and in the fall of 1870, he became the first student enrolled in the theological school at Howard University in Washington, D.C. Brawley remained only three months, then in 1871, he transferred to Lewisburg (now Bucknell) University at Lewisburg, Pennsylvania, becoming the first black student to enter the institution. He had a scholar-

Chronology

1851	Born in Charleston, South Carolina on March 18
1861	Goes to Philadelphia to attend the Institute for Colored Youth
1866	Returns to South Carolina
1869	Returns to Philadelphia and works as a journeyman
1870	Enrolls as first student in the theological school at Howard University in Washington, D.C.
1871	Transfers to Bucknell University
1872	Receives license to preach
1875	Becomes ordained and takes a position with predominately white American Baptist Publication Society as a missionary in South Carolina
1877	Forms South Carolina Black Baptist churches into an annual convention; marries Mary W. Warrick of Virginia
1878	Receives A.M. from Bucknell University
1879	Marries Margaret Dickerson of Columbia, South Carolina
1883	Becomes president of Selma University
1885	Resigns from position at Selma University due to health problems; receives honorary Doctor of Divinity from State University in Louisville, Kentucky
1887	Begins the *Baptist Tribune*, a weekly publication
1923	Dies in South Carolina

ship and he supplemented his income by giving voice lessons to students and others. In 1872, at the close of his sophomore year, Brawley was licensed to preach by a white Baptist church, and in 1875 after his graduation, he was ordained by a vote of a council of the church. The board was composed of thirty-five ministers.

The day after his graduation, June 30, 1875, Brawley was employed by the predominately white American Baptist Publication Society as a missionary in South Carolina. In his new position, he discovered there were many black churches in South Carolina, but few were organized or even had Sunday schools. There were also many associations, but they were not effective. Brawley immediately began to reorganize the associations and organized new ones. He organized a Sunday school convention in every association, and in May 1877 formed them into an annual state convention.

There were as many Sunday schools in South Carolina as there were churches, and the denomination was united and strong. Brawley raised a large amount of money for the state convention and also for Benedict Institute. It was reported that once, within a period of a few months, he raised a special collection of $1,000, an unimaginable sum for that time.

In 1883, Brawley became president at Alabama Baptist Normal and Theological school (now Selma University), succeeding Reverend William H. McAlpine. The decision to offer the job to Brawley was important to Alpine. He would not concede his position until a man with better educational credentials than he had could be

hired. The decision proved wise; Brawley completely overhauled the curriculum and brought the institution back to college status. The first class to graduate under Brawley finished in May 1884. He resigned from this position in 1885 due to health problems. Brawley returned to South Carolina. While back home he edited the *Baptist Pioneer* for three years.

Brawley married Mary W. Warrick of Virginia, a graduate of Howard University, in January 1877. They had one child, but both mother and child died. He married again, the second time to Margaret Dickerson of Columbia, South Carolina, in December 1879; and they had four children.

In the late 1880s Brawley once again was affiliated with the American Baptist Publication Society serving several years as the district secretary and financial agent for the Atlantic Coast District. Under his direction, a number of young men began preparing for the ministry and were eventually sent to Africa for missionary work. Brawley became the editor of *The Negro Baptist Pulpit*, the first collection of black theological and denominational writing ever published.

Brawley continued his education and received his A.M. from Bucknell University, his alma mater, in 1878 and an honorary degree of Doctor of Divinity from State University in Louisville, Kentucky in May 1885. Brawley was regularly asked to speak by the American Baptist Publication Society at the national anniversaries. Over the years, he had numerous positions on boards in various associations. Brawley was hailed as dedicated and self-sacrificing, determined to educate those who for so long had been denied.

Brawley was known as a refined, scholarly gentleman of mild and quiet habits. Although Brawley made considerable money, he was said to have spent it largely in aiding students who could not afford to pay for their education. One-half of his salary while president at Selma University was spent that way. He resigned from his job at Selma University due to the failing health of his second wife. He returned once again to South Carolina.

Over his lifetime, Edward M. Brawley earned a reputation as an effective and notable minister, as well as a dynamic speaker and writer. He was a champion for blacks publishing their own materials and educating their ministers. In January 1887, he began the *Baptist Tribune*, a weekly publication. It was considered one of the best papers of the South, a credit to his editorial ability and Christian labor. Though Brawley relinquished control of the National Baptist Convention, he remained an active worker and brought untold goodwill to blacks in South Carolina, Alabama, and elsewhere in the United States. Edward Brawley died in South Carolina in 1923.

REFERENCES

Books

Majors, Gerri, with Doris E. Saunders. *Gerri Majors' Black Society.* Chicago: Johnson Publishing Co., 1976.

Simmons, William J. *Men of Mark, 1887.* Chicago: Johnson Publishing Co., 1970.

Beverly E. Richards

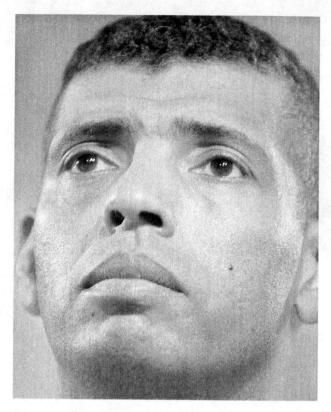

Vincent K. Brooks

Vincent K. Brooks
1958–

Army officer, spokesperson

Brigadier General Vincent K. Brooks' deft handling of the media and his outstanding performance as the United States Army's most senior spokesman during the second Iraqi War earned him international recognition and respect. Millions of people around the world observed his televised press conferences on a daily basis and listened avidly to the information he shared about the progress of the war. To many of those watching, his presence represented the increased participation of minorities, particularly African Americans, in the United States armed services and the strides that they have made toward leadership roles.

Truly a soldier's soldier, Brooks was born into a military family that was posted in Anchorage, Alaska on October 24, 1958. His father, Leo Brooks Sr. was an army officer who would himself become a brigadier general and his mother, Naomi, was a schoolteacher. On both the maternal and paternal side of his family, Brooks has deep roots in the black experience in the United States, especially in the state of Virginia. His mother is a descendant of the Quander family, a free black family which has resided in the Virginia and Maryland area for over three hundred years. Nellie Quander was one of the founders of Alpha Kappa Alpha Sorority in 1908. His father can trace his antecedents back to a slave traded in the Haymarket area in Alexandria, Virginia. Brooks is the second of three children, having an older brother, Leo Brooks Jr., and a younger sister, Marquita.

Like many military families, the Brooks led a nomadic life, relocating twenty-eight times while the father was on active duty. When Brooks and his brother were enrolled at an Alexandria, Virginia co-educational high school, as a junior and senior respectively, their father received orders that put him in charge of the Sacramento Army Depot. The family moved to California and the two brothers became students and later graduates of the all male Jesuit High School, where there were only four other black students enrolled. At six feet and five inches tall, Brooks ran track and played basketball well enough to be offered an athletic scholarship to the North Carolina State University in Raleigh. He decided instead to follow his older brother to the United States Military Academy at West Point in New York.

Joins the Military

At West Point, Brooks played basketball and excelled as a student. In May 1980, the *New York Times* noted that Brooks was the first African American in the 178-year history of the prestigious university to hold the post of captain of cadets. As a senior, he led more that four thousand cadets and was first in his class. Brooks graduated from West Point with a B.S., but without a major.

Commissioned as a second lieutenant on May 28, 1980, Brooks was first assigned as weapons platoon leader, in B Company, First Battalion (Airborne), 504th Infantry in Fort Bragg, North Carolina. Between October 1980 and December 1983, he held several successive platoon leader positions and advanced to the rank of first lieutenant on November 28, 1981. In January 1984, he was promoted to captain and attended the Infantry Officer Advanced Course at Fort Benning, Georgia prior to being stationed in Germany as adjutant and then com-

As a senior service college fellow, he studied national security issues. At the end of his academic program, Brooks was appointed a full colonel and moved on to Fort McPherson, Georgia, where he was the chief of the Plans and Program Division, G-3, Third United States Army/Army Central Command.

Chronology

1958	Born in Anchorage, Alaska on October 24
1976?	Graduates from Jesuit High School, Sacramento, California
1980	Graduates first in his class at West Point; first African American captain of cadets commissioned as second lieutenant in the U.S. Army
1981	Promoted to first lieutenant
1984	Promoted to captain
1991	Appointed major
1992	Attains master's degree in military art and science
1995	Serves as deputy chief of staff for operations and plans at the Pentagon; promoted to lieutenant colonel
1999	Attends John F. Kennedy School of Government as senior service college fellow; promoted to colonel
2000	Leads troops to Kosovo for peacekeeping mission
2002	Appointed chief operations spokesman, United States Central Command; youngest officer to be nominated for brigadier general
2004	Promoted to brigadier general; appointed chief of Army Public Affairs

Serves During Second Iraqi War

In July 2000, Brooks was put in charge of the First Brigade, Third Infantry Division (Mechanized) at Fort Stewart, Georgia. He led his command to Kosovo, where they participated in a peacekeeping mission as a part of Operation Joint Guardian. Brooks remained with the Third Infantry until 2002, when he was appointed deputy director of Military Affairs, J-5, the Joint Staff in Washington, D.C. Shortly thereafter he shipped out to the post that brought him national and international media exposure: deputy J-3, chief operations spokesman, United States Central Command ("Centcom") at Camp As Sayliyah, in Doha, Qatar.

The Central Command is one of nine combat commands that answer directly to the president of the United States and the secretary of defense and is comprised of twenty- five African countries, the Middle East, and Central Asia. Brooks remained with the Central Command from 2002 to 2004, working with the Operation Enduring Freedom and Operation Iraqi Freedom campaigns of the Iraqi War. As the chief operations spokesman, it was Brooks's responsibility to conduct daily military briefings on the progress of the coalition troops toward victory over Saddam Hussein's Iraqi Army.

The Second Persian Gulf War produced a new type of journalist, the embedded reporters, who traveled with military units on combat missions. Specially chosen for the task by General Tommy Franks, Commander in Chief of United States Central Command, Brooks had to verify and respond to information about war activity that was being reported by nearly six hundred print, online, and televised journalists. Verne Gay of the *Chicago Tribune* dubbed Brooks, "the face of the U.S. military," because it was his face and demeanor that most frequently appeared on camera to report news about the war. Brooks took notes at Centcom staff meetings and discussed with General Franks what information would be released to the press. Always calm, polite, and "on message," Brooks reported the facts and tried to provide effective sound bites. He efficiently discharged his objective of disseminating the army's war news coverage to the public and within the service, through foreign and domestic channels. In his bestselling autobiography *American Soldier*, General Franks noted that Brooks is a "brilliant young officer" and praised him for playing a "superb" role in Operation Iraqi Freedom.

Although Brooks received overall high marks for his performance before the cameras and his handling of the

mander of B Company in the Sixteenth Infantry, followed by a position as commander, Headquarters and Headquarters Company, Fourth Battalion (Mechanized), Sixteenth Infantry Division (Forward), United States Army Europe and Seventh Army in Germany.

After a stint at the United States Total Army Personnel Command in Alexandria, Virginia, Brooks attended the United States Army Command and General Staff College in Fort Leavenworth, Kansas for two years. In 1992, he earned an M.A. in Military Art and Science (MMAS). Having acquired the rank of major at this point in his career, Brooks went on to fill various positions with the First Calvary, where he came to the attention of General Wesley Clark, a Rhodes Scholar who would later command the United States Army peacekeeping mission in Kosovo and campaign for the office of Commander and Chief. He found Brooks to be a "no-nonsense leader, who had studied his profession carefully, worked hard, and delivered."

Brooks left the First Calvary Division in Fort Hood, Texas and rotated to Washington D.C. as a lieutenant colonel. He went to the Pentagon to serve in the Army's Office of the Deputy Chief of Staff for Operations and Plans in 1995 and ably performed as an infantry systems integrator. While posted at the District of Columbia, Brooks also served as an aide-de-camp to the vice chief of staff of the United States Army and held that job until April 1996, when he was sent to Korea to serve as commander of the Second Battalion of the Ninth Infantry, Second Infantry Division in the Eighth Army.

Brooks returned to the halls of academe from July 1998 to June 1999, when he attended the John F. Kennedy news media, he was not without his detractors. Several reporters openly complained about the absence of General Franks at the briefings and others took issue with the timing of the information released at Brooks's press conferences. They pointed out that in many instances Brooks's news was not really new, because the information had already been released by the Pentagon.

In 2002, Brooks became the youngest officer to be sent to the United States Senate to be nominated for promotion to general and on May 1, 2004 his appointment to brigadier general made him the first graduate of West Point's class of 1980 to attain the rank of general. His promotion to brigadier general, along with the identical rank promotion of his older brother, Leo Jr., also made the Brooks family the first African American family to have three generals in two generations, surpassing General Benjamin O. Davis Sr. and General Benjamin O. Davis Jr.

Wins Medals and Honors

When Brooks's tour of duty with Operation Iraqi Freedom terminated on April 24, 2004, he returned to Washington, D.C., to work at the Pentagon as deputy director for the war on terrorism, J-5, Joint Staff, where he participated in the formulation of national security policies and strategies to control nuclear proliferation. Although he expected to return to his command in Georgia, Brooks was appointed chief of Army Public Affairs in December 2004.

Over the course of an excellent career, Brooks, who speaks German, has been the recipient of numerous medals and badges, including the Defense Superior Service Medal, the Legion of Merit (with oak cluster), the Defense Meritorious Service Medal, the Meritorious Service Medal (with seven oak clusters), and the Joint Service Commendation Medal. His military badges include the expert infantry badge, the senior parachutist badge, and a ranger tab. He is married to the former Carol Rene Perry, a physical therapist, and the couple resides in Alexandria, Virginia.

REFERENCES

Books

Parker, Marjorie H. *Alpha Kappa Alpha: Through the Years, 1908-1988*. Chicago, Ill.: Mobium Press, 1990.

Periodicals

"Black Face of War: Brooks Family Has Long Military History Sacramento Ties." *Sacramento Observer*, 16 April 2003.

"Brig. Gen. Vincent Brooks: Newsmaker of the Year." *Precinct Reporter*, 25 March 2004.

"Brooks Brothers in Arms." *Afro-American Red Star*, April 2003.

Curry, George E. "War Against Iraq Showcases Top Black Leadership." *New Amsterdam News*, 10 April 2003.

Feron, James. "Service Academies Hail First Female Graduates." *New York Times*, 29 May 1980.

Gowen, Annie. "In Brooks Family, Ranking Values are Duty Devotion…" *Washington Post*, sec: District Extra, 29 May 2003.

Harris, Hamil R. "General Is Named Top Newsmaker Publisher Honor Vincent Brooks." *Washington Post*, 15 April 2004, sec: Prince William Extra.

Lewis, Monica. "With War, Ties that Bind: Brooks Family a Military Success . . ." *Philadelphia Tribune*, 4 April 2003.

Winsome, Morgan. "CORE Awards to African Americans." *The Weekly Gleaner*, 23 January 2004.

Online

"Brigadier General Vincent K. Brooks, Chief of Public Affairs." Army Public Affairs. http://www4.army. mil/ocpa/resources/chiefpublicaffairs.html (Accessed 2 February 2005).

Cooper, Patrick. "Military Man Brooks Steps Up to the Mike." http://www.cnn.com/2003/us/04/04/spri.irq. brooks/ (Accessed 1 February 2005).

Henry, Tanu T. "Who is Brigadier General Vincent Brooks?" http://archive.blackvoices.com/articles/ daily/bw20030409brooks.asp (Accessed 1 February 2005).

"Vincent Brooks." *Biography Resource Online*. http:// galenet.galegroup.com (Accessed 31 January 2005).

Glenda M. Alvin

Walter H. Brooks
1851–1945

Minister, religious reformer, orator, poet

One of the most widely known clergymen of his era, Reverend Walter Henderson Brooks was an eloquent orator, poet, missionary, journalist, and reformer. Brooks provided leadership and service to one of the most important African American churches and denominations. A man of letters, Brooks was a published theologian and a scholar of Black Baptist Church history, as well as a poet and composer of hymns. He made great efforts to promote education and Christian morals as a means to improve the quality of life for African Americans.

Chronology

1851	Born in Richmond, Virginia on August 30
1866	Enters Lincoln University in Pennsylvania
1872	Earns B.A. degree from Lincoln University
1873	Earns B.D. degree from Lincoln University; baptized at the Richmond Baptist Church
1876	Ordained a Baptist minister
1877-80	Serves as pastor of the Second African Baptist Church of Richmond, Virginia
1882-1945	Serves as pastor of the Nineteenth Street Baptist in Washington, D.C.
1895	Creates the National Baptist Convention
1922	Publishes histories of black Baptist churches in *The Journal of Negro History*
1929	Receives LL.D. degree from Lincoln University
1944	Receives the D.D. degree from Howard University, Washington, D.C.
1945	Publishes *The Pastor's Voice: A Collection of Poems*
1945	Dies in Washington, D.C. on July 6

Walter Henderson Brooks was born on August 30, 1851, in Richmond, Virginia, the fifth of nine surviving children of Albert Royal and Lucy Goode Brooks. He was born a slave, his parents belonging to different masters. His father, Albert R. Brooks, worked hard to earn enough money to purchase Brooks' mother for $800 and two of the younger children. His father was able to purchase the oldest son, but his oldest daughter was sold to traders and taken to Tennessee where she died in bondage. Walter Brooks often recalled in his sermons the sale of his sister on a Richmond auction block.

In the summer of 1865 Walter attended his first school, Cheeseman's in Richmond. In the fall of 1865 he entered the Wilberforce Institute at Carolina Mills, Rhode Island. He entered Lincoln University in Pennsylvania in 1866. He joined the Ashmun Presbyterian Church in 1868, while a student at Lincoln University. He and Archibald H. Grimké served as church elders when the church was organized in 1868. Completing the course for a B.A. degree in 1872, Brooks spent an additional year at Lincoln University in the theological course, earning a B.D. degree in 1873. It was his intention to enter the ministry of the Presbyterian Church, but in the spring of 1873 he changed his mind on the subject of baptism.

Receives Calling to the Church

Returning to Richmond, Walter Brooks was baptized in November 1873 at his mother's church, the Richmond Baptist Church, later the First African Baptist Church. He worked for the Richmond post office as a mail clerk from 1873 to 1874. On April 21, 1874, Brooks married Eva Holmes, the daughter of the minister who had baptized him. He worked for the American Baptist Publication

Society of Philadelphia and as Sunday School missionary for the State of Virginia. For the years 1874 to 1876, Brooks supplied homes, churches, and schools with Christian literature. He also held Sunday school institutes, teaching Christian workers. In May 1875 at a meeting of the Northern Baptists in Philadelphia, Brooks presented a speech entitled "Facts from the Field," at the request of the Publication Society. According to Adam Biggs in *American National Biography Online,* his speech "sparked controversy when he 'drew a picture of the drinking habits of preachers' in an effort to illustrate the critical need for temperance." He swept his audience, but the newspaper reports made him enemies, white and black, in his native state.

On December 24, 1876, Brooks was ordained a Baptist minister. Brooks was the pastor of the Second African Baptist Church of Richmond from 1877 through 1880. He was successful in paying off the entire debt of the church. In 1880, he attended a meeting of the white Baptists at their annual convention in Petersburg, Virginia, the first African American received by that body.

His activities as a temperance worker were noted from the beginning of his ministry. In 1875, he began his service as chaplain to the Anti-Saloon League in Washington, D.C. He was a delegate from this body to the convention that formed the American National Anti-Saloon League. In 1881, he attended the Annual Convention of Northern Baptists at Indianapolis, Indiana, where he made an address and greatly enlarged his reputation. From 1880 to 1882, at the request of the American Baptist Publication Society, he worked in New Orleans, Louisiana; however, his wife's failing health caused his return to Richmond.

In 1882, Brooks became pastor of the Nineteenth Street Baptist Church in Washington, D.C., where he remained until his death. During his tenure, the Nineteenth Street Baptist Church grew in stature, membership, and toward an ideal of a model congregation. The church was $5,600 in debt when he took charge. In four years that debt was erased and the Nineteenth Street Baptist Church began to buy more land and spent some $30,000 to repair the building, becoming one of the finest churches in Washington, D.C.

Reverend Brooks played an important role in efforts to build and maintain a national black Baptist convention. He was chairman of the American National Baptist Convention's Bureau of Education, a black organization founded in 1886, and he continuously mediated relationships with national white Baptist conventions. Difficulties between white and black Baptist conventions led to the creation of the National Baptist Convention in 1895, with which the Nineteenth Street Baptist Church was affiliated.

Along with his church work, Brooks was a member of the Board of Trustees of Nannie H. Burrough's National Training School for Women and Girls, the Stoddard Baptist Home for the Elderly, Virginia Seminary and College of Lynchburg, the United Society of Christian Endeavor, and the National Baptist Foreign Missionary Board of Philadelphia. Brooks received the LL.D. degree from Lincoln University in 1929, a D.D. degree from Howard University, Washington, D.C. in 1944, and other honors from Roger Williams University, Tennessee, and from Straight College (later Simmons Memorial College) in Louisville, Kentucky. Always active in civic affairs, Brooks served as vice-president of the Bethel Literary and Historical Association under Phi Beta Kappa educator John Wesley Cromwell. On November 2, 1938, President Franklin D. Roosevelt sent a letter of congratulations to Reverend Brooks on the occasion of completing fifty-six years as pastor of Nineteenth Street Baptist Church.

Brooks dignified the pulpit and promoted the art of respectability in his congregation, denouncing gambling, fornication, adultery, and even dancing. He preached and practiced the "Social Gospel," emphasizing the reality of collective, societal sin, such as the starvation of children and the denial of human rights, and maintained that Christian repentance of these sins must be followed by concrete actions to rectify injustice and to assist the poor. Martin Luther King Jr. was profoundly influenced by this Social Gospel movement.

A fiery temperance orator, Brooks' sermons on the evils of drunkenness contributed to the sobriety of the congregation. His poems, such as "Christ the Burden-Bear," "Why Jesus Died," and "God So Loved the World," express his religious beliefs and his lifelong commitment to temperance, faith in God, and racial progress. The Sunday School of the Nineteenth Street Baptist Church had a library of both religious and secular books. The Sunday School published Reverend Brooks' "Original Poems," a forty-page pamphlet, in connection with the fiftieth anniversary of his service as pastor. A sketch of Brooks' life is included in a forty-eight page publication on the one hundredth anniversary of the church (1839-1939) and the fifty-seventh anniversary of Reverend Walter H. Brooks' pastorate. The National Association of Colored Women was founded in 1896 at a meeting in the Sunday School room of this church.

Walter Brooks and his first wife had ten children. She died June 1912. Reverend Brooks' second marriage was to Florence H. Swann on November 27, 1915, and his third marriage in 1933 was to Viola Washington.

For many years, Brooks was honored by Lincoln University as its oldest living alumnus. He wrote several articles for publication, most notably one of the first scholarly treatments on the history of the Negro Baptist Church and one on the history of the Silver Bluff Church (Aiken County, S.C.), both appearing in the *Journal of Negro History* in 1922.

Brooks was a member of the American Negro Academy and a lifelong member of the Association for the Study of Negro Life and History, where he worked closely with Carter G. Woodson. He traveled widely in the United States and in England, Scotland, and France. In 1889, Brooks was a delegate to the International Sunday School Convention in London, England. Walter Henderson Brooks died of natural causes on July 6, 1945 in Washington, D.C. Funeral services were at the Nineteenth Street Baptist Church, and he was interned in Lincoln Memorial Cemetery in Suitland, Maryland. An obituary was published in the *Washington Evening Star* on July 8, 1945 and in the *Journal of Negro History* in October 1945.

REFERENCES

Books

"Brooks, Walter Henderson." In *Who's Who in Colored America*. Yonkers-on-Hudson, N.Y: C. E. Burckel, 1950.

Jeter, Henry Norval. "Rev. Walter H. Brooks, D.D." In *Pastor Henry N. Jeter's Twenty-five Years Experience with the Shiloh Baptist Church and Her History*. Providence, R.I.: Remington Print. Co. 1901.

Logan, Rayford W. "Brooks, Walter Henderson." In *Dictionary of American Negro Biography*. Eds. Rayford W. Logan and Michael R. Winston. New York: Norton, 1982.

Online

Biggs, Adam. "Brooks, Walter Henderson." *American National Biography Online*. http://www.anb.org/articles/08/08-00184.html (Accessed 14 March 2005).

Kathleen E. Bethel

Henry "Box" Brown
1815–?

Abolitionist, house servant, factory worker

Henry "Box" Brown got his nickname "Box" after he mailed himself from Richmond, Virginia, to the Philadelphia, Pennsylvania, antislavery office in 1849 in order to escape from slavery. His method of escape was so unusual that his story was told repeatedly. Brown, who was unlettered, got the abolitionist Charles Stearns to write down his autobiography for him. It was first published just several months after his escape and revised and reissued in England in 1851.

In his narrative Brown explains that he was born in 1815 on the Barret plantation in Louisa County, Virginia,

Henry "Box" Brown

about forty-five miles from Richmond. Brown describes the cruelties of the institution of slavery but in many ways favorably compares his youth in slavery to that of other slaves, minutely describing an encounter at a mill when he and his brother impressed other slaves with their attire. He explains that as a lad he usually worked in the master's household serving him and his wife. When Brown was fifteen years old, his master died, and Brown's family members were divided between the owner's four sons. Brown's bitterest complaint about slavery throughout his narrative is the devastation it caused in the African American family. Taken to Richmond by William Barret, Brown began to work long hours in a tobacco factory. His new master regularly set aside small sums of money as a reward for Brown's work. Brown was no spendthrift so he was able to amass some savings.

As Brown matured he became a part of the Richmond African American community and joined the choir at a local church. After several years he decided that he had earned enough resources working at the tobacco factory to be able to have a family and settle down. Brown got permission to marry a house slave named Nancy on the condition that he find a place to live. With the help of a free black man, Brown was able to procure a house and marry Nancy. Even though Brown and Nancy were happily married and had several children, Nancy regularly suffered because of the uncertainties of her enslavement.

Even while she continued to live with Brown, she was sold several times and abused by some of her mistresses. Brown was forced to try to stabilize his wife's situation with his own resources, but as a slave he had no rights to defend himself or his family. Whites repeatedly cheated him. Ultimately, his wife's owner decided to sell Nancy and her children to owners in an undisclosed location. Since children followed the condition of the mother—if the mother was a slave, then her children were owned by her master—Brown, enslaved himself, had no say over their disposition. Brown pleaded with all concerned for mercy, including Nancy's master and his owner. He tried to secure adequate resources to purchase his wife and children himself but to no avail. After twelve years of marriage Brown's wife and family were sold away and he had no idea where they had gone. To add to the calamity, some whites also took everything Brown owned out of his house.

Ships Himself to Philadelphia

In despair Brown devised a plan to get away from enslavement. He went to a carpenter to ask him to construct a shipping crate three feet and one inch long, two feet and six inches deep and two feet wide for his two hundred pound, five foot eight inch body. On March 19, 1849, with the help of two allies, James Caesar Anthony Smith, the same free black man who helped Brown to buy his home, and Samuel A. Smith, a white sympathizer, Brown was shipped in a crate marked "THIS SIDE UP WITH CARE" to William H. Johnson in Philadelphia. Sometimes during his twenty-seven hour trek to Philadelphia by sea and overland the handlers obeyed the crate directions but other times he found himself on his side and even upside down with the blood vessels bulging in his forehead. Brown had drilled several small air holes in the box and took the drill along in case he needed more air. He also took along some water with which he repeatedly bathed his face. To cool himself he was able to fan himself continually with his hat.

Brown's Philadelphia accomplices awaited his arrival at the Adams Express Company offices. They feared that his crate would turn out to be a coffin. Nevertheless, when they heard that the box had arrived, they went to get it and brought it to the antislavery offices on North Fifth Street. Several witnesses, including the African American Underground Railroad conductor, William Still, were present for the opening of the crate. To their utter amazement, Brown emerged alive.

Becomes an Abolitionist Lecturer

The abolitionists were so excited by Brown's daring escape that they broadcast news of it far and wide. Brown began speaking on the antislavery circuit about his escape and about the horrors of slavery. After spending a brief time with abolitionists in the Philadelphia area, Brown moved on to New Bedford, Massachusetts, and then to Boston. Subsequently, his two allies in Richmond were arrested and tried. Astonishingly, the free black man, J. C. A. Smith, with the aid of an expensive attorney, was acquitted. Samuel Smith, the white man, was sentenced to prison. After serving his sentence for seven years and surviving several assassination attempts behind bars, he moved to the North and was celebrated by a grateful Philadelphia African American community. At a ceremony honoring Samuel Smith, the leaders presented him with a money gift they had collected to help him get a new start.

Soon after Brown's escape, with the aid of wealthy abolitionists, Brown developed a traveling exhibit—called a panorama—which he used to expose the evils of slavery while he told the story of his escape. J. C. A. Smith moved to the North to join Brown and they continued on the speaking circuit together. After the passage of the Fugitive Slave Act of 1850, Brown feared he would be captured especially after an attempt by slave catchers to nab him and Smith in Providence, Rhode Island. Consequently, he and Smith fled to England and arrived in Liverpool in October 1850. There Brown continued to tell of his exploits and tour with his panorama. He published a revised version of his narrative in 1851 and a second English edition in 1852. Little is known of him after 1852. There the historical trail grows cold.

REFERENCES

Books

Blassingame, John W. *Slave Testimony: Two Centuries of Letters, Speeches, Interviews, and Autobiographies*. Baton Rouge, La.: Louisiana State University Press, 1977.

Brown, Henry. *Narrative of the Life of Henry Box Brown, Written by Himself*, introduction by Richard Newman and forward by Henry Louis Gates Jr. New York: Oxford University Press, 2002 (originally published in 1849 with an introduction and essay by Charles Stearns).

Still, William, *The Underground Railroad; A Record of Facts, Authentic Narratives, Letters et cetera Narrating the Hardships, Hair-Breadth Escapes, and Death Struggles of the Slaves in their Efforts for Freedom, as Related by Themselves and Others, or Witnessed by the Author; together with Sketches of Some of the Largest Stockholders, and Most Liberal Aiders and Advisors of the Board*. Chicago: Johnson Publishing Company, 1970 (originally published 1872).

Debra Newman Ham

James "Buster" Brown
1913–2002

Dancer, choreographer

According to his website, when asked by an interviewer to define "funky," tap dancer, teacher, and choreographer James "Buster" Brown would reply, "Funky? That's when you look like it smells bad." He would wrinkle his nose and do a funny dance, bringing laughter to anyone who was in the room. What the interviewer was likely getting at was that it was Brown himself who defined funky and not in the off-putting and smelly sense of the word. One of the most prominent figures in the world of tap dance, Brown is cited as an inventor of the art form, and certainly an influence on later entertainers such as Sammy Davis Jr. and Gregory Hines. Brown's career spanned more than seven decades, from vaudeville to Broadway to an appearance in the Hollywood film *Cotton Club*. Brown made his name touring internationally as a soloist with Cab Calloway, Count Basie, Dizzy Gillespie, Duke Ellington, and his own groups, the Hoofers and the Copacetics. Brown died in his sleep on May 7, 2002.

Born James Richard Brown in Baltimore, Maryland on May 17, 1913, Brown was the son of William Brown and Marie Ella Otho-Brown. He learned tap on the streets. "The guys around my time, we all learned on the street…Never classes," Brown told radio host Liane Hansen in a 1999 interview for National Public Radio. "We'd teach one another, 'If you show me your step, I'll show you this step.'" They danced, he added, to the sounds of bebop era in jazz.

Moves from the Autumn Follies to Duke Ellington

Brown began dancing for an audience at age sixteen with two friends at an annual high school show called the "Autumn Follies." The three performers, who called themselves Three Aces, began touring the United States

James "Buster" Brown

in the 1930s. His next act, the Speed Kings, also a trio, was known for its precision and rapid-fire tap dancing, acrobatics, and jive; it toured the United States and Canada for several years with the Brown Skin Models and the Rudy Vallee Show. Other acts Brown worked with included Beige & Brown and the Entertainers, sharing bills with Sarah Vaughan, among many others.

In 1989 Brown participated in a roundtable discussion with fellow African American entertainers for the PBS-TV show *Frontline*, in a segment called "Talented, Black and Blue." The group discussed the racial climate between white stars and black acts in the early days of the stage. "We (blacks and whites) couldn't be on stage together sometimes," Brown recalled. "A lot of the times…when you were on stage you couldn't touch." The group acknowledged that the arrangement was just accepted, never brought to light, because performers feared losing the opportunity to be on the stage at all.

As a soloist, Brown traveled the world. He also appeared in the 1943 film musical *Something to Shout About*, starring Don Ameche.

Around 1949 tap went dormant. Brown suggested it happened about the time that Bill "Bojangles" Robinson died. "Dancers seem to have gone out the same time that Mr. Robinson died," Brown told Hansen on NPR. "Everything about dancing went out." Dance stayed "out" until the 1970s, and Brown had to find other means

to support his family. Among his interim jobs he worked as a hotel clerk and as a janitor.

Sees Bright Lights in Europe

Though tap was out of the spotlight in the United States, Brown found audiences abroad were eager to watch him perform. He danced in jazz festivals in Berlin and other European cities in 1966 with a group called the Harlem Uptown All Star Dancers. The group, which included Jimmy Slyde, Chuck Green, and Baby Laurence, later became the legendary tap crew known as the Hoofers. The Harlem Uptown band included jazz icons Papa Jo Jones, Roy Eldridge, Illinois Jaquette, Milt Buckner, and Jimmy Woode. Brown then traveled to Africa, where he gave a command performance for Ethiopian emperor Haile Selassie and was awarded the Medal of Honor, the Lion of Judea Coin.

The long hibernation caused many of Brown's peers to walk away from the stage and follow other pursuits, but when tap came back into favor, Brown was ready to dance. He danced on Broadway in *Bubbling Brown Sugar* and *Black and Blue*. He appeared in the films *Tap* and *The Cotton Club* with Gregory Hines. His TV credits include the PBS specials *Great Performances: Tap Dance in America*, *Gershwin Gala*, and the *Dick Cavett Show*. He was featured in the tap documentaries *Great Feats of Feet*, *Fancy Feet*, and *Tap Dancin'*.

During the 1990s, Brown toured as a guest with concert tap companies. The 1995 Broadway musical *Bring in 'Da Noise, Bring in 'Da Funk* honored his influence on modern tap dancers. In 1997, Brown started hosting a weekly Tap Jam in New York City. Every Sunday, tap dancers and fans would flock to Swing 46, a Manhattan jazz club on West 46th Street. The event was marked by Brown's genial hosting skills and enthusiastic support for anyone who wanted to "hit the boards." Regulars to the club included a range from old friends from Brown's vaudeville days to throngs of children breaking in their first pair of tap shoes. He hosted the weekly event until just before his death.

In 2002 Brown was among nine tap legends awarded honorary doctorates by the School of American Dance and Arts Management at Oklahoma City University. "As we looked at the world of tap, we realized that many of its creators were still alive, ignored by society, mostly because they were black," John Bedford, the school's dean, is quoted as saying in the *San Antonio Express News* online. "We decided to recognize those who created the art form, as well as the art form itself as a reflection of American culture." The lively ceremony was filmed for a documentary called *The Doctors of Dance*.

Brown died in his sleep on May 7, 2002 at Presbyterian Hospital in New York City, just ten days shy of his eighty-ninth birthday. In a memorial on Brown's website, actor and tap dancer Gregory Hines is quoted as saying: "There are no mixed reviews when it comes to Dr. Buster Brown. He had no mean words to say about anyone. And no one had mean words to say about him. He was a role model." The memorial's author, Max Pollack, continued, "Not only did he amaze every single musician and dancer he ever worked with through his effortless artistry, he could also 'outhang' them all at the bar after the gig. Dr. Buster Brown was the quintessential Gentleman."

REFERENCES

Periodicals

"Obituaries: James 'Buster' Brown." *Variety*, 20 May 2002.

Online

"James 'Buster' Brown." TapDance.org. http://www.tapdance.org/tap/people/tapbios1.htm (Accessed 28 January 2005).

"Obituary." Dr. Buster Brown homepage. http://www.drbusterbrown.com (Accessed 28 January 2005).

"Project, film honor tap legends." *San Antonio Express-News* online. http://www.mysanantonio.com (Accessed 28 January 2005).

"Talented, Black and Blue." PBS.org. http://www.pbs.org/wgbh/pages/frontline/shows/secret/oral/rat02.html (Accessed 28 January 2005).

Other

Hansen, Liane. "Profile: Tap dancer Buster Brown and his teaching techniques." *Weekend All Things Considered*, National Public Radio, May 23, 1999.

Brenna Sanchez

Lee Brown
1937–

Mayor, police chief, federal government official

Lee Patrick Brown is one of the top law-enforcement officials in the United States. After helming the police forces of Atlanta, Houston, and New York City, Brown served as drug czar in the first Clinton administration and then headed back to Houston to run for mayor. Voters in the city—an urban sprawl equally divided between black, white, and Hispanic residents—elected him in 1997 and returned him to office two more times. Known as a level-headed, press-shy leader, Brown has been criticized sometimes for his management style, but in both his role as police chief and later mayor, Brown "was a determined agent of progress and upheaval for the nation's fourth-largest city," noted *Houston Chronicle* journalist Alan Bernstein. "As he leaves government service, his record brims with the stuff of bricks, concrete, light rail tracks and classrooms or libraries filled with children in after-school programs."

Brown was born on October 4, 1937, in Wewoka, Oklahoma. When he was of kindergarten age, his parents moved to California's San Joaquin Valley in order to work in its fertile farmlands as migrant laborers. The family took shelter in a barn at first, with another family, and Brown recalled in an interview with *Ebony*'s Kevin Chappell, "when we finally got a house, it was a one-bedroom house with seven kids and mother and father. There were six boys. We would sleep in an old army tent. The ground was a hard floor. We had to pump our water. We had to chop our wood. We had to have an outhouse."

As a youngster, Brown helped out in the fields, picking grapes, cotton, and other crops for meager piecemeal wages. Luckily, he earned a football scholarship out of high school and enrolled at Fresno State University, where he earned an undergraduate degree in criminology in 1961. Before he had even graduated, however, Brown joined the force of the San Jose Police Department as a patrol officer. He eventually moved over to the undercover narcotics and vice divisions and also took courses at San Jose State University, which granted him a master's degree in sociology in 1964. From there, he commuted to the Berkeley campus of the University of California and earned a second master's degree, this one in criminology.

Brown's break came in 1968, when he was tapped to set up Portland State University's Department of Administration of Justice. Taking a leave of absence with the San Jose police force, he spent several months on the job in the Oregon city then returned home and decided to run for a seat on the San Jose city council. Because of his time in Portland, however, his residency status was declared invalid. Shelving political office for the time

Lee Brown

Chronology

1937	Born in Wewoka, Oklahoma on October 4
1942	Moves with his family to the San Joaquin Valley in California
1960	Joins San Jose Police Department as a patrol officer
1961	Earns B.A. in criminology from Fresno State University
1964	Earns M.A. in sociology from San Jose State University
1970	Earns Ph.D. in criminology from the University of California
1978	Becomes public safety commissioner of Atlanta, Georgia
1982	Moves to Houston, Texas, to become the city's new police chief
1989	Takes over as police commissioner of New York City under Mayor David Dinkins
1993	Becomes director of the U.S. Office of Drug Control Policy under President Bill Clinton
1997	Wins election as Houston mayor
2003	Joins the faculty of Rice University in Houston as scholar-in-residence

being, Brown earned his Ph.D. in criminology from the University of California at Berkeley in 1970, making him one of the first African Americans to hold a doctorate in the subject. He spent three years in Washington D.C., teaching at Howard University. In 1975, he was appointed sheriff of Multnomah County, in which Portland was situated, but held the post for just a year. He remained there, however, as director of the county's justice services for two more years.

In 1978, Brown was named the public safety commissioner of Atlanta, Georgia, a position in which he was responsible for the city's police, fire, and emergency-services departments. The city was mired in thorny anti-discrimination lawsuits at the time due to unfair hiring and promotion practices on both the police and fire departments, and Brown quickly moved to remedy the problems by promoting and recruiting minority officers. He also put in long, eighteen-hour days to help solve a string of unsolved slayings of children and teens between 1979 and 1982 that became known as the Atlanta child murders.

The mayor of Houston, Texas, appointed Brown as that city's next chief of police in 1982, and he became the first African American to hold the post in Houston history. Again, Brown took over a force troubled by charges of discrimination and hostility toward the city's black and Hispanic residents. At the time, just 8 percent of Houston's police ranks were African American, and

white officers had been charged with using unnecessary force against minorities during arrests. But Brown took a firm hand as an outsider, enacting changes that served to permanently balance the racial makeup of the force; he also solved several internal-management issues that had kept the Houston force from moving forward. One of the most controversial features of his tenure, however, was a groundbreaking new program called community policing, which sought to improve relations between the police and residents in some of the city's more troubled neighborhoods. It was a hotly debated initiative and opposed by many police officers at first. Nevertheless, it proved to have some success and was widely copied by other U.S. cities over the following decade.

In 1989, newly elected New York City mayor David Dinkins appointed Brown as the police commissioner of the largest city in the United States. Again, Brown implemented new policies that put more officers on the streets, and the city experienced the first drop in crime in thirty-six years just months after Brown came on the job. He stepped down from the post in 1992, however, when his wife, Arlene, was diagnosed with lung cancer. She died later that year, and Brown took a job teaching at Houston's Texas Southern University. Midway through 1993, Brown suddenly gained national attention when President Bill Clinton made him the country's newest drug czar, the media catchphrase for the director of the Office of Drug Control Policy. As documented in *Weekly Compilation of Presidential Documents*, in the speech announcing the appointment, Clinton commended Brown for his community-policing strategies and expressed gratitude to the appointee for accepting "this challenge. He'd made the decision to do so at a time in his life when he might have reasonably been expected, for personal and professional reasons, to take a different course. He could clearly be making more money doing something else.... The simple fact that at this point in his life he resolved to do this says a great deal about him and his character."

Brown spent three years as the drug czar, advocating more drug-treatment and drug-prevention funds that were usually blocked by conservatives in Congress. He resigned in 1996, returning once again to Houston, and the following year made a successful bid for the mayor's office. His opponent was a wealthy Texas Republican, Robert Mosbacher Jr., but Brown—a Democrat—won endorsements from President Clinton as well as the Reverend Jesse Jackson. He was reelected two more times for two-year terms. One of his lasting accomplishments was the "Super Neighborhoods" program, which created eighty-eight districts in the city, each with its own local council. He also held regularly scheduled "Mayor's Night In" evenings, in which residents could visit City Hall to voice their complaints directly to him and his staff.

The Houston city charter's term-limit provision prevented Brown from seeking a fourth term as mayor, and in 2003 he took a post as a scholar-in-residence at the city's Rice University. He was planning to write a book on community policing, but he also recognized his place as a role model for youngsters. "When I grew up as a youngster I did not see anyone who looked like me as mayor or police chief," he told the *Houston Chronicle*'s Bernstein. "And I think that makes a big difference in terms of the aspirations of young people. If they can see me, as an African American, serve as mayor of the fourth-largest city in America, then it also serves to energize them to know that they can do the same thing, that they can achieve what they want to achieve."

REFERENCES

Books

"Lee Patrick Brown." In *Contemporary Black Biography*, Vol. 24. Ed. Shirelle Phelps. Farmington Hills, Mich.: Gale Group, 2000.

Periodicals

Belkins, Lisa. "A Chief Known for Turning Strife into Calm." *New York Times*, 19 December 1989.

Bernstein, Alan. "Bricks and Brickbats Mark Brown's Tenure." *Houston Chronicle*, 21 December 2003.

Chappell, Kevin. "Houston's Lee P. Brown: A Can-Do Mayor for a Can-Do City." *Ebony* 54 (January 1999): 96.

"Remarks at the Swearing-In of National Drug Control Policy Director Lee Brown (Bill Clinton's speech, July 1, 1993)." *Weekly Compilation of Presidential Documents* 29 (5 July 1993): 1213.

Serrill, Michael S. "The New Black Police Chiefs; Updating a Long Tradition of Ethnic Groups Rising to the Top." *Time* 125 (18 February 1985): 84.

Carol Brennan

Roscoe C. Brown, Jr.
1922–

Military officer, pilot, college president

A decorated military veteran, college president, and media personality, Roscoe Conkling Brown Jr. refused to go along with the racism of his era. Instead, he resisted discrimination and never let it stop him from pursuing and achieving his goals. He became a superior combat pilot at a time when many ranking members of the U.S. Air Corps believed African Americans lacked the ability to become pilots. As an educator he was the president of Bronx Community College and helped to restore the institution's Hall of Fame for Great Americans, the first hall of fame in the United States. Brown also hosted television programs and produced videos documenting the history and experience of black America. In later life Roscoe continued to show his commitment to equality and civil rights as he demonstrated against injustice.

Roscoe Conkling Brown Jr. was born on March 9, 1922 in Washington D.C. to a renowned black family. Brown's father, Roscoe Conkling Brown Sr., practiced medicine in Washington D.C. at the beginning of the twentieth century and served as the Negro Specialist of the United States Public Health Service and on Theodore Roosevelt's black cabinet. Brown's mother, Vivian Kemp Brown, was a teacher in the D.C. public school system. Both parents instilled a strong work ethic in Roscoe and a respect for education that he carried into adulthood.

Brown is the younger of two children and, along with his sister Portia Brown who died in 1984, attended segregated schools in Washington D.C. He graduated from Paul Laurence Dunbar High School in Washington D.C., earned his B.S. from Springfield College in Massachusetts (1943), and his M.A. (1949) and Ph.D. (1951) from New York University. During the 1940s Brown participated in the distinguished and well-established D.C. area sport programs.

Becomes World War II Pilot

Brown wanted to be a pilot when many people believed African Americans were intellectually inferior and that blacks lacked the coordination needed to fly a plane. The common belief did not dissuade him and other black men determined to become pilots and prove the prejudiced theory wrong. He and over nine hundred other black men learned how to fly in a training program at Tuskegee Institute (now University), a black college in Alabama.

In 1943, Brown joined the armed forces and became a member of the 332nd Fighter Group, a black fighter squadron whose core was the Tuskegee trained pilots, later becoming a squadron commander for the group dur-

Chronology

1922	Born in Washington D.C. on March 9
1943	Earns B.S. from Springfield College, Massachusetts
1943-45	Serves as pilot in U.S. Air Force; receives Distinguished Flying Cross, Air Medal
1945	Applies for position as pilot with Eastern Airlines; works as social investigator in New York City for six months
1946	Teaches physical education at West Virginia State College
1949	Earns M.A. from New York University
1951	Earns Ph.D. from New York University; becomes professor at School of Education at New York University, where he remains for twenty-five years
1960	Becomes director of the Institute of Afro-American Affairs at New York University, where he remains until 1967
1973	Receives Emmy award for *Black Arts* television series
1977	Becomes president of Bronx Community College of the City University of New York, where he remains until 1993
1993	Becomes director of the Center for Urban Education Policy at the Graduate Center of the City University of New York

where he had the opportunity to coach Earl Lloyd, one of the first black players in the NBA.

By 1949 Brown earned an M.A. at New York University (NYU), and in 1951 he was awarded a PhD. from the same institution. Once again Brown had a taken a triple major, focusing on exercise physiology, educational psychology, and educational research as a doctoral candidate. After completing his doctorate, Brown joined the School of Education at New York University where he became a full professor. He was a faculty member at NYU for more than twenty-five years. In 1960 while at New York University, Brown became the director of the Institute of Afro-American Affairs and remained its director until 1967. From 1977 to 1993 he served as president of Bronx Community College of the City University of New York (CUNY). In 1993, Brown became director of the Center for Urban Education Policy at the Graduate School and University Center of CUNY.

Becomes Community Servant

Brown serves on the boards of many non-profit organizations. He has served as chairman of the New York City Regional Educational Center for Economic Development, and is a member of the National Board of the Boys and Girls Clubs of America. He has also served on the boards of the American Council on Education, the YMCA of Greater New York, the Fund for the City of New York, the New York Botanical Garden, the New York City Partnership, the Museum of the City of New York, and the City Parks Foundation. Brown is chairman of the Greater Harlem Nursing Home and the Sports Foundation and is past president of One Hundred Black Men Inc., an influential group of civic-minded New Yorkers. He is vice-chairman of the Black Leadership Commission on AIDS. Brown has been appointed by the governor to the New York State Job Training and Partnership Council and the New York State Health, Fitness, and Sports Council. He chaired the Urban Issues Group, a think tank devoted to the concerns of the African American community. He is a member of the Jackie Robinson Foundation and Libraries for the Future.

A media personality, Brown hosted the television program *African American Legends*, and was awarded an Emmy in 1973 for the distinguished television series *Black Arts*. He hosted other black-oriented programs, including the *Soul of Reason*, and was co-host of WCBS's *Black Letters* and WNBC-TV's *A Black Perspective*. Brown is the co-author of widely read used references such as the *Negro Almanac* and the author of more than sixty articles in scholarly journals.

REFERENCES

Periodicals

Banks, Ann. "Doing Battle on Two Fronts." *New York Times*, May 1995.

ing the war. Brown flew his first combat mission in August 1944 and completed a total of sixty-eight missions. His assignment as a combat pilot was to escort B-17 bombers to their destinations in the Balkans, Austria, and Germany. When Brown shot down an enemy ME-262 jet fighter while he was escorting a B-17 bomber to a German tank works, he became the first pilot in the 15th Air Force to do so. He received the Distinguished Flying Cross and the Air Medal with eight oak leaf clusters. As a member of the Tuskegee Airmen, or Red-tails, known for their P-51 Mustang fighters' paint schemes, his unit's record of shooting down 111 enemy aircraft in the air and 150 enemy aircraft on the ground played an important role in changing the segregationist policies of the U.S. Air Corps. Their record during the war influenced President Harry S. Truman's decision to integrate the armed forces in 1948. The combat unit received the Presidential Unit Citation, one of the highest honors a combat unit can receive.

Before the war, Brown had attended Springfield College in Massachusetts where he majored in three areas— pre-medical, chemistry, and health physical education. Brown was awarded a B.S. upon graduation in 1943 and was class valedictorian. Instead of using his college degree to find employment after he came out of the military in 1945, Brown sought employment as a pilot with Eastern Airlines in New York City, relying on his military experience instead of his education. However, he was told Eastern Airlines did not hire black pilots. After being denied that job, he found employment as a social investigator in New York City. He remained there for about six months. Brown also worked as a physical education teacher at West Virginia State College for a short time

Boyd, Herb. "New York's Honor Roll." *New York Amsterdam News*, 18 March 1999.

Kifner, John. "Public Lives; A Pioneer in the Cockpit, Still at the Controls." *New York Times*, 30 August 2001.

Prime, John Andrew. "Tuskegee Airmen Veteran Recalls WWII Service at Barksdale Meeting."*The Baton Rouge Advocate*, 1 February 2004.

Terrell, Mary Church. "History of the High School for Negroes in Washington." *The Journal of Negro History*, July 1917.

Online

Education Makers. http://www.thehistorymakers.com/ biography/biography.asp?bioindex=487&category= educationMakers (Accessed 18 May 2005).

Mario A. Charles

Chronology

1829	Born in the District of Columbia on February 14
1833	Father dies and leaves family penniless
1844	Assigned to work with Lambert Tree, assistant postmaster for Washington, D.C., which leads to work with Samuel B. Morse on the telegraph
1852	Begins work at the Foreign Exchange Division of the Smithsonian Institute; launches career as lecturer
1855	Delivers first lecture to the Young People's Literary Society
1864	Marries wife Lucinda
1871	Elected the first of three times to District of Columbia legislature
1887	Retires from travel and lecturing
1906	Retires from the Smithsonian; dies in Washington, D.C. on June 24

Solomon G. Brown
1829–1906

Inventor, lecturer, naturalist, poet

Solomon G. Brown was as self-educated man, whose gifted intellect, hard work, creativity, and inventive spirit endowed him with a versatile public career. He helped Samuel F. Morse develop the telegraph and became the first African American employed by the Smithsonian Institute. Brown's expertise as a naturalist and his talent as an illustrator made him a highly desirable lecturer in his day. Brown was also a published poet and a local legislator. While his is not quite a rags to riches story, it is nevertheless a fascinating one about what one determined black man with meager beginnings can accomplish with a strong intellect and a willingness to seize opportunities to enhance his education and advance his professional status. As his careers developed, Brown always reached back to extend a hand to other African Americans who were less fortunate and to do what he could to improve their plight.

Solomon G. Brown was born to Isaac and Rachel Brown on February 14, 1829. The fourth son of six children, Brown was born a free black, because both of his parents were free Negroes. The family resided in Washington, D.C., living on very modest means. Brown was deprived of formal education because when his father died in 1833, his mother was left defenseless against creditors who made false claims of indebtedness on the family's estate. The year after Brown's father died, bill collectors seized all of his family's property and left the family destitute.

Begins Post Office Career

In 1844 Brown was lucky enough to be apprenticed to Lambert Tree, the assistant postmaster for the District of Columbia. The next year he was assigned to assist Joseph Henry, Samuel F. Morse, and Alfred Vail with the development of a new invention that would constitute the genesis of the modern telecommunication industry and become one of the pinnacles of the industrial revolution in the United States: the electric telegraph. Brown functioned as a technician and assisted his supervisors with installing the wiring necessary for the telegraph to perform efficiently. After Samuel F. Morse successfully transmitted his Morse code, a series of dots and dashes forming words, from Washington, D.C. to Baltimore, the telegraph became the new sensation. Brown continued to work with the new communications innovation, even after it was sold to the Morse Telegraph Company.

In the Solomon G. Brown biographical essay that appears in *Men of Mark*, the author laments that Morse went on to garner accolades, fame, and wealth, but the contribution of the "negro[sic] who materially assisted" Morse with getting the project started has largely been ignored. Robert C. Hayden, in the *Dictionary of American Negro Biography,* speculates that Brown actually wrote this essay himself, and if that is true, the passage reveals that Brown was acutely aware of the fact that his skin color may have kept him from receiving proper recognition for his contribution to the invention of the telegraph.

Brown accepted a position as battery tender with the fledgling Morse Company but later moved on to become an assistant packer at Gillman and Brothers Manufactory, a chemical laboratory. While working at the laboratory Brown discovered that he had a talent for painting and coloring maps and other illustrations. His artistic side evolved when he mounted and painted maps for two laboratory clients, the General Land Office and a book binder.

A self-taught individual in the purest sense of the phrase, Brown was one of those rare people who achieved more that one thought he could, given his social status and lack of formal schooling. He was born with a natural ability for science and art, and he was hard working and ambitious. He learned whatever he could from each of his employers and intelligently applied his education in ways that advanced him socially, economically, and politically.

Becomes Smithsonian's First Black Hire

Although he thoroughly enjoyed his work, Brown left the laboratory position in 1852 to work in the Foreign Exchange Division of the newly opened Smithsonian Institute. The first secretary of the Smithsonian was Joseph Henry, the same electrical engineer with whom Brown had worked at the post office, so the two men had a previous work relationship, and similar roles in the early days of working with Samuel F. Morse and the invention of the telegraph, all in common.

Brown holds the unique distinction of being the first African American hired to work at the Smithsonian Institute. In June 2004, during the one-hundred-year anniversary celebration of the founding of the Museum of Natural History, which was attended by some of Brown's descendants, his contributions to the Smithsonian were honored by the planting of a Lebanon tree on the museum grounds. Christian T. Samper, the museum's director, noted that Brown was present at the museum's original ground breaking.

When Brown was hired by the Smithsonian, he found his niche and his lifelong avocation. He remained with the Smithsonian for fifty-four years and held several positions. He started at the bottom rung with manual labor tasks such as building exhibit cases, was promoted to clerical positions, and finally obtained the position of naturalist. Over the years, he absorbed and compiled a plethora of information on natural history. He then synthesized his knowledge with his artistic experiences and began lecturing before various audiences in the District of Columbia area, demonstrating with his own illustrations on a variety of topics.

Brown's very first lecture occurred on January 10, 1855 at the invitation of the Young People's Literary Society and Lyceum at the Israel Church in Washington, D.C. With a dazzling display of forty-nine different drawings, Brown captivated the audience with his expertise on the subject of the social habits of insects. This lecture proved so popular he was called upon to repeat it in surrounding cities such as Baltimore, Georgetown, and Alexandria. Encouraged by the demand for his informative speaking engagements, Brown expanded his repertoire and delivered addresses on water, air, food, coal, mineralogy, fungi, plant embryos, and geology.

For his first lecture on geology, presented to a packed audience at the 1883 Annual Conference of the African Methodist Episcopalian Church in Washington, D.C., he used twenty-nine of his own large illustrations, including one on geologic strata formations. Then, too, Brown's selection of subjects was not limited to natural phenomena. He enlightened his audiences on philosophical, religious, and educational topics, including "God's Providence to Man," "Early Educators of D.C.," "Man's Relations to Earth," and the telegraph. He continued to travel and lecture until 1887.

Brown served under two other secretaries of the Smithsonian, Spencer F. Baird and Samuel P. Langley. When Baird would leave Washington, D.C. during the summers for his family vacation, Brown would conscientiously write him letters, keeping his supervisor abreast of the daily affairs of the Smithsonian, as well as events happening in the city. One letter to Baird dated July 15, 1864, reported that Confederate Army Rebels were threatening the city and that the museum had very few visitors.

On June 16, 1864, when he was a museum assistant, Brown married his wife, Lucinda, who then became his devoted companion and an enthusiastic helpmate, nurturing his enterprising spirit and aspirations. The couple had no children of their own but mentored several young women. In 1869, Brown changed Smithsonian jobs again and assumed responsibility for the registration, transportation, and storage of museum materials and resources.

A nineteenth-century renaissance man, Brown also possessed literary talent and became a published poet. He performed poetry readings and his poems were published in a local African American newspaper, the *Washington Bee*. In 1983, Louise Daniel Hutchinson and Gail Sylvia Lowe compiled his poetry into a book entitled *Kind Regards of S. G. Brown: Selected Poems of Solomon G. Brown*. It was published by the Smithsonian Institution Press.

Brown was socially active and involved in his community's political, educational, and religious activities. He held trusteeships with Wilberforce University, the Fifteenth Street Presbyterian Church, and the Washington, D.C. public school system. He was a Sunday School superintendent and helped found the Pioneer Sunday School. He was grand secretary of the District Grand Lodge of Masons, a member of the Freeman's Relief Association, president of National Union League (1866), director of the Industrial Saving and Building Association, editor of the *Sunday School Circle of the Christian Index*, and the Washington correspondent for the *Anglo-African Christian Recorder*. He served as a commissioner for the poor and, beginning in 1871, was elected three times to the District of Columbia legislature. The 1878 minutes of the Negro Society show that Brown was admitted as a member at its meeting on January 19; however, none of the subsequent published minutes demonstrates that he ever attended a meeting.

Solomon G. Brown retired from the Smithsonian Institute on his birthday, February 14, 1906. He was seventy-seven years old and had lived life to the fullest. He died at his home five months later, on June 24. A brilliant man with so many accomplishments in different fields of endeavor, Brown left a legacy of service, entrepreneurship, and embracing all life had to offer a man of his class and his race in the late nineteenth century. Brown is best remembered by many historians as the first African American employee of the Smithsonian Institute, but he made other lasting contributions with the telegraph, his natural history lectures, his poetry, and his long record of unselfish public service.

REFERENCES

Books

Brawley, Benjamin. *Negro Builders and Heroes*. Chapel Hill, N.C.: University of North Carolina Press, 1937.

Logan, Rayford W., and Michael R. Winston. *Dictionary of American Negro Biography*. New York: Norton, 1982.

Sammons, Vivian Ovelton. *Blacks in Science and Medicine*. New York: Hemisphere Publishing Corp., 1990.

Simmons, William J. *Men of Mark: Eminent, Progressive, Rising*. New York: Arno Press, 1968.

Webster, Raymond. *African American Firsts in Science and Technology*. Detroit, Mich.: Gale Group, 1999.

Periodicals

Cromwell, W., N. Thomas, and F. G. Barbadoes. "Adjourned Meeting of the Negro Society." *Journal of Negro History* 64 (Winter 1979): 63-69.

Online

Schmid, Randolph E. "Smithsonian Celebrates 100 Years." CBSNEWS.com. http://www.cbsnews.com/stories/2004/06/16/national/main623517.shtml (Accessed 31 January 2005)

"Solomon G. Brown: First African American Employee at the Smithsonian." Smithsonian Scrapbook: Letters, Diaries & Photographs from the Smithsonian Archives. http://www.si.edu/archives/documents/brown2.htm (Accessed 31 January 2005).

"Solomon G. Brown: Letter dated July 15, 1864." Smithsonian Scrapbook: Letters, Diaries & Photographs from the Smithsonian Archives. http://www.si.edu/archives/documents/brownjuly1864.htm (Accessed 31 January 2005).

Glenda M. Alvin

Hugh M. Browne
1851–1923

Educator, civil rights activist, minister

Hugh M. Browne was an influential educator and creative thinker whose ideas were a part of the early development of African American education and civil rights. Although Browne was a contemporary of both Booker T. Washington and W. E. B. Du Bois, his philosophical positions marked a middle ground between Washington's advocacy of industrial education for the masses and Du Bois's advocacy for classical, liberal education to develop the "talented tenth" for leadership and stronger agitation for political and civil rights.

Hugh Mason Browne was born in June 1851 into a prominent free Negro family in Washington, D.C. His parents, John and Elizabeth Wormley Browne, and other relatives were established members of the local black elite as a result of their entrepreneurial, educational, and political activities in the nation's capital.

After receiving his early education in the local colored public school system, Browne attended Howard University, graduating with a B.A. in 1875 and an M.A. in 1878. He also received a B.D. degree from Princeton Theological Seminary in 1878 and was ordained for ministry in the Presbyterian Church.

During the next two years Browne traveled to Germany and Scotland and pursued additional studies, then returned to the United States to pastor Shiloh Presbyterian Church in New York City for a brief period. In August 1883 he went to Liberia where he was appointed to a professorship in intellectual and moral philosophy at Liberia College. While in the country he learned about the challenges involved in assimilation of former slaves into an African setting and about the problems and cultural differences affecting Liberian social, economic, and educational development.

Theoretical and intellectual, Browne was nonetheless committed to practical application of ideas to specific needs. While he commanded the respect of more well-known thinkers and leaders such as Washington and Du Bois, Browne also spent time turning abstract ideas into tangible inventions in the manner of George Washington Carver or Elijah McCoy. He was credited with patenting a device for preventing back flow of water in cellars on April 29, 1890, and cited in the July 8, 1893 issue of *The Colored American*, which included "a partial list of patents granted by the U.S. for inventions by colored persons."

Critiques Liberian Systems and Experiences Controversy

In 1896 Browne commented that the Americo-Liberian education and economic development was totally dependent on U.S. paternalism and goodwill and other foreign influences and based primarily on outside interest in the country's natural resources. He pointed to the lack of effective Liberian leadership in developing the country's own cultural, political, and economic infrastructure to address ongoing issues and concerns, prophetic statements which were borne out in the country during the twentieth century.

Although Browne addressed these problems by developing a plan to reorganize educational and administrative systems, his candor created personal difficulties. Edward Wilmot Blyden, principal of the college, distrusted Browne after he publicly criticized Liberian culture, which added to existing problems with the Liberian government. As a result, Blyden restricted Browne's academic freedom by preventing him from teaching.

Resumes Academic Career in United States

Browne returned to Washington after nearly two years in West Africa and taught physics for the next two years at the Colored Preparatory and M Street High School in his hometown. Next, he taught at Hampton Institute in Virginia from 1898 to 1901, then served as principal of Colored High School in Baltimore, Maryland. In each of these settings, Browne sought to improve educational systems and services to African Americans through a balanced approach of theory and practice, academic with industrial training, and equal development of the mind and body through intellectual stimulation and physical education.

In 1902, Browne married Julia Shadd Purnell, a widow and member of another prominent Washington family, and the couple moved to Philadelphia where Browne became the principal of the Institute for Colored Youth (ICY). The original name of the school, the African Institute, was changed shortly after it was founded in 1837 with support from the Society of Friends (Quakers).

Browne served as the fourth principal of ICY, overseeing the relocation of the school from Philadelphia to Cheyney Station, Pennsylvania, on farmland formerly owned by the Cheyney family, prominent white supporters of Negro education. Matthew Anderson of Philadelphia assisted Browne during this transition. During his tenure as principal, Browne developed the first campus buildings, invited Booker T. Washington to speak at the formal dedication of the new campus in 1905, and secured funding for Andrew Carnegie Hall, the school's first library.

Browne maintained contacts and correspondence with Washington, Du Bois, writer Charles Chesnutt, and other prominent African Americans, and was a key participant in the January 1904 conference of African American leaders convened by Washington at Carnegie Hall in New York City. Documentation of the conference proceedings indicates that Browne was one of the signers of a resolution establishing the Committee of Safety, twelve men who would serve as a national information bureau on racial concerns, work toward cooperation among various African American organizations, and facilitate communications among African Americans in various regions and sections of the country.

Washington, Du Bois, and Browne were appointed as the first three members of the Committee of Safety and given authorization to select the other nine members. Du Bois eventually broke with Washington regarding white influence over the conference, Washington's control of the committee and organization, and other major differences of opinion. Browne remained as secretary of the committee until 1913 and a confidant of Washington while not subscribing wholeheartedly to his social and educational philosophies.

Browne was widely respected for his leadership of ICY and other intellectual endeavors until his retirement in 1913. His successor, Leslie P. Hill, became the last principal of ICY and first president when it was renamed the Cheyney Training School for Teachers in 1914. After additional transitions and name changes, the present Cheyney University of Pennsylvania was recognized as the oldest of the historically black colleges and universities (HBCUs).

Returning to his native Washington after spending time in Germany studying vocational education, Browne did not completely retire from work as an educator. He cast himself in yet another role as an educational engineer or consultant, until his death on October 30, 1923.

The District of Columbia Board of Education honored Browne posthumously when the Hugh M. Browne Junior High School was erected in 1932. The school survived through decades of change to become a nationally recognized institution, successfully incorporating many of the concepts of its namesake into the twenty-first century.

REFERENCES

Books

McGuire, Robert C. "Hugh M. Browne." In *Dictionary of American Negro Biography*. Eds. Rayford W. Logan and Michael R. Winston. New York: Norton, 1982.

Periodicals

"A Partial List of Patents Granted by the U.S. for Inventions by Colored Persons." *The Colored American*, 8 July 1893.

Online

"Browne Junior High School." http://www.exploredc. org (Accessed 16 September 2005).

"Cheyney Timeline." http://www.cheyney.edu/pages/ ?p=136 (Accessed 16 September 2005).

Harlan, Louis, ed. The Booker T. Washington Papers Web Site. http://historycooperative.press.uiuc.edu/ btw/Vol.7/384.html (Accessed 16 September 2005).

Williams, Abraham M. "President Pro-Tempore Addresses Surreptitious Liberian International Trade Conference." http://www.theperspective.org/trade. html (Accessed 16 September 2005).

"Writing for the Advancement of Colored People." http://www.eden.rutgers.edu/~c350445/lund1.html (Accessed 21 September 2005).

Collections

The Moorland-Spingarn Research Center at Howard University has some additional biographical information related to Browne in its archival materials.

Fletcher F. Moon

John Edward Bruce
1856–1924

Journalist, historian, orator, politician

The life of John Edward Bruce was marked by perseverance and fortitude. Born a slave, Bruce rose from humble beginnings on a plantation in Piscataway, Mary-

---

Chronology

1856	Born in Piscataway, Maryland on February 22
1864	Enters integrated school in Stratford, Connecticut
1874	Works as messenger for the *New York Times* at the Washington, D.C. office
1875	Works as Washington correspondent for the *Progressive American*
1880	Publishes the *Sunday Item*, the first black-owned Sunday newspaper in the United States
1895	Marries Florence Bishop
1897	Founds the American Negro Academy with Alexander Crummell
1911	Founds the Negro Society for Historical Research with Arthur Schomburg
1916	Publishes novel *The Awakening of Hezekiah Jones: A Story Dealing with Some of the Problems Affecting the Political Rewards Due the Negro*
1919	Joins Universal Negro Improvement Association
1924	Dies in New York City on August 7

land, to an adulthood in which he corresponded with friends and activists throughout Africa, the Caribbean, Central and South America, the Philippines, and Europe. While some found manumission by escaping or at the mercy of their masters, others never obtained complete liberation from slavery because they had internalized beliefs of their racial inferiority. For Bruce, however, freedom lay in his pen. With this weapon, he railed against imperialism and slavery, writing searing articles and editorials for more than 100 newspapers worldwide. Championing the proponents of cultural nationalism, he was a stalwart race man who attacked Reconstruction, Jim Crowism, lynching, the vacillations of the Republican Party, and the accommodationist stance of Booker T. Washington. Due to his aggressive, matter-of-fact writing style, he affectionately became known as "Bruce Grit," his most widely known pseudonym.

At three years of age, Bruce became fascinated with race. At that time, Bruce's father, Robert Bruce, was sold to slave owners in Georgia. He was never to hear from or see his father again. His mother, Martha Bruce, then served as his sole caretaker. Martha, having agreed to provide her master, Major Thomas Harvey Griffin, with half of her earnings, worked as tavern cook at Fort Washington, approximately one mile from their plantation, and sold goods to U.S. Marines in exchange for their used clothes which she later stockpiled and sold as a part of a secondhand clothing business she operated. As the Civil War approached, Bruce witnessed countless numbers of his playmates and their families sold into slavery, a fate he dreaded. Martha feared the same, and in 1861, she and her children (Bruce's brother died shortly thereafter) joined the band of Union soldiers, after the first battle of Bull Run, as they marched through Maryland to Washington, D.C. Based on these early memories, Bruce wrote a fictional account of a slave trade in 1916, entitled *The Awakening of Hezekiah Jones: A Story Dealing with Some of the Problems Affecting the Political Rewards Due the Negro.*

After three years in Washington, D.C., Martha moved her family to Stratford, Connecticut. There Bruce entered an integrated school and was first introduced to formal education. The family lived in Stratford briefly, returning to Washington after two years. In Washington, Bruce enrolled at the Free Library School and schools operated by the Freedman's Aid Society and the Freedman's Bureau. Although Bruce applied himself, these new schools afforded him only basic skills. In 1872, he took a three-month course at Howard University, but after the course, he never pursued formal education again. Thereafter, he relied primarily on informal means of schooling and was mostly self-taught.

Earns Prominence as Journalist

While Bruce wrote various pamphlets, poetry, plays, songbooks, essays, and several books over his career, he is best known for his work as a journalist. Living in Washington after the Civil War, where he earned odd jobs around the city to augment his mother's income from her work at restaurants and as a domestic in private homes, Bruce met famous individuals who sparked his interests in culture and politics. These individuals included Charles Dickens, Martin R. Delany, and Henry Highland Garnet.

In 1874, when he was only eighteen years old, Bruce earned a job as a messenger for L. L. Crouse, associate editor at the *New York Times* Washington office and brother of the Nebraska governor. Bruce's duties required that he obtain communications for the next day's paper from Senator Charles Sumner, the author of the 1875 Civil Rights Act prohibiting racial discrimination in public facilities. In this capacity, Bruce developed a personal relationship with Sumner, who was regarded highly in the African American community, but Bruce was also able to speak with many members of Congress who visited Crouse's office. Given this exposure, Bruce was hired in 1875 as a special Washington correspondent for the *Progressive American* in New York. His first article, titled "Distillation of Coal Tar," was published under the pseudonym, "The Rising Sun." Frederick Douglass was apparently so moved by Bruce's writing that he made him a correspondent for the *New National Era*, where he assumed another pseudonym, "Caleb Quotem." With these publications, Bruce's writing career was effectively launched.

In the subsequent years, assuming the pseudonym "Bruce Grit," Bruce contributed to dozens of newspapers, most notably the *Weekly Argus* and the *Sunday Item*, both of which he founded. Printed in 1879, the editors of the *Weekly Argus*, Bruce and Charles N. Otley, decided that the paper would "be a fearless advocate of the true

principles of the Republican Party, and the moral and intellectual advancement of the Negro American," according to William Seraille's book, *Bruce Grit: The Black Nationalist Writings of John Edward Bruce*. The following year, in 1880, the *Sunday Item* became the first black-owned Sunday newspaper in the United States. Also of significance were Bruce's contributions to the *African Times and Orient Review*, beginning in 1910, which detailed the heroism and valor of black, African, and West Indian troops in World War I. Printed in London, England, the periodical was edited by Duse Mohammed Ali.

Establishes Relationships with Activists

Bruce's writings generated a considerable amount of interest from African American communities and the world. This interest spawned a host of relationships that proved influential to Bruce. A survey of his collected papers reveals that he maintained regular correspondence with Majola Agbebi, of Lagos, Nigeria; Liberian president C. D. B. King; Liberian Judge Dossen; J. R. Archer, first black mayor in Battersea, England; Kobina Sekyi of the Gold Coast; J. Robert Love of Jamaica; Henrietta Vinton Davis; Monroe Trotter; W. E. B. Du Bois; Alexander Crummell; Edward W. Blyden; and Paul Laurence Dunbar. In these lifelong relationships, Bruce was able to question and discuss the African's position in the world with powerful thinkers.

Bruce's relationship with Alexander Crummell, an Episcopal priest who lived in Liberia for almost twenty years before returning to the United States, proved to be especially significant. After returning to the United States due to illness, Crummell envisioned an institution of scholars who would be intent on eradicating the race problem through a coalition of black intellectuals who would study and document all aspects of the African race throughout the Diaspora. The result of his vision was the founding of the American Negro Academy with seventeen other scholars, clergy, and professionals in 1897. At Crummell's request, Bruce was one of the founding members. Crummell was Bruce's mentor, father-figure, and dear friend, guiding him through his published responses to Booker T. Washington's integrationist solutions to the plight of Africans and various other arguments he asserted in his writing. A staunch supporter of racial pride, Crummell also encouraged Bruce to affirm the achievements of Africa in his writings. When Bruce considered composing a children's book on African history, Crummell was most encouraging: "If you can do anything to increase the respect of our people for their own, you will be a benefactor to the race," he said, as quoted by Seraille. When Crummell died in 1898, Bruce suffered a debilitating blow.

Bruce also worked with Arthur Schomburg and Marcus Garvey. His relationship with Schomburg, who was nearly twenty years his junior, was one of a surrogate father from which he promoted Schomburg's bibliomania and his interest in freemasonry. Eventually they founded the Negro Society for Historical Research in 1911, which was a product of their shared passion for acquiring books and artifacts revealing the contributions of the black race to world history. With Bruce's guidance, Schomburg's collections grew. They are housed in the Schomburg Center for Research in Black Culture, one of the largest collections of materials pertaining to African studies.

Later in life, Bruce realized that his lifelong hopes for the African race were succinctly articulated by Garvey. As a result, Bruce vowed his allegiance to the aims of the United Negro Improvement Association (UNIA) in 1919, writing a weekly column for Garvey's *The Negro World* as well as defending Garvey from his critics.

Although John Edward Bruce was well known, his importance never reached the level of his contemporaries, Booker T. Washington and W. E. B. Du Bois. One reason is that he refused to be connected to any white institution or to anyone who consciously sought an association with these institutions. Professionally, he never was able to sustain himself economically without relying on odd jobs, and on August 7, 1924 he died in New York City's Bellevue Hospital. When Bruce died, a pension from the Port Authority of New York was his only source of income. The UNIA, however, honored him with a state funeral that consisted of three services at the UNIA Liberty Hall in New York City on August 10, 1924. On that day, more than 5,000 people viewed his body. He was survived by his wife Florence (Bishop) Bruce, whom he married in 1895, and daughter Olive Bruce.

REFERENCES

Books

Crowder, Ralph L. *John Edward Bruce: Politician, Journalist, and Self Trained Historian of the African Diaspora*. New York: New York University Press, 2004.

Gilbert, Peter, ed. *The Selected Writings of John Edward Bruce: Militant Black Journalist*. New York: Arno Press, 1971.

Gruesser, John C., ed. *The Black Sleuth*. Boston: Northeastern University Press, 2002.

Seraille, William. *Bruce Grit: The Black Nationalist Writings of John Edward Bruce*. Knoxville, Tenn.: University of Tennessee Press, 2003.

Periodicals

Beard, Richard L., and Cyril E. Zoerner. "Associated Negro Press: Its Founding, Ascendancy, and Demise." *Journalism Quarterly* 46 (Spring 1969): 47-52.

Crowder, Ralph L. "John Edward Bruce, Edward Wilmot Blyden, Alexander Crummell, and J. Robert Love: Mentors, Patrons, and the Evolution of a Pan-African Network." *Afro-Americans in New York Life and History* 20 (July 1996): 59-91.

Collections

Bruce's papers are in the Schomburg Center for Research in Black Culture, New York Public Library.

Irvin Weathersby, Jr.

Charles Eaton Burch
1891–1948

Literary critic, educator, poet, bibliophile

Charles Eaton Burch devoted his life to teaching seventeenth- and eighteenth-century literature and studying the literary and political activities of Daniel Defoe, English author of *Robinson Crusoe*. Burch was especially known among literary scholars as an authority on the life and works of Daniel Defoe. Although Burch received international acclaim for his scholarship on Defoe among academic circles, he received very little public recognition for his literary achievements. Burch's love for teaching and studying literature continued until his death as a result of a heart attack on March 23, 1948 in Stamford, Connecticut.

Charles Eaton Burch was born on July 14, 1891 in St. Georges, Bermuda. As a young child, living in St. Georges, Burch was greatly influenced by his father's passion for seventeenth- and eighteenth-century literature. When Burch expressed interest in pursuing a career as a professor of language and literature, his father, a woodworker and entrepreneur, played a significant role in helping him reach his goal.

After passing the Cambridge junior examinations, Burch left Bermuda, with the support of his family, to explore his educational opportunities in the United States. He attended Wilberforce University in Ohio where he received his B.A. in 1914. Burch received his M.A. in English literature from Columbia University in New York in 1918. While at Columbia University, Burch expressed interest in the poetry of Burns, Whittier, and Dunbar, and he wrote a master's thesis entitled *A Survey of the Life and Poetry of Paul Laurence Dunbar*. Dunbar was one of the first persons of African descent living in the United States to receive national recognition as a poet. However, Burch's interest in Defoe overshadowed this interest in poetry.

Chronology

1891	Born in St. Georges, Bermuda on July 14
1914	Receives B.A. from Wilberforce University, Ohio
1916	Teaches English at Tuskegee Institute, Alabama
1918	Receives M.A. in English literature from Columbia University, New York; marries his second wife, Willa Carter Maye
1921	Starts twenty-seven-year teaching career at Howard University in Washington, D.C.
1927	Travels to Scotland to research the life and works of Defoe at Edinburgh University and the National Library of Scotland
1933	Becomes chairman of the English Department at Howard University; receives Ph.D. in English literature from Ohio State University
1938	Returns to Scotland for further biographical and bibliographical research on Defoe
1948	Dies in Stamford, Connecticut of a heart attack on March 22

Columbia University professor William P. Trent introduced Burch to the works of Defoe. Burch became especially interested in Defoe's literary and political influence during the writer's Scottish period. By the time Burch received his Ph.D. from Ohio State University in 1933, his interest in Defoe was firmly established. Burch's doctoral dissertation was entitled *The English Reputation of Daniel Defoe*.

Burch's research on Defoe has been acknowledged in *Cambridge Bibliography of Eighteenth-Century Literature*, *Who's Who in American Library Scholarship*, and . His writings on Defoe have also appeared in distinguished publications in the United States, England, and Germany, such as *Philological Quarterly*, *Notes & Queries*, *London Quarterly Review*, and *Englische Studien*.

While working at Howard University, Burch went on sabbatical (1927-28) to study the life and works of Defoe at Edinburgh University in Scotland with Regius Professor of Rhetoric and Literature, Herbert Greirson. Burch returned to Scotland in 1938 to conduct further biographical and bibliographical research on Defoe in the archives at Edinburgh University and the National Library of Scotland. At the time of his death, Burch was working on two major projects: a biography on Defoe and an edition of Defoe's pamphlet on the Union.

While pursuing his M.A. degree at Columbia University, Burch taught English at Tuskegee Institute in Alabama (1916-17). After receiving his degree at Columbia, Burch taught at Wilberforce University in Ohio, Morris Brown University in Georgia, Langston University in Oklahoma, and Alabama State University in Alabama. He was a faculty member of the English Department at Howard University in Washington, D.C. for twenty-seven years. Burch was appointed as assistant professor (1921-24), as associate professor (1924-36)

and in 1933 he became the chairman of the English Department, a position he held until his death in 1948.

Burch made several contributions to the English Department at Howard during his career as educator and department head. One major contribution was his introduction of the course, "Poetry and Prose of Negro Life," one of the few courses devoted to black literature in an American university in the early 1920s. Burch not only felt that cultural awareness and appreciation were important, but he strived for academic excellence. Therefore, he constantly made efforts to strengthen the department by recruiting prominent scholars and by outlining plans for the introduction of graduate-level course work that offered a broad and intensive training in several areas of English study. Some departmental guidelines and precedents set by Burch continued to be used in the English department for thirty years after his death.

Burch died of a heart attack on March 22, 1948 in Stamford, Connecticut. His funeral service was held at the Rankin Memorial Chapel, Howard University, and his body was buried in Lincoln Memorial Cemetery in Suitland, Maryland. Burch was survived by his second wife, Dr. Willa Carter Mayer Burch, whom he married in 1918; he had no children.

The legacy of Burch continues into the early 2000s at Howard University. As a tribute to his accomplishments, the English department at Howard University established the Charles Eaton Burch Memorial Fund and the Annual Charles Eaton Burch Memorial Lectures. Burch's ambition, dedication, and loving personality set an example for aspiring scholars and educators.

REFERENCES

Books

Watkins, Charlotte Crawford. "Burch, Charles Eaton." In *Dictionary of American Negro Biography*. Ed. Rayford W. Logan and Michael R. Winston. New York: Norton, 1982.

Wesley, Dorothy Porter. "Black Antiquarians and Bibliophiles Revisited, with a Glance at Today's Lovers of Books and Memorabilia." In *Black Bibliophiles and Collectors: Preservers of Black History*. Ed. Elinor Sinnette, W. Paul Coates, and Thomas Battle. Washington, DC: Howard University Press, 1990.

Periodicals

Arvey, Verna. "Charles Eaton Burch, Who Treads an Unbeaten Path." *Opportunity* 20 (1942): 245-46.

Mitchell, Velma McLin. "Charles Eaton Burch: A Scholar and His Library." *College Language Association Journal* 16 (1973): 369-76.

Dana Hammond

Harry T. Burleigh
1866–1949

Composer, singer, music arranger

Harry (Henry) T. Burleigh was a renowned scholar of African American music and a pioneer in arranging spirituals for solo voice with accompaniment. His settings of the spirituals were sung by many of the acclaimed soloists of his day, including Marian Anderson, Paul Robeson, John McCormack, Roland Hayes, and others. The tradition, which continues into the early twenty-first century, of including a set of spirituals in a recital was probably initiated in his day, and very often the arrangements were by Burleigh.

Harry T. Burleigh was born in Erie, Pennsylvania on December 2, 1866. He was nurtured with spirituals and plantation songs as a child; his maternal grandfather, Hamilton Waters, the town crier and lamplighter in Erie, sang to young Harry the songs he learned as a former slave. Harry's love of music was also supported by his mother, Elizabeth, who worked as a domestic servant in Erie. Her employer, Elizabeth Russell, frequently gave recitals at her home, featuring prominent soloists. One of these was given by the famous pianist, Rafael Joseffy, and this recital was heard by young Harry, standing outside the window in the snow. Harry was subsequently given the role of informal doorman, welcoming guests to her recitals.

Burleigh graduated from high school in 1887 and continued to improve as a musician, singing at school, in church choirs, and at the Reform Jewish Temple. He also worked at various office jobs in Erie, helping to support the family. In 1892 he decided to compete for a scholarship offered by the National Conservatory of Music in New York City. With Elizabeth Russell's help and his mother's support, he traveled to New York to take the required examinations, gaining admission upon appeal to the registrar. At the conservatory, he pursued a standard course of music studies, including voice lessons, sight-singing, and music history. He also played string bass and timpani in the orchestra, copied musical manuscripts, and served as orchestra librarian.

Burleigh Assists Dvorak

Burleigh was soon assigned the job of assisting composer Antonin Dvorak, who came to the United States in 1892 to accept the position of director of the National Conservatory. Dvorak soon learned of Burleigh's love of spirituals and African American folksongs. As a believer in a nation's musical heritage, Dvorak became enamored of these songs. He continually requested Burleigh to sing spirituals for him and wove parts of their melodies and harmonies into his Symphony No. 9, *From the New World*, which was first performed by the New York Phil-

Harry T. Burleigh

harmonic on December 15, 1893. Dvorak, in addition, championed the cause of a national music, urging American composers to incorporate indigenous traditional music into their classical compositions.

Burleigh graduated from the conservatory in 1896 and continued to teach sight-singing there from 1895 to 1898. On several occasions Burleigh gave vocal recitals and lectured on spirituals at various locations, including black colleges and universities. According to Anne Key Simpson, in her biography *Hard Times: The Life and Trials of Harry T. Burleigh*, he frequently cited the *New World Symphony* as having spiritual elements and harmonic features, including the flatted seventh degree of the major scale, and reminiscences of specific portions of "Swing Low, Sweet Chariot" in the symphony's first movement.

Transitions to Professional Career

In 1894 Burleigh's career took a decidedly upward turn, when he auditioned and was accepted for the position of baritone soloist at St. George's Episcopal Church in lower Manhattan. He was the first African American to hold this position, and he served in it with great distinction for fifty years. In addition to the regular Sunday services, he performed as a soloist in many special concerts for the community of classical cantatas and oratorios. Among the highlights of his tenure was his annual performance, for fifty-two consecutive years, as soloist on Palm Sunday in the cantata *The Palms*, composed by Jean-Baptiste Faure.

In 1900 Burleigh accepted another appointment, as a soloist at Temple Emanu-El, serving there for twenty-five years (the first African American to hold this position). Burleigh was married in 1898 to the poet Louise Alston, who authored several song texts for him, including "Just My Love and I," among his first works, popular in his day and published by the William Maxwell Company in 1904. The Burleighs had one son, Alston, born in 1899. Burleigh became professionally interested in the works of Samuel Coleridge-Taylor, including his cantata *Hiawatha*. A group of local singers soon assembled, began rehearsing the work, and on April 23, 1903, the Samuel Coleridge-Taylor Choral Society performed the cantata at the Metropolitan AME Church in Washington, D.C.

Coleridge-Taylor was delighted with the success of the concert and accepted an invitation to come to the United States in 1904 to conduct a concert of his own music. Burleigh assisted with the arrangements. The tour began with a concert on November 16, in Convention Hall in Washington, D.C., including a performance of *Hiawatha* with Burleigh as a soloist. Additional concerts in Baltimore and Chicago followed, featuring songs and works by Coleridge-Taylor, Burleigh, and others. Coleridge-Taylor returned to the United States in 1906 for another series of concerts, again featuring Burleigh as soloist, in New York, Pittsburgh, Boston, and Norfolk, Connecticut.

Coleridge-Taylor died in September 1912, and Burleigh, along with scholar and Pan Africanist W. E. B. Du Bois, singer Roland Hayes, and musician and author Maud Cuney-Hare, participated in a memorial concert in Boston on January 13, 1913. Fisk's Mozart Society (now the University Choir) performed *Hiawatha* with Burleigh as soloist at Fisk University on May 13, 1913.

Active Career Continues

Burleigh's active career as a performer, scholar, arranger, and composer continued until his retirement from St. George's Church in November, 1946. As a performer, he gave numerous recitals at private homes, churches, and educational institutions over the ensuing years. At one musical event, in about 1900, Burleigh performed at an occasion arranged under the auspices of Governor Theodore Roosevelt and stayed overnight in the governor's mansion in Albany, New York following the recital.

In arranging recitals and similar events, Burleigh received considerable support from J. Pierpont Morgan, the financier, who was a senior warden at St. George's Church. Early in Burleigh's tenure at St. George's, Morgan personally arranged private engagements in local homes of socially prominent persons for Burleigh, as well as at his own annual Christmas Eve celebrations at the Morgan mansion, which included the St. George's choir. In addition, Morgan and U.S. ambassador Whitelaw Reid were instrumental in helping to arrange a performance for King Edward VII and the Crown Princess of Sweden in 1908 during Burleigh's visit to London that year.

Burleigh's earnings from recitals and publication royalties enabled the Burleighs to travel abroad. They visited Europe seven or eight times over the years, visiting Samuel Coleridge-Taylor and other prominent persons involved in the arts. The trips included lectures, guest recitals, and scheduled business trips to Italy. There, Burleigh visited publisher G. Ricordi's home office in Milan. Burleigh was employed by Ricordi in their New York office as a music editor, and they published many of his compositions and arrangements.

In her biography, *Hard Times*, Simpson presents a catalogue of Burleigh's musical works by category. Under "Art Songs and Religious Songs," Simpson lists more than two hundred songs with lyrics by Louise Alston, Paul Laurence Dunbar, James Weldon Johnson, Rudyard Kipling, Walt Whitman, and others. Among his frequently performed solo works were the cycles "The Saracen Songs" and "Passionale," with lyrics by Fred G. Bowles and James Weldon Johnson, respectively, and "Five Songs by Laurence Hope," with lyrics by Adela L. Cory.

Gains Recognition as Composer, Arranger, Soloist

Simpson's catalogue lists more than 150 spiritual arrangements and includes the "Old Songs Hymnal," containing more than two hundred hymns. The list of spirituals includes Burleigh's well known songs "Ride on, King Jesus," "Swing Low, Sweet Chariot," "Steal Away," and "Stand Still, Jordan" (composed in 1926 and dedicated to Roland Hayes). "Deep River," probably his most famous work, was published in 1917 and dedicated to the contralto Mary Jordan, also a soloist at Temple Emanu-El. "Deep River" later acquired the status of virtually a "signature song" for the bass soloist Paul Robeson.

One of the founding members of ASCAP (The American Society of Composers, Authors, and Publishers), Burleigh was elected to the Board of Directors in 1941, becoming the board's first black member. He was awarded the Spingarn Medal by the NAACP in 1917 for his achievements in the arts. He received an honorary Doctor of Music degree from Howard University in 1920, an honorary Master of Arts degree from Atlanta University, and the Harmon Foundation Award for distinguished achievement in 1917. Among the many outstanding performers who sang his works are Marian Anderson, Carol Brice, Roland Hayes, John McCormack, Mary Jordan, Abbie Mitchell, Paul Robeson, and Evan Williams.

On February 4, 1944, a special celebration was given at St. George's Church in honor of the fiftieth anniversary of Burleigh's tenure. He was presented a scroll and a gift of $1,500 by the parishioners. His home town of Erie, Pennsylvania was represented by the president of the Erie Club, who presented the honoree with a silver-banded cane on behalf of the club. Addresses were given by Bishop William Manning, Reverend Elmore McKee, and Burleigh in honor of the occasion. The choir performed a contrapuntal ode by Burleigh, "Ethiopia's Paean of Exultation," and Burleigh sang two spirituals: "I Don't Feel Noways Tired," and "Go Down, Moses." The attendees numbered about seven hundred, including many from Erie. Burleigh served St. George's Church a short time longer and presented his fifty-second annual performance of "The Palms" in 1946. Burleigh resigned and his resignation was accepted with deep regrets in November, 1946 by St. George's Church.

Feeling that Burleigh needed additional care, his son and daughter-in-law moved him to a convalescent home on Long Island in 1947. From there, he was moved to Stamford Hall, a private nursing home in Stamford, Connecticut. There, he was honored by his family with a surprise eighty-first birthday party. A portable organ was provided, and he sang his three favorite spirituals, "Go Down, Moses," "Were You There," and "I Know the Lord Laid His Hand on Me." Then, on March 24, 1948, the Howard University Choir, on tour, presented a full concert for Burleigh and three hundred invited guests at the nursing home, including two arrangements by Burleigh, "Were You There" and "My Lord, What a Morning."

Burleigh died of heart failure at Stamford Hall on September 12, 1949. His funeral was held at St. George's Church on September 14, attended by about two thousand persons. Rector emeritus Karl Reiland gave the eulogy, stressing Burleigh's contribution to the community and his great gifts as an artist. The music was provided by two combined choirs, featuring choral works by Burleigh, and soloists Carol Brice, Ernest McChesney, and Helen Phillips.

Burleigh was once asked by a music critic whether he preferred to be known as a singer or as a composer. According to Simpson in *Hard Trials*, he replied that he preferred to be known as an arranger of spirituals, for, "In them my race has pure gold, and they should be taken as the Negro's contribution to artistic possessions. In them we show a spiritual security as old as the ages."

In his creative output, Burleigh reflected the harmonic and melodic usages of his era, basically a romantic idiom. As a widely experienced vocalist, his ear for the voice rang true in arrangements that expertly supported and enhanced the melodic line. His idiomatic writing showed a great sensitivity for the lyrics and their soulful inflections, particularly in the spirituals that he knew so well. His harmonic pallet was varied, incisive, and imaginative. His works have worn well over time and remain fresh. They reflect his proud career, pursued on four levels: as composer, arranger, performer, and scholar.

REFERENCES

Books

Krehbiel, Henry E. *Afro-American Folksongs*. New York: G. Schirmer, 1914.

Levy, Alan. "Henry Thacker Burleigh." In *American National Biography* Vol. 3. New York: Oxford University Press, 1999.

Overmyer, Grace. *Famous American Composers*. New York: Thomas Y. Crowell, 1945.

Peress, Maurice. *Dvorak to Duke Ellington*. New York: Oxford University Press, 2004.

Simpson, Anne Key. *Hard Trials: The Life and Music of Harry T. Burleigh*. Metuchen, N.J.: The Scarecrow Press, 1990.

Southern, Eileen. *The Music of Black Americans*. New York: Norton, 1997.

Online

Wichterman, Larry. "Pennsylvania Biographies." http://www.geocities.com/Heartland/4547/Burleigh.html (Accessed 6 July 2005).

Darius Thieme

George Washington Bush
c. 1790–1863

Pioneer, farmer, entrepreneur

Chronology	
1790s	Born in Pennsylvania
1812	Fights in the War of 1812
1831	Meets and marries Isabella (or Isabell) James, on July 4
1844	Bush family leaves Missouri bound for Oregon along with four neighboring families—all white
1845	Settles Bush Prairie
1852	Helps to save his community from famine
1855	Special act allows Bush to legally own the land he claims and settles
1863	Dies in Bush Prairie, Washington Territory on April 5

As a leader of the first group of United States citizens to settle north of the Columbia River in what later became the state of Washington, George Washington Bush was an important African American pioneer. Born free, Bush resolved to free himself and his family from the pervasive racism of Missouri by moving westward to the Oregon Territory. When faced with the territory's own racist provisions, Bush used his connections with the Hudson Bay Company and later local Native Americans to operate a successful farming business amid a white community. Despite the looming threat of losing his land, Bush continued to farm and support community initiatives through his generosity. Finally deeded to him through a special resolution in 1855, his settlement, also known as Bush Prairie, was owned by descendants of the Bush family into the 1960s.

George Washington Bush was probably born in Pennsylvania in the late 1700s to Mathew Bush, a black sailor from the British West Indies and an Irish American servant. Although information about his birth and rearing is scarce and often at odds, it seems that his parents were employed by the Stevensons, a wealthy Quaker family, and that young Bush was educated in the Quaker tradition. While some accounts suggest that the family moved to Tennessee when he was still a child, little is known about his life before he served in the U.S. Army in the Battle of New Orleans during the War of 1812.

Later, Bush worked as a voyager and fur trapper, first for the French-owned Robideaux Company, which was headquartered in New Orleans, and then for the Hudson Bay Company. His tenure with the latter was particularly impressive, as Bush dominated the famed company's fur trade throughout western Canada and in the Oregon Territory. After traveling throughout the Western region and even to the Pacific Coast, he settled in Clay County, Missouri. There, he met Isabella (or Isabell) James (c. 1809-1866), a German American woman whom he married on July 4, 1831. Their first son, William Owen Bush, was born in 1832. Four more sons—Joseph Talbot, Rial Bailey, Henry Sanford, and Jackson January—were born before the family ventured west in 1844.

Bush's stock-raising, farming, and nursery businesses were very successful. Still, despite the fact that he was a wealthy man and his family being relatively well-off, Missouri's unwelcoming attitude towards free African American settlement echoed the bigoted and discriminatory attitudes so pervasive in the years preceding the Civil War. Meanwhile, reports from the first American residents to settle in the western territory of Oregon surfaced in the late 1830 and early 1840s. Their reports of fertile land were attractive to Bush and others, who were inspired to follow the westward trail to Oregon. While Bush was undoubtedly encouraged by Oregon's financial possibilities, he also viewed the migration as a way to escape Missouri's increasing prejudice.

Bush Family Heads West

In May 1844, the Bush family left Missouri bound for Oregon. The caravan included four neighboring families—the Simmons, McAllister, Kindred, and Jones—all white. While Kentucky-born Michael Simmons, a longtime friend of Bush, was the recognized leader of the group, which was later named the Simmons party, it was Bush who supplied Conestoga wagons and supplies that allowed some of the other families to make the trip. As an experienced traveler, Bush knew the frontier and proved invaluable on the long journey west, helping to lead the group across the Great Plains and Rocky Mountains.

However, when the expedition reached the Columbia River in the fall of 1844, the Bushes found that the discriminatory laws that they sought to escape preceded them. Encouraged by settlers from the United States, Oregon Territory's provisional government had enacted legislation that barred the settlement of African Americans. The other members of the Simmons party decided to forfeit their own plans to settle in Oregon's Rogue River Valley. As a result of their unwillingness to separate from the Bush family, all five families spent the winter of 1844-45 on the north bank of the Columbia River, where the men found work at Hudson Bay Company's Fort Vancouver.

Founds Bush Prairie

With the knowledge that the area was beyond the reach of the discriminatory legislation, the party settled north of the Columbia River that spring. While the official position of the Hudson Bay Company was to dissuade Americans from settling north of the Columbia River, Bush's friendship with Dr. John McLoughlin, the most powerful figure in the Pacific Northwest's small non-Indian community, eased the initial potential tensions towards their settlement. McLoughlin also helped to provide the party with employment as well as supplies at good prices on credit at Fort Vancouver.

In the summer of 1845, Simmons and his family settled at the falls of Deschutes, while the Bushes and the three other remaining families settled farther up the river from Simmons' New Market community. Just a few miles south, George Bush claimed 640 acres of fertile, open plain, soon known as Bush Prairie.

Surviving the harsh conditions of the Oregon frontier would have been virtually impossible without the aid of the Hudson Bay Company and the cooperation of the Puget Sound Indians, whom they considered trading partners and allies. Like so many other Midwest migrants, the Bush family adjusted to the region because of the help they received from the Nisqually Indians, who taught them how to take advantage of plentiful seafood offerings. The closeness the communities shared led every member of the Bush family to learn the Nisqually language and engendered the regard that prompted them to treat the Nisqually Indians when epidemics carried by newcomers invaded the region. Born at the Bush Prairie in December 1847, George and Isabella Bush's youngest son, Lewis Nisqually Bush, was the Nisqually's namesake.

Despite the unusually harsh weather they faced in the earliest years of their settlement, Bush farmed effectively, securing the family with small harvests. When the farm began to thrive, Bush joined forces with Simmons to open a grist mill in Simmons' New Market community. Even with the community's successes, Bush continued to focus on the success of his farm. Grown from the seeds he brought with him across the Oregon Trail, acres of fruit trees joined his substantial grain and vegetable crops. The family freely shared their harvest. They were renown for sharing their food, seeds, and experience with new emigrants, and the Bushes worked to save their neighbors during a famine in the winter of 1852.

Fights Racism on the Frontier

Meanwhile, the racism of Missouri that Bush had hoped to put behind him by settling across the river was not removed for long. The 1846 Treaty of Oregon resolved the U.S.-British boundary dispute by fixing the line of demarcation at the forty-ninth parallel; it placed Bush in U.S. territory and made him subject to the racist dynamics of its provisional government. In spite of the dilemma and its real threat against his property holdings, Bush continued to work his farm and support the economic interests of his community. However, when Washington Territory separated from Oregon in 1853, white legislators who were friends of the Bushes and had benefited from their generosity voted unanimously for a resolution urging Congress to pass a special act confirming George and Isabella Bush's title to Bush Prairie in 1854. Its successful passage one year later allowed them to keep the land but denied George Bush citizenship. While he lived just long enough know of the Emancipation Proclamation in January 1863, he died of a cerebral hemorrhage on April 5, 1863 without ever having the right to vote in the community to which he had given so much.

REFERENCES

Books

El Hult, Ruby. *The Saga of George W. Bush*. Seattle: University of Washington Press. 1962.

Green, Frank L. "George Washington Bush." In *American National Biography*. Vol. 4. Eds. John A. Garraty and Mark C. Carnes. New York: Oxford University Press, 1999.

Greenlee, Marcia M. "George Washington Bush." In *Dictionary of American Negro Biography*. Eds. Rayford W. Logan and Michael R. Winston. New York: Norton, 1982.

Online

Oldham, Kit. "George W. Bush (1790?-1863)." *Online Encyclopedia of Washington State History*, 2004. http://www.historylink.org/essays/output.cfm?file_id=5645 (Accessed February 2006).

Crystal A. deGregory

John E. Bush
1856–1916

Organization founder, politician, activist, entrepreneur

Throughout his life, John E. Bush applied his philosophy of hard work to all of his endeavors as an African American organization founder, politician, government official, lecturer, entrepreneur, and community activist. Best known for founding the Mosaic Templars of America, Bush created a legacy that served as an example of black economic and social development.

Bush was born a slave in Moscow, Tennessee on November 15, 1856. As was the custom during the Civil War, his owner moved young Bush, his mother, and his siblings to a more secure location to keep them from being freed by the impending arrival of federal troops. Their new home was Arkansas. Because of the harsh living conditions, his mother died, leaving him an orphan and homeless at age seven. To survive, the youngster slept under bridges and in livery stables, eked out a living doing chores, and spent time getting into trouble until

Chronology

1856	Born in Moscow, Tennessee on November 15
1876	Graduates high school with honors
1879	Marries Cora Winfrey
1880	Elected to political office
1882	Founds Mosaic Templars of America
1898	Appointed as receiver of the U.S. Land Office
1903	Organizes protests against segregation of Arkansas streetcars
1905	Helps defeat measures to institute segregated school taxes
1911	Oversees construction of headquarters of the Mosaic Templars
1912	Resigns as receiver of the U.S. Land Office
1916	Dies in Little Rock, Arkansas on December 11

a concerned resident enrolled him in public school. Eventually Bush went to work in a brickyard, where during the summers he was able to earn money that enabled him to continue his education. In contrast to rural schools, the urban Arkansas high schools offered a better education for blacks, including Latin, bookkeeping, science, and higher mathematics. In 1876, Bush graduated with honors. Following graduation, the young man taught school for a short time and then was appointed principal of Capitol Hill School in Little Rock. From 1878 to 1879, he served as principal of a public school in Hot Springs, Arkansas. He returned to Little Rock in 1879 and married Cora Winfrey, daughter of a respected and wealthy Little Rock family. They bore seven children, three of whom survived Bush.

Bush's life spanned a mercurial time in black history, including the highs of the abolition of slavery and the lows of the post-Reconstruction era. The ruling by the U.S. Supreme Court in the case of *Plessey v. Ferguson* in 1896, effectively reduced African Americans to conditions and status similar to those under slavery. In the 1880s, Bush became active in Republican politics. His intense interest in politics led him in 1883 to run for a seat as representative of the Sixth Ward of Pulaski County at the Republican State Convention. Political advances continued when he became secretary of the convention the following year and was elected to an at-large position with the Pulaski County Republican Central Committee. Subsequently, the young man worked in a variety of jobs in city and county political organizations. Because of his involvement in Republican politics and unquestionable party loyalty, Bush was appointed as postal clerk in the railway mail service. In 1898, despite unwillingness in the South to appoint blacks to federal jobs, Bush's political connections led to his being selected as receiver of the U.S. land office in Little Rock. In that job, Bush handled the receipt of public money for the office. At the time, it was the highest federal appointment held by a black man west of the Mississippi River

and compensated him with a generous salary. As with many political positions, following a change in administrations, Bush's bids for reappointment made him a target of political opposition, especially from white Republicans who wanted to eliminate blacks from the party. However, known as both honest and efficient, Bush served as receiver for sixteen years, through the presidential administrations of William McKinley, Theodore Roosevelt, and William H. Taft. When the country elected Democrat Woodrow Wilson to the presidency in 1912, Bush tendered his resignation. This freed him to devote his complete attention to the Mosaic Templars of America, the fraternal organization he founded.

Founds Mosaic Templars of America

The experience of seeing a black woman begging a white man for help in burying her husband propelled Bush to find a remedy. In 1882, he co-founded the Mosaic Templars of America with Chester W. Keatts. The group's original purpose was to provide life and burial insurance for widows of black men in Little Rock. Soon the organization spread into the rest of Arkansas and surrounding states, and by 1908 it boasted a membership of about 25,000. Using the skills he learned as a government employee, Bush began to transform and modernize the organization. Over the years, services expanded to include a building and loan association, an insurance company, a business school, a nurse training school, and a publishing company. In 1911, the organization completed construction of a national headquarters in Little Rock. The *History of the Mosaic Templars of America* notes that before this time, no other African American organization had built a facility for housing their organizations. In addition to the Templars' offices, the three-story building housed other black businesses and professional offices, which augmented funds for maintenance and construction. By the early 1920s, the membership had grown to over 100,000 with chapters in twenty-six states and several foreign countries. The Templars had a social and economic impact across the country. Bush served as national grand scribe and treasurer of the Templars until his death.

As a young man, Bush began accumulating wealth by investing in real estate. Reportedly, he amassed over 120 pieces of improved property in addition to numerous parcels of unimproved property and farmland. He published a newspaper, the *American Guide*, from 1889 to about 1900. The publication is probably the predecessor of the Templars' weekly paper, *The Mosaic Guide*. In 1908, Bush took over the accounts of a bankrupt insurance company. He established Arkansas Mutual Insurance Company, which became the largest employer of African Americans in Arkansas.

In addition to his work obligations and business interests, Bush was an active participant in race and community matters. The prestige and status of his position in politics and in the U.S. land office allowed Bush the opportunity to advocate for his race. At public gatherings, Bush urged and trained blacks to acquire farmland by taking advantage of the government's homestead laws, thus increasing the number of African American landowners. He was one of the charter members of the National Negro Business League (NNBL). Founded by educator Booker T. Washington in 1900, the league set out to improve the economic conditions of African Americans. For many years, Bush served on the national executive committee of that organization. A devoted friend of Booker T. Washington and staunch proponent of Washington's philosophy, Bush believed that the key to success for Negroes was hard work, thrift, lawfulness, property ownership, self-help, and preparation for competition. Washington often sought counsel from Bush on political matters and relied on his friend for support and effective administration of the NNBL organization. In a letter to Bush, Washington stated his pleasure and satisfaction in working with him, noting that unlike his dealings with others, he could depend on Bush in all situations.

Reacting to legislative attempts to segregate Arkansas streetcars, Bush, in 1903, led protests and supported boycotts of several streetcar lines in the state. In 1905, Arkansas proposed to segregate school-tax revenues. The aim of the plan was to provide financial support for black schools exclusively from taxes paid by African Americans. Writing an emotional appeal in an open letter to the members of the Little Rock legislature, Bush helped to defeat the scheme. Using petitions, protests, and boycotts, he opposed other efforts to restrict the civil rights of blacks. In addition to the Templars, he was a member of other fraternal groups, including the Pythian Grand Lodge and the Odd Fellows. He was a supporter of the Arkansas Baptist College, and a trustee of the First Baptist Church of Little Rock.

A compelling speaker, he was sought after to address a variety of groups in and out of Arkansas. Booker T. Washington invited him to give a commencement address at Tuskegee Institute. An address delivered by Bush at the 1909 convention of the NNBL attracted attention throughout the country and was the focus of several editorials.

Bush died in Little Rock on December 11, 1916 and was buried in Fraternal Cemetery. His activities had earned him the respect of both blacks and whites in the community. Following his death, associates praised his integrity and stewardship in dealing with the finances of the Templars over thirty-three years. Little Rock officials and businesspeople commended his intelligence, leadership, and service to the African American community. Bush's life was a testament to his personal philosophy of education, hard work, self-sufficiency, and assertiveness. He was tireless in his efforts to help fellow African Americans achieve similar respect and wealth. The

Mosaic Templars headquarters, by providing a place for economic, political and social support, was for many years a tangible symbol of black initiative, achievement, and pride.

REFERENCES
Books

Bush, A. E., and P. L. Dorman. *History of the Mosaic Templars of America: Its Founders and Officials*. Little Rock: Central Printing Company, 1924.

Garraty, John A., and Mark C. Carnes. *American National Biography*. New York: Oxford University Press, 1999.

Hamilton, G. P. *Beacon Lights of the Race*. Memphis: E. H. Clark & Brother, 1911.

Harlan, Louis R., and R. W. Smock, eds. *The Booker T. Washington Papers*. Open Book Edition. Urbana: University of Illinois Press, 1984.

Hartshorn, W. N. *An Era of Progress and Promise, 1863-1910*. Boston: Priscilla Publishing Company, 1910.

Richardson, Clement. *The National Cyclopedia of the Colored Race*. Montgomery, Ala.: National Publishing Co., 1919.

Periodicals

Skocpol, Theda, and Jennifer Lynn Oser. "Organization Despite Adversity: The Origins and Development of African American Fraternal Associations." *Social Science History* 28 (Fall 2004): 367-437.

Online

Central Arkansas Library System. "Black Arkansas Newspapers from 1869 to the Present." *Arkansas Black History Online*. http://www.cals.lib.ar.us/butlercenter/abho/bib/newspaper.html (Accessed 24 February 2006).

Hamilton, Kenneth. "Introduction". *Records of the National Negro Business League*. University Publications of America. http://www.lexisnexis.com/academic/guides/african_american/nnbl.asp (Accessed 25 February 2006).

"The History of the Mosaic Templars of America." Mosaic Templars Cultural Center. http://www.mosaictemplarscenter.com/history/ (Accessed 25 February 2006).

Hope, Holly. *For the Memorable Fight: Mosaic Templars of America Headquarters Building*. Arkansas Historical Preservation Program, 2004. http://www.arkansaspreservation.org/pdf/publications/mosaic_templars.pdf (Accessed 24 February 2006).

Cheryl Jones Hamberg

Calvin O. Butts
1949–

Religious leader, activist, college president, lecturer

For more than thirty years, Calvin O. Butts, one of America's leading religious leaders and social activists, has devoted his life to service in pastoral leadership and community activism. Butts, an African American and native New Yorker, has made contributions to the Harlem, New York community that have benefited the citizens, but not without assistance and associations that transcend racial, religious, and political boundaries. His personal, professional, and community life show his lifelong commitment to public service.

Calvin O. Butts was born in 1949 in Bridgeport, Connecticut. His father was a cook at a Black Angus steakhouse and his mother was an administrator in a city welfare office. His family moved to Queens when he was eight years old, and he was bussed to school in Forest Hills in the midst of anti-busing demonstrations and widespread protests against integration. Flushing High School was mostly white, but Butts was elected president of his senior class. After high school in 1967, Butts attended Morehouse College and earned his B.A. in philosophy in 1972. As a militant and civil rights activist, Butts participated in many activities in support of rights for African Americans. A defining point occurred when fellow students from Union Theological Seminary in New York recruited Butts in 1972.

During his first year of seminary, Butts was invited to be an assistant to Samuel Proctor, the new senior pastor of Abyssinian Baptist Church in Harlem, who had replaced the deceased Adam Clayton Powell Jr. Butts earned his master of divinity degree in church history in 1975 then continued his education at Drew University where he earned his doctor of ministry degree in church and public policy in 1982. Butts taught urban affairs and served as an adjunct instructor in the African Studies Department at City College in New York. He also taught black church history at Fordham University.

In 1976 Butts became assistant pastor of Abyssinian Baptist Church under the leadership of Samuel Proctor who had become senior pastor in 1972 following the death of Adam Clayton Powell Jr. At the time, the church's finances were in disarray and the membership was waning, but Proctor rebuilt the congregation and instituted new programs and services. When Butts became senior pastor in 1987, he had the burden of living up to the accomplishments of significant others who had carried a progressive torch for Abyssinian and the community. For example, Adam Clayton Powell Sr., who took over the church in 1908, believed in pride, self-reliance, discipline, and black unity and led the congregation accordingly, combining theology with politics. He

Calvin O. Butts

built the still-standing edifice on property purchased by his parishioners in 1920 on 138th Street, the heart of the Harlem Renaissance. His successor, Adam Jr., took over the church in 1937.

Living up to the outspoken, charismatic, make-things-happen attitude set by predecessors is nearly effortless for Calvin Butts, who in his own right is a controversial, outspoken preacher-politician who addresses critical public issues and faces significant criticism. The difference between Butts and his predecessors, however, is his decision to forego public office. While Butts said he has wanted to be mayor of New York City since he was a third grader, he decided to aim his energies outside the political spectrum and deliver messages to the masses from the pulpit and lecturer podiums. His loyalty to his own race has been challenged because of his racial and political alliances in spite of significant, positive changes for citizens in Harlem, New York. Butts cites himself as an example of the new black preacher-politician, one who is taking the next steps to the work started by Martin Luther King Jr.

In 1999, Butts became president of State of New York (SUNY) College at Old Westbury. Butts has served as keynote speaker at colleges, universities, and professional and governmental organizations and associations around the world. He promotes education, which he connects to economic empowerment. Butts is the recipient of several honorary degrees and recognition awards, including

Chronology

1949	Born in Bridgeport, Connecticut on July 19
1967	Graduates from Flushing High School
1972	Earns B.A. degree in Philosophy from Morehouse College, Atlanta, Georgia
1975	Earns M.Div. in church history from Union Theological Seminary in New York
1982	Earns D.Min. in church and public policy
1987	Becomes senior pastor of Abyssinian Baptist Church
1989	Forms Abyssinian Development Corporation to improve Harlem citizens' quality of life
1999	Becomes president of SUNY College at Old Westbury
2001	Serves on the September 11th Fund Board of Directors
2004	Writes *The Harlem Cookbook: Recipes and Reflections from the Abyssinian Baptist Church*; writes *My Testimony: Stories of Faith and Good Fortune from Members of the Abyssinian Baptist Church*

"Man of the Year" from his undergraduate alma mater. He also serves on boards of directors of several civic, cleric, and business organizations. Butts was also the president of the Council of Churches in the United States.

When Butts first became pastor of Abyssinian in 1987, he was newly married and lived near the church with his family. He and his three little children often interacted with neighborhood youth, and he became familiar with residents and aspects of the torn-down neighborhood. In that setting, Buts worked as an administrator, reformer, organizer, and developer. In 1989, he formed the non-profit Abyssinian Development Corporation (ADC) to improve the lives of central Harlem citizens. He forged strong friendships and alliances with government officials and executive officers of large corporations, which helped him transform Harlem.

The ADC began with a $50,000 grant and a group of Abyssinian parishioners with its headquarters in the basement of the church. Acquiring assets totaling more than $300 million, ADC built housing in Harlem for the homeless, senior, and low-to-moderate income citizens. The non-profit, community-based organization also purchased land with the help of local government loans and developed a 53,000-square-foot Pathmark supermarket in central Harlem. Several New York politicians strongly objected to the supermarket deal because ADC does not own the supermarket and did not realize much profit from the grocery chain owners. ADC was also instrumental in starting a middle and high school in 1993. After eleven locations, the academy held its ribbon cutting ceremony in 2004 to celebrate its brand new, permanent space. The Thurgood Marshall Academy for Learning and Social Change was the first new high school built in Harlem in fifty years. Immediately after the ceremony plans began shaping up for a new lower academy.

To help promote community health awareness, ADC participated in a health expo in 1999 entitled "Break the Silence". During the expo, Butts opted to undergo multiple screenings for chronic diseases, ranging from high blood pressure to HIV/AIDS. In its continued efforts to transform Harlem, ADC led protest marches through Harlem in October 2003. In December 2004, Butts and the GreenPoint Foundation made an in-kind donation of fourteen wheelchairs to North General Hospital, a voluntary community hospital located in central Harlem. When the marches resumed in March 2005, men and women of Abyssinian marched with Butts through the streets of Harlem with the assertion to "Respect Our Women, Protect Our Children." The goal was to whitewash billboards to rid the community of negative advertising. In the first decade of the twenty-first century, ADC is nationally renowned and has one hundred employees. The nonprofit community organization commands an operating budget of over $57 million. While Butts and ADC made significant strides in revitalizing central Harlem, Butts has all along prompted controversy and criticism among African Americans regarding his stand in New York politics. Over the years many viewed him as moving from liberal Democrat toward networking among more conservative Republicans.

Back in 1992, Butts was criticized for supporting Republican candidate Rudy Giuliani in his successful bid for mayor of New York. During the U.S. crisis on September 11, 2001, Mayor Giuliani called upon Butts to support the rescue efforts. Butts later served on the board of directors of the September 11 Fund. In 2004, Butts was among the leaders who were congratulated in the September 11 final report for proficiency in fundraising and distribution of funds to the victims' families. Butts served as a member of Republican Governor Pataki's transition team as well.

Butts serves on the boards of directors of major corporations and organizations in New York, such as the Empire State Development Corporation, Central Park Conservancy, and the United Way. He has engaged in partnership with a mega developer on a commercial project. He has served as president of the Council of Churches in New York, a white-dominated body. His social circle includes the president of American Express, president of United Way, president of Time Warner, and the vice chairman of the Travelers Group. Butts sees in these relationships economic assistance for the black community, support he can access personally, one-on-one. In spite of charges that Butts has sold out to whites and Republicans, he stands by his influential style and ability to form alliances, which he believes garners support for his mission. Butts acknowledges the political shift in his thinking, but he sees it as positive and congruent with his work.

Butts is the author of *The Harlem Cookbook: Recipes and Reflections from the Abyssinian Baptist Church* and

My Testimony: Stories of Faith and Good Fortune from Members of the Abyssinian Baptist Church, both of which were sold at auction in 2004. In October 2005, the church published *Food for the Soul: Recipes and Stories from the Congregation of Harlem's Abyssinian Baptist Church*.

REFERENCES

Periodicals

Boyd, Herb. "Harlem's First New High School in 50 Years." *The Black World Today*, 2 February 2004.

Browne, J. Zamgba. "Jamaica Business Resource Center Spreads It Around." *New York Amsterdam News* 95 (16 December 2004): 9.

Friedlander, Blaine P., Jr. "Butts Outlines American Dream at Development Conference." *Cornell Chronicle*, 24 July 2003.

Moorer, Talise D. "Harlem Pastor's Wheel Deal Meets Needs at North General." *New York Amsterdam News* 95 (16 December 2004): 40.

Shelhea C. Owens

John Caesar
c. 1750–1837

Military leader, interpreter

John Caesar's military service documents the importance of freedom over oppression and how the merging of two peoples (African American and Native American) into political allies led to victories over mutual enemies. In this case, Caesar, an African Seminole, was able to lead a joint force of Native Seminoles, escaped slaves, and African Seminoles on successful raids of Florida plantations that freed slaves and gave their warriors necessary supplies in the Second Seminole War.

Written documentation about the early life of John Caesar is meager and scattered. What is known is that he was born in the mid-eighteenth century, and he became allied with the Seminole nation in Florida. In Florida during the Seminole Wars, he became known for his military leadership.

This black Seminole was probably a descendant of free African Americans or fugitive slaves. Caesar was a member of the Seminole nation. He served as an interpreter between Native Seminoles and the U.S. military; this fact indicates that during his early years he must have had some association with English-speaking people.

The African and Seminole Cultural Relationship

The African Seminoles' relationship with the Native Seminoles was unique culturally, socially and politically. During this period in U.S. history, the Spanish colonists were in competition with the English colonists over the Florida territory, so Spaniards encouraged slaves to escape from the English colony's plantations.

Slavery existed among the Native Seminoles, but much freedom was granted to the escaped slaves and free African Americans who joined the Seminoles. In some cases, the African American Seminoles were adopted into Seminole clans, enslaved for a period of time, made to adapt culturally to a new lifestyle, and then made a part of the clan. Still other African Seminoles lived in independent communities, elected their own black leaders, and could amass moderate wealth in cattle and crops. They were also permitted to bear arms to defend themselves. Intermarriage was widespread. Children born from these marriages were free citizens of the nation. Cultural exchange of the natives, slaves, and free African Americans occurred regularly.

Caesar and most of the African Seminoles adopted the language and many of the cultural traditions of their Native Seminole counterparts, and African Seminoles brought their own African cultural traditions as well, which had a significant influence on the development of Seminole culture. Because African Seminoles were faced with the threat of enslavement on southern plantations, many served on the side of the Seminole against the United States in order to prevent defeat of the Seminole nation. Many Native Seminoles were connected to African Seminoles through intermarriage and were unwilling to abandon their African Seminole families and friends to slave traders and plantation owners.

Caesar served as the head adviser and interpreter to a Seminole chief, King Philip, father of Wild Cat and leader of the St. John's River Seminoles. Caesar worked with other African Seminoles, such as John Horse and Abraham. Abraham served as the chief associate adviser and interpreter to Seminole chief Micanopy. Caesar and Abraham worked to increase discontent among plantation slaves in Florida and to develop relationships with free blacks and slaves who would assist in the war effort. Caesar was successful in convincing numerous African slaves to join the Seminoles in their struggle for freedom.

Chronology	
mid-1700s	Born (actual date unknown)
1817	Leads raids during First Seminole War
1835	Leads raids during Second Seminole War
1836	Organizes runaway slaves and Native Seminoles into raiding parties that attack plantations outside St. Augustine
1837	Killed in his attempt to raid the Hanson plantation on January 17

Seminole Wars

During the First Seminole War between the colonizers and the Seminoles that began in 1817, Caesar led raids on plantations and convinced runaway slaves and free African Americans to join the fight. Known as an outstanding military strategist, he realized that establishing relationships was the key to winning military battles. He connected with key military leaders such as the Seminole leader King Philip (Emathia), and they were able together to engage in conflict with the soldiers of the U.S. government during both the First and Second Seminole War. By the second war he was a brilliant war veteran.

Sometime in December 1835, at the beginning of the Second Seminole War, Caesar and King Philip led attacks that destroyed sugar plantations east of the St. John's River outside St. Augustine. Within two days five plantations were destroyed, and many field slaves joined in the rebellion. The targeted plantations included Rosetta, Mount Oswald, and Dunlawton. The Seminole allies wrecked mills, burned homes, confiscated livestock and corn, and at each attack, more slaves were recruited. By January, almost three hundred slaves from the St. John's region were supporting the rebellion. Months of planning by Caesar was paying off, and a mass rebellion was in the making. This alliance of African Seminoles, Native Seminoles, and escaped slaves cost the U.S. military dearly.

By late 1836, the war took on a new and disturbing dimension, under the leadership of U.S. General Clinch. Caesar continued to organize and inspire runaway slaves, effectively attacking plantations just outside St. Augustine. On January 17, 1837, Caesar and his men were attempting to steal horses from the Hanson plantation and were discovered and attacked by Hanson's men, who killed three warriors, including Caesar.

Caesar's leadership in recruiting slaves from the plantations forced the U.S. military to negotiate over the issue of African Seminoles, and this action resulted in the removal of African Seminoles along with Native Seminoles, rather than their immediate re-enslavement on southeastern plantations.

REFERENCES

Books

"John Caesar." In *African American Lives*. Eds. Henry Louis Gates Jr. and Evelyn Books Higginbotham. New York: Oxford University Press, 2004.

Online

"Rebellion." http://www.johnhorse.com/black-seminoles/relev.htm (Accessed 27 March 2006).

Mattie McHollin

André Cailloux
1825–1863

Military leader, artisan

Captain André Cailloux was the first black hero of the Civil War. Gunned down on the battlefield while leading an ill-fated charge against a Confederate Army stronghold, Cailloux's body was found forty-one days later among other black dead on a Port Hudson, Mississippi battleground. Historian Steven J. Ochs, in *A Black Patriot and a White Priest*, said of Cailloux: "For black people, he became a symbol of valor, of rocklike determination, a symbol of black manhood. He had given the lie to the notion that blacks could not fight bravely."

André Cailloux was born into slavery on August 25, 1825 on a plantation owned by Joseph Duvernay, in Plaquemines Parish. Cailloux's mother, Josephine, who had been sold four times since 1813, was purchased by Duvernay while she was pregnant with André. Josephine had already given birth to two sons by Duvernay: Moliére and Antoine who were also purchased by Joseph Duvernay. The third child that Josephine was carrying was fathered by a slave named André Cailloux, who was born to a twenty-year-old slave named Francisca on November 30, 1793. The elder André Cailloux was inherited by Aimée Duvernay Bailey and her husband, William Bailey, from Aimée's family. André's carpentry and masonry skills made him quite valuable to the Baileys. Aimée sold the elder André to her brother Joseph after her husband's death on March 12, 1827. In December of the same year, elder and younger André and Josephine all became the property of Aimée Bailey.

At age two, in July 1827, Cailloux was baptized at St. Louis Cathedral. In 1828, Joseph freed André's half brothers: six year old Antoine and eight year old Moliére. They became the wards of their aunt Aimée and were united with their half brother André and his family. Aimée Bailey sold Josephine on June 20, 1830. In the same year, Aimée moved to New Orleans, taking her two wards, Moliére and Antoine, and her slaves. For unknown reasons, the elder André left Aimée Bailey's household between the years 1834 and 1846.

Aimée married Mathieu Lartet, a French immigrant. Months after they were married, the couple asked their neighbor J. B. Glaudin, a free man of color, to train fifteen-year-old Moliére, thirteen year old Antoine, and one of their slaves, nine-year-old John in cigar making. The three children taught André the trade as they learned it themselves. André may have also later been trained by Glaudin. In 1845, the Lartets petitioned to free both twenty-one-year-old André and John. They were freed in 1846.

Cailloux soon married Felicie Coulon, who was born in 1818. Her mother, Feliciana, was a slave-concubine of sugar planter, Valetin Encalada. Felicie's father was

Chronology	
1825	Born in Plaquemines Parish, Louisiana on August 25
1827	Baptized at age two
1846	Freed at age twenty-one
1847	Marries Felicie Coulon on June 22
1849	Purchases his mother on January 22
1860	Elected secretary of the Society of the Friends of Order and Mutual Assistants in October; organizes a Confederate regiment of free blacks
1862	Organizes a Union regiment of free blacks in July
1863	Dies in Port Hudson, Mississippi on May 27

Antoine Coulon, who was most likely a slave. Encalada, nearing the end of his life, freed Feliciana and Bastien, Felicie's older half-brother, and gave them financial support. Feliciana saved her money that she made as a domestic servant and purchased her daughter and Jean Louis, the infant grandson that Felicie gave birth to in 1839, from Encalada.

In December of the same year that Cailloux became free, Feliciana emancipated Felicie and seven-year-old Jean Louis, whom Cailloux legally adopted in 1847. At this time, Felicie was pregnant with Cailloux's baby. The baby boy, Eugene, was born in early June 1847. Three weeks later on June 22, 1847, Cailloux and Felicie wed at St. Mary's Assumption in Lafayette Parish, Louisiana. The couple had three more children: Althalie Clemence, born August, 20, 1850; Hortense, born January 28, 1854, and died later in the same year; and Odile, born May 6, 1857.

On January 22, 1849, Cailloux purchased his mother, then forty-five-year-old Josephine, for $100 Cailloux owned other slaves, but he purchased his mother with the intention of emancipating her as soon as possible. No record of her emancipation exists; it is possible that Josephine died before her son could free her. As one of 156 Afro-Creole cigar makers in New Orleans, Cailloux had security in an occupation that was not accessible to free people of color in the rest of the United States. This security, however, was uncertain for the Caillouxs and most other free blacks. Times became tough for the Caillouxs in the 1850 as André had to compete with large cigar factories and as the 1850s led to the Civil War, the environment in New Orleans for free people of color became hostile. In the face of such hostility, Cailloux was proud of his heritage, describing himself as the blackest man in New Orleans.

In October 1860, Cailloux was elected secretary of the Society of the Friends of Order and Mutual Assistants. This order was one of many aid societies of the Afro-Creole population of the mid-1800s. In the same year, Cailloux helped to organize a Confederate regiment of free blacks. Cailloux served as its first lieu-

tenant. The black soldiers did not participate in battle but were assigned to training and ceremonial duties. The militia disbanded on the evening of the Union takeover and occupation in 1862.

Fights for Equality, Respect, and Freedom

In July 1862, Cailloux helped to organize a Union regiment from people in his community and he became its captain. The regiment, comprised mostly of free men of color as well as some runaway slaves, faced hostile treatment from both the government and the white members of the Union army. White soldiers were openly disrespectful to black officers. Black officers and soldiers were scapegoats for many of the real and perceived flaws in the Union army.

Despite these conditions, Cailloux was admired by both Union and Confederate sympathizers for his polished professional manner, attractive looks, and bilingualism: he, like many of the free people of color, spoke both English and French. But this admiration would slight when compared to the adulation he received posthumously.

Port Hudson and Vicksburg were the two remaining Confederate strongholds. On May 27, 1863, Cailloux led a charge on the battlefield towards the Confederate army. Two hundred yards from the Confederate lines, gunfire was exchanged. Cailloux was shot in the arm. He kept on charging. The second shot to the head instantly killed him.

Cailloux's body was retrieved from the battleground forty-one days after his death. Cailloux's bloated, disfigured corpse was identified solely by his ring from the Friends of Order. On the day of his funeral, July 29, 1863, downtown streets were crowded with thousands of people, mostly black, waving flags. Claude Maistre, a Catholic priest and abolitionist, delivered an eloquent eulogy, calling Cailloux a martyr for the cause of freedom. The New Orleans black newspaper run by Afro-Creole radicals, *L'Union*, praised Cailloux for his patriotism and sacrifice. Cailloux's courage and sacrifice contradicted the myth that black men were not capable of fighting in battle. Helen Johnson, Cailloux's great-great-granddaughter, praised her ancestor to the Associated Press: "My mother was proud of him, proud of the Cailloux name. She would beam when she would say her great-grandfather was a Civil War hero. I often think how happy she would be to know that others have remembered André Cailloux and the contributions he made."

REFERENCES

Books

Ochs, Stephen J. *A Black Patriot and a White Priest.* Baton Rouge: Louisiana State University Press, 2000.

Periodicals

Mullener, Elizabeth. "Freed Slave Fought for Union after New Orleans Fell during Civil War." *Associated Press State and Local Wire*, 15 November 1998.

Ochs, Stephen J. "Black Officer Gains Almost Mythic Status in Death." *Washington Times*, 13 May 2000.

Online

"Andre Cailloux." frenchcreoles.com. http://www. frenchcreoles.com/CreoleCulture/famouscreoles/andr ecailloux/andrecailloux.htm (Accessed 25 December 2005).

Ochs, Stephen J. "'American Spartacus': Captain André Cailloux of the 1st Louisiana Native Guards." Georgetown Preparatory School. http://www.gprep. org/fac/sjochs/Times%20article-2.htm (Accessed 25 December 2005).

Brandy Baker

Thomas M. Campbell
1883–1956

Agricultural extension agent, educator

From its beginning until the 1960s the Alabama Extension Service was racially segregated. When Thomas M. Campbell was hired in 1906, he became the first African American extension agent in the nation. He became supervising agent in 1910 and held the post until he retired in 1953. Using a "Movable School," Campbell and his agents, who worked out of Tuskegee Institute in Alabama, conducted classes for isolated farm families who were unable to attend the courses on campus. His work revolutionized black farming in the South. He also led the farmers to improve and enhance their homes and to provide better health care for their families. He addressed the needs of the woman in the home and on the farm and stressed education for children.

Thomas Monroe Campbell was born on February 11, 1883, in Elbert County, Georgia, near the small town of Bowman, about twenty-five miles from the South Carolina state line. He was the grandson of slaves and the son of William Campbell, an itinerant Methodist minister and tenant farmer. His mother, whose name is not given in known sources, died in childbirth when he was five years old. She had a long and fatal illness, exacerbated by her hard work as washerwoman and farmhand in the family's struggle to pay for their home where the parents and six children lived. They also had barely enough food.

Chronology

1883	Born in Elbert County, Georgia on February 11
1906	Graduates from Tuskegee Institute in Alabama
1906	Operates the first Jessup Wagon or Movable School of Agriculture; becomes country's first black agricultural demonstration agent
1909	Becomes district agent for agricultural extension
1918	Becomes field agent for seven southern states
1944	Studies agriculture and rural education in West Africa
1945	Publishes *The Movable School Goes to the Negro*
1956	Dies in Montgomery, Alabama on February 9

Before the Campbells lost their home due to an unpaid mortgage, they lived next to a public school where young Thomas attended briefly. William Campbell neglected his family while working as an itinerant preacher but gave way to community criticism and later hired an aunt to care for the children. The arrangement failed; William Campbell remarried and brought home his second wife and her three children. He married again and his third wife, a school teacher with some training from Spelman Seminary (later Spelman College) in Atlanta, was unsuccessful in encouraging the father to send his son Thomas to school.

Leaving Home for an Education

At the age of fifteen, Thomas Campbell left home on January 2, 1899, without his family's knowledge and headed for Tuskegee. He had ten cents in his pocket, collected twenty-five cents from Aunt Cynthia Berryman—supposedly a relative—and was on his way. En route, Campbell worked here and there and arrived on campus around April 29, 1899. He was enrolled as unclassified and took the lowest courses offered in the agriculture program. To help support himself, Campbell was assigned to the livestock division where he worked at several tasks. His brother, who had been a student at Tuskegee and helped to guide him during his early days at school, died when an epidemic of typhoid and malaria broke out at the school. Campbell caught the fever as well but recovered.

Although he worked hard to support himself, Campbell scarcely had the bare minimum of clothing. His feet were large and he had difficulty wearing the clothes offered to him by his friends; he was too proud to do so anyway. Often he refused to accept invitations to dinner in the homes of the families whom he had served as carriage driver because his clothes were unsuitable. During the seven years that Campbell was a student at Tuskegee, he received from home only two dollars in cash and one suit of clothes. But he did participate in the institute's choir, continued to work in the agricultural department, and caught the eye of the school's president Booker T. Washington, who made regular visits around the school farm each morning.

Farming as an Academic Subject

Washington knew that his students and faculty had little respect for farming as an academic program; consequently, Washington held Sunday evening talks in which he introduced the students in the department and also emphasized the importance of developing rural life for blacks in the South. Campbell also served as driver of Washington's buggy and took care of the horses that were assigned to the president. This experience put him in touch with many of the distinguished visitors who came to the campus. They included black and white people of some acclaim who came to discuss race problems.

As he approached his last two years at Tuskegee, Campbell began to set some career goals; he resolved to work in some phase of agriculture. He graduated in 1906 and had just begun advanced study when Booker T. Washington recommended him for the federal post of Negro Extension Agent. In the summer of 1910, he enrolled in the graduate agricultural program at Iowa State College, where Tuskegee scientist George Washington Carver had also studied.

The Movable School of Agriculture

Washington was so concerned with the plight of black farmers and the need to raise practical farming to a higher level that he brought Carver to the campus for that purpose. On Saturdays and Sundays, both Washington and Carver had taken demonstration exhibits to rural black communities. In 1896 Washington induced the Alabama State Legislature to pass a law creating the Tuskegee Agricultural Experiment Station which Carver directed; he traveled the county on weekends to assist farmers. Throughout his administration, Washington continued to visit black families in their homes. Tuskegee held its first annual Negro Farmers Conference in February 1892; five hundred people attended. Out of that grew agricultural extension work for blacks. Washington realized a need to reach the black masses, including those who did not attend the conferences and those in adjacent counties. He conceived the idea of itinerant demonstrations which he called the "Movable School of Agriculture."

Carver headed a committee to plan for a demonstration wagon and to determine what equipment it should carry to farmers' doors. Then he solicited philanthropist Morris K. Jesup of New York, who donated funds for the wagon. The Jesup Agricultural Wagon, as it was officially named, was equipped and put in operation on May 24, 1906, under the guidance of the agricultural faculty. The wagon was also referred to as "a farmers' college on wheels." The federal government accepted the wagon, and it became the vehicle for the demonstration agent to use in reaching black farmers. Washington was committed to addressing the needs of women who worked in fields and in homes; thus, the operator of the wagon was instructed to meet these needs. The equipment of the wagon varied according to the season; for example, in spring there was a portable garden with growing vegetables; instructions were given on how to plant the garden, how to fertilize it, and demonstrations given on how to plow the field.

Demonstration Agent

From 1902 to 1910, Seaman Asahel Knapp headed the General Education Board (GEB) of the U.S. Department of Agriculture and originated the idea of farmers' cooperative demonstration work in the South. Washington and Knapp drew up "A Memorandum of Agreement between Tuskegee Institute and the General Education Board," dated November 9, 1906 and published in the *Booker T. Washington Papers* for 1906 to 1908. The GEB would pay the salary of the agent who would serve the program, Thomas M. Campbell, and he would be paid $840 per year. Both Washington and Carver recommended Campbell for the job. He was hired on November 12, becoming the country's first black demonstration agent. Since he worked through the U.S. Department of Agriculture, he was a federal employee assigned to Tuskegee. White agents worked out of the administrative headquarters at Alabama Polytechnic Institute at Auburn (subsequently Auburn University), while the black agents were headquartered at Tuskegee. They were also responsible to the state's administrative headquarters. Although Campbell began his work in Macon County, the location of Tuskegee, he took the Movable Agricultural School throughout the state. In 1909 he was promoted to district agent and supervised and instructed other agents. Agents who followed him operated the Movable School until World War II. Use of such a school also spread to Europe, East Asia, India, and Africa. The practice of carrying education to rural people appealed to leaders in other countries, and sometimes visitors from these countries came to Tuskegee to see the Movable Agricultural School firsthand and to discuss the work of the extension program.

Field Agent

In 1918, Campbell was promoted to field agent, in which role he had responsibility for seven lower southern states. He met with state directors of extension who kept watch over extension service to black farmers and their families in Alabama, Florida, Louisiana, Mississippi, Oklahoma, and Texas. By then the black land-grant colleges in the seven southern states trained students to work as extension agents. Campbell met with the presidents of these colleges and advised them as appropriate. He aided farm and civic organizations by providing advice and giving practical help to black farmers. Continuing the focus of the farmers' conferences held earlier, he gave guidance on the improvement of life in the communities. As the work progressed, he led country agents into then-modern conveniences, such as electricity, improved water systems, and sanitary toilet facilities in the rural areas. They learned to use modern farm techniques as well as the importance of rotating crops, feeding and care of animals, poultry-raising, gardening, and growing fruits.

In 1944 the General Education Board appointed Campbell to a three-member commission to study agriculture and rural education among peoples in West Africa. Over a six-month period, he visited Liberia, Sierra Leone, Ghana, Nigeria, and Cameroon, examining farmers' methods of preparing soil, planting, and cultivating crops. He studied the work of experiment stations there and sampled local diets to learn about local health and nutrition practices. The results of the study were published in *Africa Advancing* (Friends Press, 1945).

Publications

Campbell described his extension work in several articles that were published in leading agricultural journals. He also published *The Movable School Goes to the Negro Farmer* (Tuskegee Institute Press, 1936). He had begun a history of extension work in the South, sponsored by the Ford Foundation, but died before the work was completed. Although Campbell had an interest in the black folk tradition and began to collect information from former slaves whom he met in his work, that work was also left incomplete. According to Joellyn Pryce El-Bashir, singer Roland Hayes credits Campbell for collecting the words and music for the spiritual, "He Never Said a Mumblin' Word." Hayes sang the spiritual in a 1923 concert.

Recognition and Awards

Beyond the field of agriculture, Campbell's interests included the Eugene Field Society of the National Association of Authors and Journalists, of which he was a member. His outstanding agricultural work brought many recognitions; among these, the Harmon Award for outstanding service in farming and rural life (1930); honorary M.S. degree, Tuskegee Institute (1936); and Length of Service and Superior Service Awards, USDA. On January 13, 1952, Tuskegee dedicated a marker commemorating his work and the beginning of extension activities among rural blacks.

On June 11, 1911, Campbell married Tuskegee graduate Annie M. Ayers of Virginia. They had four children: Thomas Jr., Carver, Virginia, and William. Campbell attended a meeting in Montgomery, Alabama, in 1956 and was found dead in his hotel room, on February 9, apparently of natural causes.

Although greatly influenced by Booker T. Washington and George Washington Carver, Campbell went beyond their teaching to expand the scope of the U.S. Department of Agriculture in agricultural extension service for black farmers. His work made Tuskegee the center of agricultural extension form for blacks in the Deep South.

REFERENCES

Books

El-Bashir, Joellyn Pryce. "Thomas Monroe Campbell." In *Dictionary of American Negro Biography*, edited by Rayford W. Logan and Michael R. Winston. New York: Norton, 1982, 88-89.

Harlan, Louis R., and Raymond W. Smock, eds. *The Booker T. Washington Papers*. Vol. 9. Urbana: University of Illinois Press, 1980.

Richardson, Clement. *The National Cyclopedia of the Colored Race*. Vol. 1. Montgomery: National Publishing Co., 1919.

Collections

The Thomas Monroe Campbell Papers are in the archives at Tuskegee University in Alabama.

Jessie Carney Smith

Archibald J. Carey, Jr.
1908–1981

Activist, orator, speechwriter, politician, judge

Archibald James Carey Jr. enjoyed an illustrious and influential career that spanned many spheres of public life. Following in the footsteps of his father, Archibald James Carey Sr., he began his public service in the African Methodist Episcopal Church (AME), where he became a prominent African American leader and advocate for social justice in Chicago. A talented speaker and speechwriter, Carey Jr. made both legal and political contributions. He served in political positions at the state, national, and international levels, including becoming the first African American to chair a White House committee. Continuing the family legacy, Carey Jr. used his influence, from the pulpit to the bench, to advocate for civil rights.

Archibald James Carey Jr. was born in Chicago to Archibald J. Carey Sr. and Elizabeth Hill Davis Carey. Archibald Jr. was the youngest of five children; his siblings were Eloise, Annabell, Madison, and Dorothy. The Carey family had a rich tradition of public service both religiously and politically. His father, grandfather, and great grandfather were prominent figures in the AME Church and his mother's side of the family also boasted influential figures in American politics. Carey Jr. demon-

Chronology

1908	Born in Chicago, Illinois on February 29
1924	Wins National Oratorical Contest
1927	Receives license to preach
1928	Graduates from Lewis Institute, Chicago with a B.S.
1930	Appointed to Woodlawn AME Church in Chicago
1931	Becomes an elder in Chicago, Illinois
1932	Graduates from Northwestern University, with a B.D.
1935	Graduates from Kent College of Law, Chicago, with an LL.B.
1947	Elected to the Third Ward alderman seat on Chicago's city council
1949	Appointed to Quinn Chapel AME Church in Chicago
1953	Selected as the delegate to the General Assembly of the United Nations
1954	Receives a Citizen's Award from the University of Chicago and the Abraham Schwartz Award for Human Relations; included on *Ebony*'s list of the nation's ten best black preachers
1957	Delivers speech at second anniversary of the Montgomery bus boycott; appointed chair of the president's committee on government employment policy
1966	Becomes a judge of the Circuit Court of Cook County, Illinois
1981	Dies in Chicago, Illinois on April 20

Archibald J. Carey, Jr.

strated his intellectual promise at a young age. In 1924 at age sixteen, Carey Jr. won first prize in the National Oratorical Contest, beating out eighteen thousand other competitors. Fittingly, the subject of the contest was the American Constitution, and Carey's success was celebrated in the *Chicago Daily News*. The win foretold the impact Carey would have in his professional life.

Religious Career Flourishes

Carey Jr. attended Wendell Phillips High School and then attended the Lewis Institute in Chicago, where he completed his bachelor of science degree in 1928. He continued his education at Northwestern University, where he received his bachelor of divinity degree in 1932. He went on to Kent College of Law, Chicago, where he completed his law degree in 1935. While still in college, Carey Jr. officially began his religious career. He was licensed to preach in 1927 at Institutional Church, Chicago. His father performed the ceremony, as he was to do again in 1929 when Carey Jr. was ordained as a deacon. Carey Jr. became an elder of the AME Church in 1931; Bishop Henry B. Parks presided over the service. In addition to the church services that promoted his professional career, Carey also participated in a service of a more personal nature: he married Hazel Harper, with whom he had a daughter, Carolyn Eloise Carey.

In 1930, Carey was appointed pastor for the Woodlawn AME Church in Chicago, a position he held until 1949. Woodlawn AME Church experienced great growth during Carey's tenure, particularly during the depression of the 1930s. Beginning with a congregation of approximately fifty members, the church expanded to a membership of well over seventeen hundred. Carey drew people to the church by giving powerful sermons. Moreover, he was a staunch advocate for social justice and one of Chicago's most militant black preachers. Leading his congregation in support of civil rights, Carey participated in and supported political protests that sought to address the inequalities plaguing Chicago's black community. Carey frequently spoke at rallies; he lobbied for better facilities on behalf of the Lilydale community against the school board; he fought for fair housing policies and often spoke at events conducted by other community leaders.

Always advancing his career and influence, Carey Jr. was selected as an alternate delegate to the General Conference in 1940 and as the official delegate in 1944. Carey was also recognized for his scholarship. He published a number of articles in religious periodicals such as the *Christian Recorder* and the *Negro Journal of Religion*. In 1949, Carey was appointed to Quinn Chapel AME Church, where his father had been the minister at the turn of the century.

Fights for Justice and Equality

Despite the success he enjoyed as a religious leader, Carey Jr. continued to pursue a career in the legal profession. After his graduation from Kent College of Law, Carey was admitted into the Illinois Bar in 1936. He began a private practice and ultimately became a partner in the law firm of Prescott, Taylor, Carey and Cooper. Carey was admitted into the United States district court in Illinois in 1942. Having established his legal credentials and his reputation as a community leader, Carey made a bid for the position of the Third Ward alderman's seat on Chicago's city council in 1947. Carey was elected and served as alderman until 1955, during which time he continued to increase his political influence.

Carey's role in mainstream politics never compromised his commitment to the African American community he served. He served as an intermediary between whites and blacks, being able to reach both communities through his professional and grass-roots affiliations. Not surprisingly, then, Carey played a critical role in the founding and support of the Committee (later Congress) of Racial Equality (CORE). CORE's founders were a multicultural group of Christians who advocated social justice and fought for civil rights. Carey used his own influence and the resources he could acquire through his position as minister to assist CORE. Carey raised money through his congregation, which was, at the time, politically astute and a recognized socially active entity in the Chicago community. He also allowed CORE access to rooms in the church basement for meetings to plan and organize activities. Carey remained a confidant and political ally of CORE's founding members in their collective struggle for civil rights.

Carey also played a supporting role in the political and civil upheaval that was taking place on a national level. In 1955 he went to Alabama State College to address a citizenship rally. Martin Luther King Jr., the newly appointed minister of Dexter Avenue Baptist Church, was emerging on the national scene as a leader of the African American community; King was the spokesman for the Montgomery bus boycott. Carey became one of the people Martin Luther King Jr. sought out for advice on politics and strategies. In 1957, King invited Carey to Montgomery to speak at the second anniversary of the bus boycott held at the Annual Institute on Nonviolence and Social Change. The speech was a resounding success.

Emerges on the Political Scene as a Major Player

During the 1950s Carey's political significance reached a national scale. In 1952 he got involved in electoral politics and campaigned on behalf of Republican Dwight D. Eisenhower. That same year he was a speaker at the Republican National Convention. Carey spoke so movingly and eloquently that some of his fellow ministers called for him to be vice president of the party. That never materialized, however, Carey was appointed as an alternate delegate for the United States to the eighth Gen-

eral Assembly of the United Nations. Thus Carey was able to demonstrate his commitment to equality on an international level, serving as an ambassador for his country. In 1954, his diplomatic contributions earned him recognition: That year he received a Citizen's Award from the University of Chicago and the Abraham Schwartz Award for Human Relations. The same year *Ebony* listed him as one of the nation's ten best black preachers.

Carey also found time to teach. He lectured at Roosevelt University in Chicago and taught legal ethics at John Marshall Law School, also in Chicago. Moreover, he served as a lifetime trustee of Garrett Theological Seminary and trustee emeritus of the Interdenominational Theological Center in Atlanta, Georgia.

From 1955 to 1961 Carey served as a member of the president's committee on government employment policy. In 1957 he was appointed chair of the committee, becoming the first African American to chair a White House committee. In addition, Carey became the president of the board of directors of the Illinois Federal Savings and Loan Association. He held the position from 1957 to 1966. In 1966 he became a judge of the Circuit Court of Cook County, Illinois. Given the extent to which he was involved in political and legal life, Carey was no longer able to maintain his position as minister of Quinn Chapel AME Church. He left the church but was honored for his contributions to it by being named pastor emeritus. Carey served as a judge in Cook County until 1980. After a dynamic and influential career in public life, Carey Jr. died on April 20, 1981, at the age of seventy-three.

REFERENCES

Books

Farmer, James. *Lay Bare the Heart.* New York: Arbor House, 1985.

Murphy, Larry G., Gordon J. Melton, and Gary L. Ward, eds. *Encyclopedia of African American Religions.* New York: Garland Publishing Inc., 1993.

Williams, Ethel L., ed. *Biographical Directory of Negro Ministries.* 3rd ed. Boston: G. K. Hall and Co., 1975.

Periodicals

Dickerson, Dennis C. "Pulpit Review: Ringing the Bell of Freedom: Archibald J. Carey Jr., Martin Luther King Jr., & the Transformation of African American Leadership." *The AME Church Review* 117 (January-March 2001):93-99.

———. "History: Archibald J. Carey Jr. and the Founders of CORE." *The AME Church Review* 118 (July-September 2002): 39-50.

Gabriella Beckles

Archibald J. Carey, Sr.
1868–1931

Religious leader, political activist, orator

In his religious and political career, Archibald James Carey Sr. was determined to improve the lives of African Americans in both the religious and secular domains. He came to prominence as a leader in the African Methodist Episcopal Church (AME), having worked his way up through the religious ranks in Georgia, Florida, and then Chicago. In 1920 he was elected as the forty-third bishop of the AME Church. Carey was a skilled writer and speaker, and throughout his life he used his talents to affect social and political change, particularly in the city of Chicago.

Archibald James Carey Sr. was born and raised in Atlanta, Georgia. He was one of three children born to Jefferson Alexander Carey and Anna Bell Carey. Religion and politics played a significant role in the young Carey's life; both his father and grandfather were AME ministers, and the Carey family home created an environment of commitment to social change. At nine years of age, Carey experienced a religious conversion to Christianity, joined the AME Church, and became involved in the church's activities.

Religious Career Begins to Flourish

Carey showed a talent for learning and his educational training began at an early age. He entered school at the age of four and demonstrated his aptitude at every level. At age ten he was appointed secretary of the black Republican organization of Atlanta; his father was president. Carey went on to complete his B.A. from Atlanta University in 1889. In 1888, at the age of twenty, while still in college, Carey received his license to preach and joined the North Georgia Annual Conference under Bishop Wesley John Gaines. In 1890, Carey was ordained a deacon in Washington, Georgia, and the following year he was made an elder in Monticello, Georgia. Bishop Gaines presided over all these ceremonies.

During this eventful time Carey's personal life was also moving ahead. He married Elizabeth Hill Davis, daughter of the famous Georgia Reconstruction legislator Madison Davis. The two were wed on December 18, 1890 and went on to have five children: Eloise, Annabell, Madison, Dorothy, and Archibald Jr.

Carey's first pastoral appointment was to Bethel AME Church in Atlanta, Georgia in 1891, which he later rebuilt at a cost of $2,500. After serving four years at Bethel, Carey was then appointed to Mount Zion AME Church in Jacksonville, Florida. Three years later in 1898, Carey moved to a new pastoral appointment at Quinn Chapel AME Church in Chicago, the city's oldest black church. Carey was steadily building a reputation as a powerful

Chronology	
1868	Born in Atlanta, Georgia on August 25
1877	Experiences religious conversion to Christianity
1888	Receives license to preach
1889	Graduates from Atlanta University with a B.A.
1890	Ordained a deacon in Washington, Georgia; marries Elizabeth Hill Davis on December 18
1891	Made an elder in Monticello, Georgia
1892	Receives first pastoral appointment at Bethel AME Church
1898	Appointed to Quinn Chapel AME Church in Chicago
1904	Presides over the General Conference at Quinn Chapel
1909	Appointed to Institutional AME Church, Chicago
1915	Heads the fiftieth anniversary of emancipation state celebration
1918	Appointed presiding elder of the Chicago district
1920	Elected bishop on May 13
1931	Dies in Chicago, Illinois on March 23

preacher and talented orator. Moreover, he was sowing the seeds of his political connections, which would come to fruition in Chicago. During the 1896 presidential election, Carey campaigned for the Republican Party and met candidate William McKinley.

Carey's political career took off when he moved to Chicago to pastor at Quinn Chapel. While in Chicago, Carey developed his political ties with a rising young politician, William Thompson, who was connected to the Illinois Republicans. Carey campaigned a number of times on behalf of Thompson and other Republican figures in Chicago. His political affiliations enabled Carey to bolster his own career and demonstrate his support for the church and its community, particularly by raising money for the church mortgages under his pastoral care.

By the turn of the century, Carey was becoming a prominent leader in the AME Church. In 1904 he presided over the General Conference at Quinn Chapel, which made him more visible within the denomination. Carey's appointment at Quinn Chapel ended in 1904 at which time he transferred to Bethel AME, another Chicago church, despite some opposition and rivalry from Reverdy C. Ransom, another important figure in the Chicago religious scene. Carey served as pastor at Bethel until 1909 and then moved to the Institutional AME Church in Chicago, where he remained until 1920. In 1918 he was appointed presiding elder of the Chicago district.

Political Connections Prove Invaluable

Carey embraced many roles in his religious life, as he did in his political life. He was a delegate to the General Conference in 1904, 1908, 1912, and 1916. He was also a member of the Financial Board from 1904 to 1912 and a trustee of Wilberforce University in Ohio. Carey was a member of the Commission on Federation of Methodist Churches in 1915. He was elected bishop on May 13, 1920, and was assigned to the Fourteenth Episcopal District (Kentucky and Tennessee). He was chancellor of Turner Normal College in Shelbyville, Tennessee. In 1928, he moved to the Fourth Episcopal District, which included Illinois, and from 1920 to 1922 he was a member of the Illinois Constitutional Convention.

Carey's political connections continued to enhance his ability to affect change in Chicago. Under Thompson, who was elected mayor in 1915, Carey's political influence increased. He was chaplain of the black Illinois 8th Regiment and chairman of the Second Ward draft board during World War I. Carey also received the esteemed position of delivering the oration at the centennial celebration of Admiral Matthew Perry's victory at Put-in-Bay. In addition, Carey served as the chief examiner of claims and the civil service commissioner. As commissioner, Carey had a huge impact on the hiring practices and conduct of the police force, ensuring they hired more black officers and punishing those officers who abused black prisoners. Carey also used his influence, particularly during Thompson's reign, to assure more blacks were appointed to public office—so much so, that Thompson's opponents began to refer to city hall as "Uncle Tom's Cabin."

Carey, however, was not permanently bound to the Republican Party. In 1911 and 1912 he lent his campaign support to Democrat candidates Carter Harrison II for mayor and Edward Dunne for governor. Subsequently, Mayor Harrison II appointed Carey to Chicago's motion picture censorship board. Carey also secured a position at one of Chicago's most notable celebrations. In 1915 he was appointed by Governor Dunne to head the fiftieth anniversary of emancipation state celebration.

Carey enjoyed all the political and religious power he had worked for during a thriving era of black Chicagoan politics. Carey remained active until his death on March 23, 1931, at the age of 62.

REFERENCES

Books

Murphy, Larry G., Gordon J. Melton, and Gary L. Ward, eds. *Encyclopedia of African American Religions.* New York: Garland Publishing Inc., 1993.

Periodicals

Wills, David W. "History: Archibald J. Carey Sr. and Ida B. Wells-Barnett: Religion and Politics in Black Chicago, 1900-1931." *The AME Church Review* (July-September 2004): 92-107.

Gabriella Beckles

Benjamin Carson
1951–

Neurosurgeon, writer

Benjamin Carson is the director of pediatric neurosurgery at the Johns Hopkins Medical Institutions, where he performs more than four hundred complex surgeries every year. He is a professor of neurosurgery, oncology, plastic surgery, and pediatrics. He is noted for his use of cerebral hemispherectomy to control intractable seizures as well as for his work in craniofacial reconstructive surgery, achondroplasia (human dwarfism), and pediatric neuro-oncology (brain tumors). Carson has also become a leading motivational speaker, retelling the stories of his trials and tribulations in an effort to inspire others. Carson is the author of three books that explore the spiritual and philosophical beliefs that have helped him succeed.

Carson's parents, Sonya and Robert Carson, divorced when Benjamin was eight years old. They had married when she was thirteen and he was twenty-eight and moved from Chattanooga, Tennessee, to Detroit, Michigan, where Robert got a job at the Cadillac factory. In his autobiography, *Gifted Hands*, Carson called the day his father left "the saddest day of my life." Sonya raised her sons on her own, with little education and no financial help from their father. Carson described her as "hardworking, goal-oriented...refusing to settle for less." Still, the strain occasionally became too much for her, and she sought psychiatric help. The family was bolstered by the emotional and financial support they received when they moved in with relatives in Boston. They shared a grim tenement with a loving aunt and uncle and a host of rats and cockroaches.

Despite all the changes that year, Carson has fond memories of those days: He received his first chemistry set for Christmas and became interested in the Seventh-Day Adventist church the family attended. In what he called his first religious experience, Carson was inspired by a pastor's sermon and began to believe he could become a doctor. Later in his life, Carson recalled his mother's words about God: "Bennie, if you ask the Lord for something, believing he will do it, then He will do it." He often took those words into the operating room with him. In 1961, once she had recovered financially, Sonya Carson moved with her children back to Detroit.

Legal Blindness Affects Grades

Carson's dreams of becoming a doctor were not supported by the grades he earned in his early school years. Though he excelled in science, he was at the bottom of his class in fifth grade. He was taunted by schoolmates and began to believe he was dumb, as well as poor. Carson's second-hand clothes did not help his social status

Benjamin Carson

either. A pair of glasses—Carson was discovered to be almost legally blind—inspired the boy to renew his effort in school, and with the support of his mother and teacher, he rose to the top of his six-grade class.

During his school days, in the early 1960s, Carson and his brother encountered prejudice. A gang of white boys threatened to kill the young Carsons, who attended the mostly white Wilson Junior High. After being ranked top of his class in seventh and eighth grades, Benjamin watched a white teacher berate a group of white students for "not trying hard enough," he wrote in *Gifted Hands.* "She let them know that a black person shouldn't be number one in a class where everyone else was white."

The teenage Carson eventually reacted to the racial and financial pressures. At age fourteen, he was involved in a series of serious fights. In one fight, he inadvertently gashed a friend's forehead after striking him in anger. In another, he attempted to stab a boy with a knife. The boy's large belt buckle deflected the blade from slicing into his belly. Carson was frightened by his own temper and knew it was something he had to face. He turned to his pastor and his faith to understand his anger, which he called "pathological." High school ROTC also helped him learn discipline, and he achieved the rank of ROTC colonel. After high school, he was accepted to Yale University on a ninety-percent scholarship.

In college, Carson planned to major in pre-med with a minor in psychology then go on to medical school. But he was unprepared for the academic challenges of Yale. He had skated through high school, cramming for tests. He had never learned to study. Faced with the idea that low grades would keep him from medical school, however, he quickly improved his study skills, becoming what he called an in-depth learner. Carson spent his college summers in Detroit, working. His summer jobs included package delivery, highway crew supervisor, and auto factory worker. He graduated Yale in 1973 and attended medical school at the University of Michigan in Ann Arbor.

Realizes He Has Gifted Hands

It was at one of his summer jobs at a steel company that Carson discovered something unique about himself. While spending his days operating a crane, he began to realize that he had extraordinary hand-eye coordination. He also realized that he had an innate ability to see and understand physical relationships; he described the sense in *Gifted Hands* as being able to "see...and think in three dimensions." As his career developed, Carson realized the value of this skill. "For me it is the most significant talent God has given me and the reason people sometimes say I have gifted hands."

Carson was in his third year of medical school, in his one-month neurology rotation, when he realized he excelled in the discipline. He impressed his neurology professors by coming up with a new surgical technique and became the man with all the answers as the students made their rounds to patients. Soon, exhausted fellow students were turning over their patients to Carson. He was as tired as they were, but "I loved being a medical student," he wrote in *Gifted Hands*. "It was the most fun I'd ever had in my life."

Though he had planned to pursue psychiatry, Carson decided on neurology. The way he saw it, there were three undeniable reasons for his choice: first, his interested in neurosurgery; second, his growing interest in the workings of the brain; and third, his extraordinary hand-eye coordination. Carson was awarded numerous honors for his clinical work at the University of Michigan. Carson's next step was Johns Hopkins University in Baltimore, Maryland. After a year of internship, he faced six years of residency—one more year of general surgery and five of neurosurgery. Carson spent the fifth year of his residency doing research on the areas of brain tumors and neuro-oncology.

Marries College Sweetheart

As his academic and professional life was moving along successfully, so was Carson's personal life. On July 6, 1975, he married Lacena Rustin, whom everyone called Candy. The two had met four years earlier when she was a freshman at Yale. The Carsons moved to Baltimore, where Candy became an assistant for a Johns Hopkins professor and earned her master's degree in business from the university.

The young resident quickly began to observe bothersome behavior from Johns Hopkins doctors. They were snobbish and ignored the clerks and aides who kept the hospital going. Carson saw paying attention to workers as an opportunity, and whenever he had the chance, he would visit with these workers. He quickly realized these people were more in touch with the patients and could teach the young doctor a thing or two, which they did.

Carson faced some prejudice from patients who did not want treatment from a black doctor. Carson's supervising physician very politely pointed to the door and invited these people to use it. Should they decide to stay, the head doctor told them, Carson would be handling their case. None of the patients ever left. Carson had one contentious relationship at the hospital, however, with a white chief resident who was clearly uncomfortable with a black intern at Johns Hopkins. Carson quietly endured his outbursts and caustic comments and went about his business. He knew reacting would be just what the man wanted. Carson was a resident at Johns Hopkins from 1978 to 1982.

Earns Surgical Experience in Australia

In 1983, the Carsons traveled to Perth, Australia, where Carson had accepted a position as a senior registrar. Candy was by then pregnant with the couple's first child. In addition to concerns about his wife's health,

Carson was worried about the racial climate in Australia, where segregation had been the policy until 1968. To his relief, the couple liked Australia immediately. They had a built-in extended family in the Seventh-Day Adventist Church they attended. Carson took on more than his share of surgeries at the hospital and by the end of his one-year contract had become a swift and competent brain surgeon.

Colleagues at Johns Hopkins had enough faith in the thirty-three-year old doctor that, upon his return, Carson was named chief of pediatric neurosurgery. Carson got pleasure from watching people react to the news that this young black man was their neurosurgeon. Yet, within a year of his appointment, Carson faced one of the toughest surgeries of his career.

By the time Carson met four-year-old Maranda Francisco and her parents in 1985, the family had spent three years trying to alleviate the worsening seizures that had plagued Maranda since birth. Doctors had finally told them that Maranda had Rasmussen's encephalitis, and she would continue to suffer more seizures, become paralyzed, and die. Carson decided to perform a radical, risky hemispherectomy on the girl (surgical removal of the left half of the brain). The family accepted the risks. In the face of both the major surgical risks and the unknown functional abilities of an incomplete brain, Carson was elated with the hoped-for results. Maranda recovered completely, with only limited affect to her fine motor skills and a small limp. Her brain had been able to reroute all of its needs to the remaining right hemisphere. Carson stepped away from the media spotlight after the surgery. He went on to perform many successful hemispherectomies and other radical, last-resort neurosurgical procedures.

Carson was the last hope for most of his patients. Doctors all over the world called Carson and Johns Hopkins to take cases that had exhausted their resources. Carson became the go-to surgeon for operations others could not or would not perform, and he always took his faith into the operating room with him.

Makes Surgical History

Carson met the Binder twins in 1987. The German brothers were conjoined; they were born attached at the back of the head. Because of the location of the attachment, the boys would never be able to sit, crawl, or walk. They would be bedridden, lying on their backs for life. The parents wanted their boys to live separately. The infants shared no organs but did share the major vein responsible for moving blood from the brain to the heart. Carson put together a team of seventy surgeons, anesthesiologists, technicians, and nurses who studied the details of the surgery for five months, leaving nothing to chance. The procedure took twenty-two hours. Both the surgery and the recovery were fraught with problems, and the twins had to undergo subsequent surgeries, but nothing out of order for such a complex procedure. It was the first such surgery that had produced two normal, healthy, separate boys. Carson received international acclaim for his leading role in the surgery.

The demands on Carson's time were excessive. Patients took up a great deal of his time. But as the chief pediatric neurosurgeon at a teaching hospital, Carson also had to conduct research, write papers, prepare lectures, and remain involved with academic projects. He also was heavily involved in his church and had started sharing his story in motivational talks to young people. In 1990, he published his first book, a memoir titled *Gifted Hands: The Ben Carson Story*. At the end of the book, he explained how he pared back professional and academic responsibilities to make more time for his family. Instead of fourteen- to seventeen-hour days, he committed to twelve-hour days during the week and weekends with his wife, sons, and mother. Candy Carson and the three Carson boys comprise the Carson Four, an accomplished string quartet.

Becomes a Motivational Speaker, Author

Carson's second book, *Think Big: Unleashing Your Potential for Excellence*, was more directly motivational than his first. While the book is built on his personal experience, Carson refined and outlined some concrete lessons anyone can apply. In fact, Carson divided his personal philosophies into an acrostic, in which each letter of the words, think big, represents a reminder of his principles of success: Talent, Honest, Insight, Nice, Knowledge, Books, In-depth Knowledge, God. He wrote a chapter on each word, stressing the importance of education, self-reliance, positive thinking, and faith. He liberally used Bible verses to support his ideas. His third book, *The Big Picture: Getting Perspective on What's Really Important in Life*, was a more critical analysis of Carson's philosophies and their place in the world.

Though every elective surgery is fraught with ethical quandaries, Carson's decision to operate on 29-year-old conjoined twins in 2003 was particularly tough. Successful operations are not subjected to the kind of second-guessing that plagues those that do not end well. Laden and Laleh Bijani had spent their lives attached at the head and had decided that a chance to live separate lives was more important than life itself. Adult conjoined twins had never been successfully separated. Doctors tried to dissuade the women, who were law-school graduates, but they were determined. Carson was called in to lead the surgical team and felt compelled to try to help them. "I was convinced they would seek separation no matter who performed the surgery," he told the *New York Times*. The women died. Supporters of the surgery believed it was the women's right to choose the surgery; critics argued that doctors had an ethical obligation to refuse them.

Over the course of his career, Carson has been a recipient of numerous honors and awards, including more than thirty honorary doctorate degrees. He is a member of the American Academy of Achievement, the Horatio Alger Society of Distinguished Americans, the Alpha Omega Alpha Honor Medical Society, and many other prestigious organizations. He was named by the Library of Congress as one of eighty-nine Living Legends on the occasion of its two-hundredth anniversary and in 2001 was chosen by CNN and *Time* magazine as one of America's top twenty physicians and scientists. He sits on many boards, including the board of directors of Kellogg Company, Costco Wholesale Corporation, and the American Academy of Achievement, and he is an Emeritus Fellow of the Yale Corporation, the governing body of Yale University. In addition to his academic responsibilities, he is a highly sought motivational speaker who has spoken in venues that range from high school graduations to the 1997 President's National Prayer Breakfast.

Gives Talented Kids a Hand

Early in his career, Carson and his wife developed the idea for the Carson Scholars Fund, to provide scholarships for promising young people who lack the money for school. The group recognizes young people of all backgrounds for exceptional academic and humanitarian accomplishments. Carson is also the president and co-founder of the Benevolent Endowment Network (BEN) Fund, an organization which provides grants to assist families with non-covered medical care expenses for pediatric neurosurgery patients with complex medical conditions.

In 2004, President George W. Bush named Carson to the Council on Bioethics. The group of scholars, scientists, theologians, and others was created in 2001 to produce reports on human cloning, stem cell research, and the use of biotechnology to enhance human beings. Carson and two others were selected to replace two members of the group whom Bush had dismissed. Critics noted the three replacements were more inclined toward Bush's conservative stance on these matters than the ousted members, citing Carson's public statements about God and faith. The move dismayed some critics, who saw it as "Bush stacking the council with the compliant," Elizabeth Blackburn, a renowned biologist who had been dismissed, told the *Washington Post*. Many saw it as a case of Bush putting politics ahead of science. "On all these matters," wrote a *Boston Globe* editorialist, "the president should be seeking the best information and opinions, not just ones he agrees with."

Every doctor becomes a patient at some point. In 2002, at age 50, Carson was diagnosed with an aggressive form of prostate cancer. A colleague at Johns Hopkins performed prostate surgery, and Carson did well in recovery. Before the surgery, Carson told a reporter for the *Washington Post* that he was turning the outcome of the surgery over to "the Lord, [who] can heal anything."

REFERENCES

Periodicals

Grady, Denise. "2 Women, 2 Deaths and an Ethical Quandry." *New York Times*, 15 July 2003.

Jennings, Veronica T. "A Top Doctor's Journey from Poverty to Surgery." *Washington Post*, 22 June 1989.

McCombs, Phil. "For Ben Carson, Surgery Brings Good News." *Washington Post*, 8 August 2002.

"Stem Cell Ideologues." *Boston Globe*, 3 March 2004.

Weiss, Rick. "Bush Ejects Two from Bioethics Council; Changes Renew Criticism That the President Puts Politics Ahead of Science." *Washington Post*, 28 February 2004.

Online

"Benjamin S. Carson Sr., M.D." U.S. Council on Bioethics. http://www.bioethics.gov/about/carson.html (Accessed 28 January 2005).

Brenna Sanchez

Lisle C. Carter

Lisle C. Carter
1926–

Lawyer, federal government official, college president

The high-level public positions held by Lisle C. Carter Jr. exemplify the essence of his career, which spans more than sixty years. Carter became the first African American to serve in several capacities throughout his career. His character and intelligence drew many local and federal government positions to him. Through high-level public service, Carter helped to shape policies that affect the health, education, and welfare of our nation. Carter held appointments in the Kennedy and Johnson administrations and served as chancellor and president at two black universities.

Lisle C. Carter Jr., an only child, was born on November 18, 1926 in Manhattan, New York to Lisle and Eunice Hunton Carter. His father was a native of Barbados, British West Indies, and practiced dentistry in New Jersey until his death in 1963. Carter's mother, who died in 1970, was dedicated to political activism and service. She was the first African American woman to serve as a prosecutor in 1935. Carter spent his early years at boarding school in Barbados and graduated from high school at age fifteen. He attended Cazenovia College in Cazenovia, New York for two years and graduated from Dartmouth College in 1945 with a B.S. degree in business administration. Following graduation, Carter served in the U.S. Army. He graduated with a law degree from St. John's University, Brooklyn, New York in 1951. Carter and his wife Emily had five children.

Carter became executive director of the Washington Urban League in 1951 and served until 1953. He became chief council for the Urban League of Greater New York in 1957 and remained there for two years. Carter returned to Washington in 1961 where he served as deputy assistant secretary of Health, Education, and Welfare (HEW) in the Kennedy administration. Subsequently, President Johnson appointed Carter to the position of assistant secretary of HEW. Carter's appointments were significant. Involvement in cabinet action gave him a chance to participate at the highest level in policy. Doing so, Carter followed his mother's footsteps of political activism. In both administrations, Carter's responsibilities included researching and providing analyses of important social issues. As the deputy assistant secretary, Carter reported to the assistant secretary. However, as assistant secretary of HEW, he made recommendations directly to the secretary. Several pubic policies were established during Carter's appointments that are paramount to the general welfare of U.S. citizens.

In 1965, the U.S. Congress adopted the Medicare and Medicaid health programs and established a separate Department of Education, a development to which Carter contributed. Furthermore, according to Gerald Britten, a former assistant secretary for planning and evaluation in HEW, several organizational changes were made in the assistant secretary's office, such as the creation of an office particularly to help plan research and evaluation and an office to address social service policy. The Jimmy Carter administration in 1979 appointed Lisle Carter to the president's commission on pension policy. In addition Carter was named a part-time senior advisor to the secretary of the new U.S. Department of Education. One of his principle responsibilities was to assist the new secretary in the review and selection of candidates to fill positions created by the establishment of the new department. Another major responsibility was to help make the transition from an education department within HEW to its separate departmental status.

Before moving to Georgia in 1974 to accept the position of chancellor at the Atlanta University Center, Carter was a professor of public policy and a vice president at Cornell University in Ithaca, New York. By the time Carter accepted the position of chancellor of a consortium of six predominately black colleges, he had more than ten years experience in public policy and administration.

By 1968, the District of Columbia had five public institutions of higher learning: Georgetown University, Howard University, D.C. Teacher's College, Federal City College, and Washington Technical Institute. Then the D.C. City Council passed a bill that was authorized by Congress to merge the two colleges and the institute into one university, namely the University of the District of Columbia (UDC). The plan was for one university to offer teacher education, general liberal arts, and technical education. In 1977, Carter assumed the position of president with a five-year contract.

The main responsibility of the new president was to facilitate the merger of three institutions into one munici-

pally funded university that emphasized both liberal arts and vocational training. Newspapers reported on the difficulties involved. For example, Teacher's College offered a four-year curriculum. Federal City offered a two-year liberal arts program. Washington Technical also offered a two-year program, but the curriculum was designed to make students job-ready. The merger brought cutbacks in employees. Some students feared the end of the open enrollment policies. Carter had to streamline the curriculum. For 1977-78, with a conjoined total of approximately 15,000 students, each institution retained its curriculum. Carter hired consultants who formed several committees to develop a plan to incorporate the three curriculums and strengthen the technical program. Carter submitted an acceptable plan to the trustees as required by the fall of 1978. In December 1979, the UDC won accreditation from the Middle States Association of Colleges and Schools. Also under Carter's leadership, UDC opened a restored $4.2 million library on December 11, 1980. Carter felt that he had laid the foundation for the new university by 1980 and, choosing not to remain at the university for the long-term, announced his plans to step down from his post upon expiration of his contract in 1982.

In the meantime, Carter accepted a part-time position as senior advisor to the new U.S. Department of Education in December 1979, declining the White House offer to become undersecretary of the Department of Health, Education, and Welfare. As senior advisor, Carter advised the secretary on policy and helped evaluate candidates for high-level jobs in the new department.

In 1981 Carter was appointed chairman of the Executive Committee of the United Way of America. While he joined the staff in 1981, Carter had served on the long range planning committee since 1975. A subcommittee which he chaired consisting of fifteen volunteers developed strategies for local offices to serve and support health and social service agencies. Carter resigned from the United Way in 1991. In 1995, he served as Special Assistant to the Secretary of HEW, and in 2001 he was a member of the Roundtable on Democracy Research Public Agenda. Carter has served on the Children's Defense Fund, Pension Rights Center, Aspen Institute, and New York Department of Corrections. Carter has also written several articles.

REFERENCES

Periodicals

Bowman, LaBarbara. "Council Passes University Bill." *Washington Post*, 30 July 1975.

Carter, Lisle C., Jr. "UDC: Its Importance, Its Needs." *Washington Post*, 13 October 1985.

———. "Management of Our Difficult Financial Situation." *Washington Post*, 21 May 1980.

Feinberg, Lawrence. "Atlanta Educator Named to Head University of D.C." *Washington Post*, 30 July 1977.

———."City U Head Seeks to Keep Politics at Bay." *Washington Post*, 2 August 1977.

———. "Faculty's Anxiety Stirs Unrest at UDC." *Washington Post*, 12 February 1978.

———. "Head of UDC Trustees Defends Payment on President's Behalf." *Washington Post*, 18 February 1978.

Keary, Jim. "Lawyer says warning didn't slow acrimony." *Washington Times*, 17 March 1995.

Valentine, Paul W. "UDC President Offered No. 2 Post in Education." *Washington Post*, 6 December 1979.

Weil, Martin. "Lisle C. Carter to Quit Post as UDC President." *Washington Post*, 19 December 1980.

Whitaker, Joseph D. "Speaker Calls University Symbol of Hope for Poor." *Washington Post*, 6 October 1978.

Wright, Chapin. "Carter Named to United Way Committee." *Washington Post*, 24 August 1981.

Online

Britten, Gerald. "Office of the Assistant Secretary for Planning and Evaluation: Brief History." U.S. Department of Health and Human Services. http://aspe.hhs.gov/aspehistory.htm (Accessed 27 January 2006).

Shelhea C. Owens

Stephen L. Carter

Stephen L. Carter
1954–

Lawyer, writer, educator

Stephen L. Carter, a distinguished writer and professor of law, has gained critical acclaim and notoriety for his views on the role of religion in politics and culture and has sparked debates on the role of integrity and civility in American daily life.

Born in 1954, Stephen Lisle Carter grew up in Washington, D.C.'s middle-class neighborhood of Cleveland Park. Carter was born into a family of highly educated professionals. His grandmother, Eunice Hunton Carter, was a member of the prosecuting team called Twenty against the Underworld, who were responsible for bringing to trial Lucky Luciano, one of New York's famed mobsters. Stephen's father, a lawyer, worked in the Department of Health, Education, and Welfare during the administrations of presidents John F. Kennedy and Lyndon B. Johnson. Stephen's mother, Emily E. Carter, was a college graduate who worked as an assistant to the head of the National Urban Coalition. Along with his family,

Stephen Carter, the second of five children, moved to Ithaca, New York, at the age of thirteen, after his father accepted a teaching position at Cornell University.

Growing up, Carter attended nearly all-white schools, in Washington, D.C. and in Ithaca. This racial imbalance never bothered Carter; indeed, it eventually provided the framework for his mindset into adulthood, giving him as a young African American male the opportunity to achieve and excel. When he took the SAT, and made a good score of 780 on the math section, Carter took the test over so that he could make a more acceptable score of 800. After graduating from Ithaca High School, Carter enrolled at Stanford University, in California, where he majored in history and in 1976 earned a B.A. degree with honors.

Denied Admission to Harvard Law School

During his senior year in high school, Carter applied to various law schools. He was accepted at all of the schools except Harvard. Carter decided to attend the Yale Law School, but two days after he received his rejection letter from Harvard, he received a phone call retracting the former letter. The Harvard officials explained that there was an error: they somehow misread Carter's application and thought that he was white. Of course Carter was insulted and turned down their late offer for admittance. In a book that Carter later wrote about the experience, *Reflections of an Affirmative Action Baby*, he stated, "I was told by one official that the school had initially rejected me because 'we assumed from your record that you were white.'" Carter went on to say that the school had obtained "'additional information that should have been counted in your favor'—that is, Harvard had discovered the color of my skin. ...Stephen Carter, the white male, was not good enough for Harvard Law School, [while] Stephen Carter, the black male,...rated agonized telephone calls urging him to attend. And Stephen Carter, color unknown, must have been white: How else could he have achieved what he did in college?" Carter admits that even though he was accepted to Yale, he wonders if his admittance there was also based on his race. He went on and earned his J.D. degree from Yale in 1979.

Carter landed his first job as law clerk to Judge Spottswood W. Robinson III at the U.S. Court of Appeals in D.C., and in 1980 he served as clerkship at the U.S. Supreme Court for Justice Thurgood Marshall. Carter admired Justice Marshall, looking up to him as a father figure. Carter was admitted to the bar in Washington, D.C., in 1981, and in the same year he became an associate at Shea & Gardner, a Washington law firm. He began teaching law at Yale in 1982, and three years later became the youngest tenured professor in the university's history. That same year he also married Enola Aird, a fellow Yale Law School graduate. At Yale, he became the distinguished William Nelson Cromwell professor and began writing books.

In *Reflections of an Affirmative Action Baby*, Carter discussed the positives and negatives of racial preference programs, using his own experiences as examples. He argues that affirmative action harms racial minorities more than it helps them. Carter advances three arguments in support of his thesis that affirmative action harms people of color. First, racial preferences reinforce, rather than eliminate, differences between minorities and nonminorities. Justification for affirmative action based on diversity—that is, minorities add a special viewpoint, outlook, or perspective "actually perpetuate ugly stereotypes about the different ways in which people who are white and people who are black supposedly think." The proposition that skin color always stands for a single perspective leads to troubling results. Second, affirmative action creates the assumption that people of color can be only the best in their group but never the best, period. Carter relates how he was prevented from competing for a National Merit Scholarship in high school because he had already been chosen for the National Achievement Scholarship, an award exclusively for black students. Third, affirmative action diverts attention from the people who need the most help—poor blacks who never have the opportunity to prove themselves under affirmative action in the first place. As Carter puts it, "The most disadvantaged black people are not in a position to benefit from preferential admission." Thus, he concludes, affirmative action is merely "racial justice on the cheap."

Career as a Writer

He published his second book, *The Culture of Disbelief*, in 1993. In this book, Carter attempts to analyze how law and politics trivialize the religious devotion that is so much a part of the inner culture of U.S. society. He argues that faith and religious values have an appropriate place in the nation's public life. In the 1990s, politicians were shunned for talking about God or religion, which Carter defines as public discussion in explicitly religious terms. In 1994, the book won Carter the Louisville Grawemeyer Award, one of the most prestigious prizes in the world of religion. Carter, who was amazed that he won the honor, was the first non-theologian to win the prize. Also in that year he was named by *Time* magazine as one of the "Fifty Future Leaders of America." Soon after the book was published, it received a public endorsement from President Bill Clinton, who spoke about it highly at a prayer breakfast with religious leaders. Clinton was criticized for his statements by those on the left who believed that politicians should not be speaking publicly about their religious convictions and then by those on the right who disagreed with Clinton's religious views. Carter believes that these are exactly the sorts of pressures that religious people experience all the time. He was later asked on a panel discussing the media and religion, if it bothered him that Clinton spoke about the importance of religion while facing questions about alleged ethical lapses ranging from Whitewater to extra-marital affairs. Carter responded that he was not, pointing out that people are complicated and flawed.

Carter points out that there was a time in U.S. history when religious witness in the public square was welcomed. But history altered its course when the abortion issue surfaced. After the Supreme Court's 1973 *Roe v. Wade* decision, which legalized abortion, the image of American religion was damaged. In the book, Carter uses the example of New York's controversial Roman Catholic archbishop, John Cardinal O'Connor who, in 1990, stated in an article that he wrote in a religious publication, that those Catholic politicians who support a woman's right to abortion risk excommunication. Much debate ensued, and the press had a field day. *Vanity Fair* informed its readers that O'Connor was an extremist. Carter states that there is nothing wrong with people like O'Connor, in particular, or a spokesperson for any religious group pressing a moral claim in the public square.

In 1994 Carter published his next book, *The Confirmation Mess: Cleaning Up the Federal Appointments Process*, in which he criticizes the manner in which federal appointees are confirmed. The federal confirmation process, Carter believes, has become more consumed with exposé than with objective examination of candidates' capabilities to hold the post for which they were nominated. To argue his case, Carter uses several high-profile nominations of the 1980s and 1990s, including the controversial Supreme Court candidacies of Robert Bork and Clarence Thomas and also assistant attorney general for civil rights nominee Lani Guinier. Carter believes that Bork and Guinier are prime examples of the distortion that has become an integral part of the confirmation process. The two candidates were not defeated intellectually but were rather demonized. Carter maintains that one of the most victimized federal nominees in history was Thurgood Marshall, who Carter says was called a liar, was castigated as being a subversive, had his intellect and ethics questioned, and was roundly termed unqualified during his Supreme Court hearing. "The animosity that Bork and Thomas encountered was not unprecedented. Marshall received the worst treatment. But most of what happened during Marshall's hearing was not reported unlike today where the hearings are televised," Carter wrote.

In his review essay, "Is There a Confirmation Mess? An Analysis of Professor Stephen Carter's Critique of the Federal Process," published in the January 1995 edition of the *California Law Review*, reviewer Michael Kahn objects to Carter's gloomy prognostication about the nomination of Thurgood Marshall. Kahn states that if Marshall were considered all over again, he would be nominated and confirmed again. Kahn also rejects Carter's view that the system is a mess. Many of the reviews of *The Confirmation Mess*, were mixed; some

offered praise for Carter's detailed description of the problem but skepticism about his proposed solutions.

Carter's next book, *Integrity*, was written because Carter sees a problem in raising children properly in a country which does not act on its proclaimed values. Reviewer T. Howland Sanks in the April 27, 1996 issue of *America* calls the book a "skillful combination of anecdote and analysis." *Integrity* is not a philosophical or theological treatment of the virtue of integrity, but it concerns itself with "how we Americans think, or have thought, or should think of it." In Part One, "Explanations," Carter maintains that integrity means more than just honesty. Integrity requires three steps: first, discerning what is right and what is wrong; second, acting on what one has discerned, even at personal cost; and third, saying openly that one is acting on one's understanding of right and wrong. Carter discusses the issues of integrity in marriage, politics, academia, and journalism. Carter commented in the July 1996 issue of *The Lutheran* that "Integrity is the crucial element of good citizenship. It's more important to know if someone has integrity than to know whether I agree or disagree with him. If you lack integrity, nothing else you say you believe matters."

Civility: Manners, Morals, and the Etiquette of Democracy, published in 1996, endeavors to analyze what has happened to civility in the United States, why it matters, and what can be done about it. Carter presents a list of fifteen rules intended to guide readers, within the limits of democracy, in reconstructing their civility. While clearly these rules of behavior that form the "etiquette of democracy" are difficult to practice, Carter warns that failure to implement them will lead to nothing short of barbarism. The concept of civility involves deep commitment to respect or even love fellow citizens in a way that governs actions towards them. Carter locates the genesis of the lack of civility in American life in the turmoil of the 1960s, when serious questions arose about the roles of family, religion, race, gender, and education in civic life. The 1960s introduced a kind of cultural relativism into the American experience, which tended to tear down fundamental verities without supplying anything meaningful in their place. Somewhere in the chaos, civility got lost. Carter believes that Americans are rude, selfish, and "nasty as [they] wanna be." He believes that much American incivility stems from the inability or unwillingness to discipline personal desires.

In his 1998 publication, *The Dissent of the Governed*, Carter explores how the federal courts discount religion. As a legal theorist, a citizen in a democracy, and as a Christian, Carter believes deeply in dissent, not simply as a right, but as a responsibility. He analyzes the Declaration of Independence as an example of dissent and as the criterion of government legitimacy. Carter believes that moral progress in the United States demands a richer understanding of the world and that groups need to engage in more dialogue. His principal argument for community autonomy is that individuals should be constitutionally exempt from the application of laws to which they have a religious objection unless an especially strong state interest can be shown.

In his next book, *God's Name in Vain*, Carter argues that many Americans have essentially "lost sight of the proper relationship between religion and politics." Targeting religious Americans, particularly evangelical Christians with his warning, Carter contends that religious individuals and overtly religious organizations must set "sensible limits" with regard to their involvement in the political process. According to Carter, evangelical Christians must never become disengaged from politics, but they must remain mindful of the inherent capacity of politics to corrupt genuine faith and "prophetic vision."

Carter's subsequent publication, a novel entitled *The Emperor of Ocean Park*, his first work of fiction, turned out to be his most lucrative work. The central figure of the story, Judge Oliver Garland, a distinguished black conservative federal judge who is slated for the Supreme Court is accused of having ties to a crime kingpin. After the judge dies mysteriously, his son Talcott Garland, a middle-aged law professor at an Ivy League college, is drawn into the mystery surrounding his father's life and death. According to a July 18, 2002, article by Kendra Hamilton in *Black Issues in Higher Education*, Carter stated that "the enthusiasm and even affection that has greeted the novel and the characters has overwhelmed me." Some critics doubt the book and its author deserved so much money and attention. Despite some negative attention, though, the novel turned out to be a huge success. Carter earned a reputed $4.2 million in a two-book deal with Knopf, and Warner Brothers has offered him a movie deal for the novel.

Carter teaches law at Yale, frequently publishes articles in law reviews and popular presses, and writes a monthly column in *Christianity Today*. He holds memberships in the American Law Institute and is a fellow of the American Academy of Arts and Sciences. He is a trustee of the Aspen Institute, where he moderates seminars for executives on values-based leadership. He has received honorary degrees from various schools, including Notre Dame University, Colgate University, and the Virginia Theological Seminary. He lives in Hamden, Connecticut, with his wife Enola, and their children, Leah and Andrew.

REFERENCES

Periodicals

Chimiel, Mark. "Religion—Doing Right and Resisting Wrong—Key to Curing Incivility." *National Catholic Review* 35 (6 November 1998): 3-4.

Halton, William. Review of *The Confirmation Mess*. In *Political Science Quarterly* 109 (Winter 1994-95): 252.

Hamilton, Kendra. "Writing for Pleasure and Profit: Law Professor Spins a Tale of Mystery, Sex, and Intrigue to the Tune of a $4.2 Million Book Deal." *Black Issues in Higher Education* 19 (18 July 2002): 30.

Kahn, Michael A. "Is There a Confirmation Mess? An Analysis of Professor Stephen Carter's Critique of the Federal Appointments Process." *California Law Review* 83 (January 1995): 471-84.

Kauffman, Bill. "Out of the Box." *American Enterprise* 9 (November-December 1998): 3-5.

Lane, Charles. "A Victim of Preference." *Newsweek* 118 (30 September 1991): 3-5.

Sanks, T. Holland. Review of *Integrity*. In *America* 174 (27 April 1996): 22.

Trevino, A. Javier. "Sharing Democracy's Community." *Society* 37 (July-August 2000): 78-84.

Unsigned review of *God's Name in Vain*. In *Virginia Quarterly Review* 77 (Summer 2001): 102.

Washington, Linn. "Yale School Professor Stephen Carter Tackles 'The Confirmation Mess.'" *Philadelphia Tribune* 12 July 1994.

Online

Interview with Stephen L. Carter. http://www/readersread.com/features/stephenlcarter.htm (Accessed 31 January 2005).

Miller, David L. "Integrity: Why We Need a Transfusion." *The Lutheran* (July 1996). http://www.thelutheran.org/9607/jul-con.html (Accessed 28 January 2005).

Sheila A. Stuckey

Albert I. Cassell
1895–1969

Architect, engineer, educator

Albert I. Cassell was a prominent mid-twentieth-century visionary architect who excelled in a field that was scarcely ready to accept African Americans early on. The structures that he designed, constructed, or altered were scattered from Richmond, Virginia, to Baltimore, Maryland, and were located as far away as Tuskegee, Alabama, where his career began. An educator as well, he set the tone for architectural training at Howard Uni-

Albert I. Cassell

Chronology

1895	Born in Towson, Maryland on June 25
1919	Graduates from Cornell University
1920	Joins architectural faculty at Howard University
1922	Heads Department of Architecture at Howard University and becomes university architect; begins to design campus buildings
1932	Begins Calverton development, Calvert County, Maryland
1938	Erects Founders Library, his campus masterpiece
1941	Negotiates financial settlement with Howard University; later founds architectural firm Cassell, Gray, & Sulton
1942	Begins Mayfair Mansions and other facilities
1969	Dies in Washington, D.C. on November 30

versity, providing the structure for educating black youth in the field.

The third child of Albert Truman and Charlotte Cassell, Albert Irvin Cassell was born June 25, 1895 in Towson, Maryland. The family relocated to nearby Baltimore within a year of his birth. Cassell studied in the local segregated elementary and high schools. When he was fourteen, he studied drafting with Ralph Victor Cook, a teacher at Douglas High School. Cassell completed a four-year carpentry program and graduated from that school in 1914. His interest, however, was in architecture, the field that he pursued when he entered Cornell University in 1915. Cook, a Cornell graduate, continued his interest in Cassell as a student of architecture and helped to ensure that he had a good background in architecture before entering college. While there, Cassell helped to support himself by singing in local churches.

Studies Interrupted by Military Service

Cassell studied for two years at Cornell then joined the U.S. Army where he served in the United States and in France. After he was honorably discharged in 1919 as a second lieutenant, Cornell University conferred on him a "war degree," a privilege for students who left school to fight in World War I and who were then exempt from returning to college to complete their studies.

After receiving his degree, Cassell joined William Augustus Hazel at Tuskegee Institute (subsequently Tuskegee University) in Alabama in designing five trade buildings. In 1920 he became chief draftsman for Howard J. Wiegner in Bethlehem, Pennsylvania, designing silk mills and industrial plants. Two years later the men collaborated as architects for the Home Economics Building at Howard University, Washington, D.C.

Shapes Howard University Campus

Cassell joined the Howard architectural faculty, under Hazel's leadership, in 1920, then succeeded him in 1922 as assistant professor and head of the department. He was also named university architect. He put in place a firm foundation for developing the Department of Architecture in the School of Applied Science. Then, by 1934, he developed the School of Applied Science into the College of Engineering and Architecture.

Cassell is largely responsible for developing Howard's campus, as he created in 1920 the university's "Twenty Year Plan" (or Master Plan) for expansion and designed most of the buildings around the quadrangle. In so doing, he transformed the school's physical appearance, giving it an important visual order that had been lacking. He spent eighteen years there, working as surveyor and land manager, and guiding the institution in acquisition of properties adjacent to the campus. After the Home Economics Building (1922), he designed the gymnasium (1925), armory (1925), and College of Medicine (1927). Cassell supervised the construction of three women's residence halls named for famous women: Sojourner Truth, Prudence Crandall, and Julia Caldwell Frazier. From 1930 to 1933 he was architect and engineer for the campus, leading surveys and construction of the campus heat, light, and power requirements. Cassell headed the maintenance department from 1929 to 1932 and supervised a sizeable crew in planning alterations for the Art Gallery and School of Religion.

His Jewel: Founders Library

His most durable contributions at Howard were the Chemistry Building and the classroom building, Frederick Douglass Memorial Hall (both in 1935), and Founders Library (1938). He was architect, structural designer, and supervisor of construction and interior of these buildings. Landscape architect David A. Williston (1868-1962) was in charge of landscaping. The Georgian Revival style Founder's Library was, in fact, Cassell's crowning glory; it is an impressive architectural and educational symbol for the university. Commenting on Howard's hilltop campus, the document "Albert I. Cassell and The Founders Library" calls Founders Library "its jewel"; for many years it remained the most visible element on Howard's campus. Cassell favored the Georgian style and used it in other campus buildings to create his "visual order." He took into account Howard's hilly terrain and worked to unify the campus and overcome the natural separation that divided the campus.

For some time, however, President Mordecai Johnson and Cassell had been at odds, a feud that included what Cassell called "personal vindictiveness," and each asserted that the other was guilty of various improprieties. The controversy lasted until 1938, when Johnson fired Cassell. In response, Cassell took legal action against the university and the case ended in 1941 with a small, negotiated settlement.

Building Beyond Howard

While at Howard as well as after his departure, Cassell was architect and supervisor of construction for dozens of buildings in the District of Columbia and in neighboring states. These included buildings on other college campuses, such as women's residence halls at Virginia Union University in Richmond (1923 and 1928) and the Student Christian Center (1951), women's residence buildings (1941 and 1951), and a men's residence building (1964) at Morgan State College in Baltimore.

Elsewhere Cassell built Masonic temples, churches, a hospital, commercial buildings, and private residences. His works included Provident Hospital and Free Dispensary (1928), the Masonic Temple (1930), Odd Fellows Temples (1925 and 1932), Maryland School for Colored Girls (1936), Sollers' Point War Housing Development in Baltimore (for black and war workers and their families, 1942), and the George Washington Carver War Housing Building in Arlington (1942). He did alterations to Pilgrim African Methodist Church and St. Luke Episcopal Church Parish, both in Washington, D.C. Later in life he joined other black architects to form Cassell, Gray, & Sulton. His work with that firm included the U.S. Army Installation at the former National International Airport, alterations to the Pentagon building (1964), the Washington Diocese of the Roman Catholic Church, and municipal buildings for the District of Columbia.

Depression Era Plans for Calvert County

Cassell's interest lay also in providing economic opportunities and housing for African Americans during the Great Depression, especially for the period from 1932 to 1935. He purchased a 380-acre site on the Chesapeake Bay, in Calvert County, Maryland, with the idea of building a summer resort for blacks. It was to include a motel, shopping center, beach, marina, and other facilities. After constructing roads and several homes, he was unable to continue his "Calverton" development. There are claims that racial and political problems interfered.

Historic Mayfair Mansions

After that, in 1942, he bought the old Benning Race Track and began to construct in northeast Washington the Colonial-style Mayfair Mansions (or Mayfair Gardens), Mayfair Extension Housing Developments, and Mayfair Extension commercial facilities. Elder Lightfoot Solomon Michaux (1885-1968), who founded Washington's Church of God, was a major investor of the affordable housing project. While the War years and other causes interfered, Cassell completed the development in 1946. Although Cassell managed Mayfair Mansions and received a sizeable income, he lost major ownership of the 594 units. In 1989 Mayfair Mansions was listed on the National Register for Historic Sites.

Married three times, Cassell had three children by his first wife and four by his second. His third wife, Flora B. McClarty, was a widow with two children. Cassell suffered a heart attack and died at his home in Washington, D.C., on November 30, 1969. After funeral services held at the Washington Cathedral on December 3, he was buried in Baltimore National Cemetery. He was survived by his wife and six children.

From the beginning of his career until he died, Cassell was one of the nation's most prominent architects and engineers. He left his mark at Howard University, where he created a visual order for the campus and in the facilities that he designed or whose construction he oversaw elsewhere. His interest in providing upscale, affordable housing for middle-income blacks helped him to create an enduring legacy in Washington's black community.

REFERENCES

Books

Lebovich, William. "Albert Irvin Cassell." In *African American Architects: A Biographical Dictionary 1865-1945*, edited by Dreck Spurlock Wilson. New York: Routledge, 2004.

Logan, Rayford W., and Michael R. Winston. "Albert Irvin Cassell." In *Dictionary of American Negro Biography*, edited by Rayford W. Logan and Michael R. Winston. New York: Norton, 1982.

Robinson, Wilhelmena S. *Historical Negro Biographies*. New York: Publishers Company, under the Auspices of the Association for the Study of Negro Life and History, 1967, 172-73.

Periodicals

Dozier, Richard K. "A Historical Survey: Black Architects and Craftsmen." *Black World* 23 (May 1974): 4-15.

Online

African American Heritage Trail Database. "Mayfair Mansions/Albert Cassell." http://www/culturaltourismdc.org/infp-url3948/info-url_show.hjtm?doc_id=205000&attrib_id=7966 (Accessed 4 September 2005).

"Albert I. Cassell and The Founders Library: A Brief History." http://www/howard.edu/library/Cassell/Founders.htm (Accessed 4 September 2005).

"Manuscript Collections (A-C)." http://www/howard.edu/library/moorland-spingarn/colla-c.htm (Accessed 4 September 2005).

Collections

Cassell's papers are in the Moorland-Spingarn Research Center, Howard University, Washington, D.C.

Jessie Carney Smith

Alvin O. Chambliss
1944–

Lawyer, civil rights activist

Alvin O. Chambliss Jr. is best known for his legal work over nearly thirty years in the *Ayers v. Barbour* case, which sought to remedy inequalities rooted in past segregation of higher education in his home state of Mississippi. As a result of his involvement in what has become one of the longest running civil rights cases in history, he has been described as the last original civil rights attorney in the United States, displaying unusual stamina, commitment, and determination in pursuing justice for African Americans seeking educational opportunities in traditionally white institutions as well as equitable support of historically black colleges and universities (HBCUs).

Alvin Odell Chambers Jr. was born on January 22, 1944, in Vicksburg, Mississippi, to Ledorsha and Alvin Odell Chambliss Sr. As one of twelve children, Alvin Jr.

Chronology	
1944	Born in Vicksburg, Mississippi on January 22
1967	Earns B.A. from Jackson State University
1970	Receives J.D. from Howard University
1972	Completes master of law degree from University of California
1973	Marries Josephine Johnson on December 31
1974	Begins work with North Mississippi Rural Legal Services
1975	Becomes lead attorney for plaintiffs in *Ayers v. Fordice*
1987	Argues case April 17 to June 1; ruling for defendants on December 10
1990	Continues litigation after appeals court also rules in favor of defendants
1991	Argues case before U.S. Supreme Court
1992	Wins legal victory when U.S. Supreme Court rules for retrial of case
1994	Argues case for plaintiffs in second trial
1995	Loses job; becomes law professor at Texas Southern University
2002	Wins Trial Lawyer of the Year Award; loses job at Texas Southern
2003	Appeals $503 million Ayers case settlement as inadequate
2004	Joins faculty of Indiana University as distinguished visiting professor
2004	U.S. Supreme Court denies final appeal, ending Ayers case

grew up poor in Columbia, Mississippi, located in the south central part of the state. Despite the personal and family challenges, Alvin Jr. and his siblings were instilled with a passion for education and self-improvement by their parents and especially their grandmother, Elizabeth Chambliss, who courageously provided assistance to civil rights workers in Mississippi during the 1960s.

Another important early mentor to Chambliss was his high school principal, C. J. Duckworth, an educator who later became president of both the Mississippi Teachers Association and American Teachers Association. He inspired Chambliss, as well as many other students, to go to college and beyond, believing that education was the key to survival for blacks and minorities. As a result, 85 percent of his students went to college, trade schools, or the military upon graduation.

Pursues Higher Education

Chambliss also demonstrated athletic talent in football during his high school years and continued to play the game after graduating from Columbia High School in 1962 , becoming a star linebacker at Jackson State University. Among the hometown athletes he influenced were future Chicago Bears and National Football League Hall of Fame running back Walter Payton and his brother Eddie, who also played professionally in the NFL, after outstanding college careers at Jackson State.

During his years at Jackson State University, located in the state capitol, Chambliss was directly influenced by and involved in the turmoil and change brought about by the civil rights movement. The state became the setting for historic events such as the desegregation of the University of Mississippi by U.S. Army veteran and former Jackson State student James Meredith in 1962; the murder of Medgar Evers, Mississippi field secretary for the NAACP in 1963; and the murders of volunteer civil rights workers James Chaney, Andrew Goodman, and Michael Schwerner during what became known as the Freedom Summer of 1964. Chambliss's mentors at the time included Fannie Lou Hamer and Lawrence Guyot, leaders and organizers of the Mississippi Freedom Democratic party, which championed black voting rights and challenged the segregated Mississippi delegation to the 1964 Democratic national convention in Atlantic City, New Jersey.

After graduation from Jackson State in 1967 with a bachelor of arts degree in history, Chambliss decided to forego a possible career in professional football and applied to law school in hopes of becoming an attorney. He was admitted to the law school at Howard University in Washington, D.C., where he came in contact with such noted persons as Thurgood Marshall, the legendary civil rights attorney who became the first African American appointed as a justice on the U.S. Supreme Court, and Howard Moore, the attorney who represented champion boxer Muhammad Ali and activist Julian Bond. As a law student, Chambliss assisted Howard law professor Herbert O. Reid in the successful defense of Harlem congressman Adam Clayton Powell against charges of tax evasion.

Chambliss received the juris doctorate from Howard in 1970 then continued his legal studies at the University of California at Berkeley, where he was awarded a master's of law degree in 1972. On December 31, 1973, he married Josephine Johnson. The couple had three children, Sadarie, Alvin O. III, and Alvenia. His early professional work in law included providing legal counsel to the National Conference of Black Mayors; Operation PUSH (People United to Serve Humanity); Legal Aid Society of Alameda County, California; New Orleans Legal Assistance; and the Cohon, Jones, and Fazande law firm.

Returns to Mississippi and the Ayers Case

In 1974, Chambliss began work as an attorney for North Mississippi Rural Legal Services (NMRLS), headquartered in Oxford. The agency, supported by federal funds, eventually expanded to thirteen offices serving poor and elderly residents of thirty-nine counties in the northern portion of the state. Founded in 1966, NMRLS saw its status change to an independent non-profit corporation as a result of the creation of the national Legal Services Corporation (LSC) by the government in the same year Chambliss returned to work in his home state. During its prime years, NMRLS had a budget of over $3 million and over one hundred employees, including thirty-two lawyers.

The following year, Chambliss became the lead attorney in the Ayers case, which became a landmark in civil rights and higher education litigation. The case was originally filed against the state of Mississippi in January 1975 by Jake Ayers Sr., a civil rights activist from Glen Allan, Mississippi, on behalf of his son and twenty-one other black college students representing the African American citizens of the state.

The intent of the lawsuit was to hold the state of Mississippi accountable for past and present injustices and inequities in its publicly funded, state-supported historically black colleges and universities, as compared to its traditionally white public institutions. Chambliss argued in numerous legal briefs and court appearances that the state had an obligation to make meaningful efforts to provide substantial resources to remedy the ongoing negative impact of discriminatory policies and practices on African American citizens involved in its public higher education system.

In the early and mid-1980s, efforts to reach a comprehensive, out-of-court settlement of the case were unsuccessful. The persistence of Chambliss and others led to the case finally going to trial before the U.S. District Court for the Northern District of Mississippi in April 1987. Jake Ayers died in 1986 without seeing the case named for him go to a courtroom setting, which provided an additional incentive for Chambliss and others to continue their efforts. When the trial proceedings ended after five weeks, the attorneys, plaintiffs, and defendants waited several months for the ruling of the court. On December 10, 1987, the court decided in favor of the state of Mississippi and dismissed the case. The judge agreed with the attorneys representing the state, who argued that reasonable desegregation of public higher education had been accomplished in the twenty-five years since 1962, when the University of Mississippi admitted James Meredith as its first African American student.

Chambliss and his team immediately set in motion the process to appeal the district court decision. Even with the ongoing demands of the Ayers case, Chambliss devoted time to involvement in national politics, attending the 1988 Democratic national convention in Atlanta, Georgia, as a delegate supporting African American presidential candidate Jesse Jackson.

Appeals Ayers Case to Higher Courts

Chambliss and his legal team appealed the decision to the Court of Appeals for the Fifth Circuit, which reversed and then affirmed the decision of the U.S. District Court. They eventually filed an appeal to the U.S. Supreme Court, which rendered a decision in favor of the Ayers plaintiffs in 1992, sending the case back to the U.S. District Court. The second trial took place over ten weeks in 1994. The 1995 decision by the court favored the plaintiffs on some issues and the defendants on others, including keeping all of Mississippi's eight universities open after the state indicated it was considering the closing of Mississippi Valley State University, an HBCU, and Mississippi University for Women, a traditionally white institution. Revised admissions standards for all Mississippi universities, and improvement of academic programs and funding at Jackson State University, Alcorn State University, and Mississippi Valley State University were also included as objectives to be met by the state.

The legal victory came at great personal sacrifice, as Chambliss had virtually become bankrupt. In addition to the extensive amount of time he spent on the Ayers case, his wife became ill, he had to fight to maintain his home, and he was suspended without pay before being dismissed from his job at North Mississippi Rural Legal Services. The contention was that Chambliss had used excessive amounts of NMRLS resources on the Ayers case, to the detriment of other legal activities. It was also possible that he would not be paid for his 1,300 hours of legal work in connection with the case over twenty-one years, if the ruling in the case was not upheld.

Problems for NMRLS were further compounded in 1996, when Congress cut funding for public legal services by more than 30 percent and placed additional regulations and restrictions on the types of legal services made available to citizens with federal funds. As a result, many NMRLS colleagues of Chambliss were laid off, and the number of branch offices was reduced to five locations in later years.

Recognition for Work and Relocation to Texas

Appreciation for the hard work of Chambliss came in the form of numerous awards from such diverse organizations as the NAACP, the Southern Christian Leadership Conference (SCLC), the Mississippi Education Association, the Mississippi Legislative Black Caucus, the Prince Hall Masonic Orders of North Mississippi, and the Trial Lawyers for Public Justice. Despite these many recognitions of his efforts and abilities, he still faced financial constraints and problems in providing for his family. As a result, Chambliss was forced to make career moves which brought a level of financial stability and resolve personal challenges, while still maintaining his commitment to the Ayers case.

Chambliss accepted a position as a professor in the Thurgood Marshall School of Law at Texas Southern University in 1995 and relocated to Houston, Texas. He taught courses in civil rights enforcement, federal court practice, and appellate litigation, areas in which he had both practical and theoretical knowledge. His legal expertise was called upon in the resolution of the case involving desegregation of higher education in Texas, which led to increased funding for Texas Southern University and Prairie View A&M University, the state's two public HBCUs. In addition to this work Chambliss also represented the family of James Byrd Sr. of Jasper, Texas, the victim of a hate crime-related murder in 1998 which drew international attention and developed a street law program acclaimed by the Texas Supreme Court for involving more than forty Houston schools in its mock trial activities.

Continues to Represent Ayers Family and Rejects Case Settlement

While no longer representing the NMRLS, Chambliss continued his involvement in the case as a private attorney representing Lillie Ayers, the widow of Jake Ayers, and other plaintiffs, including professors and alumni from Mississippi HBCUs. In 1996, original plaintiff Bennie Thompson, who had become the U.S. congressman for Mississippi's second district, was designated by the district court as the lead plaintiff in the case. Chambliss was replaced as lead attorney by Isaac Byrd.

After the 1995 court ruling, Chambliss walked away from a potential $3.5 million payday in legal fees because he did not agree to a proposed settlement of the case by the state. Two years later, a second offer to settle the case for $2.5 million was also rejected by Chambliss. He indicated that both offers were payoff attempts intended to end his involvement in the case, and he continued to press for his clients.

In 2000, the district court ordered the parties involved in the case to come together and work out a settlement agreement. In addition to the plaintiffs represented by Chambliss and Byrd, the United States government was an intervenor in the case against the state of Mississippi. On March 29, 2001, all of the parties, with the exception of the plaintiffs represented by Chambliss who were not included in the settlement negotiations, signed a settlement agreement in the amount of $503 million over a period of seventeen years.

More Appeals, Challenges, and Life Changes

Chambliss filed yet another series of appeals, contesting the fairness of the settlement. In 2002, shortly after he was given the Trial Lawyer of the Year award by the Trial Lawyers for Public Justice, he was told that his contract would not be renewed at Texas Southern. He had not been negatively evaluated for his work as a professor in the law school, but his continued involvement in appealing the Ayers settlement left the impression that his dismissal may have been politically motivated. The appeals were preventing the settlement agreement from going into effect and bringing a final resolution to the case.

Chambliss contended that the settlement did not do enough to provide equal educational opportunities for African Americans in all of Mississippi's public higher education institutions. He noted that it did not provide enough funding to equalize programs, facilities, and other resources in the state's three HBCUs, and contested the designation of $246 million for the purpose of attracting white students to the HBCU campuses, which the state finally acknowledged had been neglected and under funded from the era of segregation through the last decades of the twentieth century.

In 2003, Chambliss and his new legal team presented his appeal of the case before the court of appeals in New Orleans, after overcoming such obstacles as missing court records, going through unrelated documents and paperwork included in requests for specific and pertinent information, the short timeline between preparation and presentation, and inadequate funding to support his colleagues. Several attorneys volunteered to assist Chambliss and worked nearly nonstop in the thirty days before the court hearing.

Chambliss and his colleagues were successful in their efforts, and the New Orleans hearing on November 3 drew significant national media attention when students, educators, and activists from all over the nation came to the city in support of the Ayers appeal. Despite an outstanding presentation by Chambliss, in which he argued the case citing legal documents and precedents, including the Thirteenth, Fourteenth, and Fifteenth Amendments to the Constitution of the United States, *Plessey v. Ferguson*, *Brown v. Board of Education*, and Title VI of the Civil Rights Act of 1964, the court did not reverse the settlement agreement in its January 2004 ruling. Chambliss then appealed the case to the court of last resort, the U.S. Supreme Court.

Chambliss again was forced to deal with personal, professional, and financial challenges after losing his professorship. Even though he was no longer employed at Texas Southern, he still retained ties to the institution. In May 2004 he celebrated as his son and daughter in-law became graduates of the university. Alvin III received a degree in biology, and Miriam was ranked fourth of 150 receiving the J.D. degree from the law school.

While waiting on the final appeal of the Ayers case, Chambliss was interviewed by journalists from various news media and invited to speak in a variety of settings about the case and its implications. He lectured at Indiana University, where he eventually accepted a position as distinguished visiting professor in the School of Education and Department of African American and African Diaspora Studies. In October 2004 the U.S. Supreme Court refused to hear the appeal of the Ayers settlement agreement, ending the case he had been involved with for nearly thirty years.

Alvin O. Chambliss Jr. made history through his unwavering commitment to the legal and social struggle for the educational advancement of African Americans. Paula Powell of the National Association of African American Students noted that Chambliss should be considered a hero of his times, and the publication *Black Issues in Higher Education* agreed, when it recognized him as being one of the most significant African Americans in the last one hundred years.

REFERENCES

Books

Upchurch, Thomas Adams. "Ayers Case, 112 S.Ct. 2727 (1992)." In *The Greenwood Encyclopedia of African American Civil Rights*. Ed. Charles D. Lowery and John F. Marszalek. Westport, Conn.: Greenwood Press, 2003.

York, Jennifer M., ed. *Who's Who Among African Americans*. 17th ed. Farmington Hills, Mich.: Thomson Gale, 2004.

Periodicals

Brazington, John. "Black College Lawsuit." *Philadelphia Tribune*, 22 November 1991.

Brown, Riva. "'75 Ayers Suit Officially Ends; High Court Won't Hear Appeal." , 19 October 2004.

Cannon, Carole. "Supreme Court Decision Ends Ayers Case Saga."*Mississippi Link*, 21-27 October 2004.

Covington, Artelia C. "Troubles Deepen for Education Crusader Alvin Chambliss." *New York Beacon*, 9 October 2002.

Online

Indiana University Media Relations. "Alvin Chambliss, One of the Original Civil Rights Lawyers, Joins IU Faculty." September 30, 2004. http://newsinfo.iu.edu/news/page/normal/1663.html (Accessed 13 January 2005).

McBride, Earnest. "Ayers Case Now in Hands of Fifth Circuit." *Jackson Advocate*, 2003. http://www.bjmjr.com/mcbride/ayers_case_5thcircuit.htm (Accessed 13 January 2005).

North Mississippi Rural Legal Services. "History of NMRLS." http://www.nmrls.com/History.htm (Accessed 3 February 2005).

Trial Lawyers for Public Justice. "Isaac Byrd of Mississippi, Armand Derfner of South Carolina, Bob Pressman of Massachusetts, and Alvin Chambliss of Texas Win 2002 Trial Lawyer of the Year Award." http://www.tlpj.org/pr/tloy_winner_072402.htm (Accessed 13 January 2005).

Other

Chambliss, Alvin. E-mail to author, 1 February 2005.

Fletcher F. Moon

William Calvin Chase
1854–1921

Journalist, newspaper editor, publisher, political activist

William Calvin Chase is perhaps most noted for his accomplishments as the editor and publisher of a successful nineteenth-century African American newspaper, the *Washington Bee*. August Meier aptly points out in his 1963 book, *Negro Thought in America, 1880-1915*, that the historical importance of Chase and his newspaper is the insight they provide historians of the late nineteenth- and early twentieth-century protest era. Additionally, the *Washington Bee* is a rich source for information about the African American community both within the nation's capital and elsewhere in the country. The *Bee* chronicled the political, cultural, and educational goals and achievements of the African American population. During the height of the newspaper's circulation, Washington D.C. was the center of African American political power.

Early Years

Chase's father was a prominent blacksmith from Maryland. He moved to Washington, D.C. in 1835, and by 1839 he had purchased a three-story brick home at 1109 L Street N.W. The home served as his residence and workplace and was the birthplace of his six children, including William Calvin Chase. William Chase Sr. met and married Lucinda Seaton shortly after purchasing the home. Lucinda Seaton (Chase) moved to Washington from Alexandria, Virginia. She belonged to one of the most wealthy and prestigious families in the Commonwealth of Virginia. Lucinda and William Sr. were early members of the newly established Fifteenth Street Presbyterian Church. The church was established in 1841 and the Chase family joined in 1844.

Tragically William Chase Sr. died in 1863, leaving Lucinda to raise their six children alone. Lucinda Chase reared and educated all six children as a single mother. She continued to serve the church, which attracted some of the most notable members of Washington's African American community. To her credit three of her five daughters became educators. As for William, his mother's influence on his life was equally clear.

Chase first attended John F. Cook School located in the basement of the Fifteenth Street Church. His teacher, John F. Cook, received his education at Oberlin College, which was founded by abolitionists. The impact that the school's teaching had on Chase as a young child remained with him into his adult life. Chase also attended an all white school in Methuen, Massachusetts. Upon his return to Washington, Chase enrolled in Howard University Preparatory Division. Shortly after leaving Howard, he began working towards a career in journalism, politics,

Chronology

1854	Born in Washington, D.C. on February 2
1863	Father dies
1875	Begins early career as journalist
1882	Becomes editor of the *Washington Bee*
1883	Marries Arabella V. McCabe of Virginia
1883-84	Attends Howard University School of Law
1889	Begins law practice
1893	Mother dies
1900	Becomes national delegate for the Republican National Convention
1912	Elected second time as national delegate for the Republican National Convention
1921	Becomes member of the Washington branch of the NAACP
1921	Dies in Washington, D.C. on January 3Z

and law. His background alone, as a freeborn educated African American living in one of the socially prominent areas of the country, provided opportunities for him that were not shared by his largely enslaved, poor, and uneducated counterparts. Thus, he was able to become involved in journalism. He found that working for the black press provided leadership opportunities as well as exposure into the business world. Before joining the *Washington Bee*, Chase worked for the *Boston Observer*, the *Boston Cooperator*, and the *Washington Plain Dealer*.

Although he returned to Howard and enrolled in the law school in 1883-84, Chase did not complete the law degree. While a student at Howard University, Chase married Arabella V. McCabe, a Virginia native who had moved to Washington with her parents in 1871. After Chase left Howard he continued reading law and successfully passed the exam and was admitted to the bar in Virginia as well as Washington, D.C. in 1889. Chase was able to establish a law practice located at 503 D Street, NW. Nannie Helen Burroughs, black educator and leader of Baptist women, served as his first law clerk for several years.

Political Activism and the *Washington Bee*

For its forty years the *Washington Bee*'s motto read "Honey for Friends, Stings for Enemies." The line sums up Chase's approach as an editor, politician, and critic. Chase became the editor of the *Washington Bee* two months after its founding, and he remained the editor and publisher for the next forty years. Initially the *Washington Bee*'s office was in Chase's parent's home. The *Bee* began as a four-page weekly paper. Between 1895 and 1922 the paper was broadened to eight pages only to provide greater opportunity for advertisement. Chase's primary concern for the paper rested on political and social events in the nation and in the District of Columbia. In a 1914 editorial Chase proclaimed that African American newspapers respected the tradition of protest that had been espoused in the earliest press and remained a value in the early twentieth century. He credited the protest tradition with influencing the contemporary organizations of the day, such as the NAACP.

More importantly, Chase used his paper to raise the nation's awareness about racial violence, such as lynching and race riots. He was very critical of the federal government for its tacit consent to such violence. Although Chase was member of the Republican Party and used his newspaper to support the Republican agenda of the day, he did not hesitate to "sting" political leaders who were also a part of the party. From 1888 to 1920, Chase repeatedly sought to be a national delegate for the Republican National Convention. He was successful in 1900 and in 1912. In keeping with his philosophy, he continued to criticize the government for refusing to uphold the Fifteenth Amendment. He used the front pages of the newspaper to bring attention to race riots in Hemphill, Texas in 1908; Coatesville, Pennsylvania in 1911; East St. Louis, Illinois in 1917; and Washington, D.C. in 1919. Chase criticized President Woodrow Wilson and his administration for expanding segregation in federal offices.

Through the *Bee* Chase also launched attacks against certain African American organizations, intellectuals, and political leaders. He was critical of organizations such as the Afro-American League, the Afro-American Council, the Niagara Movement, and the NAACP. Chase believed many of these organizations were elitist and failed to represent most African Americans. He criticized Booker T. Washington for his accommodating views. Chase was unimpressed with journalist T. Thomas Fortune's leadership of the Afro-American League and the Council. Chase also opposed W. E. B. Dubois's leadership of the Niagara Movement (1905-10) and of the NAACP during its early years. In his last year as editor, however, Chase became a member of the Washington branch of the NAACP, and the NAACP in turn placed advertisements in the *Washington Bee*. The financial support silenced the *Bee* for awhile, particularly during the short-lived period of the Niagara Movement.

Chase also objected to back-to-Africa movements. Neither Edward Blyden nor Henry McNeil Turner received any favor from Chase for their back-to-Africa ideology. On the issue of Marcus Garvey and his Universal Negro Improvement Association, Chase and the *Washington Bee* remained silent. Perhaps in light of the wide appeal of Garvey and his organization, Chase believed his criticism would have been ineffective. Since Chase considered himself a race man and advocate for the masses he avoided losing favor with the very group he claimed to support.

Washington Bee Makes Final Run

A thorough examination of William Calvin Chase and the *Washington Bee* offers a detailed account of the African American middle-class urban community at the beginning of the twentieth century. Chase was criticized as self-interested, but he was willing to protest against violence and discrimination suffered by African Americans. Chase used the press to express his opinions regarding issues that mattered most to the African American community.

The *Washington Bee* was published weekly from 1882 to 1922. During this period it was the oldest black secular newspaper in the United States with continuous publication. Chase served as its editor until his death in 1921. Even in his final hour Chase worked on his last editorial for the news. He was found dead at his desk on January 3, 1921. Following his death, his son attempted to keep the newspaper afloat. For one year he successfully managed to operate the newspaper. The *Washington Bee* ceased publication in 1922.

REFERENCES

Books

Meier, August. *Negro Thought in America, 1880-1915: Racial Ideologies in the Age of Booker T. Washington.* Ann Arbor, Mich.: University of Michigan Press, 1963.

Periodicals

"Calvin Chase 'Bee' Editor Laid to Rest." *Baltimore Afro American*, 12 January 1921.

Chase, Hal. "William C. Chase and the *Washington Bee*." *Negro History Bulletin* 36 (1973): 172-74.

Dissertation

Chase, Hal Scripps. "Honey For Friends, Stings for Enemies: William Calvin Chase and the *Washington Bee*." Ph.D. diss., University of Pennsylvania, 1973.

Baiyina W. Muhammad

Robert Churchwell
1917–

Journalist

In 1950, Robert Churchwell became the first African American journalist on the *Nashville Banner*, a Southern daily newspaper. A 1949 graduate of Fisk University, he was hired by the paper's publisher, James Geddes Stahlman. Regarding the job with the *Banner*, people told him that he would be like Jackie Robinson, the

Chronology

1917	Born in Clifton, Tennessee on September 9
1942	Drafted in the United States Army
1946	Honorably discharged from the United States Army
1949	Graduates from Fisk University with B.A. in English
1950	Accepts position at the *Nashville Banner*, becoming the first African American journalist to work for a white newspaper in the South
1951	Marries Mary Elizabeth Buckingham of Bell Buckle, Tennessee in June
1955	Given a desk in the *Banner*'s newsroom
1974	Receives TEA's School Bell Award for the *Banner* for outstanding contributions to the interpretation of issues facing public schools
1981	Retires from the *Banner*, receives an award from the Nashville Chapter of the NAACP for achievements in print journalism and for contributions to the community
1994	Made a charter member of the National Association of Black Journalists; inducted into the association's region VI Hall of Fame
1996	Honored with wife as one of five Middle Tennessee families chosen for the Family of the Year
2002	Nashville Public Library honors Churchwell for his work as a reporter for the *Nashville Banner*; Churchwell's lifetime collection of newspapers and personal papers added to Emory University's Special Collection Department
2003	National Visionary Leadership Project honors Churchwell for his pioneering efforts in journalism

African American, who broke baseball's color line three years earlier. Because the *Banner* was considered the organ of the Old South, the antithesis of everything that Churchwell believed, he was not excited about accepting the appointment. For the first five years of Churchwell's employment as a *Banner* reporter, the paper's editor and publisher, who adhered to the South's code of racial separation, barred him from sitting in the newsroom. Churchwell wrote his news stories at home and carried them to the *Banner*'s office every day. During the 1960s, he covered the civil rights movement in Nashville. Because he carried the torch for future African American journalists, Churchwell earned the soubriquet, "the Jackie Robinson of Journalism."

Born on September 9, 1917 in the West Tennessee town of Clifton, Robert Churchwell was one of Jesse and Johnnie Churchwell's six children (two girls and four boys). Before moving to Nashville, Tennessee, the family lived in Muscle Shoals, Alabama. After moving to Nashville, to support the family, the father, a strict disciplinarian, worked for the Louisville and Nashville Railroad Company and as an auto mechanic. Churchwell's maternal grandparents lived in Nashville, where his maternal grandfather served as a Methodist minister. Adhering to the segregated arrangement of the city and the southern region, the Churchwells reared their children in an all-black neighborhood in southeast Nashville and sustained themselves

in that world within a world. Churchwell attended Cameron Junior High School where he played football, and he attended a Baptist and Methodist church in the neighborhood. In 1935, because there was only one high school for African Americans in Nashville, Churchwell attended Pearl Senior High School, where he played center position on the school's football team. He dropped out of high school for two years, but graduated from Pearl Senior High School in 1940.

A year after Churchwell finished high school, the United States found itself embroiled in World War II. He was drafted in 1942. Called up for a tour of duty in the U.S. Army, he underwent basic training camp in Ft. Belvoir in Virginia and then became a part of an engineering battalion. A non-combat soldier, Churchwell went to England, France, Holland, Germany, Belgium, and the Philippines.

Enters Fisk University

Four months after World War II ended (September 2, 1945), platoon staff sergeant Robert Churchwell was honorably discharged. The following month, with assistance from the G.I. Bill, he entered Fisk University, where he majored in English. During his first semester, the effects of having served in the war's European and Asian theaters began to manifest themselves. Although he sought medical attention from physicians at Nashville's Veterans Administration (VA) Hospital, he was repeatedly told his problem was unconnected to his military experience. Holding steadfastly to their declaration, VA physicians never changed their medical opinion and never examined Churchwell.

Refusing to give in to his bout with depression, Churchwell stayed at Fisk and completed the requirements for his degree. Attending the university in the 1940s exposed him to many personalities of the Harlem Renaissance, including Arna Bontemps, Aaron Douglas, and Charles S. Johnson, editor of the Urban League's *Opportunity* magazine and the first African American president of Fisk University (1946). It was during his college days that his desire to become a writer became clear. By attending summer school at Tennessee Agricultural and Industrial State College (or A&I, now Tennessee State University), Churchwell completed his studies at Fisk University in less than four years and earned his B.A. degree in English.

Unemployed and without funds from the G.I. Bill, Churchwell started a news magazine called *Yours*, with friends Fred Booth and James Nall. He gained some experience as a writer by contributing columns without compensation for the *Commentator*, a local tabloid-size paper published for the African American community. Although the three men were supposed to be in the business together, Churchwell served as the writer, editor, and advertising manager. However, because of the lack of sales, *Yours* lasted for only about eight weeks and after that forced its owners into bankruptcy. Again, without a means of financial support, Churchwell sat at home temporarily unemployed.

Becomes Nashville's First African American Journalist

In 1950, Churchwell received a telephone call from Coyness Ennix, an African American attorney and president of the Solid Block Organization, a civic group organized to get African Americans to the voting booth. Considered by many as one of the most influential political leaders in Nashville's African American community, Ennix received a call from officials of the *Nashville Banner*, the city's daily evening newspaper, seeking a reporter. The paper's publisher, James Geddes Stahlman, an avowed segregationist, wanted to hire a black reporter to cover black news because the paper suffered decreased circulation and was all but nonexistent in the African American community. Newspaper executives thought they could boost revenue if they attracted African American readers, especially if they and their community were covered in the *Nashville Banner*, Nashville's oldest and most conservative paper that sanctioned segregationist ideals of the Old South. Concern about the paper's profit line brought Stahlman to the decision to hire an African American reporter full-time. The task of implementing the publisher's mandate was given to Charles Moss, the paper's executive editor.

Moss turned to Ennix, explaining that the *Nashville Banner* wanted to report progressive news in the African American community. Attorney Ennix approved of the paper's so-called policy shift and agreed to search for a person to fill the position. Later, Ennix called Churchwell. Churchwell disapproved of the publisher's position on race matters. Stahlman's hegemonic attitude permeated the paper but was especially explicit in his own column, "From the Shoulder," which criticized public officials, politicians, and organizations among others, who objected to the separate-but-equal edict, especially in the South. The paper gave top priority to stories that maligned blacks as second-class citizens. Stahlman's views, which the *Banner* mirrored, were antithetical to Churchwell's viewpoint and values.

Although he had almost decided against accepting the *Banner* offer, Churchwell agreed to meet with Ennix and L. J. Gunn. Because he was unemployed and insolvent, Churchwell, without a topcoat, walked to Ennix's downtown office. The men argued for awhile, then Ennix and Gunn convinced Churchwell to agree. Approximately three days after the meeting with Ennix and Gunn, Moss offered Robert Churchwell the position as a staff reporter for the *Nashville Banner*, at $35 per week, which he accepted, thus breaking the South's journalism color line.

Hired to write on how African Americans were doing in their own community, Churchwell did not even own a typewriter or, for that matter, know how to type. He bor-

rowed a typewriter from a former high school teacher, and after he printed the stories out for her, his sister typed them. Although an employee of the *Banner*, during Churchwell's first five years of employment, Moss never assigned him a desk in the newsroom. Churchwell covered activity in the African American community: the boy and girl Scouts, the YMCA and the YWCA, the city's four African American institutions of higher education (American Baptist Theological Seminary, Fisk University, Meharry Medical College, and Tennessee A & I State College), businesses, the Masonic and Elk Lodges, and the churches. To make his 8:00 a.m. copy deadline, Churchwell's day began at 3:00 a.m. The newly assigned reporter walked from his home in southeast Nashville to the *Banner* office on Broadway, to give his copy to Moss rather than the city editor.

In June 1951, Churchwell married Mary Elizabeth Buckingham of Bell Buckle, Tennessee. They became the parents of Robert Jr., Andre, twins Kevin and Keith, and Marisa.

In 1954, when the U.S. Supreme Court handed down its *Brown v. Board of Education* decision, the *Banner* gave Churchwell the assignment of covering education throughout the city, including the Nashville Board of Education and white institutions of higher education. While still covering the African American community, Churchwell also covered the Parent Teachers Association and the Tennessee Education Association. A year later, Churchwell was given a desk in the paper's newsroom. Despite the era's social code, from the beginning a few reporters on the *Banner* staff went out of their way to be nice to Churchwell. As far as Churchwell was concerned, however, the *Banner* city room remained filled with those who shared the publisher's sentiment. Although he desegregated the paper's newsroom, including the men's room and the water fountain, Churchwell in the early days never felt a part of those who worked for the paper. There were no friendly lunches with co-workers and he and his wife were never invited to the annual Christmas party, which was held at a local segregated private club. Churchwell received a check to cover the cost of dinner somewhere else until the early 1970s, when staffers agreed that the custom was no longer acceptable.

Perhaps one of the biggest stories to emerge during Churchwell's early tenure at the *Nashville Banner* was the protest against segregated lunch counters launched by student activists. Because such demonstrations challenged the *Banner*'s mission, its reporters were prohibited from covering the students' protest. However, as a part of his ongoing coverage of the African American community, Churchwell attended mass meetings held throughout the community almost every night. Although he covered the Nashville sit-in movement and wrote stories on it, they never appeared in print. The paper refused to carry any news of a major struggle for African American civil rights.

By the 1970s, almost two decades after Churchwell joined the *Banner* staff, white colleagues began to respect his reporting acumen, especially as an education reporter. In 1972, the Gannett Corporation purchased the *Banner*, and many felt that the acquisition signaled its transition to a more racially tolerant position. However, as the veteran reporter continued his work with the paper, Churchwell did not witness any change connected to him personally. Even with the change in the paper's ownership, Churchwell, unlike the younger reporters, did not advance. According to A. Tacuma Roeback of the *Tennessean*, during his final two years at the *Banner*, Churchwell said "he went from educational reporter to writing obituaries and compiling the stock market report."

Retires from the *Nashville Banner*

Churchwell retired from the *Nashville Banner* on September 10, 1981. For more than three decades of service, he received a wristwatch, $2,000 and a cake. After retirement, Churchwell worked for Tennessee State University in its Bureau of Public Relations. Because of his experience in the media and his familiarity with TSU's program, Churchwell was appointed as its interim director in 1982.

Irby Simpkins, the new *Banner* publisher, offered Churchwell a consultant position in 1987, but Churchwell was not interested. Eight years later, when the National Association of Black Journalists (NABJ) held its convention in Nashville, *Banner* officials asked Churchwell to write a history of black journalism. The following year, in 1996, he began writing a monthly op-ed column. The paper had changed, but it only continued to operate another two years.

In 1965, Churchwell became the first African American member of the Middle Tennessee Chapter of Sigma Delta Chi (now known as the Society of Professional Journalists), a society in which he served as chapter vice president in 1969. A founding member of the NABJ and the Nashville Press Club, Churchwell was inducted into the NABJ's Hall of Fame in 1994.

Robert Churchwell paved the way for other young African American reporters to enter newsrooms of Southern newspapers. The recipient of numerous awards and honors for his outstanding service as a reporter, Churchwell knew the tribulation of being the first African American journalist in Nashville struggling to report and reporting the struggles within the confines of the Jim Crow South.

REFERENCES

Books

Conkin, Paul K. *Gone with the Ivy: A Biography of Vanderbilt University*. Knoxville: University of Tennessee Press, 1985.

Cosby, Camille O., and Renee Poussaint, eds. *Legendary African American Elders Speak: A Wealth of Wisdom*. New York: Atria Book, 2004.

Halberstam, David. *The Children*. New York: Random House. 1998.

Periodicals

"5 Midstate Families Win Awards for Strengths and Achievements." *Nashville Banner*, 22 October 1996.

"*Banner* Gets TEA Award." *Nashville Banner*, 5 April 1974.

"Churchwell Appointed TSU Interim PR Chief." *Nashville Banner*, 2 September 1983.

Embry, Pat. "Churchwell Blazed Trail at *Banner*." *Nashville Banner*, 21 July 1996.

Hance, Bill. "Pioneer at *Banner*: Veteran Newsman Robert Churchwell Retires." *Nashville Banner*, 10 September 1981.

"Nashville Young Adults to Honor *Banner* Writer." *Nashville Banner*, 15 February 1969.

Pride, Dana. "Pioneer Black Journalist Set for Hall of Fame." *Nashville Banner*, 11 March 1994.

Roeback, A. Tacuma. "Beyond the Byline." *Tennessean*, 7 April 2002.

Wadhwani, Anita. " Pioneering Black Reporter Churchwell to Be Honored." *Tennessean*, 9 October 2003.

Collections

The Churchwell Biography file is held in the Nashville Room of the Nashville Public Library. The Churchwell Papers are held in the Special Collections Department of Emory University in Atlanta, Georgia.

Linda T. Wynn

Alexander Clark
1826–1891

Lawyer, newspaper publisher, orator

Inheriting the genius of his emancipated slave father and African mother, Alexander Clark Sr. embarked on a career path that took him all over the world engaging in social and political justices.

Clark's father was freed by his Irish master and his mother was an African. They were political and social activists, often taking in fugitive slaves. At the age of thirteen, Clark moved to Cincinnati, Ohio for one year to study. At the same time, under the watchful eye of his uncle, William Darnes, Clark mastered the barber trade. Two years later Clark decided to go south for a year, landing a job as a bartender on the steamer *George Washington*. Years later, Clark sold firewood to the steamboats. In 1842, Clark's journey took him to Muscatine, Iowa. At the age of sixteen and for many years to follow, he operated a successful barbershop. With the success of his barbershop, Clark soon began to invest in real estate where he managed to acquire a small fortune.

On October 8, 1848 at the age of twenty-two, Alexander Clark was married to Catherine Griffin, a twenty-three-year-old former slave. Alexander and Catherine became prominent in Iowa. The union produced five children: John and Ellen, who died in infancy; Rebecca in 1850; Susan in 1855, and Alexander Jr. in 1858. Iowa's state founders believed that all men were entitled to freedom, but the law did not allow Negro children to attend public schools. The Clarks' home-schooled their children. In 1867, at the age of twelve, Susan was denied admission to Iowa's Muscatine public school no. 2. This event led to Alexander Clark Sr. filing a lawsuit in 1868; the Iowa Supreme Court held that separate was not equal and ordered Susan Clark, an African American, to be admitted to the Muscatine public schools. This lawsuit occurred ninety-six years before the historic *Brown v. the Board of Education* in Topeka. In 1879, Alexander Clark Jr. became the first African American to graduate from the University of Iowa's College of Law. Five years later, Alexander Clark Sr. became the second African American to do so.

Achieves in Military and Political Life

Prior to Clark, African Americans did not play an important part in Iowa history or politics. Clark, a cham-

pion of racial equality and social justice, held key positions in various organizations. In 1868 when the Iowa legislature considered eliminating the word "white" from its constitution, Clark delivered a speech, asking for the right to vote for African Americans, using the platform of the black men's service in the military and the sacrifices they made. The general assembly adopted amendments that were ratified by popular vote and proclaimed part of Iowa constitution on December 8, 1868. The momentous decision advanced the cause for equality between whites and African Americans in Iowa two years before the adoption of the Fifteenth Amendment of the U.S. Constitution.

In 1863, Clark enlisted in Iowa's first colored volunteer infantry; however, a defect in his left ankle prohibited him from military combat. Nevertheless, he held the rank of sergeant-major and was an active recruiter for the Union forces. As a recruiter, Clark worked hard for the interest of the colored infantry. As a delegate from Iowa, in 1869 he was appointed chairman of the committee to lay before the Senate and House of Representatives equity claims of black soldiers to ensure they received equal pensions and bounties to those which white soldiers received. As spokesperson for this committee, Clark was also the person who conveyed congratulations on behalf of black people to President Ulysses S. Grant and vice-president Colfax on their election. Although Clark lived in the North, he was aware of the turmoil that tormented black people in the South. An unwavering Republican, Clark urged other members of his race to stand by the party. Because of his dedication, in 1869 he was elected vice-president of the Iowa state Republican convention. A year later, he was appointed a delegate to the Republican convention. Despite being devoted to the party, Clark, in 1873, declined President Grant's invitation to be appointed consul to Aux Cayes, Haiti because the salary was too low.

In 1849, Clark along with three other men founded Muscatine's African Methodist Episcopal Church. For more than twenty-five years Clark served as a trustee and Sunday school superintendent. Clark often attended the church's general conferences. In 1881, he served as a lay delegate to the Methodist Ecumenical Conference in London. Clark's religious affiliation complimented his Masonic membership. In 1851, he joined the Prince Hall Lodge No 1 in St. Louis. In 1868, he was elected deputy grand master of the Grand Lodge of Missouri.

Life as a Lawyer, Editor, and Consular General

After graduating from the University of Iowa College of Law in 1884, Alexander Clark practiced law for a while in Muscatine and then opened a law office in Chicago. Also, Clark became a partner in the weekly newspaper, the *Chicago Conservator*. He later became the sole owner and editor of the paper. Clark used the *Conservator* to voice the protests of black people.

Clark was well known as an orator. To many blacks and fraternal brothers of the Masons, Alexander Clark was known as the "Colored Orator of the West." His eloquence as orator comes through in his writing in the *Conservator*. The *Conservator* had an audience of approximately 1,200 readers who were aware of Clark's objection to the Supreme Court decisions of 1883 that denied blacks from using public accommodations as private citizens. Clark often criticized then-President Rutherford B. Hayes for his stand on issues that limited blacks. After Clark sold the *Conservator* in 1889, he divided his time between Chicago and Muscatine.

In 1890, Clark accepted President Harrison's appointment as consul-general to the Republic of Liberia. Clark served in this capacity for a short period. Word came seven months after he took the position that Clark had died in Monrovia of a fever. His remains were returned to Muscatine where a state funeral was attended by local and national dignitaries. Alexander Clark was buried in Muscatine, Iowa, along side his wife Catherine and the two children who had died in infancy.

Alexander Clark and Catherine Griffin Clark are still remembered in Iowa. Pamela Nosek's "Historical Detective Work," in the *Iowa Griot* recounts the lives of Alexander and Catherine Griffin Clark. In 1975, the Clarks' home was moved from Third and Chestnut Street to 211 West Third Street; it was refurnished to illustrate the style in which the Clarks' lived and then opened as a museum. Efforts of the AME church of Muscatine led the mayor of Muscatine to proclaim February 25 as Alexander G. Clark Sr. Day.

REFERENCES

Books

Davis, Aldeen L. "Alexander G. Clark." In *Dictionary of American Negro Biography*. Eds. Rayford W. Logan and Michael R. Winston. New York: Norton, 1982.

Simmons, Rev. William J. *Men of Mark: Eminent, Progressive, and Rising*. New York: Arno Press, 1968.

Periodicals

Jackson, Marilyn. "Alexander Clark: A Rediscovered Black Leader." *The Iowan* (Spring 1975): 43-49.

Nosek, Pamela. "Historical Detective Work: The Story of Alexander and Catherine Clark." *The Iowa Griot* 4 (Winter 2004): 4-5.

Padgett, James A. "Ministers to Liberia and Their Diplomacy." *The Journal of Negro History* 22 (January 1937): 50-92.

Annie Malessia Payton

John Henrik Clarke
1915–1998

Historian, writer, educator

Black Nationalist, Pan-Africanist, writer, and historian John Henrik Clarke is a part of a generation of African American scholars devoted to the restoration of African history and African peoples from limited, distorted, and racist characterizations. He is known as one of the most significant contributors to the development of African and African American studies in American colleges and universities during the post-civil rights era.

John Henrik Clarke was born on January 1, 1915 to Will Ella Mayes Clark and John Clark in Union Springs, Alabama. Clarke was born John Henry Clark; he altered his name by adding an "e" to his last name and changing his middle name to Henrik in honor of Henrik Ibsen, a playwright whom Clarke admired. Clarke's parents were sharecroppers. In his oral autobiography, recorded by Barbara Adams, Clarke explains that his family was nurturing and supportive of the children. With hopes of making more money, his father decided to move his family to Columbus, Georgia. In Columbus, Clarke's mother worked as a washerwoman and his father worked in a brick yard. Clarke had two siblings, Mary and Nathaniel. Clarke's mother died of pellagra, a disease caused by deficiency of niacin, which was not curable at the time. About a year later, his father married again. His father and stepmother had three additional children. In his oral autobiography, Clarke refers to the woman his father married only as his stepmother. Clarke explained that his stepmother informed him often, "I married your father, but I am not your mother." Finding his home life intolerable, at the age of fourteen Clarke moved out of his father's home. Clarke indicates that his mother's other children soon left his father's house, too. He moved into a boarding school run by Rosa Lee Brown who was supportive of Clarke.

Harlem: An Unconventional Education

While Clarke's intellectual and creative potential were recognized by his teachers, poverty and circumstance did not permit him to complete high school. He left school in the eighth grade to work. In 1933, he and his friend James Holmes left for New York. When they arrived in Harlem, they had difficulty finding a place to live and work. But their circumstances changed when they met a man named George Victor. Victor was a communist and recruited Clarke and his friend to become members of the Lower East Side's Young Communist League. Clarke's affiliation with the communist organization gave him a number of contacts and allowed him to further his education by exposing him to new ideas and books. However,

Chronology	
1915	Born in Union Springs, Alabama on January 1
1919	Family moves to Columbus, Georgia
1929	Leaves father's house and moves into boarding house
1933	Arrives in Harlem
1941	Serves in the United States Army
1949	Works as an administrator at the New School for Social Research in New York City
1956	Works as both a student and a teacher at the New School for Social Research; establishes Center for African Studies at the New School for Social Research
1958	Travels to West Africa
1961	Marries Eugenia Evans
1962	Teaches adult continuing education at Malverne High School in Malverne, New York
1966	Publishes anthology, *Black American Short Stories, a Century of the Best*
1969	Accepts position as lecturer at Hunter College in New York City; establishes the Department of Black and Puerto Rican Studies at Hunter
1970-73	Works as a visiting professor in African Studies and Research Center at Cornell University in Ithaca, New York; promoted to associate professor at Hunter College; publishes *Slave Trade and Slavery* with Vincent Harding
1985	Retires from Hunter College
1991	Publishes lectures with Dr. Yosef Ben-Jochannan; publishes *Africans at the Crossroads*
1992	Earns B.A. from Pacific Western University in Los Angeles, California
1993	Publishes *African People in World History*, publishes *Christopher Columbus and the Afrikan Holocaust*
1994	Earns Ph.D. from Pacific Western University in Los Angeles, California
1997	Marries Sybil Williams
1998	Dies in New York City on July 16

Clarke eventually split with the communists over the issue of race. Clarke's first loyalty was to his race and his communist friends believed this to be a problem.

While Clarke worked as a dishwasher, he also participated in various educational clubs. As a member of a history club, he was in contact with well known scholars such as John Jackson and Willis Huggins. Black leaders and scholars, including the first president of independent Ghana, Kwame Nkrumah, visited the club. During this time, Clarke was mentored by scholar and librarian Arthur Schomburg. In 1931, Clarke was impressed by one of Schomburg's essays, "The Negro Digs Up His Past," and he was encouraged by this essay to meet Schomburg, which he did in 1934. At the time Schomburg was the librarian in charge of special collections at the 135th Street branch of New York City Public Libraries (which would later become the Schomburg Center for Research in Black Culture). Conversations with Schomburg gave Clarke a strong foundation for

continuing his studies in history. Arthur Schomburg died in 1938, but Clarke continued his studies of history.

From 1941 to 1945, Clarke served in the army and was successful in administrative duties. After returning to New York, he married the mother of his first child, a daughter who eventually died. The couple had difficulties and soon divorced. Despite these personal problems, however, Clarke continued to grow intellectually.

During the late 1940s, Clarke taught African and African American history at various community centers in Harlem. In 1949, he worked as an administrator for the New School for Social Research. In 1956, he began teaching at the New School. From 1958 to 1959, Clarke traveled through West Africa, spending a good portion of his time in Ghana. He met Kwame Nkrumah, who remembered Clarke from the history club in New York. Nkrumah offered him a job working for the newspaper, *The Evening News*. He also lectured in Africa at various places, including the University of Ibadan in Nigeria and at the University of Ghana.

Scholar, Educator, Advocate for Black Studies

When he returned to the United States, Clarke was certified to teach, obtaining a license from the People's College in Malverne, New York. In 1961, he married Eugenia Evans, a teacher. Clarke and Evans had two children: a daughter, Nzinga Marie, and a son Sonni Kojo. In 1964, Clarke accepted a position as director of the Heritage Teaching Program for the Harlem Youth-Associated Community Teams. He taught African and African American history in the Head Start Training Program at New York University in Manhattan. During this time, Clarke also worked as an associate editor for *Freedomways* magazine. While he had published numerous short stories, including his most famous, "The Boy Who Painted Christ Black," during this time he began to publish books on African and African American studies. He edited and published an anthology of African American short stories in 1966, *Black American Short Stories: A Century of the Best*. He also published several books on African history, including *Malcolm X: The Man and His Time* (1969), *Slave Trade and Slavery*, a book co-edited with historian Vincent Harding in 1970, and the anthology *Harlem Voices* (1970).

In the 1960s, Clarke was widely recognized as an authority in the field of African history. His books and articles on African and African American history and social issues in journals and magazines added to his reputation. In 1969, he accepted a position as lecturer at Hunter College in New York City. He helped to establish the Department of Black and Puerto Rican Studies at Hunter. In 1970, he was promoted to associate professor at Hunter College. In addition to teaching at Hunter College, from 1970 to 1973, he was a visiting professor in the Africana Studies and Research Center at Cornell University in Ithaca, New York.

In 1985, Clarke retired from Hunter College, but he continued to lecture on African history in the United States and aboard. In 1991, Yosef Ben-Jochannan, an African-centered historian, and Clarke published a collection of their lectures given in London. Clarke also published *African People at the Crossroads* (1991). In 1993 he published *Christopher Columbus and the Afrikan Holocaust* in which he argues that Columbus Day should not be celebrated. Also in 1993, he published *African People in World History.*

Clarke had taught courses in African and African American history; had helped to establish black studies programs, departments, and research centers on at least three college campuses; and had published extensively on black history and on social issues. But he did not have a high school diploma, an undergraduate degree, or an advanced degree. In 1992, this changed when Clarke earned his bachelor's degree from Pacific Western University in Los Angeles, California, and in 1994 he earned his doctorate from the same university. In 1997, Clarke married for a third time, this time to Sybil Williams. Clarke suffered a heat attack and died on July 16, 1998; he was 83.

In November 2000, the New York City Council renamed Harlem's 137th Street Dr. John Henrik Clarke Place. Students, scholars, and activists are indebted to Clarke for his life of service and commitment to African studies.

REFERENCES

Books

Adams, Barbara Eleanor, and John Henrik Clarke. *John Henrik Clarke: The Early Years.* Hampton, Va.: United Brothers and Sisters Communications, 1992.

"John Henrik Clarke." *Contemporary Black Biography.* Vol. 20. Farmington Hills, Mich.: Gale Group, 1998.

Periodicals

Clarke, John Henrik. "The Influence of Arthur Schomburg on My Concept of Africana Studies" *Phylon* 49 (Spring 1992): 4-9.

Harris, Robert L. "In Memoriam: Dr. John Henrik Clarke, 1915-1998." *Journal of Negro History* 83 (Autumn 1998): 311-12.

Kelley, Robin D. G. "Self-Made Angry Man." *New York Times Magazine* (3 January 1999): 17-19.

Thomas, Robert. "John Henrik Clarke, Black Studies Advocate, Dies at 83." *New York Times*, 20 July 1998.

Collections

Clarke's papers are available at the Arthur Schomburg Center for Research; the Africana Studies Center at Cornell University in Ithaca, New York; and at the Woodruff Library in Atlanta, Georgia.

Rebecca Dixon

Sean Combs
1969–

Rap musician, record producer, actor

Sean J. Combs, an international music mogul and celebrity, is the founder and CEO of Bad Boy Worldwide Entertainment Group, which is comprised of a variety of businesses, including recording, artistic management, music publishing, television production, film production, marketing, advertising, apparel, and restaurants. Combs' extraordinary accomplishment as a record executive and producer have helped popularize rap as well as hip-hop music; Bad Boy Records, which dominated the music charts in the 1990s, remained in the early 2000s one of urban America's most successful record labels. In addition to producing and recording the music of his generation, Combs popularized the Sean John clothing line, which reflects his ability to appeal to both hip-hop culture and mainstream society.

Combs was born on November 4, 1969 in Harlem to Melvin Combs, a board of education worker and cab driver, and his wife, Janice. When Combs was two years old, his father died. Combs believed that his father was killed in an automobile accident until at the age of fourteen, his research at the public library revealed that his father had been murdered in Central Park. In 1972, the same year as his father's death, Combs participated in a fashion show that was staged by his mother at a day-care center. A member of the audience was a Baskin-Robbins executive and hired Combs to appear in a print ad. Combs, commenting on his early years, recalled in an April 1998 *Ebony* article, "I didn't have a messed-up childhood. I had a beautiful childhood . . . I didn't have a father, but I had love. My mother was always there, making sure things were great for me, and I had my grandmother [Jessie Smalls] who did the same."

His mother worked a variety of jobs, including teaching and modeling in order to support Combs and his younger sister, Keisha. From 1970 to 1982, Combs lived in Harlem. As early as twelve years old, he would sneak out at night in order to see such rap pioneers as Run-D.M.C., KRS-One, and Grandmaster Flash. Also, when Combs was twelve years old, the family moved to a home that his mother purchased in Mount Vernon, New York. Combs, who had previously attended the Saint

Sean Combs

Charles Borromeo School in New York, attended the Mount Vernon Montessori School; an after-school program in Harlem; and the Mount Saint Michael Academy, an all-male Catholic school in the Bronx, New York.

Combs, eager to help his mother financially, was prohibited from delivering newspapers because he had not reached the minimum age requirement of thirteen. Combs made a deal with the teenager who had the local paper route and who was about to relinquish the job because he was college bound; Combs took over the route, and although he gave half of his earnings to his predecessor, the job was still quite profitable for the twelve year old. He later worked at Playland Park in Rye, New York, where he sometimes worked double shifts at a restaurant. By the time Combs graduated from Saint Michael, he had danced in music videos by Babyface, the Fine Young Cannibals, Doug E. Fresh, and Stacy Lattisaw.

Combs acquired the "Puffy" nickname during his high school years. According to some sources, Combs, who was a member of Mount Saint Michael's football team, would puff out his chest in order to appear more threatening to the opposing team; other sources state Combs gained the nickname because of his temper.

Works at Uptown Records

After Combs graduated from high school in 1988, he attended Howard University where he majored in busi-

ness administration, ran a shuttle service to the airport, promoted concerts as well as parties, and sold T-shirts and sodas. Combs attended Howard for two years.

Combs' friend from Mount Vernon, Dwight Myers, was known in the music industry as Heavy D; and his group Heavy D and the Boys recorded for the New York-based Uptown records, a subsidiary of MCA. Heavy D recommended Combs to Andre Harrell, Uptown's founder and president, and Combs was offered an unpaid internship at the company in 1990. Combs spent months commuting via Amtrak from Washington to New York each weekend to work at Uptown, and sometimes he sneaked on the train because he could not pay the fare. Harrell, who was Combs' mentor, described him in *A Family Affair: The Unauthorized Sean "Puffy" Combs Story* as "the hardest-working intern ever." Harrell promoted him to director of artists and repertoire (A&R) in 1991.

In 1991, Combs and Heavy D promoted a celebrity benefit basketball game at the City College of New York. The event, which attracted more people than expected, turned into a disaster because five thousand tickets had been sold, yet the gymnasium's capacity was less than 2,800 people. Nine people were killed, and approximately twenty-eight people were injured in a stampede at the doors of the gymnasium. Family members of the deceased sued Combs, Heavy D, the college, and the city. Combs was defended in court by famed attorney William Kunstler. The suit was settled for $3.8 million, and Combs paid $750,000. A separate lawsuit, filed by those who were injured at the event, was settled on May 24, 2000.

After the City College of New York tragedy, Combs was besieged with additional legal troubles, including three events in 1999. In 2005, Combs and Random House settled a lawsuit in which the publishing company alleged that Combs never returned a $300,000 advance for a memoir that he failed to complete in 1999. In 2001, a jury found Combs not guilty on all charges of illegal possession of a weapon and attempted bribery of a witness stemming from a December 1999 shooting in a Manhattan nightclub that wounded three individuals. In July 1999, Combs settled out of court with Steve Stoute, an executive at Interscope Records, after Combs and two bodyguards allegedly assaulted Stoute. The settlement amount was $500,000. However, Combs had to appear in New York Criminal Court in September 1999 to answer criminal charges. He pleaded guilty to reduced assault charges and was sentenced to a one-day anger management class. The New York district attorney's office reduced the charges from a felony status to a violation.

During his tenure at Uptown, Combs enjoyed his first success as a record producer. Jodeci's single, "Come and Talk to Me," the first record Combs produced, sold two million copies. His stature as a producer increased with the release of such successful albums as Jodeci's *Forever My Lady* (1991) and Mary J. Blige's *What's the 411?* (1992). In 1992, Combs was promoted to vice president of A&R and artist development; he also established Bad Boy Entertainment, a record, production, and management company and planned to distribute Bad Boy Records through Uptown. However, Combs, who was considered arrogant and a threat to his colleagues, was fired from Uptown in 1993.

Leads Bad Boy Records to Great Success

Combs, after his departure from Uptown, signed a multi-million-dollar contract with Clive Davis's Arista Records in 1993. Davis's company gave Combs a New York City recording studio and allowed him to retain creative control of Bad Boy Records. The first two artists Combs signed to his label were Craig Mack and Christopher Wallace. Wallace, who was known as Biggie Smalls, recorded under the name of Notorious B.I.G. In 1994, Bad Boy Records released Mack's *Project: Funk Da World* and Notorious B.I.G.'s *Ready to Die*; both albums were produced by Combs and were certified platinum. Bad Boy Records went on to sign artists such as Faith Evans, Black Rob, Mase, 112, and Carl Thomas, and the company produced more consecutive gold and platinum albums than Motown did in its early days. According to Robert La Franco in *Forbes*, Davis,

acknowledging Combs' remarkable achievement, commented, "Puffy is making history. He has patterned something very unique in its influence on lifestyle here and all over the world." Bad Boy Records reaped huge profits as early as its first four years in existence during which it posted estimated total sales ranging from $100 million to $200 million.

In March 1997, Bad Boy Records lost one of its stars. Combs and Smalls left a recording industry party in Los Angeles in separate cars. The vehicles stopped at a red light, and Smalls was the victim of a fatal drive-by shooting. After Smalls' album *Life After Death* was released later that month, it sold more than four million copies in the United States. Combs donated part of the profits from the album to the Christopher Wallace Foundation, an organization named in Small's honor that attempts to provide educational opportunities for youth.

Also in 1997, Combs debuted as a recording artist with two singles: "Can't Nobody Hold Me Down" and "I'll Be Missing You" as well as an album, *No Way Out*. The multi-platinum "I'll Be Missing You" was the more successful single. Combs produced it as a tribute to Smalls, and it featured Combs, Faith Evans, and 112. When the song was performed at the 1997 *MTV Awards*, Combs became more widely known. *No Way Out* sold more than 561,000 copies in its first week and went on to sell eight million copies. *No Way Out*, which featured the Family (other artists who recorded on Combs' label), was one of the first rap albums to be popular outside the United States. Combs and the Family toured in 1997, and the *No Way Out* Tour was the most successful one in rap history as it generated $15 million at the box office. It was the second biggest concert tour of 1997; only the Rolling Stones outsold Combs and the Family in concert that year. Combs' second album *Forever* was released in 2000. He subsequently released *The Saga Continues* by P. Diddy and the Bad Boy Family and *P. Diddy and Bad Boy Records Present: We Invented the Remix*. In 2004, Combs announced his retirement from solo recording.

In addition to working with the artists on Bad Boy's roster, Combs has produced hit records for an impressive list of recording stars such as Boys II Men, Mariah Carey, LL Cool J, Aretha Franklin, Whitney Houston, Janet Jackson, R. Kelly, Jennifer Lopez, Brian McKnight, Busta Rhymes, Q-Tip, Usher, and Jay-Z.

Bad Boy Entertainment and Arista Records ended their joint venture in 2002, and Combs gained full control of Bad Boy Records, its catalogue, and roster of artists. One year later, Combs signed a contract with Universal Records to distribute and promote Bad Boy Records, and Combs retained total control of his company. In 2005, Combs, who terminated his deal with Universal Records eight months before the end of the contracted period, entered into a worldwide 50/50 joint venture with Warner Music Group. As part of the approximately $30 million agreement, Combs remained CEO of Bad Boy Entertainment.

Appears on Television, in Films, and on Broadway

Over the years, Combs appeared on a variety of talk shows, specials, and award shows. Verification that his appeal extends beyond the urban youth market came with his appearance on such mainstream television programs as *Live with Regis and Kelly* and *Martha*. Combs has hosted such programs as *MTV Video Awards* (2005) and the *MTV Europe Music Awards* (2002) in Barcelona.

Combs was the executive producer of the reality television series *Making the Band 2* (2002), which was MTV's third highest rated show, and *Making the Band 3* (2005). Each series followed the creation of a hip-hop/R&B group under Combs' tutelage. He also served as the executive producer of *P. Diddy Presents the Bad Boys of Comedy* (2005) and the co-executive producer of *Run's House* (2005).

Combs, who made his acting debut on the *The Steve Harvey Show* in 1997, made his film debut with a small role in *Made (2001)*. In *Monster's Ball* (2001), he played Lawrence Musgrove, a death-row inmate and husband of Leticia Musgrove, played by Halle Berry, who in 2002 became the first African American to receive the Academy Award for best actress for her performance. Combs has also appeared in *Death of a Dynasty* (2003) and the made-for-television film, *Love in Vain* (2004).

Many people were surprised when it was announced that Combs would star in the 2004 Broadway revival of Lorraine Hansberry's play, at the Royale Theater. Combs' co-stars were Phylicia Rashad, who in 2004 became the first African American to receive the Tony Award for best performance by an actress in a play; Audra McDonald, who won the Tony Award for best featured actress in a play; and Sanaa Latham. Had he been cast in a lesser role as Bobo or George Murchison, not as many individuals would have questioned Combs' association in the play. However, he was cast as Walter Lee Younger, which was originally played by Sidney Poitier on Broadway and in the 1961 film. Although Combs was not nominated for a Tony, his theatrical effort attracted younger people to Broadway.

Establishes Restaurants, Clothing Lines, and Fragrances

As early as 1997, Combs began to pursue new ventures that would prove profitable. That year, he opened Justin's restaurant in New York City. The restaurant is named after the eldest of Combs' two sons: Justin and Christian. Two years later, Combs opened Justin's in Atlanta.

In 1998, Combs founded Sean John, a line of designer clothing for men. He began with fifty thousand black hats and T-shirts that displayed his signature. Combs directs his own designers, and Sean John, unlike apparel made under licenses by a number of other celebrities, makes 70 percent of its clothes. The clothes are sold in such stores as Bloomingdale's, Macy's, and Fred Segal. His casual men's wear line is responsible for 70 percent of Sean John's sales. According to Tracie Rozhon of the *New York Times*, teenagers spend approximately $42 billion each year on clothes, including sales for Sean John of approximately $400 million. Sean John has been acknowledged as paving the way for other entertainers to have their own clothing lines. Sean John, since its inception, has been nominated for a Council of Fashion Designers of America (CFDA) Award, and Combs won the CFDA's Top Men's Wear Designer of the Year Award in 2004.

Combs, basking in the success of his Sean John line, created a women's clothing line known as Sean by Sean Combs in 2005. The clothes are sold in such stores as Bergdorf Goodman, Bloomingdale's, and Saks Fifth Avenue. Also in 2005, Combs, in collaboration with the Estee Lauder Company, introduced Unforgivable, his fragrance for men. Givaudan, the company that created Unforgivable, mixed scents 666 times before Combs was pleased with the fragrance. The bottle is designed to look like the Sean John store on New York's Fifth Avenue and Forty-first Street. Combs introduced a limited edition of fifteen thousand bottles that contain a higher concentrated version of the fragrance for $300. In early 2006, a mass market version of Unforgivable, with a $55 price tag, was introduced.

Among Bad Boy's other enterprises are the Blue Flame Marketing and Advertising and Janice Combs Management, and Daddy's House Studios.

Known for His Opulent Lifestyle

Combs, who inherited his strong work ethic from his mother, is a workaholic who has been known to work eighteen to twenty hours a day. He continues to reap the material rewards of his labor. Combs offers no excuses for his lavish way of living; instead, he asserts in an April 1998 *Ebony* article, "I come from the kings and queens of Africa. I deserve the best. We all deserve the best. I'm not ashamed to say that I like the best in life, and I work hard every day to get it. It's not a selfish thing."

Combs possesses mansions, Bentleys, and a yacht. He is known for his extravagant parties. One thousand people attended his twenty-ninth birthday party at New York's Cipriani Wall Street restaurant, and the tab was $600,000. In the summers, he holds White Parties in the Hamptons where each guest must wear white clothing. At the party on July 4, 2004, he and his fellow *A Raisin in the Sun* cast members arrived after the matinee performance in two helicopters Combs chartered for them. On display at the party was an original copy of the Declaration of Independence, and Combs used the festive occasion to launch Citizens Change, a nonpartisan voter registration organization.

Practices Philanthropy

While Combs' enjoys a lavish lifestyle, he is also generous in helping others. In addition to his donation to the Christopher Wallace Foundation, Combs has contributed to many charitable institutions and organizations. He is the founder of the Sean "Puffy" Combs and Janice Combs Endowed Scholarship Fund at Howard University.

Perhaps Combs' most well known charitable endeavor has been his completing the New York Marathon on November 2, 2003, for which he raised $2 million for children's charities. Youths consistently benefit from Combs' largesse. In 1995, he founded Daddy's House Social Programs, Inc. Daddy's House, with Sister Souljah as executive director, offers inner-city youths academic tutoring, opportunities for high school seniors to participate in tours of colleges, international travel, Bad Boy internships, summer camping programs, and courses in the stock market as well as financial skills. Combs donated one hundred computers to public schools in Harlem. During more than one yuletide season, he has delivered gifts to children in New York City's hospitals and foster care homes. Daddy's House sponsors an annual food drive. In 2000, after the death of Rev. Hosea Williams, Combs sponsored the annual Hosea's Feed the Hungry and Homeless Thanksgiving Day dinner for more than thirty thousand in Atlanta.

Combs has garnered a variety of honors and awards. He is the recipient of the NAACP Legal Defense and Educational Fund's Equal Justice Award, 2005; Patrick Lippert Award, for his ongoing work with the Rock the Vote organization, 2004; American Society of Composers, Authors and Publishers (ASCAP) Songwriter of the Year Award, 1996, 1997, and 2000; ASCAP's Rhythm and Soul Award, 1995; Howard University's Alumni Achievement Award in Entertainment and Business, 1999; and World Music Awards for Best-Selling Rap Artist of the Year, 1998, and for Best-Selling New Artist, 1998. He has won Grammy Awards for best rap performance by a duo or group, with Nelly and Murphy Lee, 2004, and with Faith Evans and 112, 1998, and Best Rap Album, 1998. In addition, Combs had the honor of carrying the Olympic Torch through New York City's streets for one lap on June 19, 2004.

In 2001 Combs, who was then known as Puff Daddy, changed his name to P. Diddy. Three years later, P. Diddy changed his name back to his birth name—Sean Coms. Regardless of the name changes and the controversy he generates at times, Combs remains committed to his work as an entertainer, entrepreneur, and philanthropist.

REFERENCES

Books

Cable, Andrew. *A Family Affair: The Unauthorized Sean "Puffy" Combs Story.* New York: Ballantine Books, 1998.

Periodicals

Chappell, Kevin. "Back from the Brink . . . Again." *Ebony*56 (June 2001):146-50.

——. "The Puff Daddy Nobody Knows." *Ebony* 55 (January 2000): 74-82.

——. "Puff Daddy: The Man, the Music, the Controversy." *Ebony* 53 (April 1998): 54-8.

La Franco, Robert. "I Ain't Foolin' Around—I'm Building Assets." *Forbes* 163 (22 March 1999): 180-86.

McAdams, Janine. "Combs Moves Up to VP at Uptown Records: Also Establishes His Own Label-Link Company." *Billboard* (12 December 1992):10.

Rozhon, Tracie. "The Rap on Puffy's Empire." *New York Times*, 24 July 2005.

Sanneh, Kelefa. "Spring Theater Preview: The Legend and the Other Guy; Rapper, Mogul, Designer, Runner. So Why Not Broadway Actor?" *New York Times*, 22 February 2004.

Taylor, Susan L. "P. Diddy: Style and Substance." *Essence* 29 (November 1998): 140.

Wilson, Eric. "Front Row: Tracking the Scent of Self-Promotion." *New York Times,* 24 November 2005.

Linda M. Carter

John Cook, Jr.
1833–1910

Educator, government official

A multifaceted man, John Cook Jr. was a staunch supporter of suffrage, public schools for black people in Washington, D.C., and civil rights. Cook held a number of political offices that gave him influence in the Republican Party. He belonged to one of the black elite families in the district and acquired considerable wealth on his own. Cook Jr. and his family were socially exclusive, but he demonstrated his concern for the entire black community by working through various organizations in their behalf.

Born in Washington, D.C., on September 21, 1833, John Francis Cook Jr. was the son of John Francis Sr. and lector—a post that he held until 1884 when the Democratic Party and Grover Cleveland took office. He was jury commissioner in 1889. He became less prominent as a local official when be left his post as tax collector.

Takes Interest in Educating Blacks

Cook maintained a keen interest in the education of blacks in the district. From 1875 to 1910, he was a member of Howard University's board of trustees. He was a member of its executive committee as well, sometimes serving as chair. In 1873, he opposed the action of the House of Delegates for the District of Columbia, which kept blacks from establishing a normal school. Noted black leaders in D.C., including Cook, diplomat and lawyer John Mercer Langston, surgeon Charles Purvis, and orator and local office-holder Frederick Douglass, had been unsuccessful in their efforts to strike down segregation in the local public schools. When the old school board was reorganized in 1906, Cook became a member of the new District of Columbia board of education and held the post until he resigned a few months before his death.

Throughout his life, Cook worked in the interest of civil rights and the welfare of black people. He was a member of the Board of Children's Guardians beginning in 1892 and continuing for nearly two decades. He was also a member of the Board of Trustees of the National Association for the Relief of Destitute Colored Women and Children. He served on the board of trustees of the Harmony Cemetery, which his father founded. While the entire Cook family was considered class conscious, his work in various organizations testified to his concern for blacks at all social or class levels.

A number of social and cultural organizations were founded in Washington's black community beginning in the 1880s. They represented an opportunity for Washington's black aristocracy to join, further separating themselves from those of different social strata. One of these was the Diamond Back Club, to which the Cook brothers belonged, along with other prominent black men, such as politician P. B. S. Pinchback, U.S. senator Blanche K. Bruce, municipal judge Robert H. Terrell, and assistant librarian of Congress Daniel Murray. For ten terms Cook was grand master of the Eureka Lodge of Free and Accepted Masons, which Willard B. Gatewood in *American National Biography* called "the oldest and most prestigious chapter of Prince Hall Freemasonry in the Washington area." His appreciation for music led him to membership in the Samuel Coleridge-Taylor Choral Association and to its presidency. The association was chartered in 1903 and named for the Afro-British composer. He also followed his father's interest in the Harmony Cemetery Association. Cook demonstrated an interest in preserving Cedar Hill, the home of Frederick Douglass located in the Anacostia section of the district. He became a trustee of the Frederick Douglass Memorial

Chronology

1833	Born in Washington, D.C. on September 21
1853-55	Studies at Oberlin College
1855-67	Manages Union Seminary, with brother George F. T. Cook
1863	Marries Helen Appo
1867	Begins career in government service
1868	Joins Board of Aldermen
1869	Becomes city registrar
1869-72	Serves as justice of the peace
1871	Becomes city registrar for second time
1874-84	Serves as district tax collector
1875-1910	Serves on Board of Trustees for Howard University
1889	Becomes jury commissioner
1906	Becomes member of the District of Columbia Board of Education
1910	Dies on January 20

Jane Mann Cook, a woman of Afro-Indian ancestry. His father was a prominent African American clergyman, educator, and community leader. He had a younger brother, George F. T. Cook, who became the first and for many years the only black superintendent in the District of Columbia. John Cook was educated at Union Seminary, which was his father's school, located on H Street near 14th Street, NW. Then he attended Oberlin College in Ohio from 1853 to 1855. After their father died in 1855, the Cook brothers, both Oberlin students, returned to Washington to take control of their father's school, Union Seminary.

Cook Jr. taught in Union Seminary for a few years and then relocated to New Orleans where he continued to teach.. When the Civil War began, he returned home and to Union Seminary which the two Cook brothers operated until it closed in 1867. In that same year, the District of Columbia opened public schools for its African American residents, which caused Union to suffer. George Cook became superintendent of the separate school system that the district maintained for blacks, while in 1867 John Cook entered a career in government service by working as a clerk in Washington's office of the collector of taxes. In 1868 he was elected to the Board of Aldermen; this was the first election in which blacks were permitted to vote. By now he was heavily involved in Republican politics and had some political power. In 1869 he was elected city registrar. When Washington became a federal territory in 1871, he was reappointed to that post.

Cook served as justice of the peace from 1869 to 1876. In 1872 and again in 1880 Cook was a delegate to the Republican National Convention. The shrewd and tactful Cook endeared himself to influential members of Congress and to those in the White House as well. In 1874, President Ulysses S. Grant appointed him district tax col-

and Historical Association which worked to make the home an historic monument.

About 1863 Cook married Helen Appo (1837-1913), a New York native and the daughter of William and Elizabeth Brady Appo. The family relocated to Philadelphia where her father was a musician and music educator and her mother owned a millinery business. Helen Cook became a leader in the women's club movement, and she was the longtime president of the Colored Women's League and an organizer of its successor, the National Association of Colored Women. Her contemporaries were illustrious black women, such as Charlotte Grimké, Lucy Moten, Anna J. Cooper, and Mary Church Terrell. The Cooks, including their children, took seriously their membership in the Fifteenth Street Presbyterian Church which Cook Sr. had founded.

John and Helen Cook built a large home of brick and stone on Sixteenth Street in the district. At some point John Jr. owned the Langham Hotel Building in the city. Their wealth came from wise real estate investments, including property in the business district. In 1884 Cook and his wife were among Washington's black four hundred, or those worth over $70,000. Called the Elite List, this forerunner of the Social Register carried the Cooks well after the names of other black elite families were no longer listed.

Cook died of heart failure on January 20, 1910, and was buried on January 28 at Harmony Cemetery in the District of Columbia, which his father had helped to found. His legacy lay in his efforts to provide public schools for blacks, his dedication to higher education as demonstrated in his long membership on Howard University's board of trustees, and in the political offices he held in the District of Columbia.

REFERENCES

Books

Cromwell, John W. *The Negro in American History: Men and Woman Eminent in the Evolution of the American of African Descent.* Washington, DC: The American Negro Academy, 1914.

Gatewood, Willard B. *Aristocrats of Color: The Black Elite, 1880-1920.* Bloomington: Indiana University Press, 1990.

———. "John Francis Cook Jr." *American National Biography.* Vol. 5. Eds. John A. Garraty and Mark C. Carnes. New York: Oxford University Press, 1999.

Logan, Rayford W. *Howard University: The First Hundred Years, 1867-1967.* New York: New York University Press, Issued under the auspices of Howard University, 1969.

Wormley, Stanton L. Jr. "John Francis Cook Jr." *Dictionary of American Negro Biography.* Eds. Rayford W. Logan and Michael R. Winston. New York: Norton, 1982.

Collections

The Moorland-Spingarn Research Center at Howard University has additional information on John F. Cook Jr. and the Cook family.

Jessie Carney Smith

John Cook, Sr.
1810–1855

Educator, minister

John Francis Cook Sr. became an educator in the period when education was neither a right nor a privilege for African Americans. He was born a slave in 1810 and lived as a slave until his eighteenth birthday when his freedom was purchased along with that of his family. His aunt, Alethia Tanner, purchased the Cook family's freedom after purchasing her own. She used money, which she had saved from selling surplus crops from her garden to pay for these freedoms; however, Cook worked very hard as an apprentice shoemaker for five years to repay her. Cook's first job that led him into the public sphere was as an assistant messenger in the government's land office. Cook was not fulfilled in this position although it was seen as a decent position for an African American at that time. He left this job to fulfill his calling as an educator.

As for Cook's family background, information on his education is sparse. It is believed that he attended the school in which he later worked as the principal and that he was self-taught in the rudiments of education methods. He also studied in preparation for his pastoral duties.

Cook was a family man. He was married first to Jane Mann and then to Jane LeCount. These marriages produced five children, three boys and two girls. It is not clear which marriage produced which children. Two of the schools that he founded were run by two of his sons, John Jr. and George. One of his sons also became the first superintendent of Colored Schools in Washington D.C. and was later elected as an alderman in 1868.

Cook was interested in the education of African Americans. His main aim was to operate a school for freed African Americans. Cook became a teacher when a school for African Americans, which was first run by Henry Smothers, then by John W. Prout, failed as a free school and resorted to requiring tuition. Cook became the principal, and he took over from the Board of Trustees which had been in charge of the school since its inception in 1822. When Cook took charge in 1834, the school flourished as it provided quality education and was well attended. Cook

Chronology

1810	Born in Washington, D.C.
1828	His aunt, Alethia Tanner, purchases his freedom
1834	Serves as principal of Union Seminary School
1835	Flees from Washington D.C. for protection from Snow Riot
1836	Returns from Columbia, Lancaster County, Pennsylvania where he sought protection from the riot
1838	Preaches in Israel AME Church on South Capitol Street, Washington D.C.
1840	Forms 15th Street Presbyterian Church, Washington, D.C.
1843	Ordained as a minister in the Presbyterian Church
1848	Licentiate in Presbyterian Church
1855	Dies in Washington, D.C. on March 2

renamed the school (previously called the Columbia Institute) Union Seminary. Union Seminary was known as a co-educational school for African American children.

Unfortunately, Cook had to flee Washington D.C. in 1835 because he feared for his life. In this period, the Snow Riot—an anti-African American civil act—threatened the lives of African Americans, so many of them fled from the community. Despite the destruction of part of the schoolroom, Cook persevered; he reopened the school when he returned to the city in 1836. It is believed that he also taught school in Columbia, Lancaster County, where he took refuge.

Cook sought to provide religious teachings that were more relevant and meaningful to the lives of the African Americans in his community. In 1836, Cook studied to become a minister, and by 1838, he was a preacher at the Israel AME Church on South Capitol Street, Washington, D.C. Cook made two great contributions to the religious lives of the African Americans in Washington D.C., as he organized the Union Bethel Church (which later became the Metropolitan AME Church), and the 15th Street Presbyterian Church in 1840. After withdrawing his membership from Bethel Church, he started the 15th Street Church in his schoolroom, and this congregation was made up solely of Africans Americans. This church became the first African American church in Washington D.C. It was accepted into the Presbyterian community as an official member in 1842. Cook was officially ordained a Presbyterian minister in 1843 after he passed the theology examinations set by the Presbyterian Church. He also preached to white congregations who accepted his theology, and moderated at an assembly of white Presbyterian clergymen who assembled in Richmond, Virginia. Cook brought the African American presence into the church hierarchy as he became licentiate in the Presbyterian Church in Washington D.C. in 1848. He was also one of the original members of Daniel A. Payne's Ministers Council for AME Churches.

As a Christian, Cook believed in the spiritual well being of his fellow men and a good burial after death. Cook helped to establish the Colombian Harmony Cemetery in which freed African Americans could bury their dead. It was relocated at Landover, Maryland and is known as the National Harmony Memorial Park.

As a multifaceted African American, Cook also became involved in politics as he wanted to represent his people. He joined the Negro Convention Movement that was formed in 1830 by freed African Americans. The sole aim of the convention was to improve the lives of African Americans. He was nominated corresponding secretary to the District of Colombia Convention, and later, at the fifth meeting, he became the general secretary of the National Convention.

The National Convention's aim was to improve the lives of African Americans in all areas, one of which was the writing of literatures from the African American perspective. Freed African Americans were interested in writing their histories and their stories. A literary and debating society was formed to voice the opinions and views of African Americans.

Cook died on March 2, 1855 and his funeral services were held at the 15th Street Presbyterian Church. He worked to improve the lot of the freed African Americans who were not prepared for their emancipated lives. Cook provided meaningful religious, educational, social, and moral teaching for free African Americans.

REFERENCES

Books

Gates, Henry Louis, Jr., ed. *African American Lives.* New York: Oxford University Press, 2004.

Logan, Rayford W., and Michael R. Winston, eds. *Dictionary of American Negro Biography.* New York: Norton, 1982.

Denise Jarrett

Will Marion Cook
1869–1944

Composer, violinist, conductor

Will Marion Cook was a uniquely gifted composer and violinist who studied with Anton Dvorak in Europe. He was also known as a bitter, temperamental man who was convinced that he would never be taken seriously as a classical musician because of his race. So he turned from classical to ragtime, composing works

Will Marion Cook

Chronology

1869	Born in Washington D.C. on January 27
1895	Gives classical concert at Carnegie Hall
1898	Composes and produces the stage musical *Clorindy, or The Origin of the Cakewalk*, for Broadway
1899	Marries Abbie Mitchell
1903	Tours Europe with *In Dahomey*
1905	Tours Europe with Memphis Students ensemble
1912	Tours Europe with Clef Club orchestra
1918	Founds Southern Syncopaters (later American Syncopated Orchestra)
1920s	Works as music teacher and conductor
1944	Dies in New York on July 19

composer Eubie Blake as quoted in an article located at Jass.com, "Cook was a great musician, but he tried to push things down people's throats. I think he got that in Europe. He was trying to ape Richard Wagner." On his return to the United States, he studied for a brief time with Antonin Dvorak at the National Conservatory of Music. He made his musical debut in 1889 and became the director of a chamber orchestra the following year. He wrote his first composition in 1893.

Vows Never to Play Violin Again

According to Jass.com, Cook stopped playing the violin after an 1895 Carnegie Hall concert about which a reviewer wrote that he was "the world's greatest Negro violinist." Cook went to the writer's office, said "I am not the world's greatest Negro violinist, I am the greatest violinist in the world," smashed his violin on the desk and swore never to perform again.

But Cook did play the violin at least one more time, when the Clef Club Orchestra played Carnegie Hall in 1912. Cook agreed to go on stage and play with the group, given that he would not be introduced or asked to take a bow. Some members of the audience recognized him, however, and his performance was met with tremendous applause and cries for "speech." The applause lasted so long, and Cook was so overcome, all he could do was bow.

Writes and Produces Broadway Show

Cook was known for his hot-headedness; he became convinced that, despite his success, the world would never embrace an African American composer. So he decided to compose ragtime, the popular music of the era. Cook first attempted composing for theater with a series of skits called *Clorindy, or The Origin of the Cakewalk*. The show was to be written, directed, and performed by an all-African American cast, a first for Broadway. Cook and Paul Lawrence Dunbar, a well-

that drew on the popular minstrel themes of the times. At the end of the nineteenth century, he composed for leading black comic and vaudevillian Bert Williams. In 1889 Cook produced and wrote the music for *Clorindy, or The Origin of the Cakewalk*, the first musical comedy written, directed, and performed entirely by African American artists. He went on to compose the music for a number of popular black musicals. Cook led his Southern Syncopaters, a huge ragtime and concert ensemble, and composed "I'm Coming, Virginia" and "Mammy" in the 1910s. As ragtime music fell out of favor, Cook was left behind, but he became an influence on Duke Ellington's early work as a composer.

Cook was born in Washington, D.C., on January 27, 1869. He was christened Will Mercer, in honor of a close family friend, John Mercer Langston. His father, John Hartwell Cook, graduated from Howard University Law School in 1871 and became one of the first black lawyers to practice in Washington. He served as chief clerk of the Freedmen's Bureau from 1867 until 1872 and as professor and dean of the Howard University Law School from 1876 until 1878. Will studied violin at age 13 at Oberlin Conservatory where his mother had graduated four years earlier. After two years at Oberlin, he traveled to Europe to attend the University of Berlin. While in Germany, he was a student of Joseph Joachim, one of the premier violinists of the era. According to fellow African American known African American poet, wrote all the songs and the libretto in one ten-hour session.

Cook approached music publisher Isadore Witmark to help produce the show in exchange for the publication rights and all the royalties. Witmark let Cook keep the royalties for himself. Cook later recalled that, when he approached Witmark, he told him he was crazy to believe any Broadway audience would pay to listen to Negroes sing.

In a time with no air conditioning, traditional theaters in New York City closed their doors during the hot summer months. The Casino Theater Roof Garden was the first open-air venue in the city. After Cook tried unsuccessfully to gain an audition there, he lied and told his cast that he had gotten them an audition. When the cast of twenty-six African Americans showed up at the theater, the conductor of the roof garden's orchestra insisted that the theater manager give the group a chance.

Clorindy, or The Origin of the Cakewalk opened on July 5, 1898. The operetta was a mixture of comedy, songs, and dances, including the cakewalk, which was a popular dance move. For the first time in Broadway history, the performers sang and danced simultaneously. The hour-long show was a triumph, and Cook and the cast were elated. Cook later said he was "so delirious" he became drunk on a glass of water. Cook would later write, "Negroes were at last on Broadway, and there to stay. Gone was the uff-dah of the minstrel! Gone the Massa Linkum stuff. We were artists and we were going a long, long way," according to the *Washington Post*.

Though he had left his classical roots behind for popular music, Cook brought his classical training to his ragtime compositions. According to Jass.com, African American critic James Weldon Johnson considered Cook "the first competent composer to take what was then known as rag-time and work it out in a musicianly way. His choruses and finales in *Clorindy*, complete novelties as they were, sung by a lusty chorus, were simply breathtaking." Ragtime music was usually considered a lower-class form of entertainment, but the hit song from *Clorindy*, "Darktown Is Out Tonight," could be heard whistled in barbershops and on street corners around New York City.

Begins Using Pseudonym

At the beginning of the 1900s, Cook composed many popular songs. His first published song, "Darktown Is Out Tonight," appeared under the pseudonym "Will Marion" in 1899; he subsequently used the name Will Marion Cook. Later he worked as composer-in-chief and musical director for Williams and Walker's Broadway shows.

In 1899, Cook married Abbie Mitchell, a lead singer with the Memphis Students. She was also the female lead in Cole and Johnson's 1908 production *Red Moon* and

performed with her husband's orchestra when they toured Europe in 1918. She opened a musical and dramatic studio in New York after retiring from the stage. The couple had a son, Mercer Cook, who went on to teach romance languages at Howard University and served as ambassador to the Republic of Niger and special envoy to Senegal and Gambia.

Cook was known as a bitter and angry man, who never felt he received the recognition he was due. He was troubled by the belief that audiences wanted to hear only light-hearted music from African American composers. According to Jass.com, critic Mary White Ovington wrote, "I am told that Mr. Cook declares that the next score he writes shall begin with ten minutes of serious music. If the audience doesn't like it, they can come in late, but for ten minutes he will do something worthy of his genius."

Passes Torch to Duke Ellington

In 1918, Cook founded and led his own band, the Southern Syncopaters, later known as the New York Syncopated Orchestra. The group toured Europe and performed before England's George V. Band member Sidney Bechet began playing the soprano saxophone during this tour and would go on to become a jazz great. When Cook returned home to New York, he led a Clef Club orchestra, which featured vocalist Paul Robeson.

Cook first met Duke Ellington in the early 1920s and became a mentor to him. In his autobiography, Ellington wrote that he would bring his unfinished compositions to Cook for guidance. He would ask Cook, whom he called "Dad," what direction he might take to finish the piece. "'You know you should go to the conservatory,' he would answer, 'but since you won't, I'll tell you. First you find the logical way, and when you find it, avoid it, and let your inner self break through and guide you. Don't try to be anybody but yourself.'"

Cook died in New York on July 19, 1944. He and his father are both buried at Woodlawn Cemetery. Their family home in Washington became an administrative office building on the Howard University campus.

REFERENCES

Books

Handy, D. Antoinette. *Black Conductors*. Metuchen, N.J.: Scarecrow Press, 1995.

Riis, Thomas. *Just Before Jazz*. Washington, D.C.: Smithsonian Institution Press, 1989.

Sadie, Stanley, ed. *The New Grove Dictionary of Music and Musicians*. 2nd ed. New York: Macmillan, 2001.

Southern, Eileen. *The Music of Black Americans*. 3rd ed. New York: Norton, 1997.

"Will Marion Cook." *Contemporary Black Biography*. Vol. 40. Ed. Ashyia Henderson. Farmington Hills, Mich.: Gale Group, 2003.

Periodicals

Goode, Eric. "In Dahomey (review)." *Back Stage*, 16 July 1999.

Harrington, Richard. "Hitting the Historical High Notes." *Washington Post*, 18 February 2000.

Online

"Minstrelsy." PBS—JAZZ, A Film by Ken Burns: Jazz Exchange. http://www.pbs.org/jazz/exchange/ exchange_minstrel.htm (Accessed 23 March 2005).

"Will Marion Cook Family Residence." Cultural Tourism D.C.: African American Heritage Trail. http://www.culturaltourismdc.org/info-url3948/ info-url_show.htm?doc_id=204614&attrib_id=7971 (Accessed 23 March 2005).

"Will Marion Cook." G. H. Grainger. http://www. grainger.de/music/composers/cookwm.html (Accessed 23 March 2005).

"Will Marion Cook." Gold Music. http://www.gold-music.com/11111/Will%20Marion_Cook.html (Accessed 23 March 2005).

"Will Marion Cook." Jazz Roots: Early Jazz History on JASS.COM. http://www.jass.com/wcook.html (Accessed 23 March 2005).

Brenna Sanchez

Joseph S. Cotter
1895–1919

Poet

Within a brief span of four years, Joseph S. Cotter's poetry influenced future poets by exploring major social, political, religious, and racial issues of the time. Following in his father's footsteps as a poet, he attained a degree of literary merit which led some to rank his work with that of Paul Laurence Dunbar and James Weldon Johnson. In sonnet and free verse style, Cotter's works demonstrate his broad talent and versatility.

Cotter's father Joseph Seamon Cotter, Sr., was born in Bardstown, Kentucky, the son of Michael and Martha (Vaughn) Cotter. He became one of the most influential community leaders of his time. Cotter Sr. was a self-taught educator, poet, and playwright. Cotter Sr.'s mother Martha Vaughn was a slave of mixed Indian, English, and African blood who had a natural talent for storytelling and poetry. Michael Cotter, his father, was a prominent citizen of Louisville who was married to Martha by common law. The young senior Cotter's formal education

---

Chronology

1895	Born in Louisville, Kentucky on September 2
1911	Graduates from Louisville Central High School
1911	Enrolls in Fisk University, Nashville, Tennessee
1913	Released from school, stricken with tuberculosis
1913	Returns to Louisville, Kentucky
1914	Sister Florence dies of tuberculosis
1918	Publishes *The Band of Gideon and Other Lyrics*; poems published in *AME Zion Quarterly Review*
1919	Dies in Louisville, Kentucky on February 3
1920	*Out of the Shadows*, a sequence of nineteen love poems written in the English sonnet style, posthumously published in *AME Zion Quarterly Review*
1921	Two pages of poems ranging in form from the traditional Italian sonnet to free verse published posthumously in *AME Zion Quarterly Review*

---

was very limited, and he was forced to discontinue grammar school education in the third grade in order to help support his mother.

When he was twenty-two, he enrolled in a Louisville night school at the primary level. After just two sessions of formal coursework, he began teaching others. This was to be the beginning of a long career in education. He taught English literature and composition (1885 to 1887), conducted a private school (1887 to 1889), taught at the Western Colored School (1889 to 1893), was founder and principal of Paul L. Dunbar School (1893 to 1911) and in 1911 was the principal of the Coleridge-Taylor School. Like his father before him, he became influential in Louisville, serving on boards and acting as president of several organizations. Cotter married Maria F. Cox, a teacher, of Louisville, on July 22, 1891.

Early Years Reflect Father's Influence

Joseph S. Cotter Jr. was born September 2, 1895, in Louisville, Kentucky. Cotter's early years were influenced by his brilliant father's accomplishments as a nationally known poet and his involvement in community, educational, social, and cultural contributions. Being born into an environment of upper middle-class wealth with access to an extensive home library with many books of poetry influenced Cotter's literary development. His older sister, Florence Olivia, taught him how to read when he was quite young. He graduated from Louisville Central High School in 1911 and entered Fisk University in Nashville, Tennessee, that same year. At Fisk, he wrote for the *Fisk Herald* literary magazine. His tenure at Fisk was a brief two years. During his sophomore year, Cotter was stricken with tuberculosis and was forced to leave Fisk University, returning home to Louisville, but not before he had been chosen president of his class.

Upon returning to Louisville, Cotter worked for a brief time serving in an editorial capacity as journalist on the *Louisville Leader* and the *Courier-Journal* until his illness restricted him to his home.

Literary Career Begins

Florence, his devoted sister and inspiration, who was also a student at Fisk University, fell ill and died on December 16, 1914, of tuberculosis. Florence's death left Cotter distraught, and he composed "To Florence," in tribute to her. This poem marked the beginning of his brief career as a poet.

A significant childhood friend, Abraham Simpson, later became one of the youngest black officers in World War I. This friendship influenced Cotter's literary work and writing of war poetry. Simpson's friendship also kept him up to date about the controversial conflict that was World War I. Due to his illness Cotter could not serve his country in war, but he was well acquainted with the conflict and its impact upon the African American community. Cotter wrote of the horrors of world war and other devastating events and declares in his poem "O Little David" that blacks suffer like wartime victims. "O Little David" was written in free verse and technically associated with the new poetry of the period. Cotter thus contributed to World War I literature, even through his health was fragile and his lifespan brief.

Though he was given the best medical care possible, Cotter, like his beloved sister Florence, soon succumbed to tuberculosis, a leading cause of death among African Americans at the time. Cotter was to have only a little over four years as a poet; he died February 3, 1919. Within his short lifetime and despite his illness, he established himself as a poet of genuine promise and achievement.

His work is marked by bold diversity and range in techniques and theme. His early experiments with techniques associated with the new American poetry of the period led to some of his finest writing. Cotter's poetry covered a range of forms, writing effectively of nature, religious faith, love, and death and of the disparate racial situation of African Americans in his time.

One of Cotter's most quoted poems, "The Mulatto to His Critics," suggests the style of Walt Whitman in its rhythms and catalogues. Listing his various ethnic heritages, the poet observes: "Through my veins there flows the blood/Of Red Man, Black Man, Briton, Celt and Scot." As the speaker concludes, he asserts that he values his black heritage most. This affirmation recurs throughout *The Band of Gideon and Other Lyrics* (1918).

Cotter's posthumous publications include two series of poems in the *AME Zion Quarterly Review*, and the one-act play "On the Fields of France," carried in the *Crisis*. The surrealistic play presents the relationship between a black Army officer and a white Army officer in France. In this play, the two soldiers consider the dam-

aging effects of racism on America and wonder at the friendship they might have had if racism not been part of their lives. The soldiers then die hand-in-hand.

Cotter received critical recognition in his day as one of the bright rising stars. He produced three volumes of verse: *The Band of Gideon and Other Lyrics* (1918), *Out of the Shadows* (1920), and *Poems* (1921), written in the sonnet and free verse styles. Frequent themes are World War I, racism and racial identity, love, death, and nature.

His significant poems include: "Sonnet to Negro Soldiers"; "The Mulatto to His Critics"; "Is It Because I Am Black?"; "And What Shall You Say?"; "O Little David, Play on Your Harp"; and "Rain Music." His poems were published in *AME Zion Quarterly Review* (1920-1921) and *Crisis* (June 1918).

REFERENCES

Books

Franklin, John Hope. *From Slavery to Freedom: A History of Negro Americans*, 5th ed. New York: Knopf, 1980.

Hughes, Langston, and Arna Bonteps. *The Poetry of the Negro, 1946-1970.* Garden City, N.Y.: Doubleday & Company, 1970.

Nichols, J. L., and William H. Crogman. *Progress of a Race.* Naperville, Ill.: J. L. Nichols & Company, 1925.

Payne, James R. "Joseph Seamon Cotter Jr." In *Afro-American Writers Before the Harlem Renaissance.* Eds. Trudier Harris and Thadious M. Davis. Detroit, Mich.: Gale Research, 1986.

Collections

The Joseph Seamon Cotter Jr. Papers are housed in the Louisville Free Public Library, Western Branch, in Louisville, Kentucky.

Mattie McHollin

Arthur Craig
1871–1959

Engineer, educator

Arthur Ulysses Craig was one of the first African Americans to earn an engineering degree in the United States. After Craig received his undergraduate degree from the University of Kansas, he studied abroad, returned to America, pursued graduate courses at two universities, helped to design an automobile, and worked as an educator at three historically black institutions.

Craig's students as well as the members of the communities where he lived and worked were the beneficiaries of his knowledge, experience, and concern for improving the lives of others.

Arthur Craig, the son of Henry and Harriet Talbert Craig, was born in Weston, Missouri, on December 1, 1871. Craig attended public schools in Weston and Atchison High School in Kansas. He graduated from Atchison High in 1890.

In September 1891, Craig began his matriculation at the University of Kansas's School of Electrical Engineering. He was the third assistant in the physical laboratory. Craig received a B.S. in electrical engineering on June 5, 1895.

Craig traveled to Naas, Sweden. He enrolled in a Sloyd Training School at Naas that was founded by Otto Solomon, the Swedish educator. Solomon's school attracted Swedish teachers as well as educators from many other countries. The objectives of the Sloyd System were to instill in students such traits as appreciation for work, respect for physical labor, self-reliance, organizational skills, neatness, accuracy, manual dexterity, attentiveness, perseverance, patience, precision, and productivity. Craig also observed industrial education in the Swedish cities of Stockholm and Goteberg as well as in London, England. Beginning in 1901, he studied psychology, manual training, and philosophy at Columbia University, in New York. From 1909 to 1910, he enrolled in ethics, psychology, and philosophy courses at the Catholic University of America.

Improves Tuskegee's Curriculum and Campus

In 1896, Craig accepted a position as teacher of physics and electricity in the Industrial Department at Tuskegee Normal and Industrial Institute (now known as

Tuskegee University). When Craig arrived at the Alabama campus, he added electrical engineering to the curriculum. Craig and the students installed and operated Tuskegee's telephone system.

In addition, Craig designed the electrical lighting for Tuskegee's original chapel, which was constructed between 1896 and 1898. The chapel was the first building on Tuskegee's campus and the first in Macon County, Alabama, to be equipped with interior electrical lights. The town of Tuskegee also benefited from Craig's expertise because he planned its lighting system which was supplied by the institute's power plant. Under Craig's guidance, students maintained the school's power plant.

During the summer of 1900, Craig was employed by F. B. Stearns and Company. The Cleveland-based company manufactured automobiles from 1898 to 1929. Craig helped design at least one automobile. One year later, he was offered the position of head of the Industrial Department at Lincoln Institute (now known as Lincoln University) in his native state of Missouri.

Moves to Washington, D.C.

Instead of accepting the position at Lincoln, Craig decided in 1901 to teach high school in Washington, D.C. According to Frank Lincoln Mather in *Who's Who of the Colored Race*, Craig also served as a vocational counselor as early as 1904. Craig taught in the nation's capital for seventeen years. During that time, he was associated with at least two high schools: the Armstrong Manual Training Night School and the M Street High School. Craig introduced mechanical and architectural drawing in Washington's African American schools and helped develop manual training courses for schools in other cities. He also served as Armstrong's principal from 1904 to 1906. Perhaps by 1915, Craig was also teaching at M Street High School.

During his years as an educator in the public school system of Washington, Craig was involved in a number of additional activities. From 1909 to 1916, he was the superintendent of the Lincoln Temple Congregational Sunday School. While serving as Sunday school superintendent, Craig became one of the first individuals to use film as an instructional aid in churches.

Craig established public playgrounds in the city and was superintendent for three years. He was also one of the founders of Washington's Colored Social Settlement. A resident of the Anacostia section of Washington, Craig was involved in the campaign to make Cedar Hill, Frederick Douglass's Anacostia home, a national landmark. The efforts of Craig and many others were rewarded when Cedar Hill, which was opened to visitors in 1916, was added to the National Park System in 1962 and was designated a National Historic Site in 1988. In addition to his school, church, and community responsibilities, Craig ran a poultry farm and dairy.

Craig was a member of the American Negro Academy, National Association for the Advancement of Colored People, Masons, National Education Association, and the Teachers' Association of D.C. He moved to New York and was employed as a mechanic, draftsman, heating engineer, teacher and an editor of a Harlem newspaper.

Craig married Luella Cassandra Gladys Moore, a teacher at Tuskegee Institute, on August 26, 1896. They had three children. Details about Craig's life are scarce, and facts about his life after 1915 are even fewer. It is known that Craig died in 1959 and that he was survived by at least one immediate family member: his second wife, Althea, who died in 1970. Arthur Ulysses Craig's contributions are not widely known in the early 2000s. Yet he was a man who earned an engineering degree, studied abroad, and attended graduate school during a time when many members of his race could not attend high school. He dedicated decades of his life to improving education for African Americans and to improving the communities where he worked and lived.

REFERENCES

Books

Mather, Frank Lincoln. "Arthur Ulysses Craig." In *Who's Who of the Colored Race: A Biographical Dictionary of Men and Women of African Descent* 1915. Detroit: Gale Research, 1976.

Nichols, J. L., and William H. Crogman, eds. "Arthur Ulysses Craig." In *Progress of a Race or the Remarkable Advancement of the American Negro.* Naperville, IL: J. L. Nichols and Company, 1920.

Sowell, Thomas. "The Education of Minority Children." In *Education in the Twenty-First Century.* Ed. Edward P. Lazear. Stanford, CA: Hoover Institution Press, 2002.

Online

"History of the Chapel." Tuskegee University. http://www.tuskegee.edu/Global/story.asp?S=1157087&nav=menu200_8 (Accessed 18 February 2006).

Linda M. Carter

William H. Crogman
1841–1931

Educator, lecturer, college president

As churchman, Christian scholar, lecturer, and educator, William H. Crogman distinguished himself

---

Chronology

1841	Born in St. Maarten, Leeward Islands, British West Indies on May 5
1855	Begins eleven-year career on the sea
1870	Graduates from Pierce Academy; begins teaching at Claflin College
1876	Receives B.A. from Atlanta University; begins teaching at Clark College
1878	Marries Lavinia C. Mott
1879	Receives M.A. from Atlanta University
1880	Serves as lay delegate to general conference of the Methodist Episcopal Church, returning in 1884 and 1888
1883	Addresses Plymouth Church, Brooklyn, New York
1884	Addresses National Education Association convention in Madison, Wisconsin
1885	Elected secretary of the Board of Trustees of Clark College
1895	Becomes commissioner for the Cotton States Exposition in Atlanta
1903	Elected president of Clark College
1910	Resigns from the presidency and returns to teaching
1921	Moves to Philadelphia, Pennsylvania
1931	Dies in Philadelphia on October 16

---

during the latter part of the nineteenth century and the first quarter of the twentieth century. He was a master teacher as well as a staunch advocate of the education of African Americans. His work was recognized at black educational institutions in Atlanta, in the Methodist Episcopal Church, and among such prominent black educators as Booker T. Washington and W. E. B. Du Bois. A man who preferred classical training for black students but respected industrial training as a purpose for sister institution Tuskegee Institute, Crogman left a legacy that is preserved in his speeches and writings on black history.

Born free on the island of St. Maarten, in Philipsburg, on May 5, 1841, William H. Crogman was the son of William and Charlotte Chippendale Crogman. By the time he was fourteen years old both parents had died. In 1855, B. L. Boomer, of a New England ship owning family, befriended him and took him to his Middleboro, Massachusetts, home to live. The family's business enabled Crogman to gain wide experiences as a seaman, as he traveled abroad for eleven years on one of its ships. He visited primary ports in Asia, Europe, Australia, and South America. His observations provided invaluable information and broadened his experiences as well.

Crogman attended a district school near his new home. He worked and saved money to support himself in further training, and in 1868 he entered Pierce Academy in Middleboro, Massachusetts. He achieved so well that the principal placed him in a class by himself so that he might continue to excel without the presence of slower students who might hinder his progress. After graduating, in 1870 the Freedmen's Aid Society hired him as English teacher at all-black Claflin College in Orangeburg, South Carolina, where he was the school's first black teacher. He had studied Greek and Latin independently, and now, with a vision to master those subjects, he enrolled in Atlanta University in 1873 and completed with distinction a classical course. He accelerated his studies and completed the four-year program in three, becoming a member of Atlanta's first graduating class in 1876 and receiving the A.B. degree. In 1879, he received a master's degree from Atlanta.

In 1876 as well, Crogman became a founding faculty member of nearby Clark University (today a part of Clark Atlanta University), later becoming a senior professor and a master teacher. On his fiftieth birthday, friends and former students recognized him with letters of praise. According to Louis-Charles Harvey's biographical sketch of Crogman, one student wrote that "he had the ability to motivate even the dullest student." He was called "a master of his very high calling, teaching." A man of unusual ability, Crogman taught Greek, Latin, and New Testament. He had honed his speaking skills and became a master of clear and elegant style. In his lectures he mixed humor with an easy delivery and held his audience spellbound. In 1910 Clark celebrated its fortieth anniversary and at the same time recognized Crogman for his work as a master teacher and advocate for education of his people.

Those organizations and institutions that invited him to speak were the American Missionary Association and the Freedmen's Aid Society of the Methodist Episcopal church. As a layman, he was invited to speak at Plymouth Church in Brooklyn, New York, where Reverend Henry Ward Beecher was pastor. He spoke on October 14, 1883, for the morning and evening services. According to *Men of Mark*, he noted in his evening discourse that blacks had fought valiantly in all wars in defense of the United States government. They were in the Revolution and the Rebellion, and military leaders such as George Washington bore witness to their service. "The Negro fought in common with you to found this government," he said, "and to perpetuate this government." Although "hanged in the streets of New York by an infuriated mob; snubbed and mocked, buffeted and spit upon, . . . he has never for a moment deserted the Union." In spite of blacks' proven commitment to the United States, heated debates over the civil rights bill of that period showed that some members of Congress still considered blacks worthless, unmanly, and cowardly. Crogman's lecture on "The Negro's Needs" included his views on what he called "counter-education," the concern that blacks were taught one thing in church or school and given another view by mainstream white treatment of the race. These three lectures of Crogman's were printed in pamphlet form under the title *Talks for the Times* and made available for distribution.

Crogman also attended the National Association of Teachers in Madison, Wisconsin, serving as a delegate from Georgia. His address was praised in the press and was published in full in the association's report. He spoke again at many summer gatherings at a site that he called Chautauqua Island Park.

A devoted member of the Methodist Episcopal Church, Crogman was a lay delegate for the Savannah Conference at the denomination's General Conference for 1880, 1884, and 1888. He served as one of the assistant secretaries of the General Conference in 1884 and again in 1888. The Board of Bishops of the AME Church appointed him a delegate to the Ecumenical Council of Methodism held in London. Crogman was also a founding member of the Board of Trustees at Clark University and held the post until 1922.

The Methodist Episcopal Church's General Conference of 1892 established the University Senate comprised of fifteen educators selected by the bishops. The senate's purpose was to set minimum requirements for a baccalaureate degree program at the colleges and universities that the church supported. Crogman became one of the senate's initial members and apparently held the post until 1900.

In 1895 the historic Cotton States and International Exposition was held in Atlanta. Those who planned the exposition decided that, to succeed, it would need to provide some distinguishing characteristics; therefore, a major exhibit representing Negro culture would be appropriate. Crogman was the man for the task. He traveled to the leading cities in the South to gather exhibit materials and ideas for the display. Blacks eagerly supported him in his goal of presenting black history in an accurate and positive light. He responded by planning a large exhibit of significant educational and industrial importance. It was at this exposition that noted educator and Tuskegee Institute founder and president Booker T. Washington gave much of his New South philosophy in his address that many of his critics dubbed the "Atlanta Comprise." Notwithstanding criticism that his speech compromised black people, the address catapulted Washington into prominence as a national black educational leader. So successful was Crogman in his work that the exposition commissioner for blacks in the state of Georgia, which had a large and effective display, named Crogman permanent chair of the Board of Chief Commissioners for blacks all over the state.

Becomes President of Clark University

Crogman continued to teach—the occupation he enjoyed most—but accepted the post as acting president of Clark University in 1903-04 and was elected president at the Board of Trustee's meeting on July 1, 1904. (The institution was later known as Clark College, and much later, after it joined Atlanta University, the merged institutions became known as Clark Atlanta University.) After he took office, Crogman continued the agricultural program established earlier. Farmers' conferences and institutes were held, reaching scores of farmers throughout Georgia. Under his administration as well, Clark eliminated industrial and vocational education from its curriculum and raised the standards in all academic departments. In the 1880s' debate over industrial or classical education in the newly founded black college of the South, Crogman emphatically favored a classical education. Although Crogman had a lifelong friendship with Booker T. Washington, respected his leadership, and recognized Tuskegee as an important black college, he criticized the financial support and the energy that some leaders placed on vocational education. Washington, of course, favored industrial or vocational education. Crogman believed that liberal college programs were being neglected. Apparently an effective administrator, he remained Clark's president until June 1910 and then stepped down to return to full-time teaching. In that year as well, the university celebrated its fortieth anniversary. At that time the school recognized Crogman's services as both a great teacher and as president through most of the school's existence. Crogman retired eleven years later.

Although Crogman was known best as a college administrator, educator, scholar, and lecturer, he was also a race man. He protested racial segregation that prevailed in the South and refused to ride the segregated streetcars to his work place; instead, regardless of weather conditions, he walked several miles from Clark's campus to the downtown area. Crogman received an honorary Litt.D. from Atlanta University and the LL.D. degree from Clark University, both in 1901. The chapel at Clark was named in his honor.

Crogman was a charter board member of Gammon Theological Seminary (a Methodist-supported college in Atlanta), the Commission for the Unification of the Book Concern, and the American Geographical Society. Crogman belonged to the American Negro Academy (ANA), which Alexander Crummell founded in 1897. The ANA's membership included Du Bois, Frances J. Grimké, and other African American intellectuals. Crogman brought a valued balance to the organization by serving in a mediating position in the continuing debate over classical education that some educators favored and the industrial education that Booker T. Washington and his followers favored.

Crogman co-authored with Henry F. Kletzing *Progress of a Race, or the Remarkable Advancement of the American Negro from the Bondage of Slavery and Poverty to Freedom and Citizenship, Intellect, Affluence, Honor and Trust.* Booker T. Washington wrote the introduction for this work. The book was subsequently revised, enlarged, and published in 1901 as *The Colored American*, with J. W. Gibson as co-author. In 1920 it was published under its original title and subsequently reprinted.

On July 10, 1878, Crogman married Lavinia C. Mott, a native of Charlotte, North Carolina and a graduate of Atlanta University. The couple had eight children. After retiring from Clark and relocating to Philadelphia in 1921, Crogman and his wife lived quietly at 105 S. 34th Street, on the west side. He died one week before his wife, on October 16, 1931, when he was ninety years old.

Crogman's writings continue to contribute to black scholarship and black biography, while his reputation as an intellect and educator lives on. Even so, according to Grant S. Shockley, he "deserves more visibility than either black history or higher education has accorded him."

REFERENCES

Books

Brawley, James P. *Two Centuries of Methodist Concern: Bondage, Freedom, and Education of Black People.* New York: Vantage Press, 1974.

Harvey, Louis Charles. *Something More Than Human.* Ed. Charles E. Cole. Nashville: United Methodist Board of Higher Education and Ministry, 1986.

Kennedy, Melvin D. *Dictionary of American Negro Biography.* Eds. Rayford W. Logan and Michael R. Winston. New York: Norton, 1982.

Shockley, Grant S., ed. *Heritage & Hope: The African American Presence in United Methodism.* Nashville: Abington Press, 1991.

Jessie Carney Smith

Oliver Cromwell
1752–1853

Soldier

Oliver Cromwell distinguished himself in the American Revolution; he served under and was decorated by General George Washington. His longevity in the service of his country in the Revolutionary War brought Cromwell to the attention of many. When Cromwell was discharged, Washington awarded him a medal as a private in the New Jersey Battalion. In addition, Washington personally signed his discharge papers on June 5, 1783 at Newburgh, New York. During his enlistment, which began in the first days of the war, Cromwell served almost seven years in several campaigns and left the Continental Army at the close of the war.

Oliver Cromwell was born on May 24, 1752, a freeman, in Black Horse (present-day Columbus), Burlington County, New Jersey. He was raised as a farmer, working with his maternal uncle, Thomas Hutchins. William C. Nell reports in an article in the *Burlington Gazette* that

Chronology

1752	Born in Black Horse (present-day Columbus), Burlington County, New Jersey on May 24
1776	Joins the 2nd New Jersey Regiment; participates in the battles of Trenton and Princeton; crosses the Delaware with General George Washington
1777	Participates in the battles of Princeton and Brandywine
1778	Participates in the battle of Monmouth
1779	Participates in the Iroquois Expedition
1780	Participates in the defense of New Jersey
1781	Participates in the Yorktown campaign
1783	Discharged by General George Washington who signs his papers and presents him with a medal for service
1853	Dies in January and is buried in the cemetery at the Broad Street Methodist Church
1983	Oliver Cromwell Black History Society is formed in Burlington City, New Jersey

Cromwell was of mixed parentage, "just half white." There is no other recorded information on his early life. At the beginning of the war against England, Cromwell enlisted in the Continental Army and he served until the war ended.

Following his discharge, Cromwell moved back to Burlington County and farming. Some years following his discharge, he applied for a veteran's pension. In spite of the fact that he could neither read nor write, he was awarded the pension. A sign of the high esteem in which he was held, the pension was granted because the judges, lawyers, and politicians supported the request. Cromwell received $96 annually and bought a one-hundred-acre farm outside Burlington. He fathered fourteen children, seven boys and seven girls, all of whom lived to maturity. His last years (he moved around 1840) were spent at 114 East Union Street in Burlington City. He died in January 1853. Cromwell was survived by three sons and three daughters, grandchildren, and great grandchildren. He was buried in the Broad Street Methodist Church Cemetery.

Serves in Revolutionary War

Initially, General George Washington, commander in chief of the Continental Army, was against including African Americans in the army. He came from a slave owner's background and state; this was the experience he had with African Americans. When he found there were free men of color fighting, he believed they would interfere with the progress of the war. Due to the petitions of some whites and free African Americans who had been a part of the regiment, he took the problem to the Congress. The decision was to allow those free African Americans who had been in the army to reenlist. However, no new men of color were to be admitted. Ultimately, this policy was changed when the need for manpower grew; white men were not rushing to join the troops, African Americans were clamoring to join, and the British began to offer freedom to African American slaves and indentured servants who joined their forces. New England states enlisted free African Americans; oftentimes slaves were enlisted in place of their white owners, and owners often freed their slaves to fight, later rescinding the papers. Thus, there were legal ways, though not without rousing objections, for African Americans to participate in the war for independence. However, these ruses for African American involvement were not necessary in Burlington, where there was a history of African American freedom and involvement in the fight independence. Burlington had the largest number of free African Americans in the state of New Jersey, a fact attributed to the large Quaker population and influence. It was in this environment that Oliver Cromwell grew up and enlisted.

At the beginning of the war, according to the *Burlington Gazette,* Cromwell joined under the company commanded by Captain Lowery, attached to the 2nd New Jersey Regiment under the command of Colonel Israel Shreve. According to the tourism department in Burlington, Cromwell "received high praise for his military discipline, superior personal conduct, strong physical abilities, his dedication and sacrifice." He later joined George Washington's command in New York and traveled through New Jersey and Pennsylvania. In his interview in the *Burlington Gazette*, Cromwell indicates he loved General George Washington "affectionately." According to Gail Buckley in *American Patriots: The Story of Blacks in the Military from the Revolution to Desert Storm*, he was with the army at General Washington's memorable crossing of the Delaware on December 25, 1776.

Cromwell's stint in the Continental Army caused him to see action at several major battles. He was present at the battles of Trenton (1776), Princeton and Brandywine (1777), Monmouth (1778), the Iroquois Expedition (1779), the defense of New Jersey (1780), and the Yorktown Campaign (1781) where he reportedly saw the last man killed. Burlington Tourism reports Cromwell as a "battlefield drummer."

In recognition of his services in the Continental Army, General George Washington personally signed his discharge papers and presented him with the badge of merit for his outstanding dedication and service. Cromwell and another African American, Prince Whipple, both soldiers in the American Revolution, appear in the painting *Washington Crossing the Delaware* painted by Emmanuel Leutze in 1851. In spite of the debate among historians over whether the painting actually portrays Cromwell, the image of the two African Americans in the painting appears on a U.S. stamp. They are identified on the stamp as Cromwell and Whipple. Oliver Cromwell's house is the fourth stop on the African American Historic Sites Tour in Burlington City, New Jersey.

The Oliver Cromwell Black History Society, established in 1983, was organized to research and preserve black Heritage in Burlington and throughout the United States. The society works with and encourages African American youth to remember and keep alive African American history. It recognizes local residents by awarding the "Oliver Cromwell Living Heritage Award" annually.

REFERENCES

Books

Buckley, Gail. *American Patriots: The Story of Blacks in the Military from the Revolution to Desert Storm.* New York: Random House, 2001.

Online

"African American Historic Sites Part 1." http://www.co.burlington.nj.us/tourism/history/looptour/african.htm (Accessed 11 March 2006).

"Biographies of Three African American Soldiers at Monmouth." http://zorak.monmouth.edu/~afam/Military7.htm (Accessed 11 March 2006).

"Cromwell, Oliver." *The Encyclopedia of African-American Culture and Education.* http://pages.towson.edu/oali/encyclopedia_of_africanamer.htm (Accessed 11 March 2006).

"New Jersey." *The Colored Patriots of the American Revolution, With Sketches of Several Distinguished Colored Persons: To Which is Added a Brief Survey of the Condition and Prospects of Colored Americans.* William Cooper Nell. Electronic Edition. http://docsouth.unc.edu/nell/nell.html (Accessed 11 March 2006).

"Oliver Cromwell." http://08016.com/cromwell.html (Accessed 11 March 2006).

"Oliver Cromwell." http://www.co.burlington.nj.us/tourism/history/african/cromwell.htm (Accessed 11 March 2006).

"Oliver Cromwell Black History Society." http://08016.com/ocbhs.html (Accessed 11 March 2006).

Helen R. Houston

Andrae Crouch
1942–

Gospel singer, composer, minister

Andrae Crouch is one of the most important innovators of contemporary gospel music. His arrange-

Andrae Crouch

ments and production of Christian music changed the way in which music of worship is perceived in the United States. Crouch's music embraces listeners of traditional gospel recordings and diverse others who enjoy jazz, blues, and non-traditional performances. His songs have been performed by various artists, including Paul Simon and Elvis Presley. The recipient of more than sixteen Grammy Awards, Crouch as a gospel musician, recording artist, songwriter, arranger, and producer is recognized as an international music star. His message of hope, faith and joy transcends color, class, and creed.

The Crouch family welcomed on July 1, 1942 twins whom they named Andrae Edward and Sandra. The new additions to the family made a total of three siblings which included an older brother, Benjamin. Crouch and his twin sister were born into the dedicated Christian family of Catherine Dorothea and Benjamin Jerome Crouch. Crouch's father Benjamin was a lay preacher and the owner of two dry-cleaning stores. Crouch's mother managed one of the stores and his father managed the other. Their places of business also served as an opportunity to share their faith with their customers. The family was aware of all their blessings and clearly saw one of their missions as proselytizing. They were active members of the Emmanuel Church of God and Christ, with Rev. Samuel M. Crouch, Crouch's great uncle as the pastor. The church had a congregation of more than 2,000 members. Early experiences for Crouch centered on church work and singing in a trio with his sister and brother at Sunday school.

As a lay preacher, Crouch's father would be called to churches that had need of a preacher on a short term basis. Crouch's father preached at the Macedonia Church about sixty miles from their home in Los Angeles. The entire family attended the service and heard Crouch's father preach for the first time in a real pulpit and not on the street, at a hospital, or in other created spaces. He was urged to continue on an interim basis until the church secured a full-time pastor. Crouch's father was reluctant and decided to make a bargain with the Lord. Both Sandra and Benjamin had musical talent, but Andrae was dyslexic and stuttered badly. Crouch's father promised the Lord that if his son were given the gift of music, he would become a full-time minister. Crouch's mother believed in her husband's prayer and bought a cardboard piano keyboard for Crouch to practice on. Crouch, who was eleven at the time, had no real thoughts about music other than singing, but he took to the keyboard emulating music he had heard on the radio. Crouch's father called on him to attest to his musical talents. During a service at Macedonia Church, the congregation was to sing "What a Friend We Have in Jesus." Crouch came forward to accompany the church on the piano at his father's request. Not really sure of all the pedals and in particular the middle pedal, Crouch played for the congregation with both hands. Within two weeks Crouch's father gave up his dry-cleaning businesses and the ministry of the entire family had begun.

Music as Personal Mission and God-Given Talent

Music helped Crouch overcome shyness and stammering that often resulted in his twin sister having to speak for him. Crouch wrote his first song only three years after his experience in church playing the piano. At fourteen, he attended a Memorial Day celebration and was inspired by the words "Oh the blood" and as he began to sing he asked his friend Billy Preston, also a pianist, to play the chords to accompany him. The song "The Blood Will Never Lose Its Power" became the first of many inspirational songs by Crouch.

When Crouch was in junior high school, his family moved to the San Fernando Valley suburb of Pacoima. His father became the pastor of the Christ Memorial Church of God in Christ, a Pentecostal church in a predominately Hispanic town. In high school, Crouch formed the group Church of God in Christ Singers (COGICS) around 1960. The members were Gloria Jones, Frankie Karl Springs, Edna Wright, Blinky Williams, Sandra Crouch, and Billy Preston. Preston later played organ for the Beatles and received acclaim for songs such as "Will You Go Round in Circles." COGICS was the first to record the song, "The Blood Will Never Lose Its Power." Crouch realized that if the audience was to be blessed by the song, it must be self explanatory. The style and singing that COGICS offered was not always understood by traditional gospel audiences. Crouch was accustomed to racially diverse gatherings since his mother and father's background included both Jewish and German mixed marriages along with Afro-European marriages of grandparents and great-grandparents. As a member of a Youth for Christ group, headed by a young white man from the Nazarene Church, Crouch saw the need for an easily understood message to all groups. All of these influences encouraged Crouch to write songs clearly so that the gospel would be understood. Crouch's split-compositional style moved between and blended light rock, soul, and pop, combined with traditional hymns and anthems.

After high school Crouch attended Valley Junior College in San Fernando, California and pursued religious studies at Life Bible Institute in Los Angeles. He worked in the community and counseled recovering drug addicts, but music was in his heart. In 1965 Crouch founded Andrae Crouch and the Disciples, which became the vehicle for his compositions for over twenty years. After signing with Light Records in 1971, their debut album *Take the Message Everywhere* was released. It featured original compositions and arrangements that would mark the Crouch sound. The album included arrangements of the Negro spiritual "Wade in the Water"; Thomas Dorsey's "Precious Lord, Take My Hand"; and the hymn "No, Not One!" The split composition style absorbed a broad spectrum of musical forms and instruments and blurred the gospel traditions of arrangement, composition, and performance.

Crouch and the Disciples recorded and traveled extensively. Appearances included *The Tonight Show Starring Johnny Carson*, performance at the Hollywood Bowl, and sell out crowds at Carnegie Hall. The group even performed on the NBC television show *Saturday Night Live* in 1980, which continued to break new ground regarding audiences. The group's performances were key in pushing the boundaries as they included pop-style vocal arrangement, crooned vocals unlike the intense gospel style, and production techniques associated more with R&B. Musicians on their recordings included Sherman Andrus, Perry Morgan, Billy Thedford, Sandra Crouch, Ruben Fernandez, Tramaine Hawkins, Danniebelle Hall, Paula Clarin and Phyllis Swisher. Crouch's solo career began in 1972 with the LP *Just Andrae*. Under the Light label, Crouch as a soloist recorded six albums, and as lead singer of the Disciples recorded twelve. Crouch and the Disciples took home Grammy Awards in 1975 for "Take Me Back," 1978 for "Live in London," 1979 for "I'll Be Thinking of You," 1980 for "The Lord's Prayer," 1981 for "Don't Give Up," and 1984 for "No Time to Lose." There were numerous other awards, such as the Dove Awards which were given to both Crouch and the Disciples.

The sound that Crouch brought to contemporary worship in the United States reached beyond the African American traditional base and incorporated the Jesus Movement from 1969 through 1979. This movement, which came out of a counterculture in the Haight-Asbury district in San Francisco, sought a more Christian-centered life for all young Americans. The group believed that, weighted down by the Vietnam War, the death of three astronauts in an explosion, and increasing unrest by African Americans, Christian belief demanded a life that centered on the teachings of Jesus and personal relations with an emphasis on discipleship, evangelism, and Bible study. This phenomenon, which began slowly as folk music with more accessible lyrics relating to the Gospel, had a lasting effect on contemporary worship. Crouch and the Disciples offered a form of praise and worship that gave support to this movement.

Despite Crouch's success, he was criticized by some gospel purists. Many felt that his inclusion of secular elements diluted the religious content. The greatest outcry came with the 1981 release of the song "Don't Give Up." It competed with secular markets and used up-to-date technology regarding production techniques and topical lyrics. Even though the song was released by Warner Brothers label, Crouch continued to record songs for Light label that remained gospel-oriented. In 1982 more difficulties arose as Crouch was arrested on cocaine possession charges. He maintained that the substance found was instant chicken soup powder. No formal charges were ever filed by the police, but the experience took its toll on Crouch. He decided to reestablish his priorities and focus more on his family and church and produce projects with other artists.

From 1984 to 1994, Crouch took a hiatus from recording. He composed and arranged for other artists, such as Michael Jackson, Quincy Jones, Diana Ross, and Elton John. His film credits include *Once Upon a Forest*, *The Color Purple*, *The Lion King*, and *Free Willy*. He also appeared as the television voice of Dr. Seuss's Yertle the Turtle. Crouch received an Oscar nomination in 1986 for his score for the film *The Color Purple*. In 1994, he released the album *Mercy!* as inspired by the words "Mercy, have mercy on us." His message remained consistent in keeping the word of God in the music, but he enhanced the songs with a global flavor, featuring a mix of reggae and African rhythms. Crouch also was presented the McDonald's Gospelfest Golden Circle Lifetime Achievement Award and an award from the international Association of African American Music. To give honor to Crouch's contribution to gospel music, the top names in gospel and contemporary Christian music spent two years making a tribute to him. Released in 1996 the album was titled *Tribute: The Songs of Andrae Crouch*.

In the wake of his refocused life Crouch met with tragedies and the realization of a calling. Crouch's mother Catherine was the first of three immediate family members to die over a three-year period. In 1992, at the age of 72, she died of cancer. The following year, December 1993, Crouch's father Benjamin died at 76 of liver cancer. His death placed Crouch's brother Benjamin as the pastor of their father's church, Christ Memorial in Pacoima. His brother Benjamin served for five months as the church pastor, before he died at the age of 53. Crouch knew that his becoming pastor of the church was a calling his father had revealed to him. His cavalier response to this as he told *People Weekly* was, "Daddy, you'll be here forever because that's one thing I won't do!" Crouch's father told him again before he died, he should have three black suits ready at all times because he wanted his son to be ready. Crouch still resisted. Even with his sister's help the congregation was unsuccessful in finding a new pastor. After resisting the idea for a while, in April 1995 Crouch began preaching at the church and was later elevated to pastor. The congregation, who had dropped off in attendance after the death of Crouch's father, regained its membership and continued to grow.

Crouch's performances consistently sold out throughout Europe, the Americas, Africa, and the Far East, and his music was translated into twenty-one languages. His timeless classics place him firmly in musical history. Crouch is one of only three gospel artists to receive a star on the Hollywood Walk of Fame. He is in the company of Mahalia Jackson and Reverend James Cleveland. Crouch received his star on the Walk of Fame in 2004 surrounded by his sister, nephew, and aunt. His personal and evangelical ministry took him from show business to the pastor of his father's church in Pacoima. He continues his love of music and composes during his six o'clock morning prayers every day. As a sixteen-time

Grammy winner and music innovator, Crouch has set a high level of musical expression.

REFERENCES

Books

Benson, Alvin K. "Crouch, Andrae." In *The African American Encyclopedia*. Vol. 3. Ed. Michael W. Williams. New York: Marshall Cavendish Corporation, 2001.

Manheim, James M. "Andrae Crouch." In *Contemporary Black Biography*. Vol. 27. Farmington Hills, Mich.: Gale Group, 2001.

Periodicals

Monroe, Steve. "Mercy." *American Vision* 9 (August-September 1994): 48.

Rogers, Patrick, and Karen Brailsford. "In His Father's House: Gospelstar Andrae Crouch Comes Home to Lead His Family's Church." *People Weekly* 44 (23 October 1995): 103.

Online

Ramsey, Guthrie P., Jr. "Andre Crouch." *International Dictionary of Black Composers*. http://www.cbmr. org/pubs/crouch.htm (Accessed 15 January 2006).

Terry, Lindsay. "It started on a Keyboard Made of Paper." The Communicator. http://www.cbmr.org/pubs/crouch.htm (Accessed 15 January 2006).

Lean'tin L. Bracks

Daniel Wallace Culp
1845–?

Educator, editor, minister, physician

Although information on Daniel Wallace Culp is scanty, he was a versatile man who prepared himself to serve as an educator, editor, minister, and physician. At some point he became involved in politics, but the extent and success of his work in that arena are unknown. An author as well, Culp compiled a collection of essays by African American writers, published as *Twentieth Century Negro Literature* (1902).

Culp was born a slave in Union County, South Carolina. Clearly, education was important to him because he pursued a college degree. In 1876, he was the first and only student to graduate from Biddle University, the forerunner of Johnson C. Smith University, in Charlotte,

Chronology	
1845?	Born in Union County, South Carolina
1876	Graduates from Biddle University, Charlotte, North Carolina
1879	Graduates from Princeton Theological Seminary; pastors Presbyterian church in Jacksonville, Florida; becomes principal of Stanton School
1880	Enrolls in University of Michigan medical school
1891	Graduates from Ohio Medical University
1902	Publishes *Twentieth Century Negro Literature*

North Carolina. That same year, Culp enrolled in Princeton Theological Seminary and also studied philosophy, history, and psychology at the university. However, according to the title page of his book, Culp only held degrees in medicine, the A.M. and M.D. degrees. Soon after his arrival at Princeton, he learned that his schoolmates were prejudiced against black people. Those from the South were particularly annoyed by his presence and left college immediately in protest. However, apparently they were persuaded to return to school.

Within three years, Culp had created friendships among both university and seminary students, including those from the South who had protested against his presence. Fellow students must have respected Culp's excellent performance. In 1879, Culp graduated from the seminary and began work immediately as pastor under the Freedmen's Board of the Northern Presbyterian Church. He held the pastorate for several years and worked in different states as well. One of these states was Florida, where he settled in Jacksonville and was pastor at the local black Presbyterian church. Culp was also appointed principal of the state's largest black school, Stanton School, located in Jacksonville. Here, young James Weldon Johnson (1871-1938) encountered Culp. Johnson, who later criticized Culp's performance at the school, went on to become one of the nation's black luminaries, recognized for his work as writer, activist, diplomat, critic, educator, lawyer, and editor.

Jacksonville held a ceremony to honor the life of President James A. Garfield, who was assassinated on July 2, 1881. On the day after his funeral, exercises were held in the city under the auspices of federal officeholders, who asked Culp to give the opening prayer. Culp was an unseasoned speaker and gave a lengthy, boring prayer that lasted from thirty-five to forty minutes. In his book *Along This Way*, Johnson wrote about Culp: "He stammered terribly, but the length of this particular prayer could not be charged to the impediment in his speech." Rather, Johnson believed that Culp had seized the opportunity to try to impress certain leading citizens of Jacksonville. "I have heard some queer prayers but never any one prayer in which so wide a range of topics was introduced," he continued. Johnson called prayers such as the one given by Culp "officious" and "pompous."

As a teacher and principal, Culp was hardly any better. He was a poor administrator as well. Stanton was loosely run, sort of a "go-as-you-please institution," wrote Johnson. In fact, many parents removed their children from the school and sent them elsewhere for their education. Johnson's father wanted to do so but his mother, who was the school's assistant principal, protested. Thus, Johnson remained at Stanton, but he and other students there "dawdled away" their time while in Culp's class. "He seemed to have no definite plans about graduating us," wrote Johnson. As the situation worsened, parents demanded a change, resulting in Culp's dismissal. Culp's formal education, however, was far better than that of his replacement, William Artell, who lacked a college education altogether.

Gradually, Culp lost interest in teaching and perhaps the ministry as well; he became interested in the health problems of blacks and then began to study medicine. He enrolled in the University of Michigan but some time later transferred to the Ohio Medical University. In 1891 he graduated with honors.

Edits Works by Black Writers

Culp's only known book, *Twentieth Century Negro Literature: A Cyclopedia of Thought*, was published in 1902 in Toronto, Canada; Naperville, Illinois; and Atlanta, Georgia. The work covers a variety of topics relating to African Americans and is written, it claims, by "one hundred of America's Greatest Negroes." The title page lists Culp as "an author and lecturer, etc." The book is illuminated with one hundred photo engravings.

Culp's work served as an important source of information and images of black men and women during the time. In addition to the articles given on then-timely subjects, a biographical sketch—many times with a photograph—accompanies each article. Among those included are North Carolina legislator John P. Green, emigrationist and AME church leader Henry McNeil Turner, educator and college president John Wesley Edward Bowen, educator and journalist Josephine Silone Yates, activist and women's rights leader Mary Church Terrell, educator and women's rights activist Mary Burnett Talbert, sociologist and writer Kelly Miller, college president and Greek scholar William S. Scarborough, and writer George Marion McClellan. There are others of similar stature as well as lesser-known figures.

In *Along This Way*, James Weldon Johnson described Culp as "a slender young man of medium height . . . [who was] pure black." Culp's photograph, published in his own work, bears out Johnson's description. Culp deserves further study if for no other reason than that his single known contribution to early African American literature is important.

REFERENCES

Books

Burkett, Randall K., and others. *Black Biography, 1790-1950.* Vol. 1. Alexandria, Va.: Chadwick-Healy, 1991.

Johnson, James Weldon. *Along This Way*. New York: Viking Press, 1933.

Jessie Carney Smith

D

Wendell P. Dabney
1865–1952

Editor

Wendell Phillips Dabney, editor of Cincinnati's oldest Negro newspaper *The Union* for forty-six years, was known for his fearless advocacy for the rights of his people. Described by Joseph T. Beaver Jr. as "a veritable composite of brain, gift, and diligence," he was "more of a philosopher than a politician."

Dabney was born in Richmond, Virginia on November 4, 1865 to former slaves John and Elizabeth Foster Dabney. John opened his own catering business after the Civil War and was able to provide a higher standard of living for his family than most former slaves. John Dabney instilled in young Wendell a respect for religion as a means of overcoming racial injustice. He also influenced his children's political views, especially the idea that Republicans helped blacks while Democrats did not.

Dabney's youth was spent selling newspapers, doing homework, and playing guitar with his older brother. He also sometimes danced alongside future author and tap dance artist Bill "Bojangles" Robinson as they grew up together in Richmond. Dabney was a waiter at a local restaurant in summer, a job that was demoralizing to him because of the way he was treated by the white customers.

In his senior year of high school, Dabney was instrumental in protesting the separation of blacks and whites for graduation. The successful protest resulted in the first combined graduation ever held at the high school. Dabney once stated that he wanted to be a lawyer, a doctor, or a musician, or all three. He said according to Gail Berry, "Law for money, medicine to benefit humanity, and music for pleasure."

Dabney spent 1883 in the preparatory department at Oberlin College. While attending Oberlin, he was first violinist at the Oberlin Opera House and was a member of the Cademian Literary Society. He gained confidence in his abilities and decided that with equal opportunity

Chronology	
1865	Born in Richmond, Virginia on November 4
1883	Enters preparatory department at Oberlin College
1884	Begins teaching elementary school and guitar
1890	Opens music school in Boston
1893	Works with Frederick Douglass on Chicago World's Fair exhibition
1894	Moves to Cincinnati to oversee Dumas Hotel
1895	Becomes Cincinnati's first African American license clerk
1897	Marries Nellie Foster Jackson and adopts her two sons
1898	Serves as paymaster in Department of Treasury in Cincinnati
1907	Establishes his newspaper *The Union*
1915	Becomes first president of the Cincinnati branch of NAACP
1949	Attends eighty-fourth birthday party honoring his achievements
1950	Receives honor by the National Convention of Negro Publishers
1952	Dies in Cincinnati, Ohio on June 5

black Americans could succeed in spite of the racial attitudes of white Americans.

In 1884, Dabney began teaching at a Louisa County Virginia elementary school. He taught guitar as well as his regular class schedule. He had never studied a note and admittedly knew nothing about counterpoint, base or harmony, according to Joseph Beaver. As quoted by Beaver, Dvorak, the music director and composer, once said of Dabney, "You break all the rules, yet your technique, I must admit, is superb, and your style matchless."

In 1890, Dabney left Richmond and opened a music school in Boston for amateur and professional musicians. In 1893, he worked on an exhibition with Frederick Douglass for the Chicago World's Fair. In 1894, Dabney moved to Cincinnati to oversee property his mother had inherited from her aunt Serena Webb. This property, the Dumas Hotel, was built in the early 1840s and was Ohio's only hotel owned by an African American. It had served as a station for the Underground Railroad by which slaves were aided in their flight from their masters. Dabney installed a gymnasium in one part of the hotel and used the rest as a convention and meeting hall.

Dabney decided to stay in Cincinnati, and in August 1897, he married Nellie Foster Jackson. Dabney adopted Nellie's two sons. Needing additional income, Dabney used his musical knowledge to teach music courses for wealthy white Cincinnati residents. Songs he wrote were published by the George Jaberg and Wurlitzer Music companies.

He gave up his music career in 1895 when he became Cincinnati's first African American license clerk. From 1898 to 1923, Dabney served as assistant, then head paymaster in the Cincinnati Department of Treasury. He was able to save money to start his own daily newspaper.

Establishes Newspaper

Hoping to bring attention to issues of the African American community, Dabney started *The Ohio Enterprise*, then on February 13, 1907 Dabney established *The Union*. His motto for the newspaper, according to Eric Jackson, was: "For no people can become great without being united, for in union there is strength." From 1907 to 1952, *The Union* was influential in shaping both political and social opinions of Cincinnati's African American citizens. In the beginning Dabney accepted funds from the Republican Party while remaining critical of its treatment of African Americans. He decided to break with the Republicans and in 1925 became affiliated with the Independent Party.

Dabney was the first president of the Cincinnati branch of the NAACP, established in 1915. The NAACP staged several demonstrations against problems such as political injustice, racial violence, and segregated housing.

Dabney's writings reflected his interests in the experiences of African Americans in Cincinnati. He wrote that in spite of the conditions in Cincinnati, in spite of the racial violence and political injustice, African American Cincinnatians had established a lively and stable community. He wrote on race relations, discrimination, segregation, and urbanization.

Joseph Beaver, who worked at *The Union* as an office boy for several years, wrote that Dabney had on his office walls a galaxy of photos of his friends, both the famous and the not-so-famous. They included photos of W. C. Handy, "Father of the Blues"; Bill "Bojangles" Robinson, author and tap dancer; Philippa Schuyler, child protégé artist and composer; W. E. B. Du Bois, American scholar and educator; Peter Jackson, heavyweight boxer; Paul Lawrence Dunbar and Langston Hughes, poets; Madam Hattie Walker, bank president in Virginia; and General Antonio Maceo, Cuba's liberator.

In *The Union*, Dabney wrote urging blacks to be civil in conduct. According to Gail Berry, he said: "Many of us talk so much about our civil rights that we forget about our civic duties." He also said: "We fight for our rights, why not so conduct ourselves as to cause the whites to see the injustice of withholding them?" Regarding critics who complained that the paper was all about Dabney, Beaver replied, "To feature oneself is not to say one necessarily praises oneself—but rather, he presents himself, his experiences, his ideas and opinions, on a public scale, as it were, for others to weigh."

On November 4, 1949, more than four hundred people gathered to honor Dabney with a celebration of his eighty-fourth birthday. In January 1950, the National Convention of Negro Publishers honored Dabney as a pioneer and leader in African American journalism.

On June 5, 1952, Dabney died in Cincinnati. As quoted by Berry, his stepson Leo said of him, *"The Union* will live on in spirit though the soul of it has fled. Its luster left with Dabney." According to Berry, Dabney was eulogized throughout the country as "an American institution dedicated to an unending crusade against segregation and discrimination and as the foremost advocator for Negro improvement and advancement." Berry quotes George Bernard Shaw as saying, "You can lose a man like that by your own death, but not by his."

REFERENCES

Books

Beaver, Joseph T. *I Want You to Know Wendell Phillips Dabney.* Published in Mexico, D.F., 1958.

Berry, Gail Estelle. *Wendell Phillips Dabney: Leader of the Negro Protest.* Cincinnati: University of Cincinnati, 1965.

Periodicals

Horstman, Barry M. "Crusading Editor Fought Injustice." *The Cincinnati Post,* 8 February 1999.

Online

Guide to 20th Century African American Resources at the Cincinnati Historical Society Library: Wendell P. Dabney. http://library.cincymuseum.org/aag/bio/dabney.html (Accessed 12 April 2005).

Jackson, Eric R. "Dabney, Wendell Phillips." American National Biography Online. http:///www.anb.org/articles/15/15-00160.html (Accessed 12 April 2005).

Collections

Dabney's papers are at the Cincinnati Historical Society Library, Cincinnati, Ohio.

Virginia D. Bailey

John C. Dancy
1888–1968

Business executive, community activist

John Campbell Dancy Jr. served as director of the Detroit Urban League in Detroit, Michigan from 1918 to 1960. Using his own brand of personal diplomacy Dancy was able to strengthen and expand the mission of the league to provide needed services and employment opportunities for local African Americans as well as the enormous number of African Americans who were migrating to the city. Dancy's leadership resulted in employment opportunities that extended outside the servant industry into skilled jobs, which had previously barred blacks. His determination to see his community grow and prosper guided his involvement in organizations that supported and made policy for institutions such as hospitals, correctional institutions, various faith-based organizations, and groups that supported the arts. He also helped establish a summer camp to bring new experiences and learning to underprivileged children. Dancy's contributions and work in the community were rewarded with numerous awards and accolades. During his retirement in 1960, he was noted as having a more profound impact on race relations in the city of Detroit than any other community leader during that time.

Born April 13, 1888 in Salisbury, North Carolina, to John Campbell Sr. and Laura Coleman, John Campbell Dancy Jr. was welcomed into a well-to-do and educated southern home. The elder Dancy, who was born in slavery, later studied at Howard University Preparatory and held many positions of public trust. These included the positions of typesetter, schoolteacher, newspaper editor, local politician, collector of customs in Wilmington, North Carolina, and recorder of deeds in Washington D.C. The elder Dancy included among his family friends educator Booker T. Washington and politician P. B .S. Pinchback, and it is said he received a personal invitation from President Theodore Roosevelt to attend an important banquet. In this environment young Dancy was made aware of books, the power of influence, and race problems.

Until the age of fifteen, Dancy attended a private elementary and middle school run by Livingstone College in Salisbury, North Carolina. At the same time the elder Dancy was teaching printing and publishing at the college. After young Dancy completed his middle school education, his father determined it was time for him to go to school with whites. Young Dancy was subsequently enrolled at the Phillips Exeter Academy, an elite preparatory school in New Hampshire. Although many West Indian planters sent their sons to Exeter, Dancy was the first American black to attend. After graduating from high school, Dancy attended the University of

Chronology	
1888	Born in Salisbury, North Carolina on April 13
1903	Completes private elementary and middle school education at Livingston College
1904-06	Attends Phillips-Exeter Academy
1910	Graduates from the University of Pennsylvania in sociology
1911	Becomes secretary of the Negro YMCA in Norfolk, Virginia
1917	Marries Maude Bulkley
1918	Moves to Detroit to become director of the local Urban League
1920	Convinces the United Community Services to hire a Negro stenographer, making national news
1930	Retires on September 30 as director of the Urban League
1931	Death of first wife Maude Bulkley Dancy; marries Malinda Wells
1963	Awarded Amity Day Award by the Women's Division of the American Jewish Congress
1968	Dies in Detroit, Michigan on September 10

Pennsylvania where he studied sociology. He graduated in 1910.

After college, Dancy worked for a while as a waiter on boats on the Great Lakes and later took a position as the principal of Smallwood Institute in Clairmount, West Virginia. In 1911 he became secretary of the Negro YMCA in Norfolk, the only recreational center for black children at the time, and had as many as five hundred children in his care at one time. Dancy learned many valuable skills managing this institution and was eager to try his hand in larger urban centers. In 1914 Dancy left Virginia and headed to New York City. He worked as a probation officer in the Children's Court and became active in the Big Brother Movement and the Urban League. In the Big Brother Movement, he later reminisced about offering assistance to the young Countee Cullen, who was to become the great Harlem Renaissance poet. Dancy was offered a position as industrial secretary for the local Urban League. Eugene Kinckle Jones, a key person in the Urban League, influenced his acceptance of the position. Dancy also began to court his childhood sweetheart, Maude Bulkley. Her father, William Lewis Bulkley, was New York's first black school principal and a founder of the National Urban League. Bulkley had educated his daughter in Europe and was not enthusiastic with the prospect of an American let alone a black as a son-in-law. Maude Buckley's father had hoped for a life, for all his daughters, away from the racism of the United States. His other two daughters had married American white men but their race was kept a secret from the men they married. Despite her father's reservation, the couple married on October 27, 1917 and moved to Detroit in 1918. Dancy became director of the Detroit Urban League succeeding Forrester B. Washington.

Heads Detroit Urban League

As director of the Detroit Urban League (DUL), Dancy focused on employment opportunities for blacks. Under the previous leadership of Washington, the DUL was among the first in its ability to effectively serve the black community. Dancy sought to maintain this reputation and improve on it with the introduction of new programs. As a result of his efforts, in less than a year, the quarters were three-times larger and the league handled over eleven thousand people by the year's end. The DUL became the fastest growing chapter in the country. Dancy found support and developed opportunities from philanthropic individuals, existing structures, and even from whites who supported segregation. Dancy was also able to get blacks hired in skilled and even some white-collar positions which broke the color line in Detroit's public and private sectors. In 1920 he convinced the United Community Services to hire a Negro stenographer, which made national news. She was the first Negro stenographer hired by a white organization.

Dancy promoted many new ideas in the DUL and also played major roles in the community as a whole. Along with new avenues for employment in the DUL, Dancy introduced travelers' aid, recreation, education, health, and housing. He supported the construction of Brewster Homes, the first government-funded units for black Detroiters. Along with community events, such as dances and athletic events, he conceived of Green Pastures Camp for poor and working-class children, promoted National Negro Health Week, and opened baby clinics. Dancy primarily remained conservative in his dealings and recognized a low profile was important in maintaining his funding for the Urban League. In 1925, though, when the National Association of Colored People (NAACP) helped raise funds for the Ossie Sweet case, Dancy supported their efforts. But he helped to raise funds as an individual and not as director of the Urban League. Ossie Sweet, a noted black physician, was accused of shooting white rioters who had opposed his move into their neighborhood. Sweet's lawyer, the famous Clarence Darrow, called Dancy as an expert witness regarding housing conditions in Detroit but not as representative of any organization.

Dancy was a willing advocate for the community and was an active participant in numerous organizations. His memberships included the Detroit Round Table of Christians and Jews, the Board of Education, the American Red Cross, the Governor's Commission on Youth Problems, Metropolitan Planning Commission, director of the United Community Services, secretary-treasurer of the Parkside Hospital, supporter of the Detroit Symphony Orchestra, and president of the Detroit Library Commission. After the death of his first wife Maude in 1931,

Dancy married Malinda Wells; she died in 1964, and the couple had no children.

Dancy's education and experiences clearly placed him among W. E. B. Du Bois' talented tenth, but he used the concepts of gradualism and deference offered by Booker T. Washington as the philosophical basis for his many works. Over the years others had evoked militant protest and more aggressive calls for change, but none was said to be more effective or to have had a more profound impact on race relation in Detroit than Dancy. He stated in his autobiography *Sands Against the Wind* (1966) that the key to racial progress was a climate of good human relations. After forty-two years in service to the Detroit Urban League, Dancy retired on September 30, 1960. In celebration of his work in the Urban League and the community, the mayor of Detroit proclaimed "John C. Dancy Day" and over seven hundred civic leaders and other distinguished state and national guests attended a tribute to "Mr. Urban League." President Eisenhower and Vice President Nixon sent congratulatory telegrams. In subsequent years Dancy received other awards, such as the annual Amity Day Award by the Women's Division of the American Jewish Congress in 1963 and the John Phillips Award in 1967 from Phillip Exeter Academy to an alumnus whose life contributed to the welfare of the community. Dancy died September 10, 1968 in Detroit after being hospitalized in the Kirkwood Hospital for nine months.

John Dancy Jr. played a crucial role in helping to strengthen the black community in Detroit and in providing a model for others to follow. His influences helped to improve the quality of life for many blacks and opened doors that might have remained closed. His efforts prepared the way for the even greater opportunities that came with the civil rights movement of the 1960s.

REFERENCES

Books

Angelo, Frank. "Dancy, John Campbell Jr." In *Dictionary of American Negro Biography*. Eds. Rayford W. Logan and Michael R. Winston. New York: Norton, 1982.

Capeci, Dominic J., Jr. "Dancy, John Campbell, Jr." In *American National Biography*. Eds. John A. Garraty and Mark C. Carnes. New York: Oxford University Press, 1999.

Fleming, James G., and Christian E. Burckel, eds. *Who's Who in Colored America*. 7th ed. Yonkers-on-Hudson, N.Y.: Christian E. Buckey & Associates, 1950.

Levine, David Allan. *Internal Combustion: The Races in Detroit 1915-1926*. Westport, Conn.: Greenwood Press, 1976.

Thomas, Richard W. *Life for Us Is What We Make It: Building Black Community in Detroit, 1915-1945*. Bloomington, Ind.: Indiana University Press, 1992.

Collections

The Dancy papers are in the Carnegie Library, Livingston College, Salisbury, North Carolina. Career information and some personal papers are located in the Detroit Urban League Papers, housed in the Michigan Historical Collections, Bentley Historical Library, at the University of Michigan, Ann Arbor, Michigan.

Lean'tin L. Bracks

William "Billy" Daniels
1915–1988

Singer, actor

Singer, entertainer, and actor William "Billy" Boone Daniels' career spanned over fifty years. Daniels was famous for his voice and the emotions he conveyed while performing. Daniels was the first black performer to have his own weekly radio show. He was one of the first black performers to have a television show as well. His unique style and talent made him a popular entertainer in the United States, Europe, and around the world. He was so popular in Britain that he gave eight Command Performances for England's Queen Elizabeth II. Over the course of his career Daniels released over forty singles and eleven albums, appeared in at least twenty-one films, made numerous television appearances, and gave over 1,200 performances in plays and thousands of performances in nightclubs around the world. He is best known for his rendition of "That Old Black Magic." His unique voice and style continues to live on through the re-release of several of his albums.

Born in Jacksonville, Florida on September 12, 1915, Billy Daniels was a descendant of slaves and the Kentucky frontiersman Daniel Boone. Daniels was one of five children. His father worked as a railway postmaster, but Daniels was drawn to entertainment from a very young age. He sang with street performers in Jacksonville as a child as well as in a church choir. He was so good that by the time he was a teenager he was a regular performer on Jones College's WJAX AM radio station and WMBR FM radio station.

Daniels' earliest ambition was to become a lawyer. He began pre-law classes at Florida State Agricultural & Mechanical College (formerly State Normal College for Colored Students) in Tallahassee, Florida, but Daniels eventually dropped out to help his father support his brothers and sisters.

In 1932, Daniels entered a song contest in New York while visiting his grandmother. Daniels took second

Chronology

1915	Born in Jacksonville, Florida on September 12
1934	Discovered by Erskine Hawkins working as a singing waiter in New York City
1937	Leaves the Hawkins band to start solo career
1941	Releases first hit song "Dianne"
1943	Becomes famous for "That Old Black Magic"
1945	Appears on Broadway in musical *Memphis Bound*
1947	Makes first movie, *Sepia Cinderella*; first wife dies
1950	Stars in *When You're Smiling* with Frankie Laine; marries Boston socialite Martha Braun
1951	Stars in *Sunny Side of the Street* and *Rainbow Round My Shoulder* with Frankie Laine
1952	*The Billy Daniels Show* premiers on television
1954	Divorces second wife, Martha Braun
1956	Marries Pierrette Cameron
1964	Begins working on musical *Golden Boy*
1977	Plays lead in musical *Bubbling Brown Sugar*
1988	Dies of stomach cancer in Los Angeles, California on October 7

place, beating out Ella Fitzgerald who came in fifth. It was the beginning of both singers' musical careers. In 1934 Daniels stowed away on a freighter leaving Jacksonville for New York City. A former college classmate took Daniels to the Hotcha Club in Harlem. Daniels' friend insisted that he should sing a few songs. The owners of the Hotcha Club were so impressed that they hired him on the spot to become one of their singing waiters. Daniels was paid $25 per week. One evening in 1934, Daniels happened to wait upon bandleader Erskine Hawkins, who was impressed with his voice. Hawkins hired Daniels as a vocalist for the Bama State Collegians. Daniels toured with Hawkins between 1934 and 1936 before striking out on his own. By 1937 Daniels had a tremendous following with both black and white audiences. By that time, he routinely worked for at least twelve New York radio stations. Daniels ultimately paired with pianist Benny Payne, with whom he worked for over thirty years. In 1941, Daniels had his first hit song, "Dianne," his trademark song until he made it big with "That Old Black Magic," which he originally sang on a whim while performing in Atlantic City in 1948. Daniels' rendition of "That Old Black Magic" became a hit across the United States. It sold more than nine million copies.

Daniels was a fixture on the New York City club and restaurant scene for over forty years, but he also performed across the United States, Europe and Australia. Daniels made several trips to Vietnam to entertain U.S. troops. His dramatic voice, the physicality of his performance, and his good looks made an irresistible combination. Daniels performed at such New York clubs as the Copacabana, Park Avenue Restaurant, the Onyx Club,

Ebony Club, Club 845, Hunts Point Palace and the Famous Door, the Mocambo in Hollywood, The Riviera in New Jersey, and Club Harlem in Atlantic City. At the height of his success, Daniels made $26,000 per week performing in Las Vegas. Daniels was a staple at London's Palladium in the 1950s and 1960s.

Daniels made over forty songs his own, including "Them There Eyes," "Love Is a Many Splendered Thing," "Autumn Leaves," "My Blue Heaven," "You Were Meant for Me," "How Deep Is the Ocean," "The Game of Love," "My Funny Valentine," "More than You Know," and "Nothing Can Stop Me Now." However, his rendition of "That Old Black Magic" from the 1942 film *Star Spangled Rhythm* became his signature song. Not one to be out of step with the times, Daniels even made a disco version of the song in the 1970s. Over the course of his career, Daniels released at least eleven albums on the Mercury, Vocalion, Bluebird, Victor, Savoy, Decca, and Apollo labels.

Daniels' career was not without its difficulties, however. He was a frequent associate with people in the mafia. He was stabbed twice and charged with shooting a man. In the most notorious case Daniels was charged with felonious assault in the shooting of James R. Jackson. There were rumors of police bribery and cover-ups. Although Daniels was ultimately acquitted of all charges, he lost his license to perform in New York night clubs for several years.

Works in the Theater

Daniels first appeared on Broadway in the short-lived musical *Memphis Bound*, a 1945 jazz remake of Gilbert and Sullivan's *H.M.S. Pinafore*. The premise of the musical was that a black musical troupe puts on a production of the *H.M.S. Pinafore* to raise the money necessary to get their showboat off the Mississippi mudflat where it has run aground. The lyrics and music were written by Don Walker and Clay Warnick. Daniels starred with Bill "Bojangles" Robinson, Avon Long, Frankie Wilson, Sheila Guyse, and Thelma Carpenter. The show was performed thirty-six times before being cancelled.

Daniels' second foray into Broadway theater was the 1964 play *Golden Boy*. The music for the show was written by Charles Strouse and the lyrics by Lee Adams. *Golden Boy* was based on the play by Clifford Odets which made a star out of lead actor William Holden. Daniels played manager Edie Satin to Sammy Davis Jr. in the lead role of Joe Wellington. *Golden Boy* was the first Broadway musical to focus on interracial differences, exploitation of blacks, and interracial relationships. A famous song in the show, "While the City Sleeps," was sung by Daniels. *Golden Boy* was a huge hit. It opened October 20, 1964, and ran until March 5, 1966, for a total of 568 performances. The show was nominated for four Tony Awards in 1965.

Daniels' next Broadway show was an all black version of *Hello Dolly!*, in which Daniels appeared with Pearl Bailey. Daniels played the lead male role of Horace Vandergelder to Peal Bailey's Mrs. Dolly Gallagher Levi. Although *Hello Dolly!* did not enjoy as long of a run as *Golden Boy*, the show was so successful that the songs featured in the musical were made into an album.

Daniels' final theatre performance was in the 1977 musical *Bubbling Brown Sugar*, produced in London at the Palladium theatre. Daniels played the lead role. The musical was set in a Harlem nightclub, and the show featured the music by Eubie Blake and Fats Waller and several gospel selections. The inclusion of the gospel and religious music was unusual at the time and was not repeated for several years until the play *Ain't Misbehavin'* debuted. Daniels gave over seven hundred performances of this play. He received the 1978 London Critics Award for Best Musical Performance. The show included such musical greats as Elaine Delmar, Clarke Peters, Lon Satton, and Helen Gelzer. Daniels' rendition of "Honeysuckle Rose" was a show stopper.

Accomplishments in Television and Film

Billy Daniels was one of the first black men to have his own television show. Premiering in 1952, the show appeared Sunday evenings on ABC. A milestone in television history, *The Billy Daniels Show* lasted only thirteen weeks. According to Fred MacDonald, Daniels' show was on television stations in the "largest cities in the United States." Television was an extremely difficult medium for blacks to break into in the 1950s. One of the biggest obstacles faced by blacks was the unwillingness of major companies to buy commercial time. When Daniels' show was cancelled many viewers wrote in to object. Even though the show did not enjoy a long run, it paved the way for the later success of Nat King Cole's television show.

Daniels was a popular guest on the *Colgate Comedy Hour* in 1953 and 1954 and made numerous appearances on the *Ed Sullivan Show*. Then in the late 1950s Billy Daniels had a second television show, *The Billy Daniels Show II*, which broadcast on a local Los Angeles television station. This very popular show featured the Benny Payne Trio. Later Daniels made several appearances on *The Tonight Show with Johnny Carson* and the 1970s show *The Mod Squad*.

As in other entertainment fields, blacks had difficulty breaking into and succeeding in the movies. The film industry was predominantly white, and few cinemas allowed blacks inside. According to Henry Sampson, most black cinemas were owned by whites who censored the films shown in their theaters. Few blacks appeared in movies; in fact, most blacks were portrayed by whites in blackface. It was not until the 1920s that all black casts appeared in movies which had been filmed and produced by blacks, and these productions were a tremendous success. Daniels appeared in twenty-one movies during the course of his career.

Daniels' first starring role was in the 1947 all black movie *Sepia Cinderella*, in which Daniels played a talented band leader. In the film, Daniels is the Cinderella character, whose sudden singing success causes him to abandon his longtime girlfriend as he chases after fame and glory. The production quality of the film was so high that Jack Goldberg, president of Herald Pictures, felt the film could play in both black and white movie theaters.

Daniels made several films with Frankie Laine, including *When You're Smiling* in 1950; and *Sunny Side of the Street* and *Rainbow Round My Shoulder* both in 1951. In 1953 Daniels appeared in *Cruising down the River*. Other film credits include the 1956 short from Universal with Eileen Barton entitled *Mr. Black Magic*.

In 1959, Daniels appeared in three films. In *The Big Operator*, Daniels played with Mickey Rooney and Jackie Coogan. Daniels appeared in *Night of the Quarter Moon*; this film was also called *Flesh and Flame* and *The Color of Her Skin*. The movie focused on race relations and bigotry. Daniels' final film was *The Beat Generation*, which dealt with then-taboo topics of rape and abortion. The film was reissued under the title *This Rebel Age*.

Family Life

Billy Daniels was married three times. His first wife, Florence Clotworthy, committed suicide in 1947. His second marriage in 1950 to white Boston socialite and model Martha Braun created headlines across the country and ended in divorce four years later. His third marriage was to French-Canadian Pierrette Cameron in 1956. Cameron was governess to Daniels' children when they fell in love. Daniels and Cameron remained married until his death in 1988. The couple had two children of their own.

In the 1980s Daniels began to develop health problems; however, he continued to perform. He underwent heart-bypass surgery in 1982 and again in 1987. Both times Daniels returned to singing. But he was unable to overcome stomach cancer. Billy Daniels died of that disease in Los Angeles, California on October 7, 1988.

Even in death Daniels' popularity continued among fans of jazz and Big Band music. Several of Daniels albums were re-released, including the 1956 *Billy Daniels at the Crescendo* in 1993 and again in 2001 with the title *Mr. Black Magic*; the 1953 *Songs at Midnight* and *Around Midnight* in 2004; and the 1948 *Billy Daniels That Old Black Magic* in 2005.

REFERENCES

Books

MacDonald, J. Fred. *Blacks and White TV*. Chicago, Ill.: Nelson-Hall, Inc., 1983.

Sampson, Henry T. *Blacks in Black and White: A Source Book on Black Films*. 2nd edition. Lanham, Md.: The Scarecrow Press, Inc., 1995.

Periodicals

"Billy Daniels Hits the Top." *Ebony* (September 1950): 42-44.

Goss, Charles Filmore. "Billy Daniels, Big Band Singer, Dies." *Washington Post* (9 October 1988): B8.

Uhlig, Mark A.. "Billy Daniels, Who Sang in Nightclubs, Dies at 73." *New York Times* (10 October 1988): B8.

Anne K. Driscoll

Darien Dash
1972–

Entrepreneur, business executive

While others pictured the American minority community on the deprived side of the digital divide, Darien Dash saw a clientele ripe for the marketing of Internet services. As founder and CEO of DME Interactive Holdings, Dash developed the first African American-owned Internet company traded on Wall Street. Through DME's subsidiaries, Digital Mafia Entertainment and Places of Color, Dash delivered less expensive hardware and software, developed customized Internet services, and played a significant role in training minorities to use the Internet. While still a young man, he modeled leadership skills for current and future African American entrepreneurs.

Darien Dash was born in 1972 in New York City to a family involved in entertainment. His mother Linda served as general manager of DME. His sister Stacey, probably best known for her role as Dionne in *Clueless*, has appeared in a number of television shows and movies. His cousin Damon chairs New York's Roc-A-Fella record label. His step-father Cecil Holmes, a Casablanca Records executive, played a major role in inspiring Dash to work hard and live ethically. Dash is married and has three children.

During Darien's childhood in Paramus, New Jersey, Linda Dash noted her son's penchant for marketing. She described her son to *People* as "always thinking of business schemes," often renting his toys instead of loaning them. Dash himself recalled for *New York Times* a turning point during his teen years: "In the space of two weeks when I was 18, my father died, and I was one of the first ones to find him, my dog died, my stepfather's

Darien Dash

house in Paramus burned down, my mother and stepfather separated, and my girlfriend, the woman who later became my wife, left me. I was either going to turn to ice, or have faith and make something of myself."

At the University of Southern California, Dash studied political science and leadership in the Emerging Leadership Program. He became president of the Black Student Union and participated actively in the Alpha Phi Alpha fraternity. As a freshman, he started his own record company, Roc-A-Blok Records, specializing in hip-hop. *New York Times* states: "He made—and spent—$100,000 during his sophomore year of college when he and a cousin, Damon Dash, teamed up as managers and snagged inaugural record deals for the rapper Jay-Z and Original Flavor." But Dash wanted to continue his education, and during his senior year, he found himself influenced by the book *Megatrends,*, which predicted future wealth for technology entrepreneurs.

Becomes Technology Entrepreneur

After college, Dash gained experience as a consultant on new media marketing for Fortune 500 companies. He worked his way to the position of eastern region marketing and sales director for Digital Music Xpress (DMX), a company that provided digital cable television with high quality music. Dash began to understand U.S. technology trends and developed a vision for marketing Internet

services to minority clientele. He believed Internet access could improve the quality of life for American minorities, and he grew angry at the technology industry's reluctance to market its services to them.

Dash quit his job at DMX—on the day after his wedding—and started his own company in the couple's one-bedroom apartment in Hackensack, New Jersey. Money from a joint venture between Roc-A-Blok and Columbia Records funded the company's start-up in September 1994. Dash later told *FSB: Fortune Small Business*: "I thank God for my wife. She paid the bills that first year." In August 1995, Dash launched DME Interactive Holdings, with the mission to expand the hardware and software infrastructure within minority communities. He financed the company for the first four-and-a-half years.

Dash envisioned DME playing a key role in rewiring urban areas for digital Internet access and then becoming a major provider of content targeted for minorities. He focused particularly on providing music to the urban market. According to *Contemporary Black Biography*, Dash became "one of a handful of minority executives to venture into the new technology world at this level." To fund his goal, he initiated a consulting service, offering technology services to such groups as the New York Knicks, Lugz, and HBO home video.

When Dash wanted to take his private company public, Chris Kinsley, president of Manhattan's Mason Hill & Co. investment firm, suggested a reverse merger. In June 1999, DME acquired Pride Automotive Group. DME took controlling interest in the leasing company, gave its shareholders a minority interest in DME, and a new ticker symbol emerged on NASDAQ. Later that year, DME also acquired Kathoderay, a New York multimedia consulting firm, and opened an additional office in Manhattan. Dash made Kathoderay's CEO Kathleen McQuaid Packard the company's new senior vice president of interactive services. He hired his mother as general manager for a staff of around fifty people, mostly under thirty-five years of age.

Dash's marketing scheme seemed modeled after the hip-hop music industry. Using flyers, posters, stickers, and slogans like "Our thing is, get connected, get plugged in, or get shut out," he counted on the community itself to generate enthusiasm. The company's long list of clients included VISA, HBO, Motown Records, Def Jam Records, MSBET (joint venture between Microsoft and Black Entertainment Television), Microsoft, Reader's Digest, Otis Elevator, Queen Latifah, BMG North America, Sony Corp., SoSo Def Records, Maxwell, ABC Radio, Universal Records, and African Heritage Network.

Serves Community and National Ventures

In addition to commercial ventures, Dash brought technology to his local community. As technology chair of Harlem's school district 5, Dash provided thousands of New York students with access to computers. He served on the board of HEAVEN (Helping Educate, Activate, Volunteer, and Empower via the Net), a nonprofit venture helping black teenagers in New York learn computer skills. He told the Cleveland *Plain Dealer*: "I think they've got all the advantages in the world. They have a better shot than any generation that's come before. The beauty of the Internet is it's colorless. There's no black and white." He also served as board member and mentor for Making Opportunities for Upgrading Schools & Education (MOUSE). The two groups merged in 2000 under the name MOUSE.

Through his work with HEAVEN, Dash met America Online executive Ted Leonsis and engaged in a new venture. In 2000, Dash launched Places of Color. Partnering with AOL, the subsidiary of DME offered minorities a customized and less expensive version of AOL's CompuServe 2000 software. The service featured thirty channels, e-mail, instant messaging, chat rooms, news, and entertainment through 150 affiliate content providers such as the National Urban League and the Black Health Network.

The target audience included Hispanics, Native Americans, and rural whites as well as African Americans. Places of Color provided content, marketing, and advertising while AOL provided the connections and oversaw the business aspects. Dash focused on empowering people—minorities especially—through education, training, and job placement. He explained to *Billboard*, "We want people to learn how to use this technology effectively, so they can be successful and change their lives."

In 1999, Dash took part in a national summit sponsored by the Department of Commerce and hosted by Secretary of Commerce William Daley. Participants responded to the department's report, "Falling Through the Net: Defining the Digital Divide," which indicated that African Americans and Hispanics had far less access to the Internet than whites. That same year, the Department of Commerce named DME the minority technology firm of the year.

In 2000, President Bill Clinton asked Dash to accompany him on his third "New Markets" tour to seek ways to make the Internet more accessible to all Americans. Through this work, Dash met Carly Fiorina, Hewlett-Packard CEO. In October, DME partnered with HP to sell low-cost computers with free Internet access to minority residents in New York and New Jersey. HP's general manager of e-services, Doug McGowan, told *Time*, "He's blazing a trail." But the success of dotcoms took a dive in the stock market, and Dash found it necessary to lay off half his staff. He still provided the computers but had to delay content development.

Awards and Service

The Department of Commerce named DME Interactive Holdings the 2000 Regional and National Technology Firm of the Year. Dash received the *Network Journal*'s Y2K 40 Under 40 Achievement Award. New York *Daily News* named him one of "50 New Yorkers to Watch in 2000." *Ebony* magazine featured him in an article titled "Black Pioneers in the High-Tech World." Dash pointed out: "We've just scratched the surface, and if I've been able to help get people involved then I've been blessed and I'm fortunate."

As a pioneer and activist within the technology community, Dash has given speeches across the country. In 1997, he spoke for the B.A.M. (Blacks at Microsoft) Minority Student Day, the seventh event of its kind hosted by Microsoft. He also has participated in national forums such as the CEO Panel, hosted by Harvard Law School's Black Alumni, and the National Urban League's Youth Summit. In 2000, the Economic Opportunity Board invited him as guest speaker for its Micro Business Awards.

In 2002, Dash spoke at a town hall meeting, "Creating a New America," hosted by New York Representative Gregory Meeks. The forum focused on providing a chance for talking and healing in the aftermath of the terrorist attacks of September 11, 2001. Other speaking engagements included the Rainbow/PUSH Convention, the Congressional Black Caucus, and the White House briefings on the Internet and Technology. Dash has also testified before Congress's Small Business Committee on the Digital Divide.

Dash served on the International Advisory Board of Equal Access, a not-for-profit organization whose mission, according to their web site, "is to create positive change for large numbers of people in the developing world by providing critically needed information and education through locally produced and targeted content, the use of appropriate and cost-effective technology, and effective partnerships and community engagement." He also served on the boards of such organizations as Chess in Schools and the National Urban League. The University of Southern California, *KIP Business Report*, and the Abyssinian Development Corporation have granted him awards.

Dash told *FSB: Fortune Small Business* that he set clear priorities for his life: "God, my wife and three children, then work." Through his mission of empowering minorities with technology and providing education to use that technology, he has affected the quality of life for numerous Americans of many races.

REFERENCES

Books

Brennan, Carol. "Darien Dash." In *Contemporary Black Biography*. Ed. Ashyia N. Henderson. Farmington Hills, Mich.: Gale Group, 2002.

Periodicals

"Black Pioneers in the High-Tech World: Crossing the Digital Divide." *Ebony* 55 (June 2000): 42-48.

Drummond, Tammerlin. "The Multimillion-Dollar Dash." *Time* 156 (4 December 2000): 123-24.

Finn, Robin. "Pulling For, and Pushing an Urban Internet." *New York Times,* 17 February 2000.

Gajilan, Arlyn Tobias. "The Web According to Darien Dash." *FSB: Fortune Small Business* 10 (October 2000): 90-94.

Mitchell, Gail. "New AOL Service To Tap Urban Entertainment Market." *Billboard* 112 (26 February 2000): 1-2.

"Net Profits: Entrepreneurs on the World Wide Web Find it Pays to Start Young." Cleveland, Ohio *Plain Dealer*, 19 January 2000.

Seals, Kimberly. "How I Did It: Closing the Digital Divide." *Essence* 31 (November 2000): 104.

Wulff, Jennifer. "Online." *People* 53 (15 May 2000): 33-34.

Online

Equal Access. http://www.equalaccess.org/ (Accessed 3 February 2006).

Marie Garrett

Willie Davenport
1943–2002

Track and field athlete, coach, military officer

A natural athlete blessed with a superb training ethic, Willie Davenport primarily taught himself the tools needed to become a world-class hurdler. A four-time Summer Olympic Games qualifier (1964 to 1976) in the 110-meter high hurdles, Davenport brought home a gold and a bronze medal in the event's greatest showcase. After retiring from hurdling, he returned to the Olympic

Willie Davenport

stage a final time in the four-man bobsled event in the 1980 Winter Olympic Games, shattering a perceived barrier to black athletes in the process. After retiring from competitive sports, Davenport revived his military career. Having served a three-year stint in the U.S. Army during the early sixties as an enlisted man, he accepted a direct commission in the Army National Guard. In a 21-year career as an officer, Davenport earned the rank of colonel prior to his death.

Willie Davenport was born on June 8, 1943 in Troy, Alabama, the eldest of seven children. At nine years of age, his family moved to Warren, Ohio. By the time he reached Warren's Howland High School, Davenport was exhibiting ability in several sports, including basketball and baseball, but track soon became his sport of choice. Although he was endowed with sprinter's speed, he became a hurdler by accident, replacing a sick teammate in the 120-yard high hurdles at a meet one day, then winning the event with the fastest time posted in the district that year. His talent was raw—consisting of merely jumping awkwardly over the hurdles, but he knew that if he learned proper technique, he would greatly lower his 15.8-second time. By the time he graduated, he had lowered his personal best to 14.2 seconds and won a state championship. Nevertheless, Davenport's time was not so spectacular as to draw intense recruiting interest from college programs. After graduation in 1962, he entered

Chronology

1943	Born in Troy, Alabama on June 8
1962	Enters U.S. Army as paratrooper and becomes member of Army track
1964	Qualifies for Summer Olympic Games in Tokyo in the 110-meter high hurdles
1968	Wins gold medal in the 110-meter high hurdles at the Mexico City Summer Olympics
1972	Finishes fourth in the 110-meter high hurdles at the Munich Summer Olympics
1976	Wins bronze medal in the 110-meter high hurdles at the Montreal Summer Olympics
1980	Finishes twelfth in the 4-man bobsled at the 1980 Lake Placid Winter Olympics
1981	Receives direct commission in the Louisiana National Guard
1993	Becomes track coach of the All-Army men's and women's track team
2002	Dies of heart attack in Chicago on June 17

the U.S. Army to become a paratrooper but continued hurdling as a member of the Army's track team.

An Olympic Legacy Begins

Stationed in Mainz, West Germany in 1963, Davenport joined a local track club but found himself without a coach. Surprisingly, he began to lower his times while self-training. The next summer, he was brought back to the States to begin training in earnest for a spot on the 1964 U.S. Olympic team in the 110-meter high hurdles. Amazingly, Davenport discovered the key to his future success by watching television. During the final of a televised race, Davenport noted that pre-Olympic favorite Hayes Jones slowed down after clearing the final hurdle. Davenport decided to copy Jones's form through the last hurdle but then attempt to accelerate through the finish tape. His discovery soon paid off handsomely.

Davenport burst onto the national scene when he won the Olympic qualifying race in New York City, upsetting Jones and suddenly becoming a frontrunner. Unfortunately, Davenport suffered a thigh injury during a training session just four days before the 1964 Summer Olympic Games commenced in Tokyo. Nevertheless, he made it to the Olympic semi-finals of the 110-meter high hurdles before the injury proved too big an obstacle to overcome against world-class competition. Afterwards, he returned to his post in Mainz and, though disappointed with the recent results, remained focused on improving. Davenport ended the season ranked number five in the world.

Domination

The following year, Private First Class Davenport left the U.S. Army to attend Southern University (SU) in Baton Rouge, Louisiana, where he majored in physical education. Davenport tried football at SU, with some success, but it was only a short time before he again focused his full attention on his more obvious talent: hurdling. Surrounded by experienced coaches and coming into his physical prime, Davenport began dominating hurdling's short-track events, setting or tying indoor record marks at 45, 50, 60, 70 and 120 yards. He won the 110-meter highs at the U.S. Outdoor Championships from 1965 to 1967, as well as the 60-yard highs at the U.S. Indoor Championships in 1966 and 1967 and again from 1969 to1971. Along the way, he won virtually every major championship race staged in the United States, including multiple wins in the AAU and NAIA meets. Nevertheless, his most famous race occurred during the 1968 Summer Olympic Games.

A severe groin injury sidelined Davenport for two months early in 1968 and his recovery was slow. He battled back, however, finally regaining his form in late summer, winning a 120-yard race at a minor meet at the University of Tennessee with a competitive time. Davenport followed that up by winning the U.S. Olympic Trials and, in the process, becoming the favorite to win gold in Mexico City. He easily handled the pressure and ran an Olympic meet record 13.33-second time to become the Olympic champion at 110 meters. He later said that he ran the perfect race that day, knowing from his first step that he would win the race.

A year later, on July 4, 1969, Davenport tied the world record with a time of 13.2 seconds at a meet in Zurich, Switzerland. He shared that record for one year, 357 days. By that time, Davenport had left almost no short-track hurdle mark untouched and won virtually every major championship. Perhaps his greatest accomplishment during that five-season stretch from 1965 through 1969, however, was that he had an unprecedented five-year run as the world's top-ranked 110-meter hurdler, a streak that stands as the longest continuous one in the event.

"The Breeze," as Davenport was nicknamed, graduated with a B.A. from Southern University in 1969 but continued to compete internationally for nearly a decade more. His first job after graduation was as a teacher in the East Baton Rouge Parish School System in 1970. He was soon hired away from that post by his alma mater, becoming head track coach at Southern from 1971 to 1974. He took advantage of being at the university by earning a master's degree in education in 1974. He also made the U.S. Olympic team again in 1972, qualifying second in the U.S. Olympic trials, but finishing fourth at the Munich games. Despite a serious knee injury in 1975, Davenport regained form to qualify for the 110-meter hurdles a fourth and final time, again finishing second at the U.S. trials. At Montreal, the 33-year-old Davenport surprised the experts by taking the bronze medal with a very competitive 13.38-second time. He finished the season as the world's third-ranked 110-meter hurdler, his best ranking since 1969. He wrapped up his hurdling career the following season, with a still-respectable number six ranking. In all, he ranked among the top ten hurdlers in the 110-meter event 12 times covering 14 seasons.

Davenport held several appointed positions in the city governments of Baton Rouge and New Orleans, as well as for the state of Louisiana during the 1970s and 1980s. Those duties, however, did not stop him from achieving one last piece of Olympic glory. In 1980, Davenport and Jeff Gadley became the first black Olympic bobsledders in the Lake Placid Games, as well as the first African Americans to make a U.S. Winter Olympic Team. In an event in which American teams had rarely fared well, the number one American team had a credible twelfth-place finish. His five Olympic appearances rank among the most by any athlete, and he was just the eighth athlete to appear in both summer and winter Olympic festivals. His notable career achievements and considerable longevity did not go unrecognized. Davenport was inducted into the USA Track and Field Hall of Fame in 1982 and the Olympic Hall of Fame in 1990. In 1999, Davenport was voted one of Louisiana's twenty-five Greatest Athletes by the Louisiana Sportswriters Association.

The Military Beckons Again

In 1981, Davenport received a direct commission in the Louisiana Army Guard. He was an untiring advocate for sports programs within the National Guard and became coach of the All-Army men's and women's track teams from 1993 through 1996. Under Davenport, that team had an unprecedented four undefeated seasons. His later assignments included commanding the Oregon Army Guard's 741st Corps Support Battalion in Portland and serving as chief of the National Guard Bureau's Office of Sports Management in Falls Church, Virginia. He had risen to the rank of colonel at the time of his death. Davenport was returning from a National Guard adjutants general conference in Boise, Idaho when he suffered a fatal heart attack at Chicago's O'Hare International Airport while making a flight connection on June 17, 2002. He was pronounced dead at 1:39 p.m. at Our Lady of the Resurrection Medical Center.

Davenport was scheduled to retire from the Army National Guard in March 2003 and was planning to marry his fiancée soon after. Unfortunately, Davenport had not made his wishes known in the case of his death, which set off a squabble among relatives regarding where he should be buried. On one side were his former wife Marian and their adopted son Mark Davenport of Baton Rouge, while the other side included Willie Davenport Stewart of Youngstown, Ohio and Tanya Gibson Morris (who, like her father, was also an SU graduate) of Ouachita Parish, Louisiana. The latter two were born out of wedlock, but acknowledged biological children (by different mothers) of Davenport, who had signed their birth certificates. Davenport's body was on the way to Warren, Ohio for burial when Mark Davenport petitioned a Louisiana district court to release the body to him. An injunction was granted and the aircraft carrying Davenport's remains was forced to land at Fort Leonard, Missouri, where the Army controlled the body pending a court hearing. A week later, Mark Davenport was able to gain a court order to secure Davenport's body. Eventually, it was decided that a memorial service would be held in Ohio on June 28, while Davenport's funeral service would be held at Southern University's Seymour Gymnasium on July 1, with burial at Roselawn Memorial Park in Baton Rouge.

Willie Davenport had two careers: athlete and military man. Sometimes those careers converged; other times they did not. The one constant they always shared was his commitment to excellence at the highest level.

REFERENCES

Periodicals

"Five-Time Olympian Col. Willie Davenport Remembered." *Regulatory Intelligence Data* 98 (20 June 2002): 10.

Goldstein, Richard. "Willie Davenport, 59, Gold Medal Olympian in High Hurdles." *New York Times*, 19 June 2002.

Hirsley, Michael. "An Olympian for All Seasons; Hurdles Champ Helped Integrate Winter Games." *Chicago Tribune*, 18 June 2002.

Online

Dorr, Gregory P. "Q&A: Willie Davenport." http://dorrk. com/inside.asp?editorial=pl_davenport.ssi (Accessed 12 February 2005).

"Family Feud: Gold Medalist Davenport's Heirs Put Burial on Hold." SI.com. 24 June 2002. http:// sportsillustrated.cnn.com/olympics/news/2002/06/24/ davenport_wait_ap/ (Accessed 12 February 2005).

"Southern Mourns Olympian's Death." The Southern Digest Online. 28 June 2002. http://www. southerndigest.com/vnews/display.v/ART/2002/06/ 28/3d1b6fb816ef (Accessed 12 February 2005).

"Willie Davenport." The Lincoln Library of Sports Champions. 1 September 2001. http://elibrary. bigchalk.com (Accessed 11 January 2005).

"Willie Davenport." USA Track & Field. http://www. usatf.org/HallOfFame/TF/showBio.asp?HOFIDs=39 (Accessed 11 January 2005).

Kevin C. Kretschmer

Albert Porter Davis
1890–1976

Physician, surgeon, entrepreneur

Prominent physician, surgeon, and entrepreneur, Albert Porter Davis was born on November 13, 1890 in Palestine, Texas, to Louisa Craven and William W. Davis, a white physician. After graduating from high school, Davis enrolled in Meharry Medical College, a historically black college established after the Civil War in Nashville, Tennessee. It offered great opportunities for African Americans aspiring to be doctors because white medical schools rarely accepted African American students. African American doctors were much needed because African Americans were often denied treatment by white doctors and hospitals.

After receiving his medical degree in 1913, Davis moved to Kansas City where he began his family practice in medicine and surgery. He continued his studies at Sumner Junior College and at the University of Kansas. He took courses that increased his knowledge in the medical field and pursued courses in other areas as well. Davis also came to the aid of unwed mothers. In 1920, he founded the Davis Maternity Sanitarium for Unwed Mothers. The sanitarium provided a range of services, including education, prenatal care, and adoption assistance if requested. The sanitarium remained in operation for over twenty years.

Davis was a man of many talents. He served as lieutenant in the U.S. Army Medical Corps Reserve during World War I, wrote music, became a fan of jazz, and in 1921, he starred in a five-reel silent black and white film, *The Lure of a Woman*, the first black film to be produced in Kansas City. Three of the five reels of film are held in the George P. Johnson Collection at the University of California, Los Angeles.

Earns Pilot's License

Davis also made time for a social life. On September 1, 1926, he married Hazel White, a schoolteacher. Shortly after the marriage, Davis began taking flying lessons from a French instructor. In those days it was difficult to find someone who was willing to teach African Americans. Later, Davis took flying lessons at the Porterfield Flying School at the Old Richards Air Field in Kansas City, Missouri. On May 16, 1928, Davis received his license to fly. On the same day, he purchased his first plane, an American Eagle, built by Ed Porterfield, an early fan of aviation. Davis became one of the earliest persons, of any race, to be licensed. The United States Department of Commerce began licensing pilots in 1926, before that the military belief was that blacks were not intelligent enough to fly.

Chronology	
1890	Born in Palestine, Texas on November 13
1913	Graduates from Meharry College
1920	Founds Davis Maternity Sanitarium for Unwed Mothers
1921	Stars in *The Lure of a Woman*
1926	Marries schoolteacher, Hazel White
1927	Founds Red Top Taxicab Company and the Service Finance Corporation
1928	Receives pilots license and purchases first plane, an American Eagle
1929	Attends first National Airmen's Association of America in Chicago; crashes plane on return trip from Chicago
1935	Purchases second plane, Porterfield Cabin Monoplane
1939	Receives the Dwight H. Green trophy
1940	Participates in the renovation of Kansas City Municipal Airport
1944-45	Keynote speaker at NAACP convention in Junction City, Kansas
1950	Serves as deputy coroner of Wyandotte County
1953	Elected president of National Medical Association; builds Kansas Trailer Village
1956	Heads Wyandotte County Mobile Homes Association
1976	Dies in Kansas City, Kansas on September 1
1999	His home "Castle Rock" is given Historic Landmark status

In 1929, Davis flew his plane to Yackey Checkerboard Airfield, just outside Chicago, to attend the National Airmen's Association of America (NAAA), the first national aviation meet of Negro flyers. He was the only pilot out of seven that was not from Chicago. On his return home, his plane crashed into a tree. Davis was uninjured, but he had no way to get his plane home. He bought a pickup truck, loaded the damaged plane onto it, and hauled it back to Kansas City.

After the crash, Davis continued to fly for pleasure, attending speaking engagements and political rallies. He often had to land in cow pastures and wheat fields because there were few landing strips. In 1935, Davis bought his second plane, a Porterfield Cabin Monoplane.

The field of aviation began to expand for African Americans. In January 1939, a little over a decade after Davis received his license, a list was issued of eighty-one African American pilots. Of those named, forty-six were students. Approximately fifty others had allowed their license to expire.

Although Davis was an active pilot and participated in many aviation activities, his main role was that of a physician. Because he spoke Spanish he could easily serve Mexican immigrants. For a while, Davis kept an office in two states, Missouri and Kansas. Eventually, he closed his office in Missouri.

In 1926, Davis was appointed assistant health director in Kansas City. He became the first African American to be assigned to that post, a position he held until 1932. Davis also served on the staffs at Douglass Hospital in Kansas City, Kansas, and Wheatley-Provident Hospital no. 2 in Kansas City, Missouri.

In addition to his medical career and aviation activities, Davis was involved in numerous entrepreneurial endeavors. In 1927, he founded the Service Finance Corporation, a savings and loan association, and the Red Top Taxicab Company. Both were the first such African American-owned institutions of their kind in Kansas.

On August 25-27, 1939, the NAAA held a conference to which all "Race Flyers" were invited. The NAAA's aim was to provide a chance for African American pilots to get to know each other and discuss common problems. Out of the approximately forty to fifty pilots attending the conference, six flew to Chicago in their own planes, an astonishing number for African American pilots for the period. At the conference, Davis was awarded the Dwight H. Green Trophy for having contributed the most to the advancement of aviation during 1938. The trophy was named for a Republican politician and former World War I veteran who served as an army aviator and later served as governor of Illinois from 1941 to 1949. Davis was also elected one of the seven vice presidents of the NAAA. They had planned to establish local chapters. Davis also invited them to hold the 1940 conference in Kansas City. This meeting was a rare opportunity for African American pilots to gather in a national body such as this one.

Davis had the opportunity to fly in his open cockpit Porterfield monoplane as part of the festivities for the renovation of the Kansas City Municipal Airport in January 1940. His passenger was his wife, who was eight months pregnant with their daughter. On February 18, 1940, their daughter, A. Portia, was born. The following year, Davis purchased his third plane, a Porterfield Columbia 75c. By 1950, he had logged 2,200 flying hours over the twenty-three years he had spent flying since he received his license. Later, he acquired a fourth plane, a Navion. He flew it eight to ten times a month, even making professional calls at times.

Builds Mobile Home Park

Davis's reputation grew as did his public service. Davis served as deputy coroner of the Wyandotte County from 1950 to 1952. The following year he was elected president of the National Medical Association, which was established by black doctors in 1895 because African Americans were denied membership in the American Medical Association. The same year, Davis engaged in additional entrepreneurial undertakings. He built the Kansas Trailer Village, a mobile home park. He bought a plot of land that ran through highways 40, 24, and 73 for $47,000. The former owner of the land gave him the idea of creating a trailer village. Davis gave it a try and the idea proved to be successful. The land held fifty spaces for permanent and short-term tenants. It offered its tenants such amenities as sidewalks, patios, a laundromat, and much more. All of the tenants in the Kansas Trailer Village were white. When Davis realized the financial benefits of owning a mobile home park, he recommended that blacks start their own mobile home park. In 1956, Davis began serving as head of the Wyandotte County Mobile Homes Association, an all-white group. The same year, he served as the vice-president of the local branch of the NAACP.

In 1969, Davis' health began to decline. He died on September 1, 1976 at the age of 85. In March of 1999, "Castle Rock," Davis' home at 852 Washington Boulevard in Kansas City, was given Historic Landmark status in Wyandotte County, Kansas City, and Kansas. "Castle Rock" was cited for having a high integrity of design, setting, association, and workmanship. The house had unusual modern features, such as phone jacks throughout the home, and central heating, amongst other conveniences. The continued occupancy of Davis' family in "Castle Rock" has contributed to its preservation.

Artifacts relating to Davis' life as an aviator, such as a propeller from one of his planes that has been restored, his logbook, and other memorabilia can be found at the Kansas City Jazz Museum.

REFERENCES

Books

Gubert, Betty Kaplan, Miriam Sawyer, and Caroline M. Fannin. *Distinguished African American in Aviation and Space Science*. Westport, Conn.: Oryx Press, 2002.

Periodicals

"Private Plane Owners." *Ebony* (December 1950): 76, 78, 80-81.

"Trailer Park Landlord." *Ebony* (August 1956): 107-10.

Sharon McGee

Daniel Webster Davis
1862–1913

Minister, educator, writer

Daniel Webster Davis was born of slave parents, John and Charlotte Ann (Christian) Davis, in Caro-

Chronology	
1862	Born in Caroline County, Virginia on March 25
1878	Graduates from Richmond High and Normal School, Virginia
1880	Begins career as a public school teacher
1893	Marries co-worker Elizabeth Eloise Smith on September 8; trains at Lynchburg Baptist Seminary
1895	Ordained for the gospel ministry
1896	Elected to the pastorate of the Second Baptist Church, South Richmond, Virginia
1897	Publishes book of poems, *Weh Down Souf and Other Poems*
1900	Lectures in Ohio, New York, and New England on tour with the Central Lyceum Bureau
1908	Publishes a history text chronicling the accomplishments of the Negro race
1913	Dies suddenly in Richmond, Virginia on October 25

line County, Virginia on March 25, 1862. After her husband's death, Mrs. Davis moved the family to Richmond, Virginia where Davis and his sister attended public school. Davis was an excellent student, earnest and studious. He received medals for his proficiency and graduated with distinction from Richmond High and Normal School in 1878 at age sixteen.

Davis's ambition was to become a teacher. With this goal in mind, he worked in various trades until he reached the age of eligibility for the teaching profession. In 1880 at age eighteen he was assigned to teach in a colored public school on Baker Street in Richmond. Davis's career as a seventh grade teacher lasted for over thirty years. He earned high praise for his work. He was selected by the superintendent of education to teach mathematics and civics in the summer institutes for teachers in Virginia. He also conducted teacher training in West Virginia and North Carolina. It was at the Baker school, though, that he met Elizabeth Eloise Smith. They married in 1893 and were parents of three children, two sons and one daughter.

Davis was educated for the ministry at Lynchburg Baptist Seminary and Guadalupe College. Official confirmation of dates or whether his degrees were earned or honorary has not been determined. It is generally believed that he received both the A.M. and D.D. degrees. He was ordained to the gospel ministry in 1895 and was elected to the pastorate of the Second Baptist church of South Richmond. He served this church from July 1896 until his death in 1913. Davis's rhythmic preaching style and skilled oratory endeared him to his congregation and the community. Under his leadership, church membership tripled, debts were cleared, and a new, larger, modern brick building was completed in 1905.

Well-Known Lecturer

Davis was often in demand as a public speaker. He appeared on lecture circuits in the South and the Northeast. In 1900, he toured with the Central Lyceum Bureau, covering Ohio, New York, and New England. He was the first black to lecture at the Chautauqua Assembly at Laurel Park, Massachusetts. His speeches were eloquent and often passionate, delivered in clear, expressive English. He employed a mixture of Biblical quotations, storytelling, and humorous anecdotes, interspersed with snippets from his poems and songs. His oratorical style was described as flowery, flamboyant, and witty. His audiences often responded with tears, rapturous applause, and much praise.

Davis spoke on the condition of the Negro and the customs and practices of daily life on the plantation. A central subject was racial inequity. Davis expounded on how best to resolve the problems, explaining what he considered the ideal for the Negro. In a series of lectures delivered in 1902 at the Hampton Normal Institute, he proposed that the way to improve the life of African Americans was through home, church, and school. He stressed the importance of African American culture, family, religion, education, and history. He declared that African Americans ought to be proud of their accomplishments.

Davis's beliefs about the Negro situation of the day closely paralleled those of Booker T. Washington. At times, Davis seemed conciliatory in his remarks, intimating that even with political and social protest the Negro could not attain self-sufficiency or honorable work without the assistance or cooperation of whites. Many criticized him for being too compromising rather than firmly demanding racial equality, equal justice, and opportunity. Yet there are instances in Davis's writings and speeches where his thinking is as radical as that of W. E. B. Du Bois. At times, Davis accused whites of unfair practices and for withholding the privileges that should be accorded in full to blacks. He held them in full blame and accountable for every act committed under the guise of slavery. Throughout his life Davis believed that independence for blacks would come only through a slow progression of honorable work and education. He advised the wise use of protest and agitation only as a last resort. Davis wanted blacks to continue to strive for equal opportunity and fundamental rights.

Davis addressed local grand ceremonies, graduations, memorials, and reunions. He delivered commencement addresses at a number of institutions, including the Waters Normal Institute in Lawrenceville, Virginia, and the Georgia State Industrial College in Savannah, Georgia. He was one of two black speakers at the International Sunday School Convention held in Toronto, Ontario, Canada in 1905 where his speech was widely praised.

Becomes a Poet

Davis's first collection of poetry, published in 1895, was incorporated into a second volume in 1897 entitled *Wey Down Souf and Other Poems*. It is his best-known work. His poems are written in a style suited to the conventions of the late 1890s and most likely with the intention of pleasing both black and white audiences. Most were written in black dialect, which for Davis was a subject of serious study. He drew the evocative titles and stereotypical characters of his poems from the customs and celebrations of antebellum plantation life. Although his poems dealt with the burdens, trials, and distresses of blacks, they portrayed the popular minstrel style of the time that emphasized crude sentiments and character traits such as laziness, gluttony, buffoonery, ignorance, and stupidity. His poetry was criticized for helping to perpetuate negative myths about blacks in the minds of white readers. When Davis read his poems in assemblies, on tour with the Central Lyceum Bureau and on various special occasions, audiences erupted into peals of laughter. The poems were also published in the Richmond newspapers. Davis's critics believed that he espoused the same accommodationist philosophy as Booker T. Washington, with whom he was friends. In 1895 Washington invited Davis to compose an ode for the Atlanta Cotton States Exposition that was accepted. Davis read the poem at the opening ceremony in the Negro Pavilion.

Some of his poems assess the plight of the slaves in a more realistic light. Davis wrote of the unfair treatment slaves received at the hands of their masters, the breaking up of families, and the utter hopelessness inherent in slavery. He blamed white masters for slaves' bad habits. As a clergyman Davis believed that faith and moral living played important roles in self-development. Consequently, his poems provided instruction with underlying moral messages. They provided entertainment and appealed to nostalgic feelings. Davis's poetry closely parallels that of his contemporaries, James Edwin Campbell and Paul Lawrence Dunbar.

Davis frequently contributed articles on race relations to the leading black magazines. He worked collaboratively with Giles B. Jackson, a Richmond lawyer, to write a textbook, published in 1908, on the industrial history of the Negro race. It emphasized the accomplishments of the race, recounting with pride the contributions made to various professions, including religion, literature, art, education, and business. The book became a powerful incentive for black youth to model themselves after heroes of the past. For many years it was included on the list of textbooks used in the Richmond public schools.

Davis also wrote for *The Baptist Companion*, the newspaper of African Baptists of Virginia. He wrote for other church, community, and Masonic publications. Davis's passion for the betterment of youth was demonstrated in his editorship of the *Young Men's Friend*, a publication of the Young Men's Christian Association of Richmond. Its purpose was to promote the educational, moral, and religious education of young men. He also edited a weekly newspaper, *Social Drifts*.

Serves as Community Leader

Davis was a prominent and respected black leader in Richmond. He enriched the black community and promoted unity between races. He served on the boards of many local organizations, including the Virginia Teachers' Association, the Virginia Building, Loan and Trust Company, the Jonesboro Agricultural and Industrial Academy, and the Virginia Baptist Sunday-school Convention. He was president of the YMCA in Richmond, director of the Old Folks' Home, and a trustee of Virginia Seminary and College. He was a member of the Dunbar Literary and Historical Society and the Society for Better Housing and Living in Richmond.

Davis served prominently in Masonic circles, as master, grand representative, and grand warden. In 1910, in an effort to bring to public notice the worthy endeavors of the United Order of True Reformers, he published a biography of the Reverend William Browne, a successful businessman and philanthropist. Like Browne, the Reverend Davis was distinguished by his dedication to reform the community.

Richmond's citizens mourned Davis's untimely death from nephritis on October 25, 1913. In tribute to Davis, all the colored schools were ordered closed by the superintendent of schools. In addition to his work as poet, writer, and lecturer, Davis is remembered for his many years of dedicated service to the Richmond school system and the Baptist Church. Davis was honored posthumously by having three Virginia schools named after him: one in Staunton, another in Petersburg, and in 1959 a new school in Richmond was dedicated in his memory.

REFERENCES

Books

Brown, Sterling Allen. *The Negro in American Fiction, Negro Poetry, and Drama*. New York: Arno Press, 1969.

Culp, D. W., ed. *Twentieth Century Negro Literature; or, A Cyclopedia of Thought on the Vital Topics Relating to the American Negro, by One Hundred of America's Greatest Negroes*. Miami, Fla.: Mnemosyne Publishing Co., 1969.

Houston, Helen R. "Davis, Daniel Webster." In *Encyclopedia of African-American Culture and History. Supplement*. Ed. Jack Salzman. New York: Macmillan Reference USA, 2001.

Johnson, James Weldon. *The Book of American Negro Poetry, Chosen and Edited with an Essay on the Negro's Creative Genius*. New York: Harcourt, Brace, and Company, 1958.

Penn, Irvine Garland. *The Afro-American Press and its Editors*. New York: Arno Press, 1969.

Redding, J. Saunders. *To Make a Poet Black*. College Park, Md.: McGrath Publishing Company, 1968.

Sherman, Joan R., ed. *African-American Poetry of the Nineteenth Century: An Anthology*. Urbana: University of Illinois Press, 1992.

Sherman, Joan R. *Invisible Poets: Afro-Americans of the Nineteenth Century*. Urbana: University of Illinois Press, 1989.

Wagner, Jean. *Black Poets of the United States: From Paul Laurence Dunbar to Langston Hughes*. Trans. Kenneth Douglas. Urbana: University of Illinois Press, 1973.

White, Newman Ivey, and Walter Clinton Jackson. *An Anthology of Verse by American Negroes*. Durham, N.C.: Moore Publishing Co., 1968.

Wright, A. Augustus, ed. *Who's Who in the Lyceum*. Philadelphia: Pearson, 1906.

Periodicals

Harrison, Lottie Davis. "Daniel Webster Davis." *Negro History Bulletin*, 18 (December 1954): 55-57.

Sherman, Joan R. "Daniel Webster Davis: A Black Virginia Poet in the Age of Accommodation." *Virginia Magazine of History and Biography*, 81 (October 1973): 457-78.

Janette Prescod

Frank Marshall Davis
1905–1987

Journalist, editor, poet, educator

The Julius Rosenwald Foundation recognized the literary achievements of Frank Marshall Davis in its first award given in poetry in 1937; however, Davis made his living as a journalist and editor of major African American and labor newspapers in Chicago, Gary, Indiana, and Atlanta, Georgia, during the 1930s and 1940s. At a very young age, he acquired a love of jazz, which led to his formidable collection of jazz records, role as jazz critic for print media, and his success at creating and teaching perhaps the first course on jazz music in the United States.

This son of the Midwest was born near the Oklahoma border in Arkansas City, Kansas, on December 31, 1905. His middle name links him to his maternal grandfather, Henry Marshall of Wichita, Kansas. Davis knew his

Chronology	
1905	Born in Arkansas City, Kansas on December 31
1923	Attends Friends College; writes his first poem
1924	Matriculates at Kansas State
1927	Moves to Chicago; first job as journalist at the *Whip*
1931-34	Edits the *Atlanta World*, Atlanta, Georgia
1935	Black Cat Press publishes *Black Man's Verse*; becomes executive editor for the Negro Associated Press
1937	Black Cat Press publishes *I Am the American Negro*; receives Julius Rosenwald Fellowship
1938	Publishes *Through Sepia Eyes*
1948	Publishes *47th Street Poems*; moves to Hawaii
1978	Publishes *Awakening and Other Poems*
1987	Dies
1992	Autobiography *Livin' the Blues: Memoirs of a Black Journalist and Poet* published
2002	*Black Moods: Collected Poems* published

father, Sam Davis, an itinerant barber and musician, by name only, since his father disappeared after his parents divorced when Marshall was not quite one year old. When he was two, his mother, who worked as a domestic, accompanied the white family to California. For reasons not discerned, she returned to Kansas two years later where Davis had a chance to hear stories told by his great grandmother, Amanda Porter. Listening to Porter's stories of slavery, the Civil War, and his personal experiences with racism changed the way in which he saw the world. As Davis relates in his memoirs, *Living the Blues: Memoirs of a Black Journalist and Poet*, "I sat open-mouthed as she related stories she had witnessed, among them the drama of a fellow slave who took an axe, laid his right hand on a chopping block, and deliberately hacked off three fingers so he would have little market value when he learned his owner planned to sell him away from his wife and children." Davis lived with his great grandmother until he went away to college.

Davis's mother eventually married James Monroe Boganey from Oklahoma who totally accepted Davis as his son, filling the young boy's need for a father. Boganey also supported Davis's love of music, which coincidentally connected him to his absent father.

Davis called Kansas near the Oklahoma border an ambiguous racial environment. There he learned lessons in racism firsthand. Some incidences imitated those of regular occurrences in the South. In school, he was one of a very few black children. Some of the schoolmates would have lynched him as he walked home from school had he not been rescued from death by a white man. This anonymous man walked Davis over a mile to his home to further assure his safety. Growing up black, Davis recalled numerous scenes that made him feel inferior, but none as traumatic as the near-lynching scene.

Davis became an avid reader and a lover of the blues. W. C. Handy's music joyously played in his head for weeks after he heard the musician and his band, the Orchestra of Memphis, while visiting his grandfather in Wichita. From a mail-order catalogue, he received guitar lessons. At fifteen, Ma Rainey's performance so enthralled him that he scraped up money to hear her performance more than once in the week in the town in 1921. Davis spent his pennies and amassed a collection of over one hundred blues records. It is no wonder that as one of his first jobs, he became a distributor for Black Swan Record Company. Later, he added jazz to his collection.

The two career paths that defined Davis did not result from a specific plan. By default, he chose journalism as a major at Friends' University, a small school of fewer than five hundred predominantly white students. The school did not offer a major in jazz music. Ada Rice, his English teacher, surprised Davis with her admiration of a poem he submitted instead of an essay for a class assignment. Eventually, he submitted twelve poems for publication to the Ur Rhune Chapter of the American College Quill Club, a national creative writing society. Davis's collection of poems was one of the five selected. After such success, Davis could no longer ignore his poetic talent, although it took many more years for him to publish his first book of poetry. When he turned to making a living, he realized his future might lay in writing for a newspaper.

At twenty-one, Davis left college to work as a journalist. He felt confident because of his writing ability and his college training in journalism. In 1927, he hopped a train to Chicago. His only living relative, an aunt, recommended him to her former husband, Clarence W. Reynolds, who introduced Davis to Lucius Harper of the *Chicago Defender*, the paper with the widest circulation in the United States. Chicago was a center for jazz. The greatest African American musicians played in Chicago, and Davis heard them in the city's numerous jazz joints. Reynolds introduced Davis to the purported inventor of jazz, Jelly Roll Morton. He heard an impromptu concert by Fats Waller in a movie theater and heard Louis Armstrong at Chicago's Savoy.

Chicago was the best place for Davis to develop his imaginative writings and to form poetic associations. One was the Inter-Collegiate Club, whose members were college students and alumni. A poem that Davis wrote for the group allowed him to meet literary celebrities such as Gertrude Stein, whom Davis admired very much. In spite of its artistic richness, Davis discovered that Chicago lacked the sophistication, celebrity, and structure seen in Harlem during the Harlem Renaissance. In his memoir, Davis writes that he resolved "to do for the Windy City in verse what others had done in Harlem."

Davis accepted a job at the National News and Feature Service, an upstart operation, which promised to syndicate a magazine section to African American newspapers. However, the pay was very low. In his memoirs he states: "I intended to make it as a newspaperman or starve to death trying. There were moments when it seemed the alternative was winning out."

Although Davis spent time writing articles in anticipation of the magazine's eventual publication, it apparently never materialized. Another upstart newspaper, the *Evening Bulletin*, hired Davis as its night city editor and columnist with plans of carrying the *National Bulletin*. His duties expanded into detective and entertainment news writer and with increased work he had more income. He was offered a salary of $35 a week. Until funds completely dried up at the newspaper, Davis enjoyed success as a detective writer, but soon tired of the genre.

In 1928, he started working at the *Whip*. As an assistant editor, Davis learned plenty about police detail, the strength of the mob, and the court system of Chicago during the bootlegging days of Prohibition. When funds ran out at this paper, Davis found a job at the *American*, Gary, Indiana's newest newspaper started in 1927. In 1929 he returned to Kansas State. A celebrity on campus, with plenty of work to pay his school bills and succeeding academically, Davis nevertheless did not remain in school long enough to finish his degree. After a short time, he returned to *American*.

Southern Discomfort

From 1931 to 1934, Davis spent his time in Atlanta, Georgia, coaxed there by the founder of the *Atlanta World*, W. A. Scott. Scott founded the paper in 1928 and by 1931 owned papers in Birmingham, Alabama and in Chattanooga and Memphis, Tennessee. Davis's financial situation and the financial solvency of *Atlanta World* convinced him that he could survive just as other blacks did living in the South. Scott offered him a good salary of $25 a week with a promise of $35.

When Davis arrived at the office of the *Atlanta World*, he found the reporters inexperienced. As editor, he spent countless hours rewriting articles and recruiting staff from Chicago. Within a year Scott requested that Davis publish a daily. The idea both intimidated and exhilarated Davis for he would become the first editor of an African American daily. By contacting the Associated Negro Press, worldwide sources, and cartoonist and other features, Davis produced within a month a paper which satisfied Scott. Subscriptions increased especially since Davis pointed out to black Atlantans the need to support a newspaper that dignified their existence unlike the white news establishment that referred to them as "darkies" with a large coverage of black crime.

In Atlanta, Davis was introduced to black college football and the battle of the bands of the black schools in the Atlanta University complex. This music substituted for the live jazz and blues performances of Chicago. As for his poetry, his creative writing stopped for two years and then revived when Frances Manning of Chicago took an interest in his poem, "Congo," and inspired him to write. They exchanged poems and critiques of them and shared a common interest in jazz music and a bohemian life style.

Davis's Atlanta work came to a close after Scott was murdered. According to Davis, Cornelius Scott, who assumed responsibility for the paper, lacked vision and the spunk of his brother. Then too, Davis felt the negative effects of living in the South. Chicago was still Davis's favorite city and Manning was there, inspiring him to publish a first book of poetry.

From 1935 to 1948, Davis life took an unprecedented fertile turn. He published four books of poetry. His poetry called attention to U.S. racism. Davis received critical acclaim for *Black Man's Verse*, published in the summer of 1935, and for his other publications: *I Am the American Negro* (1937), *Through Sepia Eyes* (1938), and *47th Street Poems* (1948). The Detroit race riot and a lynching in Missouri were defining moments in his life and his poetry. "For the first time in my life," he writes in his memoirs, "I would quit being a loner. No matter how consuming my wrath, I could go nowhere by myself. My poetry was primarily a one-man protest." Davis joined and supported the efforts of numerous organizations fighting racism. He helped with rent strikes, became vice-chairman of the Chicago Civil Liberties Committee and lectured at Northwestern University.

In 1935 Davis became executive editor for the Negro Associated Press, where he remained until he left for Hawaii in 1948. During that time, he showed talent in his new creative undertaking—photography with prints selected for national and international exhibitions—and became one of the first teachers of jazz music in the country. Davis returned from Hawaii in 1973 for a poetry reading tour. He died in 1987.

Posthumous Writings

In 1992, five years after Davis's death, the University of Wisconsin Press at Madison published *Livin' the Blues: Memoirs of a Black Journalist and Poet*, edited by John Edgar Tidwell. Davis had begun writing his memoirs in the late sixties and early seventies from Hawaii. Davis's life as a journalist, political activist, as a jazz teacher and critic, and his connections and conversations with some of the most important figures of his time in politics, literature, entertainment, and sports, suggest the significance of his memoirs. Included in *Livin' the Blues* are excerpts of Davis's autobiographical work (under the pen name Bob Green) *That Incredible Waikiki Jungle*, which was written in the late seventies and chronicles his life in Hawaii. Davis's *Black Moods: Collected Poems* was published in 2002.

The forgotten journalist, poet, political activist, jazz aficionado, critic, and historian claims his place among African American and American writers. His writings provide a window on twentieth-century arts and politics.

REFERENCES

Periodicals

Takara, Kathryn Waddell. "Frank Marshall Davis: A Forgotten Voice in the Chicago Black Renaissance." *Western Journal of Black Studies* 26 (Winter 2002): 215-30.

Tidwell, John Edgar. "Alternative Constructions to Black Arts Autobiography: Frank Marshall Davis and 1960s Counterculture." *College Language Association* 41 (December 1997): 147-60.

Online

Miller, James A. "Frank Marshall Davis: Black Moods: Collected Poems." African American Review, Summer-Fall, 2003. http://www.24hourscholar. comp/articles/mi (Accessed 21 July 2005).

Collections

Davis's jazz records are in the Moorland-Spingarn Research Center, Howard University.

Rosa Bobia

Gordon J. Davis
1941–

Lawyer, business executive

Gordon J. Davis is a well-known attorney and former president of the Lincoln Center for the Performing Arts in New York. With a love for the arts that began at a young age, Davis was the founding chairman of the Jazz at the Lincoln Center board. According to Davis, his parents had a play reading circle that met in their living room. His early memories are of coming into his house and seeing the adults reading excerpts from dramatic productions. He even remembers Lorraine Hansberry, author of *A Raisin in the Sun,* participating in these readings.

Davis was born on August 7, 1941 in Chicago, Illinois. He was the son of a University of Chicago professor, yet he grew up near an almost exclusively all African American neighborhood. Davis credits the musical influ-

Chronology

1941	Born in Chicago, Illinois on August 7
1963	Graduates from Williamsburg College with an A.B. degree
1967	Receives law degree from Harvard University
1968	Admitted to law practice in Chicago, Illinois
1973	Begins serving as a member of the New York City Planning Commission
1978	Accepts appointment by Mayor Edward Koch to be the commissioner of Parks and Recreation for the City of New York
1989	Serves as a trustee of Consolidation Edison of New York
1990	Begins to serve as chair of the Department of Jazz at the Lincoln Center
1994	Becomes a partner at LeBoeuf, Lamb, Greene & MacRae LLP
1997	Becomes director of Consolidated Edison of New York
2001	Becomes the first black president of New York City's Lincoln Center for the Performing Arts; resigns nine months later
2002	Receives distinction as one of top U.S. black lawyers by *Black Enterprise*

ences he heard there as fostering his early love of music. Jazz was his favorite. In 1963, he received his degree from Williams College. In 1967, he received his J.D. from Harvard University.

Davis began practicing law in 1968. His specialty initially was real estate and later he expanded that to complex real estate, land development and environmental conflicts, public finance, and cultural and not-for-profit organizations. Davis soon began to work in or with state and city government. In 1973, he began to serve as a member of the New York City Planning Commission. By 1978, he was appointed by Mayor Edward I. Koch to be commissioner of Parks and Recreation for the city of New York. He served in that capacity until 1983. During his term as commissioner of parks and recreation, he established highly popular free concerts that attracted artists such as Diana Ross and Simon and Garfunkel. He was a co-founder of the Central Park Conservancy. In 1990, Davis became the founding chairman of Jazz at the Lincoln Center. He helped to raise $80 million for a building campaign for this program. His achievements did not go unnoticed, and in 2001, he was chosen to be the president of the Lincoln Center for the Performing Arts in New York City, the first African American to hold that position.

The Lincoln Center presented quite a challenge for Davis. He wanted to stress diversity in its many offerings. With much success, Davis helped to raise and manage $1.5 million for the renovation of the center and its property. He also appropriated a ten-year, $240 million grant from New York City, the largest grant of any kind to be awarded to an arts organization. But despite Davis's success, problems occurred early on in his tenure.

After working for the Lincoln Center for nine months, on September 27, 2001, Davis presented a resignation letter to Lincoln Center chair, Beverly Sills. It was one of the most difficult decisions of his career. Ongoing disagreements between different groups at Lincoln Center frustrated Davis and made it very difficult to establish unity.

Davis became a partner at LeBoeuf, Lamb, Greene & MacRae LLP, in New York in October 1994. By November 2001, he was a senior partner at the New York law firm. He served as a trustee of Consolidated Edison Inc. Holding Company in 1989 and became the director of that company in 1997. He served in the capacity of director of numerous other companies and organizations. Moreover, his list of clients is very impressive. He has represented Viacom, Pepsico, the Lincoln Center, and New York Public Library, to name a few.

Davis wrote an article for the *Wall Street Journal* and was a featured speaker for the New York historical society in conjunction with the Central Park Conversancy in honor of Central Park's 150th anniversary on October 16, 2003.

Davis continues to practice law with LeBoeuf, Lamb, Greene & MacRae LLP. He assists clients in assessing possible development options, exploring different sources of funding and finance, and negotiating correct contract provisions. He also gives counsel on zoning and planning and historic preservation and landmark. Davis continues to be active with Jazz at the Lincoln Center. Davis is married to New York University law professor Peggy Cooper Davis. They have one daughter who is an aspiring actress. Davis was the lead counsel on the $250 million development of the American Museum of Natural History Rose Center and on the over $7 billion revitalization of the World Trade Center site.

REFERENCES

Books

Smith, Jessie C. *Black Firsts*. Detroit: Visible Ink Press, 2003.

Periodicals

Bryant, Aaron. *Business of Fine Arts* 32 (November 2001): 30.

Salinas, Mike. "Davis Resigns Lincoln Center Presidency." *Back Stage* 42 (October 2001): 4.

——. "Next Lincoln Center Prez Stresses Diversity." *Back Stage* 41 (November 2000): 3.

Connie Mack

Gussie Lord Davis
1863–1899

Composer, lyricist, entrepreneur

Gussie Lord Davis's professional career covered less than twenty years (roughly from 1880 to 1899). Arguably the first black songwriter to have great success on Tin Pan Alley, New York City's foremost center for the publication and circulation of seemingly unending streams of popular songs, Davis wrote over six hundred songs in a standardized formula that was very well received by music lovers at the time. Davis's standard fare featured sentimental ballads, often in waltz time that stressed a sweet sadness. Usually, they were melodramatic songs with a lyrical twist that was capable of bringing tears to listeners' eyes. The stories fueled harmonic tension followed by a consequent relaxed mood, expressing the song's texture. The themes often sprang from ordinary experiences shared by his audience, as is clear from their titles: "Beneath the Maple on the Hill," "Down in Poverty Row," "Irene, Good Night," and so on.

Early Career Path

Davis's path to achievement was arduous; he started with little preparation as a lyricist, but a driving urge to express his thoughts and learn his craft well. Initially, he met resistance when he applied and was refused admission to study music formally at the Nelson Musical College. In a compromise, he took a job at the college as a janitor for a nominal salary and worked several years in return for private music lessons. An able student, he soon became proficient as a pianist and composer. Davis's first published song, "Beneath the Maple on the Hill," was very promising. Confident in its merit, he agreed to pay for its initial publication. Published in 1880 by the firm of F. W. Helmick of Cincinnati, the song was successful enough to encourage Davis to continue writing, and many new songs followed.

One of his first professional acquaintances was James E. Stewart of Cincinnati, composer of "Cricket on the Hearth," and "Jenny, the Flower of Kildare" (composed about 1884). Davis credits Stewart as an important influence, passing on valuable knowledge of the craft of songwriting to Davis. Stewart, unfortunately, died soon after they became colleagues.

Songwriting Successes

An important success for Davis came with the publication of "The Fatal Wedding" in 1894 by Spaulding, Koruder, & Co. of New York, with words by William Windom, a popular singer of the day. Fitting Davis's thematic model, "The Fatal Wedding" tells the story of a young mother intervening at a wedding to protest that the groom-to-be is the father of her child and asking that the wedding be cancelled. Events take a tragic turn with the announcement that the baby has died, followed by the suicide of the child's father. The tragedy has an ironic resolution, however, as the two women (the wife and the bereaved young mother) leave together in the company of the abandoned wife's parents. The song remained popular well into the twentieth century, being recorded on both OKEH and Edison labels in 1927 by country music artist Ernest Stoneman.

A somewhat similar plot is used in what was probably Davis's biggest success, "In the Baggage Coach Ahead" (1896). The lyrics tell of a baby crying aloud on a train, causing anxiety among the passengers. On inquiry, the travelers learn that the baby's tears are shed for his deceased mother, who is in "the baggage coach ahead" lying in a coffin. Davis, working for the railroad at the time, was told the story by a porter. The song was published in New York by Howley, Havilland and sold perhaps a million copies.

Another prominent songwriter who was very influential in Davis's development, George Propheter, published numerous songs by Davis, including "Irene, Good Night" (1886), "'Neath the Maples Long Ago" (1886), "The Court House in the Sky" (1887), and "Do the Old Folks Miss Me?" (1887). Incidentally, "Irene, Good Night," is similar in structure and lyrics to a song with the same title sung by several major artists, including Hudie Ledbetter, Josh White, and many others in the folk revival of the 1950s, 1960s, and later. This later song is also a waltz, and the overall theme is similar, but the melody is not the same, and the song speaks to a different era.

Davis worked under contract for George Propheter for about seven years, moving to New York with his wife, taking up residence there, and becoming well known as one of Tin Pan Alley's best composers. He was among the ten top songwriters named to compete in a song contest in 1895, sponsored by the *New York World*. Davis took second prize in the contest, winning $500 in gold for his song, "Send Back the Picture and the Ring," published in 1896 by New York Music.

Davis published several other songs, including "The Dear Folks at Home" (1881); "The Light House by the Sea" (1886); "We Never Meet, 'Tis Better So" (1897); and "Down in Poverty Row" (1896), the cover of which featured one of the divas of the day, Bonnie Thornton.

In addition to his songwriting, Davis was also an entrepreneur. He formed the Davis Operatic and Plantation Minstrels and toured with this company successfully several times during his career. His last endeavor, in fact, was a staged musical, "A Hot Time in Old Dixie." The show was rehearsed in 1899 and successfully launched on a national tour. Unfortunately, though, Davis fell ill and had to leave the remaining performances in charge of his partner, Tom McIntosh. Davis died at his home in Whitestone, New York, on October 18, 1899.

REFERENCES

Books

Floyd, Samuel A. *International Dictionary of Black Composers*. Vol. 1. Chicago: Fitzroy Dearborn, 2001.

Marcuse, Maxwell F. *Tin Pan Alley in Gaslight*. Watkins Glen, N.Y.: Century House, 1959.

Southern, Eileen. *Biographical Dictionary of Afro-American and African Musicians*. Westport, Conn.: Greenwood Press, 1982.

———. "Gussie Lord Davis." *New Grove Dictionary of Music*. 2nd ed. Vol. 7. Ed. Stanley Sadie. New York, Oxford University Press, 2001.

Periodicals

Kearns, William. "From Black to White: A Hillbilly Version of Gussie Davis's 'The Fatal Wedding,'" *Black Perspective in Music* 2 (Spring 1974): 24-36.

Wright, Josephine R. B., and Sam Lucas. "Gussie Lord Davis (1863-1899): Tin Pan Alley Tunesmith." *Black Perspective in Music* 6 (Autumn 1978): 188-230.

Darius Thieme

Richard L. Davis
1864–1900

Labor leader, coal miner

Coal miner Richard L. Davis has been called the most important black miner in the late 1800s and into the turn of the twentieth century. He was a founder of the

Chronology

1864	Born in Roanoke, Virginia on December 24
1882	Relocates to Rendville, Ohio
1890	Becomes delegate to United Mine Workers of America Convention; elected to Executive Board, Ohio's District 6, United Mine Workers of America
1892-98	Recruits blacks for union membership
1900	Dies of lung ailment in Rendville, Ohio on January 24

United Mine Workers of America (UMWA) in 1890 and a delegate to its first convention. He held leading positions with the organization twice, serving as a member of its national executive board. He was a tireless organizer whose work as union leader and ability to deal with black workers and organized labor in the 1890s command attention and discussion.

Much more is known about Richard L. Davis's activities as a coal miner and officer of the UMWA than is known about his personal life. It is known that he was born in Roanoke, Virginia, on December 24, 1864, just before the Civil War ended. The circumstances of his birth and whether his parents were slave or free are unknown. The *United Mine Workers' Journal* (*UMWJ*) refers to him as "a full-blooded colored man" and nothing more. Davis attended school in Roanoke but only during the winter months, yet he received a fair education. He was also a good reader and writer, which facilitated his work later on. When he was only eight years old he took a job in a local tobacco factory and remained there for nine years. The deplorable conditions that he endured in that factory prompted him to seek employment elsewhere, moving to a coal miner's job in the Kanawha and New River regions of West Virginia.

Davis then lived in a small, mining village of Rendville, Ohio, in 1882, located southeast of Columbus in the Hocking Valley region. There he settled down, married, and the couple had children. There are no known records giving his wife's name or the number of their children. First-hand accounts giving the little that is known about Davis's life and work are published in the *UMWJ* and the labor paper, the *National Labor Tribune*, published in Pittsburgh.

Clearly, Davis's life as a coal miner offered few amenities. For Davis and his fellow miners, the work was unsteady, resulting in recurrent unemployment. Workers in the coal-mining region of Ohio suffered from the mid-1980s depression. As cited by Jacobson in *The Negro and the Labor Movement*, Davis described the situation in a letter to the editor of the *UMWJ* dated February 28, 1895: "Times in our little village remain the same...—no work and much destitution with no visible signs of anything better." Conditions did not improve, work had all but ceased, and neither Davis nor his fellow miners knew what to do. Over a year later, on April 30, 1896, he wrote to the journal's editor: "We can't earn a living, and if we steal it we will be prosecuted." Conditions improved slightly by 1897, yet during one week the miners worked only half a day.

Becomes Union Organizer

Davis worked intermittently both as a miner and union organizer. From age eighteen until he died, he was an active participant in the labor movement. He joined the Knights of Labor and then the United Mine Workers of America. He was a delegate to the founding convention of the UMWA in 1890 and at the same time was elected to Ohio's district 6 executive board, a post that he held until 1896. His success was duly noted in the *UMWJ*, which celebrated his election by publishing a brief biographical sketch of Davis (referred to him as "Dick") and the other new officers. The *UMWJ* said that he represented his race well and that the miners were confident that blacks should be recognized on the board. Jacobson published the journal's view that, "He will in a special way be able to appear before our colored miners and preach the gospel of trade unions and at the same time will be able to prove to our white craftsmen how much progress may be made with very limited opportunities." "Dick" had merited the recognition "from either standpoint, for as a man, and more especially as a union man, he has deserved well of the miners of this country," the journal continued. The journal also praised him for his seriousness and wished him well. In 1895, he was seventh among twenty-eight candidates for one of six vacancies on UMWA's international executive board. Davis in 1897 had the highest number of votes among fourteen candidates who sought the UMWA office. With that post he held the highest position of an African American in the UMWA.

After Davis was defeated in the 1898 election, his popularity among the delegates fell dramatically. He concentrated on organizing black workers in southeastern Ohio and was successful in recruiting Ohio's black miners for union membership. While in 1892 he had recruited in West Virginia's New River field and in McDonnell, Pennsylvania, in 1894 he moved his efforts to the Pocahontas field of West Virginia. In 1897-98, Davis organized black miners elsewhere in West Virginia as well as in Ohio. In Alabama in the 1890s he had extreme difficulty combating the color line, where racial prejudice among blacks was deep and legally enforced segregation was hardening. Biracial unionism there, regardless of the advocates, presented a grim shadow over his work. Sadly convinced of the need for immediate and dramatic change, he wrote to the *UMWJ*'s editor on January 1, 1898: "As our people [the Negroes] are celebrating the emancipation proclamation, we will stop now and go out to listen for awhile. But we need another proclamation of equal importance, and that one is to emancipate the wage slaves both white and black."

Apparently Davis was a religious man. His published letters reflected religious images; Jacobson notes his letters to the *UMWJ*'s editor in 1895 through 1898 in which Davis commanded, "Let us resolve to do better. We are taught by the Holy Writ that in unity there is strength." He reminded Massillon, Ohio, miners who threatened to leave the union that "Except those abide in the ship, ye cannot be saved," quoting Paul in the New Testament.

Some believe that Davis's commitment to trade unionism hurt ordinary miners. In 1898, some black miners claimed that Davis and other miners organized a strike for the purpose of restoring a wage scale. Davis was affected by the strike and went without work while other miners were able to find work. By 1898, he lived in a pitiful condition, having been black-listed for unknown reasons. Mining companies refused to hire him and his union refused to pay him for his organizational work. Although Davis had done what he thought best, he also did so in the interest or organized labor. He had lived at risk; his life had been threatened, and he had been sandbagged, stoned, and deprived of his rights to support himself and his family.

According to Jacobson, a black miner from Congo, Ohio called "Old Dog" joined Davis's complaint about being unable to find work in the mines or work to do as an organizer. "Old Dog" knew that Davis had worked hard in the interest of black miners and had brought many Ohio workers into the union. He petitioned the *UMWJ* and its readers to provide support for Davis and his family. He deserved better treatment than he received. Others took up the cause as well, praising Davis for his work. Through it all, Davis's commitment to organized labor never waned.

Richard Davis died young, just one month after his thirty-fifth birthday, in Rendville, Ohio, of "lung fever" on January 24, 1900. Ironically the UMWA was in convention in another city at the time. His work touched local, regional, and national arenas. Both the UMWA and black miners had lost a key advocate of workers' rights. Although he was most influential in southeastern Ohio where he lived and worked, Davis had fought racial injustice within and beyond organized labor at a pivotal moment in the history of America's industrial society.

REFERENCES

Books

Fink, Gary M. *Biographical Dictionary of American Labor Leaders*. Westport, Conn.: Greenwood Press, 1974.

Foner, Philip. *Organized Labor and the Black Worker, 1619-1981*. 2nd ed. New York: International Publishers, 1982.

Jacobson, Julius, ed. *The Negro and the American Labor Movement*. Garden City, N.Y.: Doubleday, Anchor Books, 1968.

Trotter, Joe W. "Richard L. Davis." In *American National Biography*. Vol. 6. New York: Oxford University Press, 1999.

Frederick D. Smith

Drew Saunders Days
1941–

Lawyer, federal government official, educator

Drew S. Days III was the first African American to head the U.S. civil rights division of the U.S. Department of Justice when he took the position in 1977, and in 1992 he became the U.S. solicitor general under former President Bill Clinton.

Drew Saunders Days III was born on August 29, 1941, in Atlanta, Georgia. His father, Drew Saunders Days II, a graduate of Morehouse College, studied under black historian W. E. B. Dubois. Days II was an accomplished violinist and also an executive at Central Life Insurance Company, an all-black firm, founded by Mary McLeod Bethune. His mother, Dorothea Jamerson, a graduate of Talladega College, was a schoolteacher. The Days family lived in Tampa, Florida, until Days II landed a job with an insurance company in New Rochelle, New York, in the early 1950s. Days III and his younger sister attended school in both Florida and New York. He received a B.A. in English literature from Hamilton College in New York in 1963 and an LLB from Yale University Law School in 1966. While at Yale, Days was a featured tenor in the Russian Chorus.

Days was admitted to the Illinois bar in 1966 and joined the Cotton, Watt, Jones, King, and Bowlus law firm in Chicago as an associate attorney. At twenty-five, Days worked as an attorney for the Illinois Civil Liberties Union on a fair-housing lawsuit in Chicago, with Martin Luther King Jr. From 1967 until 1969, he served in the Peace Corps, setting up an agricultural cooperative in Comayagua, Honduras, that is still in operation. During that time, he also worked as an interpreter for the Rockefeller Committee to Latin America. In 1969, Days joined the staff of the NAACP Legal Defense Fund in New York City. As first assistant counsel, he litigated cases in school desegregation, police misconduct, and employment discrimination. At the age of thirty, he won a lawsuit to desegregate the Tampa schools he attended as a boy in Florida. From 1973 to 1975, Days was an associate professor of law at Temple University and taught in the summer of 1975 at the University of Ghana.

Drew Saunders Days

Becomes Assistant Attorney General and Solicitor General

Days was nominated in 1977 by President Jimmy Carter and confirmed by the Senate to serve as assistant attorney general for civil rights in the U.S. Department of Justice. Thus he became the first black to lead the civil rights or any division. His tenure was marked by an aggressive enforcement of the nation's civil rights laws in a number of areas, including police misconduct and unlawful discrimination in employment, housing, voting, and education. Days joined the Yale Law School faculty in 1981 and received tenure in 1986. In 1989 he became the founding director of the Orville H. Schell Jr. Center for International Human Rights Law, at the law school, and in 1992 was honored by being named the Alfred M. Rankin Professor of Law.

In 1992, Bill Clinton was elected president, ending the twelve-year Republican hold on the presidency. Clinton nominated Days to be solicitor general of the United States, the second leading position in the Justice Department. He argued seventeen cases before the Supreme Court of the United States as solicitor general during President Clinton's first term and oversaw a group of lawyers who made more than 180 appearances. During that tenure, Days successfully argued cases touching upon such diverse subjects as international tax, military and criminal law, and civil rights. One case, the historic

Chronology

1941	Born in Atlanta, Georgia on August 29
1963	Receives B.A. from Hamilton College (cum laude)
1966	Receives L.L.B. from Yale Law School
1966	Marries Ann Ramsay Langdon
1966	Admitted to the Illinois Bar
1966-67	Joins Cotton, Watt, Jones, King, and Bowlus law firm in Chicago; volunteers as attorney for the Illinois Civil Liberties Union; serves in the Peace Corps in Comayagua, Honduras
1969	Serves as interpreter, Rockefeller Committee to Latin America
1969-77	Serves first assistant counsel for NAACP Legal Defense Fund in New York
1973-75	Associate professor, Temple University
1975	Professor, University of Ghana (Summer)
1977-80	Assistant U.S. attorney general for civil rights, U.S. Department of Justice
1981-92	Associate professor, Yale Law School
1989-93	Founding director, Orville H. Schell, Center for International Human Rights at Yale Law School
1992	Appointed Alfred M. Rankin Professor, Yale Law School
1993-96	Serves as solicitor general of the United States
1997	Serves as counsel to Morrison and Foerster Law Firm in Washington, D.C.

term limits case, *U.S. Term Limits v. Thornton*, No. 93-1456, held that states may not constitutionally impose term limits on congressional offices. This decision was viewed as a turning point in the national debate over federal term limits.

Fails Nomination to the U.S. Supreme Court

In 1994 when President Bill Clinton began looking for a new Supreme Court justice, Days, a Yale law professor and a black man with a distinguished career in arguing civil rights cases, was his obvious choice. But Days was apparently denied the nomination because of a decision he made earlier in a case involving child pornography.

Stephen Knox, a graduate student at Pennsylvania State University, had been sentenced to five years in prison for receiving in the mail and possessing three videotapes of child pornography. Days argued that the tapes did not constitute pornography because the girls in them, aged ten to seventeen, were not nude. The 3rd U.S. Circuit Court of Appeals upheld the conviction in the *United States v. Knox*, 977 F.2d 815, agreeing with the government's position.

In a brief filed in September 1994 with the Supreme Court, the Justice Department changed its stance, arguing that the "plain meaning of the statute requires that the material must include a visible depiction of the genital or pubic area of the body" and that "the material must depict a child lasciviously engaging in sexual conduct." The High Court dropped the case and ordered the appeals court to re-examine the matter in light of the government's new position. Former anti-pornography prosecutors argued that the Knox case was an early sign that the Clinton administration was soft on crime and held radical legal views. By vote of one hundred to nothing, the Senate passed a resolution condemning the solicitor general's interpretation of the law. To put out the political fire, the president sent an icy rebuke to Attorney General Janet Reno, asking that her department work with Congress to clarify the law. Some believe that the Knox case cost Days a seat on the Supreme Court.

Days remained in the post as solicitor general until 1996, and in September 1997 he joined the law firm of Morrison and Foerster. Days leads the firm's national appellate practice with a special emphasis on the United States Supreme Court, in its Washington, D.C. office. He also teaches law in the Yale School of Law. He has published extensively, including two volumes on the Supreme Court of the United States in the third edition of Moore's *Federal Practice*, a leading treatise on federal court practice and procedure.

Days has served as guest lecturer and keynote speaker on numerous occasions. In May 1996, Days delivered the commencement address at Tennessee State University. He replaced former U.S. Secretary of Commerce Ron Brown, who was killed in a plane crash during a mission to Bosnia. He has received numerous awards and honors, including a honorary doctoral degree from the University of North Carolina at Chapel Hill in May 2003, the 1997 Spirit of Excellence Award from the American Bar Association, which recognizes minority lawyers who have achieved great distinction, and the Judge Robert F. Kennedy Memorial Human Rights Award, to name a few. Days is a member of various organizations, including the American Law Institute, the American Bar Foundation, and the American Academy of Arts and Sciences. He has been married since 1966 to Ann Ramsay Langdon, an artist and writer. They have two daughters, Alison Langdon, and Elizabeth Jamerson. The Days reside in New Haven, Connecticut.

REFERENCES

Books

Richardson, Francine, ed. *Who's Who in American Politics 2001-2002*. Vol. 1 New Providence, N.J.: Marquis Who's Who/Reed Elsevier Inc., 2001.

Periodicals

Caplan, Lincoln. "Uneasy Days in Court." *Newsweek* 124 (10 October 1994): 62.

"Cruz Reynoso among Excellence Honorees." *Human Rights: Journal of the Section of Individual Rights and Responsibilities* 24 (Spring 1997): 3.

Reske, Henry J. "A Flap over Flip-Flops." *ABA Journal* 80 (January 1994): 12.

"Solicitor General of the United States to Address TSU Graduates." *The Tennessee Tribune* 7 (30 April 1996): 7.

Online

"Drew S. Days III." Backbone Cabinet: A Progressive Cabinet Roster. http://www.backbonecampaign.org/cabinet/nominee.cfm?ID=353 (Accessed 2 February 2005).

"Drew S. Days III Joins Morrison and Foerster LLP." *Business Wire* (2 September 1997). http://static.elibrary.com/b/businesswire/september01997/drewsdayiii_ (Accessed 2 February 2005).

"FYI Carolina: News for Alumni, Parents, and Friends." University of North Carolina at Chapel Hill. http://www.unc.edu/news/FYI/fyi0503html (Accessed 2 February 2005).

Tubbs, Sharon. "Music in the Storm." *St. Petersburg Times* (November 19, 2002). http://sptimes.com/2002/11/19/news_pf/Florida_ (Accessed 6 December 2004).

Sheila A. Stuckey

William H. Dean
1910–1952

Economist, educator

William H. Dean was an economist and United Nations staff member. He overcame racial discrimination and hardships to excel academically at some of the most prestigious universities in the United States. In Haiti and Somaliland he used his expertise in economics to improve the quality of life for local people. Dean was one of the first African Americans to receive a Ph.D. in economics.

William H. Dean Jr. was born on July 6, 1910 in Lynchburg, Virginia, the third of four children to Reverend and Mrs. William Henry Dean Sr. His early years were spent in Pittsburgh, Pennsylvania; Baltimore, Maryland; Washington, D.C.; and Lynchburg, Virginia where his father was the pastor of several churches.

Dean graduated from Douglass High School in Baltimore, Maryland in 1926 as class valedictorian. He won a college scholarship from the Baltimore chapter of Alpha Phi Alpha Fraternity. During his junior year at Bowdoin College in Brunswick, Maine, he was elected to Phi Beta

Chronology

1910	Born in Lynchburg, Virginia on July 6
1926	Graduates as valedictorian of his class from Douglass High School in Baltimore, Maryland
1930	Earns B.A. from Bowdoin College in Brunswick, Maine
1932	Earns M.A. in economics from Harvard University
1933-42	Serves as economics and business administration professor at Atlanta University in Atlanta, Georgia
1938	Earns Ph.D. from Harvard University
1942-44	Serves as executive at Price Administration in the Virgin Islands
1944-46	Serves as director of Community Relations Project at the National Urban League
1949	Receives United Nations Africa Unit Chief status
1951	Directs mission to Italian Somaliland
1952	Commits suicide in New York City on January 8

Kappa and received the B.A. summa cum laude in 1930. He earned an M.A. in 1932 and a Ph.D. in economics (1938) from Harvard University. At Harvard he was a university scholar (1930-31), Henry Lee Memorial fellow (1931-32), and Edward Austin fellow (1932-33). His doctoral dissertation, "The Theory of Geographical Location of Economic Activity," was published in 1938 by Edward Brothers Inc. and used as a text in economics courses.

However, despite all his academic achievements and knowledge, Harvard refused to hire Dean to a tutorial post, an honor usually given to the top person in a specific discipline. According to the *Dictionary of American Negro Biography*, a 1939 letter from Abbot Payson, professor of economics at Harvard, to the Board of Higher Education, New York City stated: "Beyond any possible doubt he is the most talented man has at any time worked under my direction_We deeply regret that special circumstances make it impossible for us to use Dr. Dean here at Harvard. Any institution that can place Dr. Dean on its staff will be indeed fortunate. He is a man of exceptional attainment and promise."

Dean taught economics and business administration at Atlanta University in Atlanta, Georgia from 1933 to 1942. As associate professor of economics and business administration, he introduced courses on labor economics and invited workers from various occupations to visit his classes and talk about their jobs. He tried to improve opportunities for Negro workers on the Bell Aircraft bomber plant in nearby Marietta, Georgia. Dean was a realist and a perfectionist; he realized that the company and white workers resisted equal opportunity for Negro workers. He also surveyed thirteen cities for the National Urban League, thus contributing to record of urban history.

Dean lectured on economics during the summer of 1939 at the City College of New York. He was also a consultant to the National Resources Planning Board from 1940 to 1942. From 1942 to 1944 Dean served as chief economist at the Office of Price Administration, a U.S. federal agency in World War II established to prevent war time inflation, in the Virgin Islands and Haiti.

Becomes United Nations Africa Unit Chief

Dean became acting chief of the United Nations Africa Unit Division of Economic Stability and Development after serving as director of the Community Relations Project of the National Urban League from 1944 to 1946. In 1949 he was made unit chief. In 1949 he also served as secretary to the United Nations mission to Haiti. In 1950 he was appointed administrative officer and second-ranking officer of a United Nations mission to Libya.

In 1939, the City College of New York and Queens College refused to appoint Dean as a member of the faculty, despite the endorsement of Professor Frederick W. Taussig of Harvard; Walter White, secretary of the NAACP; and Mayor Fiorello LaGuardia. The discrimination was reminiscent of Harvard's earlier refusal to hire him.

In 1949, Dean went to Haiti as secretary of the United Nations technical assistance mission. The result of this trip was one of the best analyses of Haiti's problems regarding demography, health, production, transportation, trade, and finance. Its excellent recommendations, however, produced few beneficial results because of the magnitude of the problems and the failure of the United Nations and the United States to provide adequate funds.

Directs Italian Somaliland Mission

During four months in late 1951, Dean directed a six-man mission to Italian Somaliland to determine the means by which that colony could be made self-supporting. The mission to Somaliland documented the shameful legacy of colonialism. Dean returned from his trip despondent, fearing the trip had been a failure, concerned for the hardship endured by people in primitive living conditions in Italian Somaliland, and frustrated by the Italian government. Dean attempted to improve Somaliland's technical development. On January 8, 1952, shortly after his return to the United States, he committed suicide in the New York City apartment of his father-in-law Channing H. Tobias. His funeral was held at St. Mark's Methodist Church, New York City with internment in Woodlawn Cemetery in the Bronx. He was survived by his wife Mary Tobias Dean, whom he had married in 1936, a son Channing, and daughter Joyce.

REFERENCES

Books

DeWerff, Timothy J., ed. "William H. Dean." *Concise Dictionary of American Biography*. Vol.1. New York: Scribner's, 1997.

Logan, Rayford. "William H. Dean." *Dictionary of American Negro Biography*. New York: Norton, 1982.

Prudence White Bryant

Richard DeBaptiste
1831–1901
Minister, educator

Richard DeBaptiste used his talents as an educator and Christian minister to help establish the Olivet Baptist Church in Chicago, where he served as pastor from 1863 to 1882. Just prior to his death in 1901, DeBaptiste led a congregation in Elgin, Illinois, serving a community of former slaves that later became the core of the Second Baptist Church. Additionally, DeBaptiste held leadership roles within various Baptist organizations.

DeBaptiste came from a family that distinguished itself in nearly every major war in which the United States had been involved. His grandfather, John DeBaptiste, fought in the Revolutionary War; George DeBaptiste, an uncle, was in the War of 1812; and two brothers, George and Benjamin, were involved in the Civil War. Richard DeBaptiste was born a free man in Fredericksburg, Virginia on November 11, 1831. His parents, William and Eliza, devoted considerable energy and income to educate Richard and their other children.

DeBaptiste had an excellent career in Christian ministry. When he was a young man, he received basic instruction in reading and grammar at home, first from a black man and later from a Scotch-Irishman who had earlier taught in Scotland. The desire of William DeBaptiste to provide teachers for his immediate family and for a few relatives led to his being kept under surveillance and to his home being watched by police. Virginia laws were such that had it been detected that he was operating a school in his home, he would have been subject to fines and imprisonment.

Leaving the family home in Virginia, young Richard made his way north, first to Ohio and later to Michigan and Illinois, where he continued his English studies with a Quaker teacher, Richard Dillingham. DeBaptiste later learned that Dillingham died in a Nashville prison, where he was incarcerated for helping escaped slaves. The kindly Quaker died from abuse and beatings. DeBaptiste's next teacher was Samuel H. Davis, pastor of the Second Baptist Church of Detroit. With this man, DeBaptiste studied theology and several languages (German, French, Latin and Greek) in preparation for his subsequent study of theology at the University of Chicago.

DeBaptiste went to Mt. Pleasant, Ohio during the great northern migration, motivated, like others, by the desire for personal safety, freedom, and broader opportunity. After his arrival in Mt. Pleasant, he received ordination into the Baptist ministry. The ordination was approved by a representative council drawn from the notable Baptist congregations of the Union Baptist Church, the First and Ninth Street White Assemblies, the Union and Zion black churches, and the church at Lockland. From 1860 to 1863, Lowery ministered to the congregation he founded in Mt. Pleasant, Ohio, and at the same time he taught children attending local colored public schools.

Olivet Baptist Church

In 1863, DeBaptiste assumed leadership of the Olivet Baptist Church of Chicago. This church flourished under DeBaptiste's early leadership. The congregation in later years increased in membership to become, early in the twentieth century, the largest African American church in the world, eventually numbering as many as 20,000 members.

Upon its founding in April 1850, this church was known to its fifty-six members and their pastor, H. H. Hawkins, as the Zenia Baptist Church. The church building stood at the corner of Harrison and LaSalle (then called Griswold). Later it took the name Zion Baptist, and eventually it was renamed Olivet Baptist. Olivet remained under DeBaptiste's leadership from 1863 to 1882, a remarkable tenure of twenty years and a remarkable period of early growth for the church. By 1877 the membership had grown to over seven hundred. Meanwhile DeBaptiste had led his congregation in erecting a new church building, this time on Fourth Avenue (later renamed Federal Street), and when this building was consumed in the great Chicago fire of 1873, he led again, building a new structure on the same site. That building was sold in 1883, and the site became the Dearborn-Polk Street Station.

Later in his life, DeBaptiste served as pastor of the Second Baptist Church in Elgin, Illinois, for two or three years prior to his death in 1901. This historic church, years before his arrival, had originated as a community of escaped slaves, at first consisting of only women and children, brought to the location by the Reverend Benjamin Thames in October 1862. When the men of these families began to arrive, they reconnected and unified Elgin, which became the core of the Second Baptist Church, the last church DeBaptiste would serve.

Other Services

In addition to his work as pastor, DeBaptiste served his fellow Baptists in a number of capacities. He was corresponding secretary to the Wood River (Baptist) Association in 1864, recording secretary for the Northwestern and Southern Baptist Convention's organizational meeting in 1865, and corresponding secretary of the 1866 annual meeting of the organization. In addition, he held several elective positions, including that of president of the United American Baptist Missionary Convention, a post to which he was re-elected until 1877. He then assumed the role of recording secretary of the Foreign Mission Board, serving for another two years. He was elected to offices in such prestigious organizations as the Baptist Free Mission Society and the American Baptist National Convention. At the latter meeting, he revealed the encouraging, but previously undiscovered, fact that instead of the 800,000 black Baptists reported in the American Baptist Publication Society yearbook, there were, in fact, over one million black Baptists. Surprisingly, the total reported by DeBaptiste did not include the newly baptized from twenty-one out of thirty-seven states for that year.

In 1887, DeBaptiste received an honorary D.D. from the State University in Louisville, Kentucky. He died in Chicago, Illinois on April 21, 1901. DeBaptiste devoted most of his life to the Baptist ministry; he had accumulated very little money and few worldly possessions, but for him the number of souls that he saved counted for much more.

REFERENCES

Books

Sernett, Milton C. *Afro-American Religious History*. Durham, N.C.: University of North Carolina Press, 1985.

Periodicals

Crimpich, John. "The Beginning of the Black Suffrage Movement in Tennessee, 1864-1865." *Journal of Negro History* 65 (Summer 1980), 185-95.

Online

Hicks, William. "History of Louisiana Negro Baptists." The Reformed Reader. Louisiana Baptist Brotherhood: Nashville, 2000. http://www. reformedreader.org/history/hicks/bioclanton.html (Accessed 8 November 2005).

Lois A. Peterson

Chronology	
1825	Born in New York City
1840	Enters the Oneida Institute in New York
1843	Studies medicine for two years in Paris
1849	Receives his M.D. from Bowdoin College in Maine
1853	Practices medicine in New York City
1854	Becomes first African American in the Massachusetts Medical Society
1863	Volunteers in Union army; serves as assistant surgeon in the 35th U.S. Colored Troops
??	Dies in unknown circumstances

John Van Surly DeGrasse
1825–?

Physician, surgeon

John Van Surly DeGrasse was one of the first black Americans to be commissioned as surgeons in the U.S. Army. Born in New York City and educated at private, public, and undergraduate schools in New York, DeGrasse also studied in Paris and Maine. He was admitted to the Massachusetts Medical Society in 1854, at a time when this type of honor was unheard of for men of color. DeGrasse was intelligent and persevering, the most accomplished of the colored pioneers in the post-Revolutionary and pre-Civil War eras.

DeGrasse was born in 1825 in New York City, one of several children of George DeGrasse, born in Calcutta, and Maria Van Surly of German parentage. Before the Civil War only a few blacks practiced medicine in the sense of participating in a discrete professional class with mainstream established traditions. Those who did were often denied access to normal lines of professional development, including membership in medical societies, or were shunned from medical practice, but their routes of entry into the profession tended to follow their white counterparts. Three major routes were self-education, apprenticeship, and medical school attendance. DeGrasse was one of those who managed to overcome the medical school color bar and receive formal training.

DeGrasse attended private and public schools in New York City until 1840. In 1840 he entered the Oneida Institute in New York. Then from 1843 to 1845, he studied medicine at Aubuk College in Paris. In 1845 he returned to New York City and commenced the study of medicine with Samuel R. Childs. On May 19, 1849, he received the M.D. degree with honors from Bowdoin College in Brunswick, Maine.

DeGrasse went to Europe and spent time working in the hospitals of Paris, traveling periodically elsewhere in France and to England, Italy, and Switzerland. He returned to the United States on the *Samuel Fox*, working as a surgeon. After practicing medicine in New York City, he moved to Boston where he continued to practice.

Admitted to Massachusetts Medical Society

In recognition of his extraordinary ability, on August 24, 1854, DeGrasse was admitted to the Massachusetts Medical Society. According to a Boston newspaper in 1854, it was the first time that an honor of that magnitude had been conferred upon a black man in the United States. DeGrasse may have been the most accomplished physician of his era.

A volunteer with the Union Army during the Civil War, DeGrasse served as assistant surgeon with the 35th U.S. Colored Troops in 1863. He was one of the first of eight blacks to be commissioned a surgeon in the U.S. Army. In appreciation of his service, Governor John A. Andrew presented him with a gold-hilted sword on behalf of the Commonwealth of Massachusetts. The cause of and circumstances around his death are unknown.

REFERENCES

Books

Ahmed, Siraj. "John Van Surly DeGrasse." In *Encyclopedia of African American Culture and History.* New York: Norton, 1982.

Asbury, Howard D. "John Van Surly DeGrasse." In *Dictionary of American Negro Biography.* Eds. Rayford W. Logan and Michael R. Winston. New York: Norton, 1982.

"John Van Surly DeGrasse." *African American Breakthroughs*. Eds. Jay P. Pederson and Jessie Carney Smith. New York: Gale Research, 1995.

Online

African American Contributions to Science and Industry. http://www.inventions.org/culture/science/african.html (Accessed 25 February 2006).

Just Learning to be Men. Chapter Two: "They Have Been Slaves." http://www.rootsweb.com/~ncusct/shana2.htm (Accessed 25 February 2006).

Prudence White Bryant

Robert DeLarge

Robert DeLarge
1842–1874

Congressman

During his relatively short life, Robert Carlos DeLarge was very active, politically and otherwise, in his home state of South Carolina. These involvements ultimately led to his election as a U.S. congressman during the Reconstruction period, but personal and political challenges ended his career after he served only one three-year term in office.

Robert Carlos DeLarge was born on March 15, 1842 in Aiken, South Carolina. His father was a free black tailor who was also a slaveholder, and his mother was of Haitian descent. Sources indicate that DeLarge was identified as being a mulatto, but the term may have been used to indicate any person of mixed ancestry, regardless of the racial categories involved.

DeLarge went to the neighboring state of North Carolina to receive his primary education, then returned to South Carolina, where he attended and graduated from Wood High School in Charleston. During this period he also became a member of the Brown Fellowship Society, a fraternal and charitable organization that restricted its membership to mulattos.

After the firing on Fort Sumter in Charleston's harbor began the Civil War in 1861, DeLarge was employed (under duress) by the Confederate navy to assist in building fortifications for the city. Reports indicate that DeLarge also was a barber, an agricultural laborer, and, like his father, a tailor, all to support himself during the war years. When the Civil War ended in 1865, DeLarge secured employment as an agent with the Freedmen's Bureau after it was established in South Carolina during the Reconstruction period.

DeLarge became one of more than a hundred free blacks in Charleston who signed a petition asking for voting rights, which was submitted to the 1865 state constitutional convention. He also attended the convention and acknowledged the concession that "ignorant" persons of both races could still be prevented from participating in elections.

Becomes Involved in State Politics

During the same year DeLarge participated in the state black convention, which was known as the "Colored People's Convention", and chaired its credentials committee. He submitted a resolution urging that South Carolina establish public schools for all its citizens, and he made speeches in support of it that were well received by those in attendance. Although his resolution was adopted by the convention, it did not result in any immediate action at the state level.

In 1867 DeLarge chaired the platform committee at the Union Republican state political convention, where he continued to be an advocate for public schools. Other issues he supported and spoke in favor of were voting rights, tax reform, reorganization of the state court system, welfare assistance, modification of immigration laws, fair and equitable awarding of contracts for railroad and canal building projects, popular elections for all

Chronology

1842	Born in Aiken, South Carolina on March 15
1861	Works as forced laborer for Confederacy when Civil War begins
1865	Works for Freedmen's Bureau after Civil War; participates in state conventions
1867	Chairs platform committee at state Union Republican convention
1868	Becomes member of state legislature; chairs committees and land commission
1869	Attends South Carolina labor convention
1870	Runs for Congress; is declared winner of contested election
1871	Begins service as representative of South Carolina in Congress on March 4
1873	Ends congressional service when seat is declared vacant on January 24
1874	Dies in Charleston, South Carolina on February 14

political offices, the end of land monopolies, and the abolition of capital punishment.

DeLarge held a number of other positions during the Reconstruction period, including delegate to the state constitutional convention in 1868, where he chaired three standing committees and frequently gave speeches and participated in debates. While many of his ideas, petitions, motions, and resolutions were unsuccessful, the convention did pass his resolution which asked the U.S. Congress for a $1 million grant to purchase land which would then be sold to poor persons displaced from plantations and other large land tracts.

As a member of the state house of representatives, DeLarge chaired the ways and means committee during the 1868 and 1869 legislative sessions, sponsored railroad legislation, successfully argued against a proposal limiting debate on legislative issues, and served as head of the state land commission. He also served as a board member of the Sinking Fund Commission, on the board of regents for the state lunatic asylum, and as a magistrate in Charleston.

DeLarge attended the South Carolina labor convention in 1869. By this time he was well known and influential in state political circles. Apparently, DeLarge used his influence, contacts, and other resources for his own benefit as well, for the 1870 U.S. Census indicated that DeLarge owned $6,650 in real estate holdings, a considerable amount at that time. In addition, his position as land commissioner came as the result of a political arrangement; the former commissioner, C. P. Leslie, resigned and was replaced by a Negro selected by the legislature. DeLarge was the chosen person, and he benefited from the political power of Negro voting majorities in his state as well as the concessions imposed upon the South after the Civil War.

Serves as U.S. Congressman

As part of efforts by black leaders that year to gain additional political power and influence, DeLarge was nominated as a Republican candidate to represent South Carolina in the U.S. House of Representatives. He won in a closely contested election and assumed office in 1871 as one of three black congressmen from his state. One of his colleagues, Joseph H. Rainey, had the distinction of being the first black member of the House of Representatives when he was sworn in on December 12, 1870, while Robert Brown Elliot was seated at the same time as DeLarge.

Personal and political problems at home hindered DeLarge during his single term as a member of the 42nd Congress from March 4, 1871 to January 24, 1873. Charges of election fraud were brought against DeLarge by Christopher C. Bowen, his political rival and former two-term congressman for the South Carolina 2nd Congressional district, which included the city of Charleston. Although there was a Negro majority of registered voters in the district and the Board of Canvassers had declared DeLarge the winner, Bowen appealed to his former colleagues in Congress to further investigate the matter.

In a speech from the floor of the House of Representatives made on April 6, 1871, DeLarge criticized corruption in both political parties, condemned Negroes for trusting white carpetbaggers from the North and elsewhere, urged that former Confederates be allowed to return to politics, and spoke in favor of the ratification of the Fourteenth Amendment to the Constitution. One observer, Samuel Delany Smith, described these remarks as "one of the sanest and most sensible speeches ever delivered by a Negro Congressman". This was high praise, coming from a person who in general was very critical of African American politicians, and reflected the delicate balancing act DeLarge and other politicians sought to achieve in order to maintain the favor and support of various factions in their home districts.

By the time of the second session, which began on December 4, 1871, DeLarge had to devote most of his time and energy to proving that he had the right to stay in Congress. Bowen continued to put pressure on DeLarge regarding his past political and business dealings from his new positions in the South Carolina legislature and as sheriff of Charleston.

As a result, DeLarge was implicated on charges of fraud and mismanagement in connection with his period as head of the state land commission. Earlier in 1871 DeLarge had reported that nearly two thousand small tracts of land had been sold or would be occupied by new homeowners, with a period of eight years to pay for their property. This was not the case, and the controversy became a major factor in his political demise.

Leaves Congress after Controversy and Illness

DeLarge also experienced health problems, which may have been intensified by his political difficulties, and was reported as absent and sick when the House of Representatives reconvened on January 24, 1873. After the report of its Committee on Elections and a brief debate, the conclusion was reached that neither DeLarge nor Bowen had been properly elected in 1870 because of election fraud and other irregularities.

The brief period of service by DeLarge in the national government ended that day, when his seat in Congress was declared vacant. He was replaced by another African American, Alonzo J. Ransier, on March 4, 1873. Black officeholders would continue to participate in politics on the national stage with varying degrees of success throughout the Reconstruction period. South Carolina had the largest number of blacks to become members of Congress, as Richard H. Cain and Civil War hero Robert Smalls were also elected in succeeding years. DeLarge returned to his home state, where he lived for a time in Columbia, the state capital. Governor Robert Scott then appointed DeLarge to his last political position, as a magistrate in Charleston.

DeLarge's health continued to fail, and he died of consumption at the age of thirty-one on February 14, 1874 in Charleston. Reports indicate that he was survived by his wife and Victoria, a daughter. His funeral took place on February 16 at his home, 106 Calhoun Street, with burial in the Brown Fellowship Graveyard. The offices of other city magistrates closed that day in tribute to a young politician who had experienced such a spectacular rise to prominence, as well as subsequent downfall, in the brief window of political opportunity and advantage for African Americans during the Reconstruction period.

REFERENCES

Books

Foner, Eric. *Freedom's Lawmakers: A Directory of Black Officeholders during Reconstruction*. Baton Rouge: Louisiana State University Press, 1996.

Middleton, Stephen, ed. *Black Congressmen during Reconstruction: A Documentary Sourcebook*. Westport, Conn.: Greenwood Press, 2002.

Smith, Samuel Delany. *The Negro in Congress: 1870-1901*. Chapel Hill, N.C.: University of North Carolina Press, 1940.

Tobin, Sidney. "Robert Carlos Delarge." In *Dictionary of American Negro Biography*. Eds. Rayford W. Logan and Michael R. Winston. New York: Norton, 1982.

"United States Congress." *Biographical Directory of the United States Congress, 1774-1989*. Washington, D.C.: Government Printing Office, 1989.

Online

"A Timeline of Reconstruction: 1865-1877." http://chmn. gmu.edu/courses/122/recon/chron.html (Accessed 11 November 2005).

Fletcher F. Moon

Gary C. Dennis
1950–

Surgeon, educator

Gary Creed Dennis, surgeon and professor of neurological surgery, is a respected practitioner, educator, and noted healthcare advocate. He is a past president of the National Medical Association (NMA), a professional and scientific organization serving the interests of African American physicians. Dennis has an intense interest in health policy and legislative and regulatory affairs. He has spoken widely on healthcare disparities, access to health care, managed care, and diversity in medical education. As chief of the Division of Neurosurgery and associate professor of neurological surgery at the Howard University College of Medicine and Howard University Hospital, Dennis has clearly demonstrated his commitment to professional education and development.

Dennis, a native of the District of Columbia, is the son of Creed and Yvonne C. Bush Dennis. He was born December 27, 1950. He graduated with a B.A. from Boston University in 1972. In 1975 he was inducted into the Alpha Omega Alpha Medical Honor Society. In 1976, he received the Merck Manual Award, the James T.W. Grandy Award 1st Prize, the Sandoz Award and the Clarence S. Green Sr. Award when he graduated from the Howard University School of Medicine.

Begins Teaching Medicine

Dennis interned at Baltimore's John Hopkins Hospital from 1976 to 1977 and was a neurosurgical resident at Baylor College of Medicine Affiliated Hospitals in Houston, from 1977 to1981. The Kern Medical Center in Bakersfield, California, appointed him chief of neurosurgery in 1981. At the same time, he was clinical assistant professor of neurosurgery at the University of California at San Diego. In 1984, he was appointed chief of the Division of Neurosurgery and assistant professor at the Howard University College of Medicine, where he became associate professor in 1990. He became an attending physician at D.C. General Hospital in 1990.

In 1993, Dennis participated in an exchange program for the Medical Education for South African Blacks (MESAB), a nonprofit organization seeking to increase the number of black health professionals. Dennis lectured on his specialty at several medical hospitals and schools. In 2002, Dennis joined the MESAB board. He was a member of Summit '93, a coalition of health and service organizations seeking to increase the role of African Americans in the healthcare debate. The Rainbow Coalition sponsored a press conference at the NMA where the Health Insurance Association of America presented a new series of television advertisements about healthcare legislation. At the gathering, Dennis said that it was crucial that legislation should provide for physicians that serve the urban poor.

Dennis is a fellow of the American College of Surgeons, chairman of the Board of Trustees of the Medical Society of the District of Columbia, and an elected member of the Society of Neurological Surgeons. He also is an appointee to the Federation Advisory Committee of the American Medical Accreditation Programs of the American Medical Association, as well as its Minority Affairs Consortium. In 1995, he was reappointed to the Practicing Physicians' Advisory Council of the Health Care Financing Agency.

Dennis, then chief, Division of Neurosurgery, and associate professor at the Howard University College of Medicine, was installed as the ninety-seventh president of the National Medical Association (NMA) at its annual Convention and Scientific Assembly in New Orleans in 1998. For his tenure, Dennis focused on creating effective healthcare leaders through the promotion of a National African American Leadership Colloquium and creating new alliances with the federal government and corporate America to better educate patients and physicians on healthcare issues dominating the black community.

Becomes Healthcare Advocate

Speaking before the United States House Appropriations Committee in 1999, Dennis presented key health priorities. He encouraged the congressional subcommittee to provide more funds for healthcare research, particularly minority health research, and recruit more health professionals of color. He encouraged the committee to increase funding for the Office of Minority Health at the Department of Health and Human Services and raise the office's visibility inside and outside government. He requested that the government fund a national study on racism in medicine, particularly regarding issues related to medical education and healthcare delivery. He asked for greater attention to health care for the uninsured and community based public health initiatives. He would like medical school curriculum changes that expose medical students to racial and gender health issues. Dennis noted that given the extent to which racism is ingrained in the practice of medicine and in the education of health professionals, students must be understood as essential in the effort to eliminate health disparities.

Dennis has provided testimony before the Congressional Black Caucus Health Braintrust, as well as the Democratic Caucus Special Task Force on Medicare; the U.S. House of Representatives Committee on Ways and Means; the Joint Subcommittee on Labeling Information for Nonprescriptive Drugs, the U.S. House of Representatives Judiciary Committee, the U.S. House of Representatives Appropriations Subcommittee on Labor, Health and Human Services and Education, and the Food and Drug Administration, among others.

Dennis serves on a variety of professional boards and committees. He has served as the chair of the American Neurological Surgery Political Action Committee. He served two terms as a member of the Practicing Physicians Advisory Council of the Health Care Financing Administration, having first been appointed by Secretary of Health and Human Services Louis Sullivan in 1992 and later reappointed by Secretary Donna Shalala in 1996. The doctor was listed among the best doctors in the southeast area by *Washingtonian Magazine* in 1995. In August of 1999, he joined the Board of the American Liver Foundation.

In a 1999 *Emerge* magazine interview, Dennis noted that racism not only affects the health care of African Americans but that it affects biomedical research, the practice of medicine, healthcare delivery, and medical education. He expressed concern for the declining enrollment of African Americans which he attributed to anti-affirmative action efforts, particularly in Texas, Louisiana, Mississippi and California. Dennis and the NMA reprimanded health management organizations (HMOs) and managed care corporations for their consistent exclusion of African American physicians' requests to participate in provider networks panels. He also noted that health plans are not including sufficient numbers of black physicians in proportion to the racial and ethnic make-up of the communities in which they serve. He noted in the *Emerge* interview that HMOs do not have a mandate to support postgraduate education. Funds that previously supported the training of postgraduates have gone to HMOs.

Other healthcare issues promoted by Dennis during his NMA presidency include encouraging reluctant African Americans to participate in clinical trials and to follow pharmaceutical developments; teaching African Americans how to navigate the healthcare system; the under treatment of severe pain in the black community; the promotion of the Patients Bill of Rights as congressional legislation; and the promotion of lactose-free dairy foods in the food guide pyramid and dietary guidelines for Americans from the United States Department of Agriculture. Dennis promoted the *Merck Manual of Medical Information—Home Edition*, the company's first consumer reference published in 1999.

Dennis has published numerous peer-reviewed articles and book chapters and conducted various research. For example, he is a co-investigator on research projects studying the effects of cocaine on the ventral lateral medulla and the biological precursors of violence.

Power Couple Achieves

Dennis and his wife, Sharman Naomi Word Dennis, were the first husband and wife team to be named simultaneous presidents of the NMA and the Auxiliary National Medical Association (ANMA). The ANMA was formed in 1936 and consists of professional spouses, male and female, of the NMA. Each ANMA program has at least one NMA doctor on the project. The theme promoted by the auxiliary under Sharma Dennis was "We Are Who Our Ancestors Were: Looking Back as We Move Forward in Fulfilling Our Obligation to Improve the Status of Health Care through Commitment, Respect and Partnership." Sharma Dennis, an early intervention child development expert and former special education teacher in Washington D.C., worked with "Destination: Vaccination," an outreach project for child immunization. In 1999, the auxiliary met with the Congressional Black Caucus to discuss the "Gift of Giving" program that focuses on organ, tissue, bone marrow donation and enlisting organ donors in partnership with community organization.

The couple, along with Congresswoman Eleanor Holmes Norton, chaired the 1999 Duke Ellington Ball to benefit the Washington Symphony Orchestra. They are parents of three children, twins Gary and Gina, and Gregory. Dennis is a recipient of the D.C. Youth Symphony Orchestra's Distinguished Service Award, the McDonald's Black History Leaders of Today and Tomorrow, and the highest honor bestowed by Howard University Hospital, the Legacy of Leadership Award. He serves on the Mayor's Health Services Reform Commission, the Dis-

trict of Columbia Commission on Judicial Disabilities and Tenure, and on the Board of Trustees of the Delmarva Foundation. He has also chaired the NMA's Council on Medical Legislation. He continues to make frequent media appearances.

REFERENCES

Periodicals

"Dennis installed as new NMA president at Annual Convention." *Jet* 94 (7 September 1998): 8-9.

Stewart, Rhonda. "Dead on Arrival." *Emerge* 10 (September 1999): 34-39.

Online

"Gary C. Dennis." The Society of Neurological Surgeons, Senior Society. http://www.societyns.org/society/bio.asp?MemberID=80 (Accessed 10 June 2005).

"Gary C. Dennis, M.D., F.A.C.S. Docrates." http://www.docrates.net/QuickInterview/drdennisbio.htm (Accessed 10 June 2005).

Kathleen E. Bethel

James DePreist
1936–

Conductor

Symphony orchestra conductor James DePreist has been acclaimed as a rare and special artist. His extraordinary talent took him to the Oregon Symphony, which he transformed from a regional to a national orchestra. He was the first African American conductor of the Houston Symphony and was assistant conductor to Leonard Bernstein and the New York Philharmonic. Known as one of the finest U.S. conductors, DePreist continues to support the American tradition of excellence in conducting and recordings.

James Anderson DePreist was born November 21, 1936 in Philadelphia, Pennsylvania, to a family where music was important. DePreist's mother was a singer and his aunt was the world-renowned contralto Marian Anderson. When DePreist was six years old, his father died. His famous aunt came to the aid of the entire family. She helped the family purchase two adjoining rowhouses in a middle-class neighbor on the south side of Philadelphia. DePreist and his mother lived in one house and his aunt Alyce and his grandmother lived in the other. He obtained his early education in music in the Philadel-

James DePreist

phia public schools, and at the age of ten he studied piano. Because of music lessons that lasted well after the regular school hours, DePreist found most of his friends in music classes. He participated in musical activities throughout high school and played in the City-Wide High School Orchestra. Music had become a major focus in DePreist's life, but he did not choose it as a career until years later.

After graduating from high school in 1954, DePreist entered the University of Pennsylvania's Wharton School as a pre-law student. Not forsaking his musical interest, he took music classes and played in the symphony orchestra and the university marching band. He received his B.S. degree in 1958 and continued at the university to earn a master's degree. In 1959, DePreist studied composition at the Philadelphia Conservatory of Music with Vincent Persichettie, a distinguished American composer. He also studied music history and the theory of harmony and orchestration at the conservatory. While in college, DePreist formed a jazz group called the Jimmy DePreist Quintet. This band became so well-known in the East that in 1956, they appeared on the Steve Allen television show. DePreist received his M.A. degree from the University of Pennsylvania in 1961.

In 1962, the State Department sponsored a cultural exchange tour and engaged DePreist as an American specialist in music. The tour was to cover the Near and the Far East with DePreist lecturing and performing jazz. While on tour in Thailand and attending a Bangkok orchestra rehearsal, he was asked if he wanted to conduct. This experience caused DePreist to realize he wanted to be a conductor. It also marked his debut as a conductor with the Bangkok Symphony Orchestra and led to DePreist's becoming guest conductor at other locations on the State Department tour. Also in 1962 on the tour DePreist was stricken with polio. The disease paralyzed both his legs. He had to be flown home to the States in 1963 for care and therapy. After six months of intensive therapy and perseverance on his part, DePreist was able to walk with the aid of crutches and braces. In the midst of his recuperation, DePreist kept sight of his goals and prepared himself to compete in the Mitropoulos International Conductors Competition, which moved him closer to his goal of becoming a classical conductor and gave him the visibility that creates opportunities. In the competition, DePreist only made it to the semi-finals, but in the next year, he went on to win first prize. His abilities brought him to the attention of Leonard Bernstein, who asked DePreist to sign on as assistant conductor for the New York Philharmonic during the 1965-66 season.

Legacy and Marion Anderson

On June 28, 1965 DePreist conducted the farewell concert of his aunt Marian Anderson. Her concert was held at the Robin Hood Dell in Philadelphia. In later years, DePreist remarked on what a tremendous contribution his aunt had made to the world of music, part of which was that it made possible much more African American participation. DePreist realized he entered rehearsal halls which in the 1930s may well have been closed to his aunt. In fact, in 1939 the Daughters of the American Revolution refused to let Anderson perform at Constitution Hall in Washington D.C. There was a great wave of protest. First Lady Eleanor Roosevelt resigned from the organization and was instrumental in getting Secretary of the Interior Harold L. Ickes to issue an invitation to Anderson to sing at the Lincoln Memorial. On Easter Sunday, April 9, 1939, Anderson sang to an audience of 75,000 in one of the most important and significant concerts in U.S. history. Subsequently, the policy of prohibiting African American performers in Constitutional Hall was changed. But through it all, Anderson had become for DePreist his hero, godmother, mentor, and close friend. In an interview with CNN in 2002, DePreist stated: "My aunt Marion used to say that she wasn't cut out for hand-to-hand combat. Her approach to life was to lead and fight by example of personality and character." Marion Anderson spent the last years of her life in DePreist's home.

After the completion of his appointment as assistant to Leonard Bernstein, DePreist had difficulty finding a serious classical position as a conductor in the United States, where orchestra boards favored European conductors. Most of the time his letters were met with no response while others suggested pop concerts. To realize his goal DePreist decided to go abroad. He moved to Rotterdam, in the Netherlands, and called that home from 1966 to 1970. He made his debut with the Rotterdam Philharmonic in 1969, when he took over concerts scheduled to be conducted by Edo de Waart That same year he was awarded the Martha Baird Rockefeller grant, which allowed DePreist to tour in Europe and the United States as a guest conductor. From 1968 to 1970, DePreist was a guest conductor for the Symphony of the New World in New York. His home town recognized his creative talents and his success as a conductor, and he was presented with a Merit Citation from the City of Philadelphia in 1969.

The National Symphony Orchestra in Washington D.C. engaged DePreist from 1971 to 1975 as associate conductor under Antal Dorati. In 1976, DePreist became the first African American conductor of the Houston Symphony. Although he was prepared for his patrons of the Texas symphony, not all of them were prepared for him as an African American. When he stepped on stage, there was a gasp from a woman in the audience. Remembering the guidance given by his aunt, Marion Anderson, DePreist remained calm. In spite of the attendant's unexpected response, DePreist was extraordinary, a skilled conductor who impressed his entire audience.

DePreist received an honorary doctorate from the University of Pennsylvania in 1976. He also became director of the Quebec Symphony and after four years was offered, in 1980, the directorship of the Oregon Symphony. DePreist's vibrancy as a conductor and his ability to connect with the audience fostered positive relation-ships with this symphony and its audiences. People found him witty, commanding, and charismatic. DePreist would sit on a swiveling stool when interacting with his audience, as the effects of polio required him wear leg braces and use metal canes when walking. He also used podium rails to turn and make statements and comments.

DePreist directed Sweden's Malmo Symphony Orchestra in 1991. In 1999, he was diagnosed with kidney disease, and he received a kidney transplant in December 2001. The Oregon Symphony, which initially was a regional orchestra, was transformed into one of national acclaim by DePreist's directorship. Marking his twentieth anniversary, DePreist and the Oregon Symphony were awarded $1 million for recordings. The funds helped to establish the Gretchen Brooks Recording Fund named for its donor. DePreist was able to have complete artistic freedom over record labels, producing, repertoire, venue, and medium Of the fifteen-album discography that DePreist conducted with the Oregon Symphony, many received critical acclaim. The recording with Neil DePonte of Tomas Svoboda's *Concerto for Marimba and Orchestra* became the first to be nominated for a Grammy Award in 2004. After twenty-two years as director, DePreist retired from the Oregon Symphony in September 2003. In 2004, he was named laureate director for the Oregon Symphony and continued to do occasional concerts over the seasons.

Juilliard School in New York named DePreist director of Conducting and Orchestral Studies in the fall of 2004. The president of Juilliard, Joseph W. Polisi, said in a school press release by Janet Kessin that " James DePreist beings extraordinary artistry and humanity to his new post. His musical and personal integrity will exist as a model for all the members of our community." DePreist led the orchestra in concert with violinist Gil Shaham as soloist in a Mendelssohn concerto and returned nearly every season to conduct. As director of Conducting and Orchestral Studies, DePreist selects, auditions, and trains five to six young conductors annually in an increasingly global profession. When the school reached its centennial in 2005, DePreist and his orchestral ensembles and conductors were in the forefront of activities. He planned to lead four of the sixteen concerts that Juilliard performs each season.

DePreist's ongoing commitment to conducting was recognized on November 1, 2000, when he received the Ditson Conductor's Award, given annually by Columbia University. As Columbia's 56th recipient of the award, DePreist was acknowledged because of his continued advancement of American music. Other recipients include Leonard Bernstein, Eugene Ormandy, Leopold Stokowski, Joann Falletta, and Christoph von Dohnanyi. DePreist has also been guest conductor for every major orchestra in North America and the leading orchestras of Amsterdam, Berlin, Budapest, Copenhagen, Helsinki, Manchester, Melbourne, Munich, Prague, Rome, Seoul, Stockholm,

Stuttgart, Sydney, Tel Aviv, Tokyo, and Vienna. He debuted with the London Symphony Orchestra in April 2005 with a performance of Mahler's *Symphony No. Five*. In April 2005, DePreist became the new permanent conductor of the Tokyo Metropolitan Symphony.

DePreist has to his credit over fifty recordings and thirteen honorary doctorates. His compositions consist particularly of ballet scores. He has been honored as a fellow of the American Academy of Arts and Sciences and the Royal Swedish Academy of Music. He has received the Insignia of Commander of the Order of the Lion of Finland, the medal of the City of Quebec, and an Officer of the Order of Cultural Merit of Monaco. DePreist is also the author of two volumes of poetry, *This Precipice Garden* (1987) and *The Distant Siren* (1989). DePreist regularly appears at the Aspen Musical Festival, with the Boston Symphony at Tanglewood, with the Philadelphia Orchestra, at the Mann Music Center, and with the Juilliard orchestras at Lincoln Center and Carnegie Hall.

REFERENCES

Books

Gran, John. *Blacks in Classical Music: A Bibliographical Guide to Composers, Performers, and Ensembles*. Westport, Conn..: Greenwood Press, 1988.

Ploski, Harry R., and James Williams. *The Negro Almanac: A Reference Work on the Afro-American*. 4th ed. New York: John Wiley & Sons, 1983.

Southern, Eileen. *Biographical Dictionary of Afro-American and African Musicians*. Westport, Conn.: Greenwood Press 1982.

Strong, Willie. "DePreist, James Anderson." *Encyclopedia of African-American Culture and History*. Vol. 2. Eds. Jack Salzmann, David Lionel Smith, and Cornel West. New York: Simon & Schuster, 1996.

Lean'tin L. Bracks

Mathew W. Dogan
1863–1947

College president

Mathew W. Dogan was the president of Wiley College for forty six years. Wiley, a private, Methodist school, was the first black college west of the Mississippi River. Under his tenure, Wiley grew in size,

Chronology	
1863	Born in Pontotoc, Mississippi on December 21
1886	Receives A.B. from Rust University
1888	Marries Fannie Forrest Falkner on July 21
1896	Becomes president of Wiley College
1942	Retires from Wiley College
1947	Dies in Marshall, Texas on June 17

enrollment, and stature with the addition of many new buildings and programs, including a library funded by the Carnegie Foundation. With Dogan's great planning and care, Wiley became a respected institution of higher learning for African Americans.

Mathew Winifred Dogan was born on December 21, 1863 in Pontotoc, Mississippi, to William Dogan and Jennie Martin Dogan. Born and raised in poverty, Dogan took advantage of the few educational opportunities that were offered in his tiny town while working a variety of odd jobs to help out his family. Dogan saved the little money that he made shining shoes and boots in his father's shop to attend a college preparatory program at Rust University in Holly Spring, Mississippi. After completing the program, he enrolled in the university's undergraduate program, but due to financial hardship, Dogan left Rust for two years, making what turned out to be an ill-fated attempt at a career in the grocery business. Dogan also taught school, which enabled him to return to Rust and complete his studies. Dogan graduated with an A.B. degree at the top of his class in 1886. He was awarded an honorary Ph.D. from Rust College in 1904 and received a D.D. from New Orleans College in 1910. Dogan also received honorary doctorates from Walden College and Howard University. On July 21, 1888, Dogan married Fannie Forrest Falkner of Memphis, Tennessee. The couple had five children.

Sometime between 1889 and 1891, Dogan joined the faculty of Rust, leaving later to teach mathematics at Central Tennessee College (later Walden University) in Nashville. Dogan left Central Tennessee College in 1896 to become the seventh and longest seated president of Wiley University in Marshall, Texas. Wiley University, the oldest black college west of the Mississippi River, was founded by the Freedmen's Aid Society of the Methodist Episcopal Church, and in its first twenty years of existence was operated by white faculty and white administrators. Dogan was the school's second black president. Wiley's first black, Bishop Isaiah B. Scott, served as the school's president from 1892 to 1896. Under both Scott's and Dogan's tenures, black faculty and administrators were recruited, and the school's leadership and professors were soon predominately African American.

Strengthens Wiley and Becomes Involved in Civic Affairs

Between 1896 and 1906, six buildings were constructed on Wiley's campus. The first under Dogan's leadership was the central building, which was erected by the students. The students also made the bricks for the building on campus.

In 1929, Wiley University changed its name to Wiley College and dropped their high school and trade programs, focusing only on post-secondary education. Under Dogan's guidance, Wiley expanded its campus and programs. It became one of the top black universities in the United States. Science, athletics, education, and music were some of the programs added to Wiley during Dogan's tenure.

Dogan prospered financially. In 1915, he owned over $7,000 worth of property. Dogan shied away from politics, except for voting Republican, but he belonged to many civic and religious organizations. He served as president of the Standard Mutual Fire Insurance Company, the National Association of Teachers in Colored Schools at both state and national levels, as well as the Teachers State Association of Texas. He served as an executive board member of the National Association of Teachers in Colored Schools after his presidency of the organization. Dogan was a member of the following organizations: the Association for the Study of Negro Life and History, the board of education of the Methodist Episcopal Church, the East Texas Colored Teachers Association, the local and national Negro Business League, the Inter-Racial Commission of Texas, Phi Beta Sigma, an advisory member of the State Charities Committee, and the Knights of Pythias. Dogan also served as a delegate to the Methodist Episcopal Church's national conference in 1904, 1908, and 1912 and on four other occasions. He served several times as a delegate to meetings of the National Y.M.C.A. Council. Dogan also founded the Southern Athletic Conference, of which Wiley College was a member.

Dogan contributed to the 1927 book, *The Negro and Methodism* published by Eaton and Maines. Educator Warmoth T. Gibbs wrote Dogan's life story, *President Mathew W. Dogan of Wiley College: A Biography*, which was published in 1930.

Dogan retired as president of Wiley University in 1942 and spent his remaining years in Marshall, Texas. On June 17, 1947, Mathew Winifred Dogan died in his home. Little was written on Dogan after his death, but most existing biographical accounts praise his work as Wiley president.

REFERENCES

Books

"Dogan, Mathew Winifred." In *Who's Who in Colored America [1928-1929]*. 2nd ed. Ed. Joseph J. Boris. New York: Who's Who in Colored America Corp., 1929.

"Dogan, Mathew Winifred." In *Who's Who in Colored America [1941-1944]*. 6th ed. Ed. Thomas Yenser. Brooklyn: Thomas Yenser, 1942.

"Dogan, Mathew Winifred." In *Who's Who of the Colored Race*. Vol. 1. Ed. Frank Lincoln Mather. Chicago: 1915.

"Dr. M. W. Dogan." In *A Sure Foundation*. Ed. A. W. Jackson. Houston: 1940.

"Dr. M. W. Dogan, A.M." In *An Album of Negro Educators*. Ed. G. F. Richings. Philadelphia: 1900.

"Mathew W. Dogan, A.A.B.D." In *The National Cyclopedia of the Colored Race*. Vol. 1. Ed. Clement Richardson. Montgomery: National Publishing Company, Inc., 1919.

Periodicals

"Mathew Winifred Dogan." *The Journal of Negro History* 32 (October 1947): 527.

Brandy Baker

Thomas J. Dorsey
1812–1875

Caterer

Among the elite class of caterers in Philadelphia during much of the nineteenth century, Thomas J. Dorsey ranked as one of the most successful. In many ways, Dorsey's life reflects the proud history of African Americans. Dorsey, along with a number of other African Americans who were enslaved and oppressed, transcended their status as bondmen and bondwomen and created lives marked by achievement, respectability, and prosperity. Despite extremely limited options for African Americans during the nineteenth century, Dorsey used his keen business mind, culinary talents, and commitment to excellence to build a thriving catering business that eventually brought him wealth and prominence among Philadelphia's African American elite.

Dorsey was born a slave in Maryland in 1812, and he managed to escape from bondage when he was in his early twenties. Dorsey fled to Philadelphia, Pennsylvania (a free state) but he was soon captured and returned to Maryland. However, the friends Dorsey made during his short stay in Philadelphia raised funds on his behalf, and eventually Dorsey was able to purchase his freedom officially.

Chronology

1812   Born in Maryland
1836   Arrives in Philadelphia
1837   Birth of first child
1838   Works as a boot and shoemaker
1844   Works as a waiter
1861   Appears as caterer in the *Philadelphia City Directory*
1875   Dies in Philadelphia

Dorsey made what appears to be a successful transition from fugitive slave to productive entrepreneur, despite the extremely tumultuous times in which he lived. Notwithstanding the somewhat progressive decade, during which Pennsylvania enacted counter measures to the Fugitive Slave Act of 1820 to protect free blacks against kidnapping, by the end of the 1820s, it was clear the racial climate had begun to change. In his book *The Negro in Philadelphia* W. E. B. Du Bois describes the period from 1820 to 1840, as "a time of retrogression for the mass of the race, and of discountenance and repression from the whites." The increasing influx of European immigrants attracted to the new industrial jobs played a significant role in undermining the economic opportunities available to blacks living in the city at the time.

Despite shrinking economic opportunities, however, free African Americans, as well as those enslaved, continued taking up residence in Philadelphia. In fact, during the period from 1820 to 1830 alone, Philadelphia saw a 27 percent increase in the number of blacks living in the city. Abolitionist activity increased in the face of growing racial conflict, as laws were passed requiring free African Americans to carry passes. In the midst of increasing racial antipathy, poverty, and growing lawlessness, African Americans suffered through a series of riots, and many saw their homes burned and looted and their neighborhoods destroyed.

However, African Americans in Philadelphia continued their positive efforts, making progress during the 1830s, despite collective efforts on the part of the larger society to create impediments. African Americans built churches, held conventions, and established schools, which saw an increase in attendance over the course of the decade. A number of African Americans, as professional blacksmiths, tailors, morticians, and barbers, went into business, which allowed them to successfully circumnavigate the closed doors to opportunity that society had put in place.

Rise to Prominence in the Catering Industry

One of the most successful areas of entrepreneurship was in the area of food service and catering, particularly in Philadelphia, the center of the African American catering industry prior to the Civil War. Despite minimal formal education, African Americans ruled the catering business; they delivered services with such impeccable manners, taste, and elegance that they elevated themselves from underpaid cooks and waiters to self-reliant entrepreneurs who were prospered. In Philadelphia, reports indicate that some black caterers were able to command as much as $50 a plate for their dinners. Robert Bogle, a pioneer in the catering business, along with Peter Augustin, whose reputation extended beyond Philadelphia, did much to pave the way for other African Americans. Of those who would take up the profession of catering, the most prominent were Henry Jones, Thomas J. Dorsey, and Henry Minton.

These caterers, whose names were household words in Philadelphia during much of the 1800s, ran successful catering businesses and owned profitable restaurants and real estate properties as well. After securing his freedom officially, Dorsey arrived in Philadelphia in 1836, and a pamphlet published by the Pennsylvania Abolition Society indicates that he operated a boot and shoemaking business by 1838. However, by 1844, Dorsey appeared in Philadelphia's city directory as a waiter and was listed as such until 1861, when he was first listed officially as a caterer. It appears that sometime in the 1860s the term caterer came into fashion; presumably Dorsey began his catering career prior to 1861. When his catering business began remains unclear.

A man of refinement despite little education, Dorsey was one of the most sought after caterers of the time. Indeed, local newspapers declared his presence at reception banquets and balls as key for the event's success. Diverse in his culinary repertoire, Dorsey's specialties included filet de boeuf-pique, lobster salad, terrapin, deviled crabs, chicken croquettes, ladyfingers, and champagne jelly.

Dorsey married Louise Tobias, a free woman and Pennsylvania native, very shortly after he arrived in Philadelphia. Louise Dorsey gave birth to their first child, William Henry Dorsey in 1837. The couple eventually had two more children: Sarah and Mary Louise. The success of Dorsey's catering business afforded his family a lifestyle of relative privilege and comfort, eventually allowing them the luxury of a home on Locust Street, which was considered an especially prestigious address at the time.

Flourishes among Philadelphia's African American Elite

Outside the kitchen, it could be said that Dorsey well surpassed others of his profession. He owned real estate and rented to white tenants, which was most unusual. Dorsey is reported to have owned and operated at least one restaurant as well. He possessed the kind of natural sophistication that gave him influence within his community. Du Bois describes Dorsey, a former slave, as having the sway of an imperial dictator and counted him as one of those who made Philadelphia noted for its cultivated and well-to-do African American citizens. Roger Lane writes in his book *William Dorsey's Philadelphia and Ours* that when Dorsey was denied entrance to a ball honoring Russian Grand Duke Alexis, he wrote the future czar an angry letter which boldly called into question the man's character. It is reported that he even refused his catering services to one potential customer on the grounds that he was a Democrat and therefore disloyal to the government and Lincoln, a serious offense to Dorsey and many other African Americans who were Republican during the post-Civil War Reconstruction era.

Hosting such prominent men as Frederick Douglass, William Lloyd Garrison, and Charles Sumner in his home, Dorsey was one of the wealthiest and most celebrated caterers of the time. Having known the indignity of slavery, Dorsey was politically active throughout his life. He worked closely with the abolitionists and served for a time as vice president of the Sumner Club, which organized important rallies concerning desegregation and equal rights for African Americans.

By the time he died in 1875, Dorsey had accumulated enough wealth to establish a trust for his family, which was to run through two generations. The trust supplied each of Dorsey's three children with income of about $500 a year, almost a third of which was generated from their father's real estate holdings alone. In addition to the trust, Dorsey bequeathed to his family both his Dean and Locust Street homes However, after his wife died three years later, in 1878, the issue of the trust proved to be somewhat troublesome. In 1871, Dorsey's eldest daughter Sarah died, and it was determined that his other daughter Mary would be the legal guardian of Sarah's two orphaned children. This afforded Mary a controlling share of the inheritance, which was disputed by William, Dorsey's only son and eldest child, amidst much controversy. In any case, neither Mary nor William elected to continue Dorsey's catering business.

The closing of the nineteenth century witnessed the decline of Philadelphia's catering industry. Many caterers found it hard to compete with the emerging high quality luxury hotels, with their eloquent banquet halls and fine restaurants. Also contributing greatly to the decline was the liquor licensing law adopted by Pennsylvania in 1888. The new legislation, which raised the cost of a permit from $50 to over $2,000, with annual fees of as much as $900, proved much too high for many independent African American businessmen in the catering businesses.

Because of his enterprise, Dorsey was able to have a life of success and prosperity despite little education and few resources. Dorsey's story not only embodies the proud history of African Americans in the United States, but it challenges subsequent generations to overcome obstacles and strive for success.

REFERENCES

Books

Du Bois, W. E. B. *The Philadelphia Negro*. Millwood, N.Y.: Kraus-Thomson, 1973.

Lane, Roger. *William Dorsey's Philadelphia and Ours*. New York: Oxford University Press, 1991.

Walker, Juliet E. K. *The History of Black Business in America*. New York: Simon & Schuster Macmillan, 1998.

Periodicals

Conrad, Sharron Wilkins. "Nineteenth-Century Caterer Thomas J. Dorsey." *American Visions* (August-September 2000): 36-8.

Lovenia A. Leapart

George T. Downing
1819–1903

Entrepreneur, caterer, civil rights activist

A warrior for human rights and free speech, George T. Downing was a well-known caterer and businessman who favored his conviction over his livelihood. He grew up in a family business and, when still a young man, ventured out on his own as an entrepreneur. He supported civil rights as a youth, developing early a compassion for justice and human rights that never waned. He also supported education for African American youth and school integration in Rhode Island.

Thomas and Rebecca West Downing were residents of Jinketig, Accomac County, Virginia, before they started a new life in New York in the early 1800s. There Thomas Downing became a restaurant owner. The clients for his Oyster House were the aristocrats and influential politicians of New York. The Downings' oldest son, George Thomas Downing, was born in New York City on December 30, 1819. He enrolled in Charles Smith's private school and later attended the old Mulberry Street school (or African Street #2), where he established what would become lasting ties with James McCune Smith, Henry Highland Garnet, Alexander Crummell, and Charles and Patrick Reason, all black abolitionists in later times.

Chronology

1819	Born in New York City on December 30
1841	Marries Serena Leanora de Grasse
1842	Opens restaurant in New York City
1846	Opens oyster house in Newport, Rhode Island
1847	Becomes member of first board of trustees, New York Society for the Promotion of Colored Children
1850	Establishes catering business in Providence, Rhode Island
1854	Builds Sea Girt Hotel in Newport
1857	Begins fight to abolish Rhode Island's racially segregated public schools
1869	Helps organize the Colored National Labor Union
1873	Works successfully for passage of public accommodations law in Washington, D.C.
1903	Dies at home in Newport, Rhode Island on July 21

When he was fourteen years old, Downing and other young boys around his age established a literary society and discussed what they called "live subjects," or conditions of the race. The Fourth of July was meaningless to them; thus, at one of their meetings they adopted a resolution to refuse to celebrate it on the grounds that, according to *Men of Mark*, it was "a perfect mockery" for African Americans. Still in his teens, Downing established a second literary society.

During this time black children in New York City attended school at their own risk. To protect their children, however, parents or guardians often accompanied them to and from school yet the climate on the streets among crowds of insulting whites was still unsafe. Nonetheless, Downing persevered, going on to complete his education at Hamilton College in Oneida County, New York. His interest in Underground Railroad activities had begun earlier, while he was still underage. He was arrested early on for smuggling from jail "Little Henry," a fugitive slave who had been incarcerated in New York City. Downing was released after paying the jail the slave's value.

Both George Downing and his father were interested in civil and human rights. The two worked together to lobby the New York legislature for equal suffrage and were delegates to the first convention of the American Reform Board of Disenfranchised Commissioners held in 1841.

Downing was both an entrepreneur and an effective abolitionist and civil rights leader. In 1842 he opened his own restaurant and catering business in New York, and in 1846, he opened what some called a branch of his father's Oyster House in Newport, Rhode Island. He continued to expand his business and in 1850 established a catering enterprise on Mathewson Street in Providence while he maintained his Rhode Island enterprise. Now a

man of means, he built the luxurious, five-story Sea Girt Hotel in Newport in 1854 and restricted his business to white clientele. The complex also included his residence, a restaurant, a confectionery, and his catering business. A fire on December 15, 1860, destroyed the building, giving him an estimated loss of $40,000. Following that, he built a new structure on Downing Block and rented the upper floor to the federal government. That space served as a hospital for the Naval Academy.

Downing traveled extensively and before the Civil War he lived in Providence as well as Boston. His interest in the colored troops of the Civil War and their treatment in the military led him to Washington, D.C., where he organized several regiments. While there he was persuaded to manage the dining room for the House of Representatives and he did so for twelve years. His primary interest was not as much in the position as it was in the contact that he would have with political figures and opportunities to discuss race matters with them. He had strong political ties to Senator Charles Sumner of Massachusetts and to black abolitionist and orator Frederick Douglass.

Fights for Civil Rights

Race matters remained at the forefront of Downing's interests. In addition to his early interest in rescuing fugitive slaves, he had a continuing interest in the education of African American children, as demonstrated in 1847 when he became a member of the first board of trustees of the New York Society for the Promotion of Colored Children. Later on, in Rhode Island, he led a successful fight from 1857 to 1866 to abolish separate publicly supported schools in the state. For twelve years he urged the legislature to allow children to attend the school of their choice, regardless of their race.

In 1866 Downing and Frederick Douglass petitioned President Andrew Johnson to initiate a liberal Reconstruction policy, particularly in the South. The men, joined by fellow abolitionist John Sella Martin, petitioned Senator Charles Sumner to support the Fourteenth Amendment guaranteeing, among other rights, due process and equal protection under the law.

At times Downing's views on politics and race were at odds with those of other race men. For example, he questioned Frederick Douglass's manual labor school proposal because he found it racially exclusive. Downing fought for the rights of all who were oppressed, not just African Americans. He was also persistent and passionate in his opposition to the American Colonization Society's interest in having blacks migrate to Liberia. When black abolitionist Henry Highland Garnet began efforts to emigrate blacks and formed a black African Civilization Society for that purpose, Downing fought vehemently to stop the plan. He took his fight to the conventions held in 1859, 1860, and 1864, often resorting to personal attacks and threats of violence to those who took up Garnet's efforts.

Downing was a key player in the successful fight to abolish segregated cars on the Baltimore and Ohio Railroad. His efforts also led to admission of blacks to the U.S. Senate gallery and to passage of a public accommodations law in Washington. D.C., in 1873.

Downing's interest in labor issues led to his becoming an organizer of the Colored National Labor Union in 1889. He chaired the first convention and was the union's first vice president. Around this time he began to loosen his ties to the Republican party, in which he had been a longtime member, and in 1883 Downing broke with the party and supported northern Democrats.

A financially secure businessman, Downing retired in the early 1880s and devoted his time to his other interests—his dogs and a collection of memorabilia. He attended Union Congregational Church and established a close friendship with its pastor, Mahlon Van Horne who, with Downing's financial backing, was elected to the Newport School Committee and later became the first black legislator in the state's General Assembly. Downing was a member of the equal rights movement in Rhode Island and a member of several antislavery societies. He was also an organizer of the Grand United Order of Odd Fellows and for several years served as grand master. He was a Royal Arch Mason as well.

On November 24, 1841, Downing married Serena Leanora de Grasse, the daughter of George de Grasse, a prosperous landowner from Calcutta, India. He had courted her when she spent summer vacations at the home of political abolitionist Gerrit Smith, whose daughter was Serena's classmate at Clinton Seminary in Clinton, New York.

Downing, a tall, commanding figure with light complexion, had a lingering illness and then died at his Bellevue Avenue home in Newport, Rhode Island, on July 21, 1903. His three sons, three daughters, brother Peter W., and nephew Henry F. Downing survived him. His funeral services were held on July 24 at Emmanuel Church in Newport. He was remembered as a racial optimist, one who worked diligently for the cause of liberty and justice.

REFERENCES

Books

Asbury, Howard D. "George T[homas] Downing." In *Dictionary of American Negro Biography*. Eds. Rayford W. Logan and Michael R. Winston. New York: Norton, 1982.

Fishel, Leslie H. Jr. George Thomas Downing." In *American National Biography*. Eds. John A. Garraty and Mark C. Carnes. New York: Oxford University Press, 1999.

Simmons, William J. *Men of Mark: Eminent, Progressive and Rising*. Cleveland: Geo. M. Rewell & Co., 1886.

Online

DuJardin, Richard C. "George Thomas Downing." Providence Journal Company, 1997. http://www.projo.com/special/history/downing.htm (Accessed 1 October 2001).

Collections

There is a small collection of Downing's correspondence in the Houghton Library at Harvard University. Other collections in which individual letters may be found are those of Frederick Douglass (Anacostia, Virginia), John Jay at Columbia University, Blanche K. Bruce at Howard University, and Alexander Crummell in the Schomberg Center for Research in Black Culture, New York Public Library.

Jessie Carney Smith

James B. Dudley
1859–1925

Educator, college president

As teacher, school principal, and finally as president of North Carolina's historically black land-grant college, former slave James B. Dudley helped to shape the educational background of many young black people. A multidimensional man, Dudley used the press as well as his community affiliations to promote black education, black economic development, and civil rights; he did so despite racial hostilities in the state and received the respect and support of blacks as well as whites.

James B. Dudley was born a slave and an only child in Wilmington, North Carolina, to John Bishop and Annie Hatch Dudley, slaves of Edward B. Dudley who was governor of North Carolina from December 1836 to January 1841. Governor Dudley was an advocate of education and one of the state's most progressive governors. John Dudley was a highly skilled and well-respected carpenter who taught his son the carpentry trade with the aim of equipping him to become self-sufficient. Later, young Dudley used his skill for summer employment to pay his school expenses. Wilmington at that time provided no public schools for its black residents. Determined that their son would be educated, however, the Dudleys saw that their Jimmie, as he was called then, was trained by private teachers. Later he attended Wilmington

Chronology

1859	Born in Wilmington, North Carolina on November 2
1880	Becomes first-grade teacher in Sampson County, North Carolina
1881	Named principal of Peabody Graded Normal School in Wilmington
1882	Marries Susan Wright Sampson on February 23
1895	Elected secretary to the Board of Trustees, Agricultural and Mechanical (A&M) College in Greensboro
1896	Elected president of A&M (later A&T)
1896	Elected delegate to the Republican National Convention in St. Louis
1897	Receives M.A. from Livingstone College
1901	Closes female department at A&T
1912	Organizes State Farmers' Union and Cooperative Society
1917	With the federal government, offers A&T as military training site
1920	Appointed state commissioner for the national Memorial Association
1925	Dies in Greensboro, North Carolina on April 4; James Benson Dudley High School in Greensboro named in his honor

Normal School, a local institution that the Freedmen's Bureau established. There his instruction included Latin grammar; all of his teachers were white.

One of Dudley's teachers, Ella Roper, recognized his talent and encouraged him to continue his education at the Institute for Colored Youth in Philadelphia, a prestigious high school for blacks founded by the Society of Friends in 1837. Dudley attended the institute for one year and then enrolled at Shaw University in Raleigh, North Carolina, where he studied elementary education. Roper and Dudley remained in contact with each other, exchanging letters regularly. At Shaw, Dudley was often in difficulty due to his playing some mischievous prank, but he tempered his sense of humor with serious ambition. Always interested in enhancing his education, sometime later he spent summers studying at Harvard University. Still later he attended historically black Livingstone College in his home state. He was awarded an M.A. and Wilberforce University conferred on him the J.D. These degrees were probably honorary, though. In fact, Warmoth T. Gibbs states in *History of North Carolina Agricultural and Technical College* that Dudley "had limited formal education."

After his study at Shaw University, Dudley worked as a mechanic's apprentice. But he had performed well in his studies and soon, upon examination in Sampson County, received a first-grade teacher's certificate. In 1880, when he was twenty-one, he became a first-grade teacher in that county. The next year he was named principal of the Peabody Graded Normal School in Wilmington, where he remained until 1896. He became known throughout the state and was recognized as one of its most effective educators.

Dudley married Susan Wright Sampson of Wilmington on February 23, 1882; she had also attended Wilberforce University in Ohio and taught in the Peabody school when James Dudley was principal there. Susan Dudley's artistic and literary talents were recognized later on. The Dudleys had two daughters; one died at a young age, and the other, Vivian, married S. B. Jones, a vice president and college physician at the Agricultural and Technical College in Greensboro, later health officer at St. Kitts in the British West Indies.

In addition to his work in Wilmington as an educator, Dudley edited the weekly black newspaper, the *Wilmington Chronicle*. He organized the Perpetual Building and Loan Association and used both the *Chronicle* and the loan association to encourage thrift, economy, and enterprise among black people. He was active in politics as well but never sought political office. In 1891 Dudley's brother-in-law served as register of deeds for New Hanover County, which helped Dudley remain acquainted with county affairs as well as with national and foreign matters. A Republican, he represented his party at county and state conventions, and in 1896 he was elected a delegate to the Republican National Convention held in St. Louis. His interest in the educational arena continued, as demonstrated by his service on the board of trustees for the Agricultural and Mechanical College (now North Carolina Agricultural and Technical State University, or A&T) in Greensboro. From May 29, 1895 to May 27, 1896, Dudley was secretary of the board.

Becomes College President

Dudley's service on the board of trustees as well his reputation across North Carolina as a capable educator led to his election as president of A&T on May 28, 1896, a post he held for twenty-nine years. He succeeded founding president John O. Crosby and was the first black to head the school that had been founded in 1891 under the Second Morrill Act, or the Second Land-Grant Act (1890) that made it possible for southern and border states to establish or provide separate black land-grant colleges. Dudley moved swiftly to strengthen the struggling school. When he took charge, there were eight faculty members, fifty-eight students, and two brick buildings that stood on twenty-six acres. By the end of his tenure, there were forty-six faculty members, 476 students enrolled in the winter program and 500 in summer school. He increased the facility as well, increasing the buildings to thirteen and the campus to one hundred acres of land.

His concern for the quality of life for black people was constant. For example, Dudley believed that black faculty could serve the needs of black students at the racially segregated college and, therefore, instituted a gradual transition from white faculty to black. The school was founded to serve the agricultural and technical needs of blacks, hence the name A&T. But Dudley worked to strengthen the agricultural programs that were available; he stressed agricultural training rather than mechanical and industrial. He supported educator and Tuskegee Institute founder Booker T. Washington in his work to promote agriculture and public service. So devoted was Dudley to this concept that in 1901 he closed the female department of the college, claiming that women were poorly suited to agricultural pursuits. Moreover, their presence was a disservice to such programs, he reasoned, and hampered their development.

In order to secure annual appropriations for A&T, Dudley followed the tradition of inviting the college's alumni to meet with the state legislature in Raleigh each year, where they could bring political attention to the school's needs. He was a talented fundraiser himself and had winning ways with both black and white contributors. Thus, in time he was responsible for lifting the college from near bankruptcy its prestigious position in the state and in the South. He attended conventions and conferences to gather new ideas for the school, and he read widely. He even taught history and civics. His biography in Nathan C. Newbold's *Five North Carolina Negro Educators* indicates that he "became a master of detail."

His concern for black farms and farming led his joining J. H. Bluford, head of the college's agricultural department, in order to organize in 1912 the State Farmers' Union and Cooperative Society. Local unions were set up in each county in North Carolina. The union was headquartered at A&T, and aimed to discourage the credit and mortgage system that had been detrimental to the success of black farmers. According to Newbold, the organization also helped black farmers buy and sell products, "control methods of production and the distribution of farm products," as well as to "secure uniform prices." The organization succeeded in raising the standards of living among black farmers in the state.

The Smith-Hughes Act of 1917 that marked the beginning of federal funding for vocational education programs in the United States proved helpful to Dudley and the college. In 1917, he secured matching funds for the Smith-Hughes appropriations and then established a vocational agriculture department for preparing teachers of agriculture for the public rural schools in North Carolina.

Dudley's concern was for a well-rounded student. Under his administration, the school held chapel services each Sunday, led by local pastors of different faiths. There was also a flourishing temperance society.

Dudley in the Matter of Race

Dudley remained concerned with justice for his race. Never an activist, he was a man of passive resistance, who urged his people to be patient as they waited for justice to come. But the Wilmington (North Carolina) race riots of 1898 might have put his family in harm's way;

certainly they caused him concern for his family's well-being as well as for that of other black residents in Wilmington. When the riots began, he rushed to his home town to "calm the Negro population and act as mediator between black and white," wrote Kenneth Warlick in *Dictionary of North Carolina Biography*. Both the mayor and the local law enforcement officers met him and provided protection for him during his visit. He gathered his family and returned to Greensboro.

His concern for race was seen again in 1917, when a part of the college grounds was transformed into a military training camp to help meet the nation's military needs during World War I. A&T trained more men for the military than any other black land-grant college. Dudley urged his people to remain loyal to the United States. Though he was a race man who recognized the racial conflicts and grievances that he had seen in Wilmington and elsewhere, he said in a June 1917 speech, "This is not the time to discuss our racial conflicts," as reported in *Five North Carolina Negro Educators*. "In every war and conflict that our country has engaged in, we have as a race been loyal," he continued, and he called for acts of patriotism.

His interest in race matters, his speeches before interracial groups, and his work to promote racial cooperation, all led to his post as chair of the Negro division of the Greensboro Interracial Committee. By all accounts, he was a successful champion against legal segregation in the state.

James and Susan Dudley made their mark in the local and broader community; for example, Susan Dudley wrote the words for A&T's college song, and was active in drama on campus. For most of his life, Dudley was active in a variety of affairs. He was a member of the State Teachers' Association for Negroes and was its president for six years. His activities in the Farmers' Alliance movement helped bring about legislation that established A&T College. In 1920 North Carolina governor Cameron Morrison appointed Dudley as state commissioner for the national Memorial Association, a group formed to help build a memorial in Washington, D.C., to honor black soldiers and sailors who had fought in national wars. Dudley also served as trustee of the National Religious Training School and Chautauqua, chartered in 1910 and later renamed North Carolina Central University in Durham. He was an advisory member of the board of directors, Inter-State Church Association for Whites and Negroes; president of the North Carolina Anti-Tuberculosis League; honorary member of the board of trustees of Palmer Memorial Institute in Sedalia; founder of the Rural Extension work in the state; and chair of the Negro Railroad Commission.

Dudley maintained an interest in debating and encouraged intercollegiate debate. To the most outstanding debater, he presented the "Dudley Cup." He was also interested in art and literature, often referring to these subjects in his speeches. This led to honorary membership in the Oriental Organization for the Recovery and Preservation of the Literature and Art of the Ancient Peoples of the East.

He was the only black member of the committee of city extension for Greensboro. Among other memberships, Dudley belonged to the Masons (having served over twenty years as foreign correspondent of the Grand Lodge of Masons), the Odd Fellows, and Pythians. He was a member of Bethel African Methodist Episcopal Church in Greensboro and served the church as trustee and Sunday school teacher.

Dudley was an imposing figure with a massive frame, and he demonstrated great physical poise. Quoted in *Five North Carolina Negro Educators*, an editorial eulogy from the *Greensboro Daily News* of May 3, 1925 called him "a thoroughbred in every respect." He was a courteous and polite man with "a high degree of integrity, diplomacy, common sense, and courage." He had great consideration for all people, regardless of race, and he had an abiding concern for racial equality. He made a far-reaching impact on the lives of numerous young people as well as adults. In a very touching way, according to *Five North Carolina Negro Educators*, he may be remembered as a diplomat and philosopher "who forms a link between a State dominated by one race, and another race dwelling within it."

By mid-spring 1925, Dudley was physically weakened. He suffered a severe headache in his office on April 3 that year and left to rest at the president's residence, a mansion located near the college known as the Magnolias. Whatever his condition, he remained at home the next day and attended to college matters from his room. His condition worsened. After his death at the Magnolias on April 4, he was eulogized by the Greensboro press, the A&T trustees, and others. His funeral was held in Murphy Hall on campus. As his body passed under the college arch en route to the train station, taps were sounded. A second funeral was held at St. Stephens Church in Wilmington, and he was buried in the Pine Forest Cemetery, where a full Masonic ceremony was held. In his honor, the board of trustees named the administration building Dudley Hall; after it was destroyed by fire, the new administration building bore his name as well—Dudley Memorial Building. Dudley Day was established to honor him on his birthday, and the street on which he lived was renamed Dudley Street. The new high school for blacks, erected in Greensboro in 1925, was named in his honor, James Benson Dudley High School (now James Benson Dudley Senior High School and Gymnasium). Now a racially integrated school, Dudley High, as it was known for many years, was placed on the National Register of Historic Places in 2003. The state honored Dudley's memory with a highway marker on U.S. 17 in Wilmington, pointing out his grave site north of Market Street at Sixteenth.

REFERENCES

Books

Caldwell, A. B., ed. *History of the American Negro*. North Carolina Edition. Vol. 4. Atlanta, Ga.: A. B. Caldwell Publishing Co., 1921.

Gibbs, Warmoth T. *History of the North Carolina Agricultural and Technical School*. Dubuque, Iowa: William C. Brown Book Co., 1966.

Newbold, Nathan C. *Five North Carolina Negro Educators*. Chapel Hill: University of North Carolina Press, 1939.

Nichols, J. L., and William H. Crogman. *Progress of a Race, or the Remarkable Advancement of the American Negro*. Naperville, Ill.: J. L. Nichols and Co., 1925.

Paths Toward Freedom: A Biographical History of Blacks and Indians in North Carolina by Blacks and Indians. Raleigh: Center for Urban Affairs, North Carolina State University at Raleigh, 1976.

Richardson, Clement. *National Cyclopedia of the Colored Race*. Vol. 1. Montgomery, Ala.: National Publishing Co., 1919.

Warlick, Kenneth. "James Benson Dudley." In *Dictionary of North Carolina Biography*. Vol. 2. Ed. William S. Powell. Chapel Hill: University of North Carolina Press, 1986.

Who Was Who in America. Vol. I. Chicago: Marquis Who's Who, 1966.

Online

"James Benson Dudley." Biography. http://www.library.ncat.edu/info/archives/dudley.html (Accessed 14 January 2006).

Other

Pitts, Gloria. Email to Jessie Carney Smith, January 18, 2005.

Collections

Several of Dudley's speeches, financial documents, biographical sketches, and the student newspaper the *A&T Register* devoted to Dudley when he died are in the archives at North Carolina A&T State University. Correspondence from Dudley may be found in the Jackson Library, the University of North Carolina at Greensboro, in the records of Chancellor Julius Isaac Foust and Chancellor Charles Duncan McIver.

Jessie Carney Smith

Joe Dudley
1939–

Entrepreneur, business executive

Joe Dudley is a self-made millionaire who came from an extremely poor family. Dudley overcame the label of retardation and a speech impediment to become the president of one of the biggest black-owned businesses in the United States, selling beauty products to blacks around the world as well as offering educational programs in cosmetology. By age forty, Dudley was a millionaire, the father to three children, and a mentor to others. Dudley credits his success to hard work, deep faith in God, a positive attitude, and the desire to work as hard as necessary to succeed. The goal of Dudley's company is to help others achieve economic empowerment and self-sufficiency.

Joe Louis Dudley was born May 9, 1939 in Aurora, North Carolina. Dudley was the fifth of eleven children born to Gilmer and Clara Dudley. Dudley was born with a speech impediment which, in combination with the hours he missed at school because of the farm, led Dudley to discount the value in school. Dudley became the class clown telling and playing jokes. As a result he was labeled by the school as mentally retarded. Dudley was held back in two different grades. It was not until he was a junior in high school and dumped by a girlfriend because he was not smart enough that Dudley decided to take academics seriously. He set out to read all the school books from the last eleven years of school. Dudley sometimes had difficulties reading the books, but stuck with it and learned. In the process, he developed a love of reading and the knowledge that people who read hold real power.

After high school, Dudley worked in a chicken factory in Hartford, Connecticut, until he saved up enough money for two semesters of college. Dudley began classes at North Carolina Agricultural and Technical (A&T) State University. In addition to classes Dudley worked on the school's farm and did housekeeping for a professor on weekends.

In the summer of 1957, Dudley went to Brooklyn, New York, to find work to earn money for the next school year. Dudley met a young man selling Fuller Products. Dudley was so impressed by the man, that he went to the Fuller offices and bought a $10 sales kit and began working for the company. Eventually Dudley became a good salesman and saved enough money to continue school in the fall. Dudley did not stop selling Fuller Products when he returned to school; instead he sold them at school and every summer in Brooklyn for the next four years. Dudley earned a bachelor's degree in business administration.

It was through the Fuller Products Company that Dudley met his wife, Eunice Moseley. The two married in

Chronology	
1939	Born in Aurora, North Carolina on May 9
1956	Begins studying at North Carolina A&T State University
1957	Begins selling Fuller Products
1961	Marries Eunice Moseley
1969	Begins manufacturing Dudley Products
1975	Becomes a millionaire
1976	Returns to Fuller Products to try to save the company
1984	Buys the name and rights to produce Fuller Products
1988	Launches Dudley Cosmetology University
1989	Launches Dudley Beauty School
1991	Builds hotel, Dudley Inn, and launches Dudley Q+ Travel Agency
1994	Builds 80,000-square-foot plant and offices in Kernersville, North Carolina
1995	Begins training cosmetologists in Zimbabwe and Brazil
1998	Publishes *Walking by Faith I Am! I Can! & I Will! The Story of How Joe L. Dudley Sr. Walks by Faith*
2002	Becomes largest black-owned industrial and service company in the United States

1961 and began working together for Fuller. Dudley became a troubleshooter for Fuller Products in 1963, traveling to cities with poor sales and figuring out how to improve them. By 1966 Dudley decided to become a branch manager for Fuller but was disappointed when someone else received the promotion. Dudley was prepared to quit the company, but S. B. Fuller gave him the opportunity to become an independent distributor for Fuller Products in North Carolina. Being in charge of a distributorship taught Dudley that leaders must lead by example; if ge wanted the people who worked for him to do well selling Fuller Products, then he would also need to excel. Dudley's business eventually became the top procuring distributorship for Fuller Products.

Fuller Products began facing financial problems in the 1960s. By 1969, Fuller Products was increasingly unable to supply its distributors, and Dudley decided to make his own products. Dudley bought a company called Rosebud Beauty Products and began producing them in the kitchen in the evenings. Eventually the city licensing department ordered Dudley to stop making the product at home. He acquired space in a strip mall, naming the new business Dudley's Beauty Center & Salon. Business was so good that in short time, Dudley was able to open stores throughout North Carolina and in South Carolina, Georgia, Virginia and New York.

Eventually Dudley expanded the product line to include a professional line used by and sold only to cosmetologists. Dudley used the principals and business experience he had gained from S. B. Fuller, and his hard work paid off. By 1975, he was a millionaire.

Tries to Rescue Fuller

In 1976 S. B. Fuller asked Dudley to takeover as president of Fuller Products in the hopes of saving the company. Dudley sold most of the Dudley retail stores and moved Dudley Products to Chicago. He spent the next seven years running both companies simultaneously. He was able to improve Fuller Products, but eventually it became obvious that the company could not be saved. In 1984 Dudley bought exclusive rights to manufacture Fuller Products and use the Fuller name. Then he moved Dudley Products back to Greensboro, South Carolina. Eventually a new plant was built in Kernersville, which continued to produce Dudley's complete product line, including cosmetics, hair care, personal care, and books and videotapes on hair care and motivation.

In 1988 Dudley launched Dudley Cosmetology University (DCU) in Kernersville, North Carolina. The school offers advanced cosmetology programs designed to help licensed cosmetologists improve their skills, attitude, self-esteem, and earn continuing education credit. Dudley opened Dudley Beauty Schools in 1989, which provide training to would-be cosmetologists. Dudley's schools are located in Chicago; Washington, D.C.; Charlotte, North Carolina; and Durham, North Carolina. Students may take classes in cosmetology, manicuring, esthetics, and management training, or students may train to become instructors of cosmetology, esthetics, or manicuring.

In 1991, DCU Inn was built, a hotel in which students and national sales managers stay. The next step was opening Dudley Q+ Travel Agency, which takes care of the travel needs of Dudley's students and national sales managers.

It quickly became apparent that local hotels could not provide the space and time necessary for Dudley's sales and company meetings. Dudley employees helped to renovate an abandoned gym to make the 7,000-square-foot Yeates Convention Center. The convention center is named after Dudley's mother Clara Yeates.

In 1994 Dudley built an 80,000-square-feet plant, laboratory, and headquarters in Kernersville. The building received the 1995 Efficient Building Award for Building Management in a Manufacturing Facility. The design of the building was such that it has a 33 percent reduction in energy use as compared to conventional buildings.

Going Global

In 1994, North Carolina governor Jim Hunt asked Dudley to serve as an advisor to a group of business people looking at the possibility of building business relationships in Africa. Dudley agreed. In Zimbabwe, Dudley met with President Robert Mugabe. The two men thought along the same lines. Both felt that the best way for blacks to improve their lives was through economic empowerment. Upon returning from Africa, Dudley formed Dudley Products International Exchange and Development

Program. Its purpose was to find people and companies who wanted to help people in Africa become more self-supporting. Next, Dudley formed a joint venture with Zimbabwe's Harare Polytech and the Chinhoyi Technical Teachers College. Under the joint venture, Dudley Products would teach interested students hair care techniques and provide hands-on training. In 1995, Dudley Products formed a partnership in Brazil with Senac Technical School, which is part of Servi o Nacional de Aprendizagem Comercial in the Sao Palo area of Brazil.

In the early 2000s Dudley Products have expanded to Martinique, Guadeloupe, Jamaica, Canada, South Africa, and the Bahamas. By 1997, over 10,000 people had come from all over the world to be educated at Dudley Beauty Schools and Dudley University. In 2001 Dudley Products was listed on Black Enterprises 29th annual report of top black businesses. In 2002, Dudley Products was the largest black-owned service/industrial company in the United States with sales of $80 million and over four hundred employees. Dudley also formed a multimillion dollar distribution partnership with W&W Spices Ltd. of Grenada. Dudley intended to distribute a new product called GNO, which is made of 100-percent-pure distilled oil from Grenada nutmegs. The product is billed as an all-natural topical pain reliever.

Philanthropist and Mentor

Over the almost fifty years Dudley has been in business, he has been recognized many times for his work and the help he has provided to blacks in the United States and around the world. Dudley was presented the Vision for Tomorrow Award by the Direct Selling Association in 1991, and that same year President George H. Bush named him the 467th Daily Point of Light. He received the Horatio Alger Association of Distinguished Americans Award in 1995, which is given to ten people annually who have achieved success despite the circumstances in which they grew up. In 2004 Dudley received the Business Courage Award from the Los Angeles Black Expo.

As Dudley was mentored by S. B. Fuller, so he believes in mentoring other blacks. Dudley established a corporate mentoring program in Greensboro, South Carolina for students at the James B. Dudley High School. The success of the program led to the development of the Eunice Dudley Ladies Program for high school girls. Students in both programs are expected to be role models for their fellow students. Another program Dudley began is the Dudley Products Collegiate Sales Manager Trainee Program, which, according to his book *Walking by Faith I Am! I Can! & I Will! The Story of How Joe L. Dudley Sr. Walks by Faith*, is "designed to develop a strong base of young, talented black entrepreneurs for the world."

In 1991, Dudley was elected to the board of his alma mater North Carolina Agricultural and Technical State University. Dudley served as chairman of the American Health & Beauty Aids Institute in 1995 and has participated in Wendy's Enterprise Ambassador Program, sponsored by Wendy's founder, Dave Thomas. Dudley has sponsored the Black Teenage World Pageant. He also served on the board of Southern National Corporation which includes BB&T Bank from 1992 to 1998.

Dudley is committed to training leaders for today and tomorrow. According to his book, Dudley teaches blacks to "say yes to success, to maintain a positive attitude, to not consider difficulties a problem, instead to consider them as challenges, and to teach people that for every disadvantage there is an equal or greater advantage."

REFERENCES

Online

Dudley Products, Inc. http://www.dudleyq.com/ (Accessed 2 February 2006).

Holloway, Jay. "An Interview with Joe Dudley." *Black Issues Forum*, 1996-1997. http://www.unctv.org/ bif/transcripts/1996/bif1108.html (Accessed 3 February 2006).

Spruell, Sakina. "Minority Entrepreneurs: New Voices: Joe Dudley Sr." *Fortune Small Business*, December 2003. http://money.cnn.com/magazines/fsb/fsb_ archive/2003/12/01/359890/index.htm (Accessed 30 June 2005).

Anne K. Driscoll

Chronology	
1903	Born in Danville, Kentucky on February 12; moves with his mother to Somerset, Kentucky
1916	Completes elementary education
1925	Receives B.A. from Butler University
1925-30	Teaches at Louisville Municipal College for Negroes
1930	Receives M.A. from Columbia University Teachers College
1931-45	Appointed professor of voice at Howard University
1933	Debuts in Mascagni's *Cavalleria Rusticana*
1935	Performs the role Porgy in George Gershwin's *Porgy and Bess*
1938	Has lead in the *Sun Never Sets* (London)
1939	Gives concert at the White House for President and Mrs. Roosevelt
1940	Appears in the film *Cabin in the Sky*
1942	Appears in *Syncopation*
1942-43	Appears in revival of Broadway musical *Porgy and Bess*
1945	Retires from Howard University; opens his own voice studio; becomes the first African American male to sing with a major opera company, singing the role of Tonio in Leoncavallo's *I Pagliacci*; sings the role of Escamillio in Bizet's *Carmen*
1949-50	Appears as Stephen Kumalo in Weill's *Lost in the Stars*
1955	Appears in *Unchained*
1978	Seventy-fifth birthday gala held by the Washington Performing Arts Society
1998	Dies in Washington, D.C. on February 28
2005	Posthumously inducted into the Kentucky Civil Rights Hall of Fame at Kentucky State University in Frankfort, Kentucky

Todd Duncan
1903–1998

Opera singer, educator, actor

One of Kentucky's great civil rights pioneers, noted teacher, opera singer, and actor Todd Duncan was inducted into the Kentucky Civil Rights Hall of Fame at Kentucky State University in Frankfort, Kentucky, in 2005. Duncan made significant contributions on a national level, and as a voice and music teacher he influenced generations of African American musicians and vocalists. He developed a system of teaching operatic singing known as the Duncan Technique. Because of Duncan, major changes in classical musical performance for African Americans began to take place in the United States.

Born Robert Todd Duncan in Danville, Kentucky, in 1903, Todd Duncan (as he was commonly called) moved to Somerset with his mother when he was quite young. While a young child he studied piano with his mother, Nettie Cooper Duncan. He attended the Davis Chapel African Methodist Episcopal Church, singing in the choir. Duncan completed elementary school about 1916, then at the age of thirteen he moved to Louisville to attend the African American high school at Simmons University. There appears to be some disagreement on when the family moved to Indianapolis. Some sources indicated that his early education was completed in Louisville, Kentucky, and some mention that his early education was completed in Indianapolis. Sources that report that he attended high school in Indianapolis indicate that he was an industrious but not brilliant student.

Duncan continued his musical training at Butler University in Indiana, where evidence of his outstanding abilities began to manifest. He earned a bachelor of music degree in 1925. He also attended the College of Fine Arts in Indianapolis. His academic training continued with training in voice and theory at the College of Music and Fine Arts in Indianapolis.

Duncan later attended Columbia University Teachers College in New York, where he received a master's degree in music in 1930. He studied voice with Sara Lee, Edward Lippe, and Sidney Dietch in New York City. He received his L.H.D. from Valparaiso University in 1950 and the degree of Doctor of Music from Central State College in Ohio.

Success in Teaching

After earning his degree from Butler, Duncan accepted a teaching position in a local junior high school in Indianapolis. After this position he taught at Louisville Municipal College for Negroes, operated by the University of Louisville, from 1925 to 1930, as an instructor in English and music. His tenure there offered him an opportunity to gain experience directing operettas such as *The Marriage of Nanette*, *The Chocolate Soldier*, and other Gilbert and Sullivan works.

After graduating from Columbia University, in 1930, with an M.A., he was offered a teaching position at Howard University, in Washington, D.C. In 1931, he was appointed professor of voice at Howard University in Washington, D.C., a post he held until 1945. As a teacher at Howard, he was able to share his knowledge of classical European music with a mainly black student population. He taught special ways to present the music. These special ways became known as the Duncan Technique. Along with his teaching responsibilities at Howard, Duncan was also in charge of the public school music department in D.C.

In 1934, Duncan married Gladys Jackson, a teacher in the Washington, D.C. public school system. They had one son. Duncan was an avid tennis player and was often on the courts in Washington, D.C., where he made his home with his wife and son when he was not on tour.

Moves to Concert, Stage, and Film

Duncan's training prepared him to break ground where African Americans were practically unknown. African Americans are known for their jazz but not for writing or performing classical music. This was one of Duncan's contributions. Despite teaching being his main vocation, the stage performance often caused him to spend a great amount of time away for the university.

In addition to teaching, Duncan sang in several operas with all black performers. In 1933, Duncan debuted in Mascagni's *Cavalleria Rusticana*, singing Alfio at the Mecca Temple in New York with the Aeolian Opera, an all black opera company. This performance was witnessed by *New York Times* critic Olin Downes, who told George Gershwin of Duncan's talent after Gershwin had auditioned and rejected around one hundred baritones for the role of Porgy for *Porgy and Bess*. Duncan was already an established baritone and was teaching voice at Howard University when Gershwin heard of him.

According to the *Encyclopedia of Popular Music*, on their first meeting, after Duncan had sung only twelve measures of an Italian aria, Gershwin asked, "Will you be my Porgy?" Duncan, replied, "Well, Mr. Gershwin, I've gotta hear your music first." He did not know that Gershwin was such a successful composer. He also thought Gershwin wrote only popular music. Duncan almost always had sung classical works by composers such as Brahms and Schumann, and he was not sure that he wanted to sing for a popular musician such as Gershwin.

Jerilyn Watson reports in *Voice of America* that after accepting the part of Porgy, Duncan said that he found it difficult to perform because Porgy has a bad leg and cannot walk which means the person playing this part spends most of the opera on his knees. Duncan used his special methods to get enough breath to produce beautiful sound. He was able to do this even in the difficult positions demanded by the part.

Duncan was the first to perform the role of Porgy in George Gershwin's *Porgy and Bess*, which opened on Broadway on October 10,1935. Duncan played the role more than 1,800 times. In 1935, Duncan led a strike of the cast of *Porgy and Bess* at the National Theater in Washington, D.C. He refused to perform at a theater where he himself could not purchase a ticket. Although the management of the National Theater attempted to offer such things as separate all-black performances, Duncan refused. The ultimate integration of the National Theatre was not accomplished until 1947, twelve years later, by American theatre icon Helen Hayes.

While continuing to work as an educator between performances, Duncan gave concerts around the world. In 1939, Duncan gave a concert at the White House for President and Mrs. Franklin D. Roosevelt. He considered himself an opera singer, with a repertoire of hundreds of German Lieder and French and Italian songs, and preferred the concert stage more than the theater. Quoted in the *Encyclopedia of Popular Music*, Duncan said: "In the theatre, you have grease paint, sets and lights, action and people. On the concert platform it is the song alone that matters; it is a drama, a message straight from the singer to the audience. It is more personal and more concentrated than a play can ever be. There is nothing that ever quite matches the thrill of holding an audience even on your faintest note the way a violinist stroke keeps his listeners silent even on the thin last stroke of the bow they can hardly hear."

Duncan went to London in 1939 to play the leading role in the *Sun Never Sets*, at the Drury Lane Theatre. Regular concert tours took him to Europe, South America, Australia, and New Zealand. He starred in the Kurt Weill musical adaptation of Alan Paton's *Cry, the Beloved Country*, which was given the title *Lost in the Stars*. He was also the first performer for the role of Stephen Khumalo in *Lost in the Stars*. American writer Maxwell Anderson wrote the words for the music by German composer Kurt Weill.

In 1942, Cheryl Crawford's revival of *Porgy and Bess* found Duncan back in the role of Porgy. Many critics thought that this simpler version was understood by more people than the original version. Theodore Strauss wrote in the *New York Times* in 1942: "After seven years Mr. Duncan has re-created one of the winning and pathetic figures of the modern theatre. Crawling about the stage on Porgy's useless legs, he is the easiest and most relaxed figure in the play. Out of Porgy's affliction and innocent mind he has kindled a sunnily haphazard disposition that warms the stage and radiates through the reaches of the house." Another *Times* critic commented that "with the passing years Todd Duncan has grown in the part of Porgy, and his cripple has an added dignity and spiritual strength." The critic continued, "Keeping himself in good voice throughout this saga of the poor cripple and his love for wayward Bess was a hard job, for Duncan sings the entire role on his knees."

In 1944, Duncan made his debut at New York's Town Hall as a concert baritone; the following two decades he toured widely in the United States, giving solo recitals and appearing with symphony orchestras. His longtime accompanist was William Duncan Allen.

His fame as Porgy helped him to get the part of Tonio in *I Pagliacci* with the New York City Opera Company in 1945. Duncan became the first African American male to sing with a major opera company that had no other black performers. Watson of *Voice of America* writes that "no one was sure how he would be received, but the people in the theater offered loud, warm approval of his performance."

The most amazing aspect of this performance was that Duncan did not sing a black role. He portrayed and sang a role traditionally performed by a white man. This historic performance took place ten years before black singer Marian Anderson performed at the Metropolitan Opera in New York. Watson reports, "Todd Duncan opened doors for other black musicians when he appeared in *I Pagliacci*; and until that night, black singers of classical music had almost no chance of performing in major American opera houses and theaters."

In the same year he sang as Escamillio in Bizet's *Carmen* with the New York City Opera Company. One of Duncan's most memorable concerts was his rendition of the baritone part in Beethoven's Ninth Symphony with the New York Philharmonic Orchestra in 1946.

Duncan appeared in a number of Broadway musicals and films, including *The Sun Never Sets* (London production, 1938); *Cabin in the Sky* (1940); revival of *Porgy and Bess* (1942-43); and *Lost in the Stars* (1949-50). His performance in *Lost in the Stars* won him the Donaldson and New York Drama Critics awards. He also appeared in the films *Syncopation* (1942) and *Unchained* (1955). In the movie *Unchained* Duncan introduced the song "Unchained Melody" for the first time. The song, which later became a rock and roll standard, earned an Academy Award nomination for Duncan.

Resumes Teaching Career

After a twenty-five-year career on Broadway, in films, and with more than two-thousand recitals in fifty-six countries, Duncan resumed his career as a teacher. He retired from Howard University in 1945 and opened his own voice studio teaching privately and giving periodic recitals. In 1978, the Washington Performing Arts Society presented his seventy-fifth birthday gala. Duncan died upstairs at his home on February 28, 1998. He taught hundreds of students over the years, and some musicians say they can recognize his students because they demonstrate his special method of singing.

Todd Duncan was inducted into the Kentucky Music Hall of Fame. Duncan's achievements in the world of classical music were highlighted in Kentucky after the former chair of the music department of Bethune-Cookman College in Florida went to Kentucky to visit the places she had written about in her dissertation on his life. After her visit, the Duncan Celebration Team was formed to revive his memory in the state of Kentucky.

In 2003, the theater in the Center for Rural Development paid a musical tribute to the life of Todd Duncan and raised over $1,500 toward the Dunbar High School Alumni Scholarship fund. Dunbar was the former all-black high school in Somerset, Kentucky where Duncan spent his early years. He was also awarded an NAACP award for his contribution to the theater (1945), the president of Haiti's Medal of Honor and Merit (1945), and the Donaldson and the Critics Awards for his performances in musicals (1950).

REFERENCES

Books

Altman, Susan. *The Encyclopedia of African American Heritage*. New York: Facts on File, Inc., 1997.

"Duncan, Robert Todd." In *The African American Almanac*. Eds. Jessie Carney Smith and Joseph M. Palmisano. Farmington Hills, Mich.: Gale Group, 2000.

"Duncan, Robert Todd." In *International Library of Negro Life and History: Historical Negro Biographies*. Ed. Wilhelmena S. Robinson. New York: Publishers Company, Inc., 1968.

Southern, Eileen. *Biographical Dictionary of Afro-American and African Musicians*. Westport, Conn.: Greenwood Press, 1982.

——. *The Music of Black Americans: A History*. 3rd ed. New York: Norton, 1997.

Periodicals

"'Unchained': Todd Duncan makes return to screen in Hollywood film on honor prison." *Ebony* (November 1954): 107-10.

Online

"Duncan, Todd." *Encyclopedia of Popular Music*, Muze UK, Ltd, 2005. http://www.keepmedia.com/pubs/Muze (Accessed 22 November 2005).

Watson, Jerilyn. "People in America—March 3, 2002: Todd Duncan." *Voice of America*. http://www. voanews.com/specialenglish/archive/2002-03-01-2-1.cfm?CFID=18 (Accessed 7 November 2005).

Mattie McHollin

Chronology

1762	Born in Philadelphia, Pennsylvania on May 1
1775	Medical apprenticeship
1783	Purchased freedom
1788	Met Dr. Benjamin Rush
1802	Moved to Philadelphia from New Orleans

James Durham
1762–?

Physician

James Durham is recognized as one of the earliest black physicians. He was held in the highest regard by many medical practitioners of his era and by the leading physician of the period, Dr. Benjamin Rush. Durham's medical skill was acknowledged by his contemporaries, and his medical practice was profitable enough to provide him with a comfortable life in New Orleans. As an expert on the throat and diseases common in New Orleans and the surrounding area, he treated patients from different social and economic backgrounds. James Durham contributed to the abolitionist movement and to the legacy of American civil rights and culture.

James Durham (some sources say Derham) was born into slavery in Philadelphia on May 1, 1762. When he was a child he became the property of Dr. James Kearsley Jr., an expert on sore throat diseases. Durham learned how to mix medicines and how to care for patients on a small scale as an assistant to Kearsley. In this way, Durham had a medical apprenticeship that was the same as the medical training most of the 3,500 American trained physicians experienced. Durham left Kearsley when the latter was arrested for his Loyalist leanings and imprisoned for treason during the American Revolutionary War. Kearsley died in prison in 1777. During the American Revolutionary War, Durham continued to work in medicine, performing menial tasks for a new owner, George West, a surgeon linked to the Sixteenth British Regiment.

Durham's apprenticeship continued with different masters until Dr. Robert Dow (Dove), a Scottish physician of New Orleans, became his owner. Durham impressed Dow with his knowledge of medicine and continued to learn a great deal as a medical assistant to the Scottish physician. Durham worked for Dow for a couple of years until he bought his freedom just before his twenty-first birthday. His freedom cost him approximately five hundred pesos which he paid in small amounts to Dow, who afterward became his patron. James Durham served the mulatto and black residents of New Orleans as well as some of the prominent white residents of the city. He earned up to $3,000 a year, a significant amount, by the time he was in his mid-20s.

Gains Professional Recognition

In 1788, at the age of twenty-six, Durham traveled to Philadelphia where he was baptized by Bishop White of the Episcopal Church and where he met Dr. Benjamin Rush, the renowned American physician. He was married without children when he met Rush. Durham may have been traveling to meet with abolitionist groups when he visited Philadelphia since he was active in the abolitionist movement and secretary of the Pennsylvania Society for the Abolition of Slavery. At their first meeting, Rush was impressed with Durham's medical knowledge and praised him for his language skills, for at the time Durham spoke both French and Spanish.

The meeting in Philadelphia could have been prearranged. Rush, an abolitionist, may have been interested in interviewing Durham, since abolitionists in America and abroad had agreed to distribute information about intelligent blacks as a means of changing the belief that the Negro was inferior and lacking in intelligence. In Philadelphia, Durham was introduced to Rush's family, his academic colleagues, and his friends. He became somewhat of a personality in Philadelphia. After their initial meeting Rush and Durham corresponded with each other for many years.

James Durham was a courageous and a dedicated physician. During the yellow fever epidemic of the late eighteenth century, he worked long hours with the sick. During the diphtheria outbreak in the 1780s he mixed medicines to fight the disease. Apparently, his career progressed without much interruption until 1801 when city commissioners in New Orleans decided to restrict the activities of persons practicing medicine without medical degrees. According to Betty L. Plummer they wrote, "Among those prohibited from 'treating persons in the city because they are not physicians' was the free Negro[s] Derum [sic]." The commission did, however, allow him to provide care for throat ailments only. Durham apparently cooperated with the decree and worked with Dow on the patients he was not allowed to treat independently. Yet Durham was concerned about the restriction. Plummer's article on Durham's correspondence to Benjamin Rush indicates that he asked about the opportunity of earning a living in Philadelphia.

On May 20, 1801 he wrote to Dr. Rush, "Sir if you think I can get a living in Philadelphia for I want to leave New Orleanes [sic] and come and live in the states." Durham eventually set up a practice in Philadelphia and continued to have a successful medical practice and career.

REFERENCES

Books

Goodell, William. *American Slave Code in Theory and Practice: Its Distinctive Features Shown by Its Statutes, Judicial Decisions, and Illustrative Facts.* Subdivision: Part II, Chapter VI. New York: American and Foreign Anti-Slavery Society, 1853.

Low, Augustus, and Virgil A. Clift. *Encyclopedia of Black America*. New York: McGraw-Hill, 1981.

Walker, Helen Edith. *The Negro in the Medical Profession*. Charlottesville, Va.: University of Virginia, 1949.

Periodicals

Miller, Kelly. "The Historic Background of the Negro Physician." *The Journal of Negro History* Vol. 1, No. 2 (1916): 99-109.

Plummer, Betty L. "Letters of James Durham to Benjamin Rush." *The Journal of Negro History* Vol. 65, No. 3 (Summer 1980): 261-69.

Online

All about black health. http://www.allaboutblackhealth. com/historyofblackphysicians.htm (Accessed 5 May 2005).

"First Three African American Physicians." http://ohoh. essortment.com/africanamerican_rqdo.htm (Accessed 12 May 2005).

Other

Kinney, John A. *The Negro in Medicine* [microform]. Tuskegee, Ala.: Tuskegee Institute Press, 1912.

Mario A. Charles

Edward Dwight
1933–

Sculptor, astronaut trainee, research pilot

Edward Joseph Dwight Jr. was denied a place in space and eventually became a highly praised sculptor. He was born September 9, 1933, in Kansas City, Kansas to Georgia and Edward Dwight Sr. He grew up near Fairfax

Edward Dwight

Airport, a municipal airport that was turned into an Army Air Force base during World War II. Dwight's father, Edward Dwight Sr., quit school at age fifteen to play professional baseball in the Negro Leagues. While on a road trip, he met his future wife and Dwight Jr.'s mother, Georgia Baker, in Sioux City, Iowa. After a long distance courtship, he married her and they settled in Kansas City, where they raised Dwight, Jr. and their four other children.

Dwight Jr.'s parents were devout Catholics. Dwight attended Our Lady of Perpetual Help grade school. He and his sisters were taught the importance of hard work and to use time wisely. The family garden helped to provide food for the family and to instill a love for the land in young Dwight. Dwight spent a lot of time watching planes near the fence surrounding the airfield. At the age of ten, he and some friends saw a P-39 fighter spin out of control and crash in a nearby field. The live ammunition exploded in the plane causing the cockpit to catch fire and burning the pilot. Dwight believed that that would not happen to him if he were piloting a plane. At that moment Dwight decided that he would learn to fly.

After the war, Fairfax Airfield returned to its civilian status and Dwight and his friends did odd jobs around the hangars, with the hopes of being flown in exchange for the work. Eventually Dwight's hope to fly became a reality when a pilot gave him a ride in a Piper Cub two-seater, an experience he found to be both exciting and terrifying.

While in high school, the Sumner High School Majorettes caught the attention of Dwight, particularly Sue Lillian James, who gave him little initial attention, but later became his wife. Dwight's love for airplanes and all things related to that remained throughout junior high and high school during which he studied sample pilot tests in library books. He spent many hours preparing to take the real test and playing an imaginary pilot.

Although he weighed only 104 pounds, Dwight excelled at track and football. Later, he was named winner of the state 118-pound championship as a Golden Gloves boxer. In 1951, Dwight completed high school as the first African American male to graduate from Ward Catholic High School where he was a member of the National Honor Society.

Dwight later enrolled at Kansas City Junior College and became even more interested in aviation. Despite President Truman's 1948 order to desegregate the armed forces, Dwight visited a local air force recruiting office on several occasions to ask for an application to train as a pilot and was repeatedly told that the air force was no place for his kind. Years later, Dwight applied and was accepted. In 1951, not realizing that a movement to recruit aviators was occurring, he wrote to Washington and was informed that an aviation evaluation team would

be visiting his junior college campus. When the team visited the campus, Dwight and some of his fellow students were sent to Lowry Air Base in Denver to take the pilot's exam. Dwight was the only one who passed the test and everyone was upset. The pilot's exam contained the actual problems on the tests Dwight had practiced taking in the library years ago. In 1953, after graduating from Kansas City Junior College, Dwight joined the U.S. Air Force, taking his airman basic training at Lackland Air Force Base in Texas and taking primary flight training at Malton Air Base in Missouri.

Better than the first ride, Dwight's second ride, which took place in the Air Force, helped him overcome his fear of flying. In 1955, he earned his wings and was commissioned second lieutenant. The same year he married Sue Lillian James. Dwight became even more excited about flying when he began jet aircraft training at Williams Air Force Base (AFB) in Arizona. It was a fantastic experience; he loved jets and became the first pilot in his class to solo in a T-33 jet trainer. He remained at Williams AFB for a couple years, performing duty as a jet-flying instructor. At the same time Dwight attended night courses at Arizona State University, graduating cum laude in 1957 with a B.A. in aeronautical engineering. After his assignment at Williams AFB, Dwight was stationed in Japan as a B-57 bomber pilot. He then became chief of collateral training of the ground education program of the Strategic Air Command at Travis AFB.

Trains to Become Astronaut

In response to the rising civil rights awareness and challenging segregation laws of the early 1960s, the Kennedy administration emphasized the integration of government programs. At the same time the space race was emerging and the astronauts chosen for the Mercury program, the first United States manned program, were among America's new heroes. A Kennedy spokesperson questioned the Department of Defense, asking if there were any blacks in the new aerospace research pilots' course being set up at Edwards AFB and the answer was no. The question sent the Air Force on a search for an African American pilot with credentials. The search ended in 1961 with Dwight, who had more than 2,000 hours of jet flight time to his credit and a degree in aeronautical engineering. Dwight received a letter from President Kennedy offering him an opportunity to be the first African American astronaut. Excited about this opportunity Dwight submitted his application. The air force replied promptly and Dwight was sent to Edwards AFB for an evaluation. In August 1962, Dwight was enrolled into the first phase of astronaut training at the Experimental Test Pilot School at Edwards AFB.

Dwight felt his efforts to become an astronaut would be a success because Kennedy had a dream of having an African American and an Asian on the first moon mission. However, he ran into many obstacles. According to

Distinguished African Americans in Aviation and Science, Dwight heard that the commandant of the Aerospace Research Test Pilots' School, Colonel Charles Yeager, had called in several staff members and commented that Kennedy's dream would "hurt the program and destroy everything you people have been putting together." It was then that Dwight realized that there would be much resistance to his becoming an astronaut. Dwight suspected that the others did not fear him, but the number of blacks that would follow him.

Although the competition was intense at the school, Dwight initially felt camaraderie with his fellow students, but as the course progressed, it became a game of survival. Known as a "Kennedy Boy," the candidate that had been selected by NASA, Dwight encountered jealousy and the silent treatment. Dwight "caught hell" from members of the faculty, including an incident in which he was called in for a face-to-face confrontation with Colonel Yeager. According to *Distinguished African Americans in Aviation and Science*, an incident occurred in which Yeager asked Dwight, "'Who got you into this school? Did President Kennedy send down the word that you're supposed to go into space? As far as I'm concerned, there'll never be a ['colored guy'] to do it. And if it was left to me, you guys wouldn't even get a chance to wear an air force uniform!'"

Despite the intimidation, Dwight graduated eighth in his class from Phase I training in April 1963. He then enrolled in the second and last phase at the test pilot school. Graduates completing Phase II training were qualified as astronauts and ready to be selected by NASA. Members of Phase II training were encouraged by NASA to participate in public relations events. Dwight made 176 speeches that year, was awarded dozens of citations by organizations all over the nation, and was featured in a filmstrip used by the NASA Space Mobile Education Program. Yet he experienced an incredible amount of social discrimination. When the astronauts spoke at clubs and restaurants, sometimes rooms were reserved for everyone except Dwight. However, Dwight continued to speak highly of his experiences as an astronaut candidate when addressing black youngsters, a group who viewed him as a role model.

In another incident, Dwight and some of his colleagues arrived late for class and he was the only one scolded. Frustrated, Dwight complained all the way to the White House. His complaint included a fifteen-page report describing his confrontations with Colonel Yeager. The descriptions of his complaints got the attention of the United States Attorney General's office resulting in their sending investigators to Edwards AFB.

Transferred to Germany

Dwight and his eight classmates graduated from test pilot school in 1963, less than a month prior to Kennedy's November 22 assassination. As a result,

Dwight's hopes of going into space began to fade. That fall the astronaut selection board to NASA selected two of Dwight's classmates, Theodore C. Freeman and Captain David R. Scott. Freeman was killed shortly thereafter in a T-33 crash, and. Scott later participated in the Gemini 8 and Apollo 9 missions. Although Dwight was passed over, President Johnson promised him that he would serve in the space mission if he would stop talking to the press. Articles featuring Dwight's complaints about racial discrimination in the Air Force angered President Johnson. He wanted Dwight to be silenced. Nevertheless, Dwight continued to discuss his plight. Days later, President Johnson ordered Dwight to serve as a liaison officer for a non-existent German test pilot school. Dwight was never officially notified that he was no longer in the space program. Dwight was then sent to Dayton, Ohio to work in Wright-Patterson's bomber group, a place most graduates viewed as the worst possible assignment. At Wright-Patterson, his job was to sit at the desk and not be in the air. Dwight complained repeatedly about his assignment, and he visited Washington on several occasions to plead his case in vain before Pentagon officials and other influential people. Without the aid of Kennedy, Dwight had no support at all.

Dwight and his family were harassed on and off the base in Dayton. The harassment ranged from property damage to personal attacks. In an effort to find a good home for his family, he faced the same problems as other African Americans when seeking homes in predominantly white neighborhoods. At every realtor's office he was met with comments suggesting that the property was unavailable for one reason or another. Finally, a Catholic layman, who had recognized Dwight from a picture he had seen on a church publication, offered to rent him a house in Huber Heights, a Dayton suburb. On a daily basis, the family was met with hostility. Dwight finally decided to move after a brick was thrown through a window and his daughter, Tina, was sprayed with glass. As the pressures of racism escalated, Dwight's marriage to Sue ended in divorce. Upon winning custody of his son, Dwight III, and his daughter, Tina, Dwight took a second wife, a union that lasted a mere thirty days. He then took a third wife, Barbara, a childhood friend from Kansas City.

In June 1964, President Johnson signed the Civil Rights Act. Riots broke out in many cities during that summer. An Air Force Base press release in February 1964 stated that neither NASA nor the Air Force considered Dwight as a candidate for future selection in aerospace projects. Newspapers across the country picked up on the story. In 1965, an article appeared in *Ebony* magazine chronicling Dwight's troubles in the Air Force Space pilot training program. NASA issued a general statement indicating that Dwight was not omitted because he was not qualified, but because someone more qualified was selected ahead of him. NASA's public information office also reported that 2.5 percent of their employees were Negroes.

In 1966, Dwight resigned his commission in the U.S. Air Force. The following year, President Lyndon B. Johnson decided that he wanted his own African American astronaut, Robert H. Lawrence, who was killed the same year during a simulated space ship landing at Edwards AFB. Lawrence became the first designated African American astronaut.

Dwight moved to Denver, where a not-so-profitable stint with a chain of restaurants he opened led him to become a realtor. He built condominiums and other property in Denver's more exclusive areas, making him a millionaire by the early 1970s. By this time, Dwight had five children. He became the only black who could get a $100,000 loan, but that did not stop him from losing his property during the recession-torn mid-1970s. His wiser partners did not lose their properties because they sold them in time.

Dwight also co-founded the Jet Training School in 1967. One day the other six flight instructors took off in a plane without Dwight, who had stayed on the ground to complete a real estate deal. Minutes later the plane crashed, killing everyone aboard. After the accident, Dwight never flew again.

Becomes a Sculptor

By the mid-1970s, Dwight returned to a longstanding hobby, sculpting. In 1974, he created a sculpture of George Brown, the first black lieutenant governor of Colorado. Since few facts were known about early African American pioneers, Dwight used his unique artistic style to expose viewers to the unknown history of the American West. The thirty bronzes he created won him widespread acceptance and critical acclaim. In 1977, he attended the University of Denver, where he earned a master's degree of fine arts in sculpting and taught for time. His artistic success, depicting African American pioneers of the West through sculpting, led him to create sculptures of other aspects of the African culture and ancestral imagery. Dwight became an acclaimed sculptor. As of the early 2000s he heads the Ed Dwight Studios Inc. in Denver and has produced bronze sculptures for both public installations and private collectors all over the world. Dwight has created over eighty public art commissions in his 25-year career. Among his most noted works are statues of Hank Aaron and Dr. Martin Luther King Jr., in Atlanta; the Frederick Douglas Memorial in Washington D. C.; and six jazz figures at the Smithsonian Institution's National Museum of American History. In 1986 he and a team of architectural firms were commissioned to design a ninety-foot installation to commemorate the 5,000 enslaved Africans and Free persons who served and fought as African American patriots in the Revolutionary War from 1776 to 1781 and tens of thousands of slaves of that era who ran away from slavery or petitioned for liberty, intended for the Mall in Washington near the Lincoln Memorial and the Washington Monument.

His company, Ed Dwight Studios, Inc., developed into one of the largest single artistic production and marketing facilitates in the western United States. He has an innate ability to create life, breath, and mobility in his works. In 2001, he unveiled four major monuments, including the first bi-national monument in Detroit, Michigan and Windsor, Ontario, Canada dedicated to the International Underground Railroad movement on the Capitol Grounds in Columbia, South Carolina, and a memorial to the first black legislator in Ohio, George Washington Williams, installed in the state capitol in Columbus, Ohio. Since his art career began in 1976, Dwight has become one of most prolific and insightful sculptors in the United States.

Dwight believes that the death of Kennedy had everything to do with his fate as an astronaut candidate. Since Dwight grew up in mostly white environments and private schools, he was bewildered over the discrimination problems he had experienced in the Air Force Space pilot training program. In an interview in *Ebony* in February 1984, Dwight described his fall into racism: "It's like being out into a storm without knowing that it's coming." He described himself as naive, and summed up his space training as a nightmare.

REFERENCES

Books

Gubert, Betty Kaplan, Miriam Sawyer, and Caroline M. Fannin. *Distinguished African American in Aviation and Space Science*. Westport, Conn.: Oryx Press, 2002.

Periodicals

"Black War Memorial Will Open Nation's Eyes." *Los Angeles Sentinel*, 17 October 1991.

Dawson, Margaret. "Community Focus." *Columbus Times*, 28 September 1983.

"First Black Astronaut Who Turned to Sculpting 20 Years Ago After Never Making It into Space." *Jet* (2 November 1983): 47.

Sanders, Charles L. "The Troubles of Astronaut Edward Dwight, Air Force Captain." *Ebony* (June 1965): 29-36.

White, Frank, III. "The Sculptor Who Would Have Gone into Space." *Ebony* (February 1984): 54, 56, 58.

Online

Ed Dwight Studios. http://www.eddwight.com/home.htm (Accessed 9 March 2005).

Sharon McGee

Mervyn M. Dymally
1926–

Politician, civil rights activist

Mervyn M. Dymally

Mervyn M. Dymally is a native son of the Caribbean. He was born in Trinidad, West Indies on May 12, 1926, the third of nine children. His mother was a native Trinidadian; his father's family had come from India. Dymally and his second wife, former teacher Alice Gueno of New Orleans, were married in 1964. They had two children, Mark and Lynn. Dymally makes his home in Compton, California, the district he has represented in the California Assembly, Senate, and the United States House of Representatives.

Dymally's early education was received in the primary and secondary schools of San Fernando, Trinidad. After high school, Dymally was employed as a staff reporter for the Oil Workers' Trade Union newspaper, *The Vanguard*. He left Trinidad in 1946 to further his education in journalism at Lincoln University in Jefferson City, Missouri. After brief stays in Missouri, Indiana, and Illinois, he headed to California, enrolling first at Chapman College, then California State University at Los Angeles. He graduated in 1954 with a B.A. in special education. He began his career as a special education teacher in the Los Angeles Unified School District. Throughout his years in public office, he continued to further his education. He was awarded a master's degree in government from California State University at Sacramento, and a Ph.D. in human behavior from United States International University, San Diego. He is the recipient of several honorary doctorates.

Entry into California Politics

Dymally became a U.S. citizen, but his distinctive Caribbean accent remained his unique characteristic. Seeking opportunities to enter political arena at the grassroots level, he became active in the American Federation of Teachers. He joined the local Democratic Party and served as treasurer for the California Federation of Young Democrats. During the 1960 presidential election, he was a field coordinator for the John F. Kennedy campaign. These experiences were pivotal in building the support base he needed to run for the State Legislative Assembly. Two years later he easily won the historically black and solidly democratic 53rd district in Compton, an area south of Los Angeles. He was the first foreign-born black elected to the assembly.

In 1964 the Civil Rights Act was signed into law, marking the dawn of a new era for blacks and race relations in the United States. When the Watts district of South Central Los Angeles, where people were straining under the duress of high unemployment and inadequate housing and schools, erupted in violence, Dymally was there to help find solutions. In 1966, he ran for the 29th District Senate seat. His win made him the first African American to serve in the California State Senate and one of the few politicians to make the move from the Assembly to the Senate.

Dymally's political clout enabled him to capture the post of Democratic Caucus chair in the Senate. He headed the powerful reapportionment committee following the 1970 census. A number of other key committees fell under his chairmanship, including social welfare, military and veterans' affairs, elections and a select committee on medical education and health. He became a vocal advocate, fighting to improve social services for blacks and other minorities. He was the primary author and sponsor of significant pieces legislation, including the bill to ratify the Equal Rights Amendment in California and to reduce the voting age to eighteen. He sponsored early childhood education legislation to improve funding and to teach black history in the public schools. He was instrumental in the passage of the Prison Reform Act and the California Fair Plan. The latter was designed to increase the availability of property insurance to owners of property considered high risk.

Elected Lieutenant Governor

In 1970, Dymally was instrumental in establishing the Joint Center for Political and Economic Studies, founded

Chronology

1926	Born in Cedros, Trinidad, West Indies on May 12
1946	Immigrates to the United States
1954	Graduates from Los Angeles State College, B.A. special education
1956-63	Begins career as a special education teacher
1957	Becomes a U.S. citizen
1962	Elected as a representative in the California State Assembly
1966	First black elected to the California State Senate
1968	Marries Alice M. Gueno of New Orleans
1969	Receives M.A. in government from California State University, Sacramento
1974	First black elected lieutenant governor of California
1978	Receives a Ph.D. in human behavior from United States International University, San Diego, California
1980	First foreign-born black elected to the U.S. Congress, House of Representatives
1992	Retires from U.S. Congress after serving 10 years
2000	Post office building in Compton named in his honor
2002	Reelected to the California State Assembly

to provide guidance and to increase black participation in the political process. He handpicked and surrounded himself with young black aides whom he groomed for political positions. Rumors of a rivalry with Tom Bradley, the new mayor of Los Angeles, were fuelled as the two backed competing candidates for political office. In 1974, Dymally was elected as California's first black lieutenant governor at the same time and by the same slim margin that Jerry Brown was elected governor. His name was now inextricably linked to the national political agenda. When Brown announced his candidacy for president in 1976 with Dymally's endorsement, speculation grew that he was being primed for the governorship. Not everyone was singing his praises though. The 1974 campaign had raised issues regarding his ethics and integrity. Allegations of conflicts of interests were unearthed. Charges ranged from questionable use of campaign funds; authorship of legislation to benefit his businesses; nepotism in public and political positions; and multiple billings for office expenses. None of the charges was proven or advanced beyond the allegation stage. Dymally repeatedly declared that the charges were trumped up because he was a black man in high political office.

As lieutenant governor Dymally was involved at the highest levels of state government, with responsibility for governing, education, trade and the economy, law enforcement, and the environment. He is credited with raising the visibility of the office by significantly increasing the level of activity. Two important commissions fell under his jurisdiction, the State Commission for Economic Development (to develop and foster economic growth) and the Commission of the Californias (to develop favorable relations with Baja California and Mexico). As lieutenant governor, he cast the historic tie-breaking vote in 1975 that led to the passage of the first major gay rights legislation in the nation.

Dymally was defeated in his 1978 reelection bid for the lieutenant governorship by the Republican candidate Mike Curb. It was a bitter campaign with each candidate slinging accusations of criminal conduct. The old charges from the 1974 campaign were resurrected and publicized with additional claims of an imminent indictment. Dymally characterized the charges as dirty tricks. He was never indicted, and his opponent later apologized.

In 1980, Dymally entered the Democratic primary race vying for a seat representing the 31st District in the U.S. House of Representatives. He was running against the nine-term incumbent democrat, Charles H. Wilson and three other opponents. Congress had recently censored Mr. Wilson for misappropriating campaign funds. This played heavily in Dymally's favor. Although his opponents resurrected the skeletons from his closet, the record he had built in the California Assembly, particularly in social services, remained firm. He waged a positive grassroots campaign focusing on the issues of residential crime and economic development. With the support of friends like labor leader Cesar Chavez, who helped deliver the Hispanic vote, Dymally catapulted to a decisive victory and the U.S. Congress welcomed its first black foreign-born member.

Dymally broadened his experience and knowledge of both domestic and foreign affairs with membership on House congressional committees, including the Post Office, Civil Service, District of Columbia, and Foreign Affairs. In 1991 he became chair of the Subcommittee on African Affairs that reviewed World Bank and African Development Bank programs. He had long had an interest in Africa and traveled to twenty African countries during his chairmanship. African nations very much appreciated his leadership and praised his efforts and initiatives to raise awareness of the issues, particularly human rights.

Leads Congressional Black Caucus

As a member and later chair of the Congressional Black Caucus he reacted firmly and aggressively to the various issues affecting minorities. Dymally is considered the most influential African American on U.S. African affairs and foreign policy. He believed that U.S. policy has never been coherent or consistent outside protecting oil interests. Dymally saw the key to solving the political unrest in Africa, not in democracy but economic support for debt reduction, poverty, healthcare, education, and transportation. Dymally's colleagues in Congress, however, did not always support his views on Africa. He frequently sponsored relief bills for war-torn Liberia and achieved some measure of success during George H. Bush's presidency.

The Caribbean always remained near and dear to his heart. Dymally founded the Caribbean Action Lobby and the Dymally International Group Incorporated, to foster development projects in Africa and the Caribbean. He chaired the Caribbean Task Force of the Black Caucus, seeking to improve relations between U.S. blacks and their Caribbean neighbors. Dymally and the Caucus were particularly displeased with the 1983 Grenada intervention. After initial reluctance, they supported President Reagan's Caribbean Basin Initiative but remained opposed to the administration's sugar policy that negatively affected the region.

Dymally retired from public service in 1992 after a long, successful, and diverse career in education and government. Although he declared himself to be in good health, he had undergone surgery for prostate cancer. On his retirement he was praised for his leadership on Africa and was honored by African countries as their American champion. Even with his support, though, his daughter, Lynn, lost her bid to win his vacated seat.

After retiring from Congress, Dymally spent his time traveling and teaching. He visited Africa, Asia, and the Caribbean and has remained very active in educational and political affairs. A plethora of teaching appointments, including Central State in Ohio, the Charles R. Drew University in Los Angeles, and various California colleges, have kept him fully engaged.

He has founded, helped organize, or served as chair of numerous organizations, including: the Joint Center for Political Studies, the Caribbean American Research Action Inc., the Urban Affairs Institute, the National Conference of Black Elected Officials, and the Congressional Institute for Science, Space, and Technology. Dymally has authored, edited, or contributed to a number of published works. In 2000, he received the distinction of having the post office building in Compton, California, named after him.

Makes Political Comeback

In 2002, after a ten-year break, he was reelected at age seventy-six to the California State Assembly. Dubbed the comeback kid, he quipped characteristically that politics was in his blood, and he had never really retired from public service. He captured a seat in the predominately Hispanic 52nd congressional district. Dymally campaigned on his experience and attributed his win to concentrating on the issues most important to the people.

Dymally is described as industrious, aggressive, and daring. Yet many rate the accomplishments during his 40-year career as modest. Some charge that his prolonged focus on foreign nations left him little time to advocate for the needs of local constituents. He has been criticized for his public association with Marxist leaders. Allegations of fraud, bribery, and tainted campaign contributions have clouded his record. Yet Dymally assessed his own legacy not in terms of legislation but in his openness and willingness to serve all the people of his state.

REFERENCES

Books

Chandler, Trevor L. *A Conversation with Mervyn M. Dymally, Lieutenant Governor, State of California.* Seattle, Wash.: Office of Minority Affairs, University of Washington, 1975.

Clay, William L. *Just Permanent Interest: Black Americans in Congress, 1870-1971.* New York: Amistad Press, 1992.

Dymally, Mervyn M. Interview by Elston L Carr. *State Government Oral History Program.* Los Angeles, Calif.: University of California, 1997.

Evory, Ann. "Mervyn M(alcolm) Dymally." In *Contemporary Authors: A Biographical Guide to Current Authors and Their Works, 41-44.* Ed. Ann Evory. Detroit, Mich.: Gale Research, 1979.

Haskins, James. *Distinguished African American Political and Governmental Leaders.* Phoenix, Ariz.: Oryx Press, 1999.

U.S. Congress. House of Representatives. *Black Americans in Congress, 1870-1989.* 101st Cong., 2nd sess.,1990, H.Doc.117, serial 13947, 43-44.

Periodicals

Brice, Jessica. "Top Black Politician Returns to Reclaim Assembly Seat at Age 76." *Associated Press Newswires*, 9 December 2002.

Dymally, Mervyn. "IMF Policies are 'an Absolute, Total Disaster': interview with Harley Schlanger, 29 August 1997." *Executive Intelligence Review* (12 September 1997): 66-68.

Knight Ridder/Tribune Business News. "California Lawmaker Backs Herb Product for State Study." *The San Diego Union-Tribune*, 10 July 2003.

"Mervyn Malcolm Dymally." *The Associated Press*, 20 May 1989.

Robinson, Louie. "Breakthrough: Mervyn M. Dymally Takes Over California's Number Two Slot of Lieutenant Governor." *Ebony,* 30 (March 1975):128+.

Warner, Mary. "Mervyn Dymally: Expanding the Lieutenant Governor's Role." *Sepia* 27 (November 1978): 26-32.

Yacoe, Donald. "California Ex-lieutenant Governor joins Doley Securities as Vice-Chairman." *The Bond Buyer* 13 (September 1993): 4.

Online

Dymally, Mervyn M. "California State Assembly Member. Mervyn M. Dymally." *California State*

Assembly. http://democrats.assembly.ca.gov/ members/a52/ (Accessed 10 January 2005).

Collections

Dymally's papers are in Special Collections, University Library, California State University, Los Angeles.

Janette Prescod

Michael Eric Dyson
1958–

Writer, educator, lecturer, minister

Michael Eric Dyson

Michael Eric Dyson is a distinguished professor at an Ivy League University; a prolific, award-winning writer of books and articles; a social and cultural critic; a public intellectual; a popular lecturer; a frequent talk show guest; a radio show host; and an ordained minister. He has been hailed as one of the most influential and inspirational of all African Americans as he steadfastly focuses on issues of race, identity, religion, and popular culture in American society.

Dyson was born on October 23, 1958, in Detroit, Michigan, to Addie Mae Leonard, who picked cotton in Alabama before becoming a paraprofessional for the Detroit board of education. He was adopted by Everett Dyson after Leonard married him in 1960. Consequently, Dyson had four stepbrothers, and he was the second oldest of the five sons who were raised in the inner city. Everett Dyson worked at Kelsey-Hayes, an auto parts factory, for thirty-three years. When Dyson was twelve years old, he began helping his father as he worked part-time at Morton's Nursery. After Everett Dyson was laid off from Kelsey-Hayes in 1970, he refused to apply for welfare. Instead, he started Dyson and Sons Grass Cutting and Sodding. The Dyson boys also helped their father look for discarded metal in the city's alleys, which they sold to junkyards. The elder Dyson later worked as a maintenance man for a church and drug store prior to his death in 1981.

Dyson attended public schools in Detroit where three teachers greatly influenced him: Mrs. James, Dyson's fifth-grade teacher at Wingert Elementary School, who inspired him to learn about and be proud of his African American heritage; Otis Burdette, Dyson's seventh-grade English teacher at Webber Junior High School, who recognized and encouraged Dyson's potential talents as a public speaker; and Lola Black, Dyson's French teacher at Northwestern High School, who in addition to speaking French and English, spoke "the language of black self-esteem through rigorous study and linguistic excellence" (according to *Why I Love Black Women*) and encouraged Dyson to serve as a French tutor for his classmates. During his early teen years, Mrs. Bennett, who was Dyson's neighbor, gave him her late husband's set of Harvard Classics. Thus Dyson, who read each book in the collection, read such literary classics such as Richard Dana's *Two Years Before the Mast* (1840). He read great literature at an early age, and he also listened to popular African American musicians, such as the artists on the Motown record label.

Remembers the Turbulent 1960s

Two events in the late 1960s were pivotal moments in Dyson's childhood. In July 1967, a riot broke out in Detroit after police officers arrested eighty-two people who were celebrating the return of two members of the military from Vietnam at an after hours club. By the time the riots ended, more than forty people were dead, approximately four hundred to one thousand people were injured, and thousands of people were arrested. Dyson, who was eight years old, saw the destruction and the looting. In his first book, *Reflecting Black: African-American Cultural Criticism*, Dyson recalls that "[he] felt the reprimand and fear of the word that regulated our lives during that painful period and that signified the sharp division of safe and unsafe social time: curfew."

One year later, the assassination of Martin Luther King Jr. proved to be an even more traumatic time for Dyson. He acknowledged in *Reflecting Black* that King's murder "heralded the end of [his] youthful innocence" and that for months he feared standing in front of windows and doors at night. His nine-year-old mind reasoned that if a man of peace such as Martin Luther King Jr. could be assassinated, he could also be killed. King's assassination was Dyson's "initial plunge into the tortuous meanings of racial politics, and [he] began to believe that the world was largely predicated upon color, its vain and violent ubiquity becoming increasingly apparent to [his] newly opened eyes." Although Dyson did not know who King was prior to his assassination on April 4, 1968, King became an important figure in Dyson's life. Dyson, who listened to King's "I've Been to the Mountaintop" speech, aspired to become a stirring and powerful orator. In 1971 Dyson, at the age of twelve, delivered his first public speech in an oratorical contest and won.

That same year, Dyson met Frederick G. Sampson II, who was pastor of the Tabernacle Missionary Baptist Church. Sampson, who encouraged Dyson to read W. E. B. Du Bois and Bertrand Russell, became Dyson's mentor. At the age of sixteen and with Sampson's assistance, Dyson was the recipient of a scholarship to Cranbrook, a boarding school in Bloomfield Hills, Michigan that was thirty miles from Detroit. Dyson recalls in *Reflecting Black*, "That short distance had divided me from a world I had never known as a poor black inner-city youth: white wealth, power, and privilege. I had never gone to school with white kids before, much less wealthy white kids, many the sons and daughters of famous parents, a banking magnet here, a film giant there. I immediately experienced a Hitchcockian vertigo about the place, its seductive grandeur, warming grace, and old world elegance not enough to conceal the absurdity of racism that lurked beneath its breathtaking exterior." Dyson left Cranbrook near the end of his second year, returned home to Detroit, and eventually earned his high school diploma at night school.

Becomes a Licensed Minister

Dyson held various jobs such as a clerk-typist at a Chrysler plant, a manager-trainee at a fast-food restaurant, an arc welder and unloader of trains with brake drums at Kelsey-Hayes, and a substitute janitor in the Detroit Public School System. In 1977, eighteen- year-old Dyson married his pregnant girlfriend, Terrie, an actress and a waitress who was eight years older than Dyson. Their son, Michael Eric Dyson II, was born in 1978, one month after Dyson lost his job and applied for welfare. Also in 1978 Dyson, with Sampson's encouragement and assistance, became a licensed Baptist minister.

In 1979 Dyson and his wife divorced. That same year, at the age of twenty-one, he began his pursuit of a college diploma at a historically African American college. Dyson enrolled in Knoxville College in Knoxville, Tennessee before he transferred to Carson-Newman College, a Baptist and predominantly white school in Jefferson City, Tennessee, where he majored in philosophy. During his undergraduate years, Dyson earned a living by working the three o'clock to eleven o'clock shift as a cleaner and degreaser of heavy machinery at Robertshaw Factory. Although he was an honor student, Dyson did not receive a scholarship during his matriculation at Carson-Newman. Dyson graduated magna cum laude with a B.A. in 1982 and received the Outstanding Graduate in Philosophy Award.

Dyson, who was ordained as a minister in 1982, served as a pastor at three churches while he attended college and worked at the factory. He was fired from two churches: he questioned why his white congregation did not have other African American speakers, and he wanted to allow three women to become deacons at an African American church. Also in the 1980s, Dyson remarried; however, his marriage to Brenda Joyce Dyson, a nurse, ended in divorce. From 1988 to 1989, he was assistant director of a poverty project at Hartford Seminary in Connecticut. From 1989 to 1992, Dyson was instructor of ethics and cultural criticism before being promoted to assistant professor at Chicago Theological Seminary.

Becomes a Freelance Writer

In the late 1980s, Dyson began writing for professional as well as popular journals, magazines, and newspapers. Dyson's earliest works appear in various magazines, such as *Chicago Theological Seminary Register*, *Chicago Tribune Books*, *Christian Century*, and *DePaul Law Review*.

Dyson continued his education at Princeton University where he received a graduate fellowship to study in the Department of Religion. While pursuing graduate work at Princeton, Dyson was an assistant master at the University's Mathey College. Dyson received an M.A. in 1991. On June 24, 1992, he married his third wife, Marcia Louise Dyson. Also in 1992, Dyson, who had published in periodicals such as the *Atlantic Monthly*, *New Republic,* and *Vibe*, was the recipient of the National Magazine Award from the National Association of Black Journalism for his freelance writing. In 1993, he received a Ph.D. from Princeton University.

After earning his doctorate, Dyson continued teaching. From 1993 to 1995, he was an assistant professor at Brown University in Providence, Rhode Island, where he taught courses in American civilization and African American studies. From 1995 to 1997, Dyson was professor of communication studies and director of the Institute of African-American Research at the University of North Carolina, Chapel Hill, where each semester he taught a popular course on gangsta rap's effects on societal values. From 1997 to 1999, Dyson was a visiting distinguished professor of African American studies at Columbia University, in New York, where he continued to use the classroom to investigate gangsta rap.

In 1999, Dyson became the first Ida B. Wells-Barnett University Professor at DePaul University in Chicago. In 2002, Dyson became the Avalon Foundation Professor in the Humanities at the University of Pennsylvania, teaching courses in the Religious Studies Department and the African-American Studies Program. Dyson's appointment was acknowledged as the first step in the revitalization and expansion of the African-American Studies Program as it celebrates its more than three decades existence and anticipates recruiting additional scholars of Dyson's caliber. At the University of Pennsylvania, Dyson focused on gangsta rap as well as hip-hop music and taught on Tupac Shakur's lyrics and life.

Publishes Thirteen Books in Thirteen Years

From 1993 to 2006, Dyson averaged one book per year, most of them bestsellers. *Reflecting Black* (1993), a collection of essays that Dyson wrote and published during the late 1980s to the early 1990s, focuses on African American popular culture's effects on mainstream American culture, African American culture, race, gender, class, and religion. *Reflecting Black* won the Gustavus Myers Center Human Rights Award.

There are additional collections of Dyson's essays. *Between God and Gangsta Rap: Bearing Witness to Black Culture* (1996) begins with Dyson's letter to his incarcerated brother and ends with a letter to his third wife. In between is Dyson's commentary on African American athletes, political leaders, activists, rhythm and blues artists, and rap performers as he attempts to place gangsta rap in its cultural and social perspective. Dyson followed with *Race Rules: Navigating the Color Line* (1996), which focuses on African American intellectuals, leadership, and youth as well as popular culture, the black church, and sex. Dyson describes *Why I Love Black Women* (2003) as his love letter and testimony to a diverse group of unknown and famous women who have shaped his life and consequently made him a better son, brother, man, father, friend, minister, and professor. Among the women honored are Dyson's relatives, former teachers, writers, revolutionaries, and entertainers. Dyson ends the book with "How to Love a Black Woman: A Sermon." *Why I Love Black Women* won the 2004 NAACP Image Award for Outstanding Nonfiction Literary Work. *Open Mike: Reflections on Philosophy, Race, Sex, Culture and Religion* (2003) is a collection of interviews, and *The Michael Eric Dyson Reader* (2004) is a collection of essays, speeches, and interviews.

Dyson has also written books on four African American icons: Malcolm X, Martin Luther King Jr., Tupac Shakur, and Marvin Gaye. In the *Washington Post Book World*, William Jelani Cobb labeled Dyson's "abiding interest in black men who live complex, often troubled lives and die violent deaths" the Dyson Icon Project. In each of the four books, Dyson blends biography, social criticism, and cultural criticism; the end product is known as biocriticism. Dyson, in *Making Malcolm: The Myth and Meaning of Malcolm X* (1995), places Malcolm X's life in historical context and explores his legacy in terms of contemporary society. *Making Malcolm* was named Notable Book of 1994 by the *New York Times* and the *Philadelphia Inquirer* and was selected as one of the outstanding books of the twentieth century by *Black Issues Book Review*.

In *I May Not Get There with You: The True Martin Luther King Jr.* (2000), Dyson focuses on the last three years of King's life and advocates a ten-year moratorium on King's "I Have a Dream" speech in order to call attention to the ideas expressed in his less well known speeches and sermons. Dyson, in a 2003 article written for the *Washington Post*, comments: "King was a much more radical thinker than either friend or foe could abide. To say that well was the critical attention of my book."

In *Holler If You Hear Me: Searching for Tupac Shakur* (2001), Dyson, known as "the hip-hop intellectual," writes about Shakur's attainment of iconic status after his death and asserts that Shakur may be "the most influential and compelling" rap artist. The book analyzes Shakur's life, death, and lyrics as well as hip-hop culture, and Shakur's significance for African American youth.

Mercy, Mercy Me: The Art, Loves, and Demons of Marvin Gaye (2004) was published on the twentieth anniversary of Gaye's death. Dyson, who offers his personal testimony on the importance of Gaye's music in his life, reassesses Gaye's life and music and explores his ongoing influence on American music. As with Dyson's works on Malcolm X, King, and Shakur, *Mercy, Mercy Me* reveals the enigmatic figure's humanness that has been overshadowed by his legendary status.

After writing about four icons, Dyson challenged a living legend in *Is Bill Cosby Right? (Or Has the Black Middle Class Lost Its Mind?)* (2005). Dyson takes issue with Cosby's comments at the May 17, 2004 NAACP commemoration of the fiftieth anniversary of the Supreme Court's *Brown v. Board of Education* decision. Cosby's statements about lower income African Americans' lack of parenting, poor academic performance, and other problems led to Dyson's book-length defense of poor blacks as he acknowledges that class and generational tensions exist in black America.

Come Hell or High Water: Hurricane Katrina and the Color of Disaster (2006) was one of the first books published about the physical, cultural, and economic devastation caused by the 2005 hurricane. Dyson analyzed the plight of poor African Americans in the Delta before and after Hurricane Katrina. The book is Dyson's indictment of the race- and class-specific delays in the government's response to the disaster. Dyson published a second book in 2006, *Pride: The Seven Deadly Sins*, which is Dyson's elaboration of pride's dangers as well as virtues.

Hosts Radio Talk Show

Dyson served as a columnist for the *Chicago Sun Times* and *Savoy* and was a contributing editor to the *Christian Century*. He was a frequent guest on most of the major talk shows on network and cable stations as well as radio talk shows (including National Public Radio). Thus his views receive widespread media exposure.

On January 20, 2006, Dyson launched *The Michael Eric Dyson Show*, a talk show broadcast on Syndication One, which is a joint venture of Radio One (founded by Catherine Hughes) and Reach Media. Syndication One hoped to fill the void in radio talk programs for African American audiences. Marcia Dyson was anticipated to be an occasional guest on her husband's show.

Dyson and his wife live in Philadelphia. In addition to Michael Dyson II, Dyson is the father of Mwata and Maisha Dyson.

Dyson received the BET/General Motors Black History Makers Award in 2005. As educator, author, and social critic, he remains a ubiquitous figure in the United States: he eloquently addresses issues of race, identity, religion, and popular culture. Evaluating Dyson's role, Robert S. Boynton asserts in *Atlantic Monthly* that Michael Eric Dyson is a member of "an impressive group of African American writers and thinkers [who] have emerged to revive and revitalize [the role of the public intellectual]. They are bringing moral imagination and critical intelligence to bear on the definingly American matter of race—and reaching beyond race to voice what one calls 'the commonality of American concern.'"

REFERENCES

Books

"Michael Eric Dyson." In *Contemporary Black Biography*. Vol. 11. Eds. L. Mpho Mabunda and Shirelle Phelps. Detroit: Gale, 1996.

Periodicals

Arana, Marie. "Michael Eric Dyson Telling It Any Way He Can." *Washington Post Book World*, 24 August 2003.

Boynton, Robert S. "The New Intellectuals." *Atlantic Monthly* 275 (March 1995): 53-70.

Cobb, William Jelani. "Tortured Soul: An Attempt to Solve the Riddle of a Musical Legend's Complicated Life." *Washington Post Book World*, 20 June 2004.

Dyson, Michael Eric. "Shakespeare and Smokey Robinson." *New York Times Book Review*, 19 November 1995.

———. "The Writing Life: A Social Critic Reads Before He Rights the World—Just as He Reads Before He Writes It." *Washington Post Book World*, 24 August 2003.

Online

Gregory, Kia. "What's Up, Hip-Hop Doc?" http://www.philadelphiaweekly.com/view.php?id=11400 (Accessed 6 February 2006).

Linda M. Carter

William Lewis Eagleson
1835–1899

Editor, journalist, political activist

The immigration of African Americans to the Oklahoma territory, efforts to establish the all-black town, Langston City; and the founding of black newspapers in Kansas and Oklahoma were among William Eagleson's primary interests. He dabbled in politics as well, using his paper to promote black causes. Although he switched back and forth from Republican to Democratic party membership, it is doubtless Eagleson's chief interest was in finding the right niche to enable him to support his race.

Except that he was born a slave in St. Louis, Missouri, on August 9, 1835, the details of Eagleson's early life and his parents' names are unknown. Eagleson was trained as a barber and also learned the printer's trade early on, practicing both throughout his life. He lived in Illinois for a period of time, and in 1877 he relocated to Fort Scott, Kansas. In 1878 he founded the *Colored Citizen*, the first black-owned newspaper in Kansas. He was able to print the paper from an outdated press with second-hand type. Since Topeka had a burgeoning black population, he considered his chances for success much greater there; consequently, six months later he moved the paper to that city. Reverend T. W. Henderson, a prominent African Methodist Episcopal minister, became his associate editor.

Their newspaper was a strong advocate of black participation in the Republican party. Early on Eagleson had viewed Henderson with a political eye, but he was unsuccessful in his effort to have Henderson nominated for lieutenant governor. Now with a Republican victory in 1878, Eagleson stepped up his drive to put blacks in political office. As a result of the paper's strong appeal to black citizens, both Eagleson and Henderson soon had a chance at such activism themselves. Henderson was appointed chaplain of the House of Representatives—then controlled by the Republicans—and Eagleson became first assistant doorman. After the Colored State Emigration Board was organized to oversee the place-

Chronology	
1835	Born in St. Louis, Missouri on August 9
1865	Marries Elizabeth McKinney
1878	Founds the *Colored Citizen*
1879?	Suspends publication of the *Colored Citizen*
1880	Helps organize Colored Men's State Convention; founds the *Kansas Herald*
1889	Becomes officer in Oklahoma Immigration Association
1891	Recruits blacks to Oklahoma Territory; publishes the *Langston City Herald*
1895	Becomes president of the Colored Men's Independent League
1896	Becomes messenger to governor of Kansas
1899	Dies in Topeka, Kansas on June 22

ment of refugees from the South, the men became prominent members of that board.

In 1879 or 1880, Eagleson suspended publication of the *Colored Citizen* and by January 30, 1880, he became editor of the *Kansas Herald*. Later on, for legal purposes, the paper was renamed the *Herald of Kansas*. He used the paper to tout the Republican party and also to call for racial unity. This activity may be what caused a disagreement between Eagleson and his conservative partner and resulted in the paper's demise on June 11 as well as an end to Eagleson's journalistic career.

Eagleson continued his work to support the black cause. In 1880 he helped organize the Colored Men's State Convention, becoming a member of the State Executive Committee. He went to Washington, D.C., as a member of a committee to discuss the massive immigration of blacks to Kansas. His break with the Republican party came in the mid-1880s, when he shifted his membership to the Democratic party. To support himself and his family, Eagleson returned to his profession as barber but worked for a while in the city jail. In 1889, when he reemerged from virtual obscurity, he became a prime mover in efforts of blacks to colonize the Oklahoma Territory. On July 17 that year, the Oklahoma Immigration Association was organized, with Eagleson as corresponding secretary and business manager. He worked to build the all-black town Langston City, Oklahoma.

Helps Promote All-Black Town

A delegation of twenty blacks urged President Benjamin Harrison to appoint a black person as secretary of Oklahoma Territory. The ultimate goal was to make that territory a Negro state. It received large numbers of black migrants from Arkansas, Louisiana, Mississippi, and Texas. Several all-Negro towns were established in the newly-opened lands in the territory; Langston City was the first, having been founded in 1889. Eagleson worked with Edwin P. McCabe, Kansas' first black state auditor and his wife, Sarah McCabe, in promoting the all-black community, Langston City, located in Logan County. The town, now known simply as Langston, was named in honor of John Mercer Langston (1829-1897), black lawyer, diplomat, and congressman. Having moved to Langston City in 1891, Eagleson worked aggressively to recruit blacks to the territory. On May 2 of that year, he began publication of the *Langston City Herald*, the first black paper published in the Oklahoma Territory. He used the paper to call for black colonization of the Cimarron Valley, scheduled to open on September 22. Local whites became so enraged over Eagleson's work that a drunken gang invaded Langston on September 17, attempted to shoot Eagleson, and succeeded in wounding several blacks. This aggression drew Eagleson's ire, and he responded by forming a rifle-armed posse that invaded a camp of white cowboys on September 20 and gave them a stern warning. In the end, a thousand or so black families claimed land that whites controlled and now had their own homes, for which Eagleson and the *Herald* took credit.

Still in Langston until the end of 1892, Eagleson continued to edit his newspaper and held several offices as well, including that as justice of the peace and city council member. He continued to work in the interest of immigration, dabbled in partisan politics, and placed the *Herald* in the Republican camp rather than that of the Democrats. Apparently the Republicans were back in his favor.

Although he returned to Topeka, Eagleson maintained his interest in Oklahoma and its political and racial activities. Edwin McCabe was appointed territorial governor but by fall 1892 he turned over to a black group in Guthrie the agency that he owned, that would sell the city's lots as well as his interest in the *Herald*. Meanwhile, Eagleson was unsuccessful in his efforts to establish another all-black town, Sumner City. He returned to his barbershop business and remained politically active as well. He also devoted his efforts to the Democratic party. His work with black party organizations included serving as president of the Colored Men's Independent League (1895), a group that opposed Republican loyalism. After supporting the successful candidacy of Populist-Democratic fusion governor John W. Leedy, Eagleson was appointed messenger to the governor (1896-97). Leedy lost his bid for reelection in 1898.

Eagleson married Elizabeth McKinney on December 2, 1865, and they had nine children (including one adopted daughter). In 1897, the Eaglesons' oldest son, Albert, established the short-lived *Colored Citizen (2d)*, which folded in December 1900. Eagleson continued his interest in racial uplift, and in his final year he worked to establish a home for the aged to serve Topeka's black community. He suffered from dropsy and died in Topeka on June 22, 1899, leaving a legacy as a race man who worked diligently to develop the black community in the West.

REFERENCES

Books

African American Almanac. 8th ed. Eds. Jessie Carney Smith and Joseph M. Palmisano. Detroit, Mich.: Gale Group, 2000.

Bruce, Dickson D., Jr. "William Lewis Eagleson." In *American National Biography*. Vol. 7. Ed. John A. Garraty and Mark C. Carnes. New York: Oxford University Press, 1999.

Porter, Kenneth Wiggins. "William Lewis Eagleson." In *Dictionary of American Negro Biography*. Ed. Rayford W. Logan and Michael R. Winston. New York: Norton, 1982.

Periodicals

Littlefield, Daniel F., Jr, and Lonnie E. Underhill. "Black Dreams and 'Free' Homes: The Oklahoma Territory, 1891-1894." *Phylon* 34 (1973): 342-57.

Online

"Black in Oklahoma—Before the Riot." *Afro-American Almanac*. http://www.toptags.com/aama/events/oklahoma.htm (Accessed 17 September 2005).

Jessie Carney Smith

Hosea Easton
1798–1837

Abolitionist, minister, lecturer

A noteworthy abolitionist, minister, and lecturer, Hosea Easton was a prominent black man from an elite New England family. Not widely known, Easton worked to ameliorate problems caused by slavery, racial prejudices, and the need for social reform. Though he was three generations removed from slavery himself, Easton understood the plight of people of color and the devastating affects slavery had on them. Consequently, he urged white Americans to do what was ethically, morally, and spiritually correct in regard to their treatment of black people.

Easton opposed the racism and prejudice that erupted against people of color in northern cities during the 1820s and 1830s. His work disproves the simple idea that before the Civil War, the North was uniformly for equality while the South was for slavery. Easton described atrocities committed by white northerners against black people and their communities, how mobs attacked people of color as they left church and as they traveled from place to place. He also described name-calling, vandalism, looting, and the burning down of black homes, churches, and other buildings. Easton addressed white people's refusal to see black people as human beings and the way they poisoned the minds of their children about the races.

The surge of racial violence which Easton described occurred immediately after the Revolutionary War. As black people in the North were gradually emancipated, they became educated, managed their resources, and improved their financial circumstances. Black communities began to thrive. Many white Americans saw elite black communities as a threat. Such black achievers disproved the myths whites had created about black people. In addition, whites saw this class of blacks as a threat to white economic and political supremacy. Hosea Easton fought against this response. He could not reconcile the idea that people had fought together for the country's freedom, and yet they allowed race to divide them after that freedom was won. Easton's own father, James, was a veteran of the Revolutionary War.

Hosea Easton's family tree can be traced back to Africans and Narragansett Indians via the son and grandson of Nicholas Easton, one of the founders of Newport,

Rhode Island, in 1639. According to George R. Rice and James Brewer Stewart in *To Heal the Scourge of Prejudice: The Life and Writings of Hosea Easton*, during the latter half of the seventeenth century, the Eastons became Quakers, and they freed their slaves in the 1690s.

The black branch of the Easton family became members of the elite class of African Americans which developed in the years following the Revolutionary War. James Easton, Hosea's father, was a self-educated man who saw himself, his family, people of color, white Americans, and all other people from a worldwide view—a perspective that he passed on to the members of his family, especially his youngest son, Hosea. James Easton believed all people to be equal; he taught his children this belief and he demonstrated it in his own life.

Hosea Easton was first exposed to his father's stance against racism when he was about two years old. The church the Easton family attended erected a Negro gallery where all colored members of the congregation were to sit. Previously church members sat wherever they chose. James Easton refused to submit to this act of racism in the church sanctuary. He and his family continued to sit on the main floor of the church until they were literally forced out of the church. In a similar situation, at another church, Easton purchased a pew for his family from a white member who empathized with persons affected by a law relegating the colored members of the church to a segregated part of the church. When the James Easton family continued to occupy the pew against the wishes of church officials and members, the family came one Sunday to find that the pew had been painted with tar. The undaunted James Easton, his wife, Sarah, and their seven children responded by returning the following Sunday with their own chairs. This conflict continued until the Eastons were barred from the church.

Abolitionist and Minister

Hosea was groomed like his older brothers and sisters to be an abolitionist, and decided to enter the ministry. His duties as minister complemented his commitment to abolitionism since the black church was a major forum for the black protest movement. Easton saw his duties as multifaceted: most importantly he wanted to advocate black self-improvement and work to instill faith and optimism in those who suffered from racism.

In 1831, Easton attended the first annual National Convention of Free People of Color in Philadelphia. One outcome of this meeting was that Easton began working to raise money to build a manual labor school for young men of color. The plan was to build the school in New Haven, Connecticut, in partnership with Yale University. The plan failed, however, because of white resistance. Easton also served as president of the Hartford Literary and Religious Institution, one of many Negro self-improvement organizations in northern cities. The expressed purposes of these organizations was to promote education and encourage discussion of social, political, and economic issues, helping members to express themselves in a public forum. Thus, while he advocated abolition, Easton also tried to empower black people by preparing them to function as social equals to whites.

As a minister, Hosea Easton used scripture to argue for racial equality. In his "A Treatise on the Intellectual Character, and the Civil and Political Condition of the Colored People of the United States; and the Prejudice Exercised Towards Them: With a Sermon on the Duty of the Church to Them," he tried to explain the social problem in hopes of creating a change of heart in white society. According to Rice and Stewart in *To Heal the Scourge of Prejudice: The Life and Writings of Hosea Easton*, the treatise was revered for its "analytical scope and its expressive power" in these regards and for the two premises upon which the whole work stands: that people of all colors are created by God and the nobility of African American ancestry is worthy to be recognized and praised. Hosea Easton died in Boston in 1837.

REFERENCES

Books

Dick, Robert C. *Black Protest: Emphasis and Tactics*. Westport, Conn.: Greenwood Press, 1974.

Price, George R. and James Brewer Stewart, eds. *To Heal the Scourge of Prejudice: The Life and Writings of Hosea Easton*. Amherst: University of Massachusetts Press, 1999.

Quarles, Benjamin. *Black Abolitionists*. Oxford: Oxford University Press, 1969.

Online

Price, George R., and James Brewer Stewart. "The Roberts Case, the Easton Family, & the Dynamics of the Abolitionist Movement in Massachusetts, 1776-1870." http://www.historycooperative.org/journals/mhr/4/price.html (Accessed 25 February 2006).

Jewell B. Parham

James Conway Farley
1854–1910

Photographer

James Conway Farley is recognized as the first African American photographer. Photography became popular in the 1840s, but very few African Americans were involved in the early years of its introduction to the public. Farley overcame adversity and discrimination to master the photographic process and become a successful businessman.

James Farley was the son of slaves in Prince Edward County, Virginia, born on August 10, 1854. In 1861, after the death of his father, his mother moved with the young Farley to Richmond, Virginia. In order to support the family financially, Farley's mother worked as a storeroom keeper at the Columbia Hotel in Richmond, Virginia. Early on Farley worked to help support the family as well. He was an assistant in making candles by tying strings and getting the candle molds ready for the hot grease. At night, Farley would visit an old cook who taught him how to read and write. The cook used an old linen book to help Farley become literate. He was lucky enough to be given a chance to attend a public school for three years to further his education. Farley struggled to continue his education and support the family financially. He became an apprentice to learn the trade of a baker, but he worked only briefly. In 1872, he was employed in the chemical department of the photographic business of C. R. Rees and Company in downtown Richmond.

Finds His Niche

Through hard work, Farley became familiar with the photographic process. In May 1875, he became an operator for the G. W. Davis Photographic Gallery on Broad Street in Richmond. At this time, the four white men employed as operators at the gallery protested the employment of Farley because he was African American and insisted they would not work if Farley's employment continued. Mr. Davis, the proprietor of the gallery, tried to sort out the real reason for their disapproval. The men claimed that Farley was disagreeable. When confronted

Chronology	
1854	Born in Prince Edward County, Virginia on August 10
1861	Moves, along with his mother, to Richmond, Virginia
1872	Begins employment at C. R. Rees and Company
1875	Makes photographs for the G. W. Davis Photographic Gallery
1876	Marries Rebecca P. Robinson on December 10
1878	Joins the First Baptist Church in Richmond, Virginia
1879	Serves as operator of the G. W. Davis Photographic Gallery
1884	Wins first prize for his exhibit at the Colored Industrial Fair
1885	Wins a premium at the New Orleans World Exposition
1895	Opens his studio, the Jefferson Fine Arts Gallery
1910	Dies in Richmond, Virginia

with the document containing the complaint, Farley expressed his appreciation for Mr. Davis, whom he did not want to trouble. Then Davis stunned Farley by telling him that he had fired the white operators.

This benevolent act inspired Farley to use this opportunity to learn all he could about the photographic process and become a first-class operator. Together, Davis and Farley improved the business, and Davis was able to establish a gallery that was less expensive. Over the next four years, Farley continued to excel in the photographic business. At one time, Farley was said to have produced more photographs in one day than were produced in any other gallery in the southern states.

Farley's work was displayed at the 1884 Colored Industrial Fair held in Richmond. He received first prize. His work was also displayed at the 1885 World's Exposition in New Orleans. There he received numerous compliments and was awarded a premium for his achievements.

In 1895, Farley started his own photography studio, the Jefferson Fine Arts Gallery. His gallery specialized in taking the photos of individuals and groups and converting them into greeting cards. Because of the excellent work that Farley produced, he was sought after by whites and African Americans.

Farley married Rebecca P. Robinson on December 10, 1876. Their union produced seven daughters. His accomplishments afforded them a comfortable life, and he continued to be respected by others in his profession. In 1910, Farley died in Richmond, Virginia. Today little evidence remains of his amazing work. The Valentine Museum in Richmond displayed one of his photographs until 1982. A single photograph remains as a testimony to his genius and skill.

REFERENCES

Books

"James C. Farley." *Dictionary of American Negro Biography.* Eds. Rayford W. Logan and Michael R. Winston. New York: Norton, 1982.

Simmons, William J. *Men of Mark.* Chicago: Johnson Publishing Company Inc., 1970.

Online

Richings, G. F. *Evidence of Progress Among Colored People: Electronic Edition.* University of North Carolina at Chapel Hill, 2000. http://docsouth.unc.edu/church/richings/richings.html (Accessed 2 February 2006).

Connie Mack

Mel Farr

Mel Farr
1944–

Football player, automobile dealership owner

elvin Farr was born on November 3, 1944, in Beaumont, Texas, the younger of two sons of Miller and Dorthea Farr. Dorthea Farr did domestic work; Miller Farr drove a cement truck and sold used cars to provide a second income. In 1960, he had opened a car dealership, Farr's New and Used. Both sons, Miller Jr. and Melvin, worked part-time in their father's used car business. Melvin, later known as Mel, and Miller Jr. helped their father look for old cars that could be repaired and sold for a profit. They would clean cars and make an initial showing of the cars to customers while Miller Sr. handled the actual sales. From his father, Mel gained experience in running a car dealership and the belief that determination and hard work allow people to overcome obstacles and succeed.

A versatile athlete, Farr graduated from Beaumont's Herbert High School in 1963, receiving All-State honors in track and football and All-District honors in basket-

ball. Awarded a scholarship to UCLA, Farr was an outstanding tailback and was named a consensus All-American in his junior and senior years. He was inducted into the UCLA Hall of Fame in 1988. In 1967, Farr was the seventh player chosen overall in the National Football League draft and the first choice of the Detroit Lions. He was given a three-year $94,000 contract. Outstanding in his first season, he was named NFL Rookie of the Year and Offensive MVP of the Year. Farr's assumption that his first year success would enable him to earn a higher salary met with the Detroit Lion's flat refusal to negotiate. Farr's agent was unable to attract contracts for him to endorse commercial products, though he did receive $500 as Rookie of the Year.

Farr had an exceptional record with the Lions, becoming a top all-time scorer with thirty-six career touchdowns. Though an injury caused Farr to miss half of the 1968 season, he was again named MVP and chosen for the Pro-Bowl. In 1969, Farr was named co-captain of the Lions and in 1971 was again selected for the Pro-Bowl. In Farr's last season, 1973, his older brother, Miller Farr Jr., formerly an all-star in the American Football League, also played for the Detroit Lions. Traded to Houston in 1974, Mel Farr instead chose retirement from professional football.

While hospitalized at age twenty-three in his second season, Farr realized that professional football might not

Chronology

1944	Born in Beaumont, Texas on November 3
1967	Drafted by the Detroit Lions
1968	Named NFL Rookie of the Year and Offensive MVP of the Year
1971	Completes B.A in political science, University of Detroit
1974	Retires from professional football
1975	Purchases Ford franchise in Oak Park, Michigan, with John Cook
1977	Cook-Farr Ford listed as one of the Top 100 Companies by *Black Enterprise*
1978	Buys out Cook's share of the dealership
1988	Inducted into the UCLA Hall of Fame
1990	Establishes Triple M Financing Co.
1992	Named the *Black Enterprise* Auto Dealer of the Year
1999	Acquires a loan of $36.5 million
2000	Begins selling his Ford and Lincoln-Mercury franchises when his loan payments fall behind
2002	Divorces Mae Forbes
2004	Marries Linda Johnson Rice

be a long-term career or make him rich. He began to plan for a business career after football. Farr entered Ford Motor Company's dealer development program. Working in football's off season, Farr sought to identify blacks who could qualify as future Ford auto dealers but could only find a handful, none of whom had the needed financial resources. After discussion among top executives, Ford Motor Company started a black dealer development program. Farr spent several years in the program, learning the details of managing a dealership, including methods of cost accounting for each vehicle in the inventory. It was necessary to keep track of all costs associated with acquiring, maintaining, and selling each vehicle in order to determine the necessary selling price to keep the dealership profitable. Farr continued playing football in order to save enough cash to purchase an auto dealership. He also enrolled in evening classes at the University of Detroit, completing his bachelor's degree in political science in 1971.

Farr married Mae R. Forbes with whom he had three children, sons Melvin Jr. and Michael, and daughter Monet. Both sons later played football at the University of California, Los Angeles, and in the National Football League. Farr remained married to Mae for over thirty-five years, sharing interests in tennis, golf, and travel. Farr was divorced in 2002, and in 2004, he married Linda Johnson Rice, president and chief executive officer of Johnson Publishing Co., publisher of *Ebony* and *Jet* magazines and owner of the Ebony Fashion Fair cosmetic line and touring fashion show.

Becomes Automobile Dealer

Farr became an auto dealer in 1975, when he formed a partnership with John Cook, a retired dealer with whom Farr worked while in the dealer development program. Cook and Farr invested $40,000 each to purchase a Ford franchise in Oak Park, Michigan, a small town on the northern border of Detroit. When Cook-Farr Ford, Inc. opened for business, Farr took sales as his primary responsibility while Cook was in charge of the finances. In 1977, *Black Enterprise* listed Cook-Farr Ford in its top 100 companies, having $9.8 million in gross income. Its 1978 revenues of $14.6 million made it sixteenth on the list of the largest black-owned businesses in the United States.

However, problems loomed. The partners disagreed about how to run the business with Farr wanting a bigger and wider marketing approach than did Cook. Farr bought Cook's share of the business in 1978 and found out that the dealership had serious financial problems.

In 1979 an economic recession occurred in the United States due to the Iranian hostage crisis and rising oil prices. The situation caused long lines at gasoline stations and spiked the public's desire for fuel efficient cars, few of which were available from Ford automobile dealers. While many automobile dealers, black and white, went out of business, Farr took aggressive and innovative actions to survive. Farr reduced his employees by half and did both sales and janitorial work. Needing loans to keep his business operating, Farr energized other blacks to start the Black Ford-Lincoln-Mercury Dealers Association in order to lobby the federal government for loans to black auto dealers. Successful, Farr borrowed $200,000 each from the Small Business Administration and Ford Motor Company. Farr also was a co-founder of the National Association of Minority Auto Dealers, serving for a time as chairman of its board of directors.

In addition, Farr initiated a television advertising campaign, using his football persona, "Mel Farr, Superstar," to attract customers to his dealership. Lacking money to pay an ad agency, Farr planned, wrote, and appeared in each commercial, even using his own video camera to film them. Tough, low-budget, and amateurish, the commercials appealed to the public. Farr added a red cape to his business suit and imitated Superman flying through the air. His message was "Mel Farr to the Rescue," combating high prices, guaranteeing payment for any vehicle traded in, regardless of condition, and offering a "Farr Better Deal." Farr's business rebounded and the commercials became a trademark and a key to his long-term survival and to his unusual success as one of a few who owned multiple dealerships.

As Farr's success and revenues grew in his Oak Park location, he wanted to acquire ownership of franchises in other locations and become the largest African American business owner in the nation. Using loans from banks and from Ford Motor Co. credit department, Farr acquired auto dealerships in five states; most of them were either Ford or Lincoln-Mercury dealerships, located in Michigan or Ohio. In 1986, Farr purchased a Lincoln-Mercury dealership in Waterford, Michigan, and named his brother Miller Jr. its general manager. Also in 1986, he acquired a Ford franchise in Aurora, Colorado, but he sold it after thirty months because it was too far away for him to supervise adequately. After six years of effort, in 1989, Farr was awarded a Toyota franchise in Bloomfield Hills, Michigan. In 1993, he added Mazda and Volkswagen franchises to this location. Farr bought a Ford dealership in Fairfield, Ohio, a Cincinnati suburb, and appointed Melvin Jr. the general manager. Farr also acquired Ford dealerships in Grand Blanc, Michigan in 1993, and in Houston, Texas and Baltimore, Maryland in 1996. A Lincoln-Mercury franchise was bought in Dayton, Ohio in 1993. In 1996, Farr opened a Hyundai / Suzuki / Kia dealership and a Used Car Superstore on thirteen acres of land in Ferndale, Michigan.

Wins High Praise

Accolades followed. *Black Enterprise* named Farr the BE Auto Dealer of the Year in 1992, citing his ability to withstand a 1991 recession with a 16 percent increase in sales to $106 million. According to the magazine, Farr's companies had "the sixth-highest volume of any Ford dealer in 1991 and ranked second in sales in Escort and Festiva economy cars." Farr's 1991 sales placed him fifth among black dealers, but by 1998, Farr Automotive Group was number one among African American auto dealers. That year, *Crain's Detroit Business* declared Farr's automotive group "the 19th-largest privately held corporation in metro Detroit." A year later, *Black Enterprise* listed Farr's company as the number one enterprise among all African American-owned companies in the United States with gross sales of $596.6 million in 1998.

Throughout his business career, Farr had shown an unusual willingness to take risks, many of which brought him considerable success. In the 1990s, Farr decided, first, to tap the largely underserved market of those with poor credit, and, second, to open a nationwide chain of used car superstores to serve the so-called "sub-prime" market. Triple M Financing Co. was established by Farr in 1990 to support and expand his businesses. Specializing in high-risk auto loans, Triple M had eighty employees in 1999, over 12,000 clients, and almost $50 million in outstanding loans, according to the *Michigan Chronicle*. Farr sought to greatly increase the financial resources of Triple M and the number of used cars he could sell nationwide. Triple M employees were trained to monitor their clients' payment record closely. Those whose payments were two days late received phone calls. Vehicles were repossessed if payments were two

weeks late. In 1999, Farr began adding to each used car an electronic device that would automatically prevent the car from starting if the customer was not up-to-date with payments. Many praised Farr for enabling people with low incomes to have transportation while some complained about high interest rates and the electronic device, claiming it had shut the engine off while they were driving in traffic. In 2000, Farr settled lawsuits about the devices by issuing coupons worth $200 to 1,500 customers, according to *Black Enterprise*. Farr's company sponsored workshops on credit and budgeting personal finances to make his customers better consumers.

Farr's efforts to expand his sub-prime auto loan business led to the collapse of his new car dealerships. Farr sought a large loan from a consortium of Wall Street investors to expand his used car business to customers with sub-prime credit. With the help of civil rights leader Jesse Jackson, after fifteen months of negotiations, Farr was given a loan of $36.5 million in August 1999 with 4,500 signed leases of his high-risk credit customers as collateral that the loan would be repaid. By January 2000, the financial arrangements had proved unfavorable to Farr. He was not collecting enough money from his customers to keep up payments to either the Wall Street investors or to Ford Motor Co. Ford Motor Co., stating it wanted to emphasize selling new cars, pressed Farr to sell his Ford and Lincoln-Mercury franchises, all of which were sold between 2000 and early 2002. Eventually, Farr had to dispose of his foreign car franchises also, leaving him with his Triple M Financing Co, his used car superstore in Ferndale, Michigan, and dreams of expanding it into a chain of superstores.

REFERENCES

Periodicals

Bray, Hiawatha. "Mr. Touchdown." *Black Enterprise* 22 (June 1992): 154-60.

Hughes, Allen and Lloyd Gite. "Driving in a New Direction?" *Black Enterprise* 32 (April 2002): 25.

"Mel Farr Automotive Group No. 1 African American-Owned Enterprise in the United States." *Michigan Chronicle*, 2-8 June 1999: A10.

Rousch, Matt. "In the Car Game, He's Been a Superstar." *Crain's Detroit Business*, 30 March 1998: E14

Snavely, Brent. "Mel Farr Empire Falls to Earth." *Crain's Detroit Business*, 1 April 2002: 3, 32.

Williams-Harold, Bevolyn. "The Loaded Sticker Price." *Black Enterprise* 29 (June 1999): 131-32.

De Witt S. Dykes, Jr.

Arthur Huff Fauset
1899–1983

Anthropologist, educator

Arthur Huff Fauset was the fourth known African American to receive the Ph.D. in anthropology. His dissertation, *Black Gods of the Metropolis: Negro Religious Cults of the Urban North*, was first published in 1944. As a young man, he won prizes in the Urban League's Opportunity contests. He also wrote books and articles in the areas of folklore and history. He had a long career as a school principal in Philadelphia, during which time he fought for better working conditions for teachers, as well as for civil rights for blacks and other disadvantaged people.

Arthur Huff Fauset was born on January 20, 1899, in Flemington, New Jersey. His parents were Redmon and Bella Huff Fauset. Redmon Fauset was a widower with seven children when he married Bella Huff, who already had three children from her previous marriage. The couple then had three children of their own, two boys and a girl. Arthur was the second of the three.

Arthur was the half-brother of Jessie Redmon Fauset (1882-1961), the youngest child of Redmon Fauset's previous marriage. Jessie Fauset, the first known black woman to be elected to Phi Beta Kappa, was a major figure in the Harlem Renaissance both as a literary editor of the NAACP's influential magazine *The Crisis* and through her creative writing.

The Fauset family was well-established in the Philadelphia area, having lived there since the eighteenth century. Redmon was an African Methodist Episcopal minister who did not have extensive formal education himself, but he recognized the value of an education. He did not always agree with the views of his fellow ministers, and his outspokenness may have been a factor in his having to pastor many small churches, including one in Flemington, Arthur's birthplace, in order to support his family.

Bella Huff Fauset was white, of Jewish background, and was a convert to Christianity. Her previous husband had been black also. She had no patience with prejudice. Like Reverend Fauset, she stressed the value of an education, and she was a positive influence on Arthur's aspirations. Reverend Fauset died in 1903, when Arthur was about four years old. Bella Fauset survived her husband for twenty years.

Arthur Huff Fauset married Crystal Dreda Bird in 1931. The couple divorced in 1944. Crystal Bird Fauset was a community leader and activist who achieved distinction in politics. Upon her election in 1938 to the Assembly of the Commonwealth of Pennsylvania, she became the first known black woman elected to a state

Chronology

1899	Born in Flemington, New Jersey on January 20
1918	Begins career as public school teacher and administrator
1931	*Folklore from Nova Scotia* published by the American Folklore Association
1942	Receives Ph.D. in anthropology from the University of Pennsylvania
1944	Publishes *Black Gods of the Metropolis*
1946	Retires from public education career in Philadelphia
1983	Dies in Philadelphia on September 2

legislature. Among his various affiliations, Arthur Huff Fauset was a fellow in the American Anthropological Association and a member of Alpha Phi Alpha Fraternity. He died on September 2, 1983 in Philadelphia.

Prepares for Career

Educated at Central High School in Philadelphia, Fauset secured his teaching credentials after studying at the Philadelphia School of Pedagogy for Men. He received all of his higher degrees at the University of Pennsylvania: his B.A. in 1921, his M.A. in 1924, and his Ph.D. in 1942.

Fauset began to teach elementary school in Philadelphia in 1918. He performed extremely well on the principals' qualifying examinations, and he requested an immediate assignment. School officials granted his request, although they then systematically transferred all the white students from the previously integrated Joseph Singerly (elementary) School. Fauset became its principal in 1926. In 1938, when an annex was built to address overcrowding, Fauset led the intensive campaign to have the school named for Frederick Douglass. The board of education, consisting of all whites, opposed doing so, considering Douglass too radical. The black community's efforts were successful, however, and Fauset remained principal of the newly renamed Douglass Singerly School until his retirement in 1946.

During his career, Fauset provided leadership in improving the conditions of teachers, and he worked diligently for civil rights. In the early 1930s, he was vice-president of the Philadelphia Teachers' Union. He was a member of the Urban League and of the National Negro Congress (NNC), the latter an activist organization that pursued equity issues more aggressively than most civil rights groups of the time.

Also in the thirties, Fauset served as president of the Philadelphia Council of the NNC as well as its national vice president. He left the organization when he felt it was not addressing the issues most important to African Americans. Fauset did not align himself with the leftist political wing of the group, but the influence of the Communist Party in the NNC led to problems in his pursuit of opportunities later.

Starting in the late 1930s, Fauset had a regular column in the *Philadelphia Tribune* called "I Write as I See." He also wrote short pieces published in the *Philadelphia Independent*. After the United States entered World War II, he volunteered for the army despite being well beyond the draft age. In addition to believing in the rightness of the cause, he was also eager to obtain first-hand experience in order to fight segregation in the military. He attended the Officers Training School and the Administrative School in Iowa, but he was not commissioned as a second lieutenant as expected. His activism, especially his association with the NNC, was the probable reason. He nonetheless received an honorable discharge.

Upon his return to Philadelphia in 1943, Fauset continued his work to improve conditions for blacks. He joined the United Peoples' Action Committee, a civil rights organization, and served as its chairman until 1946. He also edited *The People's Voice*, a Philadelphia edition of the New York-based publication co-founded by Adam Clayton Powell.

After 1946, he traveled abroad, spending time in Europe and in Egypt. He lived for a year in Mexico, an experience which prepared him to educate Spanish speakers later. He lived in New York City beginning in the 1950s. In the era of McCarthyism, his association with the NNC and with the United Peoples' Action Committee (also considered radical for the time) led to Fauset's being expelled from the New York Public School system in 1960. Fauset continued to teach in New York, and that city was his home base into the 1960s and 1970s. However, he did not hold any long-term positions. It was during this period that he taught English at the Spanish American Institute. He also founded a school designed to teach English and business basics to Spanish speakers. Insufficiently funded, the school did not last long.

Engages in Research and Creative Writing

Fauset's initial research and publications were in folklore, a focus which grew out of his anthropological studies. In the summer of 1923, he collected folklore in Nova Scotia. The project was developed through his work with Dr. Frank G. Speck, his advisor and chairman of the Department of Anthropology at the University of Pennsylvania. Dr. Elsie Clews Parsons, an intrepid pioneer in the folklore studies, sponsored the project and served as a mentor both on and off site.

The research provided the basis for Fauset's M.A. thesis in anthropology. It also resulted in his article, "Folklore from the Half-Breeds in Nova Scotia," published in *Journal of American Folklore* in 1925, as well as the basis for his *Folklore of Nova Scotia*, published in 1931. Fauset focused on collecting stories told by Negroes or descendants of Negroes who had settled in Nova Scotia in previ-

ous generations. He reported finding few carryovers with the folklore of blacks in the United States, a major reason being that wide and thin distribution of blacks in Nova Scotia. Fauset learned personally that prejudice based on color was present in Nova Scotia when he had difficulty securing lodging and other services.

Also in the 1920s, Fauset gathered folklore in Philadelphia and in the deep South (Alabama, Mississippi, and Louisiana), and he visited the British Islands of the Lesser Antilles. In 1922, he published "A Tale of the North Carolina Woods" in *Crisis*. In 1925, his "The Negro's Cycle of Song— A Review" was published in *Opportunity*. His article "Tales and Riddles Collected in Philadelphia" was published in 1928 in *Journal of American Folklore*. His other articles dealing with folk tradition include "Jumby," which drew on his travel to the West Indies, published in *Ebony and Topaz* (1927), and "Safe in the Arms of Jesus" published in *Opportunity* (1929).

The folklore research is relevant to Fauset's links to the Harlem Renaissance. Alain Locke, a key spokesperson for the Renaissance, was also a native of Philadelphia and a friend of the Fauset family. Locke had encouraged Fauset to obtain a college degree even though Fauset had already started his full-time career in the public schools. Aware of Fauset's folklore research, Locke solicited two selections for inclusion in *The New Negro: An Interpretation* (1925), edited by Locke. Fauset's contributions are "American Negro Folk Literature" and "Negro Folk Lore: A Bibliography."

In 1926, Fauset won first prize in two of the competitions sponsored by the journal *Opportunity*: the short story division prize for "Symphonesque" and the essay division prize for "Segregation." *Opportunity*, published under the leadership of Dr. Charles S. Johnson, the Urban League's director, was a major supporter of the work of young black artists developing in the Harlem Renaissance. "Symphonesque" was republished in Edward J. O'Brien's *The Best Short Stories of 1926* as well as in the *O. Henry Memorial Award Prize Short Stories* series for that year.

In about 1924, the Ethiopian Publishing Company of Philadelphia issued *Booker T. Washington*, a brief work by Fauset. Of his books dealing with African American history, Fauset is better known, however, as the author of *For Freedom: A Biographical Story of the American Negro* (1927; rpt 1934) and *Sojourner Truth: God's Faithful Pilgrim* (1938). Although they are not limited to young readers, the books are intended for such an audience. In his introduction to *For Freedom*, Fauset notes, "It is told in the spirit of young folk because they, more than any of us, are able to re-live the lives and struggles of heroic characters with that innocence and fidelity of interpretation which are so essential to a true understanding of the elements which underlie human aspirations."

In introducing his volume on Sojourner Truth, Fauset emphasizes her revolutionary stance and notes that she was a rebel "despite her firm allegiance to Jehovah—or shall we say because of it." The book was favorably reviewed for its engaging narrative.

Fauset's major scholarly work is *Black Gods of the Metropolis: Negro Religious Cults of the Urban North*, his Ph.D. dissertation. The work was published by the University of Pennsylvania in 1944 and reissued by the press in 1971. The book considers five groups: the Mt. Sinai Holy Church of America; the United House of Prayer for All People; the Church of God, which identified itself as a group of Black Jews; the Moorish Science Temple of America; and the Father Divine Peace Mission Movement. All of the organizations were based in Philadelphia, except the Father Divine Movement, which was based then in New York.

Fauset conducted interviews and observed services and other activities by each group. At times, his status as a non-member of the sect was viewed with suspicion and he was not given full access to information. Fauset nonetheless obtained much detail to help describe each sect as objectively as possible. In summarizing his findings, Fauset states that there is no evidence to claim a "religious 'bent'" among Negroes. He cites the effects of segregation and discrimination as key in understanding emphasis on religion: "It is a fair inference that the apparent over-emphasis by the American Negro in the religious sphere is related to the comparative meager participation of Negroes in other institutional forms of American culture, such as business, politics, and industry, a condition which is bound up intimately with the prevailing custom of racial dichotomy which restricts the normal participation of Negroes in many avenues of American life." Fauset also asserts that social needs would probably receive more attention by the church in the future: "[A]s the evidence of some of the cults indicates,...the American Negro church is likely to witness a transformation from its purely religious function to functions which will accommodate the urgent social needs of the Negro masses under modern stresses of politics and economics." When the book was republished in 1971, Fauset quoted this assertion in his "Author's Note to the Paperback Edition," with the inference that he had indeed been correct.

The book was generally favorably reviewed. Reviewers praised Fauset's careful research and scholarship. A common criticism, however, was that the work could profit from being placed in a wider context, perhaps through comparative discussion and by giving more attention to analysis. Fauset recognized that he was dealing with a relatively small segment of non-traditional religious bodies even within the Negro church experience, and his purpose was descriptive more than analytical. In introducing the 1971 edition of *Black Gods*, the anthropologist John Szwed points out that the descriptive focus on an African American religious context is part of the book's singular importance.

In 1969, Fauset co-authored *America: Red, White, Black, Yellow* with Nellie Rathbone Bright, also a former Philadelphia school principal. Like *For Freedom* and *Sojourner Truth*, the work was especially meant for young readers and had been developed at the request of the Philadelphia school system's leaders. Fauset never lost interest in writing and the arts. While still based in Philadelphia before his retirement, he was co-founder of a cultural arts group called the Black Opals and was co-editor of its review of the same name.

Arthur Huff Fauset succeeded as scholar, educator, activist, and—throughout these endeavors—as author. His publications in folklore and anthropology document with clarity and without polemics the beliefs and practices of a variety of cultural groups outside the mainstream of their societies. As an activist, he wrote newspaper columns and essays attacking discriminatory practices, and while in various positions of leadership, he fought to change those practices. Despite difficulties resulting from his activism, he remained committed to the cause of social justice, the unifying principle of his life and work. In an interview with Carole H. Carpenter in 1970, Fauset fittingly characterized himself as having been "a fighting leader."

REFERENCES

Books

"Arthur Huff Fauset." *Encyclopedia of African-American Culture and History.* 5 vols. New York: Macmillan, 1996.

Carpenter, Carole H. "Arthur Huff Fauset, Campaigner for Social Justice: A Symphony of Diversity." In *African-American Pioneers in Anthropology.* Eds. Ira E. Harrison and Faye V. Harrison. Urbana, Ill.: University of Illinois Press, 1999.

Hudson, Theodore R. "Fauset, Arthur Huff." *The Oxford Companion to African American Literature.* New York: Oxford University Press, 1997.

Periodicals

"Arthur H. Fauset, Ex-Principal in Phila." *Philadelphia Inquirer*, 5 September 1983.

Mezzacappa, Dale. "Looking Back, Looking Ahead School Rededicates Itself to Douglass' Ideals" *Philadelphia Inquirer*, 19 May 1988.

Collections

Many of Fauset's papers are in the Rare Book and Manuscript Library at the University of Pennsylvania. The Papers of Arthur Huff Fauset, 1855-1983, consist of 412 folders, five scrapbooks, and one portfolio (32 boxes). Materials include correspondence; addresses; published and unpublished short stories; and the unpublished autobiographical novel. (The beginning date is 1855 because of a ledger beginning in that year for the Union Building and Loan Association, Philadelphia.) The Rare Book and Manuscript Library also contains a copy of Fauset's book *Booker T. Washington* and 1941 correspondence he had with Marian Anderson.

The Memorial University of Newfoundland Folklore and Language Archive (St. John's) has tapes of the interviews conducted by Professor Carole H. Carpenter of York University (Toronto) with AHF in New York on February 27, 1970, and on June 29, 1970. These tapes are also on deposit at the Ontario Folklore-Folklife Archives of the Ontario Folklife Center at York University (Toronto). The latter center also includes additional documentation, photographs, and works by and about AHF.

Arlene Clift-Pellow

Miles Mark Fisher
1899–1970

Minister, educator, church historian, writer

Miles Mark Fisher, a Baptist minister, educator, and writer, is best known as a church historian of the black church. He wrote several scholarly articles and monographs. His work on the origin of Negro slave songs established his reputation. Fisher's career in the church defined both his life and his teachings. Recognized as an outstanding black preacher and leader of his time, Fisher practiced a social gospel philosophy in his churches, reaching out to the community with innovative programs.

From birth, Fisher seemed destined for church ministry. As the son of a clergyman, he no doubt was encouraged to follow in his father's footsteps. His parents, Elijah John and Florida Neely Fisher, were former slaves who considered education and Christian service essential to their son's development. Fisher was born in Atlanta, Georgia, on October 29, 1899 but spent his formative years in Chicago where his father ministered at the Olivet Baptist Church.

Fisher's parents influenced both his educational and ministerial pursuits. His home environment was intellectually stimulating. Fisher and his father worked together to teach his mother to read. After receiving his elementary and high school education in the Chicago public schools, Fisher was sent to his father's alma mater, Morehouse College, in Atlanta. His undergraduate studies included basic training for the gospel ministry. He graduated with a B.A degree in 1918 and was ordained for the ministry at the same time. After college, he was

Chronology

1899	Born in Atlanta, Georgia on October 29
1914	Completes high school in Chicago, Illinois
1918	Graduates from Morehouse College with A.B.
1918	Ordained as a Baptist minister
1919	Begins career as a Baptist minister in Chicago
1922	Granted a B.D. from Northern Baptist Theological Seminary; awarded an A.M. from the University of Chicago
1923-28	Serves as English instructor at Virginia Union University then transfers to Richmond Theological Seminary as J. B. Hoyt professor of church history and New Testament Greek
1928-38	Pastor at Sixteenth Baptist Church, Huntington, West Virginia
1930	Marries Ada Virginia Foster on September 6
1933	Lectures on the history of religion at Shaw University
1933-64	Pastor at Rock Baptist Church, Durham, North Carolina
1941	Awarded an honorary D.D. from Shaw University
1948	Earns Ph.D. from the University of Chicago Divinity School
1953	His book, *Negro Slave Songs*, wins the American Historical Association's outstanding history volume of the year
1954	Listed as one of the nation's top ten black ministers by *Ebony* magazine
1958	Wins the Golden Anniversary Award from the National Recreation Association
1965	Retires from active church ministry; awarded minister emeritus status
1970	Dies in Richmond, Virginia on December 14

employed briefly as a secretary for the YMCA at Camp Sherman, in Chilicothe, Ohio.

Begins Church Ministry

Fisher devoted his life to church ministry and teaching. His career as a Baptist minister spanned several decades, from 1919 until his retirement in 1965. His early ministerial placements were short-term, probably because at the time Fisher also was in school, writing, lecturing, or on teaching assignments.

His first call to preach came in 1919 when he was assigned to pastor the International Baptist Church in Chicago. While living in Chicago, he enrolled at Northern Baptist Theological Seminary in Lombard, Illinois. He was the only black ministerial student. The excellent preparation in Greek and Hebrew that he received at Morehouse benefited him, and he was able to offer tutoring sessions in exchange for carfare and lunch money.

The Anti-Saloon League hired Fisher as a lecturer in the summer of 1920. He traveled the country representing the league and speaking on temperance and moral living. Shortly after, he took another assignment at the Zion Baptist Church in Racine, Wisconsin. While serving there, Fisher was elected president of the Baptist State Convention of Wisconsin. He served from 1921 to 1922.

In 1922 at the age of twenty-three, Fisher was awarded a B.D. from Northern and an M.A. from the University of Chicago. He also began his writing career with the publication of two works, a biography of his father, whom he nicknamed the master slave, and an article on Lott Cary in Liberia, the first American Baptist missionary to Africa.

With his graduate studies behind him, Fisher moved from Chicago to Virginia where he held a number of pastoral assignments. He served as senior pastor at the Elam Baptist Church in Charles City County and at Second Liberty Baptist in New Kent County. He also assisted at the Fourth Baptist Church in Richmond.

While serving as pastor at the Elam Baptist Church, Fisher taught at Virginia Union University. He joined the faculty in 1923 as an English instructor but later transferred to the University's Richmond Theological Seminary as J.B. Hoyt professor of church history and New Testament Greek. During his tenure at Union, Fisher joined with a group of young radical scholars, who were often embroiled in controversial disputes. He renounced biblical fundamentalism and openly espoused an evolutionist view. He also declared that the virgin birth was nothing more than symbolism. When the Baptist General Association called for his dismissal, his friend, Gordon Hancock, head of the department of economics and sociology, intervened on his behalf. In spite of the controversies that erupted from time to time, Fisher and a group of young academics at Union brought distinction to the school in the 1920s. Fisher's contributions included a history of the achievements of Virginia Union University completed 1924 and a number of papers presented at annual organizational meetings. An article on the Negro and World War II published in 1925 discussed the migration of blacks from south to north and how participation in the church affected their lives. Fisher left Virginia Union in 1928 to take up his next assignment at the Sixteenth Baptist Church in Huntington, West Virginia. He remained there for five years. On September 6, 1930 he married Ada Virginia Foster. Six children were born to the couple, four sons and two daughters.

Serves Ministry at White Rock Church

By the time Fisher transferred to the White Rock Baptist Church, Durham, North Carolina in 1933, he was a seasoned preacher and church administrator although quite young. With a wife and growing family, he was ready to settle down with church ministry as his main pursuit. His tenure at White Rock lasted over thirty years, until his retirement in 1965.

The congregation consisted mostly of middle-class, educated blacks, but Fisher attracted others with his innovative community programs and leadership. His recreation programs attracted community youth. He sponsored a Boy Scouts program, a summer football league, a table tennis club, and a boxing team. His table tennis team toured the country. In addition he started a health clinic, a day nursery, an employment bureau, an adult education and job training program, and other self-help services. Fisher was also responsible for attracting black artists and lecturers to the area. His social gospel philosophy was criticized by some church members when he permitted the tobacco workers' union to hold meetings in the church. Fisher's ideal was for the church to be the central focus of the neighborhood, addressing needs not just one day a week but on a continuous basis. He planned for the future expansion of the church by establishing a building fund.

Fisher had a bold, forceful preaching style. Music played an integral part in his service, and he often featured different choirs and soloists. For an anniversary celebration in 1948, Fisher presented a program that was a distinctive blend of black history and Negro spirituals. This program was so popular that it became a permanent feature of the church's annual celebrations. Fisher believed that slave songs were some of the most original music of the nation. When he spoke on the history of the black church, he included some aspect of black spiritual music.

His contributions to the church and community did not go unnoticed or unrewarded. In 1954, Fisher was numbered among the nation's top ten black preachers by *Ebony* magazine. The National Recreation Association awarded him their Golden Anniversary Award in 1958 in recognition of the outstanding weekday recreation programs he had created for young people.

In 1933, during his pastorate at the White Rock in Durham, Fisher returned to teaching. As lecturer in the history of religion at Shaw University, Raleigh, North Carolina, he introduced courses on African American history. Fisher maintained a rigorous and productive schedule of preaching, writing, and teaching. In 1933 he wrote a history of the Baptist denomination published by the Sunday School Publishing Board in Nashville, Tennessee. Although a history of the entire Baptist denomination, Fisher highlighted the religious development of Negro Baptists who made up the majority of non-whites within the group. Another article in 1937 discussed organized religion and cults. Additional articles published between 1937 and 1963 were on black history and religion. Shaw University presented Fisher with an honorary D.D. in 1941, and he was inducted into the International Mark Twain Society as an honorary member.

During the summers, Fisher attended the University of Chicago Divinity School where he studied with William Warren Sweet, the church historian. Fisher completed his Ph.D. in 1948. His doctoral dissertation was the first ethno-historical study of Negro spirituals: *Negro Slave Songs in the United States* became Fisher's best-known work. It offered a new and radically secular interpretation and was awarded the prize for outstanding history volume of 1953 from the American Historical Association. Fisher concluded that slave songs were manifestations of African culture and as such were not truly religious in origin but songs of protest born out of the slaves' longing for freedom. He combed through historical documents, manuscripts, song collections, and other documentary records in various collections, looking for evidence. Fisher attempted to recreate the events and situations that gave rise to the songs. He believed that religion played an important part in the lives of slaves, but it was less important than their daily labor or dreams of escape. He concluded that the American Colonization Society and other back-to-Africa movements had a profound effect on slaves. He theorized that the slave psyche was steeped in African-oriented stories that naturally flowed out in songs, describing oppression, separation, and alienation from the mother country.

Fisher also suggested that lyrics in spirituals referred to the plight of the newly emancipated slave. For instance, mention of the Promised Land was not a reference to future glory but a yearning to return to the mother country, Africa. Since there was little contact between slaves, some songs were merely communication devices to convey messages of warning or caution about escapes or rebellions.

Many were skeptical of Fisher's interpretation. Some of his conclusions were contradicted by historical writers, including James Weldon Johnson, who believed that Fisher did not present enough evidence to prove his conclusions. Scholars agreed that spirituals were born from the day-to-day experiences of the slaves but the tonal development of spirituals grew out of their religious experience. Biblical expressions, examples in nature, and personal experiences were all woven together to form the materials out of which spirituals were fashioned. However viewed by critics, Fisher's book presents a different approach to the origin of the slave songs and as such is an important contribution to the study of black history and thought.

In Durham, North Carolina, Fisher was involved in reinvigorating a branch of the NAACP. He served as its president from 1933 to 1935. He also served with the Durham Interdenominational Ministerial Alliance and was a member of the executive board of the General Baptist State Convention of North Carolina.

Fisher retired from teaching and active church ministry in 1965. Although he stepped down from the pulpit, he continued to function as an emeritus pastor until his death on December 14, 1970. After that, the Baptist State Convention's Unified Program established a scholarship fund in his name. A housing development built adjacent to the White Rock Church was named the Miles Mark Fisher Heights in his honor.

REFERENCES

Books

Bardolph, Richard. *The Negro Vanguard*. New York: Rinehart and Company, 1959.

Fry, Gladys-Marie. *Night Riders in Black Folk History*. Knoxville, Tenn.: University of Tennessee Press, 1975.

Gavins, Raymond. *The Perils and Prospects of Southern Black Leadership: Gordon Blaine Hancock, 1884-1970*. Durham, N.C.: Duke University Press, 1977.

Hill, Samuel S., ed. *Encyclopedia of Religion in the South*. Macon, Georgia: Mercer, 1984.

Melton, J. Gordon. *Religious Leaders of America: A Biographical Guide to Founders and Leaders of Religious Bodies, Churches, and Spiritual Groups in North America*. Detroit: Gale Research, 1999.

Murphy, Larry G., J. Gordon Melton, and Gary L. Ward, eds. *Encyclopedia of African American Religions*. New York: Garland, 1993.

Porter, Dorothy, ed. *Selected Black American Authors: An Illustrated Bio-Bibliography*. Comp. James A. Page. Boston: G. K. Hall, 1977.

Thorpe, Earl E. *Black Historians: A critique*. New York: Morrow, 1969.

White, James T., ed. *National Cyclopedia of American Biography*, Vol. 56. Clifton, N.J.: James T. White, 1975.

Yenser, Thomas, ed. *Who's Who in Colored America: A Biographical Dictionary of Notable Living Persons of African Descent in America*. 4th ed. Brooklyn, New York: Thomas Yenser, 1937.

Periodicals

Davis, Lenwood G. "Miles Mark Fisher: Minister, Historian, and Cultural Philosopher." *Negro History Bulletin*, 36 (January-March 1983): 19-21.

Hudson, Arthur Palmer. "Negro Slave Songs in the United States" (Book Review). *American Literature* 26 (November 1954): 453-56.

Simms, David M. "The Negro Spiritual: Origins and Themes." *The Journal of Negro Education* 35 (Winter 1966): 35-41.

Janette Prescod

Arthur A. Fletcher
1924–2005

Political consultant, civil rights activist

A staunch Republican and a civil rights activist, Arthur Fletcher advised four Republican presidents and for three years headed the U.S. Civil Rights Commis-

Arthur A. Fletcher

sion. He had a keen interest in education, personally providing financial support for the legal case *Brown v. Board of Education in Topeka, Kansas*, where he wanted to desegregate public schools. His interest in the rights and benefits of blacks was demonstrated in many ways throughout his lifetime, including his support of the Civil Rights Act of 1991. He established the framework for affirmative action; as a result, he was labeled by some as the "father of affirmative action." In so doing, he created opportunities for millions of women and minorities. He often spoke publicly on civil rights and affirmative action. Because of his views, at times, he was at odds both with his political party and with his race.

Arthur Allen Fletcher was born on December 22, 1924, in a black neighborhood in Phoenix, Arizona. He was the son of Andrew A. and Edna Miller Fletcher. At the time of his birth, his father (according to some sources his stepfather) was a career military man stationed at Camp Huachuca while serving in the all-black cavalry regiment in the U.S. Army. During his youth the family moved frequently, living in poor neighborhoods in Arizona, California, Oklahoma, and Kansas. While living in the Watts district of Los Angeles, Fletcher became a gang leader by age thirteen. Since the family moved around, young Fletcher attended seventeen different schools by the time he was in the eighth grade. Although Edna Fletcher held college degrees in education and

nursing, employment for blacks at that time was difficult to find; consequently, she worked as a live-in maid. This arrangement meant that Arthur Fletcher lived with various families, including American Indians and Mexican Americans.

Early on, Fletcher considered becoming a minister. He developed an interest in civil rights when he was in the seventh grade, after hearing educator and presidential adviser Mary McLeod Bethune speak. According to Lottie L. Joiner for *Crisis* magazine, she told students in Fletcher's school to "always carry a brief for Black folks." He followed her advice and became an activist while in high school. In 1943 Fletcher organized his first civil rights protest at the Junction City Junior/Senior High School, boycotting the yearbook because it placed photographs of black students at the back of the book. He also distinguished himself on the school's football team as a halfback and defensive end. To build up their fire before playing against white teams during that racially-charged time, Fletcher and his black teammates read accounts of black lynchings.

Fletcher married at age eighteen, and at age nineteen, after graduating from high school in Junction City, Kansas, he enlisted in the U.S. Army during World War II and served in a tank division. He was wounded while serving in Europe under General George C. Patton and was awarded a Purple Heart. He was discharged in 1945.

On his return to the states, Fletcher had football scholarship offers from Northwestern, Iowa, and Indiana universities. He had a brief stay at Indiana but the lack of suitable housing in Bloomington led him to accept a scholarship offer from Washburn University.

Fletcher enrolled in Washburn University in Topeka, Kansas and studied under the G. I. Bill of Rights and with a scholarship from the university. Fletcher excelled in football, earning Little All-American honors; he was the sixth leading rusher in small college teams through the country. A political science and sociology major, he also gained practical experience by working part-time in a state agency in Kansas as well as for legislative committees. In 1950, Fletcher graduated from the university with a bachelor of arts degree.

In 1950, Fletcher joined the Los Angeles Rams as defensive end. The Rams soon had their quota of five blacks on their team and in 1954 sold Fletcher to the Baltimore Colts, making him the Colts' first African American team member. From there he moved to the Hamilton (Ontario) Tiger Cats of the Canadian Football League. By now he had five children, so the meager salary of $5,100 was insufficient for his needs. Fletcher returned to Kansas with the hope of coaching high school football. Unsuccessful, he supported his family by working long hours in menial jobs for several years. He applied for a management trainee program with Goodyear Tire and Rubber Company in Topeka, but was turned down; instead, he was hired on in a factory job with the company. Fletcher decided to enhance his education and in 1953-54 did postgraduate work in economics and education at Kansas State University. Much later he took a law degree from Chicago's LaSalle Extension University. Still later, according to one source, he earned a Ph.D. degree in education.

Begins Political Career

Fletcher began his political career in Kansas in 1954 by working in the area of public relations on Lieutenant Governor Fred Hall's successful campaign for governor. Hall was a liberal Republican who needed Fletcher to push his candidacy in the black community. The 17,000 votes that Fletcher delivered were said to be enough to ensure Hall's victory. Hall rewarded him by giving him a post overseeing building and maintenance of the highway system. Thus, Fletcher took his first position in state government (1954-57), as assistant public relations director for the Kansas Highway Commission. There was a boom in highway construction at that time, and Fletcher positioned himself well for the benefits that he reaped for his race. He learned the details of awarding and administering lucrative government contracts and in so doing, he encouraged African American business leaders to bid for the contracts. In his view, this action was the cornerstone for aiding minorities. Some local white business leaders attacked him for working to steer highway contracts to

minorities. He was legislative liaison officer and chaired a commission on racial problems which, again, gave him an opportunity to help address racial needs. He also worked for the Kansas State Republican Central Committee as vice-chairman from 1954 to 1956. Although in the 1950s blacks in Kansas were predominantly Democratic, Fletcher was a Republican who began to fight for better opportunities for blacks. He instituted policies that Republican administrations followed.

In Kansas, Fletcher became a staunch defender of education and demonstrated a keen interest in school desegregation. While waiting for his reward from Hall, Fletcher taught in a rural elementary school and was appalled by the gross inadequacies in the black schools. With his own funds, he helped to finance the lawsuit against Topeka's Board of Education, the landmark case *Brown v. Board of Education*, which aimed to desegregate the public schools in Topeka.

After Hall lost his bid for reelection in the 1956 primaries, the administration that followed abolished Fletcher's post. To support himself and his family, Fletcher opened a used-car business in Topeka. Some claim that his involvement in the school desegregation case led city officials who disagreed with his actions to force him out of business. The determined Fletcher moved on to become assistant football coach at his alma mater, Washburn University. The appointment made him the university's first black staff member and in the national view, the first black in the country to coach at a predominantly white academic institution.

Fletcher and his family followed Fred Hall to Sacramento, California, in late 1958. There Fletcher became management control coordinator for Aerojet-General Corporation and lived in a white neighborhood. Racial prejudice was alive and well in his neighborhood, as rocks were thrown into the family's home. The family relocated to Berkeley where Fletcher worked for an Oakland tire company and for a while opened an unsuccessful restaurant business. This was a critical period in the Fletcher family's life, and in 1960 tragedy hit hard. The family had been denied a rental house in Berkeley's white section and continuing racial problems, combined with continuing economic pressures, took their toll, and Fletcher's wife, Mary, committed suicide.

In 1960 as well, the struggling Fletcher became involved in politics again, this time as a paid staff member for the Nixon-Lodge campaign. His task was to "Republicanize" the East Bay Area's strong concentration of blacks who comprised the Democratic Seventeenth Assembly District. The Republican candidate's bid for Congress in the election failed by a wide margin, but Fletcher demonstrated in his work that he had tremendous influence and organizational skills. He had built a Republican organization of some two hundred volunteers. Still interested in education, between 1960 and 1965 he taught at Burbank Junior High School located in

Berkeley. His interest in school integration continued as well, for he became a special project director for Berkeley's board of education and helped desegregate the local school system. He continued his political activities, running for the state assembly in 1962. His two-to-one- margin loss did not discourage him; he had put up a good fight for the Republicans. Fletcher remained active in politics as well as in civil rights activities. He was a member of the Alameda County Republican Central Committee from 1962 to 1964 and chaired the advisory commission on civil rights for the California Republican Assembly (1962-64). He did postgraduate work at San Francisco State College in 1964-65.

In 1967 Fletcher moved to the state of Washington, where he directed a federally funded manpower development program in East Pasco. The program addressed hard-core, semi-literate black migrants from the South, who lived on the outskirts of that small town in the southeastern part of the state. Although the program failed due to difficulties with local welfare officials, Fletcher had trained 380 men. After that, he established on his own initiative, the East Pasco Self-Help Cooperative, an urban renewal project. Again he entered the political arena and was elected overwhelmingly to the Pasco city council, serving from 1968 to 1969. He was employee relations specialist for the Nanford atomic energy facility in Richmond, Washington in 1967. He remained connected to politics and in 1968-69 he was a special assistant to Washington governor Daniel J. Evans. Around this time as well, he was alternate delegate to the United Nations General Assembly. Meanwhile, Fletcher's community help program in East Pasco caught the eye of the national Republican party and brought him an invitation to address the party's platform committee in 1968. His self-help program became the basis for the "black capitalism" program that the Republican National Convention endorsed that summer at its convention in Miami. Meanwhile, he moved forward with political activities, becoming the first black nominee for statewide office in Washington. Although he lost the election by only a few thousand votes, he had fared well in a state whose population was only 2 percent black.

Now an attractive figure in his party, President Richard M. Nixon appointed Fletcher his assistant secretary for wage and labor standards in the Department of Labor, on March 14, 1969. As the highest-ranking black in Nixon's administration, Fletcher and his career were on the national stage. He also had far-reaching power, overseeing the Office of Federal Contract Compliance, the Bureau of Labor Standards, the Women's Bureau, the Wage and Hour and Public Contract Division, the Bureau of Employee's Compensation, and the Office of Wage Determinations. He took a hard look at economic security for blacks and concentrated on using federal power to bring about equal employment opportunities. The Office of Federal Contracts Compliance (OFCC), established during the Lyndon B. Johnson administration, was the

vehicle for carrying this task. He reorganized the OFCC and set up a compliance review system that required firms receiving federal contracts to give monthly reports.

Becomes "Father of Affirmative Action"

In 1969, Art Fletcher, as he was called, concentrated on the construction industry, where a mere 2 percent of the highest paying construction jobs were held by blacks. Fletcher called for hearings in Chicago in September 1969 to learn about union activities and union resistance to job integration. Conflicts between local black groups and union workers and some five hundred white construction workers who crowded the meeting site put Fletcher in harms way, forcing him to barricade himself in his hotel room. Meanwhile, Fletcher and the OFCC revised a plan that the Johnson administration had developed early on and set goals to address employment practices for racial minorities on federal projects. Secretary of Labor George Shultz put the plan into effect in the summer of 1969. It was called the Philadelphia Plan. That summer, Fletcher held hearings in Philadelphia and found indisputably that seven different construction trade unions practiced racial discrimination. After that, he put in place a plan that required federal construction workers in Philadelphia to establish goals to hire minorities and follow this by putting forth "good faith effort" to reach these goals. If not, they would face sanctions.

Some of the projects that the Nixon administration put in place, such as the experimental home town plans that called for voluntary hiring programs, gave the black community a negative image of the administration. There was mixed reaction from the black community: black militants called for totally independent development of black communities; some blacks claimed that the plan did too little; and others claimed that the aim was to drive a wedge between black and white workers by attacking unions. Fletcher went ahead with his "Order No. Four" in February 1970, setting up more stringent rules for hiring minorities and later issued show cause orders to some firms, who had to do just that or perhaps be debarred from defense contract-bidding.

Fletcher's plan became the model for affirmative action programs elsewhere. Quoted in the *Washington Post*, he told *Fortune* magazine in 2000, "Affirmative action changed the American workplace for the better, forever." Proud of his work in this area, he said, "I'm proud to say that I set the stage for today's workplace and workforce diversity efforts." Years later, he told an audience in Peoria, Illinois, cited in the *New York Times*, that "the purpose of affirmative action is so that you can do what God intended you to do and be what he intended you to be." Even later, he urged corporations to keep affirmative action alive. At the time of Fletcher's death, Julian Bond, chair of the NAACP Board of Directors, said in an article from the NAACP that he made the Philadelphia Plan "a prototype of early affirmative action decrees. As he often said, it 'put flesh and blood on Dr. King's dream.'"

Fletcher resigned his post in the Nixon administration in December 1971 to become head of the United Negro College Fund (UNCF), then an organization of forty black colleges that came together for joint fundraising. While he was there, Forest Long of the advertising agency Young and Rubicam created the phrase "A mind is a terrible thing to waste" that became the UNCF's slogan and pierced America's conscientiousness toward financial support. Many sources, however, attributed the slogan to Fletcher. UNCF continues to use the phrase in promotional pieces. At odds with the fund's leaders, a little over a year later Fletcher stepped down, but not before he had started a management training program and had begun a grass-roots effort to reach blacks beyond the middle class.

Moving into private enterprise, in 1973 Fletcher founded and served as president of the consulting firm Arthur A. Fletcher and Associates. Its mission was to provide consulting services in government relations, management relations, and human resource development. It also conducted affirmative action technical assistance seminars and workshops at colleges throughout the country. In a joint venture with the Gray Hound Corporation, the firm provided food service and lodging for workers at the Alaskan pipeline project. In the 1980s the firm held the food services contract at Fort Belvoir, Virginia and served meals to troops stationed there. He left the firm in 1989. While with his firm, however, Fletcher testified at the hearings of the House Judiciary Committee in 1973 in support of Gerald R. Ford's nomination for vice president of the United States. Ford repaid him by appointing him deputy advisor of urban affairs. Some claim that in this post he became known as the father of the affirmative action enforcement movement.

In this position, Fletcher was responsible to James M. Cannon, the executive director for domestic affairs. He reviewed proposals, conferred with government and corporate leaders, and met with Congress and other federal officials. The black community kept in touch with Fletcher, informing him of ongoing activities. He visited these institutions and solicited their advice. He also had contact with educational, social, and political organizations. Blacks in large corporations, small enterprises, and in neighborhood groups sought his assistance in urban issues. Fletcher's service came during the Ford administration's last year—an election year—and he became active in the reelection campaign. He traveled throughout the country giving speeches and discussing Ford's domestic policies. While in the field, he met with community leaders and private citizens at the local and national levels. Those who sought funds from various federal agencies for projects dealing with the elderly, housing, mass transit, and other issues often gave

Fletcher their proposal for review. Small businesses saw him as liaison between their offices and bureaucracy.

Heads Civil Rights Commission

In 1978, Fletcher took another unsuccessful stab at political office by becoming the Republican candidate for mayor of Washington, D.C., challenging Marion Barry. He did so even with full knowledge that there were few registered Republican voters in the city.

His big chance at effecting change in civil rights came in 1990, when President Bush appointed him chair of the Civil Rights Commission, a post he held until 1993. He endorsed the Civil Rights Act of 1991 as well as the nomination of Clarence Thomas, who became the second black ever on the U.S. Supreme Court (Thurgood Marshall was the first). He was persuaded that Thomas benefited from *Brown v. Board of Education* as well as from affirmative action—and knew it. Thomas was "fortunate enough to ride them both all the way to the top," he told the *Boston Globe*, cited in the *Washington Post*.

Fletcher never lost his zeal for equal economic opportunity. By 2003, he owned and managed Fletcher's Learning System, Inc. The firm created, produced, and marketed books, training manuals, and audio and videotapes to assist companies that sought to meet governmental laws, statutes, and guidelines for maintaining equal business opportunities for minorities. Fletcher took the program to national and international audiences. He was practically a constant presidential adviser, giving support to presidents Nixon, Ford, Reagan, and George H. W. Bush. Although he was a staunch Republican, the outspoken Fletcher admonished Reagan and Bush for failing to support civil rights. Reports on Fletcher's opinions of those Republican presidents and their support of civil rights are conflicting. He denied that the Nixon administration was racially biased and claimed, if that were true, he would not have kept his post. He would not defend every action that the administration took, though. According to the *Washington Post*, he called Reagan "the worst president for civil rights in this century." When he headed the Civil Rights Commission, he was highly critical of Bush for "labeling civil rights legislation as a quota bill."

Late in life, Fletcher became an advocate of the National Black Chamber of Commerce. He belonged to various professional and civic groups, including the NAACP, and the American Legion. His numerous awards included the George Washington Honor Medal from the Freedom Foundation of Valley Forge (1969), the Russwurm Award from the National Newspaper Publishers Association (1970), and the Living Legend Award from the National Caucus and Center on Black Aged, Inc. (1995). He received honorary degrees from Allegheny and Malcolm X colleges, and Washburn, Virginia Union, and Denver universities.

Fletcher was six feet four inches tall and immensely popular, humorous, and creative. He was a devout Methodist who each morning read his favorite passages from the Sermon on the Mount in the Bible. Fletcher died of a heart attack at his home in Washington, D.C. on July 12, 2005, at the age of eighty. (Some sources claim, however, that he died at George Washington University Hospital in Washington.) His first wife, Mary Fletcher, died in 1961. His son Arthur Jr. died in 1973, and another son, Phillip, died in 1989. A daughter, Phyllis Hatcher, died in 1990. He was survived his second wife Bernyce Hassan-Fletcher, whom he married on May 5, 1965; a son, Paul; a daughter Sylvia; and a host of grand-and great-grand-children. An NAACP article called him "a friend and mentor to those in both political parties who believed in civil rights." Joe Holly for the *Washington Post* hailed him as "a maverick Republican who proudly laid claim to the title 'the father of affirmative action.'"

REFERENCES

Books

Gomes, Daniel. "Arthur Allen Fletcher." In *The Greenwood Encyclopedia of African American Civil Rights*. Vol. I. Eds. Charles D. Lowery and John F. Marszalek. Westport, Conn.: Greenwood Press, 2003.

Periodicals

Holley, Joe. "Affirmative Action Pioneer Advised GOP Presidents." *Washington Post*, 14 July 2005.

Joiner, Lottie L. "Arthur Fletcher: On the Right." *Crisis* 112 (September/October 2005): 12.

McGann, Chris. "Arthur Fletcher, 1924-2005: Mission Was Carving Out Opportunity for Minorities." *Seattle Post-Intelligencer*, 13 July 2005.

O'Donnell, Michele. "Arthur Fletcher, G.O.P. Adviser, Dies at 80." *New York Times*, 14 July 2005.

Online

"Arthur A. Fletcher: The Activist." Friends of America's Future. http://www.theenterprize.com/FRIENDS/fletcher.htm (Accessed 18 September 2005).

Good, Diane. "A Moment in Time: Arthur A. Fletcher: Father of the Affirmative Action Enforcement Movement." http://www.kshs.org/features/feat202.htm (Accessed 5 September 2005).

"NAACP Mourns Death of Arthur Fletcher." http://www/naccp.org/news/2005/2005-07-13.html (Accessed 5 September 2005).

Collections

The files of Arthur A. Fletcher as deputy assistant to the president for urban affairs are in the Gerald R. Ford Library, Ann Arbor, Michigan.

Jessie Carney Smith

Benjamin Fletcher
1890–1949

Labor activist

Benjamin Harrison Fletcher rose from obscure beginnings to become a key organizer of workers across racial and cultural lines in the early decades of the twentieth century. He was able to achieve these accomplishments at great personal sacrifice despite limited formal education, by applying socialist philosophies to address labor issues in the U.S. system of industrial capitalism. His views and approach were radical and progressive for any worker, but especially so for an African American who championed worker solidarity even above racial solidarity as a response to discrimination and other unfair practices in the workplace and the society at large.

Very little information is known about Fletcher's early life beyond the facts that he was born in Philadelphia in 1890, one of four children born to parents who migrated north from Virginia, where his father, Dennis Fletcher, was born. His mother was born in Maryland. Some biographical accounts suggest that his family may have had Native American as well as African heritage. Fletcher grew up in the African American community in Philadelphia, which was the largest outside the South during the period. He came into contact with various racial and ethnic groups that migrated to the area during his formative years.

In a practice common in many cultures, Fletcher apparently received his first and middle names after an important person in society: Benjamin Harrison was president of the United States when Fletcher was born. Fletcher's later writings and speeches indicate that he may have been educated as far as high school and that he read extensively on his own and engaged in other forms of self-education.

From Laborer to Longshoreman to Activist

At the age of twenty in 1910, Fletcher had left his parents' home to live on his own, boarding with other young black men, and had begun working on the Philadelphia docks. Records in the 1910 U.S. census identify Fletcher's occupation as "laborer," one of the few job categories open to most African Americans at the time, along with domestic service. At this time he worked in the port and shipping areas and became known as a stevedore or longshoreman.

Fletcher may have met such socialists as John Reed and Joe Hill during this period, along with other radical thinkers and activists. By 1912 he had become an active member of the International Workers of the World (IWW), also known as the Wobblies, and reportedly was also involved with the Socialist Party (SP). Very few blacks were a part of these organizations, yet Fletcher

Chronology

1890	Born in Philadelphia, Pennsylvania
1910	Listed in U.S. census with occupation of laborer
1912	Attends Industrial Workers of the World (IWW) conference in Chicago
1913	Becomes labor activist; helps to found Local 8 in Philadelphia
1917	Arrested with other IWW leaders for alleged violation of federal laws
1918	Convicted and sentenced to federal prison in Leavenworth, Kansas
1920	Released on bail from prison; continues labor activism
1923	Receives commutation of prison sentence from President Warren G. Harding
1933	Receives full pardon from President Franklin D. Roosevelt
1949	Dies in Brooklyn, New York on July 10

identified with their philosophy in support of working-class men and women.

The presence of Fletcher and D. B. Gordon from the Louisiana-based Brotherhood of Timber Workers at the 1912 national IWW convention in Chicago was highlighted in *Solidarity*, the IWW weekly newspaper, "as proof that we have surmounted all barriers of race and color." This claim was questionable at that point, since African Americans were not involved in the IWW in significant numbers nationally and had little impact on the organization as a whole.

Fletcher began to be recognized for his skills in local organizing and his speeches at worker rallies in the Philadelphia area. He became secretary of IWW Local 57 and wrote articles about labor issues which also appeared in *Solidarity* during 1912 and 1913. Other observers and commentators were impressed by Fletcher's intellect and speaking and writing skills, which along with his activism, brought him to prominence in the national labor movement.

Helps to Found Multiracial Labor Group

In May 1913 longshoremen in Philadelphia on strike in protest of intolerable working conditions and low wages were approached by both the Marine Transport Workers Union (MTWU) of the IWW and the International Longshoremen's Association (ILA) of the American Federation of Labor (AFL) to consider formal affiliation in support of their cause. At a mass meeting during the same month, the Philadelphia group chose the IWW over the AFL, influenced in part by Fletcher's connection to the IWW and the perception of racism with the AFL.

The new Philadelphia organization, which became known as Local 8, was diverse, including African Americans; West Indian, Polish, Italian, Spanish, Belgian, and Lithuanian immigrants; and Irish Americans among oth-

ers. The group numbered in the thousands during its prime years. The integrated group of workers prevented employers from using racism to play different ethnic groups against each other, and from successfully using segregated groups of strikebreakers to undermine the union.

Although Fletcher was instrumental in founding Local 8, he made certain that he was not perceived as being its only leader. Its meetings were chaired by persons of different ethnic groups on a rotating basis, and its committees and representatives in labor negotiations always reflected the diversity of the organization. The solidarity of workers across racial, ethnic, and cultural categories was essential to the success of Local 8 in its efforts to improve the status, pay, and working conditions of the longshoremen.

Controversy, Trial, and Imprisonment

The establishment of Local 8 led Fletcher and the IWW to expand their labor organizing work to Baltimore, but without the same level of success. In Philadelphia the union continued to face opposition from the city's business and government leaders and competition from the ILA, but Local 8 held strong against these attempts and became the dominant influence on the Philadelphia waterfront.

The 1913 IWW convention was held in Chicago, and Fletcher attended on behalf of Philadelphia Local 57, the National Industrial Union of Marine Transport Workers (NIUMTW) affiliate, while James H. Murphy, an Irish American, represented Local 8. Issues related to the seating of both Fletcher and Murphy were debated and resolved, in large part due to the sheer numbers and influence of Local 8 within the IWW, but tensions between the local and national organizations created problems in following years.

Fletcher continued to organize workers in Philadelphia and other cities along the East Coast from his position as secretary of the IWW District Council. Although he focused his efforts on African American dockworkers who had been excluded from the ILA, he continued to practice as well as preach racial harmony and worker solidarity. Fletcher made public appearances with IWW organizers John J. Walsh, an Irish American, and Jack Lever, an immigrant from Russia.

World War I created both problems and opportunities, as the socialist-oriented IWW could not be perceived as being anti-American, particularly when the United States officially entered the war in 1917. Workers were in demand on the home front, as many men were called into military service, and the longshoremen worked consistently in support of the war effort. As a result, Local 8 called for only one work stoppage during the war.

Even though the longshoremen's work stoppage lasted only one day (May 15, 1917, in celebration of the fourth anniversary of Local 8), during the fall of 1917 the U.S. Department of Justice raided the two IWW locations in Philadelphia and confiscated records and documents. Shortly afterwards, warrants were issued for the arrest of Fletcher and nearly two hundred other Wobblies across the country. The men were charged with interfering with the Selective Service Act, violating the Espionage Act of 1917, conspiring to strike, violating the rights of employers holding government contracts, and using the mail to defraud employers.

Ben Fletcher was the only African American among the IWW leaders and membership who were arrested. The IWW established the General Defense Committee (GDC) to raise funds and secure legal counsel on their behalf. Local 8 members sold liberty bonds and gave generously, which helped the defendants and their families.

Records of funds distributed indicated that Fletcher's wife received $10 a week from the GDC to support her and a son; she would later apply for additional assistance from a Philadelphia charitable organization. This is the earliest known documentation of Fletcher as a husband and parent. Other sources note that his wife was white, and that he also had a white stepdaughter, but no biological children. With his arrest, his family lost its primary breadwinner, and Local 8 had to operate without one of its most respected members and effective leaders.

Fletcher was again the only African American among the one hundred men and one woman who were indicted by a grand jury, tried, and convicted in Chicago; twelve others were released during the course of the trial. The presiding judge was Kenesaw Mountain Landis, who later became the first commissioner of Major League Baseball in 1920. After four months of testimony, the jury deliberated less than an hour before finding Fletcher and his co-defendants guilty on all counts. In separate trials, forty-six IWW members were also convicted in Sacramento, California, and twenty-six in Wichita, Kansas.

On August 30, 1918, Judge Landis sentenced Fletcher to ten years in prison and fined him $30,000 plus court costs, a tremendous amount of money at the time, while some of his colleagues received twenty-year sentences. Despite the seriousness of the situation, reports indicate that Fletcher maintained his sense of humor while protesting the injustice and unfairness of the trial, verdict, and sentence.

Protests to End Prison Term

African American leaders such as W. E. B. Du Bois and A. Phillip Randolph protested Fletcher's imprisonment, and Randolph launched a campaign to bring about his release through *The Messenger*, the African American socialist publication he edited along with Chandler Owen. They recognized him as making a genuine contribution to the uplift of blacks and other disadvantaged persons through his labor activism, and in the next few

years many persons from various racial groups urged President Warren G. Harding to pardon Fletcher.

While Fletcher was in prison, Local 8 managed to maintain control of the Philadelphia waterfront despite ongoing surveillance of IWW members by the government. In keeping with Fletcher's philosophy of shared leadership, other persons came forward to keep the union strong and effective in its dealings with employers and in its competition with the ILA and AFL. These leaders included Lithuanian immigrant Paul "Polly" Baker and African Americans Joseph Whitzen, William "Dan" Jones, Charles Carter, Amos White, and Alonzo Richards.

Due to direct support from Local 8, as well as the GDC, the national IWW headquarters, and other supporters from around the country, Fletcher was released after making bail during an appeal of his conviction on February 7, 1920. He went on a speaking tour to promote the IWW then returned to Philadelphia where he lived with his father and a sister, Helen Brazton, instead of with his wife and stepfamily. It is unclear why Fletcher did not resume living with his wife, but the stress of his notoriety could have contributed to his decision. Despite his personal challenges and difficulties, Fletcher remained committed to the IWW and to worker solidarity.

At great personal risk, Fletcher helped to raise money to get other convicted IWW persons out of Leavenworth on bail, and he provided leadership to Local 8 when it went on a major strike during the summer of 1920. His activities could have resulted in losing his own freedom again, as well as forfeiting the bail money already raised on his behalf. After a month on strike, Local 8 did not win any additional concessions from employers, but still managed to stand firm as the dominant labor organization representing Philadelphia waterfront workers.

Fletcher was perceived as having black power and green power years before these terms came into vogue, due to the racial and worker unity of his organization. The strength of Local 8 and the IWW was translated into economic clout, due to its influence on the shipping industry and the war effort. Persons in government and industry were threatened by the socialist leanings of the IWW and sought to weaken, then destroy the organization by prosecuting Fletcher and its other leaders and organizers.

More Controversy Leads to Demise of Local 8

The power and influence of Local 8 became a challenge to other constituents within the IWW, particularly those with communist sympathies as opposed to the socialist philosophy of Fletcher and others on issues of racial, labor, and class struggle. Fletcher refused to let Local 8 become a pawn of the Communist Party, which wanted to use its success to support the party's various agendas, and the internal struggle within the IWW led to what Fletcher and others called the Philadelphia Controversy.

Local 8 continued to operate in its own fashion, and when it did not change policies and procedures that conflicted with IWW directives, the IWW suspended the local on December 4, 1920. This action prevented Fletcher from taking his position as secretary-treasurer of the MTWU and created openings for communist sympathizers to assume leadership. Even though the factions opposed to Local 8 were gaining strength, in December 1921 the U.S. Department of Justice advised the attorney general against recommending executive clemency for Fletcher.

Another beneficiary of Local 8 problems was the rival ILA, which gained members after Local 8 went on strike for an eight-hour work day in October 1922. The employers locked them out of the workplace with the cooperation of federal authorities and brought in replacement workers. As a result, the employers were finally able to break down the local's interracial solidarity and weaken their bargaining position.

Receives Clemency and Presidential Pardon

On October 31, 1922, the prison sentences of Ben Fletcher and two other IWW leaders, Walter Nef and Jack Walsh, were commuted, with official documentation coming from President Warren G. Harding in 1923. Fletcher had served four years at Leavenworth, and ten years later Fletcher received a full pardon from President Franklin D. Roosevelt.

After his release, Fletcher began to curtail much of his Local 8 and IWW activities, although he remained committed to his principles. In January 1923 he and another African American, William "Dan" Jones, started a new organization, the Philadelphia Longshoremen's Union (PLU), in hopes of recapturing the success of Local 8 during its glory years. This effort was unsuccessful, as the continued presence of the IWW and the ILA made it impossible to unify a sufficient number of longshoremen, and the PLU disbanded in 1924. Fletcher then returned to the IWW despite his continued disagreement with the direction of the organization.

Ben Fletcher continued to speak on occasion in support of interracial unionism and worker solidarity well into the early 1930s. He no longer functioned in an official leadership role within the IWW, though, and the organization had lost nearly all of its support and effectiveness. Reports indicate that after he stopped working as a longshoreman and union official, Fletcher relocated to the Bedford-Stuyvesant section of Brooklyn, in New York City. Several of his former colleagues from the IWW and Local 8 days had also moved to the same area, and they provided assistance and support to Fletcher during his final years.

On July 10, 1949, Benjamin Fletcher died at his home in Brooklyn at the age of 59. Although he never received the fame of other African American labor leaders, such as A. Phillip Randolph, the end of his life and work did not go unnoticed. Fletcher's obituary appeared in the *New York Times*, as well as in *Solidarity, Industrial Worker*, and other labor-related publications. Many IWW Wobblies attended his funeral and offered tributes to Fletcher's unwavering commitment to industrial unionism.

Fletcher's work with the IWW and Local 8 was recognized in subsequent years as one of the earliest examples of successful interracial cooperation in the workplace and remained a fitting legacy to his life, philosophy, and efforts to create the "One Big Union" for the benefit of all persons involved in organized labor occupations.

REFERENCES

Books

Marcus, Irwin M. "Benjamin Harrison Fletcher." In *Dictionary of American Negro Biography*. Eds. Rayford W. Logan and Michael R. Winston. New York: Norton, 1982.

Periodicals

"Benjamin H. Fletcher: Labor Organizer Convicted Under Espionage Act in 1917 Dies." *New York Times*, 12 July 1949.

Foner, Philip S. "The IWW and the Black Worker." *Journal of Negro History*. 55 (January 1970), 45-64.

Marcus, Irwin M. "Benjamin Fletcher: Black Labor Leader." *Negro History Bulletin* (October 1972): 138-41.

Seraile, William. "Ben Fletcher, I.W.W. Organizer." *Pennsylvania History* 46 (1979): 213-32.

Other

Cole, Peter. E-mail message to author, 18 October 2005, with biographical essay in attached file, "Black Wobbly: Ben Fletcher and the IWW."

———. "Shaping Up and Shipping Out: The Philadelphia Waterfront During and After the IWW Years, 1913-1940." Ph.D. dissertation, Georgetown University, 1997.

Fletcher F. Moon

Barney Launcelot Ford
1822–1902

Entrepreneur

Barney Launcelot Ford, born in Virginia, rose from slavery to become a conductor on the Underground Railroad. In the 1840s he was hired out by his master to

Chronology

1822	Born a slave in Virginia
1840	Hired out by his master to work on a steam ship; escapes
1841	Encounters another escaped slave, Henry O. Wagoner
1842	Becomes a conductor on the Underground Railroad
1848	Marries Julia; moves to Central America; begins to build hotels and becomes wealthy businessman; returns to the United States and moves west; joins the gold rush
1850	Moves to Denver
1851	Opens many hotels and barbershops all over Denver
1867	His Cheyenne, Wyoming restaurant destroyed by fire
1870	Opens hotel in Cheyenne
1871	Establishes the first adult education classes for Negroes in Colorado
1873	Becomes a member of the Arapahoe County Republication Central Committee; makes unsuccessful bid for the state legislature
1880	Moves to San Francisco and rents a lunch counter and again prospects for gold
1882	Returns to Denver and opens a series of restaurants
1882	Invited as first black to a dinner for the Colorado Association of Pioneers
1885	Organizes a successful drive to pass a bill that prohibits discrimination
1902	Dies from a stroke

work on a steam ship, from which he escaped. Ford left not knowing if he would ever get caught but seeking a better life for himself. On his run for freedom, Ford encountered another escaped slave named Henry O. Wagoner. The men taught themselves to read and helped each other as well as they could as they made their way to the Underground Railroad.

Enters Business and Political Ventures

By 1848 Ford had married and left with his wife, Julia, for Central America. While there, Ford built several hotels that prospered, making him a very wealthy businessman. Returning to the United States, he lived briefly in Chicago and then headed for the West. Ford wanted to be part of the gold rush, but he encountered much racism and was driven off by white prospectors. In 1850, Ford moved to Denver and soon opened hotels and barbershops around the city. He provided food and shelter to runaway slaves escaping Colorado during the Civil War.

After the war ended, the state of Colorado proposed a law that would prohibit black suffrage. Ford traveled to Washington along with Senator Charles Sumner of Massachusetts, who led the fight for the elimination of the provision by trying to persuade President Andrew Johnson to veto in 1867 a new bill providing statehood with white suffrage only. The ratification of the Fifteenth Amendment in 1870 ended this phase of Ford's career.

This legislation delivered a painful blow to Ford and to all black people, but he refused to allow the decision to change him. Ford and Wagoner returned to Denver where they and others decided to establish the first adult education classes for blacks in Colorado. Ford was a member of the Arapahoe County Republication Central Committee and also made an unsuccessful bid for the state legislature in 1873.

While engaged in these activities, Ford continued to manage his restaurants and hotels. He operated his restaurant in Cheyenne, Wyoming from 1867 to 1870, until it was destroyed by a fire. The Cheyenne Chamber of Commerce requested that Ford open an elegant hotel there in the place of the restaurant. According to the *Dictionary of American Negro Biography,* Ford opened the hotel, boasting in advertisement that the Inter Ocean Hotel was "the largest and Finest Hotel between Omaha and San Francisco." President Ulysses Grant stopped to check out the hotel. However, Ford was unable to generate enough business to sustain the place and had to sell.

In 1880, Ford moved to San Francisco. He rented a lunch counter and again had an unsuccessful venture prospecting for gold. In 1882, he returned to Denver and opened another series of restaurants; this business venture was worse than before. As he absorbed losses in the depression of the 1890s, Ford reevaluated his business plan. He rebuilt his fortune and opened two barbershops and residential properties, which were highly successful business ventures.

Becomes First Black on Colorado Grand Jury

Ford and Wagoner remained friends through various shared experiences. Ford was the first black to serve on a Colorado grand jury. Wagoner was the first to serve as deputy sheriff of Arapahoe County. In 1882, Ford and his wife Julia were the first blacks to be invited to a dinner given by the Colorado Association of Pioneers. After the Supreme Court civil rights decision in 1883, Ford organized a successful drive for a state public accommodations bill prohibiting discrimination (1885). This action was a notable achievement for a black American at the time.

Ford's wife died of pneumonia in 1899. Ford died three years later from a stroke. They had three children: Louis Napoleon, Sadie, and Frances.

REFERENCES

Books

Logan, Rayford W., and Michael R. Winston, eds. *Dictionary of American Negro Biography.* New York: Norton, 1982.

Online

Denver History. www.denvergov.org (Accessed 3 December 2005).

African American Resource Center. www.genealogy
forum.org/ (Accessed 3 December 2005).

LaVerne Laney McLaughlin

Harold Ford, Jr.
1970–

Congressman

In 1996, Congressman Harold Eugene Ford Jr., at the age of twenty-six, became the first African American to succeed a parent in the United States Congress and the second youngest member in the annals of that institution's history. The keynote speaker at the 2000 Democratic National Convention, Ford was one of the party's candidates seeking the Senate seat of retiring majority leader Bill Frist of Tennessee.

Harold Eugene Ford Jr. was born in Memphis, Tennessee on May 11, 1970, to Harold E. Sr. and Dorothy Bowles Ford. The oldest of five children (brothers Jake, Isaac, and Andrew, and sister Ava), he spent the first nine years of his life in the environs of his native city, where he attended the public schools.

The Fords were members of one of Memphis' most well-established African American families in both business and politics. Grandfather Newton Jackson Ford, the family patriarch, was a well-known funeral home director of the N. J. Ford and Sons Funeral Home, which was founded by his father. Six months after starting the business, the elder Ford died and his son, Newton, then only seventeen, took over the business, which developed into one of the city's most prominent funeral homes. The family's political influence grew from their funeral business.

In addition to his father, Harold Ford Sr., who began his political career as a member of the Tennessee General Assembly (1970-75), Ford's uncles were also politically active and held local and state legislative positions. According to the *Congressional Quarterly Weekly Report*, when his father was sworn in as the first African American congressman from Tennessee in January 1975, Ford asserted, "This is what I want to do when I grow up." After his father won two successive congressional elections, Congressman Ford moved his family to Washington, D.C. in 1979. The Fords enrolled their son in St. Albans School, an Episcopal school for boys, where many of D.C.'s power brokers sent their sons. As a child, the younger Ford often accompanied his father to meetings of the Congressional Black Caucus. He grew up learning the ways of the Washington power structure. In

Harold Ford, Jr.

1988, he graduated from St. Albans. Afterward, he entered the University of Pennsylvania in Philadelphia.

Collegiate and Law School Years

Upon entering the University of Pennsylvania, Ford majored in history and took an active role in campus activities. Coming from one of Tennessee's most politically active African American families and imbued with some of the values that emanated from the civil rights struggle for equality and justice, he became an active campus leader and journalist. Because he discerned that the views of minority students on campus were not being heard and that they had no voice, he founded *The Vision,* an African American student newspaper. Completing his undergraduate requirements, Ford graduated from the University of Pennsylvania with a B.A. in 1992.

After graduation, Ford returned to Tennessee and coordinated his father's tenth reelection campaign for the United States House of Representatives. After that, Ford Jr. served on the 1992 Clinton/Gore transition team as a special assistant and as an aid to the Senate Budget Committee under Tennessee senator James Sasser. The following year he worked as a special assistant to the Economic Development Administration under Ron Brown, the United States secretary of commerce. Ford later entered the University of Michigan School of Law. In 1994, taking time out from law school, he again coor-

Chronology

1970	Born in Memphis, Tennessee on May 11
1979	Moves with family to Washington, D. C.
1988	Graduates from St. Albans School for Boys in Washington, D.C.
1992	Earns B.A. from the University of Pennsylvania, Philadelphia; serves as a staff aide to the United States Senate Committee on the Budget; serves as special assistant to the 1992 Clinton/Gore Transition Team; coordinates father's re-election campaign
1993	Becomes special assistant to the United States Department of Commerce under the leadership of the late Ron Brown
1996	Earns J. D. from the University of Michigan Law School; wins Democratic nomination to succeed his father as U. S. Representative for the Ninth Tennessee Congressional District
2000	Becomes keynote speaker at the Democratic National Convention; announces candidacy for House Minority Whip
2005	Announces intentions to run for the Senate seat occupied by Senate Majority Leader William H. "Bill" Frist

dinated his father's reelection campaign. Harold E. Ford Sr. won reelection and represented the people of Tennessee's Ninth Congressional District for two more years. The same year that the elder Ford announced that he would not seek a twelfth term in office, Harold Ford Jr. completed the requirements for his law degree and graduated from the University of Michigan School of Law in 1996.

Enters Race for House of Representatives

When Harold E. Ford Sr. announced in 1996 that he would not seek reelection to the U.S. Congress, he looked to his son for a successor. As asserted in *Jet*, "I want to go out on top," said Ford Sr. "I think the public polls show that I'm stronger than ever in my career . . . I went with a new vision in 1974, and I think it's time for a new vision and a new generation." Remaining true to his political roots, Ford Jr. entered the race for his father's seat. With name recognition, Ford's campaign paraphernalia merely said "Jr." Notwithstanding name recognition and the political entrenchment of the Ford family within the Memphis community, "Jr.," a Democrat, faced political opposition from Memphis mayor Willie W. Herenton, the city's first African American mayor and a political rival of the Ford family. Herenton, who assumed the mayoral position in 1992, looked for politicians to run against the younger Ford. During the Democratic primary, he faced two opponents: state representative Rufus Jones, an African American, and state senator Steve Cohen, a white liberal candidate, who hoped that Ford and Jones would split the African American vote.

Although Ford Jr. possessed name recognition and was connected to the powerful Ford political machine, he did not take that for granted. Fully cognizant that name recognition and family connection was not enough to garner the votes needed to win the election, he solicited votes throughout the Ninth District in an effort to earn the confidence of the people he would represent. Ever aware of the exploding technology and expanding systems of communication, Ford addressed issues of economic and community development, Internet access in the classrooms of his district, education, Head Start, environmental issues, juvenile crime, and affirmative action.

When the August primary votes were counted, "Jr." soundly defeated both of his opponents with approximately 60 percent of the vote. After winning the Democratic nomination, Ford faced his Republican opponent, Rod DeBerry, an African American, in the general election. Upon winning the congressional race, Ford Jr., at age twenty-six, became the first African American to succeed a parent in Congress and the second youngest (succeeding his father, who was the first) member in the annals of that legislative body's history. Ford was among a new generation of political leaders who wanted to substitute or change the partisan affairs of state of the past with fresh ideas and a practical line of attack to the challenges of the twenty-first century.

Elected to the United States Congress

Harold E. Ford Jr. was sworn into the U.S. House of Representatives on January 7, 1997, and became a member of the 105th Congress. Later that same day, he participated in a ceremonial swearing in of the Congressional Black Congress, where U.S. District Court Judge Constance Baker Motley presided. After being sworn in, Congressman Ford was elected vice president of the 105th Congress's Freshman Class. He was appointed to serve as a member of the House Committee on Education and Workforce and the House Committee on Government Reform and Oversight.

Ford was reelected in 1998 by almost 60 points; in the 2000 election, he ran unopposed. The same year, Ford was the keynote speaker for the Democratic National Convention, which supported then-Vice President Albert Gore Jr. for the Democratic presidential nomination.

Ford served on the Committee on Financial Services; the Subcommittee on Capital Markets, Insurance and Government Sponsored Enterprises, Financial Institutions and Consumer Credit; the Budget Committee; the Congressional Black Caucus; the Blue Dog Coalition On-Line; Community Solutions and Initiative Caucus; and as co-chair of the Congressional Savings and Ownership Caucus. He was also a member of the Transformation Advisory Group (TAG). A fifth-term congressman, Ford was among the more assertive young politicians to come from a growing list of black political families.

Seeks to Be Elected to the Senate

In April 2005, Ford announced his intentions to run for the Senate seat occupied by Senate Majority Leader William H. "Bill" Frist. One of five major candidates seeking to replace Senator Frist, who was not seeking reelection, Ford worked intensely to gain positive name recognition in those parts of Tennessee, especially East Tennessee (which is predominately Republican), where he is not well known.

Ford was expected to enter the 2006 August Democratic primary and the November general election; like his father who made history by becoming the first African American elected to Congress from Tennessee, Ford would be the first African American elected to the United States Senate from one of the former Confederate states since the Reconstruction era.

REFERENCES

Books

Cornwell, Ilene J., ed. *Biographical Directory of the Tennessee General Assembly.* Vol. 6, 1971-1991. Nashville: Tennessee Historical Commission. 1991.

Kalfatovic, Mary C.. "Harold E. Ford, Jr." *Contemporary Black Biography*, Vol. 42. Eds. Ashyia N. Henderson and Ralph G. Zerbonia. Farmington Hills, Mich.: Thomson Gale, 2004.

Periodicals

"Another Ford Now Seeks U.S. House Seat." *Nashville Tennessean*, 26 February 2006.

Hefner, David. "Federal Government Plays Key Education Role, Ford Says." *Nashville Tennessean*, 20 April 1997.

Lawrence, Jill. "Family Legacy Cuts Both Ways for Senate Candidate." *USA Today*, 22 December 2005.

Rhodes, Carol and Alan Greenblatt. "Harold E. Ford, Jr." *Congressional Quarterly Weekly Report*, 4 January 1997.

Online

White, Jack E. "Harold Ford Jr. Reaches for the Stars." *Time* 10 December 2002. http://www.time.com/time/nation (Accessed 18 February 2006).

Linda T. Wynn

Harold Ford, Sr.
1945–

Congressman

Harold Eugene Ford Sr. was the first African American to represent a Tennessee district in the U.S.

Harold Ford, Sr.

Congress. Elected to the Congress in 1974 from Tennessee's Ninth Congressional District, which comprises the city of Memphis, he served the district for twelve consecutive terms until he retired in 1996 and was succeeded by his son Harold E. Ford Jr.

Family Background

Ford was one of fifteen children born to Newton Jackson and Vera Davis Ford. Ford's father was the director of the N. J. Ford and Sons Funeral Home, which was founded by his grandfather on Beale Street. However, his grandfather only worked in the business for six months before his death. Refusing to let the business close, Newton took over the operation at age seventeen. It developed into one of the best known funeral homes in the Memphis African American community. In addition to working in the funeral business, for a brief period the elder Ford worked as a keeper of the Peabody Hotel's famous ducks, which into the early 2000s continued to be marched ceremoniously from the hotel's rooftop to the lobby fountain. It was during his stint at the Peabody that Newton met Vera Davis, who also worked at the hotel. Reared in modest circumstances, the Ford children attended the Ford Chapel AME Zion Church, named for their great-grandfather, Newton F. Ford, who donated the land. After making the funeral home into a successful business, Newton Ford moved his family to the suburbs of Memphis.

In 1966, Newton Ford unsuccessfully ran for a seat in the Tennessee House of Representatives. Two years after his unsuccessful bid for a seat in the Tennessee General Assembly, Vera was named Delta Sigma Theta's Mother of the Year for Tennessee and was first runner-up for the national title. All of the Ford's surviving twelve children earned their undergraduate degrees, primarily from the state's historically black public institution of higher education now known as Tennessee State University. Inspired by their father's encouragement, several of the Ford children entered politics.

Harold Eugene Ford was born in Memphis, Tennessee on May 20, 1945. He received his primary and secondary education in the schools of Shelby County and graduated from Geeter High School (which was named after the parents of Ophelia Edna Geeter Ford, the mother of Newton J. Ford) in 1963. After graduating from high school, Ford entered Tennessee State Agriculture and Industrial University (now Tennessee State University) where he earned his undergraduate degree in business administration in 1967. A year later, he received the A.A. degree in mortuary science from Nashville's John A. Gupton College of Mortuary Science. In 1969, he joined his family's funeral business as a vice president and manager and became involved in politics. The same year that he joined the family business, Ford married Dorothy Jean Bowles on February 10, and they became the parents of three sons, Harold Eugene Jr., Newton Jake, and Sir Isaac Ford. In 1970, he entered politics as a Democrat and ran for a seat in the Tennessee General Assembly's House of Representatives.

Elected to Political Office

Elected as a Democrat to the state House of Representatives in 1970, Ford served in the 87th and 88th General Assemblies, representing Shelby County's District Five and then House District 86 until 1975. During his first term in Tennessee's House of Representatives, he chaired a panel looking at utility rates and spoke against excessive late charges. In 1972, Ford was a delegate to the Tennessee State Democratic convention and to the national Democratic convention. After he served two terms, Ford's work in the Tennessee General Assembly and the nation's grappling with the Watergate scandal and improprieties within the Nixon administration emboldened Ford to seek election to the U.S. Congress against Dan Kuykendall, a four-term Republican incumbent, who had successfully defeated four opponents in the Republican primary. In addition, the 1972 redistricting gave the district a larger proportion of African American voters than in previous elections, and many political forecasters believed that the district would not remain Republican. Ford waged a tenacious get-out-the-vote campaign in the African American community. He ran on issues relating to education, fair housing, higher minimum wages, Social Security reform, and fair crime bills. At the same time, Ford went after the Republican incumbent as one with close ties to the previous Nixon administration. He also campaigned against the proposed five percent income tax surcharge recommended by President Gerald Ford. Although he received little help from most Democratic Party politicians, Ford was publicly endorsed by singer Isaac Hayes and Mayor Tom Bradley, an African American from Los Angeles. A month before the election, two white law enforcement officers of the Memphis Police Department beat and killed a young African American male. This ruthless killing and Ford's ceaseless get-out-the-vote campaign galvanized the African American community and ultimately aided Ford in his election bid for the U.S. Congress.

Tennessee's First African American Elected to Congress

On November 5, 1974, at age twenty-nine, Harold E. Ford Sr. became the first African American elected to the U.S. Congress from Tennessee. He defeated U.S. representative Kuykendall for the Eighth Congressional District, in a disputed and drama-filled election. Before Ford was declared the winner by a mere 574-vote margin, Ford's opponent appeared on WREC-TV and claimed victory, only to be informed that his 5,000-vote margin had dissipated. Ford's people were monitoring the vote tally and did not believe the vote margin. By their calculations, Ford should have been ahead by 500 votes. He and some members of his campaign staff went to the Shelby County election office to confirm election returns. There, an African American election worker counseled Ford to check the basement for uncounted boxes. Taking the election worker's advice, Ford found six ballot boxes from predominately African American districts that had not been counted. He and his people watched as the votes were counted and turned the election in his favor by more than 500 votes.

After being informed of the 574-vote turnaround, Kuykendall, who had held the seat since 1967, wanted the election results investigated. An analysis of the results revealed several interesting factors that led to his defeat in addition to a number of ballot boxes in African American districts not being counted. An independent white candidate received 987 votes. There was a light turnout in the white districts, where he received 89 percent of the vote. Mixed districts gave Ford the edge, and he received 94 percent of the African American districts. Additionally, he received 47 percent of the working-class white vote. Kuykendall was not the only Republican to fall during the 1974 elections, as voters across the country registered their disapproval of the Republican Party as a result of the Watergate scandal.

Despite Kuykendall's protestations, Ford's slim election margin stood. After being certified, he went on to serve in the 94th Congress of the United States, thus becoming not only the first African American elected from Tennessee but also the first African American elected from the country's southeastern region in the twentieth century. He remained in Congress until 1996.

The same year that Ford was elected to the U.S. Congress, constituents elected his brothers, Emmitt and John Ford, to the Tennessee General Assembly. Emmitt won election to his brother's seat in the Tennessee General Assembly's lower chamber, and John won election to a Senate seat in that legislative body's upper chamber. The Fords were well on their way to creating a political dynasty. The year before being elected to the Congress, Ford and the entire family were honored by the Chicago Civic Liberty League for their contributions.

After he was sworn into the U.S. Congress, Harold Ford Sr. became one of the youngest members elected to the country's legislative branch of government. As a member of Congress, he served as a member of the House Committee on Ways and Means, which had jurisdiction over all tax and revenue-raising legislation, and on the Social Security and Medicare programs. Ford also served on the House Select Committee on Assassinations that investigated the death of Martin Luther King Jr.

During his next three elections (1976, 1978, and 1980), although he faced well-funded opponents, Ford easily won the bid to retain his seat in Congress, which because of redistricting became the Tennessee's Ninth Congressional District. In 1981, Ford became the chairman of the House Ways and Means Subcommittee on Human Resources, which had jurisdiction over approximately $40 billion in programs, including Aid to Families with Dependent Children, Title XX and Supplementary

Security Income under the Social Security Act, Child Welfare and Foster Care, Low Income Energy Assistance, and Unemployment Compensation Insurance. While serving in the Congress, Ford entered Howard University and earned an M.B.A. degree in business administration in 1982. During the same year, he faced opposition for his congressional seat from Minerva J. Johnican, a former school librarian, who had held a seat on the Shelby County Commission since 1975.

During the Reagan administration, Ford consistently opposed Reagan's attempt to dismantle social welfare programs. He advocated welfare reform, job training and assistance, and forcing parents to pay child support. In the mid-1980s, Ford became one of his party's principal proponents of welfare reform. Because of his leadership in designing a far-reaching welfare reform bill in 1987, the Child Welfare League of America named him Child Advocate of the Year.

Later that same year, House Speaker Jim Wright appointed Ford to the Democratic Steering and Policy Committee. He also served as a Democratic zone whip, representing the states of Tennessee, Louisiana, and Mississippi. Never forgetting his constituents within the Ninth Congressional District, Ford was known for a wide range of services he provided to people within the district. He often reminded his congressional aids that his votes came from the district, not Washington.

Political Career Tarnished

While serving in the 100th Congress, Harold E. Ford Sr. was indicted with co-defendants Karl Schledwitz, David Beaty, and David Crabtree on nineteen counts of conspiracy, bank fraud, and mail fraud following the 1983 collapse of the Knoxville-based banking empire of brothers Jacob "Jake" Franklin and Cecil H. Butcher Jr., both of whom were convicted. Because of financial transactions between Ford and the Butcher brothers, prosecutors claimed that they were political bribes. Officials within the U.S. Department of Justice asserted that the secret deals dated back to 1976 and intimated that one 1978 transaction was as a payment to Ford for his endorsement of Jake Butcher in his Tennessee gubernatorial candidacy.

At first prosecuting attorneys scheduled congressman Ford's trial for the East Tennessee city of Knoxville, which was predominately white and predominately Republican. It was asserted by those associated with the Ford camp that the Knoxville site was representative of what some described as a Reagan administration political searching out and deliberate harassment of those on the opposite side of the aisle. Ford's attorneys were successful in gaining a change of venue from Knoxville to Memphis, his home base where the population was approximately 55 percent African American. Those conducting the court proceedings on behalf of the people felt that because of the defendant's political profile, along with that of his politically active family and the family's funeral home business, that it would be impossible to seat an impartial jury.

Congressman Ford's trial in Memphis federal court began on February 12, 1990 and ended with a deadlocked jury. The jury impaneled for his case consisted of eight African Americans, who voted to acquit, and four whites, who voted to convict the congressman. On April 27, 1990, U.S. District Judge Odell Horton declared a mistrial. It took three years before a second trial was scheduled. As in the first trial, prosecutors sought a change of venue. This time instead of seeking an East Tennessee venue, they asked that the trial be moved from Memphis to Jackson, which was still in the state's western division.

When the Jackson trial began in April 1993, Ford was hospitalized because of chest pains. The jury for this trial was composed of eleven white and one African American. This jury acquitted Harold E. Ford Sr. of all charges. He returned to Washington and resumed his chairmanship of the Ways and Means subcommittee and issues relating to welfare reform. Ford remained in Washington serving the constituents of Tennessee's Ninth Congressional District for another three years before resigning. He was succeeded by his son, Harold E. Ford Jr., who went on to assume his father's seat in Congress after the 1996 elections.

Memberships and Awards

Harold Ford Sr. was a member of the National Advisory Council of Saint Jude's Children's Research Hospital. He served on the board of directors of the Metropolitan Memphis Young Men's Christian Association. He was a member of Alpha Phi Alpha Fraternity, Inc., and chaired the Black Tennessee Political Convention. A member of Mount Moriah East Baptist Church, he was the recipient of numerous awards, including the Outstanding Young Man of the Year (1976) and the Tennessee Jaycees (1977).

After he retired from Congress, Harold Eugene Ford Sr. divided his time between homes in Miami and the Hamptons outside New York City. He also worked in his own consulting firm.

REFERENCES

Books

Brennan, Carol. "Harold E. Ford, Sr." *Contemporary Black Biography*, Vol. 16. Ed. Shirelle Phelps. Farmington Hills, Mich.: Gale Group, 1998.

Cornwell, Ilene J. *Biographical Directory of the Tennessee General Assembly.* Vol. 6, 1971-1991. Nashville: Tennessee Historical Commission. 1991.

Tennessee Blue Book, 1971-1972. Nashville: Secretary of State Office, 1972.

Periodicals

Baird, Woody. "Judge Declares Mistrial in Ford's Fraud Case." *Nashville Banner,* 28 April 1990.

Bradley, Carol. "Harassment and Black Politicians." *Nashville Tennessean*, 17 June 1990.

Daughtry, Larry. "Ford Trial to be a Saga of Race and Politics." *Nashville Tennessean*, 25 February 1990.

——. "Ford Trial Waits for Butcher to Hit Center Stage." *Nashville Tennessean*, 1 April 1990.

——. "Mistrial Ruled in Ford Case, Retry Vowed." *Nashville Tennessean*, 28 April 1990.

——. "Revisiting Old Butcher, Ford Alliance." *Nashville Tennessean*, 4 March 1990.

de la Cruz, Bonna. "The Fords of Memphis: Service and Scandal Define a Dynasty." *Nashville Tennessean*, 31 July 2005.

——. "Political Future of Fords Hinges on Constituents: Some Observers Wonder Whether Family Will Survive 'Waltz' Scandal." *Nashville Tennessean*, 1 August 2005.

Lewis, Dwight and Doug Hall. "State's First Black Elected to Congress." *Nashville Tennessean*, 6 November 1974.

Pratt, James. "'Been Ready from Day One,' Ford Says as Trial Date Set." *Nashville Tennessean*, 13 September 1989.

Smith, M. Lee. "Memphis Venue Big Hurdle for U. S. in Ford Case." *Nashville Banner*, 20 February 1990.

Linda T. Wynn

John R. Francis
1856–1913

Physician, educator

John R. Francis was a prominent African American medical practitioner during the late nineteenth and early twentieth centuries. He was also a distinguished educator. He worked in private medical practice and developed a private sanitarium to care for African Americans who lacked proper health care and sanitation in their homes. Francis saw the need for this facility since African Americans were prone to high mortality rate and shorter life spans because of their social conditions. He benevolently treated poor African Americans who were unable to pay for medical services. Although he is known as an obstetrics specialist, Francis worked as a general practitioner in the African American community. He also tried to educate African Americans to become self-reliant and self-supporting. Francis agreed with his close associate, Booker T. Washington, who proposed that African Americans should start at the level where they are in society and develop their skills in order to become self-sufficient. Francis served on several school boards and as a professor at Howard University in Washington, D.C. Despite the color barriers in his time, he was a prominent figure in the Washington, D.C. area, and served on many committees that worked to improve the lives and community of African Americans. Francis was also an astute businessman in the medical field.

Francis was born free in Washington, D.C. in 1856, although slavery was still a prominent feature in U.S. society. His father, Richard Francis or "Uncle Dick" Francis, was a very well-known African American caterer and bartender at the famous Hancock's Restaurant in the Senate area of the nation's capital. One of the wealthiest African Americans in the area, Richard Francis, who had owned various properties, purchased Hancock's in 1885. Mary E. Francis, his wife and the mother of Francis and four other children, was a housewife. The Francis family was ardent Christians who attended the Wesleyan (Presbyterian) Church. Young Francis was the only son, and his father encouraged him and his sister, Lulu, to do well in all areas and to be conscious of the needs of others. John Francis believed in developing the community in which he lived. He only left D.C. to attend post secondary institutions in Massachusetts and Michigan.

Francis received a good education because of his family's high social status. His father was able to send him to private schools, but he also attended public schools in Washington, D. C. His quest for further education led him to Wilbraham, Massachusetts where he attended Wesleyan Academy, a Christian institution. Francis chose the medical field, and he graduated with high honors in

the class of 1878 from the University of Michigan in Ann Arbor, Michigan.

At twenty-five years of age, Francis married Bettie, and the union produced five children—four boys and one girl. Their eldest son, Milton A. Francis, and John R. Francis, the second child and a graduate of Howard University, followed in their father's footsteps and became medical doctors. The third son, Hugh R. Francis, attended Harvard where he studied law. Dorothea was the youngest child and the sole daughter. The Francis family resided at 2112 Pennsylvania Avenue, in the capital, for a long time, but Francis and his wife moved in later years to 1102 Ninth Street, North West. They had a summer home in Uniontown, Maryland, where they were Fredrick Douglass's neighbors.

Francis believed that education was necessary for African Americans to improve their conditions in a period when most still struggled to get a quality education. He believed that education helped many African Americans to forge ahead despite the obstacles. It is also evident that he stood as a testimony in his times that African Americans could be uplifted and respected via education.

In 1886, Francis was appointed trustee of the District of Columbia's school board; however, he resigned because of lack of support for enhancing the education of African Americans. He gained teaching experience at Washington High School and the Normal School where he made great improvements. Significantly, he implemented a nursing program at the Freedman College where African American nurses were trained. At Howard University, he was a professor of clinical obstetrics and served as a member of the committee of the board of trustees and the permanent committee on the construction of the Carnegie Library.

After graduating from medical school, Francis worked as an obstetrician in the Freedmen's Hospital where he treated only African Americans. Francis was a humble man who tended to the sick in the streets, and he also appealed for guardianship for abandoned babies who were born in his care. In time, he became acting surgeon-in-chief of the Freedmen's Hospital. In this position, he instituted reforms in working standards, mainly in his specialty—obstetrics. He also trained nurses, and he participated on many committees that fought for proper medical and sanitation facilities for African American communities. Francis was also a member of the local and national boards of health where he voiced the concerns of African Americans in all area of health care.

Upon leaving public heath care services, Francis established a private practice called the Francis Sanatorium at his former home on Pennsylvania Avenue. The first of its kind in the United States, this institution offered services to poor African Americans who lived in deplorable, unhealthy conditions. Trained nurses and private care doctors rendered services in this institution, including emergency services. Patrons were treated in a medical institution that resembled a comfortable home.

Francis belonged to the upper crust of African American society. He proved that African Americans, in the height of segregation, racism, and discrimination, were able to rise above the odds, distinguish themselves, and make important contributions to society. Francis was an associate of Booker T. Washington, who was also affiliated with Howard University, and he was friends with his neighbor, Frederick Douglass. In fact, he was a pallbearer at Douglass's funeral, and he was a guest of honor at a luncheon held for Washington on February 15, 1906. Francis was also mentioned in Washington's book, *A New Negro for a New Century*.

Francis engaged in various social activities. He was a member of several social clubs and committees. He was a member of the Civic Club where he was in charge of sanitation, and he used his office to highlight the plight of African Americans in that area. When he was appointed as delegate to the National Conference of Charities and Corrections in 1909, he represented the needs of his race. He also served on ad hoc committees in a bank, where he had stocks, and the Washington Automobile Club that lobbied for better road conditions and solutions to other automobile-related problems.

Francis died, at his home, on May 23, 1913, and his funeral service was held, three days later, at Fifteenth Street Presbyterian Church. Although Francis was educated, wealthy, and socially accepted in the upper echelon of African Americans, he used his offices and social position to lobby for the welfare of his race.

REFERENCES

Books

Richings, G. F. *Evidences of Progress among Colored People*. Philadelphia: George S. Ferguson Co., 1905.

Washington, Booker T. *A New Negro for a New Century*. Manchester, Ill.: Ayer Company Publishers, Inc., 1969.

Denise Jarrett

Free Frank
1777–1854

Entrepreneur, pioneer

As a pioneer on the Kentucky and Illinois frontier, Frank "Free Frank" McWhorter coped with the hostile and desolate conditions of remote backwoods as

---

Chronology

1777	Born in Pulaski County on the South Carolina frontier
1799	Marries a slave named Lucy
1800	First child born
1810	Allowed to hire himself out to earn money
1815	Owner dies without making provisions to manumit him
1817	Purchases wife's freedom from William Denham in April for $800
1819	Purchases his freedom from the McWhorters in September for $800
1827	Wins court case validating the legality of marriage between free blacks in Illinois
1829	Purchases freedom of son Frank Jr., a fugitive slave, for $1000
1830	Leaves Kentucky for Illinois in September, settling in Pike County
1835	Purchases son Solomon's freedom for $500 with the money the family earned from the sale of its agricultural products
1836	Establishes the town of New Philadelphia under the Illinois Town Plat Act
1854	Dies on September 7

---

both a slave and freedman. Heralded for his dedication as a slave, Free Frank managed to amass enough money by hiring himself out to purchase his wife's freedom and then that of his own. As a free person of color, Free Frank owned and operated a successful saltpeter business and was a lifelong farmer. Through his extraordinary business savvy he purchased several plots of land in both states, including the town of New Philadelphia, which he purchased sight unseen. Established in 1836, the settlement was the first city founded by an African American.

Free Frank was born to a West-African-born slave named Juda sometime in 1777 on the South Carolina frontier where she was a slave of the McWhorter family. No surviving written records point to the child's paternity; however, the family's rich oral history suggests that his father was George McWhorter, his mother's owner. Sources on young Frank's childhood experiences are scarce, but there is substantial information on the activities of his probable father. Settling in Union County in 1763, George McWhorter was among a considerable population of Scotch-Irish immigrants on the American frontier. During the Revolutionary War, McWhorter volunteered and served in Colonel Henry Hampton's regiment of the light dragoons, a part of General Thomas Sumter's South Carolina Brigade. The fact that the revolution marked the beginning of the end of Northern slavery meant little to the reality of slaves in the South such as Frank, whose childhood experiences were undoubtedly defined by fear and terror.

Like most slave owners on the South Carolina frontier, the McWhorters only held a few slaves before settling in Kentucky. Reports on the conditions of Frank's arrival in the state vary, but most sources suggest that he arrived in Pulaski County, Kentucky along with the McWhorter family as their slave. During his first year on the Kentucky frontier, Free Frank met a slave named Lucy who became his wife in 1799. While the commitment of slaves like Frank and Lucy was not legally sanctioned, the pair's commitment was as real then as it was when they eventually formally married under Illinois law in 1839. Born a slave in 1771, Lucy was owned by William Denham, who lived in a distant Pulaski settlement. In 1800, the couple had their first child whom they named Juda, after her paternal grandmother. Over the next seventeen years, Frank and Lucy had twelve more slave-born children, yet only four of the thirteen lived to adulthood and freedom. Similarly, the couple later had four free-born children, only three of whom survived the harsh conditions of the Pulaski County frontier to live to adulthood.

How Industry Secured His Freedom

As a developer and defender of his owner's westward movement to settle the Kentucky Pennyroyal wilderness, Free Frank's value was immeasurable. With the initial settlement period in the late 1790s over, new laws at the turn of the century further encouraged settling on the Kentucky frontier. Slave labor was in demand by new settlers and very profitable for owners who could earn from $80 to $100 a year hiring out their slaves. Given Free Frank's skills as both a farm laborer and jack-of-all-trades, his master could benefit from the lucrative practice by hiring him out throughout the early years of the nineteenth century. Sanctioned and even encouraged by law, the lucrative practice soon became commonplace for slaveholders. However, it was against the law for owners to allow their slaves to hire out their own time.

By 1810, Free Frank was already allowed to hire himself out with the potential to earn his freedom, but the provision required him to pay his owner $10 to $12 a month. Doubtless, George McWhorter never anticipated that there was any real possibility that Free Frank would find enough time to earn his freedom, much less that of his family as well. Then too the availability of crude niter allowed Free Frank to capitalize on the growing demand for saltpeter brought on by the War of 1812. He established a saltpeter works business and was apparently the county's sole provider.

George McWhorter died in 1815 without making any provisions for Free Frank's manumission. His sons agreed to grant Free Frank's freedom in exchange for his continuing to do all the work on the Pulaski farm until he could accumulate the $500 required for his freedom. While the McWhorter brothers probably expected him to take at least another five to fifteen years before he earned the price of his freedom, they had misjudged Free Frank's resourcefulness and business shrewdness.

In April 1817, within just two years of his owner's death, Free Frank purchased his wife's freedom from William Denham for the considerable sum of $800. While the purchase price was $300 more than his own, his wife's freedom meant that any future children she bore would also be free, and the couple welcomed their first free-born child whom they named Squire that September. In September 1819, Free Frank also managed to bargain with the McWhorters for the purchase of his freedom for $800.

Free Frank and his family continued to live in Pulaski County, all the while expanding their business and receiving fame as a result of its success. The family reveled in the accomplishment of Frank, Lucy, and Squire's freedom, but their joy would be short-lived. Denham, Lucy's former owner, died suddenly living considerable debts, part of which his son and executor attempted to pay by suing Lucy for $212 in 1824. The Pulaski court ruled against the Franks and ordered Lucy to repay the debt. Even so, the Franks refused to accept the lower court's verdict and continued to pursue the case until it reached the Kentucky Court of Appeals later that same year. In a landmark decision, the Court of Appeals ruled in the Franks' favor, establishing the precedent that later allowed free blacks to marry in the state of Kentucky. After a series of attempted counter-moves by the Pulaski Court, the Court of Appeals finalized its determination in a 1827 ruling that recognized the right of free blacks to legally marry.

With the possibility of being sold away by the Denham's twenty-one-year-old, Frank Jr. fled as a fugitive slave in December 1826. In 1829, Free Frank used the continued success of his saltpeter business to arrange for the purchase of his son Frank's freedom, even though the business was worth more than young Frank's $1000 market value. This was one of the elder Frank's last business transactions before leaving Kentucky for Illinois. In preparation for his departure, Frank purchased a 160-acre tract of land for $200 without ever having seen it to circumvent a new Illinois law that required free blacks to pay a $1000 security bond to guarantee that he or she would not become a public charge. As such, the strategic purchase effectively demonstrated that he was self-supporting and unlikely to become dependent on the state.

Pioneering Illinois

By the time he was ready to leave Kentucky for Illinois in September 1830, fifty-three year-old Free Frank had accumulated several hundred dollars from the sale of his homestead and other properties. Free Frank, his wife Lucy, who steadily approached her sixtieth birthday, their newly manumitted son Frank and free-born children Squire, Commodore, and Lucy Ann, began their journey westward, well aware of the dangers posed by kidnappers despite their being free. In Illinois they found racism was pervasive.

They settled in Pike County, a community largely populated by families relocating by way of Kentucky. While settlements on the Military Tract where the Franks settled were sparsely populated, the family was able to use the agricultural equipment they brought with them from Kentucky to cultivate the land that Free Frank purchased. While they earned little from the subsistence crops in their first year, by the 1830s, Free Frank was able to increase his economic activities by diversifying his crops, raising hogs, and boarding horses in the mid-1840s.

Founding New Philadelphia

In 1835, just four years after moving to Illinois, Free Frank was able to purchase his son Solomon's freedom for $500 with the money the family earned from the sale of its agricultural products. The family continued to cultivate their 160-acre farm holdings, and in 1836, they made a critical land acquisition of five adjacent tracts totaling 280 acres for a purchase price of more than $360. In 1836, under the Illinois Town Plat Act, Free Frank established the community of New Philadelphia with 144 lots, two principal streets and several alleys, all named by him. Located just north to the plat, Free Frank remained on his farm even after founding New Philadelphia so that he could attract fellow farmers as well as townspeople to his development.

Despite the sale of at least eight lots by the early 1840s, only three houses stood during the years of depression on the Illinois frontier. Like most fledgling Pike county towns, the community experienced little growth until the end of the depression period in the mid-1940s, when the economic outlook for the entire county improved drastically. Centrally located at the intersection of several important country roads, New Philadelphia acted as a stagecoach stop and opened a U.S. Post Office branch in 1849. Free Frank also planned for the building of a private school to be called Free Will Baptist Seminary that would also serve as a church; the school never materialized. Despite being severely hampered by the relocation of a main road to the outskirts of its community, by 1850 New Philadelphia was home to at least eleven families and a population of 58 people, including 36 whites. Even so, the Illinois assembly passed a law that fined any person who brought free blacks into the state and ordered the arrest and deportment of any free black who came to the city on his or her own in 1853.

As a part of the Underground Railroad, Free Frank and his family readily assisted fugitive slaves on their way to Canada. However, legislative attempts to make the county all-white demonstrated that pioneer blacks were never far from the reach of racism. Even so, Free Frank continued to develop land through the sale of his lots and his steady agricultural efforts. By 1850, the family owned over 600 acres of land valued at more than $7,000. Free Frank purchased the freedom of his daughter Sally in 1843, and he purchased Juda's freedom shortly before 1850. Free Frank's earnings also secured the freedom of seven slave-born grandchildren and great-grandchildren as well as the freedom of Squire's fugitive wife Louisa, allowing her to return from Canada (where she had escaped to freedom) to live with the family in Illinois. When Free Frank died on September 7, 1854, he left a legacy much richer than most of his white counterparts at a time. Perhaps most impressively, Free Frank paid more than $14,000 in all to free himself and fifteen other family members in just a forty-year span.

REFERENCES

Books

Walker, Juliet E. K. *Free Frank: A Black Pioneer on the Antebellum Frontier.* Lexington: University Press of Kentucky, 1983.

Periodicals

Browning, Tamara. "Historic Revival of Town Planned." *State Journal Register*, 25 July 2005.

Davis, Ericka Blount. "Frontier Town Founded by Black Pioneer." *Crisis* 111 (September/October 2004): 11.

Smith, Wes. "Freed from Obscurity: This Ex-slave Pioneered a New Image for Blacks." *Chicago Tribune*, 28 September 1990.

Crystal A. deGregory

Charles Fuller
1939–

Playwright, screenwriter

Best known for *A Soldier's Play*, Charles Fuller was the second African American to receive a Pulitzer Prize. Fuller has written compelling social drama revolving around African American life in society. His works encompass the full range of human behavior and emotion.

Charles Fuller was born in Philadelphia, Pennsylvania on March 5, 1939. Being raised in a racially mixed neighborhood and attending integrated parochial schools provided Fuller with the self confidence he needed to pursue a writing career. Fuller's love of the written word began early in his life. As a young child, his father established his own printing business. Fuller assisted his father with proofreading galleys. The first play Fuller saw was performed in Yiddish. Fuller did not understand a word, but he was profoundly moved by what he saw.

Charles Fuller

Another influence on Fuller was the time he spent at the public library reading. Most books he read perpetuated negative stereotypes of African American culture. Reading widely made Fuller want to become a writer, so he could write about the black experience as it really is.

In 1956, Fuller began attending Villanova University located in Philadelphia, Pennsylvania majoring in English. But he was discouraged from pursuing his dream of becoming a writer by his professors. Additionally, the school magazine refused to publish his stories. In 1958, Fuller dropped out of college and joined the army.

After his discharge from the army in 1962, Fuller returned to Philadelphia, Pennsylvania and married Miriam Nesbitt. Fuller and his wife had two sons (Charles Fuller III and David). For several years, Fuller had a variety of jobs; he was a bank loan collector, a counselor for minority students at Temple University where he later became a lecturer of black studies, and a city housing inspector. Fuller returned to night school at La Salle College in 1965 where he graduated in 1968 with a B.A. degree.

Black Theater

Fuller continued to write short stories and essays, primarily in dialogue. These writings became the basis for his plays. While working as a housing inspector Fuller realized that the black communities were in bleak cir-

cumstances. In a bid to strengthen and support these communities, Fuller co-founded the Afro-American Arts Theatre in Philadelphia in 1969. Much of Fuller's early work in the theater were sketches based on community issues that he observed while serving as a housing inspector.

Over the next several years, the Afro-American Arts Theatre staged many of works by Fuller, including *The Sunflowers*, which were six one-act plays, and *The Rise*, which depicted the story of Marcus Garvey in four acts.

Fulfilling the Dream

As Fuller's plays became more intricate, he gained the attention of the McCarter Theater in Princeton, New Jersey. The McCarter Theater commissioned Fuller to write the play *The Village: A Party* in 1968. This play was a study of racial integration and conflict. *The Village: A Party* presents an idealistic look at racial integration that eventually erodes in a community in which all the couples are interracial when an African American man falls in love with an African American woman and is killed. This play was so well received that it ran off-Broadway a year later at Tambellini's Gate Theater. The play was re-titled *The Perfect Party* in 1969. Due to the success of this play, Fuller decided to move his family to New York and become a professional playwright.

Next, Fuller wrote two plays for the New Federal Theatre: *In My Many Names and Days* in 1972 and *The Candidate* in 1974. In 1974 Fuller began a long and successful relationship with the Negro Ensemble Company. However, his first play for the ensemble (*In the Deepest Part of Sleep*) was not well received.

By this time, Fuller had reached another turning point. He wanted to go beyond social issues to bring attention to the explosive racial strife in the United States. He wanted to put a different face on the common stereotypes. Fuller wrote a play that depicted the historical tragedy of the shooting spree that took place in Brownsville, Texas in 1906. An all African American army regiment was accused of the incident. The entire regiment was dishonorably discharged by President Theodore Roosevelt. The play, *The Brownsville Raid*, not only brought to light the unwavering loyalty the soldiers felt for their country, but their faith in the army. Fuller had written elegantly of the betrayal the soldiers experienced. *The Brownsville Raid* ran for 112 performances. This play marked the first time Fuller wrote about the military. In 1972, the army overturned the dishonorable discharge.

Although Fuller's next play, *Zooman and the Sign*, received mixed reviews, it garnered two Obie Awards. In 1995, *Zooman and the Sign* was adapted into a movie entitled *Zooman*.

Fuller's most noted play, *A Soldier's Play*, was written as a tribute for his friend Larry Neal, who was a poet, playwright, and critic. *A Soldier's Play* ran for more than a year off-Broadway. This work was such a successful work that Fuller was awarded the Pulitzer Prize in 1982. Fuller adapted this play for the motion picture, *A Soldier's Story*.

REFERENCES

Books

Smith, Pamela J. Olubunmi. "Charles Fuller." In *Cyclopedia of World Authors*. Ed. Frank N. Magill. Pasadena, Calif.: Salem Press, 1997.

Sussman, Alison Carb. "Charles Fuller." In *Contemporary Black Biography: Profiles from the International Black Community*. Ed. L. Mpho Mabunda. Detroit: Gale Research, 1995.

Teri B. Weil

Solomon Carter Fuller
1872–1953

Pathologist, psychiatrist

One of the nation's first African American psychiatrists, Solomon Carter Fuller became well known for his work in neuropathology and psychiatry. Early in his career, he conducted research on degenerative dis-

---

Chronology

1872	Born in Monrovia, Liberia on August 11
1893	Receives A.B. degree from Livingstone College, Salisbury, N.C.; studies medicine at Long Island College Hospital in Brooklyn
1894	Transfers to Boston University School of Medicine
1897	Receives M.D. degree from Boston University School of Medicine; begins internship at Westborough State Hospital for the Insane in Boston
1897-1919	Serves as director of the Clinical Society Commission of Massachusetts
1899	Named chief pathologist at the hospital; becomes part-time instructor at Boston University School of Medicine; becomes one of the first African American physicians to teach at a multiracial medical school in United States
1900	Establishes museum to display his research items
1904-05	Studies on leave of absence at Carnegie Laboratory in New York and the University of Munich
1909	Marries sculptor Meta Warrick
1911	Identifies one cause of Alzheimer's disease and publishes findings
1919	Resigns post at Westborough State Hospital for the Insane
1921	Named associate professor of neurology at Boston University School of Medicine
1928-33	Functions as chair of the Department of Neurology but is never named chair
1933	Retires from post at Boston University School of Medicine
1943	Receives honorary Doctor of Science degree from Livingstone College
1944	Loses eyesight
1953	Dies in Framingham, Massachusetts on January 16
1971	Black Psychiatrists of America presents his portrait to American Psychiatric Association
1973	Memorialized in all-day conference at Boston University School of Medicine

---

eases of the brain, including Alzheimer's disease, leaving a legacy to American and African American psychiatry. He endured racism in his workplace and in the community where he lived and yet late in life was finally recognized for his outstanding work.

The son of Solomon Carter Fuller Sr. and Anna Ursula James, Solomon Fuller Jr. was born in Monrovia, Liberia, on August 11, 1872. Anna James Fuller was the daughter of two doctors and church missionaries who returned to the United States from Africa. The father of Solomon Sr., John Lewis Fuller, was a coffee planter and Liberian government official—a high sheriff who specialized in land claims and the son of a repatriated former American, who started life in Norfolk, Virginia. John Fuller was an excellent cobbler with a sharp mind; thus, he was able to run his own business so well that he received part of the profits. He used the money to buy his freedom as well as that of his wife. By then the American Colonization Society made it possible for former slaves to settle in Liberia, if they wished. This option attracted John Lewis Fuller, so he sent his son Thomas to Liberia to investigate living conditions. The favorable report encouraged him to move his family to Monrovia in 1849. The experienced cobbler found that carpenters were in demand and thus changed his profession. This change provided a good living for him, his wife, and their two sons, Thomas and Solomon Jr. Fuller Sr.'s brother also served the government as treasurer of the Republic of Liberia. In June 1899, Solomon Jr. left Monrovia for the land that his paternal grandfather had left much earlier, the United States, at first studying at historically black Livingstone College in Salisbury, North Carolina, founded just ten years before. He experienced racism in the small town of Salisbury, something he had not known in the country of his birth. He survived, however, and concentrated on advancing his studies.

After receiving an A.B. degree from Livingstone in 1893, Fuller entered Long Island College Hospital in Brooklyn, New York, to pursue a medical degree. When the American Psychological Association held its fiftieth annual meeting in May 1894, Fuller attended and heard S. Weir Mitchell give the keynote address. Impressed with his speech, Fuller soon made a decision that would affect his entire professional life. Miller noted that the field of psychiatry needed transformation and that nurses and doctors needed to be better prepared to serve the field. They needed to know the causes of mental illnesses, to work in more humane conditions, and to be rigid in observing the rules of science. They needed to follow rules regarding cleanliness and record-keeping in the laboratories. Fuller soon decided that he would follow Mitchell's lead.

In 1894, Fuller transferred to Boston University School of Medicine, and he graduated in 1897 with the M.D. By then neurology was especially appealing to Fuller, a fact that attracted the attention of Edward P. Colby, one of his professors. Fuller had been disturbed by racism in the United States and knew that his grandfather had been a slave in Virginia early on, but he chose to remain in this country rather than return to Liberia. Colby introduced him to George Adams, superintendent of Westborough State Hospital for the Insane, located in west Boston. Colby also encouraged Adams to hire Fuller. Fuller accepted Adams's offer for a six-month unpaid internship at the hospital as an assistant in the pathology laboratory. He worked under E. L. Mellis, examining brain cells of psychiatric patients who had died, as he sought a link between their mental problems and their anatomy. He did research on living patients as well, gathering blood samples as he searched for other clues to mental illness. In so doing, Fuller became a trailblazer, for he connected the work of the physician and that of the laboratory researcher in the area of mental illness.

Within the year his mentor, Dr. Mellis, left for a post at Johns Hopkins University in Baltimore. Both were confident that Fuller could manage the laboratory well. He continued his research, tested his findings against what scientists knew up to that time, and documented all of his work. He also suggested areas in which additional research was needed—topics that fascinated him by then, such as paranoia, melancholia, and pernicious anemia. Fuller performed well, and two years after Mellis left, Fuller was promoted, becoming the chief pathologist for the hospital. This marked the beginning of a forty-five-year tenure there—as pathologist for twenty-two years and as consultant for twenty-three. Fuller soon built a fine reputation as a talented teacher in pathology, having accepted a part-time instructorship at Boston University School of Medicine in 1899. With this post he became one of the first African American physicians to teach at a multiracial medical school in the United States.

Fuller lived on the grounds of Westborough State Hospital, near Boston University, which allowed him long hours in the laboratory that he directed at the state hospital. While in the laboratory he photographed extremely thin sections of brain tissue from deceased psychiatric patients. His aim was to determine whether or not there were connections between mental disorder and organic disease; thus he cautiously used the camera, microscope, and microtome in his search. Later, he practiced medicine in Boston. On several occasions Fuller threatened to leave the laboratory post due to his low salary, only $25 monthly, while white physicians were paid $45 a month. With an increase in salary to $800 a year, he decided to stay on for another year. Another perk that he received was six weeks off a year.

In 1900, Fuller established a museum at the hospital where he could display what he regarded as a casual connection between diseases of the brain tissue and the behavior resulting from some mental illnesses. The photomicrograph (a way to photograph pathology slides though a microscope lens), which he invented, became acceptable in medical textbooks.

Fuller took a leave of absence from both of his posts. He did advanced study at the Carnegie Laboratory in New York and in 1904-05 studied under several well-known German medical scientists at the Psychiatric Clinic of the University of Munich. He knew that, at that time, psychiatry was more advanced in Europe than elsewhere. In Munich, he studied with neuropsychiatrist Emil Kraepelin, whose 1883 book *Compendium der Psychiatrie* was the basic text for psychiatrists. According to *Contemporary Black Biography*, the book helped to influence the setting of scientific parameters in psychiatry. It also "displayed the first attempts to classify mental diseases into two general groups: dementia praecox—later called schizophrenia—and manic-depressive psychosis." Kraepelin was also interested in objective tests that would facilitate the study of medications on mental disorders. As impressed with Kraepelin's work as he was, Fuller was equally impressed with his laboratory, the precision with which it operated, his experiments and results, and the detailed documentation that was kept. Both men knew that psychiatry and any other medical discipline should follow rigorous standards. Fuller's professional life was greatly enhanced by his year in Germany and ideas he learned from Kraepelin's lectures.

While in Germany, Fuller also met Alois Alzheimer of Hamburg, the scientist who identified progressive dementia, or Alzheimer's disease. Although Alzheimer was a poor lecturer, Fuller found him a peerless scientific researcher. Fuller also met Paul Ehrlich, the 1908 Nobel Prize winner for his work in immunology.

In 1909, Fuller attended a series of lectures by Sigmund Freud given at Clark University in Worcester, a town not far from Framingham. Later, Fuller established a private psychotherapy practice in his home, where he worked with both blacks and whites. He also continued his research and teaching, particularly on neurology. Fuller's German mentor, Alzheimer, had spurred his curiosity about the disease that bore his name, and Fuller included among his various writings several papers on the disease. In fact, in a 1911 publication, Fuller identified the ninth known cause of Alzheimer's disease.

Fuller left Westborough in 1919, when his teaching at Boston University finally brought him recognition. In that year, Fuller became associate professor of neuropathology. The title was revised in 1921, when he became associate professor of neurology. Fuller functioned as chair of the Department of Neurology from 1928 to 1933, yet was never actually given the chairmanship. He retired in 1933 but the retirement resulted from yet another act of racial discrimination. A white assistant professor was promoted to full professor, outranked Fuller, and was made the official department chair. Despite what appeared to be full acceptance of the popular, effective, and highly respected teacher, Fuller was never officially placed on the university's payroll. He was paid for his services, however inadequate his compensation. He knew that race played a part in his stay at Boston University from his first encounter with the school until the last. As well, he believed that, given his training and experience, he would have gone farther had he been white.

Fuller never fully severed his ties with the hospital: he held a succession of part-time positions there. He was also visiting neurologist at Massachusetts Memorial Hospital and a consulting neurologist for Massachusetts General Hospital. After consulting with Framingham Marlboro Hospital, Fuller moved to the Allentown, Pennsylvania, State Hospital.

In addition to his work at various hospitals, from 1897 to 1919, Fuller was pathologist and director of the Clinical Society Commission of Massachusetts. For many years he edited the *Westborough State Hospital Papers*, where the work of the hospital staff was published. He

was an accomplished scientific writer as well. Among his published papers were "Four Cases of Pernicious Anemia among Insane Subjects" (*New England Medical Gazette*, 1901); "An Analysis of 100 Cases of Dementia Precox in Men" (*Proceedings of the Society of Neurological Psychiatry*, 1908); "Involutional Melancholia" (*New England Society of Psychiatry*, 1910); "An Analysis of 3,140 Admissions to Westborough State Hospital, with Reference to the Diagnosis of Involutional Melancholia" (*Proceedings of the Society of Neurological Psychiatry*, 1911); and "A Study of the Miliary Plaques Found in Brains of the Aged" (*Proceedings of the American Medio-Psychological Association*, 1911).

While visiting Westborough State Hospital, Meta Vaux Warrick, an exceptional sculptor who had studied in Paris under Auguste Rodin, met Solomon Fuller Jr. The couple was married on February 9, 1909, and bought a house halfway between Boston and Framingham. Meta Fuller was diminutive, strikingly beautiful, with deep spiritual roots. She had sold her works at reputable galleries and was widely respected. She was also an important precursor of the Harlem Renaissance artists. Despite the prominence of both of the Fullers, the white community in which they lived rejected them. Local whites were unsuccessful in the petition to prevent the Fullers from buying their house. The Fullers persevered, ignored the racism that surrounded them, and enjoyed their comfortable home and the three sons they had.

Some writers suggest that Meta Fuller would have preferred life on the Continent, but she planned and lived her life according to social dictates for a married woman. Solomon Fuller supported her interests and became the subject of one of her most famous works. Meanwhile, Meta Fuller was impressed with her husband's knowledge and equipment and thought that he might consider engaging in portrait photography. The couple then took up portrait photography as a hobby and received great satisfaction from it in their later years, until Fuller lost his sight. When blindness came, Meta Fuller gave up the studio where she had continued her fine sculpturing and tended to her husband's needs.

Solomon Fuller had several other hobbies: he was a skillful gardener and bookbinder; and he became a leather crafter and tooled and decorated his own leather. He became a bibliophile as well, locating old, rare books found in second-hand stores and using his leather crafting and binding skills to restore the books to beautiful works that became collectors' items. Both of the Fullers loved music as well; in fact, early on Meta Fuller played the guitar.

Fuller's contribution to World War II came in the form of membership on the Advisory Medical Board No. 17. Fuller returned to his alma mater, Livingstone College, in 1943, the fiftieth anniversary of his graduation from the college. The Livingstone occasion also marked the dedication of the Price Memorial Building for science laboratories; the building honored J. C. Price (1854-93), gifted orator, temperance leader, minister, and early president of the college. During the college's celebration, Fuller was awarded the honorary degree Doctor of Science.

While at the college, Fuller also engaged in a lengthy radio interview in which he discussed the impact of World War II on the mental and nervous energies of those engaged in war and on civilians. Quoted in the *Journal of the National Medical Association*, Fuller said the federal government was taking precautions to ensure that men who suffered mental disorders saw no combat and were discharged instead. Some of the men with such disorders could be rehabilitated, he thought, due to the advances in psychiatry. After citing an example of the British population that had been heavily bombed during World War II, Fuller noted that the same could happen in American cities. If that occurred, "a certain mental strain would be the inevitable result." He thought that "the process of adjustment to such a situation would strengthen the resistance of the public to deterioration in mental health and would eventuate a stronger determination to protect their lived ones and their homeland."

Fuller belonged to several professional organizations: the Massachusetts Psychiatric Society, New York Psychiatric Society, American Psychiatric Society, American Medical Association, the Boston Society for Psychiatry and Neurology, Massachusetts Medical Society, the New England Medical Society, and the New England Psychiatric Association.

After Fuller died, the Boston Society for Psychiatry and Neurology published a number of resolutions honoring Fuller in the *New England Journal of Medicine*. In the 1970s Fuller was well recognized for his contribution to American psychiatry as well as to black psychiatrists who practiced in this country. In May 1971 the Black Psychiatrists of America presented his portrait to the American Psychiatric Association, located in Washington, D.C. His recognitions continued, and in October 1973 the Boston University School of Medicine celebrated its centennial year and included in the celebration an all-day conference to memorialize Fuller. At that time as well, Meta Fuller presented her sculpture of his bust to the library of his alma mater, Livingstone College. The Solomon Carter Fuller Mental Health Center in Boston is named in his honor.

Virginia Sammons, in *Blacks in Science and Medicine*, wrote that Fuller was acknowledged as America's first black psychiatrist. Toward the end of his life a colleague, James B. Ayer, visited him and, according to the *Journal of the Negro Medical Association*, described meeting him at his home: "though blind, his memory was excellent, his speech flawless, his interests alive. He knew he had not long to live, but accepted the fact in his usual philosophical manner, like the perfect gentleman he was."

Solomon Fuller suffered from diabetes, which began to take its toll on him soon after he retired from Boston University and led to his blindness in 1944, forcing him to sever his long association with Westborough State Hospital. Yet he continued to see patients in his private practice from time to time, practically until he died in Framingham of natural causes on January 16, 1953. His wife Meta and three sons survived him. Meta Warrick Fuller died on March 13, 1968.

REFERENCES

Books

Harkness, Jon M. "Solomon Carter Fuller." In *American National Biography*, Vol. 8. Eds. John A. Garraty and Mark C. Carnes. New York: Oxford University Press, 1999.

Hayden, Robert C. "Solomon Carter Fuller." In *Dictionary of American Negro Biography*. Eds. Rayford W. Logan and Michael R. Winston. New York: Norton, 1982.

Sammons, Vivian O. *Blacks in Science and Medicine.* New York: Hemisphere Publishing Corp., 1990.

Who's Who in Colored America, 1938-41. 5th ed. Brooklyn: Thomas Yenser, 1940.

Wolf, Gillian. "Solomon Carter Fuller." In *Contemporary Black Biography.* Vol. 15. Detroit: Gale, 1997.

Periodicals

Cobb, W. Montague. "Solomon Carter Fuller, 1872-1953." *Journal of the National Medical Association* 46 (September 1954): 370-72.

Jessie Carney Smith

Thomas O. Fuller
1867–1942

Senator, educator, entrepreneur

During the latter part of the nineteenth century and well into the twentieth century, Thomas O. Fuller made a sweeping contribution to African Americans through a variety of endeavors, ranging from teacher, to school principal, from state senator to religious leadership, and from entrepreneurship to writings. His work also spanned two states: North Carolina (where he was its first African American state senator) and Tennessee (where he became a college president). Although his vision for racial

Chronology

1867	Born in Franklinton, North Carolina on October 25
1890	Becomes ordained in the Baptist church
1892	Receives B.S. degree from Shaw University; begins teaching in public schools
1893	Establishes Colored Grade School in Franklinton; establishes Girls' Training School in Franklinton; receives M.A. degree from Shaw University
1895	Becomes principal of Shiloh Institute at Warrenton
1898	Elected first African American senator in North Carolina
1900	Moves to Memphis, Tennessee; becomes pastor of First Baptist Church
1902	Becomes principal of Howe Institute; later becomes president
1906	Receives Ph.D. degree from Alabama A&M College
1910	Receives D.D. degree from Shaw University
1942	Dies in Memphis, Tennessee on June 21

uplift was demonstrated in all of his work, he never saw himself as the racial leader that he was.

Born in Franklinton, North Carolina, near Raleigh, Thomas Oscar Fuller Sr. was the youngest child of former slave J. Henderson Fuller, a wheelwright and carpenter, who had learned to read while still enslaved. Since his services were in constant demand, he was able to earn enough money to purchase the freedom of a woman named Mary Eliza Fuller, who became his wife and mother of their fourteen children. Aunt Mary, as she became known, served as a nurse to sick blacks and whites. After the Civil War ended, the elder Fuller bought property in Franklinton and moved his family into their new home. During Reconstruction he became involved in politics, serving as delegate to various Republican conventions and as magistrate.

Achieves Academic and Divinity Degrees

When he was five years old, Thomas Fuller began his education in a private school. In 1882 North Carolina established the State Normal School in Franklinton, where Fuller continued his studies until 1885, when he enrolled in Shaw University, a black college in Raleigh. In addition to the academic course, he took simultaneously a four-year course in theology. In 1890, his senior year at Shaw, Fuller became an assistant teacher for the American Baptist Home Mission Society. He worked his way through college and graduated as valedictorian in May 1890 with a B.A. degree. Other degrees followed: M.A., Shaw University (1893); Ph.D., the Agricultural and Mechanical College at Normal, Alabama (1906); and D.D., Shaw University (1910).

Although Fuller began to preach in 1886 while in his senior year at Shaw, he was not ordained in the Baptist church until April 30, 1890. Upon graduation, Fuller taught in the public schools of Granville County, North Carolina, where he worked for $28 a month. Then he moved to a second school in that county, located in Berea. Still teaching in April 1891 he also headed Belton Creek Church near Oxford. Within the year, with donations from a white friend, he led the construction of a new facility. Within one year, Fuller was called to pastorates at eleven churches in the area.

The Baptists in Franklinton called Fuller back to his home town in 1892 for the purpose of organizing a school while he continued his pastoral work. He established the Colored Graded School and in 1893 the Girls' Training School in Franklinton, which attracted students from all over the state. He oversaw the construction of a new building for the girls' school, which was completed in 1894. In 1895, Fuller resigned and became principal of Shiloh Institute at Warrenton, which the Shiloh Association of Baptist churches owned. He also took charge of a nearby church. He became recording secretary of the North Carolina State Sunday-School Convention.

Elected to North Carolina State Senate

By now his success as school principal and pastor was so well known that he was asked to accept the nomination for state senate. Now living in Warrenton, he was in the midst of a political hotbed, a place where black Republicans had held various county offices and were in complete charge of county and district party machinery. Fuller won the election handily in 1898, representing the Eleventh District (Warren and Vance counties) and became the first African American in the state senate and the only one until 1968. The Wilmington riot, in which many people died, followed the election. The state had gone Democratic while Republicans had won in Warren and Vance counties; this outcome provoked the cry of "White Supremacy" and "Negro Domination," wrote Fuller in his memoir, *Twenty Years in Public Life*. These events marked a dark chapter in the state's political history, as Democrats used various methods to gain control of counties and cities with black Republican officials. Fuller responded in "An Address to the Colored People of the Eleventh Senatorial District of North Carolina," published in his memoir. He called for calm and assured blacks that the color of their skin could "never become legal barriers to the exercise of the right of franchise." He called himself an educator and a humble Christian worker who refused to serve in any capacity that would jeopardize what he had achieved; he would work in the interest of his constituents.

When the state assembly convened in January 1899, Fuller was the last senator to be seated, following that of all whites who were seated in alphabetical order. His seat on the outside row next to the lobby positioned him to hear comments from those outside, including such racist remarks as "Here is a Negro in the Senate—Never mind we'll fix that within the next two years," which he recorded in his memoir. He witnessed another display of racism when the senate refused to appoint him to any committees. Nonetheless, Fuller persevered and was successful in the work that he did for the benefit of both white and black races. In his judgment, the most significant service that he rendered while in the legislature clearly put him on records in political annals. He drafted and introduced a bill to enable the criminal court to meet every four (instead of every six) months, to give that court jurisdiction over the superior court, and thus decrease docket loads and result in speedier trials. He supported temperance and every move to curtail liquor traffic in Warrenton; his lobbying for the Warren County Dispensary Bill led to the closing of a local bar, replacing it with a dispensary.

For African Americans, however, Fuller's work was more notable than he acknowledged. He successfully led the political task of incorporating North Carolina Mutual and Provident Association—later known as North Carolina Mutual Life Insurance Company—making it a legitimate insurance industry in the state. Ultimately, it became a prosperous black insurance enterprise and the nation's largest black insurance company. Later on, Fuller became a vice-president of North Carolina Mutual. Next, Fuller sponsored a bill to reverse the law and allow outside labor to recruit black workers from within the state. He was unsuccessful in his protest against a bill to disfranchise blacks and to use literacy tests, a poll tax, and a grandfather clause to return blacks to the restricted legal status that they had known early on. His eloquent address before the senate fell on deaf ears.

Becomes President of Howe Institute

After a two-year term in office, Fuller moved to Memphis, Tennessee, in 1900 and became pastor of First Baptist Church on St. Paul Avenue. He continued to serve the Baptist church at both the local and national levels. In 1902, Fuller was elected principal of the coeducational and normal school, Howe Institute in Memphis, which the Baptists of West Tennessee operated. There he also taught theology, law, and other subjects. His appointment was with the understanding that he would serve only a short time, until a full-time principal could he hired. But sometime later on the school was renamed Howe Junior College, and he served as president until he retired in 1931. Fuller devoted his time to literary work in connection with First Baptist Church. Around this time Fuller wrote *Pictorial History of the American Negro* (1930).

In 1927, officials at Howe began talks of a merger with the once Nashville-based Roger Williams College, which was founded in 1864 and offered elementary classes to black Baptist preachers. This college was operated under the American Baptist Home Mission Society of New York. In 1883 it was incorporated as Roger Williams University. Mysterious fires destroyed it, and after it relocated in Nashville the school continued to

experience financial problems. By the time of merger talks, the school had no president. Roger Williams moved to Memphis and on December 29, 1929 merged with Howe Institute. Roger Williams offered college courses while Howe Junior College offered high school or academy courses. The school's trustees asked Fuller to return to the presidency of Roger Williams-Howe in 1934 and help resolve its critical financial problems.

Acknowledges Work of Baptist Women

Fuller was able to mix well his work as preacher, college president, and writer. In his writings, whether about religious work or teaching, he continued to praise women. In his book *History of the Negro Baptists in Tennessee*, Fuller praised the work of women in local churches in Women's Societies, missionary societies, auxiliaries in all of the Baptist associations, as missionaries, Red Circles Junior Matrons, and in Bible bands. He criticized the lack of definite programs of instruction for the women and called for Baptist churches to establish a special course in religious training for women. The course would include motherhood, training of children, the conduct of a Christian home, health, and morals. The female students should study noted women of the Bible. He also acknowledged national women of prominence, including Sarah Willie Layten of Philadelphia; Mary W. Parrish of Louisville, Kentucky; Nannie Helen Burroughs of Washington, D.C.; and Virginia W. Broughton of Tennessee.

Fuller also held in high esteem educator Booker T. Washington, founder and president of Tuskegee Institute (now University) in Alabama. He respected him for his "methods, meetings, ideas and policies," as he noted in his memoir. Fuller attended the farmers' conferences that Washington held at Tuskegee and supported his views on industrial education and his teachings that called for jobs, homes, and schools for African American people. On many occasions he traveled the country with Washington.

Fuller's religious work included membership in the Memphis Association of Sunday School Teachers, and he was the editor of the *Signal*, the organ of the Baptist of West Tennessee. He was also a member of the Afro-American League. He chaired the Trustee Board of the Orphans and Old Ladies' Home in 1906 and helped the home to construct a new building. Among his business ventures, he was president of Our Own Real Estate Company in Memphis and organizer of the Bunker Hill Grocery Company.

Other Publications

In addition to works previously mentioned, Fuller wrote *Bright Lights in Memory's Hall, Flashes and Gems of Oratory, Banks and Banking* (1920), *Flashes and Gems of Thought and Eloquence* (1920), *Ridging the Racial Chasms: A Brief Survey of Inter-Racial Attitudes* and *Relations* (1937), *Story of Life among Negroes* (1938), and *Notes on Parliamentary Law* (1940).

While little is known of his personal life, Fuller had four wives. The first, Lucy G. Davis, whom he married in 1890, died sometime during the time that they lived in Franklinton. He married Laura Faulkner in 1898 and had two sons, Thomas Jr. (born in North Carolina) and Erskine (born in Tennessee); Erskine died in 1909. Laura Fuller died while the boys were very young, and Fuller married a woman named Rosa, who also died; then he married Dixie Williams. Thomas Fuller died in Memphis on June 21, 1942, and was buried at New Park Cemetery in Memphis.

A former student at Howe, Lula I. Hobson wrote an account of the school entitled "Howe Institute as First I Saw It and Now; or, A Short Story of Progress." In her sketch of Fuller she wrote, "as an orator he is matchless"; he never failed "to leave his audience with rich and coveted thoughts." Although Fuller never characterized himself as a race man, he was without a doubt a civil rights leader/activist. Through his work as a North Carolina legislator, educator, businessman, orator, preacher, and writer, Fuller helped to enhance African Americans, both materially and intellectually. He helped a number of African Americans to open businesses and purchase property in North Carolina and Tennessee.

REFERENCES

Books

Edmonds, Helen G. *The Negro and Fusion Politics in North Carolina, 1894-1901.* Chapel Hill: University of North Carolina Press, 1951.

Starnes, Richard D. "Thomas Oscar Fuller." In *American National Biography*, edited by John A. Garraty and Mark C. Carnes. Vol. 8. New York: Oxford University Press, 1999.

Weare, Walter B. *Black Business in the New South: A Social History of the North Carolina Mutual Life Insurance Company.* Urbana: University of Illinois Press, 1973.

Other

Hobson, Lula I. "Howe As I First Saw It and Now; or, A Short Story of Progress." Memphis: Howe Institute Printing Department, n.d. Located in the John Mercer Langston Collection, Collected Items, Box 5, folder 32. Special Collections, John Hope and Aurelia E. Franklin Library, Fisk University, Nashville, Tennessee.

Lovett, Bobby L. "Roger Williams University." *The Tennessee Encyclopedia of History and Culture.* Online edition. Knoxville: University of Tennessee Press, 2002.

Jessie Carney Smith

Harvey Fuqua
1929–

Music producer, record label executive

Harvey Fuqua became a living legend in the entertainment industry. His rise to prominence was due to his talent and a keen eye for recognizing potential in other aspiring artists.

Fuqua was born in Louisville, Kentucky on July 27, 1929. His uncle, Charlie Fuqua, had made his mark on the music industry as a member of the singing group, The Inkspots. As a young man, Fuqua would often spend time with his friends singing on the street corner of their neighborhood. They would sing spirituals and popular songs while trying to pass the time and impress girls. These informal sessions helped Fuqua hone his skills as a singer and entertainer.

The 1950s were a time of great musical innovation, especially for black artists. About this time, Fuqua and some friends of his from his neighborhood started singing together as a group. The success of his Uncle Charlie helped fuel Fuqua's desire to perform, and a group called The Crazy Sounds was formed. The group began by performing at local clubs and events. In 1952, the group came to the attention of a radio disc jockey, who changed their name to the Moonglows. The group landed a label, Chance Records, and began recording. Fuqua shared the lead vocals with Bobby Lester. By the late 1950s Fuqua soon began to sense trouble within the group. Some band members resented the money that Fuqua made as both a band member and primary songwriter. In 1959, the Moonglows disbanded, and Fuqua made several solo recordings and two duet recordings with Etta James.

Next Fuqua met Marvin Gaye. A fledgling group, the Marquees, auditioned for Fuqua in the late 1950s. Marvin Gaye was the breakout talent of this group. Fuqua was so impressed with their talent that he decided to take on this new group, and even joined the group under the new name Harvey and the Moonglows. The group broke up in 1960, but Fuqua began managing Marvin Gaye himself. That same year, Fuqua moved to Detroit to work with Gwen Gordy, the sister of Berry Gordy, for her label Anna Records. In 1961, Gwen Gordy and Fuqua (soon to be husband and wife) started two record labels, Tri-Phi and Harvey Records. Fuqua grew wearisome of the difficulties associated with running two small independent labels that had no distribution or manufacturing advantage over major record labels. In 1963, he disbanded the labels and joined Berry Gordy's burgeoning Motown operation as a writer, producer, and promotion man. Fuqua had come to Berry Gordy's attention after he rented a room from Berry's sister Ester Gordy, where he would have lengthy practice sessions with various artists.

Chronology

1929	Born in Louisville, Kentucky on July 27
1952	Starts The Crazy Sounds with Bobby Lester; later the group changes their name to the Moonglows and are signed to Chance Records
1959	The Moonglows disbands
1961	Starts two record labels, Tri-Phi and Harvey Records
1962	Closes his labels and joins Motown to work as a writer, producer, and promotion man, later becoming head of Motown's Artist Development department
1970	Leaves Motown and forms own production company
1971	Begins working with RCA
1982	Collaborates with Marvin Gaye on his comeback album
2000	Inducted into the Rock and Roll Hall of Fame with the rest of the Moonglows; begins the Resurging Artists recording label

Berry later gave Fuqua the opportunity to head Motown's Artist Development department. This department was responsible for grooming Motown acts in their stage performances and public persona. This position allowed Fuqua to discover talent for Motown as well. Throughout the years, he had remained in contact with Marvin Gaye. Fuqua eventually introduced Marvin Gaye to Gordy and Motown history was made. Gaye went on to record a number of hits for Motown with Tammi Terrell such as "Your Precious Love" and "Ain't No Mountain High Enough". Fuqua's success at Motown was due to the attention and care that he gave the new artists for whom he was responsible. He groomed them and showed them how to entertain as well as excite. Fuqua also wrote and produced numerous hits for Motown during this time, including hit songs for the Supremes, Jr. Walker and the Allstars, and Stevie Wonder.

Begins New Independent Career

Fuqua enjoyed his work at Motown immensely, but he eventually felt the need to separate. In the early 1970s, Fuqua began a production deal with RCA. This venture allowed Fuqua to discover new talent such as New Birth, The Nightlighters, and Sylvester. In addition, he helped develop the talents of The Weathergirls, who along with Sylvester took the world of disco to new levels of popularity. Fuqua reunited with Marvin Gaye in 1982 on Gaye's comeback album to help produce several songs that went on to be huge hits, like "Sexual Healing".

In 2000, Fuqua and the other members of the Moonglows were inducted into the Rock and Roll Hall of Fame. Harvey Fuqua continued to be involved in the music industry. He worked with artists such as Smokey Robinson, The Temptations, and Gladys Knight. He started a new recording label, Resurging Artists, in April of 2000. He was an active board member of the Rhythm and Blues Foundation, which works to make sure that the American musical pioneers get medical care and treatment, financial help, and proper credit for work that they have done.

REFERENCES

Online

Marion, J. C. "Harvey Fuqua: After the Moonglows." http://home.earthlink.net/˜v1tiger/harvey.html (Accessed 30 January 2006).

Puckett, Jeffrey L. "Harvey Fuqua." http://www. thisoldsoul.com/hf.html (Accessed 30 January 2006).

Connie Mack

G

Clarence E. Gaines
1923–2005

Basketball coach

National basketball icon Clarence E. Gaines, popularly known as "Big House," was one of the country's greatest collegiate basketball coaches as well as the African American coach with the most wins in the history of the National Collegiate Athletic Association (NCAA). In his forty-seven-year coaching career, Gaines compiled a remarkable record of 828 wins and 447 losses and led his team at Winston-Salem State University to become the first historically black college to win an NCAA basketball title.

On May 21, 1923, Clarence E. Gaines was born in Paducah, Kentucky, where Illinois and Missouri meet along the Ohio River. He was the only child of Lester and Olivia Bolen Gaines. His maternal grandfather, Ambrose Bole, had been a slave on a Kentucky plantation and opened a blacksmith shop in Paducah when the Civil War ended. While Gaines's mother worked in a cooperage (a barrel factory) and his father served as a hotel cook and jackleg carpenter, young Gaines spent time with his maternal grandmother Ida Bolen, a highly religious woman who had him baptized in the Ohio River. The boy attended public schools in Paducah and graduated salutatorian from Lincoln High School, where he was an All-State football player. Gaines also had a musical background, having played the trumpet in the school band. In 1941, he enrolled in Morgan State College (later University) in Baltimore on a football scholarship. Gaines was a big man; he stood six feet five inches tall and weighed 250 pounds. As soon as James "Stump" Carter, the business manager of Morgan's athletics department, saw Gaines, Carter made a statement, part of which became Gaines's permanent nickname. Quoted in Gaines's autobiography, Carter said "Man! The only thing I've ever seen bigger than you is a house." From then on, Gaines was called Big House, which he thought "had nice style to it" and considered more appealing than Sully, his high school nickname.

Clarence E. Gaines

Gaines graduated from Morgan State in 1945 with a B.S. and continued his education at New York's Columbia University where he received an M.A. in 1950. Although Gaines's ambition was to become a dentist, after graduation from Morgan State he accepted an offer from Winston-Salem State Teachers College (later University, or WSSU), a historically black college in North Carolina, where he became football coach and later basketball coach.

Gaines joined the staff at WSSU in 1946. His was to be a temporary assignment yet his work in basketball became a lifelong vocation. During his tenure at the college, he coached every sport offered-football, basketball, track, tennis, and boxing-and taught classes as well. He spent 1946 through 1949 coaching football, compiling a

Chronology	
1923	Born in Paducah, Kentucky on May 21
1945	Receives B.A. from Morgan State University
1946	Serves as football coach at Winston-Salem State College
1949	Becomes basketball coach at Winston-Salem State College
1950	Marries Clara Berry; receives M.A. degree from Columbia University
1966-67	Leads WSSC to basketball championship in NCAA Division II
1970-74	Serves as president of the CIAA
1972-80	Serves as president of CIAA Basketball Coaches
1973-76	Serves as member of the U.S. Olympic Committee
1980-90	Member of the board of directors, Naismith Basketball Hall of Fame
1993	Retires with 828:447 record
2005	Named Kentucky Colonel at University of Kentucky basketball game; dies in Winston-Salem on April 18

20:12:4 record. Once he concentrated on basketball, beginning in 1949, he went on to build one of the Central Intercollegiate Athletic Association's (CIAA) best basketball programs and regularly won games. He headed the Department of Physical Education and also taught courses at WSSU.

Wins NCAA Championship

Among the star players that Gaines produced at WSSU was Cleo Hill, the first African American player to be drafted in the first round by the National Basketball Association in 1961. Another future professional star was Hall-of-Famer Earl "The Pearl" Monroe, who led WSSU to its Division II national championship (1966-67), making WSSU the first predominantly black school and the first college in the South to win an NCAA basketball title. With Monroe's skill and Gaines's leadership, the games drew enormous crowds of sports fans that were well-mixed racially at a time when racial barriers in the South were gradually breaking down. They wanted to see the up-tempo teams with their fast-breaking techniques and speed that overwhelmed opponents. This was without a doubt Gaines's best-ever squad. After the Monroe era, Gaines spent most of his time as athletic director while continuing as basketball coach. He also actively recruited athletes in the Midwest as well as on the inner-city playgrounds of the Northeast. Altogether, eighteen of Gaines's teams won twenty or more games. His success raised WSSU's profile to national prominence.

Gaines was CIAA president (1970-74); CIAA Basketball Coaches president (1972-80; 1990-92); a member of the U.S. Olympic Committee (1973-76); and a member of the board of directors, Naismith Memorial Basketball Hall of Fame (1980-90).

Toward the end of his legendary career, Gaines and WSSU faced the same obstacle as other historically black college athletic programs. Increasingly they became unable to attract the top players due to stiff competition from mainstream institutions that had integrated their sports programs and enticed black athletes with attractive offers. The teams no longer performed well and were less exciting to watch than they had been earlier.

In 1993, Gaines had reached mandatory retirement age in North Carolina at that time. After coaching at WSSU for forty-seven years, he retired in 1993 and was named professor emeritus. He left collegiate basketball coaching with an impressive record of 828 wins, eight CIAA conference championships, and a national title. With this record, he had the most wins in NCAA history up to that time and second only to legendary coach Adolph Rupp at the University of Kentucky. He had the most wins of any African American coach in NCAA basketball history. He had viewed basketball as a way to help young men enrich their lives.

Gaines retired from college coaching, but he did not retire from athletic service to young people. Throughout North Carolina and beyond, Gaines was known for his involvement with youth, which added to his great reputation. He founded and was administrator of the WSSU National Youth Sports Program. The sports and academic enrichment program continues in the early 2000s to influence the lives of hundreds of youth who attend the sessions each summer. As well, he co-founded the Winston-Salem Youth Baseball League. The numerous professional and civic organizations in which he held memberships included the American Association of Health, Physical Education, and Recreation; Boy Scouts of America; the Forsyth County Heart Association; the old Patterson Avenue YMCA Board of Management; and the Rotary Club. He was also a member of St. Paul United Methodist Church.

Receives Numerous Honors

Gaines received many honors during his career. He was named NCAA College Division Basketball Coach of the Year (1967) and CIAA Outstanding Tournament Coach (1957, 1960, 1961, 1963, 1966, 1970, 1972, 1979). He was honored with the joint National Association of Basketball Coaches and National Invitational Tournament Award (1978); presented the Indiana Sports Foundation Lifetime Achievement Award (1990); and given the Atlanta Tipoff Club Lifetime Achievement Award (1991). Reflecting his excellence beyond the professional arena, in 1973 the National Urban League presented the Gaines family with the Family of the Year Award.

Gaines was honored in January 2005 during the halftime ceremony of the University of Kansas and University of Kentucky game in Kentucky's Rupp Arena. Before a capacity crowd of 24,000, Kentucky governor

Ernie Fletcher gave Gaines the highest honor a native son of Kentucky can receive, the designation "Kentucky Colonel." Sometime late in his life, WSSU honored him during the WSSU Rams' Living Legend Benefit, a gala that raised funds for the Clarence "Big House" Gaines Scholarship. WSSU also named the athletic facility, the C. E. Gaines Center, in his honor; the facility was dedicated in 1975.

The legendary Gaines is enshrined in eight halls of fame: National Association of Intercollegiate Athletics (NAIA) Helms (1968); Morgan State College Sports (1973); CIAA Sports (1976); North Carolina Sports (1978); Winston-Salem State University (1980); Naismith (1982); Bob Douglas (1985); and National Association for Sport and Physical Education (1990).

For some time Gaines suffered heart problems, but he continued to lead an active life visiting shut-ins. He also participated in several research studies at Wake Forest University Baptist Medical Center. He died in Forsyth Medical Center in Winston-Salem on April 18, 2005, of complications from a stroke. He was survived by his wife Clara Berry, whom he married in 1950, and two children-Lisa Gaines McDonald of Chicago, and Clarence Edward Gaines Jr. of Los Angeles. A memorial service for Gaines was held on April 22, 2005, in the Joel Coliseum Annex, having been moved from WSSU's campus to accommodate a huge crowd.

In his lifetime, Gaines remained concerned with closing the divide that separated races and cultures. His life's story is told in his autobiography, *They Call Me Big House*, published in 2004, and in his record preserved in national sports history. Although basketball dominated his life, Gaines was passionate about his family, young people, his church, his community, and his race. His legend is summed up in the words of WSSU chancellor Harold L. Martin Sr., who was quoted in a sports article on the school's website: "Coach Gaines was an icon. . . . His contributions and accomplishments in sport were incredible, but the contributions he made to uplift so many young people during his lifetime . . . is his greatest legacy."

REFERENCES

Books

Smith, Jessie Carney, ed. *Black Firsts: 4,000 Ground-Breaking and Pioneering Historical Events*. 2nd ed. Canton, Mich.: Visible Ink Press, 2003.

Who's Who among African Americans. 18th ed. Detroit: Thomson Gale, 2005.

Periodicals

Dell, John. "Loss of a Giant." *Winston-Salem Journal*, 21 April 2005.

———. "A Shared Loss." *Winston-Salem Journal*, 21 April 2005.

Online

"Clarence 'Big House' Gaines." Basketball Hall of Fame. Hall of Famers. http://www.hoophall.com/halloffamers/Gaines.htm (Accessed 15 January 2006).

"WSSU Family, Community, State and Nation Mourn Death of Clarence 'Big House' Gaines." Winston-Salem State University Website. http://wssurams.collegesports.com/sports/m-baskbl/spec-rel/042005aac.html (Accessed 26 February 2006).

Jessie Carney Smith

Ernest Gaines
1933–

Novelist

Ernest Gaines, one of the most important writers of the twentieth century, is known for his depiction of the South, his strong characters, his historical accuracy, and his realistic use of setting. He has created a town in Louisiana, Bayonne, a sustained place like Faulkner's creation of Yoknapatawpha County. Bayonne is the setting for most of his stories; the readers come to know this part of Louisiana which is based on the place in which Gaines spent the first fourteen years of his life. Even though he uses this setting repeatedly, he adds new details each time. He often uses foil characters who present the contrast between what is and what might be. His best-known works are *The Autobiography of Miss Jane Pittman*, *A Gathering of Old Men*, *A Lesson Before Dying*, and "The Sky Is Gray," all of which have been adapted to the screen. Gaines has been a teacher and a writer in residence at several institutions, both in the United States and abroad, and he is the author of six novels, two collections of short works, and a children's book.

Gaines, the oldest of twelve children, was born on January 15, 1933, in Oscar, Louisiana, and raised on the River Lake Plantation in Pointe Coupee Parish. He says he was raised by older people, both men and women, who depended on him because he often read and wrote for them. However, in turn, he learned to respect and appreciate them and their wisdom. He grew up in a community that valued the oral tradition of storytelling. Even though he says he is not a storyteller, he has the stories and the sound of the Louisiana he knew. When he began to write, the language was true to his experience. His old

Ernest Gaines

women have more voice and are more decisive than the men, in many cases, which may result from his being reared by his aunt, Augustine Jefferson.

Gaines says that even though his mother was in the house, she often worked away from home. The guiding force in his life was his aunt who never walked, but she stood tall both morally and physically. She taught him what it means to survive with dignity, which he often portrays in his works. From reading Ernest Hemingway, Gaines came to understand what the expression "grace under pressure" means. He heard so much from the people in the Quarters; since his aunt could not travel, people came to her. The strength of his aunt can be seen in Gaines's portraits of old women, especially Miss Jane Pittman. He patterned that character after and dedicated the book to his aunt, "who did not walk a day in her life but who taught me the importance of standing."

Though bright, Gaines received limited schooling; the cycle was five to six months between the time of harvesting and the time of planting. Classes were taught in a church, which during the week served as a one-room schoolhouse. Following his time in the little church-schoolhouse, he attended a Catholic school. However, there was no high school for black children, so in 1948, Gaines joined his mother and stepfather, who had become a merchant marine, in Vallejo, California, where they had moved during World War II. There he spent a lot of time in the public library. In California he attended high school and developed his fondness for fiction.

Gaines began to look for writers who wrote about the South and the people he knew. He was constantly searching for himself, the South, his people. He read John Steinbeck and Willa Cather. Then he began to read the Russian writers of the nineteenth century, Nikolai Gogol and Anton Chekhov. In the works of Ivan Turgenev, Gaines appreciated the treatment of the peasantry, the land, and small everyday things. However, there was no black voice. At seventeen, he wrote his first novel and confidently sent it off to New York to be published; it was returned. However, he had decided to become the voice for which he had been searching.

In 1953, Gaines entered the U.S. Army where he served until 1955. When he left the armed forces, he entered San Francisco State College (now the University of California, San Francisco). There, he published his first short stories. "The Turtles" (1956) appeared in the inaugural edition of *Transfer*, the school's literary magazine; this was followed in 1957 with "Boy in the Double-Breasted Suit." Following the publication of "Turtles," Dorothea Oppenheimer contacted him and encouraged his writing and ultimately became his agent. Upon graduation in 1957, Gaines received a Wallace Stegner Fellowship (creative writing) to Stanford University where he studied between 1958 and 1959. At both universities black writers were not assigned; however, once his teachers (including Stanley Anderson, Mark Harris, and Wallace Stegner) understood what he wanted to do and that he was serious, they encouraged him. He read Eudora Welty and William Faulkner. Though Gaines had physically left the South at fifteen years of age, the South never left him; his family was still there as was his spirit and he returned frequently, both in person and in his writing.

In several interviews and the book *Porch Talk with Ernest Gaines*, Gaines identifies some of his influences and models: music, paintings, and the discipline of great athletes; Ernest Hemingway for grace under pressure; William Faulkner for dialogue; Gertrude Stein for rhythms; Leo Tolstoy for demonstrating how to put a complete story into a day; Ivan Turgenev's treatment of serfs; Anton Chekhov's handling of the significant rural past; and both Gustave Flaubert and Guy de Maupassant for style.

Gaines's first novel, *Catherine Carmier* (1964), set in the Louisiana of the 1960s, is the story of Jackson Bradley who returns to Bayonne after completing his education in California. Upon his return, he clashes with the town's traditions, which he no longer accepts; falls in love with Catherine Carmier, who is light skinned, believed by her father to be better than those darker than she and he will recognize no dark-skinned suitor; and becomes the victim of Carmier's love and the pull she feels between him and her father. The novel was coolly received, often called an apprentice novel.

Gaines's second novel, *Of Love and Dust*, set in 1940s Bayonne, is about forbidden love and racial conflicts. It is the story of Marcus Payne, who has been released from prison on bond to a white landowner and placed under the supervision of Sidney Bonbon, a Cajun overseer. The overseer attempts to break Marcus who in turn seeks revenge by paying attention to the overseer's wife, Louise. They fall in love and determine to run away, but there is a confrontation between Marcus and the overseer which ends tragically. The story is narrated by Jim, Marcus's co-worker. The black community and its reactions are more prominent in this novel and the themes are clearer.

With the folk autobiography, *The Autobiography of Miss Jane Pittman*, Gaines garnered wide public attention. Characters and events are so finely drawn and the novel is so well executed that people ask continuously if

it history, if Miss Jane Pittman is based on his aunt. The novel is, indeed, a work of fiction, though the character of Miss Jane Pittman draws upon Gaines's aunt. In the story, a young black history teacher with a tape recorder from Baton Rouge goes to a plantation to interview this lady who is upwards of one hundred years old. He wants the black students to have an authentic perspective on their past. Miss Jane tells her own story of slavery, the Civil War, Reconstruction, segregation, and the civil rights era. In this first person narrative, Gaines presents for the reader a neo-slave narrative. Though fictional, the novel was carefully researched and Miss Jane's storytelling is based on fact. Gaines read many of the 1930s Works Progress Administration (WPA) slave narratives. One theme pertains to manhood and that is addressed through three generations of men in Pittman's life: Ned, whose mother is killed and Miss Jane becomes his surrogate mother; Joe Pittman, her husband, who is independent and a hard worker; and Jimmy, "the One," the one who is seen as special and in whom the black community places its hopes and dreams. Miss Pittman at the end of the novel makes a decision to become a leader for her community and people. The novel was adapted for television in 1974 with Cecily Tyson in the role of Miss Jane Pitman; it won nine Emmy Awards.

The 1978 novel *In My Father's House* presents the relationship between father and son. It is the story of Reverend Phillip Martin, a prominent civil rights leader, who at the height of his career is forced to confront his past. This is precipitated by the appearance of a young man, Robert X, who intends to kill him. The book was not a moneymaker; but it did present the themes of manhood, struggle and sacrifice, and survival with dignity, which would remain important for Gaines.

With the 1983 *A Gathering of Old Men*, Gaines came back in the public eye. The story, set on the Marshall Plantation in the 1970s, focuses on a group of old men, much like the ones in Gaines's youth, who take a stand against injustice; the story is told in multiple first person points of view. Each man, like Miss Jane, reveals a part of his personal history. In the revelations, each voices the humiliation and exploitation he endured within the oppressive system. These men, plus a thirty-year-old white female, plead guilty to the murder of an antagonistic member of a Cajun clan. The novel was adapted for television in 1987.

In 1993, Gaines published *A Lesson Before Dying*, which created much the same stir in the reading public as had *The Autobiography of Miss Jane Pittman*. The story, set on a plantation and in a Bayonne jail in the 1940s, concerns a young man, Jefferson, wrongfully convicted of murder and sentenced to die in the electric chair. The black teacher, Grant Wiggins, intends to teach Jefferson to die with dignity and in the process discovers something about himself and reconnects with the black community. Both Jefferson and Grant learn important lessons. For this novel, which was both critically and commercially successful, Gaines received the 1993 National Book Critics' Circle Award. It was adapted for the Home Box Office cable channel by Walt Disney Television in 1994.

In 1971, Gaines published his only children's book, *A Long Day in November*. It is dedicated, says Gaines, "to all little boys who have had one long day in their lives." It is a revision of the story of this title in his *Bloodlines* collection. The story begins with the little boy waking up in the cold morning and ends with him curling up in the warmth of the bed that night. In the course of the day, he encounters and witnesses many challenges. Yet, in the course of growing into manhood, he, like his father, makes sacrifices in order to survive with dignity.

His first collection, *Bloodlines* (1968), contains five short stories that convey a sense of the novel because time progresses and characters grow. The stories begin in the 1930s and progress through to the 1960s. The male characters age from the first story to the last, which actually portrays a number of ages and a woman, Aunt Fe, who in upwards of one hundred years old. The movement in the collection is ever widening. The first story takes place on the plantation; the second is mostly set in the town, with a brief period on the plantation; the third story takes place in town; the fourth moves back to the plantation, but the main character has traveled the world; and the fifth story presents various places. The first story, "A Long Day in November," became a children's book. The second story, "The Sky Is Gray," moves the little boy toward manhood while socializing him in the traditions and ways of his culture and introducing him to the future world. "Three Men," the third in the collection, illustrates ways of approaching manhood. The title story involves a young man who returns home to claim his inheritance; he's a little crazy since he is trying to buck tradition, and yet, evidently some recognize the coming change. The final story, "Just Like a Tree," has the black community and one lone white woman coming together to see Aunt Fe leave the plantation for her safety. The violent forces of the civil rights movement have caused family members to decide Aunt Fe needs to leave the area for her own safety, but she says she will not be moved. Thus, the collection ends with the beginning of a new era, the passing from the old traditions to new ones. However, throughout, Gaines cautioned the reader that the new era must be combined with the old.

In 2005, Gaines published *Mozart and Leadbelly: Stories and Essays*. In these pieces, Gaines discusses why he became a writer, his early life in Louisiana, the inspirations behind his books, and his portrayal of the black experience in the South. In so doing, he gives valuable background information on both the artist and the man. There are six essays, five short stories, and a conversation between Gaines and fellow writers Marcia Gaudet and Darrell Bourque. Two of the short stories "The Tur-

tles" and "The Boy in the Double-Breasted Suit" represent his first published writing. "Christ Walked Down Market Street" is a moving story and his first attempt to write a story with a setting outside Louisiana. The title reflects the coexistence of similarities and differences, neither being superior to the other. In 2006, Gaines was working on a novel, which had the working title *The Man Who Whipped Children*.

REFERENCES

Books

Beavers, Herman. *Wrestling Angels into Song: The Fictions of Ernest J. Gaines and James Alan McPherson*. Philadelphia: University of Pennsylvania Press, 1995.

Gaudet, Marcia, and Carl Wooton. *Porch Talk with Ernest Gaines: Conversations on the Writer's Craft*. Baton Rouge: Louisiana State University Press, 1990.

Online

Ernest J. Gaines. http://www.louisiana.edu/Academic/ LiberalArts/ENGL/Creative/Gaines.htm (Accessed 3 February 2006).

"Major Twentieth Century Writers." http://www. princeton.edu/~howarth/557/gathering3.html (Accessed 3 February 2006).

Collections

The papers of Clarence Gaines are in the archives of the C. G. O'Kelly Library, Winston-Salem State University.

Helen R. Houston

Willie Gary
1947–

Lawyer

Trial lawyer Willie E. Gary has been called one of the most compelling courtroom orators of the modern age. Known as the "giant killer" for his legal victories against corporations and insurance companies in cases where his clients have sued to collect personal-injury damage awards, Gary has racked up some impressive statistics, including a $500 million verdict in 1995 that set a new record in American legal history. "I won't rest until I try and win a billion-dollar case," Gary told *Ebony* writers Joy Bennett Kinnon and Vandell Cobb. "It's not just the money; it's a testament to being one of the best

Chronology

1947	Born in Eastman, Georgia on July 12
1960	Moves with family to Indiantown, Florida
1968	Marries childhood sweetheart, Gloria Royal
1971	Graduates from Shaw University in Raleigh, North Carolina
1974	Earns law degree and passes Florida bar exam
1975	Opens storefront law office in Stuart, Florida
1984	Wins first million-dollar jury verdict
1991	Donates $10 million to Shaw University
1995	Successfully argues for a record $500 million jury verdict

lawyers I can be and a message—that you can't cheat poor people."

Son of Sharecroppers

Gary's rise to multimillionaire attorney seems all the more remarkable given his humble origins. He was born on July 12, 1947, in Eastman, Georgia, where his parents, Turner and Mary Gary, lived on their farm with Gary's five older siblings. His arrival was a difficult one for his mother, and a twin did not survive the birth. Resulting medical complications put Mary Gary in the hospital, and the debts that her treatment incurred, combined with other financial problems, forced Turner Gary to sign over the deed to the farm a year later. The senior Gary had an education that stopped at the second grade, and lacking any other source of income, he moved his family to Florida, where he, his wife, and the older children worked as sharecroppers in Canal Point, a small farming community in Palm Beach County. There, the Garys lived in a three-room shack with no electricity or plumbing. They headed to the Carolinas in the summer months to join the migrant-labor armies that picked cotton, corn, string beans, and other crops during the harvest season.

Gary himself began working at the age of five, carrying water to the farm workers and progressed to working in the fields himself. "By the time I was 10, I was a working man. I could pick 10 to 15 bushels of beans in a day," he told Adam C. Smith of the *St. Petersburg Times*. Eventually, his father bought a truck for selling food and water to the field workers, and Gary often worked alongside him. Because of the crop-harvest schedule, schooling was intermittent, with the children attending only half-days during the harvest months. As he grew older, Gary dreamed of a way to contribute financially to the family, and near their Florida home he convinced the local feed-store owner to let him purchase a lawn mower on credit. He set up a landscaping business, paid off the debt, and turned the remaining money over to his father, which enabled Turner to buy a produce truck.

Refuses to Return Home without Degree

In 1960, the family moved to Indiantown, Florida, and Gary made it onto his high school's football team despite his relatively small size, at just five feet, seven inches. After he graduated, he was determined to enter college and managed to win a conditional athletic scholarship to Bethune-Cookman College, a historically black school in Daytona Beach, Florida, that dated back to the era when higher education was still strictly segregated in the South. Gary had to make the football team first in order to formally enroll at Bethune-Cookman, but the fact that he was beginning college warranted a headline in Indiantown's local newspaper because he would be the first youth from the all-black town to make it that far. So in the summer of 1967, he traveled to Daytona Beach and began football tryouts. On the last day, though, he was cut and told to return home. He recalled in interviews later that he cried that day in the coach's office, but he did go back home—and straight to his high school coach, who made some calls and managed to get him a tryout at another historically black school, Shaw University, in Raleigh, North Carolina. "I wanted to go to college so bad I could taste it," he told Tony Chappelle in a *Black Collegian* profile years later.

Gary took an overnight bus to Raleigh, arriving with just $13 in his pocket, but the coach took one look at his small figure and told him to return home. He did not have enough to get back home, however, and so the coach told him to call his folks and have it sent. Pretending he was still waiting for the money, Gary began sleeping on the sofa in the men's dormitory, and befriended some football players, who sneaked food out of the school cafeteria to help him out. He also started cleaning the team locker rooms. "My daddy always said, 'If you want a job, start working for nothing. They'll end up paying you,'" Gary recalled in an interview with Jonathan Harr for the *New Yorker*. Eventually a player fell out with an injury and the coach let him onto the team. He did not have the $10 application fee to formally apply to Shaw, but the administration waived it; he also needed his high school transcripts, and he was allowed to make a collect call to the Indiantown high school principal's office to have them sent. Gary would never forget the two favors granted him that week and would later repay Shaw generously for the kindness.

Gary was a defensive back on the Shaw football team and was voted captain during his junior year. His teenage girlfriend from Indiantown, Gloria Royal, also enrolled there; the two had met while working on Carolina farms with their families when they were very young. Royal was a good student and tutored Gary to help him catch up in subjects in which he was lacking. "So much of what I am today, I owe to her," Gary told Smith in the *St. Petersburg Times* interview. "In grade school I used to wear two pairs of pants to try to cover up all the holes, but it wasn't enough. I'd walk up to the blackboard and other kids would laugh, and Gloria would get mad at them."

The couple was married during their college years, and Gary continued to work to make ends meet. He waited tables and established another successful landscaping business; his Raleigh venture proved so lucrative that he eventually hired others to do the work, and took in about $25,000 annually from it by the time he graduated—more money than some Shaw professors earned in a year. After graduating in 1971 with a degree in business administration, Gary began law school at North Carolina Central University in Durham. Academically he was somewhat unprepared for such rigors, and he earned a D, some Cs, and one A during his first year.

Opens County's First Black Law Firm

The landscaping business paid his law-school tuition, and by then he and Gloria had also started a family that would eventually number four sons. When he graduated in 1974, the couple and their two young children moved back to Florida and settled in the city of Stuart, where Gary hoped to find a job after he passed the Florida bar exam. Through newspaper ads and the telephone, he rented an apartment there while still in Durham, and when the family arrived at the rental office to pick up the keys, they were told that there was no apartment available—though Gary had already paid a deposit for one. As he recalled in the *New Yorker* interview, he told the manager, "You can keep me out. That's O.K. But I want you to know that I just graduated from law school, and I'm going to sue you to kingdom come. I contracted with you, and it's clear that you don't want me here because my face is black." The family was allowed to move in.

Gary studied eighteen hours a day to pass the Florida bar exam, which had an unusually high failure rate for African American attorney hopefuls. He took a provisional job with the local public defender's office, offering to work for free until they could pay him, but after he passed the bar exam in December of 1974, he was told that there was still no money in the budget to hire another attorney to defend the county's indigent. It would be one of the last instances in Gary's life in which race sidetracked his ambitions. A month later, in January of 1975, he opened his own law practice in a small storefront on Colorado Avenue that had the noted honor of being the first black-owned law firm in Martin County, Florida. His wife was his first secretary.

Gary made local headlines that same year after he won his first major judgment for a widow whose husband, a black North Carolina truck driver, had been decapitated in an accident in Putnam County. For many years, the $225,000 settlement was the highest personal injury settlement ever awarded in the county. The settlement was all the more remarkable given the fact that the northern Florida county had been a Ku Klux Klan hotbed for generations. Back in Indiantown, Gary was already so famous that townsfolk came to see "Lawyer Gary" when he visited his parents' home. He remembered those early days as ones in which visions of future success drove his ambitions and hunger for success. "In my first year of law practice, I said I wanted a Rolls Royce, and I was willing to burn the midnight oil to get it," he told Pamela M. McBride in a *Black Collegian* profile from 2001. "I put a photo of one on my door to keep me focused and often worked until 2 a.m., just to get it right."

In 1976, he opened a second legal office in Fort Pierce, Florida, and continued to take on personal-injury cases, where his emotional, often heart-wrenching arguments to the jury usually won them over. His courtroom opponents were tough—they were the well-funded legal teams that represented corporations, insurance companies, and hospitals—but Gary and the medical and other experts whom he hired successfully demonstrated a pattern of negligence or wrongdoing that resulted in monetary damages awarded to the plaintiff. Out of that amount, Gary's office took a cut of 33 to 40 percent. In 1984, he won his first million-dollar verdict, a benchmark for a personal-injury lawyer. A year later, another legal victory made headlines across Florida, when he successfully sued the local utility whose power line had electrocuted seven members of the same family in Jupiter, Florida. The proceeds from that settlement, reached out of court, went to the sole survivor of the family and was rumored to be in neighborhood of $40 million.

Gary continued to make headlines for his courtroom successes, and one of them, in the mid-1990s, made the national newspapers as one of the largest jury verdicts in U.S. legal history, at $500 million. In that case, Gary and his firm represented a Mississippi funeral-home owner, Jeremiah O'Keefe, who claimed that the Loewen Group of Toronto, Canada, had irreparably harmed his local funeral home and funeral insurance business. The Loewen Group owned funeral homes across the United States and Canada, and struck a deal with O'Keefe on which they later reneged. This was actually a commercial lawsuit, involving a breach of contract, and Gary rarely took such cases, but O'Keefe's plight had moved him; the O'Keefe family funeral business dated back to the Civil War era, and the Loewen Group was an aggressive new player on a determined expansion plan.

During the trial, Gary stressed to the jury the unsavory aspects of Loewen's business practices, including the price they charged for a casket. "If you really want to gouge someone," he told them, according to the *New Yorker* profile, "you catch them during that time when they've lost a mother or a father or a child. They are helpless....They are there for the picking." Gary's legal victory for O'Keefe even merited a mention in the *Wall Street Journal*.

By 1999, the Loewen Group had declared bankruptcy. The case also brought down the Reverend Henry Lyons, a pastor from St. Petersburg, Florida who was also president of the National Baptist Convention USA. Lyons offered to look into allegations of jury tampering during the trial, and he and an aide received more than $3 million from the Loewen Group to do so. A subsequent arson investigation revealed that Lyons was engaged in an extramarital affair with the aide and had secured payments from Loewen and other companies on the basis of his influence over millions of African Americans who were also church-going Baptists. After resigning in disgrace, Lyons served five years in prison on charges of tax evasion, embezzlement, and grand theft.

Repays Shaw Several Times Over

Gary's generosity with his own personal fortune has become legendary. Earlier in his career, he bought his father a farm, as repayment for the deed he signed over in 1948 to pay that hospital bill, and later built a house for his widowed mother. In 1991, he made a gift to Shaw University of $10 million, at a time when his alma mater was nearing bankruptcy. It was the largest ever for an alumnus of a historically black school to give the institution from which the benefactor had graduated, and Gary also organized a fundraising drive that netted another $17 million for Shaw's coffers.

Gary's personal bequest to Shaw put him in the same upper echelons as entertainment personalities Bill Cosby and Oprah Winfrey, both of whom had made generous donations to older schools that had helped generations of African Americans achieve a college degree. "I think we're all indebted to Black colleges," he said in the interview with Chappelle for *Black Collegian* in 1994. "But for one of our historically Black colleges, I would not be where I am. They were considerate enough to take a chance on a farm boy who'd been turned down and told he wasn't college material." Gary eventually set up a foundation bearing his family name that donates to worthy causes. It has provided scholarships to disadvantaged college-bound students in Martin County, and helped build a church back in Indiantown.

By 2003, Gary's Stuart-based law firm—officially known as Gary, Williams, Parenti, Finney & Lewis—boasted 130 employees and satellite offices in several states. His oldest son, Kenneth, runs a real-estate management company that serves as a sideline business for Gary and his thirst for good investments. His most impressive parcel of land, however, is a 25,000-square-foot, fifty-room oceanfront home on the St. Lucie River in Stuart, that reportedly cost $10 million. "Villa de Gloria," named in homage to his wife, is a lavish palace, but Gary is also proud of his personal aircraft, a Boeing 737 that he uses for business, which features 24-karat gold fixtures. He is one of the few American citizens to own a jet outright, and he calls it the "Wings of Justice." Its goal, beyond helping him win cases in other states and then make it home for dinner on time, is to intimidate his legal opponents, he told *Ebony* writer Kevin Chappell. "They know their

worst nightmare has come true," he joked. "When we land in the big bird, they know they got to pay. Stop arguing 'cause you got to pay. That's all there is to it."

Launches Cable Network

Gary has also ventured into media ownership, launching the Major Broadcasting Cable Network in 1998 with sports figures Evander Holyfield and Cecil Fielder as well as Marlon Jackson, formerly of the Jackson 5, and Alvin James, an entertainment executive. The network has a cable presence called the Black Family Channel, which presents positive, uplifting fare aimed at African American viewers. Gary hosts his own show in which he interviews others about the role faith has played in their lives. "Inspiring our children is the most important thing we can do for our country, and I guess you could say this is what's burning in my belly," he asserted in the *St. Petersburg Times* interview with Smith. "People are saying this (network) can't be done, and I feel like my reputation is on the line. When I'm determined, I won't ever give up."

Gary's own family includes several grandchildren from his four sons, Kenneth, Sekou, Ali, and Kobie. In a 1990 *Ebony* article that asked individuals to reveal their personal hero or unexpected mentor, he recalled that it was his own father who provided the greatest inspiration. "It was that guy with the second-grade education who had the greatest impact on me, who knew just what to say to motivate me," Gary wrote of his father. "He faced a lot of obstacles, but he moved each one. Watching and listening to him changed and shaped my life."

REFERENCES

Books

"Willie E. Gary." In *Contemporary Black Biography*. Volume 46. Detroit: Thomson Gale, 2005.

Periodicals

Chappell, Kevin. "Blacks Who Own Jets." *Ebony* 57 (April 2002): 144.

Chappelle, Tony. "Willie Gary, Esquire." *Black Collegian* 25 (October 1994): 63.

Clarke, Caroline V. "Champion for the Underdog." *Black Enterprise* 24 (August 1993): 68.

Desloge, Rick. "The Lawyer Who Took on the Brewery and Won." *St. Louis Business Journal* 22 (12 October 2001): 1.

Freedman, Michael. "Sugar Is Sweet." *Forbes* 164 (29 November 1999): 86

Harr, Jonathan, "The Burial." *New Yorker* 75 (1 November 1999): 70-95.

Hays, Constance L. "Some Workers Face a Tough Challenge." *New York Times* 24 June 2000.

Kinnon, Joy Bennett, and Vandell Cobb. "Superlawyer's 50-Room Mansion." *Ebony* 53 (April 1998): 38.

McBride, Pamela M. "Willie Gary: Rises from Migrant Farmer to Multi-Millionaire Attorney." *Black Collegian* 32 (October 2001): 84.

Smith, Adam C. "Soaring on Wings of Law." *St. Petersburg Times*, 1 June 2000.

"$10 Million for Shaw University." *Ebony* 47 (October 1992): 106.

"Thanks 10 Million." *People* 37 (13 April 1992): 65.

"The Love That Changed My Life." *Ebony* 45 (May 1990): 36.

Carol Brennan

Chronology

1828	Born in Philadelphia, Pennsylvania on October 28
1843	Joins the Presbyterian Church
1852	Graduates from Dartmouth College
1853-55	Studies at Princeton Theological Seminary
1855	Named pastor of Liberty Street Presbyterian Church, Troy, New York
1860	Named Pastor of First African Presbyterian Church, Philadelphia, Pennsylvania
1865-66	Serves as missionary in North and South Carolina
1868	Serves as Florida's secretary of state
1873	Serves as Florida's superintendent of public instruction
1874	Dies in Tallahassee, Florida on August 14

Jonathan Clarkson Gibbs
1828–1874

Minister, politician, educator

Jonathan Clarkson Gibbs was a noted clergyman, missionary, politician, and educator. At the height of his influence during the Reconstruction Era, he made significant and lasting contributions to the Florida educational system. Gibbs High School in St. Petersburg, Florida, and the Gibbs Campus of St. Petersburg College are named in his honor and testify to his enduring achievements regarding the education of blacks and whites in the Sunshine State. An intellectual and a gifted speaker, Gibbs ranked among the leading black abolitionists of his day and achieved wide recognition for being Florida's first black secretary of state during the Reconstruction Era.

Born a free black on October 28, 1828 in Philadelphia, Pennsylvania, Jonathan C. Gibbs was the son of a Wesleyan Methodist minister, Jonathan C. Gibbs, Sr. After his father died suddenly, Gibbs' mother, Maria Jackson Gibbs, was left to rear the couple's three sons, Jonathan, Mifflin, and Isaiah, in circumstances of dire poverty. The widow performed laundry work until it ruined her health. To subsidize the family's meager income, Jonathan and Mifflin became apprentice carpenters for James Gibbons, a reputable black Philadelphia craftsman.

Although their father was a Methodist and their mother was a Baptist, Jonathan and Mifflin became Presbyterians in 1843 and joined the First African Presbyterian Church in their hometown. Gibbs shrewdly parlayed his newly acquired membership in a Presbyterian Church into an opportunity for a more lucrative future, by gaining sponsorship from its assembly to attend Dartmouth College.

As a part of his undergraduate experience, Gibbs was active in the abolitionist movement in which he associated with Frederick Douglass, Martin Delaney, and other leading advocates of the abolishment of slavery and enfranchisement for blacks. A gifted learner with an inquisitive mind, Gibbs studied Latin, Greek, math, rhetoric, morals, and philosophy. When he finished his studies in 1852, Gibbs was only the third black to graduate from Dartmouth College.

Gibbs strengthened his preparation for the ministry by attending Princeton Theological Seminary from 1853 to 1855. He left Princeton to become the pastor of the Liberty Street Presbyterian Church, in Troy, New York. Under Gibbs' guidance, the congregation increased, and the church became more financially stable. Along with his church work, Gibbs was tirelessly active in local and state organizations. In 1855, he attended the New York Colored Men's State Convention, which focused on African American civil rights but opposed colonization, a plan to resettle former slaves and free blacks on the African continent.

As his ministerial career began to soar, Gibbs's marriage to the former Anna Amelia Harris suffered from marital disharmony. The unhappy spouses had two children, Julia Pennington and Thomas Van Renssalaer. Matters came to a head and a pregnant Anna Gibbs left her husband in 1857. She subsequently gave birth to a daughter, Josephine, but the couple divorced. Both later remarried, with Anna gaining custody of the couple's two daughters and Jonathan Gibbs retaining custody of their son.

In 1860, Gibbs accepted a post at his home church, the First African Presbyterian Church of Philadelphia. The church served as an underground railroad station for southern slaves fleeing to northern states and Canada. Gibbs signed the "Appeal from the Colored Men of Philadelphia to the President of the United States," issued in 1862. This document spoke against colonization, argued for equal rights for blacks, and expressed confidence in Abraham Lincoln. During his four years at First African Presbyterian, Gibbs participated in the 1864 Colored People's Convention that produced the National Equal Rights League, which protested against racial discrimination. Gibbs married his second wife, Elizabeth F. Gibbs, and fathered a third daughter, Anne, in 1866.

Gibbs decided to relinquish pastoring churches by 1865 and to become a missionary. In the aftermath of the Civil War, the Presbyterian Board of Missions for Freedmen sent him to North and South Carolina to work with former slaves. Gibbs was assigned to the Zion Presbyterian Church in Charleston, South Carolina, where he successfully started a school, but he annoyed white Carolinians by hosting a convention at the church which promoted more rights for the freedmen. The Presbyterian board exiled him to a smaller sphere of influence in Sumter County, South Carolina.

Serves as Secretary of State

Gibbs moved to Florida in 1866 and in an apparent effort to re-invent himself, abandoned missionary work altogether and entered politics. He was attracted to the radical wing of the Florida Republican Party, but thought it more prudent to ally himself with the moderate faction. This strategy proved wise because it led to his becoming one of eighteen blacks elected to the Florida Constitutional Convention of 1868. After much haggling and political infighting, the delegates emerged with a document that established the rights for male voting, free public education, and equal protection for African Americans under the law. W. E. B. Du Bois observed that Gibbs was the most cultured member of the convention's black delegates, describing him as a tall, slender mulatto with a prominent forehead. Gibbs's support for Harrison Reed as governor eventually positioned him for an appointment as Florida's secretary of state.

Gibbs assumed the office of secretary of state on November 11, 1868. His duties included keeping the official records of the legislative and the executive branches; protecting the state seal, returning vetoed bills to the legislature, and evaluating applicants for state office. In addition to certain corrupt, inept, and disloyal officials, Gibbs had to deal with the attempted impeachment of the governor and a chaotic statewide election. He also had to face outbreaks of violence and lack of law enforcement across the state, mostly related to the heightened criminal conduct and activities of the Ku Klux Klan and other likeminded racist groups, who were intent on intimidating blacks.

According to one of his biographers, Learotha Williams Jr., Gibbs was the target of a failed assassination plot in Marianna, Florida in 1870. Many whites did not enjoy seeing a black man in such a coveted political office and effectively wielding power. He received death threats on a regular basis and kept his home armed. Yet Gibbs sometimes served as acting governor when Harrison Reed was away from the capitol.

Becomes Superintendent of Public Instruction

In 1872 Gibbs served concurrent terms as a Tallahassee city councilman and secretary of state. When Governor Reed was succeeded by Ossian B. Hart in 1873, Gibbs was appointed superintendent of public instruction. During Gibbs's administration, Florida's public schools suffered from a shortage of certified teachers, inadequate funding, and suitable school buildings. Gibbs required thorough reports from county superintendents, attempted to have uniform textbooks for elementary and secondary pupils, and published a list of recommended textbooks.

Gibbs attempted to find funding for Florida's two schools designated for the freedman's education, Florida Agricultural College and Cookman College. Gibbs's improvements and innovations had a major impact and lasting legacy on public education in Florida. His life abruptly ended on August 14, 1874, when he suffered a stroke. The suddenness of his death, coupled with persistent death threats, fed unsubstantiated rumors that he had been poisoned.

REFERENCES

Books

Ahern, Wilbert H. "Gibbs, Jonathan." In *Dictionary of Negro Biography*. Eds. Rayford W. Logan and Michael R. Winston. New York: Norton, 1982.

Du Bois, William Edward Burghardt. *Black Reconstruction*. New York: Russell & Russell, 1935.

Periodicals

Abraham, James M. "Education Owes Its History to Black America: Two State Teaching Colleges Were Founded Out of 'Separate But Equal' Laws." *Tallahassee Democrat*, 6 February 1994.

Black, Marian Watkins. "The Battle Over Uniformity of Textbooks in Florida, 1868-1963." *History of Education Quarterly* 42:4 (April 1964): 363-68.

Clark, James C. "Florida's Only Negro Cabinet Member." *Orlando Sentinel*, 15 February 1990.

"Jonathan Gibbs." *Tampa Tribune*, 5 February 1997.

Online

"An Appeal from the Colored Men of Philadelphia to the President of the United States." http://www.learner.org/channel/workshops/primarysources/emancipation/docs/appfrom2.html (Accessed 3 February 2006).

Dissertations

Williams, Learotha, Jr. "'A Wider Field of Usefulness': The Life and Times of Jonathan Clarkson Gibbs c.1828-1874." Ph.D. dissertation, Florida State University, 2003.

Glenda M. Alvin

John Wesley Gilbert
1864–1923

Archaeologist, minister, college president

John Wesley Gilbert was a black archaeologist and a classical scholar. His work as an archaeologist made him unique among African Americans of his era. After studying at one of the nation's leading universities and studying and traveling widely abroad, he made his mark at historically black Payne College in Augusta, Georgia. His most enduring contribution may be as teacher and preacher in the South, where his students and the community benefited from his scholarship and lectures. Of equal importance is his call for blacks to write and publish their own histories and to broadcast their stories before wide audiences.

Born in Hephzibah, Georgia, on July 6, 1864, John W. Gilbert was the son of Gabriel and Sarah Gilbert. While John was still very young, his father Gabriel died, and he was raised by his mother and his uncle John, for whom he was named. As a young child, he spent half of the year on a farm and the other half in the public schools of Augusta, Georgia. It was not uncommon for blacks in rural areas to divide their time in this manner, for they were needed as a source of labor on the farm during planting and harvesting time. Sources differ on the course of his education after he completed grammar school. Some claim that Gilbert studied next at Atlanta Baptist Seminary, which became the Theological Department of Morehouse College in Atlanta; others report that he became interested in Payne College, the new institution that opened in Augusta around that time and was the first student to enroll. The earnest, studious, and capable young Gilbert completed the normal course that the school offered and his performance attracted the attention of the college's president, who paid his expenses to Brown University in Rhode Island. Whatever the course of his early college years, he did, in fact, enroll in Brown.

Gilbert was specially gifted in learning languages and achieved distinction as a classical scholar adept in Greek. He won the university-offered Athens scholarship and was able to live in Athens and study classics there at the American School, during the academic year 1890-91. He was that school's first African American student. To help support his study, Gilbert worked as a tourist guide.

Chronology

1864	Born in Hephzibah, Georgia on July 6
1890-91	Studies at American School of Classics in Athens, Greece
1891	Receives M.A. from Brown University; returns to United States and joins faculty at Payne College, Augusta, Georgia
1895	Enters ministry of the Colored Methodist Episcopal (CME) Church
1901	Represents CME Church at ecumenical conferences in London
1911	Travels in Africa with Bishop W. R. Lambuth
1913	Serves as president of Miles College, Birmingham, Alabama
1923	Dies on November 19

Gilbert traveled widely during that year; his interests and work took him on excavations throughout Greece and the Mediterranean islands. He was interested in archaeology, gaining recognition as one of the first African American archaeologists. After finding Eretria's ancient pillars, gates, and walls, he traced the walls, located the structure's towers, and then worked with his team to prepare a map of the ancient structure. He also spent a semester at the University of Berlin in 1891. After writing his thesis on the villages of Attica (or the demes) in 1891, Brown University awarded him the master's of arts degree. He traveled a lot, visiting most European countries and later much of the United States.

Gilbert returned to the United States in the fall of 1891, with a keen interest in helping blacks and whites understand, love, and help each other. In 1891 he was named chairman of Greek and German at Payne. He was dean of theology for three years, probably in the late 1880s or early 1890s. He was a vital force at Payne.

By the mid-1890s Gilbert had become interested in preaching, and in 1895 he entered the ministry of the Colored Methodist Episcopal (CME) Church. In 1901, he represented the church at ecumenical conferences held in London in September.

Helps Lead Mission to Africa

Bishop W. R. Lambuth wanted the Methodist Episcopal Church, South and the CME Church to share in a visit to Africa, and he invited Gilbert to go along to help open a mission station there. The two men and their team of nearly sixty Americans went to London, on to Belgium, and from there they sailed to Dakar, arriving on October 24, 1911. After a short stop in Dakar, they went up the Congo River and landed in Luebo. They set out further, crossing rivers, swamps, passing through villages, and altogether traveled 750 miles and visited 200 villages. Gilbert provided an important service to Lambuth and their cause, as he translated materials into French and did some work with several dialects. When he returned to the

United States, the CME Church was eager to begin its mission work in Africa, yet its zeal soon faded. At some point Gilbert was superintendent of African missions for the CME Church.

Gilbert was professionally active; he published articles on archaeology in the *New York Independent* and other scholarly journals. One of his essays "How Can the Negroes Be Induced to Rally More to Negro Enterprises and to Their Professional Men?" was published in 1902 in Culp's *Twentieth Century Negro Literature*. There he questioned the training that blacks received to support their own enterprises and other black professionals. He raised questions about the textbooks blacks study and how they are written by whites and for whites. These works suppressed information, he asserted, and suggested that blacks have not contributed to history and literature. He called for a "thorough review of our system of education," so that blacks would be encouraged to write and to discover their own worthiness.

Gilbert believed that blacks should promote their own work, particularly at conventions and national congresses. According to Culp, Gilbert said that "training in the school room, preaching in the pulpit, proclaiming in social and civic organizations, promulgation from the rostrum, and broadcast distribution of literature, all ending toward the same end" would serve well to educate blacks about their own work. He knew the importance of black business development and became an entrepreneur as well, as demonstrated by 1919, when his real estate holdings were valued at $15,000. He held several shares in a realty company in Augusta.

Whether he interrupted his tenure at Payne College is not known, but for one year, 1913-14, Gilbert was president of Miles College, a CME institution founded in Birmingham, Alabama, in 1905. Since many religious denominations used their own leaders to head the colleges that they supported, this would have been a logical transition for Gilbert, who possibly held the presidency until a permanent chief administrator could be placed.

Gilbert belonged to a number of professional and civic organizations, including the Archaeological Institute, Philological Association of America, the Masons, the Knights of Pythias (which he served as grand auditor), and the Odd Fellows.

Gilbert married Osceola Pleasant, an Augusta native, in the spring of 1899; they had four children. Gilbert's health began to fail around 1920, and he died on November 19, 1923.

REFERENCES

Books

Afro-American Encyclopedia. Vol. 4. North Miami, Fla.: Educational Book Publishers, Inc., 1974.

Culp, Daniel W., ed. *Twentieth Century Negro Literature; or a Cyclopedia of Thought.* Naperville, Ill.: J. L. Nichols & Co., 1902.

McAfee, L. D. *History of the Women's Missionary Society in the Colored Methodist Episcopal Church.* Rev. ed. Phenix, Ala.: Phenix City Herald, 1945.

Nichols, J. L., and William H. Crogman. *Progress of a Race; or the Remarkable Advancement of the American Negro.* Rev. and enl. ed. Naperville, Ill.: J. L. Nichols & Co., 1925.

Richardson, Clement, ed. *The National Cyclopedia of the Colored Race.* Vol. 1. Montgomery, Ala.: National Publishing Co., 1919.

Online

"Miles College Presidents." http://www.miles.edu/Presidents.asp (Accessed 16 January 2006).

Jessie Carney Smith

Roscoe C. Giles
1890–1970

Surgeon

Roscoe Conkling Giles's admission to Cornell University Medical School was the first in a series of firsts for the pioneering African American surgeon. He was also the first African American to receive his medical degree from the institution and was the first black certified by the American Board of Surgery. Over the span of more than fifty years, Giles was a dedicated teacher, uniquely talented surgeon, and author of dozens of highly regarded medical papers.

Roscoe Giles was born May 6, 1890 in Albany, New York. He was the son of Reverend Francis Fenard and Laura Caldwell Giles. In addition to his work as a minister in New York City, Giles's father was also an attorney. Giles was raised in Brooklyn and graduated from Boys' High School in 1907. He displayed a talent for oration while in high school, winning the B.B. Christ medal and a scholarship to Cornell University in Ithaca, New York. At Cornell, Giles majored in literature and was a member of the crew team. His fraternity brothers of the Alpha Phi Alpha fraternity recognized his natural leadership skills. In 1910, he was elected the group's national president.

Given his talent as a speaker, it seemed natural that Giles would follow in his father's footsteps. But Giles had other plans. The elder Giles had encouraged his son toward a career in medicine since childhood, and Giles

Roscoe C. Giles

Chronology

1890	Born in Albany, New York on May 6
1907	Graduates from Boys' High School in Brooklyn
1910	Elected national president of Alpha Phi Alpha fraternity
1911	Becomes first African American admitted to Cornell University Medical School
1915	Becomes first African American to graduate from Cornell University Medical School
1917	Appointed supervisor of the Chicago Health Department by Chicago mayor William Hale Thompson; receives honorary attending physician position at Cook County Hospital; becomes part of Provident Hospital's program aimed at black medical students; marries Frances Reeder on January 9
1922	Publishes first paper, "Rickets: The Surgical Treatment of the Chronic Deformities of, with Emphasis on Bow-Legs and Knock-Knees," in the *Journal of the National Medical Association*
1926	Elected to the National Medical Association
1929	Earns Rockefeller fellowship to study in Vienna, Austria
1933	Earns General Education Board and Rosenwald Foundation Fellowship, studies bone pathology at University of Chicago
1937	Elected president of the National Medical Association
1938	Becomes first African American certified by the American Board of Surgery
1945	Becomes founding member of the International College of Surgeons in Chicago
1953	Publishes "A Ten-Year Survey of Gall Bladder Surgery at Provident Hospital"
1960	Honored by the Masons for contributions to race relations
1970	Dies in Chicago, Illinois on February 19

set his sights on becoming a doctor. Upon his graduation with an A.B. degree in 1911, Giles became the first African American to be admitted to Cornell University Medical School.

When it came time to do an internship, Giles's options were limited because of his race; few medical institutions welcomed African American medical students. He was accepted to Provident Hospital in Chicago, where he studied under George Cleveland Hall, Daniel Hale Williams, C. G. Roberts, and U. Grant Dailey. Giles maintained his association with Provident Hospital for the rest of his life. He received his medical degree from Cornell in 1915, becoming the first black to do so. Race became an issue again as Giles prepared to begin his career in medicine. Despite outscoring 250 other applicants on the civil service examination, he was passed over for junior physician appointments at the Municipal Tuberculosis Sanitarium and Oak Park Infirmary because of his race.

The year 1917 was significant both professionally and personally for Giles. That year, alderman Oscar DePriest intervened on his behalf, and Giles was appointed supervisor of the Chicago Health Department by Chicago mayor William Hale Thompson. He also received an honorary attending physician position at Cook County Hospital, which was a formality, as he performed no medical duties there.

Also in 1917, Giles became part of Provident Hospital's pioneering education program aimed at black medical students. Provident was the first institution to address the needs of black, postgraduate-level medical students. Giles was named assistant attending surgeon at Provident, which made him one of the program's first teachers. According to *A Century of Black Surgeons: The U.S.A. Experience, Volume I,* Giles was well suited for the task. He has been described as being a perceptive teacher and a conscientious caregiver. He was known for visiting his patients as often as he felt was needed, "day, night, or every half hour." Giles was known for having the patience to provide thorough postoperative care, guiding even the most traumatized patients back to caring for themselves.

During this time, he was an attending surgeon for Southside hospital, and he began a private practice that continued until his death in 1970. Giles's personal life also thrived in 1917. On January 9, 1917, Giles married Frances Reeder. They eventually had three sons together: Roscoe C. Giles I (who died as a child), Oscar DePriest Giles, and Roscoe C. Giles II.

In addition to his skills as a teacher and physician, Giles kept up on literature of developing medical techniques and practices. With the help of his wife, a registered nurse, Giles read widely in medical journals, and attended medical meetings and conventions. He was able to draw upon the latest literature when assessing a patient's condition and treatment needs.

Giles published his first paper, "Rickets: The Surgical Treatment of the Chronic Deformities of, With Emphasis on Bow-Legs and Knock-Knees," in the *Journal of the National Medical Association* in 1922. His subsequent contributions to the *JNMA* included papers on pancreatic cysts, intestinal obstructions, intestinal surgery, spine fractures, tuberculosis, and appendicitis, among other topics. Giles gained stature among his medical peers and, in 1926, was elected to the National Medical Association. He remained a member of the organization until 1935.

In 1929, Giles was awarded a Rockefeller fellowship to study in Vienna. In his time abroad, he studied with Von Eiselberg at the Institute of Traumatic Surgery, with Jacob Erdheim and Rudolf Maresh. He wrote about his experiences overseas in several *JNMA* articles.

Giles's *JNMA* publications during the mid-1930s focused on bone diseases, largely because, in 1933, he was awarded a General Education Board and Rosenwald Foundation Fellowship. He spent his fellowship studying bone pathology at the University of Chicago.

In 1937, at the annual convention for the National Medical Association, a professional group of African American doctors, Giles was elected president by his peers. Among the committees to which he was appointed, one was known as the Giles committee. The Giles committee's goal was to convince the American Medical Association to removed the abbreviation "col." from its directory after the names of African American physicians. After much struggle, "col." was finally removed from the directory in 1940. Giles was later named to a special liaison committee between the National Medical Association and the American Medical Association, which then banded together on issues of mutual interest, such as health insurance. In 1938 Giles became the first African American certified by the American Board of Surgery.

Giles served the country during World War II as a member of the Army Medical Corps, and he published several papers based on his experience in the war. In 1945, he was invited to become a founding member of the International College of Surgeons in Chicago. He continued to serve as an assistant professor in surgery at Chicago Medical School (later Northwestern University) and as an attending surgeon at Westside Veterans Hospital and Cook County Hospital. He remained as an alternate attending physician in surgery at Northwestern from 1947 to 1952, then was an associate attending surgeon from 1953 until his retirement in 1959.

In 1953, Giles refuted a long-held misconception with his paper "A Ten-Year Survey of Gall Bladder Surgery at Provident Hospital," in which he stated that the disease was more prevalent in African Americans than was previously believed. Giles's last article was published in the *American Journal of Surgery* in May 1957. In December of that year, he was named one of One Hundred Outstanding Citizens of Chicago. Giles was honored by the Masons in 1960 for contributions to race relations. Giles died at Veterans Hospital in Chicago on February 19, 1970.

REFERENCES

Books

Organ, Claude H., and Margaret Kosiba, eds. *A Century of Black Surgeons: The U.S.A. Experience, Volume I.* Norman, OK: Transcript Press, 1987.

Periodicals

"The Special Liaison Committee." *Journal of the National Medical Association* 32 (1940): 260-61.

Brenna Sanchez

Hugh Gloster
1911–2002

College president

Historically black colleges and universities praised Hugh Morris Gloster as one of the celebrities among their college presidents. President of Morehouse College in Atlanta, Georgia, for twenty years (1967-87), Gloster, affectionately called "Hugh" by the student body, touched the lives of thousands of students who later held prominent positions around the country. However, in a nationwide survey conducted by the Exxon Education Foundation, peers named Gloster one of the 100 most effective college presidents in the United States. College and university English and foreign language teachers also acknowledged Gloster as the founder and first president of the prestigious association of black teachers, scholars, and writers, the College Language Association, and his outstanding achievements as author and scholar. Hugh Gloster was a visionary, a creator, and an originator. He pioneered his way to success in all areas of his career by his foresight, imagination, and bold decisions.

Gloster was born in Brownsville, Tennessee, on May 11, 1911, to John R. and Dora Gloster. Near the end of World War I, lynchings of African Americans in Brownsville forced John Gloster to move the family to nearby Memphis, Tennessee, to provide a safer environment for his family. Hugh, the last of three boys and a girl, was essentially reared as an only child. His sister, Alice,

Chronology

1911	Born in Brownsville, Tennessee on May 11
1931	Receives B.A. degree in English at Morehouse College in Atlanta, Georgia
1933	Receives M.A. degree in English at Atlanta University
1935	Founds Association of Teachers of English in Negro Colleges at Lemoyne College, Memphis, Tennessee (subsequently College Language Association)
1941	Enters New York University for doctoral studies in English
1943-46	Completes doctorate and begins work with USO as an administrator
1946	Begins teaching career at Hampton Institute
1948	Publishes *Negro Voices in American Fiction*
1967	Leaves Hampton Institute to become president of Morehouse College
1987	Selected as one of the 100 most effective college presidents in the United States
1987	Retires from Morehouse College at age of 75
2002	Dies in Decatur, Georgia on February 16

died in her teens, and his brothers, Clarence and Claudius (also known as Claude) were many years his senior.

According to the census, Gloster's parents were born during the slavery era; nevertheless, they became educators. At the end of the nineteenth century, Gloster's father attended Roger Williams University, one of Nashville, Tennessee's four colleges founded for freed slaves. The university merged in 1929 with How Institute of Memphis (subsequently Lemoyne-Owen College) where John Gloster later served on the board for several years.

Hugh Gloster later appreciated the importance his parents placed on excellence in learning. Following their parental model, all of the Gloster children pursued an education. They may be identified as Morehouse men, having all graduated from Morehouse College in Atlanta, Georgia. After Morehouse, Clarence continued his studies at Meharry Medical College in Nashville, Tennessee, and practiced medicine for many years in Tuskegee, Alabama. Claudius studied music and performed and taught private lessons in Chicago. Hugh remained in Atlanta to complete a M.A. at Atlanta University.

Founds College Language Association

Gloster began his teaching career at Lemoyne College in 1933. Four years later, the need for a venue in which to discuss issues pertaining to blacks and engage in research and scholarly discussion inspired the creation of the Association of Teachers of English in Negro Colleges. By 1941, the association had enlarged its scope to include foreign language teachers and the teaching of literature. Eventually in 1949 the group became known as the College Language Association. In the document, "The College Language Association Collection," schol-

ars acknowledged the following about the organization: "The rich tradition of Black intellectual history is incomplete without the records of the CLA. The debates, the studies, scholarly works . . . is [sic] testament to the ongoing conversation intra-internationally about the value of literature and language in the African American community." As first and fifth president of the organization and a board member for sixty-five years, Gloster served the organization with distinction. CLA honored Gloster with the President's Award in 1997 and established the Hugh M. Gloster Endowed Scholarship in 1999. CLA returned in April 2002 to Lemoyne-Owen to celebrate the sixty-fifth year of the organization and to honor its founder who unfortunately died on February 16, two months before the conference.

Gloster's creation of and work to develop CLA signaled his dedication to the profession, but his plans to do much more uprooted him from Lemoyne College. With the nation at war, Gloster left in 1941 to pursue a doctorate in English at New York University. In spite of his Ph.D., Gloster then faced military service. Leaving New York University in 1943, Gloster reported to Fort Hauchuca, Arizona, as United States organization program director at the all black military training facility. He ended his military service as associate regional director in familiar territory, Atlanta, Georgia, in 1946 to begin work at Hampton Institute.

The Hampton Institute Years

Gloster accepted a teaching position at Hampton Institute in Hampton, Virginia, culturally, professionally, and personally stimulated by the interaction with writers, artists, and intellectuals in the atmosphere of the Harlem Renaissance during his studies in New York and with experience in administration and deepened otherwise by three years of military service. At Hampton, Gloster distinguished himself as teacher, scholar, and administrator during his twenty-one years (1946-67). Gloster's authorship of numerous articles on African American literature included his groundbreaking work (the result of his dissertation) in black literary criticism, *Negro Voices in American Fiction*, published by University of North Carolina in 1948. A reviewer, Alexander Cowie, hailed the work as an "illuminating survey of little-known territory." Gloster's work as co-editor of *The Brown Thrush*, an anthology of student verse, and a college textbook, *My Life-My Country-My World* (in print since 1948) define his career as a scholar. Gloster also lectured in Hiroshima, Japan, as a Fulbright lecturer traveling extensively in Asia with his first wife, Louise, and their two daughters.

As an administrator at Hampton, Gloster pioneered a pre-college program in 1952. He was director of the summer session from 1952 to 1962. His success in administration prepared him for his role as dean of faculty. Gloster's success in fund raising ($21 million) contributed to his selection as president at Morehouse College in 1967. Hampton honored him with the Centennial Award in 1968 and an honorary degree, doctor of Humane Letters, in 1999.

Becomes College President

As recorded in the Gloster papers at Atlanta University Center Library, in his inauguration speech as seventh president of Morehouse, Gloster declared his vision for the school: "I did not come to Morehouse to maintain the status quo but to work with all in developing it as a first class institution . . . [It] will never become a mini-college with a mini-curriculum, a mini-faculty and a mini-student body." Given the typically short terms for university presidents, it is remarkable that in nearly five decades (1940-87) only two presidents, Benjamin E. Mays (1940-67) and Hugh Morris Gloster, helmed Morehouse College, a private liberal arts college and the only college for black males in the United States. Even with his outstanding credentials, many feared Gloster might lack the ability to step out of the large shadow cast by his predecessor although Gloster knew Atlanta and Morehouse well from the vantage point of a student and teacher. As reported in the article, "Morehouse Gloster: Man on a Mountain Top," Gloster recalled a barber telling him to quit because he could not replace Jesus. Nevertheless, Gloster, the first graduate to become president, transformed Morehouse College from a regional college of teachers and preachers to an internationally known academic institution.

Gloster's arrival in Atlanta from Hampton, Virginia, came within two months of the death of Morehouse's most famous alumnus, Martin Luther King Jr. Starting a new career amid a politicized and stimulating environment, Gloster challenged Morehouse men, as quoted in an article in the *Atlanta Daily World*, "to learn as much about American Negro literature and history and the race problem and race relations as I know."

After twenty years of presidential service, campus organizers celebrated him, as the recognition banquet program booklet states, "For Two Decades of Progressive Leadership." Listed among his major accomplishments was the establishment in 1976 of the Morehouse School of Medicine, the first medical school planned and opened by blacks in the United States. The School of Medicine graduated its first class two years before Gloster's retirement in 1987. Other impressive accomplishments were increasing the number of majors in the Department of Business, doubling student enrollment and faculty, quadrupling the college endowment to $20 million and overall raising more than $100 million for the college. As quoted in *The Atlanta Journal Constitution*, the president of the Robert Woodruff Foundation stated, "One always knew that an investment made in the college during his tenure was an investment well made."

Upon his retirement from Morehouse College in 1987 at the age of 75, Gloster declined numerous offers of college and interim presidencies. Instead he spent most of his fifteen years in retirement not writing books as he thought he would but consulting with major educational organizations, serving on boards such as UNCF and Lemoyne-Owen. Until September 11, 2001 curtailed his trips, Gloster traveled extensively around the world with his third wife, Yvonne King Gloster, a lawyer, who was his executive assistant at Morehouse College. Being a family man, he also enjoyed the family gatherings, which included his three children, Alice and Evelyn (by his first wife Louise), and Hugh Junior (by his second wife Beulah), four step-children and numerous grand and great-grand children.

"I wish I could have done more. But where would we be if we did not have wishes and dreams," reflected Gloster in a *Chronicle of Higher Education* interview at the end of his career. Always striving for excellence, Gloster lived a life of superlatives. He influenced the lives of many through his excellent teaching and his bold administration work. Retiring president of Tennessee State University, James Hefner, referred to Gloster in an interview with the *Tennessee Tribune*: "I have tried to adhere to the philosophy of President Hugh Gloster, who I worked for at Morehouse College. He believed that your work should speak for you." Gloster demonstrated his commitment and dedication to the education of African Americans. By all standards he met the challenge of the students at Morehouse whose letter in 1967 to the in-coming president stated: "We challenge you, Dr. Gloster, to provide powerful and dynamic leadership."

REFERENCES

Periodicals

Collision, Michele, "Morehouse's Gloster: Man on a Mountain Top." *Chronicle of Higher Education* (22 July 1987): 3.

Cowie, Alexander. Review of *Negro Voices in American Fiction. American Literature* 21 (March 1949): 134-35.

Perry, Hammond. "Gloster Inaugurated with Pomp, Pageantry." *Atlanta Daily World* (18 February 1967): 1-2.

Reid, S .A. "Morehouse Grew on Gloster's Watch." *Atlanta Journal Constitution* (19 February 2002): 1, 8.

Online

Tennessee Tribune. http://thetennesseetribune.com/news/article/article.asp (Accessed 2 June 2005).

Other

"For Two Decades of Progressive Leadership," Recognition Banquet Program April 24, 1987.

Atlanta University Center Woodruff Library Archives/ Special Collection, Atlanta Georgia.

Freeney, Charles, et al. *College Language Association Collection Guide, 1997*. Atlanta University Center Woodruff Library Archives/ Special Collection, Atlanta Georgia.

"Letter to Hugh Gloster." Atlanta University Center Woodruff Library Archives/ Special Collection, Atlanta Georgia.

Collections

The majority of Hugh Gloster's papers are housed at the Atlanta University Center Woodruff Library Archives/ Special Collection, Atlanta, Georgia.

Rosa Bobia

Peter Gomes
1942–

Minister, educator

Peter Gomes

Harvard University's professor of Christian Morals and minister to its Memorial Church, Peter J. Gomes presents to his students and readers an engaging and accessible look at biblical scholarship. As a Christian who happens also to be gay, Gomes has published two books and a collection of sermons exploring biblical perspectives on issues such as slavery, racism, homosexuality, and sexism. Gomes's ability to get to the heart of an issue with clarity and honesty appeals to a wide audience which includes non-church goers. His success as a university professor is heightened by the fact that his books reach the bestseller lists. Gomes's eloquent and scholarly sermons earned him a place among the top seven U.S. preachers in 1979 and the opportunity to participate in inaugural ceremonies for two U.S. presidents.

As the only son of Peter Lobo and Orissa Josephine White Gomes, Peter John Gomes was indulged by attentive parents. Gomes's father Peter Lobo was born in Cape Verde Island in 1908 and immigrated to the United States in the 1920s. After settling in Plymouth, Massachusetts, he worked his way up the ranks to superintendent in the local cranberry bogs. Versed in several languages, the elder Gomes willingly helped other immigrants in the area to compose letters to send home. Orison Josephine was born on Boston's wealthy Beacon Hill in 1901. She was one of nine children and the daughter of Jacob Merrit Pedford White, a well-known Baptist minister in the area. She graduated from the New England Conservatory of Music and was the first African American woman to

work in the Massachusetts State House as a clerk. Her family could be traced back to before the Civil War. Her mother and many of their family had escaped to the North via the Underground Railroad. Known as free-issue Negroes, the family faced situations of emancipation that were both disruptive and benevolent.

With the birth of their son, Peter John, on May 22, 1942, Peter Lobo and Orissa Joseph White Gomes set about to educate him well beyond the public school system. He was given music lessons and had classical literature read to him nightly by his mother. Outings to places of interest were included in his education. His parents prepared him to have a good life, recognizing that diverse life experiences and an openness to others were essential.

It was the experience of failing the second grade that motivated Gomes to excel. He became an exceptional student. He writes in his book *The Good Life* that this experience was one which made him something of an ambitious overachiever. He recognizes it as a valuable lesson in the ongoing search for the good life. Church was also an important part of Gomes's early years. As a young boy, he attended a Baptist church in Plymouth and was active in church programs to the point of preaching his own private sermons. At twelve years of age he preached his first sermon in a basement pulpit constructed of cranberry boxes. Gomes later compared the excitement of the pulpit to the unleashed freedom that

Chronology

1942	Born in Boston, Massachusetts on May 22
1954	Preaches his first sermon at twelve years of age
1961	Graduates from Plymouth High School
1965	Receives B.A. from Bates College
1968	Receives B.D. degree from Harvard University; ordained to ministry of American Baptist Church
1968-70	Teaches at Tuskegee Institute
1974	Receives D.D. degree from New England College; minister to Harvard Memorial Church and Plummer Professor of Christian Morals
1985	Delivers benediction at second inaugural for President Ronald Reagan
1989	Delivers inaugural service for President George Bush
1991	Declares status as Christian who happens as well to be gay
1996	Publishes *The Good Book: Reading the Bible with Mind and Heart*
2002	Publishes *The Good Life: Truths that Last in Times of Need*

most African American youth might associate with the basketball court. In the eleventh grade, Gomes wrote the entry on Plymouth, Massachusetts for the 1960 *American Encyclopedia* and also worked as a page for the public library, where he was responsible for the department of genealogy and research in some of New England's finest homes. These activities foreshadowed his later decision to become a scholar and a clergyman. In 1961, Gomes graduated from Plymouth High School with hopes of attending Bowdoin College in Brunswick, Maine. When this did not work out, he successfully enrolled in Bates College in Lewiston, Maine. Bowdoin College in later years gave Gomes an honorary degree. The experiences provided by his parents made it possible for him to pay his way through college by working as an organist and choirmaster at the first Congregational Church in Lewiston and at the Pilgrim Hall museum in Plymouth in the summers. He was awarded the Theodore Presser Scholarship in music for the entire four years of college.

As a sophomore at Bates College, Gomes like many students of the 1960s had reservations about religion. He took Religion 101, with John A. T. Robinson. Thanks to Robinson's instruction and an approach that enlightened and did not diminish the questions of the college sophomore, Gomes was rescued from religion of doubt. He graduated from college in 1965 and determined that history was his chosen subject. He planned to become the first curator of American Decorative Arts at the Boston Museum of Fine Arts. Before he executed his plan, though, he was persuaded to spend a year at Harvard Divinity School. If this year did not peak his interest, he would move on to his original plan as curator. After a year, Gomes decided to stay, and three years later in 1968 he earned his bachelor's of divinity degree.

Gomes was an active member of the university community because he was the chair of the Worship and Publications committee and served as proctor of Divinity Hall. He also won the Harvard preaching prize. Gomes was ordained to the ministry of the American Baptist Church in 1968 before he accepted an offer to teach history at Tuskegee in Alabama. Tuskegee, a predominately African American college in the Deep South, offered a more intense cultural experience for Gomes than life in Massachusetts. For the first time African American people were the majority. Gomes commented once in an interview for the *New Yorker*: "I saw more black people in my first half hour at Tuskegee than I had ever seen in my entire life." As well as teaching history, Gomes directed the Freshman Experimental Program and assisted in the institute chapel. He used his musical talent as choirmaster for St. Andrew's Episcopal Church in Tuskegee.

In 1970 he returned to Harvard and was appointed assistant minister of Harvard's Memorial Church. His commitment to service was again realized and he was an active participant in various organizations: member of the Royal Arts Society, London, England; director of the North Baptist Educational Society, 1973; member of the Farmington Institute of Christian Studies; and a member of Phi Beta Kappa. By 1974, Gomes was appointed minister of the Harvard Memorial Church and the Plummer Professor of Christian Morals.

Christianity and Homosexuality Debated

In November 1991 Harvard University campus was in heated dialogue over the activities of the student publication called *Peninsula*. The magazine was devoted to denouncing homosexuality as destructive for individuals as well as for society. The magazine used as the basis for its statements a fifty-six-page special issue Muslim, Jewish, and Christian scriptures. Faculty and other administrators were asked to comment at a campus protest. Gomes placed himself squarely in the controversy when he stated, on the steps of the Memorial Church, that he was a Christian who happened to be gay. Although Gomes was not the only person who declared their homosexuality, his declaration received the most vocal response. A fifty-member student committee calling themselves Concerned Christians at Harvard was formed to seek the resignation of Gomes. His resignation was not sought because of his own homosexuality but because he teaches that homosexuality is not a sin in the Christian church.

The American Baptist Church at the time had no stated policy on homosexuality, but in June 1991, it issued a statement against homosexual practices. The president of Harvard stated that it was not the school's task to apply doctrines that are a part of theological debate. It was reasonable that different religious groups have differing views. Gomes continued in his position as minister of the university chapel and vowed to address the religious causes and root of homophobia as presented through various scriptures and doctrines. Toward that goal, he published in 1996, *The Good Book: Reading the Bible with Mind and Heart.*

The Good Book, which was a *New York Times* bestseller, confronts the biblical roots of homophobia as well as other controversial topics such as racism, sexism, and anti-Semitism. He offers a scholarly and thoughtful reinterpretation of these issues and places them in the context of the times. Reviews about the book note the dual purpose that it serves. Not only does it reach the audience of those seeking spiritual engagement, but it provides an example of how the Bible still speaks to the most intellectual or sophisticated Christian. Gomes argues that the Bible is good news for gays, women, people of color, and all others who seek its wisdom. He further notes that strict fundamentalists may not see the value of his interpretation, but the text given a limited reading can become a dangerous tool. His promotion of an on-going context and a community of interpretations of the Bible serves as the key rational for the moral decisions of the church. Among those voices he concludes that feminist interpreters have much to teach others and to ignore their views sets a dangerous precedence for the scriptures and the church. Religious institutions in confronting cultural ills such as slavery and racism have used the process of interpretation to understand the scriptures of the time and of the people. Gomes places the charge of the Bible squarely in the hands of the Christian. The words, syntax, doctrines, and interpretations must be given time, commitment, imagination, and serious study by those who truly seek to know the scriptures. To do anything less is a derelict of duty.

To reach the scope of believers from the embarrassed to the exiled, Gomes published in 1998 *Sermons: Biblical Wisdom for Daily Living.* It is a collection of forty selections from sermons preached over the years to the Harvard congregations at First Memorial Church. The first eighteen sermons in the book address themes of the Christian calendar: Advent, Christmas, Epiphany, Lent, Easter, Pentecost, and Martin Luther King Jr. Day. The second group of twenty-two sermons looks at more universal topics such as identity, miracles, depression, love, death, and stewardship. The entire collection, which is very readable, offers a broad view of Gomes's approach to teaching the word.

In 2002 Gomes wrote *The Good Life: Truths That Last in Times of Need.* His goal in this text is to reclaim doctrines of virtue and lifelong moral education verses materialism, which has come to inform much of U.S. culture. Julianne Malveaux in her article in *Black Issues in Higher Education* notes that Gomes speaks about the moral agenda in education. In an interview with *The Christian Century*, Gomes states: "making a living is what most parents of my students today were brought up to do. Mak-

ing a living is supposed to be a means to an end, but it often becomes an end in itself." His book explores these issues in three parts. The first part of the book discusses the yearning for something more than material reward, for some noble purpose or destination worth living and even dying for. The second part of the book looks at what prepares people to live fully, such as successes, failures, discipline, and other character builders. In the final section the process and the means to reach the good life are placed within Christian teaching. Gomes asserts that a good life can only be called good if it exhibits in some way the four cardinal virtues and the three theological virtues. The four cardinal virtues are prudence, justice, temperance, and fortitude. The theological virtues are faith, hope, and love. The journey to a "good life" as offered in this text is ultimately an examination of what matters and gives purpose to people's lives.

Gomes, who is unmarried and celibate by choice, continues to confront issues of spiritual growth in his scholarly and ministerial work. He contributes articles and book reviews to the *New York Times*, covering various topics, such as cultural attitudes regarding tourism and African American culture in Harlem, reviews on religious texts such as Buddhism, and scholarly commentary on historic moments (for example a sermon preached by John Winthrop, governor of the Massachusetts Bay Colony in 1630). In 1985, Gomes delivered the benediction for the second inaugural address for Ronald Reagan, and in 1989 he delivered the inaugural service for George Bush. Even though his life was changed by his willingness to respond to an act of hate, Gomes seeks to expand the understanding of the scripture. His ultimate response does not rest on the issue of homosexuality, but on the doctrines of Christianity.

REFERENCES

Books

French, Ellen Dennis. "Peter J. Gomes." In *Contemporary Black Biography.* Vol. 15. Ed. Shirelle Phelps. New York: Gale Publishing, 1997.

Periodicals

Gergen, David R. "A Pilgrimage for Spirituality." *U.S. News & World Report* 121 (23 December 1996): 80.

Higgins, Richard. "Polishing the Truth." *The Christian Century* 119 (22 May 2002): 19.

Malveaux, Julianne. "Moral Education in an Immoral Society. (Speaking of Education)." *Black Issues in Higher Education* 19 (29 August 2002): 46.

McGrath, Bernandette. "Sermon: Biblical Wisdom for Daily Living." *Library Journal* 123 (1 May 1998): 106.

Olson, Ray. "Sermons: Biblical Wisdom for Daily Living." *Booklist* 94 (15 April 1998): 1397.

Ostling, Richard N. "Christians Spar in Harvard Yard." *Time* 139 (16 March 1992): 49.

Lean'tin L. Bracks

Charles G. Gomillion

Charles G. Gomillion
1900–1995

Civil rights activist

Charles Goode Gomillion is best known as a community activist with a strong interest in voter rights. His active involvement in voter rights for black Americans in the late 1950s, and eventually the lawsuit that led to the landmark Supreme Court case known as *Gomillion v. Lightfoot*, affected the nation and the South in regards to redistricting designed to circumvent the black vote.

Gomillion was born in Johnston, South Carolina in Edgefield County on April 1, 1900. His grandparents were born in slavery. His father, Charles, was born a slave in 1855 and remained a slave until the Emancipation Proclamation in 1863. His father married his mother Florence, who was twenty-two years his junior. Charles was the oldest of four children, having two sisters and a younger brother.

Gomillion's early education was limited. He attended the public schools from first to third grades only three months of each year. During the fourth, fifth, and sixth grades, he attended school for five months. The public school system paid for three months and his parents paid for two months. In the seventh grade, he attended only four weeks and decided to drop out because he had problems with arithmetic. The next year he went back and was in the eighth grade. He attended only five weeks and dropped out because he was the only student.

Although his father never attended school or learned to read or write, his mother had gone through the third grade and was very interested in her children's education. After Gomillion dropped out of the eighth grade, his mother decided he knew enough to be home schooled. She borrowed old magazines and newspapers from neighbors, and encouraged all her children to read. Gomillion saved for two and a half years in order to attend Paine High School in Augusta, Georgia, to complete eighth grade. He also attended Paine College until 1922, when he married his college girlfriend, Hermyne Jones, then dropped out to help support his parents, both of whom had become disabled. For about a year, he worked in Philadelphia as a postal worker, then moved to Georgia to teach middle school. After about a five-year absence, he returned to Paine College and received his bachelor's degree at the age of twenty-eight.

Gomillion was hired as a faculty member at Tuskegee Institute in Tuskegee, Alabama in 1928. He moved there with his wife and two daughters, Vernita and Mary Gwendolyn. After a year, his wife left him, and he received custody of his daughters, ages five and six. Gomillion's co-workers described him as an intense man who always seemed to be concentrating deeply. In addition he earned the respect of onlookers for raising children alone. He remarried in 1936 and his second wife helped in the rearing of his two daughters.

In 1933, an old Paine College professor invited Gomillion to Fisk University in Nashville, Tennessee to conduct sociological research. At Fisk, Gomillion studied under the best sociologists of the time—Bertram W. Doyle, E. Franklin Frazier, and Charles S. Johnson. Under Johnson, he learned as much as he could about working with whites in the South and trying to bring blacks and whites together in order to lay a foundation for improving race relations. He took a year's leave of absence from Tuskegee Institute and returned in the fall of 1934 when he began teaching in the college's sociology department.

Gomillion returned to Fisk in 1936 for further studies in sociology. Gomillion also studied briefly at Chicago

Chronology

1900	Born in Johnston, South Carolina on April 1
1922	Marries Hermyne Jones
1928	Graduates from Paine College in Augusta, Georgia; joins the Tuskegee faculty
1934	Additional studies at Fisk University; leads effort to register blacks to vote
1936	Remarries
1939	Registered to vote in Macon County, Alabama
1941	Creates the Tuskegee Civic Association (formerly the Tuskegee Men's Club)
1957	Sues Tuskegee Mayor Phillip Lightfoot over gerrymandering
1959	Receives doctorate in sociology from Ohio State University
1960	The Supreme Court rules that the Fifteenth Amendment rights of Tuskegee blacks are violated by the gerrymander
1970	Retires from public life
1971	Retires from Tuskegee University
1995	Dies in Montgomery, Alabama on October 4

University and later attended Ohio State University where he received his doctorate in sociology in 1959.

In 1934, Gomillion was not considered a radical or an activist. However, after his return from Fisk, Gomillion became active in the Men's Club of Tuskegee, which was established in1910 to help improve public services around Tuskegee Institute. (Under Gomillion's leadership women were included in 1941.) The Men's Club consisted of faculty members from Tuskegee, teachers from the local school, and other local professional men. Members addressed community concerns such as sewerage, drainage, streets, credit institutions, and voting issues. As a club member Gomillion encouraged people to register to vote. He believed that many problems could be solved with increased political participation. But blacks were obstructed from participating by various strategies, for example the poll tax; white primary, intelligence tests; and the voucher system.

The poll tax was enacted in 1901 by the Alabama Constitution to keep blacks from registering to vote. The intelligence test purported to measure understanding of the United States Constitution; the test asked people to read or write portions of the Constitution. In 1875, white supremacists wrote a new constitution in Alabama that supported the white primary and manipulated the black vote for nearly twenty-five years. The voucher system required one or more white persons to vouch for the character of blacks who applied to register to vote. Gomillion expended a lot of effort trying to register to vote, but he was held up since people who agreed to vouch for him started backing out. In 1939, he applied again after a white contractor approached him about building a house. Gomillion agreed to let him build the house if he would vouch for him. The contractor agreed, and Gomillion

became a registered voter after paying back poll taxes from 1928 to 1939. Gomillion's second wife became a registered voter in 1940 and also had to pay poll taxes of $1.50, covering the period from when she came to Macon County in 1936 to 1940.

In 1941, the Men's Club broadened the scope of its mission and changed its name to the Tuskegee Civic Association (TCA). Its main goals were to improve public services, to get equal opportunities for public education, and to heighten blacks' awareness of all community concerns. Gomillion believed that the citizens of Tuskegee had a civic duty to register and vote. The TCA started an active campaign to get blacks registered, pay their poll taxes, and make informed voting choices. At the start of the campaign there were about 75 registered black voters in the county. Over a period of nearly twenty years, the number increased to about 410. This increase was alarming to the white political powers of Alabama.

Gerrymandering to Eliminate Black Voters

Tuskegee is the county seat of Macon County and the home of Tuskegee Institute, which was founded by Booker T. Washington in 1881. On June 7, 1957, state representative Samuel Engelhardt convinced the Alabama legislature to redraw the boundaries of Tuskegee so that all but a handful of registered black voters were excluded from the city. (Redrawing voting districts for political purposes is called gerrymandering.) At this time the population of Tuskegee was 5,300 blacks and 1,400 whites with 410 black registered voters and 600 whites. All but twelve blacks were excluded by this line, but none of the whites were left out.

The original lines demarked a four-mile square. The new district lines had twenty-eight sides and took the shape of a sea dragon. On June 25, 1957, the Tuskegee Civic Association called a public meeting to discuss the redistricting. The decision was for blacks to boycott local merchants. The Macon Theatre was the first business to close as a result of the boycott. After a week, the protest was said to be 90 percent effective.

Gomillion and the Tuskegee Civic Association challenged the redistricting in court. A federal suit was filed seeking to bar mayor Phillip M. Lightfoot and other city officials from enforcing the state statutes on the grounds that it circumvented the Fifteenth Amendment's voting guarantees.

After losing twice in the lower courts, Gomillion took his case to the Supreme Court. In 1960, the Supreme Court ruled that the Fifteenth Amendment rights of Tuskegee blacks had been violated by the redistricting. The Supreme Court decision helped persuade Congress to pass the Voting Rights Act of 1965.

Gomillion did not initially believe in Booker T. Washington's philosophy about the future of blacks in the general society. The more he actively participated in civic concerns in Tuskegee and after his studies, he began to change his mind. However, he believed that political power was the means to the end. Gomillion briefly ventured into politics in 1964 when he ran for a seat on the school board and won.

In his lifetime, Charles G. Gomillion conducted research periodically He also was a field worker under Charles Johnson. His job was to interview Negro tenants in Mississippi and Texas to determine the extent to which they were receiving the surplus food that was being sent down for poor people and to what extent they were receiving financial support from certain acreages devoted to cotton. The study showed that some landlords were not being fair and were increasing the tenant's indebtedness rather than reducing it by the sum entitled.

Gomillion's professional career included serving as an instructor at Tuskegee High School and at the college from 1928 to 1944. From 1944 to 1949, he served as dean of the School of Education at Tuskegee. From 1949 to 1958, he was the institute's dean of students. From 1959 until he retired in 1971, he taught sociology.

Gomillion was active in many organizations at the local, state, and national levels. He was a life member of the Paine College National Alumni Association, a life member of the NAACP, and a member of the National Education Association, the Southern Sociological Association, and Omega Psi Phi Fraternity. He also served as a member of the Alabama Council on Human Relations and was a member of the Advisory Board Committee on Civil Rights in the United States Department of Agriculture. He served on the board of directors of the Highlander Folk School and Southern Conference Education Fund.

For his community participation, he was the recipient of many honors and awards. In 1958, he received the Omega Psi Phi Fraternity Man of the Year award. In 1965, Fisk University presented him with the Charles S. Johnson Award. At the Democratic conference in Alabama in 1975, he was presented the Lyndon Baines Johnson Freedom Award. In 1976, the Ohio State University Citation of Achievement was awarded to him, and in 1982, Paine College named him Alumnus of the Decade. In 1991, he was awarded the Distinguished Career Award for the practice of sociology by the American Sociological Association.

Gomillion was also the recipient of four honorary doctorate degrees, from Howard University in Washington, D.C., 1965; Ohio State University in Columbus, Ohio, 1967; Tuskegee Institute in Tuskegee, Alabama, in 1971; and Paine College of Augusta, Georgia in 1986.

President and Mrs. Bill Clinton also honored Gomillion in 1994 at a Martin Luther King Jr. birthday celebration at the White House. At age 94, he was the oldest honoree present.

Gomillion was a member of the Christian Methodist church from the age of fourteen. He was originally raised in the Baptist church but was allowed to attend the Colored Methodist Episcopal church when he and his siblings complained to their mother that the Sunday school teachers at the Baptist church refused to answer their questions. Gomillion became very active in the youth organization of the Methodist church, the Epworth League. He was so inspired by its motto, "Keep Everlastingly At It", that he adopted it as his personal credo.

Gomillion was proud of the landmark court decision, but he was more proud of the many young lives he influenced during his tenure at Tuskegee. In an interview in 1987, he stated that many of his students remained in touch with him. Gomillion retired from Tuskegee and moved to Washington, D.C. and Roebling, New Jersey. He lived there for almost twenty-five years before returning to Tuskegee. His wife Blondelia Elizabeth Graves Gomillion died in July 1992. He died on October 4, 1995 at a hospital in Montgomery, Alabama at the age of 95. A daughter, Gwendolyn, three grandchildren, and one great grandchild survived him.

REFERENCES

Books

Breling, Christor, ed. *Who's Who Among Black Americans*. Detroit: Gale Research, 1993.

Norrell, Robert J. *Reaping the Whirlwind: The Civil Rights Movement in Tuskegee*. New York: Knopf, 1985.

Salzmon, Jack, David Smith, and Cornel West, eds. *Encyclopedia of African American Culture and History*. New York: Simon and Schuster, 1995.

Taper, Bernard. *Gomillion versus Lightfoot*. New York: McGraw-Hill, 1962.

Thompson, Kenneth H. *The Voting Rights Act and Black Electoral Participation*. Washington, D.C.: Joint Center of Political Studies, 1982.

Periodicals

Booker, Simeon. "Civil Rights Heroes Honored At White House by President and Mrs. Clinton." *Jet* 85 (February 1994): 12.

Brittain, Joseph M. "Some Reflections on Negro Suffrage and Politics in Alabama-Past and Present." *Journal of Negro History* 47 (April 1962): 127-38.

Elwood, William A. "An Interview with Charles Gomillion." *Callaloo* 40 (Summer 1989): 576-98.

Online

"Charles Gomillion, 95, Figures in Landmark Remap Case, Dies." http://thomas.loc.gov (Accessed 26 January 2005).

"Death of a Town." Time Magazine Archive, November 25, 1987. http://www.Times.com (Accessed 4 February 2005).

"Gomillion, Voting Rights Pioneer, Dies in Alabama." http://lexis-nexis.com (Accessed 26 January 2005).

"Honoree Dr. Charles G. Gomillion." South Carolina African American History Online. http://scafrican americanhistory.com/currenthonoree.asp (Accessed 4 February 2005).

Tuskegee: Living Black and White. http://wwww.cptr. ua.edu/alex/studyguides/tuskegee.htm (Accessed 3 December 2004).

Orella Ramsey Brazile

Carlton B. Goodlett
1914–1997

Physician, psychiatrist, publisher, activist

When Carlton B. Goodlett—physician, psychiatrist, publisher, human rights activist—died, the residents in San Francisco renamed a street in his honor. According to his colleague and friend, Thomas Fleming, Dr. Goodlett often referred to himself as "the champion of the people." Indeed, Goodlett was dedicated to the disadvantaged. He succeeded in multiple careers, all in an effort to contribute to the development and well being of other people. Initially in the San Francisco area, Goodlett, a psychologist and physician, was known throughout the black community. After assuming ownership of the *Sun-Reporter* newspaper, Goodlett served his community by keeping its members informed. His medical and newspaper work did not limit his activism. He worked for the NAACP, advocated for peace during the cold war as a member of socialist organizations, and ran for political office.

Carlton Benjamin Goodlett was born in Chipley, Florida on July 23, 1914. He was raised in Omaha, Nebraska. His mother was a schoolteacher and his father was a sawmill worker. He attended Howard University in Washington, D.C. where he was president of the student body. He also served as editor for the *Hilltop*, Howard University's student newspaper. He graduated from Howard University with a B.A. in 1935. He then pursued his Ph.D. at the University of California at Berkeley. While at Berkeley, Goodlett continue to advocate for his peers and participated in the organization of a black student union. In 1938, Goodlett earned his doctorate in psychology from the university; he was only twenty-three years old. After completing his doctoral studies, Goodlett taught at West Virginia State College, a historically black college, in Institute, Virginia. He taught at the college for one year and then decided to get an M.D. in Nashville, Tennessee. While a medical student, he married Willette

Chronology	
1914	Born in Chipley, Florida on July 23
1935	Earns B.A. from Howard University
1938	Earns Ph.D. in psychology from University of California at Berkeley
1942	Marries Willette Kilpatrick
1944	Earns M.D. from Meharry Medical College in Nashville, Tennessee; wins rights to *Sun* newspaper in San Francisco, California
1945	Moves to San Francisco and establishes medical practice; becomes co-publisher of the *Reporter*
1947	Serves as president, San Francisco branch of NAACP; fights against racially discriminatory hiring practices of the city's public transit
1948	Merges two papers into the *Sun-Reporter*
1951	Becomes sole owner of the *Sun-Reporter* newspaper; joins the National Newspaper Publishers Association; serves as chairman of the California Black Leadership Council
1963	Moves medical office and newspaper office to one building on Turk Street
1966	Runs for governor of the state of California
1968	Divorces wife Willette Kilpatrick
1970	Attends World Peace Conference in Stockholm; awarded the Lenin Peace Medal
1983	Retires from medical practice
1994	Retires as publisher of the *Sun-Reporter* newspaper
1997	Dies in Cedar Rapids, Iowa on January 25

Kilpatrick in 1942. (They had one son, Garry M. Goodlett. Goodlett and his wife divorced in 1968, and she died in 1982.) Goodlett earned his medical degree from Meharry Medical College in Nashville, Tennessee in 1944.

In 1945, Goodlett established a prosperous medical practice in San Francisco, California. However, at the time there were very few black physicians in the San Francisco area, and black doctors were not allowed access to hospitals. Goodlett was a part of the effort to gain hospital privileges for black physicians. In spite of the demands of his medical practices and the racial tension, Goodlett engaged in another career.

In 1944, Goodlett won the rights to the *Sun*, a black newspaper, in a poker game, and became co-publisher. In 1948, he assumed ownership of *The Reporter* and merged the two newspapers. In 1951, he bought out his partner Daniel A Collins, and joined the National Newspaper Publishers Association. Goodlett purchased a number of other small newspapers and increased his circulation. The paper grew to be the most prominent African American newspaper in northern California. As publisher, Goodlett served as mentor for many young journalists. Journalists Lance Gilmore, Edith Austin, Belva Davis, and Valerie Coleman are a few of the people who were first employed by the *Sun-Reporter*. The paper's motto, "That no good cause shall lack a champion and that evil shall not thrive unopposed," defined the agenda of the newspaper and reflected Goodlett's activism. As publisher of the *Sun-Reporter*, Goodlett continued to address civil rights and to protest discrimination. He protested against the discriminatory hiring practices of San Francisco's Municipal Railway and insisted on desegregation of the municipal labor unions.

In an effort to balance his medical practice and his work as a publisher, in 1963, Goodlett moved to a building on Turk Street that would accommodate both his medical practice and his newspaper offices. The office was a center for activism and was visited by well known political leaders and celebrities, including Paul Robeson, Malcolm X, Muhammad Ali, and Dick Gregory.

Serves as Publisher, Political Leader, and Mentor

Goodlett's activism took him into various groups. He was a member of the Prince Hall Masons. In the 1940s, Goodlett participated in the establishment of a black club for the Democratic Party in San Francisco. From 1947 to 1949, Goodlett was the president of the San Francisco branch of the NAACP. As president of the NAACP, Goodlett spoke out against police harassment and physical abuse of African Americans. He insisted on improvements of public housing and called for an end to the discriminatory practices of the draft boards in San Francisco.

Goodlett was undeterred by controversy and unjust authority figures. In November 1947, Goodlett was arrested after being stopped by the police. The police demanded Goodlett step out of his car. Goodlett refused and was arrested. This incident earned Goodlett a reputation as a fierce agent for social change, a person unwilling to submit to harassment. In July 1959, a similar incident occurred. When detained by police, Goodlett became enraged. He was arrested and charged with swearing at the police. By 1959, Goodlett's influence and prominence in the San Francisco area had grown and friend and assemblyman Phil Burton came to his assistance. Goodlett was released and the charges were dismissed.

In the late 1940s, before the climax of the twentieth century civil rights movement in the 1950s and 1960s, Goodlett advocated for civil rights in an aggressive fashion In 1951, he served as chairman for the California Black Leadership Council. He organized protests of restaurants that exclusively served whites. In public speeches, he encouraged citizens in San Francisco to boycott businesses that discriminated against black people. He called for redistricting so that African Americans would be adequately represented in Congress. He insisted that elected officials recognize the rights and needs of their African American constituents. He argued that the politicians be held accountable for supporting discriminatory legislation. Following the shooting of four protesting students by National Guardsmen at Kent State

University in Ohio in May 1970, Goodlett participated in a protest march. He also was opposed to the war in Vietnam and encouraged other African American leaders to speak out against the war. In the late 1970s, he criticized Jewish involvement in apartheid South Africa and was met with harsh criticism.

From the 1950s through the 1970s, with his work as publisher and activist, Goodlett became one of the most dominant African American leaders in California. As a publisher, Goodlett often used his newspaper to support candidates for political office. He played an integral role in the election of many political leaders in California. According to San Francisco district attorney Terence Hallinan, an endorsement from Carlton Goodlett was important to the election of many political leaders. Goodlett helped to inspire and promote the political careers of Mayor Willie Brown, the late Representative Phil Burton, Senator John Burton, and Representative Ron Dellums, among others.

Although Goodlett was critical of traditional politics, in 1966, he ran for governor of California. He was the first African American to run for governor of the state since Reconstruction. Goodlett argued that then-Governor Brown was "uninspiring" and neglected to consider the representation of African Americans. Goodlett's campaign motto was, "The people are wiser—wiser than the politician thinks." He did not win the democratic primary, receiving only a marginal number of votes. However, he continued to be active in the Democratic Party and in politics through his support of other politicians and his participation in political organizations.

Affiliates with Socialist Activities

Shortly after he moved to San Francisco, Goodlett began teaching psychology at the California Labor Schools. This position was one of many direct and indirect associations Goodlett had with socialist and communist organizations. The school was founded by the International Longshoremen's and Warehousemen's Union, and Longshoremen were suspected of being communists. Goodlett's association with such organizations did not present conflict for him since they appeared to be working for the rights of the disadvantaged. Moreover, as a critic of mainstream politics, alternative venues were welcomed by Goodlett. He also served on the American Committee for Protection of Foreign Born. He invited Paul Robeson to perform and W. E. B. Du Bois to speak at his church, Third Baptist. The two leaders were controversial because of their communist associations. In the 1960s, Goodlett was a member of the World Peace Council. (The World Peace Council, founded in 1949, is an organization devoted "to peace, disarmament, and global security" as well as other issues related to human rights.) The organization supposedly had communist ties. Goodlett made several trips to the Soviet Union and was critical of the U.S. foreign policy regarding the Soviet

Union. In 1962, Goodlett participated in a disarmament conference in Moscow. During the 1960s and 1970s, his opposition to nuclear weapons and his participation in the World Peace Council led him to make several trips abroad to cities such as Stockholm, East Berlin, Prague, Budapest, and Copenhagen. In 1970, he led a delegation to the World Peace Conference and was awarded the Lenin Peace Medal by the Soviet Union for his efforts to support world peace and human rights. He also served as chairman of the board of trustees for the William L. Patterson Foundation. The foundation was named after an African American communist leader.

Commitment to Institutions Devoted to Education

Goodlett was active in the development of institutions devoted to helping African Americans. He helped to found the Morehouse School of Medicine. The school offers a scholarship in Dr. Goodlett's name. He also helped establish the Black Press Archives in 1973 at Howard University's Moorland Spingarn Research Center. This center is supported by Howard University and the National Newspaper Publishers Association. It consists of a gallery of photographs and information on African American achievements in journalism.

In 1983, Goodlett retired from his medical practice, but he remained a major voice in his community. In 1994, he retired as publisher of the *Sun-Reporter*. In the 1990s, his health began to decline, and he was diagnosed with Parkinson's disease. In January 1997, he died at his son's home in Cedar Rapids, Iowa. He was survived by his son Dr. Garry M. Goodlett and five grandchildren.

On February 7, 1997, a memorial service was held to honor Carlton Goodlett Over one thousand people attended. On February 11, 1997, Congresswoman Nancy Pelosi addressed Congress, paying a tribute to Carlton Goodlett. Amos Brown proposed unsuccessfully that Fillmore Street be renamed to honor Goodlett. Fillmore Street was originally named after Millard Fillmore who signed the Fugitive Slave Act of 1850. However, eventually a part of Polk Street was renamed Dr. Carlton Goodlett Way.

Carlton B. Goodlett dedicated his life to human progress. When he saw injustice, he was not afraid to take action and defend the disadvantaged. His achievements in medicine, journalism, education, and politics serve as examples for future generations.

REFERENCES

Periodicals

Cott, Lawrence. *"New York Times* Ignores Black Publisher's Red Record." *Human Events*, 13 April 1997.

Edward, Epstein. "Street Name Plan Faces Uphill Fight." *San Francisco Chronicle*, 21 July 1997.

La Riva, Gloria. "Dr. Carlton Goodlett: African American Pioneer." *Workers World Newspaper*, 20 February 1997.

Schatzmann, Dennis. "Hundreds Pay Tribute to Dr. Carlton Goodlett." *New York Amsterdam News*, 15 February 1997.

Taylor, Michael. "Goodlett's Mark on S.F." *San Francisco Chronicle*, 15 February 1997.

Online

Fleming, Thomas. "Carlton B. Goodlett, Champion of the People" *Reflections on Black History*, 4 June 1999. http://www.freepress.org (Accessed 7 November 2005).

Rebecca Dixon

Charles Gordone
1925–1995

Playwright, actor

The first African American to receive a Pulitzer Prize for drama was Charles Gordone in 1970 for the dramatic work *No Place To Be Somebody*. Gordone took the theater world by storm and brought a new type of race consciousness to the stage. His play came on the scene in the 1960s when people embraced the emergence of long silenced African American voices. Its truths brought many awards to Gordone and the opportunity to produce more plays, screenplays, and creative projects. Although other works of equal attention eluded Gordone for the balance of his career, he continued to contribute to both stage and screen. In his later years he was a distinguished lecturer at Texas Agricultural & Mechanical University and continued to do some acting. Gordone saw himself not as a producer of African American or black theater, as it was called, but as someone who presented human experiences not splintered by race. In an interview with Susan Smith he stated, "I don't write out of a black experience or a white experience; it's American." Gordone left a body of work that was both multiracial and cross-cultural.

Born in Cleveland, Ohio, on October 12, 1925 with a mixed race heritage, Charles Edward Fleming was the son of William Fleming and Camille Morgan Fleming. The family later moved to Elkhart, Indiana, his mother's hometown. Also in the family were two other siblings, Jack and Stanley. Charles and Camille Fleming parted

Charles Gordone

ways, and in 1930 Camille Fleming married William Lee Gordon. The entire family embraced the name Gordon and grew to include seven children. Gordone (the letter "e" was added later in life) had some challenges growing up in the Midwestern town of Elkhart. His stepfather was an auto mechanic and his mother was a former circus acrobat and dancer in Harlem's Cotton Club. William and Camille Gordon and their seven children lived on the white side of town which alienated racial identification particularly for their son and raised questions about his family's racial loyalties. Gordone often found himself rejected by the whites who dominated the town and by the blacks whom he knew. In spite of these difficulties, he excelled academically and as an athlete.

Years as an Actor

After graduating from high school, Gordone enrolled in the University of California at Los Angeles. After only one semester he left to join the United States Air Force. He earned the rank of second lieutenant. Gordone returned to Indiana after his discharge and later married Juanita Burton. The couple had two children, but the marriage failed due to Gordone's promiscuity and alcoholism. Gordone determined to make a change from Indiana as he continued to confront his identity and his place in the world. He decided to move to Los Angeles in 1945 and became a police officer. Using his G.I. Bill of Rights

he was able to complete his education and enroll in Los Angeles City College to study music. By 1952, Gordone had earned a B.A. in drama from the Los Angeles State College. He later studied at New York University, and Columbia University. Soon after receiving his degree from Los Angeles State College, Gordone moved to New York to pursue his acting career. He was discouraged by his professor who advised that African American actors had no future in New York. Nonetheless, Gordone went to New York initially as a singer and found work waiting on tables at Johnny Romero's bar. It was not long before he was back on track and among the ranks of struggling actors. In viewing the Actors' Equity membership, Gordone noticed another actor named Charles Gordon. He decided to add an "e" to his surname to set him apart. The experiences and patrons that he encountered while working in Romero's served as the basis for his future play *No Place To Be Somebody* (1967). Using his many talents, Gordone for a time managed his own theater, the Vantage, in Queens. His first acting roles were in Moss Hart's *Climate of Eden* on Broadway and in Charles Sebree and Greer Johnson's *Mrs. Patterson*. The next year, 1953, he received an Obie Award for his performance as George in an all-black production of John Steinbeck's *Of Mice and Men*. Gordone went on to play the title role in Wole Soyinka's *The Trials of Brother Jero* and in *The Blacks*, a play by Jean Genet. When the play *The Blacks* opened in 1961, Gordone was a part of the original cast. He was in the excellent company of Maya Angelou, Roscoe Lee-Browne, Godfrey Cambridge, Louis Gossett Jr., James Earl Jones, Helen Martin, Raymond St Jacques, and Cicely Tyson. It was during this period in 1959 that Gordone met and married Jeanne Warner. Eight years into the relationship the couple separated due to Gordone's heavy drinking, but they never divorced.

Gordone involved himself in various aspects of the theater and film making, which included directing, producing, and writing. As a director Gordone took on many diverse projects, such as *Rebels and Bugs* (1958), *Peer Gynt* (1959), *Faust* (1959), and *Tobacco Road* and *Detective Story* (1960). He was associate producer of the film *Nothing but the Man* in 1964, while at the same time he saw the opening of *Little More Light Around the Place*, which Gordone co-authored with Sidney Easton. The play, an adaptation of a novel by Easton of the same title, had its first performance at New York City's Sheridan Square Playhouse. As Gordone's career developed he became more interested in policies regarding his craft and the involvement of African Americans in the performing arts. Godfrey Cambridge and Gordone co-founded the Committee for the Employment of Negro Performers, while Gordone chaired a similar committee for the Congress on Racial Equality. In 1967 Gordone was appointed by President Lyndon Johnson to the research team of the Commission on Civil Disorders.

No Place To Be Somebody Brings Pulitzer

Using his experiences as a waiter in Greenwich village, Gordone wrote *No Place To Be Somebody*. He began work on the play during the same period he performed in *The Blacks* written by Jean Genet, who was a formative influence on Gordone's dramaturgy. After trying for two years to get his play produced, Gordone persuaded the New York Shakespeare Festival's Public Experimental theater to give it a preliminary run. The original cast included several actors who would go on to have high profile careers: Paul Benjamin, Nathan George, and Ron O'Neal. The play was first presented at the Sheridan Square Playhouse in New York in 1967. It was performed off-Broadway at the New York Shakespeare Festival Public Theater on May 2, 1969 and on-Broadway at the American National Theater on December 30, 1969. The play ran until October 18, 1970 for 312 performances and was met with critical as well as financial success. Gordone was heralded by Walter Kerr in the *New York Times* as "the most astonishing new American playwright to come along since Edward Albee." In 1970 Gordone became the first African American to receive the Pulitzer Prize for drama. Although the play was regarded as a pioneer form of race-consciousness that explored the black experience, Gordone saw it as an American experience. He maintained that his work should not be from only a racial perspective, for he was above all else a humanist. The play, which consists of character portraits of schemers, dreamers, and losers in a grungy Greenwich Village bar, owes as much to the saloon drama of Eugene O'Neill as it does to the African American theater renaissance of the 1960s. Critics also noted the play's relationship to Greek, Elizabethan, and Jacobean drama.

Subtitled "A Black Black Comedy" the story in *No Place To Be Somebody* centers on saloon keeper and hus-

tler Johnny Williams, who tries to take over the control of a local racket from the local syndicate. Coving a period of fifteen years, Williams becomes the victim of his own awareness of black power. Involving two prostitutes, a short-order cook, a down-and-out actor, a drugged out bartender, and other characters, the play explores the question of identity and how these people represent "everyman". Each is seeking a way to fulfill dreams. The language and experiences come from an urban jungle unleashed by the fury that surrounded black-white and black-black relationships. Johnny Williams, the main character, is unsuccessful in his plan and is ultimately shot by one of the black characters in the play, Gabriel, a light-skinned black writer/actor, seeking his own racial identity. He is rejected by blacks because he is too light and rejected by whites because he is black. Gabriel has several monologues and in some ways becomes Gordone's spokesperson. He expresses the tragedy of racism and how the negative equation of color to value and worth must be abandoned in order to achieve a more human perspective. Gabriel is more of an observer than a participant. He shoots Williams at the request of Machine Dog, a black militant, a figment of Gabriel's imagination.

Although many critics noted the play's flaws, overall it was praised for the characterization and dialogue, along with the sense of life and intimacy it conveys. The language was both rough and eloquent. Criticism from African American reviewers was favorable, but many found evidences of self-hate and contempt for black people. Most could agree that even in despair, black or white, the aspect of hope continued to be evident in the play. In addition to the Pulitzer, the play won the Critics Circle Award, the Drama Desk Award, and the Vernon Rice Award all in 1970. The universal appeal resulted in the play being translated into Spanish, Russian, French, and German.

Theatrical, Community and Educational Projects

Bolstered by his earlier success, Gordone presented a tryout performance of his play *Gordone Is a Mutha* in 1970. The work was a collection of five poems and a monologue. It was presented at Carnegie Recital Hall in May 1970, featuring Gordone. Neither this work nor any of the efforts that followed ever received the attention and acclaim that *No Place To Be Somebody* received. Gordone referred to *Gordone Is a Mutha* as a work that deals with the souls of black people. It portrays black male social castration and presents a humorous description of a mother's preparation for a visit by the welfare lady. The play, which was to be presented on Broadway in the spring of 1971, never appeared, but it was published in 1973 in *The Best Short Plays* edited by Stanley Richards. In 1971 Gordone earned a grant from the National Institute of Arts and Letters. He continued to write plays and over the years presented works such as

Worl's Champeen Lip dansuh an' Watah Mellon Jooglah
(World's Champion Lip Dancer and Water Melon Jug-
gler, 1969), performed at the Other Stage; *Willy Bignigga
and Chumpanzee* (1970), first produced in New York
City at Henry Street Settlement New Federal Theatre;
Baba-Chops (1975), performed at the Wilshire Ebell
Theater in New York City; *The Last Chord* (1976), a
melodrama about an African American church official
who becomes involved with the mafia, first performed at
the Billie Holiday Theater in New York City; *Anabiosis*
(1979), staged by the St. Louis's City Players; *Roan
Brown and Cherry*, produced in 1988; and the one act
play *The Cowmen*. Gordone also wrote poetry and produced a cassette in 1978 that included excerpts from *No
Place To Be Somebody*.

In 1975 Gordone began working with inmates in Cell
Block Theatre in Yardville and Bordentown Youth Correctional Institutions in New Jersey using theater as rehabilitation therapy. One production staged toward the
rehabilitation process was Clifford Odet's *Golden Boy*.
Returning his attention to New York in 1978 Gordone
taught at the New School for Social Research. During
this time his director credits included *Curse* (1978) and
Under the Boardwalk (1979). He also had a lead role in
Ralph Bakshi's controversial 1975 part-animated film
Coonskin, which was re-released in 1987 as *Streetfight*
on video. The video, which has the voices of Barry
White, Gordone (in the lead role), Scatman Crothers, and
Philip Thomas, is gritty and even offensive in its content
for many audiences. The story follows the exploits of a
black rabbit that comes from the rural South to New York
and ends up ruling the streets of Harlem. This animated
fantasy received nominal attention when it was first run.
By 1981 Gordone had moved to California and was writing screenplays in Hollywood for Paramount Pictures.
His credits include *Under the Boardwalk, From These
Ashes, Liliom,* and *The W.A.S.P.* Gordone continued to
support more non-traditional casting for roles. He
strongly believed that actors of different ethnic groups
could be integrated into traditionally white roles and not
lose their unique identity. Casting along this line would
offer to dramatic effect the diversity of American society
and show a cross-cultural perspective and not simply a
multiracial one. While working on *A Streetcar Named
Desire* in 1982 Gordone met Susan Kouyomjian, a stage
and film producer, who was his companion for the last
thirteen years of his life. Together they co-founded American Stage in Berkeley where Gordone directed numerous productions.

Gordone was awarded the D. H. Lawrence Fellowship
in Taos, New Mexico in 1985 and two years later became
lecturer in the theater department at Texas A&M University in College Station, Texas. This same year he had his
final movie credit in a supporting role in *Angel Heart*.
After five years and a less than tranquil experience in the
theater department, Gordone moved into teaching playwriting and literature surveys. He spent nine years at

Texas A&M. He also devoted time to traveling around
the country, directing and producing plays in community
theaters. Gordone immersed himself in Native American
culture and poetry which sparked and inspired his creativity.

Although an active participant in the performing arts
and a champion for African American participation, Gordone questioned the separation of theater into racial and
social categories. In his own casting he placed Hispanic
performers as migrant laborers in *Of Mice and Men* and
a Creole actor as Stanley in *A Streetcar Named Desire*.
He advocated for the American theater and had no allegiance to the concept of the black theater. By embracing
the universal at a time when silenced voices were struggling for recognition in many cultures Gordone felt as
though he lacked a true place of his own. In an interview
captured by *Touchstone*, cowboy poet Buck Ramsey said
it best: Gordone had "no place to be." Gordone's diverse
and eclectic approach were reflected in his work as well
as his attire. He was known for his flamboyant appearance that might feature wild hats and rainbow love beads.
Gordone died November 13, 1995 from liver cancer.

After his death his work received high regard from his
peers. He was memorialized in various places, such as
the New York Shakespeare Festival Public Theater, the
Canadian River Breaks of the Texas Panhandle, and the
Gene Autry Ranch. His uniqueness and dedication was
also celebrated by an annual Gordone Award in fiction,
poetry, and playwriting at Texas A&M University. In
song, he has been memorialized by his daughter Leah-
Carla Gordone on her CD *Butterfly Child* (1998). Gordone had four children: two daughters, Judy and
Leah-Carla, and two sons, Stephen and David.

REFERENCES

Books

Collier, Richard L. "Charles Gordone." In *The Scribner
    Encyclopedia of American Lives*. Eds. Kenneth T.
    Jackson, Karen Markoe, and Arnold Markoe. New
    York: Scribner, 2001.

Elam, Harry J., Jr. "The Black Performer and the
    Performance of Blackness: *The Escape; or, A Leap to
    Freedom* by William Wells Brown and *No Place To
    Be Somebody* by Charles Gordone." In *African
    American Performance and Theater History*. Eds.
    Harry J. Elam, Jr. and David Krasner: Oxford:
    Oxford University Press, 2001.

Lenord, Charles. "Charles Gordone." In *African
    American Writers: A Dictionary*. Eds. Michael R.
    Strickland and Shari Dorantes Hatch. Santa Barbara:
    ABC-CLIO, 2000.

Leonard, Charles. "Charles Gordone." In *The Oxford
    Companion to African American Literature*. Eds.
    William L. Andrews, Francis Smith Foster, and

Trudier Harris. New York: Oxford University Press, 1997.

Page, Yolanda W. "Charles Gordone" In *African American Dramatists*. Ed. Emmanuel S. Nelson.Westport, Conn.: Greenwood Press, 2004.

Peterson, Bernard L. Jr., ed. "Charles Gordone." In *Contemporary Black American Playwrights and Their Plays: A Biographical Directory and Dramatic Index*. Westport, Conn.: Greenwood Press, 1988.

Smith, Susan Harris. "Charles Gordone." In *Speaking on Stage: Interviews with ContemporaryAmerican Playwrights*. Eds. Philip C. Kolin and Colby Kullman. Tuscaloosa: University of Alabama Press, 1996.

Periodicals

Barnes, Clive. Review of *No Place To Be Somebody*, by Charles Gordone. *New York Times*, 5 May 1999.

Kerr, Walter. "Not Since Edward Albee." *New York Times*, 18 May 1969.

Pogrebin, Robin. "Charles Gordone Is Dead at 70; Won a Pulitzer for His First Play." *New York Times*, 19 November 1995.

Online

Costa, Richard H. "The Short Happy Afterlife of Charles Gordone." *The Touchstone*, February-March 1996. http://www.rtis.com/reg/bcs/pol/touchstone/February96/costa.htm (Accessed 18 January 2006).

Lean'tin L. Bracks

Chronology	
1897	Born in Jacksonville, Florida on August 10
1917	Graduates from Cambridge High and Latin Preparatory School; enters Harvard University
1920	Becomes the National AAU's junior 100-yard champion
1921	Establishes a new world record on July 23 with his broad jump of 25 feet 3 inches; wins the National AAU Pentathlon Championship; sets a new collegiate long jump record with 24 feet 6 inches
1922	Wins the National AAU Pentathlon Championship
1923	Marries Amalia Ponce of Cambridge, Massachusetts on May 10
1924	Wins a silver medal in the long jump (the first African American to win this medal) in Paris, France, at the VIII Olympiad; graduates with the LL.B. from Harvard
1925	Joins the Student Training Corps and enlists in the National Guard; admitted to the Massachusetts bar
1929	Becomes a member of the federal bar
1936	Appointed assistant U.S. attorney by Franklin Delano Roosevelt
1941	Assigned to the 372nd Infantry and becomes the commanding officer
1942	Appointed colonel
1947	Discharged from the army; rejoins the National Guard
1952	Appointed justice of Roxbury District Court
1958	Sworn in as the first African American on the Massachusetts Superior Court
1959	Retires from the National Guard with the rank of brigadier general
1966	Dies in Quincy, Massachusetts on July 22; buried in Cotuit, Cape Cod, Massachusetts
1997	Recognized on May 1, Law Day, with the posthumous unveiling of Gourdin's portrait, painted by Robert Freeman, in Boston's Old Suffolk County Courthouse

Edward O. Gourdin
1897–1966

Athlete, soldier, judge

Edward Orval Gourdin was an exceptional athlete, soldier, and judge. In all of his endeavors he proved to be a barrier breaker. He was the first man in history to long jump 25 feet and the first African American to win a silver medal in the Olympics in the long jump event. In 1921, he set a new collegiate long jump record with his leap of 24 feet 6 inches. In both 1921 and 1922, he won the Amateur Athletic Union (AAU) National Pentathlon Championship. Gourdin was the first African American appointed to the Supreme Court of Massachusetts. He served in World War II as Commanding Officer of the 372nd Infantry and retired from the National Guard with the rank of brigadier general.

Edward Orval Gourdin was born on August 10, 1897, one of nine children born to Walter Holmes Gourdin, a meat cutter, who was part African American and Seminole Indian, and Felicia (Garvin) Gourdin, an African American. There are few details about his life prior to graduation from high school. However, it is evident that he was the child chosen to be the one in the family who would be committed to education. The family would do all they could make it possible for Edward to excel. While the family's finances were meager, their belief in education was rich. They recognized in their son the intellect and the ability to succeed.

Edward Gourdin excelled in academics and in sports at Stanton High School in Jacksonville, Florida, and he was valedictorian of his graduating class. In Cambridge, Massachusetts, at age nineteen, he entered Cambridge High and Latin Preparatory School where he completed one year prior to his entry into college. In the fall of 1917, Gourdin entered Harvard University. In 1923, he married Amalia Ponce of Cambridge, Massachusetts. They subsequently became the parents of four children (Elizabeth, Ann Robinson, Amelia Laindal, and Edward

Orval Jr.). Gourdin graduated from Harvard in 1921 with a B.A. and from Harvard School of Law in 1924 with the LL.B. In 1925, he was admitted to the Massachusetts bar, and in 1929, he was admitted to the federal bar.

Star Athlete

Gourdin entered Harvard in pursuit of a law degree and with the idea of playing baseball. He lettered in both baseball and basketball at Harvard. However, he made his lasting mark in athletics in the long jump. Gourdin ran for Harvard during the school year (September to June) and for clubs in the summer which had been formed by middle-class African Americans. Gourdin ran for the racially integrated Dorchester Athletic Club of Boston, Massachusetts. The year 1921 was a stellar period for Gourdin. At the Harvard-Yale meet, he won the long jump at 24 feet and 14 inches; the 100-yard dash in 10.4 seconds; and finished second in the 200-yard dash. Against Princeton, he won the long jump, the 100-yard dash, and the 200-yard dash. His long jump of 24 feet and 6 inches set a new collegiate record. In a Harvard-Yale and Oxford-Cambridge track meet, he established a new world record by jumping 25 feet and 3 inches. He became the National AAU champion in the pentathlon in both 1921 and 1922 by achieving the combined requisite points in the long jump, 100-meter dash, discus, and 1500 meters. In 1924, after completing the law school exams at Harvard and missing the graduation activities, he went to Paris, France, to participate in the games of the VIII Olympiad men's athletic event. He came in second in the long jump event with 23 feet and 10 inches and became the first African American to win a silver medal in this event. Ironically, the day following the event, he jumped 25 feet and 8 inches which exceeded the jump of the gold medalist by 1 foot and 3 inches; but it took place as a part of an exhibition event and did not count.

As a sophomore at Harvard, Edward Gourdin joined the Student Training Corps and in 1925 enlisted in the National Guard. In 1941, he entered World War II where he was assigned to the 372nd Infantry Regiment, a segregated unit, and served as its commanding officer both in the United States and abroad. He rose to the rank of colonel, serving until 1947. Gourdin excelled within the limits of the segregated army as he had in athletics. After the army, he resumed his law practice. Upon his discharge, he rejoined the National Guard and served in it until 1959. He retired having earned the rank of brigadier general, the first African American to earn this rank in the state of Massachusetts.

Life in the Legal Arena

While pursuing his law degree at Harvard University, Gourdin worked as a postal clerk. Following graduation, even after attaining his law degree in 1924, he retained his postal clerk job. It was difficult to find a position with a law firm. Like many African Americans, he found that the post office was a viable source of revenue. Despite his talent, degree, and his admission to the Massachusetts bar in 1925, he found it necessary to retain the job of postal clerk until 1927.

While working as a postal clerk, he strove to establish a private practice. In 1929, he was admitted to the federal bar and began to work in politics. He began as a Republican, but in the 1930s, he switched to the Democratic Party. This activity led to his association with many prominent and influential individuals in Boston. One of these was Francis J. W. Ford, who had been named U. S. attorney for Massachusetts. He encouraged Franklin Delano Roosevelt to appoint Gourdin assistant U. S. attorney, and he was named to this post in 1936. He held this position, excluding the years he was in the National Guard, until 1951.

Following his years in the National Guard and his return to the assistant attorney's position, he was promoted to chief of the Civil Division. In 1951, he was appointed justice of Roxbury District Court. In 1958, Gourdin became the first African American to be seated on the Massachusetts Superior Court. Thurgood Marshall, a future Supreme Court justice, was present when Gourdin was sworn into the court. Gourdin retained his judgeship until his death in 1966.

As a result of the efforts of his son Edward Jr., Gourdin was honored on Law Day, May 1, 1997, in the Old Suffolk County courthouse in Boston; at this time, jurists and legislators, African Americans and whites, came together to honor his achievements as athlete, soldier, and judge, and his portrait was unveiled.

During his life time, Gourdin worked with and supported the NAACP, the Roxbury Youth Program, and the New England Olympians. His papers, photographs, scrapbooks, and records are housed in the Department of Special Collections in Mugar Memorial Library at Boston University.

REFERENCES

Books

Ashe, Arthur R. Jr. *A Hard Road to Glory—Track & Field: The African American Athlete in Track & Field*. New York: Amistad, 1993.

Online

Abeel, Daphne. "Edward Orval Gourdin—Brief Life of a Breaker of Barriers: 1897-1966." http://128.103.142.209/issues/nd97/vita.html (Accessed 11 March 2006).

Dean, Amy. "Edward Gourdin: Olympic silver medalist, but a man of firsts." *B. U. Bridge*, Vol. V, No. 23, 15 February 2002. http://www.bu.edu/bridge/archive/2002/02-15/connect.htm (Accessed 11 March 2006).

Frenette, Gene. "Athletes of the Century: Discover Jacksonville's hidden treasure." http://www. jacksonville.com/special/athletes_of_century/stories/ gourdin.shtml (Accessed 11 March 2006).

Helen R. Houston

Meredith C. Gourdine

Meredith C. Gourdine
1929–1998

Physicist, engineer

Before Meredith "Flash" Gourdine became a world-renown engineer and physicist, he was a silver medalist in the 1952 Olympic Games. Ultimately better known for his work in thermal management technology than for his 24-foot long jump, he specialized in research relating to electrogasdynamics, which is a method used to disperse fog and smoke. Other applications of electro-gasdynamics include refrigeration, desalination of seawater, and pollutant reduction in smoke. The companies he founded worked on purifying the air and converting low-grade coal into inexpensive, transportable, and high-voltage electrical energy. They produced a commercial air-pollution deterrent, a high-powered industrial paint spray, and a device to eliminate fog above airports. He died in 1998 with seventy patents to his name.

Gourdine was born in Newark, New Jersey, on September 26, 1929. He was raised in Brooklyn, New York, where his father was a painter and a janitor. After school at Brooklyn Tech High School, he worked eight hours a day on painting jobs with his father. Gourdine once told the *New York Times*, "My father said, 'If you don't want to be a laborer all your life, stay in school.' It took." He earned a bachelor's degree in engineering from Cornell University in Ithaca, New York. In 1960, on a Guggenheim fellowship, he earned a doctorate in engineering science from the California Institute of Technology.

Gourdine was a swimmer in high school and did not start running until his senior year, when he joined the track team. He never won a race there, but he did earn a swimming scholarship offer from the University of Michigan. Instead, he went to Cornell and paid his way most of the first two years. His sports career flourished at Cornell, where at 6 feet and 175 pounds he earned the nickname "Flash." He competed in the sprints, low hurdles, and the long jump. He earned four titles in the championships of the Intercollegiate Association of Amateur Athletes of America and five titles in the Heptagonal Games. In 1952, he was on the five-member Cornell team that finished second to Southern California,

which had thirty-six athletes, in the National Collegiate Athletic Association championships.

After his successful track career at Cornell, Gourdine experienced his greatest achievement and greatest frustration in the 1952 Olympics in Helsinki, Finland. He finished second in the long jump, an inch and a half behind American team member Jerome Biffle. Biffle won the gold medal in the long jump at 24 feet 10 inches. "I would have rather lost by a foot," he said as he recalled the event years later, according to the *New York Times*. "I still have nightmares about it." After graduation from Cornell and the Olympics, Gourdine became an officer in the United States Navy.

Founds Own Research Lab

When he was out of the Navy, Gourdine went into research in the private sector. He got a job on the technical staff of the Ramo-Woolridge Corporation in 1957. In 1958, he became a senior research scientist at the Caltech Jet Propulsion Laboratory. He was a lab director of the Plasmodyne Corporation from 1960 to 1962 and was chief scientist of the Curtiss-Wright Corporation from 1962 to 1964. In 1964, he served on the president's panel on energy. After years working in other people's labs, Gourdine scraped together $200,000 from friends and opened his own research and development laboratory,

Chronology

1929	Born in Newark, New Jersey on September 26
1952	Wins silver medal at Olympics in Helsinki, Finland; joins Navy
1957	Takes job on the technical staff of the Ramo-Woolridge Corporation
1958	Becomes a senior research scientist at the Caltech Jet Propulsion Laboratory
1960	Receives Guggenheim fellowship; takes job as lab director of the Plasmodyne Corporation
1962	Serves as chief scientist of the Curtiss-Wright Corporation
1964	Serves on the president's panel on energy
1965	Founds Gourdine Systems, in Livingston, New Jersey
1971	Earns first of seventy career patents
1973	Founds Energy Innovations in Houston, Texas
1987	Patents method of removing fog from airport runways
1998	Dies in Houston on November 20

Gourdine Systems, in Livingston, New Jersey. The company grew to employ 150 people.

In 1973, Gourdine founded Energy Innovations in Houston to produce direct-energy conversion devices. He built Energy Innovations into a multi-million dollar company and was the chief executive there until his death. Later in his career, he focused his efforts on heating and cooling systems based on the conversion and transfer of thermal energy. His work in this field is represented by his collection of patents from 1989 to 1996.

Makes Name in Electrogasdynamics

Gourdine was one of the first, and one of the most respected, scientists in electrogasdynamics (EGD), which is the generation of energy from the motion of gas molecules which have been ionized, or electrically charged, under high pressure. Gourdine had a great talent for inventing practical applications for this complex procedure. He is best known for his invention of various electrostatic precipitator systems, for which he earned his first patents in 1971 to 1973.

Gourdine's patents include an application called Incineraid, which helps remove smoke from burning buildings. He patented a method of removing fog from airport runways in 1987. These systems clear the air by introducing a negative charge to airborne particles: once negatively charged, the particles are electromagnetically attracted to the ground, and so drop down, to have their former place taken by clearer air. Gourdine also won patents for applications of EGD to circuit breakers, acoustic imaging, air monitors and coating systems, as well as the Focus Flow Heat Sink, which is used to cool computer chips.

As Gourdine aged, he suffered multiple strokes and complications from diabetes. He gradually went com-

pletely blind. He died in Houston, Texas on November 20, 1998 at age 69. He was serving as the president of Energy Innovation, Inc. of Houston, Texas at the time of his death. He was survived by his wife, Carolina Baling Gourdine, a son, three daughters from a previous marriage, and five grandchildren.

REFERENCES

Periodicals

Litsky, Frank. "Meredith Gourdine, 69, Athlete and Physicist." *New York Times*, 24 November 1998.

"Meredith Charles Gourdine." *Los Angeles Times*, 16 July 1986.

Online

"Meredith C. Gourdine." Mathematics Department, University of Buffalo. http://www.math.buffalo.edu/mad/physics/gourdine_meredithc.html (Accessed 23 March 2005).

"Meredith C. Gourdine." Princeton University. http://www.princeton.edu/˜mcbrown/display/gourdine.html (Accessed 23 March 2005).

"Meredith Gourdine." About.com. http://inventors.about.com/library/inventors/blgourdine.htm (Accessed 23 March 2005).

"Meredith Gourdine." Massachusetts Institute of Technology. http://web.mit.edu/invent/iow/gourdine.html (Accessed 23 March 2005).

"Meredith Gourdine, Ph.D., 48." Brooklyn Technical High School Alumni Association. http://www.bthsalum.org/hall_inductees%2098.htm (Accessed 23 March 2005).

Brenna Sanchez

John Patterson Green
1845–1940

Politician

At a time when blacks in the North were unable to provide a population base to support an African American political candidate or to provide a voting block to draw attention to their community's issues, John Patterson Green became the first African American elected to the Ohio Senate. His success was preceded by his appointment to other governmental positions such as justice of the peace and state representative and followed by appointments as U.S. postage stamp agent and acting superintendent of finance for the Post Office Department.

Chronology

1845	Born in Newbern, North Carolina on April 2
1857	Moves to Cleveland after the death of his father
1866	Publishes book *Miscellaneous Subjects by a Self-Educated Colored Youth*
1869	Graduates from Central High School in Cleveland; marries Annie Walker
1870	Graduates Union Law School in Cleveland; moves to North Carolina
1872	Elected as justice of the peace; elected as delegate to the state Republican Convention
1881	Elected to the Ohio House of Representatives
1890	Re-elected to the Ohio House of Representatives
1892	Elected to the Ohio Senate
1893	Sponsors Labor Day legislation for the state
1897	Appointed U.S. postage stamp agent
1905	Named acting superintendent of finance for the Post Office Department
1912	Marries Lottie Mitchell Richardson
1920	Publishes autobiography
1940	Dies in Cleveland, Ohio on August 30

As a successful lawyer and loyal Republican, Green was able to enter the Ohio political system. Tempered by cautiousness and conservatism, he never criticized Republican leaders on civil rights issues or the increasing tide of racism in the post-Reconstruction Era. In some ways, Green's role in Ohio politics may show a racial liberalism by white voters, but his approach toward accommodation, as defined by Booker T. Washington, let many whites escape being accountable for equal rights among and protection of all citizens.

John Patterson Green was born April 2, 1845 in Newbern, North Carolina, to John R. and Temperance Green, free blacks with mixed ancestry. Green's fraternal grandfather was John Stanley, a Yankee privateer during the Revolutionary War, and his grandmother was Sarah Rice, an African and servant to North Carolina representative Jesse Speight. Green's father was a tailor and his mother was a seamstress. Many free blacks learned a trade through an apprenticeship at an early age, to assure their ability to take care of themselves and their families. When Green was five, his father died, which left the care of Green and his two siblings to his mother. Initially, using her skill as a seamstress, she was able to maintain the family in North Carolina, but in 1857 she moved the family to Cleveland, Ohio. First, Green attended a private school for free blacks run by John Stuart Stanley in North Carolina. After arriving in Cleveland, Green was sent to Oberlin, Ohio to learn a trade and live at the home of John Patterson, a bricklayer and plasterer. He subsequently was apprenticed to John Scott, a harness maker. When this did not work out, Green returned to Cleveland.

There he spent a year and a half in the Mayflower School before leaving in 1859 because of family financial difficulties. In order to assist his mother, Green took on various jobs: he caned chairs, did odd jobs, and hired himself out as an errand-boy for $4 a month. In 1862 he found employment at the East Cleveland Street Railway, and he also tried his hand as a tailor and as a waiter.

Green realized the importance of education and continued his studies on his own. He was learned independently about Latin and algebra. To earn money for his education, Green wrote the 1866 pamphlet *Essays on Miscellaneous Subjects by a Self-Educated Colored Youth*. As a result of spending a year doing lecture tours and promoting the essays, Green sold more than 1,500 copies in Ohio, Pennsylvania, New Jersey, Delaware, Maryland, New York, and the District of Columbia. He subsequently enrolled in Cleveland Central High School and completed a four-year classical program in two years, two terms and two months. He graduated from Cleveland Central High School in 1869 at the head of his class of twenty-three students, married Annie Walker, and enrolled in Cleveland's Union Law School. Green graduated in 1870, receiving his LL.B and he and his wife started a new life in North Carolina.

Green was only in North Carolina for a short time, however. He worked as a clerk in a local grocery store and then moved to South Carolina to run his own grocery business. In South Carolina in 1870 Green was admitted to the bar and began a lifelong relationship with the Republican Party. This relationship made it possible for him to be elected in 1872 as a delegate to the State Republican Convention in South Carolina and as an alternate delegate to the Republican National Convention in Philadelphia. In the fall of 1872 Green decided to return to Cleveland because of health reasons. He became a practicing attorney and began a lecture tour. In the spring of 1873 he was elected as justice of the peace in Cuyahoga County. This position, which had both judicial and police power, made Green one of the first elected African Americans in the North. Green served three terms and in those eight years decided more than 12,000 cases. He was very popular with both black and white voters and was nominated in 1877 to the Ohio House of Representatives. Initially he was elected by a sixty-two vote margin but after a recount his Democratic opponent was elected. Green unsuccessfully claimed that the recount was fraudulent and that he had won the election.

In 1881 Green was elected to the Ohio House of Representatives. He served during the 65th session (1882-13) and was on the library and corporation committees. While in the House, Green presented a resolution condemning the contract-labor system in the Ohio penitentiary system. When it came time for reelection in 1884, Green was defeated, but he was called to serve as an alternate delegate-at-large for the Republican National Convention in Chicago. While attending the convention he shared the platform at one point with Frederick Douglass. Green continued practicing law and as a loyal Republican gave speeches and spoke on behalf of party candidates. In 1890 Green again secured a nomination for the Ohio House of Representatives and was elected by a wide margin. He served during the 69th session (1890-91). During this term he was on the turnpike committee and supported legislation on behalf of civil rights and veterans benefits.

Green developed relationships with influential Republican leaders and prominent persons of the day, including John D. Rockefeller; Marcus Hanna, a national Republican leader; and George A. Myers, a barber and confident of Hanna as well as the most influential African American in Ohio Republican politics. Bolstered by his powerful connections and the racial liberalism of white Clevelanders, Green became the first African American to be nominated for a seat in the Ohio Senate. He was elected from a majority white district and became the only African American from the North to be elected to a state senate before World War I. While he served in the 70th session (1892-93) of the Ohio Senate General Assembly, Green contributed to the sponsorship of legislation which established Labor Day as a holiday in Ohio in 1893. When the Ohio legislation was used as a model for Congress in making Labor Day a national holiday, Green became known as the Father of Labor Day. He also secured funding for an Industrial Department at Wilberforce University.

When Green's term in the state senate ended, he continued his law practice and traveled extensively in Europe. He spoke throughout Ohio for Republican Party candidates and wrote articles for the Afro-American News Syndicate which supplied over two hundred papers. He again served as the delegate-at-large for the Republican Party at the 1896 National Convention and was among those considered for the appointment as the recorder of deeds. In 1897 he was chosen to be U.S. postage stamp agent in the District of Columbia. Green retained this position, which entailed the supervision of the printing and distributing of postage stamps for the nation, until 1905. His final governmental position was in 1905 as the acting superintendent of finance for the Post Office Department. After a year in this position he again returned to his Cleveland law practice.

A Loyal Republican

In the decades following the Civil War, there were African American groups in the community designed to perpetuate a particular social status. Such community affiliations reflected members' philosophy. Green was an influential member of one of the community's elite groups, the Social Circle. Membership in this organization, which dated back to 1869, consisted of light-skinned, old-Negro elite, who for many years refused to associate with darker-skinned, less-educated people. The old elite, of which Green was a key member, sought to emulate the lifestyle of the affluent white middle class. Green was also a member and co-founder of St. Andrews Episcopal Church, one of Cleveland's wealthiest African American congregations. From this prominent position in the community and in the Republican Party, Green could have been an important voice toward equality for African Americans. Instead, Green stood for accommodation and extreme caution. His philosophy rejected militant protest, which he considered unnecessary.

Kenneth Kusmer in *A Ghetto Takes Shape: Black Cleveland, 1879-1930* (1976) assesses Green's political career. Kusmer describes Green as a person who did not disturb the status quo, a man who was loyal to the Republican Party leadership. To an audience in 1890, Green declared that Negroes were ostracized not because of the color of their skin but because they were poor. He saw success for the Negro through acquiring wealth, which in turn would bring power and status. As a lawyer Green defended those who were victimized by racism, but he did not challenge it in his political career. Green had a wide network of political and social contacts with important whites, which reflected local white liberalism. But his success was also connected to his benign and often silent response to growing problems of racial inequality.

In 1912 after the death of his first wife, Green married Lottie Mitchell Richardson who became the mother of his six children. In his later years Green continued to practice law and speak in support of the Republican Party and its candidates. When African Americans switched to the Democratic Party in 1936 to have more of their issues addressed, Green remained steadfast with the Republican Party. At the time of his death on August 30, 1940, when he was struck by an automobile, Green was the oldest practicing lawyer in Ohio.

REFERENCES

Books

Kusmer, Kenneth L. "Green, John Patterson." In *American National Biography.* Vol. 9. Eds. John A. Garraty and Mark C. Carnes. New York: Oxford University Press, 1999.

———. *A Ghetto Takes Shape: Black Cleveland, 1879-1930.* Chicago: University of Illinois Press, 1976.

Levstik, Frank R. "John Patterson Green." In *Dictionary of American Negro Biography.* Eds. Rayford W. Logan and Michael R. Winston. New York: Norton, 1982.

Nichols, J. L., and William H. Crogman. *Progress of a Race.* Naperville, Ill.: J. L. Nichols & Company, 1929.

Williams, George W. *History of the Negro Race in America from 1619-1880.* New York: G. P. Putnam's Sons, 1883.

Online

"Documenting the American South." *Fact Stranger than Fiction. Seventy-Five Years of a Busy Life and Reminiscences of Many Great and Good Men and Women.* http://docsouth.unc.edu/southlit/greenfact/green.html (Accessed 4 February 2006).

Collections

Green's papers are located in the Western Reserve Historical Society. His correspondence with George A. Meyers, a prominent black Clevelander, are in Meyers's papers, which are housed in the Ohio Historical Society in Columbus, Ohio. His upbringing, family life, and political career are discussed in his book *Recollections of the Carolinas*, 1881.

Lean'tin L. Bracks

Frederick D. Gregory

Frederick D. Gregory
1941–

Astronaut

The National Aeronautics and Space Administration (NASA) has had its share of influential African Americans involved in its program, but only a few have risen to high ranking administrative positions. Colonel Frederick D. Gregory is one of those few.

Gregory was born in Washington D.C. on January 7, 1941, at the Freedmen's Hospital. His parents are Francis A. Gregory and Nora Drew Gregory. Gregory was born into a family of distinction and accomplishment. His great-grandfather was enrolled at prestigious Howard University and became a member of the university's first graduating class. Added to that legacy, Dr. Charles Drew is Gregory's uncle on his mother's side. Charles Drew is known throughout the world as an innovative surgeon who assisted in the development and introduction of blood banks for use during World War II.

The accomplishments and fame of the Gregory family allowed Frederick to have a relatively privileged childhood, much like many American boys at that time. He was a member of the Boy Scouts and his family enjoyed summer vacations at their cabin located on Lake Erie. Gregory was not immune, however, to segregation and the Jim Crow laws of the day. The Boy Scouts were segregated, so he attended a scout camp for African American boys. The family vacations provided a way to involve the Gregorys in activities outside the city where there were little to no activities for African American families.

During the late 1950s the racial barriers slowly began to unravel. Gregory was in a good position to take advantage of opportunities that were once denied to African Americans. He attended integrated Anacostia High School, graduating in 1958. That same year, he entered the Air Force Academy. Gregory studied military engineering there and received a B.S. in 1964. After his graduation, he was admitted for pilot training at Stead Air Force Base in Nevada. While he attended Stead, Gregory also attended undergraduate helicopter training. His hard work and determination earned him his wings in 1965. His first assignment from October 1965 to May 1966 was to serve as an H-43 helicopter rescue pilot at Vance Air Force Base in Oklahoma.

Gregory's military expertise was called upon in June 1966, when he was assigned to be an H-43 combat rescue pilot at Danang Air Base in Vietnam. This assignment involved flying search and rescue missions over the demilitarized zone in Vietnam. He returned to the United States in 1967, where he did more training as a fixed-wing pilot, traveling to Air Force bases in Texas and Arizona. He attended the United States Naval Test Pilot School in Maryland from September 1970 to June 1971. After he finished this training he traveled to Wright Patterson Air Force Base in Ohio, where he served as an operational test pilot.

Chronology

1941	Born in Washington, D.C. on January 7
1958	Graduates from Anacostia High School in Washington D.C.; enters Air Force Academy
1964	Graduates from Air Force Academy with a B.S. in military engineering
1965	Receives his wings
1966	Works as an H-43 combat rescue pilot in Vietnam
1970	Attends Naval Test Pilot School in Maryland
1974	Becomes detailed to the NASA Langley Research Center in Virginia
1977	Earns a master's degree in information systems from George Washington University
1978	Selected for the Astronaut Program
1985	Becomes the first African American to pilot a spacecraft
1989	Becomes the first African American to command a space mission
2002	Accepts position as deputy administrator of NASA
2003	Receives Presidential Award for Distinguished Executives
2005	Resigns as deputy administrator

Changes Direction and Makes History

Gregory's next stop was the NASA Langley Research Center in Hampton, Virginia in June 1974. He pursued a master's degree in information systems from George Washington University in 1977. His service at the Langley Research Center involved being a research test pilot until he ultimately was selected for the Astronaut Program in January 1978. Gregory went on to fly three shuttle missions after his training and actually made history with two of these missions. On April 29, 1985 he became the first African American to pilot a spacecraft. In 1989 Gregory made history again when he became the first African American to command a space mission.

Gregory continued his service with NASA, serving as associate administrator for space flights and associate administrator for the Office of Safety and Mission Assurance. He retired as a colonel in the U.S. Air Force in December 1993. In 2002, Gregory was nominated by President Bush to serves as deputy administrator of NASA. With the backing of the Senate, he accepted this nomination and served as the agency's chief operating officer. His responsibilities included management and direction of many of NASA's programs and daily operations and activities.

Gregory's military honors are many, including two Distinguished Flying Crosses, sixteen air medals, three space flight medals, two Outstanding Leadership Medals, plus the Legion of Merit, Distinguished Service Medal, Defense Superior Service Medal, and Air Force Commendation Medal.

In 2003, Gregory received the Presidential Award for Distinguished Executives. He has received numerous awards such as the National Intelligence Medal, the U.S. Air Force Academy Distinguished Graduate Award, the National Society of Black Engineers Distinguished National Scientist Award, the President's Award, the George Washington University Distinguished Alumni Award, and honorary doctorates from the College of Aeronautics, the University of the District of Columbia, and Southwestern University.

Gregory and his wife Barbara are the parents of two children and four grandchildren. Their son, Frederick Jr,. is a captain in the U.S. Air Force and graduate of Stanford University. Heather Lynn, their daughter, is a social worker and graduate of Sweet Briar College.

In 2004 and 2005, Gregory was designated as one of the 50 Most Important Blacks in Technology. In 2005, Gregory announced his retirement from his position as deputy administrator, ending a career that demonstrated excellence and great achievement.

REFERENCES

Online

Gugliotta, Guy. "Backed by History, Looking Ahead." *Washington Post*, March 2005. http:www.washington post.com/wp-dyn/articles/A18422-2005Mar8.html (Accessed 23 January 2006).

NASA. "Colonel Frederick D. Gregory (USAF, Ret.) Biography." http://space.about.com/od/former astronauts/a/gregoryfbio.htm (Accessed 21 January 2006).

Connie Mack

Greg Gumbel
1946–

Television sportscaster, radio broadcaster

Known for his seemingly effortless delivery style and standout work as a television sportscaster, three-time Emmy Award winner Greg Gumbel was born on May 3, 1946 in New Orleans, Louisiana to Rhea Alice LeCesne Gumbel, a housewife, and Richard Dunbar Gumbel, a county probate judge for the Cook County Court in Illinois. The family—which included Greg, a younger brother, Bryant, and two younger sisters, Rhonda and Renee—moved to a middle-class neighborhood in Chicago's Hyde Park when the children were very young.

Greg Gumbel

Chronology	
1946	Born in New Orleans on May 3
1967	Graduates from Loras College
1968-73	Works as sales representative for American Hospital Supply Company
1973-81	Begins broadcasting career as weekend sports anchor for WMAQ-TV in Chicago
1981-89	Becomes co-anchor of ESPN's *SportsCenter*
1986	Leaves ESPN; joins Madison Square Garden Network
1987-88	Hosts morning programs on WFAN Radio in New York
1989-94	Joins CBS as play-by-play announcer
1990-93	Co-anchors *NFL Today* on CBS television
1992	Covers the Winter Olympics in Albertville, France; hosts Super Bowl XXVI (Minneapolis)
1993	Announces the American League Championship Series (play-by-play)
1994	Hosts *NFL on NBC*; prime-time anchor of Winter Olympics in Lillehammer, Norway
1994-98	Works for NBC Sports
1996	Hosts Super Bowl XXX (Tempe, Arizona); hosts Summer Olympics in Atlanta
1998	Hosts Super Bowl XXXII (San Diego)
1998-2003	Returns to CBS; hosts *NFL on CBS*
2001	Becomes first black play-by-play announcer of a major sports championship broadcasting the Super Bowl XXXV (CBS network)
2004	Hosts *NFL Today* (CBS); hosts Super Bowl XXXVIII (Houston)

In Chicago, Greg and Bryant attended major league baseball games at Comiskey Park and Wrigley Field. They were devoted athletes who played football, as well as Little League and Pony League baseball. As a child Greg was chubby, but his body became more muscular in high school as he participated in sports. He enjoyed playing outfield in baseball and softball. Greg would stand in front of a full-length mirror pretending to be a radio announcer calling baseball games with his brother. The brothers would grab gloves, stand in front of the mirror, wind up, pitch, and announce entire imaginary games, taking turns at every half inning. Although the brothers had similar interests, they loved different baseball teams. Greg was a White Sox fanatic and Bryant favored the Cubs, a rivalry that remained into their adulthood.

Gumbel's father taught his children by example and suggestion, stressing the value of education and speaking skills. To broaden his children's horizons, Richard Gumbel organized family outings to the Industry Field Museum of Natural History, Shedd Aquarium, and the Museum of Science and Industry, among other places. Gumbel attended St. Thomas the Apostle Grammar School in Hyde Park. He and his brother served as altar boys at the local Catholic Church.

After graduating from De La Salle High School in 1963, Gumbel enrolled at Loras College, in Dubuque, Iowa, where he played baseball. During his senior year in college, he batted .378, winning honors as the team's most valuable player. While in college, Greg considered becoming a teacher. However, after graduating in 1967 with a B.A. in English, he took a succession of sales and other business-related positions in Chicago. The following year, he moved to Detroit where he worked in hospital supplies sales as a representative for the American Hospital Supply Corporation. In 1972 when Gumbel was twenty-five, while he was still working for the hospital supply company, his father died after having a heart attack outside his court chambers. In an interview with *TV Guide*, Gumbel said his greatest regret was that his father died before he and Bryant had begun careers in television broadcasting. It was a great disappointment for both him and his brother.

Begins Career in Broadcasting

Gumbel began his broadcasting career in 1973 as a weekend sports anchor for WMAQ-TV in Chicago. He landed the job under the urging of Bryant, who was in Los Angeles making a name for himself as a newscaster. It took Gumbel some time to learn the craft; he even admits that as a novice he was so frightened about going on the air that he would perspire profusely, earning him the nickname "Waterfall" from the boys in the booth.

Gumbel was once demoted to sports anchor because he made mistakes due to his inexperience. He finally got over his fright and his on-air performance again earned him the weekend anchor's chair; eventually he was promoted to the station's top weekday sportscaster. His hard work and dedication earned him two Emmy awards while at WMAQ.

By 1981, Gumbel had earned the position of anchor for the Entertainment and Sports Programming Network's (ESPN) *SportsCenter*, a flagship program that aired twice nightly. During that time, ESPN was a new, all-sports cable network with headquarters in Bristol, Connecticut. Gumbel's experience there was helpful, but at times it was hectic. Because the announcers were responsible for the content and there was no floor director or teleprompter to assist them, there was a lot of ad-libbing and improvisation. His numerous responsibilities at ESPN allowed Gumbel to gain overall experience in broadcasting, which in turn led to awards as Outstanding Sports Personality for 1982 and 1983 given by *On Cable Magazine*.

As ESPN's reputation grew, so did Gumbel's. In 1986, Gumbel decided to leave ESPN to work for Madison Square Garden (MSG), a New York City-based sports network. Some thought it odd for Gumbel to leave during a period of growth for him and ESPN. But MSG gave him the opportunity to do play-by-play broadcasting. At MSG, Gumbel began serving as an announcer for some New York Knicks basketball games, and later he called New York Yankees baseball games. During this time, Gumbel also served as the anchor for three weekly programs: *Sports Forum*, *Jets Journal*, and *High School Sportsweek*. The following year, Gumbel began hosting a morning show on WFAN, an all-sports radio station in New York. His four-hour morning segment on WFAN included updates on sports news from the previous evening with post-game comments from athletes at the arena and interviews with news personalities. The show became a hit with sports fans.

Ted Shaker, the executive producer of CBS Sports, became a fan of Gumbel's radio show. He was impressed with how Gumbel would take the listener from one sport to the next. Shaker hired Gumbel in 1988 to do play-by-play announcing for NFL games. Once Gumbel was on board at CBS, his duties expanded to include covering professional and college games for the network. In 1990, Gumbel was given the job of anchoring the network's major league baseball broadcasts, a job that included game analysis, score updates, and occasional interviews. Later that year, Gumbel was surprised to learn that he had been given an even more high-profile assignment, hosting the Emmy Award-winning *The NFL Today*, a pre-game show that aired prior to Sunday football games. As host of *The NFL Today*, he succeeded Brent Musburger, a veteran sportscaster who had been fired by CBS. CBS executives wanted to redesign the program by replacing Musburger's hard news style with Gumbel's laid-back

delivery style. CBS teamed Gumbel with Terry Bradshaw, a former Pittsburgh Steelers quarterback known for his rough-edged, wise-cracking style. Although the pair's on-air relationship didn't quite mesh at the beginning, the chemistry between the two eventually began to work and resulted in Gumbel becoming quite popular.

Anchors Olympics

In the early 1990s, Gumbel added another assignment to his undertakings. He began working as a sports commentator for CBS's *This Morning*, a competitor of NBC's *Today Show*, co-hosted by his brother. In 1992, Greg became co-anchor of CBS's weekday-morning broadcasts of the 1992 Winter Olympics in Albertville, France. Gumbel was not wild about going to Albertville because of the cold weather, but he ended up loving the role and he received praise from many television critics.

Following his coverage of the Olympics, Gumbel resumed covering professional sports, including baseball. In October 1993 he was the play-by-play announcer for the CBS broadcast of the American League Championship series between the Toronto Blue Jays and his favorite team, the Chicago White Sox. This opportunity was a pleasant surprise for Gumbel. It came at a time when he had experienced some disappointments in his four years at CBS, including the network's loss of broadcast rights to televise professional basketball games.

In December 1992, Rick Gentile, the senior vice-president of the production of CBS Sports, announced that Gumbel would anchor another Olympics, the 1994 Winter Olympics in Lillehammer, Norway. This time Gumbel would be serving as the network's sole primetime host of the Olympics. According to Gentile, Gumbel was the perfect fit for the job. Driven by a fear of making a fool of himself, Gumbel spent months preparing by studying reports on Olympic events and athletes. He went to Lillehammer determined to be as unobtrusive an anchor as possible. Gumbel realized that his job as general host required him to simply set up the scenes and tell people what they were going to see.

On February 23, 1994, Gumbel and CBS covered the women's figure skating competition. The public had a keen interest in the event because earlier in the year a person associated with American skater Tonya Harding was charged with attacking fellow American skater, Nancy Kerrigan, with a club. Kerrigan recovered in time to compete in the Olympics, but there was still a flood of publicity about the women that turned the skating competition into a melodrama. CBS realized that broadcasting too much of the incident could be counterproductive and turn viewers off, so Gumbel decided to use the low-key approach and used only one piece of melodrama in his broadcast during the introduction of the women's figure skating competition. Gumbel's approach proved successful. Leonard Shapiro, a sports columnist for the *Washington Post*, commented that Gumbel had finally set himself apart from his brother after his excellent coverage of the 1994 Olympics. Shapiro also referred to Gumbel as a smooth operator with a pleasant interviewing style.

After the Olympics, Gumbel left CBS. He made his NBC debut as host of the pre-game show for the 1994 baseball All-Star game. The next fall, he began working as co-host of the *NFL on NBC*. He was excited to rejoin the Sunday morning airwaves with Ahmad Rashad and analysts Joe Gibbs and Mike Ditka. In the 1995 baseball season, Gumbel served as play-by-play announcer for both regular season and post-season games. Gumbel also served as the pre-game host for NBC's coverage of Super Bowl XXX in 1996. Later that year, Gumbel had the opportunity to cover another Olympics competition, this time in a warmer climate, when NBC appointed him to be the daytime anchor for the 1996 Summer Olympics in Atlanta.

Gumbel resides with his wife, Marcy, a former nurse, whom he met in Detroit while selling hospital supplies. He and Marcy have a daughter, Michelle, whom he adopted from his wife's previous marriage. Gumbel returned to CBS's *NFL Today* in 2004. When he is not announcing for CBS, he speaks at business gatherings, conventions, universities, and other venues. Gumbel is a strong supporter of the March of Dimes, and has been a member of the March of Dimes National board of trustees since 1996.

Few in the business have earned more respect than Gumbel. His low-key broadcasting style cannot be matched, nor can his affable personality. In 2001, Gumbel made history when he became the first network broadcaster to call play-by-play for a Super Bowl when he broadcasted Super Bowl XXXV on the CBS network.

In addition to the hosting roles that he is best known for, Gumbel has covered a variety of sporting events, such as the College World Series and the Daytona 500. When asked about the secret of his success in an interview with the *Daily Record*, he replied that people should not take themselves too seriously and that they should enjoy a good joke. He also mentioned that having a good education was invaluable in his career.

REFERENCES

Books

"Greg Gumbel." *Who's Who Among African Americans*. 18th ed. Detroit: Gale Research, 1996.

Johnson, Anne Janette. "Greg Gumbel." *Contemporary Black Biography: Profiles from the International Black Community*. Ed. L. Mpho Mabunda. Vol. 8. Detroit: Gale Research, 1992.

Periodicals

Friedman, Jack. "Cable sportscaster Greg takes after brother Bryant in the race for most-famous-Gumbel-on-TV." *People Weekly* (5 December 1983): 93.

Martzke, Rudy. "Warm Weather Guy Gumbel Prefers to Come in from the Cold." *USA Today*, 16 January 2004.

——. "Gumbel in Announcing Heaven." *USA Today*, 18 March 2005.

——. "Greg Gumbel Returns to 'NFL Today'." *USA Today*, 20 June 2004.

Meyers, Kate. "The Humble Gumbel." *Entertainment Weekly* (18 February 1994): 1c.

Miller, Jill. "Greg Gumbel Delivers Humorous Keynote at Compeer's Luncheon." *Daily Record* (Rochester, N.Y.), 1 November 2004.

Noden, Merrell. "Nice and Easy Does It On 'The NFL Today': Self-effacing Greg Gumbel Brings a New Style to CBS's Revamped Football Show." *Sports Illustrated* (19 November 1990): 16.

Sherman, Ed. "Gumbel about to Make Broadcasting History as a Black Announcer." *Chicago Tribune*, 25 January 2001.

Online

Harry Walker Agency: America's Leading Lecture Agency. "Greg Gumbel." http://harrywalker.com/speakers_template_printer.cfm?Spea_ID=123 (Accessed 20 November 2005).

Keppler Speakers on Campus. "Greg Gumbel." http://www.keppleroncampus.com/speakers/gumbelgreg/asp (Accessed 28 December 2005).

Sports Stars USA. "Greg Gumbel: CBS Sportscaster." http://www.sportsstarsusa.com/sportscasters/gumbel_greg.html (Accessed 15 December 2005).

Sharon McGee

Thomas Hamilton
1823–1865

Journalist, activist

Thomas Hamilton was a successful and respected black journalist and antislavery activist during the mid-1800s. His publications the *Anglo-African Magazine* and the *Weekly Anglo-African* informed and uplifted black Americans. Periodicals such as these that supported the antislavery movement were crucial to the political and social strategy of blacks. Hamilton's role as editor, publisher, and activist greatly influenced the actions and reaction of blacks during this difficult period.

Thomas Hamilton was born in New York City on April 26, 1823, and was the youngest of two sons born to William Hamilton, a black abolitionist. His mother's name and occupation are not known. The elder Hamilton, who was a carpenter by trade, was well known as an activist both on a local and national level. He was one of the original trustees of the African Methodist Episcopal Zion denomination and attended the four national conventions for blacks held annually between 1831 and 1835. When William Hamilton died in 1836, he was eulogized as an active and effective member of organizations who supported moral and intellectual elevation for his people. Thomas Hamilton received a rudimentary education in African Free Schools and the African Methodist Episcopal Zion Church, but it was the Hamilton household, which was alive with abolitionist ideas and reform press, that made a lasting impression on him. With the death of his father in 1836 Hamilton went to work in 1837 for the *Colored American*, a local African American weekly. Hamilton was a carrier for the paper, which was read in many black communities in the North. He later worked as a bookkeeper and mail clerk for the religious journal the *New York Evangelist*; the official periodical of the American Anti-Slavery Society, the *National Anti-Slavery Standard*; and the leading Congregationalist weekly, the *Independent*.

Chronology	
1823	Born in New York City on April 26
1836	Goes to work for the *Colored American*
1841	Establishes the newspaper *People's Press*
1843	Closes the newspaper *People's Press*
1844	Marries Catherine Anne Leonard of New York; Leonard dies shortly thereafter
1852	Marries Matilda Ann Africanus of Brooklyn
1859	Publishes the *Anglo-African Magazine* and the *Weekly Anglo-African*
1860	Last printing of the *Anglo-African Magazine*
1861	Sells the paper *Weekly Anglo-African* to the Haitian Emigration bureau; re-inaugurates *Weekly Anglo-African* five months later
1865	Dies in Jamaica, Long Island on May 29

Establishes the *People's Press*

In October 1841 Hamilton started his own paper, the *People's Press*. He learned a lot from his early experiences with the black press and sought to support the movement for equal rights. Hamilton's paper was said to replace the *Colored American*, which had been discontinued in the spring of 1841. For two years the paper was edited by Hamilton, and he received support from his brother Robert, as well as from Samuel I. Wood and John Dias. The paper, although reaching a limited black audience, was considered almost militant in its tone. The paper called for independent efforts toward the abolition of slavery, along with the organized efforts of other groups. It also went so far as to question black allegiance to the United States.

When the *People's Press* was closed down in 1843, Hamilton decided to go back to a supporting role in the black press and again worked for the *New York Evangelist* and the *National Anti-Slavery Standard*. He also worked for the *Independent* and supplemented his income by becoming a bookseller. He distributed antislavery, cultural, and temperance literature. He operated out of the Anti-Slavery Society offices in New York. His brother Robert, after leaving the *People's Press*, earned recognition as a spokesman for black issues in the community between the 1840s and 1850s. In 1844 Hamilton married Catherine Anne Leonard, who died not long afterward. In 1852 Hamilton married Matilda Ann Africanus of Brooklyn, and they had a daughter.

In 1859 Hamilton inaugurated the two publications that established his reputation as a journalist. The goal of his publications was to give a black view of what was happening in America because the coverage of white journalists was often racist. In January 1859 Hamilton launched the *Anglo-African Magazine*, which was printed monthly. Hamilton at this time lived in Brooklyn with his family, and his publication office was in New York, at the same address as the National Anti-Slavery Standard, 48 Beekman Street. The magazine was to function like the *Atlantic Monthly*, consisting of printed articles, essays, short stories, and poetry by up-and-coming African Americans along with those who were already well established in their area. Some of the well-known contributors were Frederick Douglass, Sarah Douglass, John Mercer Langston, and Alexander Crummell. Francis Ellen Watkins Harper had her short story "The Two Offers" printed, and Martin R. Delaney's novel *Blake* was serialized in the publication. The magazine gave detailed accounts of John Brown's Raid and the confessions of Nat Turner. The *Anglo African Magazine* lasted for fifteen printings; its last issue appeared in March 1860.

On July 23, 1859, Hamilton launched the *Weekly Anglo-African*. The periodical became one of the most influential journals of its time. The publication's motto was "Man must be Free!—if not through Law, why then above Law." Hamilton organized many unpaid writers from Boston to San Francisco to report on black life and culture. The paper presented issues that confronted the African American community, and Hamilton's editorials further explored the ramifications of these issues, which encompassed topics from slavery and secession to Darwinism. The scope of his journal gave it national appeal. Because of financial problems Hamilton sold the paper in March 1861 to the Haitian Emigration Bureau. This organization advocated and resettled American blacks to Haiti. The paper was subsequently renamed the *Pine and Palm*.

With the coming of the Civil War and concern about activities in Haiti, Hamilton and his brother Robert, only five months after selling their paper, began a second run of the *Weekly Anglo-American*. For the next four years, Hamilton worked behind the scenes, and his brother Robert took the role of editor. There was optimism about the possibilities of equality for blacks. The war was a frequent topic of the paper's editorials, but overall, the paper had a pro-Union slant. When blacks became eligible to enlist in 1863, Hamilton made sure the paper encouraged enlistment. To help bolster black pride and show blacks as positive and capable, Hamilton became a book publisher and seller. He published *A Pilgrimage to My Motherland: An Account of a Journey Among the Egbas and Yorubas of Central Africa, in 1859-60* by Robert Campbell; *The Black Man: His Antecedents, His Genius, and His Achievements* (1861); and a collection of biographical sketches (1863) by William Wells Brown.

Hamilton died in 1865 from typhoid fever at his residence in Jamaica, Long Island. Although a quiet and modest man, Hamilton was well known and respected. According to Penelope L. Bullock in *The Afro-American Periodical Press, 1838-1909*, his friends in New York spoke of him as "one of those untiring heroes, who, however quietly they labor, lift the people as they lift themselves."

REFERENCES

Books

Bullock, Penelope L. *The Afro-American Periodical Press, 1838-1909*. Baton Rouge: Louisiana State University Press, 1981.

Finkenbine, Roy E. "Hamilton, Thomas." In *American National Biography*. Vol 9. Eds. John A. Garraty and Mark C. Carnes. New York: Oxford University Press, 1999.

Ripley, C. Peter, ed. *The Black Abolitionist Papers*. Vol. 5. Chapel Hill, N.C.: University of North Carolina Press, 1992.

Lean'tin L. Bracks

Bernard A. Harris
1956–

Astronaut, scientist

The first African American astronaut to walk in space, Bernard A. Harris, born on June 26, 1956 in Temple, Texas to Gussie and Bernard A. Harris Sr., was the first of three children. Bernard's parents divorced when he was very young. His mother moved with her children to San Antonio, a large city plagued with drugs and violence. When Harris was about seven, his mother found work with the Bureau of Indian Affairs. The family moved again, first to Arizona and then to New Mexico, into the heart of the Navajo Indian Reservation. The Harrises were one of two black families on the reservation. At first the diverse groups of children (black, Native American, white, and Mexican) exchanged insults, but after a few weeks of becoming accustomed to each other, they became friends. When the children got older, they enjoyed going on hiking excursions in the mountains, which helped fuel Harris's desire for explo-

Bernard A. Harris

Chronology

1956	Born in Temple, Texas on June 26
1974	Graduates from Sam Houston High School in San Antonio, Texas
1978	Earns B.S. in biology from University of Houston
1982	Earns M.D. from Texas Tech University
1985	Completes residency in internal medicine at Mayo Clinic
1988	Trains as flight surgeon at the Aerospace School of Medicine, Brooks Air Force Base, San Antonio, Texas
1991	Becomes a NASA astronaut; assigned as mission specialist for STS-55; marries
1995	Serves as payload manager aboard STS-63, February 2 to 11
1996	Leaves NASA and becomes chief scientist and vice-president of Science and Health Services

ration. Childhood experiences living among different ethnic groups taught Harris to respect the diverse cultures in the United States.

Harris moved back to Texas to attend Sam Houston High School in San Antonio. There his fascination for space grew. He was captivated by NASA's space flights, especially the 1969 flight in which Neil Armstrong walked on the moon. Harris drew rocket ships in his notebooks and became an early "Trekkie," a nickname for ardent fans of television's science-fiction program, *Star Trek*. Although Harris was enamored with space, he was unsure of the career path he would take when he graduated from high school in 1974. Harris then attended the University of Houston where he received a B.S. in biology in 1978. Interested in medicine, he entered the Texas Tech University School of Medicine. As his summer job, Harris played the saxophone in a group called Purple Haze (named from the Jimi Hendrix song). He also played in the band at football games during the school year. In 1982, he earned his M.D., and by 1985, he had completed a three-year residency in internal medicine at Mayo Clinic in Rochester, Minnesota.

At the Mayo Clinic, Joseph Combs, a rheumatologist, spoke about the obstacles of sending the first man into space, which rekindled Harris's interest in space. It was then that he realized that the combination of space and medicine suited him. Harris went to the NASA Ames

Research Center in Moffett Field, California, where he completed a National Research Council Fellowship. At Ames, he conducted research in the field of musculoskeletal physiology and disuse osteoporosis. He completed his fellowship in 1987 and joined the NASA Johnson Space Center as a clinical scientist and flight surgeon with the Medical Science Division. His duties as the project manager of the Exercise Countermeasures Project included conducting clinical investigations of space adaptation and developing countermeasures for extended duration space flight. The studies included examining ways to offset the deconditioning of body tissues that occurs in space and may result in muscular atrophy, smaller heart, and bone absorption. The same year, he applied for the astronaut-training program, but he was not selected.

Receives Astronaut Status

Harris reapplied for the astronaut-training program. In September 1989, Harris was selected as one of 106 astronaut candidates selected from a pool of 2,500 applicants. The year-long training program included intellectual exercises as well as rigorous physical activities. His official astronaut status was conferred in July 1991, making him eligible to be assigned as a mission specialist on future space shuttle crews. While he waited to join a space shuttle mission, he helped design exercise equipment and routines for astronauts who remain in space for long periods of time and are at risk for musculoskeletal weakness. The same year, Harris married Sandra Fay Lewis, a systems analyst. On August 3, 1992, Harris and his wife became the proud parents of Brooke Alexandria.

By mid-July 1992, Harris began serving as mission specialist aboard the Columbia, flight STS-55, on a trip that lasted from April 26 to May 6, 1993. It was a collaborative effort between Germany and the United States. During the mission, Harris and Hans W. Shlegel of Germany conducted scientific experiments using a wall-mounted laboratory. Numerous medical experiments were conducted, including growing tiny cells to study how the lack of gravity would affect them. As busy as he was, Harris made note of the speed of the shuttle and the beauty of colors of the atmosphere. During this flight, Harris logged over 239 hours and 4,164,183 miles in space.

First African American Astronaut to Walk in Space

Harris's next mission was aboard the space shuttle Discovery, flight STS-63. During the trip (February 2-11, 1995) Harris served as the payload commander. This trip was the first flight in the new collaboration between Russia and the United States. On February 9, Harris made history when he became the first African American to perform an extra vehicular activity, which means he walked in space. Harris and C. Michael Foale, an astrophysicist, stepped out to see if their spacesuits could handle temperatures of 90 to 125 degrees Fahrenheit below zero. Other experiments were conducted, but their space walk had to be cut short by twenty-five minutes because the astronaut's gloves were not insulated well enough and both astronauts were beginning to exceed the frostbite safety limits that had been set by NASA. During this visit to space, Harris had brought along a Navajo flag to pay tribute to the diverse U.S. cultures.

Harris retired from NASA in April 1996. Throughout his career there, he logged 438 hours and flew over 6 million miles in space. After retiring, he joined Spacehab Incorporated, a private corporation that facilitates the commercial use of space by providing access to crew-tended microgravity research environments. Harris moved to Spacehab's Houston office, where he served as vice president and chief scientist.

Harris, a veteran of two space flights, will always be remembered for being the first African American to walk in space. He serves as a role model for all Americans for his contributions to space and medicine.

REFERENCES

Books

Kaplan, Betty Gubert, Miriam Sawyer, and Caroline M. Fannin. *Distinguished African Americans in Aviation and Space Science*. Westport, Conn.: Oryx Press, 2002.

Phelps, J. Alfred. *They Had a Dream: The Story of African-American Astronauts*. Novato, Calif.: Presidio Press, 1994.

Periodicals

Coleman, Dana. "Reach for the Stars: In the NASA Space Shuttle and Space Station Programs." *Afro-American Red Star* (13 September 1997): A6.

Stone, Sherry. "Black Astronaut Made History During Space Shuttle Mission." *Philadelphia Tribune* (13 February 1996): 3-J.

Online

National Aeronautics and Space Administration: Lyndon B. Johnson Space Center. "Astronaut Bio: Bernard Harris 1/99.": 1-2.http://www.jsc.nasa.gov/Bios/htmlbios/harris.html (Accessed 3 December 2004).

Sharon McGee

E. Lynn Harris
1955–

Novelist

Since the 1990s, E. Lynn Harris has reigned as one of the most popular U.S. novelists. Over the years, more than three million copies of his novels have been sold, and he is greeted at bookstore readings by long lines of fans. Harris has been acknowledged as the first African American male novelist to achieve the same level of success as African American female novelists who are his contemporaries.

Everett Lynn Harris was born in Flint, Michigan in 1955, but from the age of three, he was raised in Little Rock, Arkansas with his three sisters. Harris attended Bush Elementary School, received good grades, and dreamed of becoming a teacher. When his father, Ben Odis Harris, a sign painter and sanitation truck driver, caught an eleven-year-old E. Lynn playing school with neighborhood children on the Harris's front porch, he kicked all the books and fake report cards off the porch before asserting that only boys who were sissies wanted to teach. Ben Harris was both verbally and physically abusive to his wife, Etta Mae Williams Harris, and to his children. There were many nights when Etta Mae would arouse her children from their beds and take them to their grandmother's house in order to escape the violence. In his autobiography, *What Becomes of the Brokenhearted* (2003), Harris writes that school and the Little Rock Public Library were his refuge from the pain and fear Ben Harris generated.

Although the verbal taunts and beatings continued after Harris's twelfth birthday, they had less impact after he learned that Ben Harris was not his biological father. Such knowledge, Harris writes in his autobiography, provided him with an "omnipotent shield" that protected him. Even greater relief came one year later when his mother, who worked two jobs during most of her son's childhood and attended business college, divorced her

E. Lynn Harris

Chronology

1955   Born in Flint, Michigan on June 20

1958   Moves to Little Rock, Arkansas

1973   Graduates from Hall High School

1977   Graduates with honors with a B.A. in journalism from the University of Arkansas at Fayetteville; as *Razorback* editor, is the first African American yearbook editor at a major southern university

1977   Begins career as a computer sales executive; is employed by IBM, Hewlett-Packard, and AT&T

1990   Attempts suicide and later in Howard University Hospital's emergency room, decides he wants to live

1991   Ends his career as a computer sales executive; writes first novel *Invisible Life*; publishes and distributes it after publishers reject it

1994   Signs a contract with Doubleday which represents the official start of his writing career

2002   Edits *Gumbo: An Anthology of African American Writing* with Marita Golden

2003   After writing eight novels, writes his autobiography, *What Becomes of the Brokenhearted*; returns to the University of Arkansas at Fayetteville as writer-in-residence

2005   Edits *Freedom in the Village: Twenty-Five Years of Black Gay Men's Writing, 1979 to the Present*

husband. Two years later when he was fifteen years old, Harris returned to Flint where he spent the summer with a relative and met his father, James Jeter. Their attempts at establishing a father-son relationship did not extend beyond that season because Jeter died in an automobile accident in April of the following year.

Succeeds in Educational Endeavors

Regardless of the adversities in Harris's young life, school always remained important to him. After he graduated from Bush Elementary, Harris enrolled in Booker Junior High, which was six blocks from his house. However, he transferred to West Side Junior High, which was integrated (70 percent of the student body was African American). In order to get to West Side, Harris walked thirteen miles. Instead of enrolling in his neighborhood school, the historic Little Rock Central High School that two years prior to Harris's birth became infamous during efforts to block nine African American students from enrolling, Harris chose Hall High School. During the summer of 1972, he attended the Arkansas Boys State, the same one-week program to prepare young males for government leadership that former President Bill Clinton had attended years earlier when he was a teenager. Later that summer, Harris participated in a similar, six-week government program at George Washington University in Washington, D.C.

After graduating from Hall High School in 1973, Harris matriculated at the University of Arkansas at Fayetteville where he was the editor of the 1977 *Razorback* yearbook; thus he was the first African American to edit a publication at the school. This achievement, according to *Jet* magazine, marked the first time an African American edited a yearbook at a major southern university. Also at the University of Arkansas, Harris was president of his fraternity, vice-president of Black Americans for Democracy, and the first African American male Razorbacks cheerleader. He graduated with honors with a B.A. in journalism in 1977 and later pursued business classes at Southern Methodist University.

Prior to graduating from the University of Arkansas, Harris considered enrolling in law school. He met a white recruiter for IBM who advised him to take the company's technical aptitude test. The recruiter assumed that Harris would not do well on the test because of his liberal arts background and told Harris that he would recommend him to IBM Office products which sold typewriters, yet after Harris scored the highest of any minority student on IBM's technical aptitude test, he was hired by IBM in Dallas in computer sales. Since IBM's starting salaries were significantly higher than the starting salaries in journalism, Harris planned to work at IBM for a few years, save money, and then enroll in law school or journalism school. However, Harris sold computers for thirteen years for IBM, Hewlett-Packard, and AT&T while living in Dallas; New York; Chicago; Washington, D.C.;

and Atlanta. By the time Harris was twenty-six, he was earning $100,000 a year.

Hits Nadir in Personal Life

Although Harris's career was flourishing, his personal life was in shambles. In August 1990, living in Washington, D.C., he attempted suicide by swallowing sleeping pills and drinking vodka. In *What Becomes of the Brokenhearted*, Harris writes that when he woke up the next day, he "realized that [his] suicide attempt had failed, that God was in control and not ready for [him] yet." Consequently, Harris called a taxi and went to the emergency room at Howard University Hospital where he realized that he wanted to live and that there was a reason his attempted suicide had failed. Following several months of therapy, Harris returned to Little Rock.

In January 1991, he moved to Atlanta, walked away from his career in computer sales and began writing. In his autobiography, Harris writes, "I wanted to write a story that would capture the pain and joy of being black and gay. I wanted it to be a love story . . . I wanted my story to be one where women, if they decided to read it, would think about the choices they made when it came to men." Harris's writing endeavors fulfilled a promise he made in the late 1980s to his friend, Richard Coleman. While Harris visited Coleman, who was dying of cancer, he told Harris that he should write a book; Harris promised his friend he would consider the idea. Harris had also met Maya Angelou in 1983 when she was a guest speaker at a corporate conference sponsored by the company where he worked. When Harris told Angelou he wanted to be a writer, she advised him to write every day even if he only wrote a single word.

In July 1991, Harris completed his first novel, *Invisible Life*. He sent copies to New York publishing companies, and by September, all of them had rejected the novel. Undaunted by the rejection letters, Harris created his own company, Consortium Press, and published and distributed his novel. In early December 1991, 5,500 copies of *Invisible Life* were printed, and Harris drew upon his sales experience to promote and sell it. Harris loaded the trunk of his car with boxes of *Invisible Life* and sold his novel at African American beauty salons, bookstores, book clubs, etc. Harris's perseverance paid off because other bookstores requested his book after their customers began inquiring about it. *Essence* proclaimed it one of the magazine's ten best books of the year, and by the time he had sold ten thousand copies of his book, Harris signed a contract with Doubleday, which released *Invisible Life* as an Anchor Books paperback in 1994. Five years later, Doubleday, paying tribute to Harris's phenomenal success as a writer, published a special fifth anniversary, hardcover edition of *Invisible Life*.

Harris's first book established a precedent that each of his subsequent novels as well as his autobiography have met—achieving bestseller status. Doubleday published *Just As I Am* (1994), which was the first work by an African American male to rank number one on Blackboard's bestsellers list; Harris's second novel received Blackboard's 1996 Novel of the Year Award and along with *Invisible Life*, received a film option from Showtime. Harris's third novel, *And This Too Shall Pass* (1996) was optioned by Pam Grier for her production company. His novels have consistently appeared on the bestseller lists and been reviewed in various publications. Harris's next novel, *If This World Were Mine* (1997), was nominated for a NAACP Image Award and won the James Baldwin Award for Literary Excellence. Harris's fifth novel, *Abide with Me* (1999), is the last novel in the trilogy of Harris's character, Raymond Taylor, that began with *Invisible Life* and continued with *Just As I Am*: *Abide with Me*, for which Doubleday paid Harris more than $1 million, was also nominated for a NAACP Image Award.

Harris's sixth novel, *Not a Day Goes By* (2000), debuted in second place on the *New York Times* bestseller list and ranked as *Publisher's Weekly*'s top bestseller for two consecutive weeks. In 2004, an adaptation of his novel, *Not a Day Goes By: The Play*, was performed nationwide; the play starred Jackee Harry, Trenyce, and Gary Owens. Harris followed his sixth novel's success with "Money Can't Buy Me Love," a novella that was published in *Got to Be Real: Four Original Love Stories* (2000); the book also contains stories by Colin Channer, Eric Jerome Dickey, and Marcus Major. His next novel, *Any Way the Wind Blows* (2001), was the first book after Harris signed a new contract with Doubleday worth between $5,000,000 and $6,000,000. The book, a sequel to *Not a Day Goes By*, debuted in second place on the *New York Times* bestseller list. It was also named Blackboard's Novel of the Year (2002). When Harris was awarded Blackboard's Novel of the Year (2003) for his subsequent novel, *A Love of My Own* (2002), he became the first writer to receive the award three times and the first author to receive it in consecutive years. *A Love of My Own* was also nominated for an NAACP Image Award. His autobiography, *What Becomes of the Brokenhearted* (2003), won the 2003 Lamda "Bridge Builder" Literary Award.

In addition to his novels, collection of short stories, and autobiography, Harris edited two compilations: *Gumbo: An Anthology of African American Writing* (with Marita Golden, 2002) and *Freedom in This Village: Twenty-five Years of Black Gay Men's Writing, 1979 to the Present* (2005). Various other writing have also appeared in such periodicals as *American Visions*, *The Advocate*, *Essence*, *Savoy*, and the *Washington Post Sunday Magazine* as well as such anthologies as *Brotherman: The Odyssey of Black Men in America* (1995).

Pursues Additional Endeavors

Harris's extraordinary success in the literary world has provided him with opportunities to showcase his talents in other areas. In 2003, Harris returned to his alma mater, the University of Arkansas at Fayetteville, where, as writer-in-residence, he taught creative writing as well as literature, served as the cheer coach for the Razorback cheerleading team, and remained a fan of the Razorback football team. Harris has lectured at many colleges and universities throughout the United States, including Carnegie Mellon University, College of William and Mary, Florida A & M University, George Washington University, Hampton University, Harvard University, and others.

Harris, who acknowledged that the Broadway hit, *Dreamgirls*, is his favorite musical, appeared as the emcee in a fall 2001 benefit performance of *Dreamgirls* that starred Lillias White, Heather Headley, and Audra McDonald. Harris also appeared on Broadway in a special one-night performance of *Love Letters to America*, with Rosie Perez, Annabella Sciorra, and others. Harris's talents have reached the motion picture screen; three of his novels have film options, and Harris has written a screenplay for a remake of the popular 1970s African American film *Sparkle*.

Harris is a member of the Board of Directors of the Evidence Dance Company and the Board of Directors of the Hurston/Wright Foundation, an organization founded in 1990 by novelist Marita Golden to support writers of African descent. In addition, Harris has established the E. Lynn Harris Better Days Literary Foundation in order to assist new authors. Proceeds from the fifth anniversary edition of *Invisible Life* were earmarked for the foundation.

Harris, who was inducted into the Arkansas Black Hall of Fame (2000), is the recipient of a variety of additional awards and honors, including the University of Arkansas at Fayetteville's Distinguished Alumni Citation (1999), Poets & Writers' Writers for Writing Award (2002), Sprague Todes Literary Award, Harvey Milk Honorary Diploma, *SBC* Magazine Brother of the Year Literature Award, Harlem Y. Mentor Award, and GMAD (Gay Men of African Descent) Award. Harris remains one of the most influential and inspirational literary voices in the United States.

REFERENCES

Books

Weaver, Kimberly. "E. Lynn Harris." In *Oxford Companion to African American Literature*. Eds. William L. Andrews, Frances Smith Foster, and Trudier Harris. New York: Oxford University Press, 1997.

Linda M. Carter

Wesley L. Harris
1941–

Educator, scientist

Wesley L. Harris is the head of the Department of Aeronautics and Astronautics at the Massachusetts Institute of Technology (MIT). Prior to this position, he served as associate administrator for aeronautics at the National Aeronautics and Space Administration (NASA), vice president and chief administrative officer of the University of Tennessee Space Institute (UTSI), and dean of the School of Engineering and professor of Mechanical Engineering at the University of Connecticut. Harris's life work paved the way for NASA to acquire more powerful supercomputers and advanced minority student concerns as well as programs. He is an exceptional role model for his students. His many honors and achievements indicate the high quality of his work.

Harris was born in Richmond, Virginia on October 29, 1941 to William and Rosa Harris, who worked in Richmond's tobacco factories. As a child, Harris was intrigued by airplanes and learned to build different models. Some of his airplanes were made of balsawood or plastic and were powered with rubber bands. In the fourth grade, Harris won an essay contest about career goals with a paper on how he wanted to become a test pilot. Harris's parents were convinced that education would give their three children entry into a better life, and Harris proved it. Harris received his B.S. with honors in aeronautical engineering in 1964 from the University of Virginia, Charlottesville, Virginia. He received his M.A. in 1966 and his Ph.D. in 1968, both in aerospace and mechanical sciences from Princeton University.

Harris initially wanted to study physics in college after he graduated high school; unfortunately, at that time the University of Virginia did not allow African Americans to major in it. He settled for a major in aeronautical engineering. In addition to his studies Harris had married in 1960 and had family responsibilities. He was often lonely on campus because there were only five or six other African Americans at the university. Moreover, most facilities in Charlottesville were segregated, and there were only a few places black students could go.

After completing his Ph.D. at Princeton, Harris was hired by the University of Virginia, as assistant professor of aerospace engineering. Harris believed that black educators should encourage promising African American students. He took a one-year leave of absence to teach physics at Southern University in Baton Rouge, Louisiana, a university that has a predominately black student body. He returned to Virginia as associate professor and met Leon Trilling of MIT who eventually became his mentor. In the mid-1960s, Trilling started a program to take some students from Boston's inner city areas and

Wesley L. Harris

place them in suburban schools. In 1972, Trilling persuaded Harris to take another temporary leave from the University of Virginia and work with him. In 1973 MIT offered Harris the position of associate professor of aeronautics, astronautics, and ocean engineering. Harris accepted this position and remained with MIT until 1979.

At MIT Harris developed many programs to assist African American students and other minorities. He established MIT's first Office of Minority Education in 1975 in order to help retain minority students and improve their performance. Harris created methods for measuring the students' achievements and developed ways for the school to help them improve. He also started other programs to acquaint faculty members with the special needs of African American students.

In 1979, Harris joined NASA headquarters in Washington, D.C., pioneering the use of computers to solve problems concerning high-speed air movement. His success in complex ventures paved the way for NASA to acquire more powerful supercomputers. In 1985, Harris accepted the position of dean of the School of Engineering at the University of Connecticut in Storrs. During his five years at the University of Connecticut, Harris developed a partnership between the university and local companies, namely, Pratt & Whitney, an aircraft engine maker, and United Technologies, an aerospace giant. When he first arrived at the University of Connecticut,

the School of Engineering recruited only five or six African American or Hispanic students each year. When Harris left in 1990, the number of new minority students accepted each year had risen to about forty. Harris also established the first University of Connecticut research center for grinding metals and an institute for environmental research.

Harris joined the University of Tennessee Space Institute (UTSI) in Tullahoma as the vice president and chief administrative officer. In 1992, Harris was encouraged by NASA administrator Dan Goldin to assist in the revival of aviation studies in the United States. Harris accepted Goldin's invitation to return to NASA as associate administrator for aeronautics. In this capacity Harris directed the NASA research and development efforts to support of the domestic aeronautics industry. He was also in charge of several projects, including research on technology for a new supersonic transport plane. In addition, he directed the National Aero-Space Plane (NASP) program, which works to develop aircrafts that can reach orbital altitudes by themselves.

Harris's research interests focused on demonstrating what happens when an object travels at or above the speed of sound. For example, Harris studied how the shape of an object influences its high-speed movement through space. He investigated other effects as well, such as noise generated by high-speed travel. Harris also studied the problems of air flow in supersonic conditions.

Harris returned to MIT as a Dr. Martin Luther King Jr. Visiting Professor in 1995 and rejoined the faculty the next year. He received a Leadership Award at MIT's annual MLK Celebratory Breakfast in 2001. He was named head of the Department of Aeronautics and Astronautics in 2003.

Harris has published more than one hundred reports on his research and has been recognized by professional organizations and engineering institutions. In research works co-authored with his students, Harris always put the name of his students ahead of his own.

Harris was the first African American to become a member of the Jefferson Society, the University of Virginia's famous debating group. He was also the first African American to receive a tenured faculty position at the University of Virginia and was the first to teach engineering at that school.

Harris has received numerous awards. For example, the American Institute for Aeronautics and Astronautics (AIAA) named Harris a fellow for his work on helicopter rotor noise, air flows above and below the speed of sound, and the advancement of engineering education. Harris has served as chair and member of various boards and committees: the National Research Council, the National Science Foundation, the U.S. Army Science Board, and several state governments. He is a member of the National Academy of Engineering, the Cosmos Club, and the Confrerie Des Chevaliers Du Tastevin.

REFERENCES

Books

Kessler, James H. et al. *Distinguished African American Scientists of the Twentieth Century*. Arizona: Oryx, 1996.

Periodicals

Thompson, Garland L. "19 Engineers Told to Broaden Their Reach. A NASA View: People, Economics as Important as Technical Mastery." *Black Issues in Higher Education* 11 (11 August 1994): 25.

Online

"Face to face with Wesley Harris." *Aerospace America* 31 (September 1993). http://vnweb.hwwilsonweb. com/hww/results/results_single.jhtml?nn=20 (Accessed 13 January 2005).

"MIT professor celebrates 60th birthday with scholarship fund." http://web2.infotrac.galegroup. com/itw/informark/954/778/60339620w2/purl=rcI_ GRG (Accessed 13 January 2005).

Nkechi G. Amadife

Andrew T. Hatcher
1923–1990

Presidential aide, press secretary

The varied communications career of Andrew Hatcher took him from the East Coast to the West Coast and back again and led to his history-making appointment in 1960 as the first African American associate press secretary to the president of the United States. His service during the administrations of John F. Kennedy and Lyndon B. Johnson made him a participant in, as well as eyewitness to, the internal operations of the executive branch of government during a decade of great changes and upheavals in America and the world.

Andrew T. Hatcher was born on June 19, 1923 in Princeton, New Jersey. As a youngster he attended the Witherspoon School for Colored Children, an educational institution founded by Betsy Stockton, a former slave, as early as 1830 in connection with the Witherspoon Street Presbyterian Church. The school and church were located in the section of Princeton nicknamed African Lane for its concentration of black residents.

Hatcher went on to Princeton High School, where he graduated in 1941. He continued his education at Springfield College in Massachusetts, beginning in September 1941. After the Japanese bombing of Pearl Harbor on December 7, 1941 brought the United States into World War II, Hatcher interrupted his college studies to join the U.S. Army in November 1943. During most of the war years Hatcher was stationed at Camp Lee, Virginia, where he received basic and branch training. He also participated in the Officer Candidate School (OCS) at Camp Lee and was eventually promoted to the rank of second lieutenant. Hatcher also served at the Oakland Army Base in northern California and remained there until he received his honorable discharge in June 1946 after nearly three years of active duty.

Hatcher returned to Springfield College in September 1946 and was noted in the school's 1947 yearbook as the editor of *The Student*, the college newspaper. As a former soldier and military officer who was a few years older than the typical college student, Hatcher was a "non-traditional student" as well as a member of a racial minority on campus. It is unclear if Hatcher graduated from Springfield, but sources indicate that in later years he served as a member of the college's alumni council.

Pursues Careers in Journalism and Politics

Hatcher made the decision to return to the northern California area and became a journalist for the San Francisco *Sun-Reporter*, an African American newspaper. He also attended the Golden Gate Law School between 1952 and 1954, but it is unclear whether he received a degree,

Andrew T. Hatcher

Chronology

1923	Born in Princeton, New Jersey on June 19
1941	Graduates from Princeton High School; enters Springfield College
1943	Joins United States Army in November
1946	Receives honorable discharge from Army as second lieutenant in June; returns to Springfield College in September
1952	Attends Golden Gate Law School after relocating to California
1959	Becomes California assistant secretary of labor
1960	Receives appointment as associate White House press secretary
1963	Helps to found One Hundred Black Men organization
1964	Resigns from White House after presidential assassination and transition
1977	Confronts criticism as public relations executive doing business with South Africa
1990	Dies on July 26; interred in Suffolk County, New York

as available sources do not indicate that Hatcher ever actively pursued the practice of law.

Hatcher soon made the transition from journalism to politics and became actively involved with the Democratic Party. As a result, he received a political appointment in 1959 as assistant secretary of labor in the administration of California governor Edmund G. "Pat" Brown. Hatcher's abilities did not go unnoticed by other leading Democrats, and he became a speechwriter for New York governor Adlai Stevenson during his two unsuccessful campaigns for president during the 1950s.

Along with his close friend Pierre Salinger, Hatcher joined the presidential campaign of Massachusetts senator John F. Kennedy in 1960 as a speechwriter and member of the campaign press staff. By this time Hatcher was a veteran of the campaign trail and helped considerably with the numerous details and logistics involved in presentations by the candidate around the country. His presence on the team also helped Kennedy in his efforts to appeal to African American voters in particular, whose support provided the margin of victory over vice president Richard M. Nixon in the closely contested election.

One of Kennedy's first appointments after winning the presidency was his selection of Hatcher as White House associate press secretary on November 10, 1960. Salinger had been appointed to the President's cabinet as press secretary, so the two friends and colleagues were

able to continue to work as a team during the Kennedy administration.

Hatcher was the first African American to serve in such a high-ranking position, being involved in the inner workings of the executive branch on a daily basis. The symbolic importance of this achievement was underscored when television cameras showed only Salinger and Hatcher seated behind the president during his first news conference after taking office in January 1961.

Represents Kennedy Administration

Among the many issues and concerns faced by the Kennedy administration were the testing of nuclear weapons by the Soviet Union and the Bay of Pigs incident in Cuba in 1961, the Cuban missile crisis, civil rights demonstrations and the desegregation of the University of Mississippi in 1962, and responses to the March on Washington and the Birmingham church bombing in 1963. Hatcher was directly involved in briefing the national and international media on the president's policies, decisions, actions, and other activities, and conducted news conferences and press briefings in place of Salinger as necessary.

The job responsibilities also involved extensive national and international travel with the president and other government officials, as well as coordinating schedules and logistics for public appearances, interviews, and media updates. On several occasions, Hatcher even accompanied the president on holidays in order to accommodate the constant press coverage of the charismatic Kennedy and his family.

Hatcher endured criticism and skepticism from some quarters regarding his qualifications and expertise for such a high-level position. It was assumed that Hatcher was not as knowledgeable about international and domestic issues beyond civil rights, which placed him in the position of proving his capabilities on a regular basis. Any mistakes he made were magnified because of his status as the first African American in his position, yet Hatcher realized that this was part of the job and continued his work.

Black leaders also confronted Hatcher regarding civil rights policies and initiatives and the speed with which they were being implemented by the Kennedy administration. While he was sensitive to their concerns, Hatcher remained focused on representing the views and actions of the White House on these and other issues in a fair and objective manner.

Hatcher also managed to balance his professional responsibilities with being a husband and father of seven children. When First Lady Jacqueline Kennedy set up the first White House kindergarten for the children of employees in the executive branch, Hatcher's son Avery, who was the same age as Caroline Kennedy, was included in the class. This discreet yet symbolic gesture in support of civil rights for African Americans was not openly publicized by the Kennedy administration for its political and public relations benefits, but it was acknowledged when it became a news item.

The presence of Hatcher on the White House press staff also increased access for African American journalists and newspaper organizations, which in past years had not been given the same opportunities as mainstream media. The National Newspaper Publishers Association (NNPA), which represented editors and publishers of African American newspapers from around the country, presented Hatcher with an award in 1961. The Capital Press Club (CPC), an organization of black journalists in Washington, showed their appreciation by awarding President Kennedy, Hatcher, and Salinger honorary CPC memberships. Hatcher was on his way to Paris, France at the time of the presentation, and President Kennedy accepted their awards while hosting the group at the White House.

Hatcher also became a member of the National Press Club, in no small part due to his high-level position and profile as part of the Kennedy administration. In addition, sources indicate that Hatcher was a member of the American Academy of Political and Social Science, and received an honorary doctorate from Miles College in 1962.

Continues Work in Aftermath of Kennedy Assassination

Hatcher did not accompany Kennedy on his fateful trip to Texas, and was in Washington on November 22, 1963 when the president was assassinated in Dallas. Despite his personal feelings about the tragic event, Hatcher maintained his professionalism and continued to work with the new president, Lyndon B. Johnson, as well as with Salinger, Kilduff, and other officials to coordinate activities and provide information during the presidential transition and period of national mourning. His involvement in one of the defining periods of the second half of the twentieth century was not widely recognized at the time or in later years but remained significant nonetheless.

Hatcher was a key figure involved in another important development during 1963, which was the founding of a men's organization devoted to concerns in the African American community. Along with Livingston Wingate and David Dinkins, who would eventually become the first African American mayor of New York City in November 1989, Hatcher created the concept for One Hundred Black Men (OHBM), Inc.

From its beginnings as a local organization in New York City formed to address injustices and other issues facing blacks in Harlem and other city neighborhoods, the organization expanded in following years to include chapters in all regions of the country. The OHBM would not only bring black men together to strategize, organize, and network to address community issues and problems, but would also become a vehicle for black men to serve as positive role models and mentors to African American children.

Hatcher resigned from his White House position on March 19, 1964, and became a consultant for P. Ballentine and Sons, a brewery based in Newark, New Jersey. During the same year, he wrote the introduction to *The Kennedy Years and the Negro: A Photographic Record*, a book published by the Johnson Publishing Company, the Chicago-based business owned by African American John H. Johnson.

Hatcher remained based in the metropolitan New York area for the remainder of his professional career, moving on to executive public relations and communications positions in a variety of settings. These included the Hill and Knowlton public relations firm, the national Young Men's Christian Association (YMCA), and the New York State Assembly.

By 1976 Hatcher was employed by the international public relations firm of Sydney S. Baron and Company as a vice president. His work for the company became controversial when it was made known that the firm was involved in public relations for the apartheid regime in South Africa, and recognized as a registered agent for the South African government. Hatcher expressed the viewpoint that he thought his work would help create a climate of change in the country from the inside, much as he felt he had done in the United States during the Kennedy years.

The company and Hatcher were criticized by anti-apartheid activists and others opposed to continued U.S. business relationships and investments in South Africa, and Hatcher eventually left the firm. Sources differ as to the date of Hatcher's resignation, but the timeframe of his departure was between 1977 and 1979.

Very little definite information on Hatcher's final years is available. Records from Calverton National Cemetery in Suffolk County, New York indicate that an Andrew T. Hatcher born on June 19, 1923, and deceased on July 26, 1990, is interred at that location. If this information is related to the same person, Hatcher would have been sixty-seven years old at the time of his death.

It is ironic, yet somehow fitting that Andrew Hatcher managed to make history as a trailblazer in the field of communications, yet remained behind the scenes and became somewhat "invisible" while advancing the agendas of his people as well as colleagues and employers. His understated approach made him very effective in the many high profile and high visibility positions and situations he experienced during his life and career.

REFERENCES

Books

Germany, K. *The Presidential Recordings: Lyndon B. Johnson: The Kennedy Assassination and the Transfer of Power, November 1963-January 1964.* New York: Norton, 2005.

Matney, William C., ed. *Who's Who Among Black Americans. 1977-1978.* 2nd ed. Northbrook, Ill.: Who's Who Among Black Americans, Inc. Publishing Company, 1978.

Saunders, Doris, ed. *The Kennedy Years and the Negro: A Photographic Portrait.* Chicago: Johnson Publishing Company, 1964.

Periodicals

Booker, Simeon. "Ticker Tape: Civil Rights Legacy of Kennedy Family." *Jet* 96 (16 August 1999): 56.

Giglio, James N. "Kennedy: The Tide Turns (African Americans Enter the Executive Ranks)." *American Visions* 10 (February/March 1995): 36-37.

Hoagland, Jim. "Black Opposition Mounts to U.S. Investment in South Africa." *Washington Post*, 14 January 1977.

Pincus, Walter. "South Africa is Waging Extensive Publicity Drive." *Washington Post*, 27 January 1977.

Online

"Hatcher Cemetery Records: New York." http://homepages.rootsweb.com/~nhatcher/hatcemNY.htm (Accessed 1 December 2005).

"The History of Princeton-Noteworthy People." http://athena.prs.k12.nj.us/groups/phs/pulse/people/people.html (Accessed 23 November 2005).

"One Hundred Black Men (Informational Paper)." http://www.learningtogive.org/papers/index.asp?bpid=170 (Accessed 23 November 2005).

"Transcript of News Conference with Assistant White House Press Secretary Andrew Hatcher: September 30, 1962." http://jfklibrary.org/meredith/days_e_01.html (Accessed 23 November 2005).

Other

Paige Roberts (College Archivist, Springfield College), e-mail message to author, 5 December 2005.

Fletcher F. Moon

Palmer Hayden
1890–1973

Painter

As one of the premiere artists of the African American folk experience, Palmer Hayden painted ordinary aspects of twentieth-century black life and helped pioneer candid representations of everyday existences in American modern art. While his work has been widely celebrated since the mid-twentieth century, his incorporation of African American folkloric themes and images was more widely debated than celebrated for its novelty. Characterizing his work as black primitivism, his critics denounced Hayden for his use of minstrel-like forms, which they felt played to racist stereotypes of black people. Even so, several of his contemporaries, including Harlem's poet laureate Langston Hughes, disagreed. In the early 2000s, his contemporary supporters joined scores of art critics who celebrate Hayden's work as an invaluable representation of the common American experience.

Hayden was born on January 15, 1890 to John and Nancy Hedgeman in Widewater, Virginia; his given name was Peyton Cole Hedgeman. Growing up on the banks of the Potomac River as one of twelve children, he was inspired by an older brother to begin drawing as a child. Though he also had private dreams of becoming a fiddle player, his family could not afford a fiddle and certainly could not afford fiddle lessons. Hence, he decided to pursue drawing, his true childhood passion in the rumbling town's surrounding countryside.

Educated in public schools, Hayden moved to Washington, D.C. as an adolescent to find work. Working as an errand boy and porter, he spent his spare time sketching boats on the Potomac. Emboldened by his love and natural talent the aspiring artist placed an advertisement in a

Chronology

1890	Born in Widewater, Virginia on January 15
1914	Enlists in the U.S. Army's 24th Infantry Regiment, an all-black company; assumes the moniker Palmer Hayden
1918	Re-enlists and is posted at West Point where he begins a correspondence course in drawing
1919	Settles in New York at the close of World War II; begins studying at Cooper Institute under the tutelage of Victor Perard
1926	Enters the Harmon Foundation's contest and is awarded the first place prize of $400 and its Gold Medal in Fine Arts
1927	Receives $3,000 grant from Alice M. Dike to study art in Europe
1928	Solo show at the Bernheim-Jeune Gallery in Paris, France
1932	Returns to New York City with the financial aid of the American Aid Society of Paris
1933	Hayden's *Fetiche et Fleurs* (Fetish and Flowers) is exhibited at the Harmon Show of 1933 as a part of the "Exhibition of the Works of Negro Artists," where it wins the Mrs. John D. Rockefeller Prize
1936	Briefly lives in Paris, France
1937	Returns to New York; marries Miriam Huffman
1944	Begins his John Henry Series
1973	Dies in Manhattan, New York on February 18

local newspaper seeking employment as an artist's assistant. When Hayden showed up for an interview with the white artist who responded, the artist turned him down because he was black.

Life as Serviceman and Fledgling Artist

After a series of odd jobs, including a stint as a laborer with the Buffalo Bill Circus (later known as the Ringling Brothers Circus), Hayden enlisted in the U.S. Army's 24th Infantry Regiment, an all-black company in 1914. While there are two different versions of how his name was changed from Peyton C. Hedgeman to Palmer Hayden, both accounts suggest that the name change occurred during his time as a serviceman. In the most popular account, his white commanding officer mispronounced his name, giving him the moniker Palmer Hayden. He used the name from that time forward and legally changed his name nine years later.

In addition to affording an opportunity to earn a decent living, the army also gave Hayden ample time to draw surrounding land- and seascapes. With more time to draw, Hayden began receiving tutorials from his white second lieutenant Arthur Boetscher, who drew maps as a hobby. While he was assigned to the 10th Cavalry at West Point after re-enlisting in 1918, he was not a cadet but was instead assigned as a caretaker of the cadets' training horses. Although it required more than half of his $18 per month salary, Hayden was able to enroll in a correspondence course in drawing for $10 each month.

The Renaissance Artist Paints Seascapes

At the close of the war in 1919, Hayden settled in New York. While working nights at the post office, Hayden studied charcoal drawing at Columbia University. Since the job required too much of his time, he quit the post office to begin part time work as a janitor in a Greenwich Village apartment building. Luckily, the first tenant he assisted was Victor Perard, then instructor at Cooper Institute (later called Cooper Union); Perard hired Hayden as a helper in his studio, while continuing to nurture his artistic talent.

Living in New York, Hayden was in the midst of the artistic, cultural, and social burgeoning of African American literary expression from the 1920s to the early 1930s, referred to as the Harlem Renaissance. Even so, Hayden's training was always more closely related to painting scenery, especially seascapes. In 1925, he began study under Asa Randall at the Boothbay Art Colony in Maine. The association served as a major turning point for Hayden, who demonstrated his increased understanding for the relationship between color and composition in several paintings of Boothbay Harbor.

In another chance meeting while moving furniture as a paid laborer, Hayden met Alice M. Dike, a wealthy daughter of a prominent judge. After explaining to Dike that he was an artist, Dike showed him a brochure from her church advertising the Harmon Foundation Awards for Distinguished Achievement among Negroes. Founded in 1922 by white real estate developer and philanthropist William E. Harmon, the foundation, in conjunction with the Commission on the Church and Race Relations of the Federal Council of Churches, recognized achievement in literature, music, drama, and visual arts.

Early Accolades for a Promising Career

Hayden submitted five of his paintings depicting various water scenes in Portland, Maine, and Haverstraw, New York, to the 1926 contest. Citing his work as unusual for an artist with little training and limited opportunity as handicaps, the foundation awarded Hayden the first place award of $400 and its gold medal in fine arts. Hayden was among a distinguished list of Harlem personalities to be awarded, including black bibliophile Arthur A. Schomburg, poet Countee Cullen, and writer James Weldon Johnson.

The following year, Hayden received a $3,000 gift from Dike, who wished to remain anonymous. Combined with the monetary award he had received, Hayden planned to use Dike's contribution for a two-year art study in Europe, in spite of his precarious financial state.

African American Artists Experience Paris

Hayden settled in Paris, among a cadre of other renaissance African American artists, including other Harmon grant awardees such as Cullen, William H. Johnson, and Lois Mailou (later Jones). "They felt unhindered by the constraints imposed upon their lives in the United States," according to the 1966 *Time* article. In Paris, "they could study at prestigious academies, exhibit at respected salons, and feel confident that their art would receive serious critical attention." Like other expatriate artists who found training available through a system of ateliers, Hayden began privately working under M. Clivette Le Fevre at the École des Beaux-Arts.

Despite financial constraints, which led him to end his lessons late in 1928, Hayden showed at the Bernheim-Jeune Gallery. As a solo show, the exhibit should have served as a major achievement but was marred by the disapproval of Le Fevre. As Hayden's former teacher, an angry Le Fevre felt that he was not prepared. The two men never saw each other again.

While in Paris, Hayden socialized in the circle of Harlem Renaissance artists, artisans and activists, including Alain Locke, an African American philosopher and writer. Locke, who had long-called for black artists to incorporate more African themes in their art, was among a group of Harlem personalities who either teased Hayden for his primary use of seascapes in his paintings or chastised him for his choice of black imagery.

With funds borrowed from the American Aid Society of Paris, Hayden returned to New York City in 1932, after five years abroad. Soon, he began work with the Works Progress Administration, during which time he mostly painted buildings and landscapes of New York City.

At the Helm of the "Africanist" Movement

Painted sometime between 1926 and 1932, Hayden's *Fetiche et Fleurs* (Fetish and Flowers) was exhibited at the Harmon Show of 1933 as a part of the "Exhibition of the Works of Negro Artists." The small still-life composition of a vase of lilies, an ashtray, and a Gabonese Fang head on a table covered with a Kuba textile from Zaire, clearly linked Hayden with the African-Cubist tradition of Harlem and Paris. As one of the earliest works by an African American artist to incorporate actual African imagery, the painting won the coveted Mrs. John D. Rockefeller Prize.

The 1930s proved to be the decade of Hayden's most productive and most controversial work. Having moved away from depicting the land and seascapes for which other Harlem artists teased him, Hayden sought to capture the folk culture of Harlem and the wider black American experience from his vantage point. Impressed by the black character of his newer paintings, Locke described Hayden's new style in *Negro Art: Past and Present* as "more modernistic . . . more decorative, high-keyed and in broken color."

Hayden moved briefly to Paris in 1936, but he returned to New York where he married Miriam Huffman in 1937. Throughout the 1930s Hayden exhibited his work at various shows throughout New York, including the Independent Artists in New York, Cooperative Art Market, Commodore Hotel, and the Nicholas Roerich Museum as well as the Smithsonian Institution and Howard University Gallery of Art in Washington, D.C., and the Colonial Exposition in Paris.

Protest in the Midst of Controversy

Hayden began one of his most noted and most contentious paintings, *The Janitor Who Paints*, in 1939-40. The composition depicts a black janitor busily working on a portrait of an attractive woman and a small child. The artist's studio is actually a bedroom, furnished with bed, nightstand, and alarm clock with a modest portrait of a cat on its wall. While the humble nature of the apartment suggests that the green beret-wearing artist is working-class, the rendering conveys the dignity with which he pursues his art.

An x-ray of the canvas reveals an earlier version of the composition in which all three figures have enlarged lips. The janitor's beret and hair are absent and his head is bald and cone-shaped. His hands are noticeably large and a portrait of Abraham Lincoln hangs in the background. Many critics gave this version scathing criticism, charging that Hayden's employment of minstrel-like features was stereotypical and re-enforced the use of racist images in art.

While Hayden altered the painting in response to mounting criticism, he would later defend the earlier rending as a "protest painting." In a 1969 interview, Hayden cited his friendship with Cloyd Boykin, an older African American painter who supported himself as a janitor, as its source of protest. "I painted it because no one called Boykin the artist," said Hayden. "They called him the janitor."

The Janitor Who Paints was only one of several paintings in which Hayden drew on themes that resonated from his own life. Hayden portrayed his childhood dilemma—the fiddle or his love of drawing—in an oil painting titled *Midnight at the Crossroads* (1940). Similarly, the painting *Michie Stadium* represents a time in Hayden's life. Recalling his time as a serviceman at West Point, it depicts cadets filing into the stadium to watch a football game while a single black person looks on from his perch up in a nearby tree. Critics would ridicule Hayden's *Midsummer Night in Harlem* (1936) for its flat forms and stylized figures; nevertheless, later art critics heralded the painting for evoking the mood of Harlem's residents congregating outside to escape the heat inside the tenements.

Hayden insisted that he was not striving for satirical effects in his African American folk paintings but that he wanted to achieve a new type of expression. In a February 1947 interview with Nora Holt, Hayden explained, "I decided to paint to support my love of art, rather than have art support me."

In 1944, Hayden began a three-year effort to create the John Henry series, which became his most famous group of paintings. Drawing heavily on his childhood remembrances of the "steel drivin' man," Hayden sought to create images of the African American folk hero. His twelve-part series, based on the true story of John Henry as a strong man who used a hammer to create railroads and hammer tunnels through mountains, was hailed for successfully capturing the soul, the spirit, and the strength of a hero as no artist had done before.

Hayden continued to paint throughout his life, returning often to the land and seascapes with which he began. Just two weeks after being awarded a grant from the Creative Arts Project to complete a series of twelve paintings about an African American solider from World War I to World War II, Hayden died on February 18, 1973, in the Veterans Administration Hospital in Manhattan, New York. He was 83.

REFERENCES

Books

Driskell, David. *Two Centuries of Black American Art.* New York: Los Angeles County Museum of Art, 1976.

Glickman, Simon. "Palmer Hayden." *Contemporary Black Biography.* Vol. 13. Detroit, Mich.: Gale Research, 1997.

Lewis, Samuella. *African American Art and Artists.* Berkley: University of California Press, 1990.

Miers, Charles, ed. *Negro Artists: An Illustrated Review of Their Achievements.* The Black Heritage Library Collection. Freeport, N.Y.: Books for Libraries Press, 1971.

Periodicals

"African-American Artists in Paris." *Time* 24 (30 June 1996): 32.

Hanks, Eric. "Journey from the Crosswords: Palmer Hayden's Right Turn." *International Review of African American Art* 16 (Fall 1999): 30-42.

"Negro Artists." *New York Times*, 25 December 1927.

"Negro Artist Wins Prize for Paintings." *New York Times*, 8 December 1926.

"Negro Worker Wins Harmon Art Prizes." *New York Times*, 2 January 1927.

"Palmer Hayden." *New York Times*, 20 February 1973.

Crystal A. deGregory

Michael Healy
1839–1904

Naval officer

A distinguished captain in the U.S. Revenue Service, Michael Healy was the only African American to have command in any service that predates the establishment of the U.S. Coast Guard. He began his career as a seaman at age fifteen without any seafaring experience, and just ten years later, he was ascending through the ranks of the Revenue Service. By the time the service promoted him to the rank of captain in 1883, Healy had already amassed years of experience on cutters that braved the menacing weather conditions of the Arctic and Bering seas to rescue distressed ships and their crews as well as to ensure maritime law and order. While his temper and harsh leadership tactics helped him to maintain the respect of his men, it was also the source of much unrest, and throughout the 1890s he was tried several times for conduct unbecoming an officer.

Born just across the Ocmulgee River near the town of Macon, Georgia on September 22, 1839, Healy was one of nine children born to Michael Morris Healy, an Irish immigrant, and Eliza Clark (also referred to as Mary Eliza Smith), his father's mulatto slave. Having arrived in Georgia in the second decade of the nineteenth century, the senior Healy was a very wealthy man by mid-century. In addition to farming fifteen hundred acres of land, he owned forty-nine slaves worth $34,000, the equivalent of an estimated $500,000 in the early 2000s. While Georgia law made it impossible for Healy to lawfully marry Clark, the couple lived together in common-law from 1829 until their deaths within months of each other twenty years later.

Because the children of an enslaved mother invariably took the condition of their mother, the Healy children were each sent north as they became school age. Their father's 1844 chance meeting with John Fitzpatrick, Roman Catholic bishop of Boston, led to the enrollment of the older boys at the newly opened Holy Cross College in Worcester, Massachusetts. Sent to join them at Holy Cross in 1848, young Michael was only nine years old when he ventured north. Uninterested in academia, he quickly grew restless and in 1854 ran away from school to become a cabin boy to the dismay of his older brothers. Together, they managed to bring him back in 1855 and resolved to send him to school in Paris, where brother James, who assumed the role of guardian since their parents' death five years earlier, was completing seminary.

Begins Seafaring Career

Healy ran away from the French school in the summer of 1855, this time to England. Perhaps frustrated with his

Michael Healy

Chronology

1839	Born near Macon, Georgia on September 22
1855	Becomes a cabin boy mate on board the clipper ship *Jumna*
1865	Commissioned as a third lieutenant in the U.S. Revenue Marine by President Abraham Lincoln on March 4; marries Mary Jane Roach
1866	Promoted to second lieutenant, serving as a junior officer on board the cutters *Reliance*, *Vigilant*, *Moccasin*, and *Active*
1870	Promoted to first lieutenant
1874	Becomes second officer on the cutter *Rush*
1877	Obtains his first command on the cutter *Chandler*
1880	Assumes the second-in-command post on board the *Thomas Corwin*
1883	Promoted to the rank of captain
1886	Takes command of the ship *Bear*, designated as the flagship of the Bering Sea Force
1890	Court-martialed for charges of drunkenness and cruelty but acquitted of all charges
1896	Court-martialed a second time and found guilty of seven charges; suspended for a period of four years
1900	Temporarily given the command of the cutter *McCulloch*
1902	Given command of the cutter *Thetis*
1903	Retires from the service
1904	Dies in San Francisco on August 30

determination to be at sea, his brothers decided to let him pursue seafaring. Taking a berth as cabin boy on the American East Indian clipper *Jumna*, bound for Calcutta from Boston that same year, he spent the next several years roaming the world, from India and Africa to Europe, the Mediterranean, Asia, and to the Americas.

Healy weathered several years on the high seas. He was in Australia when the American Civil War broke out. He was back in Boston with much of the rest of his family for its duration. Still, he was anxious to return to his life at sea, and he got his chance in 1863 as a part of the Revenue Cutter Service. As the forerunner to the present-day Coast Guard, Alexander Hamilton, the first secretary of the Treasury, founded the service in 1790 as an armed maritime law and enforcement service.

In 1864, just one year after his enlistment and at twenty-five years of age, Healy made a formal application for commission and an appointment to the U.S. Revenue Marine. The captains under whom he served attested to his ability and promise. Despite the fact that Healy did not perform well on his written exam, the power his brother James wielded as the de facto leader of Boston's growing Catholic community strengthened his case. With the benefit of James's influence and the impressive political endorsements it secured, Healy was commissioned as third lieutenant in January 1865, serving on cutters operating out of Boston. A week later, on

January 31, his brother James officiated at his marriage to Mary Jane Roach, the daughter of Irish immigrants to Boston. Five years his senior, Mary Jane would experience eighteen pregnancies, but only a single child named Frederick was born to the couple in 1870.

Promoted to second lieutenant in 1866, Healy saw duty as a junior officer and commander aboard the cutters *Reliance*, *Vigilant*, *Moccasin*, and *Active* across the East Indies. In 1870, he was promoted to first lieutenant and began his Alaskan tour as the second officer of the cutter *Rush* in 1874. Two years later, Healy began serving as commanding officer of the cutter *Chandler*.

In 1881, Healy was ordered to assume service as second-in-command of the *Thomas Corwin* under Captain C. L. Hooper. The cutter cruised up and down the North Pacific, performing rescue operations and facilitating exploratory operations of the Arctic territory later known as Alaska. Documented by renowned naturalist John Muir, the 1917 book *The Cruise of the Corwin* details the convoy's search of the Siberian and Arctic Alaskan coasts for the steamer *Jeannette* and two whalers, *Mount Wollaston* and *Vigilant*. Healy made important connections with Siberian communities the following year while searching for distressed ships. His meeting with the Chukchi people, who raised reindeer to sustain themselves, later served as the impetus for Healy's plan to transplant reindeers in Alaska.

Becomes King of the Arctic and Bering Seas

Promoted to the rank of captain on March 3, 1883, Healy had his wife, son, and brother Patrick accompany him aboard the *Corwin* to the Arctic. While his family and friends dispute reports that suggested he drank heavily, drunkenness was common among sailors, particularly those who endured the cold, damp weather of the Bering Sea. He continued his service on the *Corwin* until 1886, publishing reports of its activities both in 1884 and in 1885, in which he expressed the difficulty of cruising two grounds separated by one thousand miles.

Captain Healy was ordered to take command of the sailing vessel *Bear* in February 6, 1886. Purchased by the navy in 1883, the *Bear* had rescued Greenly and the survivors of its expedition, successfully returning them to safety. The *Bear* was designated as the Arctic Ocean cruiser as well as the flagship of the Bering Sea Force, and Healy led its command from 1886 to 1895.

Having been acquired by the United States in 1867, the new territory of Alaska would have been entirely remote and isolate were it not for the U.S. Revenue Service. As a result, Healy and cutter crews often acted as liaisons between the territory and the federal government. Over the course of their service, they developed relationships with Alaska's 25,000 natives. Consequently, when the decline of whales and seals, their principal food sources, threatened the Eskimo with starvation, Healy began working on a plan to save the Arctic natives. As early as 1890, he and Dr. Sheldon Jackson, Presbyterian missionary and general agent for education in Alaska, traveled to the Steward Peninsula to arrange for the acquisition of the Chukchis' domesticated reindeer. Using his own funds, Healy was able to negotiate the purchase and transport of the initial group of reindeer aboard the *Bear* for resettlement on Alaskan shores in 1891. Continuing to transport about twenty or more at a time throughout his command of the cutter, he helped secure the future of the Eskimo by lobbying for federal funds to acquire more reindeer, ensuring the growth of its population over the course of the next decade.

"Hell-roaring" Mike Faces Prosecution

During his nine-year leadership, Healy was unyielding in his charge, which earned him a reputation as an unswerving defender of the law in Arctic and Bering waters, who crushed any sign of mutiny. Dubbed "Hell-roaring Mike Healy," he was quick-tempered and authoritarian, an attitude which earned him a legendary reputation in the maritime and Arctic circles. Standing before the mask, he barked orders, calling his tough-minded crew into action in the midst of the harshest weather conditions imaginable. He was also infamous for "tricing" officers, a technically permissible but long abandoned form of nautical punishment. The procedure required that a man be suspended by his hands above his head until his feet were just above the deck's surface for about five minutes. While the position caused great pain, it was not life-threatening and did not leave any lasting injury.

However, it was not the captain's controversial disciplinary methods alone that led to a string of charges against Healy. Beginning with his first court martial in 1890, the allegations leveled against him included the brutality of tricing and the charge of being drunk when he did so. The case may have been trumped up by the temperance advocates (especially those of the Women's Christian Temperance Union, or WCTU), and Healy was acquitted, at least in the first case.

Healy was less fortunate during his second trial in 1896, although a great deal of its fabricated accusations were an extension of the crusade of junior officers and the WCTU. Healy was charged with spitting in the face of one of his junior officers while in a drunken stupor. This case was well-supported by a host of witnesses. In spite of their sympathy, the panel of Revenue Service officers had no real choice but to find him guilty. He was punished with demotion to the bottom of the captain's list, permanent removal from his command of the *Bear*, and a four-year suspension from active service.

The loss was only one of many which Healy soon faced. His health had begun to fail one night prior to the 1896 trial, when an inebriated Healy reportedly walked home after learning of the impending case. After more than four decades of courageous sea-fearing, he had already suffered from a severe case of influenza on his lass cruise aboard the *Bear*. The walk home caused severe congestion, which degenerated to lung hemorrhages during the following night, but Healy rallied his strength enough to face trial.

In a strange twist of fate, the demotion provided the time he so desperately needed. Supported by his wife Mary and a host of friends, he gradually regained his strength and eventually returned to active duty aboard the *McCulloch* in 1900. However, his jubilation was short-lived. A series of losses followed. First, Captain Hooper, his oldest and most loyal friend, died. Shortly thereafter, his brother James died as well. Then he was directed to turn over his command to one of the judges in his court martial, only to be reassigned to the *Seminole*. Removed from the Arctic to which he had dedicated his life, Healy descended into depression, drunkenness, and suicidal behavior.

Restored to Rightful Place

Even so, a 1902 administrative change in Washington prompted a review of his 1896 trial; the trial had been perjured and Healy believed to have been treated too harshly. As a result, he was restored to number three in the captains' list and was assigned to command of the *Thetis*. His dignity and self-respect restored, Healy led the cutter through Alaskan cruises in 1902 and 1903.

Having reached the mandatory age for retirement, Healy left the Revenue Service on September 22, 1903. Less than a year later, Michael Healy died of a heart attack in San Francisco on August 30, 1904. Buried in the Holy Cross Cemetery there, he was survived by his widow Mary Jane Roach Healy and their son Frederick Healy.

While Michael Healy's career was as controversial as it was courageous, it does not appear as though his mixed-heritage was ever an issue. He was light-skinned, his siblings held powerful positions in the Catholic Church, and Healy seemed to self-identify as a white person. The fact that the U.S. Revenue Service relegated its black servicemen to menial jobs as stewards, cooks, and seamen was undoubtedly known to Healy, who would have been barred from advancing in the service if his mixed heritage was known. Even so, Michael Healy's achievements are among the most legendary in American nautical history.

As one of ten children born to the interracial Healys, Michael Healy succeeded differently than his siblings. With "firsts" in their own right, his siblings included Bishop James Healy, who served as the bishop of Maine; the Reverend Father Sherwood Healy, who served as the rector of the Boston's Holy Cross Cathedral; and his brother the Reverend Patrick Healy, who served as the president of Georgetown University in Washington, D.C. His three sisters Martha, Josephine, and Eliza were all nuns; Eliza was a mother superior.

In 1997, the U.S. Coast Guard Service recognized the achievements of Michael Healy by naming of a new Polar-class icebreaker in his honor. At 420-feet and weighing 16,300 tons, the *Healy* is part of continued efforts to memorialize Healy's career. Additionally, a grant from the Alaska Humanities Forum funded the production of *The Odyssey of Captain Healy*, a film of the life and work of Michael Healy.

REFERENCES

Books

Bixby, William. *Track of the Bear.*. New York: D. McKay Co., 1965.

Evans, Stephen H. *The United States Coast Guard, 1790-1915: A Definitive History with a Postscript, 1915-1949*. Annapolis, Md.: United States Naval Institute, 1949.

Muir, John. *The Cruise of the Corwin*. Boston: Houghton Mifflin Co., 1917.

O'Toole, James M. *Passing for White: Race, Religion, and the Healy Family, 1820-1920*. Amherst: University of Massachusetts, 2002.

Williams, Albert E. *Black Warriors: Unique Units and Individuals in African American Military History*. Haverford: Infinity Publishing Co., 2003.

Periodicals

Johnson, Paul H. "Portrait of Captain Michael A. Healy, Part II." *The Bulletin, U.S. Coast Guard Academy Alumni Association* 41 (March/April 1979): 22-27.
——. "Portrait of Captain Michael A. Healy, Part III." *The Bulletin, U.S. Coast Guard Academy Alumni Association* Vol. 41 (March/April 1979): 26-30.

Murphy, John F. "Portrait of Captain Michael A. Healy, Part I." *The Bulletin, U.S. Coast Guard Academy Alumni Association* 41 (January/February 1979): 14-18.

O'Toole, James M. "Racial Identity and the Case of Captain Michael Healy, USRCS," Prologue, *The U.S. Archives & Records Administration* 29 (Fall 1997): 191-200.

Online

O'Dell, James. "Captain 'Hell Roaring' Michael A. Healy, U.S.R.C.S.," www.uscg.mil/hq/g-cp/history/FAQS/Healy_Odell_Article.html (Accessed 3 January 2005).

Collections

The Michael A. Healy Papers (1865-95) are held at the University of Alaska, Anchorage's Archives and Manuscripts Department of the Consortium Library in Anchorage, Alaska.

Crystal A. deGregory

Jimi Hendrix
1942–1970

Guitarist, rock musician, composer, songwriter, singer

Jimi Hendrix became recognized during his short life and music career as a brilliant innovator on the electric guitar and arguably the greatest rock musician of all time. His music combined elements of blues, jazz, folk, pop, rhythm and blues, rock and roll, country, classical virtuosity, electronic experimentation and manipulation of noise, volume, feedback, sound delay, repetition, and other special effects in live and recorded performances. His songs and instrumental compositions expanded the vocabulary of his instrument, and his showmanship helped to define and draw attention to rock as a separate and unique musical art form.

Johnny Allen Hendrix was the given name of the first child born to James Allen (Al) Hendrix and Lucille Jeter

Jimi Hendrix

Hendrix on November 27, 1942, in Seattle, Washington. His paternal grandparents, Ross and Nora Hendrix, had been members of a vaudeville performing company that went broke in Seattle in 1910.

Al Hendrix was drafted into the U.S. Army in early 1942, and at age twenty-two decided to marry Lucille on March 31 of that year before leaving for basic military training. When their son was born in Kings County Hospital, Lucille was unprepared to raise a child on her own. Al did not get to see his son until his discharge in 1945. In 1946, Al Hendrix changed his son's name to James Marshall Hendrix.

Al had difficulty making a steady living from a variety of temporary, low-paying jobs in the Seattle area. Lucille was frequently absent from the home, but she gave birth to a second son, Leon, in 1948. As a result, young James (Jimmy) and his brother were often shuttled among various relatives and friends in Seattle and as far away as Texas. Jimmy also spent time with his grandmother Nora Hendrix in Vancouver, British Columbia (Canada), who shared stories of her vaudeville days and their Cherokee Indian ancestors in Georgia and Tennessee.

In 1951 Lucille separated from Al, but Jimmy and Leon would often sneak away for secret visits with their mother and half-siblings from her other relationships. She died at age thirty-two in 1958.

Discovers Music and Guitars

While his father was away from home for long periods seeking and finding work, Jimmy spent considerable time listening to music from his father's jazz and blues record collection. He was drawn to the sound of the guitar in particular, as played by Muddy Waters, T-Bone Walker, B. B. King, John Lee Hooker, and others. Hendrix convinced his father to buy an acoustic guitar for five dollars from the son of their landlord.

The left-handed Jimmy reversed the order of the strings on the instrument, but later became adept at playing right-handed guitars upside down with their strings in regular order, a unique approach to the instrument. At age twelve he began playing the acoustic guitar, and he continued to learn from records, radio, and local musicians. His first electric guitar, a white Supro Ozark model, was purchased by his father from the Myers Music Store in Seattle, and in the summer of 1959 Hendrix joined a teenage group called the Rocking Kings. He did not own an amplifier, so he plugged into a borrowed unit and played bass guitar parts for the band on his lead guitar.

The group's first performance was at a National Guard armory, where they were paid thirty-five cents each for their musical efforts. After his electric guitar was stolen from Seattle's Birdland nightclub, his father got a white Danelectro model, which was painted red by Hendrix. The Rocking Kings went through a period of local popularity before the group disbanded.

Hendrix continued to lose interest in academics and dropped out of Garfield High School in October 1960, only a few months before graduation. He helped his father by working with him in his landscaping and gardening business but soon became bored and restless.

Shortly afterwards he got into trouble, was arrested in May 1961, sent to a juvenile detention center, and given a two-year suspended sentence. With a criminal record and no high school diploma, Hendrix had few options. At the age of eighteen, he decided to enlist, instead of waiting to be drafted into military service. Hendrix followed in his father's footsteps and signed up for three years of active duty.

Hendrix was sent to Fort Ord, California for basic training but could not bring his guitar. He was then sent to Fort Campbell, Kentucky, the base of the 101st Airborne Division, called the Screaming Eagles. The nickname was apt and somewhat prophetic for Hendrix, in light of his future guitar exploits. He was jumping out of airplanes weeks later and enjoyed the experience of flight and freefalling. In January 1962 he wrote his father and asked for his guitar, which he named Betty Jean after a Seattle girlfriend and played as often as possible.

Another soldier, Billy Cox, was a bass player, and the two musicians started playing together on a regular basis. They formed a band named the King Kasuals and began working at military service clubs, in the nearby community of Clarksville, Tennessee, and traveled to other locations in surrounding states.

Leaves Military for Nashville Music Scene

Hendrix received an honorable discharge from the army in summer 1962. Reports vary as to the reasons for his early exit, but music became his main occupation. Hendrix decided to establish himself in Nashville, which had developed a strong rhythm and blues music scene in addition to its reputation for country music.

The King Kasuals played on a regular basis at black nightclubs, where Hendrix also participated in jam sessions and so-called battles with other guitarists, including Larry Lee and Johnny Jones, who played alongside Hendrix and Cox on *Night Train,* a Nashville rhythm and blues television program. Hendrix said later that Nashville was where he actually learned how to play the guitar.

Despite the variety of playing opportunities, Hendrix and his fellow musicians made little money and often relied on friends, club owners, and other associates for financial assistance, food, and shelter. He worked infrequently as a backing musician for nationally known entertainers visiting Nashville, and eventually Hendrix went on the road with Sam Cooke, Jackie Wilson, and Curtis Mayfield, a singer, songwriter, and guitarist whose approach also influenced Hendrix.

These persons and promoter "Gorgeous George" Odell exposed Hendrix to showmanship and versatility in playing different musical styles. After a package tour with Curtis Mayfield and the Impressions in late 1962, Hendrix returned to the Seattle/Vancouver area, where he spent time with his grandmother and briefly joined another soul group, Bobby Taylor and the Vancouvers. He returned to Nashville in the spring of 1963 then went back out on the road with other artists. In his spare time he continued to write his own songs, poetry, and lyrics.

Moves to New York to Advance Career

In late 1963 Hendrix moved to New York City, where he hoped to find more performing opportunities. He had little money and pawned his guitar for food and lodging. When these funds ran out, he managed to survive, redeem his instrument, and work with local bands. He won the $25 first prize at the Apollo Theatre talent competition and met Fayne Pridgeon, who helped him get established in the Harlem music scene at the Palm Cafe.

By March 1964 Hendrix was touring and recording with the Isley Brothers, who let him have solos and indulge his showmanship. Hendrix in turn became a major influence on their younger brother, guitarist Ernie Isley, who joined their group in later years. Hendrix decided to leave the Isleys when they performed in Nashville and reunited briefly with old friends and colleagues.

He went out on another tour promoted by Odell and made a short-lived connection with rhythm and blues/rock and roll legend "Little Richard" Penniman in Atlanta, who needed musicians for his new group. During several performances Hendrix upstaged his employer, who was not pleased and imposed fines. Shortly afterwards Hendrix quit the band, returned to New York, quickly landed another job in 1965 with Curtis Knight and the Squires, freelanced with other New York groups, and did some recording studio work.

Hendrix also began to investigate the predominantly white music scene centered in the Greenwich Village section of Manhattan, gained inspiration to sing his own songs, and in summer 1966 formed a group and a new stage name, as Jimmy James and the Blue Flames. The group began appearing in small Village cafes. His talent continued to draw attention but provided meager financial rewards.

All this changed after an English musician, Chas Chandler, heard Hendrix playing at Café Wha? on July 5. Chandler, a former bass guitarist, was now involved in the business side of the music industry. He talked to Hendrix, confirmed that he did not have any legal obligations, and offered his services.

Travels to England to Further Develop Music Career

Hendrix was more than ready to make a move and accepted the offer made by Chandler. On September 23, 1966, Hendrix and his new manager began the next phase of his career. When they arrived in England, problems developed with officials, but Hendrix was granted a tourist visa. The new band highlighted the guitar and vocals of Hendrix, with bass guitarist Noel Redding and drummer Mitch Mitchell. Chandler changed the spelling of Hendrix's nickname to the more exotic-looking "Jimi," and the band was named the Jimi Hendrix Experience (JHE).

The JHE played its first performances in France in October 1966 and made its London debut on November 25, two days before Hendrix celebrated his twenty-fourth birthday. The group recorded its first single, "Hey Joe," performed the song during its first British television appearance on December 13, and it became the band's first hit record. As a result, the JHE became an overnight music sensation, with the top British rock stars and guitarists as audience members and fans. Hendrix became the talk and toast of London, with all the excesses of celebrity, including sudden wealth, access to exclusive parties, alcohol, drugs, and sexual favors.

The British press did not quite know what to make of Hendrix and created controversy by demeaning his appearance and performances. Business partner Mike Jeffrey returned from the United States in January 1967 with a $150,000 recording contract from Warner Brothers Records, a considerable amount for a band unknown to the American public.

The band continued to perform at packed theaters, concert halls, and other venues throughout Europe. Hendrix wrote the band's next hit, "Purple Haze," with the subtitle, "Jesus Saves," but its spiritual message was edited out in the final version. "Purple Haze" climbed to the top five on the British music charts, replacing "Hey Joe," which had peaked at number four a few months earlier. By the end March 1967, the JHE had added additional songs to their performances, including "Fire," where Hendrix shocked the audience by literally setting his guitar on fire with lighter fluid.

At first, the concert promoters and press were dismayed by his antics and his sexually suggestive motions, playing the instrument in numerous positions, including between his legs and behind his back, picking the strings with his teeth, and destroying his guitar and stage equipment on occasion. Hendrix later felt that his showmanship may have detracted from the music, but it also added to his mystique as an artist.

The group recorded additional songs for its first record album, *Are You Experienced?*, on the Reprise/Warner Brothers label. The album went on sale in May and yielded another hit single, a ballad called "The Wind Cries Mary." This song proved that there was more to Hendrix than loud volume, amazing guitar technique, and outrageous showmanship.

The JHE appeared at the first Monterey (California) International Pop Festival before over 30,000 people in June 1967. A memorable performance by Hendrix included "Wild Thing," where he set his guitar on fire, smashed it to splinters, and then threw the pieces into the audience. The response in America was the same as in Europe, and *Are You Experienced?* quickly became a bestseller, creating additional demand for live performances. They became the opening act for the Monkees pop group but were dropped from that tour after only eight performances and returned to England.

The success of the JHE led to nearly non-stop activities for the remainder of 1967 with the recording of the second album *Axis: Bold as Love* and various performances. Hendrix was voted the best musician in the world that year by *Melody Maker*, the top British music journal.

By early 1968 the band was preparing for another American tour, which included a February 12 concert in Seattle where he reunited with his father and brother and met his new stepmother and stepsister. He returned to Garfield High School the next day for recognition from local officials. Tensions escalated between Hendrix and his bandmates, while their managers continued to control the band's large revenues and expenses. Hendrix never obsessed about money, but his music and his time were constantly being drained by numerous people and activities demanding his attention.

Becomes Symbol of Counterculture

Hendrix reflected the turmoil of the times in his music, as the civil rights movement, youth and sexual revolution, and Vietnam War era all were a part of his personal experience as an African American musician, military veteran, and expatriate. He tried to avoid direct commentary on political and social issues, but his status made him a hero or target for others who approved or disapproved of his music and lifestyle.

Hendrix canceled a scheduled performance after Martin Luther King was assassinated and gave $5,000 to a memorial fund but received criticism for not speaking out against the riots and upheaval that followed. He chose to respond through his music and began work on his third record album, *Electric Ladyland*, the same month in New York. Hendrix used numerous musicians, full studio technical capabilities, spent huge sums for studio time, and finished it in October 1968. The album rose to number one on the music charts, but its success created additional problems.

Disbands JHE; Performs at Woodstock Festival

The year 1969 began with erratic behavior and performances by Hendrix, now a music superstar. Chandler quit and Jeffrey was now in charge of his business matters, while Redding led his own band in addition to his work with Hendrix. The JHE was the highest-paid band in the world, performing to large audiences in stadiums and arenas, but Hendrix still faced numerous offstage issues.

His personal problems were complicated by a May arrest for drug possession in Toronto, and on June 29 Hendrix announced in Denver, Colorado, the end of the JHE. Hendrix contacted old friends Billy Cox and Larry Lee, formed a new group called Gypsy Sun and Rainbows, convinced Mitchell to stay on, and added percussionists Juma Sultan and Jerry Velez.

Over 400,000 people came to a large dairy farm in Bethel, New York, in August 1969 for the Woodstock Arts and Music Festival. Hendrix insisted on being the last performer of the festival, even though the new group was not well-rehearsed. Technical and weather problems caused numerous delays, so Hendrix did not take the stage until Monday morning, August 18. The festival was originally supposed to end on Sunday, and most fans had left or were leaving by that time.

The estimated 80,000 that remained became witnesses to another legendary Hendrix performance, including his solo version of "The Star-Spangled Banner" on his trademark white Fender Stratocaster guitar. He transformed it into an electronic masterpiece, and many persons interpreted his performance as a brilliant musical commentary or protest regarding the war in Vietnam.

After Woodstock, the band was reduced to a trio, consisting of Hendrix, Cox, and new drummer Buddy Miles, and was renamed Band of Gypsys. Their sound was more blues and soul-oriented. Hendrix also received good news in December 1969 when he was cleared of drug possession charges in Toronto.

In 1970, Miles was replaced by Mitch Mitchell, and the group began the "Cry of Love" tour in April. In July Hendrix got to see his family in Seattle for the last time. He went on to Hawaii, to New York for the opening of his Electric Lady recording studio on August 26, then to England for the Isle of Wight Festival on August 30.

The nonstop pace continued with performances in Sweden, Denmark, and in Germany where Hendrix gave his final public performance on September 6. His last press interview was on September 11, and on September 16 Hendrix played his instrument for the last time.

Hendrix was in the apartment of girlfriend Monika Dannemann after dinner and late drinking, where he took some sleeping tablets before going to bed. She could not wake him later and called for an ambulance. Hendrix was rushed to St. Mary Abbotts Hospital, where he went into cardiac arrest and was pronounced dead at 12:45 p.m. on September 18, 1970, at the age of twenty-seven. It was later determined that the unintentional combination of sleeping pills and alcohol caused his death due to choking on his own vomit, putting to rest rumors of suicide.

His body was returned to Seattle for the funeral on October 1, 1970. Dunlap Baptist Church was filled with his family, fellow musicians, and hundreds of fans and news media covering the event. Hendrix was buried in the city's Greenwood Cemetery.

Years of legal battles ensued over his estate, with his father gaining legal ownership in the late 1990s. Hendrix was posthumously inducted into the Rock and Roll Hall of Fame in 1992 and honored with a 1993 Grammy Lifetime Achievement Award as his record sales, influence, and popularity continued undiminished into the twenty-first century among several generations of admirers.

REFERENCES

Books

Floyd, Samuel A. Jr., ed. *International Dictionary of Black Composers*. Vol. 1. Chicago: Fitzroy Dearborn Publishers, 1999.

George-Warren, Holly, and Patricia Romanowski, eds. *The Rolling Stone Encyclopedia of Rock & Roll*. 3rd ed. New York: Rolling Stone Press, 2001.

Glickman, Simon. "Jimi Hendrix." In *Contemporary Black Biography*. Vol. 10. Ed. L. Mpho Mabunda. Detroit: Gale Research, 1996.

Henderson David. *Scuze Me While I Kiss the Sky: The Life of Jimi Hendrix*. Toronto: New York: Bantam Books, 1983.

Piccoli, Sean. *Jimi Hendrix*. Philadelphia: Chelsea House Publishers, 1997.

Southern, Eileen. *Biographical Dictionary of Afro-American and African Musicians*. Westport, Conn.: Greenwood Press, 1982.

Online

Official Jimi Hendrix Web Site. http://www.jimi-hendrix.com (Accessed 2 March 2006).

Fletcher F. Moon

Aaron Henry
1922–1997

Civil rights activist, state government official

Aaron Edd Henry dedicated his life to the uplift of the people in the state of Mississippi and of the nation. Henry's service extends to the NAACP, the Free-

Aaron Henry

dom Riders, and the Mississippi House of Representatives. Protest and personal involvement brought him shoulder to shoulder with the great leaders such as Martin Luther King Jr. and longtime friend Medgar Evers. Although Aaron Henry is not known widely outside Mississippi, his service to his community had a direct impact on all communities that struggled for equality.

Aaron Edd Henry was born on July 2, 1922, in Dublin, Mississippi, on the Flowers Plantation. Sharecropping was a well-established system in the South, and Henry's father was a sharecropper with forty acres to farm. When he was three, Henry's mother died and two years later his father also died. Henry was raised by his mother's brother Ed Henry and his wife Mattie. In his younger years Henry worked on the Flowers plantation and later as a shoeshine boy and a porter. The elder Henry tried his hand at shoe cobbling and was quite successful. In 1927 the family moved to Webb, Mississippi, to set up a cobbler shop. Within a year the family moved again to Clarksville and bought a home. In Clarksville, Henry was not allowed to become a Boy Scout. Because the organizers of the Boy Scout troop taught the boys to march, which was viewed as a means toward protests, the troop was asked to leave. The white community was concerned that the troop might promote actions that they would not condone. Henry came to realize that whites were the authority and they would not risk anyone or any group undermining that authority.

In high school Henry was greatly influenced by his teacher, Thelma K. Shelby. She taught English and economics and was a member of the NAACP. She encouraged Henry and other students to realize their own self worth. Henry wrote in his autobiography that the lesson they learned from Shelby and other teachers was, "You are as good as anybody. You must believe in your personal worth and that you are equal to any other man. Racial superiority is a myth."

Henry completed high school in 1941 and in 1943 was drafted into the army. He was discharged after three years of service, and attended Xavier University in New Orleans on the G. I. Bill. He served as student body president and president of his junior and senior classes. In 1950 with a pharmaceutical degree in hand, Henry returned to Clarksville. He opened up the only black pharmacy in the local community. Henry was successful in his business and became a leading voice in the community. He married Noelle Michael and they had daughter, Rebecca.

Civil Rights Activism and Leadership

In 1954, Henry joined the local chapter of the NAACP. He saw a need to organize and manage the various organizations that were associated with the NAACP. In order to coordinate these activities, inclusive of the Congress of Racial Equality (CORE), the Student Nonviolent Coordinating Committee (SNCC), and the Southern Christian Leadership Conference (SCLS), Henry and others developed a management organization called the Council of Federated Organizations (COFO). The organization, which was started in 1955 but remained dormant until the 1960s, took on the large-scale initiative toward adult education and voter registration. The voter registration project was to have several headquarters in order to support the community while registering persons to vote. Most blacks that tried to register suffered all types of abuse, threats, and violence. Many were arrested on fake charges, beaten, fired from their jobs, threatened, and some were run out of town. COFO played a key part in educating and supporting the black communities in Mississippi.

Henry's commitment as a leader along with his unflinching determination to fight segregation earned him the position of president of the state chapter of the NAACP in 1960. In December 1960 the Supreme Court ordered the integration of all bus stations and terminals serving interstate travelers. When blacks tried to use terminals and front seating in busses they were often thrown off, beaten, or jailed. Henry and COFO supported the Freedom Riders and their efforts to openly challenge and protest such treatment. The Freedom Riders' travels across the South were met with violent attacks. They arrived in Mississippi in May 1961. Henry was among the group arrested at Jackson, Mississippi. Along with Stokely Carmichael (later known as Kwame Toure), Jim Forman and other protestors, he was taken to the Parchman State Penitentiary. Many could have paid the fines and been released, but they chose not to in order to dramatize the racism and segregation and also not give their money to the racist state. By the end of the summer over three hundred protesters had been arrested and were being held at the penitentiary. Henry by his own account had been arrested over thirty-eight times in the struggle for equal rights.

One of Henry's plans for fighting segregation in the local community was a 1961 boycott of businesses in Clarksville, Mississippi, which discriminated against black customers and did not hire blacks. The boycott, which began in 1961, saw the city respond by arresting Henry and six other protestors for conspiring to withhold trade. Although the protesters were convicted, the ruling was overturned on appeal, and the boycott continued. Henry was then arrested for sexually harassing a white female hitchhiker and was convicted in March 1962. The appeals count overturned the conviction, and Henry was exonerated. As the boycott continued, Henry claimed that the local prosecutor and the police chief falsified the sexual harassment charges against him on the basis of his civil rights activities. The prosecutor and the police chief sued Henry and were awarded $80,000, but the verdict was again reversed by an appeals court. The city officials had done all they could to terrorize Henry, including fire bombing his pharmacy and having his wife fired from her teaching position. Henry remained steadfast in his work for equal rights. The boycott continued for three years with decreasing effect because of transportation prob-

lems in trading in other places. The boycott was called with the passing of the 1964 Civil Rights Act.

The year 1963 was a difficult time for the movement and for Henry. Henry's close friend and colleague in the movement, Medgar Evers, was killed at his home in June. Henry had gone to see Evers in Jackson, Mississippi, regarding their testimony to the House Judiciary Committee in Washington D.C. the next day. Henry had a speech to give the next morning in Houston to the Texas Pharmaceutical Association and planned to meet Evers in Washington that afternoon. Evers took Henry to the airport after their meeting. Back at home, Evers was murdered in his driveway. Henry heard the report of Evers's death the next morning as he dressed for his speech. Evers and Henry had been friends since the early 1950s. They had investigated cases of racial violence to obtain affidavits for witnesses. At the time Henry was supporting Evers in his bid as field secretary of the Mississippi NAACP. They both were aware that each day could be their last. Henry lost a friend, and the country lost a courageous fighter for the movement. Henry later learned it was a coin-toss to determine whether Henry or Evers would be the target of the murder. Henry was quoted in his *New York Times* obituary as having said that once Evers was murdered, he made "sure he didn't die in vain."

Although before 1963 there had been some success in getting blacks registered to vote, there was a need to increase efforts. Senators James O. Eastland and John Stennis told Congress that blacks did not vote because they were too lazy and unconcerned about political issues. In response to these erroneous statements, under Henry's guidance COFO orchestrated a mock election for the governor of Mississippi in 1963. The plan was to show the nation that blacks would vote if given the opportunity. The plan was also to stress the important issues that the actual campaign ignored, in deference to an aggressive racist agenda. In the mock campaign, Henry was the candidate for governor and Edwin King, a white Methodist minister from Tougaloo College, a historically black college in Jackson, was the candidate for lieutenant governor. The two men traveled around Mississippi, giving campaign speeches and operating as an official campaign. After the election and the votes were counted, eighty thousand blacks had voted which was nearly three times the official number of black registered voters. As a result of the mock election, the officially elected governor of Mississippi stated that the state would no longer be divided based on race, color, or creed. For black voters this was a start.

Representation and 1964 Democratic Convention

The summer of 1964 was designated as Freedom Summer by COFO. The campaign to register black voters was accelerated with the aid of eight hundred volunteers, which included many white college students. To come one step closer to political access, Henry co-founded and served as chairperson of the Mississippi Freedom Democratic Party (MFDP). This coalition of blacks and whites sought to challenge the exclusion of black voters from the Democratic Party. The MFDP selected sixty-eight delegates to attend the Democratic Convention in Atlantic City, New Jersey. President Lyndon Johnson said the MFDP delegates could not participate, and the attorney general of Mississippi issued an injunction threatening the delegates with jail if they tried to attend. The MFDP candidates, including Henry, attended the convention in spite of the injunction. They requested to be seated at the convention and received support for their request from other delegates. After three days of both sides standing their ground, a compromised was offered. The MFDP delegates were offered at-large status, which did not allow them to vote or represent any state. Henry and the delegation refused this offer. Another compromise was offered which would allow at-large seating only for Henry and King. Unknown to the MFDP delegation, James Farmer, Martin Luther King Jr., Roy Wilkins, and Bayard Rustin reluctantly agreed to the compromise and settled for political expediency. Still not informed of the acceptance, on the first day of the convention the delegates took seats on the floor, causing quite a stir. The next morning Henry and Martin Luther King Jr. tried to persuade the delegation to accept the compromise, but they refused. They felt that blacks always had to compromise. The young black veterans labeled the compromise as back-of-the-bus. They fiercely believed that the MFDP should not place politics over principle. When the delegation went to the convention that afternoon to again take seats again they found that all the chairs had been removed except three. The three remaining seats were for white delegates, and they were surrounded by security. The sixty-eight MFDP delegates stood up throughout the evening.

Elected to the House of Representatives

Henry eventually moved away from the MFDP since their views seemed to become more radical over time. He instead helped to form the Loyalist Democratic Party and chaired the delegation for the 1968 and 1972 Democratic National Conventions. Henry attempted to run for Congress in 1964, but he was accused of not having the required number of signatures to do so. In 1965 in another Freedom Vote mock election, Henry won a U.S. Senate seat. He was actually elected to the national board of directors of the NAACP. Unification of the Democratic Mississippi parties was completed in time for the 1976 Democratic National Convention. Henry was the co-chair with another delegate. In order to allow more blacks to be elected to the Mississippi legislature Henry filed suit in 1980 for redistricting. This change resulted in blacks being elected, including Henry's election to the Mississippi House of Representatives. Henry held the position from 1982 to 1996.

Although Henry's name and accomplishments are more well-known in Mississippi, his work for integration and equality for blacks was felt around the nation. He operated from grass roots to administrator, and from marching to planning in the fight against segregation and for equal rights. He directed much of his efforts to Coahoma County, but his relationships with national civil rights leaders and his fierce dedication had long-range impact. He maintained his position as president of the Mississippi NAACP until 1994 when his wife Nicolle died. Henry died in 1997 of heart failure in Clarksville, Mississippi.

REFERENCES

Books

Escamilla, Brian. "Aaron Henry." *Contemporary Black Biography*. Ed. Shirelle Phelps. Vol. 9. Farmington Hills, Mich.: Gale Group, 1999, 103-06.

Lowery, Charles D., and John F. Marszalek. *Encyclopedia of African-American Civil Rights*. New York: Greenwood Press, 1992.

Nossiter, Adam. *Of Long Memory: Mississippi and the Murder of Medgar Evers*. Reading, Mass.: Addison-Wesley Publishing Company, 1994.

Walter, Mildred Pitts. *Mississippi Challenge*. New York: Bradbury Press, 1992.

Williams, Juan. *Eyes on the Prize: America's Civil Rights Years, 1954-1965*. New York: A. Robert Lovelle Book, Viking Press, 1987.

Periodicals

Dittmer, John. "Dr. Aaron Henry: Mississippi freedom fighter." *Crisis* 104 (July 1997): 25.

Thomas, Robert M. "Aaron Henry, Civil Rights Leader Dies at 74." *New York Times*, 21 May 1997.

Collections

Information on Aaron Henry may be found in the Mississippi Civil Rights College, Tougaloo College, Tougaloo, Mississippi.

Lean'tin L. Bracks

Josiah Henson
1789–1883

Abolitionist, minister, writer

During the period of slavery in the United States and afterward in the ongoing struggle for equality and opportunity for people of African descent, Josiah Henson

Josiah Henson

Chronology

1789	Born a slave in Port Tobacco in Charles County, Maryland on June 15
1807	First exposure to Christianity and the abolitionist movement
1811	Marries Charlotte, a slave
1828	Becomes a preacher in the Methodist Episcopal Church
1830	Escapes slavery with wife and four children and settles in Dresden, Canada; becomes involved in the Underground Railroad and the abolitionist movement
1837-38	Serves as captain of Afro-Caribbean troop in the Canadian Rebellions
1842	Founds a settlement and begins the British American Institute as a refuge for escaped slaves
1849	Publishes the first of three editions of his autobiography *The Life of Josiah Henson, Formerly a Slave, Now an Inhabitant of Canada, as Narrated by Himself*, makes first of three journeys to England
1850	Meets Harriett Beecher Stowe who has read his autobiography
1852	Wife Charlotte dies
1856	Marries Nancy Gambles
1883	Dies in Dresden, Ontario, Canada on May 5

was a man who lived his conviction of being honest in both word and deed. Even while a slave and enduring violence, when given the choice of defiling his word or gaining freedom, Henson kept his word. When Harriet Beecher Stowe read *The Life of Josiah Henson, Formerly a Slave, Now an Inhabitant of Canada, as Narrated by Himself* (1849), she was determined to meet Henson. They met in 1851 and Henson's life became the basis for the character Uncle Tom in her 1852 novel *Uncle Tom's Cabin*. After escaping from slavery and finding freedom in Canada, Henson learned to read and write and became a religious and community leader both there and in the United States. He traveled throughout the United States, Canada, and England, preaching and speaking for the abolition of slavery. He became a conductor of the Underground Railroad and had an audience with Queen Victoria. In all, Henson was a man of integrity and determination whose life far exceeded the limits that society had placed on him.

Josiah Henson was born into slavery on June 15, 1789, in Port Tobacco, Charles County, Maryland. He was given the Christian name of his master Dr. Josiah McPherson and the surname of his master's uncle. During his life as a slave Henson witnessed beatings and other abuses to his family and to others. In his 1849 autobiography Henson describes the beating his father received for striking a white man who was trying to rape his mother. As his father endured the sentence of one hundred lashes, "a feeble groan was the only response to the final blows. His head was then thrust against the post, and his right ear fastened to it with a tack; a swift pass of a knife, and the bleeding member was left sticking to the place." Henson's father was never the same after this and was later sent to Alabama away from his family; neither Henson nor his mother ever knew what happened to him. Later, when Henson was five years old, his master died. Henson's brother and sisters were sold off one by one as property in an estate sale. When Henson's mother was sold to Isaac Riley of Montgomery County, Maryland, she begged that he purchase Josiah, her baby and last remaining child. She was brutally rebuked by Riley, her new owner. Henson was sold to Adam Robb, a tavern keeper in Rockville, Maryland. Robb later sold Henson to Riley in exchange for a horse-shoeing job.

Henson was tall, strong, and quick minded. Riley took full advantage of Henson's abilities by moving him from plow and horse boy to overseer to market man. Since Henson could not read or write, his having the responsibility of market man, which was most often delegated to white men, proves that Riley recognized his intelligence. This job required Henson not only to bargain for the best price for his master's produce but to bring the money back to his master. Henson's obedience and moral high ground had been proven to his master. On one occasion he came to the aid of his master in a fight when a man named Bryce Litton got the better of him. Litton retaliated against Riley by ordering his house slaves to ambush and beat Henson. They broke Henson's shoulder blade by hitting him with an oak fence post. It took five months for Henson to heal, and he could no longer raise his hand above his head. Although Henson had not been raised in a religious environment, he found an immediate connection with Christianity and began to embrace its teachings in 1807. Around the same time, Riley allowed Henson to attend a sermon by an anti-slavery preacher, and he was exposed to the abolitionist movement. These experiences gave greater meaning to Henson's life. Henson married Charlotte, a slave, in 1811. In 1825, Riley went bankrupt and had to sell his farm. Henson and twenty-two other slaves were to be transferred to Riley's brother, Amos, in Davies County, Kentucky. Riley made Henson give his word that he would deliver himself and the other slaves to Kentucky. The trip took them through Ohio, a free state, but Henson kept his word and all were delivered.

In 1828, Henson became a preacher for the Methodist Episcopal Church and was able to earn money while in Kentucky. He was able to save $350 toward his freedom. His master Amos Riley took the money but reneged on the agreed amount of $400. Riley raised the price to $1,000 and then decided to sell Henson to a new planter in New Orleans. Henson accompanied his master's son to New Orleans while he transacted some business, which included the final transaction of the sale of Henson. When the master's son got seriously ill, rendering him weak and helpless, he begged Henson to take him home safely to his father. Henson could have left his master's son and made a run for his freedom, but he instead brought him safely home to his father. Henson's act of kindness was met with no reward or appreciation. Henson was so outraged by this experience along with his growing desire for freedom, he decided to escape along with his family to Canada.

In the summer of 1830 Henson, his wife, and their four children fled Kentucky. They endured sickness, wolves, starvation, and the ever-present fear of being captured, punished, and returned to slavery. A tribe of Native Americans and the Underground Railroad helped Henson and his family. After traveling through Cincinnati, Buffalo, and New York, they crossed the U.S. border into Canada on October 28, 1830. Henson and his family settled in Dresden, Ontario, near Lake St. Clair and south of the Sydenham River. For four years Henson worked as a farm laborer and preacher in the area. To better himself he had his oldest son teach him how to read and write. Only a short time passed before Henson got involved in the Underground Railroad. As a conductor he made several trips south and led over two hundred slaves to Canada to freedom. During the Canadian Rebellion of 1837-38, Henson served as a captain in a troop of Afro-Caribbean volunteers.

In 1834, Henson and a dozen of his associates rented government land in Colchester, and with the help of sponsors from the United States and England, Henson began plans for an Afro-Canadian community and indus-trial school. Henson's plans for an exclusive black settlement was aided by Hiram Wilson, the missionary sent by the American Anti-Slavery Society, and James Cannings Fuller, a Quaker philanthropist of Skaneateles, New York. Henson formally organized the Afro-Canadian community in 1842 when he, Wilson, and another partner purchased two hundred acres in Dawn Township, Upper Canada. The land that was purchased in Chatham, Ontario, was a place in which escaped slaves were taught various skills such as how to clear land for farms and how to support themselves and their families. The institute did not exclude whites or Indians. Also in 1842, Henson bought two hundred acres of adjoining land and moved his family to this site.

In 1849, Henson published his autobiography, *The Life of Josiah Henson, Formerly a Slave, Now an Inhabitant of Canada, as Narrated by Himself*. It was reprinted in 1858 and renamed *Truth Stranger than Fiction: Father Henson's Story of His Own Life*, and published in 1879 as *Truth Is Stranger Than Fiction; An Autobiography of the Rev. Josiah Henson*. The last two editions had forwards by Harriet Beecher Stowe. Stowe read Henson's 1849 autobiography and was interesting in talking with him. The opportunity came in 1850 after Stowe had moved to Maine. Henson was passing through on an anti-slavery tour and met her. Stowe was so interested in Henson's story and his life that she wanted to know of other peculiarities regarding slaveholders. Henson shared more experiences. Stowe's book *Uncle Tom's Cabin* published in 1852 was met with claims of misrepresentation and anger from the South. In response to this Stowe wrote *A Key to Uncle Tom's Cabin*. This book referred to the actual slaves who were the basis for her characters and events in the book. The most benevolent of her characters was Uncle Tom whom Stowe states in her book was based on Josiah Henson. For a few years Henson made lecture tours as the "real Uncle Tom."

As an active abolitionist, Henson traveled through New England, Canada, and England, preaching against the evils of slavery and sharing his life story. In England in 1849 and 1851, he met the archbishop of Canterbury, was honored at a private party by Prime Minister Lord Jim Russell, and was invited by Lord Gray to travel to India. Henson's first wife died in 1852, and he married a Boston widow, Nancy Gambles, in 1856. On Henson's last visit to England in 1876 he visited the World's Fair and became the first ex-slave to have an audience with Queen Victoria. The queen gave Henson a personal gift of her photograph in a gold frame.

Henson died on May 5, 1883, in Dresden, Ontario. His contribution to the cause of freedom and equality touches both the United States and Canada. The state of Maryland named an underdeveloped state park site in Montgomery County after Henson in 1991. Henson became the first black person to be featured on a Canadian stamp and honored by the government in 1999 with a plaque designating Henson as a Canadian of National Historical Significance.

REFERENCES

Books

Stowe, Harriet Beecher. *A Key to Uncle Tom's Cabin.* Boston: John P. Jewett & Co., 1853, pp. 19, 26-27.

Vicary, Elizabeth Zoe. "Henson, Josiah." In *American National Biography.* Vol. 10. Eds. John A Garraty and Mark C. Carnes. New York: Oxford University Press, 1999, pp. 621-22.

Periodicals

Richman, Michael. "Uncle Tom's Montgomery Cabin," *Washington Post*, 10 December 1997.

Online

The African American Registry. "Josiah Henson, a true abolitionist." www.aaregistry.com/african_american_history/954/Josiah_Henson_a_true_abolotionist (Accessed 12 March 2006).

The National Archives Learning Curve. "Josiah Henson." www.spartacus.schoolnet.co.uk/USAShenson.htm (Accessed 12 March 2006).

Richman, Michael. *Uncle Tom's Montgomery Cabin.* www.innercity.org/columbiaheights/newspaper/cabin.html (Accessed 12 March 2006).

Lean'tin L. Bracks

Angelo Herndon
1913–1997

Labor activist, editor

Angelo Herndon moved from menial laborer to radical labor activist, which resulted in his becoming a Communist in the 1930s who sought to organize black and white workers in the South during the era of segregation. He was tried, convicted, and imprisoned in Georgia because of his activities, and his case became the focus of international attention. Herndon endured mistreatment while incarcerated and eventually regained his freedom and continued his activism through writing, speaking, organizing, and other pursuits.

Eugene Angelo Braxton Herndon was born on May 6, 1913, in Wyoming, Ohio, a suburb of Cincinnati, to Paul and Hattie Herndon, who had come north from Birmingham, Alabama. His father was a coal miner who died

Angelo Herndon

from miner's pneumonia when Eugene was very young, leaving his mother to raise a large family, including seven sons and two daughters. She began doing housework for wealthy white families; the older boys sought work in mines, steel mills, and other industries; and the younger children helped out by doing a variety of odd jobs, all in efforts to support the family.

It was hoped that Angelo would be the one to leave the working class for better opportunities through education, but the family was unable to save money to assist him. In 1926 when he was thirteen Angelo left home with his brother Leo for Lexington, Kentucky to work at a mine owned by the DeBardeleben Coal Corporation. Here Herndon experienced the Jim Crow system firsthand, as well as dangerous working conditions, very low pay, high prices for food and necessities at the company-owned store, and squalid living conditions.

Begins Activism in Birmingham

When the company cut the pay of its workers due to large overhead expenses, Herndon and his brother quit the Kentucky mine and headed south to Birmingham. With relatives in the area as well as mining sites, Herndon was able to survive until he was hired by the Tennessee Coal and Iron (TCI) Company. He did surface work at the company's Docena mine, cutting the right of way for wiring and transformation lines.

Chronology

1913	Born in Wyoming, Ohio on May 6
1926	Leaves home with brother to work in Lexington, Kentucky coal mine
1930	Becomes labor activist and Communist after moving to Birmingham, Alabama
1932	Organizes multiracial protest in Atlanta, Georgia; is arrested and jailed
1933	Tried and convicted of inciting insurrection; returns to prison
1934	Released on bail after case becomes international cause for activists
1937	Publishes autobiography; conviction is overturned by U.S. Supreme Court
1938	Marries Joyce M. Chellis
1942	Edits *Negro Quarterly* publication with writer Ralph Ellison in New York City
1950	Lives quietly in Chicago after leaving Communist Party and other activism
1997	Dies in obscurity on December 9

After an accident which resulted in the death of a fellow worker, Herndon surprised the management by speaking up about a foreman's negligence and other safety issues. The other men supported Herndon's account of the incident, and the widow received some compensation from TCI. Herndon then realized that organizing workers would help to improve their pay, working, and living conditions, and the present system was designed to divide as well as exploit employees for the benefit of owners and management.

When the Great Depression hit the United States in late 1929 after the stock market crash in October of that year, unemployment rose sharply and those fortunate enough to still have jobs endured continued problems with many employers. In June 1930 Herndon attended a meeting of the local Unemployment Council, where he heard Communist Party (CP) members speak about black and whites working together and being treated as equals.

This idea appealed to Herndon. Shortly afterwards he joined both organizations, became a recruiter for the National Miners Union, and was elected a delegate to the National Unemployment Convention being held the same year in Chicago. Once Herndon began to associate with the Communists, however, his relatives asked him to move out and not return, fearing for their safety. Their concerns were justified, as the Ku Klux Klan left a message for Herndon on the same day he went to the convention.

Continues to Organize Workers

In June 1932, Herndon and other members of the Unemployment Council organized black and white workers in Atlanta, Georgia to petition the city, county, and state governments for relief after 23,000 families

were dropped from the welfare rolls, action that could have led to widespread hunger and starvation. A large number of persons from both racial groups came to the Fulton County court house on July 7 to demonstrate their concerns to the county commissioners and other authorities, with white workers being allowed in, while blacks were kept outside.

The attempt to use Jim Crow to divide the protestors was unsuccessful, as the commissioners only made excuses and told the white workers that no money was available, leaving them in the same position as the black workers. On the next day $6,000 suddenly appeared to fund unemployment relief for workers regardless of race.

The success of the peaceful demonstration made Herndon a marked man at age nineteen. On the following Monday (July 11, 1932) he was arrested by detectives when he went to get mail from the post office, and he was held in custody for eleven days without any formal charge placed against him. Herndon refused to talk despite attempts to intimidate him, and he smuggled a letter out by another prisoner to the International Labor Defense (ILD), the legal arm of the CP, requesting assistance and legal representation.

When a judge threatened to release Herndon, the county's assistant solicitor, John Hudson, charged him under 1804 and 1861 laws used to prosecute slaves for "inciting to insurrection," which included a death sentence, and cited him for possession of Communist literature. As a result, he was indicted by an all-white grand jury and held for nearly six more months in the Fulton County Tower prison. While there he was forced to stay in a cell with a dead body, was given spoiled food to eat, became sick himself, and was denied medical treatment.

Becomes Known Internationally During Trial

On Christmas Eve, 1932, Herndon was finally released from custody, with his trial date set for January 16, 1933. The ILD had to come up with $25,000 for bail, a tremendous increase from the original amount of $3,000. In the meantime, news of Herndon and his case spread from Georgia to national and international levels.

The courage of the young Herndon galvanized progressive and radical intellectuals, leaders, and activists in the black and white communities, and inspired persons from many different backgrounds to speak out, write, and provide financial support. The progressive rhetoric and action of the CP and the ILD in support of Herndon increased their visibility and credibility, yet also increased others' resolve to oppose their activities. The NAACP and other civil rights organizations were concerned about the CP use of blacks to publicize and advance its agenda, as well as the possible loss of their own members, while white and black conservatives, such as *Pittsburgh Courier* columnist George S. Schuyler, commented that Herndon was a pawn for CP anti-Americanism.

African American literary figures such as Jean Toomer and Langston Hughes came out in support of Herndon, with Hughes later writing a political play in 1936, *Angelo Herndon Jones*, which dramatized his case. Richard Wright and Ralph Ellison reflected the influence of Herndon in some of their best-known writings, and Ellison worked directly with Herndon in founding and editing the short-lived but influential publication, *Negro Quarterly*, from 1942-43. Hughes and Wright were among the writers who contributed work to the journal, and Herndon published his own essay, "Frederick Douglass: Negro Leadership and War" in its pages.

Noted historians John Henrik Clarke, C. Vann Woodward, and Herbert Aptheker have cited the personal impact of the Herndon case on their lives and careers. Aptheker became a member of the Communist Party in part due to his relationship with Herndon and later collaborated with Herndon and Richard B. Moore in establishing the Negro Publication Society. Jewish American poet Aaron Kramer wrote "To Angelo Herndon," which was published in 1934, and radical activist women such as Lucy Parsons and Claudia Jones were vocal supporters of the "Free Angelo Herndon" movement.

The defense attorneys hired by the ILD to represent Herndon were local lawyers Benjamin J. Davis Jr. and John H. Geer, the first time that blacks were lead attorneys on a major civil rights case in the South. The trial became a platform for addressing injustice on a larger scale, as well as the defense of the specific person involved in the proceedings. Herndon himself eloquently addressed the jury during the trial, indicating that the larger problems of discrimination, unemployment, and worker rights would not be solved with his conviction or death.

Herndon was convicted by the jury hearing his case, but they recommended that mercy be shown and sentenced him to prison for a period from eighteen to twenty years. The international attention and media coverage of his case made Herndon into a cause celebre, even as he began serving his sentence and continued the appeals process.

Herndon remained behind bars in Atlanta until August 1934, when he was released on bail due to the efforts of the ILD. He then went on several national speaking tours and participated in numerous rallies in support of his case, and eventually he settled in New York City.

In 1935 Herndon told his story in an autobiographical booklet, "You Cannot Kill the Working Class," which was published by the ILD. Later that year Herndon was employed by the *Amsterdam News*, a Harlem-based black newspaper, but this did not prevent him from continuing to organize workers and participating in a strike against the paper when its ownership resisted efforts by the workers to join the Newspaper Guild. Herndon continued his labor activities the following year as a vice president on the national executive board of the Workers Alliance of America, and he was also involved with the National Negro Congress, chaired by African American labor activist A. Philip Randolph.

Herndon published a full-length autobiography, *Let Me Live*, in 1937 with assistance from a ghostwriter, and in April of that year the U.S. Supreme Court overturned his conviction by a 5-4 vote. He decided to remain in New York, where he stayed active for a time with the CP and wrote articles for their publication, the *Daily Worker*. Herndon married the former Joyce M. Chellis, an Alabama native, in 1938, and began to make additional changes in his lifestyle.

Leaves Communists and Activism for Quiet Life in Chicago

By the mid-1940s Herndon had become disillusioned with the CP; he left both the party and New York for a very private existence in Chicago. He shared details from his radical past with only a few close friends and consistently declined public appearances and interview requests.

Angelo Herndon died on December 9, 1997. His notorious life as a young man stood in sharp contrast to his obscurity in middle and later years, but he made an important contribution to the African American community with his courage and great personal sacrifice. The Chicago-based playwright OyamO staged a production based on Herndon's life, *Let Me Live*, in 1991 and 1998, demonstrating that Herndon's life and activism continued to have significance.

REFERENCES

Books

Broderick, Francis L., and August Meier, eds. *Negro Protest Thought in the Twentieth Century.* Indianapolis, Ind.: Bobbs-Merrill Company, 1965.

Marable, Manning, and Leith Mullings, eds. *Let Nobody Turn Us Around: Voices of Resistance, Reform, and Renewal.* Lanham, Md.: Rowman and Littlefield Publishers, 2000.

Martin, Charles H. "Angelo Herndon." In *African American Lives.* Eds. Henry Louis Gates Jr. and Evelyn Brooks Higginbotham. New York: Oxford University Press, 2004.

———. *The Angelo Herndon Case and Southern Justice.* Baton Rouge, La.: Louisiana State University Press, 1976.

Periodicals

Griffiths, Frederick T. "Ralph Ellison, Richard Wright, and the Case of Angelo Herndon." *African American Review* 35 (Winter 2001): 615-36.

Herndon, Angelo. "Frederick Douglass: Negro Leadership in War." *Negro Quarterly* 1 (Winter/Spring 1943): 303-29.

Martin, Charles H. "Communists and Blacks: The ILD and the Angelo Herndon Case." *Journal of Negro History* 64 (Spring 1979): 131-41.

Online

D'Amato, Paul. "The Communist Party and Black Liberation in the 1930s." *International Socialist Review* Summer 1997. http://isreview.org/issues/01/cp_blacks_1930s.shtml (Accessed 12 December 2005).

Collections

Microfilm of International Labor Defense organization records from 1925-1946, including materials on Angelo Herndon, are housed in the Kheel Center for Labor-Management Documentation and Archives, Martha P. Catherwood Library of the School of Industrial and Labor Relations, Cornell University, Ithaca, New York.

Fletcher F. Moon

Dennis Fowler Hightower
1941–

Business executive, educator

Dennis Fowler Hightower ascended to one of the highest echelons in the U.S. entertainment industry when he was named the president of Walt Disney's Television and Telecommunications unit in 1995. By climbing the corporate ladder and strategically changing jobs in order to advance his career, Hightower built a solid portfolio of innovative achievements in global marketing, planning, and management which brought remarkable results. Upon retirement from corporate work, Hightower parlayed his decades of leadership skills, global management knowledge, and business acumen into an academic career at the Harvard University Graduate School of Business. As a professor, he invested his energy in training another generation of African American entrepreneurs and corporate executives.

A native of Washington, D.C., Hightower was born to Virginia Fowler Hightower and Marvin William Hightower on October 28, 1941. He spent most of his formative years in the LeDroit Park area of the District of Columbia and graduated from McKinley High School in 1957. At the age of sixteen, Hightower entered nearby Howard University, a historically black university. He completed his studies and graduated with a B.S. in 1962. He was commissioned into the U. S. Army as a second lieutenant on June 15, 1962, through the Howard Univer-

Chronology

1941	Born in Washington, D.C. on October 28
1957	Graduates from McKinley High School
1962	Graduates with B.S. from Howard University; commissioned into the United States Army
1962-69	Trains and serves with Army Intelligence Units; serves in Vietnam
1970	Separates from army with rank of major; accepts position with Xerox Corporation
1972	Leaves Xerox to attend Harvard University Graduate School of Business
1974	Graduates with M.B.A. from Harvard; takes position with McKinsey and Company
1978-81	Holds vice-president positions at General Electric
1982	Takes over as vice-president of corporate planning at Mattel, Inc.
1984-87	Holds executive positions at Richard Reynolds Associates, Inc.
1987-94	Holds vice president and president positions for Walt Disney Company in Europe
1995	Named president of the Walt Disney Company's Television and Telecommunications
1996	Retires from Disney; joins faculty of Harvard University Graduate School of Business
2000-02	Becomes CEO of European Online Networks
2003	Retires; becomes lecturer; serves as member on various boards of directors

sity ROTC program, in which he was cited as a "Distinguished Military Graduate."

Hightower served as an officer in the United States Army for eight years. From 1962 to 1965, he was an infantry platoon leader and company commander, and he also served as an assistant S-3 at the battalion level. During six months of 1965, Hightower attended the Army's military intelligence school at Fort Hollabird, Maryland. He was briefly assigned to the 502nd Military Intelligence Battalion of the Eighth Army for a few months in the winter of 1965-1966, but resumed training at the army's intelligence school at Fort Hollabird from September 1966 through May 1967.

The following year, Hightower went to the United States Defense Department and served in the Soviet Office. From 1968 through 1969, he was assigned to the 199th Infantry Brigade, and then he was stationed with the 179th Military Intelligence Detachment (MID). When he left the army in 1970, Hightower was twenty-seven years old, held the rank of major, and had served in Vietnam. An army ranger and parachutist, he also earned a Purple Heart, the Vietnam Honor Medal First Class, five army commendation medals with "V", three air medals, and two bronze stars.

After Hightower left the military, he accepted a managerial position with the Xerox Corporation's Research and Engineering Group. He was awarded a fellowship and left Xerox after two years to attend the Harvard University Graduate School of Business. Hightower earned his M.B.A. from Harvard in 1974 and was immediately hired by McKinsey and Company, Inc. as a senior associate and engagement manager.

Seizing an opportunity for advancement, Hightower went to work for the General Electric Lighting Business Group in 1978 as manager of operations and planning, and was subsequently promoted to vice-president and general manager of General Electric's subsidiary in Mexico. When he left General Electric in 1981, Hightower became vice-president of Corporate Planning at Mattel, Inc. Three years later, he was hired by Richard Reynolds Associates, Inc, a consulting firm, where he held the positions of executive director from 1984 to 1986 and managing director of the company's Los Angeles office from 1986 to 1987.

The Disney Years

In 1987, Hightower made his smartest career move when he accepted the highly coveted position of vice-president of consumer products at the Walt Disney Company division for European, African, and Middle Eastern markets. Hightower and his family moved to Paris, France, where he was promoted to executive vice-president of consumer products in 1989 and then promoted to president of the Walt Disney Company's European Unit in 1992.

As president of Walt Disney in Europe, Hightower was responsible for increasing the sales of Disney consumer products such as book and magazine publications, character merchandise (also known as Disneyana), licensing, software, and children's recorded music and sheet music. He was also charged with sales campaigns to promote Disney films, such as *The Lion King*, and gaining television sponsorship. During his tenure as president of Walt Disney's European operations, he expanded the company's 120 magazines and comics, which were published in sixteen languages, to 180 periodicals published in twenty-eight languages in thirty-two countries. Hightower proved that he was the right man for the job by increasing his unit's sales from $650 million to $4.5 billion. He remained at the helm of Disney Europe from 1987 to 1995, widely viewed as running a highly successful operation.

However, in the mid-1990s, the Walt Disney Company, under the leadership of its chief executive officer, Michael Eisner, started to undergo major staff changes at its executive levels. After a fatal helicopter accident took the life of Frank Wells, Disney's president in early 1994, his successor, Jeffrey Katzenberg, resigned in August 1994 to form a new entertainment company named Dreamworks with Steven Spielberg and David Geffen. Katzenberg's departure was rapidly followed by other Disney executives, prompting widespread speculation among entertainment industry analysts and insiders about Disney's future and its stability.

According to an article in *Black Enterprise*, Michael Eisner telephoned the fifty-four-year-old Hightower at his Paris residence at midnight on March 8, 1995 and offered him the position of president of Walt Disney Television and Communications. Hightower accepted the promotion and in so doing assumed responsibility for all facets of Disney's television projects, including network, animation, the Disney Channel, syndicated programs, pay-per-view television, international home video, and interactive media. Disney Television and Telecommunication formed roughly one fourth of the media conglomerate's $12 billion profits in 1994, and industry analysts were predicting that it was positioned for even more revenue growth.

Hightower's main tasks were to broaden international production and marketing for all Disney televised products and services. He launched the Disney Channel in Taiwan, the first of its kind beyond the United States coastline, and followed up on his success with Disney Channels in Great Britain and Germany. Hightower also entered into a multi-million dollar cooperative enterprise with telecommunications giants Ameritech, Southwestern Bell, Bell South Corporation, and GTE Corporation. The deal was designed to allow telephones to deliver television programming.

Retirement and Academic Career

Hightower stayed at the helm of Disney's Television and Telecommunications unit for one year before resigning in the wake of his company's merger with another entertainment company, Capital Cities. Hightower announced his intention of teaching at Harvard University's Graduate School of Business and Howard University, both of his alma maters. The transition to university teaching took place in 1996, when Hightower joined Harvard's faculty as professor of management and senior lecturer. He taught aspiring entrepreneurs for four years and then, in 2000, briefly returned to corporate life as the chief executive officer of Europe Online Networks, a satellite based broadband internet company, located in Luxemburg.

Since 2003, Hightower has capitalized on his thirty years of business leadership by accepting speaking engagements and serving on boards. A limited partner in Washington Baseball Club, he serves on the board of directors of Brite Smile, Inc., the Gillette Company, Pan Am Sat Corporation, Domino's, Inc., Accenture, Ltd., Northwest, and TJX. He is a trustee of Howard University and chairman of the board of the Andrew Young Center for International Affairs at Morehouse College.

Over the course of his stellar business career, Hightower has received many awards, including the Alumni Achievement Award from Howard University (1984) and the Harvard Business School Alumni Achievement Award (1992). *Black Enterprise* selected him to be one of the Top 25 Black Managers in Corporate America in 1988. He is married to the former Denia Stukes, and the couple has two children.

African American achievements in U.S. corporations are in the early 2000s more and more noticeable. While many mega corporations, such as American Express, Sears Retail, Young & Rubicam Brands, and the Merrill Lynch Company, have hired African American chief executives, when Dennis Hightower became president of Walt Disney Television and Telecommunications in the 1995, it was a rarity. His achievements in business and at Harvard not only demonstrate intelligence, ambition, and determination, but also a desire to make a difference for African Americans in the corporate setting and signal that blacks should consider the advantages in international opportunities for advancement.

REFERENCES

Periodicals

"Dennis Hightower Picked to Head Disney TV, Telecommunications." *Los Angeles Sentinel*, 5 July 1995.

"Disney Names New TV Unit President." *Michigan Chronicle*, 14 June 1995.

Milloy, Courtland. "Rising above Racism." *Washington Post*, 29 October 1995.

Scott, Matthew S. "Wonderful World at Disney." *Black Enterprise*, December 1995.

Smith, Eric L. "A 'Magical' Ride Comes to an End." *Black Enterprise*, July 1996.

Online

Dennis F. Hightower: Former Executive Officer Europe Online Networks S.A. http://www.accenture.com (Accessed 13 March 2005).

Dennis F. Hightower: Limited Partner. http://baseballindc.com/about_us/bios/dennis_f_hightower.asp (Accessed 13 March 2005).

Dennis Hightower. http://www.podiumprose.com/topics/hightower.html.(Accessed 13 March 2005).

Department of Army. U.S. Army Center of Military History. The Separate Brigade S-2 In Vietnam: VNIT-398. http://www.army.mil/cmh-pg/documents/vietnam/vnit/vnit398.htm (Accessed 6 December 2005).

Domino's Welcomes Dennis Hightower, Robert Ruggieo to Board of Directors. http://domino.com (Accessed 13 March 2005).

Glenda M. Alvin

Peter Hill
1767–1820

Clockmaker

Peter Hill was the first known African American clockmaker in America, and the only one of his race to have worked in this trade in the late eighteenth and early nineteenth centuries. While there were other black entrepreneurs of that period, they were barbers, restaurateurs, caterers, merchants, and tailors, but not clockmakers. Although he was not an inventor, Hill was certainly a pioneer.

Quaker clockmaker Joseph Hollinshead Jr., of Burlington Township, New Jersey, held slaves in the seventeenth century. Presumably, Peter Hill was born to slave parents that Hollinshead owned. Hill was born on July 19, 1767 and lived his boyhood and youth in Hollinshead's home. His master followed the custom of local Quakers, who firmly believed in teaching their slaves certain skills to enable them to enhance their lives. Since Hollinshead was a clockmaker, he taught that skill to young Peter Hill. Thus, from age fourteen until he was twenty-one, Hill served some form of apprenticeship with his master and provided assistance in his clock-making shop. Then he was paid for his work in service as a shop assistant or journeyman in clock-making. Eventually, Hill saved enough money to buy his freedom. Hollinshead manumitted Hill, his mulatto slave, in 1794, when Hill was twenty-seven years old. Following local laws, a committee comprised of two overseers and two justices of the peace were required to examine the slave before he was liberated. Thus, the committee considered Hill and declared him fit to live as a free man. As noted in *Dictionary of American Negro Biography*, the committee certified in a document dated May 1, 1795, that Hill appeared to be of sound mind and "not under any bodily incapacity of obtaining a support and also . . . not under twenty-one years of age nor above thirty five."

Hill married on September 9, 1795, four months after his manumission took effect. Thomas Adams, who had served on his manumission board, performed the marriage ceremony between Hill and Tina Lewis, describing Lewis in the official records as a spinster from Burlington Township. Peter Hill purchased Tina Lewis's freedom as well. She had been linked to the Society of Friends of Burlington. Again, the Friends were strong advocates of free schooling for blacks; accordingly, they saw that Lewis received some education, and she made considerable progress in a short time.

Sometime before Hill's manumission process began in 1794, he opened his first shop. The date and location of his businesses are unknown. Records confuse the different locations in which Hill maintained a shop; however, he lived and worked out of his home in Burlington for a while. In this shop on the east side of High Street and below Broad Street, he was almost opposite the Friends' Meeting House. George Deacon operated a cabinetmaking shop nearby and built many of the cases for Hill's clocks. Some sources claim that Hill maintained his Burlington business for twenty-three years.

Between 1795, when Burlington tax records show Hill with a tax levy, and 1808, Hill's estate increased in value. He owned one head of cattle in 1796 and on March 3, 1801, he bought a two-and-one-half-acre lot and later that year he bought a horse. He acquired other properties at various times, each time increasing the value of his estate. By 1814, the Hills sold some of their property, but on February 20, 1820 they had bought a new brick house and several buildings in Mount Holly, a village some seven miles from Burlington in Northampton Township.

Hill continued to develop his clock-making business. Although he kept his Burlington property, sometime after 1814 he also opened a business on Main Street in nearby Mount Holly. Quakers had settled Mount Holly earlier, as they emigrated from England. They developed the area as a farming community with iron works and a paper mill. Apparently the community could support a clock-making business, for it served others who flocked there from Philadelphia after a yellow fever epidemic. Those who came included French refugees. Hill continued his clock and watch-making business and was listed in local records by 1820. His business appeared to thrive, but he was deeply in debt by the time he died in December 1820. To settle the sizeable debt that he owed, Hill's properties, including his personal estate, were sold. Tina Hill may have died shortly thereafter. Hill was buried in the Society of Friends' Burial Ground in Burlington, adjacent to the residence and shop that he maintained there earlier.

Five clocks made by this early black clockmaker are extant. They contain eight-day striking movements. One of Hill's creations—a tall case clock—may be found in the Smithsonian Institution's National Museum of History and Technology, located in Washington, DC. This item documents his skill in a craft that was extremely rare

for an African American during this early colonial period in the United States.

REFERENCES

Books

Bedini, Silvio A. "Peter Hill." *Dictionary of American Negro Biography.* Eds. Rayford W. Logan and Michael R. Winston. New York: Norton, 1982.

Hine, Darlene Clark, and Earnestine Jenkins, eds. *A Question of Manhood.* Vol. 1. *"Manhood Rights": The Construction of Black Male History and Manhood, 1750-1870.* Bloomington: Indiana University Press, 1999.

Jessie Carney Smith

Gregory Hines
1946–2003

Dancer, actor, singer

Gregory Hines, an actor and veteran performer, is considered the greatest tap dancer of his time. He began dancing at three years of age, and his style and presentation were perfected over the years. Hines took his craft as an accomplished dancer to the stage and screen and brought renewed attention to tap. His warm eyes, easy charm, and comedic style earned him many awards for his performances, and his contribution to the development of tap dancing both preserved this art form for the next generation and took it to greater heights.

Hines was born in New York City, New York on February 14, 1946. He was the second son born to Alma Iola and Maurice Robert Hines. The family lived in Washington Heights, an integrated neighborhood on Manhattan's Upper West Side, near Harlem. Hines's father was a club bouncer at night and sold soda during the day. His mother had great hopes for Gregory and his older brother Maurice and encouraged them to learn tap dancing. She signed Maurice up for tap dance lessons when he was just four and a half. Gregory, who was just over two, and his mother attended Maurice's first lesson. Wanting to participate in the lessons, the toddler Gregory cried until he was allowed to join his brother. With one hand holding his brother's hand, and the other with his thumb in his mouth, Gregory followed along by mimicking his brother's movements. He was too young to take lessons, but he already showed a talent for tap dancing. Gregory was eventually enrolled in lessons. Both he and his brother took lessons from the famed Broadway choreog-

Gregory Hines

rapher Henry LeTang, considered the greatest tap-dancing teacher in the world.

Young Hines and his brother became professionals at the ages of five and eight. They used the stage name "The Hines Kids," developed a song-and-dance act, and toured in nightclubs around the United States and abroad. They regularly performed jazz tap at the renowned Harlem's Apollo Theater in New York. As regular performers they also had the opportunity to see other Apollo regulars such as Bill "Bojangles" Robinson, the dance duo Buck and Bubbles, and other great performers such as Sammy Davis Jr., Bessie Smith, Billie Holiday, and Ethel Waters. Wednesday was amateur night and greats such as Ella Fitzgerald, Sarah Vaugh, and James Brown began their careers there. The theater often served somewhat as day care for the boys. Their mother took them to the Apollo after school and picked them up after the last show. Often they would watch tap legends such as Honi Coles, Sandman Sims, and the Nicholas Brothers. It was tap-dance great Teddy Hale who inspired Hines the most. Teddy Hale and Sandman Sims during breaks in the show would pass on steps and techniques to the young dancers. Hines noticed that Hale would do one performance and return and do a second show that was completely different. He came to realize that Hale did not have a set act but made up his performances as he went along. Hines saw this as a challenge which encouraged his interest in improvisation.

Hines's family had a mixed heritage. His father was black, and his grandmother on his father's side was Ora Hines, a showgirl at the Cotton Club. Performers at the Cotton Club were required to be light skinned which denoted a mixed heritage. His mother's ancestry was also mixed and included Irish, Jewish, Panamanian, and Portuguese, along with her African American heritage. For Hines there was no ambivalence about his ethnicity. He knew he was black. Hines and his brother attended Willard Mace, a school for professional children. They were the only blacks. They also attended Quintano School for Young Professionals where other future performers such as Patty Duke and Bernadette Peters attended. Hines became quite aware of his race while traveling in the South. Segregation was part of the times in 1957 when Hines almost made the mistake of drinking from a whites only fountain. He quickly learned what it meant to be black in the deep South.

Hines and his brother performed in night clubs on weekends during the school year and more extensively during the summer. They also earned roles in the musical comedy *The Girl in Pink Tights*. When Hines was nine, he fell on a tree stump that penetrated his right eye. The accident affected his vision for the rest of his life. Fortunately it did not stop his tap dancing, which he greatly enjoyed. As "The Hines Kids" got older they billed themselves as "The Hines Brothers." In 1963 their father Maurice Hines Sr., who had learned how to play the drums, joined the group and their name changed to "Hines, Hines, and Dad." With the arrival of Hines Sr., the family would be together when touring. Hines in 1966 married and later divorced Patricia Panella, a dance therapist. They had one child, Daria, who was born in 1971. The group went on to play on numerous television shows, such as *The Tonight Show* and *The Ed Sullivan*

Show. While touring Europe they performed at London's famed Palladium and at the Olympia Theatre in Paris. As the 1960s saw tap lose its audience, "Hines, Hines and Dad" continued to perform as a musical comedy group with Maurice as the straight man and Gregory as the comedian. Frustrated by the stagnation of the group, Gregory Hines began to reassess his career goals.

Ventures Away from Dancing and Family

The group was enjoying moderate success, but Hines was extremely unhappy. Money was short, his marriage was falling apart, and he often used cocaine to try and escape a way of life that he had maintained for twenty-five years. Hines's relationship with his brother was also strained, and they often did not speak to each other. Hines knew the partnership was over when he and his brother Maurice had an argument that nearly ended in blows.

In 1973 Hines moved to Venice, California. He took to the hippie lifestyle and experimented with sex, drugs, and rock 'n' roll. He became a black belt in karate and during the day worked as a busboy, waiter, and karate instructor. At night he played in a jazz-rock group he formed called Severance. While in Venice, Hines met Pamela Koslow, a producer who later became his wife. The time spent in Venice gave Hines a renewed sense of himself as he learned to be self-reliant and further embrace his role as a father. He joined a group of men who discussed how men treated women and the expression of one's feelings. He also took a class for single fathers. In 1978, Hines returned to New York to be closer to his daughter.

Home and the Revival of Tap

Once in New York and having already reconciled with his brother, Hines got back to performing. Maurice convinced his agent to submit his brother's name for an audition for a role in *The Last Minstrel Show*. Hines got the job and in 1978 put his tap shoes back on after eight years. When the show closed in Philadelphia, Hines teamed up with his brother for the Broadway production *Eubie*. The play, which honored composer Eubie Blake, opened in 1978 with Hines as a tap dancer and singer. His performance earned him the first of four Tony Award nominations as outstanding featured actor in a musical. His successful run in *Eubie* was followed by the play *Comin' Uptown* in 1979, which earned him a second Tony Award nomination. This musical was an all-black version of Charles Dickens' *A Christmas Carol* in which Hines played Scrooge. In 1980 he appeared in the show *Black Broadway*, which traced the history of black musicians through the first half of the twentieth century. The stars in the musical were seasoned performers and dance greats including John W. Bubbles of the tap duo Buck and Bubbles. *Sophisticated Ladies* (1981) earned Hines a third Tony nomination. *Sophisticated Ladies*, a revue of Duke Ellington's songs, helped to showcase his talents as a dancer, singer, and comedian. Although Hines's co-star was renowned dancer Judith Jameson, it was his performance that stood out because of his quick movements involving jumps and turns and the lightening speed of his tap. In 1981, after a year's run with *Sophisticated Ladies*, Hines left the musical while on the West Coast. He also married Pamela Koslow, who had a daughter Jessica from a previous marriage. Two years later they had son Zachary.

Film and Other Performing Arts

On the West Coast Hines began his film career. An early role was in the Mel Brooks film *History of the World Part I*. Hines played a Roman slave. The next role was as a medical examiner investigating a series of deaths in the film *Wolfen* (1981). When producer Robert Evans began casting for the major film *Cotton Club*, Hines went after a role. He set his sights on the part of Sandman Williams, an upwardly mobile dancer at the Cotton Club. Hines told *Ebony* magazine: "I started calling [Evans] every day and going over to his house telling him how perfect I was for the part." Hines had a personal interest in the film since his grandmother had been a Cotton Club performer. Also in the film was an impressive group of tap dancers, including Charles "Honi" Coles. Frances Ford Coppola, the director, wanted to present old-fashion tap dancing. Hines particularly liked working with Coppola since he researched tap and viewed endless footage of tap dancing. Once he had the role he wanted, Hines found himself reflecting on real life as the character breaks up with his brother, just as Hines had broken up with his brother Maurice. Hines and Maurice were cast as dance partners and brothers in the film. When the scenes regarding the breakup were finished, both Hines and Maurice were in tears along with their parents who were on the set that day. When the film came out in 1984 Hines's performance was seen as a bright spot in the film.

Hines's film career continued to blossom as he appeared in *White Nights* in 1985 with Mikhail Baryshnikov and Isabella Rossellini. Baryshnikov, an acclaimed ballet dancer who defected from the Soviet Union in real life, plays a similar role in the film. Hines plays a dancer who flees to the Soviet Union to protest the racism functioning in draft practices during the Vietnam War. Together the actors performed incredible dance routines. In 1986's *Running Scared* Hines co-starred with Billy Crystal, and in 1987's *Off Limits* he co-starred with Willem Defoe. One film that combined the talents of tap dancing and acting for Hines was *Tap*, which opened in 1988. This film was the first to merge tap with the musical styles of funk and contemporary rock. The film had a host of tap greats, including co-star Sammy Davis Jr., Sandman Sims, Jimmy Slyde, Harold Nicholas, Bunny Briggs, Arthur Duncan, Steve Condos, and Pat Rico. In the television documentary *Bojangles*, Hines played the role of tap great William "Bojangles" Robinson. Hines stepped behind the camera in 1994 and directed the film

White Man's Burden. Making full use of his talents Hines released a singing duet with Luther Vandross in 1986 called "There's Nothing Better Than Love" and an album released in 1988 entitled *Gregory Hines*.

After completing the film *A Rage in Harlem* (1991), which starred Eddie Murphy, Redd Fox, and Richard Pryor, Hines returned to the stage. In 1992 he earned a fourth nomination and received a Tony Award for the musical *Jelly's Last Jam*. The musical portrayed the life of jazz musician "Jelly Roll" Morton. Hines's mesmerizing performance in *Jelly's Last Jam* showed the brilliance of Hines as a singer, dancer, and actor, and changed the ways in which African American musical theater was presented. Previously musical productions focused on African American music with the exception of the musical *Dreamgirls*. *Jelly's Last Jam* celebrates the life of "Jelly Roll" Morton and provides a look at the individual challenges and complexities of his life. Morton, who was a light-skinned Creole, was known to have denied his African American heritage while at the same time being drawn to the rhythmic and passionate music of African American ancestry. Hines originally did not like the character of "Jelly Roll" and rejected the part. Encouraged by his wife (who was also the show's co-producer), he attended a workshop performance where he met writer and director George Wolfe. Impressed with Wolfe and recognizing the risk of this new approach to the African American musical he signed on. Hines did have some difficulty delivering some unusually negative lines, but he overcame it and immersed himself in the character. Recognizing that "Jelly Roll" was a piano player, Hines expressed the piano through his dancing. During this production Hines danced for the second time with eighteen-year-old Savion Glover who played "Jelly Roll" as a young man. Glover became a protégé of Hines. Hines's performance was a high point in his stellar career.

Hines appeared in several other successful films relevant to the African American experience, such as *Waiting to Exhale* (1995) and *The Preacher's Wife* (1996). His talents also took him into television. He earned an Emmy nomination for his performance in *Motown Return to the Apollo*. His PBS special *Gregory Hines: Tap Dance in America* also received an Emmy Award in 1989.

"Improvography" and His Teachers

Hines became enormously popular because of his style. He coined the word "improvography" to explain his style because he took liberty with rhythms and made up steps as he went along. The first time he remembered experimenting was on *The Tonight Show* in 1963. He would dance on tempo and then stop in the step and go to another tempo. Other dancers thought something had been wrong with Hines after viewing the show. Hines took their comments as encouragement and a challenge to do more to invigorate tap as an art form. He called the move he improvised on *The Tonight Show*, "No Time."

His style was often likened to that of a jazz musician with the abilities of a composer, who creates lines of melody that come through the sounds of the tap and mirror the precision of a drum. Hines's performances were legendary. He expressed through "improvography" the most respected tap dancing art, the creative and immediately brilliant choreography of a tap master. It was because of Hines that tap dancing moved into the twenty-first century with style and grace. Hines learned a great deal from idols, such as Sammy Davis Jr. who saw Hines's extraordinary talent. Hines was nine years old when he met Davis. He learned a lot about tap from Davis, but he was also touched by his generous, honest, and sincere attitude as a person and an artist. Davis died in 1990 from throat cancer. Hines was at Davis's side when he passed. Hines told the press that Davis made the gesture of passing a basketball to Hines who understood the message and caught it. The passing of the ball was symbolic of carrying on the art of tap dancing.

Hines was always involved in the arts. He participated in the 1991 *Kennedy Center Honors: A Celebration of the Performing Arts*, his own television show in 1997 called *The Gregory Hines Show*, the 1999 film *Once in a Life* and numerous other appearances. After suffering from liver cancer, Hines died on August 9, 2003, in Los Angeles, California. A tribute to Hines was held at Harlem's Apollo Theater hosted by Phylicia Rashad and his brother Maurice. Many stars came out to celebrate the great dancer, a kind and generous man who remained true to himself on and off the stage.

REFERENCES

Books

De Angelis, Gina. *Gregory Hines*. Philadelphia: Chelsea House Publishers, 2000.

Kram, Mark. "Gregory Hines." *Contemporary Black Biography*. Vol. 1. Detroit: Gale Research, 1992, pp. 102-104.

Periodicals

Randolph, Laura B. "Gregory Hines on Fame, Family, and His Years of Living Dangerously." *Ebony* 46 (January 1991): 132-136.

Online

Bridget Byrne. "Tap Star Gregory Hines Dies." E online. http://www.eonline.com/News/Items/0,1,12299,00.html (Accessed 13 March 2006).

"Gregory Hines." Apple Hot News. http://www.apple.com/hotnews/articles/2003/08/hines/ (Accessed 13 March 2006).

Lean'tin L. Bracks

William H. Holland
1841?–1907

Soldier, politician

William H. Holland was born a slave in Marshall, Texas. There are conflicting dates for Holland's birth. In *Negro Legislatures of Texas*, Brewer records his birth year as 1849 while other sources such as the *Dictionary of American Biography* records Holland's birth year as 1841. Holland was reared as the son of Captain Byrd (Bird) Holland, former onetime secretary of the state of Texas. In the late 1850s, Byrd purchased William and his brothers Milton and James. Upon Byrd's death, William and his brothers were taken to Ohio to attend school. Albany Enterprise Academy, a school owned and operated by blacks, provided William and his brother Milton with their early education.

Holland's military service began with his enlistment on October 22, 1864 in the Union Army 16th Regiment of U.S. Colored Troops, which was organized in Clarksville, Tennessee and continued in Nashville. This regiment included enlisted black men from Ohio and runaway slaves from Kentucky. Colonel R. D. Mussey served as the commissioner for the regiment of colored troops, which had as many as 24 officers and 504 men before mustering out on April 30, 1866. The 16th U.S. Colored regiment participated in the Nashville and Overton Hill battles in pursuit of John Bell Hood to the Tennessee River and in garrison duty in Chattanooga, Tennessee. Holland, like many other black soldiers that volunteered, saw combat and served behind the lines. Holland's brother Milton received the Congressional Medal of Honor for his heroic service in the Battle of New Market Heights on September 29, 1864.

After serving in the military, Holland turned his attention to pursuing a college education. In 1867, he entered Oberlin College in Ohio. It is believed that it was Holland's time at Oberlin that prepared him intellectually and socially for challenges he later encountered. It is not known if Holland graduated. However, after two years at Oberlin, Holland returned to Texas to become principal in the Austin Doublehorn community. Holland's passion for education and the education of children later led him to sponsor legislation that sought the educational interest of children.

The congressional reconstruction of Texas brought with it African Americans and carpetbaggers. Holland, like many other African Americans, joined the Republican Party, which was mostly made up of white men. Their presence was more collaboration than control of the party. Nevertheless, Holland's affiliation with the party gained him an appointment with the post office. The exact date of Holland's move to Waller County is not known, but in 1876 he won election to the fifteenth legislature as a representative from Waller County. It was during this time when the legislature convened that Hol-

Chronology	
1841?	Born in Marshall, Texas (some sources say 1849)
1850	Captain Byrd (Bird) Holland purchases William and his brothers
1864	Enlists in the Union Army's Sixteenth United States Colored Troops
1867	Enters Oberlin College
1876	Wins election to the Fifteenth legislature and sponsors bill to create Prairie View A&M University
1887	Sponsors bill to create and is appointed superintendent of Texas Institute for Deaf, Dumb, and Blind Colored Youth
1907	Dies in Mineral Wells, Texas on May 27

land sponsored a bill to establish an agricultural and mechanical college for the white and colored youth of Texas. On August 14, 1876 the Fifteenth Legislature passed an act to establish an Agricultural & Mechanical College of Texas for the benefit of Colored Youth.

Other than the credit given to Holland in the *Handbook of Texas Online,* very little information is credited to him as the father of Agricultural & Mechanical College of Texas for Colored Youth. However, the Second Morrill Act of 1890 links Holland to what is known today as Prairie View Agricultural & Mechanical University. The Morrill Act of 1890, which passed in the Fifteenth Legislature, provided for the creation of land grant schools of higher learning for African Americans. As a result, seventeen land grant institutions were created in the southern states. African Americans were much disfranchised during the 1890s by state and federal constitutional laws that prohibited equal access. The establishing of the seventeen land grant institutions gave strength to the separate but equal doctrine.

After he was chosen as a delegate to the Republican National Convention in 1876 and 1880, Holland sponsored a bill in the Texas legislature to establish a school for the deaf and mute. Six months later, on April 5, 1887, the Deaf, Dumb, and Blind Institute for Colored Youth was opened. Approximately $50,000 was appropriated to construct on a 100-acre site two miles outside Austin. The institute offered the children instruction in trades and industries such as broom making, mattress making, shoemaking, and repairs and cooking. Governor Lawrence S. Ross appointed Holland as its first superintendent on August 15, 1887. This appointment made Holland the first black man in the United States to head a public institution. For the next eleven years Holland remained as superintendent and was later joined by his wife Eliza, in 1890, as an instructor of the deaf.

The institute was governed by an all white board of trustees that had complete faith and trust in Holland's leadership. In 1898, another African American, S. J. Jenkins, succeeded Holland as superintendent. At the death of Jenkins, on April 21, 1904, Holland was again appointed superintendent where he remained until his death on May 27, 1907, at his home in Mineral Wells, Texas, having suffered a heart attack.

Living up to Oberlin's motto and spirit to live large and unselfish led to Holland's establishing an organization in the Negro community known as the Friends in Need. This organization provided financial assistance to Negro students who were unable to meet their educational expenses. While Holland was very generous with his finances, he never looked for praise. Reaching out and helping others was the epitome of his life.

Not much is known about Holland and his personal life other than the fact that he married Eliza H. James, a school teacher. Eliza worked with Holland for a short while at the Texas Institute of Deaf, Dumb, and Blind Colored Youth as an instructor. Holland and Eliza had two daughters.

REFERENCES
Books

Brewer, J. Mason. *Negro Legislators of Texas and Their Descendant*. Dallas, Tex.: Mathis, 1978.

Logan, Rayford W., and Michael R. Winston, eds. *Dictionary of American Negro Biography*. New York: Norton, 1982.

Periodicals

Levstik, Frank R. "William H. Holland: Black Soldier, Politician, and Educator." *Ebony* (October 1955): 135-38.

Online

Markham, James W. "Texas Blind, Deaf, and Orphan School." *Handbook of Texas Online* http://www.tsha.utexas.edu/handbook/online/articles/HH/fho30.html (Accessed 25 August 2005).

Thompson, Nolan. "Holland, William H., 1841-1907." *Handbook of Texas Online*. http://www.tsha.utexas.edu/handbook/online/articles/HH/fho30.html (Accessed 8 August 2005).

Annie Malessia Payton

Dwight Oliver Wendell Holmes
1877–1963

College president

Dwight Oliver Wendell Holmes was born on November 18, 1877 in Lewisburg, West Virginia. He was the son of a minister in the Washington D.C. and New

Chronology

1877	Born in Lewisburg, West Virginia on November 18
1901	Earns B.A. from Howard University; is valedictorian of his class
1902	Teaches at the Sumner High School in St. Louis; teaches science at the High School of Baltimore (Douglass High School)
1903	Enrolls in art and education classes at Johns Hopkins University
1909	Serves as vice principal of Douglass High School in Baltimore
1912	Granted honorary M.A. from Howard University
1917	Teaches education and psychology at the Miner Normal School in Washington, D.C.
1918	Becomes registrar and professor of education at Howard University
1928	Increases enrollment by one thousand students in the School of Education at Howard
1934	Publishes *The Evolution of the Negro College*
1934	Heads the graduate school at Howard University
1937	Installed as the sixth president of Morgan College
1963	Dies on September 7

York conferences of the Methodist Church. Holmes spent his formative years in Annapolis, Maryland; New York; and Staunton, Virginia. His secondary schooling was obtained in the preparatory department of Howard University.

After completing his secondary schooling, Holmes continued at Howard University. As an undergraduate Holmes was an athlete, playing quarterback on the football team and serving as captain of both the baseball and football teams. He established and was the president of Howard's first tennis team. He earned nine letters for athletics. In addition, Holmes organized Howard's very first debate competition. He also led Howard's college Mandolin and Glee Club. Holmes earned a B.A. in 1901. He was the valedictorian of his class.

The next year Holmes began his post-graduate work at Howard and then became an instructor at Sumner High School in St. Louis. In the fall of 1902 he was appointed to teach science courses in the High School of Baltimore in Maryland. While teaching high school, he simultaneously enrolled at Johns Hopkins University for classes in art and education. Holmes continued his education, earning both his M.A. and Ph.D. at Columbia University. Howard University awarded Holmes an honorary M.A. degree in 1912.

Holmes served four institutions for almost four decades as an educator. He taught at what is now Douglass High School in Baltimore, Maryland, for fourteen years, chairing the Science Department for eleven years and serving as vice principal for eight years. He left Baltimore in April 1917 to teach psychology and education at the Miner Normal School of Washington, D.C. In 1919, Holmes returned to his alma mater to serve as

Howard's registrar and to teach education courses. He was later appointed dean of Howard's College of Education. It was in this capacity that Holmes first began to distinguish himself as a university administrator.

Becomes Morgan State's First Black President

At the time of his appointment to the College of Education, Holmes inherited one of Howard's most challenged programs. During his tenure at this post, however, Holmes developed the College of Education into one of the best programs at the university, enrolling approximately one thousand students in 1928. Six years later, Howard's board of trustees began to organize for the establishment of graduate programs. In 1934 Holmes was appointed the first dean of Howard University's Graduate School. By May 1937, there were almost four hundred students enrolled in graduate study at Howard. It was this success that encouraged the trustees of Morgan College to offer Holmes the presidency by unanimous vote in July 1937. Holmes became the first African American president of Morgan College in Baltimore, Maryland.

At the time of his inauguration, Maryland was one of the remaining seventeen states which still maintained a segregated system of public education. A state commission was appointed, did research, and then recommended that the state should assume ownership of Morgan College. Morgan's board of trustees concurred, and in 1939, Morgan State College came into being.

Holmes led Morgan from 1939 to 1975. Under his leadership, Morgan's faculty increased from thirty to eighty-five members, and from four to twenty-five holding the Ph.D. The total annual salary of all faculty members increased from $33,728 to $512,000. Holmes improved working conditions, establishing the first benefit programs to include sabbatical leave; pension, and retirement benefits, and an academic ranking system. The student body grew from 752 to 1,595 students. Three buildings were erected during his presidency and two additional facilities were under construction increasing the value of the physical plant from $858,879 to $3,321,579.

In addition to his successful administrative career, Holmes was an active member of many civic and educational organizations. In Baltimore, Holmes was the first president of the Schoolmaster's Club and served for several years as the president of the Baltimore Education Association. For four years, he was president of Howard University's General Alumni Association. During his tenure at Howard, Holmes represented the university at the American Association of Collegiate Registrars, the Association of Colleges and Secondary Schools of the Middle States, and the Association of American Colleges. Holmes was president of the Association of College for Negro Youth and chairman of the Committee on Rating Negro Colleges. It was the latter committee that in 1928 persuaded the United States Bureau of Education to

survey and report on Negro colleges. The Southern Association of Colleges and Secondary Schools agreed to take on the rating of Negro colleges as a direct result of the committee's efforts.

Holmes was a member on many boards and commissions, including the following: the National Consultation Committee on Religious Life among the Colleges; the National Advisory Committee on Negro Education under the United States Office of Education; the Division of Corporation and Education in Race Relations of the State Department of Education of North Carolina with Duke University and the University of North Carolina; the Advisory Board of the Educational Outlook among Negroes; and the Editorial Board of the *Journal of Negro Education*. He held memberships in the National Educational Association, the American Education Association, the American Association of School Administrators, the Association of Colleges and Secondary Schools for Negroes, the National Society of College Teachers of Education, the Sigma Pi Phi National Graduate Fraternity, the Kappa Mu Honorary Scholarship Fraternity, the Phi Gamma Mu National Social Science Honor Society, and the Alpha Phi Alpha Fraternity.

Holmes was a popular speaker and published many scholarly articles. He is best known for his book *The Evolution of the Negro College*, which was published in 1934. Holmes died on September 7, 1963.

REFERENCES

Books

Morgan State University 1976 Yearbook. Baltimore, Md.: Morgan State University.

Parham, Alice Warner. *I Remember Morgan in the Twenties: Reflections of An Alumna*. Baltimore, Md.: Morgan State University, 2002.

Wilson, Edward N. *A History of Morgan State College: A Century of Purpose in Action, 1867-1967*. New York: Vantage Press, 1975.

Edwin T. Johnson

Albon L. Holsey
1883–1950

Organization executive, writer

According to Albon L. Holsey, slavery deprived blacks of the opportunity to learn the art of business. Through his efforts with the National Negro Business League, the Colored Merchant's Association, and

Chronology

1883	Born in Athens, Georgia on May 31
1906	Marries Basiline Boyd on October 3
1914	Joins staff of Tuskegee Institute
1929	Expands Colored Merchants' Association nationally
1930?	Receives Harmon Foundation Award for achievements in business
1950	Dies in Tuskegee, Alabama on January 16

writings about black business topics, Holsey attempted to assist African Americans in competing and succeeding in the world of commerce.

Holsey was the son of Albon Chase Holsey and Sallie Thomas Holsey. As a boy, he attended Knox Institute in Athens, Georgia, and later he matriculated at Atlanta University in Atlanta, Georgia.

Begins Work at Tuskegee Institute

Holsey joined the staff of Tuskegee Institute in 1914, during the time that the famous educator, Booker T. Washington, headed the institution. He was hired as an assistant to Washington's secretary, Emmett J. Scott. During his tenure, Holsey worked as secretary to president Robert R. Morton and assistant to president Frederick D. Patterson, served as associate editor of the *Tuskegee Student* and possibly acted as director of public relations. Between 1938 and 1944, Holsey was also on loan to the U. S. Department of Agriculture. While working for the government, he was involved in projects related to black farmers. Holsey worked at Tuskegee for thirty-six years.

Expands the Colored Merchants' Association

Following the *Plessy v. Ferguson* ruling in 1896, African Americans were subjected to escalating racial discrimination. To develop economic self-help opportunities for blacks, Booker T. Washington founded the National Negro Business League (NNBL) in 1900. Similarly, in 1928, A. C. Brown of Montgomery, Alabama established the Colored Merchants' Association (CMA), a cooperative organization of black grocery stores. The purpose of the organization was to reduce the operating costs of black retailers through cooperative buying. The CMA model was markedly successful. Associated stores reported increases in business and profits. The CMA in Montgomery was affiliated with the NNBL. Holsey, secretary of the NNBL, led the effort to expand the CMA into a national organization. Holsey believed that if the purchasing power of the black community could be channeled through black-owned wholesale and retail business, thousands of jobs would be created for African Americans. He also realized that in order for black busi-

nesses to succeed, they had to offer competitive pricing and service. In addition, Holsey was concerned that black college graduates had insufficient employment opportunities, except in overcrowded professions or in limited fields in industry and welfare. The association spread, and eventually there was a CMA store in nearly eighteen cities, including Chicago, Philadelphia, Nashville, and New York. The CMA built its national headquarters in New York City in October 1929, a time of apparent prosperity and favorable economic environment. Unfortunately, it was also the same month as the stock market crash.

Similar to franchise ownership in the early 2000s, CMA members paid a weekly fee to the headquarters and were required to meet designated standards. In return, members received support services from the association. The association recognized that the grocers needed intensive training in merchandising techniques. CMA provided sales training, advertising, and management resources such as market analysis, inventory and bookkeeping systems, and collection and credit procedures. Holsey arranged frequent instructional sessions that incorporated speakers such as James A. Jackson, the African American advisor on Negro affairs in the U. S. Department of Commerce, who discussed waste elimination and cost control. Other discussants included Gorton Jones, editor of *Business Week*; F. R. Snapp, assistant sales manager at Royal Baking Company; and George Loomis, cashier at Dunbar National Bank. As CMA store purchases increased, grocery wholesalers began to hire African American workers. With the cooperation of the NNBL and the New York Urban League, a group of black women organized the Housewives' League. The purpose of the group was to support black businesses and to give preference in their buying to the CMA stores and other businesses that employed blacks. Although the CMA flourished for a time, several internal and external factors during the 1930s negatively affected the organization. The Great Depression, which began in 1929, limited the amount of capital available for spending and operating. Holsey explained that perspective CMA members were in debt to wholesalers. In addition, Holsey stated that the members did not attend the training sessions that were designed to help them effectively manage their businesses. Though there were many contributing factors for its demise, the CMA could not continue its work because the grocers could no longer pay the membership dues. As a result, the organization failed around 1934.

The Harmon Foundation, established in 1922, held competitions for black achievement awards in nine fields. Holsey's significance in the business arena can be inferred from the fact that in 1930 or 1931, he received the Harmon Award for achievement in business. Other historical giants who, at various times, had been considered for the award include labor leader A. Philip Randolph, banker Maggie L. Walker, and insurance executive Charles C. Spaulding. According to *The Colored Situation*, Eugene Gordon, a black journalist at the *Boston Globe*, rated Holsey as one of the thirteen most important and gifted African Americans in the United States.

Writes Numerous Publications

Holsey wrote numerous articles, most related to business topics, including the article "Learning How to be Black," in which Holsey described the experiences of African American children that triggered their consciousness of color and the "deadly toll" on the manhood of the race. In "Public Relations Intuitions of Booker T. Washington," Holsey described Washington's common sense approach to keeping good relationships with various constituencies involved with Tuskegee Institute. The *Public Opinion Quarterly* published Holsey's lengthy review of a book on the subject of black newspapers in 1948. Holsey, in a chapter in *The Progress of a Race*, recapitulated the first twenty-five years of the NNBL. He was business manager of *Crisis*, the official publication of the NAACP, during the time that W. E. B. Du Bois edited the periodical.

Holsey was a member of the Masons and Phi Beta Sigma fraternity. The 1928-29 edition of *Who's Who in Colored America* lists his political and religious affiliations as Republican and as African Methodist Episcopal.

After a brief illness, Holsey died on January 16, 1950, in John Andrews Memorial Hospital in Tuskegee, Alabama, at 67 years of age. Funeral services were held on January 26 in the Tuskegee Institute chapel. His wife, Basiline Boyd Holsey, whom he married on October 3, 1906, survived him. A sister, Annie Holsey of Baltimore, and brothers, Augustus J. Holsey and Crosby Holsey of Baltimore and Cleveland, respectively, also survived him. He was buried in Tuskegee.

REFERENCES

Books

Boris, Joseph J., ed. *Who's Who in Colored America*. New York: Who's Who in Colored America Corp., 1929.

Everett, Faye Philip. *The Colored Situation: A Book of Vocational and Civic Guidance for the Negro Youth*. Boston: Meador Publishing Company, 1936.

Harris, Abram. *The Negro as Capitalist: A Study of Banking and Business among American Negroes*. New York: Haskell House Publishers, 1970.

Newman, Debra. *Black History: A Guide to Civilian Records in the National Archives*. National Archives Trust Fund Board: Washington, DC, 1984.

Oak, Vishnu V. *The Negro's Adventure in General Business*. Yellow Springs, Ohio: The Antioch Press, 1949.

Walker, Juliet E. K. *The History of Black Business in America: Capitalism, Race, Entrepreneurship*. New York: Twayne Publishers, 1998.

Cheryl Jones Hamberg

Lucius Henry Holsey
1842–1920

Bishop

In his early youth Lucius Henry Holsey felt compelled to enter the ministry. Fulfilling this desire, he converted to the Methodist religion and rose through the ranks as pastor, delegate, elder, and bishop. He served as the fourth bishop of the Colored (now Christian) Methodist Episcopal Church. With dedication to the services of the church Holsey served in that position for almost fifty years. He was an advocate for both religion and for the education of freed slaves. His influence and commitment to the black community remained steadfast throughout his lifetime.

Holsey was born July 3, 1842 near Columbus, Georgia. His parents were Louisa, a slave woman of pure African heritage, and James Holsey, her slave master. After the death of his father, Holsey was separated from his mother and became the property of James Holsey's cousin, T. L. Wynn in Hancock County, Georgia. A few days prior to his death, Wynn allowed Holsey to choose his next owner; he requested Richard Malcolm Johnston, a planter and an educator. When Johnston accepted a position as an English professor at the University of Georgia and relocated to Athens, Holsey accompanied the family to serve as the house servant, carriage driver, and gardener. He lived with the family from 1857 until the abolition of slavery.

As a fifteen-year-old slave, Holsey could not receive an education, but his thirst for knowledge and initiative allowed him other avenues for learning. His first collection of books consisted of two Webster blue back spellers, a common school dictionary; John Milton's *Paradise Lost*; and a Bible, which were acquired by collecting and selling rags to a junk house in the city. These books constituted his library, which he thoroughly studied in order to master reading and writing.

On November 8, 1862 Holsey married Harriett Turner, a fifteen-year-old servant who lived in the home of George Foster Pierce. Pierce was a bishop of the Methodist Episcopal Church, South (now United Methodist Church). The couple was favored by the bishop who presided over their elaborate wedding at his

Chronology

1842	Born near Columbus, Georgia on July 3
1862	Marries Harriett Turner
1868	Receives license to preach
1869	Ordained as an elder
1873	Elected as the fourth U.S. bishop of the Colored Methodist Episcopal Church
1883	Founds Paine College
1891-1904	Compiles and publishes *Songs of Love and Mercy*
1894	Revises *A Manual of the Discipline of the Colored Methodist Episcopal Church in America*
1898	Publishes *Autobiography of Bishop L. H. Holsey*
1920	Dies on August 3

residence. Their union produced fourteen children but only nine of them survived. To make a living, Holsey farmed on land given to him by his last owner, Richard Malcolm Johnston. During the Civil War, Johnston had returned to Hancock County to open and direct a boarding school named Rockby Academy. Harriett Holsey provided laundry services for the students at the academy.

Bishop Pierce assisted Holsey in his desire to become a minister in the Methodist Church. In 1868, Holsey received his license to preach and was assigned to the Hancock circuit in Georgia. A year later he was ordained an elder during the Colored Conference of Georgia. He was elected as a delegate to the first General Conference when the Colored Methodist Episcopal Church in the United States became a separate denomination from the Methodist Episcopal Church, South. It was during this conference that Holsey was appointed to be the pastor of Trinity Colored Methodist Episcopal Church in Augusta, Georgia. This church was in the forefront of the conference, and Holsey served as the pastor for two years and four months.

In 1873 at the General Conference assembly in Augusta, Georgia, the thirty-year-old Holsey was elected a bishop. Holsey played a significant role upon his election by assisting the presiding Bishop Miles with the preparation of the bishop's message and assuming leadership roles in other works of the conference. He was ordained bishop by Miles and assisted by an honored guest, Bishop George Foster Pierce.

With a fixed salary of $800 Holsey was assigned to serve in Texas, Arkansas, Alabama, and Tennessee. The first ten years was a struggle for the Holsey family. There was little or no way to organize the charges whom he served. The necessities of life, including food, shelter, and clothing, were almost out of reach for the family. The family vegetable garden prevented starvation. The family of eleven resided in a two-room house that was heated with coal. Holsey did not complain about his family's

plight, but he believed that with faith and determination, his struggles would be rewarded.

Service as Bishop

As a bishop, Holsey traveled and ministered throughout the southern states, expressing a keen interest in the establishment of the Colored Methodist Episcopal Church in America. This denomination was organized in 1869 as a method to separate the black and white worshippers and attract the black Methodists who attended Southern white churches. As the leader of this denomination, Holsey recruited Georgia black Methodists to join. Other congregations in Georgia were founded under his leadership. Holsey served as the secretary of the College of Bishops for over twenty years. He was also the statistician and the corresponding secretary for the denomination during those years.

As bishop, Holsey continued to serve the denomination conscientiously, and in 1881 he was selected as a delegate to represent the church at the Ecumenical Conference in London, England, making him the first and only representative from the denomination to function outside the United States.

In 1882, Holsey and other leaders of the Methodist Episcopal Church, South and the Colored Methodist Episcopal Church founded Paine College located in Augusta, Georgia. He had advocated that the school be established to train black teachers and preachers to address the educational and spiritual needs of freed slaves. However, Holsey faced much opposition from other blacks who did not approve of such an establishment. He nonetheless refused to give up in the face of opposition and continued his crusade to establish the school. Holsey traveled throughout the states and made many speeches explaining his ideas. At the General Conference of the Methodist Episcopal Church, South approval had been given in 1881 for the school to be established. The school commenced a year later with approximately thirty students. It was noted that Holsey gave the school its first $100. Holsey became the first vice-president of the board of trustees at Paine College. He also founded Lane College located in Jackson, Tennessee, the Holsey Industrial Institute in Cordele, Georgia, and the Helen B. Cobb Institute for Girls in Barnesville, Georgia.

Holsey revised *The Book of Discipline* and its companion *The Manual of Discipline* in 1894. These served as guidebooks for governing the administration of the Methodist Episcopal Church. In 1898 Holsey published his autobiography *The Autobiography of Bishop L. H. Holsey*, which included sermons, addresses, essays, and a volume of poems. The General Conference granted him the authority in 1891 to compile the hymnal of the Colored Methodist Episcopal Church in America. The hymnal, *Songs of Love and Mercy*, was published in 1904.

For many years, Holsey was the editor-in-chief of the periodical, *The Gospel Trumpet*, the church paper.

During the late nineteenth century and the beginning of the twentieth century, Bishop Henry McNeal Turner of the African Methodist Episcopal and other African American ministers started a "Back to Africa Movement." This movement would entice African Americans to leave the United States, settle in parts of Africa, and regain their civil rights. They would conduct their own government and business affairs among themselves. Numerous leaders in the church balked at this movement, but in 1895 and 1896 two ships arranged by Bishop Turner sailed African Americans to Liberia to start a new way of life. Bishop Holsey and some other African American leaders had a different separatist idea: they advocated that the federal government create a separate state from Native American territories for African Americans. Even though this movement supposedly promised African Americans equal status with whites the idea was met with much skepticism.

Undaunted by opposition to his views on separation of the races, Holsey continued to work with black and white church leaders. His lifetime achievements, along with his skills of leadership, influence, and commitment, were interwoven throughout the Atlanta black community. Holsey died in 1920.

REFERENCES

Books

Angell, Stephen W. "Religion." *The African American Almanac*. Ed. Jeffrey Lehman. Farmington Hills, Mich.: Thomson Gale, 2003.

Online

"Paine College 2003-2005 Catalog." http://www. collegesource.org (Accessed 18 January 2005).

Sharon D. Brooks

James Walker Hood
1831–1918

Minister, activist

As one of the major developers of independent black churches and an active promoter of black fraternal orders, James Walker Hood is an example of nineteenth- and early twentieth-century beliefs that Christian faithfulness and racial justice are inseparable in the mission of the black church. Hood was a successful advocate for the rights of emancipated slaves after the Civil War. During

---

Chronology

1831	Born in Kennett Township, Chester County, Pennsylvania on May 30
1852	Decides to become a preacher; marries Hannah L. Ralph, who dies three years later
1856	Receives license to preach in a branch of the Union Church of Africans in New York City
1857	Begins affiliation with the African Methodist Episcopal Zion Church
1858	Marries Sophia J. Nugent of Washington, D.C.
1859	Serves on trial basis in the New England Conference of the African Methodist Episcopal Zion Church
1860	Ordained a deacon of the African Methodist Episcopal (AME) Zion Church on September 2; appointed to the Nova Scotia Missions
1862	Becomes an elder on June 15
1868	Elected as delegate to the Reconstruction Constitutional Convention in the state of North Carolina; appointed agent of the state board of education
1870	Elected grand master of the Prince Hall Masons in North Carolina
1872	Consecrated as bishop at the AME Zion General Conference on July 3
1875	Second wife Sophia dies
1876	Serves as temporary chairman of the Republican State Convention
1877	Marries Keziah Price McKoy, a widow from Wilmington, North Carolina
1916	Retires after forty-four years of service as bishop of the AME Zion Church
1918	Dies in Fayetteville, North Carolina on October 30

---

the operation of the Freedmen's Bureau, he served as an assistant superintendent of education and had helped place 49,000 black children in schools. As a minister and later bishop of the African Methodist Episcopal Zion Church (AMEZ), Hood helped to establish well over 366 churches in the coastal areas of North Carolina, as well as in South Carolina and Virginia. He was the founder of North Carolina's denomination newspaper, the *Star of Zion*, and helped to establish the Zion Wesley Institute which later became Livingstone College. As the superintendent of the southern jurisdiction for the Prince Hall Masonic Lodge of New York, Hood helped to establish numerous lodges and became grand master of Masons of North Carolina. Given his political and social influence, his views on subjects such as slavery, lynching, segregation, education, and even politics regarding the president of the United States were important factors in state government and Reconstruction in North Carolina.

James Walker Hood's parents, Levi Hood and Harriet Walker Hood, had strong religious affiliations. Levi Hood was a minister in the Union Church of Africans in Delaware and Harriet Walker was a member of Bethel African Methodist Episcopal (AME) Church in Philadelphia. When the couple married in 1813, Harriett Walker Hood transferred her affiliation to the Union Church of Africans to support her husband. Even though Levi Hood remained a minister with this denomination for over forty years with his wife at his side, Harriett Hood continued to support and sometimes attend Bethel AME. Contrary to most women of the time, Harriett Hood was very outspoken. She was interested in ecclesiastical affairs and gave public lectures on antislavery. She was never ordained as a minister, but her role as the minister's wife and church mother gave her an audience. Her active role may have influenced her son's decision years later to champion the ordination of women. When James Walker Hood was born on May 30, 1831, the family lived on a rented farm in Kennett Township, Chester County, Pennsylvania. Hood was one of twelve children, six boys and six girls. His position among his sisters and brother is not known. Hood had a year and eight months of training in a rural school between the ages of nine and thirteen. His mother taught him grammar and got him interested in public speaking. He delivered his first abolitionist speech at the age of fifteen. Hood's feelings about slavery and the abolitionist movement were influenced by the disenfranchisement of blacks and the hostile racial climate in Pennsylvania toward free blacks, the close proximity of Delaware, a slave state, and the influence of Quakers. Active in the abolitionist movement, the Hood family's role in the secret network of the Underground Railroad is unknown. Hood saw many slaves, fleeing from the South to the North and to Canada. These early years set the spiritual and moral agenda of Christian faithfulness and racial justice that Hood championed in his career.

Hood was converted and convinced of his salvation by the age of eighteen. He experienced a call to preach the gospel in 1852 and later married Hannah L. Ralph of Lancaster City, Pennsylvania. Sadly, three years later, Hannah Hood died of consumption. After receiving his license in 1856, Hood moved to New York City to preach in a branch of the Union Church of Africans. After a year in New York, Hood moved to Connecticut but found no branch of the Union Church of Africans. Having some experience with the African Methodist Episcopal Church (AME) Hood pursued and received an acceptance of his license and established an affiliation with the African Methodist Episcopal Zion Church (AMEZ) in 1858. He also was appointed on a trial basis to an AMEZ Church in Connecticut and as a missionary to Nova Scotia Canada. Hood had to supplement his small salary from parishioners in order to support himself and his new wife, Sophia J. Nugent of Washington D.C., whom he married in 1858. He took a job as the headwaiter at the Torntine Hotel in New Haven. He converted hotel coworkers and influenced religious colleagues, bringing in over seventy-two new members to the AMEZ church.

In 1860 Hood secured funding to make his missionary sojourn to Nova Scotia. As a result of his efforts he was ordained a deacon in 1860 and in 1862 ordained as an elder by the AMEZ Church. Later in 1863 Hood assumed the pastorate of a congregation in Bridgeport, Connecticut. After six months he was appointed missionary to the freed people in the South. With the outbreak of the Civil War in 1861 and the Emancipation Proclamation in 1863, which liberated slaves in Confederate states, freed slaves needed a lot of support. Hood arrived in 1864 at his southern assignment in New Bern, North Carolina. The congregation of Saint Andrews in New Bern was initially organized as a Methodist Episcopal Church, South. Hood was successful in securing the denominational allegiance of this pre-Civil War black congregation to the AMEZ Church even with the convergence of other representatives from the AME Church seeking to gain their affiliation.

Freed Slaves and Activism

In 1865 Hood was selected president of a convention of free blacks in North Carolina, which met in Raleigh, North Carolina, and called for full citizenship and rights for all blacks. Hood was involved in many North Carolina political and social arenas that affected blacks. When Radical Reconstruction began nationwide in 1867, Hood along with other blacks in the state participated in the state convention to redesign the constitution. As required by the victorious Union, Confederate states were to bring the rights of their black citizens in accordance with Congressional Reconstruction. Hood as a convention delegate successfully promoted homestead laws, public education, and women's rights, which laid the foundation for black equality and benefited whites as well. Hood was so dynamic that the constitution, once ratified in 1868, was referred to as the Hood Constitution. To support the education component in the constitution, the position of agent of the state board of education was created. Hood held that position for three years. The position was eliminated in 1870 when the Democrats took control of the state legislature and amended many of the advances that Reconstruction had established.

General Otis O. Howard of the Freedmen's Bureau commissioned Hood as assistant superintendent of public instruction of North Carolina, with special duties for black children and temporarily as a magistrate. By 1870 Hood had placed 49,000 black children in public school and had established a department for the deaf, dumb, and blind. He also played a supporting role in establishing Fayetteville State University. The end of Reconstruction in North Carolina was imminent as Democrats eliminated Hood's position and went after other plans that supported black citizens. The educational plan and other advances that Hood helped develop were well established by the end of Reconstruction and did not fall easily to Democrats' and white Southerners' efforts to dismantle them. Hood served as a delegate to the National Republican convention in 1872 and as temporary chairman of the convention. The state constitution was amended in 1872 and no longer could be referred to as the Hood Constitution. With the election of Rutherford B. Hayes as president of the United States and the withdrawal of federal troops, Reconstruction came to an end in other parts of the South as well. In addition to suffering political loss, Hood experienced two personal losses: his father died in 1872, and his second wife, Sophia, died in 1875.

Affiliated with Fraternal Orders

Hood left few references to his affiliation with the fraternal order of Prince Hall, in line with the enforced secrecy of this society. Secret societies as well as the origins of the black church can be traced back to post-Revolutionary America when both groups served blacks as a means for finding autonomy and a sense of racial strength against racism in both the North and the South. Hood had become superintendent of the southern jurisdiction of the Prince Hall Masonic Grand Lodge of New York. A common goal of both the church and the societies was to uplift blacks through the art of social organized life. Although there were clear differences between these groups, the mutual benefits were recognized by blacks of the time. As many as two-thirds of the most prominent blacks in the United States in the early 1900s held memberships in both a fraternal order and the black church. Hood served as a moving force in bringing black Masonic lodges to the North Carolina region. In a trip to the fifth annual proceedings of the Prince Hall Grand Lodge of Free and Accepted Ancient York Masons for the state of North Carolina, Hood was honored as the "Most Worshipful Grand Master." From his 1864 arrival in North Carolina until 1874, eighteen Prince Hall lodges were established in the state with 478 members. Hood served as the "Grand Master of Masons of North Carolina" for fourteen years and as "Grand Patron of the Order of Eastern Star" for nineteen years.

Church Progress and Later Years

As the Reconstruction planning came to a close for North Carolina state government, Hood continued to move forward in the AMEZ Church. He was ordained as the seventeenth bishop of the AMEZ Church in 1872, and he married his third wife Keziah Price McKoy, a widow from Wilmington, North Carolina, in 1877. As a northerner and church organizer, Hood found that freed slaves were influenced by white religion that supported slave masters' beliefs in submission and subservience. Hood sought to transform these beliefs and to support social equality.

From 1864 to 1874, Hood oversaw the organization of 366 churches with over 20,000 members. He also helped lay the foundation for what became the denomination newspaper, the *Star of Zion*. In an effort to provide equal opportunities and training for roles in the church, Hood successfully advocated for women's equal rights in the denomination and for starting an institute for ministerial candidates. The church discipline was amended in 1876

to secure women's equal religious rights. The Zion Wesley Institute, a school for training ministers, was established in 1879 in Concord, North Carolina. Initially the institute lasted only three brief sessions and then it closed. Then in 1881 Hood and Joseph C. Price began raising money to re-establish the institute. The college was reopened due to a generous donation from the town of Salisbury, North Carolina, just twenty miles north of Concord, as well as the invitation to locate the college there. Price became the school's first president. Zion Wesley Institute was renamed Livingston College by an act of the legislature in 1887. Hood remained active with the college throughout his life and remained on the trustee board.

Hood published his first book in 1884, *The Negro in the Christian Pulpit*, a collection of sermons written and delivered primarily by Hood. As the black Baptists organized their first nationwide organization, the National Baptist Convention, Hood published *One Hundred Years of African Methodist Episcopal Zion History* in 1895. Hood continued as a key voice in the church and published *The Plan of the Apocalypse* in 1900, *Sermons* in 1908 and *Sketches of the Early History of the AMEZ Church* in 1914, which is a second volume of the church history.

Hood served churches in New Bern, Fayetteville, and Charlotte, North Carolina. He often moved and received less pay for his ministerial duties, but he did so because he recognized the needed growth of the AMEZ Church and was committed to the faith and racial uplift. In Fayetteville, he was the minister of Evans Chapel from 1867 to 1870. Hood was successful in bringing this congregation into the AMEZ Church. He was then transferred to Charlotte. He was working for the board of education at the time and would leave his office in Raleigh on Saturday and make the 175-mile trip to his church in Charlotte. This would get him to Charlotte in time to preach three sermons on Sunday and make the trip back to Raleigh on Monday. His involvement in so many aspects of the community enabled Hood to interact with some of the greatest leaders of the AMEZ Church, including Peter Ross, Christopher Rush, and J. J. Clinton. Hood was also advisor to Theodore Roosevelt on issues concerning African Americans. His opinion as bishop was called into play in particular as the AMEZ Church saw the ordination of Mary J. Small in 1898 as an elder. This event created a debate over the role of women, but Hood continued to advocate for women to receive the same religious rights as men.

Those who knew Hood characterized him as warm and generous, deliberate in his discourse, and frugal as he maintained meager circumstances but gave generously to public charities. In addition to his work, Hood's family life was full. He fathered ten children with six living past infancy. His third wife Keziah Hood was a kind and loving stepmother to Hood's children from his previous marriages. She was energetic and resourceful as she paid for their home from money she earned from sewing. She was a strong and supportive partner. All six of the Hood's children were educated at Livingston College. In 1916 Hood was placed in mandatory retirement but was called into active Episcopal service with the death of a key bishop. James Walker Hood died October 30, 1918 in Fayetteville, North Carolina. He served as bishop of the AMEZ Church for forty-four years and as a minister for approximately sixty years. He contributed to uplifting the black race as a religious, political, and social servant of his people. Study of his life shows how thoroughly he practiced what he preached.

REFERENCES

Books

"James Walker Hood, 1831-1911." In *Paths Toward Freedom: A Biographical History of Blacks and Indians in North Carolina by Blacks and Indians.* Illus. James and Ernestine Huff. Raleigh, N.C.: North Carolina State University Center of Urban Affairs, 1976.

Kletzing, H. F., and W. H. Crogman. *Progress of a Race.* Atlanta, Ga.: J. L. Nichols & Co., 1898.

Martin, Sandy Dwayne. *For God and Race: The Religious and Political Leadership of AMEZ Bishop James Walker Hood.* Columbia, S.C.: University of South Carolina Press, 1999.

Periodicals

Hackett, David G. "The Prince Hall Masons and the African American Church: The Labors of Grand Master and Bishop James Walker Hook, 1831-1918." *Church History* 69 (December 2000): 770.

Hildebrand, Reginald F. "For God and Race: The Religious and Political Leader of a AMEZ Bishop James Walker Hood." *Journal of Southern History* 66 (November 2000): 872.

Online

Documenting the American South, University of North Carolina Library. http://docsouth.unc.edu/church/hood100/bio.html (Accessed 6 February 2006).

Evans Metropolitan AME Zion Church. http://www.evansmetropolitan.org/bishopjameswalkerhood/ (Accessed 6 February 2006).

Collections

The Carter G. Woodson Collection, Chicago Public Library, Chicago, Illinois, has some of Hood's papers consisting of his unfinished autobiography and correspondence from leaders of his day. Related information can be found through collection of AMEZ Church Histories.

Lean'tin L. Bracks

John Lee Hooker
1917–2001

Blues musician, guitarist

John Lee Hooker was an influential blues artist who played a role in the development of the genre from the late 1940s through the 1990s. Playing both electric and acoustic guitar, Hooker's distinctive vocal and instrumental style also shaped the development of rock and folk music during the 1960s and 1970s.

John Lee Hooker was born on August 22, 1917 (some sources say 1920), in Clarksdale, Mississippi, the fourth of 11 children born to William and Minnie Hooker. Hooker's father was a sharecropper and Baptist minister who did not like the blues, referring to it as the "devil's music." Hooker's parents separated when he was five and divorced when he was 11 years old.

While Hooker received a limited formal education, music was an important component to his life. He first became exposed to it at church and constructed his first instrument out of a piece of string and an inner tube. Soon after her divorce, Hooker's mother was remarried to William Moore, a blues musician. Hooker credited Moore with mentoring him as a musician.

Moore taught Hooker how to play guitar, showing the boy his minimalist but very rhythmic style of playing. Soon Moore and Hooker were playing together at house parties and dances near their hometown. Though Hooker enjoyed playing with his stepfather he was unhappy living in Mississippi and when he was 14 years old he ran away from home.

Travels to Tennessee and Midwest

Hooker first tried to join the U.S. Army, in part because during World War II a young man in uniform would attract attention from women. He made it through basic training and after three months was stationed in Detroit before it was discovered that he was underage and he was kicked out. Hooker then moved to Memphis, Tennessee. Supporting himself with day jobs such as movie theater usher, Hooker also worked as a musician at house parties because he could not get into clubs. Among the musician he played with was Robert Lockwood.

In his late teens Hooker moved to Cincinnati, Ohio, where he continued to work menial day jobs like dish washer and steel mill worker while establishing his music career at night. Because he was still a minor, Hooker could only play the blues at house parties. However, he also sang in gospel quartets like the Delta Big Four, Fairfield Four, and the Big Six. By working frequently in front of a crowd, Hooker learned the ropes of performing on stage and entertaining an audience.

John Lee Hooker

Chronology

1917	Born in Clarksdale, Mississippi on August 22
1948	Records first single, "Boogie Chillen," which climbs to the number-one spot on the R & B charts
1949	Follows up with ten other top-ten songs
1951	Releases "In the Mood"
1959	Releases his first record album, *I'm John Lee Hooker,* on Riverside Records
1971	Records *Hooker 'n' Heat* with the group Canned Heat
1980	Appears in *The Blues Brothers*; inducted into the Blues Foundation Hall of Fame
1989	Records *The Healer*
1990	Inducted into the Rock and Roll Hall of Fame
1991	Records *Mr. Lucky*
1995	Retires from performing on a regular basis
1997	Opens blues club in San Francisco called John Lee Hooker's Boom Boom Room; releases *Don't Look Back*
2001	Dies in Los Altos, California on June 21
2003	Album *Face to Face* is released posthumously

In 1943 Hooker moved to Detroit, where jobs were plentiful because so many men were overseas fighting in World War II. He held day jobs washing dishes and working as a janitor in a Chrysler automobile plant until 1951. Now a legal adult, Hooker was now able to perform at the many blues clubs located near Detroit's Hastings Street.

While living in Detroit Hooker's style changed: from the country/rural folk-type blues played primarily on an acoustic guitar, he shifted to a more urban style played on an electric guitar. Part of the change was due to his encounter with Elmer Barber, a local record-store owner. Barber had heard Hooker perform and he made several primitive recordings of the young musician in the makeshift studio located in the back of his store.

Barber's recordings soon found their way to Bernie Besman, owner of a small record label, Sensation Records. It was Besman who suggested that Hooker should switch to electric guitar and include faster-paced material in his gigs at local clubs. Taking this advice, Hooker soon became one of the leading musicians in the Motor City, which at this time was witnessing a booming economy due to the men and women living there who had become wealthy due to the rise in wartime manufacturing.

Records First Hit Single

Hooker made his first single for Besman in 1948. "Boogie Chillen," recorded in a basement in Detroit, fea-

tures only Hooker's vocals, his electric guitar, and the sound of his foot tapping the beat. When "Boogie Chillen" was released on Sensation it sold so well that the small label could not handle the demand. The single was then released on Modern Records and quickly climbed to the number-one spot on 1949's prototype R & B charts, selling a million copies.

Although Hooker did not receive the royalties he was entitled to for this and future songs, his success with "Boogie Chillen" came as a surprise to him. In 1949 he followed up his first single with ten other top-ten songs. Many of these early recordings feature only Hooker and his guitar, although fellow guitarist Eddie Kirkland sometimes appeared on recordings with him.

One reason that Hooker often recorded alone was that his beat was hard for accompanying musicians to follow. By recording alone, it was easier to achieve a clean take, and the recording session took less time. Describing his sound, Hooker once told John Collis of the *Independent,* "I don't like no fancy chords. Just the boogie. The drive. The feeling. A lot of people play fancy but they don't have no style. It's a deep feeling—you just can't stop listening to that sad blues sound. My sound."

Despite becoming involved in conflicts regarding royalty issues, Hooker continued to record for Modern in the late 1940s and early 1950s, and some of his hits of the period include "Rock House Boogie," "Crawling King Snake," and "In the Mood." One of his most popular recordings of the period, "In the Mood," was released in 1951 and sold a million copies. To ensure that he would earn enough to support his family, Hooker recorded and released material under several other names for over two dozen other labels. Some of his pseudonyms included John Lee Booker, which he used for Chess recordings, Johnny Lee, used for DeLuxe, and Texas Slim and John Lee Cooker, which he used on his recordings for the King label.

Many of Hooker's early releases influenced other bluesmen such as Buddy Guy and are considered to be early precursors to rock and roll. His blues songs incorporated the traditional blues sound with jump and jazz rhythms. Although Hooker recorded his music with little backup, he also performed with a live band at clubs in Detroit and beyond. Due to his talent, hard work, and determination, Hooker was a success on the R & B circuit throughout the 1950s.

In 1955 Hooker signed on with VeeJay Records of Chicago. For this label he changed his recording style; his subsequent recordings becoming a better reflection of his live show. Because solo blues performance was waning in popularity, Hooker started recording with a band, producing such hits as "Dimples" and "Boom Boom."

Becomes Hit on Folk Circuit

Even though Hooker found success performing on electric guitar, he discovered a new audience for his acoustic blues during the late 1950s. Folk music was now undergoing a revival of interest, and groups like the Weavers and blues singers like Odetta were increasingly becoming popular among young white college students. Hooker began appearing in folk clubs, coffeehouses, on college campuses, and at folk festivals as a solo artist, and did several recordings accompanying himself with acoustic guitar. Many of his songs written and recorded during this period reflect his background in Mississippi.

In 1959 Hooker released his first record album, *I'm John Lee Hooker*, on Riverside Records, his new label. This new turn in the career of the 42-year-old bluesman earned him an even wider audience, not just among white folk fans but in international markets where his records were also released.

Hooker once discussed his change from electronic band to solo folk music with Peter Watrous, telling the *New York Times* interviewer: "I played solo for a long time, so I know how to tap my feet so it sounds like a drum. It wasn't any problem to start playing the coffeehouses. I can switch to any style, you have to be versatile as a musician. I knew the white audience was out there but I didn't know how to get it. As the years go by, thing change and to me they were just people. I had no thought that British singers would start singing my songs, I had no idea what would come with that. People got more civilized."

In the 1960s Hooker began touring internationally, and the popularity of his music spread throughout the world, particularly among the more sophisticated audience. His songs also influenced emerging British rock bands such as the Rolling Stones and the Animals. Hooker continued to record on VeeJay, although he did not end his practice of laying down tracks for other labels as well.

Returns to Electric

By the mid- to late 1960s Hooker once again moved away from performing acoustic solo blues when the trend toward electric blues prompted him to put together a new band. In 1965 he recorded an album with British group John Mayall and the Groundhogs. Many of Hooker's recordings during the late 1960s were albums rather than singles, and many were recorded in collaboration with bands composed of younger musicians. While many of these recording sessions produced mixed results due to Hooker's unique rhythmic stylings, his sessions with the group Canned Heat is considered one of the best. The resulting album, 1971's *Hooker 'n' Heat*, was a hit.

Though Hooker continued to record a little and play a lot during the late 1970s and 1980s, the blues had declined in popularity and demand for his music had declined. He still toured as a way to pay the mortgage on the house he owned in San Francisco, often performing with his Coast-to-Coast Blues Band and sometimes coming under fire for letting other musicians carry him musically. Many of his early recordings were also repackaged and released for blues collectors.

Considered one of the top blues performers in the United States, Hooker was given a small role in the blockbuster movie *The Blues Brothers* in 1980. That same year he was inducted into the Blues Foundation Hall of Fame. In the late 1980s and 1990s his songs regained popularity, even appearing as part of film soundtracks. In the 1990s, Hooker himself began appearing in ads for Lee Jeans, Pepsi, various brands of liquor, and other products.

Records *The Healer*

In 1989 Hooker returned to the studio after a decade's absence and recorded *The Healer*. He was joined by several contemporary blues artists, including Bonnie Raitt and Robert Cray, as well as Latin artists Los Lobos and Carlos Santana. Produced by Hooker's former guitarist Roy Rogers, *The Healer* became one of the biggest-selling blues records of all time, selling 1.5 million copies. Hooker also won a Grammy Award for the song "I'm in the Mood," which he performs on the album with Raitt.

Hooker was inducted into the Rock and Roll Hall of Fame in 1990 and was the focus of a tribute concert at Madison Square Garden that same year. With the success of *The Healer*, he started recording again, again in collaboration with other blues artists. His 1991 recording *Mr. Lucky* was a hit on the album charts in the United Kingdom. Among the musicians he worked with on this recording were Johnny Winter, Keith Richards, Van Morrison, and Santana.

Hooker continued to perform and record into his late 70s and early 80s and found himself even more popular than he had been earlier in his career. He continued to perform live with the Coast-to-Coast Blues Band into the 1990s, but had the added security of royalty income to rely on. Unlike many other blues and R & B artists of his generation, Hooker continued to earn royalties from his early recordings because he had wisely saved his contracts and, with the proper legal advise, went to court to ensure that recording companies continued to honor them.

After a hernia operation in 1994 made it painful for Hooker to perform, he slowed down. After the release of *Chill Out* in 1995 he retired from performing on a regular basis, although he still made occasional appearances on stage. In 1997 he opened a blues club in San Francisco called John Lee Hooker's Boom Boom Room. One of his final releases was the album *Don't Look Back* (1997), which features a cover of Jimi Hendrix's "Red House."

Hooker died in his sleep of natural causes on June 21, 2001, at his home in Los Altos, California. At the time of his death, Hooker was working on the album *Face to Face,* which was released in 2003. During his lifetime he had recorded more than 500 tracks, making him one of the most recorded blues musicians of all time. Married and divorced four times, Hooker was survived by eight children. Late in his life he had contemplated his eventual passing, telling Ben Wener of *Tulsa World*: "We all got to go one day. We live out this life as long as we can and try to make the best of it. Simple as that. That's what I've done. All my life, just try to make the best of it."

REFERENCES

Periodicals

Independent, July 1, 1990.
New York Times, October 16, 1990; June 22, 2001.
Tulsa World, August 30, 1997.

Online

E! Online, www.eonline.com, September 15, 2003.

Annette Petrusso

Daniel M. Jackson
1870–1929

Gambling house owner, funeral director

Daniel M. Jackson was undoubtedly the most powerful African American vice lord ever known to Chicago's black community. He was educated, thoroughly criminal, generous to African Americans in need, political, and civic-minded. Jackson, a quiet, savvy man, ran several gambling houses out of his funeral parlors; at the same time he sacrificed his own profits to help blacks that lacked money for a proper burial.

Donald McKee Jackson was born September 9, 1870 in Pittsburgh, Pennsylvania. He came to Chicago in 1892 with his father Emanuel, and brother, Charles, and together they opened a funeral parlor at 26th and State streets in Chicago's Second Ward.

By the time Jackson arrived in Chicago, he had graduated from Lincoln University, in eastern Pennsylvania. He and the family ran the Emanuel Jackson Undertaking Company until tension developed with his father. Because of the increased population and the concurrent lack of public health regulations, a variety of professional groups developed. Within the ranks of embalmers, casket manufacturers, funeral directors, and burial policy agents, professional associations formed to insure that funeral industry standards were met. Jackson was one of the first African Americans to use the most up-to-date undertaking techniques in his business. Standardization in the funeral business did not lead to impersonal or ethnically identical services. Black funeral companies even benefited from the prejudice of some white funeral parlors that did not like to handle blacks.

Engages in Legitimate and Illegitimate Businesses

Jackson relied on gambling for a large part of his income. A crackdown on gambling in 1923 by a new face in the mayor's office, Democrat William Dever, severely reduced Jackson's profits. Because of the Great Depression and a deteriorating economy, Jackson sought a partner, and he and Otto Stevenson, a black entrepreneur,

Chronology	
1870	Born in Pittsburgh, Pennsylvania on September 9
1892	Moves from Pittsburgh to Chicago with his father and brother; family opens the Emanuel Jackson Undertaking Company
1919	Works in William Hale Thompson's mayoral campaign
1923	City crack-down on vice depletes Jackson's operating capital
1925	Marries Lucy Mott, sister of gangster Robert T. Mott; establishes the Metropolitan Funeral Home Association with Robert M. Cole
1927	Sells the Metropolitan Funeral Home Association to Cole for $500; retains position as MFHA's funeral director
1928	Appointed as the acting Republican committeeman for Second Ward
1929	Appointed to the Illinois Commerce Commission; dies in Chicago

joined forces to provide a burial insurance service to Chicago's Bronzeville residents. Jackson did the funeral services and Stevenson sold insurance. The Metropolitan Funeral System Association (MFSA), as the company was called, continued an earlier tradition of mutual aid and beneficial societies to provide funerals to those with limited incomes. Working-class citizens received affordable funerals, prompt payment of claims, and inexpensive premiums (15 cents paid in for each dollar paid out), and the arrangement allowed recent immigrants the opportunity to return their deceased to the South for burial.

The premium that subscribers paid per policy was inexpensive and did not provide enough money to cover the cost of a funeral. When the MFSA started to falter, Stevenson lacked the personal income needed to keep the company solvent. When Stevenson departed, Jackson was unwilling to let the company dissolve, believing that it provided a useful service to needy clients. Jackson perhaps owed his solvency to the money that came his way when he married Lucy Mott, the sister of gangster Robert T. Mott, in 1925. As a result, Jackson subsidized the company until Robert M. Cole joined it in 1926.

Jackson hired Cole, former railroad porter-in-charge, to manage his mortuary business. The two probably became friends as a result of their mutual interest in

351

gambling. Jackson and Cole established the Metropolitan Funeral Home Association (MFHA) in 1925. After Cole joined the business as manager, Jackson continued to tend the service end of the business himself. In 1927 Cole asked Jackson to sell him the business which he did—for $500.

Cole reorganized the MFHA and later renamed it the Metropolitan Mutual Assurance Company. He hired two former associates of Jackson, professionals who restructured the company's policies. First, premium charges were restructured and college-trained businessmen managed the accounts. Between 1927 and 1931, Cole had poured $18,000 of his gambling profits into the business to keep it afloat. Although Jackson retained his position as MFHA's funeral director, Cole, until his death in 1956, was the real force behind the company. The firm narrowly survived the Depression, but, by the end of World War II, it was a profitable and smoothly operating business.

If Jackson viewed the MFHA as his own private charity, he had no such view of others' businesses. In the Second Ward and parts of the Third, he was known as the uncontested vice-lord of Chicago's African American settlement. Throughout Prohibition, except for two brief periods, Jackson controlled blind pigs (speakeasies or places that sold alcohol illegally), prostitution, gambling, and policy (betting) wheels. From Second Ward operations in liquor and gambling, Jackson's bagmen collected about $500,000 per year—and from the Third Ward and adjacent areas, another $200,000. Jackson's secretary, Carter Hayes, collected protection money—approximately 40 percent of the proceeds—from each of the illegal games in operation. Jackson's men also shook down pool halls, saloons, and cabarets that operated craps, poker, and blackjack games and sold gin and whiskey on the premises. The quiet, shrewd Jackson ran several gambling houses. Two were located in his funeral parlors and a third in the Pekin Theater building.

Becomes Interested in Politics

During the racial strife of 1919, Jackson began to take an interest in politics. Shortly before the 1919 victory of William Hale "Big Bill" Thompson, Jackson became active in politics. Thompson was not unknown to Jackson since Thompson had lived near the Jackson family mortuary. Jackson was impressed with Thompson's address to Second Ward voters during his first run for mayor. The thrust of his campaign hinged on his willingness to provide jobs and stay out of vice operations (mostly controlled by Jackson) in exchange for votes in the ward.

Jackson campaigned for Thompson in Chicago's African American community. Since Jackson consistently donated a percentage of his gambling profits to the less fortunate in the community, he helped secure votes for Thompson, who claimed that African Americans had

the right to self-determination. Thompson's campaign rhetoric aimed at black gambling gained him the staunch support of voters and ward-level political candidates. So successful was Thompson at securing local offices for his constituents that his detractors began to call him the "Second Abraham Lincoln" and referred to city hall as "Uncle Tom's Cabin."

Republican Mayor Thompson, like Jackson and partner Cole, believed that African Americans should have access to wide-open gambling, prostitution, saloons, and policy betting. Since such entertainment was generally segregated, many Second Ward voters believed that this was reason enough for them to run their own vices wide open. After an investigation of his operations, Jackson was summoned to city hall and forced to shut down; however, many of his establishments soon reopened and started to thrive again under the protection of local law enforcement.

In 1923 the state attorney's office dispatched another team to investigate South Side vice. The investigation resulted in the second closing of all illegal vice operations. Although most gambling parlors, saloons, and policy games closed, Jackson's stayed open, and most of Jackson's cohorts returned to business. Thompson decided not to run for mayor again in 1923; so Jackson's supporters urged him to back Democrat William Dever, hoping to negotiate a deal with him that would protect Jackson's gambling interests. The mayoral race in 1923 was complicated by harsh accusations against Arthur Lueder, the Republican candidate, from both the Jackson syndicate and the Dever faction. The Dever faction tried to undercut Lueder, by accusing him of Ku Klux Klan sympathies, prejudice against blacks, and other race-related activities. The bad publicity Lueder received may have influenced Jackson's decision to vote for Dever. In the 1923 election, emotions ran high and Jackson, feeling insecure perhaps about Dever's policies, may have forced his way into polling booths and may have threatened voters and Second Ward voting officials.

After Dever's election, Jackson's supporters saw their worst nightmare come true. Dever closed Jackson's operations for the duration of his term in office. Jackson and his cohorts threatened to oust Dever—which in effect they did—by reelecting Thompson to a second term in 1927. By this time, voters and gamblers alike were becoming disaffected. The prices they paid Jackson for protection were draining them since they often took in less than they paid out. Much of the money they paid was used by Thompson for his America First cronies who were running in the 1928 primaries. The America First Party goals were to keep American troops out of Europe and other foreign countries and to encourage self-determination.

Thompson's second and third terms brought back and reinforced the South Side's former open gambling policy and rewarded Jackson's efforts on behalf of Thompson.

Jackson, who had never held a political office, was appointed acting Republican committeeman in 1927 for the Second Ward and was then elected to the position in 1928. He also received from Governor Len Small an appointment to the Illinois Commerce Commission, shortly before his death, in 1929. When Jackson died, an indictment for fraud and gambling was still on file against him.

Jackson, the Anomaly

Jackson was an anomaly—a soft-spoken man who ran a mortuary and did so even after the business lost money so his clients could receive just the kind of funerals they wanted. He was kind to his associates and gave them help in starting businesses, and he stood up for those he believed in. As an example of that faith, Jackson remained a supporter of Thompson long after others believed that Thompson used them for his own political advancement. Jackson was also persuasive and not above using his political power to get what he wanted. He had ties to mobsters and his business and political dealings were outside the law, yet Jackson seems to have believed in certain positive values, such as self-determination.

REFERENCES

Books

Drake, St. Clair, and Horace Cayton. *Black Metropolis: A Study of Negro Life in a Northern City.* New York: Harper&Row, Publishers, 1962.

Gosnell, Harold F. *Negro Politicians: The Rise of Negro Politics in Chicago.* Chicago: University of Chicago Press, 1967.

Online

Adkins, Brian. *Black Business in the Black Metropolis: The Chicago Metropolitan Assurance Company, 1925-1985.* http://www.eh.net/bookreviews/library/0055.shtml (Accessed 13 March 2006).

Cogwell, Henry. "By the Numbers: A Look at Chicago's Policy Racketeers Part I." http://www.geocities.com/jiggs2000_us/article.html (Accessed 13 March 2006).

Ruth, David E. "Crime and Chicago's Image." *Encyclopedia of Chicago.* http://www.encyclopedia.chicagohistory.org/pages/352.html (Accessed 13 March 2006).

Wilson, Mark R. "Funeral Service Industry." *Encyclopedia of Chicago.* http://www.encyclopedia.chicagohistory.org/pages/491.html (Accessed 13 March 2006).

Lois A. Peterson

Isaiah Jackson
1945–

Conductor

Isaiah Jackson, a brilliant and renowned conductor, has been guest conductor for many of the world's greatest orchestras. He was the first American and the first African American to serve as principal conductor and later music director for the Royal Ballet, Covent Garden, in London, England. Jackson is credited with helping the London orchestra achieve a higher level of performance.

Jackson was born on January 22, 1945, in Richmond, Virginia. Jackson's family lived in a middle-class, segregated neighborhood, and his friends were the children of doctors and lawyers. Among his childhood friends was the famous tennis player Arthur Ashe. Education was an important part of Jackson's family goals as his father and grandfather were both surgeons. His family believed that education was the only useful response to a racist society. Jackson's first introduction to music came as a result of an early childhood accident. When Jackson was two years old, he fell on a milk bottle and severed the tendons of his wrist. His father, who was an orthopedic surgeon, prescribed music lessons for therapy. Jackson took to his lessons with such dedication and obvious aptitude that music became a permanent part of his life. Jackson was a good student, but to make sure that he would meet academic challenges and also be happy, his parents decided to send him to Putney, a progressive and academically intense private boarding school in Vermont. Putney was integrated, and the students were socially conscious. In the 1960s Jackson and his friends picketed the local Woolworth's near Brattleboro in support of the lunch counter sit-ins that were happening in the South for equality and equal access for African Americans.

Jackson enrolled at Harvard University after graduating from high school. Although he wanted to pursue music as an adolescent, his parents had hoped he would join the diplomatic corps once he graduated from college. Jackson's father had taken a diplomatic post in the Agency for International Development in 1967 and saw opportunities there for his son. Jackson chose to major in Russian history and literature, which reflected the international politics of the times. Even though he chose an international subject, Jackson committed himself to a career in music. While at Harvard he had the opportunity to conduct the Mozart opera *Cosi fan tuttle*. Jackson was so taken by the experience that he decided at that point to pursue music as a career. Subsequently, he went to Stanford University and received his M.A. in music in 1969. He spent a summer in Fontainebleau, France, with Nadia Boulanger, a renowned teacher, before going to the prestigious Julliard School of Music. While still a student at Julliard, Jackson was named music director of the New York Youth Symphony. He became the founder and con-

Chronology

1945	Born in Richmond, Virginia on January 22
1949	Begins music lessons as therapy for wrist injury
1959	Attends Putney, a private boarding school in Vermont
1966	Graduates from Harvard (cum laude) with a degree in Russian literature and history
1967	Receives M.A. from Stanford University
1969	Receives M.S. from Julliard School of Music
1973	Receives D.M.A. from Julliard School of Music
1973-87	Serves as associate conductor, Rochester Philharmonic Orchestra, Rochester, New York
1978	Begins serving as guest conductor for numerous orchestras from New York to Berlin
1986	First American and African American appointed principal conductor, Royal Ballet, Covent Garden, London, England
1987	First African American music director appointed Dayton Philharmonic Orchestra
1987-90	First American and African American appointed music director, Royal Ballet, Covent Garden, London, England
2000	First African American music director appointed to Pro Arte Chamber Orchestra of Boston

ductor for the Julliard String Ensemble (1970-71), and was appointed assistant to the renowned conductor Leopold Stokowski with the American Symphony Orchestra (1970-71). He served as assistant conductor for the Baltimore Symphony (1971-73). Jackson received his M.S. in 1969 and his D.M.A. in 1973 from Julliard.

After completing his education at Harvard in 1973, Jackson became associate conductor for Rochester Philharmonic Orchestra, Rochester, New York. He maintained this position for fourteen years while engaging in other orchestral opportunities. Also during this time Jackson met and married Helen Tuntland, president of Hochstein Music School. With an active career in place even before graduation, once he completed his studies Jackson was invited as a guest conductor for many important American orchestras, such as the New York Philharmonic (1978), San Francisco Symphony (1984), Detroit Symphony Orchestra (1983, 1985), Cleveland Orchestra (1983-84, 1986-87, and 1989-92), and the Boston Pops (1983, 1990-92).

Makes Orchestral Debut in Europe

In Europe, Jackson made his orchestral debut with the Vienna Symphony in July 1973. He also conducted the Orchestre de la Suisse-Romande, the Helsinki Philharmonic at the Helsinki Festival, the R.A.I. Orchestra in Rome, and many other prominent orchestras. Jackson performed with the Dance Theater of Harlem at the Spoloeto Festival in Italy. While he was conducting with the Dance Theater of Harlem, the group performed in the Royal Opera House in London in 1981. The management

of the Royal Opera House carefully observed Jackson. As a result Jackson was invited to serve as guest conductor for the Royal Ballet, Covent Garden, in London in 1986 and became the music director for the Royal Ballet in 1987. Jackson became the first American and first African American to have a chief role with the Royal Ballet. To meet the needs of this London post, he moved his family from New York to London. By this time his family had grown to include his children, Benjamin, Katharine, and Caroline. Jackson expressed regret that his schedule had increasingly allowed less time with his children and his wife. Once coming to London, Jackson came to love England and its culture and said that it reminded him of Richmond. He was quite successful with the Royal Ballet and was credited with developing the Royal Ballet orchestra into a disciplined and eloquent ensemble. Also in 1987 Jackson was appointed music director of the Dayton Philharmonic Orchestra.

Jackson became the first African American to serve as music director of the Dayton Philharmonic Orchestra. Jackson is one of only a few African American conductors and one of the very few who make a living at this profession and have a permanent post. Jackson has an extraordinary talent which consists of a keen ear, fine touch, and the ability to reveal the subtle points of a score. Fluent in five languages, Jackson is further enhanced by his broad knowledge of music, spanning from European composers to African American ones. Jackson has said that works of art are capable of transcending cultural differences.

Jackson has also been active in the recording industry. He made three recordings with the Berlin Symphony: string music by the film composers Bernard Herrmann, Miklo's Ro'zsa, and Franz Waxma; dance music by William Grant Still; and a live-performance CD of the orchestra's 1991 New Year's Eve concert. Also among his recordings is one of harp concertos of Ginastera and William Mathias for Koch with the English Chamber Orchestra and Ann Hobson Pilot as soloist. Another CD features Jackson conducting the Louisville orchestra and gospel choirs from the Louisville, Kentucky area under the direction of Alvin Parris III. The CD grew out of a project between Jackson and Parris. The project opened the Brisbane Biennial Festival of Music and was presented in fourteen U.S. cities.

Jackson is the music director of the Pro Arte Chamber Orchestra of Boston and the Youngstown Symphony Orchestra. He is also the musician in residence at the Memorial Church at Harvard University. His contributions to the orchestral community have been rewarded with numerous awards, including the Signet Society Medal for Achievement in the Arts from Harvard University in 1991. Jackson joins past recipients such as T.S. Eliot, Robert Frost, and Robert Lowell. He remains in great demand by orchestras and music organizations around the world.

REFERENCES

Books

Burgess, Majorie. "Isaiah Jackson." In *Contemporary Black Biography*. Vol. 3. Ed. Barbara Carlisle Bigelow. Detroit: Gale Research, 1993.

Periodicals

Story, Rosalyn. "Have Baton—Will Travel." *American Visions*. Vol. 8 (February-March 1993): 42-5.

Online

"Isaiah Jackson Biographical Information." http:// maximaltd.com/ijbio.htm (Accessed 30 March 2006).

"Isaiah Jackson." *Pro Arte: Isaiah Jackson*. http://www. proarte.org/concerts/Pro%20Arte%20Isaiah%20 Jackson.htm (Accessed 30 March 2006).

"1992 Honorees—Isaiah Jackson." *Dominion*. http:// www.dom.com/about/education/strong/1992/ isaiahjackson.jsp (Accessed 30 March 2006).

Lean'tin L. Bracks

Chronology	
1878	Born in Bellefonte, Pennsylvania on June 20
1896	Leaves home to study and support himself; joins Ed Winn's Big Novelty Minstrels around this time
1900	Becomes journalist for *Today* newspaper in Detroit
1902	Becomes first black bank clerk with the Chicago Jennings Real Estate and Loan Company
1904	Joins U.S. Railroad police around this time
1912	Heads investigation and inspection for Standard Life Insurance Company; begins newspaper work for the New York *Globe*
1919	Becomes editor of the Negro Department of *Billboard* magazine; writes "Jackson's Page"
1920	Writes articles for the New York *Sunday Herald*
1921	Writes articles for *Chicago Defender*
1927	Becomes first head of Negro Affairs for U.S. Department of Commerce
1934	Becomes first black marketing specialist for Esso Standard Oil Company
1940s	Becomes first black member of the American Marketing Association
1960	Dies in New York City on November 15

James A. Jackson
1878–1960

Editor, journalist, promoter

A versatile man, James A. Jackson worked through three highly visible arenas to promote black cultural and economic development. As editor of the Negro Department of *Billboard* magazine, he was a major influence in promoting black theatricals during the Harlem Renaissance of the 1920s. He was also well-connected with black and white professional, commercial, and industrial groups and, due to his work with the U.S. Department of Commerce, was regarded as an eminent advisor on African American business activities. He traveled widely and aided and encouraged black commercial development and encouraged industrial training to prepare youth for commercial enterprise. As a public relations specialist of Standard Oil Company, Jackson became one of the first African American salespersons of the mid-1930s to promote his business in the African American market.

In 1773 a group of Quakers who had bought the Jackson family's freedom from Portuguese traders in Portsmouth, England, brought the Jacksons to America. They settled in the area later known as Centre County, Pennsylvania. Before his marriage, James Jackson's father, Abraham Jackson, was engaged in show business as a member of the McMillen and Sourbeck Jubilee Singers, a commercial singing group formed in Bellefonte. Later on, but before the group became widely known as the Stinson's Singers, Abraham Jackson left the singers and married. James Albert Jackson was born in Bellefonte (sometimes spelled Belfonte), Pennsylvania, on June 20, 1878, to Abraham Valentine and Nannie Lee Jackson—the oldest son of their fourteen children.

James A. Jackson was educated in Bellefonte's public schools and Bellefonte High School. In 1894-95 he worked as a reporter for two local newspapers, the *Bellefonte Daily Gazette* and the *Daily News*, apparently over the objections of his mother. Jackson is quoted in *The Colored Situation* as saying that, when he was fourteen years old, his mother refused to permit him to learn newspaper work. She also refused to allow him to work with a local white doctor who wanted him to learn medicine, for "she was sincere in her belief that there was no place for a Negro in either calling," he said. His mother was familiar with only four African American newspapers, and they were small, two-sheet publications for which she had no respect. Likewise, she knew little about the accomplishments of blacks in medicine and had known of only two doctors—one in Washington, D.C., and another in Chicago. "I longed to be an editor," he continued, and his persistence toward fulfilling his ambition paid off. Meanwhile, the large Jackson family put a strain on the family's income. James Jackson left home around 1896 to earn money on his own and to continue his education. He appears to have moved to Cleveland, Ohio where he continued to write. He also worked as a bellboy and dining room employee in Cleveland's Hollender Hotel. There he met Richard B. Harrison, later a dramatist and college arts instructor, who taught him elocution.

Around this time Jackson became an advance man for Ed Winn's Big Novelty Minstrels and also sought out feature players. When Winn's show closed, Jackson had to find other ways to support himself and pursue his education. It is unclear if he attended college. He spent his winters earning enough money to support his summer school work. With a firm knowledge of show business and some education, he became a good representative for the minstrel shows. He appears to have traveled with minstrels between 1896, when he first left home, and 1900. In that year he worked with Richard and Pringle's Georgia Minstrels, featuring Billy Kersands. Around 1900 as well, he was a journalist for *Today*, an afternoon newspaper in Detroit. He left for Chicago a year later and took a civil-service examination. Since the results were slow to come, he spent much time in Daddy Love's place, located at the corner of 27th and State Street. Actors gathered there between seasons, and Jackson met and became friendly with many of them.

In 1902, Jackson accepted a post as bank clerk with the Chicago Jennings Real Estate and Loan Company, becoming the first person of color in the state to hold such a post. When off duty, he was part-time usher at the famous Pekin Theater and on hand for its historic opening in 1904. It was the first black-owned theater in the country and became important for stage productions and concert series. It was also the home of the Pekin Stock Company, the first black theatrical stock company.

Jackson passed the civil-service examination and for a number of years was a member of the U.S. Railroad police. As a road officer, he traveled throughout the country to investigate various cases; one of them was the infamous Harrison Gang. Headed by Jeff Harrison, the Harrison Gang was involved in what was called the "World's Greatest Train Robbery."

In 1912 Jackson was in charge of investigation and inspection for Standard Life Insurance Company. Jackson went on to engage in newspaper work for the *New York Globe* (1912), the New York *Sunday Herald* (1920), and the *Chicago Defender* (1921). According to Henry T. Sampson in *Blacks in Blackface*, his two best serial works were published in the *Globe*: "The Negro at Large" in 1912 and "The Underlying Cause of Race Riots" in 1919. The New York *Sun* published several of his feature stories in 1921 and the New York *Herald* carried others in the magazine section of its Sunday edition. He collaborated with other authors and published in national magazines and foreign newspapers. During World War I, Jackson was one of the two agents-in-charge of the U.S. Military Intelligence Bureau and worked in the "Plant Protection" section.

Promotes Black Entertainment in *Billboard* Magazine

According to *Blacks in Blackface*, at some time in the 1920s Jackson was owner/manager of two theaters in Columbus, Ohio—the Empress (for motion pictures) and the Dunbar (for vaudeville, or road shows). By age forty in 1918, Jackson had joined the editorial staff of *Billboard* in New York City, then the largest theatrical paper in the world, and was so prominent in his work as editor of the Negro Department that he was given the nickname "Billboard." Jackson was the first African American reporter hired by a major white theatrical magazine. *Billboard* hoped to increase its circulation by tapping a new market, and Jackson helped make the magazine popular among black entertainers. Beginning with the November 6, 1920 issue, he wrote a regular column called "Jackson's Page"; the black press copied his articles, adding the byline "Billboard" Jackson. According to Bruce Kellner for *The Harlem Renaissance*, "by 1919 he had become the most widely read black show-business newspaperman in America." His work brought him in contact with many black luminaries, including those of the Harlem Renaissance.

Through the magazine Jackson celebrated the achievement of blacks in the entertainment industry and also helped them to set high moral standards. He encouraged performers to join theatrical organizations. He exposed the conditions surrounding those involved with the Theater Owners Booking Association (TOBA), a large employer of black entertainers, by airing the unfair treatment they received. His writings stimulated the formation of several professional organizations, such as the Colored Actors' Union, the National Association of Colored Fairs, and the Deacons. For his page, Jackson collected information on all aspects of entertainment, including the circus, burlesque, music and opera, street fairs, and vaudeville. He published several annual surveys of the industry, presenting data that he compiled. Thomas Fletcher wrote in *100 Years of the Negro in Show Business* that "his record of achievements . . . [was] one of the most imposing anywhere." He served *Billboard* from 1919 to 1925 when lack of advertising forced retrenchment. While in that post, he was also executive correspondent in New York for Claude Barnett's Associated Negro Press, which led to his next post, this time in the business arena.

Heads Black Affairs for the Commerce Department

African American businesses grew rapidly during the first three decades of the 1900s. Thus, there was a need to find a person who could work with the U.S. Department of Commerce to help make its publications and activities meaningful to black entrepreneurs. Claude A. Barnett (1889?-1967), founder of the powerful Associated Negro Press (ANP), persuaded the Republican administration to hire Jackson as "Negro information specialist" to serve this need. While the Republicans were no great friends of black America, they knew that the National Negro Business League had strong ties to the Republican Party and, of course, the presidential election of 1928 was coming up. Thus, in May 1927, Barnett notified the administration and Secretary of Commerce Herbert Hoover that he had a candidate for the post, "Billboard" Jackson.

In *Enterprise & Society*, Robert E. Weems Jr. and Lewis A. Randolph chronicled James Jackson's life as promoter of "Negro Affairs" for the U.S. Department of Commerce beginning November 1927 and ending in 1933. They wrote that, although Jackson failed to "generate the direct financial assistance to black entrepreneurs" associated with later federal initiatives, he pioneered in efforts "to provide black businesspeople with useful information," and he "helped to positively reshape contemporary African American entrepreneurs' belief about the role of government in their lives."

Jackson's appointment was surrounded by racial issues and began and ended in the midst of political maneuverings. His duties began on November 15, 1927, and his race was withheld to avoid criticism from whites in the department. Thus, he was referred to as a dark-skinned foreigner, whom whites could accept over a black American. While Jackson passed a civil service examination and was hired for the position of commercial agent, the Commerce Department's "Daily Bulletin" listed him as an assistant business specialist. Jackson and the department remained at odds over how his post would be publicized, particularly in the African American business community that he was hired to serve. Political overtones arose when the department envisioned the forthcoming presidential election with Hoover in the race and again feared negative reaction from whites. Finally, the department officials resolved the matter of title and called him special agent; a commercial agent designation was reserved for the department's foreign staff.

Jackson attended a meeting of African American leaders from the field of business, education, religion, and elsewhere in the community, which was held in Durham on December 7-9, 1927. Called the Durham Fact-Finding Conference (also known as a Stock-Taking and Fact-Finding Conference on the American Negro) the session provided Jackson's introduction as a Department of Commerce official. The conference dealt with a number of issues, including black business organizations, health conditions of the race, religious progress, political progress, insurance (including fraternal, mutual, and life), educational progress, and black relations everywhere. In his address to the audience, Jackson noted that there were no African American organizations on the bureau's list of contacts.

By early 1929, both the Department of Commerce and Hoover, who was now in office, displayed some sensitivity toward racial parity, at least in the matter of business. Some of the changes were due to the pressure brought to bear on Hoover by Barnett, who was also secretary of the Colored Voters Division of the GOP as well as wielder of the power of the Associated Negro Press to give positive news coverage to the administration. Barnett's efforts were partly devoted to ensuring that Jackson was treated fairly. Jackson traveled widely in 1929 and 1930, visited 34 cities, and gave presentations to nearly 30,000 people. He also held numerous interviews in his Washington office and responded to inquiries regarding research. According to Weems and Randolph, "the primary message Jackson presented to the black business community was that of self-help." He also attended the second Durham Fact-Finding Conference on April 17-19, 1929, and told the audience that the general public expected black entrepreneurs to bear full responsibility for themselves.

As he called for efficiency in black business operations, he criticized blacks for patronizing non-black businesses but fell short of endorsing the "buy black" practice that was gaining in popularity around that time. The Colored Merchants Association (CMA), however, embraced Jackson's call for business efficiency, for it, too, advocated such practice. The CMA, organized in Montgomery, Alabama in 1928, spread rapidly across the country and was especially active in Harlem. Albon L. Holsey, National Negro Business League secretary, organized chapters across the country. The CMA advocated cooperative purchasing and advertising in an effort to keep costs low for black consumers. Jackson aided the CMA movement by holding a three-month training course in Harlem for grocers on issues such as business efficiency and modern management. He also compiled extensive data about black businesses for the Department of Commerce, and surveyed national, state, and local African American organizations, thus providing the department extensive information about black enterprises.

Hoover and his administration never took Jackson's work seriously but appeared to use him for whatever political gains they could garner. The African American community, according to Weems and Randolph, linked Holsey's and Jackson's interest in Hoover and the Republicans to "class considerations." The black masses, who were hit hard when the Great Depression of the 1930s worsened, began to oppose Hoover and the Republican Party and later embraced Franklin D. Roosevelt and his New Deal public assistance. After the presidential election of 1932, Republicans Hoover and Jackson were out of office; Democrat Eugene Kinckle Jones (1885-1954), a National Urban League official, replaced Jackson.

Holds Marketing Post with Standard Oil

Jackson had indeed performed well, yet he was unemployed for two years. His skills and connections then led him to a post with Esso Standard Oil Company of New

Jersey, which he served as special representative to the African American community. At that time, Standard Oil was perhaps the largest business enterprise in the world. Beginning in 1934, Jackson was one of the few blacks working in such a capacity for a major white company. He became an asset to Standard Oil and was promoted several times. He knew the African American market very well—something that proved beneficial to Standard Oil—and he helped aspiring young blacks prepare for service as filling station-operators. He also prepared them for other business ventures. Writing in *Crisis* magazine for 1935, Jackson noted that Standard Oil had always maintained a substantial number of blacks on its payrolls; the company "has given every reason for the Negro to look upon the company and its affiliates with favor." His work with Standard Oil made him nationally prominent. Originally hired for six months, he served the company altogether for twenty years. When he was eligible for retirement in 1941, the company kept him on as a special representative in public relations, on a yearly basis, until he retired in 1954.

Jackson was a member of the National Association of Market Developers (NAMD), founded in 1953. By then, many large companies in the United States hired "Negro Market" specialists to help them attract African American consumers. These specialists were never included in the companies' meetings where marketing and strategic issues were discussed and, in fact, were isolated from white market developers. The black specialists reacted by forming a mutual support organization and social network. NAMD's early membership read like a "Who's Who" of African Americans in the business arena, and included one of the most well-known men of such stature, James "Billboard" Jackson. Jackson was also a member of the American Marketing Association, which he joined in the mid-1940s, becoming its first and only black member. He spoke at its 1947 annual convention. He was an advisory board member of Friendship College in Rock Hill, South Carolina. Other memberships included board of director, the National Negro Business League; National Negro Press Association; Brotherhood of Sleeping Car Porters; Association of Special Agents; NAACP; National Fair Officials Association; Business Men's Exchange; the Elks; League of Teachers in Business Education; American Teachers Association; founding member, Association of Business Education; board of trustees, Pioneer Business Institute (in Philadelphia); Clef Club (which he also served as honorary vice president); Florence Mills Club; and Negro Actors Guild. As well, he was a 33rd degree active Mason and at one time grand historian, United Supreme Council of the Masons. His social organizations included the Hiawatha Club (Los Angeles); Red Caps (Chicago); DePriest Fifteen (Washington, D.C.); and founder, Tri-Esso Club of Standard Oil Company. In addition to his membership in the Republican Party, he belonged to Phi Beta Sigma Fraternity According to his obituary in the *New York Times*, he was an active or honorary member of over thirty-seven fraternal and business organizations.

In *Pages from the Harlem Renaissance: A Chronicle of Performance*, Anthony D. Hill described Jackson as "bright, confident, self-motivated, and [a] indefatigable journeyman." Hill said also that he was "a tall, clean shaven, full-faced, fair-complexioned man with a receding hair-line." By age forty-two, Hill described him as stout and neatly dressed "in his usual professional attire—a dark suit, white shirt, and a tie that exuded the air of a distinguished gentleman." He married Gabrielle Bell Hill on April 6, 1909. Jackson was devoted to his wife, and she accompanied him on many of his early travels for the railroad police. They had one son, Albert, who became an actor on the black stage. While their early addresses are unknown, at least in later life the Jacksons lived at 312 Manhattan Avenue in New York City. Jackson died on November 15, 1960, and was survived by his wife, his son, a brother, and two sisters. His funeral was held at the Grace Congregational Church in Harlem, where he was a member. It was also the church of choice for many show business people, whose profession was not considered honorable unless in performance for the church. Gabrielle Jackson's funeral was held there as well, in 1961. The accounts of Jackson's life show that he was successful in every major assignment that he undertook and that he became known for his work in these areas, chiefly in promotional work in entertainment, business, and advertising, and in transcending racial barriers

REFERENCES

Books

Everett, Faye Philip. *The Colored Situation: A Book of Vocational and Civic Guidance for the Negro Youth.* Boston: Meador Publishing Company, 1936.

Fletcher, Thomas. *100 Years of the Negro in Show Business.* 1954. New York: Da Capo Press. 1984.

Hill, Anthony D. *Pages from the Harlem Renaissance: A Chronicle of Performance.* New York: Peter Lang, 1966.

Oak, Vishnu V. *The Negro's Adventure in General Business.* Yellow Springs, OH: The Antioch Press,1949.

Ottley, Roi, and William J. Weatherby, eds. *The Negro in New York: An Informal Social History 1626-1940.* New York: Praeger Publishers, 1967.

Sampson, Henry T. *Blacks in Blackface: A Source Book on Early Black Musical Shows.* Metuchen, N.J.: Scarecrow Press, 1980.

Weems, Robert E., Jr. "National Association of Market Developers (NAMD)." In *Encyclopedia of African American Business History.* Ed. Juliet E. K. Walker. Westport, Conn.: Greenwood Press, 1999.

Who's Who in Colored America. 7th ed. Eds. G. James Fleming and Christian E. Burckel. Yonkers-on-

Hudson, N.Y.: Christian E. Burckel & Associates, 1950.

Periodicals

Jackson, James A. "Big Business Wants Negro Dollars." *Crisis* 42 (February 1935): 45-46.

"James Jackson, 83, Ex-Esso Publicist." *New York Times*, 18 November 1960.

Weems, Robert E. Jr., and Lewis A. Randolph. "'The Right Man': James A. Jackson and the Origins of U.S. Government Interest in Black Business." *Enterprise & Society* 6 (2005): 254-77.

Collections

Letters to and from Jackson and other documents related to his work are in the Claude A. Barnett Papers, Chicago Historical Society in Chicago, Illinois; the General Records of the Department of Commerce, Record Group 40, National Archives and Records Administration, College Park, Maryland; and the Hoover Presidential Papers, Herbert Hoover Presidential Library, West Branch, Iowa. Personal information is in the National Personnel Records Center, St. Louis, Missouri.

Jessie Carney Smith

Jesse L. Jackson, Jr.

Jesse L. Jackson, Jr.
1965–

Politician, minister

Representative Jesse L. Jackson Jr. began service in the United States House of Representatives on December 12, 1995, as a member of the 104th Congress. He was the ninety-first African American ever elected to Congress. The elder son of well-known activist Jesse Jackson Sr., Jackson Jr. was rapidly making a name and a place for himself in U.S. politics.

Jesse Jackson Jr. is the second of five children (the first son) born to Jesse Jackson Sr. and Jacqueline Jackson. He was born on March 11, 1965 in Greenville, South Carolina. On that date, his father was in Alabama with Martin Luther King Jr. participating in the Selma to Montgomery civil rights march.

Jackson grew up on the South Side of Chicago, where his mother was a dominant force in his early life. His father was away the majority of his early life participating in the civil rights movement. When his father was home, the two of them worked together for the non-profit

organization PUSH (People United to Save Humanity, later changed to People United to Serve Humanity) that was founded by Jackson Sr. in 1971.

Jackson Jr. spent his early school years at LeMans Military Academy, a private junior high school located in Rolling Prairie, Indiana, and at St. Albans preparatory school, located in Washington, D.C., where he excelled academically and on the football team. Jackson attended North Carolina Agricultural and Technical State University in Greensboro, North Carolina, the same school where his mother and father met. In 1987, he graduated magna cum laude earning a B.S. degree in business management after only three years at the university. Three years later, he earned an M.A. in theology from the Chicago Theological Seminary in 1990, and in 1993, he received his J.D. from the University of Illinois College of Law.

Jackson spent his twenty-first birthday with his famous father in a jail cell in Washington, D.C. They had been arrested for taking part in a protest against apartheid staged at the South African Embassy. In 1987, Jackson met the woman he later married; Sandra Jackson, a lawyer and former television reporter, was politically active, working for Michael Dukakis's 1988 presidential campaign while Jackson Jr. was working for his father's campaign. She also worked for U.S. representative Cleo Fields. Prior to becoming involved in politics she worked for NBC in Toledo, Ohio. The couple married in 1991.

Chronology

1965	Born in Greenville, South Carolina on March 11
1987	Earns B.S. (magna cum laude) in business management from North Carolina Agricultural and Technical State
1988	Introduces his father at the Democratic National Convention
1990	Earns M.A. in theology from the Chicago Theological Seminary
1991	Marries Sandra Jackson
1993	Receives J.D. from the University of Illinois College of Law
1995	Elected to House of Representatives on December 12
1996	Co-authors *Legal Lynching: Racism, Injustice, and the Death Penalty* with his father
1999	Co-authors *It's About the Money!* with his father and Mary Gotshall
2000	Member of the Abraham Lincoln Bicentennial commission; member of the Harvard University John F. Kennedy School of Government's Institute of Politics Senior Advisory Board
2001	Co-authors *Legal Lynching: The Death Penalty and America's Future* with his father and Bruce Shapiro

Jesse Jr. and his wife settled in the Second Congressional District of Illinois. They had two children, Jessica Donatella and Jesse L. Jackson, III.

Before becoming an elected official, Jackson served as the national field director of the National Rainbow Coalition. In this role, he instituted a national non-partisan program that successfully registered millions of new voters. He also created a voter education program to teach citizens the importance of participating in the political process, including how to use technology to win elections and more effectively participate in politics. He also helped create *JaxFax*, a weekly facsimile and online weekly newsletter of the Rainbow Coalition.

His famous father influenced his career choices. Jackson watched his father's political activities and the results of the elder Jackson's social actions impressed him; he knew that he wanted a career in public service. This desire was also influenced by many of the political decisions made during the 1990s, such as the Supreme Court's efforts against affirmative action and proposed cuts in Medicare and Medicaid that made him question the government's care for the elderly. He told *Ebony* magazine: "There's something wrong about a government that would try to balance its budget on the backs of people who cannot defend themselves."

Wins Bid for Office

On September 9, 1995, Jackson entered the special election held in Illinois' Second District. In 1992 Mel Reynolds had defeated Gus Savage, who was well known in Congress for his chronic absenteeism and for his anti-Semitism. Reynolds, who was the first African American Rhodes Scholar, was highly praised by the press as a coalition-builder. But approximately halfway through his first term, he was in court being tried for having had sex with an underage campaign worker. In September 1995, the court found him guilty of criminal sexual assault and obstruction of justice, and he resigned from Congress. This vacancy led to Jackson's successful first run at politics.

Although he was young, Jackson had the experience of working with his father to prepare him. He had traveled with his father and had met every president since Jimmy Carter, as well as many other influential individuals, such a Pope John Paul II; Fidel Castro, Cuba's head of state; Yasir Arafat, the Palestinian leader; and Yitzhak Rabin, the prime minister of Israel. Also, at the 1988 Democratic National Convention, he had spoken briefly before introducing, along with his brothers and sisters, his father at the Democratic National Convention, a moment that gave him wide public exposure.

Jackson won a hard fought special election for the seat, representing south Chicago industrial neighborhoods and the racially diverse communities surrounding them. He ran in the primary in a district that was primarily Democratic against three political veterans. Jackson discovered that his youth served to his advantage, and he targeted those voters between the ages of 18 to 45, who were disheartened by the current system. Jackson's campaign efforts led to some 5,000 new voters being registered within thirty days. He accomplished this increase by visiting churches, as well as those areas that attract younger people.

On December 12, 1995, Jackson defeated his Republican opponent, T. J. Somer. Two days later, he was administered the oath of office by House Speaker Republican Newt Gingrich. The event was witnessed by Jackson Sr., who, at that time, represented the District of Columbia as a nonvoting member of the U.S. Senate.

Being a black liberal but fiscal conservative increased Jackson's popularity among the middle class. His voting record proves his support for labor unions, abortion rights, and environmental issues. Moreover, he has expressed his feelings that most racial debates are really economic ones.

Jackson sat on the following committees and subcommittees: the House Appropriations Committee; Subcommittee on Labor, Health and Human Services, and Education; and on the Subcommittee on Foreign Operations, Export Financing, and Related Programs. During his tenure, he proposed constitutional amendments to ensure that public education and universal healthcare are seen as human rights for all Americans.

Jackson's legislative initiatives also included the HOPE for Africa Act of 1999, which addressed the HIV/AIDS epidemic and set a framework for trade in sub-Saharan Africa. He worked to improve domestic healthcare needs in underserved communities by leading the successful effort to establish the National Center on Minority Health and Health Disparities at the National

Institutes of Health in 2001. He served as a member of the Harvard University John F. Kennedy School of Government's Institute of Politics Senior Advisory Board starting in 2000 and as a member of the Abraham Lincoln Bicentennial commission starting in 2003.

Jesse Jackson Jr. is a member of the "Keep Hope Alive" Political Action committee; Democratic National Committee; and Operation PUSH. Jackson has received many awards, including honorary doctorate degrees from Chicago Theological Seminary, Governors State University, North Carolina A & T State University, Charles R. Drew University of Medicine and Science, Meharry Medical College, and Morehouse School of Medicine.

REFERENCES

Periodicals

Norment, Lynn. "Introducing Jesse L. Jackson Jr." *Ebony* (February 1996): 156-58.

Online

"Congressman Jesse L. Jackson, Jr." http://www.house. gov/jackson (Accessed 2 December 2005).

"Jesse Jackson Jr." Fair Vote. http://www.fairvote.org/ (Accessed 2 December 2005).

Mattie McHollin

Reggie Jackson

Reggie Jackson
1946–

Baseball player

Reggie Jackson became known as "Mr. October" for his outstanding athletic performances in baseball, particularly during post-season playoff competition and the World Series. A member of five world championship teams with the Oakland Athletics and the New York Yankees, Jackson is best known for hitting three home runs in one game of the 1977 World Series. His efforts matched the record of Yankee legend Babe Ruth, made him the first player to ever hit five home runs in one World Series, and secured his place in the Baseball Hall of Fame.

Reginald Martinez Jackson was born on May 18, 1946, in Wyncote, Pennsylvania, a suburb of Philadelphia. He was the fourth of six children. His father, Martinez Clarence Jackson, was the son of a white Spanish woman and black man who operated his own tailoring and dry cleaning business after being a second baseman with the Newark Eagles in Negro League baseball from 1933 to 1938.

Clara Jackson, his mother, was a homemaker, but split the family and moved to Baltimore, Maryland, when Reggie was six years old. Reports vary on how many children went with her, but Reggie and some of his siblings remained with their father. The abandonment by his mother affected him deeply, yet it forced him to mature early and become an independent, self-reliant child.

When not in school, the younger Jackson helped out in the family business, gaining skills in tailoring, cleaning, and other aspects of clothing maintenance. His father demanded excellence and also inspired his son to show initiative and pursue worthwhile goals.

Shows Promise in Baseball and Other Sports

At the age of thirteen, Jackson was already recognized as the best baseball player in town and the only black athlete on the Greater Glenside Youth Club baseball team. He experienced racism in sports for the first time while playing against a team from Fort Lauderdale, Florida, and failed in trying to impress observers with his ability. The disappointment motivated Jackson to improve, with the goal of becoming a professional athlete.

In 1960 Jackson entered Cheltenham Township High School in Philadelphia, where he became an outstanding

Chronology

1946	Born in Wyncote, Pennsylvania on May 18
1966	Named College Player of the Year and drafted by Oakland Athletics
1967	Hits first major league home run on September 17
1968	Marries Juanita Campos
1972	Goes on injured list while Oakland wins World Series; divorces
1973	Plays in first World Series and wins MVP Award
1974	Helps Oakland win third straight world championship
1977	Hits three home runs in World Series game; wins championship and MVP with New York Yankees
1978	Helps New York win second straight world championship
1982	Leaves New York for California Angels
1987	Returns to Oakland Athletics for last season of baseball career
1993	Inducted into Baseball Hall of Fame
2005	Survives potentially fatal automobile accident

athlete in football, basketball, and track, as well as baseball. As a senior, the left-handed Jackson pitched three no-hit games, had a batting average of .550, and ran the hundred-yard dash in 9.7 seconds.

When college recruiters began contacting the Jackson home, his father was as concerned about academic and educational opportunities for his son as athletics. As a result, Jackson followed his father's advice to go to college instead of pursuing professional baseball when he was drafted by the Kansas City Athletics.

Attends College; Begins Baseball Career

After Jackson graduated from high school on June 20, 1964, he attended Arizona State University (ASU) in Tempe, Arizona, on an athletic scholarship. He was recruited to play football for the university, but freshmen could not play in games. This was not the case in baseball, and after his first year at ASU, Jackson spent the summer of 1965 playing baseball for a team in the Baltimore Orioles organization.

Jackson returned to ASU, broke nearly every school record by the end of the baseball season, and was named the national College Player of the Year in 1966. On June 12 of that year Jackson was selected again during the second baseball free agent draft by Charles O. Finley, owner of the Kansas City Athletics (A's), and signed to an $85,000 contract with a new Pontiac automobile as an extra incentive. At the time Finley commented that Jackson would help him win a World Series, a prophecy that proved to be true.

At the age of twenty, Jackson left college to fulfill his dream, beginning with the Lewiston (Idaho) Athletics and the Modesto (California) Reds. During this period Jackson was trained as a fielder and continued to develop

his powerful hitting swing. In nearly seventy games played with Lewiston and Modesto, Jackson hit twenty-three home runs with sixty runs batted in, but also struck out eighty-one times. When unsuccessful, he often exploded in anger and lashed out.

Jackson's talent still earned him a quick promotion to the A's minor league team in Birmingham, Alabama, where he led the Southern League with eighty-four runs scored despite his eighty-seven strikeouts. As a result, he was named the Southern League Player of the Year.

Becomes Major League Player

During the same year Jackson was promoted to the Kansas City Athletics major league team for the rest of the baseball season. The A's were in tenth place with no prospects for postseason play, but Jackson served notice of things to come when he hit his first major league home run on September 15, 1967.

In his first full season with the team, which became the Oakland A's after the organization relocated to California, Jackson became a national sensation by hitting twenty-nine home runs and driving in seventy-four runs. He also married his Mexican-American college sweetheart, the former Juanita (Jennie) Campos on July 8, 1968, and finished the season with the unfortunate distinction of 171 strikeouts, the second highest total for a season in major league history.

During the 1969 baseball season Jackson hit forty-seven home runs, and his number of runs scored and walks led the major leagues. His home runs, runs batted in, and slugging average that year became personal and career bests, but he also led the majors in strikeouts for the second of four straight years.

Jackson continued his personal development by playing winter baseball in San Juan, Puerto Rico between the 1970 and 1971 seasons, with coach and teammate Frank Robinson, who became the first African American manager (head coach) in major league baseball with the Cleveland Indians in 1975. At the 1971 All-Star Game in Detroit, he added to his fame with a home run that hit a light tower, preventing it from going completely out of Tiger Stadium.

Owner Charles Finley's dreams came true in 1972, as the A's won the first of three straight world championships that year. Jackson injured himself in the AL championship series against the Detroit Tigers and did not play in the World Series as his teammates defeated the Cincinnati Reds in seven games. In addition to his physical injury, Jackson saw his marriage end in divorce the same year.

In 1973 Jackson led the AL in home runs and runs scored, won the league's Most Valuable Player Award as the A's repeated as AL champions, and was named Major League Player of the Year by *Sporting News*, a national publication. Jackson played in his first World Series against the New York Mets, helping his team to win with several key hits in the sixth game and his first World Series home run in the seventh game. He also led the A's with six runs batted in (RBIs), and was named the most valuable player in the championship series.

Oakland won its third straight title the following year, against the Los Angeles Dodgers; however, the following season ended in disappointment. Even though he tied for most home runs in the AL with thirty-six in 1975, the team lost the AL championship series to the Boston Red Sox in three straight games.

Jackson's personality often made for difficult relationships with teammates, but that was not the only reason the team lost its chemistry. His increased salary demands and holdouts led to clashes with Finley and team management during and after the 1975 season. As a result, Finley traded Jackson to the Baltimore Orioles in 1976. After one year in Baltimore, Jackson became a free agent, with offers from several teams for his services.

Takes Right Field and Center Stage in New York

Jackson turned down a five-year, $5 million contract to play for the Montreal Expos and was quoted in *African American Sports Greats: A Biographical Dictionary* as saying, "if I played in New York, they'd name a candy bar after me," comparing himself to legendary Yankee home run hitter Babe Ruth. After personally negotiating a nearly $3 million contract for five years and the bonus of a $60,000 Rolls Royce automobile with Yankee owner George Steinbrenner, Jackson signed a hotel napkin with the words, "I will not let you down. Reginald M. Jackson."

His huge salary, ego, reputation, and the high expectations of Yankee supporters created controversy immediately after he arrived in New York. Problems developed with several of his teammates and fans, especially after a sportswriter quoted Jackson as saying that "he was the straw that stirs the drink" during spring training before the 1977 season, according to *Contemporary Black Biography*. He also frequently clashed with Yankee manager Billy Martin, who was known to have as explosive a temperament as Jackson.

Hits Three Home Runs in One World Series Game

Despite these problems, Jackson made good on his promises during his first year with the Yankees. He drew sellout crowds to Yankee Stadium and major league ballparks all over the country, causing him to make the statement, "I could put meat in the seats," as quoted in *Contemporary Black Biography*. Jackson fans, haters, and hecklers relished opportunities to see what the controversial athlete would do both on and off the baseball diamond.

Jackson's crowning achievement in baseball came on October 18, 1977 during Game 6 of the World Series

against the Los Angeles Dodgers. He hit three consecutive home runs in three at-bats in Yankee Stadium, each on the first pitch from three different Dodger pitchers (Burt Hooton, Elias Sosa, and Charlie Hough). His efforts not only clinched another world championship for the Yankees but also matched a feat that previously had only been accomplished by Babe Ruth in Game 4 of the 1923 World Series against the St. Louis Cardinals. Jackson was named the most valuable player of the series, becoming the first player to win this distinction with two different teams.

Jackson stated that his three home runs in that game were the ultimate highlight of his baseball career. His prediction also came true in 1978, when the Standard Brands Company marketed the "Reggie Bar" to the public. His teammate with both the A's and Yankees, pitcher Jim "Catfish" Hunter, was quoted in *Contemporary Black Biography* as saying, "When you unwrap a Reggie Bar, it tells you how good it is."

Endures Stormy Season to Win Second World Series with Yankees

The 1978 baseball season began with great anticipation and expectations of Jackson and the Yankees to repeat as world champions. The number of egos involved with the team increased, and despite many heated arguments, meetings, and other distractions (including Jackson's five-game suspension after a racially charged argument with Steinbrenner and disobeying Martin during a game), the talent of the Yankees prevailed and put the team back into contention for postseason play.

The Yankees were tied with their hated rivals, the Boston Red Sox, on the last day of the regular season with 99 wins each. The teams met in Boston's Fenway Park for a one-game playoff, with the winner moving on to the AL championship series. Jackson hit a home run in the eighth inning which provided the margin of victory, as they defeated the Red Sox by the score of five to four.

The team went on to defeat the Kansas City Royals in the AL championship series, as Jackson lived up to his "Mr. October" nickname with a .462 batting average in the four games. His output included two home runs and six RBIs, leading Baltimore Orioles manager Earl Weaver to say, according to *October Men*, that Jackson "was simply the best late-season hitter ever."

The World Series rematch against the Los Angeles Dodgers provided more drama, as Jackson struck out at a critical point in the second game. The Dodgers then led the series two games to none, before the Yankees won Game 3 behind ace pitcher Ron Guidry. Jackson was involved in a controversial base-running play that eventually turned Game 4 into another Yankee win to tie the series.

Jackson and the Yankees went on to win the fifth game in New York, and the sixth and final game in Los Angeles for a second straight world championship. Jackson hit a home run against the same pitcher who had struck him out in Game 2, but Yankee shortstop Bucky Dent was named the most valuable player for the series.

Tragedy and Turmoil During Final Years in New York

Exactly two weeks after the World Series ended, the son of Yankee manager Bob Lemon died on October 31 of injuries sustained in an automobile accident. Lemon resigned midway through the 1979 season. The team was in fourth place when Billy Martin returned as manager, but did not improve afterwards.

Jackson remained on the team due to contract obligations, despite his past history with Martin. The Yankees suffered another tragedy when catcher and team captain Thurman Munson died in an aircraft accident on August 2, 1979. Ironically, it was Munson who gave Jackson the nickname "Mr. October" during the 1977 World Series. The following year Jackson batted .300 for the only time in his career and hit 41 home runs during the regular season, but he and the Yankees lost three straight games to the Kansas City Royals in the AL championship series.

Jackson had only fifteen home runs during the 1981 season, which was shortened by a player strike. The Yankees made it back to the World Series against the Dodgers, after a five-game AL eastern division series and the AL championship series. Jackson hit two home runs against the Milwaukee Brewers in the division series but was not a factor in winning the AL championship over his old team, the Oakland Athletics.

The Yankees lost the 1981 World Series in six games to the Dodgers, as Jackson had four hits in only twelve at-bats, including his last World Series home run in Game 4. Steinbrenner did not sign Jackson to a new contract, making Jackson a free agent.

In 1982 Jackson headed west to play for the California Angels and owner Gene Autry, the singing cowboy and actor in Hollywood westerns and other films. During his first year with the team, Jackson tied for the AL lead in home runs and helped the Angels get as far as the AL championship series. He also got some satisfaction when he hit a home run against the Yankees the first time he returned to Yankee Stadium as a visiting player.

On September 17, 1984, Jackson reached another milestone when he hit home run number 500 during a home game against the Kansas City Royals. The date had double significance, in that he hit his first major league home run on the same day in 1967. Jackson continued with the Angels through the 1986 season, with the team again only getting to the AL championship series in the postseason. A personal highlight was passing Yankee legend Mickey Mantle when he hit home run number 537, putting Jackson in sixth place among major league play-

ers (at the start of the 2006 baseball season, he had moved down to tenth place).

After his contract with the Angels ended, Jackson returned to the Oakland Athletics for his last season in 1987. Jackson hit his last home run in Anaheim Stadium (the same place where he hit his first one and home run number 500) and a single in his last at-bat against the Chicago White Sox in Comiskey Park, ending his career after twenty-one seasons with 563 home runs and the dubious record of the most strikeouts (2,597).

Enjoys Business Success, Honors, and Life after Baseball

In retirement, Jackson continued a number of business pursuits, including work as a part-time field reporter and color commentator for *ABC Sports*, cameo appearances in movies, and commercials as a spokesperson for various companies. He remained connected to the game by lobbying for increased involvement of minorities in baseball as front-office managers and executives, served as a consultant to the Oakland Athletics from 1988 to 1993, then reconciled with Steinbrenner and became a special assistant and liaison in the Yankee organization.

Jackson also turned his passion for automobiles into a multi-million dollar personal collection and ownership of several car dealerships. He also worked with the Upper Deck baseball card company, developed his own successful sports memorabilia company, invested wisely in real estate, fine art, and antiques, and avoided the financial problems faced by many former professional athletes.

In 1993 Jackson was elected to the Baseball Hall of Fame in Cooperstown, New York, the first year he was eligible for consideration. He received 396 out of 423 ballots (93.6%), and was the twenty-ninth player to enter on the first vote. At his induction ceremony, Jackson thanked his father, paid tribute to African American baseball trailblazers Jackie Robinson and Larry Doby, and quoted Yankee legend Lou Gehrig in expressing appreciation for his baseball career.

The Yankees retired Jackson's number 44 in a ceremony at Yankee Stadium on August 14 of that year. In 1999 Jackson placed forty-eighth among "The 100 Greatest Baseball Players" by *The Sporting News*, and his plaque was added to Yankee Stadium's Monument Park on July 6, 2002. The Oakland Athletics followed suit several years later, when they retired Jackson's uniform number 9 on May 22, 2004.

On two occasions, Jackson led a team of investors in attempts to gain ownership of a major league baseball franchise. His groups were outbid when the California Angels and Oakland Athletics were for sale, yet he continued efforts to become the first African American owner in major league baseball.

In March 2005 Jackson was spared serious injury after an automobile accident in Tampa, Florida, while there for spring training with the Yankees. In the account of the accident posted on his official website, he began with the words, "Thank God for having a hand on my shoulder." In terms of his life and career achievements, past and present, it is obvious that this indeed has been the case.

REFERENCES

Books

Kahn, Roger. *October Men: Reggie Jackson, George Steinbrenner, Billy Martin, and the Yankees' Miraculous Finish in 1978.* New York: Harcourt Books, Inc., 2003.

Light, Jonathan Fraser. *The Cultural Encyclopedia of Baseball.* Jefferson, N.C.: McFarland and Company, Inc., Publishers, 1997.

Porter, David L., ed. *African American Sports Greats: A Biographical Dictionary.* Westport, Conn.: Greenwood Press, 1995.

Reichler, Joseph L., ed. *The Baseball Encyclopedia.* 7th ed. New York: Macmillan Publishing Company, 1988.

Reynolds, Victoria. "Reggie Jackson." In *Great Athletes.* Vol. 4. Eds. Dawn P. Dawson et al. Pasadena, Calif.: Salem Press, 2002.

Strumolo, Amy Loerch. "Reggie Jackson." In *Contemporary Black Biography.* Vol. 15. Ed. Shirelle Phelps. Farmington Hills, Mich.: Gale Group, 1997.

Online

Reggie Jackson Web Site. http://www.reggiejackson. com (Accessed 1 April 2006).

Fletcher F. Moon

Robert R. Jackson
1870–1942

Politician, entrepreneur, soldier

At a time in American politics when African Americans had a difficult time in getting elected and exerting any political influence, Robert Raymond Jackson was able to find a path into Chicago politics and gain recognition for African American voters. His experiences in the military during the Spanish American War and his efforts toward improved race relations supported his move into politics. Jackson became alderman for two Chicago wards and promoted issues important to the community. Once leaving politics his entrepreneurial interests took him into printing and into cooperative grocery work.

Chronology

1870	Born in Malta, Illinois on September 1
1888	Joins the National Guard, "Famous Eight Illinois," attaining the rank of major
1889	Becomes postal service clerk
1909	Retires from postal service as assistant superintendent
1912	Wins election to state legislature as a Republican
1913	Secures funding for Emancipation Golden Jubilee
1918	Becomes alderman, Second Ward District for Chicago City Council
1931	Becomes alderman, Third Ward District for Chicago City Council
1939	Leaves politics and becomes commissioner of Negro American League
1942	Dies in Chicago, Illinois on June 12

Jackson's service as a joiner, leader, and military man made it possible for him to have an impact on the political visibility of African Americans in Chicago politics.

Robert Raymond Jackson, the son of William and Sarah Cooper Jackson, was born on September 1, 1870 in Malta, Illinois, but most of Jackson's childhood was spent in Chicago. As a youth Jackson sold newspapers and shined shoes in the business district to help him get as far along in school as possible. He eventually left school during the eighth grade and pursued full-time employment. In 1888, Jackson joined the National Guard as a drummer in the Eighth Regiment of Illinois volunteers. These soldiers fought in Cuba during the Spanish American War and came to be known as the "Famous Eight Illinois" infantry because of their African American commanding officer. During that time Jackson is noted for his organization of the Manana Club to improve relations between Cubans and African American officers. Jackson moved through the ranks and eventually earned the title of major.

Apart from the National Guard, by the time Jackson was eighteen he had secured a position as clerk in the post office. This was a much-coveted position for African Americans in 1889, since most jobs for blacks were in the service industry or as laborers. Jackson passed the civil service exam with an unusually high mark of 98.16 and maintained this level of performance on future tests. He worked as a stamping clerk and as a letter distributor. On May 31, 1885, he married Annie Green of Chicago and they had two children, Naomi and George Earl.

After over twenty years with the postal service, Jackson resigned in 1909 having earned the position of assistant superintendent of Armour Station. Next Jackson started a printing and publishing business, the Fraternal Press. He pursued other ventures, too, such as secretary of the Chicago Giants Baseball Club; director and auditor of the African Union Company, which dealt in

African merchandise; director of the Fraternal Globe Bonding Company; and military writer and authority for text books issued by U.S. officers. He and partner Beauregard F. Mosley co-founded in 1910 the Leland Giants. Jackson later went on to own the Columbia Giants professional baseball team.

In addition to his successful postal career, military career, and publishing business, Jackson became very active in fraternal and volunteer organizations. He was listed in the city directory in 1923 with memberships in nearly all of Chicago's fraternal orders, including the Appomattox Club, Elks, Knights of Pythias, Dramatic Order of Knights of Omar, the Odd Fellows, the American Wood, the Royal Arch, and the Masons. He participated in establishing the first cooperative grocery in the African American community in Chicago. He also participated in over twenty-five volunteer organizations, such as the Boy Scouts and the Young Men's Christian Association. White and African American candidates would speak to members of these organizations during primary and election campaigns to secure votes. Jackson's involvement and exposure in these groups along with his career in postal service and the rank of major in the National Guard provided the network and credentials for him to enter politics in 1912.

Chicago Politics

After defeating two Democrats, a fellow Republican, and a Progressive candidate, Jackson was elected as a Republican to the state legislature from the Third Senatorial District. Getting elected was an accomplishment in itself as discriminatory practices in the election process made it difficult for African Americans to enter the political arena. Once Jackson was elected, the same limitations made it difficult for him to influence decisions that were not specifically related to racial issues. He spoke out against prohibiting intermarriage and helped to stop legislation that reduced African American workers on the railroads. He was able to ban from Illinois theaters racist films such as *The Clansman* and *The Birth of a Nation*. Jackson secured funding for Chicago's 1913 Emancipation Golden Jubilee celebration. However, beyond issues regarding race, Jackson had little to no influence on the state legislature.

In February 1918, after six years as a state legislator, Jackson ran for alderman for the Second Ward District to the Chicago City Council. He ran against former county commissioner Oscar DePriest who even though acquitted on charges of conspiracy and bribery, still had six other indictments unresolved against him. DePriest was a race man and was well liked by the community, while Jackson had the backing of the state senator George F. Harding and Congressman Madden. Jackson won by a narrow margin. In 1931 with the rezoning of Chicago's wards, Jackson had to move south to secure a legal residence.

With this change he was elected to alderman for the Third Ward District to the city council.

Jackson's role as alderman in the Republican Party and the overall political scene regarding African Americans made far reaching reform difficult. Leadership in the Republican Party, headed by Mayor William Hale Thomson (1915-23 and 1927-31), promoted vice and corruption, which allowed even less opportunity for reform. The result for most African American politicians was a style of politics that catered to white dominated organizations and public work projects. Jackson was able to secure major projects such as a park, a library, a playground, and minor improvements in services such as a system of milk inspection. With the migration of African Americans to the North in the 1920s and 1930s, the ability to provide voting blocks to various parties was essential.

Southern African Americans still identified Republicans with Abraham Lincoln, and Democrats with the Old South. Although this alignment gave more influence to Republican African American politicians, it did not allow for any further opportunities for reform. Jackson and other African American politicians continued to have minimal impact on issues other than race. As more African Americans moved into the Democratic Party, Jackson eventually lost his seat on the city council in 1939. The style of politics in Chicago at that time was seen by activists in the 1960s as plantation politics, which resulted in votes for recognition and power within the African American community but few changes that imparted political and social opportunity and equality. Although reform was not accomplished on a level that most had envisioned for African Americans during the time, politicians such as Jackson were able to secure some consideration in an environment of staunchly imposed limits.

After leaving politics, Jackson returned to his love of baseball. He became commissioner of the Negro American League for two years. He was elected president of the league for three terms and was serving as president of the New Negro Baseball League at the time of his death. Jackson continued to pursue opportunities for the African American community as he sold the city on the idea of erecting a tablet commemorating Chicago's first citizen, Jean Baptiste Point De Sable, a person of African descent. On June 12, 1942 Jackson suffered a stroke and died. He was survived by his wife Hattie Ball Lewis and son George Earl.

REFERENCES

Books

Drake, St. Clair, and Horace R. Clayton. *Black Metropolis: A Study of Negro Life in a Northern City*. New York: Harcourt, Brace, & Company, 1945.

Gosnell, Harold. *Negro Politicians: The Rise of Negro Politics in Chicago*. Chicago: University of Chicago Press. 1935.

Grossman, James R. "Robert R. Jackson." In *American National Biography.* Vol. 11. Eds. John A. Garraty and Mark C. Carnes. New York: Oxford University Press, 1999.

Who's Who of the Colored Race. Vol. 1. Chicago: Who's Who in Colored America Publishing, 1915.

Yenser, Thomas, ed. *Who's Who in Colored America.* 6th. ed. Brooklyn: Thomas Yenser Publisher, 1942.

Periodicals

Obituary. *Chicago Defender*, 20 June 1942.

Lean'tin L. Bracks

Samuel L. Jackson
1948–

Actor

S amuel L. Jackson is the quintessential example of a steady rise to success, and his work ethic serves as a model of perseverance. After having a showy role in Spike Lee's film *Jungle Fever*, Jackson continued to work as if each new role might be his last. From *Pulp Fiction* to *Unbreakable* to *Coach Carter*, he showed versatility and willingness to take chances.

Samuel Leroy Jackson was born on December 21, 1948 in Washington, D.C. to a mother, Elizabeth, a clothing buyer, and a father who would soon abandon them. Without support from Samuel's father, Elizabeth had difficulty trying to raise her son, an only child. While he was still very young, she sent Samuel to Chattanooga, Tennessee, to live with his grandparents and an aunt. She joined them in Chattanooga a few years later.

Living in that segregated southern city had a lasting effect on Jackson. Once, at five years of age, while sitting on the front porch, he whistled at a pretty white girl walking by on the sidewalk. Immediately, his mom, grandmother, and aunt were out on the porch scolding him. They worried that such an innocent act might result in somebody getting killed; such was the brand of bigotry practiced by whites on blacks at the time. There were always things that he could not do or places he was not allowed to go, based on the color of his skin.

At an early age Jackson began appearing in the local children's productions staged by his aunt. He starred as Humpty Dumpty and the Sugar Plum Fairy in two of those productions. His stutter, however, made him self-conscious about being the center of attention. Fearing that Samuel was not getting enough opportunity to

Samuel L. Jackson

develop in the male world, his mother insisted that he play Little League baseball when he was ten. Baseball proved the beginning of his love affair with sports in general. By high school, he had developed into a talented all-around athlete. At Chattanooga's all-black Riverside High, he participated on the swimming and track teams. He also played in the school's marching band and was popular enough to be elected senior class president.

Pushing the Limits at College

After high school, Jackson enrolled at Atlanta's Morehouse College, majoring in architecture. At Morehouse, no longer under the rule of his mother, Jackson pushed the limits of personal freedom. Sporting a giant "black is beautiful" afro, he dressed like a hippie, often wearing an army fatigue jacket, set off by a flamboyant headband, a la rock star Jimi Hendrix, and little, dark-lens glasses, like those worn by Clarence Williams III on the television show *The Mod Squad*. While immersed in the anti-establishment culture at Morehouse, Jackson was introduced to the drug culture. In addition to heavy alcohol use, he experimented with marijuana, cocaine, and heroin. Though he later described himself as a weekend, recreational drug user in those days, it was the start of what would become a very serious drug dependency. Jackson also became a political activist at Morehouse, primarily participating in protests opposing the Vietnam War.

It was a protest much closer to home, however, that made Jackson front-page news in 1969. Upset that Morehouse, a historically black institution, did not offer a black studies program, Jackson and some fellow activists decided to stage a media event to air their demands. Using chains they had acquired from the school grounds and padlocks bought at a local hardware store, the protesters stormed a board of trustees meeting and locked board members in for two-and-a-half days. Among the trustees was Martin Luther King Sr., the father of the civil rights icon. Although there were police officers outside waiting for an opportunity to rush the students, the incident was resolved peacefully. Jackson, however, who had made speeches from the steps of the building during the takeover, was expelled. After moving to Los Angeles, where he worked as a social worker for a year and a half, Jackson was allowed to reenroll at the college.

Jackson's change of major from architecture to drama was serendipitous. A speech professor who offered his students extra credit for appearing in the school's musical production encouraged Jackson to audition to help him overcome his persistent stutter. Jackson auditioned and managed to snag a role. Once Jackson smelled the greasepaint and heard the roar of the crowd, he was ready for more. Despite the objections of his family, Jackson pursued an acting career. He became involved with the theater program at Spelman, a nearby women's college, where he met LaTanya Richardson, who also dreamed of an acting career. Richardson soon became his girlfriend, and they pursued their goals together.

Jackson's television debut came in commercials for the Southern fast-food chain Krystal Hamburgers in Atlanta. While still at Morehouse, Jackson made his movie debut in a supporting role in the film *Together for Days*, with Broadway and television star Clifton Davis and Lois Chiles, a future Bond girl. That movie, released in 1972, doubtless was very encouraging for the young actor, but it was Jackson's last motion picture credit for nearly a decade. Jackson graduated from Morehouse with a dramatic arts degree in 1972 but remained in Atlanta another four years while Richardson earned her dramatic arts degree (1974) and he learned his craft appearing in local theater. He landed his first television series appearance in 1974 in *Moving On*, an NBC action drama about truck drivers.

In 1976, Jackson and Richardson moved to New York City, where they both hoped to work on Broadway, as well as break into television. Jackson kept busy performing, be it Broadway, off-Broadway, off-off-Broadway, or children's theatre. The size of venue or type of production made no difference, because Jackson believed that if a person is going to be an actor, then he had better be working. In 1977, he returned to the small screen when he was cast in an hour-long TV adaptation of Flannery O'Connor's story *The Displaced Person*, starring John Houseman. A year later, he appeared in *The Trial of the Moke*, shown on the long-running PBS anthology series, *Great Performances*. In 1980, after ten years together, Jackson and Richardson married. Their only child, a daughter, Zoe, was born two years later.

Nine years after his motion picture debut in *Together for Days*, Jackson had his second flirtation with the big screen when he was cast in director Milos Forman's 1981 film version of the best-selling E.L. Doctorow novel *Ragtime*, starring the previously long-retired Hollywood legend James Cagney. Jackson was convinced that the film would serve as a springboard to success in Hollywood. His minor role as a gang member, however, did not turn out to be the career boost he envisioned. Several more years passed before Hollywood came knocking again.

In the meantime, Jackson went where the work was, appearing in plays throughout the United States. He became a mainstay of the Negro Ensemble Company, both in New York City and as part of their touring company. He starred in the company's *A Soldier's Play* and *Home*, both in 1981; in *District Line* in 1984; and later in *Burners Frolic* and *Jonquil*, both 1990. While appearing in *A Soldier's Play* Jackson had a fortuitous meeting with the young film director, Spike Lee, who came backstage after the performance. Subsequently, Lee, a fellow Morehouse grad, cast Jackson in several of his early films. During the eighties, Jackson also worked with Yale Rep and the Shakespeare Festival.

Starting in the mid-1980s, Jackson began acquiring regular small screen work. His most regular work for television, however, did not result in any actual airtime. For three seasons, starting in 1985, Jackson served as Bill Cosby's stand-in on the enormously popular NBC comedy named for its star. Concurrently, Jackson managed guest roles in such series as the ABC action drama *Spenser: For Hire* (two appearances as different characters), that show's spin-off: *A Man Called Hawk* and the NBC "dramedy" *The Days and Nights of Molly Dodd*. He also had minor roles in two television movies: the 1987 television version of *Uncle Tom's Cabin* and the 1989 drama *Dead Man Out*.

Spike Lee gave Jackson's big screen career a boost in 1988 when he cast him in *School Daze*, set on the campus of a black college not unlike Morehouse. In 1989, Jackson appeared in Lee's commercial breakthrough *Do the Right Thing* and the next year in *Mo' Better Blues*, starring Denzel Washington. Aside from the films for Lee, Jackson also appeared in a number of other films in the late 1980s. Among those was the little-seen cult flick *Magic Sticks* (1987); two Eddie Murphy movies, *Eddie Murphy: Raw* (1987) and *Coming to America* (1988); and the Al Pacino police drama *Sea of Love* (1989). By 1990, Jackson was working frequently in motion pictures. In that year alone (besides the Lee film) he had roles in *A Shock to the System*, *Def by Temptation*, *Betsy's Wedding*, *The Exorcist III*, *Goodfellas*, and *The Return of Superfly*.

Overcoming Addictions

Unfortunately, during the entire period of his emergence as an actor, Jackson never worked without an illegal or controlled substance in his body. He drank alcohol to excess, always willing to be the life of the party and show that he could imbibe more than his colleagues. That was the public side of his substance abuse, but the private side was even worse. He smoked marijuana, dropped acid, snorted cocaine, and used anything else that would get him high. Worst of all, he did not confine his drug use to non-working hours: he later admitted that anytime he went on stage he had some sort of drug in his body. It got even worse in that latter half of the 1980s when Jackson began smoking crack cocaine. In addition to his drug problems, Jackson was also a perpetual womanizer. Through it all, his wife LaTanya remained by his side, trying to help him become the man she believed that he could be. With the support of his family, Jackson finally sought treatment for his addictions in early 1991 by entering rehab. Over the next several years, he spent countless hours attending Narcotics Anonymous and Alcoholics Anonymous meetings learning how to live a life of sobriety. He also recommitted himself to LaTanya and their daughter.

In early 1991, Jackson returned to series television as a guest in a first-season episode of NBC's long-running crime drama *Law & Order*. He also appeared that fall in a first-season episode of the Fox comedy *Roc*. His breakthrough role, however, came on the big screen, in Spike Lee's interracial love story *Jungle Fever*. In that film, Jackson portrayed the character Gator Purify, the brother of the character played by Wesley Snipes, the star of the

film. While still in rehab, Jackson, who had been cast earlier, pleaded with Lee not to recast the role due to his personal problems. Two weeks after completing rehab, Jackson began acting the role of the intense, crack-addicted Gator, bringing an unusual amount of realism to his portrayal. At the Cannes International Film Festival, Jackson was awarded a rare special jury prize for his outstanding performance in a supporting role. Later that year, he also earned the New York Film Critics Circle Award for best supporting actor. The expected Academy Award nomination never came, but the visibility of the performance greatly enhanced his employability.

Over the next two years, though his was not exactly a household name, Jackson was developing into a star. Continuing his philosophy of working as much as possible, he took the best offers that came his way, not concerned about the size of the role or magnitude of the production. In television series, made-for-television movies, and roles in minor flicks and major motion pictures, Jackson was always working. Among the highlights of his many credits was the acclaimed television series *I'll Fly Away*; the movies *Juice*, *White Sands* and *Patriot Games*, both in 1992; and the movies *Loaded Weapon 1*, *Amos & Andrew* (in which he received top billing for the first time), *Menace II Society* and the blockbuster *Jurassic Park*, all in 1993.

In 1994, Jackson and Richardson switched coasts when they moved from their Harlem brownstone to a Tudor-style home in Encino, California. The move was meant to benefit the television and motion picture careers of both Jackson and Richardson, whose career was also on the rise. She had landed roles in such popular movies as *Fried Green Tomatoes*, *Malcolm X* and *Sleepless in Seattle*, as well as TV roles in such hits as *Law & Order* and *Cheers* during the early 1990s. The move also resulted in Jackson's introduction to golf. He quickly became an avid enthusiast, replacing his former addictions with a new, socially acceptable one. Within a few years, once he had garnered the necessary sway, Jackson was having tee times written into his movie contracts, so that his passion for the game could be balanced with his work schedule.

In Hollywood, Jackson continued working at his usual, frenetic pace. In 1994, his credits included the film *Fresh*, and the television movies *Assault at West Point: The Court-Martial of Johnson Whittaker* and *Against the Wall*. The move to the A-list, however, came via a medium-budgeted action feature directed by Quentin Tarantino, who had just one previous directorial credit. Tarantino's *Pulp Fiction* became the sleeper hit of the decade, a watershed film in terms of story construction and a boon to the careers of everyone involved. In addition to Jackson, the latter was also particularly true of John Travolta, a seemingly washed-up actor, who starred alongside Jackson as a pair of hit men who propel much of the action in the highly episodic film. Jackson, as the Jheri-curled, scripture-quoting tough guy Jules Winnfield, provided the perfect companion to Travolta's loopy killer.

Playing for months with steady business, *Pulp Fiction* became a cultural phenomenon. The movie went on to win numerous critics awards and was nominated by the Academy of Motion Pictures Arts & Sciences for the best picture Oscar. For Jackson, it also meant his first Oscar nomination, as he was nominated in the supporting actor category. On March 21, 1995, just prior to the Oscar telecast, Jackson appeared on *The Late Show with David Letterman* and proved a very natural, yet lively guest. It was not long before Jackson was a regular guest on many talk shows. Ultimately, he lost the Oscar to Martin Landau, for his portrayal of Bela Lugosi in *Ed Wood*, but Jackson had become a star.

Due to the lag time between a movie's production and its actual release date, some of Jackson's film credits for the following year did not yet reflect his rise in status brought on by *Pulp Fiction*. For instance, 1995 saw the release of the kids' flick *Fluke*, in which Jackson voiced the title character, a dog. Likewise, neither *Raising Isaiah* (in which LaTanya Richardson also appeared) nor *Kiss of Death* did big business that year, but *Die Hard: With a Vengeance* certainly did. Playing sidekick to Bruce Willis, Jackson received rave reviews for his portrayal of Zeus Carver, adding a human dimension to a big-budget, special effects-laden crime thriller sequel that could easily have just been played by the numbers.

Among the higher profile projects in which Jackson appeared during 1996 were the comedy *The Great White Hype* and the action thriller *The Long Kiss Goodnight*. Sandwiched between those disappointing productions was the release of the courtroom drama *A Time to Kill*, in which Jackson starred as Carl Lee Hailey, a Mississippi man accused of murdering the two white men who raped his 10-year-old daughter. Based on the John Grisham novel, the film was one of the top hits of the year. The following year he starred in the high school/gang violence drama *187*, before adding a new credit to his resume, that of producer, for the period drama *Eve's Bayou*.

Set in 1962 Louisiana, Jackson also co-starred, playing a womanizing doctor and head of a family keeping many secrets. *Eve's Bayou*, the writing and directing debut of actress Kasi Lemmons, garnered critical raves (including Roger Ebert's naming it his top film of 1997), but had a lukewarm box-office reception. Jackson's final screen appearance of the year was in the crime drama *Jackie Brown*, in which he teamed again with *Pulp Fiction* director Quentin Tarantino. As vicious arms dealer Ordell Robbie, Jackson's dialogue is sprinkled with curse words and the heavy use of the "n-word." Spike Lee publicly denounced Jackson for agreeing to repeatedly say the "n-word" in the movie, especially because Tarantino, a white filmmaker, penned it. Jackson defended Tarantino whole-heartedly, saying that the dialogue was true to

the character. He further stood up for Tarantino's right to exercise creative license. Though they strongly disagreed on the issue, he and Lee remained friends. *Jackie Brown* did not prove the box office bonanza that *Pulp Fiction* was, but it did moderate business and received excellent critical notices.

Four more movies hit the big screen for Jackson in 1998: *Sphere, Out of Sight, The Negotiator* and *The Red Violin*. On January 10, 1998, Jackson took his celebrity status to a new level when he hosted NBC's sketch-comedy institution *Saturday Night Live*. He followed that up by hosting the 1998 *MTV Movie Awards*. With his standard Kangol cap (always rakishly worn backwards) and flashy but nattily tailored suits, Jackson was quickly becoming the ambassador of cool. Soon, in addition to talk shows, Jackson was a regular guest on award and entertainment magazine shows, as well as a favorite interview subject for Hollywood documentaries and celebrity profiles. Among the programs he has hosted are *From Star Wars to Star Wars: The Story of Industrial Light & Magic* (1999), *Comic Books & Superheroes* (2001) and *The ESPY Awards* (2002).

Jackson was among many celebrities who lent their voices to *My Friend Martin*, a one-hour cartoon based on the life of Martin Luther King Jr., which was nominated in the Outstanding Animated Program category of the 1999 Emmy Awards. His two other major projects for 1999 were supporting roles. He played a rich businessman who finances an Alzheimer's research project at an underwater laboratory in the sharks-versus-humans thriller *Deep Blue Sea*. He was also cast as Jedi Master Mace Windu in George Lucas's *Star Wars: Episode I— The Phantom Menace*. His role grew in importance and his screen time increased in the next two episodes of the series: *Star Wars: Episode II—Attack of the Clones* (2002) and *Star Wars: Episode III—Revenge of the Sith* (2005). In the latter, he had an exhilarating light saber duel to the death with the saga's ultimate evildoer, Darth Sidious.

By the end of the 1990s, Jackson was believed to have appeared in more Hollywood films during the decade— over forty—than any other actor. His extraordinary pace did not slow upon the arrival of the new millennium. In addition to *Rules of Engagement* and *Unbreakable* (playing a demented, yet fragile villain) in 2000, Jackson starred in the title role of *Shaft*, playing the nephew of the character from the 1971 version played by Richard Roundtree. For playing police detective John Shaft, Jackson reportedly earned $10 million. In 2001, Jackson served as an executive producer on two movies in which he starred: *Formula 51* (donning kilts) and *The Caveman's Valentine*. The following year he appeared in such titles as *Changing Lanes, The House on Turk Street* , and *xXx*. In 2003, Jackson teamed again with John Travolta for the military drama *Basic* and starred in the film version of the 1970s television series *S.W.AT.*

Jackson appeared on screen in several movies during 2004, including *In My Country* (in which he engages in a love affair with French actress Juliette Binoche), *Twisted*, and *Kill Bill 2*. He also served that year as the voice of superhero Frozone in the blockbuster animated film *The Incredibles*. *Coach Carter*, which had Jackson portraying a real-life high school basketball coach who positively affected the lives of the students at an inner-city school, got 2005 off to a fine start. *xXx: State of the Union*, *The Man* and *Freedomland* rounded out another year in the career of the prolific actor.

Samuel L. Jackson had arrived. He has had a career doing what he loves, and he is so good at it that in an often-iffy business, he manages to work as much as he wants, which is constantly. And he has the love of a good woman, who has helped him in becoming a good husband and father.

REFERENCES

Periodicals

Cohen, David S. "Jackson Career a Tour de Force." *Variety: Film Fest Guide Special Issue 2000* 380 (28 August-3 September 2000).

Collier, Aldore. "Samuel L. Jackson: Talks about His Marriage, the Oscar Snubs, and Why He Works So Hard. *Ebony* 58 (August 2003):10.

Fretts, Bruce. "The Making of a Hit Man." *Entertainment Weekly* 250 (25 November 1994).

Lee, Elyssa. "Man of Style: Samuel L. Jackson." *INSTYLE* 9 (May 2002): 6.

Morgan, Joan. "You're Still the One: LaTanya and Samuel L. Jackson." *Essence* 33 (May 2002).

O'Neill, Tom. "Samuel L. Jackson." *Us* (March 1998): 242.

"Samuel L. Jackson, with 64 Movies to His Credit, Is Featured in 'Star Wars the Phantom Menace.'" *Jet* 96 (7 June 1999): 1.

Schoemer, Karen. "The `L' is for Lucky." *Newsweek* 125 (5 June 1995): 23.

Smith, Kyle, Michael Fleeman, and Ivory Clinton. "Action Jackson." *People Weekly* 54, 3 July 2000.

Online

"Samuel L. Jackson." Hollywood.com (Accessed 28 September 2005).

"Samuel L. Jackson: How Did an Average Boy Become One of the Biggest Actors in Hollywood?" Hollywoodfirm.com (Accessed 28 September 2005).

"Samuel L. Jackson." IMDB.com (Accessed 28 September 2005).

Kevin C. Kretschmer

T. D. Jakes
1957–

Minister, television show host

Bishop Thomas Dexter (T. D.) Jakes Sr. has become a world-renowned minister and broadcaster. He is the founder of the Potter's House mega-church in Dallas, and established T. D. Jakes Ministries to help the homeless, people with AIDS, and prisoners.

Born on June 9, 1957 in South Charleston, West Virginia, Jakes was the last of three children born to Ernest and Odith Jakes. His father ran a janitorial company. His mother taught home economics which was beneficial to Jakes and his siblings because they learned how to cook, sew, and clean up after themselves. Jakes' childhood was nurtured in a strong, close-knit community.

Known as "Bible Boy"

Jakes possessed strong character traits at an early age. His drive for preaching was witnessed during his childhood. He often preached to an imaginary congregation and always carried his Bible to school. Due to his early habits, he was nicknamed "Bible Boy." As he grew up, he also worked as a part-time music director at the Baptist Church.

Throughout his college career, Jakes attended several institutions. In 1972, he was enrolled at Center Business College. In 1976, he became a student at West Virginia State College. However, he earned both his bachelor of art and master's degree from Friends University. He received his doctor of ministry degree in 1995.

Jakes married Serita Ann Jamison in 1980. The couple have five children: Jamar, Jermaine, Cora, Sarah, and Thomas Dexter Jr.

Becomes Full-Time Pastor

Jakes founded Greater Temple of Faith Church in 1979 in Montgomery, West Virginia with only 10 members. In 1982, his father died of kidney disease, and he was terminated from his day job at the Union Carbide plant in Charleston. Then his unemployment ran out. During this year, he struggled to survive as a full-time pastor. He eventually began to work with his brother and preach at revivals. His wife Serita worked as a disc jockey for a local Christian radio station at night to contribute to their income.

In 1983, Jakes began a radio program called *Back to the Bible*. People had begun to spread the word about his powerful messages. As a result, Jakes became known as an inspiring speaker, and his congregation grew. In 1990, he decided to move his church to his hometown of Charleston. His congregation increased from 100 to 300 with forty percent of his congregants being Caucasian.

Chronology

1957	Born in South Charleston, West Virginia on June 9
1972	Enrolls at Center Business College
1976	Enrolls at West Virginia State College
1979	Founds Greater Temple of Faith Church in Montgomery, West Virginia
1980	Marries Serita Jamison
1982	Loses day job at Union Carbide plant in Charleston; father dies of kidney disease
1983	Begins radio program *Back to the Bible*
1990	Relocates Temple of Faith Church to Charleston
1993	Begins television program *Get Ready with T. D. Jakes*
1994	Establishes T. D. Jakes Ministries
1995	Receives doctor of ministry degree
1996	Moves to Dallas, Texas; founds Potter's House mega-church in Dallas
1998	Launches 232-acre City of Refuge and new 14,000-seat Potter's House
2006	Named one of the Top 20 Worship Leaders by *The Church Report* magazine

During the 1990s, Jakes' congregation continued to grow. In 1993, he developed a weekly television program called *Get Ready with T. D. Jakes* which aired on both the TBN (Trinity Broadcasting Network) and BET (Black Entertainment Television) networks. In 1994, Jakes established T. D. Jakes Ministries and added counseling conferences for men and pastors.

The turning point of Jakes' career was in May 1996 when he relocated his family and fifty other families to Dallas, Texas. Jakes founded the Potter's House mega-church which grew from 7,000 worshipers to 14,000 within two years and which continued to grow into the early 2000s. The church, located in the Oak Cliff area in Dallas, has a diverse congregation. In 1998, Jakes launched the 232-acre City of Refuge and new 14,000-seat Potter's House. In 2006, *The Church Report* magazine listed Jakes as one of the Top 20 Worship Leaders.

Influences Many Different People

Jakes became a highly influential pastor. His kind gesture notes that God does not duplicate people. More importantly, Jakes' goal is to be the best that he can possibly be, and he strives every day to make it happen. Through his ministry, he displays the will of God. His keen spirit can be seen through the lives of others. For instance, he has helped women to overcome the hardships of divorce. He assures them that the road to recovery is through spiritual guidance. Along with divorce, he has become an advocate for women who are victims of molestation, depression and discrimination. Throughout his endless efforts, he has remained humble and grateful.

Jakes strives to be a vessel for the Lord because he knows that the harvest is truly plenteous, and the laborers are few. His extraordinary gifts have been shared throughout the world through television and literature. Although he may be classified as an entertainer, he is a believer in Jesus Christ trying to bring others closer to eternal life. Aside from Potter's House, he runs ministries for the homeless that provide them with regular haircuts, meals and showers. His endeavors are continuous with creating special programs for people with AIDS, drug addicts and prisoners.

Jakes has written more than 16 books, including *Woman, Thou Art Loosed!; The Lady, Her Lover, and Her Lord; Ten Commandments of Working in a Hostile Environment; So You Call Yourself a Man?: A Devotional for Ordinary Men with Extraordinary Potential; He-Motions: Even Strong Men Struggle* and many others. His gospel album *Live at The Potter's House* has received nominations for both the Grammy and the Dove Awards. His accomplishments have truly categorized him as a prestigious individual.

REFERENCES

Books

Phelps, Shirelle, ed. *Contemporary Black Biography: Profiles from the International Black Community.* 17 vols. Detroit: Gale, 1998.

Online

"Top 20 Worship Leaders." *The Church Report.* http://www.thechurchreport.com/content/view/1081/32/ (Accessed 6 June 2006).

Clarence Toomer

John Jasper
1812–1901

Minister, orator

Although John Jasper started life as a slave working at whatever odd jobs his owners, the Peachy family, desired, he became famous for his scripture-based, charismatic preaching. His sermons had the power to persuade even the most skeptical among the congregation and brought both blacks and whites together. Though a passionate preacher, Jasper was dogmatic in his views and that dogmatism produced a great deal of dissension within the Baptist fellowship.

Chronology

1812	Born on a plantation in Fluvanna County, Virginia on July 4
1825	Hired out to work in several industries
1839	Experiences a religious conversion; subsequently unites with the Baptist church
1840	Begins ministry in the Baptist fellowship
1844	Marries Candus Jordan after annulment of his first marriage to Elvy Weaden
1860	Works at the Rolling Mills recycling iron and preaches to mill workers
1863	Marries third wife Mary Ann Cole
1865	Preaches his last sermon before Richmond falls; answers call to return to the Third Baptist Church of Petersburg, Virginia
1866	Founds the First Colored Baptist Church of Weldon, North Carolina
1867	Organizes the Sixth Mount Zion Church known as Jasper's Church
1874	Third wife Mary Ann Cole dies
1878	Gives sun sermon "De Sun Do Move" for the first time, launching controversy with some of the scientific community
1901	Dies

John Jasper was born into slavery on July 4, 1812 on a plantation in Fluvanna County, Virginia, to Phillip and Tina Jasper. Jasper was the youngest of twenty-four children born to the two. Phillip, an esteemed Baptist minister, was committed to spreading the gospel. Although legal and social attitudes toward race hindered his ministry, Phillip continued preaching against the white preachers' message to obey. Jasper's mother, Tina, tilled the fields for the Peachy family until the slaves were transferred to another plantation. She became a house slave and worked as a seamstress along with an older daughter.

Young Jasper's early jobs were as cart-boy, gardener, and yardman. Over a nine-year period beginning in 1825, Jasper was hired out to work in several industries. As he grew older, he worked off the Peachy plantation for Patrick McHenry, Dr. Woldridge, and Samuel Cosby (the latter for approximately seven years). Around 1833, Jasper worked as a stemmer at Sam Hargrove's tobacco plant, removing the stems from plants and thus readying them for final shaping into plugs.

Between 1832 and 1839, three events occurred that propelled Jasper toward his future role as preacher. Jasper, who throughout his life had watched the stars and planets, was the first of his factory co-workers to catch site of a brilliant star shower. So awed were the workers that they fell down to pray. The second extraordinary event that followed was the cholera outbreak in 1833. The slaves, including Jasper, saw these events as bad omens—forecasting the end-of-days—appeasable only by prayer and increased devotion to church and scripture. The deaths of Mrs. Peachy, his old retainer, followed

shortly by the death of her son, John Blair Peachy, who planned to take his inherited portion of slaves to his Louisiana cotton farm, saved Jasper from being moved South, something all slaves greatly feared. Jasper again went to work for Hargrove. On July 4, 1839, Jasper felt guilty for his sins; his distress heightening for a number of days, on July 25 he confessed and found his faith. By 1840, he believed that he had been called to preach.

About four years after the Peachy estate was divided, Jasper was married to Elvy Weaden, a slave from Williamsburg. Jasper left Williamsburg immediately after his marriage and returned to Richmond. Since many slaves were then escaping North, Jasper was not allowed to return to Williamsburg or to see his wife ever again. She wrote to tell him that if he could not or would not come to see her again, she should be allowed to remarry. He replied that he would be unable to come again and that she should marry again if she desired to. Although marriage between slaves was seldom recognized or recorded, churches did offer some guidance for members. Jasper went to the membership of the old African Baptist Church in Richmond, seeking guidance on the status of his marriage. The elders told him that since his wife had remarried, he, too, should have the option to marry again if he chose. With the granting of the request, he was again free to marry and did so in 1844. His second marriage to Candus Jordan, who bore Jasper nine children, also ended in divorce. From the beginning the two were never on particularly good terms. Often when Jasper was out of the house, gossips came to Mrs. Jasper with stories about her husband's behavior. Gossips were generally motivated by jealousy, since Jasper frequently took parishioners away from other ministers or alienated them from their home churches. In 1863, Jasper married again. Jasper's third wife was Mary Anne Cole, a widow with one child, Mary Elizabeth. This union produced no children and the marriage ended with her death in 1874.

Decision for Ministry

During Jasper's first marriage, he made the decision to preach. He presented himself to the African Baptist Church and was found fit enough in his beliefs and knowledge of scripture to preach. Then he set out to minister to his people. Much of his first ministry was spent preaching at the funerals of dead slaves, but because of very rigid slave laws, he was required to ask for permission of his master and the approval of a committee of white preachers. Also, a fine of one dollar per day was charged for days missed (except Sundays) from labor. Ways were found around these requirements, and slave preachers often performed funeral services, particularly since slaves wanted to have fellow slaves officiate. As a result, Jasper was called to the plantation of a Dr. Winnfree who had several slaves to bury. The justice of the peace in attendance on this occasion tried to prevent Jasper from conducting the service but was put down by the arrival of Dr. Winnfree, who had invited Jasper and insisted that he be allowed to preach, offering to accept responsibility if anything went wrong. Thus agreed upon, the service began with the white preacher speaking for two hours—using up most of the two and a half hours allotted. Jasper, who understood the maneuver, took the stand and preached a sermon that even had many detractors under his spell. As his reputation grew, his ministerial range expanded, and before his ministry was over he had preached in all the cities of Virginia, had toured Washington, Baltimore, Philadelphia, and several cities in New Jersey, and had spoken before the Virginia Legislature.

The Sun Sermon and Controversy

The speaking tour resulted from the notoriety that Jasper achieved in 1878 with his sermon on the rotation of the sun, entitled "De Sun Do Move." A parishioner and an unknown white man argued the question of the sun and its rotation around the earth as described in Exodus 15:3. Failing to agree, they put the question to Jasper to preach on. His sermon prompted so much interest by both blacks and whites that Jasper was requested to give the sermon again and again—possibly 250 times before his death. However, at the time of its delivery, the sermon caused a great controversy between Jasper and Reverend Richard Wells, pastor of the Ebenezer Church, regarding the theory of the rotation of the sun. Wells then released a newspaper dispatch that denounced Jasper and his theory. Jasper replied to it and apparently bested Wells in his response. However, after returning from his northern tour, Jasper learned that Wells had asked that a Baptist Council be convened to settle the troubles that had developed between them. At first Jasper refused to appear, responding that the council was not legal. The council immediately selected a new committee; they informed Jasper if he came to the council, he could make charges against Reverend Wells and be assured of a fair hearing, and that justice would be given to both, according to Baptist doctrine. When Jasper did appear before the council, he brought charges against Wells (in reference to the rotation of the sun sermon) for alleging that his reading and interpretation of biblical text was completely made up. Jasper stated that all he wanted from the hearing was an apology from Wells. Wells in turn denied writing anything that was unflattering to Jasper. The council concluded its business by stating that although they did not share Jasper's views on the sun's rotation, they did apologize for stating their position too strongly. Both Jasper and Wells signed the council's resolution, and the secretary was instructed to have everything that Wells had said about Jasper sent to the newspaper for retraction. However, the secretary failed to do so, and the retraction was apparently never published. The tension between the two ministers and their followers did not end, either. Outside elements wrote and published treatises on Jasper's theory of the sun's rotation and various Baptist congregations censored each other in the press.

Throughout his life Jasper earned a reputation as an effective speaker, a faithful interpreter of scripture, and a devout individual who thought and acted for himself. He was described as intelligent and gifted, possessing a keen memory, but he was also described as dogmatic and unwilling to alter his attitudes. Although he had an incomparable knowledge of scripture, he did not seek to broaden his knowledge in other areas. He was vain about his dress and he smoked. His supporters viewed him as a holy, nearly infallible authority on the gospel; his detractors saw him as arrogant and unbending. He died in 1901 at the age of eighty-nine.

REFERENCES

Books

Smith, Edward D. *Climbing Jacob's Ladder.* Washington: Smithsonian Institution Press, 1988.

Online

Hatcher, William E. "Jasper: The Unmatched Negro Philosopher and Preacher." New York: Fleming H. Revel Company, c. 1908. http://docsouth.unc.edu/church/hatcher/summary.html (Accessed 13 March 2006).

Matthews, Terry. "Religion of the Slaves." The Religion of the Slaves. Winston-Salem: Wake Forest University, Department of Religion, 1995. http://www.wfu.edu/~matthetl/perspectives/twelve.html (Accessed August 24, 2005).

Randolph, Edwin Archer. *The Life of Rev. John Jasper, Pastor of the Sixth Mt. Zion Baptist Church, Richmond, Va., from His Birth to the Present Time, with His Theory on the Rotation of the Sun.* Richmond: R.T. Hill & Co., 1884. http://docsouth.unc.edu/neh/jasper/jasper.html (Accessed 13 March 2006).

Woodson, Carter Godwin. *The History of the Negro Church.* Washington, DC: The Associated Publishers, 1921. http://docsouth.unc.edu/church/woodson/woodson.html (Accessed on 13 March 2006).

Lois A. Peterson

Charles Johnson
1948–

Novelist, journalist, screenwriter, cartoonist

Charles Johnson is a multitalented, versatile, and prolific African American teacher, writer, screenwriter, and martial artist. He has been creating and producing since the age of seventeen. Johnson is best known for his

Charles Johnson

Chronology

1948	Born in Evanston, Illinois on April 23
1967	Works as political cartoonist for *The Southern Illinoisian*
1968	Interns for *The Chicago Tribune*
1969	Works as teaching assistant, Southern Illinois University
1970	Marries Joan New
1970-84	Broadcasts *Charlie's Pad*, a 52-part series on PBS
1973	Receives M.A. in philosophy from Southern Illinois University
1977	Works as assistant professor at the University of Washington in Seattle
1978	"Charlie Smith and the Fritter-Tree" televised on PBS
1981	Named journalism alumnus of the year by Southern Illinois University; promoted to associate professor at the University of Washington
1982	Promoted to professor at the University of Washington
1983	Receives Governor's Award for Literature from the State of Washington; wins *Callaloo* Creative Writing Award for short story "Popper's Disease"
1984	Receives a citation in Pushcart Prize's Outstanding Writers section for short story "China"; receives Black Filmmaker's Festival Award for PBS film "Booker"; receives "Best Film in the Social Studies Category," National Education Film Festival for PBS film "Booker"
1985	Receives the Prix Jeunesse Award for the screenplay "Booker"
1988	Receives Ph.D. in philosophy from State University of New York at Stoney Brook, New York
1990	Wins National Book Award for *Middle Passage*; holds the S. Wilson and Grace M. Pollock Professorship for Excellence in English
1998	Named a MacArthur Foundation Fellow
1999	Awarded honorary doctorate from State University of New York at Stoney Brook
2000	Receives the Lifetime Achievement in the Arts Award from the Corporate Council for the Arts
2001	Receives the 2001 Pacific Northwest Writers Associations' Achievement Award
2002	Receives the American Academy of Arts and Letters Award for Literature

novels *Middle Passage* and *Dreamer* and the short story collection *Soulcatcher*. He has been teaching at the University of Washington in Seattle since 1976 and holds the S. Wilson and Grace M. Pollock Professorship for Excellence in English (the first chair in writing at the University of Washington) and teaches fiction. He has to his credit four novels, two collections of short stories, two books of political cartoons for which he did the drawings, numerous essays and interviews, over twenty screenplays, and translations of his work into several languages, including Japanese, Dutch, Russian, and Italian.

Johnson, a Buddhist, a philosopher by training, and a writer of historical, philosophical fiction, can be aptly called a Renaissance man. In 1990, Johnson won the National Book Award for *Middle Passage*, his third published novel, and became the first African American male to receive that award since Ralph Ellison in 1953 for *Invisible Man*. The American Academy of Arts and Letters says, "Charles Johnson is a storyteller with a philosopher's intellect and a historian's belief in the power of the past to shape the present. But he is before all else a true storyteller. In his short stories, he ingeniously braids history, philosophy, and imagination in making postmodern fiction of the highest order."

Charles Richard Johnson was born on April 23, 1948 in Evanston, Illinois to hard-working parents, Benjamin Lee and Rudy Elizabeth Jackson Johnson. His mother was a voracious and eclectic reader who liked the unique, exotic, and beautiful. As a result, Johnson was exposed to diverse reading material and grew up reading widely. He read on such subjects as yoga (the beginning of his interest in Buddhism), dieting, Christian mysticism, Victorian poetry, and costume design; such works as James T. Farrell's *Studs Lonigan Trilogy*, Daniel Blum's *Pictorial History of the American Theatre 1900-1956*, and *Candide*; and such authors as Rilke, Richard Wright, Shakespeare, Mary Shelley, Sartre, P. G. Wodehouse, and Dickens. He and his mother often shared and discussed books.

While in Evanston Township High, an integrated school, Johnson read, wrote, and drew. Even at this early point in his life, he was self-disciplined. He challenged himself to read one book a week and increased it to three when he found how easy it was. Writing was for fun; when he was twelve, his mother gave him a blank book and from that time on he kept a diary and later he kept a journal. His career goal was to become a cartoonist and illustrator. For him drawing was his main pleasure. By the time he entered Southern Illinois University in 1966 as a journalism major, he had published three short stories in addition to some artwork. The best of his early works appears in Paul Mandelbaum's *First Words: Earliest Writing from Favorite Contemporary Authors* (1993), Tonya Bolden's *Tell All the Children Our Story* (2001), and John McNally's *Humor Me: An Anthology of Humor by Writers of Color* (2002).

At Southern Illinois University, he drew both for the school and town newspapers. At this time he developed his lasting love for philosophy; in 1971, he earned his bachelor's degree in journalism and moved directly into the master's program in philosophy. When he was a graduate student in philosophy and working on his seventh novel, he met John Gardner (writer, teacher, critic, and cartoonist). Gardner was to become his literary guide and his friend. Johnson says he was inspired by Gardner's concept of moral fiction, demanding that the writer make a commitment to technique, imagination, and ethics. Gardner encouraged the writer to know form and technique, to try new forms, styles, and techniques, and always to stretch beyond the last work and not to be repetitious. In 1973, Johnson earned a master's degree in philosophy and in 1988 he earned his Ph.D. in philosophy at the State University of New York at Stoney Brook.

Begins Serious Writings

Johnson began seriously writing novels to fill the void he saw in black literature; there were in his estimation very few writers creating black philosophical fiction. In his view, the black writers of philosophical fiction were Jean Toomer, Richard Wright, Ralph Ellison, and later Albert Murray. These were the only black writers who recognized the connection between fiction and philosophy. Johnson's writing is informed by his training in philosophy, martial arts, and Buddhism. His stories are filled with layers that come from character names and allusions to history, philosophical systems, philosophers, and literary works and artists, both Eastern and Western. The central philosophy in his fiction is phenomenology, which is developed in *Middle Passage* and expressed by the fictional tribe, the Allmuseri. In an interview with Michael Boccia of *African American Review*, Johnson stated the central theme in his opus "is the investigation of the nature of the self and personal identity."

Johnson challenges the reader to be open to new possibilities, to be engaged by the work and to stretch. He demands no less of himself or his craft. One indication of this is that he set himself to learning Sanskrit by studying the holy texts of Hinduism and Adaita Vedanta in the original Devanagari script with a Vedic priest.

Draws Cartoons

At the age of fourteen, Johnson informed his parents he was going to be an illustrator and cartoonist. By age seventeen, he had earned his first professional paycheck from a Chicago company which sold magic tricks and bought six of his drawings to use in their catalog. He spent the next seven years studying with Lawrence Lariar (cartoonist for the *Parade* magazine in the 1960s, editor of the annual *Best Cartoons of the Year*, and author of over one hundred books). He won two awards in national high school competitions sponsored by journalism organizations for cartoonists. Johnson published over one thousand drawings in such diverse publications as *Black World* and the *Chicago Tribune* and scripted for Charlton comic books.

Johnson says it was a public reading given by Amiri Baraka in which he called on black people to "take [their] talent back to the community" which moved him to focus his cartooning and illustrating on the history and culture of black America. He began to research and draw; at the end of seven days, he had created a collection of comic art entitled *Black Humor* which was published in 1970. This was followed in 1972 by *Half-Past Nation Time*. The cartooning led Johnson to television work.

Johnson has not given up his cartooning or illustrating. He drew a regular cartoon feature "LitCrits" for *Quarterly Black Review*; a two-page comic strip on Bruce Lee for *Seattle Laughs* (1994); regular cartoon feature "Literarte" for *Literal Latte*; regular cartoon feature for *Black Issues in Higher Education*; and seven Zen cartoons for *Buddha Laughing* (1999). In the early 2000s, he still liked to draw and accepted assignments.

Cartooning led Johnson to creating, hosting, and co-producing an early PBS show, *Charlie's Pad*, a fifty-two part series on cartooning and how to draw. His "Charlie Smith and the Fritter-Tree," a 90-minute fictionalized biography of Charlie Smith, the oldest living American, was written for PBS in 1978. He wrote "Booker," another PBS program. It won the international youth prize Prix Jeunesse Award and the Writers' Guild Award for "outstanding script in the television category of children's shows." "Booker" was released for home video in 1996. In 1992, Johnson wrote a screenplay, *Tuskegee Men* for Columbia Pictures. In all, Johnson has written over twenty screen- and teleplays and has had his own works optioned. He was working on a movie project based on *Middle Passage* for which he had written two screenplays; it has been optioned three times.

Charles Johnson has contributed to, written, and co-edited numerous books. He wrote the introduction or preface to the commemorative edition of Ralph Ellison's *Invisible Man*; Mark Twain's *What Is Man?*; the preface essay entitled "A Capsule History of Blacks in Comics" for Roland and Teneshia Laird's *Still I Rise*; "On the Nature of Tales," preface for *A Treasury of North Ameri-*

can Folktales edited by Catherine Peck; a statement on fiction in *Free Within Ourselves: Fiction Lessons for Black Writers*, edited by Jewell Parker Rhodes; and the introduction to *On Writers and Writing* by John Gardner.

Johnson and John McCluskey Jr. co-edited *Black Men Speaking* (1997) in which eleven men discuss race, racism, and values. Included is a wide range of men who talk about the way they see themselves and their experiences in a variety of forms. Speakers include Don Belton, Yusef Komunyakka, Ellis Marsalis, Joseph Scott , and both Johnson and McCluskey. Johnson and Rudolph P. Byrd have edited *I Call Myself an Artist: Writings by and about Charles Johnson* (1999). It provides an overview of Johnson's opus, including examples of his writings and cartoons, and ends with eight critical articles.

Johnson's *Being and Race: Black Writing Since 1970* (1988) is his doctoral dissertation, which became a book and is "devoted to the creation of a phenomenological aesthetic for black fiction." He examines the works and artists of black literature from the position of philosophy and ideology. In this text, he criticizes black women writers, especially Toni Morrison and Alice Walker. He sees them as limiting their work to criticism of social problems. In a later nonfiction text, *Turning the Wheel: Essays on Buddhism and Writing* (2003), Johnson explores connections between Buddhism and creativity, discusses the role of Eastern philosophy in the quest for a free and thoughtful life, links Martin Luther King Jr. and W. E. B. Du Bois with Buddhism, and looks at basic Buddhist principles and practices. He sees the "Buddhist dharma as the most revolutionary and most civilized of possible human choices." He links Buddhist practices with the civil rights movement.

Johnson wrote six apprentice novels before he began to write seriously. These novels were naturalistic, in the style of those writers he was reading at the time, such as James Baldwin, John A. Williams, and Richard Wright. He says these were easy for him to write, but they did not express his vision or purpose: to expand the body of philosophical fiction by black writers. Once he was clear on his purpose, to write out of a philosophical sensibility, he wrote his seventh novel, the first to be published, *Faith and the Good Thing*.

Faith and the Good Thing (1974), the novel he was working on when he met John Gardner, necessitated his reading over seventy books on magic as a part of his research. At this point in his writing career, he was still trying to work out how to use philosophy and philosophers in the fictional form. Thus, the philosophy is not as smoothly fused as in his later novels. *Faith and the Good Thing* is a folktale which recounts the quest of Faith Cross for the "good thing." She travels from the South to Chicago and home again. The novel is rife with philosophical speeches, myths, folk material, and allusions. In 1995, *Faith and the Good Thing* was adapted by Keli Garrett and staged as a play by the City Lit Theater and

Chicago Theater Company (March 16-April 20) and by the Chicago Theater Company (April 21-May 28).

His second novel, *Oxherding Tale* (1982), took five years to write; Johnson received the 1983 Washington State Governor's Award for this novel. In preparation for the writing of this novel, Johnson read many books on slavery. The novel uses myths, folk material, allusions, philosophy, and history to tell a complex slave narrative and coming of age story set in the antebellum South. One night Jonathan Polkinghome, a plantation owner, and his man-servant, George Hawkins, were drinking to excess. Neither wanted to face his wife, so they agreed to swap wives for the night. The result was the impregnating of Anna Polkinghome and the birth of Andrew Hawkins. Anna refuses to acknowledge the child; therefore, he is raised by Mattie Hawkins, George's wife. He receives a privileged education, one which exposes him to Eastern mysticism, Plato, Schopenhauer, and other philosophers. Johnson says this novel deals with many forms of slavery—psychological, sexual, and metaphysical. This novel, like his first, includes a quest. According to Johnson, the catalyst for this novel was the "Ten Oxherding Pictures" of Zen artist Kakuan-Shien which he had viewed as a child.

Johnson calls his third novel, *Middle Passage* (1990), a "classical sea story." It grew out of the second of his apprentice novels. Johnson read seafaring works and material on the sea, even nautical dictionaries, along with the fiction of Melville and Conrad. In the novel, there are allusions to *Moby Dick*, *The Odyssey*, and Coleridge's "The Rime of the Ancient Mariner." In this novel, the fictional tribe the Allmuseri, which had been mentioned in earlier works ("The Education of Mingo" and *Oxherding Tale*), is fully developed. This is the story of Rutherford Calhoun, who in 1830 was a recently freed slave and rogue. In a desperate attempt to escape creditors and marriage, he hops the first boat leaving New Orleans. Calhoun discovers this boat, *The Republic*, is a slaver on its way to bring back African slaves, the Allmuseri. For this work, Johnson received the 1990 National Book Award in fiction and the Northwest Booksellers Award; in 1991, the book was nominated for the Florentine Literary International Prize "Chianti Ruffino Antico Fattore."

In 1998, Johnson's fourth novel, *Dreamer*, was published. Its focus is the last years of the life of Martin Luther King Jr. In his research, Johnson came to see King as both a civil rights leader and a philosopher. He says it is necessary for people to demythologize King in order to understand what he actually had to say. King spoke about the oneness of life and the potential unity of mankind. The novel has a King look-alike, Chaym Smith, who was not raised as King was, but has the same physical features and training in religion and philosophy. Johnson explores the nature of the self and what forces shape man. In 1999, the novel was selected as a *New York Times Book Review* "Notable Book of the Year" and in 2000 as second book in the *Kansas City Star*'s Book Club.

Johnson's first three short stories were published in 1967. His stories appear in such works as *Breaking Ice, Calling the Wind, O. Henry Prize Stories,* and *Best Short Stories of the Eighties.* His first collection of short stories, *The Sorcerer's Apprentice: Tales and Conjurations* (1986) contains eight stories which address African American history and the magical. "The Education of Mingo," the first story and one frequently anthologized, explores the master-slave relationship and asks the question, Who is the slave? The story alludes to Aristotle and *Frankenstein.* The story has been called an antebellum parable about education and slavery and a twentieth-century Frankenstein story. Like his other works, this one is multilayered.

Soulcatcher and Other Stories (2001), his second collection, contains twelve stories that grew out of a television series entitled "Africans in America" which aired on PBS in 1998. The stories represent moments occurring in the historical span of time from the slave trade to the Civil War. Each of the stories is in a different literary form, including the epistolary, dramatic monologue, fairy tale, and newspaper article. Historical events such as the Plague, Back-to-Africa debate, and the American Revolution, and historical figures such as Phillis Wheatley, Frederick Douglass, Richard Allan, and Martha Washington are highlighted. The work begins with "The Transmission," which describes the Middle Passage and the passing on of history (the griot in the story) to remind the enslaved that they must continue to record history and ends with "Murderous Thoughts." This story brings the work full circle with the words, "One of the most important things we can do young man, is never forget."

In 2005, Johnson's third collection *Dr. King's Refrigerator, and Other Bedtime Stories,* which contains nine stories, appeared. The title story shows a pre-Montgomery King thinking about a sermon topic and being reminded of the interdependence of things. "Kwoon," which was selected for the 1993 *O. Henry Prize Stories,* has martial arts as its subject. Included also are "Sweet Dreams," a world where dreams are taxed and a man and his dreams are being audited; "The Gift of Osuo," and "Cultural Relativity," a fairy tale. The short stories, like his longer works and interviews, reflect Johnson's philosophical training, his concern with the human condition (how it can be improved and understood), and his use of allusions to both Western and Eastern culture.

REFERENCES

Books

Byrd, Rudolph P. *Charles Johnson's Novels: Writing the American Palimpsest.* Bloomington: Indiana University Press, 2005.

Little, Jonathan. *Charles Johnson's Spiritual Imagination.* Columbia: University of Missouri Press, 1997.

McWilliams, Jim, ed. *Passing the Three Gates: Interviews with Charles Johnson.* Seattle: University of Washington Press, 2004.

Periodicals

Boccia, Michael. "An Interview with Charles Johnson." *African American Review* 30 (1996): 611-18.

Griffiths, Frederick T. "Sorcery Is Dialectical: Plato and Jean Toomer in Charles Johnson's *The Sorcerer's Apprentice.*" *African American Review* 30 (1996): 527-38.

Rushdy, Ashraf H. A. "The Phenomenology of the Allmuseri: Charles Johnson and the Subject of the Narrative of Slavery." *African American Review* 26 (1992): 373-94.

Scott, Daniel M., III. "Interrogating Identity: Appropriation and Transformation in 'Middle Passage'." *African American Review* 29 (1995): 649–59.

Selzer, Linda. "Master-Slave Dialectics in Charles Johnson's 'The Education of Mingo'." *African American Review* 37 (2003): 105–14.

Online

"Buddhism is the Most Radical and Civilized Choice." *Shambhala Sun* (January 2004). http://www.shambhalasun.com (Accessed 6 February 2006).

"Charles Johnson Vita." http://depts.washington.edu/engl/people/vita/johnson—cha.html (Accessed 6 February 2006).

"Essay by Charles Johnson." National Book Foundation Archives. http://www.nationalbook.org/authorsguide_cjohnson.html (Accessed 6 February 2006).

Mudede, Charles. "The Human Dimension: An Interview with Writer-Philosopher Charles Johnson." http://www.realchangenews.org/pastarticles/interviews/fea.cjohnson.html (Accessed 6 February 2006).

Helen R. Houston

Fenton Johnson
1888–1958

Poet

Writing primarily between 1913 and 1920, Fenton Johnson produced a group of memorable poems expressing despair about race relations. Other significant poems use language to convey the power of spirituals. Johnson was part of the new imagistic poetry of the early

Chronology

1888	Born in Chicago on May 7
1913	Publishes first book, *A Little Dreaming*
1918	Founds *The Favorite Magazine*
1920	Publishes *For the Highest Good* and *Tales of Darkest America*
1930s	Works for the Federal Writers' Project
1958	Dies in Chicago on September 17

twentieth century, which had Midwestern and specifically Chicago roots. A self-published writer and founding editor of two short-lived periodicals, Johnson struggled to earn a living as a writer. Although these efforts and his attempts at social reform failed, his works have remained in print in anthologies from the 1920s into the early 2000s.

Around 1918 Johnson married Cecilia Rhone, whom he called "the woman of his dreams" ("The Story of Myself"). He was a member of the Authors League of America and of Alpha Phi Alpha Fraternity.

In the 1930s, Johnson was employed in the Works Progress Administration and his final poems draw upon that experience. He did not publish beyond that period. Any known remaining additional works were destroyed when a basement storage area was flooded prior to his death in 1958.

Fenton Johnson was born in Chicago on May 7, 1888 to Elijah H. and Jesse Taylor Johnson. Elijah Johnson's work as a railroad porter enabled him to provide his family with relative financial security, which included owning the State Street building in which they lived. In a 1963 biographical note, Arna Bontemps described Fenton Johnson as "a dapper boy who drove his own electric automobile around Chicago."

Johnson completed high school in Chicago, after having attended both Englewood High School and Wendell Phillips High School. He studied at Northwestern University in 1908-1909 and at the University of Chicago more briefly thereafter. He worked as a messenger and in the post office in Chicago before teaching English at State University (later Simmons College) in Louisville, Kentucky in 1910-1911. The Louisville experience was disappointing: Johnson was not paid even the promised meager salary. He returned to Chicago to concentrate on his literary ambitions.

Johnson began his literary efforts when he was quite young, and he published his first poem in 1900 in a Chicago newspaper. By the time he was nineteen, he had written plays which were performed at Chicago's Pekin Theatre. According to Elizabeth Englehardt, Johnson

wrote plays at least through 1925, the year that *The Cabaret Girl* was staged at Chicago's Shadow Theatre.

Johnson's main genre was poetry. In 1913 he published his first volume, *A Little Dreaming*, which, like all his work, was self-published. He dedicated the book to his grandmother, Ellen Johnson, who may have been the book's sponsor. Johnson expressed his appreciation to her as one "whose life was a poem full of tender sympathy and wholesome striving."

Johnson moved to New York, where, with financial support from another benefactor, he studied journalism at Columbia University's Pulitzer School. He wrote for the Eastern Press Association and was the acting drama editor of the *New York News*. He also published two poetry volumes, *Visions of the Dusk* (1915) and *Songs of the Soil* (1916).

Encouraged by positive reviews, Johnson returned to Chicago, where he continued his work as a journalist. He was the founding editor of *The Champion* in 1916, a monthly magazine which focused on black achievements. It included articles seeking reform, which he called "The Reconciliation Movement." His goal was to bring about racial harmony and in the process to address issues related to stability and order in society. *The Champion* folded in 1917, and although Johnson still spoke of reform in his later endeavors, his Reconciliation Movement had little impact.

Johnson founded his next venture, *The Favorite Magazine*, in 1918. Looking back on the origin of *The Favorite*, he observed in "The Story of Myself": "I had nothing save a meager allowance from a relative but I was determined to have a magazine and conceived the idea that I could accomplish a large number of reforms and the creation of a new literature through a magazine of my own." *The Favorite* lasted until 1920, when Johnson published *For the Highest Good* (essays) and *Tales of Darkest America* (short stories and brief sketches), both volumes using materials Johnson had written for *The Favorite*.

Johnson's work received attention in a wider context between 1918 and 1921 when several of his poems were published in *Poetry: A Magazine of Verse*, edited by Harriet Monroe. He also had several poems published in 1919 in *Others*, edited by Alfred Kreymborg. These periodicals presented the new poetry. Johnson's style fit in well with those of other Midwestern poets and writers, such as Carl Sandburg and Edgar Lee Masters.

In the 1930s, Johnson worked for the Federal Writers' Project, part of the Works Progress Administration (WPA) in Chicago. Arna Bontemps directed the unit, which focused on writing about the Negro in Illinois. Bontemps was Johnson's literary executor.

Johnson's poems published between 1913 and 1916 often feature thick plantation dialect or use what Shirley Lumpkin has termed "genteel, imitative Victorian diction," in exploring commonplace themes. Even so, Johnson was interested in a range of topics, as illustrated by "The Song of the Titanic Victim" and "The Plaint of the Factory Child" in *A Little Dreaming*. That volume also demonstrates Johnson's use of ballad themes related to Scottish, German, and Jewish traditions as well as to classical and medieval settings. Like Paul Laurence Dunbar, the subject of praise in one of the poems in *Dreaming*, Johnson did not want to be limited to dialect poetry presenting simple expressions about plantation life.

Even though *Songs of the Soil* includes many poems that use artificially literary diction, Johnson did not use this language in the poems he identified as Negro spirituals. He explains in his introduction to *Songs* that dialect could not do justice to the spirituals' " barbaric splendor." The contrast in language is evident by comparing "Plantation Prayer" and "Shout, My Brother." Of the two, Johnson identifies only "Shout" as a spiritual. "Plantation Prayer" begins "No othah joy, O Lawd, but jes' to wu'k,/ No othah joy but jes' to love mah folks." Such sentimentality and diction contrast sharply with lines from "Shout, My Brother, Shout": "Hoeing cotton t°ll day of Judgment/ We will reign with God in Heaven/ Shout, my brother! Shout!" The elements of pain and hardship integral in Johnson's most memorable poems are also seen in "Harlem: The Black City" in *Songs of the Soil*: "We ask for life, men give us wine,/ We ask for rest, men give us death."

In *The Book of Negro Poetry* (1922; 1931), James Weldon Johnson noted that Fenton Johnson's expression of "fatalistic despair" brought a new element to African American poetry. This despair is illustrated in "Tired," which includes the directive: "Throw the children in the river; civilization has given/ us too many. It is better to die than to grow up/ and find out that you are colored." Pioneering critic of African American literature J. Saunders Redding found these lines "false to the emotion of despair as the Negro feels it." Redding preferred Johnson's more positive "Children of the Sun." In any case, as Redding points out, Johnson's despairing stance is distinctive in African American literature.

Fenton Johnson worked valiantly for several years to support himself as a writer. His most memorable poetry has its roots in African American culture and experiences. These poems demonstrate the lean, carefully honed verse characterizing American poetry which gained importance through the work of many other Midwestern-based poets and critics in the early decades of the twentieth century.

Johnson's lasting significance despite a relatively small output is demonstrated in his continued presence in anthologies. In the 1920s, in addition to appearing in James Weldon Johnson's *Book of American Negro Poetry*, his work was published in Harriet Monroe and Alice Corbin's *The New Poetry: An Anthology of Twenti-

eth Century Verse in English* (1923) and in Countee Cullen's *Caroling Dusk* (1927).

Other anthologies which include Johnson's work are Arna Bontemps' *American Negro Poetry* (1963); Ruth Miller's *Black American Literature: 1760-Present* (1971); Abraham Chapman's *Black Voices: An Anthology of African American Literature* (1968); Richard Barksdale and Kenneth Kinnamon's *Black Writers of America: A Comprehensive Anthology* (1972); Robert Hayden's *Kaleidoscope* (1982); Arthur P. Davis, J. Saunders Redding, and Joyce Ann Joyce's *The New Cavalcade* (1991); the Library of America's *American Poetry of the Twentieth Century* Volume I (2000); and Henry Louis Gates Jr. and Nellie McKay's *Norton Anthology of African American Literature* (2004).

REFERENCES

Books

Bell, Bernard W. "Johnson, Fenton." *Dictionary of American Negro Biography*. Eds. Rayford W. Logan and Michael R. Winston. New York: Norton, 1982.

Bontemps, Arna, ed. *American Negro Poetry*. New York: Hill and Wang, 1963.

Brown, Sterling. *Negro Poetry and Drama and the Negro in American Fiction*. New York: Atheneum, 1969.

Davis, Arthur P. *From the Dark Tower: Afro-American Writers, 1900-1960*. Washington, DC: Howard University Press, 1981.

Engelhardt, Elizabeth Sanders Delwiche. "Johnson, Fenton." *The Oxford Companion to African American Literature*. Eds. William L. Andrews, Frances Smith Foster, and Trudier Harris. New York: Oxford University Press, 1997.

Lumpkin, Shirley. "Johnson, Fenton.." *Dictionary of Literary Biography*. Vol. 45: American Poets, 1880-1945. First Series. Ed. Peter Quartermain. Detroit, Mich.: The Gale Group, 1986.

Redding, J. Saunders. *To Make a Poet Black*. Chapel Hill, N.C.: University of North Carolina Press, 1939, rpt. College Park, Maryland: McGrath, 1968.

Redmond, Eugene B. *Drumvoices: The Mission of Afro-American Poetry: A Critical History*. New York: Anchor/Doubleday, 1976.

Worthington-Smith, Hammett. "Johnson, Fenton." *Dictionary of Literary Biography*. Vol. 50: Afro-American Writers Before the Harlem Renaissance. Ed. Trudier Harris. Detroit, Mich.: The Gale Group, 1986.

Other

Breman, Paul, ed. "Fenton Johnson: The Daily Grind." Heritage Black Poetry Pamphlet 2. London: Parchment, 1994. Limited Printing (100 copies).

Collections

The John Hope and Aurelia E. Franklin Library at Fisk University has in its Special Collections Department a manuscript of forty-two poems associated with Johnson's WPA years. Other sources for works by Johnson are in the papers of Harriet Monroe at the Joseph Regenstein Library at the University of Chicago and in the Cullen-Jackman Memorial Collection in the Robert W. Woodruff Library of the Atlanta University Center. The Cullen-Jackman Collection includes correspondence between Johnson and Arna Bontemps.

Arlene Clift-Pellow

John V. Johnson
?–1907

Gambling house owner

Long before the lottery became legal in Illinois, John V. "Mushmouth" Johnson owned several gambling houses in Chicago, the first African American to do so. By delivering votes, Johnson influenced Chicago politics, thus providing protection for his enterprises. He gave generously to philanthropic endeavors to help his race, establishing a precedent that other gambling tycoons would follow. Personally, the "Negro Gambling King of Chicago" declined to engage in gambling.

The details of Johnson's early life remain obscure. Accounts of his death mention a mother and two sisters. Born in St. Louis, Johnson moved to Chicago in 1875. For about six years, he worked as a waiter at the Palmer House. In 1882, he became a floor man in Andy Scott's gambling house at 205 South Clark Street. Scott eventually gave Johnson an interest in the business.

Later, Johnson partnered with white men, George Whiting and Al Bryant, to open a gambling house at 311 Clark Street. Herbert Asbury characterizes this venture as "the best-known cheap resort in Chicago" for nearly ten years. The resort welcomed people of all races and social status to play its full complement of games. Unlike other gambling houses that required higher stakes, Johnson's business welcomed bets as low as a nickel. According to Harold Gosnell, "'Craps' and draw poker almost eliminated the more aristocratic games of faro and roulette" in the Clark Street establishment.

Gosnell describes Johnson as "a hard-headed business man and at the same time something of a sentimentalist." Johnson showed no mercy when people pleaded for the return of lost money. But when the sons of distinguished black families came gambling, he often gently advised the young men about gambling's dangers. "Whether this

Chronology

?	Born in St. Louis, Missouri
1875	Moves to Chicago; works at Palmer House
1882	Takes job in gambling house
1890	Opens Emporium Saloon
1903	Mayor revokes Johnson's license
1906	Opens Frontenac Club
1907	Dies in Chicago on September 13

action was motivated by race pride, a desire to avoid personal embarrassment, class consciousness, or a carry-over of early religious training cannot be ascertained," states Gosnell.

Johnson eventually sold his interest in the partnership with Whiting and Bryant. In 1890, he opened his own saloon and gambling house, the Emporium Saloon, at 464 South State Street, in the midst of Chicago's Whiskey Row. Gosnell describes the Emporium as "a meeting-place for railroad men, waiters, porters, and professional gamblers—Chinese, Negro, and white." The gamblers bet each other, rather than the house, but the gamekeeper claimed a portion of each winning.

Johnson also owned the Bad Lands, the Little Cheyenne, and other gambling halls. For seventeen years, he reigned as king of Chicago's gambling czars. The city's best-known gamblers frequented Johnson's saloons, often playing tournaments that lasted for days.

Gains Political Power

Johnson knew the importance of developing a network of friends. Some accounts indicate that he supported the Republican and Democratic parties equally. Although he declined direct involvement in politics, he attended conventions, gained a reputation for political power, and encouraged blacks to register and to vote.

For delivering votes, First Ward Democrat Roger C. Sullivan ensured protection of Johnson's businesses. Under Sullivan's direction, "Hinky Dink" Mike Kenna and "Bathhouse" John Coughlin, a local alderman and committeeman, usually kept Johnson's properties free from police raids—or at least forewarned him.

According to Robert Lombardo, Johnson "held the distinction of being the 'man to see' in Chicago's Chinese quarter. He reportedly sold protection to over twenty Chinatown opium dens and gambling halls where *Fan Tan* and *Bung Loo* card games were played." Asbury states that Johnson charged three dollars per week per table.

When the game policy, a precursor of lottery, was introduced into Chicago, Johnson was "probably the first important black gambler to see the potential of policy," according to Lombardo. Players usually placed a "gig," a three-numbered bet, or sometimes a "saddle," only a two-numbered bet. Policy writers recorded the numbers in a book. Drawings took place at least once a day, usually three or four times a day, allowing twenty-four numbered balls to come into play from a total of seventy-eight.

Nathan Thompson observes that "by the turn of the century, Policy was becoming good business. Everybody was playing—society folks, teenagers, housewives, the poor and the wealthy; and for church folks Policy was a welcome change from Bingo." Through the late 1890s, Johnson promoted policy. With Tom McGinnis, he operated two policy companies known by the names "Union" and "Phoenix." Asbury comments that "The Citizens' Association procured a hundred and fifty indictments against Mushmouth Johnson and others for operating policy games, but none went to jail."

The city council's graft committee, however, watched Johnson carefully. People testified that they found it nearly impossible to win at the Emporium and that, if they did win, the gamekeepers tried their best to collect these winnings. According to Lombardo, the committee saw Johnson "as a 'card cheat' who robbed patrons 'stone blind' at his craps, hand faro, and draw poker tables." In 1903, Mayor Carter Harrison revoked Johnson's license.

Survives Anti-Policy Legislation

In 1903, the Reverend Reverdy Cassius Ransom, pastor of Chicago's Institutional AME Church and Settlement House, denounced policy and its evils from the pulpit. After the firebombing of Ransom's church, Edward Morris, a prominent black lawyer, helped Ransom lobby Republican representative Edward Green to introduce anti-policy legislation. Johnson's rival Bob Motts may have also encouraged Green. According to Thompson, the 1905 law imposed sanctions on "all persons involved in the game from the policy racketeer to the caretaker of the building in which the gambling was conducted."

Johnson closed the Emporium, but on May 1, 1906, with Tom McGinnis and Bill Lewis, Johnson opened Frontenac Club on Twenty-Second Street. This gambling hall, near the city's Levee red-light district, catered only to white men. Admittance consisted of a ready display of at least ten dollars. During the first year, the owners took in about two hundred dollars a day and divided the profit.

According to Thompson, Johnson's "exceptional gift for profanity" earned him the nickname "Mushmouth." But his generosity to Chicago's black community gained him respect. He funded the local Old People's Home and helped the needy. Through his mother, he contributed generously to Chicago's Bethesda Baptist Church. Other black gambling czars would follow Johnson's tradition of philanthropy.

Johnson died on Friday, September 13, 1907. A huge crowd attended his funeral at the Institutional AME Church, including police inspector John Wheeler. Johnson's mother, Ellen Johnson, and his sisters, Louise Ray and Eudora Johnson, came for the funeral. Some accounts indicate that Johnson's money may have helped establish Binga State Bank, the nation's first black-owned bank, in 1908. Eudora Johnson had married Jesse Binga, the bank's founder.

Some sources speculate that Johnson acquired a fortune of $250,000. But shortly before his death, he estimated his assets at under $15,000. Asbury quotes Johnson as telling a friend, "I have spent more than $100,000 for fines...and a huge sum for police protection. I have had to pay out four dollars for every one I took in at the game."

REFERENCES

Books

Asbury, Herbert. *The Gangs of Chicago: An Informal History of the Chicago Underworld.* New York: Thunder's Mouth Press, 1986.

Drake, St. Clair, and Horace R. Cayton. *Black Metropolis: A Study of Negro Life in a Northern City.* Rev. and enl. ed., Vol. 2. New York: Harcourt, Brace & World, 1970.

Gosnell, Harold F. *Negro Politicians: The Rise of Negro Politics in Chicago.* Chicago: University of Chicago Press, 1967.

Thompson, Nathan. *Kings: The True Story of Chicago's Policy Kings and Numbers Racketeers, An Informal History.* Chicago: Bronzeville Press, 2002.

Periodicals

Lawrence, Curtis. "Bronzeville's Policy Kings Were Early Venture Capitalists." *Chicago Sun-Times,* 7 July 2003.

Lombardo, Robert M. "The Black Mafia: African-American Organized Crime in Chicago 1890-1960." *Crime, Law, & Social Change* 38 (2002): 33-65.

Marie Garrett

William Johnson
1809–1851

Diarist, entrepreneur

William Johnson, in his efforts to keep orderly records of his business transactions and the events in Natchez, Mississippi, wrote one of the most

Becomes Successful Businessman

In 1828 Johnson acquired a barbershop in Port Gibson, Mississippi. Two years later Johnson sold his Port Gibson shop to purchase Miller's shop in Natchez when Miller moved to New Orleans. The Natchez barbershop served a predominately white clientele and was very popular. Johnson and his staff provided haircuts, shaves, fitted wigs, and sold fancy soaps and oil. He was so enterprising that in 1833 he was able to purchase a brick building on Main Street. The following year he opened a bathhouse at this location and was able to pay it off within two years. Johnson owned several rental properties, rented rooms for office and retail use, as well as loaned money in small amounts for short periods of time. He speculated on farmland and owned as many as fifteen slaves before his death. As a smart businessman, he also kept abreast of social issues that were important to his status. Johnson dressed fashionably, read newspapers, and purchased books. Though not belonging to one particular denomination, Johnson did attend church. His hobbies supported his competitive side: he enjoyed sports such as hunting, fishing, and horse racing, and participated in lotteries, cards, checkers, raffles, and shuffleboard. He recorded his wins and losses for these activities as well as his business transactions in his diary.

In 1833, Johnson spent two months visiting New York, Philadelphia, and other cities. In a search for a potential bride, he began traveling to New Orleans, St. Francisville, Louisville, as well as other lower Mississippi towns to vacation. After traveling widely, he settled for a local woman. In 1835 Johnson married Ann Battles, the daughter of a family friend and a hometown girl of Natchez. Both Battle and her mother were freed slaves who were emancipated in 1826. Battle was perceived as catching the most eligible bachelor in her class in Natchez. The couple spent sixteen years together and had ten children, with the last child born only a month before Johnson's death.

In 1835 with his new wife, Johnson completed a three-story brick home only half a block from the Adams County Courthouse. His other ventures included a toy shop, engaging in wallpaper sales, and providing cart rentals for transporting goods. He also expanded his money-lending operations, agricultural holdings, and slave ownership. However, even as the most respected and successful free Negro in Natchez, Johnson was still subject to racism. He had access to the courts, but he could not vote, sit on a jury, or bare arms in the local militia. At the theater he was still relegated to the balcony. On Sundays he stood outside to hear sermons at white churches where Negroes were not allowed to enter. The only time he truly crossed the line of segregation was in death: he was buried in the local white cemetery. His mother and one of his daughters were also buried there.

Chronology	
1809	Born into slavery in Natchez, Mississippi
1820	Freed and apprenticed to brother-in-law James Miller
1828	Acquires barbershop in Port Gibson, Mississippi
1830	Purchases Miller's Barbershop in Natchez
1830-50	Keeps diary of business transactions and life in the Antebellum South
1833	Expands business to include money lending, land and slaves
1835	Marries Ann Battles of Natchez
1851	Murdered by Baylor Winn in Natchez, Mississippi on June 17
1951	Johnson's diary is published by family

important historic documents of Antebellum America. His diaries constitute one of the few records that give extensive insight into this part of U.S. social and economic history. As a slave who had been freed, Johnson became a successful businessman and a slaveholder. He began with a barbershop and expanded into various business as well as land ownership. Johnson's diary records how he negotiated a society of racial limitations and discrimination while embracing many white aristocratic values. Although Johnson's experiences serve as an example of the complex role of a free person of color and a slaveholder, his ability to negotiate amicable relations with whites in the pre-Civil War period marked a unique instance for the times. Johnson was able to rise to a level of prominence in Natchez and was respected by both black and white persons in his community.

William Johnson was born in 1809 to Amy Johnson, a slave in Natchez, Mississippi. Amy Johnson and her children were owned by William Johnson of Adams County. Although the child bore the status of his mother, his father ultimately determined his condition. Amy Johnson never openly said that her master, William Johnson, was the father of her children but it was known to be true. When young Johnson was five years old, his mother was emancipated by her owner. Four years later, in 1818, Amy's daughter, a mulatto girl named Delia, was also emancipated by Johnson. It was not until 1820, when young Johnson was eleven years old, that he was freed through a petition submitted also by his master to the Mississippi General Assembly. Johnson was apprenticed to his brother-in-law James Miller, a Philadelphia-born free Negro barber in Natchez. Miller was a well-established and respected local businessman. He taught Johnson the barber business, and he took the place of a father by imparting ethical principals and behaviors that shaped Johnson's character. Miller also initiated him into the ways of upper class free Negroes and the vaguely marked boundaries of economic and social status in the white Natchez community. The lessons that Johnson learned became a key part of his business and social practices throughout his life in Natchez.

Life in Natchez

Embracing the genteel white tradition of keeping a diary, Johnson recorded his view of the antebellum South. With no formal education, Johnson learned about his community and its social rules from his brother-in-law. Politically and socially, Johnson had unusual relationships with whites. He was able to conduct business on a fairly equal basis. As a freed person, Johnson knew both enslaved and free Negroes, as well as the white aristocrats and the white lower class. He loaned money to whites, employed them in some of his businesses, and even sued them in court. He did not write much about religion, and he left political issues such as slavery as a whole to others. Although he could not vote, he was interested in politics and was sympathetic to the Democratic Party. He was in favor of universal suffrage and education. Johnson did offer an opinion on some local issues. Business transactions were a key part of Johnson's dairy, and he also made notes regarding his slaves and related transactions. He vacillated between scorn and pity for other blacks. Regarding his role as slaveholder, Johnson recorded the circumstance of one problem slave. He determined that the slave, Stephen, who drank excessively, was to be sold. He agonized over the decision but came to no other solution. Johnson took the slave system as it was.

In 1851 at the age of forty-two Johnson was murdered over a land-border dispute. Baylor Winn, a long time neighbor, had recently been at odds with Johnson over land and timber rights. Winn ambushed Johnson after he lost the dispute. Johnson lived until the next day and left a statement that Winn was the person who shot him. The fact that Winn claimed to be a white man was the central issue in the trial. Although legally Winn had passed for white, the Johnsons were able to get documentation with certification from the governor of the state that showed Winn and his family to be free Negroes from King William County. The defense was able to have this information left out due to legal technicalities. This ruling, which allowed Winn's claim that he was white, prevented the crucial eyewitness testimony to be given. All three witnesses for the case were Negroes and by Mississippi law Negroes were legally barred from testifying against whites. The case continued through two trials and at two separate locations and was abandoned after two years. Local papers all over the state followed the case as it unfolded. Until her death in 1866, Johnson's wife maintained the family. Her sons and employees maintained the barbershop through the Civil War and afterwards. By 1872, the family name had been changed to Johnston and as members of the family died over the years, the local Natchez press continued to refer to their lineage as one of the most respected local families.

William Johnson, in his efforts to succeed and achieve acceptance, tried diligently to conduct himself as an honorable human being. At the time of his death Johnson had acquired 350 acres of farmland and timberland, several buildings and businesses, and fifteen slaves. Johnson's diary, which was cherished and preserved by his family for nearly a century, contains over two thousand pages in fourteen volumes. The diary of life in Natchez, Mississippi from 1835 to 1851 gives accounts of antebellum Southern life, race relations, economic and social conditions, political affairs, and a unique look at a freed slave's rise to a level of prominence.

REFERENCES

Books

Davis, Edwin Adams. "William Johnson." In *Dictionary of American Negro Biography*. Eds. Rayford W. Logan and Michael R. Winston. New York: Norton, 1982.

——, and William Ransom Hogan. *The Barber of Natchez*. Baton Rouge: Louisiana State University Press, 1954.

Lissek, Deborah. "William Johnson." In *American National Biography*. Vol. 12. Eds. John A. Garraty and Mark C. Carnes. New York: Oxford University Press, 1999.

Salzman, Jack. *Encyclopedia of African-American Culture and History*, Supplement. New York: Macmillan Reference USA, 2001.

Collections

William Johnson's original diary and 1,310 additional items are housed in the Department of Archives at Louisiana State University in Baton Rouge, Louisiana.

Lean'tin L. Bracks

Bobby Jones
1938–

Television show host, musician

Gospel music was not popular on television before the advent of Bobby Jones and his TV program *Bobby Jones Gospel Hour*. In 2004, he celebrated his twenty-fifth season as one of the most popular shows on Black Entertainment Television (BET). As host and executive producer of the number one syndicated gospel television program, seen by millions of viewers, Jones is synonymous with gospel television. Over the years, he established himself as a major principal in the gospel music industry by providing a medium for new talent while reaching a broader audience. Fundamen-

Bobby Jones

Chronology

1938	Born in Henry, Tennessee on September 18
1959	Graduates from Tennessee A & I State University
1965	Receives M.A. from Tennessee State University
1967	Serves as educational consultant, McGraw-Hill, St. Louis, Missouri
1973	Co-hosts *Fun City Five* TV show, Nashville, Tennessee
1975	Instructor, Tennessee State University; forms the gospel group Bobby Jones and the New Life Singers
1976	Introduces the *Nashville Gospel Music Show*, which later becomes *Bobby Jones Gospel Hour*; Bobby Jones and the New Life Singers record first album, *Sooner or Later* on Benson Records
1978-84	Hosts *Bobby Jones's World*, a community-affairs talk show
1980	Receives doctorate from Vanderbilt University; *Bobby Jones's World* wins Gabriel Award; *Bobby Jones Gospel Hour* appears on Black Entertainment Network (BET); Gospel Opera *Make a Joyful Noise* airs on PBS
1982	Bobby Jones and the New Life Singers win a Grammy for best performance by a black contemporary gospel group for album *Soul Set Free*; appears in the NBC-TV Movie of the Week *Sister, Sister*
1984	Receives Dove Award from the Gospel Music Association for the black contemporary album of the year *Come Together*; receives Grammy Award for duet with country music singer, Barbara Mandrell, "I'm So Glad I'm Standing Here Today"
1989	*Video Gospel* premieres on BET
1990	Receives the GMA's Commonwealth Award for outstanding contribution to gospel music; the Bobby Jones Gospel Explosion is founded
2000	St. Martin's Press publishes memoir *Make a Joyful Noise: My 25 Years in Gospel Music*
2002	Receives the Chairman's Award from BET
2005	Receives Next Level Award at About My Father's Business conference
2006	Receives the Trumpet Award for Television

tally, he changed the gospel music industry. An award-winning artist and host of the first and only nationally syndicated African American gospel television show and *Video Gospel*, Jones has worked with and introduced some of the most noted artists in the industry. Considered an icon in gospel music, Bobby Jones has received numerous awards, including the Grammy, the Gospel Music Association's (GMA) Dove Award, the National Association for the Advancement of Colored People's (NAACP) Image Award, and the GMA's Commonwealth Award for outstanding contribution to gospel music, to list only a few.

Born into a family of sharecroppers on September 18, 1938 in Henry, Tennessee, Bobby Jones was the youngest of Jim and Augusta Thorpe Jones's three children. Delivered by his paternal grandmother, Lydia Jones, he spent his early years in Henry, which is in the western division of the state, just south of Paris, Tennessee. A shy child, Jones was reared in a three-room, wood-framed house, with no electricity or running water, and at times barely enough food to eat. Although his early life was somewhat traumatic because his parents abused alcohol and his father verbally abused him, his paternal grandmother, who was responsible for his formative years and provided a much needed support system, strongly influenced Jones and gave him the love and guidance he needed.

In 1943, Jones began attending Caton Elementary School, which only operated during the winter months, since the spring and fall were reserved for crop harvesting. Caton, an all black, one-room schoolhouse, catered to children in grades one through eight. Because of his ability to read and do mathematical computations, the teacher moved him to the second grade.

Jones attended Central High School in Paris, Tennessee. He walked a mile to meet the school bus by 7:00 A.M. and then rode at least an hour on the back roads as the bus driver picked up other students. Because of his parents' breakup, the family moved to Paris during his second year of high school. While in high school, Jones participated in extracurricular activities, and he worked as a dishwasher at the Paris Landing State Park restaurant, where he advanced to being a waiter. In the top five of his class, Jones graduated from Central High School in 1955. Influenced by the class valedictorian, who planed to pursue a college degree, Jones decided to do the same.

Pursues Degree in Elementary Education

With the help of his uncle, Johnny Thorpe, who lived in Nashville, Jones entered Tennessee Agricultural & Industrial State University (now Tennessee State University) in the fall of 1955. Thorpe provided his nephew with a place to stay and paid his tuition. While standing in the registration line to select classes, he struck up a conversation with a fellow student who asked him what major he was going to pursue. It was during this dialogue that the freshman decided to major in elementary education.

While living with his uncle and attending Tennessee A & I, Jones learned to play the piano and became interested in gospel music. Unlike his hometown, which primarily played country music, the radio stations in Nashville played gospel music. With his aunt's tutelage and his persistent practicing, Jones learned to play a few church songs. Practice paid off when he answered a First Street Baptist Church radio ad seeking a piano player for its Sunday school. Although his repertoire was limited, he was hired. Soon Jones played for the Sunday school and for the senior choir, and later he became responsible for the church's entire musical department. All of these factors caused Jones to identify with gospel music, which held the path to his future career.

Jones stayed with the Thorpes for approximately nine months, and as promised he repaid his uncle. While there, he worked with his uncle doing construction, played the piano at a number of churches, and waited tables. Although Sundays were full and exciting, Jones had trouble adjusting to college and urban life. He missed family and friends. Those to whom he was closest were still in high school. At the end of the second quarter, he dropped out and returned home to Paris, where he remained until the fall of 1956.

Jones returned to the university when one of his friends and a cousin entered in the fall. Their presence made college bearable for him. They facilitated his reentrance, and they also helped him make the transition to an academic environment. Jones's grade point average began to improve, and he made the honor roll. Although he made the impulsive decision to major in elementary education as a freshman, he now knew for sure that he wanted to teach and help mold the minds and character of elementary age students. In 1959, at the age of nineteen, Jones graduated from Tennessee A & I State University with a bachelor's degree in elementary education.

Enters Teaching Profession

In 1959, Jones began his teaching career at Farragut Elementary School, in St. Louis. Assigned to teach fifth grade students, he found that they were only a few years younger than he. Observing that other teachers were strict disciplinarians, he knew he faced a challenge. The new teacher used music to bring discipline into his classroom by teaching his students to sing in addition to their other coursework. It was an imaginative tactic and it worked well. As he had done in Nashville, Jones found a way to continue his gospel music interest. He affiliated himself with a small Baptist church in Braden, where he played gospel music.

Jones taught in the St. Louis school system for seven years before returning to Nashville to accept a teaching position there. While in St. Louis, Jones pursued a master's degree. However, the teaching position may not have been the only thing that persuaded Jones to return to Nashville. Crime permeated St. Louis. Being from the rural South, Jones was naive about people, and it caused him problems. On more than one occasion, people he knew broke into his apartment and stole his possessions. During another incident, a male attacker jumped into his car, put a knife to his throat, and demanded money. Escaping unharmed, these incidents aided Jones in making the decision to return to Nashville.

In 1965, Jones earned a master's degree in education from Tennessee A & I State University. The same year, Jones returned to Nashville to accept a teaching position at Lakeview Elementary School, a predominately white school. Nashville was in the midst of desegregating its school system and hired Jones to assist in that process. The only African American teacher at the school, he taught fifth grade students. Later, he transferred to Head Elementary School, which was located in north Nashville where all the students were African American. There Jones taught math and science courses. McGraw-Hill then hired him as an educational consultant in 1967. Although it meant returning to St. Louis, Jones accepted the position.

A year after he moved to St. Louis for a second time, in 1968, the April 4 assassination of Martin Luther King Jr. shattered the country. That night as Jones traveled to be with friends, the police stopped his car, made him get out, and searched him. One of the officers butted him with his weapon. They held him in custody and carried him to jail. Once Jones reached the jailhouse, he was fingerprinted, handcuffed, and shackled. His emotions ran the gambit from being afraid and angry to being devastated by King's assassination. With his one phone call, he telephoned his godmother and was ultimately released.

Jones continued to work for McGraw-Hill as a traveling educational consultant, but after approximately eight years of traveling, Jones grew weary of living out of a suitcase. He returned to Nashville and accepted a position at Tennessee State University.

Soon after his return to Nashville, Jones became actively involved in the community. Ever true to gospel music, he organized the Love Train Choir, which had 350 members from all socio-economic groups, occupations, professions, and lifestyles. He organized Project Help, a program designed to assist the elderly. On the first Sunday of each month, the Love Train Choir performed in concert, the proceeds from which went to Project Help. Project Help fed the poor, paid utility bills, and purchased medicines for Nashville's poor senior citizens. Jones also became involved in Nashville's Black Expo, an organization that gave exposure to the city's African American intellectual and artistic individuals. He became the organization's first president. Under Jones's leadership, Nashville's Black Expo was a success.

Hosts Television Show

After his tenure with the Black Expo ended, Jones became affiliated with Channel 4 (WSMV), a local affiliate of the National Broadcasting Company (NBC). However, this was not Jones's first appearance as a television host. In 1973, he co-hosted *Fun City Five*, a Saturday morning children's show on Channel 5 (WTVF), the local Columbia Broadcasting System (CBS) affiliate. *Fun City Five* allowed the aspiring news reporter to put his acquired skills from working with McGraw-Hill to use in a different venue.

In 1976, Theresa Hannah, an assistant of Nettie Stowers, who hosted an African American community-affairs program, approached Bobby Jones about doing a regular gospel music show for television. Thrilled about the possibility, Jones put together a pilot. Accepted by the station, the *Nashville Gospel Music Show* was born. The pilot was given a thirteen-week trial. To produce the show, Jones received an expense account of approximately $500. The *Nashville Gospel Music Show* aired on Sunday mornings at 9:00. Featuring known gospel artists as well as local artists, the *Nashville Gospel Music Show* eventually captured the highest ratings during that time slot. Within two years, officials at the city's public broadcasting station asked Jones to produce a community-affairs talk show. *Bobby Jones's World* aired on Nashville Public Television's (NPT) Channel 8, the Public Broadcasting System's (PBS) affiliate, and remained on the air for approximately six years.

Blazes a Path in Television for Gospel Artists

Through his magazine-style program, Jones met noted authors, entertainers, and national leaders. While working with both television programs, Jones continued in his position at Tennessee State University and pursued his doctorate degree at Vanderbilt University. It was in his position at Tennessee State University that he met the African American poet, novelist, and educator Maya Angelou. Later, the two became friends and she asked him to do a benefit for her aunt's church in California. By 1980, the *Nashville Gospel Music Show*, now known as the *Bobby Jones Gospel Hour* was picked up by Robert Johnson's Black Entertainment Network (BET), which was also established in 1980. One of the first programs on BET, the gospel show aided the new cable enterprise in gaining a substantial television audience, as well as providing a considerable viewing audience for the musi-

cal genre. The same year that the *Bobby Jones Gospel Hour* appeared on BET, Jones received his doctorate in Curriculum Leadership from Vanderbilt University. Additionally, his gospel opera, *Make a Joyful Noise*, which is the same title of his 2000 memoir, aired on PBS. Jones, who starred in the opera, won a Gabriel Award and an International Film Festival Award for his writing and performance.

It was through Angelou that Jones and his choral group, the New Life Singers, appeared in the 1982 NBC Movie of the Week, *Sister, Sister*. Written by Angelou, *Sister, Sister* featured such stars as Diahann Carroll, Paul Wingfield, Irene Cara, and Rosland Cash. The same year that he and the New Life Singers appeared in the NBC-TV movie, the Recording Academy nominated their album, *Soul Set Free*, for a Grammy Award for the best performance by a black contemporary gospel group. One year after he appeared on the NBC Movie of the Week, he was a guest on country music star Ronnie Milsap's television special, *In Celebration*.

Seven years after his appearance in *Sister, Sister*, Jones's *Video Gospel* premiered on BET. *Video Gospel*, which he produced, was the only national television outlet that gospel artists had for showing their videos.

Jones recorded a number of releases, including *There is Hope in this World* (1978); *Caught Up* (1979); *Tin Gladje* (1981); and *Come Together* (1984), which the Gospel Musical Association awarded a Dove Award for the black contemporary album of the year. The same year, "I'm So Glad I'm Standing Here Today," a duet with country music star Barbara Mandrell, received a Grammy Award. Jones and the New Life Singers later released *I'll Never Forget* (1990); *Bring It to Jesus* (1993); and *Another Time* (1996). Two years later, Jones and a new group, the Nashville Super Choir, released *Just Churchin'*. This 1998 release featured gospel music artists Vanessa Bell Armstrong, Donald Lawrence, James Moore, and Vicki Winans. In addition, Angelou rendered her talents to the *Just Churchin'* album.

Bobby Jones has received many awards and accolades. The GMA awarded him the Commonwealth Award for outstanding contributions to gospel music in 1991. In 1994, he was nominated for the National Cable Television Association's Cable Ace Award. In June 2001, Bob Clement, the U.S. representative from Tennessee's Fifth Congressional District, paid homage to him in Congress. When BET held its Second Annual Awards program in June of 2002, Jones received the Chairman's Award. In 2003, he received a number of honors and awards. Xernona Clayton presented him with the Trumpet Award on January 4, in Atlanta, Georgia. On April 25, the St. Louis Heart Association honored him with the Citizen's Award. On May 9, at the Brooklyn Museum of Art, the Tom Joyner Foundation honored Jones as "The Hardest Working Man." During the first week in June, 100 Black Men of America, Inc. presented Jones with the "Uplifting God through Song and Praise" Award. On June 22, Texas State representative Al Edwards honored him with the Unsung Hero Award at the Juneteenth Celebration in Dallas, Texas. The government of the Turks and Caicos Islands honored him for outstanding service in gospel music in July 2003. The same month, President George W. Bush invited Jones to the White House for an update on his trip to Africa. On September 19, he was inducted into the National Black College Alumni Hall of Fame. In January 2005, the Stellar Music Awards paid tribute to the legendary gospel music entertainer by presenting him with the first ever Legendary Award. Eight months later, the About My Father's Business conference honored Jones with the Next Level Award. He was also the recipient of the 2006 Trumpet Award for Television.

Through his BET television show, the *Bobby Jones Gospel Hour*, Jones has given gospel artists the opportunity to present their music before millions. One of the first programs and the longest-running weekly show in cable-television history, it was the only syndicated black gospel television show that affords gospel performers the chance to gain national exposure.

REFERENCES

Periodicals

Schmitt, Brad, and Ryan Underwood. "Gospel Star Bobby Jones Likes the Sound of Florida Overture." *Tennessean*, 22 January 2006.

Linda T. Wynn

Edward P. Jones

Edward P. Jones
1950–

Writer

Edward P. Jones began by publishing short stories in magazines such as *Essence*, *Callaloo*, and the *New Yorker*. However, it was his two books that brought him acclaim. The works were written ten years apart but when published, each made an impact. The first, *Lost in the City*, is a collection of fourteen short stories set in Washington, D.C. The second work, *The Known World*, is a novel about slavery.

For these two works, Jones has received recognition and awards, including a National Book Foundation Award and the PEN/Hemingway Award for *Lost in the City* in 1992. In 2004, he received a MacArthur Foundation grant, the National Book Critics Circle Award for fiction, and the Pulitzer Prize for fiction for *The Known World*. In spite of this success, Jones has remained low-keyed and committed to honesty in writing. He presents strong, realistic characters who survive despite the reality of racism.

Edward P. Jones was born in Washington, D.C. on October 5, 1950. He was raised in a single parent home and attended kindergarten and part of the first grade in a Catholic school. Due to the family's financial limitations, he then transferred to the local public schools. Until he was thirteen years of age, Jones mostly read comic books. Then he discovered two influential novels: Ethel Water's *His Eye Is on the Sparrow* and Richard Wright's *Native Son*. He became an avid reader and began unconsciously to educate himself in the craft of writing. He attended Holy Cross College in Worcester, Massachusetts, on scholarship, earning a B.A. in 1972. In his sophomore year at Holy Cross, he began writing fiction, but it was not until much later that he considered fiction writing for a career. Following graduation and while caring for his terminally ill mother, he held various jobs, including a job with *Science* magazine. In 1975, his first story appeared in *Essence* magazine. In the same year, his mother died. After working three years in Washington, he entered graduate school at the University of Virginia in 1979.

While at the University of Virginia, Jones studied under and was encouraged by John Casey, Peter Taylor, and James Alan McPherson. At the university, he wrote

Chronology

1950	Born in Washington, D.C. on October 5
1972	Earns B.A. from Holy Cross College
1975	Publishes first story in *Essence* magazine
1981	Earns M.F.A. from University of Virginia
1992	Publishes *Lost in the City*; wins National Book Foundation Award and Ernest Hemingway Foundation/PEN Award for *Lost in the City*
1994	Receives a Lannan Foundation grant
2003	Publishes *The Known World*
2004	Wins National Book Critics Award and Pulitzer Prize for Fiction for *The Known World*; wins 2004 MacArthur Fellowship
2005	Wins 2005 O. Henry Prize for short story "A Rich Man"

assignments and pursued his own writing, too. Literature classes, including one in the Bible, helped him more than creative writing classes. He received the M.F.A. from the University of Virginia in 1981.

In an interview with *African American Review*, Jones stated that he developed his own style while being influenced by the work of Richard Wright and Zora Neale Hurston. He uses the 1950s and 1960s in his short stories, a time he knows firsthand. In his discussion of his craft and his philosophy about writing, Jones stated that he is an African American writer, and he cannot drop this description until people in the United States have transcended race. He has taught creative writing at both George Washington University and Princeton University.

Lost in the City

After reading James Joyce's *Dubliners*, Jones realized that no one had provided this treatment for Washington and a collection of short stories on this order could explore the capitol's diversity. Stories in *Lost in the City* (1992) present a fresh and candid view of the city. It portrays the Washington beyond the monuments, Capital Hill, and politicians. It took three years to write the fourteen stories; however, the characters and storylines had been germinating in his head for years. The city of Washington itself becomes a character in these stories. As is true of any locale, some individuals are literally lost in the city, while others are able, after a time, to move on.

Set in the 1950s and 1960s, such stories as "The Girl Who Raised Pigeons," "The Night Rhonda Ferguson Was Killed," and "The First Day" (originally published in *Callaloo*) are set in a time when adults knew children in the neighborhood, were free to reprimand them, and knew the child would receive another reprimand upon his arrival home. In presenting the diversity of the city and its people, Jones also writes about the criminal side of the city in "Young Lions" and in "His Mother's House."

These stories present ordinary working-class African Americans living their lives, struggling to survive.

The Known World

Jones' novel *The Known World* tells the story of Henry Townsend, who goes from slave to freeman to slave owner in the course of the work. The story is set in Manchester County, Virginia. The town and the characters in the book are fictional. In creating a town, Jones follows in the tradition of William Faulkner's Yoknapatawpha County and Ernest Gaines's Bayonne, Louisiana. The creation of place requires detailed history. Jones refers to real places, real historical people (for example, President Fillmore), and actual historical events (for example, the Civil War). Added to this historical information, he presents population statistics: number of Indians, blacks, and whites in the county at a given time. He even accounts for the inability of the reader to locate Manchester County; it was absorbed into surrounding counties. This woven history frames the story, giving it a sense of accuracy and credibility.

The novel, like *Lost in the City*, which begins with the epigraph, "My soul's often wondered how I got over," has strong characters and character development. The characters struggle through hardships, face the tenuousness of life (free today and slave tomorrow, part of a family unit today and sold the next), and challenges. The novel has many characters, and each has his or her own story. However, the central subject in *The Known World* is the institution of slavery as is the city in *Lost in the City*.

Jones' female characters are strong and independent. There is Caldonia Townsend, who is left to run the plantation upon Henry Townsend's death; Fern Elston, a free black woman who chooses not to pass for white as many of her family have, who remains in Manchester County with her husband, Ramsey, and teaches the young; Celeste on the Townsend plantation, Minerva, the Skiffington's wedding present; and Alice Night, an artist. Through these women, Jones pays homage to black women in their disparate, challenging situations.

Edward P. Jones is at work on another collection of short stories, which evolve and use characters from his earlier collection. Two of the stories have been published: "In the Blink of God's Eye" and "All Aunt Hagar's Children." In 2005, Jones won the O. Henry Prize for "A Rich Man."

REFERENCES

Periodicals

Jackson, Lawrence P. "An Interview with Edward P. Jones" *African American Review* 34 (Spring 2000): 95-103.

Online

"Robert Birnbaum Converses with Edward Jones."
    January 21, 2004. http://www.identitytheory.com/
    interviews/birnbaum138.php (Accessed 6 February
    2006).

                                        Helen R. Houston

Edward Perry Jones
1872–1924

Activist, minister

Chronology

1872	Born in Hinds County, Mississippi on February 21
1880	Enters Alcorn Agriculture and Mechanical College at eight years of age
1888	Graduates from public high school
1894	Graduates from Rust University with his doctorate in divinity
1894	Ordained a minister on June 17, in Tunica County, Mississippi
1896	Marries Harriet Lee Winn of Greenville, Mississippi, on November 19
1900	Serves as grand master, Odd Fellows of Mississippi fraternity
1915	Becomes first president of the National Baptist Convention of America, Unincorporated
1923	Ends presidency in National Baptist Convention of America, Unincorporated
1924	Dies in Mississippi

Born in 1872, Edward Perry Jones made a stunning contribution to the society when African Americans had many barriers that often prevented them from excelling. Jones was born at the end of the Reconstruction period when the many freedoms that African Americans enjoyed in that period were being revoked by the black codes and ultimately, the Jim Crow laws. Jones was born in Hinds County, Mississippi, on February 21, 1872. He was active in the social, educational, political, and religious affairs that propelled the lives of African Americans at that time. In all these spheres, Jones defended his beliefs as he voiced his opinions and planned and implemented programs that benefited blacks. Jones was involved in the education of his fellowmen. He promoted the good life for the African American community by challenging fractions in the society that tried to deter the growth of blacks.

In his early years Jones had a good role model in his father, George P. Jones, who was a prominent pastor. He performed his minister's duties at the King Solomon M.B. Church in Vicksburg, Mississippi, and he was also an elder at the Missionary Baptist Church in Mississippi. Reverend Jones was very involved in the education of his sons, Edward Perry and St. Paul, especially after the death of his wife Louvenia. Edward was the older of the two boys, and his father sought the best education for him.

When Jones was eight years old, he was enrolled in the Alcorn Agricultural and Mechanical College in 1880. Jones remained at Alcorn College for one and a half sessions before enrolling in the public school, Vicksburg High, where he graduated as valedictorian of his class. Sadly, Jones's father died before providing him with the total education that he needed. Fortunately, the Baptist Church sponsored Jones in furthering his studies. He attended the Baptist College for a short time, then he continued his studies at the Natchez College where he received his B.S. and was valedictorian of his class. After

his graduation from Natchez, he entered Rust University where he gained his doctor of divinity degree in 1894.

After his graduation from Natchez, Jones made his mark as an educator. Jones was the principal of the Rolling Fork School in Mississippi for approximately five years. In this capacity, Jones developed educational programs for African Americans who were able to attend the segregated school. He promoted high quality education for African Americans, despite their being marginalized in white society. Jones joined the board of trustees for Natchez College where he unlocked the way for many African Americans who were not able to pay for their tuition.

Moves from Business to the Ministry

Jones was also a leader in the business world. He saw the need to protect the properties owned by African Americans. Jones became an insurance salesman and eventually was president of Union Guaranty Insurance Company. He sold insurance to African Americans, and he purchased property, which gave him financial clout. He owned real estate in the prime area in Tunica, Mississippi. At the beginning of the twentieth century, Jones' property in the Mississippi area was valued at over $40,000, which was very high for an African American's assets in that era.

Jones was also involved in the African American division of the Baptist Church. After working as a principal, he followed in his father's footsteps, entering the ministry. He was ordained a Baptist minister on June 17, 1894, in Tunica County. He fulfilled pastoral duties at the Forest Sale Missionary Baptist Church in Mississippi where his father had served as an elder. His next assignment was with the Fredonia Baptist Church, in Tunica, where he served for over three years. Within that time, Jones had built a modern worship facility for his congregation. He also served as a pastor for the congregation at the Mount Horeb Baptist Church in Greenville, Mississippi, and for King Solomon Baptist Church in Vicksburg, Mississippi. Jones was even a pastor in Chicago, Illinois, for some time. The African American arm of the Baptist Church valued Jones for his dedication and service, and he was appointed to many positions in the organization. In fact, he became the recording secretary of the General Mississippi Baptist State Convention.

His name is adjoined to the National Baptist Convention of America, Unincorporated as Jones was given the privilege of being its first president. The National Baptist Convention of America, Unincorporated was formed after a disagreement aroused between E. C. Morris and Richard H. Boyd. Boyd was the head of the publishing board, and he fought for the independence of the publishing board from the National Baptist Convention—the African American Baptist organization. Boyd and his supporters formed the National Baptist Convention of America that later became the National Baptist Convention of America, Unincorporated. Jones was appointed president on September 15, 1915 because he supported Boyd wholeheartedly. In the dispute, he spoke effectively to build support for Boyd who was managing the publishing board that published all materials for the organization, and this entity was the most profitable arm of the organization. As president, Jones approached both African Americans and whites in the South and the North in order to improve the organization's unity and to gain support. Jones adeptly led the National Baptist Convention based in Nashville, Tennessee, for eight years, and it was the most productive African American division of the Baptist organizations for that era. In 1923, a year before his death, Jones was succeeded by J. E. Woods during the eighth annual National Baptist Convention of America in Fort Worth, Texas.

Figures Prominently in Fraternal Societies

Jones played a prominent role in the social organizations. He was involved in several fraternal societies that were run by African Americans. He joined the Odds Fellow of Mississippi Fraternity. In 1901 he was elected grand master to this social organization. He was further elevated as he became grand director of the United Order of Odd Fellows of America. As a delegate of the organization, in 1907, Jones represented Odd Fellows of the United States in Burslem, Stoke-on-Trent, London, and in Paris, France. In addition, Jones was the supreme master of the Unified Reformers of America, Europe, Asia, and Africa. Jones served for five terms in this position. In the early 1900s, the Unified Reformers was the fastest growing African American fraternity. In addition, he was also a member of the Mason Lodge, Knights of Pythias.

Jones was also a force in the political arena. He represented his people and aired their views in the many political forums that he attended. Jones, a Republican, was a delegate at large to the National Convention in Chicago in 1908 and 1912. He was a Republican because the Republican Party was credited with the emancipation of slaves. He chaired the Mississippi State Convention in 1913. Jones encouraged African Americans to vote despite barriers, such as the poll tax and literacy tests, aimed at preventing African Americans from exercising their right to vote.

Jones was married to Harriet Lee Winn, a native of Greenville, Mississippi, on November 19, 1896. The union produced three boys. Jones died in Mississippi in 1924.

REFERENCES

Books

Mather, Franck Lincoln, ed. *Who's Who of the Colored Race: A General Biographical Dictionary of Men and Women of African Descent.* (1915, repr.) Vol. 1. Detroit: Gale Research, 1976.

Thompson, Patrick H. *The History of Negro Baptists in Mississippi.* Jackson, Miss.: R. W. Bailey Printing Co., 1898.

Who's Who in America. Vol. 5. Chicago: Marquis Who's Who, 1993.

Denise Jarrett

John Jones
1816–1879

Activist, politician, tailor, entrepreneur

A former slave who learned the trade of tailoring, John Jones made his mark in Chicago; he arrived in the city almost penniless and amassed a fortune to become one of black America's wealthiest entrepreneurs. His Chicago home was a station on the Underground Railroad, as he helped runaway slaves who were en route to Canada. He held political office and participated in the black convention movement. He strenuously opposed Illinois Black Laws as well as the Fugitive Slave Act of 1850, and worked hard at the local and national level to repeal both.

Born on November 3, 1816, on a plantation in Greene County, North Carolina, John Jones was the offspring of a racially mixed couple. He was the son of John Bromfield, a German, and a free mulatto mother whose name was noted simply as "Jones." His mother feared that, despite the fact that he was considered free by virtue of her status, his father might try to enslave him. While he was still very

Chronology

1816	Born free in Greene County, North Carolina on November 3
1844	Marries Mary Jane Richardson; files for certificate of freedom
1845	Relocates to Chicago with wife and child; opens tailoring shop
1847	Appeals to Illinois State Constitutional Convention for repeal of Black Laws
1848	Elected delegate to Colored National Convention
1850	Attends black rally at Quinn Chapel; appointed to resolutions committee; helps set up vigilance committee to monitor whites' actions toward blacks; circulates petition to repeal Illinois Black Laws
1853	Elected a vice president of the Colored National Convention; elected president of first Black Illinois State Convention
1861	Helps to found Olivet Baptist Church
1864	Publishes pamphlet, *The Black Laws of Illinois and a Few Reasons Why They Should Be Repealed*
1871	Loses some of his wealth in the great Chicago fire; becomes first black elected a Cook County commissioner
1872	Re-elected a commissioner for three-year term
1874	Begins successful fight to dismantle segregated schools
1879	Dies in Chicago on May 21

young, she apprenticed her son to a man named Sheppard, who taught him the tailoring trade. Sheppard took young Jones with him to Tennessee and apprenticed him to Richard Clere, a tailor who lived about fifty miles from Memphis in Somerville, Fayetteville County. Since Jones knew the trade well, when his business was slow, Clere often hired him out to different tailors throughout Tennessee. While working in Memphis, in 1841 John Jones met Mary Jane Richardson, the daughter of free blacksmith Elijah Richardson. The Richardson family moved to Alton, Illinois, while Jones remained in Memphis for three years to complete the requirements of his apprenticeship and to secure himself financially.

Jones knew that during slavery, he was required to have free papers with him at all times. Thus, with permission, he returned to North Carolina, secured his free papers from the state, and on return to Tennessee he petitioned the Eleventh District Court to release him from Clere's service and custody. He was already on his way to financial security, having saved approximately $100 by 1844, when he was twenty-seven years old. Now that he was economically and legally free, he could join his future wife.

Jones moved to Alton, Illinois, and married Mary Jane Richardson. Some sources say that they met Illinois laws and yet, although they were free, in 1844 John and Mary Richardson Jones obtained a certificate of freedom, posted a $1,000 bond in Madison County, and gained the privilege of traveling and living in the state. Although little else is known about their life in Alton, the couple remained there for a while then in March 1845 relocated to Chicago, only twelve years after the city was founded. The couple

sought a climate that was favorable to blacks and also wanted to become active in the abolitionist movement. They believed that opportunities for blacks were greater in Chicago than in Alton. Although Chicago was still a frontier town, it was becoming an urban city. When it became a port of entry in 1846, it attracted people from throughout the country and abroad. With only $3.50 in their pockets, the Joneses and their only child Lavinia moved to Chicago. They took a circuitous route, traveling first by stage to Ottawa, then by canal to Chicago. Throughout the journey, they feared slave catchers, who were on the lookout for fugitive slaves. They were also harassed due to their race and detained at one point, until the stagecoach driver vouched for their free status.

On March 11, nearly one week after they set out on their journey, the Jones family reached Chicago and settled in the Second Ward, bound by State Street, Clark Street, and the Chicago River. They rented a one-room apartment, or cottage, on the corner of Madison Street in what was then called Fifth Avenue but known later as Wells Street. A few blocks away, on the west side of Clark Street between Randolph and Lake, John Jones set up his small tailoring shop. That site later became the entrance to the Sherman House. Later the Joneses lived at 119 Dearborn, where John Jones also established a business that became one of Chicago's first black establishments. It was advertised in the city directory as "J. Jones, Clothes Dresser & Repairer." The highly skilled tailor soon had a thriving enterprise; he catered to many of Chicago's elite. His announcement in the city directory, cited in the *Illinois Historical Journal*, noted: "I take this method of informing you that I may be found at all business hours at my shop, ready and willing to do all work in my line you may think proper to favor me with, in the best possible manner. I have on hand all kinds of trimmings for repairing Gentlemen's clothes."

By 1860 Jones's business was advertised as the Clothes Cleaning and Repairing Room. He called it the city's oldest and best business enterprise. He had strengthened his financial base as well, now having accumulated between $85,000 and $100,000. The great Chicago fire of 1871 affected his wealth, yet he was left with enough money to be called one of the country's wealthiest African Americans and Chicago's undisputed black leader.

From his early days in Chicago, Jones obtained the aid of two local abolitionists: physician Charles V. Dyer, and noted attorney Lemanuel Covell Paine Freer. These men kept a steadfast friendship throughout Jones's life. Since Jones was not a learned man, he needed the assistance of one who was; thus, Freer wrote all of his letters and also taught Jones to read and write—basic skills that he needed to maintain his business and to operate in abolitionist activities when the time came. Jones learned well and later became the first black notary public in Illinois. He entered politics as well, and in 1871 he became the first black elected as Cook County commissioner. He was reelected to a three-year term in 1872. From then on, Jones played an important role in the black convention movement and in the black abolitionist movement.

After he moved to 43 Ray Street, Jones opened his home to fugitive slaves, making it the second major station on the Underground Railroad in the city. The first stop was located at Quinn Chapel, the oldest African Methodist Episcopal church in Chicago. The ardent abolitionist hosted such luminaries as John Brown and Frederick Douglass. Mary and John Jones opposed Brown's radical views and plans, including his proposed raids in Pennsylvania and Virginia. Jones played a leadership role for three hundred blacks who met at the church on Wells Street which was later renamed Quinn Chapel. They met to protest the Fugitive Slave Law of 1850. Jones also joined the local Vigilance Committee and became one of its leaders.

Protests Illinois Black Laws

John Jones bitterly opposed Black Laws, calling them the reason for poverty among blacks. Obsessive fear of slave insurrections led many states to adopt Black Laws early on. Illinois Black Laws were adopted in 1819 and made it clear that blacks had no legal rights. They could neither sue nor be sued; they could testify against another slave or a free black but never against whites; they could own no property or merchandise; their oath was worthless; they could not become educated; no more than three could come together for dancing, unless a white person was present; and so on.

Illinois became notorious for restricting blacks' rights. When the state's Constitutional Convention was held in 1847, Jones was there to call for repeal. He wrote a series of articles in Chicago's *Western Citizen* in that year, defended black rights, and noted, among other accomplishments, the record of blacks in the Revolutionary War. He insisted that blacks had a right to equal representation and equality before the law. Still, Illinois passed Article XIV of the 1848 Illinois Constitution, which prohibited blacks from immigrating to and settling in Illinois. After that, Jones became well known as a spokesman for black rights.

Jones and other black Chicagoans met at Olivet Baptist Church on August 7, 1848, where Jones and Reverend Abraham T. Hall were elected delegates to the forthcoming Colored National Convention to be held in Cleveland. Members of the convention consisted of black freemen. The delegates were to report on the moral and intellectual development of blacks in Illinois. In September, between fifty and seventy-five men assembled for the convention, most of them self-made men who were carpenters, blacksmiths, editors, painters, dentists, farmers, grocers, or clergymen from the United States and Canada. Frederick Douglass was elected president and Jones vice president. The delegates were mainly interested in improving the status of blacks in the United States. They promoted such issues as education, temperance, and community cooperation. While Jones supported mechanical trades, business, farming, and the professions, he opposed menial labor, perhaps equating it with the experiences he had seen as a slave, and the work to which Black Laws relegated black people. The convention nearly became one of political action, as the delegates entertained the idea, but fell short of endorsing a presidential candidate.

Back in Chicago, Jones and other prominent local blacks met on September 11 to work further to repeal the state's Black Laws. They formed a correspondence committee to determine the feasibility of circulating a petition to repeal the laws and to identify all blacks in the Fourth Congressional District. But the 1849 session gave no further hope for repeal. Adding fuel to the racial unrest was the Fugitive Slave Act which Congress passed in September 1850, further preventing black emancipation. This act gave the federal government almost unlimited power to seize and return fugitive slaves, to deny the slave a trial by jury, and to enable slave owners to provide a single affidavit to claim their slaves. Those who failed to follow the law could be subjected to heavy penalties. The law produced great fear and alarm in blacks everywhere, for this was a dehumanizing act that gave whites license to engage in man-hunting schemes.

Jones and his followers were relentless in their work. On September 30, 1850, over three hundred black Chicagoans rallied at Quinn Chapel to determine their course of resistance to the new law. Jones was appointed to the resolutions committee and brought the committee's report to the mass meeting before the session ended. The committee was resolved to resist any attempt to return blacks to bondage and, at the risk of imprisonment or even death, to defend each other. There was no doubt that the Fugitive Slave Act was designed to re-enslave blacks. Then the group formed a vigilance committee that would become a black police force and would serve as long as needed. There were seven divisions in the force and six people within each division. The force patrolled the city each night and kept watch for so-called interlopers.

In December 1850, Jones circulated another petition— signed by black residents of the state—for state legislators to repeal the Black Laws. In fact, subsequent petitions were circulated throughout the 1850s but to no avail. Chicago's black leaders had a double fight—state and federal laws that restricted blacks. Jones moved his campaign outside Illinois, as he and Frederick Douglas took an anti-slavery tour throughout the West. By now, leaders saw a need to revive the black national convention movement. Thus, in 1853 Douglass called a meeting of free blacks, and nine states responded by sending 140 delegates. They met in Rochester, New York, on July 6, 1853, and elected Reverend James W. L. Pennington of New York as president. Among the vice presidents elected were Jones and Douglass. The group was known as the Union of Colored

People of the Free States, later called the Colored National Convention. There were six councils in each state. Jones and James D. Bonner led the Illinois movement. Four standing committees were appointed as well: the Manual Labor School, Protective Unions, Business Relations, and Publications. The idea of an industrial school was not new and had been endorsed as early as the 1830s. Jones, Douglass, and other leaders, such as James McCune Smith, endorsed the idea, contending that white artisans refused to accept black apprentices and that blacks needed to learn the skilled trades necessary for social and economic independence. The institution would be called the American Industrial School, to be located in western Pennsylvania. It would admit students regardless of gender or complexion. In 1855, however, the national black convention abandoned the plan.

In October 1853, Chicago hosted the meeting of the first Black Illinois State Convention, where Jones was elected president; later he became chair of the colonizing committee. Both the Illinois and Rochester conventions were unsuccessful in bringing about equal opportunities for blacks. Even so, the black convention movement was significant. The Fugitive Slave Act prompted a black exodus to Canada, factional disputes emerged, financial support for the efforts was inadequate, but the local work had to continue. National black leaders emerged from the movement; they wrote, spoke, and petitioned for black rights and kept the issues before governing bodies. The leaders were firm believers in the race and its rights.

In 1864, the *Chicago Tribune* published—at his expense—Jones' pamphlet, *The Black Laws of Illinois and a Few Reasons Why They Should Be Repealed*. Jones continued to agitate against the Black Laws by distributing his pamphlet, making speeches, writing other articles, and lobbying in the state legislature. But it was not until 1865 that Illinois repealed the provision of its Black Laws.

Repeal of the Black Laws

The Illinois General Assembly seemed ready to repeal the Black Laws in January 1865. Outgoing governor, Richard Yates, who had resigned to become a United States senator, urged the legislature to remove the laws from the statute as quickly as possible. He was one the few whites in the legislature who had always found slavery abominable. In 1864 Yates openly stated that he favored the abolition of slavery because he supported humanity, and he knew that the U.S. Constitution gave all Americans independence. He agreed with Jones, who had said all along that both the state and federal laws were in conflict with state and federal constitutions. Bills to repeal the laws were introduced in the Illinois general assembly on January 2, 1865. Petitions poured in from throughout the state, asking for the repeal of the now infamous Black Laws. Concurrently, the U.S. Congress debated the Thirteenth Amendment. Congress acted on February 1 and Illinois became the first state to ratify the amendment, abolishing slavery and involuntary servitude. On February 7, 1865, after the Senate and House had voted overwhelmingly in favor of the repeal, Governor Richard J. Oglesby signed the repeal of the Illinois Black Laws. The black celebration that followed in Springfield included recognition of Jones, who ignited the fuse in a cannon that blacks fired sixty-two times—one for each member of the Senate and House. Following, Jones and the group went to the local African Methodist Episcopal Church to continue the celebration, concluding with a speech by Jones.

As Chicago's black population increased and the civil rights bill was passed in 1866, providing equal protection under the law, segregation was still alive and well in the city. Even so, blacks were now eligible to hold public office. In 1869, Governor Palmer appointed Jones a notary public, making him the state's first black to hold that office. When the state ratified the Fifteenth Amendment in March 1870, blacks could then vote in Illinois elections, and they did so. From 1872 to 1875, Jones served a short term and a full term as member of the Cook County Board of Commissioners. He was one of the first blacks in the North to win such an office and the first black in Chicago elected to public office. In 1874, Jones was successful in his fight to dismantle segregated schools. A public-spirited citizen, he donated the site of the Jones School, located at Harrison Street and Plymouth Court. Named in his honor, the school educated some of Chicago's most distinguished business leaders, politicians, educators, and social and civic leaders.

Jones was gratified that, finally, the legal system in Illinois and throughout the United States recognized blacks and gave them their rights. Five years before he died, Jones referred to the progress of blacks in the *Chicago Tribune*, cited in the *Illinois Historical Journal*: "Everywhere the black man has sprung of his own free will and determination, in spite of Church and State, from the position of slavery and its consequences, to the bar, the pulpit, the lecture-room, the professorship, the degrees of M.D. and D.D."

The Joneses were active in the Chicago community. They were among the founders of Olivet Baptist Church in 1861, an important early black church that boasted a 128-volume library—the first of its kind that was open to black residents. Jones contributed significantly to black charitable institutions and various philanthropies.

After a lengthy illness, Jones died on May 21, 1879. He was buried in Graceland Cemetery. Both Jones and his wife were interred near the graves of two white abolitionists whom Jones met early in his Chicago days and who remained his lifelong friends—Alan Pinkerton and Charles Dyer. Throughout his life, Jones demonstrated a commitment to human justice and persevered in his fight to see that his race was given what was already legally his right. He was an acknowledged leader of black liberation.

REFERENCES

Books

The Black Abolitionist Papers. Vol. IV: *The United States, 1847-1858*. Ed. C. Peter Ripley. Chapel Hill: University of North Carolina Press, 1991.

Bontemps, Arna, and Jack Conroy. *Anyplace But Here*. New York: Hill and Wang, 1966.

Branham, Charles. "John Jones." In *Encyclopedia of African American Business History*. Ed. Juliet E. K. Walker. Westport, Conn.: Greenwood Press, 1999.

Drake, St. Clair, and Horace R. Cayton. *Black Metropolis: A Study of Negro Life in a Northern City*. New York: Harcourt, Brace and Co., 1945.

Gatewood, Willard B. *Aristocrats of Color: The Black Elite, 1880-1920*. Bloomington: Indiana University Press, 1990.

Gliozzo, Charles A. "John Jones." In *American National Biography*, Vol. 12. Eds. John A. Garraty and Mark C. Carnes. New York: Oxford University Press, 1999.

Intercollegiate Wonder Book, or The Negro in Chicago, 1779-1927. Vol. I. Chicago: Published by the Washington Intercollegiate Club of Chicago, 1927.

Logan, Rayford W.. "John Jones." In *Dictionary of American Negro Biography*. Eds. Rayford W. Logan and Michael R. Winston. New York: Norton, 1982.

Spear, Allan H. *Black Chicago: The Making of a Negro Ghetto, 1890-1920*. Chicago: University of Chicago Press, 1967.

Periodicals

Gliozzo, Charles A. "John Jones: A Study of a Black Chicagoan." *Illinois Historical Journal* 80 (Autumn 1987): 177-88.

Collections

The papers of John Jones are in the Chicago Historical Society. The Jones collection also includes oil portraits of Jones and his wife, Mary Jane Richardson Jones, which hung in their home.

Jessie Carney Smith

Robert Elijah Jones
1872–1960

Bishop, editor

Active participation in the African American community was an important commitment that Robert

Chronology	
1872	Born in Greensboro, North Carolina on February 19
1891	Serves as pastor in Leaksville, North Carolina
1892	Ordained Methodist Episcopal (M.E.) minister, deacon
1895	Receives A.B. from Bennett College, Greensboro, North Carolina
1897	Receives B.D. from Gammon Theological Seminary, Atlanta, Georgia
1897-1900	Becomes assistant manager, *Southeastern Christian Advocate*
1898	Receives M.A. from Bennett College
1901	Marries Valena C. MacArthur on January 2, who dies in 1917
1904-20	Becomes bishop in the M.E. Church
1911	Receives L.L.D. from Howard University, Washington, D.C.
1920	Marries H. Elizabeth Brown
1960	Dies in Waveland, Mississippi on May 18

Elijah Jones made to his church and his community. Early on he was ordained as a Methodist Episcopal minister and later became the first elected African American bishop of the Methodist Church. In his role as bishop Jones supported efforts to give African Americans a voice in the activities and decisions of the Methodist Church. The church previously did not allow African Americans in any major role. Jones played a key role in the relationship between African American and white Methodist churches of the time. As a clergyman, he offered strong and eloquent words to bring many to religious awareness. His opinion was sought by persons of influence not only because of his role as editor of the *Southeastern Christian Advocate* but as a person of character and commitment to the community.

Robert Elijah Jones was born on February 19, 1872 to Sydney Dallas and Mary Jane Holley Jones in Greensboro, North Carolina. While many in his community left to receive their education elsewhere, Jones stayed close to home. He attended public school and upon graduation attended Bennett College which is a historically black college that at the time was coeducational. (Bennett later became an all African American women's college.) Jones received his A.B. degree from Bennett College in 1895.

Jones began his career as a preacher in Leaksville, North Carolina in 1891 and was ordained into the Methodist Episcopal ministry in 1892. His first church assignment was Reidsville, North Carolina, where he earned the rank of elder in 1896. While preaching and meeting the needs of his church, he attended Gammon Theological Seminary in Atlanta, Georgia and received a bachelor of divinity degree in 1897. He returned the following year to Bennett College and received his M.A. in 1898.

The *Southeastern Christian Advocate* appointed Jones assistant manager in 1897. After four years of service, Jones left the magazine and took an appointment as field secretary of the Board of Sunday School of the Methodist Episcopal Church. That same year he married Valena C. MacArthur, whom he shared sixteen years with before she died. (On February 4, 1920 Jones married H. Elizabeth Brown.) In 1904 Jones returned to the *Southeastern Christian Advocate* as its editor and maintained this role until 1920. During this time he was a popular speaker. Recognizing Jones's character and influence in the community, Booker T. Washington also sought his views.

In the early 1920s the Methodist Church saw the African American membership as separate from the white congregation. The Southern Church Commissions were supportive of African Americans leaving the Methodist Church and becoming a part of the African Methodist Episcopal Church, the Colored Methodist Episcopal Church, and the African Methodist Episcopal Church Zion. The Northern Church Commissioners supported an independent church for African Americans only. The Northern Churches already had in place separate African American churches, schools, and annual conferences. The Methodist Church decided to support the northern structure of the African American congregation. The groups were segregated and many considered the African American Methodist as a church within a church. In 1920 Jones became the first elected African American bishop of the Central Jurisdiction which served African Americans. The bishops were to have full membership in the church's Council of Bishops. Jones became one of fourteen African American bishops covering an immense geographical area, including Liberia, West Africa. He fully understood the magnitude of these elections and was quoted in *Black People in the Methodist Church* as saying, "We of the Central Jurisdiction of the Methodist Church have an advantage for the promotion of interracial Christian brotherhood which is not held by any other religious group of people." African American bishops had a key role in the development and growth of Methodist African American communities. Rather than separate, Jones saw the role of the African American bishop as supporting the working together of the races in the Methodist Church.

Jones's commitment to community was reflected in a speech he made at Tuskegee Institute on May 29, 1913 entitled "A Few Remarks on Making a Life." In his speech he told the graduates: "prove to the world what you are by what you can do—that you let your achievements point to your diploma." Jones was the president of the Board of Trustees for Wiley University, Samuel Houston College, New Orleans University, and Haven Institute and Conservatory of Music; he was the chairman and board member of Flint-Goodbridge Hospital and Training School and a trustee of Gammon Theological Seminary and Bennett College; he was the president of the Colored YMCA in New Orleans and vice president of the International YMCA. He was the president of Gulfside Association; the president of the Travelers' Protective Association; the first vice president of the National Negro Press Association; and chairman of the Executive Committee of the National Negro Business League. Because of his distinguished service, Howard University in Washington, D.C. conferred upon him the honorary LL.D. in 1911.

Jones continued to travel and give sermons and speeches well into his eighties. He died May 18, 1960 and was buried in the Gulfside Assembly in Waveland, Mississippi.

REFERENCES

Books

McClain, William. *Black People in the Methodist Church. Whither Thou Goest?* Cambridge, Mass.: Schenkman Publishing Co., 1984.

Nelson, Alice Dunbar. "A Few Remarks on Making a Life." *Masterpiece of Negro Eloquence* New York: Bookery Publishing Co., 1914.

Nichols, J. L., and William H. Crogman. *Progress of a Race*. Naperville Ill.: J.J. Nichols & Co., 1925.

Yenser, Thomas. *Who's Who in Colored America.* Brooklyn: Thomas Yenser Publisher, 1940.

Online

Historic Register—Louisiana Conference—United Methodist Church. http://www.iscuo.org/no_mtzion.htm (Accessed 19 January 2006).

Washington, Booker T. The Booker T. Washington Papers. Vol. 10. 129-30. June 1909. University of Illinois Press. http://www.historycooperative.org/btw/Vol.10/html/129.html (Accessed 19 January 2006).

Lean'tin L. Bracks

Tom Joyner
c. 1949–

Radio host

Tom Joyner has used his talents and opportunities to redefine the role of radio host beyond the traditional perception of disc jockey (DJ) throughout his media career. Joyner expanded his influence to the national level, used his media platform to inform as well as entertain his audiences, supported a variety of causes related

Tom Joyner

Chronology

1949?	Born in Tuskegee, Alabama
1970	Graduates from Tuskegee University
1970	Begins radio career in Montgomery, Alabama
1983	Settles in Dallas, Texas after several radio jobs in other states
1985	Works two daily radio jobs by flying between Dallas and Chicago
1994	Begins nationally syndicated Tom Joyner Morning Show (TJMS)
1996	Establishes Tom Joyner Foundation
1998	Becomes first African American in Radio Hall of Fame
2000	Marries fitness expert Donna Richardson
2002	Receives major support for foundation from corporate America
2003	Gains ownership of TJMS through his company, REACH Media, Inc.
2004	Increases wealth when REACH Media is acquired by Radio One, Inc.

to the African American community and others, and generated financial support as well as publicity for historically black colleges and universities (HBCUs).

Tom Joyner was born in Tuskegee, Alabama around 1949. His father, Hercules L. Joyner, was a former Tuskegee Airman, a member of the first group of African American pilots during World War II, and his mother was a secretary for the military. One of two children, his only sibling is his brother, Albert Joyner.

Joyner attended nursery school through college in Tuskegee with Lionel Richie, who went on to fame and superstar status as a singer, songwriter, and musician. Joyner was also a singing member of the Commodores, the local band formed at Tuskegee Institute (now University) which included Richie and others. He left the group before they went on to fame with Motown Records in the 1970s and later said (in jest) that it was his greatest mistake in life.

Begins Radio Career

Joyner remained in Tuskegee through his college years and married his first wife, Dora. Two sons, Thomas and Oscar, were born in the course of their relationship. Joyner began his career by accident a few years earlier, when he was involved in a protest of the only radio station in town, which would not play records by black artists. When the station agreed to do so, he volunteered his services, even though he had no experience.

Joyner also worked as a student announcer, which helped with his college expenses, and kept a weekend job at the local station. After he graduated from Tuskegee in 1970 with a B.A. in sociology, his next position was as a radio newsman and disc jockey at WRMA-AM, an African American-owned station in Montgomery, Alabama. While working there, Joyner was first influenced to use media to positively impact the African American community, and he continued to do so as he developed his radio career.

Joyner left his home state to pursue additional opportunities as his career progressed, working at WLOK in Memphis, Tennessee; KWK in St. Louis, Missouri; and KDKA in the Dallas-Fort Worth, Texas area. By the early 1980s he had settled in Chicago, where he worked at several radio stations, including WJPC (owned by John H. Johnson, publisher of *Ebony* magazine), WVON, WBMX, and WGCI. In 1983 Joyner was hired to do the morning program at KDKA in Dallas, and his show became the second most popular radio broadcast in the area.

In 1985 Joyner found himself renegotiating his contract with KDKA when he was approached by one of his former employers, WGCI in Chicago, about doing an afternoon radio program. After researching travel arrangements and weather patterns, he took the unprecedented step of signing contracts with both stations. While neither knew about Joyner's decision to do both jobs at first, he convinced executives at KDKA and WGCI and his family that the unique arrangement would work.

From 1985 to 1993 Joyner hosted the morning show in Dallas, flew to Chicago, did the afternoon show there, and returned to Dallas by late evening. His exploits drew national attention, and within three years, both shows became first in their markets and time slots (program schedules). As a result of his on-air and in-air schedule totaling ten shows and eight thousand miles each week, Joyner became known as the "Fly Jock" and literally one of the hardest working men in the media and entertainment industry.

The stamina demonstrated by Joyner in handling the stress and fatigue involved in maintaining his two-city commute was attributed to his easygoing personality, as well as good general health, consultations with doctors, and wise time management, which included rest and relaxation. He made it clear to observers that his work of talking and playing records was not stressful, as compared to other occupations.

Joyner's personality was also considered his greatest asset in terms of the success of his radio programs, presented in the urban contemporary music format, which featured recordings by African American singers, groups, and bands in a variety of musical styles. He was also gifted with the ability to relate to all types of people from all walks of life and used his broadcasts to inform as well as entertain the audience.

In the late 1980s Joyner explored radio syndication for the first time, with a weekly show called "On the Move," highlighting the most popular current recordings in a countdown format. This show reinforced his reputation of travel and awareness of the latest issues and trends in African American communities and prepared him for the next major phase of his media career.

In 1993, ABC Radio Networks approached Joyner with an opportunity to do a syndicated morning show, which would allow his program to be carried by a number of radio stations throughout the nation from a single base of operations. Joyner accepted and made history by becoming the first African American to host a nationally syndicated radio program. When he ended his airline commute, he had accumulated over seven million frequent-flyer miles with American Airlines, paying a $30,000 annual fee. The airline also retired two seats in his honor, in appreciation for the favorable publicity received from the "Fly Jock" arrangement, to be used in his radio studio.

The first broadcast of "The Tom Joyner Morning Show" (TJMS) took place in January 1994, and was heard in nearly thirty radio markets from north to south and coast to coast, including Chicago, Miami, Los Angeles, and Washington, D.C. While the music focus remained on the urban contemporary format, Joyner's new show incorporated some different elements, including a live band in a Chicago radio studio, Joyner and his crew of announcers in Dallas, comedy segments, and a variety of celebrity guests.

Key members of Joyner's on-air team were comedians J. Anthony Brown, Myra J., Ms. Dupree, and news anchor Sybil Wilkes. The show's daily format included news, commentary on current events, politics, guest interviews,

sports, and comedy, as well as music. Previously taped introductions by Joyner led to traffic and weather segments by local announcers, which provided useful information to listeners regardless of their location.

The show was an immediate success, and in its first two years of syndication grew to include over sixty radio stations. From a marketing standpoint, Joyner's program usually drew its highest ratings and response from black-oriented radio stations, whose local ratings also were helped as they added TJMS to their programming. The successful track record of the program interested additional station owners and executives, and by the late 1990s TJMS had expanded to outlets in nearly 100 radio markets, with an audience of eight million listeners. The TJMS theme, "Oh, Oh, Oh, It's the Tom Joyner Morning Show", became a catchphrase in the African American community and further evidence of the show's appeal.

Expands Influence with Advocacy and Philanthropy

Joyner's profile and influence grew to new levels after the president of the United States, Bill Clinton, appeared on his program. Joyner was also introduced to Tavis Smiley by Clinton during a White House conference in 1996. Smiley had also worked in radio, prior to landing a position as a talk show host with Black Entertainment Television (BET) during the same year. Shortly afterwards, Joyner began featuring Smiley's commentaries twice weekly on TJMS broadcasts, bringing yet another dimension to his radio program.

The Tom Joyner Foundation, established in 1996, became widely known for its efforts to assist historically black colleges and universities (HBCUs) and African American students attending these institutions. Joyner was sensitive to these concerns as a graduate of Tuskegee, one of the flagship HBCUs, and used a number of creative approaches to bring attention to the schools and raise much-needed funds for them. He stated at the time that assisting HBCUs was the primary and only purpose of the foundation.

Joyner partnered with the United Negro College Fund (UNCF), an organization founded by Frederick Patterson, a former Tuskegee president, and eventually established relationships with a number of corporations to support his efforts, along with his use of TJMS to encourage direct giving to the foundation from his listening audience. His oldest son, Thomas Joyner Jr., a graduate of Howard University, another HBCU, was installed as chief executive officer (CEO) of the foundation. Oscar Joyner, his younger son, earned an M.B.A. from Florida A&M University, and assisted his father with other aspects of his business enterprises.

Joyner and Smiley used the national platform of TJMS on numerous occasions to address political and social concerns facing the African American community, including campaigns with the NAACP to encourage and increase voter registration and participation in the political process. They decided to literally take TJMS on the road, using the theme, "Party with a Purpose," broadcasting the show live and free of charge from selected cities, requiring the audience to provide proof of voter registration or register on-site for admission.

In recognition of his many accomplishments, Joyner received numerous honors, including the Mickey Leland Humanitarian Award from the Congressional Black Caucus (CBC), the NAACP President's Award, Best Urban Contemporary Air Personality from Billboard magazine (four times), the 100 Black Men Man of the Year award, and the Harold Washington Award, named for the first African American mayor of Chicago.

Joyner won the Best DJ of the Year Award from *Impact* magazine so many times that it was renamed the Tom Joyner Award, in addition to the publication's Joe Loris Award for Excellence in Broadcasting. He made history again in 1998, when he became the first African American ever inducted into the Radio Hall of Fame in Chicago.

The response from fans of TJMS led Joyner to expand the concept to an ongoing series of thirty shows each year. Southwest Airlines signed on as a corporate sponsor in 1999, and he became the "Fly Jock" again with the "Tom Joyner Southwest Airlines Sky Shows." He also continued to stress voter registration, featured African American musical artists in live performances, and tied the Sky Shows in with the work of his foundation by using HBCU campus venues in areas where they were located, and establishing the "HBCU of the Month," where different schools would receive funds generated from contributions during the time period.

TJMS continued to balance fun and entertainment with serious concerns, such as support and criticism of African American celebrities and leaders during times of controversy and protests of corporate policies and activities that were insensitive to African Americans and other ethnic groups. Among the companies singled out were Christie's International Auction House for plans to sell items related to slavery, Katz Media for refusing to buy advertising time on black radio stations, and CompUSA, the computer and technology retail company, for insensitivity to African American consumers of its products.

Joyner's involvement in certain activities caused a good deal of criticism and controversy of him as well, especially when all the facts about a situation were not known before taking action. This was the case with CompUSA in 1999, where negative information about African Americans attributed to the company turned out to be false, and Joyner came under pressure from the company's lawyers and his own employer, ABC Radio Networks, for rushing to judgment and launching a protest. At one point the network threatened to take TJMS off the air, but Joyner still held firm, with the support of Smiley and his audience. As a result, the company did make changes in its marketing to African Americans and advertising in black-owned media.

The year 2000 brought major life changes for Joyner, even as he continued his many ongoing commitments with TJMS, the Tom Joyner Foundation, and other business and professional obligations. He launched another new venture, the Tom Joyner Fantastic Voyage cruise, another "party with a purpose" where fun and entertainment were mixed with serious information, while a portion of the proceeds were given to the foundation to benefit HBCUs.

Divorced from his first wife some years earlier, he married fitness expert Donna Richardson after a three-year courtship. They met when she was a guest on TJMS in 1997 and was very outspoken to Joyner about his personal health and physical fitness. Despite the initial friction, he was intrigued and asked her to develop a diet and exercise program suitable for his lifestyle.

The relationship was all business, until they spent time together in Italy and Tahiti and discovered their mutual interests. Donna Richardson Joyner continued her career as a health/fitness expert, appearing on cable sports channel ESPN, NBC's *Later Today* and *Weekend Today* shows, and also served on the board of directors for the Tom Joyner Foundation.

Joyner returned to work and teamed with Smiley for "Black Agenda 2000," a special radio broadcast to encourage voter registration, education, and participation in the November 2000 elections. The town hall format included participants such as Kweisi Mfume, executive director of the NAACP; Maynard Jackson, the first African American mayor of Atlanta, Georgia; famed attorney Johnnie L. Cochran Jr.; Randall Robinson, founder of the TransAfrica Forum; Rev. Al Sharpton of the National Action Network; and Iyanla Vanzant, author and inspirational speaker.

Takes Activities to New Levels

Not all of Joyner's relationships with corporate America were confrontational, as his national influence translated into advertising revenue and sponsorships for TJMS, contributions to the Tom Joyner Foundation, and financial support for new undertakings. These activities included the BlackAmericaWeb.com Internet site he launched in June 2001, with links to web sites for TJMS and the foundation, along with a variety of health, educational, financial, inspirational, and cultural information. Joyner also continued his annual Tom Joyner Fantastic Voyage cruise in partnership with Walt Disney World Resort in Orlando, Florida and numerous other corporate sponsors. In 2002 General Mills Inc. presented a $600,000 donation to the Tom Joyner Foundation, the largest single gift in the history of the organization to that point, and Kellogg supported fund-raising galas for HBCUs featuring Joyner with a $110,000 contribution.

In January 2003 Joyner founded his own multimedia company, REACH Media, Inc., and made more history when he purchased TJMS from ABC Radio Networks. In February of the same year, Joyner celebrated Black History Month by promoting his new book, *Interactive Guide to Historically Black Universities*, which was developed in partnership with the William J. Clinton Foundation and included an accompanying compact disk (CD) with detailed information on 104 HBCUs.

To publicize the book and CD, Joyner and former president Clinton appeared on CNN as guests on *Larry King Live* and used the occasion to emphasize the continuing importance of HBCUs. Joyner indicated that the CD was being sent to every public high school in New York, Los Angeles, and Washington, D.C., and to every public school with more than fifty black students in the rest of the country. *Black Enterprise, Essence*, and *Vibe* magazines also distributed the CD to their subscribers.

Despite his many involvements, Joyner managed to balance his career and his marriage, as more opportunities continued to come in his direction. McDonald's, the world's largest fast food company, featured Joyner in commercials promoting his "365 Black" concept celebrating African American history throughout the year. Proctor and Gamble also entered into major advertising and sponsorship agreements with Joyner, which were incorporated into TJMS, BlackAmericaWeb.com, and other enterprises under the REACH Media umbrella. The company successfully launched the first annual Tom Joyner Family Reunion during the 2003 Labor Day weekend, again partnering with Walt Disney World and attracting more than 7,000 people to Orlando for the event.

In 2004 Joyner continued to use his celebrity and success to positively impact and influence individuals, HBCUs, and the larger community. The foundation established a $700,000 challenge to raise funds for student scholarships at HBCUs, and later in the year offered $500,000 to help Barber-Scotia College, one of the smaller HBCUs with serious financial problems. In 2005, the foundation made available scholarships of $1,000 each to students from Xavier, Dillard, and Southern University in New Orleans who were forced to leave their schools during the tragic consequence of Hurricane Katrina in 2005 and who, the interim, transferred to other colleges. Other activities included "Take a Loved One to the Doctor Day," with cooperation from the U.S. Department of Health and Human Services and the March to Vote rally in Miami, Florida prior to the November elections. Joyner continued to receive honors, as the National Association of Broadcasting presented him with the 2004 Marconi Radio Award as the nation's top syndicated radio personality. He was also inducted into the Texas

Radio Hall of Fame, as he had made Dallas his home and base of operations some years earlier.

Joyner signed a contract with TV One during the same year, a new cable network targeting African American viewing audiences. As a result, the TJMS Sky Shows would broadcast live on both radio and television. In November 2004 REACH Media, Inc. was acquired by Radio One, Inc., for $56 million in cash and stock, making Joyner a very wealthy man. Radio One was also black-owned, founded by Cathy L. Hughes in 1980, and had become the seventh largest radio broadcasting company in the nation.

Joyner's personal financial resources became such that when he offered to buy Morris Brown College, an HBCU in Atlanta that had been closed due to financial and accreditation problems, it was not assumed that he was being humorous. While he no longer needed to work, Joyner remained committed to his extensive broadcasting schedule out of love for his audiences and the sheer fun of doing his programs.

The Tom Joyner Foundation continued its valuable work, partnering with the National Education Association in 2005 to increase the number of minority teachers in urban and rural public school systems. Joyner remained the man in the forefront as well as behind the scenes, "partying with a purpose," making invaluable contributions through his entrepreneurship and philanthropy because of his passion for life and people, particularly those in the African American community.

REFERENCES

Books

Eggert, Mike. "Tom Joyner." *Contemporary Black Biography*, Vol. 19. Ed. Shirelle Phelps. Farmington Hills, Mich.: Gale Group, 1999.

Lehman, Jeffrey, ed. *African American Almanac*. 9th ed. Farmington Hills, Mich.: Thomson Gale, 2003.

York, Jennifer M., ed. *Who's Who Among African Americans*. 17th ed. Farmington Hills, Mich.: Thomson Gale, 2004.

Periodicals

Bachman, Katy. "When Tom Joyner Speaks, People Listen." *MEDIAWEEK* 12 (1 July 2002): 19-22.

Larson, Megan. "TV One Taps Tom Joyner: New Black Network Launches Today with Run of Radio Show." *MEDIAWEEK* 14 (19 January 2004): 8.

Malveaux, Julianne. "Finding the Key to Make a Difference." *Black Issues in Higher Education* 20 (3 July 2003): 82.

Norment, Lynn. "Tom and Donna: The Wildest, Wettest Wedding Ever." *Ebony* 55 (October 2000): 82-93.

Sims, Muriel L. "The Fly Jock: Tom Joyner, a Radio First." *Black Collegian* 29 (February 1999): 36-41.

White, Jack E. "Racism in Advertising? Two Radio Stars Score a Victory for Black-Run Media." *Time* 154 (1 November 1999): 90.

Online

BlackAmericaWeb.com. "About the TJMS Sky Shows." http://www.blackamericaweb.com/site.aspx/tjms/skyshowch/about (Accessed 2 March 2005).

——. "About Us." http://www.blackamericaweb.com/site.aspx/misc/aboutus (Accessed 2 March 2005).

North Carolina Central University. "Legacy Gala: Tom Joyner Biography." http://www.nccu.edu/legacygala/joyner.htm (Accessed 1 March 2005).

Texas Radio Hall of Fame. "2004 Inductee: Tom Joyner." http://www.texasradiohalloffame.com/tomjoyner.html (Accessed 1 March 2005).

Tuskegee University. "Tom Joyner." http://www.tuskegee.edu/Global/story.asp?S=1147444&nav=CcWzEUvo (Accessed 7 March 2005).

Fletcher F. Moon

Hubert Julian

Hubert Julian
1897–1983

Pilot, parachutist

Hubert Fauntleroy Julian was one of the first blacks in aviation. He was the first black parachutist and the first black to fly across the United States. Some called Julian a showman, a fraud, full of big talk. To others, Julian was a hero who did much to advance black aviation. Some labeled Julian a gun runner who dealt with less than scrupulous characters if the price was right. Other people knew him as a man who would fly to rescue people in need all over the world. Julian is also warmly remembered by the people of the West Indies, where he was born, and to whom Julian donated a medical van, hospital equipment, food, and clothing. Julian was tall, handsome, and elegantly dressed, reported to be a ladies man but also a man who deeply loved his wife of forty-eight years.

Hubert Fauntleroy Julian was born January 5, 1897 in Port of Spain, Trinidad. Julian was the only child of middle-class parents Henry and Silvira Julian. Julian's father managed a cocoa plantation, which gave Julian many opportunities that less fortunate children did not have. Julian attended the exclusive Eastern Boys' School in Trinidad. He was scheduled to go to England to finish school when World War I broke out. Instead Julian was sent to Canada to high school. Julian decided at age four-teen to become a pilot. Much of Julian's spare time was spent at Montreal's St. Hubert Airfield. Julian earned a Canadian pilot's license at age nineteen. He moved to New York in 1921 and married Essie Gittens in 1927. They had one child.

In New York Julian sought a patent for an airplane safety device he had invented called a "parachutta-gravepreresistra." The device was activated by the pilot if the plane developed trouble. A horizontal blade would be activated, which would blow open a huge umbrella to slow the plane's descent to twenty feet per second. Julian was able to obtain a U.S. patent, but later sold the device to a Canadian aircraft corporation.

The Aviator

Aviation was a field mostly closed to blacks. Those who wanted to learn to fly faced many barriers, including segregation and racial discrimination. The U.S. military and most private aviation schools would not teach blacks to fly. Many airports also refused to let black pilots land their planes. Thus black aviators in the 1920s and 1930s started their own flight schools or went to Europe to learn to fly. Julian defied the odds to become famous in American black aviation circles and around the world. Many of Julian's flights within the United States were made prior to his acquisition of a U.S. private pilot's license.

Chronology

1897	Born in Port of Spain, Trinidad on January 5
1919	Becomes first black aviator
1922	Becomes first black parachutist
1927	Marries Essie Gittens
1929	First black to fly transatlantic solo
1930	Awarded the rank of colonel in the Ethiopian Air Force
1931	First black to fly coast to coast in the United States
1931	Sets record for longest flight without refueling
1934	First black to land on French soil; becomes first black man to obtain a pilot's license in England
1935	Flies to Ethiopia and is hired by Emperor Haille Selassie to head his airforce
1939	Produces film *Lying Lips*
1940	Fights in Finland's Winter War with the Finnish Air Force Regiment 2
1949	Founds Black Eagle Enterprises, Ltd.; becomes munitions dealer
1974	Attempts to secure freedom of Ethiopian emperor Haile Selassie
1983	Dies in the Bronx, New York on February 19

In 1924 Julian proposed to make the first solo flight to Africa in a hydroplane. All previous attempts at international flight had been conducted by pairs of pilots. Julian stated he would fly down the East Coast of Florida then across the Caribbean to Brazil. The next leg of the journey would be to Monrovia, Liberia, up Africa's Gold Coast and finally down the Nile to Ethiopia. Julian raised funds in a variety of ways, including selling shares in the plane. He eventually acquired a plane, which Julian named Ethiopia I. Julian took off from New York; unfortunately, about five minutes into the trip, the right pontoon fell off, and the plane crashed into Flushing Bay.

Despite the fierce opposition faced by black aviators, some people supported black aviation. One such person was Giuseppe M. Bellanca, a leading airplane designer, who pledged $3,000 to the Julian Fund, for construction of a plane which Julian proposed to fly to Paris.

In 1929 Julian became the first black to make a transatlantic flight. Julian was immortalized by Calypso singer Sam Manning in a song entitled "Lieutenant Julian" (1947).

The Parachutist

Julian became the first black parachutist in 1922 when he performed at the Long Island Air Show. Called the Ace of Spades, Julian performed parachute stunts to supplement his income.

Julian also invented a motorized parachute, which allowed him to play the saxophone as he floated through the sky. Julian called the device the "Saxophoneparachuttapreresistationist." During one performance, Julian blew

off course and landed on the roof of a New York police station. It was at this point that the *New York Telegram* bestowed the name Black Eagle of Harlem on him.

On another occasion Julian was scheduled to parachute into Atlantic City. At the last minute the wind blew Julian over the Atlantic Ocean. Not wanting to ruin his clothing, Julian calmly held the parachute with his teeth. Julian removed all his clothing except his undershorts. Another strong blast of wind blew Julian's undershorts off, thus making Julian the first nude parachutist.

Despite some mishaps, Julian was in fact a skilled parachutist. His prowess with a parachute brought him to the attention of Ethiopian emperor Haille Selassie, for whom he performed. This jump was the beginning of a new chapter in Julian's life.

Joins Ethiopian Air Force

In 1930 Julian went to Ethiopia at the invitation of emperor elect Haile Selassie to perform a parachute exhibition. Emperor-elect Selassie was so impressed with Julian's parachuting skills that he bestowed the rank of colonel on Julian and gave him Ethiopian citizenship. Julian became the emperor-elect's confidant and advisor. It was Julian's idea to start an Ethiopian shipping line and commercial airline. In July 1930, Julian returned to the United States to recruit black pilots and technicians for the Ethiopian air force. Unfortunately few people took Julian seriously and he was unable to recruit any pilots. He returned to Ethiopia only to crash the emperor-elect's prized de Havilland Gypsy Moth airplane the day before Selassie's coronation. Julian reduced the Ethiopian air force by one fourth and was expelled from Ethiopia.

Despite the circumstances under which Julian left Ethiopia, he rushed to their aid when the Italians invaded Ethiopia in 1935. Julian so impressed Selassie that in August 1935, Julian was reinstated as the commander of the Royal Ethiopian Air Force. This trip to Ethiopia ended badly, though. Amid rumors that Julian had tried to embezzle funds from the Ethiopian army, he was asked to leave the country after fighting with another black aviator.

In 1931 Julian began flying bootlegged whiskey from Canada to the East Coast. However, Julian discovered that the Mafia was adding drugs to the whiskey shipments.

By July 1931 Julian had passed the Board of Aeronautics pilot's test. Julian's next step was to organize the all black flying circus called *The Five Blackbirds*. Their debut in Los Angeles on December 16, 1931 marked the first time so many black pilots were in the air together.

In 1939 Julian became an official correspondent for the *New York Amsterdam News*, reporting on the deteriorating situation in Europe. Julian returned to the United States when France declared war on Germany.

Julian decided to take a break from aviation and parachuting to become a movie producer. His first picture was *The Notorious Elinor Lee*, which premiered in 1940. It told the story of a woman falsely accused of murdering her aunt.

In 1940 as war continued to rage in Europe, Julian volunteered to help Finland resist invasion by the Russians in what was called the "Winter War." Julian was made a captain in the Finnish Air Force Regiment 2. Upon returning to the United States, Julian promptly challenged Nazi Air Marshall Hermann Goring to an aerial duel over the English Channel. Julian's purpose was to avenge and lay to rest Goring's insults to the black people. The challenge was never accepted.

After the United States entered World War II, Julian volunteered to train for combat with the 789th Tuskegee Airmen. He wore a non-regulation colonel's uniform, despite not holding that rank in the United States Armed Forces. He was discharged before graduation then he turned to the United States Army. Julian served the remainder of the war as an infantryman and was honorably discharged in May 1945.

Julian was able to put his aircraft expertise to use, serving out the remainder of the war as an administrator in Detroit at Ford's Willow Run Aircraft Plant. Once the war ended Julian founded Black Eagle Airlines, Ltd. The company chartered international freight flights and owned several aircraft plants in Europe.

Becomes Munitions Dealer

In 1949, Julian founded Black Eagle Enterprises, Ltd. and registered with the U.S. State Department as a munitions dealer. He became involved in the arms business in 1950. Julian eventually became a purchasing agent for the Guatemalan government. Unfortunately for Julian, the Guatemalan government was Communist and was in the midst of a civil war. When Julian returned from a trip to Europe in 1954, the United States government seized Julian's passport and accused him of selling arms to communists. Julian maintained the whole thing was a big mistake threatening to renounce his U.S. citizenship. One month later Julian was cleared of the charges, and his U.S. passport was returned.

Julian became involved in the Congolese War in 1960. He was arrested in the Congo, labeled a mercenary, and expelled by the United Nations for smuggling arms to Moise Tshombe, who declared the Katanga region of the Congo an independent state. Julian was held in the Congo for approximately four months. Essie Julian appealed to President Kennedy, the United Nations, and

U.S. attorney general Robert Kennedy. He was finally released in June 1960.

Julian remained connected to Ethiopia and its emperor Haile Selassie. In 1974, Julian, who had settled into the tame existence of running a sugar brokerage firm in New York, learned of Selassie's imprisonment during the Dergue Coup by the Ethiopian military. Julian offered $1.45 million cash to the Ethiopian government. Julian felt he was honor bound to try to free Selassie as, according to *Distinguished African Americans in Aviation and Space Science*, Julian "owed his prominence and stature to the benevolence of His Imperial Majesty."

Julian lived in the Bronx for the remainder of his life. Essie Julian died in 1975. Julian later married Doreen Thompson. He and his second wife had one son. Julian died quietly at the Veterans' Hospital in the Bronx, New York, on February 19, 1983. He was survived by his second wife, the son from his second marriage, a daughter from his first marriage, and two grandsons.

Despite Julian's failures, there is no doubt that he achieved many firsts in aviation and as a parachutist. He used publicity and self-promotion to further his career and advance the field of aviation.

REFERENCES

Books

Gupert, Betty Kaplan. "Hubert F. Julian." In *Invisible Wings: An Annotated Bibliography on Blacks in Aviation, 1916-1993*. Westport, Conn.: Greenwood Press, 1994.

——, Miriam Sawyer, and Caroline M. Fannin. "Hubert F. Julian." In *Distinguished African Americans in Aviation and Space Science*. Westport, Conn.: Oryx Press, 2002.

Hall, Herman. "Hubert Julian: The Black Eagle of Harlem." In *200 Years of West Indian Contributions*. Brooklyn, N.Y.: Herman Hall Associates, 1976.

Nugent, John Peer. *The Black Eagle*. New York: Stein & Day, 1971.

Scott, Lawrence P., and William M. Womack. *Double V: The Civil Rights Struggle of the Tuskegee Airmen*. East Lansing, Mich.: Michigan State University Press, 1998.

Scott, William R. "The Eagle and The Lion." In *The Sons of Sheba's Race: African Americans and the Italo-Ethiopian War, 1935-1941*. Bloomington, Ind.: Indiana University Press, 1993.

Anne K. Driscoll

Preston King
1936–

Educator, writer

In 1956, the U.S. military draft required all males at the age of eighteen to register to be drafted in the event of war. At this time, Preston King was a student at Fisk University in Tennessee. King received a deferment because of his student status. He completed his studies at Fisk with high honors, and he was given a scholarship to the London School of Economics, England to pursue graduate studies. The draft board at Tennessee had requested that he make his request to his hometown board in Albany, Georgia. His draft deferment application was accepted in Georgia, and he was given two years deferment to pursue his studies in London, England.

When he returned from London, he visited his family in Albany, Georgia, and before returning to London to complete his studies, he visited the draft board in his hometown. When he went to express his gratitude to the staff in the office and check his paperwork for correctness, the people of the draft board realized that he was black. King continued his studies in London, but the respectful addresses in his early correspondences from the draft board were absent in his later correspondences. After two years of graduate studies in London, King was awarded yet another scholarship to pursue doctoral studies. King had to ask for another extended deferment of his draft. He was eligible for the extended deferment, but his request was refused in a very insulting manner. He received a letter commanding him to report for a physical examination before his induction. King was not anti-war, but he was insulted by the tone of the letter that threatened him. King addressed the order by commanding the same respect that was given to his white counterparts when they were invited to report to duty. This led to his prosecution on four counts of draft evasion as was expressed in a letter from the draft board.

King had addressed the racism that was practiced by the draft board. He also stated that he would not submit to the injustice that was being meted out to him, and that he would prefer to be jailed than to submit to the degra-

Preston King

dation because of his race. In 1961, when King visited his family, federal marshals arrested him. When the trial commenced in the spring of 1962, his brother, C. B. King, a civil rights attorney, defended him. His main defense was that refusing an African American student deferment to study when he was fully eligible and changing the salutation in correspondences to King constituted racism and inequality. In the Jim Crow South, a jury of all white males gave a guilty verdict, and King was sentenced to eighteen months in prison. King's appeal was made and his bail bond was set at an enormous figure. However, the King family and many members of the Albany community pooled the money, so King was not detained in jail. On his father's advice, he fled to London to evade the jail sentence, and to continue his studies. King was fully aware that he could not re-enter the

United States without threat of imprisonment because he was now guilty of evading federal prosecution.

The Kings of Albany, Georgia

Preston King was born in Albany on March 3, 1936. His parents Clennon and Margaret King were well known in the society. King had five brothers—Allen, Clennon Jr, Chevene (C.B.), Slater and Paul—and one sister, Muriel. The King family was no stranger to racism as Clennon Jr. felt the brunt of racism when he was refused admission to graduate school at the University of Mississippi. His application actually led to his incarceration, when the state deemed him insane and forced him into the state asylum on the premise that any African American who tried to gain admission to such a prestigious white institution must be insane. After this saga, Clennon Jr. was accepted into another university where he gained his M.A. Clennon's case opened the eyes of all his siblings to the struggles that African Americans had to face in a society that decried their race.

The Kings were educated African Americans who were aware of their rights as U.S. citizens. Their parents instilled in them the idea that African Americans should use education to better themselves. The King boys were all college graduates who excelled in their respective fields. Mr. King was the first African American restaurateur in Georgia, and he was also the head of Albany's National Association for the Advancement of Colored People (NAACP). Mr. King was concerned with the civil liberties of his people, and he fought for these liberties, which might have attributed to the blatant discrimination his boys faced. King's mother was a teacher, and both of his parents attended Tuskegee Institute where they met. Clennon King worked as a coachman for Booker T. Washington when he attended Tuskegee Institute. He used his wages to supplement his fees for his tuition.

Life in Exile

By 1969, King had gained his doctoral degree in political science from the London School of Economics. Then he did post graduate work at the University of Vienna, University of Strasbourg, and University of Paris. He taught in many parts of the world, including Cameroon, New Zealand, and Uganda. He was a visiting lecturer to the London School of Economics, England; McGill University, Canada; and Bellagio, Italy. He was also the chair at the University of Lancaster in the Political and International Relations Center Department. In 1999, he was awarded an honorary Doctor of Humane Letters Degree from Fisk University.

In exile, King married a British citizen, Murriel Hazel Stern. His first child, his daughter, Oona was born in 1967. His second child, Slater, was born in 1968. His son was named after his brother who had been killed in a car accident, the year before King's son was born. King did not attend the funeral because he was unable to return to the States. King and Murriel divorced, but he maintained close ties with his children. After King moved to northeastern England in 1986, he married his second wife Raewyn Stone, and King's third child Akasi Peter was born. King's daughter Oona became a politician, and she was elected into the British Parliament and was a member of Parliament (MP) in the House of Commons. Oona was the second woman of African decent to be elected in the British Parliament. Her mixed race and her father's experiences helped her learn to deal with race relationships, and this special ability gave her the edge in her political life. She was elected to Parliament for a majority Muslim constituency.

Despite his achievements, King suffered emotionally during his exile. Several family members died, but he was unable to attend their funerals. First, his brother, Slater, then his father, followed by his mother and brothers, Allen and C. B. King became resolute, and he was determined to see his oldest brother, Clennon, Jr. when he heard that he was very sick. The United States was evolving into a less racially charged society, and King was willing to take a chance in returning.

King's love of family prompted him. In his absence, he did everything to maintain family ties with his relatives in Albany, Georgia, and all over the United States. They often met in family gatherings outside the United States. They enjoyed the tropical climates of the Caribbean and Africa, but King felt an emptiness as he wanted to do something great for his country and his race. He had to enter his country to make his contribution.

Bringing Him Home

In 1977, President Jimmy Carter pardoned the persons who evaded the draft when the Vietnam War was fought in 1960. However, King was not pardoned because he was also charged with avoiding federal prosecution. King's case was appealed regularly and was presented in vain to three presidents—Carter, Reagan, and Bush—requesting amnesty. Despite these failures, King's family remained vigilant in their campaign. His nephew, Clennon King, used his position as a journalist to air his uncle's story to gain support for his pardon. At about the same time, Oona was invited to Atlanta, Georgia, to participate in a documentary about the civil rights movement and she brought up her father's situation at a news conference. President Bill Clinton was drawn to King's story. Major television programs such as the *Today Show* and *60 Minutes* gave time to King's story as they interviewed Oona. Subsequently, she accompanied her father on a risky visit home when his oldest brother was dying. She believed that the federal government would find it difficult not to pardon her father because of widespread support for him in the United States.

On February 21, 2000, President Clinton announced that King was pardoned. King entered the United States after thirty-nine years in exile, now a free man. He remained concerned about social, economical, and political issues in the world, especially in Africa. He was also engaged in preparing his autobiography.

After being pardoned in 2000, he became scholar-in-residence at the Leadership Center at Morehouse College, and distinguished professor of political philosophy at Emory University. King was also the founding editor of *Critical Review of International Social and Political Philosophy* (CRISPP). He is a director of the Black Leadership and Ideologies in the South since the Civil War (BLIS).

King writes on various subjects, including politics, economics, and sociology. His first book *Fear of Power* was published in 1967, and his writings span four decades. Some of the most popular titles are *Federalism and Federation*, *Ideology of Order: A Comparative Analyses of Jean Bodin and Thomas Hobbes*, *Thinking Past a Problem: Essays on the History of Ideas*, and *Tolerations*. In 2004, King co-edited a volume titled *Black Leadership*. King's books educate Americans and expose injustices in parts of the African continent.

REFERENCES

Books

Henderson, Ashyia, ed. *Contemporary Black Biography.* Detroit: Gale Group, 2001.

Online

"Dr. Preston King's Desktop." http://www.prestonking.net/ (Accessed December 21, 2005).

Thornell, Richard Paul. "The Case and Pardon of Professor Preston King." *The New Crisis,* September/October 2000.http://www.findarticles.com/p/articles/mi_qa3812/is_200009/ai_n8927402(Accessed December 21, 2005).

Wilkerson, Isabel. "The Exile And His Daughter—Preston King, scholar, author, draft evader, 40 years in waiting for a pardon." *Essence,* February 2001.http://www.findarticles.com/p/articles/mi_m1264/is_10_31/ai_69795112(Accessed December 21, 2005).

Denise Jarrett

Simmie Knox
1935–

Painter

Simmie Knox became the first African American commissioned to paint the official portrait of a president of the United States. The oil on linen portrait was unveiled in the White House on June 18, 2004, and earned Knox a place in American history. Initially an abstract painter, he changed his subject matter early on, became a portrait painter, and for more than twenty-five years has painted likenesses of people of different races and various positions in life. He has concentrated successfully on capturing the real personality, lifestyle, likenesses, and experiences of his subjects.

Born in Aliceville, Alabama, on August 18, 1935, Simmie Knox is the son of Simmie Knox Sr., a carpenter and mechanic, and Amelia Knox. His parents divorced when Knox was three years old. While still a toddler, he moved to Leroy, Alabama—near Mobile—and lived on a farm of sharecroppers with his grandfather Ben, his paternal aunt Rebecca, and her eight children. The family worked on the farm from daybreak to sundown. School was not an option, only work on the farm. This arrangement was necessary because, until he was nine, his father lived and worked in another city. Then he moved to Mobile and lived with his father and his stepmother Lucille Knox.

Early on Knox demonstrated an interest in drawing. To entertain his family and friends, he drew funny renditions of Batman and Superman. Playing baseball was also one of the youngster's favorite pastimes; he played the game with friends, one of whom was Hank Aaron, a neighbor. When he was thirteen years old, an eye injury that resulted from being hit by a ball forced Knox to avoid the game for over a year. Concerned about his difficulty in focusing his eyes, a doctor recommended that Knox concentrate on drawing to retrain his eye muscles. The nuns at Heart of Mary School, which he attended in the community, provided drawing experiences for him. Among his early renditions were the Stations of the Cross, which impressed the nuns considerably. Knox became the one to provide art images whenever they were needed. No formal art instruction was available;

Simmie Knox

Chronology

1935	Born in Aliceville, Alabama on August 18
1956	Joins the U.S. Military service
1962	Enrolls in Delaware State College
1963	Transfers to University of Delaware
1970	Receives B.F.A. degree from Tyler School of Art, Temple University
1972	Receives M.F.A. degree from Tyler School of Art
1974	Directs Museum of Art, Washington, D.C.; paints portrait of Martin Luther King Jr.
1975	Paints portrait of Frederick Douglass
1981	Specializes in portraiture
1989	Paints portrait of Thurgood Marshall; later includes many others
2004	Unveils portraits in White House of Bill Clinton and Hillary Rodham Clinton
2005	Unveils portraits of John Hope and Aurelia E. Franklin

instead, the nuns arranged for impromptu drawing sessions with the postal carrier on Saturday mornings.

Knox graduated from Mobile's Central High School in 1956. Later, he volunteered for military service, where he remained for three years. In an interview with the author, Knox said that he "wanted to be eligible for the benefits that the military provided."

On leaving military service, Knox went to Milford, Delaware, where his parents had then lived. In 1962, he entered historically black Delaware State College in Dover and majored in biology. For his classes he drew anatomically correct figures and demonstrated an interest in floral watercolors. His images depicted such skill that he changed his major to art education; however, Delaware State could not meet his needs.

In 1961 at twenty-six years of age, Knox attended university in the morning, and in the afternoons he worked in a textile factory in Milford. He persuaded a friend to sit for him in his dormitory at night so Knox could practice sketching. He also sat before a mirror and painted his first self-portrait, a pastel. He concluded that he wanted to become an artist.

Referring to racial segregation, he told Jose Antonio Vargas for the *Washington Post* that he was "suffering for silly reasons." He began to question who he was and what he wanted to be. "Once in your life...you'll sit

and...really look at yourself, and ask: Who am I? What am I? What kind of person do I want to be? I knew, deep within me, that I wanted to be an artist." The piece helped to secure a place for him in Tyler School of Art later on.

In 1963 Knox transferred to the University of Delaware in Newark and majored in art education, but later he changed his major to fine arts. While at the university he taught at local high schools for a while. On recommendation from a faculty member at the University of Delaware, Knox continued his studies at Temple University's Tyler School of Art in Philadelphia, where in 1970 he earned the B.F.A. degree magna cum laude. He enrolled in the graduate program at Tyler and taught part-time at historically black Lincoln University in Lincoln University, Pennsylvania. Knox completed graduate work in 1972 and was awarded the M.F.A. degree. When he left Tyler, Knox, like many other artists of that period, was an abstract painter. Although he had been taught the elements of design and the principles of composition, he had no formal training in figure painting. In truth, he had originally wanted to become a portrait painter; but his professors at Tyler had encouraged him to work in an abstract style. His interest in portrait painting never ended, though; now he saw it as a new challenge in art, and he wanted to develop his talent in that area. He read widely and applied what he had learned to his native talent, thus evolving his art of self-portraiture. Because he honed his skill on his own, sometimes he refers to himself as a self-taught portrait painter.

Knox had a continuing desire to teach art in public schools and did so for eighteen years. After graduating from Tyler, he taught at historically black Bowie State College in Bowie, Maryland. For one year (1974) he was director of the Museum of African Art in downtown Washington. He left for the Duke Ellington School of the

Arts in Washington, where he taught for five years, until 1980, when the Ellington school eliminated the art department.

Whenever Knox participated in art shows, he did so as an abstract artist. In 1971 Knox participated in the Thirty-Second Biennial of Contemporary American Painting at the Corcoran Gallery in Washington, D.C., in which his abstract art was exhibited. During this time he painted incessantly, producing still lifes such as pots with cherries, strawberries, and pears. For several years he did large-scale abstracts and exhibited his work at the Corcoran and the Kreeger Museum, also in Washington. In 1972, he moved to the Washington area, and beginning in 1981 he specialized in oil portraiture full time. Although he found portrait painting complicated, he found no other form of painting more challenging and interesting than creating a likeness of the human face.

Knox and his family lived in cramped quarters in the Adams Morgan section of the city. Their two-bedroom apartment provided one bedroom for the family and another for Knox's studio. His wife, Roberta Knox, and their children took his paintings to Eastern Market on the weekends, leased a small space (five by seven feet) and displayed his still lifes for sale. Though his works sold in this humble fashion, one of them, a portrait of Frederick Douglass, has been in the Smithsonian Institution since 1975.

Knox credits comedian Bill Cosby for jump-starting his career. For twenty years Cosby saw that Knox received commissions to paint family and friends. Knox painted Cosby's son Ennis, who was murdered in January 1997. The portrait, a gift from Knox, hangs over the fireplace in Bill and Camille Cosby's Manhattan home. "It is a portrait that projects every inch and every centimeter of our son," Cosby told Jose Antonio Vargas for the *Washington Post*.

Paints President's Portrait

Although Knox had painted portraits of a number of celebrities and famous officials, he earned a highly visible place in history on June 18, 2004, when his oil portrait of President Bill Clinton was unveiled during a White House ceremony in the East Wing. He had become the first black artist to paint an official portrait of a U.S. president. He also painted the portrait of former first lady and later senator Hillary Rodham Clinton. The portraits are oil on linen and took two years to complete. Although official portraits of U.S. presidents and first ladies have been unveiled at the same time, rarely has the same artist created both. When Clinton sought a portrait painter for the work, he was referred to Knox and visited his office. U.S. Supreme Court Justice Ruth Bader Ginsburg, whose portrait Knox had done early on, told the Clintons that she liked Knox's portrait of her. Ginsburg had seen Knox's portrait of Spottswood Robinson, who once served as chief judge with the U.S. Court of Appeals for

the District of Columbia Circuit. The fact that he had painted many of Clinton's friends helped to spur the president's interest in Knox.

Shortly before Christmas of 1992, Knox was invited to the White House. He took his portfolio with him but had misgivings about his being selected. The president inspected Knox's portfolio and asked Knox to do a study of him; later he did the final portrait. During the visit Knox snapped photos of Clinton, as Clinton described what the portrait should include. He wanted specific props, such as an American flag and several military medallions. Knox worked through the Christmas holidays and returned with a still-wet study in oil showing Clinton in five different poses. Clinton selected a three-quarter-length standing image. Clinton especially liked the way Knox captured his hands, showing a confident and pleasant look.

Paints Other Famous Subjects

In addition to his first two figure paintings—Martin Luther King Jr. in 1974 and Frederick Douglass in 1975—the long list of portraits that Knox has painted includes educator Mary McLeod Bethune, writer Alex Haley, comedian Bill Cosby and family (twelve portraits between 1983 and 1991), boxer Muhammad Ali, early black U.S. senator Blanche Kelso Bruce, singer Paul Robeson, voting rights activist Fannie Lou Hamer with civil rights activist Ella Baker, baseball player Hank Aaron and wife Billy, lawyer Johnny Cochran, New York mayor David Dinkins, Dorothy Height (then of the National Council of Negro Women), Department of Energy secretary Hazel O'Leary, historian John Hope Franklin, and Supreme Court justices Thurgood Marshall and Ruth Bader Ginsburg. Franklin also commissioned Knox to paint a portrait of himself and his wife, Aurelia Elizabeth Franklin, whom he met at Fisk University in Nashville while they were students. In 2005 Knox unveiled the portrait for the couple at Fisk in the library renamed in their honor.

After more than twenty-five years as a portrait painter, Knox remains convinced that it is challenging and interesting to paint a human face. To be good at the task is difficult for an artist who wants to be successful. He believes that the painting must present an accurate likeness of the subject. It must tell a story; it tells the artist about that person's experiences and the things that helped to shape the subject as a person. "One must communicate a subject's character, spirit, and personality, and everything must speak the energy of the subject," he told the *Washington Post*.

Knox works from his single-car garage studio of his home in Silver Spring, Maryland, where he lives with his wife Roberta. He has three children—Amelia, Zachary, and Sheri. Daughter Sheri was born during his marriage in 1961 to Marceline Ward. He loves music, especially jazz, and saw a connection between President Clinton's love for the saxophone and his love for jazz. To relax, the soft-spoken, humble man listens to jazz and paints; sometimes he is up as early as 2:00 a.m. to begin his favorite pastime. Knox is on demand for interviews with journalists who are on a tight deadline, who want an interview, a photograph, or a piece of his work. As successful as he is, Knox has one unfilled passion—to paint a portrait of former South African president Nelson Mandela. He also plans to paint historical themes, including the Civil Rights movement.

The Clinton portraits, unveiled in a White House ceremony in 2004, introduced Simmie Knox to thousands of people, and he continues to inspire countless artists who want to become known, who now have new hope, and who now know the beauty of what can be created with oil and canvas. In the *Louisville Scene*, Robert Hall of the Anacostia Museum and Center for African American History and Culture (of the Smithsonian Institution) sums up the work of Knox at the White House and the lasting impression that he has made: "It's very special when you're asked to do a White House painting. What you're doing is painting your place in history."

REFERENCES

Periodicals

"Now, Painter to the President." *Newsweek* (26 February 2001): 9.

Vargas, Jose Antonio. "A Painter Draws Attention at Last." *Washington Post* (16 June 2004): C1.

Interviews

Knox, Simmie. Interview with Jessie Carney Smith, 29 April 2005.

———. Interview with Jessie Carney Smith, 30 November 2004.

Online

Jennings, Peter. "Person of the Week: Simmie Knox." http://abcnews.go.com/WNT/PersonOfWeek/story?id=1317225 (Accessed 23 November2004).

Klug, Foster. "Portrait Artist Does What He Likes: Listens to Jazz and Paints." *Louisville Scene*, 4 July 2004. http://www.louisvillescene.com/2004/07/04arts_portrait.html (Accessed 27 November 2004).

"Simmie Knox, an Exceptional Portrait Artist." *African American Registry.* http://www.aaregistry.com/african_american_history/1642Simmie_Knox (Accessed 23 November 2004).

"Simmie Knox 'Takes Five.'" (Milwaukee) *Journal Sentinel Online.* 16 June 2004. http://www.jsonline.com/news/gen/june04/236882.asp (Accessed 28 November 2004).

Simmie Knox Website. http://www.simmieknox.com/bio2.htm (Accessed 23 November 2004).

Jessie Carney Smith

Sam Lacy

1903–2003

Sportswriter, journalist, editor

Perhaps it was prophetic that Sam Harold Lacy was born in October 1903, the month and year of the first World Series. For over sixty years, he used his pen and his persistence as a sports journalist to become a crusader for the integration of major league baseball and other sports.

Samuel Lacy was born in Mystic, Connecticut on October 23, 1903. His father, Samuel Erskine Lacy, and his mother, Rose Lacy, moved the family to Washington, D.C., when he was two years old. Perhaps his interest in newspapers began when, at age eight, he began working for two dollars a week as a printer's helper. It was there that he learned to set type and run a rotary press. As a youth, he also shined shoes, set up pins in a bowling alley, sold newspapers, waited tables, and lugged heavy golf bags at a country club. Living near Griffith baseball stadium, Lacy took advantage of the opportunity to meet professional players by fielding batting practice balls for the Washington Nationals. In addition, he earned cash selling merchandise at the ballpark. The youngster attended Garnet Elementary School, and, for a short time, he attended Dunbar High School. At Dunbar, several future prominent African Americans were his classmates, including Charles Drew, William Hastie, Allison Davis, and W. Montague Cobb. A budding rebel, Lacy eschewed the middle-class intellectuals of Dunbar and transferred to Armstrong Technical High School which his sports-playing friends from the local YMCA attended. There he played basketball, football, and in multiple roles as star pitcher, third baseman, and captain, he helped the baseball team win three straight city championships from 1922 to 1924. Lacy dreamed of becoming a professional baseball player. During the 1920s, while still in high school, he pitched for a couple of black sandlot teams in the District of Columbia, the Buffalo A.C. and the LeDroit Tigers. Although in his autobiography, written when he was ninety-five, Lacy claimed that he played with the semi-pro Atlantic City Bacharach Giants, a

black professional team, there is no supporting documentation for that claim.

After graduating from high school in 1924, he coached men's and women's basketball teams, refereed games, and promoted and announced sporting events. Again rejecting an icon of black middle class, he left Howard University in 1926 after one year. Subsequently, the young man made several irresponsible decisions. Lacy's obsession with betting on racehorses led to money problems. His illicit efforts to earn quick money by writing bad checks resulted in close encounters with the police; however, he managed to correct his mistakes before he became a convict instead of a reporter.

Even as a teenager while he pursued a baseball career, Lacy had another occupation. When he was a sophomore in high school, he began writing sports for the *Washington Tribune*. The *Tribune* hired Lacy as a full time journalist in 1926. His assignment was to cover high school and amateur sports. Within two months, the newspaper promoted the young man to sports editor. He married Alberta Robinson in 1927 and their son, Samuel Howe (Tim) Lacy, was born in 1938. However, tempted again by baseball, Lacy left the *Tribune* in 1929 to play in Connecticut. After finally accepting the reality that a profes-

Chronology	
1903	Born in Mystic, Connecticut on October 23
1920s	Works as sportswriter at the *Washington Tribune*
1934-37	Serves as managing editor and sports editor of the *Washington Tribune*
1940-42	Works as assistant national editor for the *Chicago Defender*
1943	Becomes columnist and sports editor for the *Afro-American*
1945	Begins travel to report first-hand on the Jackie Robinson experience
1948	Accepted as first African American member of the Baseball Writers Association of America
1997	Wins the J. G. Taylor Spink Award
1998	Becomes first Baseball Hall of Fame sportswriter inductee who spent entire career with a black newspaper
2003	Dies in Washington, D.C. on May 8

sional baseball career was not in his future, he returned to reporting full-time for the *Washington Tribune*. From 1934 to 1937, Lacy was both managing editor and sports editor of the paper.

Begins Crusade to Integrate Major League Baseball

The mid-1930s was a time when the NAACP was soliciting for anti-lynching legislation. Black newspapers took advantage of their influence to fight segregation. A product of his times, Lacy used his column to highlight racial disparities in sporting facilities and opportunities. Lacy began campaigning against policies that banned black players from major league teams. From 1937 to 1939, he was sports editor for the Washington *Afro-American*. In October 1937, Lacy exposed a Syracuse University scheme to pass off their black star player, Wilmeth Sidat-Singh, as a Hindu so that he could play in a game with the University of Maryland. As a result, Syracuse yielded to Maryland's refusal to participate if a black played in the game. The controversial story produced criticism of Lacy, even from African Americans. Nevertheless, he stood behind his story. Lacy thought that it was a reporter's responsibility to be honest, and he believed racial progress required candor. Soon after the Sidat-Singh episode, Lacy met with Clark Griffith, owner of the Washington Senators, to discuss the hiring of African American players. Griffith's refusal to cooperate apparently fueled Lacy's resolve to integrate baseball. In a column "Pro and Con on The Negro in Organized Baseball," Lacy printed the diverse opinions of white sportswriters as well as letters of support from black Washingtonians. In 1940, Lacy left Washington to work as assistant national editor for another black newspaper, the *Chicago Defender*. There he began a letter-writing campaign to the major league owners.

Lacy returned to Baltimore in 1943 to work as a columnist and sports editor for the weekly *Afro-American* newspapers, a position he held for almost sixty years. Still committed to the cause, he continued to write on the subject of integrating baseball in his column. He also urged baseball owners to set up a committee to discuss integration. The full membership of Major League Committee on Baseball Integration never met, but member Branch Rickey, owner of the Dodgers, broke the color barrier when he signed a black player, Jackie Robinson, in August 1945.

Travels with Jackie Robinson

Aware of the historical implication of Jackie Robinson's signing, Carl Murphy, publisher of the *Afro-American*, assigned Lacy to follow Robinson and cover the story. Lacy began to travel in order to give detailed reports on the treatment of Robinson and other black players and on the progress of the integration of baseball. As a result, he was exposed to indignities similar to those endured by many other blacks. For example, Lacy was not allowed to sit in the press boxes of ballparks in Texas. As a compromise, the president of the National League gave permission for Lacy to set in the dugout. On one occasion, according to Lacy, he and Jackie Robinson were not admitted into a stadium in Florida. In order for Robinson to play that day and for Lacy to do his job, they had to get in through a loose plank in the stadium fence. Asking for directions to the colored restroom in a Florida stadium, the usher directed him to a tree about thirty-five yards away from the right field fowl line. Another time, when Lacy was refused admission to a press box, he decided to view the game from the roof. Several sympathetic white peers joined him on his perch declaring as a joke that they wanted to get a tan. Ironically, in order to segregate Lacy from the other reporters, park authorities placed him in a separate field box, which resulted in a better seat for him than for many of the white fans. Lacy viewed his race-based encounters as representative of the humiliations suffered by many other blacks in countless other jobs. Like others, he did not let the innumerable confrontations interfere with the tasks he set out to accomplish.

Though remembered mainly for his battle to eliminate obstacles faced by black, major league baseball players, Lacy also reported about the achievements of African Americans in other sports. While he felt obliged to confront the individuals and institutions that resisted extending equal opportunities to players, his professional honesty also required him to query athletes about personal and sensitive issues.

Receives Recognition for Work

Hard work, sports, and writing were constant factors throughout his life. Although his goal was to be a star professional player, rather than reporting the feats of other athletes, Lacy won acclaim and shaped society through his writing. During his lifetime, he received numerous awards and tributes. *Sports Illustrated* presented Lacy with the Lifetime Achievement Award in Journalism in 1989 and the National Association of Black Journalists presented him with a similar honor in 1991. He was inducted into the Society of Professional Journalists Hall of Fame in 1994 and honored at the All Sports Hall of Fame dinner in New York City in 1998. In 1948, Lacy was the first African American admitted to membership in the Baseball Writers Association. In 1997, he won the J. G. Taylor Spink Award, the highest award given by the Baseball Writers Association to its members. According to Lacy, the most important award was induction into the writers' wing of the National Baseball Hall of Fame in 1998. He was only the second African American to receive the honor and the first Baseball Hall of Fame sportswriter inductee who spent his entire career with a black newspaper.

Following his divorce from his first wife in 1952, Lacy married Barbara Robinson in 1953. She often traveled with him and her fair complexion sometimes led to embarrassing incidents when they were mistaken as an interracial couple. Lacy credited Barbara with teaching him responsibility. He remained a widower after her death in 1969.

Lacy died on May 8, 2003, in Washington, D.C., at age 99. The Baseball Hall of Fame notes, "it was as a crusader in the 1930s and 1940s, when Lacy's columns were devoted to desegregating baseball in the major leagues, that he made his greatest impact as a journalist." Lacy's pen and typewriter were truly mightier than a sword.

REFERENCES

Books

Nathan, Daniel A. "Sam Lacy." In *African American Lives*. Eds. Henry Louis Gates and Evelyn Brooks Higginbothan. New York: Oxford University Press, 2004.

Snyder, Brad. *Beyond the Shadow of the Senators: The Untold Story of the Homestead Grays and the Integration of Baseball*. New York: McGraw-Hill, 2003.

Online

National Baseball Hall of Fame. "1997 J.G. Taylor Spink Award Winner Sam Lacy." http://www.baseballhalloffame.org/hofers%5Fand%5Fhonorees/spink%5Fbios/lacy_sam.htm (Accessed 6 February 2006).

Cheryl Jones Hamberg

Lunsford Lane
1803–?

Slave, entrepreneur

Lunsford Lane, a nineteenth-century slave, went from slavery in North Carolina to a free man serving as a steward in Wellington Hospital in Worcester, Massachusetts. He wrote and self published the story of his life as a slave and his efforts to extricate himself and his family from slavery; the narrative has as part of the subtitle "Embracing an Account of His Early Life, the Redemption of Himself and Family from Slavery, and His Banishment from the Place of His Birth for the Crime of Wearing a Colored Skin." In the note to the reader, Lane indicates that he is writing in response to requests from

Chronology	
1803	Born in Raleigh, North Carolina on May 30
1828	Marries Martha Curtis
1829	First child born
1835	Makes arrangements to purchase himself and is taken to New York to receive his manumission papers
1842	Publishes *The Narrative of Lunsford Lane* in Boston; returns to Raleigh to purchase his family
1863	Prior to this year listed as steward at Wellington Hospital in Worcester, Massachusetts; no Lunsford Lane listed in the city directory after this date

friends and to garner income for his large family (seven children, a wife, and parents). Even though his stated aim is not to speak out against the institution of slavery, the narrative was used as a tool in the fight against slavery.

Lunsford Lane was born May 30, 1803, to Edward and Clarissa Lane (whose names were acquired from their previous owners) in Raleigh, North Carolina. Lane and his mother were the slaves of Sherwood Haywood, a planter and banker. His father was a slave on a neighboring plantation. His mother was a house servant; as a result, Lane was born and lived in the kitchen, the accommodations for the house servants. His childhood was fairly happy and he was not aware of a difference between him and the white children until he was about ten when he was actually assigned tasks to complete. He became a driver for his owner, came in contact with many personalities (legislators, speakers, other influential individuals) of the day, and grew in his knowledge of the world and the rights of men. In spite of what appears to be a life of ease when compared to the slaves in the field, he understood the tenuousness of a slave's life and he had a thirst for freedom.

Lane came to the conclusion that the only way to gain freedom was for him to purchase himself. He pondered ways this could be executed; his father provided him with the catalyst and later the method for earning money for his freedom. One day, he provided him with a basket of peaches, which Lane sold for a profit. From that point on, Lane began to work and save towards his future freedom. He often acquired tips from the men who visited Haywood; he cut wood after a day's work and sold it the next morning. However, the plan which proved most profitable for him again was the result of his father's action. He had devised a way of making smoking tobacco different from any other. Lane improved on the tobacco and made it sweeter; he also constructed a smoking pipe better than any others. Sales were lucrative and his smoking clientele grew to include smokers in other cities and members of the legislature. He became known as a tobacconist and later labeled his tobacco, Edward and Lunsford Lane.

As his business grew, so did his relationship with white men in power. With his prosperity, he decided it was time to marry. He married in 1828 and began his family in 1829. His wealth increased; however, there were many demands on it, including providing for his family when the owner did not. Before he could purchase his freedom, his owner died, and the bank placed a claim against the estate. This action forced Haywood's widow to sell some of the slaves. However, she retained Lane and allowed him to hire out his time and pay her a fee. Through this boon and his various means of making money, he was finally able to pay his owner $1,000 for his freedom and to make a deal with the owner of his wife and children to buy them for $2,500 on an installment plan. In 1835, Lane made arrangements to be purchased in Raleigh; he could not legally purchase himself or receive his freedom except for meritorious service, and he had to be taken to New York to receive his manumission papers.

Early Life as a Free Man

Lane received his papers and returned to Raleigh to his family and to work. Through an agreement with his family's owner and the purchase of a house, he and his wife were allowed to live together. He returned to his businesses and worked in the office of governor Edward B. Dudley. As he prospered and moved towards the purchase of his family, he received a letter telling him to leave the city and reminding him of a North Carolina law which prohibited free men from other states to reside in North Carolina. Even though many individuals supported his efforts to remain in Raleigh and the legislature was petitioned, Lane had to leave.

He left with one of his daughters for whom he paid $250 and went to New York and Boston where he lectured and earned money to aid in the purchase of the remainder of his family. Lane returned to Raleigh on February 23, 1842, to buy his family. He had been assured his entry, purchase (paying the remaining $1,380), and exit would take place without incident. However, there were complications and he wound up being captured, jailed, and tarred and feathered. Even though he encountered these obstacles and men who were jealous of his success, there were those who tried to save him and aid in the completion of his business. Once he was freed, he was reunited with his family, the transaction was completed, and Lane was able to leave with his family. His former owner Mrs. Haywood gifted his mother to him, provided her with free papers, and told Lane that if he were ever able to pay for her, the price would be $200. The ten (mother, wife, seven children, and Lane) lived in Philadelphia; New York; Boston; Oberlin, Ohio; and Worcester, Massachusetts.

Later, they were joined by Lane's father who had gained his freedom through legacy. Lane expressed his appreciation to friends and others who helped their initial progress in freedom. Lane continued to lecture on the subject of slavery. In his book on Lane, William Hawkins reports that two of Lane's sons were at Port Royal, South Carolina doing their part in the Civil War. During the Civil War Lunsford Lane served as a steward at Wellington Hospital in Worcester where he, his wife, and daughters cared for sick and wounded soldiers. According to Sande Bishop, they cared for one hundred soldiers prior to the closing of the facility in 1863. According to the *Dictionary of North Carolina Biography*, there is no record of Lane in the city directory of Worcester after 1863, although there is a Lunsford Lane Jr. mentioned in 1865.

REFERENCES

Books

Cotton, Alice R. "Biography of Lunsford Lane (30 May 1830-ca. 1863)." In *Dictionary of North Carolina Biography*. Vol. 4. Ed. William S. Powell. Chapel Hill, N.C.: The University of North Carolina Press, 1991.

Franklin, John Hope. *The Free Negro in North Carolina 1790-1860*. New York: Russell & Russell, 1943.

Hawkins, William G. *Lunsford Lane: Another Helper from North Carolina*. New York: Negro University Press, 1969.

Online

Bassett, John Spencer. *Anti-Slavery Leaders of North Carolina*. Ed. Herbert B. Adams. Baltimore: The Johns Hopkins Press, June 1898. http://www.webroots.org/library/usablack/aslonc00.html (Accessed 8 February 2006).

Bishop, Sande P. *Dale Hospital: A Civil War Hospital with Community Support*. http://www.ci.worcester.ma.us/cco/history/dale_hospital.htm (Accessed 28 February 2006).

Helen R. Houston

William Henry Lane
1825–c. 1852

Dancer

William Henry Lane is "probably the first famous figure in tap dancing," according to *Smithsonian* magazine. Also known as "Master Juba," he got his stage name from a word that signified a rhythmic dance that came over to America with Africans on slave ships. According to the *Smithsonian*, in the 1840s theater handbills proclaimed Lane as "The Wonder of the World, Juba . . . the King of All Dancers" and declared, "No conception can be formed of the variety of beautiful and intricate steps exhibited by him with ease."

In his 1842 book *American Notes* English novelist Charles Dickens describes a dancer many believe to be Lane. "Single shuffle, double shuffle, cut and crosscut," Dickens wrote, "snapping his fingers, rolling his eyes, turning in his knees, presenting the backs of his legs in front, spinning about on his toes and heels like nothing…dancing with two left legs, two right legs, two wooden legs, two wire legs, two spring legs—all sorts of legs and no legs—what is this to him?" Until Lane came along, a free black in the time of slavery, whites portrayed African Americans on stage. Their act was called minstrelsy—these white dancers performed "authentic Negro dances," smudging their faces black with burnt cork, and entertaining crowds with their mocking, denigrating portrayal of African Americans as goofy caricatures. Lane is credited with being the first black to darken his own face with burnt cork and perform in the American minstrel shows.

Lane was born a free black in 1825 in Providence, Rhode Island. He spent his teenage years in the Five Points area of New York City. It is said that Lane learned to dance as a teen from a well-known black saloon dancer, "Uncle" Jim Lowe. Lowe, best known for his jigs and reels, initially encouraged Lane to become a "Buck and Wing" dancer. The phrase came from "buck," a term used by whites for African American males, and "wing," a nineteenth-century minstrel dance routine. Before long, Lane developed his own style, won several challenge dances, dancing an Irish jig against white competitors. Twice he beat the best white dancer in Five Points, an Irishman named John Diamond who was famous for jig dancing. Lane was declared the best.

Minstrel Shows Aped Blacks

White minstrelsy became popular during the Civil War era, and audiences enjoyed the shows, depicting African Americans as acrobatic, dancing clowns. After the war, blacks had to step into the roles created for them by whites if they wanted to find work on the stage. As African American minstrel troupes began to form—Sam Lucas, the Georgia Minstrels, Lew Johnson's Plantation Minstrel Company, Haverly's Mastodon Genuine Coloured Minstrels, the Great Nonpareil Coloured Troupe, James Bland, W. C. Handy, and others—they had to perform the Jim Crow dance if they wanted to please audiences and fill theater seats.

To compete with established white minstrels, blacks had to advertise themselves as real, or bona fide Negroes. Also, though many black performers were already dark-skinned, they blackened their faces and painted clownish lips on their faces with red and white, making their mouths twice normal size, because that was what audiences were used to.

Lane's style was unique, and one awestruck critic declared that his performance reflected the dance style of an entire people. Even though his talents set him apart from both black and white minstrels, Lane still had to conform to the derogatory minstrel act if he was to work. Nonetheless, Lane has been described as the "most influential single performer of nineteenth-century American dance," according to PBS Television.

Becomes Master of Dance

The dance Lane became famous for, the Juba, has a rich tradition. West Africans on slave ships danced for exercise, on occasion, to the hornpipe, banjo, or fiddle, unfamiliar instruments played in an unfamiliar march-time beat by members of the ships' Europeans crews. As the ships pitched and lurched, the Africans did a foot stomp. Rhythmic clapping sometimes went along with the steps. This tradition was known as patting Juba. Settled on American plantations in the South, the Africans kept dancing and became adept at copying Irish jigs, quadrilles, Virginia reels, and Lancashire clogging. They were even called into their masters' homes to entertain white guests. On their own, the transplanted people of Dahomey, Congo, and Senegal were more apt to dance giouba, described as "an African step-dance which somewhat resembled a jig with elaborate variations, [which] occurred wherever the Negro settled," according to the *Smithsonian*.

By 1845, Lane was making his name with his version of the Juba. Lane's style focused on rhythm and percussion over melody and built heavily on improvisation. He may have been the first to add syncopation to his dancing.

In 1846, Lane became the only black dancer of his time to receive top billing in an otherwise all white minstrel company who, in blackface, called themselves the Ethiopian Minstrels. He toured with the group through the United States and the United Kingdom, where he was very popular. In 1848 he danced at Vauxhall Gardens and before Queen Victoria at Buckingham Palace.

Lane's popularity in England led him to found a school in London, where he lived after touring there. According to PBS Television, he inspired in whites a desire to search "for inspiration among the Negro folk "as they sought to copy his complicated steps. Details of Lane's death are somewhat obscure, but he is thought to have died young, at the age of twenty-seven somewhere in England.

REFERENCES

Periodicals

Santiago, Chiori. "Ziggedy bop! Tap dance is back on its feet." *Smithsonian*, May 1997.

Online

"Great Performances: Free to Dance—Behind the Dance—From Minstrel Show to Concert Stage." PBS Television. http://www.pbs.org/wnet/ freetodance/behind/behind_minstrel.htm (Accessed 23 March 2005).

"Juba—William Henry Lane." The Vauxhall Society. http://www.vauxhallsociety.org.uk/Juba.html (Accessed 23 March 2005).

"William Henry 'Juba' Lane." Dancer History Archives. http://www.streetswing.com/histmai2/d2juba1.htm (Accessed 23 March 2005).

Brenna Sanchez

James M. Lawson, Jr.
1928–

Civil rights activist, minister

The Reverend James Morris Lawson Jr. made significant contributions to the modern civil rights movement in Tennessee and in the South. A leading proponent of the philosophy of direct nonviolent protest, he was the movement's leading theoretician and tactician in the black American struggle for freedom, justice, and equality. The product of a politically active family, he continued his family's heritage by using his intellect and talent for the betterment of humankind.

Reared in a household of ten children (nine biological and one adopted), James Morris Lawson Jr. was born in Uniontown, Pennsylvania on September 22, 1928 to the Reverend James Morris Sr. and Philane May Cover Lawson. His father was born in Guelph, Ontario. Lawson's paternal great-grandfather, an escaped slave from Maryland, made his way to Ontario via the Underground Railroad. The surname Lawson is the family name that his

James M. Lawson, Jr.

great-grandfather assumed to honor a man who worked on the secret escape route and aided the family in its flight from the South. Lawson's mother was born in St. Anne's Parish, Jamaica. During her late teens, she left Jamaica and migrated to the United States in search of better opportunities. Lawson's father came to America as an African Methodist Episcopal (AME) Zion minister. To Lawson Sr., religion and education were of prime importance. An itinerant minister, he was one of the first persons of African descent to graduate from Canada's McGill University. Imbued in the Wesleyan tradition, the Lawsons often traveled from place to place, setting up new congregations. In addition to being a man of the cloth, Lawson Sr. was an activist. Wherever he resided, he organized and established both a chapter of the National Association for the Advancement of Colored People (NAACP) and the Urban League. As a gun-toting AME Zion minister, he advocated a gospel of liberation. A strong activist, he did not adhere to or believe in the tenet of nonviolence. He instructed his children to fend off any assault, be it physical or verbal. By contrast, Lawson's mother did not adhere to her husband's position. She believed that force never settled any problem.

A Youthful Social Activist

Lawson grew up in Massillon, Ohio, a predominately white town. He received his primary and secondary education in the Massillon public schools. While growing

Chronology

1928	Born in Uniontown, Pennsylvania on September 22
1947	Enters Baldwin-Wallace College in Berea, Ohio
1949	Refuses to be drafted into the Korean War
1951	Convicted and sentenced to three years in prison for violating the draft laws; enters federal prison on April 25
1952	Paroled from Ashland Federal Prison; graduates from Baldwin-Wallace College
1953-56	Serves as a Methodist minister in India and teaches and serves as a coach at Hislop College in Nagpur
1956	Returns to the United States; attends Oberlin College Graduate School of Theology
1958	Moves to Nashville, Tennessee; transfers to Vanderbilt Divinity School from Oberlin College; serves as southern secretary for the Fellowship of Reconciliation for two years
1959	Begins nonviolent action training workshops in Nashville; marries Dorothy Wood on July 3
1960	Expelled from Vanderbilt University on March 3; gives the keynote address at the founding session of the Student Nonviolent Coordinating Committee; receives master's degree in theology from Boston University; serves as director of the Southern Christian Leadership Conference
1961	Participates in the final stage of the Freedom Rides
1962	Appointed to the pastorate of the Centenary Methodist Church in Memphis, Tennessee
1968	Invites Martin Luther King Jr. to come to Memphis to draw attention to the plight of the striking sanitation workers
1973	Becomes board member of the Southern Christian Leadership Conference
1974	Begins serving as pastor of Holman Methodist Church in Los Angeles, California, until 1999
1994-2000	Serves as president of the Fellowship of Reconciliation
2002	Receives the Walter R. Murray Distinguished Alumnus Award; serves as visiting professor for UCLA's Labor Center
2003	Receives the Ralph J. Bunche Trailblazer Award
2006	Receives the 2005 Vanderbilt University's Distinguished Alumnus on January 18; appointed distinguished visiting professor for the 2006-2007 academic year

up, Lawson was exposed to the views of Mohandas K. Gandhi, who demonstrated the effectiveness of passive resistance for fighting injustice. This philosophy was discussed in editorials of the *Cleveland Defender* and the *Pittsburgh Courier*. Before graduating from high school, he and a schoolmate, provoked by the unjust treatment of African Americans, entered a Massillon eating establishment and insisted that they be served. Reluctantly serving Lawson and his friend, the eatery's management ordered them not to return. That was his first sit-in. The youthful Lawson continued his protest activity by testing white-only restaurants at different Methodist youth meetings in small Midwestern cities. From his protest encounters, he discerned that the region's mindset was not unlike that in the South.

In high school, Lawson proved himself scholarly, and his intellectual talent was not to be wasted. For the student scholar, college was a given. During his last two years in high school, Lawson leaned toward the ministry. Offered several scholarships after high school, he entered Baldwin-Wallace College in Berea, Ohio in 1947.

Becomes a Conscientious Objector

As a freshman at the Methodist liberal arts institution of higher education, Lawson felt his activism strengthen. He joined the local chapter of the Fellowship of Reconciliation (FOR) and also became a member of the Congress of Racial Equality (CORE). Both organizations promoted nonviolent passive resistance to racism.

At Baldwin-Wallace, Lawson met A. J. Muste, the founder of FOR. The formidable pacifist became a significant person in Lawson's life. He introduced Lawson to the intellectual and historical basis for his beliefs. Additionally, because of Muste, Lawson encountered others of similar beliefs, including James Farmer, Bayard Rustin, and Glenn Smiley.

Within two years of entering Baldwin-Wallace, Lawson was firmly grounded in the principle of nonviolence and became a conscientious objector just as the United States began to engage in the cold war. Although he registered for the draft at age eighteen, Lawson indicated he did so with misgivings. He did not believe in the draft and as a Christian did not know if he could serve in the armed forces. In 1949, the draft board sent him a second classification form that he refused to complete.

Five months after the Korean War erupted in 1950, Lawson and his pacifist beliefs came under attack. Although he could have taken a student or ministerial deferment, Lawson remained steadfastly committed to his beliefs. Having been warned that there was a warrant for his arrest, he turned himself in to the authorities, who subsequently charged him with violating the country's draft laws. After posting bond, Lawson returned to Baldwin-Wallace and worked toward completing his academic program, as he expected to be a member of the 1951 graduating class.

Enters Federal Prison

FOR assigned an attorney to represent Lawson at his trial. A senior, he went to trial in April 1951. The judge sentenced him to three years in federal prison. On April 25, 1951, he entered prison at Mill Point, West Virginia.

Lawson was not prepared for the Baldwin-Wallace faculty's action. Withholding his degree, they ruled that he would have to come back when he completed his sentence and retake his final course work. The consciousness objector served thirteen months in prison. However, before his early release, just before Christmas in 1951, officials moved Lawson from the West Virginia penal complex to a maximum-security institution in Ashland,

Kentucky, under the trumped-up charge of being a troublemaker. Earlier in the month, President Harry S. Truman issued an order desegregating all federal prisons. That action caused a racial storm in the prison. Whites who wished to maintain the status quo identified Lawson as the leader of the would-be integrationists. In reality, Mill Point prison officials transferred Lawson and the five white inmates because of desegregation.

In May of 1952, Lawson was paroled from federal prison. He took the summer off and returned to Baldwin-Wallace in the fall to complete his undergraduate degree. Lawson earned his B.A. in 1952. Years later, however, as a prominent figure in the civil rights movement and one of the college's distinguished alumni, when the college asked him to return to receive an honorary degree, Lawson requested that his original undergraduate degree be listed with the class of 1951. Baldwin-Wallace's administrators honored his request and listed him with the class of 1951.

Studies Principles of Nonviolent Direct Resistance in India

Because of an opportunity provided by the Methodist Church, Lawson went to India to serve as a missionary in April 1953. Arriving in Nagpur, Lawson was assigned to Hislop College, a Presbyterian school in the British system. While in Nagpur, he continued to study satyagraha, the principles of nonviolent resistance. There until 1956, in addition to his teaching and coaching responsibilities, he continued his study of Gandhi and even visited with Prime Minister Nehru. Before returning to the states in the spring of 1956, Lawson traveled to parts of Africa, where he also discerned the growing intensity of anti-colonial feeling.

When he returned to the United States, Lawson entered Oberlin College's Graduate School of Theology in 1956. In February of the following year when Martin Luther King Jr. spoke on campus, they met and talked. During the course of their conversation, King praised Lawson's experience and understanding, and encouraged him to come to the South.

Becomes Involved in the Nashville Movement

A. J. Muste arranged for Lawson to become the organization's southern secretary. For two years, from 1958 to 1960, he served as a troubleshooter, moving in and out of southern cities such as Little Rock, Columbia, Jackson, Memphis, Knoxville, and Greensboro among others. Based in Nashville, Tennessee, he enrolled in Vanderbilt University's School of Divinity and became a member of the Nashville Christian Leadership Conference (NCLC), founded by the Reverend Kelly Miller Smith, a local affiliate of King's Southern Christian Leadership Conference (SCLC). As chair of the Action Committee, Lawson launched a process to demonstrate that the success of the Montgomery bus boycott could be repeated in Nashville. That fall, with Lawson serving as organizer and teacher, NCLC sponsored weekly nonviolent action workshops

bringing together students, clergy, and laity. During the workshops Lawson met, mentored, and nurtured a cadre of students who became leaders within the movement across the South.

Soon after arriving in Nashville, Lawson met Dorothy Woods, a graduate of Tennessee A & I State University. In December 1958, Lawson asked Woods to be his wife. They married on July 3, 1959 and ultimately became the parents of three sons, John (who, as a toddler, desegregated the public parks in Memphis), Seth, and James Morris III.

In November and December 1959, the Reverends Lawson and Smith and students Diane Nash, Marion Berry, John Lewis, and James Bevel, conducted "test sit-ins" at downtown Nashville department stores, two months prior to the students in Greensboro, North Carolina. Approximately two weeks after the Greensboro sit-ins, on February 13, 1960, Lawson and other students began full-scale sit-ins at Nashville downtown stores. Because of its discipline, the Nashville student movement became the model for other movements across the South. However, Lawson's involvement with Nashville's desegregation movement brought him into direct conflict with Vanderbilt University board of trustees member James Geddes Stahlman, publisher of the *Nashville Banner*. On March 2, 1960, the Vanderbilt trustees met and gave Lawson the choice of withdrawing as a student or being dismissed from the university. He refused to withdraw and the following day, university's officials expelled him from Vanderbilt.

Between April 15 and 16, 1960, at Shaw University in Raleigh, North Carolina, Lawson and the Nashville student contingent were leading supporters in the establishment of the Student Nonviolent Coordinating Committee (SNCC). The Nashville group's dedication to nonviolence and the Christian ideal of community helped determine SNCC's initial direction. SNCC's statement of purpose, written by Lawson and endorsed by a student conference held in Atlanta on May 13 and 14, 1961, emphasized the religious and philosophical tenets of nonviolent direct action.

After being expelled from Vanderbilt's School of Divinity, Lawson went on to Boston University and received his master's of theology in August 1960. In that same year, he served as the pastor of the Green Chapel Methodist Church in Shelbyville, Tennessee. A year later, when the Freedom Riders were going through the Deep South testing the region's compliance with the U. S. Supreme Court's edict in the *Boynton v. Virginia* case, Lawson participated in the rider's last journey. In 1962, officials of the Methodist Church appointed Lawson to the pastorate of the Centenary Methodist Church in Memphis, Tennessee. The following month, King asked Lawson to serve as director of nonviolent education for SCLC.

Brings Martin Luther King, Jr. to Memphis

Lawson supported a number of civil rights organizations, mostly conducting workshops. He worked with FOR from 1957 to 1969; SNCC from 1960 to 1964; and the SCLC from 1960 to 1967. After moving to Memphis, he participated in the Bluff City movement. Lawson pressed the NAACP to confront the city's governmental agencies. He organized Community on the Move for Equality (COME) and initiated action groups to address high poverty rates, inadequate healthcare facilities and services, indecent housing, and unequal education. Lawson persuaded local clergy to support the striking sanitation workers in their protest for better wages and improved working conditions. Lawson, who emboldened the refuse workers to think of themselves as men, led them to employ the well-known "I am a Man" signs. In 1968, COME spearheaded an economic boycott, and Lawson asked King to come to Memphis to draw attention to the plight of striking sanitation workers. Arriving on March 18 and moved by the crowd, King promised to return on March 22 and lead a march. Postponed because of inclement weather, King returned to Memphis on March 28. Because the march ended in violence, the civil rights leader returned to Memphis on April 2. The following day he gave his "I've Been to the Mountain Top" speech at Mason Temple, the last speech he made. The following day, King was murdered. After King's April 4 assassination, Lawson pleaded for calm in the black community.

Heads Holman United Methodist Church

Remaining in Memphis for six more years, Lawson continued to work with various civil rights groups. In 1972, he returned to Vanderbilt University on a one-year fellowship. The following year, he became a board member of the SCLC. In 1974, Lawson and his family moved to Los Angeles, California, when he was appointed pastor of the Holman United Methodist Church. Serving the Holman congregation for twenty-five years, he continued his application of the gospel for all human issues. In the 1980s, Lawson became a nonviolent consultant and conducted workshops for organizers and staff in civil disobedience and demonstrations. In the 1990s, he was one of the founders of Clergy and Laity United for Economic Justice (CLUE) in Los Angeles. Since its founding in 1996, he served on the special advisory committee of the National Interfaith Committee for Worker Justice. As chairman of CLUE, Lawson stood with workers and labor leaders in any number of efforts, including civil disobedience.

Retired in the early 2000s, Lawson, an unwavering activist, campaigned against violence, demonstrated for equal rights of gays and lesbians, and worked to promote community diversity and solidarity. As an activist, he saw the inside of jails and prisons in numerous states. As a pastor, he participated in a wide range of ministries on the local, national, and international levels.

Lawson was awarded Vanderbilt University's 2005 Distinguished Alumni Award. Within the same week, almost forty-six years after the university expelled him for his civil rights activism, Vanderbilt appointed him as its distinguished visiting professor for the 2006-2007 academic year.

Born just four months before Martin Luther King Jr., Lawson was the understated leader of the civil rights movement. His impact was enormous and long lasting. He became noted in the struggle for African American civil rights by teaching Gandhi's nonviolent civil disobedience techniques and philosophy, which became the movement's most compelling and effective political weapon.

REFERENCES

Books

Arsenault, Raymond. *Freedom Riders: 1961 and the Struggle for Racial Justice*. New York: Oxford University Press, 2006.

Branch, Taylor. *Parting the Waters: America in the King Years, 1954-1963.*. New York: Simon & Schuster, 1988.

Burns, Stewart. *To the Mountain Top: Martin Luther King Jr.'s Sacred Mission to Save American, 1955-1968*. New York: Harper Collins, 2004.

Clayborne, Carson. *In Struggle: SNCC and the Black Awakening of the 1960s*. Cambridge, Mass.: Harvard University Press, 1981.

Conkin, Paul K. *Gone with the Ivy: A Biography of Vanderbilt University*. Knoxville: University of Tennessee Press, 1985.

Halberstam, David. *The Children*. New York: Random House. 1998.

Riches, William T. Martin. *The Civil Rights Movement: Struggle and Resistance*. New York: Palgrave, 2004.

Sumner, David. "James Lawson, Jr." *Tennessee Encyclopedia of History and Culture*. Ed. Carroll Van West. Nashville: Rutledge Hill Press, 1998.

Zinn, Howard. *SNCC: The New Abolitionists*. Cambridge, Mass.: South End Press, 2002.

Periodicals

"James Lawson Named 2005 Vanderbilt University Distinguished Alumnus." *Tennessee Tribune*, 22 December 2005.

Mielczarek, Natalia. "Vanderbilt Hires Ex-student It Expelled for Civil Rights Activism." *Tennessean*, 19 January 2006.

Summer, David E. "The Publisher and the Preacher: Racial Conflict at Vanderbilt University." *Tennessee Historical Quarterly* LVI (Spring 1997): 34-43.

Wynn, Linda T. "The Dawning of a New Day: The Nashville Sit-Ins, February 13, 1960-May 10, 1960."

Tennessee Historical Quarterly L (Spring 1991): 42-54.

Online

"Interview: Rev. James Lawson." A Force More Powerful: Nashville 1960. http:www.pbs.org/weta/forcemorepowerful/nashville/interview.html (Accessed 10 July 2005).

Linda T. Wynn

Chronology

1835	Born in Fayetteville, North Carolina on March 17
1857	Moves to Oberlin, Ohio
1857-58	Marries Mary Sampson Patterson sometime during these years
1859	First and only child is born; meets John Brown and agrees to help him raid Harpers Ferry Arsenal; killed at Harpers Ferry

Lewis Sheridan Leary
1835–1859

Abolitionist

Lewis Sheridan "Shad" Leary accompanied John Brown on the raid of the Harpers Ferry arsenal (October 1859), where he was killed during the gun fight with federal troops. Leary was said to be handsome and to wear his wide-brimmed hat at a rakish tilt, which was the first sign of his reckless, yet courageous nature.

Leary was born of free parents in Fayetteville, North Carolina, in 1835. He had never been enslaved and was without slave ancestors. His father reportedly was Jeremiah O'Leary, an Irishman, who fought in the American Revolution under General Nathaniel Greene. His mother was of mixed heritage, partly African, partly Croatan Indian tribe of North Carolina that is believed by some to be descended from the colonists left by John White on Roanoke Island in 1587. Lewis grew up in Ohio, where he learned from his father how to make harnesses and saddles. In his father's home, he was privately tutored and attended the free colored people's school in Fayetteville. He later dropped the "O" from his name, going by the last name Leary.

Though he was himself free, Leary hated slavery. The story is told that as a young man he witnessed a white man beating a slave. He decided to defend the slave by beating the white man. As would be expected, his actions caused so much distress in the community that he was forced to escape across the Cape Fear River under the cover of darkness. Leary then traveled northwest until he reached Oberlin, Ohio.

Arrives in Ohio

In 1857 he arrived in Oberlin, Ohio. He spent some time studying at Oberlin College and was able to support himself by designing and decorating saddles. Leary also displayed unusual musical talent and learned to play several instruments.

While in Oberlin, sometime during the years 1857 and 1858, he met and married Mary Sampson Patterson, who also attended Oberlin College. (Patterson was the grandmother of Langston Hughes.) Leary, for reasons known only to him, did not inform her or his sister who also lived in Oberlin of his plans to join the infamous white abolitionist John Brown. He left his wife and their six-month-old child to rendezvous with Brown in Virginia. Leary did, however, manage to send his family messages before he died of gunshot wounds at Harpers Ferry. After his death his wife also received the torn and blood-stained cape in which he died. In 1899, the body of Leary was disinterred at Harpers Ferry. It was reburied at North Elba, New York, near the grave of John Brown.

Harpers Ferry Experience

Leary accompanied John Brown on the raid of the Harpers Ferry arsenal in October 1859, where he was killed during a gun fight with federal troops. He had first met the abolitionist's son who recruited him in the spring of 1859. The elder Brown had come to Ohio on his way to Harpers Ferry. He was visiting his son, John Brown Jr., at his home in West Andover, Ohio, and he wanted him to recruit and direct young volunteers to the elder Brown's secret rendezvous point in Virginia. John Brown Jr. went to Oberlin and met John Langston who suggested that Lewis Sheridan Leary and John Copeland Jr., Leary's nephew, might be persuaded to join the elder Brown. Copeland was born in Raleigh, North Carolina, and moved to Oberlin in 1834 where he, too, attended Oberlin College. The young men were invited to meet John Brown Jr. and, after a lengthy discussion, agreed to join John Brown's raiding party. Both Leary and Copeland were involved with John Langston in the Oberlin Anti-Slavery Society.

Leary was one Brown's first recruits who committed directly to the raid at Harpers Ferry. Copeland and he departed for Virginia on September 1859, to fight to free slaves. Leary, age twenty-five, and Copeland, age twenty-three, joined Brown's small band on a farm near Harpers Ferry in Virginia. They received about three weeks of training. The company was made up of twenty-two men, including John Brown and three of Brown's sons. Seventeen of the men were white. Five were African Americans and one of these, Shields Green, was a fugitive slave of pure African ancestry.

Green was acquainted with Frederick Douglass, the black abolitionist. He joined him in Chambersburg, Pennsylvania, where John Brown was to be the speaker. Brown was primarily interested in recruiting Douglass to be a part of the raid but was unsuccessful. However, he did recruit the young fugitive slave to join the party. Green was captured at Harpers Ferry and later executed. It was reported that he, like Copeland, was twenty-three.

Near midnight on Sunday, October 16, 1859, Leary and others under Brown's leadership entered the town of Harpers Ferry and seized the federal rifle factory, the armory where heavy military equipment was made, and the arsenal where guns and ammunition were stored. Leary, Copeland, and John Henry Kagi, a white raider, became isolated in the armory called Hall's Rifle Works. When things began to go wrong with the raid, the three men made a run for it, heading down to the Shenandoah River. But they were caught in crossfire. Kagi was killed, and Leary was shot several times. He was captured, but his wounds were so severe that he died the following morning. Before his death, he was able to dictate messages to his family. Copeland, too, was captured alive. Although he was tried, convicted, and sentenced to death, he impressed many with his courage. His dignity continued to the gallows.

A monument was erected by the citizens of Oberlin in honor of Leary, Copeland, and Shields. The eight-foot marble monument is located in Vine Street Park where it was moved in 1971. The Leary child would subsequently be educated by James Redpath and Wendell Phillips.

Family Legacy of Fighting Slavery

Leary also had other relatives who fought to end slavery. One was Aaron Revels, a soldier of African descent who fought in the American Revolution. His daughter, Sally Revels, was Lewis Leary's grandmother and Hiram Revels' aunt. Reverend Hiram Revels was an African Methodist Episcopal minister and a militant abolitionist. He eventually discontinued his connection with the African Methodists and joined the Methodist Episcopal North denomination. In 1870, he later became the first African American to be elected to the U.S. Senate.

Leary's relatives in North Carolina joined the Civil War effort and supported the Union troops. Seven family members, including Leary's brother John S. Leary, attached to James Montgomery's Brigade when the 1st North Carolina Colored Infantry became the 35th Regiment Infantry, U.S. Colored Troops (U.S.C.T.). James Montgomery was a former Kansas guerilla fighter associated with John Brown—one who was on his way to assist at Harpers Ferry until the battle ended too soon.

Brother John S. Leary became a representative of the North Carolina legislature in 1868. He then earned a law degree from Howard University and became the first African in America to be a member of the bar of North Carolina.

REFERENCES

Books

"Leary, Lewis (Sheridan)." In *Dictionary of American Negro Biography*. Eds. Rayford W. Logan and Michael R. Winston. New York: Norton, 1982.

Periodicals

"Blacks in the Harper's Ferry Raid." *Negro History Bulletin* 34 (October/November 1971): 315.

Online

"The 1859 Raid on the Federal Arsenal at Harpers Ferry." http://www.kouroo.info/page5.html (Accessed 2 December 2005).

"Charles Henry Langston and the African American Struggle in Kansas." Excerpt from *Kansas History* 22 (Winter 1999/2000): 268-83.http://www.kshs.org/publicat/history/1999winter_sheridan.htm (Accessed 2 December 2005).

"John Brown's Black Raiders." http://www.pbs.org/wgbh/aia/part4/4p2941.html (Accessed 2 December 2005).

"John Brown: The Conspirators Biographies." http://www3.iath.virginia.edu/jbrown/men.html (Accessed 2 December 2005).

Mattie McHollin

J. Kenneth Lee
1923–

Lawyer, civil rights activist

J. Kenneth Lee helped to chart the course of civil rights in the United States, particularly in the state of North Carolina. One of the first two blacks admitted to the University of North Carolina (UNC) at Chapel Hill's School of Law, he helped to open doors for others who followed him into the law profession in that state. He was legal counsel for over seventeen hundred civil rights lawsuits, including suits to integrate public elementary and secondary schools in North Carolina, and he defended students who began the sit-in movement in Greensboro. In

Chronology

1923	Born in Charlotte, North Carolina on November 1
1931	Moves to Hamlet, North Carolina
1944	Joins the U. S. Navy
1946	Receives B.S. from North Carolina A&T College
1949	Enrolls in law school at North Carolina College; joins in suit to desegregate law school at the University of North Carolina (UNC) at Chapel Hill
1950	Enrolls in UNC's law school
1957	Files successful suit to integrate Gillespie Park elementary school
1959	Opens American Federal Savings and Loan Association
1960s	Represents over 1,700 civil rights cases in North Carolina, including sit-in case in Greensboro
1973	Becomes first black member of North Carolina's banking commission
1985	Becomes first black inducted into Greensboro Business Leaders Hall of Fame

addition to his civil rights activities, he was a businessman who founded or helped to establish shopping centers, a nursing facility, rental and commercial property enterprises, and the state's first federally chartered savings and loan association. His efforts made it possible for blacks in Greensboro to secure enough money to build their own homes and establish businesses.

The thirteenth of fourteen children, John Kenneth Lee was born in Charlotte, North Carolina on November 1, 1923, to Henry Franklin Lee, a Church of God minister, and Sara Bell Lowdner Lee. The family was poor and lived on the $11 his father earned each week. When young Lee was six years old, the family moved to Hamlet, a small town in Richmond County, located near the South Carolina state line. Feeding the sizeable family was a struggle; sometimes young Lee watched his mother limit herself to tiny food portions so that there would be enough to go around. His father was determined that his children would be self-sufficient. For this to occur, his sons would learn to use their minds as well as their hands. To ensure that his daughters would not have to work in the kitchen for anyone, he saw that they became educated.

J. Kenneth Lee graduated from a small school with four grades that met in a Baptist church in Hamlet. There was no library to serve the students. As class valedictorian of Capital Highway High School in Hamlet in 1941, he had no difficulty being accepted as an electrical engineering student at North Carolina Agricultural and Technical (A&T) College, located in Greensboro. As poor as his family was, his father managed to save $33 for Lee's first semester expenses. Lee had never lived in a place with running water and electricity until he moved into a residence hall at A&T. Nor had he been in a laboratory

until his chemistry professor asked him to retrieve a Bunsen burner for him.

He attended college year round, but World War II interrupted Lee's undergraduate education when he was six weeks from graduation. He joined the U.S. Navy in 1944 and, while in training, married Nancy Young, a senior at nearby Bennett College for Women. Having grown up in a racially segregated society, Lee experienced segregation again in the navy. He went to the Pacific and served as a second mate electrician on the *USS Dade*, an attack transport vessel that had separate sleeping and dining facilities for the sailors. He was honorably discharged in 1946, returned to A&T, and received a B.S. in electrical engineering in that same year.

Lee continued to feel the effects of racial segregation, this time in employment. The South of the 1940s was not ready for a black engineer. Although engineering firms ran full-page advertisements for electrical engineers, black applicants were denied an opportunity for interview. Lee could find no engineering position in the local area and would not consider offers for employment that he received from around the country. He joined the faculty at A&T as professor of engineering but could not avoid the obvious restraints that a racially segregated community imposed. "Black people were doing all kinds of crazy things to exist," he told the *Greensboro News & Record*. At this time, blacks sat at the back of the bus, used the back door of restaurants if they were served at all, and those with college or graduate degrees were relegated to lesser jobs than their qualifications prepared them. Lee found conditions "hell certified by law," he said. "We knew that if you stayed on your side of the fence you could avoid the nastiness of segregation...but who wanted to live that way." He saw the legal system as a path toward a solution, and he considered becoming a lawyer.

In North Carolina blacks who sought a law degree had only one option—North Carolina College for Negroes (now North Carolina Central University) in Durham. Although the NAACP had attempted to integrate the law school at the University of North Carolina at Chapel Hill, the case was long and slow to weave its way through the courts. In 1949, he enrolled in the program at North Carolina College but signed on as a plaintiff in the NAACP's case against Chapel Hill. Floyd McKissick and several other blacks filed the suit but graduated from law school, which meant that no other plaintiffs were left. Lee intervened as a plaintiff in 1948-49. The case was heard in 1950, with Thurgood Marshall, later U.S. Supreme Court justice, as chief counsel for the NAACP's Legal Defense Fund (LDF). The blue-ribbon legal team of twenty-five or thirty lawyers also included Howard University's dean of the law school, Jack Greenberg of the LDF, and Constance Baker Motley (later a federal appeals court judge). The judge ruled against them and added, "I know ya'll should be admitted to the UNC law school, but someone other than me will have to sign it," Lee told the *News &*

Record. "It was the times," Lee said. On appeal, the court sided with the plaintiffs and the U.S. Supreme Court would not hear the case. Lee said in an interview for the Greensboro Public Library that "this was the initial integration of the law schools in the South." The case attracted national coverage. It also brought harassing statements from prominent white citizens from Greensboro who wrote to the plaintiffs as well as to the local press. After the case was settled, several members of the school's board of trustees resigned in protest. Eighteen months passed before desegregation took place.

Integrates Law School

In June 1950, Lee and Harvey E. Beech of Kinston, North Carolina, entered UNC and as a contingent of law enforcement officers escorted them into the dining hall, "everybody stopped, forks in mid-air," Lee said in his interview with Eugene E. Pfaff Jr. Their escorts continued for several months. Soon they moved about with little attention, but continued to face racism. At the football games, they were given tickets for the "colored" section behind the goal posts but went back to court and won the right to sit in the general student section. Chancellor Carmichael sent the tickets to them but cautioned, "I hope that you have sense enough not to use them." He said that the university would not be responsible if they were hit with a rock or if a riot occurred. Racism also worked itself into the law school courses at UNC. In one of Lee's classes, students sat in alphabetical order and were addressed by the professor as "mister," but the professor never addressed Lee, simply pointing to recognize him. "It hurt every time," said Lee. Lee passed the bar examination before his graduation in summer 1952 and was licensed in September; he deliberately missed the ceremony to work in Greensboro.

In 1953, Lee saw the peculiar way the state's legal system worked for blacks. He served as attorney for a black man in Alamance County who was accused of "reckless eyeballing" a white woman who walked by a field where the man was working. The woman and the worker did not speak to each other. When the case was heard, the judge, dressed in bibbed overalls and working without legal training, disregarded Lee's contention that there was "no such thing as reckless eyeballing" and sentenced him to two years. The case was reversed on appeal. As Lee handled many other civil rights cases, the road was always rough.

The court room was often a hostile environment for Lee, one filled with total lack of respect for him as a black lawyer. He recalled in the *News & Record* that on many occasions when he argued a case, jurors would look out the window. During his first jury case, involving five black men charged with killing a white sheriff's deputy in Moore County, the judge and other attorneys ignored a white spectator who had a double-barreled shotgun in easy view. Although the men had committed

the crime and Lee wanted to spare them the death penalty, Lee argued that their arraignment was improper. In the end, the man who actually pulled the trigger was sentenced to life in prison, and Lee was on his way to becoming a successful lawyer.

The late 1950s and early 1960s was a time of numerous civil rights cases in North Carolina and elsewhere. Whether a lawyer was white or black, anyone who advocated the rights of minorities was in danger. Lee became assistant legal counsel for the state NAACP; the other thirty to forty black lawyers in the state would not accept such a post. Lee became local counsel for the first suits to dismantle racial segregation in the state's public elementary and secondary schools. With his steady and compelling voice, he successfully represented five black children who, in 1957, sued to enter all-white Gillespie Park elementary school in Greensboro. As result, Josephine Boyd won admission to Greensboro Senior High School and the five black children were the state's first black students to attend previously all-white schools.

Defends Students of the Sit-In Movement

Beginning in 1960, Lee represented most of the seventeen hundred civil disobedience cases in the state. The movement began with the sit-ins at Woolworth's store in Greensboro, now the site of the International Civil Rights Museum; it was the first such civil disobedience to receive widespread notice at that time. Lee's son, Michael, was among those arrested. Lee's legal work with these cases was always pro bono. NAACP Legal Defense Fund attorney Thurgood Marshall reminded him that the fund spent $500,000 to enable Lee to integrate UNC's law school; therefore, what he did was simply payback. In time, the integration suits that Lee argued expanded to include swimming pools, golf courses, and other public venues.

Cross-burnings and fires disturbed Lee's family, who wondered if Lee would be harmed while out at night. The family also suffered from telephone calls claiming that Lee had been shot or was staked and unable to free himself. As Lee endured, he also saw contradictions in race relations. He had a strange relationship with Clyde "Hammer" Webster, the Grand Klud in charge of enforcement and security for the Ku Klux Klan. Webster, a carpenter, displayed KKK banners as he marched when Gillespie Park School was integrated and threw bottles though the glass in Lee's office windows. After Webster was convicted of vandalism and served a jail sentence, he came to Lee's office and announced that he had been fired from his job as chief carpenter for the firm hired to build Lee's new home. Lee hired Webster, who claimed to be a fine carpenter and one who would save Lee money. According to Lee in the *News & Record* article, Webster said "You and me ain't gonna never agree on race." When Webster's case was appealed and Lee was subpoenaed to talk about their time together, Webster's sentence was suspended. Outside the court room, Webster, surrounded by his KKK members, expended his hand to Lee and assured him that if "anybody in this town ever messes with you, all you got to do is call us." This was, in Lee's view, an "unholy alliance," but clearly it was meaningful for the telephone calls and threats ceased. Webster continued to picket Gillespie School the next fall.

Lee was partner in the Lee, High, Taylor, Dansby, and Stanback law firm. He decided to put to test his business acumen beyond the legal profession. In the 1940s he opened a theater in Salisbury, North Carolina, to give blacks a place to attend concerts by black performers; they had been denied access to the performances in Greensboro. In 1947, Lee opened a radio and electronics trade school in nearby Winston-Salem to prepare black veterans who wanted an education through the G.I. Bill. Successful in business, he was able to support his family well and to build homes in Greensboro, on a golf course in Pinehurst, and on the oceanfront in the Caribbean. With the help of his wife, Nancy, he maintained his businesses while in law school.

Later Lee tried to borrow $20,000 to build a $55,000 home in one of Greensboro's upscale black neighborhoods and was refused on the grounds that banks would lend no more than $13,000 to blacks. He researched mortgage loans granted in the city and found that only one bank had made a $13,500 loan to a black person. Immediately he set out to charter a savings and loan association to serve the needs of his race. After considerable planning, in 1959 he opened American Federal Savings and Loan Association, the state's first black, federally chartered savings and loan association. Now home-building opportunities for blacks boomed, and blacks could build sizeable homes if they wished. They used their homes as collateral on loans and established businesses of their own.

Through Lee's ingenuity, in 1960 President Richard Nixon persuaded the chair of the A&P grocery chain to anchor the Cumberland shopping center that Lee was developing near his alma mater, A&T College. This may have been the first time the chain was anchored in such a black business enterprise in the South. In addition, Lee helped to develop in Greensboro the Lincoln Grove Shopping Center and founded the Carolina Nursing Center. The nursing facility was the largest black-owned nursing home in the state. He also helped to build the North Carolina Mutual Building in Greensboro. In 1973, he became the first black to serve on North Carolina's banking commission. Through his efforts, the state issued a $2.2 billion tax exempt bond that financed more than 55,000 new homes for low-to-moderate-income families. In honor of his mother, who died when he was a college freshman, Lee helped to build the Sarah Lee Fitness Center at the Hayes-Taylor YMCA located on the corner of A&T's campus. The Dudley-Lee Complex, a modern office complex facility in the vicinity of A&T, honors his son Michael as well as the founders of Dudley Products, a thriving cosmetics and hair care products business based in Kernersville.

A Republican, in the early 1950s Lee made a successful bid in the primary election for city council but withdrew when another black and a local doctor, William Hampton, also ran. He felt Greensboro was not ready for two blacks on its council.

Lee was honored in 1985 when he became the first black inducted into the Greensboro Business Leaders Hall of Fame. He has received numerous other recognitions, as attested to by the plaques that once lined his office walls: one honoring him as a founding member of the Southeastern Lawyers' Association (for blacks in the legal profession), and others honoring his influential work in law, civil rights, business, and community.

Among the organizations in which he held office or had an association are the North Carolina Housing Finance Agency (vice-chair); Southeastern Lawyers' Association (founding member); A&T Alumni Association (founding member); and North Carolina Banking Commission (board member).

In later years, Lee's personal life began to suffer; his wife, Nancy Young Lee, who was an elementary school teacher in Greensboro, was for several years confined to a highly skilled nursing home until she died in July 2005. The stroke that Lee suffered on September 11, 2001 made him unable to care for his wife. Their son Michael, an attorney, died in 1995. Lee's granddaughter, Michele Bonds, carried on the legal legacy. Lee continues some involvement in legal matters. He likes to recall the events that shaped the direction that civil rights took in North Carolina and in the nation, and he wants people to remember that there was a time when there was no recourse for blacks in the eyes of the law. He was never deterred by the legal system that worked against him. To survive, however, he turned to real estate ventures and banking. He also worked to bring about social change—not by demonstrating hostility and anger but by quiet resolve and deliberate moves that resulted in his having a place in history as a civil rights legend.

REFERENCES

Periodicals

"Kenneth Lee: Dismantling the Walls of Prejudice." [Greensboro] *News & Record*, 24 March 2002.

Online

Humphrey, Lillian L., and Winona L. Fletcher. "Offshoot: The H. F. Lee Family Book." www.offshoots-hfleefamilybook.info/menu.htm (3 September 2005).

Interviews

Lee, J. Kenneth. Interview with Eugene E. Pfaff Jr. Oral History Collection, Greensboro (N.C.) Public Library.

——. Interview with Helena Carney Lambeth, January 1, 2004.

——. Interview with Jessie Carney Smith, August 5, 2005.

Collections

J. Kenneth Lee donated his papers to the International Civil Rights Museum to be housed in Greensboro when completed. The Southern Historical Collection, at the University of North Carolina at Chapel Hill, contain papers related to Lee's lawsuit to attend the university's law school; they include copies of court papers, photographs of Lee and Harvey Beech registering and attending class, and news clippings describing the court battle and the university's reactions. A portrait of Lee and his four classmates hangs in the law school at the university.

Jessie Carney Smith

LaSalle Leffall
1930–

Oncologist, surgeon

LaSalle Leffall is one of the leading cancer surgeons in the world. The first black president of the American Cancer Society and the American College of Surgeons, Leffall, born and raised in the Jim Crow South, has broken many racial barriers with his research, work as a surgeon, and teaching. Leffall has won numerous awards and has earned the admiration of those in and out of the medical establishment around the world for devoting his career to the study of cancer, particularly its high rates among African Americans.

LaSalle Leffall was born in Tallahassee, Florida to educators LaSalle Leffall Sr. and Martha Jordan Leffall, who met when they were students at Alabama Teachers College. LaSalle Leffall Sr. was the only child in his family out of eleven children to attend college. As a child, Leffall Jr. was urged by his father to go into the field of medicine. "My folks, particularly my father, said that he and my mother as teachers were doing something imparting knowledge but a physician could do so much more," Leffall Jr. told the *Washington Post*. Leffall Sr. always told his two children, LaSalle Jr. and Delores, "With a good education and hard work combined with honesty

Chronology	
1930	Born in Tallahassee, Florida on May 22
1945	Graduates from high school as valedictorian
1948	Graduates summa cum laude from Florida A&M College
1952	Graduates at the top of the class from Howard University Medical School; interns at Homer G. Lewis Hospital in St. Louis
1953	Serves as an assistant surgical resident at the Freedman's Hospital in Washington D.C.
1954	Serves as assistant surgical resident at Washington D.C. General Hospital
1956	Serves as chief surgical resident at Freedman's Hospital
1957	Serves as a senior fellow in cancer surgery at Memorial Sloan-Kettering Hospital
1960	Serves as chief general surgeon in U.S. Army while stationed in Germany
1962	Joins Howard University's faculty
1970	Appointed chairman of the Department of Surgery at Howard University
1978	Testifies before the Health Subcommittee of the Senate Human Resources Committee about his research on cancer rates among African Americans
1979	Becomes the first African American president of the American Cancer Society
1994	Becomes the first African American president of the American College of Surgeons
1996	Howard University establishes an endowed chair of surgery in Leffall's name
1997	Donates $350,000 to Florida A&M University, the largest donation from a single contributor in the university's history
2005	Releases autobiography, *No Boundaries: A Cancer Surgeon's Odyssey*

and integrity, there are no boundaries." The younger Leffall, who was growing up in the segregated South in Quincy, Florida, was skeptical of this advice. Leffall's father acknowledged his son's skepticism but urged his son to heed this advice, which he repeated to his children until they were grown.

Skipping second grade and completing high school in three years enabled Leffall to graduate high school in 1945 as valedictorian and start college at Florida Agricultural & Mechanical College (now University and known as FAMU) at age fifteen. Leffall, who was bound for medical school, was also part of the college's basketball team. His heroes in college were Joe Louis and Paul Robeson, and he enjoyed the writings of Frank Yerby.

As a senior, Leffall applied to Meharry Medical College in Nashville, Tennessee and Howard University in Washington, D.C. His first choice, Meharry Medical College, was the school that Dr W. S. Stevens, the only black physician in Quincy and the husband of Leffall's godmother, urged him to attend. Leffall was not accepted to Meharry. His grades were excellent, but he only did slightly better than average on his admissions test, since he had not been exposed to much of its content in his undergraduate career. Leffall and George Rawls, another student at Florida A&M who had a 4.0 GPA and was a good friend of Leffall's, were both denied admission to Howard University. Dr. William H. Gray Jr., Florida A&M's president, went to Washington, D.C. and demanded to know from both the Howard president and dean why Leffall and Rawls were not accepted. A week later, Leffall and Rawls received acceptance letters. Leffall graduated summa cum laude from Florida A&M in 1948 and both he and Rawls went on to Howard University Medical School.

Attends Medical School, Begins Career

In October 1951, while Leffall was in medical school, his father died of a massive stroke. Not long before his death, Leffall Sr. told his son that he and the family would attend Leffall Jr.'s graduation in June 1952. The death of Leffall's father resulted in his not having tuition money to continue his medical education. Leffall contacted Walter Beneke, a wealthy businessman whom he had met while working as a waiter and bartender at a golf club on Nantucket in the summers of 1950 and 1951. He asked Beneke for a $500 loan; a few days later, Beneke sent the young medical student a check for $500 with a note stating that the money was not a loan, but a gift and asked Leffall for two things: to help someone else out financially someday and to become a fine physician. Also during Leffall's final year of medical school at Howard, he met his future wife, Ruth McWilliams, who had recently graduated from Virginia Union College. She met Leffall in the emergency room of Howard University's hospital. Leffall and McWilliams married on August 18, 1956. Their only child, LaSalle Doheny Leffall III, was born on January 6, 1963.

After graduating first in his class at Howard Medical School in 1952, Leffall interned at Homer G. Phillips Hospital in St. Louis. He served as an assistant surgical resident at the Freedman's Hospital in Washington, D.C. from 1953 to 1954. Then he went on to be an assistant surgical resident at Washington, D.C. General Hospital from 1954 to 1955. Leffall returned to Freedman's Hospital where he was by then a chief surgical resident from 1956 to 1957. From 1957 to 1959, Leffall was a senior fellow in cancer surgery at Memorial Sloan-Kettering Hospital. He served a year in the army as chief of general surgery from 1960 to 1961. Leffall came back to the United States and joined Howard University's faculty in 1962 and became involved in the local American Cancer Society in Washington, D.C. In 1970, he was appointed chairman of the Department of Surgery. In 1992, Leffall was named the Charles R. Drew professor of surgery. This position was the first endowed chair in the surgery department's history. Leffall became the first African American president of the American Cancer Society in 1979, and in 1994, he became the first African American president of the American College of Surgeons. In 1996,

Howard University established an endowed chair of surgery in Leffall's name.

In 1978, Leffall testified before the Health Subcommittee of the Senate Human Resources Committee about his research on cancer rates among African Americans. Leffall told the subcommittee that African Americans have higher incidences of lung, colon, rectum, and prostate cancer than their white counterparts, and African American males have the highest prostate cancer rate in the world. Leffall stresses prevention by encouraging African Americans to get tests such as colonoscopies in order to detect the disease early.

Bedside Manner

Leffall's personality has won over many. During his senior fellowship at Memorial Sloan-Kettering Hospital, Leffall encountered a challenging incident with a wealthy, white female patient who had advanced uterine cancer. The patient refused to let Leffall examine her. The chief surgeon, Dr. Brunswick, who was scheduled to operate on her the next day, threatened to immediately discharge the woman unless she allowed Leffall to examine her. After her operation, the woman apologized to Leffall for her prejudice and the two became good friends.

Despite achieving such a distinguished career, Leffall did not become arrogant. In bestowing the first Society of Surgical Oncology's Heritage Award to Leffall in March of 2001, Edward M. Copeland III recalled the first time he met the cordial Leffall on a tennis court and how surprised he was when Leffall knew his name. Leffall's sister, Dorothy, a librarian, proudly recounted to the *Washington Post* the time in childhood when her brother healed an injured bird.

Dr. Leffall in his busy life has found time to go to schools and talk to students in both primary and secondary schools on the matter of achieving their dreams by focusing on their education. Having already become a fine physician, Leffall was to grant Walter Beneke's other request for the favor that Beneke did for him so many years ago. In 1997, Leffall gave the profits of a very successful investment to Florida A&M University for a scholarship fund. The $350,000 gift was the largest donation from an individual in the university's history. The only criteria that he established was that applicants were not to be discriminated against on the basis of race, religion, or gender.

Celebrates Life and Work

Leffall serves on the boards of many civic and profession organizations, including the medical advisory board of the Cancer Research and Prevention Foundation, as a trustee of the National Health Museum, and a member of the Scientific Advisory Committee of the Lance Armstrong Foundation. He has authored or co-authored over 130 articles and chapters. His autobiography, *No Bound-*

aries: A Cancer Surgeon's Odyssey was published in 2005 by Howard University Press.

REFERENCES

Periodicals

Copeland III, Edward M. "LaSalle D. Leffall, Jr., MD, FACS: The First Heritage Award Winner, Society of Surgical Oncology." *Annals of Surgical Oncology* 8 (2001): 477-79.

"Dr. LaSalle Leffall Jr. Chair Established at Howard University Medical School; Dr. Clive Callender Named to the Chair." *Jet*, 1 April 1996.

Trescott, Jacqueline. "The Special Spirit of the Surgeon: Howard's Dr. LaSalle Leffall." *Washington Post*, 5 February 1986.

Online

"About Us: Board of Directors" Cancer Research and Prevention Foundation. http://www.preventcancer. org/about/board.cfm (Accessed 1 November 2005).

"Dr. LaSalle Leffall: Biography." The Historymakers. http://www.thehistorymakers.com/biography/ biography.asp?bioindex=758&category=medical Makers (Accessed 1 November 2005).

"The Museum: Our Board." The National Health Museum. http://www.nationalhealthmuseum.org/ themuseum/board.html (Accessed 1 November 2005).

"Scientific Advisory Committee." The Lance Armstrong Foundation. http://www.livestrong.org/site/c. jvKZLbMRIsG/b.736603/k.BDAF/Advisory_ Committee.htm (Accessed November 1, 2005).

"Testimony of LaSalle D. Leffall, Jr., M.D. President-Elect, American Cancer Society Before the Health Subcommittee of the Senate Human Resources Committee." Tobacco Documents Online. http:// tobaccodocuments.org/lor/03603570-3576.html (Accessed 1 November 2005).

Brandy Baker

Theophilus Lewis
1891–1974

Drama critic

Theophilus Lewis was a drama critic of the Harlem Renaissance era. Lewis was passionate about theater and thought that it should reflect the values of the black culture. In an article on Lewis, Theodore Kornweibel stated that Lewis wanted to provide "an ideology for the

Theophilus Lewis

development of a national black theater which would be both a source of a racial ethos and repository of the race's genius." He wrote a monthly review in the periodical the *Messenger*, one of the first periodicals to have a regular column devoted to theater. For many years, he wrote for several black and Catholic periodicals. Lewis wrote short stories, poetry, and book reviews.

Theophilus Lewis, a native of Baltimore, was born March 4, 1891. He attended the public schools in Baltimore and New York City. He served in the American Expeditionary Force overseas during World War I. As a young teen, Lewis developed a love for theater and attended shows whenever he could afford them. Lewis was a self-taught man who received no formal training.

Lewis's affiliation with the *Messenger* had an interesting beginning. Upon moving to New York, Lewis met A. Phillip Randolph and Chandler Owen, who later became the publishers of the *Messenger*. During this period, the 1920s, there were two prominent theaters in Harlem, the Lincoln and Lafayette, which Lewis attended. He shared his review with the publishers and they were very impressed. They asked him if he would write a monthly column for their new publication. The publishers had no money, but they offered to purchase the theater tickets for Lewis. Lewis accepted this arrangement.

Although Lewis was passionate about theater and wrote a column in the *Messenger* from 1923 until 1927,

Chronology

1891	Born in Baltimore on March 4
1923-27	Drama critic for the *Messenger*
1933	Marries; ultimately fathers three children
1939	Converts to Catholicism; begins writing in Catholic magazines
1974	Dies on September 3

he was never compensated for his work. He supported his passion with manual labor jobs and later became a postal worker in New York City.

Uses the *Messenger* as a Voice

Lewis reviewed plays and discussed the importance of black culture in his column. He wrote about black theater productions and voiced his concerns regarding the portrayal of blacks in black theater and how white playwrights portrayed blacks. Many early plays reviewed by Lewis were written by white playwrights and had little or no black representation.

Lewis was very critical of certain trends during this era. While he liked comedy and the musical revues, he viewed them as having a lower standard than drama. He disapproved of racial stereotypes or the portrayal of light-skinned women in many black theater and white productions. He wanted the productions to reflect a serious perspective of the life of blacks and the culture. He blamed the playwrights for not using the considerable talent of the few black actors in a more productive manner.

Lewis thought that with the development of a national African American theater many of the stereotypes would disappear. It was his perception that an African American theater would be different in terms of materials and audience, and plays would be based on the experience and culture of African Americans. He hoped that such work would establish the worth of the African American playwright.

In 1924, Lewis stated that the play, *Rosanne*, was one of the first plays to present blacks in a human manner. He was impressed with the quality of this play and how it depicted a black character with realism.

Family Life and Writings

Lewis married in 1933 and became the father of three children: Selma Marie, Alfred Charles, and Lowell Francis. While the literature contains no information about his wife, Lewis periodically made reference to his children in his column "Plays and Point of View" in the magazine *International Review*.

In 1939, Lewis converted to Catholicism and began writing in many Catholic magazines including *Catholic World*, *Commonweal* and *America*. Lewis also wrote for many Negro presses and periodicals, including the renowned *Pittsburgh Courier* and *People's Voice*, for over fifty years. Lewis appreciated drama that presented an honest, realistic portrayal of the culture of African Americans. He was especially fond of Eugene O'Neil's *The Emperor Jones* and *All God's Chillun Got Wings*.

While Lewis was known mostly for his reviews of drama, he also wrote and coauthored short stories. Of notable interest is his work with George S. Schuyler. They coauthored a satirical column entitled "Shafts and Darts."

In spite of his talent and love of theater Lewis was never ever able to make his living solely as a critic. He continued to work and ultimately retired as a postal worker. He also continued to write reviews for many Catholic publications until a few years before his death in 1974. His legacy will be that of a dedicated self taught critic who made an indelible impression on African American theater.

REFERENCES

Books

Black Writers. Detroit: Gale Research, 1989.

Contemporary Authors. Vol. 125. Detroit: Gale Research, 1989.

Kornweibel, Theodore Jr. "Theophilus Lewis and the Theater of the Harlem Renaissance." In *The Harlem Renaissance Remembered*. Ed. Arna Bontemps. New York: Dodd, Mead, 1972.

Online

Scally, Sister Mary Anthony. "Theophilus Lewis." *Negro Catholic Writers, 1900-1943*. http://www. nathanielturner.com/negrocatholicwriterssources3. htm (Accessed 26 February 2006).

Theodosia T. Shields

J. W. Loguen
1813–1872

Minister, abolitionist

Jermain Wesley Loguen was born into slavery, and had no formal education skills when he and a friend decided to run away from Tennessee. Having to rely on the help of others to complete their journey northwards, the two runaways soon realized how poorly prepared they were to successfully navigate the journey they had undertaken. As soon as Lougen reached Detroit, he was

Chronology

1813	Born on a plantation near Nashville, Tennessee on February 5
1834	Runs away; escapes to Canada after a lengthy and dangerous journey
1836	Moves from Canada to New York
1837	Enters the Oneida Institute, Utica, New York
1839	Becomes minister in the African Methodist Episcopal Zion Church
1840	Marries Caroline Storum
1848	Buys half-acre of ground on which to build a school house
1851	Involved in the Jerry Rescue; flees to Canada to avoid indictment
1852	Returns from Canada without pardon
1859	Publishes autobiography *The Reverend J. W. Lougen, as a Slave and as a Freeman: A Narrative of Real Life*
1868	Elected to the office of bishop at the American Methodist Episcopal Zion General Conference
1872	Dies in Saratoga Springs, New York on September 30

determined to get an education and then set out to teach others and promote abolition through his efforts with the Underground Railroad. He later became a bishop in the American Methodist Episcopal Zion Church and wrote articles for African American journals.

Jermain Wesley Loguen began life as a slave February 5, 1813, near Nashville, Tennessee, on a plantation/distillery belonging to David Logue. "Jarm," as he was called on the plantation, was the son of a slave named Cherry (formerly Jane) from Ohio and David Logue, a Tennessee plantation owner. Jane remembered being hoisted into a wagon filled with many other terrified children and afterward being sold to three very rough and crude men: David, Manasseth, and Carnes Logue. Initially, she lived on the rundown plantation and distillery with them and their mother. After the other two brothers sold their shares to David, Cherry worked only for him.

Cherry, like most slaves, knew little of her lineage or heritage, since slavery had separated her from family and identity. Slave marriages were seldom recorded and master to slave marriage was forbidden because of miscegenation laws. But if master-slave intercourse occurred, the relationship and the offspring were usually not publicly acknowledged. During childhood, Jarm, the son of the master, did receive recognition and kindness from his father, primarily because he resembled his father so strongly. As Jarm grew older, however, he was frequently beaten and misused, and suffered life-threatening injuries at the hands of his father and uncles.

The destiny of slaves was entirely in the hands of their masters and such was the case with Jarm. He, his mother, and her other children were placed with Manasseth Logue even though Dave had promised that he would not sell them. When he was about to lose the family planta-

tion, Dave failed to stand by that promise. Soon all of the black Logues were living at Manasseth's plantation and distillery. Manasseth's slaves, including Cherry and her children, were constantly subjected to beatings and torture as a result of his liquor-induced rages.

Life at Manasseth's

Like that of his brother, Manasseth's property consisted of a plantation and distillery. Distilleries by their very nature were subject to fire, and soon after the black Logues arrived at Manasseth Plantation, the distillery burned to the ground, leaving the white Logues short on cash. Even though Manasseth had promised his brother to keep Cherry and her children together, he began to feel his losses after the distillery burned and, determined to turn a profit, he arranged for the sale of Jarm's younger siblings to traders.

The events that followed the sale and the break up of the family ushered in the worst of times for both Cherry and Jarm. Cherry was beaten like an animal when she tried to prevent her children from being taken and was devastated by the separation when she failed. Jarm, as he was still called, was nearly beaten to death (so painful was his suffering that he cried out, "Kill me, Kill me"). Manasseth regretted the beating, once he had sobered up, and his treatment of Jarm improved markedly. Jarm was then mortgaged to one Mr. Preston—a name invented in his autobiography for a well-known man that he did not want to expose. It was after his experience with the Preston family that Jarm began to plot his escape from Manasseth and slavery.

Jarm was keenly aware of his own worth and this coupled with a newfound hatred of all servitude made him determined to seek freedom or die trying. Sometime during 1834, he heard from a childhood friend that there was a free state nearby called Illinois and that he could get there on horseback in less than a week. Jarm and two friends—John Farney and Jerry, a slave—decided to flee. Before they set off, however, Jerry decided he could not leave his wife and children. His withdrawal, which took away a third of the resources, put the enterprise in jeopardy, but despite shortness of funds, John and Jarm departed.

Flight North

Although the two had planned to arrive in Illinois within the week, a series of misadventures plagued the travelers and extended the journey. First, they narrowly missed recapture by slave catchers and nearly drowned while crossing the partly frozen Ohio River into Indiana. Later they lost their way and wandered back south toward their starting point in Tennessee where they were again in danger of being retaken. Finally, after many days of hunger, cold, and fear, they again reached Indiana. Here they spent three very comfortable weeks in a Quaker village and received advice and directions for fleeing north into Canada. Following the North Star, as instructed by one of the Quakers, they continued their northward journey. Passing through thick woodlands, they came upon Indians—some of whom were helpful, while others merely ignored them. From this point on, they asked no one for directions. Meeting a hunter during their ramblings in the wild, Jarm and John learned that they were lost again. Though weather conditions had frequently obscured the North Star, the two were heading toward the North Pole, but drifting westward. As the hunter directed, Jarm and John traveled southeasterly and arrived in Detroit, Michigan, with about fifty cents between them. Jarm and John separated to find obscure, affordable lodgings. Jarm crossed over into Canada and John stayed in Detroit; here John lodged with several unscrupulous men who took his horse and Jarm's saddle. The men knew no action would be lodged against them because John was obviously a runaway. Distraught over the loss of the horse and saddle and obsessed by the desire to get them back, John and Jarm parted ways, never seeing each other again.

Life in Canada

Jarm's fortunes took a happier turn when he settled in Hamilton, Ontario, Canada, where he took a $10-a-month job clearing land for a nearby farmer. Neighbors were impressed with Jarm's diligence and hard work, and as a reward he was admitted to the Sabbath School to learn to read and subsequently attended Ancaster where he received the title of Bible reader. Jarm, now about twenty-four years old, took on a new name to match his new station in life. He added an "n" to his father's sir name and used Jarmain instead of Jarm (his slave name), and he took Wesley as his middle name to satisfy his Methodist friends.

In 1836, Loguen moved from Canada to New York and worked at a variety of positions: farmer, proprietor, porter, and confidential servant at the Rochester House, the grand hotel of Rochester, New York. Talking to hotel patrons, Loguen began to gain a broader knowledge of freedom, slavery, and politics. Realizing his own lack of knowledge, Loguen decided to enter Oneida Institute around 1837, to study with the distinguished Reverend F. P. Rogers. Following his third winter under Rogers' tutelage, Loguen had grasped the larger issues of slavery and gone to Utica to investigate the situation of fellow blacks and to establish a school for their children.

While teaching a class of Sunday scholars, Loguen made the acquaintance of Caroline Storum, who was there visiting friends. The two grew close and married in 1840. By then Loguen had become a minister in the African Methodist Episcopal Zion (AMEZ) Church and preached throughout the area around Bath and Ithaca. He also represented the Liberty Party, an abolitionist group that developed in 1840. Its supporters wanted to put an immediate end to slavery. By 1844, Loguen was an anti-slavery lecturer and in 1846, when he returned to Syracuse, he began preaching to the African Methodists.

Loguen bought a half-acre of land in 1848. A house may have already occupied part of the land, but the rest was reserved for a schoolhouse. Mrs. Loguen joined her husband in Syracuse around this time, and they built an apartment for runaway slaves that became an important station on the Underground Railroad.

After passage of the Fugitive Slave and the Compromise Acts of 1850, a biracial committee was formed to protect fugitives entering Syracuse. Loguen spoke strongly against the acts and explained the danger that he and all runaways would face if the legislation passed. In October 1851, the Vigilance Committee and the Onondaga County Agricultural Society were meeting in Syracuse. Suddenly the church bells started to toll, a signal that slave catchers were present. Soon it was announced that a fugitive, Jerry, had been taken. Jerry was handcuffed and taken to the commissioner's office where he learned the reason for his arrest. Loguen, coordinating a rescue effort, urged fugitives and blacks, if whites would not help, to strike down officials or die trying. A great mob formed and the Jerry Rescue, as it was called, got underway. Violence soon broke out and several people were injured, including Jerry himself. Afterwards Jerry was moved continuously to avoid being retaken. He stayed a while in Mexico but returned to New York and sailed on a British boat to Canada where he remained until his death from tuberculosis on October 8, 1853.

In the weeks following, twenty-five persons were charged for their role in the Jerry Rescue. All but seven of the men fled to Canada, including Loguen. From Canada, Loguen wrote the governor of New York asking for permission to return to Syracuse and promising that he would stand trial for his role in rescuing Jerry but asking for a guarantee that he would not be tried as a fugitive slave. Governor Hunt refused, but Loguen returned to his family during the spring of 1852 anyway.

By 1855, Jermain and Caroline Lougen had six children ranging in age from one to thirteen. Additionally they housed three other adults. Loguen, despite his full household, continued to operate the Syracuse Underground Railroad, reputed to be the central depot for the entire state of New York, and Loguen was dubbed the "Underground Railroad King."

Prior to the Civil War, Loguen distinguished himself in other ways. He became the general agent of Syracuse's Fugitive Aide Society, he sought employment for slaves, and in 1868 he was elected bishop at the AMEZ General Conference. Once the war broke out, he was able to field a company of African Americans called the "Lougen's Guards." Lougen published articles in several African American newspapers and had his own autobiography, *The Reverend J. W. Lougen, as a Slave and as a Free-*

man: A Narrative of Real Life, published in 1859. In 1872, he planned to begin new mission work on the Pacific Coast. But learning that he had tuberculosis, he went to Saratoga Springs for a cure at the mineral springs. He died there on September 30, 1872 and was buried in the Oakwood Cemetery.

REFERENCES

Online

Hunter, Carol M. "The Rev. Jermain Loguen: A Narrative of Real Life." Afro-Americans in New York Life and History 13 (July 1989), 33-46. http://www.math.buffalo.edu/~sww/0history/loguen. jermain.wesley.html (Accessed 13 March 2006).

Lougen, Jermain Wesley. *The Reverend J. W. Lougen, as a Slave and as a Freeman: A Narrative of Real Life*. Syracuse, N.Y.: J. G. K. Truair & Co., 1859. http://docsouth.unc.edu/neh/loguen/loguen.html (Accessed 13 March 2006).

Lois A. Peterson

Chronology	
1922	Born in Valdosta, Georgia on August 16
1939	Attends Paine College, Augusta, Georgia
1942	Receives B.A. from Paine College
1943	Receives M.A. from American University
1947	Receives Ph.D. from Yale University; returns to Georgia, teaches philosophy at Georgia State University; becomes newspaper reporter for the *Baltimore Afro-American* and the *Chicago American*
1958	Leaves the *Baltimore Afro-American*
1959	Becomes a freelance writer for the *Amsterdam News* and *Harper's Magazine*
1960	Publishes first book entitled *The Reluctant African*
1962	Publishes *The Negro Revolt*
1963	Publishes *When the Word Is Given: A Report on Elijah Muhammad, Malcolm X, and the Black Muslim World*
1964-68	Hosts weekly television talk show in Los Angeles, California
1965	Co-hosts with Mike Wallace *The Hate that Hate Produced*, a documentary on Malcolm X and the Nation of Islam
1968	Publishes *To Kill A Black Man*
1970	Dies in car accident near Santa Rosa, New Mexico on July 30

Louis E. Lomax
1922–1970

Journalist, civil rights activist

Louis E. Lomax is perhaps best known for his journalism and books. His commitment to the civil rights struggle of the 1960s is reflected in his work and should be considered a notable achievement for a journalist. Through his news editorials in such publications as the *Baltimore Afro-American*, the *Chicago American*, and *Harper's*, his impact on the movement continues. Of equal importance are his books: *The Reluctant African*, *The Negro Revolt*, *When the Word Is Given: A Report on Elijah Muhammad, Malcolm X, and the Black Muslim World*, *Thailand: The War that Is, The War that Will Be*, and his final work *To Kill a Black Man*. For his scholarly contributions and tireless effort in the human struggle for civil rights, Lomax should be counted among the notable African American scholar activists of his time.

Louis E. Lomax was born on August 16, 1922 in Valdosta, Georgia. His parents were Sarah Louise Smith Lomax and Emanuel C. Lomax, both of Georgia. As the nation entered the Second World War, Lomax chose to take a different route from many African Americans he knew. Instead of enlisting, Lomax entered Paine College in Augusta, Georgia. After completing his B.A. at Paine, Lomax left the South to pursue graduate studies. He

received an M.A. in 1944 from American University, and by 1947, he had attained a Ph.D. from Yale University.

The Early Years with the Black Press

Immediately after completion of his doctorate, Lomax returned to Georgia to teach philosophy at Georgia State College in Savannah. His tenure at the college was short, though; he left academia to for the world of journalism. His first job as a journalist was with the *Baltimore Afro-American* and the *Chicago American*. He worked as a reporter for ten years for both newspapers. During those years he covered lynchings, riots, and leadership conflicts within the African American community.

In 1955, Lomax covered the murder of Emmett Till, the Chicago youth who was slain in Mississippi for his alleged disrespect toward a white woman. Emmett Till was murdered while he was visiting relatives during the summer of 1955. Lomax's coverage drew the attention of the Federal Bureau of Investigation (FBI). The FBI was also suspicious of Lomax because of how he covered the murder of several other African American men during the same period, raising questions about the FBI agents who seemed according to Lomax to be disinterested in solving the crimes. The cases pertained to Reverend George Wesley Lee, Gus Courts, Lamar "Ditney" Smith, and Amos Reece. Lee, Courts, and Smith were killed while trying to recruit black voters in Mississippi. Amos Reece, a resident of Cobb County, Georgia, was convicted of raping a white woman. Lomax gave each case attention in articles he wrote for the *Baltimore Afro-American* and the *Chicago American*.

In the 1960s Lomax was a freelance writer, working in both the mainstream and black presses. He also was publishing books with topics that ranged from political controversy in the black community to the crisis in Thailand. Then, too, Lomax's coverage and increasing criticism of black leadership began to extend beyond his editorial statements. In 1962, he published *The Negro Revolt*, an elaboration of earlier articles in which he examined black leadership. Lomax believed that the Negro revolt involved more than active resistance against white domination. It also included a revolt of the Negro masses against their own leadership and goals. He analyzed leading civil rights groups of the day, including the NAACP, Urban League, Southern Christian Leadership Conference (SCLC), Student Non-Violent Coordinating Committee (SNCC), and the Nation of Islam (NOI). In Lomax's view the revolt expressed black frustration with the traditional leadership organizations whose tactics had grown obsolete by the mid-1950s. Younger, more radical leadership tended to reject the elitist thinking of its leadership. Many young people in the civil rights period wanted to adopt a militant stance against segregation. Leaders such as Whitney Young of the Urban League and Malcolm X of the Nation of Islam attracted young radical activists. In Lomax's view established leaders such as Roy Wilkins of the NAACP, labor leader A. Philip Randolph, and SCLC leaders needed to broaden their ideology as well as their tactics.

In the 1960s Lomax was involved with Malcolm X and Martin Luther King Jr.. He co-hosted with Mike Wallace the documentary *The Hate that Hate Produced,* which focused on the Nation of Islam, its leadership, and the black community. In 1963 he published *When the Word Is Given: A Report on Elijah Muhammad, Malcolm X, and the Black Muslim World*. The book provided details about the Nation of Islam leader Elijah Muhammad and his appeal to a segment of the black population.

Tragically Lomax died in a car accident. The accident happened two years after the 1968 release of his book *To Kill a Black Man*, which examined the lives and assassinations of his close friends Malcolm X and Martin Luther King Jr. Lomax named the people he suspected to be the killers, and some people speculated that his death was the consequence of his investigation.

REFERENCES

Periodicals

"Funeral Services Held for Writer Louis Lomax," *Baltimore Afro-American*, 4 August 1970.

Collections

The Louis Lomax Papers are in the Ethnicity and Race Manuscript Collection at University of Nevada at Reno.

The Louis Lomax File at Federal Bureau of Investigation, Freedom of Information Privacy Library is available online at www.fbi.gov.

Baiyina W. Muhammad

Michael L. Lomax
1947–

Association executive, college president

A versatile man who appears to have been groomed early on for the life he led in later years, Michael L. Lomax has been a leader in politics, arts, and education. As a political leader, Lomax was the first African American to lead a major county government in Georgia, having become chair of the Fulton County Board of Commissioners. As a patron of the arts and arts administrator, he founded the world-class National Black Arts Festival in Atlanta. As a teacher, he enhanced the education of hundreds of students in colleges and universities in Atlanta and Athens, Georgia. As an educational leader, he headed and strengthened historically black Dillard University. Through his position as president and chief executive office of the United Negro College Fund, Lomax continues his support of historically black colleges and universities and their students, faculties, and leaders.

Born in Los Angeles on October 2, 1947, Michael Lucius Lomax and his family relocated from Los Angeles to Atlanta in 1964. When he was only sixteen years old, Lomax enrolled in Morehouse College, a historically black college for men in Atlanta, Georgia. He excelled there, graduating in 1968 magna cum laude with a bachelor of arts degree in English and membership in Phi Beta Kappa. He continued his studies at Columbia University where he was awarded a master of arts degree in English literature. Later, he enrolled in Emory University and in 1984 received a Ph.D. in American and Afro-American literature.

By the 1970s Lomax had become interested in public service and began his work in that area in Atlanta. The posts that he held early on included director of research and special assistant to Mayor Maynard Jackson. He became speechwriter for Jackson in 1973, during Jackson's first campaign for mayor of Atlanta. From 1975 to 1978, Lomax was director of parks, libraries, and cultural and international affairs for Atlanta. He was successful in his bid for a seat on Fulton County's Board of Commissioners in 1978. His interest in the arts led to his success in sponsoring legislation in 1979 to create the Fulton

Chronology

1947	Born in Los Angeles, California on October 2
1968	Graduates magna cum laude, Phi Beta Kappa, from Morehouse College; later earns M.A. from Columbia University
1969	Marries Pearl Cleage
1973	Becomes speech writer for Maynard Jackson's first mayoral campaign
1975-78	Directs parks, libraries, and cultural and international affairs for city of Atlanta
1978-81	Serves as member at large of the Fulton County Arts Council
1979	Sponsors legislation to create the Fulton County Arts Council
1981-93	Chairs the Fulton County Board of Commissioners
1984	Receives Ph.D. in African and African American literature from Emory University
1986	Marries Cheryl Ferguson
1988	Founds and serves as first chairman, National Black Arts Festival in Atlanta
1989	Runs unsuccessfully for mayor of Atlanta against Maynard Jackson
1993	Runs unsuccessfully for mayor of Atlanta against Bill Campbell
1994-97	Becomes president of the National Faculty headquartered in Atlanta
1997-2004	Serves as president of Dillard University in New Orleans
2004	Becomes president and CEO of the United Negro College Fund

County Arts Council. Continuing service on the Fulton County Board of Commissioners, from 1981 to 1993 he served as its chair. In that post, he was responsible for a healthy operating budget of $500 million. He also oversaw some five thousand employees. Lomax worked with others to bring the 1988 Democratic National Convention to Atlanta, and he also spoke at the convention. Then he played a role in the success of the 1996 Olympics, which were held in Atlanta. To meet the needs of a growing community, he spearheaded several major construction projects, such as building Georgia's Interstate 400, a major highway on the outskirts of Atlanta; expanding and renovating the historic Grady Hospital; and building the new Fulton County government center.

Although he was too young to participate in a meaningful way in the sit-ins and marches that occurred during the civil rights movement, Lomax was a college student in Atlanta as the movement subsided and racial segregation began to give way. The experiences left their mark on him; thus, by the time he decided to run for public office, he looked back at the civil rights movement and recognized that he had a legacy to fill. "I was old enough to be a part of the revolution which really realized the goals of the civil rights movement," he told John D. Thomas for *Emory Magazine*. "There was never any

question in my mind that I would do that. It was an extraordinary period when the first black mayor got elected in a major Southern city," he said in reference to Maynard H. Jackson who, on January 7, 1974, became Atlanta's mayor. "And I was the first African American to lead a major county government in Georgia. So there was the sense of the compulsion of history," he said.

John D. Thomas for *Emory Magazine* wrote that Lomax "led a grueling double life," referring to his exhaustive schedule as the top elected official in the state's largest and most populated area—Fulton County—as he taught literature at Morehouse College, Spelman College, Georgia Institute of Technology, and the University of Georgia. Sometimes he carried a full teaching load. Lomax told Thomas: "It was an eighteen-hour-a-day, seven-day-a-week effort, and it was very difficult to keep in balance." From a classroom with thirty people, he would "jump in a car, and go preside over a public hearing that might have three hundred people screaming and yelling about taxes or some zoning issue," he said. After teaching for twenty years, he left the classroom in 1989 for a new position at Dillard and a quieter life.

Lomax made an outstanding contribution to the arts as well as to politics, becoming a staunch supporter of the National Black Arts Festival (NBAF), which he founded in 1988, becoming its founding chair. In *Emory Magazine*, Dwight D. Andrews, a professor of music at Emory and artistic director of the festival, is quoted as saying: "His understanding of the power and potential of art as a vehicle for building a strong community has been a benefit to us all." Lomax had great vision, foresight, and commitment to black arts; therefore, he easily nurtured the NBAF as it became the world's largest and most comprehensive showcase of African Diaspora arts. In addition, Lomax's involvement of local government helped to strengthen the city's cultural and educational environment overall.

Lomax was twice an unsuccessful candidate for mayor of Atlanta, first in 1989 against Maynard Jackson and again in 1993 against Bill Campbell. Lomax left the political arena for good in 1993 and turned his energies back to education. From 1994 to 1997, Lomax was president of the Atlanta-based National Faculty. The National Faculty links scholars in the arts and sciences who are on college and university faculties to teachers from kindergarten through the twelfth grade. By his involvement with the issues then-current in higher education, he was in position to meet leaders of foundations and philanthropies, a relationship that would serve him well later on.

On leaving Atlanta, however, he left an impressive legacy. His name is on sixteen public libraries, and he was the force behind countless Fulton County projects. When asked to comment on his legacy as an Atlanta politician, Lomax told Gary M. Pomerantz for the *Atlanta Journal-Constitution*: "Believed in the arts, supported them. Believed in libraries, supported them.

Believed in the important role of government and stuck by it. And lived to talk about them all."

Black College Leader

Lomax had long been attracted to leadership positions in historically black colleges. He was an unsuccessful finalist for the presidency of his alma mater, Morehouse College. After that, he was presented with an offer that took him from Atlanta. In search of the best possible presidential candidate to lead the institution, Dillard University in New Orleans named Michael L. Lomax its president; on July 1, 1997, he succeeded Samuel Du Bois Cook in that post. Many Atlantans were unhappy to see one of its most distinguished citizens go. "What a pity it is for Atlanta to lose him," wrote Colin Campbell for the *Atlanta Journal-Constitution*.

Lomax sought the college presidency of a historically black institution, located in a city, and possessing a solid financial base. Dillard, one of the premier small, black, liberal arts colleges in the South, met these criteria. The school enjoyed a rich history. It was founded in 1935 when the financially strapped Straight University merged with New Orleans University to create an academically and fiscally healthier academic institution. Strait had been one of seven institutions founded shortly after the Civil War by the American Missionary Association for the express purpose of educating African American students; their charters prescribed a racial mix of students. These schools and other historically black colleges and universities (HBCUs) became the first producers of this country's black educated, professional, and leadership class. In his "Testimony Before the House Subcommittee on Twenty-first Century Competitiveness and Select Education," Lomax mentioned such black luminaries as Ruth Simmons, a Dillard alumna and now president of Brown University, and Martin Luther King Jr., a Morehouse graduate. He challenged others to invest in education, saying that education is the most important single investment one can make, telling Colin Campbell for the *Atlanta Journal-Constitution* that people who talk about apologizing for slavery could do something better—offer better schooling for blacks. "The 40 acres and a mule should be traded in for a four-year college scholarship," he said.

His interest in HBCUs may have grown out of a familial relationship with these institutions. The Lomax family had been educated at HBCUs over a period of one hundred and thirty years. Michael Lomax saw the HBCUs in a positive light and believed in their importance in society. They played an important role in the future of black Americans and the shaping of the United States. The private ones in particular "are experiencing a renaissance," he told John D. Thomas for *Emory Magazine*. He saw a resurging interest among students in the HBCUs. He believed that educators finally realized that there is "no cookie-cutter education in America" and that people require different approaches to education. "An experience which celebrates their racial heritage at the same time that it introduces students to a rigorous academic environment" worked well at Dillard and other places as well.

On assuming the presidency, Lomax took with him what he called a small "Atlanta mafia," including people who had worked with him in Fulton County and on the Atlanta Olympics. Lomax undertook an ambitious repositioning at Dillard as he challenged his new academic and development teams to assist him in re-imagining and reinventing Dillard's role as an HBCU. He wanted the team to continue to honor and respect the tradition and excellence that the school had known in the past, and his approach to leadership was student-focused. Lomax's first initiative was an aggressive multi-million-dollar renovation program. This initiative resulted in the building of the first new academic facility the college had seen since 1993—the Dillard University International Center for Economic Freedom. Seeing that the living and learning environment needed to change, he was determined to find ways to do this, such as to build more residence halls and classrooms. His primary goal, however, was to build a more qualitative than quantitative Dillard. He sought to increase the school's endowment from about $45 million to over $100 million, by the time of his then-undetermined departure. He successfully tripled giving from alumni, individuals, corporations, and foundations.

Lomax wanted no excuses of racial heritage as a reason for underdevelopment. He wanted Dillard's students to be competitive; they should come well prepared but leave exceptionally trained. Lomax recruited a strong faculty to enhance an academic program already regarded as excellent. His leadership brought nearly a 44 percent increase in enrollment, reaching 2,225 students from across the nation, the Caribbean, and Africa. Increasingly, Dillard's students were academically competitive as they came with strong high school grade point averages and high scores on standardized tests. From Dillard they went on to earn advanced degrees at some of the country's best universities. By 2002, the *U.S. News & World Report* rated Dillard twentieth in the top tier of comprehensive colleges of the South.

Heads Historic United Negro College Fund

Michael Lomax has a compassion for the HBCUs, as expressed in his writings and demonstrated in his service to black higher education as teacher and college president. He showcased his interest in a policy paper on "African Americans, Education, and Opportunities." He cited black abolitionist and orator Frederick Douglass who said, "education is the pathway from slavery to freedom" and concluded that black people must find a way to the pathway or make one themselves. Part of "making our own way," Lomax wrote, is to continue to support the HBCUs' important role of producing leaders. "Here, the record is clear, that HBCUs have been the most effective institutions in the academy in producing black college graduates." To him, diversity in U.S. institutions of higher education means also "making sure that these institutions do not merely survive but prosper." This way "they will continue to be a part of the American higher educational landscape that serves an array of different needs differently."

It was perhaps Lomax's views on the HBCUs as much as his stellar record in Atlanta and at Dillard that caught the eye of officials at the United Negro College Fund (UNCF). After seven years as president of Dillard University, Lomax became the ninth president of the United Negro College Fund, immediately succeeding William H. Gray III, who headed the organization for almost thirteen years. He was appointed in February 2004 and took office in June of that year as president and as chief executive officer of UNCF, whose headquarters are located in Fairfax, Virginia.

Lomax, who according to the biography on his website at Dillard University is "as comfortable in the classroom as the board room," and the UNCF were an easy fit. UNCF is the nation's oldest and most successful organization that assists African American higher education. Established in 1944 by presidents of private HBCUs, it aids in educating more than 65,000 students each year. There are thirty-eight member schools in the organization; the schools receive funds for advanced training for their administrators and faculties. To some, Lomax was groomed for his new post from his career as a college student. His foundation was set at an HBCU, and he built on that foundation both by advancing his education and by going back to the HBCUs to teach and to serve as chief officer. He also had a well-founded career as educator, politician, and fundraiser/volunteer.

Lomax took the helm of the UNCF as it celebrated its sixtieth anniversary amid major challenges to higher education for black Americans. For *Ebony* magazine, Lomax identified them as "the triple threat of an Affirmative Action backlash in higher education, an economic downturn poised to dwindle major corporate contributions, and the continuing debate over the role and the significance of Historically Black Colleges and Universities in an 'integrated educational' era." Notwithstanding his concerns, Lomax was firm about what he saw as the continued role of the black colleges. They had educated the "Martin Luther Kings, Thurgood Marshalls, and Toni Morrisons" when other colleges refused them. He still saw them as having an indispensable role of preparing thousands of young people for a place in the world of work who would not receive a college degree were it not for the HBCUs.

Lomax came to UNCF with admitted apprehension. At first a little overwhelmed by the underlying significance of his new position, he told *Ebony* magazine, "It's a deep honor on the one hand and a little scary on the other because this is a tremendous responsibility." But clearly Lomax was equal to the task and soon set ambitious goals in the area of fundraising for UNCF. He

wasted no time in declaring that, over the next ten years, he wanted the UNCF endowment to reach $1 billion. No other institution in the country that concentrates its energies on the African American community has such an ambitious goal. He wants the African American community to demonstrate to the world and to the UNCF that they can build and manage a billion-dollar operation.

Lomax has an additional role at UNCF. He chairs the Board of the United Negro College Fund Special Programs Corporation (UNCFS)—an organization that supports colleges and universities and helps them to build relationships and establish partnerships with the federal government and other organizations as well. By the time Lomax began his tenure at the organization, UNCF was administering some 450 programs that included the "Gates Millennium Scholars Program" under a $1 billion grant from the Bill and Melinda Gates Foundation. With the Gates grant, Lomax and the UNCF intended to address the digital divide that Lomax referred to in his testimony to the House Subcommittee on twenty-first century competitiveness. He wrote that the term "represents something distinct to us as an HBCU." For example, the technology gap seen on HBCU campuses "is a visible reminder of the unresolved legacy of separate but equal systems of education." At Dillard, he knew the importance of incorporating advanced technology in the classroom and noted Dillard's collaboration with the University of Colorado at Boulder to share course materials and classroom activities through distance learning technology. He noted the financial problems of black schools as they "are challenged to keep up with the steady torrent of upgrades that give students the competitive edge in the career world." In coming to UNCF, Lomax remained committed to increasing access to technology for the students and faculty of HBCUs.

As head of UNCF, Lomax chairs the UNCF Advisory Board for the Frederick D. Patterson Institute. An email from his office to the author described the Patterson Institute as "the first African American-led research institute in the country to design, conduct, analyze, interpret and disseminate research to the public, policymakers, and educators."

Because of his role in the arts, Lomax became a board member of the Studio Museum of Harlem and a member of the Council of National Museum of African American History and Culture. His board memberships include Emory University, the Carter Center of Emory University, the United Way, Teach America, Foxfire in Atlanta, and the Amistad Research Center. President George W. Bush appointed him to the President's Board of Advisors on Historically Black Colleges and Universities.

In 1969 Lomax married Pearl Cleage, later well-known as a poet and playwright; five years later their daughter Deignan Njeri was born. Divorced in 1979, Lomax married Cheryl Ferguson, a financial manager with Coca-Cola, in 1986. In addition to his daughter

Deignan, who graduated from Dillard, Michael and Cheryl Lomax have two daughters—Michele and Rachel. A grandfather as well, Lomax has two grandchildren. Atlanta is still home for Michael Lomax, as he commutes there each weekend; his wife, three daughters, and grandchildren are there as well.

His private life also includes tennis, to which he admits an addiction. He told *Ebony* magazine that he is "a Venus and Serena groupie." His exercise routine includes a workout four or five days a week. His spare time, which is rare, is spent reading fiction and history. An avid book collector as well, Lomax has over five hundred first-editions of African American works, the oldest of which is a book of slave narratives published in 1850.

While he balances his personal life with the enormous task he has set before him as head of UNCF, Michael Lomax has already demonstrated that he has the tools for success. As he leads UNCF in its continuing mission of enhancing the quality of education for black people, he continuous to demonstrate that he is articulate, a strategic thinker, a strong manager, and a successful fundraiser. Although UNCF keeps him busy, rather than complain, Lomax told the *New York Times*, "As long as I have breath, a beating heart and working mind I'll be doing it, because after all a mind is a terrible thing to waste."

REFERENCES

Books

Who's Who among African Americans. 18th ed. Farmington Hills, Mich.: Thomson Gale, 2005.

Periodicals

Campbell, Colin. "Michael Lomax Easing into His Collegiate Role." *Atlanta Journal-Constitution* 26 June 1997.

"Center Stage: Dr. Michael Lomax: UNCF President." *Ebony*. 59 (September 2004): 24.

Jones, Andrea, and Andrew Mollison. "Lomax: UNCF Taps Former Chief." *Atlanta Journal-Constitution*, 9 February 2004.

Pomerantz, Gary M. "Lomax on Leaving Atlanta." *Atlanta Journal-Constitution*, May 1997.

Rochell, Anne. "Politics Didn't Bring Out My Best." *Atlanta Journal-Constitution*, 8 February 1998.

Stanford, Duane D. "Dillard U Hires Lomax as President." *Atlanta Journal-Constitution*, 23 March 1997.

Online

Dillard University Presidential Transition Site. News. http://www.didllard.edu/presidentialtransition/press/pr_uncfl.asp (Accessed 21 January 2005).

Lias, Shaka. "Former Dillard President Settles in as UNCF Head." *New York Times*, Student Journal Institute 2005. http://www/nytimes-institute.com/20lomax.html (Accessed 5 November 2005).

Lomax, Michael L. "African Americans, Education, and Opportunity." Policy Paper. American Association of University Administrators, Assembly 2001 Wrap-Up. http://www.aaua.org/pub/wrapUp2001/index.php?page=paperLomax (Accessed 21 January 2005).

———. "Testimony Before the House Subcommittees on Twenty-first Century Competitiveness and Select Education." http://edworkforce.house.gov.hearings//107th/sed/hbcu91902/lomax.htm (Accessed 21 January 2005).

Michael L. Lomax Website, Office of the President, Dillard University. "Biography." http://www.dillard.edu/LomaxSite/presbio.htm (Accessed 21 January 2005).

"Michael Lucius Lomax of Louisiana—Member of the President's Board of Advisors on Historically Black Colleges and Universities." Ed.gov. http://www.ed.gov/about/inits/list/whhbcu/edlite-lomax.html (Accessed 1 November 2005).

Thomas, John D. "The Education of Michael Lomax." *Emory Magazine*. (Spring 1998) http://www.emory.edu/EMORY_MAGAZINE/spring98/lomax.html. (Accessed 21 January 2005).

Other

"Dr. Michael L. Lomax, President and CEO, United Negro College Fund." Biography. Email from Ayana Canty to Jessie Carney Smith, 8 December 2004.

Jessie Carney Smith

Eddie L. Long
1953–

Bishop

Born in 1953 in Charlotte, North Carolina, Eddie L. Long is one of four sons born to Hattie and Reverend Floyd Long. He received his basic education in the Charlotte public school system. According to Long, when he was in the seventh grade, a guidance counselor told him that he was too dumb to go to college. However, in the last week of his high school senior year, another guidance counselor told him that he could and would go to college, and she helped him apply to North Carolina Central University in Durham.

Eddie L. Long

His early interest in a position in the corporate world led him to pursue a B.S. in business administration, which he received from North Carolina Central University in 1976. He worked for brief periods with the Ford Company in Richmond, and with Honeywell in Atlanta. His upbringing in a Christian home gave spiritual meaning to his life and helped him reach the decision to study theology. Long became licensed in the ministry in 1981 and sometime later was ordained as pastor of Atlanta's Morning Star Baptist Church. He received a master's of divinity degree from Atlanta's Interdenominational Theological Center in 1986. Additionally, in 1998 he received honorary doctorates from North Carolina Central University and Beulah Heights Bible College of Atlanta, and still later from the Morehouse School of Religion.

Ministry Emerges

In 1987 Long became pastor of New Birth Missionary Baptist Church with a congregation consisting of a little more than three hundred members. After his installation, the church's membership quickly multiplied to well over 25,000, with 40 percent of his congregation being African American males. Under his leadership, the church facility grew from a chapel seating five hundred to a sanctuary in 1991 which seats 3,700; a 5,000-seat Family Life Center in 1999; and finally a Mega Worship Center with a capacity of 10,500 in 2001. This magnifi-

Chronology

1953	Born in Charlotte, North Carolina
1976	Receives B.S. from North Carolina Central University
1987	Becomes pastor of New Birth Missionary Baptist Church
1991	Constructs a 3,700-seat sanctuary
1999	Constructs a Family Life Center
2001	Constructs a 10,000-seat complex
2005	Maintains over 25,000 members in the New Birth Missionary Baptist Church

cent worship edifice is located in the heart of De Kalb County, Georgia, in the city of Lithonia. It houses countless outreach programs and community-empowering projects all orchestrated by Long.

Long's ministry reaches far beyond his mega-congregation. He is a leader among the fast growing throng of popular televangelists with skyrocketing mega-churches and traveling religious shows. His church has ministry outreach programs for drug addicts and prisoners and has started its own credit union. Bishop Long's ministry outreach has taken him to religious revivals as far away as New Zealand and Kenya. He has also attracted an abundance of young black single professionals who attend his services. He has started a school, a fitness center, and built a sanctuary to meet the needs of his fast growing congregation.

Long works tirelessly for charitable and civic causes and faces socioeconomic issues. He challenges the underprivileged by enlightening them with educational and life-changing opportunities that are intended to strengthen them spiritually and help them gain their independence. He says in his book *Taking Over*, "we're not just a church, we're an international corporation. We're not just a bumbling bunch of preachers who can't talk and all we're doing is baptizing babies. I deal with the White House and the British Prime Minister, Tony Blair."

Long deals with heads of state around the world. Close association with the political elite earned him an invitation to have breakfast with President George W. Bush and some of the nation's best-known and most influential black clergy to craft a new role for U.S. churches in Africa. Reverend T. D. Jakes, Donnie Mc Klurkin, Andrew Young, and Bishop Charles E. Blake were among more than two dozen religious leaders who met with Secretary of State Condoleezza Rice and other senior White House officials.

Bishop Long's ministry is not without controversy, however. This was amplified after he voiced his opposition to the debated issue of same-sex marriage. He along with Reverend Bernice King, daughter of the Martin Luther King Jr., led a march promoting an array of causes among which the divisive issue of same-sex marriage was central.

Honors and Awards

Honored worldwide, Bishop Long has been named one of America's 125 most influential leaders. He has received numerous awards in recognition for his world-changing ministry. In 1999, Big Brothers and Big Sisters of Metro Atlanta awarded him the prestigious Legacy Award. Long began serving as co-chair for the "Hosea Feed the Hungry" project in 2001. In 2002, he became a member of the North Carolina Central University Board of Trustees. In 2003, he received the Faith/Community Leadership Award from 100 Black Men of America, the Religious Contemporary Award from IRC's "Portraits of Sweet Success," the Champion Award for Spiritual Enlightenment from "All Children Are Special, Inc.," and he was selected by *Savoy Magazine* as one of the Most Influential Leaders in Black America. In 2004, Long and New Birth's Television Production team were awarded an Emmy for *The Face of Homelessness*. In 2005, he was honored at the Trumpet Awards for leadership, dedication, and service around the world. He is the vice-chair of the Morehouse School of Religion board of directors; he is affiliated with the Traditional Values Coalition in Washington, D.C.; and he has served as area moderator of the American Baptist Churches of the South. He is founder and CEO of Faith Academy, New Birth's school of excellence. He has a daily radio program in Atlanta, Los Angeles, Miami, and London, England.

Long broadcasts his message in 172 countries; doing so has earned him numerous awards for excellence in broadcasting, including the New York Festival's Silver World Medal and the World Media Festival's Intermedia Golden Globe. Long and his church received worldwide attention when the funeral of Coretta Scott King was held there in February 2006.

Bishop Long and his wife Vanessa have four children: Eric, Edward, Jared, and Taylor. The couple has also served as surrogate parents for many other children in the church and the surrounding Atlanta community.

REFERENCES

Books

LaBalle, Candace. "Eddie L. Long." In *Contemporary Black Biography*. Vol. 29. Farmington Hills, Mich.: Thomson Gale, 2002.

Periodicals

Blake, John. "Bishop's Charity Generous to Bishop." *Atlanta Journal-Constitution*, 28 August 2005.

Moorer, Talise D. "Giant Bash Celebrates Life of Bishop Eddie Long." *New York Amsterdam News*, 15 May 2003.

Oral Moses

Glen C. Loury
1948–

Economist

Glen Cartman Loury is a distinguished economic theorist who has taught and lectured at numerous universities in the United States and abroad. He has written many books and scholarly articles on welfare, economics, game theory, natural resource economics, industrial organization, and the economics of income distribution. He is also a prominent social critic and public intellectual.

Glen Cartman Loury was born September 3, 1948 in Chicago, Illinois, on the city's south side to Everett Loury and Gloria (Cartman) Roosley. Loury received his B.A. degree in mathematics from Northwestern University in 1972 and his Ph.D. in economics from the Massachusetts Institute of Technology in 1976. His thesis was entitled "Essays in the Theory of the Distribution of Income."

Loury's first marriage to Charlene ended in divorce. He married Linda Datcher on June 11, 1983. Lisa, Tamara, Alden, Glen II, and Nehemiah are their children.

In 1976 Glen Cartman Loury began work as assistant professor in the Department of Economics at Northwestern University in Evanston, Illinois and continued his employment there until 1979. From 1979 to 1980 he was an associate professor and from 1980 to 1982 he was professor of economics at the University of Michigan in Ann Arbor, Michigan. He served as professor of economics and Afro-American studies from 1982 to 1984 and professor of political economy from 1984 to 1991 at Harvard University in Cambridge, Massachusetts. From 1991 to 1994 he served as university professor and from 1994 to 2005 as university professor and director of the Institute on Race and Social Division at Boston University in Massachusetts. He served as visiting lecturer at colleges and universities in the United States and abroad, including Oxford University, Tel Aviv University, and the University of Stockholm. He has been a guest on radio and television programs, including *Firing Line Group* and *Think Tank*. He testified before the U.S. Senate and the House of Representatives and served as consultant to the Federal Trade Commission, Center for Naval Analyses, and American Telephone and Telegraph Company. He is also an elected

Glen C. Loury

Chronology

1948	Born in Chicago, Illinois on September 3
1972	Receives B.A. in mathematics from Northwestern University
1976	Receives Ph.D. in economics from the Massachusetts Institute of Technology
1976-79	Assistant professor, Department of Economics, Northwestern University
1979-80	Associate professor, Department of Economics, University of Michigan
1980-82	Professor, Department of Economics, University of Michigan
1982-84	Professor of economics and Afro-American studies, Harvard University
1984-91	Professor of political economy, Harvard University
1991-94	University professor, Boston University
1994-2005	University professor and director of the Institute on Race and Social Division, Boston University
1995	Authors *One by One, from the Inside Out: Essays and Reviews on Race and Responsibility*
1996	Serves as Boston University lecturer
2000	Serves as Harvard University, Du Bois Lecturer
2002	Authors *The Anatomy of Racial Inequality*
2005	Begins work as Merton P. Stolz Social Science Professor at Brown University; receives John Von Neumann Award; co-editor of *Ethnicity, Social Mobility and Public Policy*

member of the Committee on Foreign Relations and fellow of the American Academy of Arts and Sciences.

Publishes on Various Themes

Loury has published widely, writing on such topics as negative stereotypes, self-censorship, and race. Loury is editor of and a contributor to *From Children to Citizens*, published in 1987. He is a contributor to *Mending Fences: Renewing Justice between Government and Civil Society*, by Dan Coats and edited by James W. Skillen, published in 1998. He is the author of *One by One, from the Inside Out: Essays and Reviews on Race and Responsibility* (1995) and *Anatomy of Racial Inequality* (2002), and co-editor of *Ethnicity, Social Mobility and Public Policy* (2005).

He has also contributed to *American Society: Public and Private Responsibilities* (1986), *The Question of Discrimination* (1989), and the *Constitutional Bases of Political Change in the United States* (1990).

Loury has contributed more than one hundred reviews and articles in professional journals, including *Rationality and Society, Annals of the American Association of Political and Social Science, Review of Economic Studies, Review of Black Political Economy, Journal of Family and Culture*, and *The American Economic Review*. He has also served as contributing editor to the *New Republic* and served as a member of the editorial advisory board for *First Things: The Journal of Religion, and Culture, and Public Life*.

Loury enjoys playing chess, billiards, and pool, listening to jazz music and reading. He is the recipient of numerous honors and held prestigious positions, including the James A. Moffett '29 Lecturer in Ethics in November of 2003 and the W. E. B. Du Bois Lecturer at Harvard University in April of 2000, and he was elected Fellow of the Economic Society in 1994. In 2005 he was the recipient of the John Von Neumann Award given annually by the Rajk László College of the Budapest University of Economic Science and Public Administration.

On September 1, 2005 Loury was appointed Merton P. Stolz Professor of the Social Sciences in the Department of Economics at Brown University in Providence, Rhode Island, where he lectures, publishes, and shares his multitude of academic talents with administration, faculty, and students and other academicians in the United States and abroad. He ranks among notable black American men nationwide.

REFERENCES

Books

Smith, Jessie Carney, "Glen Cartman Loury." In *Black Firsts*, 2nd ed., Canton, Mich.: Visible Ink Press, 2003.

Who's Who Among African Americans. 18th ed. Farmington Hills, Mich.: Thomson Gale, 2005.

Prudence White Bryant

Neal Vernon Loving
1916–1998

Airplane designer, aeronautical engineer

A distinguished airplane designer, aeronautical engineer, flight instructor, and co-owner of a flight school, Neal Vernon Loving was diligent in his pursuit of a career in aviation. Despite the challenges of racism and a crippling air disaster, he had a successful career as an airplane designer. The designs of his airplanes stand as a testament to him and to those who cherish the humble home-built plane. He later enjoyed a distinguished career as an aerospace research engineer.

Loving was born February 4, 1916 in Detroit, Michigan to Alma and Harding Clay Loving. He had two brothers, Barney and Robert, and one sister, Ardine. His father worked full time as a conductor, while at the same time studying optometry at the Columbia Optical College in St. Paul and supporting the whole family. In 1925, his father became the first black to pass the Michigan State Board Examiners in the field of optometry. Loving later realized that his father, a tall fair-skinned man with dark wavy hair and gray eyes, must have been passing for white because blacks during that time were restricted to less skilled jobs.

Loving's life was changed at age ten when he saw a de Havilland DH-4 biplane while arguing with his fourteen-year-old brother, Barney, about where to place two radio antennae across the backyard. Barney noticed Loving's excitement over the silver and blue biplane overhead and suggested Loving study aviation instead of radio. At the sight of that plane, Loving found his life-long passion. After that incident, he raced out of the house every time a plane flew over, and he was soon able to identify planes, simply by the engine sound. The 1927 solo transatlantic flight that Charles Lindbergh took to Paris further inspired his interest in aviation.

Loving's family failed to support his interest in aviation since during this time, aviation was a field limited in its advancement opportunities for African Americans, and they were skeptical of his being able to succeed in it. His mother suggested he visit the nearby public library in Detroit to find a new interest. He did visit the library, but he did not find a new interest. Instead, he found loads of aviation and aircraft books and he studied them ardently.

Chronology

1916	Born in Detroit, Michigan on February 4
1931	Enters Cass Technical High School in auto-aero department
1935	Receives Project of the Month Award from *Mechanix Illustrated*
1935	Begins taking flying lessons
1939	Takes first solo flight; organizes the St. Antoine YMCA Glider Club for boys fourteen and older
1944	Airplane crash crushes both legs and rehabilitation begins
1946	Forms Wayne School of Aeronautics with Earsly Taylor
1949	Begins construction of WR-1 (*Loving's Love*)
1954	Wins Most Outstanding Design award for *Loving's Love*
1955	Marries Clare Therese; enrolls at Wayne State University to study aeronautical engineering
1961	Graduates Wayne State University
1968	Wins Meritorious Civilian Service award
1982	Retires from Wright AFB, aerospace engineering position
1991	Wins Distinguished Achievement award, Organization of Black Airline Pilots
1991	Stops flying
1994	Publishes autobiography
1995	Wins Major Achievement award, Experimental Aircraft Association
1996	Gets inducted into the Michigan Aviation Hall of Fame
1998	Dies in Yellow Springs, Ohio on December 19

Loving saved his money to purchase model airplane materials and aviation magazines. At fourteen, he had saved the three dollars necessary for an airplane ride. Loving's first flight was in the front seat of a Waco biplane. The flight took him from Detroit City Airport over downtown Detroit and up the Detroit River. The fifteen-minute ride was an unforgettable experience.

In 1931, Loving enrolled in the auto/aero department at Cass Technical High School to specialize in aeronautics. Shortly after enrolling, he was called to the department head's office and told that there were no opportunities for blacks in the field of aeronautics. It was suggested to Loving that he transfer to the auto department where he could learn skills that would allow him to earn a living. When Loving replied that he loved airplanes and did not care to be that practical, permission was granted reluctantly for him to remain in the program.

Loving attempted to join the Cass Aero Club, but his application was turned down because blacks were ineligible. However, shortly after that, he joined the all-black Ace-flying club, an organization committed to teaching African Americans to fly. Months later, the Ace-flying club came to an abrupt end when the founder, Don Pearl Simmons, and his wife were killed in a plane crash. Nonetheless, Loving met a life-long friend at the first meeting. Her name was Earsly Taylor, a tall young woman who had served as the club's secretary. She and Loving were friends and business partners for many years to come.

Loving graduated from Cass Tech in January 1934 and began cleaning streets for the Detroit Welfare Department. He developed frostbite on the job, so he decided to discontinue working outside as a manual laborer and was more determined than ever to pursue a career in aviation. Subsequently, Loving began working voluntarily for his former Cass Tech aeromechanics instructor, George Tabraham. The job allowed him to gain the experience necessary to obtain an aircraft mechanics license.

In 1935, after being inspired by articles in *Modern Mechanix* and *Popular Mechanics* magazines, Loving designed and built a ground trainer, a nonflying airplane for children who want to imagine they are flying. The ground trainer was his first "big" project. Loving was given the "Project of the Month" award by *Mechanix Illustrated* for the airplane. The Junior Birdmen of America invited him to exhibit the plane at the Annual All-American Air Show at Detroit City Airport. Attending the air show as an exhibitor made Loving extremely proud; just seven years prior, he had visited the show as a spectator.

In the fall of 1935 during the Great Depression, Loving began to design a full-size glider. In order to raise money for materials, he started looking for a job. It was difficult for an African American to find a job during this time. However, the following year he found a job teaching model aircraft building for the Detroit Department of Recreation. Loving completed the glider, designated N15750. The N15750 had structural problems, and he was never able to fly it. However, the experience he gained from it helped him in designing other aircraft. Loving began taking flying lessons in 1938 and took his first solo flight in 1939. His friend, Earsly Taylor, was also beginning to fly. The same year, Loving founded the St. Antoine Young Men's Christian Association (YMCA) Glider Club for boys fourteen and older. In 1940, he completed the construction of his second glider designated the Wayne S-1 and was registered with the Department of Commerce as NX27775.

In order to improve his skills, Loving enrolled in a six-month accelerated course in engineering and drafting at Highland Park Junior College and began applying for a job with the Detroit Board of Education. His old Cass Technical High School mentor, George Tabraham, called him to work as an aircraft mechanics instructor at the newly founded Aero Mechanics High School. Tabraham, the principal at the new school, had been a supporter of Loving's early efforts in aviation and had inspired Loving to achieve when others told him not to try. Loving became the most popular instructor at the school.

Co-founds Aircraft Company and School of Aeronautics

In late November of 1941, the NX27775 made its last glider flight because a week prior to this, the Japanese attacked Pearl Harbor and gasoline rationing and emergency rules grounded most private aircraft. Loving built a larger version of the plane and designated it the S-2. Loving and Earsly Taylor then formed the Wayne Aircraft Company, the first black aircraft factory, in Detroit. Work proceeded slowly because both partners had other full-time jobs. However, they were determined that their company would be a commercial success.

With a Waco biplane and the S-2 glider, Loving and Taylor applied to join the Civil Air Patrol (CAP), a volunteer civilian branch of the United States Army Air Force in which airplane owners provided pre-military and preflight training to young people to be used in air-sea rescue missions. After being turned down by the white squadrons in the Detroit area, they were granted permission to form Squadron 639-5 (63rd Wing, Group 9, Squadron 5), an all-black squadron. Loving served as executive officer of Squadron 639-5, and Taylor served as commanding officer. They offered standard preflight, pre-military training, and training in parachute jumping. Squadron 639-5 became known informally as the Parachute Squadron.

Loving's position at Aero Mechanics High School was terminated in 1943. He then began working as an engine assembler on the assembly line at the Ford Motor Company. Shortly thereafter, Loving received a draft notice, and he began increasing his efforts to complete the design of the S-2 while still working his seven days per week job at Ford and continuing his CAP duties. As a result of his many hours of hard work, Loving began experiencing long-term fatigue, a condition that would cause him later health problems.

In February 1944, Loving was called to the draft. He had passed all of his exams, except the cardiology exam. Although he had received a medical certificate and his pilot's license, the military physician classified him 4-F (unfit for service) and stated adamantly that his heart was bad. Loving gave up on his hopes of serving in the military and felt that he would never get an engineering position at Ford. He appealed to the War Manpower Commission for a Statement of Availability (SA) in order for him to be able to use his drafting skills elsewhere. With an SA, Loving planned to enroll at Wayne State University in the fall of 1944.

Scheduled for a routine CAP training session on July 30, 1944, Loving, already experiencing long-term fatigue, set out to fly the S-2 at Wings Airport in Utica, Michigan, north of Detroit, with only two hours sleep the previous night. In addition to his poor physical condition, he failed to see indications of the loss of altitude. As he was preparing to land, the glider stalled and crashed.

Both of Loving's legs were crushed, so doctors had to amputate his legs just below the knees. He recuperated at the St. Joseph Hospital in Mt. Clemens, Michigan, where he remained until Valentine's Day 1945. During his recovery, he and Taylor made the decision to close the Wayne Aircraft Company. Within months, Loving was fitted with wooden legs, and by 1946 he was driving, walking, and flying again. The same year he and Taylor opened the Wayne School of Aeronautics, the first flight school for black pilots, equipped with an Air Force training plane. They had no problem recruiting students for the school because black veterans rejected by white schools and returning war veterans could attend. Also, accepting students of all races helped to increase the number of recruits. The school was in full operation by early 1947.

Receives Outstanding Design Award for *Loving's Love*

Loving once again began designing planes. He had an interest in midget-class racers, a new category intended to be affordable to builders and pilots with average incomes. Loving began working on a midget racer, designated the WR-1, which later became known as *Loving's Love*. In 1948, the Professional Racing Pilots Association (PRPA) approved the general design of the WR-1. Loving began constructing the gull-winged plane in January 1949. On August 7, 1950, he took the plane out for a nearly flawless test flight. The following year, he began to enter it in races, earning a racing pilot's license at the National Air Races. The engine on *Loving's Love* could reach over 3,800 rpm in level flight resulting in a top speed of approximately 215 to 255 mph. Loving became the first black pilot and the first double-amputee to qualify as a racing pilot with the National Aeronautic Association and the PRPA.

Between 1953 and 1954, Loving flew *Loving's Love* on a 4800-mile round-trip between Detroit and Kingston, Jamaica to the location where Earsly Taylor Barnett and Carl Taylor Barnett had founded a flight school. The following year, at the second annual fly-in of the Experimental Aircraft Association (EAA) at Rockford, Illinois, Loving won the "Most Outstanding Design" award for *Loving's Love*. The following year, Loving married Carl Barnett's sister, Clare Therese. Later, they adopted a son, Paul Leslie, born in 1958 and a daughter, Michelle Stephanie, born in 1959. In the fall of 1955, Loving was finally able to enroll at Wayne State University as a student in the aeronautical engineering program at the age of 39. In 1957, he closed the Wayne School of Aeronautics and devoted himself full-time to his studies. He graduated from Wayne State University in 1961 with a degree in aerospace engineering.

After receiving his aerospace engineering degree, Loving went to work as an aeronautical engineer in the Flight Dynamics Laboratory at Wright-Patterson Air Force Base (AFB) in Ohio. He became known for his diplomacy and his work in clear-air turbulence measurement techniques. While serving as a project engineer for the Air Force's High Altitude Clear Air Turbulence Project, Loving coordinated agreements with other nations for worldwide operations bases for the Lockheed U-2 spy plane and traveled oversees to discuss potential turbulence problems a supersonic transport (SST) might face.

In 1982, Loving retired after twenty years of service at Wright AFB and devoted his time to his family. He continued to fly a "roadable" aircraft, kept at his garage at Yellow Springs, Ohio, where he and his wife lived. He stopped flying in 1991, when he had an aneurysm in his lower aorta and the Federal Aviation Administration revoked his medical certificate. In 1994, his autobiography, *Loving's Love: A Black American's Experience in Aviation*, was published. He also became a motivational speaker.

On October 18, 1997, Loving was enshrined in the Michigan Aviation Hall of Fame for his long and memorable career. He died in 1998 at the age of 82. He will go down in history as one who overcame the odds and made major contributions to the black aviation community and the aerospace industry. *Loving's Love* is on permanent display at the Experimental Aircraft Association's Air Education Museum in Oshkosh, Wisconsin.

REFERENCES

Books

Gubert, Betty Kaplan, Miriam Sawyer, and Caroline M. Fannin. *Distinguished African Americans in Aviation and Space Science*. Westport, Conn.: Oryx Press, 2002.

Online

Orndoff, Bill. 2003. "Pilot overcame prejudice, built experimental plane." *Hilltop Times*. http://www.hilltoptimes.com/story.asp?edition=113&storyid=3136 (Accessed 24 January 2005).

Sharon McGee

Samuel R. Lowery
1832–1900

Minister, lawyer

Samuel R. Lowery was born approximately thirty years before the outbreak of the Civil War, but,

Chronology

1832	Born in Davidson County (near Nashville), Tennessee on December 9
1840	Free Cherokee mother, Ruth Mitchell, dies
1849	Becomes minister at Nashville's Church of the Disciples
1856	Leaves Nashville to avoid race riots
1858	Marries Adora Robinson
1859	Organizes Christian Churches in Canada
1862	Returns to the United States, settling in Fayette County, Ohio
1863	Begins law studies around this time in Rutherford County, Tennessee
1867	Founds the Tennessee Manual Labor University with his father
1875	Moves to Huntsville, Alabama; establishes cooperative community, Loweryvale, in Jefferson County; establishes S. R. and R. M. Lowery Silk Culture and Manufacturing Company
1880	Gains admission to practice law before the United States Supreme Court
1884	Wins first prize for silk at the World's Fair
1900	Dies in Loweryvale, Alabama, at his own cooperative community

unlike many other blacks of his time, he was never a slave. Lowery, though a free man at birth, did not fully escape the prejudice, discrimination, and neglect that most of his fellow blacks endured. In the 1884 World Exposition in New Orleans, for example, Lowery entered his mulberry leaves (food for silkworms) in the competition. His rival from France received $1,000 to produce an exhibit. Lowery, who received no such aid, had to pay for and construct his own exhibit. Despite this handicap, Lowery won the competition. His mulberry leaves were the largest. Not only that, they far surpassed the competition in usefulness, since they stimulated, on site, the growth of 100,000 worms and cocoons, while the competition failed to generate any. Not all Lowery's experiences of discrimination ended in triumph, however. After the Civil War, for example, the school he had established in Rutherford County, Tennessee, near where he had studied law, was completely destroyed by the Ku Klux Klan.

Although Lowery did suffer from discrimination because of his skin color, his mother, Ruth Mitchell, was actually a Cherokee Indian. She had purchased the freedom of the slave Peter Lowery, Samuel's father, and was thus responsible for Samuel's being born free. She had freed not one man, but two. Lowery was born on December 9, 1832 in Davidson County (near Nashville), Tennessee. Unfortunately, his mother died in 1840, when he was only eight. His father worked at various times as a hack driver, a farmer, a livery stable operator, and a janitor at Franklin College. It was at Franklin that Samuel was able to study for the ministry, in classes separate from the white students.

Begins Ministry

Lowery began his preaching career in 1849 at Nashville's Church of the Disciples, where he remained until 1857. At that time, prior to the Civil War, during Lincoln's 1856 election campaign, great unrest broke out over the issue of slavery, causing the less fortunate whites, especially, to resent the wealthier, free blacks and to attack their businesses and force the closing of free black schools. In Nashville, twenty-four free blacks were jailed, though they were later released. In 1856, both Lowery and his father decided to flee to the North.

Lowery married Adora Robinson in 1858. The couple had two children, Ruth and Annie. In 1859, Lowery moved to Canada, where he stayed for three years, avoiding the racial turbulence in the United States during that time. In Canada he established Christian Churches (Disciples of Christ). The Lowerys' flight north to free regions was part of that large and continuing pattern of migration by blacks seeking freedom. Many blacks felt that there was less racial prejudice in Canada.

Returning to the United States around 1862, Lowery and his family settled on a farm his father had given him in Fayette County, Ohio. In 1863, when Lincoln issued the Emancipation Proclamation, Lowery returned to Nashville, where he preached and attended to the spiritual needs of free men and the soldiers of the Fortieth U.S. Colored Troops under the command of Colonel R. K. Crawford. Later, after losing his bid to be chaplain to that unit, Lowery was attached to the Ninth U. S. Heavy Artillery as chaplain. He also taught basic educational skills to soldiers of the Second U. S. Colored Light Artillery.

Pursues Interest in Law

After the war, Lowery settled with his family in Nashville, where he felt called to teach and preach—and to undertake a new career. He soon began to study law in Rutherford County with a white attorney, and subsequently he established his own practice. Lowery's interest in law may have begun much earlier, since an 1850 letter of legal advice from Abraham Lincoln, a lawyer then himself, is addressed to "Samuel R. Lowry." Lincoln's letter apparently advises Lowery on the lack of real estate rights by occupants being evicted from a residence. At the time Lowery himself began to practice law, he was also active in several organizations, such as the State Colored Men's Convention, the National Emigration Society, and the Tennessee State Equal Rights League. In 1875, after the closing of a school he ran in Nashville, he moved to Huntsville, Alabama, where he continued his law practice and his preaching. His eventual success as lawyer was such that on February 2, 1880, Lowery was nominated by Belva Lockwood to practice law before the U. S. Supreme Court. Lowery has the distinction of being the first African American to earn this honor.

On December 10, 1867, prior to his Alabama move and long before the Supreme Court event, Lowery and his father had established the Tennessee Manual Labor University. The school was located on Murfreesboro Road in Smyrna, Tennessee, near the black settlement Ebenezor. Like the Franklin College where both Lowerys had studied, the newly founded school was designed to provide its students with basic knowledge in agriculture, mechanical arts, and Christian ethics, all practical knowledge that would allow the freedmen to thrive in their new and changing environment. To support the school, Lowery traveled frequently to raise funds in various communities. Unfortunately, a scandal arose concerning money related to a fundraising trip for the university, a trip undertaken by the Reverends Lowery and Wadkins. The fault in the scandal was not Lowery's, however. Wadkins raised $1,632, but appropriated all but $200 for expenses. Although Wadkins was the culprit, Lowery, head of the school, received the blame. The white Christian Church excommunicated Lowery and withheld crucial support, resulting in the school's closing in 1872.

Establishes Loweryvale Community

After moving to Huntsville, Alabama in 1875, Lowery undertook several projects, including the establishment of a cooperative community, Loweryvale, in Jefferson County and the editing of the *Southern Freeman*. Most notably, he founded three new enterprises. One was Lowery's Industrial Academy, founded on the same principles as the earlier Nashville school and established to provide training in silk production. It was allied with the two other business enterprises, the Birmingham Silk Company (founded with the backing of several business leaders), and the S. R. and R. M. Lowery Silk Culture and Manufacturing Company. Lowery's daughter Ruth, who died in 1877, just two years after the company began, was the "R. M." of the company name. It was Ruth who first grew interested in silkworm culture, when she visited an exhibit dedicated to it. Her father bought her some worm eggs at the exhibit, which she carried home and fed on mulberry leaves. His daughter's project sparked Lowery's own interest in silkworm cultivation, and he began to see its business potential. Her interest in and expertise with silkworm growing had both inspired her father and provided him an outlet when he became discouraged with politics. The daughter's death did not dampen Lowery's devotion to her dream of silk production. In fact, following Ruth's death, Lowery visited two notable silkworm growers, John Kyle of New Jersey and Fred Cheney of Connecticut. Kyle was the first successful silk manufacturer in the United States, and Cheney was the biggest grower of silkworms in the country. Both urged Lowery to begin work in the business, and Cheney predicted he would succeed within ten years.

Prospers with Silkworm Cultivation

Lowery, because of his industry and knowledge, was given forty acres of land near Birmingham to develop the silkworm enterprise. After the meeting with Kyle and Cheney, he returned to Alabama, ordered French mulberry seeds, and started a hardy stand of trees, trees that produced the world's largest mulberry leaves. Lowery, carrying before him the vision of his daughter's work with silkworm cultivation and silk production, threw himself into the project. He viewed the silk industry as the successor to cotton for American blacks, offering a profitable income, better working conditions, and shorter hours. He envisioned that the new industry would provide more refined employment for black women and children. He died in Loweryvale, Alabama in 1900.

The Reverend William J. Simmons, a friend and contemporary, in 1886 described Lowery as "an intelligent, conservative man, steadily refusing to mix up in any way with the disturbing element of his race." Simmons also quotes Lowery as saying, "Hope is a large faculty in my organization. I have tried to abandon it and become indifferent to its inviting fields. When I do, I am really not myself; yet I know I do not hope vainly or recklessly." Simmons remarked that Lowery "constantly devotes his time to the advancement of the colored people of the South." Indeed, though Lowery's career was quite varied, a consistent theme and preoccupation sustained him. As educator and editor, he aimed to elevate the abilities and aspirations of his race. As lawyer, he sought to defend their interests. As preacher, he ministered to their spirit. As entrepreneur, he worked to provide opportunity for a better economic future for them. At the core of Lowery's efforts was the deeply felt desire to improve conditions for black Americans.

REFERENCES

Books

Childs, John Brown. *The Political Black Minister: A Study in Afro-American Politics and Religion.* Boston, Mass.: G. K. Hall & Co., 1980.

Online

Simmons, William J. *Men of Mark: A Eminent, Progressive and Rising.* Cleveland, Ohio: Geo. M. Rewell & Co., 1887. http://docsouth.unc.edu/neh/simmons/simmons.html (Accessed 13 March 2006).

Lois A. Peterson

Bernie Mac
1957–

Comedian, actor

Bernard Jeffrey McCullough, better known as Bernie Mac, garnered acclaim as a stand-up comic, actor, and the co-creator and star of a popular television series.

Bernie Mac was born on October 5, 1957 in Chicago's South Side. He was the son of Mary McCullough and Bernard Harrison. Mac grew up in a household with his mother, a personnel supervisor at Evangelical Hospital; his grandfather, a janitor at General Motors; his grandmother; aunt; and older brother. The family lived in at least four homes in Chicago during Mac's youth.

In his first book, *I Ain't Scared of You* (2001), Mac recalls that his family ate cereal with forks. His grandfather would pour milk in Mac's bowl, and after Mac ate the cereal, he would pour the milk in Darryl's bowl; after Darryl ate, he would pour the milk for the next person. Other weekday food staples included bologna, potted meat, and beans. The best meals of the week were served on Sundays; after church, the family dined on roast beef, mashed potatoes, gravy, macaroni and cheese, rolls, and cake. In his second book, *Maybe You Never Cry Again*, Mac puts his childhood in perspective: "When I think back on it, I think about all the good things I had, not the hardships. I had the luxury of being a little boy, and that's really something. Lots of kids today don't have that luxury. Grow up too fast. Don't have time to have their kid thoughts and dream their kid dreams and use their imagination."

Announces His Career Goal

In both of his books, Mac recounts an important childhood incident. When he was approximately four years old, he noticed that although his mother was crying, she started laughing when she saw an African American male on television. As she continued to laugh, Mac realized the man had the power to make Mac's mother laugh despite her woes. He asked his mother who the man was, and when she responded that he was Bill Cosby, a comedian, Mac decided that he would become a comedian so he would never have to see his mother cry again. In *I Ain't*

Bernie Mac

Scared of You, he elaborates: "That's a true story, man. That's what made me want to do this, even after my mother passed. That's what inspires my humor. I don't want nobody to cry."

Mac grew up watching many comedic stars on television: Lucille Ball, Jack Benny, Carol Burnett, Tim Conway, Bill Cosby, Redd Foxx, Stu Gilliam, Jackie Gleason, Harpo Marx, Richard Pryor, Red Skelton, The Three Stooges, and Flip Wilson. He also saw such talents as Moms Mabley and Pigmeat Markham perform their stand-up routines at Chicago's Regal Theater. As early as his childhood years, Mac displayed a talent for being able to hold an audience's attention. In 1966, when he was eight years old, Mac told jokes at a church banquet. Although Mac's jokes generated much laughter, his

Chronology

1957	Born in Chicago, Illinois on October 5
1974	Mother dies in August
1977	Marries his childhood sweetheart, Rhonda, on September 17
1978	Becomes a father
1990	Wins the Miller Lite Comedy Search
1992	Makes film debut in *Mo' Money*
1995	Stars in the HBO series *Midnight Mac*
1997	Begins *The Original Kings of Comedy* tour with Steve Harvey, Cedric the Entertainer, and D. L. Hughley
1998-2000	Has reoccurring role on the television sitcom *Moesha*
2000	Stars with Harvey, Cedric, and Hughley in Spike Lee's film *The Original Kings of Comedy*
2001	Stars in the sitcom *The Bernie Mac Show*; publishes *I Ain't Scared of You*
2003	Publishes *Maybe You Never Cry Again*
2005	Announces in February that he was diagnosed with sarcoidosis in 1983
2006	Celebrates the one hundredth episode of *The Bernie Mac Show*

grandmother berated him for telling family business, and dragged him from the banquet by his ears. Mac's ability to entertain extended to his public school classrooms. Miss Ford, one of Mac's teachers, allowed him to narrate stories to his classmates on Friday afternoons. Mac was so successful that when his classmates misbehaved and Ford threatened to cancel Mac's Friday session, the students behaved.

While in high school, Mac performed his Michael Jackson impression during open mike at the Regal and was unsuccessful. The emcee told him to return when he was funny. Yet a few weeks later, Mac performed his impressions of James Brown and *The Dick Van Dyke Show*'s husband and wife as African Americans, and told jokes about the elderly at the High Chaparral's Amateur Night. When Mac left the stage, the audience was still laughing. Consequently he won the $50 prize. Mac writes in *Maybe You Never Cry Again* that after his performance at the High Chaparral, he could not get the audience's laughter out of his head and that he wanted to hear it for the rest of his life. He adds that comedy was not a career or a choice; it was a "calling."

Faces the Unexpected

Chicago Vocational High School's graduation day for Mac was bittersweet because his mother was not in the audience. Mary McCullough, the person Mac acknowledges who believed in him before he believed in himself and who worked overtime while she was battling breast cancer to provide a better life for her family, died in August 1974. One year later, on the anniversary of his

mother's death, Mac's brother died at the age of twenty-seven. Still later, Billy Staples, who was more like Mac's brother than a friend, was murdered.

On September 17, 1977, less than a month before his twentieth birthday, Mac married his high school sweetheart, Rhonda, and on January 21, 1978, their daughter, Je'Niece, was born. Rhonda McCullough, a former nurse, became vice president of her husband's production company.

Establishes Career as Comedian

After Mac earned his high school diploma, he held a variety of low-paying jobs and attended Kennedy-King Community College in Chicago. However, he remained focused on fulfilling his childhood dream of becoming a comedian. In his quest to establish himself in the entertainment industry, he told jokes on the subway and continued to participate in amateur night contests at local clubs. After a successful weekend and a paycheck from Chicago's Cotton Club, Mac called a local agency looking for representation and sent a demo tape only to be told he was out of style and not good enough. He continued to perform at the Cotton Club and started performing at such venues as the Comedy Cottage.

During the early stage of his career, Mac and his wife vacationed in Las Vegas and purchased tickets to see Redd Foxx. They met the legendary entertainer before the show, and he offered to let Mac perform for five minutes in his show. Mac went on stage and made people laugh. After five minutes, Foxx motioned for him to continue, and Mac performed for at least another ten minutes. Afterwards, Foxx complimented him and told Mac what he already knew; Foxx advised him that he should not worry about being liked, failing, or taking risks as a comedian.

Mac entered the 1990 Miller Lite Comedy Search held at the Regal, hosted by Damon Wayans. Mac won the contest and deposited the entire $3,000 in a bank account in his daughter's name. Mac then gained greater exposure by appearing as an opening act for such entertainers as Gladys Knight and the Pips, the O'Jays, and the Temptations. Mac appeared in two HBO series: Russell Simmons' *Def Comedy Jam* (1992), and his own series, *Midnight Mac* (1995), which was nominated for a Cable Ace Award. From 1998 to 2000, Mac appeared as Uncle Bernie in the television sitcom *Moesha*.

Mac made his film debut as a club doorman in *Mo' Money* (1992), a film written by its star, Damon Wayans. He then appeared in *House Party 3* (1994), *Above the Rim* (1994), *Friday* (1995), *Get on the Bus* (1996), and *Life* (1999). Mac, along with Steve Harvey, Cedric the Entertainer, and D. L. Hughley began the *Original Kings of Comedy* tour in 1997. The show, which was initially booked in smaller venues, soon moved to larger arenas and stadiums as more than forty million people saw what became the highest grossing comedy tour. When Spike

Lee filmed the show and released the highly successful movie, *The Original Kings of Comedy* (2000), Mac gained even greater exposure.

Celebrates Sitcom's One Hundredth Episode

Mac, enjoying the success of the tour and Lee's film, appeared in additional movies, including *Ocean's Eleven* (2001); *Head of State* (2003); *Charlie's Angels: Full Throttle* (2003); *Mr. 3000* (2004), which was Mac's first starring role; *Bad Santa* (2003); *Ocean's Twelve* (2004); and *Guess Who* (2005), which is a remake of the 1967 classic *Guess Who's Coming to Dinner?*

In 2001, *The Bernie Mac Show* debuted on the Fox television network, and five years later on February 3, 2006, the one hundredth episode aired. Mac's show was one of the few African American sitcoms to appeal to crossover audiences since *The Cosby Show*. In the show, Mac plays a successful comedian who lives in Los Angeles with his wife. The childless couple becomes responsible for Mac's nieces and nephew when his sister enters rehab. *The Bernie Mac Show* is another example of art imitating reality because in the 1990s, Mac and his wife allowed his sixteen-year-old niece and her two-year-old daughter to move into their home. Since its inception, the show has consistently won awards, including an Emmy for outstanding writing in a comedy series (2002), and BET and NAACP awards for outstanding comedy series (2004 and 2005). Mac is the recipient of outstanding actor in a comedy series awards from BET in 2004 and 2005 as well as the NAACP from 2003 to 2006.

In February 2005, Mac announced that he had sarcoidosis, which is a rare autoimmune disease that causes inflammation of the body's tissues. Mac revealed that he was diagnosed with sarcoidosis in 1983. Although the disease is sometimes life-threatening, Mac asserted that he has not altered or limited his lifestyle and that he planned to establish the Bernie Mac Foundation in order to provide funds for sarcoidosis organizations.

Many years have gone by since Bernie Mac was a little boy who realized that comedy could uplift people's spirits, yet he has consistently remained true to what he views as his calling—making people laugh. He continues to enjoy the adoration of fans as he performs his comedic routines, acts in films, and stars in his critically acclaimed television show.

REFERENCES

Books

"Bernie Mac." In *Who's Who Among African Americans*.18th ed. Ed. Katherine Nemeh. Farmington Hills, Mich.: Thomson Gale, 2005.

Periodicals

Norris, Chris. "Bernie Mac Smacks a Nerve." *New York Times Magazine,* 12 May 2002.

Linda M. Carter

Victor-Eugene Macarty
1821–1890

Pianist, actor, composer, civil rights activist

Victor-Eugene Macarty was talented and ambitious. He was born into a society that afforded him privileges that were usually not accessible for men of color. Macarty used these opportunities to develop his musical talent. He was subjected to many injustices but sought ways to fight inequality and racism.

Victor-Eugene Macarty was born in 1821 in New Orleans, Louisiana. His mother was a free woman of color named Eulalie de Mandeville. He never knew his father, but he was a relative of a family of free African Americans named Macarty. The descendants of this Macarty family were wealthy, educated, and refined. The history of this family could be traced to a Scottish family named McCarthy who later changed the spelling of this name to Macarty.

Many of the white males in this family had liaisons with free women of color. The liaisons between these white males and free women of color became known as "placage", a derivative of the French word "placer", which means "to place". Populations of these free people of color were quite numerous from the 1760s through the 1790s. Generations of free girls of color were reared with the expectation of finding white men who could support and protect them, although these unions were not recognized as legal. These women were expected to be faithful to these white men until the men entered legitimate marriages to white women or the men died. This placage system was unique to Louisiana; it provided some independence and power in which free women of color could provide opportunities to their children that were unavailable before. It is unknown how many women of color were involved in these liaisons, but records from the late 1760s through 1800 reveal dozens of them as holding prime real estate in their own names. These women often were awarded property and money after the death of their wealthy white lovers. They were able to educate their children and pass on estates to them. Some court records from the 1800s show white men leaving inheritances for their illegitimate children of color.

Chronology

1821	Born in New Orleans
1840	Gains admittance to the Imperial Conservatoire in Paris
1854	Composes "Fleur de Salon"
1865	*La Tribune de la Nouvelle-Orleans* praises Macarty
1866	Publishes "La Fleur Indiscrete" on July 22
1869	Macarty challenges discriminatory seating at the St. Charles Theater
1869	Accepts appointment as a city administrator of assessments
1890	Dies

Free people of color were increasingly wealthy as they began to establish businesses and acquire property. Eulalie de Mandeville was a descendent of one of the most prominent white Creole families in New Orleans. Mandeville was the daughter of a wealthy woman of color named Marigny de Mandeville who worked a union between the young Eulalie and Eugene Macarty, a white man of wealth and privilege. After Eugene Macarty's death in 1845, Eulalie received property from his estate valued at $12,000. Eulalie was an intelligent and enterprising woman who eventually increased her fortune to about $155,000. She used her wealth to ensure that her children were well educated.

During his youth, Macarty took piano lessons from a person named J. Norres. He demonstrated musical talent early on and had numerous abilities. He had a wonderful singing voice in addition to his skills at the piano. Macarty was also a talented thespian and orator. In 1840, he was sent to Paris, and with the aid of Pierre Soule, a prominent member of the New Orleans elite class, and the French ambassador to the United States, Macarty studied at the Imperial Conservatoire. He studied vocal music, harmony, and composition.

Wins Fame and Praise

When Macarty returned to New Orleans, he garnered fame and praise as a pianist and amateur thespian. In time, he became known as a composer and also a civil rights leader. He was frequently the lead actor in theatrical productions presented by free colored people.

In 1869, Macarty took a seat in the white section of the St. Charles Theater. A light-skinned person, Macarty was not immediately recognized as being colored. When he was discovered, he was ordered to vacate the theater. He brought a suit against the theater because of their discriminatory seating policies, but the suit was dismissed and the manager resumed his practice of segregating blacks and whites. In protest, Macarty and others boycotted the theater. Their boycott ended in 1875 after the national civil rights act was passed.

Later that year, he was appointed city administrator of assessments by Governor Henry Clay Warmoth. Macarty also distinguished himself as a wealthy businessman. He held several important positions in the Republican administrations in the late 1800s. His alignment with this party helped him to promote the cause of civil rights. The militant *La Tribune de la Nouvelle-Orleans* characterized him as a talented man who brought much pride to the community. Not much is known about the last days of Macarty's life, beyond the fact that he died in 1890.

REFERENCES

Books

Christian, Marcus B. "Victor E. Macarty." In *Dictionary of American Negro Biography*. Eds. Rayford W. Logan and Michael R. Winston. New York: Norton, 1982.

Gehman, Mary. *The Free People of Color of New Orleans: An Introduction*. New Orleans: Margaret Media, 1994.

Trotter, James M. *Music and Some Highly Musical People*. New York: Johnson Reprint Corporation, 1968.

Connie Mack

Manning Marable
1950–

Historian, lecturer

Scholar and author Manning Marable is considered an expert on the black experience. Marable was born in Dayton, Ohio on May 13, 1950. His adolescent years were influenced by the civil rights movement. The segregation he witnessed as a child and the movement for integration had enormous impact on his development. As a senior in high school in Dayton, Ohio in 1968, Marable was a writer of a newspaper column, "Youth Speaks Out," for the local black weekly. When Martin Luther King Jr. was assassinated on April 4, 1968, Marable's mother decided to fly him to Atlanta to cover the funeral for the black newspaper. He was the first person at the Ebenezer Baptist Church, where the funeral was held. Marable was able to witness the funeral in its entirety and was invited into the press room that overlooked the ceremony. At this moment Marable felt that he was a participant in history as it unfolded, and he decided that day that he wanted to be a part of black history in the making.

Manning Marable

Marable came of age during the 1960s and like many at that time, he was involved in protests and marches against the Vietnam War and civil rights protests. He continued writing for student newspapers during college, and in 1971, Marable graduated from Earlham College. In 1972, he received his master's degree from the University of Wisconsin-Madison. After receiving his Ph.D. in American history from the University of Maryland in 1976, he became active with the black freedom movement. In 1976, he became active in the National Black Political Assembly, a network of community organizers, elected officials, and political activists. The National Black Political Assembly was an offshoot of the Gary convention of March 1972, which illustrated the pinnacle of the Black Power phase of the black freedom struggle in the 1960s and 1970s. At the Gary convention, thousands of African American activists and political figures discussed measures to expand black power in the political world, and to encourage the formation of independent political institutions committed to black liberation. In 1977, Marable joined the New American Movement. His involvement in these organizations shaped his views of politics and its relationship to race and class.

In 1980, Marable served as the senior research associate of Africana Studies at Cornell University, and in 1981 he became professor of history and economics and direc-

tor of the Race Relations Institute at Fisk University. From 1987 to 1989, he was the chairperson of the Department of Black Studies at Ohio State University, and from 1989 to 1993, he was a professor of history and political science at the University of Colorado at Boulder. Beginning in 1993, he was professor of history and political science at Columbia University. During his time at Columbia, he served as the founding director for the Institute of Research in African American Studies. Under his leadership, the institute became a leading center for scholarship and research on the black American experience. He has written and edited over twenty books and anthologies, and almost two hundred articles in academic journals and edited volumes as well.

In 1976, Marable began writing a political commentary series called "Along the Color Line," which continued thirty years later to appear in hundreds of newspaper and journals worldwide. In the early 2000s, Marable remained a very popular lecturer and was widely requested for guest appearances on numerous television and radio shows. He was co-founder of the Black Radical Congress, a coalition of African American activists. In 2002, Marable established the Center for Contemporary Black History at Columbia University, and in 2005, he designed the content for a multimedia educational kiosk featured at the Malcolm X and Dr. Betty Shabazz Memorial and Educational Center. Also in 2005, he published *Living Black History*. Marable continued to donate time and energy to causes involving civil rights, labor, religion, and social justice groups.

REFERENCES

Online

Crawford, Franklin. "Marable to Give Sage Sermon, MLK Lecture, Feb. 22 and 23." http://www.news.cornell.edu/Chronicle/04/2.19.04/Marable.html (Accessed 11 January 2006).

Overturf, Laura. "Manning Marable to Speak Feb. 24." http://www.udel.edu/PR/UpDate/99/20/manning.htm (Accessed 11 January 2006).

South End Press. "Being Left: A Humane Society is Possible Through Struggle; An Interview with Manning Marable." http://www.zmag.org/zmag/articles/marableint.htm (Accessed 11 January 2006).

Connie Mack

Chronology

1755	Born in the colony of New York on June 15
1759	Father dies; mother moves family to Florida and Georgia before settling in Charleston, South Carolina
1768	Converts to Christianity at the age of thirteen
1772	Runs a church school in South Carolina
1776	Serves the British Navy at the start of the Revolutionary War
1782	Discharged from military
1785	Ordained a minister; travels to Nova Scotia to minister to North American black refugees
1787	Publishes *A Narrative of the Lord's Wonderful Dealings with John Marrant, A Black*
1789	Publishes *A Sermon Preached on the 24th Day of June 1789...at the Request of the Right Worshipful the Grand Master Prince Hall, and the Rest of the Brethren of the African Lodge of the Honorable Society of Free and Accepted Masons in Boston*
1790	Publishes *A Journal of the Rev. John Marrant, from August the 18th, 1785, to the 16th of March, 1790*
1791	Dies in Islington, London, England

John Marrant
1755–1791

Writer, minister

The legacy of John Marrant lies in his published writings. Marrant contributed to religion, literature, and the progress of African Americans in the midst of slavery.

Born June 15, 1755 in the colony of New York, Marrant eventually traveled to the South with his mother, after his father's death in 1759. The family settled in Charleston, South Carolina, after stays in St. Augustine, Florida and in Georgia. Marrant was able to read and to spell by the age of eleven. Thereafter Marrant received an education in the arts; he learned to play the French horn and violin in eighteen months. Like many African American men at the time, he entertained white gentry at balls and other events. As Julien-Joseph Virey noted in his eighteenth-century work, *Natural History of the Negro Species Particularly*, the sensual and artistic human characteristics were considered to be a temperament divinely bestowed to Africa and its descendants; hence African Americans' musical talent was respected in spite of the fact that musicians themselves were denied basic human rights. In spite of his artistic skills, Marrant was required to be an apprentice in order to learn a pragmatic trade—carpentry. Eventually he returned to his pursuit of music, which indirectly led to his fame.

Marrant had an extraordinary conversion at the age of thirteen. While playing a prank on the renowned evangelist George Whitefield, Marrant was stopped by the words of the preacher and converted to Christianity.

Persecuted by his own family, Marrant sought comfort with a Cherokee tribe. Marrant remained with the tribe for some time before returning to Charleston in 1772 to teach slaves. He joined the navy late in 1776. After serving Britain for six years, he was injured in the Dutch Anglo War and discharged in 1782. The years after that were spent in ministerial training under the Huntington Methodist Connexion, which was sponsored by Selina Hastings, who was one of the benefactors of Phyllis Wheatley. In 1785 he was ordained a minister and traveled to Nova Scotia to minister to over three thousand African American refugees who fled slavery by fighting in the war.

Marrant's marital status remains unclear. The New York City Inspection Roll of Negroes in 1783 identifies Marrant as the owner of Melia Marrant and her two children. Devona Mallory, in *African American Lives*, argues that there is no reason to believe that the woman and children were not Marrant's family. However, Joanna Brooks and John Saillant, in *Face Zion Forward*, suggest that it is possible that Marrant owned slaves since he needed to avoid offending his Huntington Methodist Connexion.

Literary Influence

In 1785 Marrant published *A Narrative of the Lord's Wonderful Dealings with John Marrant, A Black* with the assistance of Reverend William Aldridge, who transcribed it. It has been argued by some critics that Marrant could not write at this time. Presumably Marrant had learned to write before he published his journal five years later, entitled *A Journal of the Rev. John Marrant, from August the 18th, 1785, to the 16th of March, 1790*. In his review of Marrant's writings in *American Writers before 1800*, John C. Shields notes that the *Journal* is written in a more conservative tone than the *Narrative*. This difference may substantiate the idea that the first work was transcribed by someone else. Arthur P. Davis, in *Dictionary of American Negro Biography*, also notes differences in the tone of the two works. He argues that the *Narrative* is sensationalized with the incredible accounts of divine intervention in Marrant's life. The *Journal*, in Davis' opinion, is monotonous. Perhaps Henry Louis Gates Jr. articulates it best in *The Signifying Monkey* when he notes that many of the early African American narratives were dictated to white editors, who possibly revised them in some ways.

In an article in *African American Review*, Cedrick May contends that Marrant's work is based on a theology rooted in black religion, which is founded on tradition and ambitious social change. Marrant's work is also an Indian captivity narrative; it was one of the top three Indian captivity narratives in circulation during the eighteenth century.

Antislavery Contributions

In spite of Marrant's popularity and influence as an African American writer, some critics still hold that Marrant failed to communicate much on behalf of his race. In his *A Sermon Preached on the 24th Day of June 1789...at the Request of the Right Worshipful the Grand Master Prince Hall, and the Rest of the Brethren of the African Lodge of the Honorable Society of Free and Accepted Masons in Boston*, Marrant focused the text on love and virtue against evil. In relation to race, he does clearly note that blacks have a place of honor as the descendents of Cush, who were responsible for the creation of some of the ancient wonders and mathematics.

Marrant died in Islington, London, England in 1791. As Shields aptly argues, Marrant's life modeled liberty in mind, body and soul, which he desired for all humankind regardless of color; this desire for universal freedom only heightened his example for eighteenth century African Americans who were denied these liberties and thought to be less than human. Marrant was a man who stood in three worlds without limitations: the literary world, the religious world, and the world of progress for African Americans.

REFERENCES

Books

Brooks, Joanna, and John Saillant. *Face Zion Forward: First Writers of the Black Atlantic, 1785-1798*. Boston: Northeastern University Press, 2002.

Carretta, Vincent, ed. *Unchained Voices: An Anthology of Black Authors in the English-Speaking World of the Eighteenth Century*. Lexington: University of Kentucky Press, 1996.

Davis, Arthur P. "John Marrant." In *Dictionary of American Negro Biography*. Eds. Rayford W. Logan and Michael R. Winston. New York: Norton, 1982.

Gates, Henry Louis Jr. *The Signifying Monkey: A Theory of African-American Literary Criticism*. New York: Oxford University Press, 1988.

Mallory, Devona. "John Marrant." In *African American Lives*. Eds. Henry Louis Gates Jr. and Evelyn Brooks Higginbotham. New York: Oxford University Press, 2004.

Shields, John C. "John Marrant." In *American Writers Before 1800..* Eds. James Levernier and Douglass R. Wilmes. Westport, Conn.: Greenwood Press, 1983.

Virey, Julien-Joseph. "Natural History of the Negro Species Particularly." Trans. J. H. Guenebault. *Race: The Origins of An Idea, 1760-1850*. Eds. Hannah Frankziska Augstein and Andrew Pyle. Bristol: Thoemmes Press, 1996.

Walker, James W. St. G. "John Marrant." In *Dictionary of Canadian Biography*. Trans. J. F. Flinn. Toronto: University of Toronto Press and Les Presses de l'université Laval, 1979.

Periodicals

May, Cedrick. "John Marrant and the Narrative Construction of an Early Black Methodist Evangelical." *African American Review* 38 (Winter 2004): 553-72.

Althea Tait

Branford Marsalis
1960–

Saxophonist, jazz musician

Branford Marsalis is a famous saxophonist who comes from a famous musical jazz family. Marsalis has been more adventurous in his musical career with his various styles than his very famous and more traditional trumpeter brother Wynton. Marsalis has enjoyed mainstream success with his brief stint on *The Tonight Show with Jay Leno* but focuses more on musical artistry than commercial success.

Branford Marsalis, born August 26, 1960, is the oldest out of six sons born to music teacher and jazz pianist Ellis Marsalis Jr. and Dolores Ferdinand Marsalis. He and his brother Wynton are the two most famous musicians of the Marsalis family. Two more of the Marsalis brothers are talented musical artists: Delfeayo is a producer and a trombone player, and the youngest son, Jason, is a drummer. Ellis Marsalis III is a poet and photojournalist and is publicly known by the pen name, t. p. Luce. Mboya is autistic and lives with his parents. The

Branford Marsalis

Chronology

1960	Born in New Orleans, Louisiana on August 26
1979	Begins studies at Berklee Music College in Boston
1982	Joins brother Wynton's band
1984	Releases debut album *Scenes in the City*
1985	Partners with Sting; performs at Live Aid
1992	Wins Grammy for Best Jazz Instrumental Performance for album *I Heard You Twice the First Time*; begins working on *The Tonight Show with Jay Leno*
1993	Wins Grammy for Best Pop Instrumental Performance for single "Barcelona Mona" with Bruce Hornsby
1995	Leaves *The Tonight Show with Jay Leno*
1996	Teams with father, Ellis Marsalis, to do album *Loved Ones*
2000	Wins Grammy for Best Jazz Instrumental Album *Contemporary Jazz*
2002	Begins own record label, Marsalis Music
2005	Co-founds *Operation Home Delivery* with Harry Connick Jr.

family has done charity work to raise funds and awareness for autism. Grandfather Ellis Marsalis Sr. worked as a poultry worker until he opened the Marsalis Motel in 1943 in Jefferson Parish, Louisiana. Exposure to musicians' lodging in the motel partly inspired Ellis Jr. to pursue a career in music.

Though he wanted to go to New York as a young man to pursue a music career, Ellis Jr. stayed in New Orleans and supported his large family on a music teacher's salary and did not try to pursue or dissuade his sons from playing music. "Everybody thinks our family was, 'Oh, let's play jazz for breakfast, jazz for lunch, jazz for dinner'," Branford told *Ebony*. "But Wynton didn't like jazz until he was 12 years old. I despised jazz until I was 19." He may not have pressed his sons to become musicians, but when his sons developed the vocation on their own, Ellis Jr. expected them to play their instruments well.

Shortly after taking up the saxophone in 1979, Marsalis began his studies at Berklee Music College in Boston, Massachusetts. While at Berklee, he worked at Burger King. The store manager was so impressed with young Marsalis that he wanted to recommend him for the fast food chain's management school, but Marsalis had bigger plans. The career decision was one that he did not regret.

Begins Successful Career

After his studies at Berklee were completed, Marsalis played baritone sax with Art Blakely's band while they toured Europe. He also briefly worked with the Lionel Hampton Orchestra in 1980 and Clark Terry in 1981 before working again with Blakely. In April 1984, Marsalis's debut album from Columbia Records, *Scenes in the City*, was released. Marsalis also worked with Herbie Hancock and Miles Davis during this stage of his career. He played with Wynton's band between 1982 and 1985 as well.

In March 1985, Marsalis was introduced to Sting and left Wynton's band to work with the singer. The work that Marsalis and Sting did together (along with fellow band members Kenny Kirkland, Daryl "Munch" Jones and Omar Hakim) resulted in the 1985 album *Dream of the Blue Turtles*. In this same year, Marsalis performed at the 1985 mega-concert, Live Aid.

In 1986, baby Reese was born to Marsalis and his then-wife, actor Theresa Reese. That same year, the rock documentary *Bring on the Night*, profiling Sting and the band, was released. Marsalis also released a solo album at the end of 1986, *Royal Garden Blues*, which earned him a Grammy nomination. Marsalis's 1987 solo album, *Renaissance*, was produced by his brother, Delfeayo.

Sting and his band's follow-up album to *Turtles*, *Nothing like the Sun*, came out in 1987. In January 1988, Marsalis toured internationally with Sting and performed at the Freedom Concert that was held in order to help free then-jailed South African political prisoner Nelson Mandela. Between 1988 and 1990, Marsalis released the albums *Random Abstract*, *Trio Jeepy*, and *Crazy People Music*. Marsalis also co-wrote the single "Jazz Thing" for the Spike Lee film *Mo' Better Blues*. All three albums and the single earned Grammy nominations. In 1991, Marsalis released *The Beautiful Ones Are Not Yet Born*. The next year, he became the musical director for *The Tonight Show with Jay Leno*, elevating his celebrity to the level of his brother, Wynton.

Marsalis's job at *The Tonight Show* did not slow him down. During his three-year stint with the show, Marsalis worked on various television and film projects as well as releasing three albums: a 1992 Grammy-winning blues album, *I Heard You Twice the First Time*; the live album *Bloomington*; and the album *Buckshot LeFonque* with the band of the same name that he formed for the project. Buckshot LeFonque was a pseudonym that was used by legendary 1950s musician Cannonball Adderly. *Buckshot* was released in the summer 1994, a few months after Marsalis won a Grammy with singer Bruce Hornsby for their single "Barcelona Mona." The pair received another Grammy nomination for their rendition of "The Star Spangled Banner," which they performed for the Ken Burns documentary, *Baseball*.

Leaves *Tonight Show* and Goes Non-Stop

In 1995, Marsalis left *The Tonight Show* to do a global tour for with Buckshot LeFonque. Marsalis later admitted one reason why he left *The Tonight Show* when he told the *York Dispatch*, "I needed to realize that I'm not an entertainer, I'm an artist." Marsalis, who worked on the show in California, also did not want to be away from son Reese, who resided in New York. Marsalis and his wife divorced in the same year that he left *The Tonight Show*. He later remarried and had two children with his second wife, Nicole.

In 1996, Marsalis and his father together recorded the album *Loved Ones* in two days. The project was initially going to be a solo project for the elder Marsalis, but he invited his son to play on the album with him. In March of the same year, Marsalis wrote the score to the Showtime movie *Mr. and Mrs. Loving*, starring Tim Robbins and Lela Rochon. In the fall, Marsalis began the Catherine Herrick Cobb Distinguished Lectureship position at Michigan University. After the year lectureship ended, Marsalis stayed on as an adjunct faculty member until the spring of 2000.

In October 1996, Marsalis released *Dark Keys*. He defended his multi-genre music in light of criticism from jazz purists: "If you listen to a lot of jazz records, all the songs have a tendency to sound exactly the same," Marsalis told the *Memphis Commercial Appeal*. "And that's something I've always hated. I've seen many reviews saying that my music lacks focus. Because to most people the concept of focus is about sameness."

In April 1997, Buckshot LeFonque released *Music Evolution*. In November, Marsalis appeared in a cameo role in the film *Eve's Bayou*. In February 1999, Marsalis's radio program *Jazzset*, received the Achieve-ment in Radio Award (AIR) for Best Syndicated Show. The next month, he released the album, *Requiem*, which garnered a Grammy nomination. Marsalis won his third Grammy for the 2000 release, *Contemporary Jazz*. Later that year, he became a part-time faculty member of San Francisco State's music department. In March 2001, Marsalis's album and collaboration with the Orpheus Chamber Orchestra, *Creation*, was released. Marsalis and the orchestra toured the United States and Japan to promote the project.

On August 4, 2001, Louis Armstrong's 100th birthday, Marsalis teamed up with brothers Wynton, Delfeayo, and Jason as well as Harry Connick Jr. for the benefit concert honoring father Ellis, *Satchmo to Marsalis: A Tribute to the Fathers of Jazz*. The benefit took place at the Kiefer UNO Lakefront Arena in New Orleans.

Makes Music on His Own Terms

Columbia Records, the record company to which both Branford and Wynton were signed, drastically cut back their production of new jazz music and began to steer towards repackaging catalog material. In response, Marsalis, wanting to practice his art without the pressures of the profit-driven music industry, founded an independent record company, Marsalis Music, in 2002.

Marsalis continues to serve his community. In the aftermath of Hurricane Katrina in 2005, Marsalis and Connick teamed up with Habitat for Humanity and announced *Operation Home Delivery*, a plan for a Musicians' Village. This village was intended to provide homes for New Orleans musicians displaced by the tragedy. In the center of this new community, the Ellis Marsalis Center for Music was to be built. This center would help to educate and nurture the musicians who live in the new neighborhood. Marsalis continues to make music and continues to co-chair *Operation Home Delivery* with Connick. Marsalis shows that one can be true to his art and himself in a business that increasingly focuses on profit.

REFERENCES

Periodicals

Ellis, Bill. "'Jazz Must Go in a Northerly Direction,' Branford Marsalis Says." *Memphis Commercial Appeal*, 18 February 1997.

Gans, Charles J. "Branford Marsalis Embraces the Jazz Tradition." *York Dispatch*, 28 January 2005.

Hadju, David. "Wynton's Blues." *Atlantic Monthly* 291 (March 2003): 43-48.

Mazza, Jay. "Marsalis Patriarch Dies at 96." *Louisiana Weekly*, 27 September 2004.

Schoettler, Carl. "Playing His Own Tune: In Poetry and Photos, Ellis Marsalis III Makes a Different Kind of Music." *Baltimore Sun*, 5 December 2004.

Waldron, Clarence. "Branford Marsalis: Blowing his Own Horn." *Ebony* 44 (February 1989): 66-67.

Online

"Blowing Up a Storm." *The Guardian*. http://www. guardian.co.uk/arts/features/story/0,11710,881770, 00.html (Accessed 23 January 2006).

"The Marsalis Family: A Jazz Celebration." Marsalis Music. http://www.marsalismusic.com/content.cfm? selection=doc.15 (Accessed 24 January 2006).

Brandy Baker

Johnny Mathis
1935–

Singer

Johnny Mathis

Johnny Mathis, best known as a romantic balladeer, is one of the most successful recording artists of all time, exceeded only by Frank Sinatra and Elvis Presley. His vast discography consists of jazz, pop, soul/R&B, soft rock, Broadway, Brazilian, Spanish, and numerous Christmas albums. As an accomplished and trained musician in jazz and opera he has captured the attention of the world's audiences for soul/R&B, soft rock, and Broadway for almost five decades. His smooth tenor voice delivers romantic ballads and brings to them a natural quality that has inspired audiences of all ages. This extraordinary ability along with the angelic quality of his voice touches the adolescent love in his listeners. Mathis is expressly recognized as one of the few artists who have recorded original material and continues as a popular concert attraction which began in the 1950s. His success was so swift and magnetic that his record and album sales place him as one of the first African American millionaires in the United States. Mathis is said to exemplify the best in musical artistry.

John Royce Mathis was born on September 30, 1935 in Gilmer, Texas. He was the fourth of seven children born to Clem and Mildred Mathis. Mathis's father, who briefly was a vaudeville performer playing piano and singing, moved his family to San Francisco, California. In his early years, Mathis and his family lived in a basement apartment in the Filmore District of San Francisco. Both of his parents worked as domestics for a San Francisco millionaire. His father was a chauffeur and handyman and his mother was a housekeeper. Even though the family was poor, Mathis's father saw the potential in his son. The elder Mathis purchased a second-hand upright piano for $25 when Johnny was eight. The piano would not fit through the front door of the small apartment so

Johnny stayed up all night watching his father disassemble and reassemble the piano in their small living room. "My Blue Heaven" was the first song taught to young Mathis by his father. With encouragement and guidance young Mathis began to participate in local church choirs, school functions, talent competitions, and other musical activities. By the time Mathis was thirteen, he had attracted the attention of Connie Cox, an Oakland-based opera singer and voice teacher. She agreed to give Mathis voice lessons in exchange for doing odd jobs around the house. A year later Mathis had won several talent shows and was singing at weddings and other events. He studied classical voice technique with Cox for six years and continued their communications for years after.

Although shy, Mathis was an excellent student. He was the first African American president of the student body at Roosevelt Junior High School and later treasurer for his high school class at George Washington High School. He also excelled in athletics in the areas of track and field and basketball. Because of his success as an athlete in high school and earning four athletic letters, he was able to attend San Francisco State College on an athletic scholarship. Mathis hoped to become a physical education teacher or a track coach. While in college he was a basketball teammate of future Boston Celtic Bill Russell. He also ran hurdles and set a record of 6 feet 5 inches in the high jump. In 1956, Mathis was invited to the Olympic track trials held in Berkeley. Instead, Mathis gave up his chance for the U.S. Olympic team in the high jump to pursue a musical career.

While in college Mathis heard famous jazz musicians who performed at the renowned Blackhawk nightclub in San Francisco. He began performing in 1955 with a sextet led by Virgil Gonsalves, a local baritone saxophone player, and other students. During one performance at the Blackhawk nightclub, the co-owner of the club, Helen Noga, and her husband were so impressed by Mathis's "jamming" that she became his manager. Noga realized the magnitude of Mathis's vocal talent and appeal and was determined to make him a success. At an informal appearance at the 440 Club in San Francisco George Avakian, a well-known jazz producer and executive of Columbia, discovered Mathis. He had been repeatedly invited to see Mathis perform by Noga. After Mathis's performance, Avakian sent a telegram announcing that he had found an exceptionally talented nineteen-year-old boy. Avakian not only arranged for Mathis to perform at the Village Vanguard and the Blue Angel in New York, but he convinced Columbia records to sign him. Mathis's first album, recorded in New York in 1955, was titled *A New Sound in Popular Song*. It included jazz standards such as "Angel Eyes" and "Easy to Love." It also featured Gil Evans and pianist John Lewis of the Modern Jazz Quartet. The album used the kind of arrangements that Mathis had admired while at San Francisco State, but it did not do well commercially. Avakian teamed Mathis with producer and arranger Mitch Miller, who pointed Mathis toward singing lush ballad string arrangements, an approach that had worked before for Columbia records.

Mathis had his first big hit in July 1957 with the album *Wonderful Wonderful*, fourteenth on the charts, which sold in the millions. He followed this with the hits:

"Chances Are" (1957), first on the charts and a million-selling single; "It's Not for Me to Say" (1957), fifth on the charts; "Twelfth of Never" (1957), ninth on the charts; "Misty" (1959), twelfth on the charts and Mathis's signature song; and "What Will Mary Say" (1963), ninth on the charts. His singles were produced on the 45rpm which was the premier music medium of the day. The string sound on his album *Warm* in 1957 began the longstanding success of Mathis as an album seller. In 1958 the album *Greatest Hits* remained on the charts for 490 weeks, or nine and a half years. Similar chart success was achieved with *Heavenly* in 1959 which stayed on the charts for 295 weeks, or over five and a half years. With the release of *Misty* in 1959, Mathis became a major concert performer and appeared in films and television shows. He appeared in films, singing the title songs, such as "Lizze" in 1957 and "A Certain Smile" in 1958. With the network television show *American Bandstand* devoted to rock 'n' roll, Mathis's appearance gave some alternative to the show's musical style.

Mathis's popularity came from his extraordinary vocal skill and his naturally smooth tenor voice. His sound was immediately recognizable, laden with soft romantic appeal, depth and technique. His wavy hair and California good looks placed him in no immediate ethnic group, thus allowing him to transcend social and racial barriers. His music reached all types of audiences. In his first successful year when he was twenty-one he earned $100,000 and by age twenty-nine he was earning $1 million per year. He is ranked among the first African Americans in the United States to become millionaires. Mathis spent the first six years of his career with Helen Noga as his manager, and he also lived as a guest in the Noga home. Although appreciative of the excellent business skill and the development of his career, Mathis decided to manage his own legal and personal life and moved out of town. Noga was known to be overbearing and domineering. Mathis launched his own company, Jon Mat, in 1964 to produce his records, and Rojohn Productions to handle his appearances. The Hollywood Hill area became Mathis's new home in the mid-1970s. Most of Mathis's early hits appeared in the 1950s and 1960s, and his marketing strategies were primarily aimed toward middle-of-the-road white audiences. During these years Mathis struggled with drug addiction, but he was able to overcome it.

In the United States Mathis depended on concept albums to support his career as the pop music of the 1960s made ballads even more difficult for commercial success. Concept albums became the major focus with themes, such as *Away from Home* (1965), concentrating on songs of European countries; *Ole'* (1965), sung in Portuguese and Spanish for a Latin-American audience; and *Wonderful World of Make Believe* (1964), which consisted entirely of songs based on fairytales and albums dedicated to composers, such as Bert Bacharach and Bert Kaempfert. In 1974, the United Kingdom's singles chart included Mathis's song "I'm Still in Love with You," and two years later Mathis had the number one Christmas song in the U.K., "When A Child Is Born." His sales were always within market success levels but a fresh look was needed.

In an effort to connect with the African American audience, Mathis sought out original material from African American composers, such as Thom Bell and Linda Creed. In a duet with African American rhythm-and-blues singer Deniece Williams, the hit "Too Much, Too Little, Too Late" rose to number one on the pop and soul charts in 1978. Her vocal virtuosity matched his and resulted in the successful album *That's What Friends Are For* in 1981. The duo also recorded "Without Us," which was used as the theme song for the television show *Family Ties*. In the late 1980s, after several attempts at disco and other rock forms, Mathis returned to his signature romantic ballad style and continued to do more duets with other popular female stars. This work resulted in considerable chart success as he teamed with artists such as Dionne Warwick, Gladys Knight, Angela Bofill, and Barbara Streisand.

Personal Life and Choices

Mathis's songs, which have been so popular with the baby boomers ever since the 1950s, shed little light on his personal life. The only biography of Mathis is the British work published in 1983 as *The Authorised Biography of Johnny Mathis* by Tony Jasper. Respectful of Mathis's privacy, this biography presents the only book-length look at Mathis's life as a whole.

In a 1982 interview with *Us* magazine, Mathis commented on his sexuality. Previously he had deflected questions regarding his bachelor status. During the interview he spoke about his first love at age sixteen and said that being gay was "a way of life that he had grown accustomed to." In 1993 in an interview with the *New York Times*, Mathis stated that the 1982 interview with *Us* magazine was to be off the record. Mathis has declined any further comments regarding his sexuality.

In the 1990s, Mathis was still going strong, headlining in Atlantic City and Las Vegas resorts and selling out three concerts at Carnegie Hall in New York in October 1993. He also received critical acclaim for his album *Personal Collection*, which is a compilation of 86 popular ballads. Mathis's music, which spans every decade from the 1950s to the early 2000s, has consistently pleased listeners from all over the world. Mathis sang for the president of Liberia in 1973. In 1978 he sang for the British royal family in "A Command Performance" at the London Palladium, and in 1987 he performed for the prime minister of Japan. United States presidents Ronald Reagan and Bill Clinton have also heard Mathis perform. One of Mathis's special performances was in May 1994, when he sang to President Clinton, along with his wife and five former first ladies.

In 2000 Mathis returned to a thematic album of contemporary materials, focusing on Broadway. He included selections from *Rent*, *Les Miserables*, and *Phantom of the Opera*, and updated versions of some of his original material. He also included *Mathis on Broadway*, updates on *Life Is Just a Bowl of Cherries* with the cast of *Forever Plaid* and Leiber-Stoller's *On Broadway from Smokey Joe's Café*. In September 2005 Mathis told John Benson of the *Cleveland Plain Dealer* that a Brazilian album was planned. Some fifteen years earlier he had recorded with Sergio Mendes and famed Latin songwriter Don Caymmi, but the record was never released. Again, the idea of a Latin recording appealed to Mathis.

Mathis has received numerous awards over the years. In June of 1972, he received his own star on the famous Hollywood Walk of Fame. He has received two Grammy nominations. His first Grammy nomination was for "Misty" in 1960 in the category of Best Vocal Performance on a Single Record or Track Mate and the second was in 1992 for "In a Sentimental Mood Sings Ellington" in the category of Best Traditional Pop Performance. Mathis was inducted into the Grammy Hall of Fame twice. He received his first induction in 1998 for the song, "Chances Are" (1957) and again in 2002 for "Misty" (1959). In 2003 Mathis was presented with the Lifetime Achievement Award by the Academy of Recording Arts and Sciences.

Mathis performed a duet with Ray Charles in 2004. They sang "Over the Rainbow," which was released on Charles's album *Genius Loves Company*. At Ray Charles's request, the song was played at his funeral. Over the years, Mathis still commands attention for his international superstar status. He joins a distinguish group of Columbia and Epic artists who have been inducted into the Essential Series of double-CD's. He is in the company of artists such as Tony Bennett, the Byrds, Johnny Cash, Miles Davis, Neil Diamond, Mahalia Jackson, Janis Joplin, Simon & Garfunkel, Sly & the Family Stone, Luther Vandross, and Earth, Wind & Fire. With two LP's listed in the Top 10 as well as the Top 25 on historian Joel Whitburn's *Albums of Longevity* chart, Mathis has set new heights in record sales. He has recorded more than one hundred albums of original music, sold more than 215 million albums and singles worldwide, and has approximately $130 million in sales in the United States and $50 million in sales from the United Kingdom. The term "Greatest Hits" was a marketing tool created for Mathis in 1958 and is now used throughout the industry.

Even after choosing music as his career, Mathis remained a sports enthusiast. He is an avid golfer and has a minimum of five holes-in-one. He also hosts several golf tournaments, such as the Johnny Mathis Seniors PGA Classic held in Los Angeles and The Shell/Johnny Mathis Golf Classic in Belfast, North Ireland. Mathis's other favorite pastime is cooking. He is a gourmet cook. In 1981 Mathis published the cookbook *Cooking for You Alone*. The book contains Mathis's favorite recipes and is designed for people who do not want to spend hours in the kitchen.

Mathis continued to tour and maintain a vigorous schedule of appearances in the early 2000s. The year 2006 marked the 50th anniversary of Mathis's singing career. He released on average one album a year and had two or three concerts a month with time for golf. His concerts appeal to longstanding fans and a new generation of listeners, all of whom enjoy "the holy trinity" as Mathis calls them: "Chances Are," "The Twelfth of Never," and "Misty." As the magical quality and smooth tenor voice of Mathis continues to interpret the music of love, "chances are" he will remain one of the twentieth century's most cherished and loved singers.

REFERENCES

Books

Collins, Willie. "Johnny Mathis." In *St. James Encyclopedia of Popular Culture*. Eds. Sara Pendergast and Tom Pendergast. Vol. 3. Detroit: St. James Press, 2000.

George-Warren, Holly, and Patricia Romanowski. "Johnny Mathis." In *The Rolling Stone Encyclopedia of Rock & Roll*. New York: Rolling Stone Press, 2001.

Manheim, James. "Johnny Mathis." In *Contemporary Black Biography*. Vol. 20. Ed. Shirelle Phelps. Detroit: Gale Group, 1999.

Periodicals

Berry, William Earl. "Millionaire Mathis Comes Home to Black Music." *Jet* (10 January 1974): 56-63.

Carpenter, Bil. "How Johnny Mathis Keeps the Music Playing." *Goldmine Magazine* (28 May 1993): 14-28.

Petrucelli, Alan W. "Celebrity Q & A." *Us* (22 June 1982): 58-60.

Online

George, Iris Gross. *The Mathis Chronicles*. http://www.themathischronicles.net/jonbio.html (Accessed 20 January 2006).

Lean'tin L. Bracks

John E. Maupin, Jr.
1946–

College president, dentist

John E. Maupin Jr. became the ninth president of Meharry Medical College in 1994. He was the first alumnus and the second dentist to lead the historically

---

Chronology

1946	Born in Los Angeles on October 28
1968	Ends undergraduate experience at San Jose State College
1972	Graduates from Meharry Medical College with a D.D.S. degree
1979	Earns M.B.A. from Loyola College in Baltimore
1980	Establishes himself as oral health professional in Baltimore
1989	Appointed executive vice president of Morehouse School of Medicine in Atlanta
1994	Appointed president of Meharry Medical College
2001	Leads celebration of Meharry Medical College's 125th anniversary
2006	Resigns as president and chief executive officer of Meharry Medical College; becomes president of Morehouse School of Medicine in Atlanta

---

black academic health center, located in Nashville, Tennessee. Before arriving at Meharry, Dr. Maupin was executive vice president of the Morehouse School of Medicine in Atlanta, Georgia from 1989 to 1994. In 2006, Maupin resigned as president and chief executive officer of Meharry Medical College, returning to the Morehouse School of Medicine as president.

Immediately prior to joining Meharry, Maupin was chief executive officer, from 1987 to 1989, of Southside Healthcare, Inc., a federally qualified community health center in Georgia's capital city. From 1981 to 1987, Maupin served the Baltimore City Health Department, first as assistant commissioner of clinical services and finally as deputy commissioner of health. Prior to the municipal appointments, he established the first dental clinic at the West Baltimore Community Health Center while serving there as dental director.

Education

Born in Los Angeles on October 28, 1946, to a prominent dentist and a revered public school educator, John E. Maupin Jr. completed his secondary education in Los Angeles and then pursued undergraduate training at San Jose State College. He earned the D.D.S. at Meharry's School of Dentistry and, subsequently, was awarded an M.B.A. in 1979 at Loyola College in Baltimore.

Having succeeded in dentistry, academia, community public health, and business, Maupin acknowledged that Meharry Medical College changed his life. He accepted the 1994 mandate to nurse his ailing alma mater back to health. A glance backwards offers context for the renaissance sparked by John Maupin's passion for the institution that took him in and thoroughly prepared him for what became his true calling.

Mainstream professional schools did not interest John Maupin of South Central Los Angeles. But Meharry Medical College took a chance on this underachieving campus activist. Spotting real potential beyond a so-so undergraduate transcript, Meharry accepted Maupin and immersed him in its culture of compassion, competence, camaraderie, and intellectual rigor.

A mature and focused John Maupin graduated from Meharry on time—in 1972—and then completed a general dentistry residency at Provident Hospital in Baltimore. He maintained a successful dental practice in that city for a few years but then decided to enter health care management. He took on leadership positions at community-based health care facilities and municipal public health agencies in Baltimore and in the U.S. Army Dental Corps in Washington, D.C.

Maupin moved to Atlanta and worked in injury prevention and health promotion, a high-profile job which brought him to the attention of faculty that once tutored him and college trustees who had been tracking his postgraduate progress. He excelled at Atlanta's Southside Healthcare, Inc., the community health center. His performance at the Morehouse School of Medicine was exemplary; in fact, he flourished under Louis Sullivan's leadership.

Moreover, he constantly sought the advice of three seasoned educators known for spotting and nurturing fast-track talent: Johnnetta Cole, then-president of Spelman College and later chief executive of Bennett College for Women in Greensboro, North Carolina; Thomas Cole, former president of Clark-Atlanta University; and Dean Emeritus Joe Henry of Howard University's College of Dentistry.

Meharry sought its distinguished alumnus when its academic and fiscal vital signs pleaded for life support. Its trustees turned to a reluctant John Maupin. Joe Henry reminded Maupin of the rare opportunity Meharry was offering. After some thought, Maupin agreed to be a candidate. The trustees determined his strengths matched the college's needs going forward, and they were correct.

Strong Doses of Discipline

When Maupin arrived in Nashville in 1994, Meharry was grappling with a $49 million cumulative operating deficit; seriously deteriorated campus facilities resulting from years of deferred maintenance; poor performance of students on national qualifying examinations; limited clinical resources and training sites for students and residents that contributed to the loss of three residency programs; a threatened loss of institutional and professional accreditations; inadequate information technology infrastructure and outdated administrative and clinical management systems; and significantly undercapitalized research and clinical enterprises.

With Maupin at the helm, Meharry launched a series of bold initiatives that reconfigured the college's external relationships and dramatically transformed its operating economy. The college committed itself to uncompromising excellence, embraced an institutional culture that values niche-focused competencies, and aggressively forged strategic partnerships to expand institutional capacity and leverage opportunities for advancement.

The results during Maupin's tenure as president were impressive and quantifiable. He earned good marks for effectively executing a financial restructuring plan that erased the college's $49 million operating deficit; investing more than $70 million in renovating and constructing campus facilities, including a hospital building, campus housing, research laboratories, classrooms, and parking sites; and strengthening the curriculum and executing new academic enrichment programs to dramatically improve student performance on national qualifying examinations—from 40 percent first-time taker pass rates to more than 90 percent pass rates.

On his watch, the college also achieved full accreditation for the maximum period afforded by the college's various accrediting bodies. It established in 1999 a nationally acclaimed academic alliance with Vanderbilt University Medical Center and initiated and completed a $125 million capital campaign, the largest advancement effort in the college's history. It increased the number of endowed chairs and professorships from six in 1993 to thirteen by 2003 and significantly enhanced the overall research infrastructure. Research funding increased from $9 million in 1994 to $26 million in Fiscal Year 2003, highlighted by important new initiatives in cancer, HIV/AIDS, women's reproductive health, oral health, and unintentional injuries.

Maupin's leadership commanded the attention and enormous respect of peers in America's health science community and elsewhere. He was elected president of the National Dental Association. He is active in various scientific advisory groups. He is a member of the National Committee on Foreign Medical Education Accreditation of the U.S. Department of Education and of the National Advisory Research Resources Council of the National Center for Research Resources, National Institutes of Health.

In the corporate sector, Maupin has been appointed to seats on the boards of several publicly traded companies, including Pinnacle Financial Partners, Inc., a bank holding company; LifePoint Hospitals, a non-urban acute care hospital company; HealthSouth Corporation, a national health services provider; and the Variable Annuity Life Insurance Companies I and II, a mutual fund complex of American International Group, Inc.

As an active leader in hometown civic affairs, Dr. Maupin has chaired the boards of the Community Foundation of Middle Tennessee and the North Nashville Community Development Corporation. He held memberships on the Board of Overseers of the Vanderbilt-Ingram Cancer Center, in 100 Black Men of Middle Tennessee, and in the Rotary Club. He has been a chairman and a board member of the United Way of Middle Tennessee, vice chairman of education for the Nashville Area Chamber of Commerce, and board member of the Middle Tennessee Council of Boy Scouts of America.

John Maupin was awarded an honorary doctor of science degree in 1995 from the Morehouse School of Medicine and an honorary doctor of laws degree in 1996 from Virginia Union University in Richmond. He is a member of the Omicron Kappa Upsilon National Dental Honorary Society. The Middle Tennessee Boy Scout organization presented its Silver Beaver Award to Maupin for his distinguished service to youth; in 2002 he received the Education Award presented by the Urban League of Middle Tennessee, and the Middle Tennessee unit of the American Diabetes Association named him Father of the Year in 2003.

Precisely because he was the lone male in a single-parent household for several years of his early life, John Maupin never waited for role models to materialize; he aggressively sought them. He found one in his beloved stepfather, a postal worker who grounded him and taught him respect for all humanity; his uncle, a dentist who beckoned him toward the oral health profession; his cousin, a hospital administrator who sparked his interest in health care management; and even his estranged biological father, who advised him early to acquire an MBA degree, advice that ultimately won him the presidency of Meharry over rivals without that credential.

In 2006, Maupin resigned as president and chief executive officer of Meharry Medical College, returning to the Morehouse School of Medicine as president. According to an article in the *Atlanta Daily World*, Morehouse Board Chairman Anthony Welters announced the selection of Maupin as president, stating, "The Board is delighted to have a person as skilled and experienced as John Maupin to lead the Morehouse School of Medicine. . . . Dr. Maupin comes to us following his 12 years as president of Meharry Medical College, where he led with distinction. His compassionate and commanding stewardship of Meharry directly relates to the mission of the Morehouse School of Medicine."

REFERENCES

Books

Roman, Charles V. *Meharry Medical College: A History*. Nashville, Tenn.: Sunday School Publishing Board of the National Baptist Convention, 1934.

Summerville, James. *Educating Black Doctors: A History of Meharry Medical College*. University, Ala.: University of Alabama Press, 1983.

Periodicals

Massaquoi, Hans. "Fifty Years of Black in Medicine" *Ebony* (July 1995): 120-125.

Maupin, John E., David Schlundt, Rueben Warren, et al. "Reducing Unintentional Injuries on the Nation's Highways: Research and Program Policy to Increase Seat Belt Use."*Journal of Health Care for the Poor and Underserved* 15 (February 2004): 4-17.

Online

"Dr. John E. Maupin Is New President Of Morehouse School Of Medicine." *Atlanta Daily World*. http://www.zwire.com/site/news.cfm?newsid=16274770&BRD=1077&PAG=461&dept_id=237813&rfi=6 (Accessed 29 March 2006).

"John E. Maupin, Jr., D.D.S., President." Morehouse School of Medicine. http://www.msm.edu/Executive/Maupin.htm (Accessed 29 March 2006).

"Meharry president to lead Morehouse med school." AJC.com. http://www.ajc.com/services/content/metro/atlanta/stories/0301morehouse.html?cxtype=rss&cxsvc=7&cxcat=13 (Accessed 29 March 2006).

Interview

Britton, John H., Jr. Interview with John E. Maupin Jr., Meharry Medical College, Nashville, Tenn., 12 April 2005.

John H. Britton, Jr.

Henry C. McBay
1914–1995

Scientist, chemist

Henry C. McBay was born in 1914 in Mexia, Texas, to Roberta Ransom and William Cecil McBay. His parents only had seventh-grade educations, but they had high expectations with regard to education for their children. Henry was the second of five children and all of them eventually received college degrees. His father began as a barber, and through self-study and the help of a local undertaker he passed the Texas state examination for licensed embalmers. He then opened a funeral home with an older brother. The following year he started a drugstore with a younger brother.

The discovery of oil under the city of Mexia in the early decades of the twentieth century made the town wealthy enough to provide an excellent high school education for African American students. In particular, the high school had outstanding teachers in the areas of science and mathematics, subjects in which Henry McBay excelled. Henry also took advantage of the well coached

Chronology	
1914	Born in Mexia, Texas on May 29
1934	Receives B.A. from Wiley College
1936	Receives M.A. from Atlanta University
1936-38	Teaches at Wiley College
1938-39	Teaches at junior college in Quinduro, Kansas
1939	High school teacher in Huntsville, Texas
1940	Joins research team at Tuskegee Institute
1942	Begins full time graduate enrollment at the University of Chicago
1945	Receives Ph.D. from University of Chicago; joins faculty at Morehouse College
1951-52	Appointed technical expert on science education to the Republic of Liberia by UNESCO
1969-70	Visiting research professor at the University of Minneapolis
1976	Visiting research scientist at the National Research Council, Ottawa, Canada
1978-84	Serves as member of the executive committee of the Georgia Section of the American Chemical Society
1979-82	Serves on board of trustees of Morehouse College
1981	Retires from Morehouse College
1982-86	Joins faculty of Atlanta University as Fuller E. Callaway professor of chemistry
1986-95	Emeritus professor of chemistry at Atlanta University/Clark Atlanta University
1990-95	Serves as co-director, PRISM-D Program at Clark Atlanta University
1992-95	Serves on board of trustees at Morehouse College
1995	Dies in Atlanta, Georgia on June 23

football team and, as quarterback, led the team to a championship in the school's regional conference tournament.

Graduates from Wiley College and Atlanta University

After graduating from the Paul Lawrence Dunbar High School at the age of sixteen, Henry entered Wiley College in Marshall, Texas. During his study at Wiley, he worked part-time, for the first two years in the dining hall, and for the last two years at the college post office. McBay had excellent teachers in the subjects that interested him most: science and mathematics. During many courses with these teachers, he became aware of organic chemistry and the possibilities associated with having a career in this area. He quickly realized that to do so required additional education.

After graduating from Wiley College in 1934, with highest academic honors, McBay entered the graduate chemistry program at Atlanta University. There he worked under Kimuel A. Huggins on a research project concerned with creating new forms of plastics having properties similar to those of natural rubber. In 1936, McBay completed the requirements for the master's degree; that same year

Professor Huggins received his doctorate in organic chemistry from the University of Chicago.

During the next several years, McBay taught at Wiley College (1936-38); Western University (1938-39) in Quindaro, Kansas; and as a high school teacher in Huntsville, Alabama (1939-40). The primary reason for not continuing his graduate education was lack of funds. Another restriction was that his parents expected his help in financing the college expenses of his younger brother and sister. However, in 1939, he enrolled at the University of Chicago as a summer student and took a course taught by the chairman of the chemistry department. McBay was one of the outstanding students in the course.

From 1941 to 1942, McBay was invited to work on a research team at the Carver Foundation of Tuskegee Institute, which was searching for a substitute material for the fiber obtained from jute, a plant native to India, but now in short supply because of the outbreak of World War II. The team focused on okra as a possible replacement. However, after a year of work, the idea was abandoned and McBay's position there ended in 1942.

McBay wrote to the University of Chicago and requested admittance to the graduate program in chemistry as a full time doctoral student. Although their response was noncommittal, he appeared on campus in September 1942 and was given the position of departmental assistant. This job was essentially reserved for racial minorities since it prevented blacks from having direct authority over white students. However, several advantages did accrue with the position: it carried a stipend, allowed experience to be obtained in various laboratory techniques, and provided a military draft deferment.

McBay began his doctoral research work in 1944 under Morris Kharasch. McBay had the necessary laboratory skills for handling dangerous chemical compounds. His selected research involved extremely volatile materials, and for this work he was placed in a private laboratory. McBay's outstanding work on this assignment earned him the Elizabeth Norton Prize for Excellence in Chemical Research in both 1944 and 1945. Based on this research, he was awarded the doctoral degree in chemistry from the University of Chicago in 1945.

Works at Morehouse College

After receiving his doctorate in chemistry, McBay accepted in 1945 a position as assistant professor in the chemistry department at Morehouse College. During his thirty-six year tenure at the college, he rose through the academic ranks to ultimately become the David Packard professor of chemistry. For twenty-five years, he served as chair of the department. However, his most significant contributions to education at Morehouse College were to instill in all his students a love for chemistry and an awareness of the important role that mathematics plays in the sciences, and to provide fundamental scientific training so that they could successfully complete doctoral studies at the major research universities. More than fifty of McBay's students went on to earn a Ph.D. or M.D. Until 1995, he had educated more African Americans who attained the Ph.D. in chemistry than any other teacher in the country.

In both his classroom management and teaching style, McBay was rigorous and rigid. No excuses were acceptable to him for not being prepared for classroom work. He openly intimidated students who did not live up to his academic standards but was always open to those who were prepared and rose to his challenge. His legacy was felt among both chemistry majors and students who took him for the basic courses and then went on to major in other areas.

In 1981, McBay retired from Morehouse College after thirty-six years of teaching, mentoring, and service to the college. The following year, he accepted an appointment as Distinguished Fuller E. Callaway professor in the chemistry department at Atlanta University. In 1986, he became professor emeritus of chemistry at Atlanta University, and in 1988 he was honored by the Morehouse College Board of Trustees with the title distinguished professor of chemistry.

The Atlanta University and Clark College consolidated in 1990 to form Clark Atlanta University (CAU). This super-university would permit increased research opportunities for interested faculty and students and allow a huge savings in administrative costs by employing fewer staff and other non-academic personnel. In 1990, McBay was invited to join a new program set up at CAU whose purpose was to help increase the number of African Americans earning the Ph.D. in engineering, mathematics, and the physical sciences. Accepting this offer, he served asco-director of PRISM-D (Program for Research Integration and Support for Matriculation to the Doctorate) from 1990 to 1995. His guidance and educational philosophy helped make the program a huge success.

At CAU McBay had a large laboratory for his research. With financial help from several former students, he was able to equip his laboratory and obtain the services of graduate students to assist in his research activities. One of his last major efforts was devoted to a theoretical and experimental investigation of how chirality arose in the molecular processes involved in the formation of life on the earth.

Receives Honors, Leaves Legacy

Henry C. McBay had a long and distinguished career in administration, teaching, mentoring, and research. His efforts in all four areas have been amply recognized. These honors include the Elizabeth Norton Prize for Excellence in Research in Chemistry, University of Chicago, 1944 and 1945; election to Sigma Xi, the Scientific Research Society, 1944; elected, Foundation Member of Delta Chapter of Phi Beta Kappa, Morehouse College, 1968; and the Charles H. Herty Award for Outstanding Contribution to Chemistry, Georgia Section of the American Chemical Society, 1976. McBay received three honorary doctorates: Atlanta University, 1987; Emory University, 1992; and, Bowie State University, 1993. In 1994, the United Negro College Fund announced the establishment of the Henry C. McBay Research Fellowships to be held by faculty members of United Negro College Fund (UNCF) institutions. McBay Fellows may conduct research in any field of their choosing as described in their research proposal.

One of the most touching events in McBay's list of honors was his selection to be the first Martin Luther King Jr. visiting scholar at the Massachusetts Institute of Technology (MIT) in 1991. There, friends, colleagues, and thirty-five former students gathered to honor him in a two-day celebration featuring interviews by the press, a symposium of scientific presentations, a luncheon hosted by the MIT provost, a testimonial session, and a celebratory banquet attended by the MIT president and the United States secretary of health and human services, Dr. Louis W. Sullivan, a former McBay student.

McBay's legacy includes his dedication to students, his firmness of beliefs, his love of teaching, his contributions to organic chemistry, and his lifelong relations with family, friends, colleagues, and former students. However, his most significant legacy rests with the hundreds of students that he influenced to pursue distinguished careers in teaching, scholarship, administration, and scientific research.

REFERENCES

Books

Kessler, James, et al., eds. *Distinguished African American Scientists of the Twentieth Century.* Phoenix: Oryx Press, 1996.

Krapp, Kristine, ed. *Notable Black American Scientists.* Farmington Hills, Mich.: Gale Group, 1999.

MIT Special Symposium Publication. *Henry C. McBay, Martin Luther King Jr. Visiting Scholar, 1991.* Cambridge, Mass.: MIT Press, 1991.

Sammons, Vivian O. *Blacks in Science and Education.* New York: Hemisphere Publishing, 1990.

Spangenburg, Ray, and Kit Moser. *African Americans in Science, Math, and Invention.* New York: Facts on File, 2003.

Periodicals

Chandler, David L. "Black Chemist Steers Students to Achievements." *Boston Globe*, 25 January 1991.

Frierson, Chaundra. "Henry R. C. McBay, 81, Professor of Chemistry at Atlanta Colleges." *Atlanta Constitution*, 2 June 1995.

"Profile of Academician." *The Nucleus* 57, No. 4 (1979): 5-7.

Ronald Elbert Mickens

George Marion McClellan
1860–1934

Writer, poet, minister

George Marion McClellan wrote poetry and short stories in standard English, taught school, and served as a Congregational minister between 1892 and 1934. His reputation rests on his sentimental and conservative poetry. While some of his poetry expresses racial pride and race consciousness, most of his poetry does not express protest or polemics. This fact suggests the tension experienced by African American writers between racial consciousness and adherence to the dominant white literary trends. However, McClellan was concerned for his people and promoted the value and success of African Americans. He wrote within white literary mainstream in order, perhaps, to illustrate the humanity of the African American.

George Marion McClellan was born September 29, 1860 in Belfast, Tennessee to George Fielding and Eliza (Leonard) McClellan. There is little information about his early life. However, he entered Fisk University about 1881 and earned a bachelor's degree in 1885 and a master's degree in 1890. Perpetually short of fund, he was constantly seeking and soliciting money. He often worked while pursuing his education. In 1888, he married Mariah Augusta Rabb of Columbia, Mississippi. She graduated from Fisk University and served on the faculty while McClellan pursued both the master's at Fisk University and the bachelor of divinity degree at Hartford (Connecticut) Theological Seminary. He received the divinity degree in 1891.

After attaining his B.D., McClellan became a minister in Nashville, Tennessee, and from 1892 until 1894, he served as financial agent at Fisk University. As the agent, he traveled extensively. He moved from Nashville to Louisville, Kentucky where he became a teacher and chaplain of the State Normal School in Normal, Alabama (1894-96). Between 1897 and 1899, he served at a Congregationalist church in Memphis, Tennessee. Throughout his adult life, he moved in and out of Louisville, Kentucky where he worked as a teacher and principal. In 1899, he taught geography and Latin at Central Colored High School. Then in 1911, he left teaching and became the principal of the well known Paul Dunbar School.

Chronology	
1860	Born in Belfast, Tennessee on September 29
1885	Earns B.A. from Fisk University
1887-90	Serves as Congregational minister in Louisville, Kentucky
1888	Marries Mariah Augusta Rabb on October 3
1890	Earns M.A. from Fisk University
1891	Earns B.D. from Hartford Theological Seminary
1892-94	Serves as minister in Nashville, Tennessee; works as financial agent at Fisk University
1894-96	Serves as chaplain and teacher at the State Normal School in Normal, Alabama
1895	Publishes *Poems*
1896	Publishes *Songs of a Southerner*
1897-99	Serves as pastor at a Congregational church in Memphis, Tennessee
1899-1911	Teaches geography and Latin at Central Colored High School, Louisville, Kentucky
1906	Publishes *Old Greenbottom Inn and Other Stories*
1911-19	Serves as principal, Paul Dunbar High School, Louisville, Kentucky
1916	Publishes *Path of Dreams*
1921-25	Lives in Los Angeles, California; attends the University of California Extension Division
1929	Publishes second edition of *Path of Dreams*
1934	Dies on May 17

He later lived in Los Angeles, California, where he attended the University of California Extension Division. The McClellans had two sons: Lochiel (b. 1892) and Theodore (b. 1895). Theodore died of untreated tuberculosis. George Marion McClellan died in May 1934.

Writing Career

Throughout his writing career, McClellan was constantly trying to find the time and space to write and the money to support his family and the publication of his works. *Poems* (1895), his first published work, contained fifty-seven poems and five sketches, two of which are "The Goddess of the Penitentials" and "A Farewell." In "The Goddess," McClellan explores the function of poetry. Two of the works appear to be autobiographical. The works in this collection show his effort to conform to the formal styles and themes or subjects of the day and simultaneously maintain his racial identity. He selected twelve poems from *Poems* a year later and published them under the title *Songs of a Southerner* (1896).

In 1906, he published for $500 a novella and four stories, *Ole Greenbottom Inn and Other Stories*. The stories demonstrate his awareness of the literary richness and potential of African American life. Through the use of African American characters and places familiar to him, he was also able to show that this life contained material worthy of serious literature. The title story of the collection, "Old Greenbottom Inn," is about interracial love. His final publication was *The Path of Dreams* (1916, reissued in 1929), which contains poetry from *Poems*, all but one of the stories from *Old Greenbottom Inn*, ten poems and a tribute to his son ("To Theodore"), and one new story ("Gabe Yowl").

McClellan's poetry is congruent with the themes, elements, and practices of the late nineteenth and early twentieth century. At the same time, there is a covert treatment of racial issues. He writes about his home state, the seasons, and art. "A January Dandelion" begins "All Nashville is a chill" and his poem "The Hills of Sewanee" details his nostalgia for home: "And, far away, I still can feel/Your mystery that ever speaks." Romantic themes are evident in such poems as "Love Is a Flame," "Dogwood Blossoms," and "In the Heart of a Rose." In "The Feet of Judas," McClellan responds to a humiliating incident which took place but which led to affirming his belief in God and purging himself of his anger and pain.

"The Feet of Judas" and other poems demonstrate the tension between white American and African American identities. In "The Color Bane," McClellan shows how "caste should force this Negro queen/To cold and proud disdain." He shows, also, overt joy in his people in "A September Night": "joyous shouts/of Negro songs and mirth awake hard by/The cabin dance." African American history, which is inextricably bound to American history, is detailed in "A Decoration Day." In spite of what appears to be a quite and passive voice in some poems, McClellan vents his feelings with force but remains optimistic. For instance, in "Day Break" printed in *Path of Dreams*, there is a call to action and a note of optimism: "Oh! Men of my race, awake! Arise!/ Our morning's in the air./ There's scarlet all along the skies./ Our day breaks everywhere." The tone here and in other poems raises the issues and responses to race as those seen before and after his era. Like many African American artists, George McClellan donned a mask in his pursuit of art and fight for racial justice.

REFERENCES

Books

Bruce, Dickson D. Jr. "George Marion McClelland." In *Dictionary of Literary Biography: Afro-American Writers Before the Harlem Renaissance.*. Vol. 50. Ed. Trudier Harris. Detroit, Mich.: Gale Group, 1986.

Robinson, Jr., William H. *Early Black American Poets*. Dubuque, Iowa: Wm. C. Brown Company Publishers, 1971.

Sherman, Joan R. *Invisible Poets: Afro-Americans of the Nineteenth Century*. Urbana: University of Illinois Press, 1974.

Helen R. Houston

James E. McGirt
1874–1930

Poet, writer, publisher

Though he never won widespread critical acclaim as a major African American writer, James Ephraim McGirt left his mark in the literary field as a poet, fiction writer, and publisher during the first decade of the twentieth century. Then, for almost two decades, he prospered as a pioneering beauty products entrepreneur and realtor. Over time, however, failed business dealings, dissipation, and poor health took their toll on McGirt, and he died in 1930. The accolades for his literary achievements, which he longed for during his lifetime, came more than seventy years after his death. The North Carolina Writers' Network inducted McGirt into their Literary Hall of Fame in 2004, praising him as one of the earliest and greatest of North Carolina poets.

McGirt was born near Lumberton, North Carolina, a rural, Coastal Plains community in the southeastern region of the state. The month and day of McGirt's birth in 1874 are unknown. He was one of four children born to farmer Madison McGirt and his wife Ellen Townsend McGirt. Early in his life, his parents moved the family to another rural community near Rowland, North Carolina. A few years later, the McGirts moved once again, to a house in a community called Warnersville, just outside the city limits of Greensboro, North Carolina, In that more urban setting, his mother worked as a laundress and his father became a drayman. Ellen McGirt, a strong-willed, zealous Christian, proved one of the most influential figures in her son's life. She instilled in young James the vision and determination to take himself beyond the limits set for African Americans in the Jim Crow South. She isolated her children from others in their community, perhaps in an effort to thwart the potentially debilitating effects of racism. Subsequently, McGirt and his three siblings became loners; none of them ever married.

Young James attended the Allen Private School for African Americans in Lumberton and later the public schools in Greensboro. When he was not in school, he performed odd jobs to earn money. In 1892, McGirt entered Bennett College in Greensboro, at the time a co-educational, historically black college. The bright student earned his bachelor's degree in 1895 after just three years of study.

Early Published Work

McGirt began to write poetry while a student at Bennett. Four years after he graduated from college, he published his first volume of poetry, *Avenging the Maine*. A number of the selections in this slim volume of lyrical, and often didactic, poetry are written in the style and structure of European, British, or American verse of the

Chronology

1874	Born in Roberson County near Lumberton, North Carolina
1892	Enrolls in Bennett College
1895	Earns B.A. from Bennett College
1899	Publishes his first volume of poetry, *Avenging the Maine*
1901	Publishes volume of poetry *Some Simple Songs*
1903	Moves north to Philadelphia, Pennsylvania; establishes *McGirt's Magazine*
1906	Publishes volume of poetry *For Your Sweet Sake*
1907	Publishes *The Triumph of Ephraim*, a collection of short stories
1910	Returns to the South to help support his parents; launches Star Hair Grower Manufacturing Company in Greensboro with his sister
1918	Leaves company to buy and sell real estate
1930	Dies in Greensboro, North Carolina on June 3

eighteenth and nineteenth centuries. McGirt included in his volume poems in "Negro dialect," the most popular form at the time for poetry about black people. His contemporary, Paul Laurence Dunbar, ultimately became the most celebrated poet of the day through his dialect poetry. But some critics considered McGirt's dialect poetry inauthentic.

Much of McGirt's poetry dealt with pastoral images of life in the South. However, a significant number of the poems in his debut collection focused on issues of race, class, and gender. The title poem, for example, recounts the valor of black soldiers in spite of the racism they faced while serving in Cuba during the Spanish American War. Another, "Slavery," protests the denigration of African American women in bondage. "A Drunken A. B." touches on themes that would cloud McGirt's own life—unrequited love and the decline of a well-educated black man as a result of self-destructive behavior.

McGirt published a total of three editions of *Avenging the Maine*. The second, enlarged edition appeared in 1900 and the third in 1901. None of the editions received much critical attention. McGirt also published the volume of poetry *Some Simple Songs* in 1901 to mixed reviews. Two years later, the struggling writer appealed to white southern writer Thomas Nelson Page for help. "If you need a man to do anything around your house, please give me the place. Give me a trial," he wrote to Page in a letter.

Success as a Publisher

It is not known whether Page responded to the young poet's plea. By the end of 1903, however, McGirt had moved north to Philadelphia, Pennsylvania, where he established *McGirt's Magazine*, an illustrated monthly "race publication" featuring stories about art, science,

and literature as well as articles focusing on the social and political issues that confronted African Americans. It also highlighted the accomplishments of African Americans and their institutions. *McGirt's Magazine* thrived for six years—an incredible feat for an independent black publication in any time period. The magazine predated by several years similar publications edited by W. E. B. Du Bois: the *Moon* (1905-06), *Horizon* (1907-10), and the NAACP's *Crisis* magazines (1910 to present). Du Bois may even have been inspired by McGirt's example. Du Bois once urged his Horizon readers to subscribe to McGirt's, pointing to the veracity of its content: "Not a yellow [journalism] line in it," he once wrote. McGirt expanded his publishing venture in 1905 by establishing McGirt's Publishing Company.

In 1906, McGirt published *For Your Sweet Sake*, his third and, arguably, best collection of poetry. One critic noted that his poem "Born Like the Pines," in particular, captured buoyancy, intensity, and a genuine lyric quality. Yet this collection barely made a ripple in the literary world. Ironically, McGirt's publishing enterprise provided the kind of opportunities for other black writers that were not offered to him. For example, over a two-year period (1907-09), he serialized historian and Pan-Africanist John Edward Bruce's work of fiction "The Black Sleuth." The magazine, therefore, introduced the world to one of the earliest works by a black writer to portray an African American detective. *The Black Sleuth* was later published as a novel.

McGirt published his fourth book under his own imprint in 1907. *The Triumph of Ephraim*, a collection of short stories, yielded no more recognition than his three collections of poetry. Two years later, McGirt's publishing company suffered hard times and closed permanently.

An Entrepreneur in Greensboro

In 1910, McGirt returned to the South to help support his parents. He launched another business in Greensboro. He and his sister bought a ten-room house and the Star Hair Grower Manufacturing Company. Over a period of eight years, the enterprise became so successful that the McGirts added a range of beauty products and distributed them to markets in the United States and elsewhere. In 1918, McGirt left the company to buy and sell real estate. Although he was successful for a time, he lost interest in his work and his business failed. None of his business endeavors ever extinguished his thirst to be a renowned poet. His excessive drinking led to poor health, and McGirt died in near obscurity in 1930. Decades later he was inducted into the North Carolina Literary Hall of Fame, and the Horton-McGirt Public Library in Greensboro is named in his honor.

REFERENCES

Books

Johnson, Abby Arthur, and Ronald Mayberry Johnson. *Propaganda and Aesthetics: The Literary Politics of Afro-American Magazines in the Twentieth Century.* Amherst: University of Massachusetts Press, 1979.

Periodicals

Parker, John W. "James Ephraim McGirt; Poet of 'Hope Deferred,'" *The Negro History Bulletin*, March 1953.

Zane, J. Peder. "Hall of Fame Inducts Fine Crop," *The Raleigh News & Observer*, 24 October 2004.

Online

North Carolina Writers' Network Literary Hall of Fame, 2004 Inductees. http://www.ncwriters.org/services/lhof/induct2004.html

Collections

A short 1952 essay about McGirt by John W. Parker is included in the Richard Gaither Walser Papers, Southern Historical Collection, Manuscripts Department, Wilson Library, University of North Carolina at Chapel Hill. A longer article by John W. Parker written for *The Negro History Bulletin* is in a vertical file for McGirt in the Greensboro Public Library.

A letter from James Ephraim McGirt to Thomas Nelson Page, dated May 12, 1903, is in the Thomas Nelson Page Papers, Rare Book, Manuscript, and Special Collections Library, at Duke University, Durham, North Carolina.

Clarissa Myrick

Robert G. McGruder
1942–2002

Journalist, editor

R obert G. McGruder was best known by his colleagues first as a passionate diversity advocate and second as a newspaper pioneer. In his sixty years McGruder attained the title of "first" perhaps more than many of his notable coworkers. His achievements as diversity advocate and news executive afford him the honor of being included among some of the most notable African American men of his era.

Robert G. McGruder

Robert McGruder was born on March 31, 1942 in Louisville, Kentucky. As a young child he lived in Dayton, Ohio and in Campbellsburg, Kentucky. At the age of six, McGruder battled and overcame polio. Although McGruder was not raised in a two-parent household, he was positively influence by both his mother and grandmother. His grandmother was an educator during the early twentieth century. She taught in rural segregated areas of Indiana and Kentucky. His mother began her career as a classroom educator as well and later became a librarian. Her love for children's literature inspired her to develop a library club for children. McGruder believed that the experience of observing two smart, strong black women provided him insight into how to overcome indifference, hostility, discrimination, and adversity. Through their experience McGruder learned a lot about how much African Americans had to endure as well as how much more work lay ahead in order for African Americans to achieve the level of success he hoped to realize one day.

Journalism Career

While living in Ohio, McGruder enrolled in the School of Journalism at Kent State University. By 1963 he graduated with a B.A. degree in journalism from Kent State. Immediately after completing his degree, McGruder was employed as the first African American journalist with the *Dayton Journal Herald* in Ohio.

Chronology

1942	Born in Louisville, Kentucky on March 31
1963	Graduates from Kent State University; works for *Dayton Journal Herald*; becomes first African American reporter to work for *Cleveland Plain Dealer*
1964-66	Serves two years in the U.S. Army
1966	Returns to the *Plain Dealer*
1969	Marries
1971-73	Serves as assistant city editor
1981	Becomes managing editor
1986	Joins *Detroit Free Press* as Deputy Managing Editor
1991-92	Becomes Knight Ridder fellow at Duke University, Durham, North Carolina
1993	Becomes managing editor
1995	Becomes first African American president of Associated Press Managing Editors
1996	Becomes first African American executive editor of news operations at *Detroit Free Press*
2001	Receives John S. Knight Gold Medal, the highest honor given to an employee of Knight Ridder, parent company of *Detroit Free Press*
2002	Dies at age 60 in Detroit, Michigan on April 12

McGruder left the *Dayton Journal Herald* in 1963 and joined the *Cleveland Plain Dealer* in the same year. The journalist position with the *Plain Dealer* would be another added to the many "first" titles that McGruder would soon claim. His position as the first African American journalist at the *Plain Dealer* was shortened due to the United States military draft. McGruder served in the U.S. Army from 1964 to 1966. He eventually returned to the *Plain Dealer*, and by 1971 he became the first African American assistant city editor at the newspaper. Not surprisingly, McGruder continued to climb the journalist ladder, and in 1978 he became city editor. McGruder became managing editor in 1981. McGruder's twenty-three-year tenure with the *Plain Dealer* was monumental for any journalist. His news coverage focused on a broad range of issues, including the urban riots and rebellion of the 1960s. During the 1970s, McGruder editorialized about the anti-busing battles in Boston, Louisville, and other cities throughout the country. While working for the *Plain Dealer* he also covered sports, arts, and entertainment, along with other topics such as diversity in the workplace.

In 1986, McGruder accepted the position of deputy managing editor of the *Detroit Free Press*. The *Free Press* had been scouting McGruder for twenty years before he accepted the position which required him and his wife Annette to relocate to Detroit. Under his direction, the *Free Press* focused on child abuse, corrupt police officers, and Michigan labor unions. Most importantly, McGruder successfully guided the *Free Press* through two strikes and a series of near business closures.

When McGruder arrived in Detroit in 1986, the *Free Press*'s main rival was the daily, Gannett's *Detroit News*. The *Free Press* was considered a failing newspaper, while the Gannett thrived. The papers eventually accepted a joint operating agreement. One editor recalled how McGruder reminded everyone to concentrate on the primary mission of the *Free Press*: to produce great journalism, treat people fairly, and provide balanced reporting. McGruder's leadership helped the newsroom function during the months following a bitter strike against the two newspapers several years later. McGruder excelled at crisis management.

McGruder experienced many highs and lows in the business. In a speech delivered at the James R. Batten Knight Ridder Excellence award ceremony in 2001, it was noted that in many cases McGruder did not always receive positive treatment from his colleagues. Excerpts taken from an editorial in the Knight Ridder company newsletter were read to the audience. In the editorial McGruder discussed his early experiences in journalism. He noted that being the first black reporter on staff at the *Plain Dealer* in Cleveland was a high point, but it was also difficult for him. Moreover, as an African American, it was not always comfortable to cover or report news that had a particular effect on the African American community.

McGruder promoted a number of African Americans to jobs that had never been held by blacks. He cited managing editors at several newspapers. He only hoped to have had a positive influence on them, he noted. He felt great pride in watching people whom he helped achieve greatness. Those were career high points for McGruder. Additionally, his unwavering commitment to diversity has made an impact well beyond Detroit. In 1999, he led a task force that compiled a diverse list of candidates for Knight Ridder to pursue for top editing posts. Under his leadership, more than fifty people were identified, and ultimately six were hired.

As the executive editor of the *Detroit Free Press* McGruder was challenged by crisis situations. His passion for journalism kept him abreast of the news. Proper news analysis was important to him as well. For McGruder, it was equally important to focus on who offered the analysis, from whose perspective did they offer it, and whether it was fair and balanced reporting. He was relentless when it came to diversity in the news business, and he gained considerable respect and support from his colleagues for his commitment. McGruder served on the board of directors of the American Society of Newspaper Editors and on the advisory board of the Institute for Minority Journalism at Detroit's Wayne State University. He was a member of the National Association of Black Journalists and the National Association of Minority Media Executives. He was also past president of Associated Press Managing Editors (APME).

Honors and Accolades

Prior to his death in 2002, McGruder received several noted honors, including the John S. Knight Medal. The recognition was the highest honor an employee of the Knight Ridder Company could receive. On January 26, 2002 McGruder received the Helen Thomas Spirit of Diversity award from Wayne State University. He accepted the William Taylor Distinguished Alumni award from Kent State School of Journalism in 2002.

On April 12, 2002 Robert G. McGruder died of cancer at the age of sixty. In recognition of his commitment to bringing diversity into the newsroom, several awards were named in his honor. In 2003 the National Association of Black Journalists awarded Robert McGruder the lifetime achievement award for his efforts to promote diversity and for the positive impact he had on the lives of journalist throughout the country. McGruder's wife of thirty-three years, Annette McGruder, and his stepdaughter, Tanya A. Martin, accepted the award on his behalf.

Charles Eisendrath, Michigan journalism fellow director, and James Naughton, president of Poynter Institute, both spoke about McGruder's mentorship during their early career and the positive impact he had on their lives. Countless other journalists spoke about his character as a journalist and news executive. Although he was said to have a competitive nature, it was also noted that he was committed to developing young talent and to encouraging them to pursue greater opportunities in the field of journalism. In his final acceptance speech just months before he died McGruder spoke of the major challenge that lay ahead for the *Detroit Free Press*. He stated that he was proud of the company for its accomplishments in four major areas: creating a diverse newsroom, increasing minority representation in top management positions, establishing apprenticeship and mentorship programs for high school students as well as minority students from Wayne State's Journalism Institute, and finally creating a diversity handbook in 2000. However, his challenge to the company was to extend itself beyond its current initiatives. McGruder offered this closing: "People who work to bring diversity to enterprise talk about the need to bring people of different voices and backgrounds to the workplace, school or neighborhood. We're working on building source lists that go beyond the usual white male sources to allow other voices to emerge. For a newspaper I think that means things like fairness, equal access and opportunity, accuracy in terms of our ability to honestly report on our citizens and communities . . . It is not, I want to add, something to pursue because it is good for business. It's about doing what is right."

REFERENCES

Periodicals

McGruder, Robert G. "Battle Against Racism Better Fought in Present." *Detroit Free Press*, March 2001.

Online

The African American Registry, "Robert G. McGruder, A Detroit Newspaper Icon!" http://www.aaregistry.com (Accessed 4 February 2005).

McGruder, Robert G. Acceptance Speech, "Helen Thomas Diversity Award." Wayne State University. 26 January 2002. *Detroit Free Press* http://www.freep.com (Accessed 4 February 2005).

———. Acceptance Speech, "John S. Knight Gold Medal Award." October 22, 2001. *Detroit Free Press* http://www.freep.com (Accessed 4 February 2005).

Baiyina W. Muhammad

George McJunkin
1851–1922

Cowboy

It was not until fifty years after his death that George McJunkin, a respected cowboy of Folsom, New Mexico, was acknowledged as having uncovered one of the most important archeological finds made in North America. His discovery offered proof that Indians had arrived in the New World more than 7,000 years before the previously determined date of 1,000 B.C. McJunkin, a former slave who became a voracious reader of scientific data, tried to bring his discovery of ancient bones to the attention of archeologists. He wrote and invited several archeologists to his site but was not successful. McJunkin knew his discovery was unusual and important. Because of McJunkin's respected role in the community and his dedication to his scientific interests, the effort to have his discovery researched was continued by others. Although his role in the archeological find was overlooked for many years, his contribution was finally recognized.

George McJunkin was born a slave in 1851 on a ranch in Midway, Texas. His master Fergesen also owned George's father who was known by the nickname "Shoeboy." Shoeboy was a very fine blacksmith and he did work for many of his master's neighbors; the money he made, he was allowed to keep. After buying his freedom Shoeboy began saving up to buy his son George's freedom. Before he had saved enough, the Civil War ended, and Union soldiers arrived to tell the slaves they were free. McJunkin was then fourteen years old. With his new freedom he worked at driving oxen and taught himself to read and write. McJunkin spent three more years on the ranch.

Chronology

1851	Born a slave in Midway, Texas
1865	Becomes free as notified by Union soldiers
1868	Secures a job on a cattle drive to Dodge City, Kansas
1908	Discovers prehistoric bones in Dead Horse Gulch
1922	Dies in Folsom, New Mexico on January 21
1926	Bones from McJunkin's site are taken to the Colorado Museum of Natural History
1927	Discovery of second spear-point caught within the bones is offered again to the scientific community
1928	Discovery recognized as changing the established date of man's presence in America
1972	Recognition of McJunkin as the discoverer of the bones that resulted in a scientific revolution

At seventeen McJunkin got a job on a cattle drive to Dodge City, Kansas. He adopted the last name of one of his former masters, John McJunkin. After taking several jobs with various outfits, McJunkin finally settled in the valley of the Dry Cimarron River in northeastern New Mexico. It was such a beautiful valley he often referred to it as "my promised land." In the Cimarron Valley there was a racially mixed population of Anglos, Hispanic, and Indians, which gave some ease to this lone black man. McJunkin took a job working for Gideon Roberds, who raised horses. Although McJunkin had never been to school and did not read or write, he was proficient in riding, roping, and other skills of the range. McJunkin was asked to teach Roberds' sons to rope and ride, and the boys in turn taught McJunkin how to read and write. He would also get help from the cow punchers when they sat around the campfire at night. McJunkin took to reading enthusiastically and read everything he could find. He excelled in reading as he did with his many other talents. McJunkin was a master shot, hunted buffalo, and was known as the first man in the West to create barbed-wire fenced pastures. He was an expert bronco rider and one of the best ropers and cow hands in the country. He was by no means a typical cowboy as he was intensely interested in science and often traveled with a telescope on his saddle. Along with his interest in archaeology and history, he spoke Spanish and played the fiddle and the guitar.

As Roberds' sons came of age McJunkin was hired by Ben Smith for the Pitchfork Ranch. He worked on this ranch for thirteen years before going to work for William "Bill" H. Jack on the Crowfoot Ranch in New Mexico. As foreman of the Crowfoot Ranch and the top cowboy in the country McJunkin was highly respected. He had white and Hispanic cowboys under his leadership. His honesty was held in high regard and his ability to speak Spanish allowed him to serve as a bridge between Anglo and Hispanic communities.

Discovers Important Bone Pit

In September 1908 McJunkin found a gap under a barb-wired fence. The gap was the result of a flash flood, which tore a ten-foot gully in the bottom of Wild Horse Arroyo. The flood was so severe that seventeen people in the nearby town of Folsom were killed. While trying to determine how to repair the fence, McJunkin saw bones exposed at the bottom of the gully. He went into the gully and dug out the bones. Over time he found more bones and even a skull. He placed these bones with his collection that he kept at his ranch house. He had a museum of sorts in his cabin that included skulls, rocks, minerals, arrowheads, and other bones. As an avid reader of scientific books, McJunkin knew the bones from the gully were from a bison but their size and the fact that they were mineralized and thirteen feet under the surface told him this find was an important one. McJunkin wrote to several bone collectors about the place he called the bone pit. He initially wrote to a man in Las Vegas, Nevada, about his find, but he could not persuade him to come. He informed Carl Schwachheim, a blacksmith, and Fred Howard, the local banker, who once dug up a woolly mammoth. Neither was interested in making the thirty-mile trip to see the bone pit.

As McJunkin grew older nothing came of his letters and efforts to have others see his find. When the Crowfoot Ranch was sold he moved to a cabin in an isolated part of the ranch. His cabin was struck by lightening and burned to the ground, destroying all of his collection of bones, fossils, books, and his telescope. When McJunkin became ill he moved into a room at the Folsom Hotel. Unable to get out of bed his friends helped him to sustain himself by setting up rubber tubing to drink from. McJunkin could only drink raw bootleg whiskey. His friends took turns visiting him and telling stories or reading from the Old Testament. On January 21, 1922 McJunkin died. He was buried in the Folsom cemetery with a large gravestone to mark his resting place.

It was four years after McJunkin's death that the bones dug out of his bone pit by Howarth and Schwachheim were shown to a scientist. Among the bones were spear points whose discovery challenged an established belief regarding Indians in the New World. The first scientific report of the discovery was published in 1927 in the *Natural History* magazine. Although some were skeptical, the site was visited by many scientists and further proof of the antiquity of man was found. Although McJunkin's bone pit was one of the most important discoveries in America, not one time was McJunkin mentioned. Howart and Schwachheim were given full credit.

Curious about the myth that the bones were found by an ex-slave, George Agogino, a Paleo-Indian archeologist at Eastern New Mexico University, researched the origins of the find. After numerous interviews and conversations with persons in Folsom he learned of McJunkin. Fifty years after his death McJunkin finally had his discovery and his efforts to share that discovery recognized. He was an extraordinary black cowboy who with telescope and scientific books helped to establish the presence of man in the New World 7,000 years before scientists originally thought.

REFERENCES

Books

Folsom, Franklin. *The Life and Legend of George McJunkin: Black Cowboy*. Nashville: Thomas Nelson, Inc., 1973.

Periodicals

Preston, Douglas. "Fossils & the Folsom cowboy— George McJunkin dug out bones that led to questions on the New World's notions of human antiquity." *Natural History* 106 (February 1997): 16-22.

Online

"1851—History: George McJunkin 1851-1922." *Soul of New Mexico*. http://www.soulofnewmexico.com/ 1851.html (Accessed 13 March 2006).

"Cowboy George McJunkin" netfirms. http://folsom museum.netfirms.com/cowboy_george.htm (Accessed 13 March 2006).

Lean'tin L. Bracks

John Willis Menard
1838–1893

Politician, poet

John Willis Menard was the first African American elected to the U.S. Congress. Though elected, he was not seated for this office. Menard went on to become a state legislator for Florida and to hold a number of civil service positions. Menard began various news publications throughout the course of his life that advocated for African American rights. Menard was also a poet; he wrote and published *Lays in Summer Lands*. Menard made many contributions as an activist, politician, writer, and publisher.

Joins Post-Civil War New Orleans

John Willis Menard was born in Kaskaskia, Illinois on April 3, 1838. Details of his early life and family background are scarce, but it is known that he and his family were not slaves. It is believed that both of his parents

John Willis Menard

were born in Illinois, yet they were also believed to be of French Creole descent and to have had ties with New Orleans, Louisiana. Menard spent his first eighteen years in the small historic village of Kaskaskia. He worked on a farm in or around Kaskaskia during his adolescence. Menard attended an abolitionist school in Sparts, Illinois before attending Iberia College where James Monroe Trotter was a fellow classmate.

In 1859, twenty-one-year-old Menard delivered a speech at an event in Springfield, Illinois celebrating the end of slavery in the West Indies. In 1860, Menard penned and published *An Address to Free Colored People of Illinois*. During the Civil War, Menard became the first African American to work as a clerk in the Bureau of Immigration at the Interior Department in Washington D.C. The government sent Menard to the South American country of Belize to investigate the country as a possible foreign land for African Americans to relocate. Menard personally favored African Americans' immigration to foreign lands. The journey rendered fruitless for his original search, but while traveling, he met and soon married Elizabeth, a young Jamaican woman. They had three children.

Wins in Louisiana but Not Seated

Menard left the Interior Department for New Orleans, Louisiana to be active in Reconstruction of the state after the Civil War. He founded and edited two newspapers: first, the *Free State*, then the *Radical Standard*. In 1868, he won the Republican nomination for Louisiana's Second Congressional District. On the day of the election, November 3, 1868, it was immediately clear that Menard won, but his opponent, Caleb S. Hunt, contested the results. Menard was the first African American to stand on the floor of the United States House of Representatives during legislative proceedings in February 27, 1869 when he made the case for his victory in Louisiana. It is reported that his audience was captivated; still, the Committee of Elections for the House of Representatives refused to seat him. Menard was financially compensated. He received the same amount of pay that he would have received if he would have been seated.

Menard sold the *Radical Standard* in 1871 and moved to Jacksonville, Florida. He was appointed a clerk in the city's post office and he served as a state legislator between 1873 and 1875 while editing the newspaper, the *Sun*. Menard was appointed a collector of revenues position with the state after his term expired. In 1876, he was appointed as a delegate to the 1876 Republican Convention in Cincinnati. Menard was very unhappy with the white leadership of the Republican Party and sharply criticized them for exploiting the black community in order to get votes. This led Menard to coalition build with anyone who shared his agenda, no matter what their party affiliation. He would sometimes break with his own party and support Independents running for office. On a few occasions, he supported Democrats.

In 1876, Menard joined many, including Josiah Walls, in opposing the reelection of incumbent Florida governor Marcellus L. Stearns. Menard supported Stearns's opponent, Democrat George T. Drew, for governor, though Menard did support Republican Rutherford B. Hayes for president. Both Drew and Hayes won the 1876 election. In appreciation of Menard's support, Drew reappointed Menard to the position of justice of the peace in Duval County, a position that Stearns had initially given to him. African Americans in Florida criticized President Hayes

for abandoning the South to the Democrats, but Menard promoted working with whoever was in office.

In 1879, Menard wrote and published *Lays in Summer Lands*, a book of poems covering a wide range of topics such as politics, Catholicism, and love. Menard's poems had been published in various issues of the *Christian Recorder*, a Philadelphia black newspaper, in 1863 while Menard was working in the Interior Department in Washington D.C.

In 1882, he began the *Key West News*, which was also known as the *Island City News*, after he had moved to Key West to work in the city's customs house. He covered the local black community, had some public exchanges with other black publications throughout the country, and the paper had a Washington D.C. correspondent, Howard University medical student Lemuel W. Livingston. In the fall 1883, the paper was renamed the *Florida News* and was expanded from four to eight pages. The focus shifted from local to state issues. In May 1884, the paper's run was cut from weekly to semiweekly.

Though Menard supported the Republican presidential ticket in 1884, he lost his customs job in Key West. Accused of having pro-Cuban sympathies, Menard was asked by the Chester Arthur presidential administration to resign. Menard admitted attending the meetings of Cuban revolutionaries, but he denied supporting any anti-Cuba actions.

Menard returned to Jacksonville in 1885 and restarted the *Florida News* there. He enlarged the paper's staff and opened a printing shop. His son, Willis T. Menard, was the new publisher and his son-in-law, Thomas V. Gibbs, was the associate editor. Gibbs was the son of black politician Jonathan Gibbs.

Menard remained involved in Jacksonville's black political and civic life and continued to work with all who supported civil rights regardless of race or political affiliation. He changed the name of the *Florida News* to the *Southern Leadership* in January 1886. The paper was widely read in the South in the few years after the name change, but it was most popular in Florida. Menard drifted further away from party politics, advocating self-help for blacks in the pages of his publication. The white press of Florida applauded this position, but Menard and Gibbs were taken to task many times for this philosophy.

Menard was close to T. Thomas Fortune, the editor of the vocational black newspaper the *New York Tribune*. Fortune, a native of Florida, kept an eye on events in his state. He and Menard often exchanged pleasantries, but the two severed their friendship over Fortune's support of the Afro-American League, a black organization that sought to take a more militant stand for black rights. Menard did not want divisiveness and a race war to erupt. He felt that racism should be gently handled, that conditions would improve over time. Fortune shot back that demanding one's rights was not an act of violence and that if black people did not demand their rights, they would never receive them.

Support for black voting rights deteriorated as a poll tax was instituted in Florida, keeping many blacks from voting. In a letter to the *New York Tribune*, Menard's son-in-law Thomas Gibbs lashed out against the new law that he and Menard before did not think would pass in the 1887 Florida legislative session. T. Thomas Fortune commented in the paper on Gibbs's letter, stating that he could not understand why the editors of the *Southern Leader* still could not see the need for the Afro-American League.

While Menard and Gibbs denounced the violence against blacks in the South, they continued to advocate a non-confrontational approach to politics and in seeking black rights. In July 1888, Menard applauded Florida governor Edward Perry for enforcing the law that only black teachers could teach in black schools. Menard asserted that this law provided employment for black teachers. The editors of the *Southern Leadership* criticized Frederick Douglass for an April 1888 speech that he made deploring the conditions for blacks in the South. They felt that his speech harmed blacks in light of the progress that blacks made in Florida with the 1888 elections of black judges, a city marshal, and a board of police commissioners. But a month later, Menard lamented the violence and intimidation of blacks that followed the 1888 election in Florida.

In the fall 1888, the *Southern Leader* forever suspended publication in the face of a devastating yellow-fever epidemic. After Benjamin Harrison won the 1888 presidential election, Menard returned to Washington D.C. where he was appointed to a clerical position in the United States census office. Menard had a change of heart about the Afro-American League and wrote a letter to Fortune's paper, now called the *New York Age*, praising the organization. Menard also asked President Harrison to allocate some land for blacks in the West so that they could move out of the South. In 1890, Menard launched one final publication: a monthly magazine called the *National American*.

John Willis Menard died on October 8, 1893 at the age of fifty-four in Washington, D.C. The *Tampa Bay Press* reissued the *Lays in Summer Lands* in 2002 with commentary provided by editors Larry Eugene Rivers, Richard Mathews, and Canter Brown Jr. On February 23, 2004, Illinois governor Rod Blagojevich proclaimed February 25, 2004, to be John Willis Menard Day in Illinois.

REFERENCES

Books

Shofner, Jerrell H. "Florida." In *The Black Press in the South 1865-1979*. Ed. Henry Lewis Suggs. Westport, Conn.: Greenwood Press, 1983.

Online

"IGNN: History Press Release. Pierre Menard Home Program February 22 to Recognize Nineteenth-Century African-American Poet and Activist." Illinois Government News Network. http://www.illinois.gov/PressReleases/ShowPressRelease.cfm?SubjectID=27&RecNum=2763 (Accessed 23 December 2005).

"Proclamations." 2004 Illinois Register of Governmental Agency Rules, Volume 28, Issue 11. 12 March 2004. http://www.sos.state.il.us/departments/index/register/register_volume28_issue11.pdf (Accessed 27 February 2006).

Stone, Spessard. "John Willis Menard" Rootsweb.com. http://freepages.genealogy.rootsweb.com/~crackerbarrel/Menard.html (Accessed 20 December 2005).

Collections

The oldest existing copy of *An Address to Free Colored People of Illinois* is housed at the Illinois State Library.

Brandy Baker

John Henry Merrick
1859–1919

Insurance agent, entrepreneur

John Henry Merrick is proof that slavery and the Jim Crow laws did not deter some African Americans from making a significant mark. Merrick was born a slave in Clinton, North Carolina, on September 7, 1859. Despite the limited education offered to African Americans at that time, he learned to read, write, and do arithmetic. His drive to excel was fueled by his quest for knowledge and his will to help his fellowmen. Merrick was the founder or co-founder of many businesses that served the African American communities in which he lived. Although Merrick is known as an insurance agent, his influence in the African American business community spans a wide range of organizations and firms in North Carolina.

Information on Merrick's family life is somewhat limited. Merrick lived with his mother, Martha, and a younger brother. His father was absent from his family. With the 1863 Emancipation Proclamation and then the Union victory in the Civil War, Merrick at six years of age and his family were freed. When he was twelve, his family moved to Chapel Hill, North Carolina where he gained employment in a brickyard as a helper. He was the

Chronology

1859	Born in Clinton, North Carolina on September 7
1865	Freed at six years of age when Civil War ends
1880	Moves to Durham, North Carolina, and becomes co-owner of Merrick and Wright barbershop
1881	Purchases his first property on Pettigrew Street in the section that he called the Hayti
1883	Purchases the Royal Knights of David with other African Americans
1890	Produces Merrick's Dandruff Cure
1892	Owns barbershop after John Wright sells him all his shares
1898	Co-founder of North Carolina Mutual
1908	Co-founder of Bull City Drug Company
1919	Dies in Durham, North Carolina on August 6

breadwinner of the family, and he took his responsibilities seriously. When he was eighteen, the family of three—Merrick, his mother, and brother—moved to Raleigh, North Carolina. Merrick worked as a brick carrier and then as a brick mason, laying bricks in the construction of Shaw University's first building. He worked as a shoe shine boy in a barbershop where he also learned the trade of barbering.

Ventures into Barbershop Business

Merrick first worked as a barber, in Raleigh, for W. G. Otey. In 1880, he joined his dear friend and fellow barber, John Wright, who was migrating to Durham, North Carolina to venture in his own business, a barbershop. After six months, the thrifty Merrick bought shares in the barbershop that gave him the title of co-owner. The partnership between Merrick and Wright continued until 1892 when Merrick became the sole proprietor of the Merrick and Wright Barbershop after Wright sold him his shares and moved to Washington D.C. Merrick eventually owned about nine segregated shops. He accommodated African Americans and white Americans in different shops as he warily upheld the Jim Crow standards, but he exploited his interaction with white patrons, asking them to contribute to several benefit funds for his race.

In addition, Merrick developed Merrick's Dandruff Cure, which he marketed with catchy advertisements around 1890. In promoting this product, Merrick showed considerable knowledge of hair health and treatment.

As a frugal businessman, Merrick used his profits from the barbershops to buy real estate. First, in 1881 he bought property on Pettigrew Street, in the area that he called the Hayti. He became a master builder in this area, as he purchased other lands and built other houses for rent to the increasing African American population. Merrick did all the calculations and purchases, and hauled all the materials for his constructions. He became one of the largest

landowners in the Hayti. Merrick helped with the Durham infrastructure, too. Later, Merrick expanded his real estate interest as he sought to protect his properties. He joined with Moore and Spaulding, two colleagues from an insurance company, to form the Merrick-Moore-Spaulding Land Company that protected the lands of African Americans and the North Carolina Mutual properties.

Merrick and the Royal Knights of King David

Merrick, John Wright, W. A. Day, J. D. Morgan, and T. J. Jones, all African American businessmen, purchased the fraternal order lodge, the Royal Knights of King David, in 1883 from a Reverend Morris of Georgia. Instead of becoming just a part of a larger group, these African Americans bought the sole right to this order and established it under the principle of David versus Goliath—African Americans who were preparing to fight the giant of discriminatory and racist laws. This order became widespread as branches were opened in 1887 in Virginia and South Carolina, Florida in 1910, Georgia in 1916, and the District of Columbia and Pennsylvania in 1918. Merrick purchased the major portions of the order, and he remained the largest shareholder until his death. In 1918 the order had 21,000 members, $22,000 worth of bonds, and $40,000 in real estate. This purchase launched Merrick into the insurance field as the order provided insurance plans for its members.

Merrick realized inadequacies in the insurance that the lodge provided for African Americans, so in 1898, he founded the North Carolina Mutual Insurance Company with Aaron McDuffie Moore, P. W. Dawkins, D. T. Watson, W. G. Pearson, E. A. Johnson, and James E. Shepard who contributed $50 each to purchase the shares. Merrick was elected as the president and operations began in 1899. This company declined after six months, but its rebirth gave rise to the stallion insurance company North Carolina Mutual and Provident Life Insurance, which was later shortened to North Carolina Mutual Insurance Company. Merrick and Moore were the only owners at the rebirth as they purchased all the shares from the others. The members traveled all over the state trying to get people to buy their policies, but this was not very successful. Advertisements in the *Blade*, an African American newspaper in Raleigh, brought in the most clients. Initially, the company sold only industrial policies, but it expanded rapidly to other policies. It also covered African American men and women equally, and both sexes were also equally employed in the company. In 1918, shortly before Merrick's death, the company grossed over $1 million. The company's large office building also served as a reservoir for other African American businesses.

The *Durham Negro Observer* was a spin off from the North Carolina Mutual Insurance Company. The newspaper was reorganized and was later called the *North Carolina Mutual*, and was the sole African American newspaper for decades in that area. Merrick and some associates also founded Bull City Drug Company in 1908. This drug company established drugstores in the Hayti where most African Americans lived. Another undertaking was the short-lived Durham Textile Mill in 1914 that employed many African Americans. Merrick assisted in establishing the Lincoln Hospital in 1901. Merrick was also instrumental in the formation of the Mechanics and Farmers Bank in Durham that served the banking interests of African Americans. He later served as vice president and president. This bank grew to become the main source of capital for African Americans who wanted to purchase properties or to venture into new businesses.

Booker T. Washington lauded Merrick for his role in developing African American businesses. Washington invited Merrick to be a guest speaker at the Tuskegee Institute after he saw Merrick's success in Durham. Merrick exemplified Washington's ideals as he used "what he had" to develop organizations and businesses that would benefit African Americans. He also proved that African Americans contributed to their societies despite the barriers that the Jim Crow laws presented.

Wife and Family Life

Merrick married Martha Hunter, who was still living at the time of his death on August 6, 1919. Edward, Merrick's eldest son, followed in his father's footsteps; he was the treasurer of the North Carolina Mutual for many years. Moreover, his other two sons worked in the company for some time. Merrick also had at least two daughters. Merrick moved his family into a large house that he built on Pettigrew Street in 1881 and then to an even larger house on Fayetteville Street in 1887 where he remained until his death.

Merrick forged unity among his people and relationships between the races. He showed what collective action could do to the African American people. Merrick also promoted self-help in the African American society. The Jim Crow laws prompted many African Americans to develop businesses to help sustain their communities. The law of separate but equal forced African Americans to create their equal place in the society, which the law ironically denied them. Merrick made many African Americans equal in a time when the races were believed to be unequal. Merrick implemented and organized structures that benefited the social, economical, and physical well-being of many African Americans.

REFERENCES

Books

Andrews, R. McCants. *John Merrick: A Biographical Sketch*. New York: Seeman Press, 1920.

Gates, Henry Louis Jr., ed. *African American Lives*. New York: Oxford University Press, 2004.

Logan, Rayford W., and Michael R. Winston, eds. *Dictionary of American Negro Biography*. New York: Norton, 1982.

Denise Jarrett

Solomon Lightfoot Michaux
1884–1968

Evangelist

Solomon Lightfoot Michaux was an evangelist and founder of the Church of God. In the 1930s, he realized the potential of using the media in spreading the gospel around the world. Much public opinion of Solomon Lightfoot Michaux was focused on his charismatic preaching, his mass annual baptizing, and his colorful radio ministry, including his cross choir. The media often focused on his legal problems, considering him to be a cult leader, faith healer, and conservative in his racial views.

Michaux was born November 7, 1884, in Newport News, Virginia. His father John was of mixed French, Indian, and black heritage. John and Henry, his younger brother, became merchant seamen. They eventually settled in Newport News. John Michaux married May Blanche, whose ancestry was African, Indian, and French Jewish. Michaux became a fish peddler and grocer located on Jefferson Street, where many other Jewish and white non-Jewish merchants operated their businesses. The family lived in quarters above the family's store.

John Michaux was considered a successful, prominent businessman in the black community. Enhancing his status as a black man, he had light skin and straight hair, both considered marks of distinction, within the black community. His influence was felt as far as the neighboring town of Hampton, Virginia. All of this impacted his young son Solomon Lightfoot, who would spend most of his adult life trying to ignore the crippling realities of being treated as black in a white capitalistic society.

Early Years

When Solomon Lightfoot was a young boy the family moved into quarters above their grocery store. His father's successes influenced his behavior and could be seen in his future business ventures and his religious life. To his son Solomon, John appeared to be accepted as equal among his fellow shopkeepers, but within a desegregated part of town; he could not escape the effects of racism that blanketed this period in the history of the South. Inequality in business black and white relation-

Solomon Lightfoot Michaux

Chronology

1884	Born in Newport News, Virginia on November 7
1904	Opens his own store
1906	Marries Mary Eliza Pauline
1917	Answers call to preach
1918	Licensed and ordained in the Church of Christ (Holiness)
1921	The Michaux congregation secedes from the Church of Christ to establish an independent church
1922	Arrested for singing on the streets of Newport News during early morning hours
1924	Begins to establish branch churches in cities along the East Coast
1929	Begins radio ministry at station WJSV in Washington, D.C.
1934	Purchases 1,800 acres of land along the beachfront in Jamestown, Virginia, to develop a National Memorial to the Progress of the Colored Race in America
1938-61	Holds baptisms in Griffith Stadium
1940	Purchases the old Benning Race Track in Washington, receiving $3.5 million from the Reconstruction Finance Corporation to construct Mayfair Mansions, a 594-unit housing development
1942	Collaborates with Jack Goldberg to make one commercial film
1964	Acquires $6 million in FHA loans to build Paradise Minor, a 617-apartment complex adjacent to Mayfair Mansions
1968	Dies in Washington, D.C. on October 20

ships was quite noticeable during this period; it was extremely difficult for blacks to profit.

The influence of skin color also was paramount in Solomon Lightfoot's early formative years. His mother, May Blanche, a woman with dark skin and black features, was practically unknown in the community. Her role was to make sure the household responsibilities were maintained and that the surviving ten of her fifteen children were taken care of. She suffered from a nervous condition. When Michaux was twenty-one his mother suffered a nervous breakdown and was sent to the black mental institution, located in Petersburg, Virginia. After she returned home, marital problems continued to plague the family. Despite her illness, she influenced her son's future career by reminding him of his importance and that he was born to head a special mission. Even his name made him feel special: Solomon, for his paternal grandfather's Jewish heritage, after the wise and wealthy Old Testament king Solomon; and Lightfoot, in honor of his mother's Indian heritage.

As a youth Solomon Michaux participated in religious activities, studying in both the Baptist and Presbyterian Church, but was considered a loner who kept to himself, unable to develop lasting friendships. Unfortunately, he quit school in the fourth grade, going to work fulltime with his father and becoming a fish peddler before he was able to read and comprehend well enough to be comfortable with his future life role.

Business Opportunities and Marriage

Like many ambitious young men, Michaux believed that he could work hard, save his money, and become rich. He worked hard, long hours each day, and saved at the local black-operated Sons and Daughters of Peace Penny, Nickel, and Dime Savings Bank, planning one day to open his own seafood and poultry store.

Michaux opened his own store around 1904, including a dancing school. There he met his wife, Mary Eliza Pauline, a beautiful fair-skinned, fine-featured young woman who possessed slightly wavy long hair. She was a volatile, illiterate woman of undetermined family origins. Her father was a white man and she had given birth to a child from a previous marriage. No children survived her previous marriage. Once divorced, she and Michaux were married around 1906.

After marrying Michaux, Mary became a fanatical convert to holiness, and the couple began attending Saint Timothy Church of Christ (Holiness), where he was selected secretary-treasurer.

Mary was ambitious and complemented her husband well in financial matters with her qualities of diligence and thrift. Working together she and her husband accumulated enough savings by 1911 to build a large three-story house on Ivy Avenue at Pinkey's Beach, over looking the Chesapeake Bay.

The couple had no children of their own to occupy that big house with them, but Jenny and Ruth, Michaux's two little sisters, lived there to help ease the burden on their ailing mother and to lessen Mary's anxiety about being without a child.

Their marriage developed out of an arranged courtship that was convenient for both. Michaux, like so many aspiring black men before him, had taken a light-colored, white-looking woman to be his wife, according himself more status in the black community. By marrying this aspiring man of good reputation, Mary agreed to an image of respectability, a good address, and comfortable living conditions. Michaux did not need a continuously intimate and physically passionate attachment; his primary passion was the pursuit of business interests.

Michaux never fought in World War I. He obtained government contracts to furnish food provisions to defense establishments. This enterprising businessman took advantage of every opportunity to make money. Because of profits, he was able to invest in branch stores in nearby Norfolk and in the Petersburg-Hopewell area. In 1917, he closed down operations in Newport News and Norfolk and moved his business headquarters to Hopewell, Virginia.

Religious Experience

After moving to Hopewell and with the success of the business, Michaux's wife became concerned regarding their spiritual state. She felt that the worldly environment that existed in Hopewell led to corruption. Spiritually she became somewhat fanatical, praying and evangelizing throughout the day. The Michauxs became dissatisfied with the churches in Hopewell and in order to satisfy her, Solomon built a church where she would be able to conduct the type of services she wanted.

The church that was built had a small, white frame. The DuPont Company donated the land for the church. The church was interracial, nondenominational, and evangelical. She named it "Everybody's Mission." This church was very successful in its nightly worship service, conducted by visiting elders and Mary Michaux.

Receives the Call to Preach

At his wife's insistence, Michaux began attending church again on a regular basis. To him religion and business were not in harmony, according to his experiences that were rooted in the Protestant tradition. However, in 1917 and in 1918 he was licensed and ordained in the Church of Christ (Holiness) U.S.A, receiving counsel from Elder W. C. Handy, a Church of Christ preacher, advising him on scriptural interpretation, pastoral duties, and church doctrine and practices. As an ordained evan-

gelist, he had the authority to pastor Everybody's Mission, and the church became a Church of Christ affiliate.

With the guidance of his wife Michaux was steered back to the Church of Christ (Holiness) which they had attended in Newport News before going to Hopewell. Both were impressed with the teaching of Bishop C. P. Jones. The Holiness movement, which was popular among southern whites late in the nineteenth century, encouraged excitable religious experiences of conversion. Mary influenced Michaux to become affiliated with the black, southern-based Holiness convention.

Makes a Fresh Start

With the signing of the armistice in 1918, World War I came to an end. There was an immediate decline in Michaux's business ventures. Early 1919 saw a decline in employment in the Hopewell area and a rapid decline in population. There had been rapid growth in Newport News during the war and greater opportunities awaited him; he returned and went into business with his father.

His business interests and his ministry began to conflict regarding his time. He decided to leave the business with his father and to organize a local Church of Christ (Holiness) mission. This would take care of the concerns of his wife, and he and Mary would subsist on savings and income from church offerings.

In 1919, Michaux pitched a tent for his first revival on the corner of Jefferson Avenue and Nineteenth Street, in the heart of the black community. He and his wife held revivals there for three months, where at least 150 people became members of his church. These 150 poor, non-property owners and mostly uneducated individuals formed the nucleus of his congregation.

Michaux believed that his own intellectual abilities far exceeded the intelligence of his congregation, and he felt comfortable leading this group. By the end of December, Michaux had managed to gather enough money to move the church into a rented storefront, one block east of Nineteenth Street and Ivy Avenue.

Organizes Church of God

In 1922, when the Church of Christ (Holiness) met in Jackson, Mississippi, Michaux notified the bishop that he was seceding. When he returned he surprised the congregation with the news of their secession from the Church of Christ (Holiness). He proceeded to establish an independent church, calling it the Church of God. He chose this name, because in his view that was what holy assemblies were called in the Bible. This church, along with its other related operations, was incorporated under an umbrella grouping known as the Gospel Spreading Tabernacles Building Association. Michaux had been planning this move for some time; the corporation purchased the building, a three-story structure built by Benson Phillips, who was an acquaintance from Michaux's childhood.

During this year Michaux experienced two personal losses, his father died and he no longer had the support and relationship that he had established with Bishop Jones, the man who had been his spiritual father for many years. Still, Michaux's mission was to build this new church and establish a chain of churches, which would eventually be an empire unsurpassed by other religious groups. Also in 1922, Michaux and several of his members were arrested for singing on the streets of Newport News, during the early morning hours, while inviting people to join the church. For his action he was fined; he later appealed in vain to the Virginia Supreme Court.

As members migrated north in search of employment after World War I, Michaux began to establish branch churches in the cities along the east coast. In 1922, Michaux was a thirty-eight-year-old, mission-oriented preacher. His many successes in business, combined with the growth of his ministry, made him believe in himself and his purpose. He embarked upon a plan of action that merged the religious, social, and economic interests he had pursued before. He also discovered that he had the ability to appeal to the masses, articulating their most intimate feelings and concerns.

Michaux traveled from city to city as an evangelist. He, organized churches, and used the media and his talent for showmanship to spread the gospel, believing that combining religion with entertainment would result in the most conversions to his church.

In 1929, Michaux ventured into radio programming at station WJSV in Washington, D.C., and became famous as a radio evangelist, despite being denied an opportunity to broadcast by most stations. It was through determination and perseverance that he succeeded. The broadcast moved to the Columbia Broadcasting System (CBS) in 1932, the eve of radio's golden era. As a result of the radio program's signature song, "Happy Am I," Michaux became known from coast to coast and overseas as the "Happy Am I Preacher." His fundamentalist sermons of hope and good neighborliness caught the attention of millions, appealing to all classes of people. His wife continued to be a powerful influence in his ministry, an exhorter and the lead broadcast soloist. She was a regular on the radio program, too. The radio program became so popular that local, national, and foreign dignitaries attended his live, theatrically staged radio broadcasts. To Michaux's surprise even the British Broadcasting Corporation (BBC) contracted with him for two broadcasts in the United Kingdom, in 1936 and 1938. A third broadcast was considered but because of Michaux's legal problems it was cancelled. Michaux was sought after by booking agents and movie directors, who offered him contracts, but all were refused by Michaux. In 1942 he collaborated with Jack Goldberg to make one commercial film, *We've Come a Long, Long Way*.

Michaux's political activities and other business endeavors continued to grow. He used his preaching via the radio to offer free housing and employment services to poor people, both black and white. In return for meals at the Happy News Café, he invited them to sell copies of *Happy News*, the church's paper.

Michaux became actively involved in the political arena when President Herbert Hoover evicted the Bonus Army (fifteen thousand unemployed World War I veterans and their families who converged on the capital in 1932 to demand immediate payment of bonuses that were not due until 1945) for which Michaux had been holding worship services. Then too Michaux used the radio to campaign for Franklin Delano Roosevelt in 1932, 1936, and 1940. He is now credited with influencing some of the first African Americans to leave the Republican Party and enter the Democratic fold in 1932.

Yet, in 1952, Michaux switched sides and campaigned as vigorously for Republican candidate Dwight Eisenhower as he had for Roosevelt and Harry Truman. This led many to believe that Michaux was an exploiter and opportunistic in his religious and business practices.

Michaux's annual baptisms were considered one of the highlights of the season. Crowds would attend these ceremonies. Because of his knack for taking advantage of entertainment opportunities, he moved the ceremony, from the Potomac riverbank in 1938 into Griffith Stadium until 1961. The significance of this move was that this was the first time that an all black organization was permitted to use Griffith Stadium. These patriotically elaborate stadium services were full of pageantry, fireworks, and enthralling precision drills and choral singing from the 156-voice Cross Choir. Singing was accompanied by the church band, while hundreds were baptized center field in a canvas-covered tank.

Michaux had made lucrative deals in real estate, such as the 1934 purchase of 1,800 acres of land along the beachfront in Jamestown, Virginia, where he intended to develop a National Memorial to the Progress of the Colored Race of America. His plans for selling investment shares, however, fell through when lawsuits that alleged mismanagement of monies were filed against him.

Michaux moved his church's headquarters to the nation's capital in 1929 mainly due to the success of his radio ministry there. He bought the old Benning Race Track in Washington sometime in 1940 and received $2.5 million from the Reconstruction Finance Corporation to construct Mayfair Mansions, a 594-unit housing development. This project was completed in 1946. In 1964, he was granted $6 million in FHA loans to build Paradise Manor, a 617-unit apartment complex adjacent to Mayfair Mansions. This growth shows just how well received and favored he was because in the 1950s he had come under investigation for favoritism from federal lending agencies. These successes were due in part to his friendship with prominent people in Washington, some of whom were honorary members of his church.

While Michaux initially preached race consciousness and stated that all races were brothers, he became more and more conservative as he aged. He criticized the civil rights and black nationalist movements in the 1960s, and preached that the activities of Elijah Muhammad and Martin Luther King Jr. contributed to racial polarization.

During the forty-nine years of his career he established seven churches and several branches, and membership numbered in the thousands. By the time he died in 1968, he had acquired and left to his church a considerable estate of temples, apartment dwellings, cafes, tracts of land, and private residences in several cities. His worth was estimated to be in excess of $20 million. When Michaux died in Washington, D.C., his radio program was estimated to be the longest continuous broadcast in radio history. The religious institution, the Church of God, which he founded, continued to operate into the early 2000s. He made a significant contribution in religious broadcasting by using electronic and print media for worldwide evangelism.

REFERENCES

Books

Ashcraft-Webb, Lillian. *About My Father's Business: The Life of Elder Lightfoot Michaux*. Westport, Conn.: Greenwood Press, 1981.

Logan, Rayford W., and Michael R. Winston, eds. *Dictionary of American Negro Biography*. New York: Norton, 1982.

Williams, Ethel L. *Biographical Directory of Negro Ministers*. New York: Scarecrow Press, 1965.

Mattie McHollin

Arthur W. Mitchell

Arthur W. Mitchell
1883–1968

Civil rights activist, educator, politician

During a time of great injustice, Arthur W. Mitchell demonstrated courage and ingenuity in using the justice system to address civil rights violations in the United States. A civil rights activist, he was also an educator, politician, and administrator. His career is a testament to the rewards of hard work and determination.

Mitchell was born on a farm, in the city of Lafayette, in Chambers County, Alabama. The son of slaves, he was educated in the public schools of the South. In 1897, at fourteen years of age, he left home to attend the Tuskegee Institute in Tuskegee, Alabama. Even at this early age, Mitchell distinguished himself and served as an office assistant to Booker T. Washington during his stay at the institute. In addition, he worked as a laborer to help pay for his education. He went on to attend Columbia University in New York City and Harvard University. Then he managed to qualify for the bar, thus opening the door to a legal career.

Mitchell began practicing law in 1927. His legal practice grew in Washington, D.C., during the late twenties. By 1929, Mitchell was established as both an educational administrator and a lawyer. He also began dealing in real estate opportunities in Chicago, Illinois. Mitchell moved to Chicago, hoping to try his hand at politics and possibly be elected as a representative for Illinois.

Mitchell's career developed during a time of great change. In the 1920s, African Americans began to play an active role in American politics, and Mitchell aspired to join them. While living in Chicago, he began working for the Republican Party. Soon he realized that party did not reflect his views. He switched to the Democratic Party, which was the party of choice for the majority of African Americans during the Great Depression of the 1930s. Mitchell worked closely with the Democrats and after the sudden death of Harry Baker, saw his chance to seek election to the House of Representatives. In 1935 he was

Chronology

1883	Born near Lafayette, Alabama on December 22
1897	Enters Tuskegee Institute
1927	Gains admittance to the bar and begins practicing law in Washington, D.C.
1929	Moves to Chicago, continuing to practice law and engaging in the real estate business
1935	Wins election as a Democrat to the seventy-fourth Congress
1937	Travels to Arkansas and later brings a suit against the Chicago and Rock Island Railroad
1941	Wins a case that he argues himself, which declares the Jim Crow practices regarding interstate travel illegal
1942	Retires from Congress
1968	Dies in Petersburg, Virginia on May 9

able to defeat Oscar DePriest by 3,000 votes to be elected to the seventy-fourth Congress.

Serves in Congress

During his term in the seventy-fourth Congress, Mitchell spoke out against injustice. He disapproved of the Italian invasion of Ethiopia and the fascist regime of Benito Mussolini. He challenged the legality of the Jim Crow laws that served to suppress the civil rights of African Americans throughout the South. Jim Crow laws emerged in the years after Reconstruction as a way to deny African Americans their rights. These laws gained popularity after the rulings of the Supreme Court in the late 1880s that supported the concept of separate-but-equal accommodations and services. Southern states readily enacted laws that prevented whites and African Americans from riding in the same railroad cars, using the same washrooms, or eating in the same restaurants. Mitchell, himself, was not immune to these restrictive conditions. Even though Mitchell led a very accomplished life in the relative safety of the northern city of Chicago, all people of African American descent in the South had to conform to the stifling conditions and injustice of Jim Crow laws.

In 1937, while Mitchell was traveling to Hot Springs, Arkansas, he was forced to leave his first-class seat aboard a train. He was then ordered to continue the trip aboard a Jim Crow train. As was the case throughout the South, accommodations for African Americans were inferior. Often they faced substandard conditions and the decrepit train that Mitchell was forced to ride was no exception. Mitchell immediately set out to legally challenge the transportation system in the South, by bringing a suit against the Chicago and Rock Island Railroad. This action was not taken very seriously, as the Interstate Commerce Commission set his complaint aside. Mitchell then filed a suit in the federal court system. The Supreme Court heard the long and expensive case. Mitchell argued

that he was sold a first-class ticket and then was forcibly removed from a first-class railroad car and that removal was a violation of his constitutional rights. With his legal experience and education, Mitchell was capable of arguing and presenting his own case to the Supreme Court.

The Supreme Court finally ruled on Mitchell's case on April 28, 1941. The Court ruled that the separate-but-equal coach laws of the southern states did not apply to interstate travel and were in violation of the Interstate Commerce Act. This was a significant ruling and victory for the burgeoning civil rights movement. In reality, even though this case was a civil rights victory, the southern states continued to operate just as they always had. It would take further court battles and challenges to truly overthrow the Jim Crow system.

However, Mitchell had accomplished what he had set out to do and that was to remedy an injustice that he saw and could not accept. After the Supreme Court ruled on his case, Mitchell continued to fight civil rights injustices against African Americans. He proposed that states that were discriminatory in their accommodations and provisions for African Americans should have less congressional representation, and he staunchly recommended harsh penalties for states that did not prosecute lynching. He worked to promote a provision that would remove the required poll tax that southern blacks were required to pay before casting their vote. After World War II, Mitchell argued that African Americans fought in that war and they should be free to vote in elections. Mitchell had the distinction of being the only African American to maintain a seat in the House of Representatives between 1935 and 1943. His tireless work and dedication to the civil rights movement inspired many.

In 1942, Mitchell chose not to seek re-election and retired from Congress. During his retirement, Mitchell moved to Virginia where he resumed his law practice, continued his civil rights activities, lectured, and farmed twelve acres near Petersburg. On May 9, 1968, Mitchell died at his home in Virginia.

REFERENCES

Books

"Arthur W. Mitchell." In *African American Almanac.* Ed. Jeffrey Lehman. 9th ed. Farmington Hills, Mich.: Thomson Gale, 2003.

Reardon, Karen E. and Durahn Taylor. "Arthur Wergs Mitchell." In *Encyclopedia of African American Culture and History.* Eds. Jack Salzman, David Lionel Smith, and Cornel West. New York: Simon and Schuster Macmillan, 1996.

Smith, Jessie Carney, ed. *Black Firsts: 4,000 Ground-Breaking and Pioneering Historical Events.* Canton, Mich.: Visible Ink Press, 2003.

Connie Mack

Isaiah T. Montgomery
1847–1924

Politician, entrepreneur

Called a black accommodationist and entrepreneur, Isaiah T. Montgomery walked a dangerous tightrope to become a wealthy and influential leader in Mississippi. He helped to found the all-black town of Mound Bayou, making it possible for blacks to own homes and businesses and to become educated in the private schools that were established in the colony. At the same time, his endorsement of legislation to disfranchise many blacks and some whites, though ill conceived, may have been the only way he knew to try to bridge a racial divide.

Born on the Hurricane plantation of Joseph Davis at Davis Bend, Mississippi, situated on the Mississippi River below Vicksburg on May 21, 1847, Isaiah Thornton Montgomery was the son of Mary Lewis, the daughter of Virginia slaves. His father, Benjamin Thornton Montgomery, the plantation's business manager, was born in 1819 in Loudon County, Virginia. Benjamin Montgomery was sold in 1837 to Joseph Davis, the older brother of Confederate president Jefferson Davis. His new owner was a benevolent man who encouraged his slaves to learn to read and write. Benjamin Montgomery learned well and later opened a store on the plantation, worked as an engineer repairing broken levees and cotton gins, and became a planter as well. In addition to managing Hurricane plantation, where some 350 blacks were enslaved, when Joseph Davis was absent Montgomery managed his plantation known as Brierfield.

The Montgomerys lived above their retail store where the mother cared for the four children. The Montgomerys gave their children far more parental guidance and attention that most slave parents at Hurricane. They also had generous amounts of food and clothing and lived in comfortable quarters. Benjamin was prominent among the slaves and therefore his son, Isaiah, at the age of nine or ten, became personal secretary and office attendant to his owner Joseph Davis. He also lived in Joseph Davis' home where he filed letters and papers. In his new role, Isaiah had full access to the Davis' fine library, and was able to study and to strengthen his education. His father and another slave had already given him some training.

In 1863, when he was just sixteen years old, Montgomery met Admiral David D. Porter, who commanded a Union naval operation that ran past Vicksburg. Porter enlisted Montgomery as his cabin boy, giving him the opportunity to serve on ships and to help General Ulysses Grant seize Vicksburg and remove Mississippi from Confederate control. Six months later, Montgomery became ill from dysentery and Porter sent him to Cincinnati to join his family who lived there temporarily. Montgomery

Chronology

1847	Born on Hurricane plantation in Davis Bend, Mississippi on May 21
1865	Becomes cabin boy in Union naval operation
1866	Purchases Hurricane and Brierfield plantations with father and brother
1871	Marries Martha Robb
1877	With cousin Benjamin Green, founds all-black town, Mound Bayou, Mississippi
1881	Hurricane and Brierfield plantations sold
1888	Elected founding mayor of Mound Bayou
1890	Elected the sole African American delegate to the Mississippi constitutional convention; supports amendment to disfranchise blacks and some whites
1900	Co-founds National Negro Business League
1902	Resigns as mayor; appointed federal post as receiver of public monies in Jackson, Mississippi
1903	Resigns from federal post
1904	Elected candidate to the Republican National Convention
1909	Co-founds Farmer's Cooperative Mercantile Company
1911-13	Helps develop Mound Bayou Oil Mill & Manufacturing Company
1924	Dies in Mound Bayou on March 6

spent most of 1863 in military service. When the Civil War ended, he and his family returned to Hurricane and father and sons reopened the store they owned, but now called it Montgomery & Sons. Benjamin Montgomery returned to his management post at the Davis plantation.

Benjamin Montgomery and his sons William and Isaiah bought the two plantations in 1866 for $300,000 and apparently owned another as well. According to Janet Sharp Hermann in *Black Leaders of the Nineteenth Century*, the Montgomerys planned to establish "a cooperative community of freed people." Isaiah, then only twenty-five years old, was already a respected and important leader at Hurricane. It was the largest of the three plantations that Montgomery & Sons now owned. Although their crops brought the Montgomery family prizes and high ratings during the next fifteen years, toward the end of that period they struggled to make the investment profitable. They were also unable to predict the difficulties that would arise by 1876. As the cost of cotton declined, crops failed, and tenants neglected to pay their debts to them, the Montgomerys were unable to meet their own financial obligations and approached bankruptcy. The strain led to Benjamin Montgomery's death on May 12, 1877; he had died intestate. Mortgage holders foreclosed on the mercantile business of Montgomery & Sons in 1879, and in 1881 the two plantations were auctioned; the Jefferson Davis family and the grandchildren of Joseph Davis became owners.

Founds All-Black Town

Isaiah Montgomery was a resident of Vicksburg by 1887. Around that time a representative of the Louisville, New Orleans, and Texas Railroad (LNOT) approached him with the idea of establishing a black settlement in the Delta Country located in the Yazoo delta. The company owned massive portions of the delta, over one million acres. Although the area was subject to malaria, had become a forest of great timber thickened with cane and briers, and was scorched by the delta's hot sun, it was supposedly appropriate for a black development but unsuitable for whites. As well, the LNOT Railroad sought black farmers to settle the land around the new tracks that now existed between New Orleans and Memphis. The company hired Montgomery as land agent and authorized him to select the site of his choice. Friends and family, including those from Davis Bend, joined in the search, resulting in the founding of Mound Bayou in 1877. Following its incorporation, Isaac Montgomery was elected the town's first mayor in 1898. He and his cousin Benjamin Green, were, in fact, the co-founders. The town was named after a nearby Indian mound, where American Indians held ceremonies and escaped rising waters. Among those who had an important role in founding and/or developing the town were men such as John W. Francis, founder in 1894 and president of Mount Bayou Bank; and Charles Banks, cashier at the bank and later an officer in the state and National Negro Business League.

Montgomery knew that any early black settlers in the Mississippi delta were freedmen who had begun to own their own land after the Civil War. As an agent for the railroad, he sold plots to the colonists. Obviously this was a profitable venture for him, as were the large retail store, cotton gin, lumber yard, and post office that he established in Mound Bayou. Thus, he was well secured financially. Janet Sharp Hermann wrote in *Black Leaders of the Nineteenth Century* that Montgomery spent "his later years comfortably established as the patriarch in a twenty-one-room red brick mansion which dominated the village scene." The railroad was good to him and his family as well, providing them access to state rooms and enabling them to avoid segregated railroad passenger cars.

Montgomery followed his father and former master in their belief that education is important for any group of people. Soon after the town was founded, he donated a track of land to be used to establish Mound Bayou Normal and Industrial Institute. He knew that the American Missionary Association (AMA) was active in the South and that it supported the founding and development of many schools. He persuaded the AMA to provide the new normal school with teachers and to fund it. Then the Colored Baptist Church of Bolivar County opened a school in the village and drew students from surrounding colonies. The state of Mississippi barely supported public education for blacks and gave only enough money to keep schools open four months a year. Private schools for blacks became the town's only options.

Montgomery realized the importance of black business development in Mound Bayou and did all that he could to encourage his people to establish businesses and employ sound business practices. In 1900 he joined Tuskegee Institute founder and president Booker T. Washington in founding the National Negro Business League (NNBL) and attended its initial meeting in Boston in August that year. When the NNBL held its second meeting in Boston the next year, Montgomery spoke on "The Founding of a Negro City." He had also served as one of the black commissioners at the Atlanta Exposition held in 1895. It was at that event that Washington delivered his accommodationist speech that brought the ire of blacks who had a different view of black/white interactions.

The founders had achieved well and in time had a town that, according to Hermann, was "self-contained, black-owned and black operated" and "white interference seemed negligible." The lynching of blacks and racial uprisings seen throughout the state and elsewhere were not a part of that community. In fact, violence barely existed. The leaders and the townspeople themselves supported temperance. To provide for the religious life of the townspeople, six churches were established. Mound Bayou had become a thriving agricultural center by 1905, with a total black population of 4,000. In 1909, Montgomery joined his son-in-law, E. P. Booze, in founding the Farmers' Cooperative Mercantile Company in Mound Bayou. Between 1911 and 1913, he helped to develop the Mound Bayou Oil Mill & Manufacturing Company. Concerned with educational opportunities for his people, Montgomery was a key figure in establishing, developing, and improving the town's educational institutions. By 1940, however, the town had become dilapidated and depopulated.

Endorses the Disenfranchisement of Blacks

Montgomery was active in local and state politics. A Republican, he was the only black delegate elected to the Mississippi constitutional convention in 1890. Montgomery and his family had for a long time become skilled in pleasing whites and in receiving their patronage. He believed, however, that blacks needed a segregated colony where they could promote their own interest. It was at that convention that efforts to disenfranchise blacks were put in motion. While Montgomery had the confidence of many whites, clearly he was acquainted with the racial climate in late nineteenth and early twentieth-century Mississippi. Since he was a man with accommodationist sympathies and beliefs, he saw nothing wrong in delivering an hour-long speech in which he conceded that it would be in the best interests of both races to reduce black vote to a total far less than that of whites. He saw nothing wrong with disenfranchising 123,000 blacks and some 12,000 whites. This would help race relations, he thought, and blacks would have to increase their education and acquire property, then reenter politics themselves. The amendment also imposed a poll tax as a requirement to vote and exclude those who were illiterate or who were convicted of certain crimes. Montgomery's action brought mixed reaction from black leaders: Abolitionist Frederick Douglass thought that he had been tricked into taking such a stance; New York lawyer T. McCants Stewart called his advocacy a move to enfranchise illiterate whites and disfranchise illiterate blacks; and Mississippi Republican John R. Lynch called his action more dishonest than the practice of stuffing ballot boxes, which Mississippi knew well.

The state adopted the amendment, and by 1915 other former Confederate states followed. Within a twenty-year period after the convention, Montgomery admitted that all was not well in his state. Hermann quotes his prediction that "the dominant spirit of the south will be satisfied with nothing less than a retrogression of the Negro back towards serfdom and slavery." And clearly, by 1904, he admitted to the work of whites who terrorized and intimidate black Mississippians.

Montgomery resigned as mayor of Mound Bayou in 1902 when, on endorsement from Booker T. Washington, President Theodore Roosevelt, who forgave him for his political transgression, appointed him as receiver of public funds in Jackson, Mississippi. Sometime in 1903, he was accused of placing $5,000 of government money into his own account. He met secretly with Washington's secretary in New Orleans in 1903, who told him that he must resign his post. Montgomery stayed in office a few months longer, then resigned and returned to Mound Bayou. He had been reluctant to accept the post in the first place, but deferred to the wishes of his friend Washington. His primary concern had been for the development of his colony, Mound Bayou, and he had considered Washington his connection to northern white philanthropy to fund more ambitious projects and businesses there. He also faced hostility from his white staff in Jackson. Continuing in politics, however, in 1904 he was Mississippi delegate to the Republican National Convention.

Isaiah and Martha Robb Montgomery, who married in 1871, had twelve children, eight of whom reached adulthood. One daughter, Mary Booze, became a committeewoman for the national Republican Party. Martha Montgomery, who had become an important business partner, died in 1923, seven months before Montgomery's death in Mound Bayou on March 6, 1924. The Montgomerys' residence is listed on the National Register of Historic Places; it is one of the nation's most historic black culture sites.

To his credit, Montgomery had been involved in nearly every project of interest to the Mound Bayou area; he also worked diligently to promote black self-sufficiency and to enhance the quality of life, especially for those blacks who lived in Mound Bayou. But, as Hermann wrote, Montgomery finally admitted that he could not forgive himself for standing by, "consenting and assisting in striking down the rights and liberties of 123,000 freedmen."

REFERENCES

Books

Hermann, Janet Sharp. "Isaiah T. Montgomery's Balancing Act." In *Black Leaders of the Nineteenth Century.* Ed. Leon Litwack and August Meier. Urbana: University of Illinois Press, 1988.

Logan, Rayford W. "Isaiah Thornton Montgomery." In *Dictionary of American Negro Biography.* Eds. Rayford W. Logan and Michael R. Winston. New York: Norton, 1982.

"Mound Bayou, Miss.: A Town Owned and Controlled Exclusively by Negroes." In *An Era of Progress and Promise, 1863-1910.* Ed., W. N. Hartshorn. Boston: Priscilla Publishing Co., 1910.

Nichols, J. L., and William Crogman. *Progress of a Race, or the Remarkable Advancement of the American Negro.* Naperville, Ill.: J. L. Nichols & Co., 1925.

Silver, David Mark. "Isaiah Thornton Montgomery." In *American National Biography.* Vol. 15. Eds. John A. Garraty and Mark C. Carnes. New York: Oxford University Press, 1999.

Online

"Mound Bayou." Cleveland: Crossroads of Culture in the Mississippi Delta. http://www.visitclevelandms.com/Templates/moundbayou.htm (Accessed 16 January 2006).

Collections

Papers of Isaiah Montgomery are in various collections. Those in the Benjamin Montgomery Family Papers and the Booker T. Washington Papers are in the Library of Congress. Papers relating to the town of Mound Bayou are in the Mississippi Department of Archives and History located in Jackson.

Jessie Carney Smith

Henry Lee Moon
1901–1985

Journalist, editor, civil rights activist

Henry Lee Moon was an advocate for civil rights and dedicated servant and leader to the African Ameri-

Henry Lee Moon

Chronology

1901	Born in Pendleton, South Carolina on July 20
1922	Graduates with B.A. from Howard University in Washington, D.C.
1924	Receives M.A. degree in journalism from Ohio State University
1926-31	Becomes press agent for Tuskegee Institute in Alabama
1931	Joins the *New York Amsterdam News* as a journalist
1932	Travels with twenty-one prominent African Americans to the Soviet Union to produce a film about the history of blacks in the United States
1933	Dismissed from the *New York Amsterdam News* for union activities
1938-44	Serves on staff at the Federal Public Housing Authority as race relations advisor
1944-48	Serves as director of Political Action Committee of the Congress of Industrial Organizations
1948	Publishes *Balance of Power: The Negro Vote*
1948-64	Becomes director of public relations for the NAACP
1965-74	Becomes fourth editor of the NAACP's magazine, *The Crisis*
1973	Edits *The Emerging Thoughts of W. E. B. Du Bois: Essays and Editorials from "The Crisis"*
1974	Retires from NAACP and as editor of *The Crisis*
1985	Dies in New York City on June 7

can community. Henry Moon's career, beginning in 1926 as press agent for Tuskegee Institute through 1974 as editor of the prominent magazine, *The Crisis*, spanned nearly fifty years. Through his work as a journalist, editor, author, and civil rights advocate, Moon must be counted as one of the major African American activists of his time.

Henry Lee Moon was born on July 20, 1901 in Pendleton, South Carolina to William J. Moon and Georgia Bullock. The Moon family soon moved to Cleveland, Ohio where young Moon spent most of his childhood years. Moon's parents became active in and Moon's father served as the first president of the local Cleveland branch of the NAACP.

Much of the Moon family's social and political activism would impact young Moon and remain with him throughout his life. When he was only nine years of age the NAACP launched its premiere magazine, *The Crisis*. With W. E. B. Du Bois, noted scholar and activist, as its editor, *The Crisis* had a huge influence on many people within the African American community. Moon was certainly influenced by Du Bois and the NAACP so much so that he would later become public relations director of the NAACP and fourth editor of this journal. Ultimately he edited and published a collection of Du Bois' works entitled *The Emerging Thoughts of Du Bois*. Moon's academic training at Howard University and at Ohio State

University provided him the training he needed to work in journalism. He entered Howard University with a major in journalism in 1918. By 1924, he had earned an M.A. in journalism from Ohio State University.

From Journalist to Film Producer

Following graduation from Ohio State University, Moon was hired as the director of press relations at Tuskegee Institute in Alabama in 1926. Moon's tenure at Tuskegee would last for the next seven years. In 1931, Moon left Tuskegee for his first newspaper job in New York City. He began writing for the *New York Amsterdam News*. Shortly afterward his editorials began appearing in both African American newspapers and mainstream white newspapers. Moon wrote for the *New York Times*, *New Republic*, *London Tribune*, *Chicago Defender*, and *Cleveland Herald News*. Moon also published articles in the Urban League's *Opportunity* magazine, as well as Atlanta University's journal, *Phylon*. Remaining true to the cause of human justice and equality for the racially oppressed, Moon editorialized about politics, corrupt labor laws, public housing, and race relations in the United States.

As a journalist Moon extended his interest beyond domestic policy into international news. He traveled throughout the United States and to other parts of the world, many times on special assignment. In 1932, Henry Moon, Langston Hughes (the prominent African American literary figure), and twenty other notable African

Americans traveled to the Soviet Union for a film project depicting the African American experience in the United States, but the film project was never completed. As reported in the *New York Times* on June 8, 1985, Moon reportedly told the *New York Amsterdam News* that the project was aborted "because of fears that it might wound American sensibilities at a time when the Soviet Union was seeking diplomatic recognition by the United States." Following the cancelled film project, Moon was dismissed by the *New York Amsterdam News* reportedly for his support of union activities.

In 1938 Moon joined the Federal Public Housing Authority as a regional advisor on race relations. His tenure with Public Housing lasted until 1944. During this six-year period Moon continued to advocate for fair housing and the abolition of race-based discriminatory practices. Also, in 1941, Moon studied public relations and public administration at American University in Washington, D.C. In 1944, Moon was selected as an assistant to Sidney Hillman, director of the Political Action Committee. The committee served under the umbrella of the Congress of Industrial Organizations (CIO). Moon assisted director Hillman until 1948.

By 1948, Moon had published his first book, *Balance of Power: The Negro Vote*, which was well received and touted throughout the black press as a definitive study of the effect of African American voting habits since Reconstruction. Although Moon had his share of critics, the book brought him national attention.

Moon's goal was to examine the process African Americans experienced in order to gain use of the ballot. He studied trends in African American party affiliation and its impact on the group's ability to attain full equality. In Moon's assessment full equality is determined by freedom of political action, the acquisition of property, and the attainment of an education. Although African Americans did not have full equality when the book was published, Moon was convinced that the tide was shifting in a positive direction. For example, despite intimidation tactics, fraud schemes, and efforts made by some legislators to deter African American voter turnout in the 1940s, the numbers of African Americans qualified to vote continued to increase. Moon further estimated that the voting campaign of 1948 was to be one of the most mean-spirited campaigns in U.S. history.

Moon concluded that in the World War II era, the main objective most African Americans shared was the elimination of Jim Crow laws and full and equal access to the rights of U.S. citizenship. The desire to achieve those goals was the binding force for African Americans, explained Moon. He pointed out that the demands were not imagined but universal among blacks, but he admitted only militant blacks and noted black leaders expressed them openly. Consequently, white Americans' unwillingness to acknowledge African Americans' commitment to

their objectives led to underestimating the political and racial challenges that lay ahead for the country.

Moon, the NAACP, and *The Crisis*

Between 1948 and 1964 Henry Moon served as the director of public relations for the NAACP. In this role Moon helped the organization increase its national and international visibility. He used his press background to strengthen the NAACP's relationship with the press. In 1955 Moon was the NAACP representative on a tour of Radio Free Europe in Munich, Germany. For a brief period between 1964 and 1965 Moon was appointed deputy director of public information for New York City's Housing and Development Board. He returned to the NAACP as its public relations director and accepted a dual position as editor of the organization's magazine, *The Crisis*. Moon was regarded as one of "The Big Four," who guided the development and execution of the NAACP. Moon followed on the heels of three great predecessors: W. E. B. Du Bois; Roy Wilkins, NAACP leader and former editor of *The Crisis*; and James W. Ivy, writer, activist, and former *Crisis* editor. For the next ten years Henry Moon served as chief editor of *The Crisis*.

Moon was privileged to become acquainted with Du Bois, a man he had idolized since childhood. In fact in his first editorial as chief editor of *The Crisis*, Moon highlighted the successes of the magazine under its venerable founder and leader, Du Bois, and the new path he hoped to establish for the publication. In the January 1965 issue of *The Crisis* Moon noted: "Under the editorship of its founder, the late W. E. B. Du Bois, the magazine enjoyed high prestige as the authentic voice of the civil rights movement. It was in the words of the founder, a record of the darker races. Its informative and often provocative editorials and articles were widely read and frequently quoted . . . It will not be the magazine it was under Dr. Du Bois, first because only he could give *The Crisis* his unique editorial flavor."

Moon was interested in broadening the magazine's circulation to reach beyond the organization's membership to enlist the support of a wider base. He wished to entice well noted authors both black and white to submit writings to the magazine, as well as to expand the range of content in the journal. He felt that the magazine's coverage should reflect changing U.S. conditions. Moon strongly believed that it was no longer the sole responsibility of *The Crisis* to shoulder the responsibility of reporting Negro news. The success of well edited and widely circulated "Negro" magazines helped to lighten the load that *The Crisis* shouldered for a long time. Nonetheless, Moon hoped to retain the prominent position of *The Crisis*.

Moon continued to keep a close eye of African American political progress and track racial voting trends. Alongside his first editorial in *The Crisis* as its new editor Moon wrote about the "Negro's Political Future." He also published an articled entitled, "How We Voted and Why?" Moon highlighted the phenomenal turnout of African American voters in the 1964 presidential election of Lyndon B. Johnson as well as editorialized about the then-recent ruling by the Democratic National Convention to ban racial discrimination in the selection of state delegations to all future national democratic conventions. Moon also articulated his hope for an increase in African American party leadership as well as an increase in the number of black mayors elected in major cities. As editor of *The Crisis* Moon emphasized the need for the magazine to highlight African American achievers and major achievements in the civil rights struggle, creating a historical record of those events.

Moon's dedication to the NAACP and to the magazine lasted throughout his reign as editor. One year prior to his retirement in 1974, Moon edited and published *The Emerging Thoughts of W. E. B. Du Bois*, an extensive collection of Du Bois's works with an introduction by Moon. By its publication Moon had become an expert on Du Bois.

In 1974, after a seventeen-year career with the NAACP, Henry Moon retired. He had witnessed numerous changes in U.S. social and political structure, and he took great pride in the work he and the organization he proudly represented contributed to bringing about progress for the oppressed. His impact on the organization lasted beyond his lifetime.

On June 7, 1985, after a prolonged illness, Henry Moon died at the age of eighty-four at Mount Sinai Hospital in New York City. His surviving relatives were his wife, Mollie, and his daughter, Mollie Moon Eliot of Manhattan. In a fitting tribute to his legacy many newspapers and *The Crisis* wrote editorials about Moon. The *New York Amsterdam News* wrote: "Henry was an effective and unusual advocate of freedom and equality for the racially oppressed. He dedicated much of his life to the NAACP, which represented and symbolized his own beliefs in human dignity and freedom . . . We will miss him but we are also assured that he departs from this world after having lived a rewarding and successful life."

In tribute to Moon for his dedication to the NAACP, many of his colleagues supported and funded the establishment of the Henry Lee Moon Library at the association's archives in Baltimore, Maryland. The association noted that Moon's accomplishments were much greater than his quiet character and modesty may have indicated. However, for his achievements in public relations, journalism, and for furthering the cause of the civil rights movement he deserves to be noted and affectionately remembered by all.

REFERENCES

Periodicals

"Henry Lee Moon Dead at 84; Ex-NAACP Spokesman." *New York Times*, 8 June 1985.

"Moon *Crisis* Editor Was Famous Journalist." *New York Amsterdam News*, 15 June 1985.

Online

NAACP Henry Lee Moon Library web page, http://www.naacp.org/library (Accessed 4 March 2005).

Baiyina W. Muhammad

Alonzo G. Moron
1909–1971

College president

Alonzo Graseano Moron was the first black president of Hampton University, influencing the civil rights movement as he worked to upgrade Hampton Institute from a trade school to a college. He proved that a school for African Americans could be successful with a black man in charge. Moron's influence was significant in many fields. An outstanding scholar, effective administrator, and advocator for civil rights, he held many groundbreaking posts, all with distinction.

Moron was born in the Virgin Islands on April 12, 1909 to Caroline Louisa Brown and Joseph Metjunto Moron. His parents were both native to the Virgin Islands, which were a Danish possession at the time. His mother was a seamstress and his father was a Jew who had migrated to the Caribbean Islands from Spain. As a young man, Moron's scholarship was so exceptional that a group of supporters raised money to send him to Hampton Institute in Hampton, Virginia. Although circumstances prevented most of the money from reaching him, he was determined to attend Hampton Institute, and he enrolled in September 1923. In Norfolk, Virginia, Moron experienced the segregated South firsthand. Attempting to buy food at a restaurant near the base he was told it was for whites only.

At fourteen, he was alone and practically destitute when he enrolled at Hampton. To support himself he worked odd jobs at homes near the yacht club in downtown Hampton. At the time Moron attended Hampton Institute (1923-27), the school offered high school level training in the trades. In 1927, Moron received a degree in upholstering, which was the highest level of education available at Hampton Institute at the time. After graduation, he accompanied the well-known Hampton Quartette on tour as spokesman and promoter for the group.

Moron entered Brown University in 1928 to study sociology. At Brown, he joined the Alpha Phi Alpha Fra-

Alonzo G. Moron

Chronology

1909	Born on St. Thomas Island on April 12
1923	Arrives in United States; enrolls at Hampton Institute
1927	Graduates from Hampton Institute with certificate in upholstering; travels on fundraising tour with Hampton Quartette singers
1928	Enrolls at Brown University
1932	Marries Leola Rowena Churchill; receives bachelor of philosophy degree from Brown University
1933	Receives M.A. in sociology from University of Pittsburgh; appointed commissioner of public welfare, Virgin Islands
1936	Returns to United States
1936-39	Becomes housing manager for Public Works Administration project
1944	Enrolls at Harvard Law School
1947	Receives LLB from Harvard Law School
1948	Appointed acting president at Hampton Institute
1949-59	Serves as president at Hampton Institute
1959	Returns to Virgin Islands
1960-66	Serves as commissioner of education and administrator in Virgin Islands
1966	Appointed deputy regional administrator for region, Virgin Islands and Puerto Rico
1971	Dies in Puerto Rico on October 1

ternity, the Liberal and Spanish Clubs, and he played tennis. He was a cum laude Phi Beta Kappa graduate in 1932. That same year he married Leola Rowena Churchill, whose family lived in the Hampton area. After marriage, Moron continued to the University of Pittsburgh on a scholarship from the Urban League, earning a master's degree in 1933.

After earning his M.A., Moron was selected as the first black man to serve in the Emergency Relief Commission of Baltimore. In 1933, Moron was selected commissioner of public welfare for the Virgin Islands at the crucial time when the Federal Emergency Relief Program was initiated. He developed welfare in this country where three-fourths of the population was unemployed or underemployed.

Moron left the Virgin Islands in 1936 to work at Atlanta University. He was soon offered a position at the Federal Public Works Administration, where for four years he managed a 675-unit housing project for African Americans. During this time, he also taught courses and lectured in sociology.

Moron entered Harvard Law School in 1944 as a Rosenwald Fellow and was awarded his law degree in 1947. At Harvard, Moron served as an advisor to the board of trustees at Hampton University, and upon receiving his law degree he joined Hampton Institute as general business manager.

First Black President of Hampton Institute

Moron displayed considerable administrative abilities during his first years at Hampton Institute. When the board of Hampton needed to appoint a new president, Moron was nominated. On April 29, 1949, the board announced the appointment of Moron as the first black president of this historically black university. This event was extremely significant to the African American community in Virginia. Local African American newspapers such as the *Norfolk Journal and Guide* wrote glowing editorials predicting a new age for African Americans. Moron's efficiency and astuteness helped the school attract benefactors. His exceptional writing style helped persuade potential contributors.

Moron's official documents as president of Hampton Institute reflect his resolve to maintain an interracial faculty at Hampton and to resist the repressive social climate of that time. He abandoned the practice of requiring faculty to swear an oath of loyalty, which he felt was too authoritarian. Moron achieved fiscal security for Hampton Institute. He was conservative politically, but believed in civil rights.

Among his most notable contributions to the civil rights movement was offering Rosa Parks a job when she was unable to find work after the Montgomery bus boycott. Parks and her husband were also having some disagreements with Martin Luther King Jr. and some other civil rights leaders. In 1957 she accepted Moron's offer of a job as hostess at the Holly Tree Inn dining hall, which paid $300 a month.

Moron believed in political action to advance civil rights. With the backing of the NAACP and Hampton Institute he opposed a movement among white Virginia legislators to support private schools at taxpayer expense. The measure passed the legislature, but Moron raised an awareness of the power of black political organizations. However,Moron had some difficulties at Hampton Institute with the Board of Trustees and the students. Moron displayed impatience and imperiousness that made him unpopular with some people, but these characteristics also gave him the drive and determination for change. He felt the Board of Trustees were not supportive of his fundraising activities and that they bypassed proper channels in dealing with faculty and student grievances. He resigned as president of Hampton Institute in 1959.

Returns to the Virgin Islands

In 1959, Moron returned to his native Virgin Islands to serve as acting commissioner of education. There he was named deputy regional administrator for an entire region that included the U.S. Virgin Islands and Puerto Rico and advised the governor on assistance grants and legislation to help the Virgin Islands gain federal assistance.

Moron was active in many organizations, including the Urban League Board of Trustees, NAACP, Phi Beta Kappa, Alpha Phi Alpha, Sigma Pi Phi, and the Rotary Club. He served as consultant to the Fund for the Advancement of Education, the American Association of Colleges and Universities, the U.S. Department of State, and others. Moron was an administrator, scholar, lecturer, author of numerous journal articles, and a dynamic force in the civil rights movement. He and his wife Leola retired to Puerto Rico where they lived for many years. Moron died in Puerto Rico on October 1, 1971.

REFERENCES

Books

Carnes, Mark C., ed. *American National Biography*. 2nd supplement. New York: Oxford University Press, 2005.

Periodicals

"The Tradition of White Presidents at Black Colleges." *Journal of Blacks in Higher Education* 16 (Summer 1997): 93-99.

Zaki, Hoda. "Man with a Mission." *Daily Press* (25 July-1 August 2004): Section J: 1-2.

Online

Brown University. Alpha Gamma History: Alonzo G. Moron, Class of 1932. www.brown.edu/Students/ Alpha_Phi_Alpha/Moron.html (Accessed 20 January 2006).

Collections

The Alonzo Moron Collection is housed in the Hampton University Archives, at Hampton University, Hampton, Virginia. This collection includes a letter dated September 5, 1957 from Moron to Rosa Parks inviting her to work at Hampton Institute.

Elizabeth Sandidge Evans

Ferdinand Q. Morton
1881–1949

Politician, lawyer, baseball commissioner

From World War I through the Great Depression, Harlem had among its first black politicians Ferdinand Q. Morton, who seemingly had absolute control over the political machine known as Black Tammany. Although he practiced law for a while, Morton was primarily interested in Democratic politics, as leader of the United Colored Democracy and perhaps more importantly as head of Black Tammany. For the Democratic mayors of New York, he became the sole spokesperson for black democracy and one of Harlem's most powerful black political leaders in his time. When appointed to the New York Municipal Civil Service Commission, he became its first black member and held the power to increase the number of black employees in New York City.

Born on September 9, 1881, in Macon, Mississippi, Ferdinand Quinton Morton was the son of Edward James Morton and Mattie Shelton Morton, who were former slaves. Edward Morton moved his family from Mississippi to Washington, D.C., in 1890, when he became a clerk in the U.S. Treasury Department. Young Ferdinand was educated in the Washington public schools before enrolling in Phillips Exeter Academy in Exeter, New Hampshire. After graduating in 1902, he enrolled at Harvard University, where he achieved well and participated in intercollegiate debate, which previously gave students credit toward graduation. During his senior year, the university changed its policy on allowing such credit and told Morton that he needed one-half course credit more to complete his degree, the amount that the debating experience would have provided. Rather than take a course to make up this work, he left school. Another interpretation of his departure is given by Francesco L. Nepa, Morton's biographer in *American National Biography*. Nepa claims that Morton left Harvard in 1905 "probably

Chronology

1881	Born in Macon, Mississippi on September 9
1902	Enrolls at Harvard College
1905	Enrolls in Boston University Law School
1910	Passes the New York Bar; enters law practice
1916	Heads United Colored Democracy; begins tenure as head of "Black Tammany Hall"; appointed assistant district attorney for New York County's Indictment Bureau
1922	Becomes first black member of the New York Municipal Civil Service Commission
1933	Leaves his post with the United Colored Democracy
1935	Becomes commissioner of baseball for the Negro National League
1946	Elected president of the Civil Service Commission
1949	Dies in Washington, D.C. on November 8

because of monetary problems." Whatever the case, Morton made a similar choice at Boston University Law School, which he entered in the fall of 1905 and after a year and a half of studies left without taking his degree. Nepa asserts again that financial problems contributed to this decision. Apparently Morton maintained his interest in law, though, for he worked as a law clerk for two years and in 1910 passed the New York State Bar without having a law degree.

Heads Black Tammany

Morton developed an interest in politics while studying for his law degree. In 1908, after he relocated to New York City, he worked in William Jennings Bryan's Democratic campaign for president. He spoke publicly on Bryan's behalf. After Bryan lost the election to Republican William Howard Taft, Morton continued his interest in the Democratic Party. At this time, Harlem had not opened up to blacks. In 1910, for example, there were no black policemen in the city. There were no blacks in state or municipal legislative branches either. Blacks in city employment, other than school teachers (who were not called political), were relegated to the Street Cleaning Department Morton joined the United Colored Democracy (UCD), which was formed to convince blacks in New York to switch from the Republican to the Democratic Party. New York was believed to be a promised land for many black migrants from the South. An unprecedented number of blacks lived in Harlem, where the community became active in politics. Their vote, however, was divided between two assembly districts, the Nineteenth and Twenty-first. Robert N. Wood especially liked Black Tammany and made the young and inexperienced Morton his right-hand man. The party also respected Wood. Thus, in 1915 the UCD, with its special black organization within the city's Democratic Party, took Ferdinand Morton as its leader and the leader of Black Tammany.

Some worried that individual blacks could impede the progress of an entire group. Morton's position as head of UCD meant that there was no struggle for leadership in the organization of Harlem's Democratic ward. Morton used his authority to quiet local demands for black Democratic leaders in the Nineteenth and Twenty-first alderman districts (ADs). But as this change took place, some thought that Morton's control of "Black Tammany" weakened. Claims were that Black Tammany consisted largely of men who were janitors and held small jobs supplemented by bribes on Election Day. There arose mixed reaction to Morton and his efforts. Gilbert Osofsky wrote in *Harlem: The Making of a Ghetto* that dissident black Democrats found Morton "haughty", "secretive", and "exclusive", a man who acted like an "overlord." He was criticized for being "utterly without the social qualities which make a leader easily accessible to his constituents and responsive to their needs." He was said to be "arrogant", "cynical", and "vindictive." On the other hand, the NAACP's *Crisis* magazine for July 1925 endorsed Morton, calling him "a strong, skillful, courageous man, cynical surely, but honest and sound." The magazine said that he deserved respect. Further, he was described as "avowedly a party politician" who argued that "a determined and resourceful Negro inside the Northern Democratic Party could do more to stop Southern domination than all the Negroes herded as Republicans." Morton believed that the future of black America would be worked out in the North rather than the South and West. It was, therefore, important for blacks to have civic and political equality. In his view, blacks in urban and industrial centers of the North should align themselves with the dominant political party.

Morton practiced law in New York for six years. He was appointed assistant district attorney for New York County in 1916. He continued in public office and in 1921 headed the office's Indictment Bureau. Charles F. Murphy, who headed mainstream Tammany Hall, admired Morton's speaking and leadership abilities and in 1915 sought Morton's support as Harlem's black Democratic leader. He knew that Morton headed Black Tammany, was the city's most recognized Democrat, and had "almost dictatorial control of Negro patronage," wrote Osofsky in *Harlem: The Making of a Negro Ghetto*. Morton worked with Harlem's white Democratic bosses through the 1930s. Morton's assistance made him recognized as the most powerful black Democrat in the city. Until 1932, blacks in Harlem had given unwavering support to Republican presidential candidates, but after World War II they were more politically independent where local politics was concern. They trusted Democratic mayoral candidate John F. Hylan, whom they believed was an honest leader. When elected mayor in 1921, Hylan responded to Morton's support during the election and on January 1, 1922, appointed him chair of the Municipal Civil Service Commission, a lucrative and important post. With this appointment Morton became the first black to head any department in the city.

Hylan went out of office, succeeded by James J. Walker, who reappointed Morton to the cabinet-rank post. Morton joined the Republican alderman, the NAACP, and the North Harlem Medical Society in persuading Walker to appoint five black physicians to racially segregated Harlem Hospital's regular staff, making them the first blacks in such a position. Walker also saw that a training school for black nurses was established there. In 1930, Walker made sweeping changes, reorganized the hospital, and saw that it was open without restrictions to black doctors. By 1932, over seventy black interns and physicians worked at the hospital.

The segregated UCD was called into question and in the 1920s was said to have outlived its usefulness. The Democratic mayors used Morton "as a vehicle of city patronage," wrote Osofsky, and blacks who were opposed to what was going on politically could do no more than hope for relief. Those who held local jobs also controlled the party and were fired if they complained too loudly or defiantly. For example, a clerk in Harlem's municipal court, a superintendent in the state employment office in Harlem, and a deputy sheriff in New York County criticized Morton's leadership and refused to give 10 percent of their salaries to UCD, only to be summarily dismissed due to incompetence. Morton's dictatorship ruled until 1933, when Republican Fiorello H. LaGuardia was elected mayor. A liberal politician, LaGuardia eliminated Morton's patronage, and the UCD functioned no longer. LaGuardia gave Morton an ultimatum: break with the Democratic Party or lose his appointment on the Civil Service Commission. Morton saved himself, gave up the party, left Tammany, and joined the American Labor Party, the party of choice of the mayor. For financial reasons as well, Morton would keep his post and the $10,000 per year that he made as one of the city's highest-paid blacks at the time. After that, Harlem Democrats were no longer under his control; they took over local district organization and removed the old white bosses from the Nineteenth AD in 1935 and the Twenty-first AD in 1939.

Morton left the political arena in 1935 and became baseball commissioner for the Negro National League that Andrew "Rube" Foster, the "Father of Black Baseball," founded in 1920. He held that post for four years. His tenure covered the final two years of the Negro National League as the only black league and the first two years of the rival Negro American League. It is said that his role was purely ceremonial. He had no power or influence in the league and fell prey to the efforts of the powerful Gus Greenlee, who owned the Pittsburgh Crawfords, and who saw to it that other owners boycotted the 1938 meeting of the league that Morton called. The commissioner's post was abolished later that year.

Morton held on to his Civil Service Commission contact, and on July 16, 1946, he was elected president of the commission, a position that he held until his retirement on July 10, 1948. By then he suffered from Parkinson's disease. Morton, who never married, returned to Washington, D.C., where he died when his hospital bed caught fire from a burning cigarette. His sole survivor was his brother Frederick Morton, of Washington. After his funeral was held in New York, he was buried in Woodlawn Cemetery. Ferdinand W. Morton led a colorful life in Harlem, controlling the black Democratic machine known as Black Tammany and serving as the designated leader of the United Colored Democracy.

REFERENCES

Books

Nepa, Frencesco L. "Ferdinand Quinton Morton." In *American National Biography*. Vol. 15. Eds. John A. Garraty and Mark C. Carnes. New York: Oxford University Press, 1999.

Osofsky, Gilbert. *Harlem: The Making of a Ghetto: Negro New York, 1890-1930.* New York: Harper & Row, 1963.

Ottley, Roi, and William J. Weatherby, eds. *The Negro in New York: An Informal Social History 1626-1940.* New York: Praeger Publishers, 1967.

Peterson, Robert. *Only the Ball was White.* Englewood Cliffs, N.J.: Prentice-Hall, 1970.

Who's Who in Colored America. 5th ed. Brooklyn: Thomas Yenser, 1940.

Periodicals

"Ferdinand Q. Morton." *Crisis* 30 (July 1925): 115-16.

"F. Q. Morton, 67, Civil Service Aide." *New York Times*, 9 November 1949.

Rouzeau, Edgar T. "Harlem seeks Political Leadership." *Crisis* 42 (September 1935): 268, 274.

Jessie Carney Smith

Nathan Mossell
1856–1946

Physician

Nathan Francis Mossell was one of the first generation of university-trained black physicians in the United States. After earning his degree from the University of Pennsylvania in 1882, Mossell practiced in that city for several years before co-founding its Frederick

Douglass Memorial Hospital, the first such institution dedicated to meeting the healthcare needs of Philadelphia's African American community which carried on its work until the early 1970s.

Nathan Mossell was born in Hamilton, Ontario, Canada, on May 15, 1856, the son of Aaron Albert Mossell and Eliza Bowers Mossell. By 1870, the family, which included his brothers Aaron and Charles and sisters Alvaretta and Mary, had moved to Lockport, New York, in Niagara County. Lockport was a mostly Quaker community and had been known as a haven for runaway slaves as far back as the 1820s. The Quakers, a Protestant pacifist sect, formally known as the Society of Friends, embraced not only religious tolerance but the expansion of civil liberties for all. Many Quakers were well-known abolitionists in pre-Civil War America.

Mossell attended Lincoln University, located in Chester County in southeastern Pennsylvania. The school was founded as the Ashmun Institute in 1854 as the first historically black college in the United States for men and was renamed in honor of slain U.S. President Abraham Lincoln after the Civil War. Mossell excelled in his studies and took the school's Bradley Medal in natural science. After earning his undergraduate degree from Lincoln in 1879, he went on to the University of Pennsylvania in Philadelphia. This prestigious school had been founded in 1740 by Benjamin Franklin and boasted the country's first school of medicine. Mossell was its first black graduate, finishing second in his class in 1882.

Joins County Medical Society

Mossell underwent a period of training under D. Hayes Agnew at University Hospital in Philadelphia and then went on to London, England, for further study. He interned at Guy's, Queens College, and St. Thomas hospitals there, and by 1888 had returned to Philadelphia and was elected a member of the Philadelphia County Medical Society. He was the first African American to earn this distinction. He was part of a small but growing list of

black physicians in the United States that dated back to James Derham. Born in 1762, Derham was a slave who was trained by the Philadelphia physician who owned him and was later sold to a doctor in New Orleans, where he had a thriving practice in that city for many years. In 1837, James Smith became the first black American physician to obtain a medical degree, but he earned it at the University of Glasgow in Scotland. A decade later, David Smith became the first black to graduate from an American medical school when he completed his training at Rush Medical College in Chicago.

Mossell practiced in Philadelphia and was a member of the city's black elite. He had wed Gertrude Emily Hicks Bustill in 1880, a teacher and journalist whose father had been a conductor in the Underground Railroad. They had two daughters, Florence and Mary, and Gertrude Mossell continued to write for a number of prominent black publications after the marriage. She served as the woman's editor of the *New York Freeman* and wrote a nationally syndicated column aimed at African American women. She also wrote *The Works of the Afro-American Woman* (1894), as well as a Sunday school book for children.

In August 1895, Mossell co-founded the Frederick Douglass Memorial Hospital and Training School in Philadelphia with some other black doctors in the city. The hospital, established to serve the city's black population, was funded with donations from wealthy Philadelphians both black and white, and with the help of renowned African Americans such as Madame C. J. Walker. It followed the Freedmen's Hospital in Washington, D.C., founded during the Civil War and later a part of the Howard University medical system, and Provident Hospital of Chicago, established in 1881. At the time, U.S. hospitals did not grant African American physicians staff privileges, and black doctors like Mossell often had to operate on patients in their homes or in small clinics.

Douglass Memorial trained doctors as well as nurses for several generations. Mossell served as its medical director and chief of staff until 1933, when he retired. He died in 1946. Two years later, Douglass combined operations and staff with another facility that had also been serving the black community, Mercy Hospital. The merged entity operated in West Philadelphia until it closed its doors in 1973.

Mossell was one of dozens of distinguished graduates of Lincoln University in the nineteenth and early twentieth centuries. For a hundred years after its 1854 founding, a stunning 20 percent of all black physicians in the United States had Lincoln degrees, and 10 percent of African American lawyers were Lincoln alumni, too, including the first black U.S. Supreme Court justice, Thurgood Marshall.

The list of achievements for the distinguished Mossell family and its relatives by marriage is a lengthy one.

Mossell's brother Aaron earned his law degree from the University of Pennsylvania Law School as its first black graduate. Gertrude Mossell was a co-founder of the Philadelphia chapter of the National Afro-American Council in 1899, which was the forerunner of the National Association for the Advancement of Colored People (NAACP). Mossell's marriage made him the uncle of actor and activist Paul Robeson, whose mother was Gertrude's sister, Maria Louisa Bustill. Mossell's brother Aaron wed Mary Louise Tanner, the sister of acclaimed painter Henry Ossawa Tanner. Their daughter, Mossell's niece, was Sadie Tanner Mossell Alexander, the first African American woman to earn a doctorate degree in economics as well as the first black female graduate of the University of Pennsylvania law school.

REFERENCES

Online

"A Gallery of African American Alumni and Faculty." University Archives and Records Center, University of Pennsylvania. http://www.archives.upenn.edu/histy/features/aframer/gallery.html#Mossell (Accessed 20 December 2005).

"Nathan Mossell Gave Much to Philadelphia." The African American Registry. http://www.aaregistry.com/african_american_history/1536/Nathan_Mossell_gave_much_to_Philadelphia (Accessed 20 December 2005).

Carol Brennan

Chronology

1889	Born in Baltimore, Maryland on January 17
1911	Receives B.A. with honors from Howard University in Washington, D.C.
1913	Receives M.A. from Harvard University
1914	Travels to Gena University in Germany
1914	Returns to the United States and teaches German at Howard University
1916	Marries co-founder of Delta Sigma Theta Sorority Vashti Turley in Washington, D.C.
1918	Moves to Baltimore, Maryland
1922-67	Becomes head of the *Baltimore Afro-American* newspaper
1929	Moves to Morgan Park Community in Baltimore, Maryland
1935-66	Becomes Head of Baltimore Branch of NAACP Legal Redress Committee
1939-53	Serves as Charter member of Board of Trustees at Morgan State College
1940	Becomes member of the Robert R. Moton Commission to Haiti
1942-49	Serves as member of Maryland Council of Defense
1948	Receives honorary doctorate from Lincoln University, Philadelphia, Pennsylvania
1953-67	Serves as chairman of the Board of Trustees at Morgan State College
1954-55	Serves as president of the National Newspaper Publisher Association (NNPA)
1955	Awarded the Spingarn Medal by the NAACP
1960	Receives honorary doctorate from Wilberforce University in Ohio
1967	Dies in Baltimore, Maryland on March 3

Carl J. Murphy
1889–1967

Editor, civil rights activist, educator

In a lifespan of seventy-eight years Carl James Greenbury Murphy managed to achieve major success in three areas. He is most noted for his career as president and chief editor of one of the nation's leading black newspapers, the *Baltimore Afro-American*. However, his works as a civil rights activist as well as an educator are equally notable.

Carl Murphy was born in Baltimore on January 17, 1889. He was one of ten children born to John Murphy Sr., and Martha Howard Murphy. His parents believed that the education of blacks was vitally important in the struggle for racial equality. Martha believed that Carl was her most scholarly child primarily because he had graduated second in his class of forty at Baltimore's Douglass High School. Beginning at an early age Carl became engaged in the national debate among African American leaders regarding the best methods of educating the race and providing leadership in a segregated society. While one faction of the leadership supported education for the masses, others supported the idea of limiting resources for the "talented tenth" of the race. The Murphy family's position was that all African Americans needed proper training in both academics as well as in trade skills. Issues about education, race relations, and leadership roles in charting a new direction for the African American community would later resurface for Murphy while he was the head of the *Baltimore Afro-American* newspaper.

While this debate continued at the national level, Murphy and his friend Jimmy Waring Jr. were receiving tutorial lessons by a fellow named Paul Brock. Waring's father, who was principal of Douglass High School, brought Brock into the school to work with selected students. Brock would often times refer to Carl, Jimmy, and two other students as the "talented tenth." The title gave Murphy the desire to pursue higher education. He believed that the most educated among African Americans had the responsibility to assist in the improvement of the race. Brock's belief in Murphy's ability to succeed prompted Murphy to consider college. In the early 1900s Murphy entered Howard University. He graduated in 1911 with a B.A. in German. He then had the opportunity to study at Harvard University. He was one of only two blacks in Harvard's Graduate School, and by 1913 he was awarded an M.A. in German. Murphy left the United States before the outbreak of the First World War to study at Jena University in Germany; the outbreak of the war, however, caused him to return home in October 1914.

Prior to joining the *Baltimore Afro-American* newspaper, Murphy became a German professor at Howard University. Murphy taught Vashti Turley, an education major at the university and co-founder of Delta Sigma Theta, the sorority for black professional women. The two courted and eventually married in 1916. Vashti Murphy began a career as an elementary school teacher in Washington, D.C. Between 1916 and 1918 Carl Murphy worked part-time for the *Afro-American* as an associate editor, while he taught full-time at Howard. Later John Murphy Sr. wrote a letter to Carl asking him to leave Howard and return to work for the *Afro-American* full-time. During the summer of 1918 both Carl and Vashti left Washington for good to join his father and his brothers at the *Afro-American* news organization.

Carl Murphy replaced George F. Bragg as editor of the newspaper. Murphy's presence and immediate success at the *Afro-American* won him his family's faith and support. Following the death in 1922 of their father, Carl Murphy was elected by his family as president and chief editor of the newspaper.

Murphy's forty-nine year tenure as editor and head of the Afro-American Company began in 1918 and ended in 1967. During his term Murphy covered a range of issues both at the national and international level. He used the editorial page to challenge local, national, and international injustices ranging from lynching, race and gender discrimination, poor housing, and poor schools, to full citizenship for all Americans. He launched an editorial attack against the U.S. government for its military occupation of Haiti. Murphy sent *Afro-American* reporters abroad to describe the experiences of black soldiers during the Second World War. Following the war, he wrote in support for the decolonization of Africa. He frequently communicated with prominent leaders and the many organizations they represented. These included Thurgood Marshall, the NAACP legal counsel and later U.S. Supreme Court Justice; NAACP leader Walter White; Urban League executives Eugene K. Jones and Lester Granger; Mary McLeod Bethune of the National Council of Negro Women; scholars W. E. B. Du Bois, Carter G. Woodson, Rayford W. Logan; and countless others.

In a 1992 interview with Fern Ingersoll, Frances L. Murphy II, Murphy's youngest daughter, gave a description of her father's dedication to civil rights struggles and to the leadership of the newspaper. She provided detailed accounts of conversations that took place between Murphy and influential black leaders such as *Crisis* editor and scholar W. E. B. Du Bois; former newspaper editor for the *Kansas City Call* and NAACP executive secretary Roy Wilkins; educator and activist Mary McLeod Bethune; and African American congressman Oscar DePriest. Breakfast meetings were conducted away from the *Afro-American*'s main office often in the Murphy home to avoid interruption. NAACP campaigns, political conferences, and political hopefuls sought support from Murphy through the *Afro-American* news.

Murphy and the NAACP

Frances Murphy recounted numerous occasions when her father and Du Bois would walk through their Baltimore neighborhood, Morgan Park, discussing strategies for handling civil rights cases and fund raising. The Morgan Park neighborhood was developed in 1917 and attracted African American faculty and staff of Morgan College. While living in this community, Murphy was credited for organizing fourteen people in the *Afro-American* office in 1935 to form an active Baltimore branch of the NAACP. Two of the most noted group members were Thurgood Marshall and Lillie Jackson. Marshall served as solicitor general while Jackson held the office of branch president for more than thirty years.

Murphy's role in the NAACP was chairman of the Legal Redress Committee during the early tenure of Thurgood Marshall. Murphy's main role was to raise money to fund court cases and pay attorney fees. Murphy was noted for giving his own money when he was unable to raise enough funds to cover legal fees and court costs. Frances Murphy recounted a statement made by Thurgood Marshall regarding Murphy's commitment to civil rights and his support of the NAACP. Marshall said that if it were not for Carl Murphy, there would not have been any money to file court cases such as those for equal salaries for Baltimore teachers, integration of the fire and police department, and challenges against the University of Maryland's Law School admission policies. The groundwork for the Supreme Court's push for school desegregation was laid in 1935 with the Donald Murry case. The success of that case opened the university's Law School to all citizens. Murphy continued to give freely of money and talent. By the time of his death the Baltimore Branch of the NAACP was so successful that it had supported two young African Americans who won office in Maryland's House of Delegates. The two senators were Clarence Mitchell III and Verda Welcome.

Murphy's leadership style had a profound impact on others. In 1939, he was able to persuade the Methodist Church to hand over control of Morgan College to the state of Maryland. His devotion to Morgan as both a trustee and chairman of the trustee board won him considerable favor among his colleagues. His leadership as chairman helped Morgan develop into one of the nation's leading institutions of higher education.

Legacy with the *Afro-American* Newspaper

Murphy wanted to broaden the circulation of the *Afro-American* beyond Baltimore's black community. Under his leadership the newspaper continued its growth by establishing bureaus in Washington, D.C., Philadelphia, New York, Newark, and Richmond. There were even some subscribers in Africa. The superior guidance of Murphy won the *Afro-American* the title of most successful black publication in the mid-Atlantic region. Frances Murphy noted that the only differences between the national edition of the *Afro-American* in Baltimore and the other city editions was that local news in various other cities was covered along with the national news coverage. The front page incorporated local news but the editorial page remained untouched. She also stated that Carl Murphy was very interested in providing readers with an understanding of the connection between local experience and national occurrences such as civil rights cases that were being filed in the courts, school integration, and equal pay and employment. He would often outline during meetings how major stories would impact each other. Therefore, managing editors and city editors were asked to keep those issues in mind when deciding on the layout of the paper.

Like his father, Carl Murphy believed in equal rights for both men and women. He encouraged all five of his daughters to learn the business, particularly since they were to inherit it. They were also encouraged to pursue academic careers in journalism and work for the *Afro-American*. Two of Murphy's daughters, Frances L. Murphy and Elizabeth Murphy Moss, became chief officers of the Afro-American Company after his death. Frances was chair of the board and chief executive officer from 1971 to 1974, and Elizabeth became vice-president and treasurer of the company. Elizabeth was the first black female war correspondent for the *Afro-American* during World War II. Murphy's vision for the business also included equal pay and equal rights for both male and female reporters. Frances Murphy stated, "We had a fight going on for survival. The people in the white press did not have that kind of fight; they were just out there doing a job. Ours was more than a job, people depended on us."

Alongside its astute journalists, the *Afro-American* newspaper also relied upon prominent black intellectuals for news reports and for their insightful political commentary. For example, Rayford W. Logan, one of the most distinguished historians of the African Diaspora, was asked by the *Afro-American* to provide an exclusive report on his travel to Haiti as well as to provide political commentary on the experience of Haitians under U.S. occupation.

Sending its reporters worldwide in search of news and commissioning reports from noted black scholars and leaders made it possible for the *Afro-American* to provide its readers with firsthand information. The editors believed that sending their own reporters to report news firsthand could create unity among African descendents worldwide. They hoped to create a Pan-African solidarity that would facilitate the black struggle for social, political, and economic justice. During the occupation of Haiti, Murphy traveled to Haiti along with the Moton Commission members and reported Haitian news to the paper. In 1933, William N. Jones, *Afro-American* editor, received an invitation from Liberian minister Barclay to travel to Liberia as its goodwill ambassador. Jones reported his findings to the *Afro-American* and also developed an economic plan for Liberia entitled the "Save Liberia Plan." The plan was designed to develop networks between Liberians and African Americans.

The use of black intelligentsia to report, analyze, and disseminate news regarding the plight of Africans abroad was another strategy adopted by the *Afro-American*. Contributing writers such as Logan, Nnamdi Azikiwe, and several others added to the paper's sophistication and integrity. Key leaders chosen were major proponents of a Pan-African ideology, which the paper wholeheartedly supported. The publisher, editors, and writers for the *Afro-American* supported and developed plans for political networks and economic ties with blacks in Haiti and Liberia. Regarding the crisis in Ethiopia, the *Afro-American* encouraged African American participation in the war, black migration to Ethiopia, and political networks between Diaspora communities. Clearly, the *Afro-American* response to identity questions was answered in its weekly coverage of Diaspora news.

Through his forty-year tenure as the head of the *Afro-American*, Murphy used the pages of the newspaper to respond to the misrepresentation of blacks in the mainstream press and to tell the story of the black experience from the black perspective. Along with other black publishers, he highlighted the living conditions of blacks, their concerns, their problems, and most important, their achievements. His achievements as newspaper man, civil rights activist, and educator illustrate what influence newspapers can have in shaping public opinion.

REFERENCES

Books

This Is Our War. Baltimore: Afro-American Company, 1944.

Periodicals

"Delta Co-Founder." *Baltimore Afro-American*, 5 December 1972.

"Publisher Thought of 'Little People,'" 80th *Baltimore Afro-American*, Anniversary Addition, 20 August 1972.

"Remembering Mr. Carl during Black Press Week."
Baltimore Afro-American, 16 March 1971.

"The Afro: Seaboard's Largest Weekly." *Baltimore Afro-American*, 17 March 1971.

Interviews

Murphy, Frances Louise II. "Women in Journalism."
Interview by Fern Ingersoll. 25 October through 3
December 1992. Washington Press Club Foundation,
Washington D.C.

Dissertations

Farrar, Hayward. "See What the Afro Says: The
Baltimore Afro-American, 1892-1950." Ph.D. diss.
University of Chicago, 1983.

Muhammad, Baiyina W. "'What is Africa to Us?': The
Baltimore Afro-American's Coverage of the African
Diaspora, 1915-1941." Ph.D. diss., Morgan State
University, 2004.

Baiyina W. Muhammad

Walter Dean Myers

Walter Dean Myers

1937–

Writer

Given his background, Walter Dean Myers seems an
unlikely literary success. He was a troubled child
living with foster parents in Harlem. It seemed more
probable that he would end up a "demographic disaster
waiting to happen," according to the *Los Angeles Times*,
than a renowned writer of more than seventy-five critically acclaimed works for children and young adults.
Myers is the acclaimed author of *Monster*, *Handbook for
Boys*, *Bad Boy*, *Malcolm X: By Any Means Necessary*,
and *Harlem: A Poem*, among others. He is the first winner of the Michael L. Printz Award, a National Book
Award finalist, and a Coretta Scott King, Boston Globe-
Horn, Newbery, and Caldecott honoree. He speaks
frankly about his difficult childhood and how he chose to
take responsibility for his life and make something of it.

Myers was born in poverty in Martinsburg, West Virginia on August 12, 1937 to a father who had "many children by almost as many mothers," according to the *Los
Angeles Times*. After his mother died, he was handed over
at age three by his father to a foster family, the Deans,
who loved him dearly. They informally adopted him and
raised him in Harlem. His new mother, a half-German,
half-Indian woman who was minimally educated herself,

taught him to read by reading *True Romance* magazine to
him. Eventually he was able to read magazines and newspapers to her. When Myers' teacher caught him reading
comics in class, she tore them up and gave him a pile of
classic books from her own collection. "That was the best
thing that ever happened to me," Myers told the *Times*. He
also found a sanctuary in the local public library: "Books
took me, not so much to foreign lands and fanciful adventures," he is quoted as saying at TeenRead.com, "but to a
place within myself that I have been exploring ever since.
The public library was my most treasured place. I could-
n't believe my luck in discovering that what I enjoyed
most—reading—was free."

Feels Alienated by Classic Works

But little of what Myers read reflected his own reality.
Growing up in Harlem in the 1950s, Myers listened to the
music of Motown and heard Billie Holliday and Duke
Ellington when they performed at the Apollo Theater. It
was common to see boxer Sugar Ray Robinson driving
through town in his huge pink car or to see author
Langston Hughes being interviewed on the street. "What
Myers read ... was largely limited to white authors, frequently British, and often about rich people," according
to the *Sarasota Herald Tribune*. "I began a quiet devaluation of myself," he told the *Sarasota Herald Tribune*.
"Books transmit values, so when a young person goes to

Chronology

1937	Born in Martinsburg, West Virginia on August 12
1954	Drops out of high school and joins Army
1968	Wins Council on Interracial Books for Children Award for *Where Does the Day Go?*
1970	Takes job as an editor at the Bobbs-Merrill publishing company
1977	Laid off from publishing company; begins to work full-time as a writer
1993	Writes biography *Malcolm X: By Any Means Necessary*
1999	Writes novel *Monster*
2001	Writes memoir *Bad Boy*
2003	Writes *Handbook for Boys*
2004	Writes *Harlem: A Poem*

school or a young person picks up a book, they should find things of value. But I could not find myself in those books." That changed when he picked up James Baldwin's *Sonny's Blues*, a story about Harlem and the world in which Myers grew up.

Myers may have loved going to the public library, but he was not a typical bookworm. Along with speech problems, he had a bad attitude and was constantly clashing with his parents, school administrators, and local authorities. "I had this very severe speech difficulty, and I arrived in school ready to conquer the world, but no one could understand a thing I was saying. That was very frustrating for me, and I responded by being angry," Myers wrote at TeenReads.com. His sixth grade teacher, a former Marine, decided to take Myers on. He spent the entire school year encouraging Myers, telling him he was smart, rather than focusing on his bad behavior. It worked. By the time he reached high school, Myers had "decided he was an intellectual," according to the *Los Angeles Times*. However, no matter how bright he was, college was not on the horizon for the low-income kid from Harlem. Myers dropped out of high school at age seventeen and joined the U.S. Army.

Myers, at 6-foot-2-inches tall with some talent, found himself a star on an army basketball team. When his team lost a finals tournament on which a colonel had heavily bet, the colonel shipped the entire team to the Arctic as punishment. Myers did not see it as punishment, however; he loved the frozen adventure.

Decides to be a Writer

Once out of the army, Myers worked dead-end jobs. "So I decided to try writing. It was cheap, no overhead," Myers told the *Los Angeles Times*. "You didn't have to have success. I could think of myself as a writer, even a would-be writer, rather than a truck-loader." He decided he would become a Great American Novelist. Instead, he was paid $15 or $20 per article by tabloids such as the

National Enquirer. He later wrote fiction and nonfiction for men's magazines. "It was the early 1960s, a dicey time in the country's color consciousness," he stated, according to the *Los Angeles Times*. But since he was writing, and not meeting his editors face to face, "I was facing absolutely no color line," Myers said. But he was not yet making a living as a writer.

Myers finally found success in 1968, when he won a contest run by the Council on Interracial Books for Children, for the text of a picture book, *Where Does the Day Go?* It was his first book. From there, he worked as an editor at the Bobbs-Merrill publishing company while continuing to write and achieve recognition, particularly for his teen novels. After 1977 he wrote full-time for a living and did not have another job.

Myers wrote about what he knew. In *Hoops* (1981), a basketball coach tries to keep a talented teen on the right path. In *Fallen Angels* (1988), a Harlem teen fights in Vietnam and begins to question both the war itself and why black soldiers draw many of the dangerous assignments. *145th Street Stories* (2000) and his memoir *Bad Boy* (2001) are about his childhood neighborhood and his troubled youth. His *Handbook for Boys* (2003) can be read as a guidebook about how young men fit into the larger society around them, and *Harlem: A Poem* (2004) is among his many works that reflect on his childhood home.

Looks to Himself for Inspiration

Myers' writing also reflects his intense interest in history and culture. *Malcolm X: By Any Means Necessary* (1993) is a biography of the late civil rights activist for preteens. For *At Her Majesty's Request: An African Princess in Victorian England* (1999), Myers pored over historical documents and letters and pieced together the true story of an orphaned African girl given to Queen Victoria as a gift.

Myers writes fairy tales, historical novels, and biographies. But his "streetwise, honest, empathetic stories about African American teens facing challenges and making difficult decisions have made him a lion in his field," according to the *Milwaukee Journal Sentinel*. "Over the years, he has reclaimed or transformed nearly everything that hurt or touched him into a book." Myers's 1999 novel *Monster*, in which a teen tells the story of his trial for robbery and murder, was his most commercially successful work, and increased Myers' freedom to write about most anything he wants.

Myers lives with his family in Jersey City, New Jersey. He helped establish the Walter Dean Myers Publishing Institute, part of the Langston Hughes Children's Literature Festival, and makes frequent appearances with the National Basketball Association's "Read to Achieve" literacy program.

REFERENCES

Periodicals

"Former 'Bad Boy' Taps into Youths' Minds, Struggles." *Milwaukee Journal Sentinel*, 24 May 2002.

"Harlem Writer Myers Repays a Debt."*Sarasota Herald Tribune*, 21 April 2002.

Mehren, Elizabeth. "Fountain of Stories for Youth; Walter Dean Myers Writes Books for Young People. But Their Realism and Richness Have Adults Reading Them Too."*Los Angeles Times*, 15 October 1997.

Online

"Walter Dean Myers." Rutgers School of Communication, Information, and Library Studies. http://www.scils.rutgers.edu/~kvander/myers.html (Accessed 7 October 2005).

"Walter Dean Myers." TeenReads. http://www. teenreads.com/authors/au-myers-walterdean.asp (Accessed 23 March 2005).

"Walter Dean Myers biography." Walter Dean Myers. http://www.walterdeanmyersbooks.com (Accessed 23 March 2005).

Brenna Sanchez

Samuel Nabrit
1905–2003

Biologist, college president

The third of eight children, Samuel Milton Nabrit was born in Macon, Georgia on February 21, 1905 to James Madison and Augusta Gertrude (West) Nabrit. His father was a Baptist minister and a graduate of Morehouse. He also taught at the Central City College in Macon. The Nabrit family moved to Augusta, Georgia in 1912 because the father had become the pastor of the Springfield Baptist Church and a teacher at the Walker Baptist Institute.

Nabrit was a pupil at the Walker Baptist Institute where his father taught. His studies included Latin, Greek, and physics, which he learned under his father. He was the valedictorian of the 1921 graduating class. After high school, he continued his post-secondary education at Morehouse College majoring in biology. He was an active member of sports and social organizations such as football and Omega Psi Phi fraternity. He also managed the student paper. He graduated with a B.A. in biology with honors in 1925.

Nabrit's success allowed him to remain at Morehouse as a teacher in the Zoology Department. Within his college career, he had taken summer courses at the University of Chicago in Chicago, Illinois. Afterwards, he took up his post at Morehouse and retained a faculty appointment for six years (1925-31). Nabrit furthered his studies in biology at Brown University in Providence, Rhode Island during the year 1927-28. He had been granted a leave of absence from Morehouse to continue his education on a general education board fellowship. As a result, he received his M.S. degree in biology in 1928. Nabrit married Constance Crocker on August 8, 1927. They had no children.

Higher Achievement

In addition to earning his master's degree, Nabrit conducted research at the Marine Biological Laboratory at Woods Hole, Massachusetts, every summer from 1927 to 1932. Although other things were interesting to him, he

Samuel Nabrit

primarily studied the regeneration of the tail fins of fish. The *Biological Bulletin* published the results of Nabrit's work. He used this work as the basis for his doctoral dissertation. Not only did Nabrit earn his doctorate in 1932, he became the first African American to earn a Ph.D. in biology from Brown University. After receiving his doctorate, he did postdoctoral work from 1943 to 1950 at the following institutions: Teachers College, Columbia University and the University of Brussels in Belgium.

Nabrit chaired the Biology Department of Atlanta University from 1932 to 1947. Later, he was appointed dean of the graduate school of arts and sciences of Atlanta University in 1947; he served as dean for eight years.

Nabrit was vital to the establishment of the National Institute of Science, which was founded in 1943. Nabrit and others sought to explore the teaching and research problems of Negro scientists. He strongly advocated for science and mathematics teachers to study in research centers where they can get the best facilities and contact other scientists in their field. Consequently, Nabrit served as the third president of the National Institute of Science from 1945 to 1946. The membership mainly consisted of science teachers in Negro colleges and universities.

Presidential Leadership

During the summer of 1955, Raphael O'Hara Lanier resigned as president of Texas Southern University, and the board of directors of the school appointed Nabrit second president. He committed to the duties of the executive office on September 1, 1955, and his inauguration was held on March 18, 1956. Nabrit wanted to develop a basic skills workshop to prepare students for successful performance in leading universities.

Honors and Memberships

Nabrit received an honorary LL.D. degree at Morehouse College and an honorary D.S. degree at Brown University. He was involved in several organizations such as the American Association for the Advancement of Science, the American Society of Zoologists, the New York Academy of Science, and the Society for the Study of Growth and Development. He was also a member of the Beta Kappa Chi and Sigma Pi Phi fraternities. Nabrit died on December 30, 2003, in Atlanta, Georgia.

REFERENCES

Books

Smith, Jessie Carney, ed. *Black Firsts: 4,000 Groundbreaking and Pioneering Historical Events.* 2nd ed. Canton, Mich.: Visible Ink Press, 2003.

Online

Emory University. http://www.emory.edu/ (Accessed 8 December 2005).

Clarence Toomer

John E. Nail
1883–1947

Entrepreneur, real estate developer

It was the vision of master businessman and visionary real estate developer John E. Nail that the vitality of middle-class African American communities become commonplace across the United States. Less than a decade after the turn of the twentieth century, Nail, along with his partner Henry G. Parker, opened the realty firm Nail &Parker, Inc. Together, Nail & Parker foresaw the transition of Harlem into a black community and ardently encouraged African Americans to acquire and retain property. Later known as the "Little Fathers" of Harlem, Nail and Parker helped engender a demographical environment in which the Harlem Renaissance, the landmark period of black cultural, literary, and musical expression during the 1920s could take place. Despite the collapse of his firm under the weight of the Depression, Nail remained committed to charitable, political, and benevolent organizations until his death in 1947. While much of his dream for black middle-class home ownership was marginalized for public housing, the usefulness of his vision for and commitment to African American financial empowerment remains relevant in the early 2000s.

Born on August 22, 1883 to John Bennett and Elizabeth Nail in New London, Connecticut, John E. Nail and his sister Grace were reared in New York City. Having migrated from Baltimore in 1863, the elder Nail, who first worked in a gambling house, had become the owner of a tavern that served as a restaurant, hotel, and billiard parlor. As a member of the earliest African American entrepreneurial group that capitalized on Harlem's growth and inflated real estate market, he owned a few rental properties in the community. Inspired by his father's strong business acumen, Nail first worked for his father after he graduated from a New York City public high school. After a stint as a self-employed real estate agent, young Nail began working for the Afro-American Realty Company of Philip A. Payton Jr., one of the most prominent African American owned New York real estate firms of its time.

Philip A. Payton Jr. recognized the economic prospects of a steady flood of African American migrants to the North from the last decade of the 1890s to the 1920s. Shut out from other New York communities open to blacks, the mass migration strained spatial resources as well as race relations. Black Southern migrants soon found themselves relegated to the ever-growing Harlem community. Payton had capitalized on these trends by learning the intricacies of New York City's segregated housing market; Nail did the same.

The Birth of Nail & Parker

Nail left Afro-American Realty in 1907 (it went bankrupt in 1908) after the exposure of its financial and internal difficulties. Parker, his colleague, also resigned. In the same year, the pair co-founded Nail & Parker, their own realty firm. After witnessing Payton's early successes, they undoubtedly learned from his signature business strategy, encouraging black homeownership while acquiring considerable profits.

Parker served as secretary, while Nail, as the firm's president, proved to be its guiding force. Despite its modest beginnings, the company succeeded, soon surpassing that of Payton. With the help of a dynamic advertising campaign, Nail & Parker diversified and expended its services to include mortgages as well as the purchase, selling, appraisal, and management of properties to African Americans.

Nail recognized that African American property ownership offered security as well as the opportunity for blacks to counteract the discriminatory real estate practices of white landlords and banks. He insisted that

African Americans acquire property in Harlem and invest in the prospect of a black community there in the future. When an unwritten agreement sought to prevent blacks from renting or owning property on certain blocks of Harlem and attempted to prohibit black firms from controlling its housing market, Nail & Parker fought against the discriminatory measures. Much to its credit, after a difficult battle, the firm successfully dismantled the block.

Early Successes and Growth

By 1911, Nail foresaw the rapid growth of Harlem properties following the shift of Manhattan's population farther north. Together with his pastor, the Reverend Hutchens C. Bishop of St. Phillip's Episcopal Church, Nail designed a real estate venture in which the church purchased several Harlem properties totaling $1,070,000. Not only did the deal secure land for the building of a new edifice, it also provided several apartment buildings for the church to rent. Prominently placed at the center of the lucrative acquisition, Nail & Parker began to negotiate the purchase of more Harlem properties. As the steady departure of whites increased both the market and the demand, Nail continued to urge blacks in the Harlem community to expand their property holdings.

As a leader in the Harlem business community, Nail & Parker served as the agent for the colored YMCA, the Wage Earners' Savings Bank, and the Copeland Realty Company. Madam C. J. Walker was among the firm's most recognizable clients. Having also shared the era's black capitalism spirit, Walker used her fortune to purchase a $200,000 property in Irving-on-Hudson.

In 1916, Nail leveraged his relationship with his brother-in-law James Weldon Johnson, a prominent scholar and activist, to garner his financial support as well as that of his affluent friends. Johnson married Nail's sister, Grace, in 1910. That same year, Nail married Grace Fairfax and though they had no children, both couples vacationed in their Great Barrington, Massachusetts, summer homes.

Nail & Parker as Black Harlem's "Little Fathers"

By 1925, Nail & Parker managed almost fifty apartment complexes and boasted an annual income of $1 million. Its growth continued into 1929, when the firm managed the Metropolitan Life Insurance Company, Harlem's largest and most luxurious apartment building. The company's ever-expanding list of wealthy clientele and important institutions earned both Parker and Nail, as black Harlem's "Little Fathers," famed reputations as successful businessmen.

As the firm's president and most visible personality, Nail particularly enjoyed increased notoriety as one of the most influential black realtors in the city. Because Nail was well respected by both blacks and whites, New

York City officials readily called on his expertise as an authority on property accommodation. In addition to being the first African American member of the Real Estate Board of New York and the sole black member of Housing Committee of New York, Nail was also a member of the Harlem Board of Commerce, the Uptown Chamber of Commerce. His achievements were so renown that President Herbert Hoover appointed Nail as a consultant to his Commission on Housing during the Depression.

Concurrently, Nail used his financial and professional successes to serve political, charitable, and racial uplift causes, including the Republican Business Men's Club of New York, the YMCA of which he served as chair of the Finance Committee, the NAACP, and the New York Urban League serving as its vice president. A leader of Harlem's Colored Merchants Association, Nail was also a proponent of Booker T. Washington, leading him to join the self-dubbed Committee of Eight which leveled an effective campaign to discredit black nationalist Marcus Garvey.

Disgruntlement, Financial Woes, and Closure

Nail knew that prestige and power did not prevent criticism. Some tenants believed that they were overcharged and accused Nail of exploiting them as tenants. Because their disgruntlement posed a serious threat to Harlem renters throughout the 1920s and early 1930s who feared a mass exodus of unsatisfied tenants, the firm reluctantly lowered some rents. At the time, Harlem was a bustling and vibrant community of middle-class African Americans who enjoyed both property ownership and entrepreneurship. Nail, in his defense, noted that rentals were high across the city.

Unfortunately, the prosperity of the roaring twenties and the thriving black Harlem community that it helped create was short-lived. A drastic downturn of the U.S. economy in 1929 marked the beginning of the Great Depression. Despite temporarily weathering the period, the future of Nail & Parker, like other realty firms, was uncertain as communities like Harlem deteriorated. Finally collapsing in 1933, Nail and Parker shared forty-five company shares and apportioned its remaining ten shares to their silent white partner Isador D. Brokow.

New Horizons Short-Lived

That same year, Nail established his own firm, the John E. Nail Company, Inc. at 249 W. 135 Street. Nail again served as president and had David B. Peskin, a white real estate agent, serve as secretary and treasurer. The fledging firm's first contact was to lease apartments for the also cash-strapped St. Phillips Church. The deal allowed the church to lease ten six-story apartment houses to Louis B. Lipman for an aggregate rental of $1 million. The following year, Nail tried to secure a multi-million dollar grant from the federal government for New Deal funding to help renovate the degenerating urban community that once thrived as black Harlem. Despite the help of his influential brother-in-law James Weldon Johnson to secure its funding, the plan never came to fruition.

In the coming years, Harlem continued to decline, particularly following a 1943 riot. Incited by the arrest and murder of an African American World War II veteran, a two-day insurgence caused approximately $500,000 to $1 million in property damage, and left hundreds injured and arrested and five dead.

By the time of his death, Nail had lost his dream; Harlem as a middle-class community of black home and business ownership was increasingly displaced by economic despair and aesthetic disrepair. Disillusioned with the failure of the black capitalism dream he first learned as a boy from his father and sharpened during his tutelage under Payton, Nail saw his vision for black economic self-sufficiency replaced by public housing projects throughout Harlem and across the United States.

Nail died in New York City's Lenox Hill Hospital on March 6, 1947. Two days later, his funeral was held at St. Phillips, the church he had so faithfully served throughout his professional life. Nail was survived by his wife Grace, his sister Grace Johnson, his aunt Josephine Miller, and Gertrude Berry, a cousin.

REFERENCES

Books

Dailey, Maceo Crenshaw Jr. "Nail, John [Jack] E." In *Dictionary of American Negro Biography*. Eds. Rayford W. Logan and Michael R. Winston. New York: Norton, 1982.

Feldman, Lynne. B. "Nail, John E." In *American National Biography*. Vol. 16. Eds. John A. Garraty and Mark C. Carnes. New York: Oxford University Press, 1996.

Johnson, James Weldon. *Along This Way: The Autobiography of James Weldon Johnson*. New York: The Viking Press, 1993.

———. *Black Manhattan*. New York: Alfred A. Knopf, 1930.

Osofsky, Gilbert. *Harlem: The Making of a Ghetto*. New York: Harper & Row, 1966.

Periodicals

"John E. Nail, Headed Harlem Realty Firm." *New York Times*, 6 March 1947.

Crystal A. deGregory

Stanley Nelson
1951–

Filmmaker

Chronology

1951 Born in New York City on June 7

1976 Receives B.F.A. degree in film from Leonard David Film School at City College

1987 Produces first independent film

1990 Begins series of documentaries for PBS

1999 Receives funding from National Endowment for the Arts for *Black Press: Soldiers Without Swords*

2001 Receives best non-fiction film award by Black Filmmakers Hall of Fame for *Look for Me in the Whirlwind*

2003 Produces *The Murder of Emmett Till*, which causes U.S. Justice Department to reopen legal case; earns George Foster Peabody Award, Primetime Emmy Award, Distinguished Documentary Achievement Award, and Sundance Film Festival Special Jury Prize for film

Stanley Nelson, a premier filmmaker, has transformed the filmmaking industry by sharing true experiences. Combining interviews, photographic stills, and real footage, Nelson raises the awareness of the African American experience. As director, producer, and writer at Firelight Media/Half-Nelson Films, Nelson motivates, uplifts and moves audiences across the world.

Stanley Nelson was the second of four children born to Stanley E. Nelson and the former A'Lelia "Liel" Ransom. The elder Nelson was a Howard University trained dentist and the outspoken Ransom was a librarian. Their union produced four children: Lynn, Stanley, Jill, and Ralph.

The family grew up mostly in Harlem but later moved to the Upper West Side of Manhattan. In an effort to instill the importance of perfection and excellence, the Nelson children attended mostly private schools and enjoyed summers vacationing at Martha's Vineyard. The Nelsons enjoyed their stay at their property that overlooked the ocean. This was one of the few places where they seemed to escape the issues of race.

Nelson saw *Sweet Sweetback's Baadasssss Song* as a teenager, and it gave him a keen awareness of cinema and its power of persuasion. *Sweetback* was the big screen's first black ghetto hero and star of Melvin Van Peebles' groundbreaking 1971 film. The movie opened doors for films about strong black characters. While some blacks did not embrace the genre, it paved the way for many African American writers, directors, and crewmembers. Nelson immediately wanted to create productions that evoked a sense of reaction. He saw filmmaking as a voice to highlight injustices and to calm pain.

During difficult times, such as his parents' divorce or personal battles, a collection of film cans, videocassettes, and lighting equipment always lurked in the shadow as a sign of strength. All of his early life experiences set the foundation for his filmmaking projects.

Changing the World Through Film

After high school, Nelson attended five colleges: Beloit College, Atlanta University, New York University, Hunter College, and City College in New York City. He earned a B.F.A. in film from the Leonard Davis Film School at City College in 1976.

His first real contact with a seasoned film industry professional was with William Greaves. It was during this apprenticeship that he learned the intricacies of documentary filmmaking.

Nelson eventually became a chief producer of motion pictures for the United Methodist Church. While they appeared to be simple productions, the church-related topics brought about cinematic awards. One of the films won a CINE Golden Eagle, which is an award that recognizes excellence in non-theatrical movies and videos.

The United Methodist Church's film service was an excellent initiation for Nelson. His first independent film was *Two Dollars and a Dream: The Story of Madame C. J. Walker and A'Lelia Walker*. This biography explored the social, economic, and political history of black America from the 1860s to the 1930s. A black woman with humble beginnings, Sarah Breedlove (1867-1919) took the name of Madame C. J. Walker in 1906. She never again used the name Sarah, preferring to build her new life—with this new identity—as the head of a company specializing in cosmetic products for black women. She was one of the first African American women to become a millionaire. Nelson's maternal grandfather, F. B. Ransom, had been a lawyer and manager of Walker. This film was named best production in 1988 and best production of the 1980s by the Black Filmmaker Foundation.

After this initial work, Nelson created a special series for PBS. PBS produced several of his stellar films during the 1990s, and continued to uphold its mandate of diversity in the sponsorship and broadcast of films by African Americans. His first PBS production, *Freedom Bags*, chronicled the life of black domestic workers and their movement to the North during the 1900s. This production earned him first place for nonfiction at the 1991 Black Independent Film, Video and Screenplay Competition. The following PBS films, *Methadone: Curse or Cure* (1996) and *Shattering the Silences: The Case for Minority Faculty* (1998), earned him several awards, including Best Cultural Affairs documentary by the 1997 National Black Programming Consortium.

While most of Nelson's films garnered little financial support, his *Black Press: Soldiers Without Swords* was funded by the National Endowment for the Arts, the Corporation for Public Broadcasting and the Ford Foundation. In this documentary, Nelson chronicled the rise of the black press from the founding of *Freedman's Journal* in lower Manhattan in 1827 until the 1960s.

Through this span of coverage, Nelson was able to show how the black press served as a voice for various social and intellectual drives. On the social front, the black press drove several of the campaigns against racism. This coverage was aimed at the black consumer, and it was written by leading black writers. These papers indicated that blacks existed in a world filled with inequalities. On the intellectual front, the black press had columnists such as W. E. B. Du Bois, Langston Hughes, Zora Neal Hurston, and Marcus Garvey. The film showed a vibrant community of black intellectuals and activists.

During production of *Black Press: Soldiers Without Swords*, Nelson became intrigued by a newspaper, *The Negro World*, published by Marcus Garvey. Garvey's story served as a basis for his next film, *Look for Me in the Whirlwind*. Marcus Garvey, born in Jamaica in 1887, founded the Universal Negro Improvement Association, which spread to the United States in 1916. The movement sought to achieve dignity and civil rights for black people by preaching pride of race and economic self-sufficiency. Garvey was widely known for his Back-to-Africa movement to establish a black-governed country in Africa. While dispelling myths often associated with Marcus Garvey, Nelson presents a unique side of Garvey, whose unknown aim was to build an empire of black business. Garvey had purchased property and owned several businesses. At his financial zenith, Garvey employed over one thousand people. As in most of his films, Nelson presented rarely seen coverage, complete with supported testimony of relevant individuals familiar with Garvey and his legacy.

The Black Filmmakers' Hall of Fame chose *Look for Me in the Whirlwind* as its first place overall winner in 2001, and at the Black International Cinema Festival in 2002, it was named best film/video documentary production in 2001.

Having an ability to look beyond usual subjects, Nelson produced *The Murder of Emmett Till*, a documentary that reawakened public interest in the 1955 murder of Emmett Till. Nelson's 2003 film used archival material to bridge the gap between racial divisions established in the Mississippi Delta since 1955. Emmett Till, a fourteen-year-old African American visiting relatives in the South, was lynched because he was suspected of whistling at a white woman. The accused, two white men, were charged with murder, tried, and found innocent. The documentary highlighted the events that led to Till's death, the trial of his murderers, and the national and international outrage over the killing. Realistic details, vivid photographs, and interviews of relatives and witnesses in the film served as a catalyst for renewed public and legal interest in the case. The U.S. Justice Department cited the presence of witnesses unearthed in the film as a major factor in its decision to reopen the case. In conjunction with the film, Nelson's production company engineered a massive card and letter-writing campaign. That film earned Nelson the George Foster Peabody Award, the Primetime Emmy Award, the Distinguished Documentary Achievement Award, and the Sundance Film Festival Special Jury Prize, all in 2003.

Nelson lives in Harlem in New York City with his wife, Marcia, their twin daughters, Kay and Nola, and Nelson's daughter from a previous relationship. Nelson remains executive producer of Firelight Media, a nonprofit documentary company dedicated to giving voice to people and issues that are marginalized in popular culture.

REFERENCES

Books

Nelson, Jill. *Volunteer Slavery.* Chicago: Noble Press, 1993.

Periodicals

Jacques, Geoffrey. "The Black Press: Soldiers Without Swords." *Cineaste* 24 (15 December 1998): 74-77.
Soukup, Elise. "We Owe It to Emmett." *Newsweek* 143 (24 May 2004): 6.
Steward, Rhonda. "Like Father, Like Son: The Making of a Milestone." *New Crisis* 111 (July/August 2004): 49-50.

Janet Walsh

Richard Bruce Nugent
1906–1987

Writer

Richard Bruce Nugent was part of the Harlem Renaissance. While he did not produce a vast body of work, he is connected to others in this period through his experimentation, candor, freedom, collaboration, creativity, and attitude. Given his longevity, he was able to serve as a resource for information on the Harlem Renaissance in the latter years of his life. Nugent was as at home in the African American community of Harlem as he was in the white community of Greenwich Village. He used the name Bruce Nugent or Richard Bruce to avoid embarrassment that might have come from the content of his work.

Richard Bruce Nugent was born on July 2, 1906 in Washington, D.C., to a socially prominent family. His mother, Pauline Minerva Bruce Nugent, was a trained schoolteacher and his father, Richard Henry Nugent Jr., initially was a Pullman porter, but later became an elevator operator at the Capitol building in Washington. He attended the famous Dunbar High School where he studied with Angelina Grimké. He was a frequent visitor of the salon hosted by the writer Georgia Douglas Johnson; it was here he met Langston Hughes who became a force in the literary and artistic career of Nugent. Growing up, Nugent was surrounded by art; the family often attended plays performed by the Lafayette Players (an African American theatre group) and hosted artists in their home. His father was a member of the Clef Club and an avid reader. Nugent was able to read at the early age of five years old.

At the age of thirteen, he had to leave Washington and the life he had known. His father died of tuberculosis and asthma; his mother moved their family to New York where she passed for white for economic reasons. In spite of her talents and training, she sought work as a domestic and waitress. Nugent augmented their income by working as an errand boy and a bellhop. He also worked at the Martha Hotel (an all women's establishment) as an ironworker, a designer, an elevator operator, and a secretary to a modiste. On one of these jobs, he even experimented with passing for white using the name Ricardo Nugent di Dosceta.

Writings

Nugent's first short story "Sadhji" was published in Alain Locke's *The New Negro* in 1925. The short story grew as a result of a drawing Nugent had completed.

Locke asked for an explanation of the drawing and liked the explanation more than the drawing. Nugent's first published poem, "Shadows," was rescued from the trash by Hughes and was published in *Opportunity* that same year and reprinted in Countee Cullen's *Caroling Dusk* in 1927. Locke and Nugent collaborated to create a one-act play, "Sadji: An African Ballet," which was published in Locke's *Plays of Negro Life: A Source Book of Native American Drama* in 1927 and produced in 1932.

In 1926, Nugent and other African American artists (Wallace Thurman, Zorro Neal Huston, Langston Hughes, Aaron Douglas, John P. Davis, and Gwendolyn Bennett) collaborated on a new quarterly that was to provide a vehicle for the work of young artists. This magazine, *Fire!!*, was edited by Wallace Thurman and contained two brush and ink drawings and a short story by Nugent. The short story, "Smoke, Lilies, and Jade," the first overtly homosexual work by an African American writer, made its author famous. Nugent used ellipsis to emulate speech and thought and the stream of consciousness technique, prevalent in his day, in this story of a young artist's discovering homosexual connection with a stranger. *Fire!!* lasted one issue and was followed by *Harlem: A Forum of Negro Life*, edited by Thurman with illustrations and theatre reviews by Nugent, under the pseudonym Richard Bruce.

Nugent is depicted in Thurman's satirical novel, *Infants of the Spring*, as Paul Arbian, a painter of the "bizarre and erotic." Nugent wrote an unpublished parallel to Thurman's novel, titled *Gentleman Jigger*. He utilizes the ellipses again in his short story, "Geisha Man," which presents a Japanese American protagonist and describes his encounters with other men. Like "Smoke, Lilies, and Jade," the emphasis is on male beauty and sensuality and not on sexual contact or affairs. In the 1930s, he wrote biographical sketches of African American historical figures and articles on African American history for the Federal Writers Project, and in 1937, he published "Pope Pius the Only" in *Challenge*. He continued to be candid about the gay experience in his writing. In 1970, he published "Beyond Where the Star Stood Still" in *Crisis*.

The Arts

Nugent's illustrations and later artwork show the influence of artists such as Aaron Douglas, Oscar Wilde, Aubrey Beardsley, and Erté. He worked with Douglas on a series of murals on the walls of Harlem nightclubs. His illustrations are marked by full-bodied women; explicit, sensuous, and attractive men; and backgrounds that are rife with suggestion. In 1928, he produced the *Salome* series which portrays images of female bodies, many of them named for biblical characters. This series also contains a painting of *Lucifer* with a full erection. Nugent's drawings were frequently used in *Opportunity* by Charles S. Johnson and he included Nugent's *Drawings for*

Mulattoes series in his *Ebony and Topaz*. In 1931, the Harmon Foundation presented four of his works in an exhibition.

In addition to writing and drawing, Nugent engaged in dance and acting. He appeared in a non-speaking role with Wallace Thurman and Dorothy West in Dubose and Dorothy Heyward's play *Porgy* in 1929. He joined several African American dance companies and appeared as a dancer in the play *Run, Little Chillun* (1933) and became a member of the Wilson William's Negro Ballet Company in the 1940s. In 1984, he was interviewed in *Before Stonewall*, a gay documentary.

Impact on Black Culture

Nugent's work became more erotic and explicit as the years progressed. In spite of the fact that he did not conform to the Harlem Renaissance's emphasis on racial uplift and his output was small, he made a lasting contribution. With Romare Bearden and others, he founded the Harlem Cultural Council, which sponsored the Jazzmobile and the Dancemobile, where major artists performed on stages on the flatbeds of trucks. His small artistic output helped define and describe the Harlem Renaissance.

In 1952, Nugent married Grace Elizabeth Marr; she committed suicide in 1969. Nugent died of congestive heart failure in Hoboken, New Jersey on May 27, 1987.

REFERENCES

Books

Garber, Eric. "Richard Bruce Nugent." In *Dictionary of Literary Biography*. Vol. 51. Ed. Trudier Harris. Detroit, Mich.: Gale Research, 1987.

Schwarz, A. B. Christa. *Gay Voices of the Harlem Renaissance*. Bloomington: Indiana University Press, 2003.

Wirth, Thomas H., ed. *Gay Rebel of the Harlem Renaissance: Selections from the Work of Richard Bruce Nugent*. Durham: Duke University Press, 2002.

Helen R. Houston

O

Barack Obama
1961–

Politician

Barack Obama appeared on the national political scene in 2004 and brought with him a renewed sense of unity and focus regarding the needs of all Americans and in particular African Americans. Steeped in a complex racial history, Obama embraces all those aspects of mixed race origins which influence who he is, while being fully aware of the blessings and challenges that come with his heritage. He wrote his autobiography which was prompted by his selection as the first African American editor of the *Harvard Law Review*. A community activist, he served as an Illinois State senator for seven years, and later as the only African American senator in the 109th United States Congress. His skillful speech at the 2004 Democratic Convention and his call for all Americans to unite brought speculations about his national political future. Some envisioned him as the first African American U.S. president.

Barack Hussein Obama was born on August 4, 1961, at the Queen's Medical Center in Honolulu. His parents, Ann Dunham and Barack Hussein Obama Sr., met as students at the University of Hawaii at Mano. Ann Dunham was from Wichita, Kansas, and a descendent of Jefferson Davis, the only president of the Confederate States of America, while Barack Hussein Obama was from Kenya, Africa with family ties to the Luo tribe. Obama Jr. was an only child. The family began to deteriorate when the elder Obama won a scholarship to Harvard to earn a Ph.D. Since the funding was not enough to support his family, he had to go alone. After completing his Ph.D. the elder Obama returned to Kenya and took a job as an economic planner for the country's government. The couple determined it was best to divorce. The elder Obama continued to write to his son and remarried, adding more siblings to share the family name. He came to see his son only once, before he died in an automobile accident in Kenya in 1982. On an extended holiday when Obama was ten, his father briefly shared his life.

Barack Obama

In the years after his parents' divorce, Obama and his mother remained in Honolulu. Even though his grandparents did not cater to racist ideas and sought to protect him, Obama still chose to call himself Barry. His given name Barack means "blessed" in Swahili, but he chose a name that would allow him to fit in. In an environment of only seven or eight African American students in his school, this was important. Obama, in his autobiography *Dreams from My Father: A Story of Race and Inheritance*, writes about being puzzled by his grandparents' resistance to racism. He was simply told by his grandmother, "your grandfather and I just figured we should treat people decently, Bar. That's all." Their mid-western small-town values had a direct affect on the person he was to become. Although their openness secured him in many ways, he came to understand himself as a person of

Chronology

1961	Born in Honolulu, Hawaii on August 4
1967	Moves to Djakarta, Indonesia with family
1971	Returns to Honolulu to live with grandparents and later mother; attends prestigious Punahou Academy
1982	Travels to Kenya because of father's death
1983	Receives B.A. from Columbia University in political science with specialization in international relations
1985	Moves to Chicago as community activist
1991	Graduates magna cum laude from Harvard Law School; becomes first African American editor of *Harvard Law Review*; returns to Chicago; accepts position as senior lecturer at University of Chicago Law School in constitutional law; practices law at Miner, Barnhill and Galland
1992	Marries Michelle Robinson
1995	Publishes autobiography, *Dreams from My Father: A Story of Race and Inheritance*
1996-2003	Elected to Illinois State Senate from south side Hyde Park neighborhood
2000	Makes unsuccessful run in Democratic primary for First Congressional District
2004	Elected to United States Senate for Illinois; gives keynote address at Democratic National Convention in Boston; autobiography is reprinted

mixed heritage. In 1967 when Obama was six years old, his mother remarried and the family moved to Djakarta, Indonesia. She married an Indonesian oil company executive and Maya Soetoro-Ng, Obama's half sister, was born. When Obama was ten, he returned to Honolulu where he had better educational opportunities. He earned a place at Punahou School, a very prestigious school, and initially lived with his grandparents. He later lived with his mother and sister once they returned to Honolulu. Obama's teenage years were troubled because of his confused sense of identity. He experimented with drugs and gave more attention to basketball and bodysurfing than to academics. He was a black man within the school's small minority population, and the expectations regarding his success were low. As he stated in his memoirs, *Dreams from My Father*, people were quite satisfied that he did not move or speak too loudly, "Such a pleasant surprise to find a well-mannered young black man who didn't seem angry." In spite of obstacles, Obama graduated from high school with honors.

As a young adult Obama moved to the mainland. For two years he attended Occidental College in Los Angeles, then transferred to Columbia University. From Hawaii to Columbia, Obama found that racial tension infected the environment. By this time he came to know that activism was the way to effect change. He graduated in 1983 from Columbia University in political science with specialization in international relations. He spent a year in the financial sector, while writing letters to com-

munity service organizations all over the United States, asking what he could do to help. Obama moved to Chicago and went to work with a church-based group that focused on the city's economically troubled neighborhoods. He became a community organizer in the Altgeld Gardens housing project on the south side of Chicago. Various experiences caused a change in his thinking and he became a Christian. Obama joined the Trinity United Church of Christ.

Next, Obama enrolled at Harvard Law School, where he became the first African American editor of the student-run academic journal *Harvard Law Review* in 1990. This honor is bestowed on a law student who demonstrates exceptional academic abilities, excellent writing and editing skills, and strong leadership qualities. As a result of this work Obama was offered a publishing deal for a book about his life, which was to include optimistic messages regarding the racial situation in the United States. After graduating from Harvard Law School, magna cum laude, in 1991, Obama wrote his autobiography, which was published in 1995 and re-released in 2004. Also in 1992 while working in a corporate law firm, Obama met Michelle Robinson, a Harvard Law student from Chicago. Robinson, who also graduated from Harvard Law school, and Obama were married in 1992.

Chicago and Politics

Passing up an opportunity from a top Chicago law firm, Obama decided to practice civil rights law with the small public-interest law firm Miner, Barnhill and Galland. He also became a lecturer of constitutional law at the University of Chicago. Continuing his role as activist, Obama took on the management of a statewide voter registration drive as director of the Illinois Project VOTE. The aggressive organizational plan that Obama helped develop was effective in registering over 100,000 voters. The result aided in the election of Democratic President Bill Clinton and Senator Carol Mosely Braun.

In 1996 Obama stepped into the political ring. His goals were clear as he turned down a chance to apply for a tenure-track teaching position at the University of Chicago. Obama, who identifies himself as an African American, ran for Illinois state senator from Hyde Park, the thirteenth legislative district. His work in the community and his role as a professor and civil rights lawyer set the tone for a successful election. As state senator, he served as chairman of the Public Health and Welfare Committee, passed bills to increase funding for AIDS prevention and care, and introduced legislation to curb racial profiling. Working-class people and those issues that impact the quality of their lives were key concerns for Obama.

In 2000 Obama ran unsuccessfully for the first Congressional district against incumbent Bobby Rush, a former Black Panther. Criticism regarding Obama during his unsuccessful run centered on his biracial background and his having been too associated with the ivy league (in essence, not black enough). His autobiography is the source for these comments from the community. He hoped his book would show the process of self-awareness and the fact that mistakes and challenges can be overcome. Obama continued in the role of state senator until 2004. The debate on his background subsided and the stage was set for future political opportunities to aid the African American community and the community at large.

Enters U.S. Senate Race

The seat for United States senator from Illinois was vacated by Peter Fitzgerald in 2004 and Obama decided to run. He was supported by South Side residents as well as Bobby Rush. In spite of early competition from Danny Hynes, a favored Democrat, and Blair Hull, who personally spent $29 million on his campaign, Obama won the Democratic primary with an outright majority of 53 percent. His victory was attributed to volunteers, his coalition of white Chicago voters, and other supporters in the state. The Republican Party had fervently tried to find a candidate to run again Obama. They needed someone to meet political scrutiny and withstand the growing appeal of Obama. In a last effort to locate such a candidate, Alan Keyes, a former ambassador and African American conservative residing in Maryland, was chosen. Keyes was in trouble from the start as he first had to establish residency. He had recently criticized former First Lady Hilary Clinton for having to establish residency in order to run in the New York primary. Keyes also alienated both parties as well as voters by making politically incorrect statements. Hypocrisy, radical statements, and extreme positions promoted by Keyes fueled the almost frantic campaign in favor of Obama. In an election that was surrounded by false starts, candidate withdrawals, and questions of other candidates' integrity, Obama stood heads above the confusion with name recognition and a clear connection to Illinois voters. With a landslide victory of 70 percent of the votes, Obama became the third African American to be elected in the U.S. Senate since Reconstruction and the fifth African American to be elected in U.S. history. Obama also became the only African American senator in the 109th Congress.

Obama is a charismatic and forceful speaker, who captures the hearts and minds of Americans of diverse racial and social backgrounds. His campaign was so successful that he was invited to give the keynote address at the 2004 Democratic National Convention in Boston, Massachusetts. Obama became the third African American to provide the convention speech. *Time* called Obama's speech, "one of the best in convention history," and Obama told *Ebony* all he was trying to do was to "tell the stories of the hopes, fears, and struggles of what ordi-

nary people are going through every day." His ability to connect with the voters and exert a sense of healing for the racial divide in the United States sets Obama apart as one politician who truly represents the people.

Obama's journey is one of self-discovery, empowerment, and confrontation with the U.S. promise to all of its citizens. In 2004 he signed a $1.9 million deal for three books, seizing the opportunity to again tell his story and his experiences. The first of three books, due out in 2006, was expected to include Obama's political views. The second was expected to be a children's book co-written by wife Michelle and the couple's two daughters, Malia Ann and Natsha, with the proceeds to go to charity. The content of the third book was undetermined.

REFERENCES

Books

Manheim, James M. *Contemporary Black Biography.* Vol. 49. Farmington Hills, Mich.: Thomson Gale, 2005.

Periodicals

Graff, E. J. "Dreams from My Father: A Story of Race and Inheritance." *American Prospect* 12 (10 September 2001): 42.

Kinnon, Joy Bennett. "Barack Obama: New Political Star Attracts National Attention." *Ebony* (November 2004) : 196.

Mitchell, Mary. "Memoir of a 21st-Century History Maker." *Black Issues Book Review* 17 (January-February 2005): 18-21.

Ripley, Amanda. "Obama's Ascent: How Do You Leap from Neighborhood Activist to U.S. Senator to Perhaps Higher Office?" *Time* (15 November 2004): 74.

Roach, Ronald. "Obama Rising: All but Assured to Become the Fifth Black American to Hold a Seat in the U.S. Senate, Obama Represents to Many the Emergence of a New Generation of National Political Leadership" *Black Issues in Higher Education* 21 (7 October 2004): 20.

Zeleny, Jeff. "Sen. Obama's Allure Transcends Black and White." *Chicago Tribune*, 30 June 2005.

Online

Leibovich, Mark. "The Senator's Humble Beginning." *Washington Post*, 24 February 2005. http://www.lexis-nexis.com (Accessed 10 October 2005).

Lean'tin L Bracks

Rod Paige
1933–

Secretary of education, school superintendent

Advancing his way through the education system and overcoming racial barriers, Rod Paige became the first African American and the first school superintendent to serve as the U.S. secretary of education. His extensive knowledge and practical experience in the field of education was most evident through the drafting of the No Child Left Behind Act of 2001, an education reform legislation.

Roderick Raynor Paige, born June 17, 1933, in Monticello, Mississippi, was the oldest of five children. Paige's father, Raynor C. Paige, was a school principal and a barber. His mother, Sophie, was a librarian who made books a central part of life in the family's four-bedroom house. "My earliest memories were associated with books," Paige told *People* in an interview. As a young boy, Paige led debates and animated discussions around the dinner table about favorite books and literary characters.

Paige attended Lawrence County Training School in Monticello. A segregated school, the two-story building served black children from the first through the twelfth grades. Paige learned early in life the hardships faced in a segregated educational system. In an interview in *Humanities*, Paige said: "The first thing that caused me to start getting angry was the fact that they had a nice gym and we didn't have a gym." He gained an appetite for proving he was as good as white students, a feeling that continued through college and graduate school.

After high school graduation in 1951, Paige enrolled at Jackson State College in Jackson, Mississippi. He was an honor student and earned a spot on the football team. His football coach, Harrison Wilson, encouraged him to go to graduate school. Following graduation with a B.A. in physical education in 1955, Paige began teaching at a high school in Clinton, Mississippi. Shortly thereafter, he was drafted and joined the Navy, moving to San Diego, California. In July 1956, he married his college sweetheart, Gloria Crawford. Only a few days following his

Rod Paige

wedding, Paige was sent to Okinawa, where he worked as a medical corpsman.

When he returned home to his family, Paige was anxious to resume his education. Paige served as head football coach at Utica Junior College in Mississippi until 1962 when he returned to coach at his alma mater, Jackson State University. Paige's career aspirations went beyond the football field to the classroom. Because no graduate schools in his home state of Mississippi would accept blacks, Paige enrolled at Indiana University. His academic deficiencies from his background at segregated schools made graduate education extremely challenging. However, Paige overcame his deficiencies to earn an M.A. in 1962 and then a doctorate in physical education

509

in 1970. His dissertation topic was the response time of offensive linemen.

After a brief tenure as an assistant football coach at the University of Cincinnati, he applied in 1971 for the job as head coach and athletic director at Texas Southern University in Houston. Granville Sawyer, then president of Texas Southern, interviewed Paige for the job. He later told *Time* that "[he] was convinced by the end of [their] conversation that this was a great mind and great educational leader in the making." Paige accepted the job offer with the stipulation that he also have faculty status. In hindsight, Paige told *Texas Monthly*, this was one of the most important decisions that he ever made.

As the years went by at Texas Southern, Paige became more interested in education than football. Paige admitted to *People* that he was "increasingly disturbed by the growing commercialism of college sports." At the same time, his family life experienced hardship with the ending of his marriage to Gloria in 1982. Paige was considered for assistant coaching positions in the NFL but chose to stay in academics. In 1984, Paige left coaching to become dean of the College of Education at Texas Southern.

As dean, Paige established the Center for Excellence in Urban Education, a research facility that focuses on issues related to instruction and management in urban school systems. Texas Southern University's education program thrived under Paige's leadership, boasting that 33 percent of teachers and administrators in the Houston Independent School District graduated from the program.

In 1989, Paige decided to run for the Houston Independent School District (HISD) School Board. Despite his inexperience in local politics, his academic credentials and definite ideas about education helped him gain the support of both Republicans and Democrats. John

Bettencourt, Harris County tax-assessor and campaign worker, told the *Houston Chronicle*, "We had a great candidate. He was the newcomer that was already the hot property . . . He had a vision of what education could be. He was helped by the environment. In 1989, people wanted a change."

The school board elections of 1989 did indeed bring change. Four of the nine members were new that year. The new members wanted to restructure the school district. The board chose to draft a vision statement for the district. The board chairperson appointed Paige to chair the committee that drafted the new statement. On June 18, 1990, the board of education unanimously approved the Declaration of Beliefs and Visions. Beliefs and Visions proposed a radical reform in educational policy and administration from a centralized hierarchy to a student-teacher centered approach. The document also called for district policies to be based on educational outcomes rather than the educational process. Finally, Paige and the other board members insisted that a common core of academic courses based on high standards be established to prepare students for college or the workforce.

The superintendent of the Houston Independent School District, Joan Raymond, was strongly opposed to the board's implementation of Beliefs and Visions. After a year-long battle with the school board, Raymond was fired from the superintendent's post in 1991. Her replacement, Frank Petruzielo, moved forward with the reforms outlined in the document, but not to the extent that was satisfactory to Paige, who was elected board president in 1992. In his book *Fighting to Save Our Urban Schools*, Donald McAdams quoted Paige as saying that Petruzielo's reforms were "just traditional 'fix the parts' school reform. It's not systemic change."

Heads Houston's School System

When Petruzielo left in 1994, Paige became the prime candidate for superintendent. A majority of the school board expressed their desire to hire Paige while he was still serving on the board without going through a national search process. The Hispanic Education Committee expressed strong opposition to the appointment of Paige and the hiring process that followed. A lawsuit was filed by the committee against the school district. The federal courts vindicated the school district of all charges in the suit, freeing Paige to concentrate on fully implementing the reforms that were outlined in the Beliefs and Visions document.

Paige began his administration in 1994 by focusing on the reform of the district's administration. He sought to work in partnership with leaders in the business community. At his request the school district formed numerous task forces made up of outside experts to recommend ways to improve efficiency. Business leaders were impressed with Paige's management style and straightforward approach to solving problems. Many of the recommendations were implemented by the district, and Paige called the reform program a huge success.

However, some of Paige's reforms were not well received by teachers and employees in the district. When principals were granted more authority to make personnel decisions on their campuses, Gayle Fallon of the area union told the *Houston Chronicle*, "We didn't see a check and balance on what we considered unbridled power." Several employees argued against the decentralizing of student services and special education from the district offices to the schools. Despite the criticism and the failure of a $390 million bond election, Paige stayed the course of his Beliefs and Visions plan.

In 1996, the state of Texas, led by comptroller John Sharp, conducted a full-scale audit of HISD. Paige was able to utilize the audit to accelerate his plan for decentralization and reorganization of the district. He privatized several of the district's services, including food service, school maintenance, and employee benefits. The district launched an overhaul of curriculum management and instructional training, implementing standardized testing for all students third grade and up. The district contracted with private secular schools to relieve overcrowding and take children that were struggling academically. Teacher and administrator evaluations were modified to focus on individual performance. Sharp praised Paige for his assistance with the auditors and credited him and his colleagues with the turnaround of HISD.

By 2000, Paige's reforms were making a real difference. *Education Week* reported that between 1994 and 1999, the proportion of students passing the Texas Assessment of Academic Skills rose from 49 percent to 74 percent. Brad Duggan of the watchdog group "Just for Kids" told the *Houston Chronicle* that 26 percent of HISD's elementary schools were performing better than comparable schools elsewhere in the state. The public's endorsement of Paige's leadership came in 1998 with the approval of a record $678 million bond issue to launch the largest building program in the district's history.

Becomes U.S. Secretary of Education

In December 2000, Texas governor and U.S. president-elect George W. Bush asked Paige to accept the position of U.S. secretary of education. Paige became acquainted with the Bush family during the 1970s when he was active in community groups helping the poorer neighborhoods in Houston. Paige volunteered for the George Bush presidential campaign of 1980 and became one of the delegates to the Republican national convention that summer. As governor, George W. Bush showed great regard for Paige and his reforms, frequently citing Houston as an exemplary urban school district to be emulated in other cities.

On January 24, 2001 Paige was sworn in as secretary of education. With the strong support of the Bush administration, Paige began his tenure by pushing the No Child Left Behind (NCLB) Act. The NCLB Act focused on many of the same issues that Paige had successfully implemented in Houston: greater choices for parents and students attending low-performing schools, standardized testing, and greater accountability and local control for school administrators and teachers. Paige was successful in gaining bi-partisan support of the U.S. Congress for the bill. The act was signed on January 8, 2002.

As the year progressed, however, Paige was harshly criticized for his performance as secretary and for the problems arising from the NCLB Act. Funding was a critical issue for the bill, and circumstances following the September 11, 2001 terrorist attacks diverted key funds from the provisions of the NCLB Act to other programs related to homeland security. Also, some political analysts questioned Paige's role in the development of the NCLB Act. White House education advisor Sandy Kress conceded in an interview with the *Wall Street Journal* that Paige was "a little bit on the periphery" because a large portion of the legislation had been drafted during the campaign before Paige took office.

The most significant criticism came from education organizations and state legislatures which opposed the strict testing and high achievement standards required by the act. The National Education Association expressed its disapproval of the law for its impairment of the education process through emphasis on standardized testing. Paige abruptly responded, calling the association a "terrorist organization," but later apologizing for the remark. Lawmakers in twenty states introduced resolutions opposing all or part of the NCLB Act. Former "blue-ribbon" schools found themselves on the failing list under the new standards imposed by the act. Several states, including Vermont, threatened to refuse federal funds rather than comply with the new guidelines. The *Christian Science Monitor* quoted governor Howard Dean's objection as "the one-size-fits-all unfunded mandate . . . What's good in Houston is not necessarily good in Iowa or Minnesota or Vermont."

In 2002, Paige went on a twenty-five city tour to gather support for the NCLB Act and encourage more active involvement of parents, teachers, principals, and administrators in the educational process. Paige started the tour in April 2002 in Albuquerque, New Mexico and finished in Bronx, New York in September of that year. At each stop on the tour he toured facilities, met with key politicians, and held town hall meetings with the various constituencies.

Throughout the remainder of his term as secretary, Paige was the administration's public voice on the No Child Left Behind Act. On November 15, 2004, Paige announced his resignation, stating that "No Child Left

Behind is indelibly launched" and that he was interested in pursuing personal interests at home.

In March 2005, Paige accepted a position as public policy scholar at the Woodrow Wilson Center in Washington D.C. to work on the "Academic Achievement Gap" project, including a book on the achievement gap and African American leadership. Paige also joined the Thomas B. Fordham Foundation, an education think tank, as a trustee.

REFERENCES

Books

McAdams, Donald R. *Fighting to Save Our Urban Schools—and Winning!: Lessons from Houston*. New York: Teachers College Press, 2000.

Periodicals

"After Two Years on the Job, HISD Chief Converts Skeptics." *Houston Chronicle* (3 March 1996): A-1.

Bryant, Salatheia. "From Humble Beginnings." *Houston Chronicle* (20 January 2001): 21.

Cole, Bruce. "Good Teacher and a Willing Student." *Humanities* 25 (September/October 2004): 6-9, 50-54.

Cook, Glenn. "The Ultimate Insider: Changing of the Guard at ED." *American School Board Journal* 192 (January 2005): 6-8.

Fields-Meyer, Thomas, and Linda Kramer. "Class Act." *People* 56 (19 November 2001): 151-55.

Johnston, Robert C. "Boosters Call Houston's Chief 'A Good Thing, and We Know It'." *Education Week* 20 (4 October 2000): 1.

Kronholz, June. "Education Secretary Gets a Schooling in Politics." *Wall Street Journal* (5 June 2001): A-28.

Markley, Melanie. "A Team-Spirit Challenge." *Houston Chronicle* (6 February 1994): A-1.

Mason, Julie. "Paige Deflects Criticism As He Tries to Reach Goal." *Houston Chronicle* (4 August 2003): A-3.

"Paige on Paige: A Talk with the Secretary." *Education Week* 20 (11 July 2001): 34-37.

Paulson, Amanda. "True Believer." *Christian Science Monitor* (10 September 2002): 15.

Richard, Alan and Joetta L. Sack. "Paige Asserts He'll Smooth Early Bumps." *Education Week* 20 (11 July 2001): 1.

Sweany, Brian D. "Rod Paige." *Texas Monthly* 28 (September 2000): 149, 238.

"Turning a Paige." *Houston Chronicle* (19 January 2001): A-1.

Winters, Rebecca, Alice Jackson Baughn, and Michelle McCalope. "Teacher in Chief." *Time* 157 (12 February 2001): 74-76.

Mark L. McCallon

Barrington D. Parker
1915–1993

Judge

Barrington Daniels Parker Sr. was appointed to the U.S. District Court for the District of Columbia by President Richard Nixon on December 19, 1969. He is probably best known for presiding over the case that found John Hinckley Jr. not guilty by reason of insanity of attempting to assassinate President Ronald Reagan. After the acquittal, Parker ordered Hinckley committed to a mental hospital. This case was not the first and it would not be the last in which Parker's judgment was questioned. Still, he was not one to be swayed by popular opinion, and he ran his courtroom the way he wanted and allowed no one to question that.

Parker was born on November 17, 1915, in Rosslyn, Virginia, the only child of George A. and Maude Daniels Parker. His father was a bricklayer and mailman, who later became a part-time preacher and lawyer. He also became a practicing attorney and teacher in both the fields of religion and law. In 1931, he was the founder and dean of the Robert H. Terrell School of Law, a night school for African American students. The school was named in honor of the first African American appointed justice of the peace and the first African American judge on the Municipal Court of the District of Columbia. The school closed in the 1950s. His mother worked in the Bureau of Engraving and Printing and was a former school teacher.

Parker's family moved to the District of Columbia when he was quite young, and he grew up at 24th and M streets, N.W. He received his early education in the District of Columbia. He graduated from Dunbar High School in 1932. He graduated from Lincoln University, Pennsylvania, in 1936, with an A.D. degree; the University of Pennsylvania in 1938, with an M.A. degree in economics; and the University of Chicago Law School in 1947, with a J.D.

In 1939, Parker married Marjorie Holloman, the daughter of a well-known minister, the Reverend J. L. S. Holloman, from North Carolina. The Holloman family moved to the District of Columbia when she was a child, and she graduated from Dunbar High School in 1932, where the two met. Marjorie Holloman Parker became a prominent D.C. educator and community leader. She served as chairman of the University of the District of Columbia Board of Trustees and was an appointed member of the old, pre-home rule D.C. city council. The couple became the parents of two sons, Jason H. Parker and Barrington D. Parker, Jr. and three grandchildren. Marjorie Holloman Parker died of heart disease on January 16, 2006 in Washington, D.C.

Barrington D. Parker

Chronology

1915	Born in Rosslyn, Virginia on November 17
1939	Marries Marjorie Holloman
1947	Admitted to the D.C. bar and joins father's law practice
1969	Appointed to the U.S. District Court for the District of Columbia by President Richard Nixon
1975	Struck by a car and has left leg amputated
1982	Presides over the John Hinckley Jr. trial; receives the Professional Achievement Award from the University of Chicago
1988	Chosen Judge of the Year by the National Conference of Black Lawyers
1990	Retires from the bench on February 9 for health reasons
1993	Dies in Washington, D.C. on June 2

Pursues Career in Law

Before attending law school, Parker for a short period of time worked as a government economist and taught economics at Dillard University in New Orleans. He was greatly influenced by his father to pursue a career in law. In 1947, he was admitted to the District of Columbia bar. He served as adjunct professor at the Robert H. Terrell Law School and at the American University's College of Law.

Upon passing the District of Columbia bar, Parker joined his father's law firm as a practicing attorney where he remained until 1968. Parker participated in and presided over several significant cases in his career as a practicing attorney and sitting judge. Very early as a young practicing attorney, in association with another attorney, Julian Dugas, Parker was assigned to do the research for the team of Gorge A. Parker, George E.C. Hayes, James A. Cobb, and others who represented Paul Robeson in defeating a state department attempt to recall Robeson's passport. In 1955, the team also assisted in the defense of W. E. B. Du Bois, one of the founders of the NAACP; the Peace Information Center; and several other defendants who were charged as agents of a foreign government. The charges were later dismissed upon the defendants' motion for judgment of acquittal.

In 1969, Parker was appointed to the U.S. District Court for the District of Columbia by President Richard

M. Nixon. Until his appointment to the judgeship, he practiced in the law firm of Parker and Parker. Although he was known for his conservative views, Parker was deeply concerned with the challenges to affirmative action plans that were being mounted by the Reagan administration in his latter years on the bench. Parker viewed the Reagan administration attempts to turn back the clock on affirmative action with disdain.

Runs a No-Nonsense Courtroom

Parker's impressive courtroom entry and his aggressive no-nonsense approach to courtroom procedures gained him a reputation as a crusty, highly independent and cantankerous judge. He made sure all knew who was in charge of his courtroom. Lawyers knew what he would and what he would not tolerate in his courtroom.

Despite Parker's reputation for being strict, outside the courtroom he was considered to be a man of compassion. He was also considered to be a modest, independent man who made his share of unpopular rulings. He liked to explain his approach to the law by quoting from Micah 6: "And what doth the Lord require of thee but to do justly and to love mercy and to walk humbly with thy God." Since he was the only child of a man who was both preacher and lawyer, combining the Scriptures and law books came naturally for this judge.

Physical disability also did not distract Parker. In 1975, Parker was crossing Connecticut Avenue, N.W. to buy a pack of cigarettes when he was struck by a car. As a result, his left leg was amputated; he learned to walk again with the aid of metal crutches. The only thing he gave up after the accident was smoking, and he continued to drive himself to work from his home in the district's Forest Hills neighborhood.

Parker's Independent Rulings

For twenty years as judge, Parker presided over many highly publicized criminal and civil cases, the most famous being the John W. Hinckley Jr. case. Hinckley was the presidential assailant found not guilty by reason of insanity. Hinckley Jr. was charged with attempting to kill President Ronald Reagan and the president's press secretary, James Brady. Significantly, the Court of Appeals affirmed Judge Parker's ruling that officials, who interrogated Hinckley after his arrest, violated his rights by continuing the interrogation after Hinckley indicated that he wanted an attorney present. The Appellate Court also affirmed Parker's determination that prison guards who seized and read handwritten notes prepared by Hinckley for the benefit of his counsel violated his rights to privacy. After ruling on the case, Judge Parker ordered Hinckley's indefinite commitment to a mental facility, meaning that Hinckley would be subject to periodic hearings to determine his fitness for release.

Other high profile cases included: Richard Helms, the former Central Intelligence Agency director accused of lying to a Senate committee; former representative Otto E. Passman, Democrat of Louisiana, charged with accepting a bribe from a South Korean businessman; and two Cuban exiles and a Chilean security agent accused of murdering Orlando Letelier, a former Chilean ambassador. Parker acknowledged that he had his share of reversals, and his biggest came in the Letelier case. An appeals court overturned the conviction of the two anti-Castro Cubans.

In a 1973 ruling, Parker barred the Nixon administration's attempt to impose certain price controls. In another case, he ruled against a National Guard attempt to bar long-haired guardsmen from wearing short-cropped wigs when on duty; and in 1978, in connection with a merger between the National Student Marketing Company and an insurance holding company, he ruled that federal securities regulations did not require lawyers to disclose fraud by their clients.

In 1979, Parker blocked President Carter from issuing wage and price guidelines. In 1982, he ruled invalid a congressional amendment that barred Communists from job training programs; in 1979, Parker refused to accept a plea bargain worked out between the Justice Department and Westinghouse Electric Company in a foreign bribery case until attorneys revealed the name of the official—a deputy Egyptian prime minister—who received the bribes.

In 1987, in response to a class action suit filed by the Mental Health Law Project and the District of Columbia Public Defender Service on behalf of patients involuntarily committed to St. Elizabeth's Hospital, Parker ruled that the patients were entitled to full and complete due process hearings to determine if they were being held unconstitutionally. The ruling affected about six hundred patients. Some of the patients had been committed for twenty-five or more years.

When he was not involved in the drama of the courtroom, Parker enjoyed reading historical fiction—James Michener was a favorite—and he listened to progressive jazz and classical music to relax.

Memberships, Civic Activities, and Awards

Parker held memberships in several organizations, including D.C. Human Relations Council (1963-67); American Bar Association; National Bar Association; Bar Association of D.C.; D.C. Committee on Judicial Disabilities and Tenure; and local chapter of the ACLU. He co-chaired the United Negro College Fund. Parker served on the Board of Visitors of the Law School of the University of Chicago and the Pace University Law School.

In 1982, Parker received the Professional Achievement Award from the University of Chicago, given in recognition of those alumni whose efforts in their vocational fields have brought distinction to themselves, credit to the university, and enhanced the lives of their fellow citizens. Around 1988 Parker was chosen Judge of the Year by the National Conference of Black Lawyers.

Parker and his wife, Marjorie H. Parker, were among the first blacks listed in one of Washington's most hidebound institutions, the Green Book, a social register for the elite. On February 9, 1990 Parker retired from the bench for health reasons. Barrington Parker died in Washington, D.C. on June 2, 1993.

REFERENCES

Books

"Barrington Daniels Parker." In *The Negro Almanac*. Eds. Harry A. Ploski and James Williams. Detroit: Gale Research, 1989.

"Parker, Barrington D." In *Who's Who Among Black Americans*. 7th ed. Ed. Christa Brelin. Detroit: Gale Research, 1992-1993.

Periodicals

"Black Federal Judge Slaps Down Carter's Decision." *Jet* 56 (21 June 1979): 13.

Feinberg, Lawrence. "From Hinckley to Helms, He's Heard Them All." *Washington Post*, 17 November 1985.

Gailey, Phil. "Hinckley's Crusty Judge: Barrington Daniels Parker." *New York Times*, 1 May 1982.

Hevest, Dennis. "Barrington D. Parker, 77, Is Dead; Trial Judge for Reagan's Attacker." *New York Times*, 5 June 1993.

"Judge Voids Rule on Federal Pay." *New York Times*, 11 December 1981.

"Washington Notebook." *Ebony* 34 (February 1979): 29.

Mattie McHollin

H. G. Parks
1916–1989

Entrepreneur, business executive

Pioneering businessman Henry Green Parks Jr. led the way for the sale of stocks in black businesses on Wall Street. As the founder of H. G. Parks Inc., Parks was the driving force behind the popular sausage company for over two decades. Established in 1951, the company flourished under his guidance and work ethic, and its cutting-edge marketing campaigns ushered in sales techniques that are widely used to market American goods. Most notably, the company's radio and television ads popularized "More Parks sausages, Mom, please," and boasted impressive earnings before the close of its first decade. In 1969, Parks led the public sale of Parks, Inc.'s stocks on the NASDAQ. The achievement was the first-ever of its kind for an African American-owned company.

Henry Green Parks Jr. was born on September 29, 1916 in Atlanta, Georgia to Henry Green Parks Sr. and a domestic laborer whose name is unknown. The elder Parks was also a domestic and soon the family moved together to Dayton, Ohio, in search of a better life. The father was hired as a hotel bartender and later as a wine steward in a private club, and both parents worked long hours, leaving the family very little time together. At just six months old, young Parks was left in the care of his maternal grandmother.

Graduating from Dayton public schools, Parks opted not to enter a historically black college or university. Instead, he applied to Ohio State University, the state's leading university. Although he was aware of the difficulties that being an African American student at a traditionally white institution posed, Parks believed that a degree from Ohio State would increase his chances of professional success. While there, he did encounter racism but endeavored to succeed, working to pay his way through college. A trailblazer in his own right, Parks became the first black on the university's swim team, and he roomed with future Olympic gold medal winner and world record holder Jesse Owens.

Parks began his collegiate career as an accounting major, but by his graduation in 1939, he had changed his major to marketing. Having graduated with honors and as the only African American in his class, Parks showed a natural talent for salesmanship both in and out of the classroom. In fact, so much so, that a counselor advised him to spend some time in South America where he could acquire an accent and then change his name. The professor reasoned that when Parks returned to the United States, he could assume a new identity. According to him, this was a perfect equation for Parks to succeed as a businessman of color in America. Parks disagreed; the example set by his father included diligence, perseverance and making difficult choices, they did not include dishonesty.

Gains Needed Marketing Experience

Accordingly Parks sought employment, and after several months, he secured a job at the National Youth Administration in Cincinnati. Later, his mentorship with renown educator Mary McLeod Bethune, founder of Bethune-Cookman College in Florida, landed him employment with the Resident War Production Training Center in Wilberforce, Ohio. In his first experience in business management, Parks was responsible for overseeing fifty staff members and training several hundred persons for jobs in industry. While in Wilberforce, he also met world champion boxer Joe Louis, with whom he later joined forces in several business projects. One such venture included Parks' management of the singing career of Louis' wife. Another collaboration entailed his heading a soft drink company that manufactured Joe Louis Punch, which, although it was not particularly successful, afforded Parks valuable management experience.

Beginning in 1940, Parks worked as a beer salesman for Pabst Brewing Company. By the end of his two-year tenure, Parks had risen to the position of national salesman and had devised several lucrative marketing campaigns for the company. His plan to displace Budweiser as the exclusive supplier for the nation's railroads solicited the cooperation of railroad porters, dining car attendants, and waiters to increase the company's sales. To market to the black community, Parks employed famous African American personalities such as Lena Horne, Duke Ellington, and Cab Calloway in Pabst's marketing campaign. Both plans were successful, far exceeding the company's expectations.

In 1942, Parks and W. B. Graham, a co-worker, resigned from Pabst. Together, they founded a public relations and advertising firm, W. B. Graham and Associates, in New York. While the company enjoyed moderate success, Parks left Graham and Associates, to co-partner in launching the Crayton Southern Sausage company in 1949. The company's slow expansion over the course of the next two years did not discourage his partners from wanting to close. Objecting to the closure, Parks allowed the other partners to buy him out.

Launches H. G. Parks Inc.

Parks had moved to Baltimore at the suggestion of Baltimore businessman and civic leader William L. Adams, whom he met on a train to Boston in 1948. Impressed by Parks' academic credentials and professional potential, Adams initially gave him a job at his real estate firm. Getting the support necessary to start a company was difficult. In the interim, he also worked as a drugstore manager and owned a cement block manufacturing company. After his efforts to secure a bank loan proved futile, Parks used the profits he yielded from the sale of Crayton to establish a new business.

With Adams' financial backing, he opened Parks Sausage Company in 1951. Its concept was to manufacture distinctive and tasty Southern-style foods that were less expensive than most cuts of meat. Parks and his two staff members made sausage one day and sold it the next. Relying on the marketing experiences he gained while at Pabst, Parks began an exhaustive campaign to attract buyers in the African American community. Eventually, he expanded his target market to include white-owned businesses, and he was one of the first food manufacturers to offer cooking demonstrations and taste tests in grocery stores. As one of the most multi-dimensional marketing promotions of its time, the company's mascot "Porky the Pig" also gave out children's gifts and conducted a "Customer of the Day" program.

Even after these successes, Parks lamented in a 1977 interview with the *New York Times*, "I nearly lost it all in the first couple years, it was difficult to borrow." Repeatedly rejected for loans by bank officers who could not even offer him a reason for their denial, Parks sold his house and borrowed against his life insurance to purchase reconditioned equipment and a few delivery trucks. Nevertheless, the business still struggled to stay afloat until he was extended two loans in 1964. Issued by the Maryland National Bank, the first loan financed the construction of a modern-structured manufacturing plant in the south Baltimore's Camden Industrial Park. Monumental Life Insurance Company provided the second, which financed the building's mortgage.

The company grew under Parks' leadership, building a national reputation for high quality. Most notably, its unique marketing strategies successfully image-branded the company with its famous radio and television campaign. As early as 1964, the plaintive voice of a child rang out with "More Parks sausages, Mom," on American radio airwaves. Devised by marketing executive Leon Shaffer Golnick, the company added "Please" to the slogan two years later, after complaints that the child sounded rude. Reproduced on television and billboards for decades to come, this ad featured a white child. In a 1995 interview with *The Baltimore Sun* Raymond V. Haysbert, one of Parks' first employees, explained the company's position: "If a person with a Negro voice said something in a commercial...there would be an immediate downplaying of the product."

Parks Goes to Wall Street

After years of financial success, Parks took the company public in 1969, making it the first black-owned business in the United States to do so. Its triumph was undoubtedly due to his constant presence as the company's guiding force. After all, he personally sampled its product everyday for more than two decades. In the process, Parks' partner Haysbert succeeded him as president after Parks began to suffer from Parkinson's disease in the mid-1970s. In 1973, the company's sales topped $13.8 million and stood seventh among the top 100 black-owned businesses as listed by *Black Enterprise* magazine in 1976.

By the following year, Parks Inc. boasted three hundred employees, but with Parks' health difficulties looming, he and Adams sold their interests in the company to the Norin Corporation. Each held 158,000 shares, which were valued at approximately $1.58 million at the time. Although Haysbert became the company's chief executive officer, Parks continued to serve as chairman. Parks also became a member of Norin's board of directors and signed a seven-year contract to serve as a consultant to the parent-company.

Unfortunately, trouble began almost immediately as the company's sales began to lag behind rising production costs. The company's 1976 profits, which had totaled $860,000, fell sharply to $424,000 the following year. Sighting the company's difficulties, the Canadian Pacific Corporation conglomerate, which acquired Norin in 1979, quickly planned to liquidate Parks Inc. While a group led by Haysbert purchased the company in 1980, the company struggled to remain open into the 1990s. Even after its sale to former National Football League greats Franco Harris and Lyndell Mitchell in the mid-1990s, the company's financial woes continued. The pair sold the company to the Philadelphia-based deli meat producer Dietz & Watson in 1999, which offered Parks' employees severance retirement packages instead of jobs, effectively ending one of Baltimore's most inspiring business legacies.

The Parks Legacy

From 1963 to 1969 Parks served on the Baltimore city council, pushing bills to open public accommodations to African Americans and easing bail requirements for people accused of crimes. His 1963 defeat of James H.

"Jack" Pollock's political machine was an impressive personal accomplishment and the implications of Parks' victory reverberated in Baltimore local politics for a long time afterward. Due to his tenure, the level of black influence in city politics increased, ultimately helping to make it possible for the elections of both William Donald Shaefer and Marvin Mandel as Maryland's governor.

Parks believed that it was his duty to share his influence and business acumen as well as to provide financial support to deserving initiatives. Accordingly, he served on the boards of W. R. Grace & Co., Magnavox, Warner Lambert, and First Pennsylvania Corporation. He was also the first African American appointee to serve as president of the Baltimore board of fire commissioners. Always supportive of efforts to extend racial uplift, Parks gave freely to the National Association for the Advancement of Colored People, United Negro College Fund, and Urban League. "We've gone beyond the time of protest marches against discrimination," remarked Parks. "I want to see that young people and other minorities of whatever race—including women—are not frustrated in their expectations of acceptance and advancement." In recognition of his lifelong achievements, Temple University awarded him an honorary doctor of laws degree in 1975.

In an awkward twist of fate, Henry Green Parks Jr. died of complications from Parkinson's disease on April 24, 1989 in Towson, Maryland, on the same day that the company broke ground for a new plant. He was survived by his two daughters, Grace C. Johnson of Baltimore and Cheryl V. Parks of Atlanta; a sister, Vera Wilson of Washington, D.C.; and three grandchildren. According to an article in *Newsday*, Parks once remarked, "I think that I proved that black businessmen not only can be successful, but that they can be successful on the same terms as anybody else." He proved that and so much more.

REFERENCES

Books

Pride, Marseille M. "Henry Green Parks Jr." In *American National Biography*. Vol. 17. Eds. John A. Garraty and Mark C. Carnes. New York: Oxford University Press, 1999.

Periodicals

Freeny, Lawrence. "For Henry Parks...More than Sausages." *New York Times*, 10 April 1977.

———. "Parks Sausages Is Back for More." *New York Times*, 20 December 1981.

"H. G. Parks, Sausage Firm Founder." *Newsday*, 26 April 1989.

Koshetz, Herbert. "'Top 100' Black Businesses Listed." *New York Times*, 13 June 1973.

Mullanet, Timothy J. "Founder's Vision Helped Firm to Overcome Adversity." *The Baltimore Sun*, 8 July 1995.

Narvaez, Alfonso A. "Henry Green Parks Jr. Dies at 72; Led Way for Black Entrepreneurs." *New York Times*, 26 April 1989.

Reed, Keith. "Wall Street Pioneer." *Baltimore Business Journal* 18 (21 July 2000): 21.

Crystal A. deGregory

James A. Parsons, Jr.
1900–1989

Inventor, scientist, educator

James A. Parsons Jr. was a scientist, inventor, and university professor, whose research with rust resistant metals and iron alloys is credited with leading to the development of stainless steel. During his lifetime, he received several patents pertaining to metals for his achievements. Parsons was highly respected among his peers in the scientific community and widely regarded as one of the nation's leading metallurgists.

James Albert Parsons Jr. was born in Dayton, Ohio on May 30, 1900. His father was a butler in the home of an executive at the Duriron Company, a metals manufacturing firm. When Parsons was young, his extraordinary ability in mathematics came to the attention of his father's employer. Parsons attended Steele High School in Dayton and after graduating in 1917, turned down an opportunity to attend the United States Naval Academy at Annapolis, Maryland. Instead, he took an interim job at the Duriron Company as foundry laborer and in 1918 began his undergraduate studies at the highly competitive Rensselaer Polytechnic Institute in Troy, New York. Duriron provided Parsons with summer employment while he was in college. The 1922 Rensselaer yearbook describes Parsons as hard working, ambitious, and popular with his peers. His love of music gave him the nickname "Jazz," and his dormitory room was a hub for aficionados like himself. His was also known for his love of smoking a big black pipe and being generous with sharing his tobacco with friends. The yearbook notes that Parsons spent a lot of his spare time at the pool and was such a skillful and enthusiastic swimmer that some of his classmates call him "Fish Parsons." He studied electro-chemistry and electro-metallurgy while majoring in electrical engineering and was a member of the AIAA club.

After Renesselaer, Parsons returned to his hometown and was hired by Duriron in 1922 for the job of analytical chemist, a position that was certainly more befitted to his credentials and intellect than foundry laborer. He worked with aluminum bronze and made a lasting contribution to the Aluminum Bronze Foundation. In 1927, Parsons won the prestigious Harmon Foundation award in science, the first of its kind, for the advances he made with rust-resistant or non-corrosive metals. His gold medal was presented by Orville Wright, one of Ohio's most famous sons, and Charles Kettering, an acclaimed engineer, gave the address for the event. During the early 1930s, Parsons continued to rise through the Duriron company ranks.

In 1935, Duriron had a reputation as the sole world manufacturer of specific kinds of non-corrosive metals. A 1939 article in the *Journal of Negro Education* mentions that the president of Duriron wrote Parsons a laudatory and appreciative letter praising his performance and his "valuable development work," as well as commending him for the patents the firm had been credited with because of Parsons' accomplishments. Citing Parsons' "executive ability," the letter indicated that he was not only superlative in his chosen field of electrical engineering but could hold his own in chemistry and metallurgy.

Between 1929 and 1949, Parsons received eight patents pertaining to the development and application of non-corrosive metals, which were credited to the Duriron Company. In 1929, he received Patent Number 1,728,360 on an iron alloy, and four years later he acquired Patent Number 1,819,479 for discovering a way to make silicon iron compounds. In 1934 and 1935, Parsons acquired Patents Number 1,912,103 and CA 348312 for inventing a process for treatment of silicon alloy castings. During the two-year span between 1938 and 1940, Parsons received three patents (2,134,670; 2,185,987; and 2,200,208) on corrosion-resisting ferrous alloy. Not one

to rest on his laurels, he achieved Patent Number 2,318,011 on a cementation process for treating metals in 1943. Parsons was awarded his final patent, Number 2,467,288, in 1949 for a nickel-based alloy.

According to Margaret Peters, who interviewed Stevens and has written extensively about notable black Ohioans, six of the patents were issued solely to Parsons, one was issued to Parsons and Earl Ryder (2,318,011), and another was credited to Parsons and Guy Baker. All of the patents were assigned to the Duriron Company. Parsons' scientific achievements did not go unnoticed by the African American academic community. Wilberforce University, a historically black Ohio university, awarded Parsons an honorary doctorate of science at its June 1941 commencement.

In the 1940s, Parsons became the chief metallurgist and a laboratory manager at the Duriron Company. Parsons' department, which was comprised of an entirely African American staff with chemical expertise, researched aluminum bronze and tested treating iron and steel to be resistant to the corrosiveness of acids, such as sulphuric and hydrochloric. Parsons was so successful in discovering new measures for testing and protecting metals from corrosion that by 1950 he was widely recognized as one of the nation's leading scientists, an expert on rust-resistant metals.

Begins Teaching Career

In 1951 or 1952, Parsons retired from Duriron and made a transition from the corporate arena to academe. During the 1952-53 school year he accepted a faculty position in the Department of Metallurgy at Tennessee Agricultural & Industrial University in Nashville, Tennessee, now known as Tennessee State University. During his thirteen years at the institution, Parsons served as chairman of the Department of Metallurgy and as acting dean of the College of Engineering. He resigned from the university during the 1966-67 school term. In an interview with the author, Professor Yvonne Y. Clark, a junior faculty member in the Metallurgy Department during the time of Parsons' tenure, praised him as a "brilliant man." His daughter, Ann Parsons Shipp, said in a letter to Homer Wheaton that he "thoroughly enjoyed his commitment to his students" and he cherished the time he spent training African American students to become engineers.

After leaving Tennessee Agricultural & Industrial University, Parsons returned to his native Ohio. He later came out of retirement: he became an adjunct professor at Ohio State University where he taught until 1971 and also an instructor at the Garfield Skills Training Center. In fact, he continued to teach until he was 87. He was a member of Trinity United Presbyterian Church, Alpha Phi Alpha fraternity, and the Sigma Pi Phi fraternity Boulé. The highly selective Sigma Pi Phi is the oldest black fraternity in the United States. At the time of his death, on March 4, 1989, Parsons had been married to his wife, Blanche, for sixty-one years and the couple had two daughters and one son.

James A. Parsons was dedicated to excellence. His patents are a testament to his abilities to achieve beyond the ordinary in his chosen field. His career as a college professor shows his willingness to share his knowledge and skills with a future generation of engineers, scientists, and inventors.

REFERENCES

Books

Brawley, Benjamin. *Negro Builders and Heroes*. Chapel Hill, N.C: University of North Carolina Press, 1937.

Foster, Vera Chandler. *Negro Year Book: A Review of Events Affecting Negro Life, 1941-1946*. Tuskegee, Ala.: Dept. of Records and Research, Tuskegee Institute, 1947.

Henry, Deane, ed. *The 1922 Transit: Yearbook of Rensselaer Polytechnic Institute*. Pittsfield, Mass.: Eagle PTG & BDG. Co., 1922.

Peters, Margaret. *Dayton's African American Heritage: A Pictorial History*. Virginia Beach, Va.: Donning Company, 1975.

Sammons, Vivian Ovelton. *Blacks in Science and Medicine*. New York: Hemisphere Publishing Corporation, 1990.

Sluby, Patricia Carter. *The Inventive Spirit of African Americans: Patented Ingenuity*. Westport, Conn.: Praeger, 2004.

The Tennessean: The Stage Is Set at Tennessee A & I University. Nashville: Bureau of Public Relations in cooperation with Department of Art, 1953.

Periodicals

Batz, Bob. "Area Black History: A Tale of Courage and Struggle." *Dayton Daily News*, 22 February 1994.

"Dr. James A. Parsons, Jr.: Inventor and Scientist (b. 1900)." *Dayton Daily News*, 26 February 2004.

Downing, Lewis K. "The Negro in the Professions of Engineering and Architecture." *Journal of Negro Education* 4 (January 1950): 135-149.

Drew, Charles Richard. "Negro Scholars in Scientific Research." *Journal of Negro History* 35 (April 1950): 135-49.

Haynes, George Edmund. "Negro Technicians in American Progress." *Journal of Negro Education* 8 (January 1939): 50-57.

Hundley, Wendy. "Matriarch of Black History Writing Book." *Dayton Daily News*, 5 February 1995.

"Migration to Dayton: The Story of Blacks in Dayton Dates Back to the City's Very Beginning." *Dayton Daily News*, 2 February 1996.

"Negro Scientists." *Ebony* (September 1950): 15-20.

Other

Clark, Yvonne Y. Interview by author. 26 January 2005.

Email from Margaret Peters to Jonas Bender and Jacqueline Brown. 31 January 2005.

Letter from Ann Parsons Shipp to Homer Wheaton. 3 February 2005.

Glenda M. Alvin

James Benton Parsons
1911–1993

Judge

Modest, hardworking James Benton Parsons was the first African American appointed for life as an Article III judge. His 1961 appointment marked a pivotal point for African Americans involved in the legal system. Through his dedication and perseverance, Parsons prospered in various roles: he graduated from high school as valedictorian, worked as a teacher, and ultimately served as a judge.

Parsons was born August 13, 1911 in Kansas City, Missouri, the youngest of four children. His father was an evangelistic minister and his mother a schoolteacher. Parsons moved to Decatur, Illinois as a young child. As a teenager, Parsons dreamed of becoming an attorney; however, it was a dream which would take many years to realize. Parsons worked his way through Millikin University as a composing room helper at the Decatur *Herald Review*. Parsons earned a B.A. in music in 1934. Parsons could not afford law school, so he joined the faculty of Lincoln University in Jefferson City, Missouri where he taught music and political science. Parsons served as acting head of Lincoln University's Music Department from 1938 to 1940. He also continued his education, earning a B.A. in political science from the University of Washington (Saint Louis) in 1940. Parsons then accepted a job with the Greensboro, North Carolina public school system as supervisor of instrumental music for the black schools.

In 1942, Parsons enlisted in the United States Navy. He served as a bandmaster from 1942 to 1945. In addition he completed a tour of duty in the Pacific. Before 1942, African Americans were not able to serve in any area of the navy other than as mess attendants. In 1946, Parsons left the navy using the G.I. Bill to earn an M.A. in political science from the University of Chicago. His only son was born in 1947. Parsons belonged to several fraternities, including Kappa Alpha Psi as an undergraduate and Sigma Pi Phi as a graduate student. He was also

James Benton Parsons

Chronology

1911	Born in Kansas City, Missouri on August 13
1934	Earns B.A. in music from Millikin University
1934	Begins teaching music and political science at Lincoln University in Jefferson, Missouri
1940	Earns B.A. in political science from George Washington University
1942	Serves in U.S. Naval Reserves
1946	Earns M.A. in political science from the University of Chicago
1947	Son Hans-Dieter Parsons born
1949	Earns J.D. from the University of Chicago Law School; begins private practice with Gassaway, Crosson, Turner & Parsons
1949-51	Serves as assistant corporation counsel in Chicago
1951-60	Serves as assistant U.S. attorney for the northern district of Illinois
1952	Marries Amy Margaret Maxwell
1961	Appointed judge for the Superior Court of Cook County, Illinois; begins Federal Judicial Service for the U.S. District Court, northern district of Illinois
1975	Becomes chief judge for the U.S. District Court, northern district of Illinois
1981	Assumes senior status for the U.S. District Court, northern district of Illinois
1992	Retires as chief judge emeritus
1993	Dies in Chicago, Illinois on June 19
1996	James B. Parsons ceremonial courtroom in Chicago's Dirksen Federal Building is dedicated

a member of the Phi Beta Phi Honor Society and an honorary member of Phi Alpha Delta law fraternity. In 1949, at the age of 38, Parsons became an attorney upon receiving his law degree from the University of Chicago.

Law and the Judicial System

Parsons began his legal career in private practice. In addition, from 1949 to 1950 he taught constitutional law at John Marshall Law School. Parsons served as assistant corporate counsel for the city of Chicago from 1949 until 1951, and his hard work paid off: Parsons was appointed assistant U.S. district attorney for northern Illinois in 1951. With his education complete and a bright future, Parsons was able to focus on his personal life. In 1952, he married Amy Margaret Maxwell. They remained married until her death in 1967. Parsons served as assistant U.S. district attorney until 1960 when he was elected to the office of Cook County Superior Court judge. Almost immediately after assuming the Superior Court judgeship, Parsons was handed the Summerdale police conspiracy case. Chicago had long been known for political and police corruption. But the Summerdale scandal rocked the city when the public discovered that for over one year eight police officers had worked with a burglar named Richard Morrison to rob north-side retail stores. Most of the officers received sentences from two to five

years. The Summerdale scandal resulted in the reorganization of the Chicago police department.

Early one Sunday morning in August 1961, Parsons received a phone call from President John F. Kennedy stating that he was naming Parsons as the first African American U.S. district court judge. Parsons was to take the seat of Judge Philip Leo Sullivan who had died in June 1960 after twenty-six years on the bench. While Parsons was not the first African American appointed as a federal judge, he was the first to receive life tenure. Judges Irvin C. Mollison, William Henry Hastie, and Scovel Richardson were appointed to judgeships prior to Parsons, but they received fixed term appointments. Parsons served as a U.S. district court judge for over thirty years, progressing to chief judge of the court in 1975, then to senior judge in 1981, and finally to chief judge emeritus in 1992 when he retired.

Parsons made headlines for his outspokenness, ethics, humility, and selflessness. He was scrutinized inside and outside court. In 1969, Parsons caused a tremendous stir when he gave an interview to the *New York Times* in which he stated that African Americans should not get involved in "white man's crimes" such as counterfeiting, mail fraud, embezzling, and other similar crimes which require a level of skill which most African Americans did not possess given their limited career opportunities especially in those professions which required a high degree of technical skill.

In his early years as a U.S. district court judge, Parsons was accused of being soft on crime when he gave a bank president who had embezzled $58,000 a ninety-day jail term. In 1971, as reported by Gary Green in *Federal Probation*, Parsons made legal history when he placed the Atlantic Richfield Company on probation "so that he could monitor the company's progress in complying with his order to develop an oil spill response program." Parsons ruled in 1985 that United Airlines could continue to employ flight attendants who were hired during the pilot's strike, which caused a tremendous stir, also. As quoted by James Warren in the *Chicago Sun-Times*, Parson stated that United Airlines "must pay full fringe benefits including reinstatement of group insurance and medical benefits to all flight attendants who refused to cross the pilots' picket lines." United was also required to give "immediate seniority accrual to the flight attendants, even if they did not return to work immediately." In November 1988, Parsons overturned an appeals court ruling against the display of religious symbols on public property. In his decision, Parsons argued that the previous court's ruling was a violation of the First Amendment which guarantees freedom of speec,h not a violation of the separation of church and state. According to Adrienne Drell, Parsons further stated, "The Public Building Commissions opposition to the créche and menorah is discrimination in its rankest form. It goes against the very grain of Americanism to see discrimination against anyone particularly against people because of their religion." Another key decision made by Parsons was his upholding the city of Chicago's Tenants Bill of Rights in 1987. He also drew attention for the role he played in the 1970 air traffic controllers' strike.

Recognition of Service

Parsons received many honors for his work as a judge. In 1967, the entire state of Illinois observed James B. Parsons Day. In addition, an elementary school in Decatur, Illinois was named after him that same year. In 1975, he was unanimously elected by the judges of the Seventh Circuit Court to represent them at the Judicial Conference of the United States. He also served for six years on the Judicial Conferences' Committee on Probation and Sentencing Seminars. In 1981, he received a citation for outstanding service as a chief judge of the district court from the Chicago Bar Association. In 1984, he received "The Outstanding Service Award" from Chicago University. Parsons served for three years as the vice chairman of the Chicago Commission on Police and Community Relations and for four years on the Council of Criminal Law Section of the American Bar Association. Parsons was cited by Operation PUSH (People United to Serve Humanity) for a quarter century of service as the first black Article III judge. Parsons was hon-

ored several times by *Ebony* magazine; in 1991 he was named one of the 100 Most Influential Blacks in America. Parsons also received academic recognition for his work. He received honorary degrees from Lincoln University, Millikin University, and De Paul University Law School. The honorary degrees included a Doctor of Letters and Doctor of Laws.

When Parsons retired in 1992, several judges, former law clerks, and attorneys decided to have a dinner in his honor. Parsons vetoed the idea, stating instead that it should be a celebration of all African American Title III judges. It became a weekend-long event called "Just the Beginning," which evolved into a foundation whose goals include education of the public about the role of African Americans in the judicial system as well as scholarships to promising law students. Parsons donated $35,000 to the scholarship fund which bears his name. Even after Parsons retired from trial work, he did not completely give up his judicial duties; he continued to swear in new United States citizens and other similar duties.

Parsons not only provided leadership in a professional capacity but was an active member of the community. Parsons was a member for twenty-eight years of the Chicago-area Council for the Boy Scouts of America as well as nine years on the Boy Scouts' National Advisory Council. Parsons served for almost twenty years on the Executive Board of the Citizenship Council of Metropolitan Chicago. He served as a member of the advisory board of the Illinois Masonic Hospital for fourteen years. Parsons served for six years as a member of the Illinois Commission on Education for Law and Justice of the State Board of Education. Parsons served eight years on the board of directors of Chicago's Harvard-St. George School and one term on the President's Council of St. Ignatius College Preparatory School. Parsons continued to serve on various committees at the University of Illinois, University of Chicago Law School, and Loyola University Law School. During the early 1960s Parsons helped found the Chicago Conference on Religion and Race which worked with interfaith groups to form housing information centers, to hold employment training programs, and to help people find work.

Parsons died after a prolonged illness on June 19, 1993. He was 81 years old. He was survived by his son, Hans-Dieter Parsons, a grandson, and one sibling, his sister Amy Margaret Maxwell. The legacy left by Parsons was such that three years after his death the ceremonial court room in Chicago's Dirksen Courthouse was named in his memory.

REFERENCES

Periodicals

Benson, Christopher. "The Super Summit of Black Federal Judges." *Ebony* 48 (December 1992): 110-13.

Drell, Adrienne. "City Get O.K. for a Créche, Menorah." *Chicago Sun-Times*, 20 June 1993.

Green, Gary S. "Organizational Probation under the Federal Sentencing Guidelines." *Federal Probation*, December 1988.

Johnson, Mary A. "James Parsons Dies 1st Black Federal Judge." *Chicago Sun-Times*, 20 June 1993.

Pace, Eric. "James Parsons, 81, A Black Trailblazer as a Federal Judge." *New York Times*, 22 June 1993.

Rossi, Rosalind. "1st Black U.S. District Judge Retiring." *Chicago Sun-Times*, 13 June 1992.

Warren, James. "United Wins on New Attendants Judge Won't Bar Employment of Strike Breakers." *Chicago Sun-Tribune*, 28 June 1985.

Online

"History of Just the Beginning Foundation." *Just the Beginning Foundation*. http://www.jtbf.org/jtbfhistory.htm. (Accessed 3 December 2004).

"James Benton Parsons." *Just the Beginning Foundation*. http://www.jtbf.org/five_firsts/Parsons_j/htm. (Accessed 3 December 2004).

"James Parson, an Influential Judge!" *The African American Registry*. http://www.aaregistry.com/african_american_history/1791/James_Parsons_an_influential_judge. (Accessed 3 December 2004).

Anne K. Driscoll

Richard Parsons

Richard Parsons
1948–

Corporate executive

Richard Dean Parsons, CEO and president of the AOL-Time Warner Corporation, emerged through academic and corporate circles to become one of the most successful African Americans in corporate America.

Parsons was born in the economically disadvantaged Bedford-Stuyvesant neighborhood of Brooklyn, New York on April 14, 1948 to Lorenzo Locklair, an airline technician (who installed and repaired electronic navigation systems for the Sperry Rand Company), and Isabelle Judd Parsons (a homemaker). He was raised in the rough neighborhood of Jamaica, New York, a city in Queens County. Parsons was a bright child with a gift for charming people by telling entertaining stories.

Parson changed his attitude dramatically (from negative to positive) and reached a turning point when he met and later married Laura Ann Bush, a child psychologist,

on August 30, 1968. To this union three children were born (Gregory, Leslie, and Rebecca). Parsons credits his father with teaching him to concentrate on achievement rather than dwell on race. Parsons' grandfather, Judd, was a groundskeeper on Pocantico, part of the Rockefeller estate, long before Parsons became a protégé of Nelson Rockefeller. Parsons later lived in a guesthouse on the estate.

Excels in Academics

Parsons skipped two grades and graduated from high school at the age of sixteen. He received a B.A. in history from the University of Hawaii in 1968. He was involved in sports at the University of Hawaii; the six-foot-four-inch Parsons played basketball, was the social chairman of his fraternity, but was unenthusiastic about academics. Parsons worked at various odd jobs, including in a parking garage and gas company to support himself while at the University of Hawaii. He received a juris doctorate from the Union University, University of Albany Law School in 1971. He paid his law school expenses by working as a part time janitor and later as an aide in the New York State Assembly. He graduated at the age of twenty-three, number one of more than 100 students and received the highest score among 3,600 lawyers in 1971 who took the state bar exam.

Chronology

1948	Born in the Bedford-Stuyvesant neighborhood in Brooklyn, New York on April 14
1968	Earns a B.A. from University of Hawaii
1971	Graduates from Albany Law School
1974	Begins career with New York governor Nelson Rockefeller's legal staff
1977	Joins firm of Patterson, Belknap, Webb & Tyler
1979	Becomes partner with Patterson, Belknap, Webb & Tyler
1988	Appointed chief operating officer of Dime Savings Bank
1990	Receives honorary LL.D. from Adelphi University
1991	Becomes chairman and CEO; receives honorary LL.D. from Medgar-Evers College
1995	Becomes Time Warner president
2000	Guides the merger of Time Warner with America Online (AOL)
2001	Replaces Gerald Levin as CEO of the AOL-Time Warner Corporation
2003	Awarded honorary doctor of humane letters by the Board of Regents of the University of Hawaii

Career Develops

Parsons began his career as a member of New York governor Nelson Rockefeller's legal staff where he served when Rockefeller became vice president of the United States under President Gerald Ford in 1974. He served as assistant counsel to Governor Rockefeller from 1971 to 1974 and was called to the New York State bar in 1972.

Under President Gerald Ford, Parsons became a senior White House aide and served as a general counsel and an associate director of the Domestic Council. Parsons joined the Domestic Council staff in March 1975, serving both as legal council and as an associate director. As counsel to the Domestic Council, he worked closely with the Counsel to the President in providing legal guidance in the formulation of domestic policy.

As associate director, Parsons succeeded Geoffrey Shepard in handling general government, which included justice, treasury, commerce, the postal service, civil rights, and drugs. In the May 1975 reorganization, his area of responsibility was divided, and Parsons became associate director for justice, crime, civil rights, and communications (communications was transferred to F. Lynn May in January of 1976). In April 1976 when Kathleen Ryan left the Domestic Council, responsibility for consumer affairs was given to Parsons' office. Parsons served with the Domestic Council until the end of the Ford administration and returned to New York to work for Governor Nelson Rockefeller.

From March 1975 to January 1976, Parsons was assisted in his duties by Lyn May, who had worked for Geoffrey Shepard. Dawn Bennett-Alexander assisted Parsons from March 1976 until the end of the administra-tion. Kathleen Ryan served as an assistant to Parsons for a few weeks after she joined the Domestic Council in April, 1975.

Parsons and his staff were responsible for providing advice to the president and formulating domestic policy in the areas of affirmative action, busing, civil rights, communication, consumer affairs, crime, drugs, illegal aliens, Indians, justice, postal service, Puerto Rico, privacy, regulatory reform, sex discrimination, and voting rights.

Becomes CEO of Dime Savings Bank

Parsons was urged by Harry Albright Jr. to become the chief operating officer of the Dime Savings Bank in 1988 with a salary of $525,000 annually. Harry Albright Jr., Rockefeller's executive assistant in Albany, New York and previous chairman of the Dime Savings Bank, cited Parsons as a great member of Rockefeller's staff and one who has great judgment and leadership skills. Parsons was left in control of a bank that was apparently dying. The Dimes' nonperforming assets were nearly 11 percent of the total assets by year 1991 in addition to $1 billion in bad debt. The bank suffered many losses due to New York City real estate devaluation in the 1980s and during the previous year had lost $92.3 million. Parsons dealt with unhappy regulators. He also earned staff respect at Dime with his fair treatment of personnel. In a *Black Enterprise* article, Fonda Marie Lloyd and Mark Lowery stated that "colleagues say Parsons' management style helped smooth painful layoffs (two thousand of the four thousand employees) that he had to make." They credit him with keeping employees informed every step of the way, producing videos for employee distribution. He became the first African American male to manage a financial institution of Dime's size and reduce the bank's debt from $1 billion to $335 million.

Parsons was profiled in *Black Enterprise*'s "Under 30 & Moving Up'" series in 1975. In 1977 deputy attorney general Harold R. Tyler Jr. requested Parsons to come aboard at Patterson, Belknap, Webb, & Tyler where he became a partner in two years, a move that usually demands seven years. During his eleven years with the firm he was successful in both corporate law and civil litigation.

Parsons chose to support Rudolph Giuliani in the New York City mayoral race instead of Democrat black mayor David Dinkins. In a *Black Enterprise* article, he openly rejected the Democrats' philosophy of taking from one group to give to another. In contrast, he embraced the Rockefeller Republicans' philosophy of equipping a group with skills so they can achieve what they need on their own. Parsons was chosen by Mayor Giuliani to head the Transition Council and later in 1993 to be the deputy mayor for economic development. Parsons refused the position but consented to work as the Economic Development Corporation chairperson.

Parsons became a board member for Time Warner, Inc., Phillip Morris, Tristar Pictures, Harvard University, and the Metropolitan Museum of Art. As a result of his involvement with Time Warner, he developed close ties with Robert W. Morgado, the chairman of the Warner Music Group, and Michael J. Fuchs, chairman of HBO.In the fall of 1994, Parsons was requested by Gerald M. Levin to become the president of Time Warner. On October 1, 1995, Parsons was appointed president of Time Warner with a salary of several million dollars per year. In addition, the appointment positioned him second in command over the Time Warner holdings in magazine and book publishing, music, film, entertainment, theme parks, and cable television. He was the first black president and one of the highest-ranking blacks in corporate America. Parsons' responsibilities at Time Warner included corporate finance and legal affairs activities and membership on the board of directors as well as the boards of TriStar Pictures and the Cable Group, American Television, and Communication (now Time Warner Cable).

Merges Time Warner with America Online

In 2000, Parsons guided the merger of Time Warner with America Online (AOL). An article in *Business Week Online* stated that after accepting the Time Warner presidency, "Parsons gradually made himself indispensable to Time Warner by taking on tough assignments that the increasingly insular Levin could not do himself." On May 16, 2001, Parsons replaced Gerald Levin as CEO of the AOL-Time Warner Corporation.

In 2001, President George W. Bush appointed Parsons along with former U.S. senator Daniel Moynihan to a commission to strengthen Social Security Program changes. Parsons also served as chairman of the Apollo Theater Foundation, Inc. and sat on the boards of several arts, educational, and commercial organizations, including the Metropolitan Museum of Art, Citigroup, and Esteé Lauder, Inc. Parsons served as trustee of numerous Rockefeller entities, including one that holds stock in all of the family businesses.

In 2003 the University of Hawaii awarded Parsons the honorary doctor of humane letters degree. This degree is awarded by the Board of Regents to individuals distinguished by their national or international reputation or accomplishments in scholarship, public service, profession, industry, or other areas. Parsons credits his experiences at the University of Hawaii as preparation for his future in corporate America.

Parsons and his wife Laura own a vineyard in Montalcino, Italy. In his spare time he enjoys shooting pool and listening to music. Errol Garner and Miles Davis are his favorite musicians. In a *Black Enterprise* article Parsons stated: "What motivates me is a sense of accountability to people who are important in my life." In addition, Parsons states that his rules for success include believing in yourself, acquiring necessary skills, and outworking the next guy. "That's what makes you different from your competition," he maintains.

REFERENCES

Books

Bell, Gregory S., "Richard Dean Parsons." In *African American Lives*. Ed. Henry Louis Gates Jr. New York: Oxford University Press, 2004.

Decker, Ed. "Richard Dean Parsons." In *Contemporary Black Biography*. Vol. 11. Eds. L. Mpho Mabunda and Shirelle Phelps. Detroit, Mich.: Gale Research, 1996.

Smith, Jessie Carney, ed. *Black Firsts*. Farmington Hills, Mich.: Thomson Gale, 2003.

Periodicals

Landler, Mark "Watch Your Back, Mr. Parsons" *Business Week* (14 November 1994): 38-39.

Lloyd, Fonda Marie, and Mark Lowery. "The Man Behind the Merger." *Black Enterprise*, 25 (October 1994): 69-76.

Online

"Can Dick Parsons Rescue AOL Time Warner?" *Business Week Online*. http://www.buisnessweek.com/magazine/content/03_20/b3833001_m2001.htm (Accessed 2 December 2005).

"Honorary Degrees Conferred by the University of Hawaii." *University of Hawaii System*. http://www.hawaii.edu/offices/bor/honorary/php?person=RP (Accessed 2 December 2005).

Richard D. Parsons, Counsel and Associate Director for Justice, Civil Rights, Drugs and Consumer Affairs: Files, 1974-77. http://www.ford.utexas.edu/library/GUIDES/Finding%20Aids/Parsons,%20Richard%20%20Files... (Accessed 7 December 2005).

Prudence White Bryant

Deval Patrick
1956–

Lawyer, corporate executive

Deval Laurdine Patrick was raised by his mother and grandparents in a poverty-stricken neighborhood on Chicago's South Side. His father, a saxophone player, left the family when Patrick and his sister were still very young. Patrick attended the Mary C. Terrell School in the 1960s. Because the school was located in a rough neighborhood bordering a housing project, each student was required to slide a pass under the door to gain entry. Patrick's teachers and counselors quickly realized his academic potential and recommended him for the scholarship program, A Better Chance. In 1970, he received a scholarship to prestigious Milton Academy. The school provided an environment that young Patrick had never before experienced. He bloomed academically, intellectually, and socially. An English teacher took him on trips with his family. The Milton experience changed Patrick's entire perspective on life and propelled him into a successful career in civil rights and corporate litigation.

Patrick was the first in his family to go to college. Accepted to five Ivy League colleges, he chose Harvard without hesitation. He majored in English and American literature and graduated cum laude from Harvard in 1978. His stellar academic performance won him a Rockefeller fellowship for a year's travel and study abroad. Patrick chose to work in the Sudan, as he wanted to learn more about the geography, cultures, and languages of Africa. In Khartoum, he received his acceptance letter to Harvard Law School. At Harvard he continued to excel academically. He worked for the school's legal clinic and was a member of the winning team in the Moot Court competition. He took the best speaker award.

After his graduation from law school, he was given a coveted clerkship with Stephen Reinhardt, a federal judge, U.S. Court of Appeals, 11th Circuit, Los Angeles. In 1983 Patrick married Diane Bemus and moved to New York City to work as a staff attorney for the NAACP's Legal Defense and Educational Fund. He wanted to specialize in voting rights cases but instead was assigned to litigate cases dealing primarily with capital punishment.

He traveled the country, mostly the Deep South, handling appeals for death penalty cases. Patrick and Lani Guinier, another NAACP lawyer, were successful in challenging a number of capital punishment cases using the racial discrimination defense. They also won some high-profile voter registration cases, most notably one against Bill Clinton when he was governor of Arkansas.

In 1986 Patrick had started a family and was ready to curtail his excessive traveling. He was hired at Hill & Barlow in Boston where he joined another Harvard graduate Reginald Lindsay, Hill & Barlow's first black partner. Patrick became a partner in 1990. He represented black defendants who were pressured into taking high interest home improvement loans through the use of excessive and overbearing sales tactics. Patrick's efforts resulted in initiatives to improve financial lending to low-income, black communities in Boston. He was known for accepting cases bypassed by the legal community. People praised him for advocating fair and equitable outcomes in his cases.

Becomes Civil Rights Advocate

Patrick had garnered enough public mention and name recognition to be considered for public office in Massachusetts. In 1994, he was nominated to be the Justice Department's assistant attorney general for civil rights. President Clinton, stinging from previous failed attempts to fill the position, wanted a candidate with a moderate stance on civil rights issues that was unlikely to stir controversy. Patrick's writings and previous caseload provided little evidence that could be used against his confirmation. He sailed though the Judiciary Committee's confirmation hearings with nearly unanimous confirmation. Patrick's supporters believed that his leadership would restore credibility to the department and boost the morale of its legal staff. He assumed his new responsibilities with an emotionally stirring speech, promising to move the nation back to a consensus on civil rights.

Expectations were that Patrick, as the nation's civil rights advocate, would concentrate heavily on enforcement in the areas of voting and civil rights. Patrick believed in strong and aggressive action tempered with compassion and fairness. Although he strongly pushed enforcement cases on many fronts, he did not shy away from more contentious and controversial cases involving racial preferences; in fact, he aggressively prosecuted them. His enforcement actions encompassed a wide spectrum of discrimination cases covering public accommodations, zoning, lending, employment, housing, and voting rights. Patrick's ruling in one of his first cases resulted in an outcry from bankers. In an attempt to battle lending bias, he forced the Chevy Chase Federal Savings Bank to spend $11 million to build branches and dispense low-interest loans in black neighborhoods. Bankers disagreed with Patrick's interpretation of the intent of the law particularly since there had been no previous discrimination complaints against the bank. Patrick argued that although the bank gave fair treatment to individual loan applicants, its service to the entire black community was inadequate. The case proved that Patrick was not deterred by the industry's complaints and was well able to negotiate an agreeable compromise. His efforts ended amicably, and his skills in consensus building were highly praised.

Another case that had garnered strong support from the previous administration of George H. Bush presented a more formidable challenge for Patrick. The case involved a white teacher who had been fired in 1989 by the school board in Piscataway, New Jersey. When cutting staff from its declining business program, the school board had been forced to make a difficult choice between a black and a white teacher with equal qualifications and seniority. Patrick supported the school board's decision to retain the black teacher. In essence, he reversed the EEOC decision on the case made during the Bush administration. When conservative Republican critics protested, Patrick argued that employers should be free to use affirmative action goals in termination decisions when candidates held equal qualifications. His critics viewed the case as a radical policy shift towards quotas. Both Patrick and President Clinton were opposed to quotas, but Patrick supported the more traditional approach of giving preference to women and other minorities. In the 1992 final ruling on the case, the judge found that the school board had violated the law. The fired teacher was awarded lost wages with interest plus compensation for pain and humiliation.

The Piscataway case generated talk of abolishing all affirmative action programs. President Clinton himself appeared to be shifting from race and gender-based programs towards programs based on economic need. Patrick refused to let his frustration interfere with his commitment to equality. He forged on with vigorous enforcement actions, including a racial discrimination case against the Denny's restaurant chain that ended with a settlement of $54 million against the company. Patrick was also confronted with the rash burnings of black churches in the South and bursts of violence at abortion clinics. However strained the situation was, Patrick did not seem deterred by political ramifications or repercussions and continued to steadily oppose any policies that would impose limits on affirmative action.

In 1997, Patrick resigned his position with the Justice Department. He had been commuting to Washington from his home in Milton and wanted more time with his family. In addition he cited the financial limitations of federal government employment. He was ready for new challenges and experiences and was looking for a position that would offer him the opportunity to practice law on a national level. Boston's elite law firm, Day, Berry, & Howard made him an offer that matched his expectations. He was hired as a full partner with the opportunity to continue active participation in public affairs. His responsibilities involved litigating and advising companies on disability, fair lending, and other civil rights employment issues. Patrick was in such high demand for consultation on diversity that instead of a lighter schedule, he was traveling as much as before. In addition to his duties at the law office, he was teaching at Harvard University and Boston College. He was also named a distinguished visiting professor at Stanford University where he taught a civil rights course.

Enters Boardroom of Multinational Corporations

In December 1998, Patrick was named vice-president and general counsel at Texaco Inc. At 42 years of age, he became the company's first black vice-president. In mid-1997, while still a partner at Day, Berry, & Howard, Patrick had consented to chair Texaco's independent Equality and Fairness Task Force on diversity. The seven-member task force was responsible for reviewing and overseeing the company's hiring and employment practices. It was created by court order as part of the settlement in a racial discrimination lawsuit filed by the company's black employees. In its first evaluation report, the task force approved of the company's internal efforts to address race relations and improve career mobility for its minority employees. Patrick resigned from the task force, not wanting to compromise the group's independence. Some questioned the appointment; others saw it as a sign that Texaco was sincere in its diversity efforts. Patrick served for two years at Texaco as vice-president, general counsel, and executive council member.

Coca-Cola hired Patrick away from Texaco in February 2001. He was appointed as general counsel to settle a class action, racial discrimination lawsuit filed against Coke by its black employees. With his new position, Patrick became the company's highest-ranking black executive. In 2004, a series of resignations cascaded down the executive ladder at the Atlanta-based soft drink company. Patrick was among the casualties. He resigned days before his third anniversary as executive vice-president, general counsel, and secretary. Although speculations surfaced that Patrick was forced out because the company was unhappy with his handling of its legal troubles, he said he resigned voluntarily for personal and professional reasons. He had revamped Coke's diversity program but along the way encountered a number of challenging cases. One was a whistleblower suit, filed in 2003, that resulted in Coke's admission of accounting mistakes. The case precipitated investigations by the U.S. attorney's office in Atlanta and the Securities and Exchange Commission. In another suit, investors alleged that Coke committed fraud in Japan by rigging marketing tests to inflate sales. Patrick departed in December 2004 with a generous severance package.

Future Role in Politics

Patrick's star rose steadily through prominent corporate management positions. His name was included on the list of the nation's highest-paid lawyers and top-ranking African American executives. Despite his increasing responsibilities, he continued in an advisory and consulting role to numerous boards and organizations. He served on the board at Coca-Cola, Reebok, and other large corporations. He was a trustee at Milton Academy. In 1991 Patrick was appointed as vice-chairman and member of the Massachusetts Judicial Nominating Council Executive Committee. The council recruited, screened, and recommended candidates for judgeships to the Republican governor of Massachusetts, William F. Weld. He visited South Africa in 1997 to assist the government in drafting civil rights legislation.

Patrick dabbled in politics but stayed mostly on the sidelines. In 1997, the attorney general of Massachusetts, Scott Harshbarger, named Patrick as the general chairman of his campaign in the race for governor. Many expected that if Harshbarger won, Patrick would be named to his cabinet. Failing that, he would at some point run for political office. Patrick took the leap of faith in 2005 when he announced that he was testing the waters for a potential run in the Massachusetts governors' race. Patrick certainly has plenty of what it takes to win a campaign: money and brains. His future in politics may be secure.

REFERENCES

Books

Strumolo, Amy Loerch. "Deval Patrick." *Contemporary Black Biography: Profiles from the International Black Community*. Ed. Shirelle Phelps, Detroit: Gale Research, 1996.

Periodicals

Bolick, Clint. "Rule of Law: Coronation of a Quota King at Justice." *Wall Street Journal*, 31 August 1994.

Caplan, Lincoln. "Serenely against the Tide." *U.S. News & World Report* 121 (25 November 996): 45.

———. "A Civil Rights Tug of War". *Newsweek* 125 (13 February 1995): 34.

George, Grace. "Coke Loses Top Black Executive and General Counsel."*Black Enterprise* 35 (August 2004): 28.

Gest, Ted. "The Man in the Line of Fire."*U.S. News & World Report* 116 (14 February 1994): 26-27.

Haygood, Will. "Partners in Power: Deval Patrick and Reginald Lindsay Took Different Paths from Poverty to a Top Boston Law Firm." *The Boston Globe*, 23 September 1993.

Moore, W. John. "Legal Affairs: Collision Course." *National Journal* 26 (3 December 1994): 2830-34.

Phillips, Frank. "Ex-Rights Enforcer Eyes Governorship; Some Say He Could Energize Democrats."*Boston Globe* 17 January, 2005.

Shao, Maria. "Patrick Lands with Day Berry." *Boston Globe*, 31 January 1997.

Yang, Catherine. "The Education of Deval Patrick." *Business Week* (12 September 2003): 92-93.

Other

Patrick, Deval. *Addresses*. Washington, D.C.: U.S. Department of Justice, 2001.

Janette Prescod

Thomas Paul
1773–1831

Minister, missionary

Thomas Paul served as a pioneer in the organization and development of the independent African American church. Paul was in the forefront of this movement in the North, and reached out to other congregations who sought similar goals. His missionary work and his desire to improve the conditions of the African American community took him to congregations as far away as Haiti. He opened a way for religious freedom for Boston's black Baptists and the development of the Abyssinian Baptist Church in New York. Paul used his eloquence as a preacher and teacher of the Gospel to influence the opinions of white congregations in the North and to effect religious freedom for all African Americans.

Thomas Paul was born on September 3, 1773, in Exeter, New Hampshire. The names of his parents and their role in the community are not known. In 1789, at the age of sixteen, Paul converted and was then baptized by the Reverend Mr. Locke, and he began preaching at the age of twenty-eight. He traveled and preached for three years before settling down. In 1804 he made Boston, Massachusetts his home. A year later on May 1, 1805, Paul was ordained at Nottingham West, New Hampshire, and during the same year he married Catherine Waterhouse. The couple had three children: Susan, Anne Catherine, and Thomas Jr. Catherine Paul and the three Paul offspring became teachers; Susan Paul became an abolitionist and also wrote the first black biography published in the United States.

Chronology

1773   Born in Exeter, New Hampshire on September 3

1789   Converts and is baptized by Reverend Mr. Locke

1805   Ordained at Nottingham West, New Hampshire on May 1; marries Catherine Waterhouse

1806   Installed as pastor of independent African American church, First African Church, Boston, Massachusetts, on December 2

1808   Organizes independent black church in New York, later known as the Abyssinian Baptist Church

1823   Performs missionary work in Haiti

1829   Resigns from First African Church due to poor health

1831   Dies in Boston, Massachusetts on April 13

Organizes Independent Black Churches in Boston and New York

As a clergy in Boston, Paul recognized that African American worshipers had limited participation in church matters. White Baptist churches seated their African American parishioners in the galleries and did not allow them to vote on church affairs. In response to this racism, Paul conducted nondenominational gatherings in Franklin Hall on Nassau Street and in historic Faneuil Hall. These meetings set the foundation for the formation of the first independent African American Baptist church in Boston. On August 8, 1805, twenty-four African American members met in Master Vinal's schoolhouse and formed the congregation known as the First African Church. The white church members' response to the separation of African American members was minimal. Boston's two white Baptist churches assisted the congregation in its early stages and encouraged its growth. Finally, on December 4, 1806, Thomas Paul was installed as pastor of the First African Church, which was later renamed the Joy Baptist Church. The congregation occupied a three-story brick building in Smith Court, near Belknap Street. The church building was dedicated two days after Paul's installation, which marked the creation of the first independent African American church in the North. During his twenty-five years of service to this congregation, Paul baptized over one hundred people, and the church became a charter member of the Boston Baptist Association. The congregation reached 139 members by the time Paul resigned in 1829.

In order to continue to improve the conditions of African Americans Paul traveled to other congregations to preach and support religious freedom. He traveled to New York in 1808 to assist and organize an independent movement that had begun in 1807. African American members of the First Baptist Church on Gold Street asked Paul to come to their aid. While visiting the city between June and September, Paul preached to large congregations and was well received by the many white churches in New York. His competence as a pastor and manager influenced white Baptists' decision regarding the separation of African Americans members from the First Baptist Church on Gold Street. The approval of separation finally came on July 5, 1809. Honorable letters of dismissal were granted to four men and twelve women of the African American membership. This group plus three others became the first independent African American Baptist congregation in New York under the name Abyssinian Baptist Church. Paul returned to Boston and his congregation, leaving the care of the church in the competent hands of Josiah Bishop and other members. This key institution in New York's African American community had a profound impact on both religious and political life in the community.

Missionary Work in Haiti

Paul presented a plan in 1823 to the Baptist Missionary Society of Massachusetts, to improve the moral and religious condition of the people of Haiti. His plan was enthusiastically accepted and he was sent as a missionary for six months. During his stay, President Boyer of the Republic of Haiti gave Paul permission to preach at public gatherings. He successfully reached many through his missionary work, but because of his lack of knowledge regarding French languages his overall success was limited.

The First African Church was an important part of the African American Boston community as it addressed issues and concerns of the day. The church hosted religious and civic activities and presented activists, such as William Lloyd Garrison, the American abolitionist; Maria Stewart, a noted abolitionist and the first American woman to give a public lecture; and other reformers of the day. Controversy erupted in the church in 1835 as a result of David Walker's *Appeal* in 1829. Walker, a member of Boston's African American Baptist community, advocated armed insurrection as a response to slavery. He also was critical of those churches and clergy who did not take a stronger stance. Paul avoided taking a direct stand on his friend Walker's *Appeal*. As questions of religious and civic nature became more prevalent, Paul faced differences of opinion over the appropriate degree of church participation. This, along with his noticeable absences on missionary trips and the onset of poor health, set the stage for Paul's resignation, which occurred in 1829. Opinions regarding the degree of participation in political protest and reform and questions regarding whether integration or separation was the most effective position resulted in splitting the church and the formation of the Twelfth Baptist Church in 1840. But by this time, Paul had ceased his involvement in church matters. Thomas Paul died in Boston on April 13, 1831.

REFERENCES

Books

Lincoln, C. Eric, and Lawrence H. Mamiya. *The Black Church in the African American Experience.* Durham, N.C.: Duke University Press, 1990.

Sernett, Milton C. *African American Religious History: A Documentary Witness.* 2nd ed. Durham, N.C.: Duke University Press, 1999.

——. "Thomas Paul." In *American National Biography.* Vol. 17. Eds. John A. Garraty and Mark C. Carnes. New York: Oxford University Press, 1999.

Lean'tin L. Bracks

Chronology

1876	Born in Westfield, Massachusetts on February 27
1899	Moves to New York City
1900	Marries Maggie (maiden name unknown); forms Brown and Payton real estate company
1903	Forms Afro-American Realty Company partnership
1904	Incorporates Afro-American Realty Company
1906	Afro-American stockholders file lawsuit against Payton
1907	Company issues first dividend
1908	Court finds company liable for prospectus misrepresentations; company ceases to do business; forms Philip A. Payton Jr. Company
1917	Dies in Allenhurst, New Jersey on August 29

Philip A. Payton
1876–1917

Real estate developer

In a career that spanned less than twenty years, Philip A. Payton Jr. became known for providing African Americans in New York City with an opportunity to live in quality housing in the northern Manhattan community of Harlem. As a real estate broker, property manager, and owner, Payton gained a national reputation among African American business leaders during the first decade of the twentieth century.

Philip A. Payton was born February 27, 1876, in Westfield, Massachusetts, the eldest of four children of Philip A. Payton and Annie Ryans Payton. Although both of Payton's parents were entrepreneurs (his father owned a barbershop and his mother operated a hairdressing business), Payton Jr. did not seem destined for a career in business. He attended public schools in Westfield but later noted that he had the least education of his siblings. In a profile in Booker T. Washington's 1907 work *The Negro in Business*, Payton characterized his aimless teen years as highlighted by his dropping out of high school during his senior year due to a football injury. Thereafter he decided to follow his father's trade and worked as a barber.

In 1899 Payton moved to New York City where he had a series of jobs and eventually found work as a porter in a real estate office. Exposed to the real estate profession, in less than a year he decided to start his own real estate business with a partner. The real estate partnership of Brown & Payton struggled, and Brown left during the first year. Payton, who had married in 1900, eventually began to get contracts to manage houses.

A real estate boom occurred in the northern Manhattan community of Harlem after 1900. The predominantly white community of Harlem, settled in the 1600s, had initially been a Dutch farming community. It became a residential community as transportation links with the lower Manhattan business districts improved in the second half of the 1800s. Merchants and other businessmen who worked in lower Manhattan were able to move their families to the developing community in upper Manhattan. By the 1880s and 1890s sections of the community were lined with four-story brownstone row houses and the area was known as a prosperous residential neighborhood. In 1900 construction began on the subway line extending from New York's City Hall in lower Manhattan north to 145th Street in Harlem. The line had been discussed since the 1880s. Real estate developers responded to the construction start by building apartment houses in close proximity to the line. Philip Payton recognized an opportunity for African Americans in these developments.

After 1890, the African American community in New York had begun to grow substantially as migrants from southern states relocated in New York for better opportunities. By 1900 African Americans in Manhattan were primarily dispersed throughout midtown Manhattan in an area approximately from 23rd Street north to the numbered streets in the low 60s (a smaller number lived in Harlem). A race riot in the midtown area in 1900, sparked by the murder of a police officer by an African American man, made the area less than hospitable for African Americans. Compounding their problems was the demolition of the residential community at 34th Street and Eighth Avenue to make way for the construction of the Pennsylvania Railroad Station. Payton recognized an opportunity to link African Americans seeking housing with the white Harlem property owners.

The Afro-American Realty Company

In 1903 Payton formed a partnership with nine African American businessmen to acquire five-year leases on Harlem properties owned by whites with a plan to rent the properties to African Americans. Payton indicated that the idea for the company had come to him while attending the annual meeting of Booker T. Washington's National Negro Business League in 1902. The league had been founded in 1900, and its annual meetings served as a gathering place for African American businessmen. Since the league was led by Washington, Payton's involvement in it most likely provided him with valuable access to the most powerful African American in the United States. Payton's real estate business was incorporated in 1904 as the Afro-American Realty Company with authorization to issue 50,000 shares of stock at $10 per share. According to Gilbert Osofsky, the company's prospectus stated that it would "buy, sell, rent, lease, and sub-lease, all kinds of buildings, houses…lots; and other…real estate in the city of New York…."

In 1904, when the subway opened, Payton's observations of potential opportunity proved to be accurate. The number of new apartments built in Harlem far exceeded the residential demand of white New Yorkers. Residential segregation, while not the law in New York City, became more a part of the city's tradition as the African American population of the city increased. African Americans were not a logical alternative tenant group for white Harlem property owners. The Afro-American Realty company facilitated occupancy by African Americans of these properties. The company eventually leased and managed buildings in which it placed African American residents. Yet the process was not without obstacles. There was organized resistance by white property owners to the incursion of African Americans into Harlem. White property owners formed organizations such as the Anglo-Saxon Realty Corporation and the Save-Harlem Committee promising not to lease or sell to blacks and justifying their activities as efforts to prevent a decline in property values. But the economic pressure of continuing to hold vacant properties that were not generating income proved too much for some white Harlem property owners, and Payton continued to receive contracts to manage buildings. He also purchased buildings. As he prospered Payton and his wife Maggie purchased a home in the community as well, an eleven-room brownstone at 13 West 131st Street.

The African American movement to Harlem continued through the first years of the twentieth century, and to meet the demand, the Afro-American Realty Company continued to sell stock advertising in the black press with promises of 10 percent profit. Payton continued to expand operations to meet the growing demand, leasing and purchasing buildings using high interest financing. The Afro-American Realty Company's board of directors advised caution but the expansion continued although the company did not issue a dividend to stockholders. In 1906 a lawsuit was filed by forty-three disgruntled stockholders. The suit, filed in the name of stockholder Charles Crowder, claimed that in the prospectus used by the company to generate stock sales, the realty company had exaggerated the amount of property it owned and also had failed to disclose that much of this property was mortgaged. At a 1908 trial the court concluded that 37 of 134 allegations had been proven, including a finding of guilt in the company's misrepresentations in its prospectus. The stockholders recovered their initial investments, plus damages and legal costs.

The Afro-American Realty Company declared its first dividend in June 1907, but the negative publicity associated with the trial led to a devastating loss in investor confidence. The recession of 1907-08 exacerbated the company's problems, reducing the demand for housing in Harlem. Payton searched for ways to keep the company afloat, appealing to Booker T. Washington to intercede with philanthropist Andrew Carnegie. Washington refused and Payton approached Carnegie on his own, but was turned down. In 1908 the company ceased to do business. In spite of appeals from Emmett Scott, a shareholder, and Booker T. Washington's secretary, for Payton to formally communicate the end of the company's operations, Payton never formally announced its having closed.

Payton's confidence did not seem dimmed or his reputation tainted by the lawsuit or by the end of the Afro-American Realty Company. He continued in real estate work doing business as the Philip A. Payton Jr. Company, owning and managing buildings in Harlem identifiable by signs containing his "PAP" logo. Newspapers continued to seek his opinion on matters related to Harlem real estate. Payton continued to appeal to African Americans' heritage in naming his properties. A Payton advertisement for Harlem apartments included buildings with the names Attucks Court, Toussaint Court, and Wheatley Court.

Philip A. Payton, Jr. died of liver cancer on August 29, 1917 at his summer home in Allenhurst, New Jersey. His funeral took place at St. Marks Methodist Episcopal Church on West 53rd Street in Manhattan. He was survived by his wife Maggie and his sister Susan Payton Wortham. His brothers James and Edward had predeceased him. William Wortham, Susan Payton's husband, continued to operate the Philip A. Payton Jr. Co. at least until the early 1940s.

Although the Afro-American Realty Company was short-lived, the company and its leader Philip A. Payton played a significant role in the racial transition of Harlem. By the time of Payton's death a substantial area of Harlem was occupied by African American residents and businesses, setting the stage for the Harlem Renaissance of the 1920s when the community became known as the "Negro Capital of the World" with Payton remembered as the "Father of Colored Harlem."

REFERENCES

Books

Anderson, Jervis. *Harlem: The Great Black Way, 1900-1950*. London: Orbis Publishing, 1982.

Johnson, James Weldon. *Black Manhattan*. New York: Knopf, 1930.

Lewis, David Levering. *When Harlem Was in Vogue*. New York: Random House, 1982.

Osofsky, Gilbert. *Harlem: The Making of a Ghetto: Negro New York, 1890-1930*. New York: HarperCollins, 1966.

Washington, Booker T. *The Negro in Business*. Wichita, Kan.: Devore and Sons, Inc. 1992, originally published by Hertel, Jenkins & Co., 1907.

Watkins-Owens, Irma. *Blood Relations: Caribbean Immigrants and the Harlem Community, 1900-1930*. Bloomington, Ind.: Indiana University Press, 1996.

Periodicals

Gray, Christopher. "'Father of Harlem' Called It Home." *New York Times* (16 June 1991): 6.

"Local Realty Men Doing Big Business." *New York Age* (6 December 1912):1.

"Payton Buried at Westfield." *New York Age* (6 September 1917): 1.

"The World's Finest Housing Proposition." *New York Age*, 16 August 1917.

Collections

Documents associated with the case of Charles J. Crowder against Afro-American Realty Company and Philip A. Payton Jr. are in the archives of the New York County Surrogate's Court.

Kevin McGruder

George Peake
1722–1827

Inventor

Living to the ripe age of 105, George Peake was the first African American to be a part of the colonial settlement that became Cleveland, Ohio. He also invented a hand mill to be used in agricultural work.

Peake was born in Maryland in 1722. His family traveled to Pennsylvania, presumably where he was raised. In 1754 at the age of thirty-two, Peake was reported as a soldier for England. After participating in the battle of

Chronology

1722	Born in Maryland
1754	Fights in Battle of Quebec; later steals comrades' pay and deserts the British Army
1809	Arrives in Cleveland as the first African American settler with two of his sons; his wife, Hannah, and other two sons arrive later
1811	Purchases over 100 acres of land; later invents a hand mill
1816	Divides and allots his land to three of his sons
1827	Dies in Cleveland at the age of 105

Quebec, he stole his comrades' pay and deserted the military. Little is known about his life until 1809, when at the age of eighty-seven he arrived in Cleveland, seven years after the first census was taken. According to Russell Davis in *Black Americans in Cleveland from George Peake to Carl Stokes, 1796-1969*, two sons accompanied Peake to Cleveland; his wife, Hannah, and other two sons followed later. Local records suggest that as of 1811 Peake owned 100 acres of land and that he was a freeborn African American. Thus, he inaugurated the black middle class in Cleveland.

Landownership and Membership in the Community

Peake's early crime in stealing military funds when he deserted from the army gave him the money he needed to purchase land. Why he deserted can only be guessed, but it suggests the possibility of tensions between black and white soldiers in colonial times. Nonetheless, by the time he was a landowner, Peake, as a rare black man in a virtually all-white community, apparently got along well with other settlers. As the town developed, he lived among whites on the west side while most other blacks lived on the east side of the city. Peake may have blended in because of his mulatto traits and those of his sons.

In his book, *Black Image in the White Mind*, George Frederickson explains the mid-nineteenth-century attitude towards mulattoes: they were fortunate because they had the mother's brute strength from Africa and their father's intellect from Europe. This perception may explain the social acceptance of miscegenation and thus the opportunities afforded to biracial individuals because they were more acceptable than darker individuals.

African American Inventor

In addition to his positive status as a mulatto, Revolutionary War veteran, and a landowner, Peake was respected for his invention, a timesaving labor device for crops. Peake's invention allowed settlers to replace the tiring manual pestle and mortar derived from the Native Americans with his hand mill, which was made of two round stones nearly nineteen inches wide. Stone-milled corn achieved a smoother consistency. Though no record of a patent connects the hand mill to Peake, the invention is still traceable to him via an article from the November 8, 1858 *Cleveland Leader* (noted in *Black Americans in Cleveland from George Peake to Carl Stokes, 1796-1969*); this was an unusual instance, since African American inventors of the time were rarely credited. In fact, many African Americans invented tools, but they did not receive public acknowledgment; they were also unable to patent or protect their inventions from others or to finance the production and distribution of the product. Peake's connection to the hand mill is undoubtedly a testimony to his character.

Family

Little is known of George Peake's wife, Hannah, except that she was a woman of means, possessing apparently a half-bushel of silver dollars. Davis notes that most women used barter to conduct business. It would be very unusual for a woman to have cash, and that she is reported to have had money suggests she had separate class distinction from her husband. Nonetheless, her name rarely appears in early accounts. Peake's alliance with such a woman would have contributed to his standing in the community. He and his wife had four sons, which was definitely an asset in an agricultural community. Peake's son, Henry, entertained people by playing the fiddle. Later records show that in 1816 Peake issued his land in three portions for three of his sons. The fourth son is not noted.

Cleveland became a center for African American ingenuity, industry, and promising wealth, certainly resulting from the legacy of Clevelanders such as George Peake. He died in Cleveland at the age of 105, but his burial place is unknown.

REFERENCES

Books

Davis, Russell. *Black Americans in Cleveland from George Peake to Carl Stokes, 1796-1969*. Washington D.C.: Associated Publishers, 1972.

Fredrickson, George M. *The Black Image in the White Mind: The Debate on Afro-American Character and Destiny 1817-1914*. Middletown, Conn.: Wesleyan University Press, 1987.

James, Portia T. "Inventors and Inventions." In *Encyclopedia of African-American Culture and History*. Eds. Jack Salzman, David Lionel Smith, and Cornel West. New York: Simon & Schuster 1996.

Johnson, Crisfield. *History of Cuyahoga County, Ohio...with Portraits and Biographical Sketches of its Prominent Men and Pioneers*. Philadelphia: D. W. Ensign, 1879.

Kusmer, Kenneth L. *Ghetto Takes Shape: Black Cleveland 1870-1930*. Urbana: University of Illinois Press, 1976.

Periodicals

Davis, Harry E. "Early Colored Residents of Cleveland." *Phylon* 4 (July 1943): 235-36.

Online

History of African Americans in the Western Reserve. Western Reserve Historical Society. www.wrhs.org/library/template.asp?id=275 - 12k (Accessed 1 March 2006).

Althea Tait

Benjamin Pelham
1862–1948

Politician, newspaper publisher

A lifelong Republican, lawyer, political organizer, and expert on Detroit's Wayne County government administration, Benjamin Pelham founded the first black political machine in Detroit, Michigan. He was an astute politician who influenced Detroit politics, and he was one of the founders of the influential Midwest black daily newspaper, the *Plain Dealer*. Benjamin Pelham also held a number of patents for automation of manual procedures.

Benjamin Pelham was the youngest of six children born to Robert Pelham, a plasterer and mason, and Frances Butcher. His father's profession as a plasterer and mason allowed his family a comfortable life. The Pelhams were free blacks, and they owned a farm in Virginia but decided to sell it when they were told by the local authority that only whites or slaves could purchase a dog license. After this incident and additional prejudice, Robert Pelham decided to move further north, taking his family to Columbus, Ohio, and Philadelphia, Pennsylvania. The Pelhams eventually settled in Detroit, Michigan, where Benjamin was born on February 7, 1862.

In Detroit, young Pelham attended public schools and took accounting courses at a local business college. He began his career in journalism as a newsboy for the *Detroit Post* while he was still in high school. Later the *Detroit Post* was renamed the *Post-Tribune*, and it soon garnered the reputation as Michigan's foremost Republican daily. While a newsboy Pelham learned the mechanics of typesetting, which led to his having a position as apprentice typesetter for the *Post-Tribune* when he grad-

Chronology

1862	Born in Detroit, Michigan on February 7
1883	Joins brother Robert and two associates in founding *Plain Dealer*
1884	Successfully manages campaign to place an African American as an at-large delegate to the Republican National Convention
1894	Appointed clerk in Internal Revenue Service
1895	Marries Laura Montgomery
1900-06	Holds position in Office of the Registrar of Deeds
1905	Patents the tabulation device
1906	Named chief accountant, board of supervisors, the highest non-elected office in Wayne County
1913	Patents the tallying machine
1942	Becomes editor of *Washington Tribune*; creates Capital News Services
1948	Dies in Detroit, Michigan on October 7

uated from Detroit High School. In 1883, Benjamin and his older brother, Robert Jr., started the *Plain Dealer*. W. H. Anderson and W. H. Stowers worked with the Pelham brothers on the publication. With offices in the *Post-Tribune* building, the team along with a staff of five published the newspaper. Robert Jr. and Benjamin continued to work as typesetters as they published the newspaper.

The *Plain Dealer* was a successful, widely read publication which became a leading African American newspaper in the United States. Many of the articles were written by well-known blacks. It supported black pride and was a harbinger for the concerns of African Americans living in the Midwest, using the term African American in place of Negro. As with most newspapers, politics was an important subject. The paper offered a Midwestern, African American view on the subject. As the managing editor, Benjamin Pelham became one of the most recognized black Detroit figures of the period. By 1884, his influence was such that he managed a successful campaign to elect a black man as an at-large delegate to the Republican National Convention in Chicago. In 1889 the first nationwide civil rights organization, the Afro-American League, was started by Pelham. However, his newspaper, the *Plain Dealer*, ceased publication in 1894, a result of financial loss.

Enters Public Service

The end of the *Plain Dealer* did not affect Benjamin Pelham's success. He was appointed to serve as clerk in the Internal Revenue Service by James H. Stone, a former owner of the *Post-Tribune*. Pelham began to work at the office of the registrar of deeds in Detroit in 1900 and remained there until 1906. Charles Buhrer, another associate of the *Post-Tribune*, appointed Pelham to the highest non-elective office in the county government, chief accountant of the board of supervisors of Wayne County. Later he was elected to be the auditor of Wayne County. Soon Pelham was recognized as an expert on Wayne County government administration, and he was asked to serve, at the same time, as chief accountant and clerk to the board of auditors, Detroit's governing body. He set the agenda for the board.

Although he was a busy man, Pelham found the time to form a black political machine by fostering a reputation as a smart politician. His organization became a governing, powerful agent in the politics of Wayne County. Pelham's influence grew to the point where he could affect political careers in Wayne County. A diverse community composed of newly arrived Europeans reduced his power, though, and broke his well-organized black political organization. Nonetheless, Pelham continued to work in city government and with the county even after a Democrat was elected to office in 1934. He retired as county accountant in 1942, after forty-seven years of continual public service.

Becomes Inventor

During the early years of the twentieth century, Pelham became an inventor. He created a device to automate the pasting process of statistical sheets. He devised a method for automating the pasting process and set out to create a device that could accomplish it. Starting with a rolling pin, cigar boxes, wooden screws, and other miscellaneous items, Pelham developed a working model. The apparatus would go on to save the department more than $3,000. He patented two items—the tabulation device in 1905 and a tallying machine in 1913. After retiring from the Census Bureau, Pelham edited a black newspaper called the *Washington Tribune* and later created the Capital News Services, a news agency devoted to black issues.

Benjamin Pelham and Laura Montgomery of Sandwich, Ontario, married in 1895; they had two children—Frances and Alfred M. On October 7, 1948, Pelham died in Detroit leaving behind him a list of accomplishments.

REFERENCES

Books

McCain, Rea, Aris A. Mallas, and Margaret K. Hedden. *Forty Years in Politics: The Story of Benjamin Pelham*. Detroit: Wayne State University Press, 1958.

Nepa, Frances. "Benjamin R. Pelham." In *American National Biography*. Vol. 17. Eds. John A. Garraty and Mark C. Carnes. New York: Oxford University Press, 2004.

Online

Plain Dealer. http://www.living-library.com/Freedom Tour/Plaindealer.html (Accessed 20 January 2006).

Mario A. Charles

Clarence M. Pendleton, Jr.
1930–1988

Politician

Clarence Pendleton Jr. was an enigma, thought by some to be a role model to blacks and by others to be a traitor to blacks and black issues. Pendleton is best known as the conservative Republican chairman of the U.S. Commission on Civil Rights. Pendleton began working for black issues and ran a record-setting program as head of the San Diego Model Cities Program. Broadly stated, Pendleton believed in changing institutions rather than providing jobs or money on an individual basis.

Pendleton, who liked to be called Penny, was an only child, born in Louisville, Kentucky, on November 10, 1930 to middle-class parents, Clarence Pendleton Sr. and Edna Marie (Ramasur) Pendleton. The Pendletons moved to the District of Columbia when Pendleton was young. His father was the swimming coach at Howard University, the assistant director for the D.C. recreation department, and a lifeguard at the Banneker Recreation Center in the family's neighborhood. Pendleton's parents encouraged him to work; one of the jobs he regularly had was washing the steps of his neighbor, Mrs. Marshall, the mother of Thurgood Marshall. In high school, Pendleton was an exceptional athlete who dreamed of becoming a football player. While he did play center for the football tem, his strength was swimming. Pendleton's tenacity in the pool could not be beat.

Howard University was a family tradition; both Pendleton's father and grandfather had graduated from there. His grandfather graduated from Howard with a degree in law in 1896 and practiced law in Baltimore while Pendleton was growing up. His maternal grandfather graduated from St. Augustine College. Pendleton served as an altar boy for fifteen years at the Episcopal Church where his great-uncle was the rector. Pendleton grew up surrounded by exceptional role models who had great expectations of him. His goal was to follow in his father's footsteps.

Pendleton graduated from Howard University with a B.S. He worked briefly for the D.C. recreation department while going to graduate school, but class work was interrupted when Pendleton joined the army. He served his time in a medical unit as a specialist third class at Fort Monmouth, New Jersey. Pendleton received an honorable discharge from the army in 1957. He returned to Howard and worked as a physical education instructor while completing his master's degree in education in 1961.

Career in Physical Education

Pendleton became a swim coach at Howard like his father, thus fulfilling his lifelong dream. He was head coach of the swim team, winning championships ten of

Chronology

1930	Born in Louisville, Kentucky on November 10
1954	Earns B.S. from Howard University
1961	Earns M.A. in education from Howard University
1961-68	Coaches at Howard University
1968-70	Works as recreation coordinator, Baltimore's Model Cities Agency
1971	Serves as director of the Urban Affairs Department of the National Recreation and Parks Association; marries Margrite Krause
1972	Moves to San Diego to work for the San Diego Model Cities Program
1975	Becomes president of San Diego's Urban League
1981	Appointed chairman of the U.S. Commission on Civil Rights
1987	Resigns from U.S. Commission on Civil Rights
1988	Dies in San Diego, California on June 5

the eleven years he worked at Howard. In 1964 and 1965, he also coached the Egyptian swimming teams, which had also won national championships. Pendleton served as head coach of the basketball and rowing teams and as assistant football coach. During this time he married and eventually divorced. There were two children born from Pendleton's first marriage.

In 1968, with two children to support from his previous marriage and earning only $7,500 per year at Howard, Pendleton jumped at the chance to become recreation coordinator for Baltimore's Model City Program. In 1970 Pendleton married Margrit Krause. He became director of the Urban Affairs Department of the National Parks and Recreation Association (NPRA) in Baltimore in 1971. In this position, Pendleton advocated for creating new parks, for open spaces, and for making recreational activities available to everyone. While at the NPRA, he worked to convince the federal government of the need for year-round parks and recreation planning instead of the short-term summer programs for which the federal government traditionally planned. Pendleton also pushed with communities in Baltimore for increased community involvement in the establishment of community recreation programs.

In 1972, mayor Pete Wilson of San Diego, California, offered Pendleton the chance to direct the Model Cities Program. In this capacity, Pendleton served on the Community Education Advisory Council, at the U.S. Office of Education, and on the Governor's Task Force on Affordable Housing for the State of California.

In 1975, Pendleton became president of the San Diego Urban League, a position he held until 1982. He pushed for increased real estate investments and economic development programs over the social programs traditionally supported by the Urban League. During his tenure at the Urban League, the league's land holdings increased from $218,000 to $3 million. Pendleton spearheaded packaging loans for small business as well as managing and upgrading small apartment units. Hearing of black Marines' subjection to Ku Klux Klan attacks at Camp Pendleton, he enlisted support for them. Another time, Pendleton stirred things up at the Urban League by arranging a $5 per plate soup and cornbread dinner for senior citizens as the annual Urban League fundraiser. However, Pendleton's time at the Urban League was not entirely peaceful. He was accused of mismanaging league funds, but was eventually cleared of all charges.

At the Urban League Pendleton began to shift political beliefs. He served as the first president of the New Coalition for Economic and Social Change. The coalition was a black conservative group that had formed in San Francisco in 1980. Among the attendees were Henry Lucas Jr., Thomas Sowell, Clarence Thomas, Walter Williams, and Randolph Bromery. The purpose of the meeting was to discuss alternatives to affirmative action and welfare. The coalition worked with the Heritage Foundation, the president of the San Diego Local Development Corporation, and the chairman of the San Diego Transit Corporation. At this same time, Pendleton also served as president of the San Diego Coalition Dedicated to Economic and Environmental Development.

During Pendleton's time with the San Diego coalition there was a lot of excitement in one black neighborhood about the construction of a veterans' hospital. The hospital would have provided many jobs for the neighborhood; however, Pendleton supported the hospital being built at Balboa Park which was the location favored by his friend Edwin Meese III. The hospital was built in Balboa Park. It was a decision which came back to haunt Pendleton quickly.

By 1970, Pendleton had come to believe that money was the great equalizer and that if blacks earned more money and became more economically self-sufficient they would assume a greater role in society. The 1970s also saw a dramatic shift in Pendleton's politics. Until this point Pendleton had been a liberal Democrat; however, he switched to the Independent Party and then the Republican Party. San Diego mayor Pete Wilson and Edwin Meese, a confidant of Ronald Reagan, who was governor of California at that time, were believed to have influenced Pendleton's switch. At least part of the decision was made based on the fact that power and profit were more common in the Republican Party than in the Democratic Party. When Reagan ran for president, Pendleton was one of only 150 Urban League directors to endorse his candidacy.

Heads U.S. Commission on Civil Rights

Pendleton's endorsement of Reagan's presidential campaign brought him to national attention. In 1981, President Reagan appointed Pendleton to replace Arthur S. Fleming, whom Reagan had fired for defending civil rights initiatives that the Reagan administration wanted to reduce or eliminate. During confirmations hearings, NAACP leaders testified against Pendleton's confirmation. Colleagues from the Urban League also testified against Pendleton. Pendleton's backing of the location of the San Diego veterans' hospital was brought up as well as questions about his political views and taxes. In the end, Pendleton was approved by Congress and assumed the chairmanship in 1982.

Some say that Pendleton's appointment was a means by which Reagan attempted to pacify critics who felt his administration was insensitive to minority concerns and that Reagan was trying to reverse hard-won civil rights progress. Regardless of Reagan's motives, Pendleton was firm in his stance against affirmative action, hiring quotas, comparable worth, and school busing to end segregation. Pendleton's number one priority was to investigate instances of reverse discrimination. In a 1985 speech Pendleton said he wanted the commission to spearhead the effort to achieve "a color-blind society that has opportunities for all and guarantees for none." He believed affirmative action was a "bankrupt policy" which did not allow people to succeed on their own merits. He felt hiring quotas caused minorities entering the workforce to think they did not have to acquire the skills necessary to fairly compete against others in the same arena. Pendleton opposed busing because it defeated the purpose of neighborhood schools. He also felt no one had the right to say white schools were better than black schools.

The political situation at the Civil Rights Commission quickly heated up. Syndicated columnist Carl Rowan wrote that Pendleton had single-handedly turned the commission into one of the most anti-civil rights units in federal government. According to Rowan, "If Congress wants to show President Reagan that it is sincere about reducing spending and the federal deficit, it might vote swiftly to abolish the U.S. Civil Rights Commission. Under the leadership of Clarence Pendleton, the Civil Rights Commission has become an arrogant enemy of the most abused, most miserable, most helpless people in the land. Pendleton, his deputy Morris Abrams, and a majority of the commission are waging war on the civil rights movement."

The Reagan administration sought to strengthen Pendleton by unilaterally replacing the three democratic commissioners with three Reagan appointees. The commission members would serve fixed terms, and Pendleton was appointed the chair for six years. One of the first things the committee did in January 1984, under Pendleton's leadership, was to vote five to three to cancel a study on the effects of budget cuts on primarily minority colleges. The five committee members argued that budget cuts were not innately discriminatory thus outside the scope of the commission. This action was quickly followed by the approval of a study of the problems caused for people of southern or eastern European descent by affirmative action. The Commission's next step was to denounce the use of quotas by the Detroit police department to increase the number of promotions by black police officers.

In 1985 on *Face the Nation*, Pendleton said there was going to be an order signed eliminating preferential treatment and that the imbalance in the workforce would not be blamed on discrimination. Speaking at Cornell University that year, Pendleton stated that the Civil Rights Commission should be dismantled in 1989 when it came before Congress for reauthorization. When the Reagan administration failed to back Pendleton's comments, Pendleton told Reagan to stop talking one way and acting another.

Pendleton's biggest problem arose because of the minority set-aside programs. Designed to give minority business owners the opportunity to compete for government contracts, the minority set-aside programs had been riddled with corruption since their inception in 1968. Some of the problems concerned white-owned companies employing blacks as fronts to get contracts; actual minority firms winning the contracts then subcontracting them out to white-owned businesses; and contracts going to minority businesses which were already successful rather than those minority businesses which would truly have benefited from the contracts. Pendleton felt there was little evidence that the set-asides helped to create legitimate minority business.

Pendleton was accused of being a hypocrite for opposing set-asides based on the fact that when he worked at the Urban League, he advised minority-owned businesses how to take advantage of Small Business Administration loans. Still others asked how Pendleton could go from believing in federal funding of social assistance programs to abandoning government support of the private sector. Pendleton's stance on set-aside programs so incensed blacks in Congress that twenty-eight black Republicans called for his resignation as chairman of the Civil Rights Commission.

While Pendleton was a staunch backer of the Reagan administration, he still had conflicts with it. For example, he was openly against the tax exemptions given to racially discriminatory private schools and criticized the slowness of the Reagan administration's endorsement of the Voting Rights Act.

Not all the changes Pendleton made at the Civil Rights Commission were looked on negatively. Pendleton increased the speed of the commission meetings, thus cutting back on some of the pontificating for which the commissioners were famous. Pendleton valued efficiency. Following the Reagan administration rule of budget trimming, Pendleton asked that the commission's budget be reduced. Pendleton closed two regional offices and trimmed the level of responsibility of the commission's state advisory committees.

The final straw for Pendleton came in 1987 when an audit of the Civil Rights Commission's records from October 1982 to January 1986 showed discrepancies in hiring practices, travel expenses, and record keeping. The commission was unable to account for $175,000 of its budget. It was also discovered that Pendleton had billed $70,000 in salary to a position which was traditionally part time. Ultimately, Congress cut the commission's budget from $11.6 million to $7.5 million. Ironically, when the budget cuts were made and were followed by recommendations to dismantle the Civil Rights Commission, Pendleton resigned.

During his tenure with the Civil Rights Commission, Pendleton continued to work in San Diego commuting to Washington, D.C. for commission meetings. He remained chairman of San Diego Transit and president of Pendleton and Associates, a business development and investment firm. Pendleton was also a trustee for the Scripps Clinic and Research Foundation and served on the board of the Greater American Federal Savings and Loan Association. He continued as chairman and president of the San Diego Local Development Corporation.

Following his resignation in 1987, Pendleton returned to his home in La Jolla, California. Thanks to his many business interests in San Diego there was much to keep him busy. Pendleton died of a heart attack while exercising at a health club on June 5, 1988; he was fifty-seven years old. He was survived by his wife, Margrit; a son and two daughters.

REFERENCES

Books

Banner-Haley, Charles Pete T. *The Fruits of Integration: Black Middle-class Ideology and Culture, 1960-1990*. Jackson, Miss.: University Press of Mississippi, 1994.

Walton, Hanes, Jr. *When the Marching Stopped: The Politics of Civil Rights Regulatory Agencies*. Albany, N.Y.: Albany State University of New York Press, 1988.

Periodicals

Pendleton, Clarence M., Jr. "Comparable Worth Is Not Pay Equity." *Vital Speeches of the Day* (1 April 1985): 382-85.

Rowan, Carl T. "Abolish the Civil Rights Commission." *Washington Post*, 19 March 1985.

Trescott, Jacqueline, and Eve Ferguson. "Chairman Clarence Pendleton, Jr.; the 'Wild Card' of the Civil Rights Commission." *Washington Post*, 12 November 1982.

Anne K. Driscoll

James Perkins, Jr.
1953–

Mayor

On March 7, 1965, Selma, Alabama was thrust into international headlines. Approximately six hundred voter rights activists organized a march from Selma to Montgomery. As the activists crossed the Edmund Pettus Bridge, they were met by sheriff deputies and Alabama state troopers who sprayed the marchers with tear gas and beat them with nightsticks as they left the bridge. The term "Bloody Sunday" was used to describe the incident, which later became the catalyst for the passing of the federal Voting Rights Act of 1965, which enabled far wider registration of black voters.

On that fatal day in March, James Perkins Jr. was only twelve years old, and as he remembers, he was safe and secure in the Brown Chapel African Methodist Episcopal Church, with eyes filled with tears because his mother would not permit him to join the marchers. Thirty-five years later, Selma, Alabama would elect Perkins as its first African American mayor. A Selma businessman, Perkins defeated the incumbent Joseph Smitherman, the seventy-year-old white former segregationist who was seeking his tenth consecutive term as mayor and who had been mayor of Selma during the 1965 march.

Perkins' parents, James Perkins Sr., a teacher in the Selma school system, and Etta Perkins, a nurse, were active community leaders. James Perkins Jr. was among the first group of black students to enter Selma High School, formed from the merger of R. B. Hudson and A. G. Parrish high schools. He received a bachelor's degree in mathematics from Alabama Agricultural and Mechanical University. Perkins' professional experience included that of a computer programmer and systems analyst for Caterpillar Tractor in Peoria, Illinois, and project manager for Martin Marietta. In 1980, he returned to Selma and opened his own technology-consulting firm, Business Ventures Inc.. Perkins married Cynthia Page, a parent facilitator in the Selma public school system, in 1984 and they are the parents of four children.

Becomes Politically Active

Perkins became impatient with the progress of integration in Selma. Smitherman had made token progress by appointing several African Americans to government administrative positions. Perkins decided that becoming involved in the political system was the most effective means for radical change. This decision led him to seek the office of mayor of Selma, challenging Smitherman's political machine. In 1964, at the time of his first election as mayor of Selma, there were only about 150 blacks registered to vote in the city, and he opposed African Americans voting in large numbers. After that time, the population of Selma had changed from being almost entirely white to about 65 percent African Americans. Somehow, Smitherman managed to retain his position as mayor by gaining all the white votes along with support from some blacks. Smitherman was also an early friend and protégé of the late former Alabama governor George Wallace, who was a key segregationist of the 1960s.

In 1996, Perkins ran for the second time against Smitherman and was defeated. Because there were two black opponents, the vote was split and Smitherman managed to survive once again. With his second defeat, Perkins was ready to call it quits because he felt that it was impossible to win. A group of community supporters convinced him to reconsider his decision while attending a dinner reception. In addition, Perkins' wife encouraged him.

Perkins challenged Smitherman again in 2000, campaigning under the slogan, "Joe's Gotta Go!" Perkins was victorious, receiving 57 percent of the votes. The figures verified that more than 75 percent of the city's estimated 14,000 registered voters went to the polls. His supporters flooded the streets, honking horns, shouting and singing.

The victory election was the result of a broad-based coalition of black churches, community organizations, labor, and youth. The NAACP was also in the forefront, testing out its voter empowerment project in Selma. The result of the election noted that there were a heavier percentage of white voters voting against Smitherman, who had been afraid to vote against him in the past. Some thought that the race was about black and white. Perkins said that it was about faith and fear. Faith won this campaign, Perkins told about five hundred of his supporters.

At the time of Perkins' third attempt, Smitherman apologized for his past and openly campaigned for black votes, appointing blacks to jobs in the town administration. Although considered a moderate segregationist when he was first elected in 1964, at the end of his thirty-fifth year, his last act as mayor was to push through the Selma city council funding for a statue of Nathan Bedford Forrest, the Confederate general who founded the Ku Klux Klan. He recommended it to be placed on public property in front of the Smitherman Museum.

Perkins' Plans for Selma

Perkins inherited a city with a high unemployment rate and falling population. His ambition was to turn the city around, making Selma a tourist spot for families, letting the world know that the Selma of 2000 was very different from the Selma of 1965. One of Perkins' first acts as the new mayor was to push through a bill canceling funding for the Nathan Bedford Forrest monument to white supremacy.

Ebony magazine quoted Perkins as saying that he wanted "to put the ominous event of the Edmund Pettus Bridge into perspective. It is a part of Selma's history, the nation's history, but it will no longer be the first thing people think of when they mention this city." In 2004, Perkins was re-elected mayor of Selma, Alabama.

Perkins was a member of the Drug Advisory Council to the Selma public school system, the Alabama New South Coalition, the Board of Directors of the Auburn University African-American Enterprise Commission, and the Selma-Dallas County Economic Development Authority. Perkins served as treasurer of Fathers Active in Children's Education, and he was one of the co-founders of the Selma-Dallas County Selma-to-Montgomery National Historic Trail Friends Association. He was also vice president of the Kappa Alpha Psi Fraternity in Selma and a Little League baseball coach.

REFERENCES

Periodicals

Hughes, Zondra. "Selma's First Black Mayor." *Ebony* 56 (December 2000): 66-70.

Online

CBS News. "Civil Rights Hot Spot Gets Black Major." http://www.cbsnews.com/stories/2000/09/13/politics/main232998.shtml (Accessed 14 February 2006).

Cose, Ellis. "Back on the Bridge." Newsweek National News (8 August 2005). http://www.msnbc.msn.com/id/8769929/site/newsweek (Accessed 14 February 2006).

Mattie McHollin

Channing E. Phillips
1928–1987

Minister, civil rights activist

Channing Emery Phillips was a noted clergyman and civil rights activist. Intellectually gifted and attuned

Channing E. Phillips

to the needs of the urban poor, he was deeply committed to helping black and low-income families improve their circumstances. He attained national recognition at the Democratic National Convention in Chicago in 1968, when he became the first black man to be nominated for president of the United States.

Descended from Native American, African American, and Caucasian people, Phillips was from a prominent upper-class black family whose family tree and achievements were profiled in the *Negro History Bulletin*. His father, Reverend Porter W. Phillips Sr., held an honorary doctorate of divinity degree and was the pastor of the Carrone Baptist Church in Pittsburgh, Pennsylvania, for twenty-five years. His mother, Dorothy Fletcher Phillips, was a schoolteacher, church organist, and choir director. The couple had five sons: Porter Jr., Channing, Treadwell, Wendell, and Fletcher, as well as one daughter, Marie.

Phillips was born in Brooklyn, New York on March 23, 1928. Like their father, Channing and his brothers earned their undergraduate degrees at the historically black Virginia Union University in Richmond, Virginia. All of the Phillips brothers were members of Alpha Kappa Alpha fraternity, and all but one was a minister or had been employed by a church.

Chronology

1928	Born in Brooklyn, New York on March 23
1945-47	Serves in the United States Air Force; leaves with rank of sergeant
1950	Graduates from Virginia Union with A.B. degree in sociology
1953	Receives B.D. from Colgate Divinity School, Rochester, New York
1954-55	Studies as doctoral fellow in New Testament Studies at Drew University
1956	Marries Jane Celeste Nabors
1959	Serves as pastor, Lemuel Hayes Congregational Church
1961	Serves as pastor, Lincoln Memorial Congregational Temple United Church of Christ
1967	Serves as executive director, Housing Development Corporation
1968	First African American nominated for president by a major political party, Democratic National Convention in Chicago
1968-72	Serves as Democratic committee member
1971	Loses election to House of Representatives from Washington, D.C.
1974	Resigns from Housing Development Corporation
1982	Serves as minister of planning and coordination, Riverside Church, New York
1987	Dies in New York City on November 13

Academic Career and Preparation for the Ministry

As a young man, the multi-talented Phillips had trouble deciding upon a career. He served in the United States Air Force from 1945 to 1947 and left with the rank of sergeant. He won a scholarship in painting and sculpture to attend the Carnegie Museum and Carnegie Institute of Technology. From there, he went to the University of Utah to study electrical engineering. Phillips ended up at his father's alma mater, Virginia Union University, where he majored in sociology and finished an A.B degree in 1950. He then went on to earn a B.D. from Colgate Divinity School in Rochester, New York, in 1953. Phillips advanced to Drew University Graduate School in New Jersey with a fellowship to study the New Testament from 1955 to 1957 as a doctoral candidate.

After he left Drew, Phillips was an instructor on the New Testament at Howard University in Washington, D.C. from 1956 to 1958; visiting lecturer in Greek at the Protestant Episcopal Seminary in Alexandria, Virginia in 1958; and visiting lecturer in New Testament at the American University in Washington, D.C. from 1957 to 1958, where he also held a interim minister position at the Plymouth Congregational Church. He met and married Jane Celeste Nabors in 1956. Eventually they became the parents of five children: Channing, Sheila, Tracy, Jill, and John.

During 1958, Phillips returned to New York City for an appointment as associate minister at Grace Congregational Church and later served as pastor at the Lemuel Haynes Congregational Church in Jamaica, Long Island, New York from 1959 to 1961. Phillips relocated to Washington, D.C. in 1961 when he accepted the senior pastor position at the historic Lincoln Memorial Congregational Temple United Church of Christ, where he remained until 1970.

Phillips reportedly left Lincoln Memorial when some church members complained about the amount of time and energy he was investing in critical social problems. The disaffected church members may have felt that Phillips was neglecting his ministerial duties to focus on his job as executive director for the Housing Development Corporation of Washington, D.C., a post he had retained since 1967. Phillips was also active in religious and fraternal organizations. In 1964, he held memberships in the National Association of Bible Instructors, the Society of Biblical Literature and Exegesis, Alpha Phi Alpha fraternity, and the National Association for the Advancement of Colored People (NAACP).

Phillips was against the Vietnam War, and he protested against it and participated in peace movement programs. He ardently supported the civil rights movement and marched with Martin Luther King Jr. in Selma, Alabama in 1964. A staunch Democrat, he worked as a committeeman from 1968 to 1972. His high profile activism brought him to the attention of Robert F. Kennedy, who requested that Phillips chair his presidential campaign in the District of Columbia. Phillips proved the candidate's confidence in him by capturing all of the Democratic delegates for Kennedy.

Kennedy's presidential bid came to a tragic end when he was assassinated while campaigning in California in June of 1968. When the delegates who had pledged to support Kennedy assembled at the Democratic National Convention in Chicago to nominate a president and vice president, many were still in mourning. Kennedy, who had represented the liberal wing of the party, had put together a strong coalition of minorities, labor interests, anti-war protesters, and civil rights activists. These delegates were in no mood to ally with the remaining democratic presidential candidates, Eugene McCarthy and Hubert Humphrey.

The 1968 Democratic National Convention was an important watershed in black political history. It had the highest attendance of black delegates up until that time, 209, and these blacks, bolstered by gains made in the civil rights struggle, asserted themselves. They challenged the credentials of the regular party delegates from several southern states. Only the contesting of the Georgia delegation was successful. It divided its votes between a racially mixed liberal coalition and a regular (all white) delegation.

Nominated for President of the United States

In this racially charged atmosphere Channing E. Phillips was nominated as a favorite son candidate from the District of Columbia from the floor of the convention. He was nominated by Philip M. Stern, a white D.C. delegate who admired Phillips' courage and honesty. Phillips received sixty-seven and a half votes. Twenty-one votes came from the D.C. delegates and the remaining votes were cast by African American delegates in seventeen other states. Julian Bond, a twenty-eight-year-old Georgia state legislator, was nominated for vice president of the United States and received forty-eight and a half votes but declined because he was not at the constitutionally required age of thirty-five. Amid all of the highly publicized tumult, Hubert Humphrey emerged as the Democratic Party's candidate for president.

Phillips's nomination, although symbolic, brought him instant fame. In a *New York Times* interview that described him as a "new Negro leader," Phillips said he thought that the nomination of a black man for president was worthwhile and that it had been an experiment to see if black peoples' problems could be solved by working with major political parties. He expressed the hope that his nomination had laid the foundation for a black man to be considered as a serious candidate at a future convention.

In 1971, Phillips lost an election to Walter Fauntroy, a charismatic Baptist minister, as the District of Columbia's non-voting delegate to the House of Representatives. He resigned from his job at the Housing Development Corporation in 1974 with mixed success. The corporation built over 1,000 homes for low income families, who in turn sold them to middle-class buyers, thereby not relieving the city's low-income housing shortage. There was also a scandal associated with an apartment complex renovation that went bankrupt.

Phillips accepted a vice president for university relations position at his alma mater, Virginia Union University, and relocated to Richmond, Virginia in 1974. An apparent personality clash with the university's president, however, led to charges of non-performance, and he was terminated. Phillips denied the allegation, sued both the president and university, and settled out of court.

He returned to Washington, D.C. as director of Congressional Relations for the National Endowment for the Humanities. He donned a clerical collar in 1982 for the last time, when he moved to New York and became the minister of planning and coordination for the Riverside Church. He remained in that position until his health began to fail, first with a heart attack and then with cancer. He died of cancer, at the age of 59, on November 13, 1987 at the Columbia Presbyterian Hospital in New York City.

A brief 1982 *Washington Post* article posed the question: "Whatever Happened to Channing Phillips?" Reflecting on his political activism in the 1960s and 1970s, a plainly disenchanted Phillips told the reporter:

"At the time I got involved, I thought I could make some social change, but in fact politics is designed to maintain the status quo."

After Phillips left his job as a Democratic committee member in 1972, he left the political stage and his opportunity to parlay his triumph as a "Negro First" into some more lucrative or high profile endeavors. Both Channing Philips and Julian Bond were sons of well-known fathers in the black community and came from upper middle-class families that could be considered black aristocracy. Coming from a somewhat privileged family, with strong academic credentials, the handsome and eloquent Channing Phillips was blessed with having spent time in the national limelight. Yet, unlike Julian Bond, who used his unsuccessful nomination as a springboard for speaking engagements that brought wider national recognition, accompanied by financial benefits and more political clout that in turn solidified his status a black leader, Phillips appeared to not want to take the time or have the temperament to pursue exploiting his presidential nomination for greater fame and fortune. This left some observers with the impression that he had squandered an opportunity.

Phillips left some of his jobs under a cloud of controversy and while his supporters admired his intellect and ability to argue his point, he was criticized for being distant and hard to get along with. He appears to have had an understanding and genuine sympathy for the suffering of the urban poor and dedicated his life to serving others, but perhaps he did not possess the patience or people skills to funnel that understanding and sympathy into accomplishments that might significantly improve their lot or his own.

REFERENCES

Books

"Phillips, Channing E." In *Who's Who Among Black Americans*. 3rd ed. Northbrook, Ill.: Who's Who Among Black Americans Publishing Company, 1981.

Periodicals

Apple, R.W., Jr. "Dr. King Aide Takes Lead in Capital." *New York Times*, 13 January 1971.

Barnes, Bart. "The Rev. Channing Phillips, Civic Activist, Politician, Dies." *Washington Post*, 12 November 1987.

Barnes, Clive. "Negro in Presidential Ballot Foresees Rise of New Breed of Leaders." *New York Times*, 30 August 1968.

"Channing Phillips Dies in New York." *Richmond Times-Dispatch*, 12 November 1987.

"Channing Phillips: Nominated for President at '68 Convention." *Los Angeles Times*, 13 November 1987.

"Channing Phillips Settles Suit with College that Fired Him." *Washington Post*, 21 January 1977.

"The Family of Porter William Phillips, Sr." *Negro History Bulletin* 27 (January 1964): 81-84.

Harris, Janette Hosten. "Political History." *Negro History Bulletin* 31 (November 1968): 8.

Walton, Hanes, Jr., and Gray, C. Vernon. "Black Politics at National Republican and Democratic Conventions 1868-1972." *Phylon* 36 (Third Quarter 1975): 276.

"Whatever Happened to Channing Phillips?" *Washington Post*, 4 February 1982.

Whitaker, Joseph D. "College Fires D.C. Civic Figure." *Washington Post*, 12 September 1975.

Glenda M. Alvin

Chronology

1848	Born in Troy, New York on June 26
1865	Graduates from the New Jersey Collegiate Institute
1868	Marries Elizabeth M. Hughes
1869	Begins career as an educator at an African American school in Leesburg, Virginia
1870	Establishes a school for African Americans in Alexandria, Virginia
1875	Becomes principal of a school in Bordentown, New Jersey
1881	Accepts job as bookkeeper in the Fourth Auditor's Office of the United States Treasury
1884	Becomes superintendent of schools in Camden, New Jersey's fourth district
1886	Teaches at Camden High and Training School
1897	Accepts appointments as envoy extraordinary and minister plenipotentiary to Haiti as well as chargeé d'affaires to the Dominican Republic
1899	Marries Jane B. Shepard
1905	Returns to Camden
1907	Becomes an editorial writer for the *Philadelphia Tribune*
1920	Dies on January 23 (approximate date)

William Powell
1848–1920

Educator, diplomat

William Powell gained prominence in New Jersey as a teacher and educational leader prior to attracting the attention of several presidents of the United States who offered Powell opportunities to become an American envoy. Powell, after rejecting two consular assignments, ultimately served as a diplomat to Haiti and the Dominican Republic.

William Frank Powell, the son of William and Julia Crawford Powell, was born on June 26, 1848, in Troy, New York. His father's ancestors were Native Americans. Powell attended public schools in Brooklyn, New York, and Jersey City, New Jersey. He also attended the New York School of Pharmacy and Ashmun Institute in Pennsylvania (later known as Lincoln University) and the New Jersey Collegiate Institute (NJCI). In 1865, Powell graduated from NJCI. Three years later, he married Elizabeth M. Hughes, who was from Burlington, New Jersey.

In 1869, Powell began his career as an educator when the Presbyterian Board of Missions hired him to teach at an African American school in Leesburg, Virginia. In Alexandria, Virginia one year later, Powell founded a school for African American children and led the school for five years.

Powell became principal of a Bordentown, New Jersey, school in 1875. In 1881, he interrupted his career as an educator and was employed as a bookkeeper in the Fourth Auditor's Office of the United States Treasury.

Also in 1881, Powell was offered a diplomatic assignment in Haiti, but he rejected it.

In 1884, Powell resumed his career as an educator when he became superintendent of schools in the fourth district of Camden, New Jersey. Under Powell's leadership, attendance increased, manual training was included in the curriculum, and a new school for industrial education was built. In 1886, Powell relinquished his position as superintendent and taught at Camden High and Training School, a predominantly white school. This career move probably made Powell one of the first African Americans to teach in a predominantly white school in Camden as well as the rest of New Jersey. He remained at Camden High until 1894. He rejected a second diplomatic appointment in 1891 during the administration of Benjamin Harrison.

Becomes a U.S. Diplomat

When Powell was offered a diplomatic assignment a third time, he accepted. On June 17, 1897, President William McKinley appointed Powell envoy extraordinary and minister plenipotentiary to Haiti, and Powell was the first American diplomat to Haiti to receive the title. Eleven diplomats to Haiti preceded Powell; the first two were designated commissioner/consul general while the remaining nine diplomats were appointed minister resident/consul general. At least six African American minister residents/consul generals were appointed to Haiti before Powell: Ebenezer D. Bassett, who was the first U.S. black diplomat; John M. Langston; George W. Williams, who took the oath of office but did not serve;

John E. W. Thompson; Frederick Douglass; and John S. Durham. On the same day as Powell was appointed to Haiti, he received a second one; Powell became the sixth U.S. diplomat to Haiti who concurrently served as chargeé d'affaires to the Dominican Republic. His appointment to the Dominican Republic ended on July 23, 1904, and his appointment to Haiti ended on approximately November 30, 1905. Thus Powell maintained his diplomatic status during the first three years of Theodore Roosevelt's presidency. The year that Powell began his career as a diplomat, 1897, was the first year of McKinley's presidency, and as Benjamin Justesen points out, at least twenty African Americans were appointed consuls during the administrations of McKinley and Roosevelt, which was a period of twelve years.

During Powell's first year in Haiti, a Haitian court fined and imprisoned a German man for assault and battery. As a result, Germany issued an ultimatum. Two German warships would bombard Port-au-Prince, Haiti's capital, on December 6, 1897, unless within three hours, President Simon Sam agreed that Haiti would pay $20,000. Sam acquiesced, yet it is interesting to note that Powell was the lone member of the diplomatic corps who advised the president not to pay the indemnity. The United States government did not consider the incident in violation of the Monroe Doctrine, and when Powell urged the U.S. government to make Haiti a U.S. protectorate, Secretary of State John Sherman rejected the idea in a January 11, 1898, letter to Powell.

Also in 1898, the Haitian government, heeding Powell's advice, ended the practice begun on October 1, 1897 of imposing a tax on U.S. merchants and clerks. Such efforts by Powell were aimed at improving relationships between the two countries' governments as well as facilitating American business in Haiti. Among the highlights of Powell's diplomatic efforts in 1899 was the release of a U.S. vice-consul general who had been arrested. One year later, Powell successfully defended Haiti's sovereignty against the German minister's plan to create special courts to try foreigners. Also in 1899, Powell married a second time; he wed Jane B. Shepard, who was from Camden. In 1902, Powell witnessed President Sam's forced resignation, the anarchy that followed, rule by a provisional government, and the election of Nord Alexis as Haiti's next president. Powell remained in Haiti through most of 1905.

When Powell ended his diplomatic career, he returned to Camden. In 1907, Powell was awarded an honorary LL.D. degree from Lincoln University, one of the schools he attended in his youth. In 1909, he accepted a position as an editorial writer for the *Philadelphia Tribune*, an African American newspaper that was founded in November 1884. His approximate death date is listed as January 23, 1920. A posthumous tribute took place when the Tenth Street School, built in Camden in 1926, was renamed the William F. Powell Elementary School.

Although Powell's accomplishments as a teacher, educational administrator, diplomat, and editorial writer are not widely known, he remains an important historical figure who dedicated his life to educating African Americans as well as others and for eight years served the United States as a member of the diplomatic corps.

REFERENCES

Books

Logan, Rayford W. *Haiti and the Dominican Republic*. New York: Oxford University Press, 1968.

Marquis, Albert N., ed. "William Frank Powell." In *Who's Who in America*. Vol. 7.: 1912-1913. Chicago: A. N. Marquis and Company, 1912.

McNeill, Lydia. "William Frank Powell." In *Encyclopedia of African-American Culture and History*. Vol.4. Eds. Jack Salzman, David Lionel Smith, and Cornel West. New York: Macmillan Library Reference, 1996.

Phillips, Glenn O. "William Frank Powell." In *Dictionary of American Negro Biography*. Eds. Rayford W. Logan and Michael R. Winston. New York: Norton, 1982.

Wright, Marion M. T. *The Education of Negroes in New Jersey*. New York: Teachers College, Columbia University, 1941.

Periodicals

Justesen, Benjamin J. "African-American Consuls Abroad, 1807-1909."*Foreign Service Journal* 81 (September 2004): 72-76.

Linda M. Carter

Richard Pryor
1940–2005

Comedian, actor, screenwriter

Richard Pryor transcended the turmoil of his personal life to become one of the greatest comedians and performers in the history of American entertainment. Although he achieved great fame, success, and wealth, Pryor challenged conventions and generated controversy with his daring use of language and subject matter considered off-limits for the general public. Pryor also suffered the consequences of several difficult marriages and divorces, dangerous lifestyle choices, and debilitating illness in his final years.

Richard Pryor

Chronology

1940	Born in Peoria, Illinois on December 1
1958	Leaves Peoria to join U.S. Army
1960	Returns to Peoria to work as local comedian
1963	Moves to New York seeking greater career opportunities
1964	Makes first national television appearance as comedian on the *On Broadway Tonight* program with Rudy Vallee
1967	Lands first movie role in *The Busy Body*
1969	Suffers a nervous breakdown during a show in Las Vegas
1970	Moves to northern California and takes a break from show business
1971	Returns to New York
1972	Showcases dramatic ability in *Lady Sings the Blues*, a film on the life of Billie Holiday
1974	Collaborates with Mel Brooks on the screenplay for *Blazing Saddles*; receives a Writers' Guild Award and the American Academy of Humor Award for his contributions
1974-76	Wins three consecutive Grammy Awards for Best Comedy Album
1977	Stars in first leading film role in *Greased Lightning*; suffers first heart attack
1980	Suffers severe burns after drug-related accident; endures a series of skin graft operations and grueling physical therapy; later establishes the Richard Pryor Burn Foundation to assist other burn victims
1983	Receives highest fee ever for black actor in single film, for *Superman III*
1986	Discovers symptoms of multiple sclerosis and other health problems
1990	Suffers second heart attack
1992	Performs new material before a sold-out audience at the Circle Star Theater near San Francisco, his first live concert appearance in almost six years; awarded the American Comedy Awards Lifetime Achievement Honor
1995	Publishes his autobiography, *Pryor Convictions and Other Life Sentences*
1996	Inducted into the NAACP Hall of Fame
1997	Makes final film appearance in *Lost Highway*
1998	Becomes the first recipient of the Mark Twain Prize for American Humor
2005	Dies at home in Encino, California on December 10

Richard Franklin Lennox Thomas Pryor was born on December 1, 1940, in Peoria, Illinois. His mother, Gertrude Thomas, was a local prostitute, and his father LeRoy Pryor Jr. (also known as Buck Carter) was a bartender, boxer, and veteran of World War II. Although his parents' relationship was far from typical and often violent, they understood the realities of their situation, eventually divorced, and moved on to other relationships. Pryor continued to have intermittent contact with his parents for the remainder of their lives.

Pryor had a traumatic childhood, being raised primarily by his grandmother and legal guardian Marie Carter, who was the madam of a local brothel on North Washington Street. Along with three other children, he experienced and witnessed the seamy lifestyles and poverty of that environment, and continued to be influenced by these factors and situations. In his 1995 autobiography *Pryor Convictions and Other Life Sentences,* Pryor said that he "lived in a neighborhood with a lot of whorehouses. Not many candy stores or banks. Liquor stores and whorehouses." Despite the lifestyles of his immediate family, his grandmother tried to instill some discipline and values in the young Pryor by insisting he go to a local church.

Pryor was raped at the age of six by a teenaged neighbor, molested by a Catholic priest during catechism, and watched his mother perform sexual acts with the town mayor. Despite this abuse, he earned high marks at a Catholic grade school until he was expelled at age ten when his family's occupations were discovered, and his mother abandoned him. Attending movies at the local theater became a way to escape the harsh realities of his life, even though he could only sit in the seats designated for African Americans. He fantasized that he was in the movies he was watching and developed an ambition to become an entertainer himself.

Begins Performing Career on Local Stage

At age twelve, Pryor was cast in a local production of the classic children's tale *Rumpelstiltskin* by Juliette Whittaker, who was a supervisor at the Carver Community Center, a Peoria public recreation facility. Whittaker was so impressed by his performance and comic talent that she sought talent shows and other venues to showcase his ability and potential, and she continued to influence Pryor in the development of his career. In junior high school he was known for telling jokes and entertaining his teachers as well as classmates, but he did not do as well academically as he had in elementary school.

After being expelled from school for a petty offense at age fourteen, Pryor worked an assortment of odd jobs, including shining shoes, attending to billiard halls, and meat packing. Despite his young age, he also worked as a janitor in a local strip club, tried his hand at playing drums, and did some truck driving, with limited success. Pryor became a father for the first time, with the birth of his daughter, Renee, in 1957.

Joins Military, Returns, and Continues Performing

From 1958 to 1960 Pryor served in the U.S. Army, stationed at one point in Idar-Oberstein, West Germany. He was involved in an altercation in which he came to the assistance of another black soldier in a bar fight with a white soldier, but avoided being jailed for his actions. Pryor returned to Peoria when he was discharged from the army, and shortly afterward he began working at Harold's Club, trying to sing and play piano, and quickly discovered that the audience preferred his jokes over his musical efforts. In 1960 he married Patricia Price, but this union ended the following year. His first son, Richard Jr., was also born in 1961.

Pryor experienced his first taste of professional success and drugs, including marijuana and amphetamines, when he began working beyond Peoria as a comic act in nightclubs throughout the Midwest and parts of Canada. Inspired by other black comedians, such as Bill Cosby, Dick Gregory, and Redd Foxx, who had received recognition for their talent beyond the African American community, Pryor moved to New York in 1963 and began to attract national attention.

In New York, Pryor became part of the downtown Greenwich Village entertainment scene, sharing stages with musicians such as Bob Dylan and Richie Havens and being influenced by other working comedians such as Woody Allen, Flip Wilson, George Carlin, and Joan Rivers. He also worked uptown at the legendary Apollo Theater in Harlem, long known as a proving ground for black entertainers. At this point, he patterned his performances after other comedians, which made his acts quite different from the radical approach he came to be known for later, a style which was already being used with mixed success by the controversial comedian Lenny Bruce.

Pryor's private life continued to be tumultuous: he began using cocaine while dating a prostitute, one of his various and numerous sexual liaisons. Despite the erratic unpredictability of his behavior off-stage, Pryor's talent on stage opened the door for his first national television appearance, on August 31, 1964. After his performance as part of the *On Broadway Tonight* program with Rudy Vallee, Pryor worked on other shows such as the *Kraft Summer Music Hall*, and made the first of numerous appearances on *The Ed Sullivan Show, The Tonight Show with Johnny Carson*, and *The Merv Griffin Show*.

Unfortunately, Pryor's success provided more money for his addictions, philandering, and other personal excesses. Nevertheless, his talent continued to keep him in demand, and by 1967 Pryor was working in Las Vegas venues such as the Flamingo Hotel, where he opened for singer/actor Bobby Darin. The same year Pryor landed his first movie role, a small part in *The Busy Body*, a film starring comedy legend Sid Caesar. Pryor also fathered another daughter, Elizabeth, married for the second time to Shelly Bonus, and received word that his mother had died before the year ended.

In 1968 he appeared in another film, *Wild in the Streets*, and began making comedy album recordings, in which he exercised the freedom to use profanity in graphic, yet funny and honest descriptions of his life and the lifestyles of others. The long-playing (LP) record format enabled Pryor to go far beyond the acceptable fare and limited time frames of most of his television, film, and Las Vegas stage performances, which were as frustrating as they were lucrative. His father also passed away during the year, leaving his grandmother as his closest relative.

The following year, Pryor suffered a nervous breakdown and walked off the stage during a show in Las Vegas. His second marriage also ended during 1969, and he fathered another daughter, Rain, who would eventually follow her father into the entertainment business.

Develops Other Aspects of Talent

Pryor moved to northern California in 1970, continued his drug use and erratic behavior, but also gained new insight while taking a break from big-time show business. While living in the Berkeley area near San Francisco, he came in contact with several African American intellectuals and activists such as Ishmael Reed, Angela Davis, Huey P. Newton, Claude Brown, and Al Young. Pryor also read the writings of Malcolm X and listened to message music such as Marvin Gaye's *What's Goin' On* album. As a result, Pryor began to add an edge of biting political and social commentary to his comedic use of profanity while working in small Bay Area clubs. He was unafraid to use explosive racial epithets, before all types of audiences, in an effort to minimize their negative impact and turn them into terms of pride and defiance.

In 1971 he returned to New York, first to Harlem and the Apollo, then to the Improv comedy nightclub to present his new concepts as performance material for his first comedy film, *Live and Smokin'*, and his second record album, *Craps (After Hours)*. His new focus extended into comedy writing for himself and other artists, and collaborating with another comedy legend, Mel Brooks, on the screenplay for *Blazing Saddles*, about a black sheriff in the Old West. The studio refused to cast Pryor in the lead role, but the film was still a hit with Cleavon Little as the sheriff.

Pryor demonstrated yet another facet of his talent with his critically acclaimed dramatic performance in *Lady Sings the Blues*, a 1972 film based on the life of jazz singer Billie Holiday, starring Diana Ross and produced by Berry Gordy of Motown Records fame. His role as *Piano Man*, a drug-addicted musician, proved to viewers that there was much more to Pryor's ability than his gift for comedy.

Pryor also wrote for television shows such as *Sanford and Son*, starring Redd Foxx, and the *Flip Wilson Show*, and helped his fellow black comedians as they found great success in the early 1970s. His work as a writer as well as a performer on two 1973 TV specials featuring comedienne Lily Tomlin led to a Writers' Guild Award, and he shared a 1974 Emmy Award for outstanding variety program writing with Tomlin and eleven other contributors. Remembering his Peoria roots, Pryor gave his Emmy to Juliette Whittaker and the Carver Center. Pryor won another Writers' Guild Award and the American Academy of Humor Award in 1974 for his contributions to the *Blazing Saddles* screenplay.

During that year Pryor also teamed with Academy Award winner Sidney Poitier, Harry Belafonte, and Bill Cosby in the cast of another successful comedy film, *Uptown Saturday Night*. The film was a departure for Poitier and Belafonte, better known for more serious performances, yet the presence of Pryor and Cosby brought balance and guaranteed laughter during production and in the finished product viewed by the public.

Recognized as Comedian and Actor

By the middle of the 1970s, Pryor had become a household name and was considered by many "the funniest man alive." He won Grammy Awards for Best Comedy Album three years straight (1974 to 1976), while also accomplishing the amazing feat of five gold (500,000) and two platinum (1 million) copies sold among his nearly two dozen recordings. Pryor's achievements took on additional significance in that his recordings did not feature music, just the man using a microphone in a studio or in front of a live audience.

Pryor also hired David Franklin, an African American attorney based in Atlanta, to provide legal counsel and serve as his agent in negotiating contracts and other business aspects of his career. Franklin helped Pryor through his numerous legal entanglements resulting from his personal as well as professional activities and assisted in his transition to superstar status in the entertainment world, but their business relationship became more strained in future years.

Makes Impact in Television and Film

In television, Pryor contributed to the early success of *Saturday Night Live*, the long-running NBC comedy show, appearing frequently during its first season in 1976 as a host and guest with original cast members John Belushi, Dan Aykroyd, Chevy Chase, Gilda Radner, Garrett Morris, and others. He also appeared in three movies that year, including teaming with Gene Wilder for the comedy film *Silver Streak*, which became a major hit with the viewing public. During the next year his career as a film actor also blossomed, with leading roles as pioneer African American race car driver Wendell Scott in *Greased Lightning*, and portraying multiple characters in *Which Way Is Up?*

Pryor married for the third time in 1977, to Deborah McGuire, and starred briefly in his own TV series on NBC, *The Richard Pryor Show*. He challenged the status quo and censors from the opening segment of the first broadcast, in which he used a body stocking and visual/camera distortion to appear nude. The series was canceled after only five shows, but Pryor remained undaunted by this setback and continued his stage, film, and recording careers with great success. One setback was his first heart attack which he experienced on November 9, 1977, while in Peoria to celebrate his grandmother's birthday.

In 1978 Pryor turned in another outstanding dramatic performance as Zeke, a Detroit auto worker, in the film *Blue Collar*, but overall Hollywood producers sought to restrict Pryor to supporting roles which softened his cutting-edge approach to life and humor. He continued his string of movie appearances that year, including his role as the title character in *The Wiz*, an African American remake of *The Wizard of Oz*. The production reunited Pryor with Diana Ross and also included Michael Jackson, Nipsey Russell, and a special appearance by the legendary Lena Horne. Despite the collection of superstar talent, the film met with mixed reviews and only moderate success.

His private life continued to reflect his hectic schedule, personal problems, and addictions, including his heavy use of cocaine. Pryor's third marriage ended that year after a dangerous and highly publicized incident in which he fired a pistol at his wife, then "killed her car" with additional shots in the course of a heated argument.

He then began dating Jennifer Lee, who was at his side in Peoria when his grandmother died in December 1978. She stayed with Pryor through his subsequent depression, drug and sexual binges, detoxification, and therapy. After a psychiatrist recommended he change his behavior and surroundings, Pryor traveled with Lee to Kenya, where he decided to stop using racial epithets after observing the country's racial diversity and harmony. Surprisingly, he received a backlash from some quarters for his decision and was accused of "going soft" because of his increasing fame, wealth, and relationship with Lee, a white woman.

Pryor's greatest film success to that point came at the end of the decade, with *Richard Pryor—Live in Concert* in 1979. He came to full life on screen, as he carried the filming of his stage performance with numerous skits, characterizations, and impersonations, including his classic Mudbone character, who humorously and sensitively depicted life as experienced by alcoholics, addicts, hustlers, the homeless, and other persons generally considered as undesirables.

Nearly Dies after Drug Accident

While Pryor continued to abuse drugs, alcohol, and other intoxicants, cocaine had become his primary addiction. In the course of freebasing cocaine at his California home on June 9, 1980, Pryor set fire to himself, suffering third-degree burns over half of his body. Pryor's Aunt Dee, who was visiting him, acted quickly to put out the flames, stabilized him after he ran out of his home while on fire and disoriented, and saved her nephew's life.

The accident drew international publicity, given Pryor's high visibility as an entertainer, and many thought he would not survive. Amazingly, Pryor endured a series of skin graft operations and grueling physical therapy and then turned his personal tragedy into positive action. In appreciation of the care he received from the Sherman Oaks Hospital Burn Center, he established the Richard Pryor Burn Foundation to assist other burn victims, and he did not hesitate to turn this experience into both comedy and commentary as part of his performances.

Makes More Movies and Money

The previously completed film *Stir Crazy*, which reunited Pryor with Gene Wilder, was released in December 1980 and earned over $100 million at the box office. Before the accident, Pryor had been working on *Bustin' Loose*, a film with Cicely Tyson, the noted African American actress and former Academy Award nominee. With his clout as a major Hollywood star and producer of the film, Pryor included three children from Peoria selected by Juliette Whittaker as cast members in the production and continued to generously support her private school, The Learning Tree.

After his recovery from the accident, Pryor returned to complete the film in 1981. He also wed Jennifer Lee on August 16 of that year at his home in Hawaii, but his fourth marriage ended the next year, as he returned to cocaine and other self-destructive behavior. He became paranoid about his money, among other things, and sued David Franklin for mismanagement and misappropriation of funds in 1982. Franklin did not take this challenge seriously, but the California labor commissioner ruled in Pryor's favor, ending their business relationship.

Despite his ongoing personal problems, Pryor also made what many critics and fans consider his best concert film, *Richard Pryor—Live on the Sunset Strip*. In his own inimitable fashion, he turned his near-death experience as well as his drug use, relationships, and other issues into hilarious comedy. This success proved to his fans and the general public, as well as to Hollywood executives, that he was not only a survivor but still "the funniest man alive" and now ready to continue his career. During that year he also directed himself in the movie *Richard Pryor—Here and Now*, and co-starred with legendary comedian Jackie Gleason in *The Toy*. While on a live performance tour, Pryor began yet another relationship, with twenty-year-old Flynn BeLaine, after meeting her in Washington, D.C.

Continues Film Career and Excessive Lifestyle

Pryor continued to be frequently cast in films during the rest of the 1980s, but his performances lacked the edge of his best earlier work. Poor scripts and parts were also a factor, but Pryor could still manage to make a film do well at the box office by his very presence. For the 1983 movie *Superman III*, he commanded a fee of $4 million, to that point the highest amount ever earned by a black actor for a single film. His appearance as a comic villain was disappointing, yet he made $1 million more than Christopher Reeve, the star of the film.

During the same year Pryor secured a $40 million deal with Columbia Pictures and established his own company, Indigo Productions, to develop entertainment projects showcasing his talents as an actor, producer, director, and writer. He hired former football star and actor Jim Brown to run the day-to-day operations but fired him before the year ended. Many observers in the African American and film communities were disappointed, as Pryor's personal success did not translate into as many increased opportunities for other blacks in Hollywood as anticipated.

In 1984 Pryor developed a short-lived children's show for television, *Pryor's Place*, and received the Black Filmmakers Hall of Fame Award. Around the same time as the award presentation he received news that Flynn BeLaine was pregnant with his child. Pryor became a father again, as his son Steven was born on November 16 of that year. He did not marry BeLaine at that time but still was required to provide large amounts of money in child support. Although Pryor made millions of dollars as an entertainer, he also spent millions to support his Hollywood lifestyle and its excesses, business associates, children from other marriages and relationships, and other family members, along with a variety of legal and other expenses.

Completes Film Version of Life Story

In 1986 Pryor co-wrote, produced, directed, and starred in *Jo Jo Dancer, Your Life Is Calling*, an autobiographical film which was only moderately successful. Because so much of Pryor's art was based on his life, many critics and viewers already knew much of his story, and a re-creation could not possibly top his real-life experiences. He also tried to defuse criticism of Indigo Productions by hiring a number of African Americans to work behind as well as in front of the camera, including longtime friend and collaborator Paul Mooney, but this did not have much impact on the overall employment of blacks in Hollywood.

In the summer of 1986 Pryor began experiencing symptoms of fatigue, sudden loss of muscle control, and noticeable weight loss. After extensive tests by his doctor and a visit to the Mayo Clinic in Minnesota, he was diagnosed as having multiple sclerosis (MS). While still a serious health problem, the medical findings helped put to rest worries and rumors that Pryor had contracted AIDS in the course of his philandering and drug abuse.

Pryor tried to carry on with his life and career as in the past but began to realize his mortality with the progression of the disease. On October 10, 1986, BeLaine became his fifth wife, but in January 1987 Pryor and BeLaine divorced after less than three months of marriage. This was in part because another son, Franklin Matthew Mason Pryor, had been born as a result of Pryor's earlier affair with actress Geraldine Mason. BeLaine was also pregnant and gave birth to their daughter, Kelsey, later that year.

By 1988 a younger comedian/actor, Eddie Murphy, who had patterned much of his style on Pryor, was the new black superstar in Hollywood, and a younger generation of African American film artists emerged to challenge the mainstream film industry, including Spike Lee, John Singleton, Robert Townsend, Keenan Ivory Wayans, and others. All of these artists, and many others, acknowledged the influence of Pryor on their development. Murphy recruited Pryor and Redd Foxx to appear with him in the 1989 film *Harlem Nights*, but the historic on-screen meeting of three generations of black comedians provided less humor than expected.

Tries to Continue Working as Health Fails

Pryor suffered another heart attack in March 1990 and eventually underwent quadruple-bypass heart surgery in addition to living with the effects of MS. Determined not to give up, he continued doing "stand-up" comedy now sitting down at places like the Comedy Store nightclub in Los Angeles, the scene of many past triumphs. He also

remarried Flynn BeLaine in April of that year, but they divorced again in 1991. By the time of his fiftieth birthday in December 1990, Pryor had appeared in over forty films, was past his prime as an entertainer and in ill health, yet he still made his best effort to continue his career.

On October 31, 1992, Pryor performed new material before a sold-out audience at the Circle Star Theater near San Francisco, his first live concert appearance in almost six years, using a walking cane for support. Encouraged by positive reviews, he tried to take his act on the road but had to cancel the tour after a few performances.

As Pryor came to grips with the end of his active performing career, he received a number of awards and recognition from peers in the entertainment industry. These included the American Comedy Awards Lifetime Achievement Honor in 1992, several all-star tributes, and retrospectives of his many career highlights.

While he maintained contact with his ex-wives and children, Jennifer Lee became his primary companion and caretaker in 1994. The following year he co-wrote and published his autobiography, *Pryor Convictions and Other Life Sentences* with Todd Gold, was inducted into the NAACP Hall of Fame in 1996, and in 1997 made his final film appearance with a small role in the David Lynch film, *Lost Highway*. In 1998 Pryor became the first recipient of the Mark Twain Prize for American Humor, presented by the John F. Kennedy Center for the Performing Arts in Washington, D.C.

Final Years

Even though his deteriorating health forced him into seclusion and the use of a wheelchair, Pryor responded to premature reports of his death through his official Internet web site. He also campaigned for animal welfare through letters and Christmas card messages and was honored by People for the Ethical Treatment of Animals (PETA) for his efforts.

In June 2001 Pryor and Lee re-married, and she continued to manage Pryor's business affairs as well as tend to his personal and medical needs. They gained legal rights to much of Pryor's earliest comedy work on small record labels, then edited and re-issued the recordings. A 2003 television documentary featured archival footage of Pryor performances, with commentary and testimonials from a number of comedians, and in 2004 the Comedy Central cable television channel named him the best stand-up comedian of all time. The same year the first Richard Pryor Ethnic Comedy Award was presented at the Edinburgh Fringe Festival in Scotland, and a 2005 British poll voted him the tenth greatest comedy act ever.

On December 10, 2005, nine days after reaching age sixty-five, Pryor died of cardiac arrest at his home in Encino, California. His wife attempted to revive him without success but indicated later that his last days were peaceful, and at the end he was smiling. Black Entertainment Television aired a Richard Pryor special on December 19 in tribute, as his death was noted by major media outlets around the world.

Pryor's last project was another film based on his life, co-written with his last wife. The comedian/actor Mike Epps was personally selected by Pryor to portray him, and the film, when completed, was intended to add to the legacy and legend of a man who exhibited the survival of the human spirit through tragedy with comedy and creativity.

REFERENCES

Books

Bogle, Donald. *Blacks in American Films and Television: An Encyclopedia.* New York: Garland Publishing, Inc., 1988.

Johnson, Anne Janette, and David G. Oblender. "Richard Pryor." In *Contemporary Black Biography*. Vol. 24. Ed. Shirelle Phelps. Farmington Hills, Mich.: Gale Group, Inc., 2000.

Robbins, Fred, and David Ragan. *Richard Pryor: This Cat's Got Nine Lives*. New York: Delilah Books, 1982.

Smydra, David F. Jr. "Richard Pryor." In *African American Lives*. Eds. Henry Louis Gates and Evelyn Brooks Higginbotham. New York: Oxford University Press, 2004.

Williams, John A., and Dennis A. Williams. *If I Stop I'll Die: The Comedy and Tragedy of Richard Pryor.* New York: Thunder's Mouth Press, 1993.

Online

"An Authentic Life: Richard Pryor's Official Biography." Richard Pryor Web Site. http://www. richardpryor.com/history.cfm (Accessed 14 March 2006).

"Comedian Richard Pryor Dies at 65." Cable News Network Web Site. http://www.cnn.com/2005/US/12/ 10/pryor.obit/index.html (Accessed 14 March 2006).

Fletcher F. Moon

Charles Burleigh Purvis
1842–1929

Surgeon, physician, educator

A physician, educator, and community leader, Charles Burleigh Purvis was ahead of his time in several ways. He was one of eight black surgeons in the

Chronology	
1842	Born in Philadelphia, Pennsylvania on April 14
1860-63	Studies at Oberlin College
1864	Serves as military nurse
1865	Receives M.D. degree from Wooster Medical College; joins Union Army as acting assistant surgeon
1869	Joins medical faculty of Howard University faculty
1870	Co-founds interracial National Medical Society of the District of Columbia
1871	Marries Ann Hathaway
1871-72	Holds Thaddeus Stevens Chair at Howard medical school
1881	Becomes surgeon-in-chief of Freedmen's Hospital; attends President James Garfield when he is shot on July 2
1897-1904	Serves as member of Board of Medical Examiners
1899-1900	Serves as president of medical school faculty at Howard
1900	Elected dean of medical school, but declines
1904	Becomes licensed to practice medicine on Massachusetts; accepted into Massachusetts Medical Society
1905	Relocates to Boston, Massachusetts but maintains affiliation with Howard
1907	Resigns teaching position at Howard University
1908	Elected to Board of Directors at Howard University
1926	Resigns from Howard University Board of Directors on June 1
1929	Dies in Los Angeles, California, on December 14

Union Army during the Civil War and was the first African American on the faculty of a U.S. medical college. He became the surgeon-in-charge at Freedmen's Hospital and provided medical services to the black community of Washington D.C.

Charles Burleigh Purvis was born in Philadelphia, Pennsylvania to a well-to-do abolitionist family on April 14, 1842. His grandfather, William Purvis, a cotton broker, had left England around 1790, becoming a naturalized American citizen. His grandmother, Harriet Judah, was free-born, although she was the daughter of a slave, Dido Badaraka, who had been kidnapped from her native Morocco at the age of twelve and sold into bondage. Given her freedom when she was nineteen, Dido had married a German, Baron Judah. Their daughter, Harriet Judah, and William Purvis had three sons; one of them was Robert Purvis, Charles' father. Charles' mother, Harriet Forten, was the daughter of James Forten, a wealthy black businessman, sail maker, and abolitionist. Harriet was an abolitionist and an ardent supporter of women's rights. In December 1833, she became a founding member of the Philadelphia Female Anti-Slavery Society, along with her mother and sisters. Robert Purvis was a major force in the formation of the Anti-Slavery Society in Philadelphia; he was also an abolitionist and supporter of women's rights. He assisted in the efforts of the Underground Railroad. Robert Purvis and Harriet Forten were married in 1831; they had eight children. Charles Purvis was the fifth child born to the couple.

When Charles was about two years old, his family moved to Byberry, a small farming community near Philadelphia. He and his brothers and sisters attended local Quaker schools. As he matured, Purvis worked on the farm and was exposed to local anti-slavery and abolitionist activities. Charles and his brothers and sisters were accustomed to life on a farm, and as he grew older he continued in this occupation for a number of years. Many of the farmers supported the anti-slavery movement and admired and respected his father's devotion and work toward this effort.

Attends College and Joins the Military

Charles Purvis attended Oberlin College from 1860 to 1863. He transferred to Wooster Medical College (later incorporated into Western Reserve University) in Cleveland as the rumblings of the Civil War began. He received his medical degree in 1865, when he graduated from the medical school.

In 1864 Purvis served as a military nurse at Camp Barker, a contraband hospital in Washington, D.C. The site was later the foundation of Freedmen's Hospital. Purvis provided medical assistance to many slaves who had either been freed by Union soldiers in the South or had escaped their masters. These freemen were referred to as contraband. The relief center, located in the Camp Barker barracks, was a model for Freedmen's Hospital, where Purvis would spend twenty-five years as a surgeon. While at the relief center, Purvis contracted typhoid fever, but after recovering in 1865, he joined the Union Army as an acting assistant surgeon. He continued to serve in that capacity until 1869.

Upon graduation from medical school Purvis petitioned the United States Volunteers to become an assistant surgeon for the Union Army. When his petition was accepted, he became one of only eight African Americans accepted as surgeons during the war. Purvis was a first lieutenant from 1865 to 1869, assigned to the Washington, D.C. area. After the Civil War, when the Bureau of Refugees, Freedmen, and Abandoned Lands took on the responsibility for medical services for blacks, Purvis, like many African American physicians, contracted his services.

Joins the Medical Faculty at Howard University

In the seven years between 1860 and 1867, the black population of Washington D.C. grew from some 14,000 to nearly 39,000, but the city had only six black physicians. Purvis was one of the physicians who served this community. The responsibility of providing medical services to the Washington, D.C. black population may have intensified for Purvis after Howard University was founded in 1867. While he continued to work as an assistant surgeon in the outdoor clinic, by March 15, 1869, he was on

Howard University's faculty. In the 1860s, Howard's students and faculty were predominantly white, and at the time Purvis was only the second African American to hold a faculty position at a U.S. medical college. (The first was Alexander T. Augusta.) Charles Purvis was a learned man. Between 1869 and 1873, he lectured on many topics related to medicine, including material medica, a branch of medical science dealing with the use of drugs to treat illnesses; therapeutics; botany; and medical jurisprudence. A successful academic, he held the Thaddeus Stevens Chair for a year (1871-72). He was also a professor of obstetrics, gynecology, and diseases of women and pediatrics from 1873 to 1889. The Board of Trustees conferred an honorary degree on Purvis in 1871, and he received a LL.D. in 1914.

Purvis's wife Ann Hathaway, whom he married in April 13, 1871, was white—a marriage which probably caused the couple some anguish in response to the reactions from members of both the black and white communities. They had two children, a boy and a girl, both of whom chose medical careers: Alice became a physician; Robert became a dentist.

In 1873 Howard University, like the rest of the country, faced an economic crisis. The medical faculty was told they would have to resign or work without pay. Charles Purvis was among those who elected to work pro bono until 1907, when the crisis ended. He and some of his colleagues, including Alexander Augusta and Gideon Palmer, were most likely able to do this because of their private medical practices. According to Michael Winston in *Dictionary of American Negro Biography*, in 1873 Purvis wrote to General Otis Howard, the university president for whom the institution is named: "While I regret the university will not be able to pay me for my services, I feel the importance of every effort being made to carry forward the institution and to make it a success." Purvis was also a powerful lobbyist who was able to influence Congress to appropriate $600,000—a vast sum at the time—for a new building to house the Freedmen's Hospital.

During this period, Purvis became secretary pro tempore of the medical department at Howard. He remained in this position until 1896. Under his direction, the department was reorganized and the staff was reminded to keep abreast of recent medical developments. His leadership helped to insure that African Americans and women would have the opportunity to receive a medical education and become physicians. Purvis was also president of the faculty from 1899 to 1900, and in 1900 he was elected dean of the medical school but declined.

Treats President, Denied Admittance to Medical Society

On July 2, 1881, President James Garfield was mortally wounded by an assassin. Charles Purvis was one of the physicians asked to give the president medical treatment. He became the first and only African American to provide assistance to a sitting president. In acknowledgement of his service President Chester A. Arthur appointed him surgeon-in-chief of Freedmen's hospital, the facility affiliated with Howard University's medical department. This act made Purvis the first black to head a hospital under civilian authority. Charles Purvis remained in the position until 1894. Racism still existed, however, and Purvis was denied admittance to the Medical Society of the District of Columbia, a branch of the American Medical Association, because of his race. This caused great concern among white physicians who supported his application and opposed the racist policies of the organization. In response, in 1870 he and other black physicians formed the interracial National Medical Society of the District of Columbia.

Charles Purvis was active in community institutions in Washington and served on the board of education, the board of health, and the board of medical examiners in the Washington D. C. area from 1897 to 1904. He was also on the board of trade. Purvis was licensed to practice medicine in Massachusetts in 1904 and in that same year was admitted to the Massachusetts Medical Society. He relocated to Boston in 1905 and continued to practice medicine; he also maintained his affiliation with Howard. He resigned his teaching position at Howard in 1907 and became a member of the board of directors in 1908. He remained on the board until 1926. Charles Purvis died in Los Angeles, California on December 14, 1929. He was an important leader in the medical profession and a pioneer black medical educator as well.

REFERENCES

Books

Logan, Rayford W. *Howard University: The First Hundred Years, 1867-1967*. New York: New York University Press, issued under the auspices of Howard University, 1969.

Newby, M. Dalyce. "Charles Burleigh Purvis." In *American National Biography*. Vol. 17. Eds. John A. Garraty and Mark C. Carnes. New York: Oxford University Press, 2004.

Spradling, Mary Mace. *In Black and White: A Guide to Magazine Articles, Newspaper Articles, and Books Concerning More than 15,000 Black Individuals and Groups*. Detroit, Mich.: Gale Research, 1980.

Winston, Michael. "Charles Burleigh Purvis." In *Dictionary of American Negro Biography*. Eds. Rayford W. Logan and Michael R. Winston. New York: Norton, 1982.

Periodicals

Miller, Kelly. "The Historic Background of the Negro Physician." *Journal of Negro History* 1 (February 1916): 99-109.

Miller, Sammy M., and C. B. Purvis. "An Unpublished Letter from Dr. Charles B. Purvis to Judge Robert Heberton Terrell." *Journal of Negro History* 63 (July 1978): 235-37.

Online

All About Black Health. http://www.allaboutblack health.com/historyofblackphysicians.htm (Accessed 21 July 2005).

Bankard, Bob. "The Underground Railroad In Bucks, Burlington, and Montgomery County." Phillyburbs. com http://www.phillyburbs.com/undergroundrailroad/ purvis.shtml 2005 (Accessed 1 March 2006).

Purvis Family. http://www.geocities.com/Heartland/ Pointe/6765/purvisfam.html (Accessed 1 March 2006).

Mario A. Charles

R

Franklin Raines
1949–

Federal government official, lawyer

Franklin Delano Raines was born on January 14, 1949, in Seattle, Washington. Raines was named after his father, Delno, but the hospital mistakenly recorded his name as Franklin Delano, assuming he was named after President Roosevelt. Having the initials F.D.R seemed to mark Raines for a special role in public service and government. Both his parents were employed as janitors. His mother held a steady job at Boeing, a fact Raines proudly acknowledged when he joined the company's board of directors. His father, who suffered from severe bouts of depression, worked intermittently for the Seattle parks department. During his frequent hospitalizations, the family was forced to seek welfare assistance. Raines is the fourth of six children. The family included a seventh child, a nephew under the guardianship of his parents. Although his childhood years were tough economically, the family managed to stay together. His parents taught by example, instilling core values of hard work and determination in their children. When his father was out of work, he would head to the fields south of Seattle to harvest beans. Raines would often accompany him, working alongside his father all day. His earnings from a job at the local grocery store also helped to supplement the family's income.

In his speeches, Raines often talks about the importance of home ownership. Owning a home allowed his family to meet their basic needs. He tells the story of how his father painstakingly built the family home over a five-year period with accumulated scrap materials salvaged from a home slated for demolition. At that time, his father's only option as a low-income wage earner was a high-interest loan. There were no special programs or agencies that offered affordable financial assistance. The experience taught Raines important lessons about home ownership and setting goals. When he became chairman of Fannie Mae, in charge of the company's overall financial policies, his perspective was deepened by his family's experience. It increased his sensitivity to people's

Franklin Raines

needs and filled him with a determination to ease the burden of home ownership for low-income wage earners.

Just as his father had to arrange finances and gather materials and all the necessary tools to build his home, so it took education, experience, and integration into the power establishment for Raines to realize his goals. During the early years, he attended predominately black public schools. In high school Raines participated in a wide range of activities from academics to sports. He was captain of the football team, student government president, and a member of the debating team that won the state championship. Although he loved sports, he realized that academics had to be ranked higher. Franklin High School in Seattle, Washington was a racially diverse educational institution with an established tradition of praising stu-

551

dent achievements. Raines was privileged to have good teachers and mentors who steered him in the right direction. He graduated with a perfect academic record in 1967. The philosophy espoused by the school was one he embraced and upheld throughout the years.

Raines's early career plans included law school but winning a scholarship and going to Harvard far exceeded his future expectations. Fortuitously, Harvard was recruiting students from the region to boost the school's status as a national university. Raines and his family were elated when he was awarded a Harvard national scholarship. During the summers he gained valuable government experience by working in various civic positions in the state of Washington. Raines, a moderate, joined the Young Democrats and the Young Republicans clubs on campus often participating in the rallies and protests on campus. In 1969, he was invited to intern for Senator Daniel Patrick Moynihan, who had been one of his college professors. Moynihan was serving in the Nixon administration as the adviser on urban affairs. Raines was asked to survey college campuses and report on the state of anti-war demonstrations. His middle ground centrist approach to the war was not always a popular one on the Harvard campus. He also served that year as a delegate to the White House Conference on Food, Nutrition and Health.

Raines believes that he is fortunate in birth order, as only the three youngest members of his family received a college education. He was the first to graduate from college when he matriculated magna cum laude in government studies from Harvard in 1971. He was a Rhodes scholar at Magdalen College, Oxford University, where he studied for a year. When he returned to the United States, he took a position as associate director of the

Seattle Model Cities Program. After a year with the program, he entered Harvard law school, graduating with honors in 1976.

From Law Practice to Government Service

After law school, Raines took a position as an associate attorney for the Washington law firm of Preston, Thorgrimson, Ellis, Holman & Fletcher. Outside his law practice, he participated in a number of civic activities in the Seattle community that gained him public exposure. As expected he was invited to run for public office. He declined the offer, instead accepting a position with the Carter administration in 1977. He served for two years, first as the assistant director of the White House domestic policy staff, then as associate director for economics and government in the Office of Management and Budget. Although Raines moved back to the private sector in 1979, his brief entry into government service had spanned two administrations. With his reputation on the rise, it was expected that he would return to the government at some future point in his career.

From 1979 to 1991, Raines was employed at Lazard Freres & Company, a New York investment-banking firm. During his tenure at Lazard he progressed through the ranks from general vice president to senior vice president, and from general partner to limited partner. He was the first African American partner in a Wall Street firm in the 1980s. His responsibilities at Lazard included helping states, cities, and public authorities with the management of financial crises and advising on the financing of large capital programs. In particular, he worked closely with black mayors in large cities helping with financial management and cost reduction strategies. He proposed an innovative plan to strengthen District of Columbia government finances by replacing the city's federal subsidy with a better package of federal services. Raines garnered a lot of praise from this effort.

Raines married Wendy Farrow in 1982 and with a growing family wanted to spend more time at home. The opportunity came in 1991 when he was hired as vice chairman of Fannie Mae. Formerly known as the Federal National Mortgage Association, Fannie Mae had been rebuilt into the nation's largest home mortgage financing business. Its mission was to make home ownership possible for every American, and Raines wanted to help realize this dream for groups traditionally excluded from home ownership. Fannie Mae especially targeted minorities, immigrants, and single-parent families. Raines was given responsibility for the company's credit and finance policy and other corporate legal functions. As a shareholding company, Fannie Mae provided financial products and services to stimulate the availability and affordability of housing for low-income to middle-income Americans. With status as a quasi-governmental agency, Fannie Mae enjoyed virtual guaranteed market protection. Government charter also covered its nearest competitor, the Federal Home Loan Mortgage Corporation, or Freddie Mac. Raines stayed with the company for five years.

Becomes Budget Mogul

Raines had declared as a Democrat but worked well with both political parties. His association with vice president Al Gore through alumni work at Harvard pinpointed him as a possible Clinton cabinet appointee. After President Clinton's reelection in 1996, Raines was persuaded to leave his lucrative position at Fannie Mae to join the administration as director of the Office of Management and Budget (OMB). Some speculated that Clinton wanted to pad his cabinet with another minority appointment. Others were of the opinion that perhaps Fannie Mae's management wanted Raines in a position to protect the company's unique government status from scrutiny. Whatever the case, Raines took a drastic cut in pay and returned to an executive position. Raines's confirmation hearings unearthed no negatives in his record. With his varied experience in the private sector he was hailed as best qualified for the position and was confirmed without difficulty. The first African American to serve as OMB director, he was faced with the burden of negotiating a balanced-budget deal before the burgeoning deficit got out of control. Although well known in Wall Street circles, he was viewed as a Washington outsider. Yet he was well respected by both African American and white colleagues. Raines's bi-partisanship and diplomacy on Capital Hill were seen as great advantages to the fiscal restraint required during the financial management reform process.

While the main task at hand was to advise the president on strategies to balance the budget and help shape economic and domestic policy matters, there were other areas of responsibility as well. These included the management and preparation of the administration's budget and increasing government efficiency and effectiveness through improved management policies and revenue expenditures, regulations, and legislation. During congressional budget negotiations Raines worked equally well with both parties. He became one of the first directors in recent history to succeed in moving the budget from a deficit to a surplus balance, a feat that seemed almost unattainable. His success led to speculation that were he to remain in government, he would be a contender for chief of White House staff, or perhaps secretary of the treasury. In 1998, after a brief two-year stint at OMB, he was offered what he considers the opportunity of a lifetime to return to Fannie Mae as its president and CEO.

Returning to Fannie Mae was the realization of a dream for Raines. He realized that the agitations of the 1960s had put systems in place that now made it possible for his generation to rise to the top. He also recognized the importance of gaining access to property as well as education and civil and political rights. He saw his appointment not only as a personal best but also as an opening for other qualified blacks to move into top-level positions. He regarded successes of this type as catalysts to provide positive role models outside professional sports for minority youth. With mentoring and other programs in place to recruit, train, and develop minority staff, Fannie Mae had built a reputation as a leader in the areas of diversity and minority recruitment. Under his leadership, minority hiring increased, filling more than a third of the highest paid positions.

Raines believed that Fannie Mae, as the nation's largest source of home mortgage financing in the country, should set the standard for socially responsible lending. As mortgage rates fell to the lowest in forty years, the housing market ballooned, pumping billions of dollars into the economy. One of Raines's main goals at Fannie Mae was to address the problems facing low-income families caused by years of economic repression. For him the key was to keep expanding horizons not just personally but also for others. His responsibility was to make people aware of the housing opportunities provided to benefit them. He strongly believed that affirmative action is a commitment necessary to the process of catching up. Like the analogy of the miracle of compound interest, success for one means success is possible for many more if they desire it. To increase home ownership affordability, Raines introduced creative financing, new lending programs, and cooperative partnerships with housing development projects such as Hope VI. He realized that society and neighborhoods benefited from increased home ownership and resulting in improved communities, better schools, more jobs, less crime, and more participation in the political process.

Raines encouraged lenders to reach out into poor neighborhoods, even the ones with high default rates. For those lenders who were hesitant to venture into such markets, Raines believed it was Fannie Mae's responsibility to help them with the marketing. Raines mounted an aggressive campaign to expand housing opportunities to entice minorities to enter the home ownership market. He believed the minority housing market was the key to Fannie Mae's continued growth. He was instrumental in developing the Access Program, designed to increase minority participation in Fannie Mae's securities business. He urged promotion of additional incentives to neighborhoods through financing incentives, such as the timely payment reward system that would offer families with slightly impaired credit a mortgage rate two points below the sub-prime rate. Another program introduced to increase affordable home buying was called Fannie's Neighbors.

Raines is very proud of his accomplishments at the company, especially since many more families in the early 2000s could afford to purchase a home. The company's earnings have risen each year and its share prices have remained at the same level since he rejoined the company. New and existing home sales reached record highs under his leadership, and the market remained strong and well able to meet the demands for home ownership. Under his leadership, the company experienced double-digit growth and expanded benefits to families with lower incomes. A leader in mortgage technology, Fannie Mae committed more to investments to increase affordable rental housing and home ownership for more families.

Faces Accounting Scandal

In 2003 regulators found irregularities in the accounting at Fannie Mae's partner company Freddie Mac and accused the company of understating its profits. The scandal aroused fears that the U.S. housing market and the economy would be adversely affected. Fannie Mae's accounting became the subject of intense scrutiny as lawmakers responded by calling for an investigation into practices at both companies. A special investigation by Fannie Mae's regulatory agency, the Office of Federal Housing Enterprise Oversight (OFHEO) alleged that company executives manipulated accounting rules to hide earnings acquisitions and executive compensation. The $245 million in cash bonuses doled out to executives was viewed suspiciously, eliciting much criticism about the company's special status as a government-sponsored enterprise. Raines denied the charges that accounting irregularities existed in the company in testimony before the congressional subcommittee on banking. He termed the charges unfair since OFHEO had no documents or proof to substantiate them. He pledged that if any irregularities were found he would hold himself personally responsible. The Securities and Exchange Commission (SEC) and the Department of Justice also conducted inquiries.

Unfortunately, Raines was unable to weather the storm of controversy and was forced to leave Fannie Mae in late December 2004. The SEC's report determined that the accounting irregularities, originally thought to be slight, were in actuality significant. Also resigning were Fannie Mae's chief financial officer, Timothy Howard, and Leland Brendsel, the CEO of Freddie Mac. The blowout was perhaps inevitable in the wake of increasing criticism echoing from banking competitors shut out of the mortgage market. Government officials were also concerned about Fannie Mae's growing mortgage portfolio. Some believed that Raines's continued focus on consistent earnings growth contributed to the company's problems and his subsequent downfall. Raines continued firm in his defense of the company's accounting. Critics viewed his performance with skepticism, but Raines's supporters believed he was fair in his dealings and acted with integrity by taking the responsibility for the misstatements. Raines was expected to face more legal battles over whether the company's action to permit him to retire was proper. His lifetime pension was also thought to be in jeopardy. Some think that politics was partly to blame for Raines's ouster since he was a Democrat in a Republican administration. In 2006 Fannie Mae remained under ongoing investigations by OFHEO, the Justice Department, and the Securities and Exchange Commission.

Raines is credited with instituting technological improvements to help lenders streamline the processing of mortgage applications, creating the Desk Top Home Counselor, an electronic system to help prospective homebuyers with finance preparation before purchasing. Raines also established new mortgage standards and instituted a series of incentives and perks to reduce the costs associated with the acquisition of mortgages.

Raines serves on numerous corporate boards, including Boeing, Pfizer, PepsiCo, the National Urban League, and AOL Time Warner. Raines has acted as a financial advisor to several states, cities, commissions, and other authorities. From 1994 to 1995 he served on the Commission on the Roles and Missions of the Armed Forces that examined the important issues surrounding the future of the United States armed services. He was elected a Fellow of the American Academy of Arts and Sciences and a member of the Council of Foreign Relations, the Trilateral Commission and the National Academy of Social Insurance.

REFERENCES

Books

Betzold, Michael. "Franklin Raines." *Newsmakers: The People Behind Today's Headlines.* Ed. Sean R. Pollock. Detroit, Mich.: Gale Research, 1997.

Gates, Henry Louis, Jr. *Behind the Color Line.* New York: Warner Books, 2004.

Johnson, Anne Janette. "Franklin Delano Raines." *Contemporary Black Biography: Profiles from the International Black Community.* Eds. L. Mpho Mabunda and Shirelle Phelps. Detroit, Mich.: Gale Research, 1997

Periodicals

Cope, Debra. "Talking with Fannie Mae's Franklin Raines." *Community Banker* (October 2003): 14-20.

Davenport, Todd. "What's Next For Fannie? A Primer on the Issues." *American Banker* 189 (30 September 2004): 1-2.

Dymi, Amilda. "Raines Most Proud of Fannie Low-Moderate Effort." *National Mortgage News* (9 June 2003): 8.

Harris, Hamil R. "Franklin Reigns" *Black Enterprise* 29 (August 1998): 103-06.

McClean, Bethany, and Oliver Ryan. "The Fall of Fannie Mae." *Fortune* 151 (24 January 2005): 122-33.

Peterson, James. "Fannie Mae's Franklin Raines: 'We Believe in Big Goals.'" *ABA Banking Journal* 92 (January 2000): 35-39.

Superville, Darlene. "Fannie Mae CEO's Ouster Surprised Many." *The Toronto Star*, 2 January 2005.

Other

U.S. Senate. Committee on Governmental Affairs. *Nomination of Franklin D. Raines.* Washington, D.C.: Government Printing Office, 1997 (GPO microfiche Y4.G74/9:S.HRG.104-715).

Janette Prescod

Joseph Rainey

Joseph Rainey
1832–1887

Congressman

Born a slave in Georgetown, South Carolina, on June 21, 1832, Joseph Hayne Rainey was able with his father's help to attain his freedom. Rainey grew up to become a Reconstruction congressman during the forty-first, forty-second, forty-third, forty-fourth and forty-fifth Congresses. He was the first African American to be seated in the United States House of Representatives. Other African Americans were elected to Congress before Rainey, but the congressmen refused to recognize them.

Not too much is known about Rainey's youth. His father Edward, a barber by trade, was able to buy his own freedom and that of his wife Gracia and their children sometime in the mid-1840s. The family then moved to Charleston. By 1860, Edward worked at the elite Mills House Hotel and had become prosperous enough to own two slaves. Joseph Rainey went to Philadelphia in the late 1850s. There he married Susan and the two returned to South Carolina in 1859.

Rainey worked as a barber until 1862 when he was forced to work for the Confederate States of America building fortifications and serving as a steward on vessels called blockade-runners. The couple was able to escape from the Confederates on one of the ships that traveled between Georgetown and the island of Bermuda. In Bermuda, Rainey once again plied his trade as a barber in St. George and Hamilton. The Raineys stayed in Bermuda until the end of the Civil War. When Rainey returned, he soon was involved in Republican politics in South Carolina.

Enters Politics in South Carolina

For fourteen years, from 1865 to 1879, Rainey was active on many levels with both his community and the Republican party. He and his brother, Edward, attended the Colored People's Convention at the Zion Presbyterian Church, which focused on advancing the interests of African Americans. He served as the county chairman for Georgetown and was a member of the State Executive Committee from 1868 to 1876. From January 14 to March 18, 1868, he served as the Georgetown delegate to the South Carolina constitutional convention held in Charleston, along with a white delegate, Henry W. Webb. Rainey was a political conservative who sometimes sided with white politicians and favored a degree of leniency toward ex-Confederates. He regularly demonstrated compassion for the mistreated—especially the newly freed black population. As a representative to the South Carolina constitutional convention he supported amnesty for the Confederates and debt relief for those made destitute by the war. He opposed radical land reform and supported poll taxes if the proceeds were used for public education. Rainey served in the South Carolina state militia and was an agent of the State Land Commission. When he attended the state labor convention in 1869, he supported legislation to protect African American workers who were suffering at the hands of former masters who wanted to relegate them to near-slavery status. Once

Chronology

1832	Born to enslaved parents in Georgetown, South Carolina on June 21
1840s	Father buys his freedom
1850s	Marries Susan (maiden name unknown) in Philadelphia, Pennsylvania
1859	Returns to Georgetown; establishes barbershop
1862	Drafted by the Confederate Army to build fortifications and serve on board vessels
1862	Escapes with family to Bermuda
1865	Returns to Georgetown and becomes active with Republican party politics
1868	Serves as a delegate to the South Carolina Constitutional Convention but is asked to fill a vacancy in the U.S. Congress
1870	Elected to the South Carolina State Senate; becomes the first African American seated in the U.S. Congress
1870-79	Serves in the 41st through the 45th Congress as the representative of the first district of South Carolina
1879	Becomes an Internal Revenue Service agent for South Carolina
1881	Goes into private business
1887	Dies in Georgetown, South Carolina on August 1

Rainey was elected to the state senate in 1870, he became chairman of the Finance Committee. He resigned soon after joining the state senate to fill a seat in the House of Representatives.

Rainey was elected to Congress from South Carolina's first congressional district to fill a vacancy caused when the House of Representatives declared B. Franklin Whittemore's seat vacant. Whittemore was guilty of selling West Point commissions. Rainey served from December 12, 1870, to March 3, 1879. Records relating to his tenure appear in both the *Congressional Record* and the *Congressional Globe*. He supported civil rights legislation, an anti-Ku Klux Klan act, and laws advocating Indian and Chinese rights.

In an April 1, 1871 speech relating to the necessity of the enforcement of the Fourteenth Amendment to the U. S. Constitution, Rainey stated that freed men and women in South Carolina were being subjected to enormous crimes that found "no parallel in the history of this Republic in her very darkest days," according to the *Congressional Globe*. He argued: "even now, after the great conflict between slavery and freedom, after the triumph achieved at such a cost, we can yet see the traces of the disastrous strife and the remains of disease in the body-politic of the South. In proof of this witness the frequent outrages perpetrated upon our loyal men. The prevailing spirit of the southerner is either to rule or to ruin. Voters must perforce succumb to their wishes or else risk life itself in the attempt to maintain the simple right of common manhood." Rainey was fighting a los-

ing battle because by 1877, the end of Reconstruction, almost all attempts at U. S. government enforcement of rights for African Americans would be abandoned for many decades.

The *Congressional Record* for March 2, 1875 records the Honorable Joseph H. Rainey's protest about the mistreatment of former slaves by the disastrous Freedman's Savings and Trust Company which collapsed in 1874. He lambastes the leadership of the bank as having been determined to "deceive the inexperienced and credulous former bonds men and women." In spite of protests by Rainey and many others, nothing stopped the malpractices of the bank's administrators. Few depositors ever retrieved their hard-earned funds.

Life after Congress

After Rainey left Congress he was appointed as an Internal Revenue agent in South Carolina on May 22, 1879, and served until July 15, 1881. Rainey, a businessman before he was a politician, maintained an active interest in investments during his career. He held stock in the Greenville and Enterprise Railroads and tried to manage an unproductive banking and brokerage business in Washington, D.C. When his health failed he left Washington, D.C., and returned to Georgetown where he died on August 1, 1887. He was buried at the Baptist Cemetery.

REFERENCES

Books

Foner, Eric. *Freedom's Lawmakers: A Directory of Black Officeholders during Reconstruction.* Baton Rouge, La.: Louisiana State University Press, 1996.

Holt, Thomas. *Black over White: Negro Political Leadership in South Carolina during Reconstruction.* Urbana, Ill.: University of Illinois Press, 1977.

——. "Joseph Hayne Rainey." *Dictionary of American Negro Biography.* Eds. Rayford W. Logan and Michael R. Winston. New York: Norton: 1982.

Middleton, Stephen, ed. *Black Congressmen during Reconstruction: A Documentary Sourcebook.* Westport, Conn.: Praeger, 2002.

Periodicals

Work, Monroe N., Thomas S. Staples, H. A. Wallace, et al. "Some Negro Members of Reconstruction Conventions and Legislatures of Congress." *Journal of Negro History* 5 (January 1920): 63-119.

Online

Biographical Directory of the United States Congress, 1774 to Present. http://bioguide.congress.gov (Accessed 12 December 2005).

Other

Congressional Globe. 42nd Cong., 1st sess. (1871): 393-395.

Congressional Record, House of Representatives, 43rd Cong., 2nd sess. (1875): 184.

Debra Newman Ham

Chronology

1834	Born in Charleston, South Carolina on January 3
1840	Works as shipping clerk in Charleston
1865	Becomes registrar of elections in Charleston
1866	Participates in South Carolina's first Republican convention
1868	Serves in the South Carolina state legislature
1870	Wins election as South Carolina lieutenant governor
1872	Becomes delegate to Republican National Convention
1873-75	Serves in the U.S House of Representatives
1882	Dies in Charleston on August 17

Alonzo J. Ransier
1834–1882

Politician

Alonzo J. Ransier was one of twenty African Americans elected to the U.S. House of Representatives during the Reconstruction era. Ransier represented his South Carolina district in Washington between 1873 and 1875, where he spoke eloquently on the House floor in favor of federal civil rights legislation.

Alonzo Jacob Ransier was born on January 3, 1834, in Charleston, South Carolina, as a free black. He had some education and by the age of sixteen was working as a shipping clerk in Charleston, which was a prosperous and bustling trade port. He was in his early thirties when the Civil War ended in 1865 and won an appointment as registrar of elections in the city. In 1866, Congress passed the Reconstruction Act, which dissolved the Confederate state governments and placed Southern states under federal military jurisdiction.

The other hallmarks of the Reconstruction era were the passage of the Thirteenth, Fourteenth, and Fifteenth Amendments to the U.S. Constitution. The Thirteenth Amendment abolished slavery, while the Fourteenth Amendment granted citizenship to any naturalized American or person born in the United States, including blacks, and further specified that no state shall abridge those rights by making or enforcing any law which denied the privileges or immunities of citizens of the United States. Ransier participated in the first Republican convention held in South Carolina in 1866, and two years later served a term in the state house. He also attended the state constitutional convention and in 1868 was one of the presidential electors who voted to approve the election of Ulysses S. Grant as president and Schuyler Colfax as vice president.

The Fifteenth Amendment, ratified in 1870, gave all qualified adult males the right to vote. Suddenly, some southern states that had relied heavily on slave labor before the Civil War found themselves with large black voting populations, and Ransier's South Carolina, along with Mississippi, was one of two states that actually had a majority black electorate. That same year, Ransier was elected lieutenant governor on the Republican ticket along with Ohioan and former Union Army commander, Robert Kingston Scott.

Takes Seat in House

In 1872, Ransier was a delegate to the Republican National Convention and supported the party faction loyal to Grant, the incumbent. That same year, Ransier won a seat in Congress and began his term in March 1873 as a member of the forty-third U.S. Congress. He supported several Republican-sponsored pieces of legislation, including a tariff bill and an attempt to adopt a six-year presidential term. He also tried to obtain federal funds to improve the war-damaged Charleston harbor.

Two speeches survive that Ransier made on the House floor during his time on Capitol Hill. Both were in favor of the Civil Rights Bill of 1875, which guaranteed both free blacks and recently freed slaves equal rights everywhere in the United States, including in schools and social settings. This was a hotly contested piece of legislation, and its opponents argued that it was unconstitutional and infringed upon the states' authority. The term "social equality" was a common political catchphrase of the day used by pro-segregationist southern whites who feared full civil rights for blacks would mean the end of the white population's dominance of the South.

The U.S. House delegation from Kentucky was entirely Democrat, at a time when that party's southern adherents were still fiercely segregationist. In a speech made on January 5, 1874, Ransier mentioned the opposition to the Civil Rights Bill voiced by one of those Kentucky colleagues and asserted: "I would most certainly oppose the passage of the pending bill or any similar measure if I believed that its operation would be to force upon me the company of the member from Kentucky, for instance, or anyone else. These Negro-haters would not open school-houses, hotels, places of amusement, common conveyances, or the witness or the jury box to the colored people upon equal terms with themselves, because this contact of the races would, forsooth, 'result injuriously to both.' Yet they have found agreeable associations with them under other circumstances which at once suggest themselves to us."

Ransier noted in the same speech that a Georgia representative in the House had argued in favor of letting the states decide civil rights matters instead of Congress. He responded to this by reminding the House lawmakers that the Georgia state assembly had recently prevented its newly elected black representatives from taking their seats in that chamber. The Civil Rights Bill passed on March 3, 1875, just as Congress was about to adjourn for the term. It specified that every American, regardless of race, color, or previous condition of servitude, was entitled to the same treatment in inns, public conveyances on land or water, theaters, and other places of public amusement.

Returns to Charleston

Ransier's stint in Washington was finished. He had run for a second term from South Carolina's Second Congressional district, but lost. His wife Louisa died not long after he returned to his hometown, Charleston, and he spent his final years in the city. He was employed by the Internal Revenue Service but fell on hard times as the city, and much of the South, reverted to its segregated practices after Union troops departed and the Reconstruction era ended. Some reports note that he worked as a day laborer before his death on August 17, 1882, in Charleston.

A year later, the U.S. Supreme Court overturned the Civil Rights Bill of 1875, supporting the challenge to its constitutionality and agreeing that Congress did not have the power to regulate the conduct of individuals.

REFERENCES

Online

"Alonzo J. Ransier Jan. 5, 1874." Neglected Voices: Speeches of African-American Representatives: Addressing the Civil Rights Bill of 1875. http://www.law.nyu.edu/davisp/neglectedvoices/RansierJan051874.html (Accessed 11 February 2006).

"An Honest Politician: Alonzo Ransier." The African American Registry. http://www.aaregistry.com/african_american_history/8/An_honest_politician_Alonzo_Ransier/ (Accessed 11 February 2006).

"Ransier, Alonzo J.—Biographical Information." Biographical Directory of the United States Congress. http://bioguide.congress.gov/scripts/biodisplay.pl?index=R000060 (Accessed 11 February 2006).

Carol Brennan

John H. Rapier, Jr.
1835–1865

Physician, dentist

John H. Rapier Jr., frustrated by the racial climate in the United States, pursued professional opportunities in the Caribbean. However, he returned to the United States to complete a medical degree and became one of the first acting assistant surgeons at the Freedman's Hospital in Washington, D.C.

Rapier was born on July 28, 1835, one of four sons. Around 1831, John Rapier Sr., a barber, married Susan, a nineteen-year-old free black from Baltimore, Maryland. From this marriage, six children were born. John's three brothers were Richard, Henry, and James, who became a member of the U.S. House of Representatives from Alabama during Reconstruction. According to Loren Schweninger, six years after John's birth, Susan, his mother, died in childbirth at the age of twenty-nine along with her twin infants, Jackson and Alexander.

After the death of Susan, John Sr. acquired a slave woman named Lucretia to help care for the four boys. However, in 1848, although not formally married due to the law that restricted free blacks from marrying slaves, he started a second family. Their five children were Rebecca, Joseph, Thomas, Charles, and Susan. Attempting to secure the freedom of his second family, John Sr. applied to the Lauderdale County Court, but to no avail. His family remained in bondage, technically speaking, until the passage of the Thirteenth Amendment to the U.S. Constitution.

Always concerned about the welfare of his children, John Sr. set aside funds for their education. The barbering business, after forty years, had been lucrative, and John wanted his sons to have good educational opportunities. Therefore, he sent them to Nashville, Tennessee to stay with their slave grandmother, Sally. Because Sally had lived in Nashville for so long and she had operated as a free black in an entrepreneurialcapacity, whites thought she was free. In Nashville, John and his brothers received a rudimentary education for six years. John had learned to write poetry at the age of ten. After completing this education, the boys moved back to Alabama. Upon the advice of his father, John Jr. left Alabama, intending to emigrate to Liberia.

Views on Emigration and Civil Rights

Disillusioned with the racial climate in the United States, in late 1854 and early 1855, John Rapier Jr. contacted the president of the American Colonization Society. After two inquiries and no reply, he abandoned the idea of going to Liberia and decided to join his uncle, James P. Thomas, who was making arrangements to emigrate to Central America. After arriving in Central America, Rapier realized that the poverty and misery for blacks in Central America was worse than for U.S. blacks. According to Philip Alexander, this factor prompted Rapier, after a few months, to return to the United States and initiate a freelance career in journalism in Minnesota, where his father had some real estate interests there. During the next four years, Rapier wrote more than one hundred articles for five different Minnesotan newspapers, including the *Little Falls Pioneer and Democrat* and the *St. Paul Times*. His themes varied but one interesting subject he elaborated on was the civil rights of colored children in St. Paul, especially regarding the absence of educational facilities, particularly since blacks paid school taxes. Elsewhere in his writing he chided federal officials for not accepting homestead applications submitted by blacks. Frustrated and upset, in 1858, he wrote an electrifying address urging blacks to leave the United States because of its unwillingness to provide liberty and equality to black Americans.

Sojourns in the Caribbean and Returns to United States

Still searching for social and professional opportunities, Rapier left Minnesota in 1860 for Haiti, the first free black island in the western hemisphere. For more than a year, he taught English to mulatto children in Port-au-Prince. Through careful observation, he realized that Haitian society, like that in the United States, was based on color. Rapier was very light-skinned and perhaps could be mistaken for white. In Haiti, skin color could work as a social stigma and/or cause one physical danger. There was a deep chasm between light- and dark-skinned Haitians. Perhaps this irony reminded him of the same relationship between dark- and light-skinned blacks in the United States. Thus, what Rapier was partially fleeing from, he encountered in Haiti. In addition, he was frightened by the political instability and potential threat of violence provoked by international pressures. Sensing the threatening mood of the country, he traveled to

Kingston, the capital of British Jamaica in 1861, where he studied dentistry for two years. Alexander quotes from a letter Rapier wrote his uncle James Thomas, in which he described the profession of dentistry, the patient's "scream of agony" and the extracted tooth with parts of "the jawbone sticking" to it. In the letter, Rapier offers upon his return to the United States to extract two of his uncle's front teeth to demonstrate.

The sadistic tone underlying this description was an in-house joke. As a young boy, Rapier had seen both his father and uncle James offer dental services such as tooth extraction to their barber customers. Because the field was so primitive—at the time dentists were thought of as little more than tooth-pullers—their practice was totally unregulated and barbers often offered dental services as an appendage to hair trimming. In Jamaica, the field of dentistry was becoming more respectable among the learned professions. Rapier was of the opinion that he could master the profession and earn a fair amount of respectability. After completing his dental studies, he contemplated starting his own dental practice. However, he did not have the money that would require. His uncle advised him to return home, but Rapier was adamant about not returning to the United States. Hoping that his uncle would quickly provide financial assistance, Rapier devised a plan to practice dentistry and medicine. It was a very common practice through the end of the nineteenth century to acquire credentials and work simultaneously in dentistry, medicine, pharmacy, and other related fields. Rapier planned to use funds earned from dentistry to support his medical studies. Thinking that this plan would impress his uncle, he began to solicit funds from him to set up a dental office in rural Jamaica.

After repeatedly being prodded, his uncle sent only half of the money Rapier requested. Without sufficient money, Rapier decided to abandon dentistry and study only medicine. So, with different professional aspirations, he left Jamaica in 1862 and returned to the United States. Not having enough funds to immediately enroll in medical school, he began teaching school. Having saved enough funds, without the help of his uncle, Rapier enrolled at the University of Michigan in Ann Arbor in the fall of 1863 in the department of medicine and surgery. As the first black to be accepted in the program, he met with adversity. This adversity was not due to a lack of qualifications. He had impressed the faculty with his knowledge of Latin, natural and mathematical sciences, and current medical techniques and prescriptions. Both the faculty and students were hostile toward him for presuming that he had a right to study there, much less to be accepted on an equal basis with whites.

Only a few months after being admitted to the university, Rapier withdrew in the autumn of 1863 and enrolled in the medical school at Iowa State University in Keokuk. The following June, he completed his medical degree and applied to the U.S. Army for the position of acting assistant surgeon at the Freedmen's Hospital in Washington, D. C. At the hospital he noticed the respect that enlisted white men gave to the black army officers. Although working long hours at the hospital, Rapier was able to talk to both Frederick Douglass and Abraham Lincoln about the condition of blacks in the South. Between work and what he perceived as his social obligation to blacks, he never had enough rest.

Although there are discrepancies about the year of his death, Alexander indicates that Rapier served in this acting position until his death in 1865, at the age of twenty-nine. If this is the correct year for his death, then he died at the same age as his mother. It is ironic that he spent his life traveling in search of peace, which he ultimately found in military service during the American Civil War.

REFERENCES

Books

Schweninger, Loren. *James T. Rapier and Reconstruction.* Chicago: University of Chicago Press, 1978.

Periodicals

Alexander, Philip. "John H. Rapier Jr. and the Medical Profession in Jamaica, 1861-1862." *Jamaica Journal* 24 (February 1993): 37-46.

——. "John H. Rapier Jr. and the Medical Profession in Jamaica, 1860-1862." *Jamaica Journal* 25 (October 1993): 55-62.

Schweninger, Loren. "A Slave Family in the Antebellum South." *Journal of Negro History* 60 (January 1975): 29-44.

——. "The Dilemma of a Free Negro in the Antebellum South." *Journal of Negro History* 62 (July 1977): 283-88.

Collections

Rapier's papers are in the Moorland-Spingarn Research Center at Howard University, Washington. D.C.

Patricia A. Pearson

Charles B. Ray
1807–1886

Abolitionist, editor

Charles B. Ray was born a free man but devoted most of his life to the antislavery movement and to the

---

Chronology

1807	Born in Falmouth, Massachusetts on December 25
1832	Enters Wesleyan University as an aspiring minister
1832	Opens boot repair shop in New York
1833	Joins the American Anti-Slavery Society
1834	Marries Henrietta Regulus
1837	Works as a traveling journalist and subscriptions promoter for *The Colored American*
1839	Becomes owner and editor of *The Colored American*
1840	Marries Charlotte Augusta Burroughs
1841	Suspends publication of *The Colored American*
1843	Serves as corresponding secretary for the Committee on Vigilance; helps to organize the Negro National Convention held in Buffalo, New York
1846	Installed as pastor of Bethesda Congregational Church in New York
1847	Co-founds Society for the Promotion of Education Among Colored Children with Charles L. Reason
1850	Serves as executive member of the New York State Vigilance Committee
1859	Serves as president of the Society for the Promotion of Education Among Colored Children; calls for a thorough review of city-run schools in New York
1886	Dies in New York on August 15

---

advancement of the African American race. During the nineteenth century, Ray endeavored to uplift his race by working as an integrationist at Wesleyan University, an abolitionist, an editor, and a preacher.

Ray was born December 25, 1807 in Falmouth, Massachusetts, to Joseph Aspinwall Ray, a mail carrier, and Annis Harrington, a well read and religious woman. Ray claimed a mixed ancestry of African, English, and Native Indian. Ray was educated in Falmouth before he relocated to Westerly, Rhode Island, where he worked on his grandfather's farm. He later settled on Martha's Vineyard, Massachusetts, where he mastered the boot making trade at Vineyard Haven and began his studies at Wesleyan Seminary in Wilbraham, Massachusetts.

In September 1832, at the age of twenty-five, Ray enrolled as the first black student at Wesleyan University as an aspiring minister. Upon his enrollment, Ray met resistance from members of the student body who did not want black students attending an all white university. Because of the overwhelming negative reaction of students towards Ray's enrollment, the trustees of the university resolved that Wesleyan University would only accept white male students and consequently revoked Ray's admission. Three years later, in 1835, Wesleyan reversed its decision, allowing students of all races to enroll. The university later established the Charles B. Ray Scholarship to assist students of color with the cost of tuition and later opened the scholarship to all students in need of financial assistance.

Leaving the university, Ray traveled to New York where he continued to work in his trade as a boot maker. While there, he became acquainted with Presbyterian pastor and abolitionist Theodore S. Wright. Ray opened a shoe making and repair shop in Lower Manhattan, close to the Wright residence, and the business began to flourish. In need of assistance for his thriving shop, Ray hired Samuel Cornish who later became a business partner.

Joins Anti-Slavery Movement

Influenced by Wright, Ray became involved with the anti-slavery movement in 1833. Around this time, Ray began working with the Underground Railroad. As a conductor, Ray guided slaves to Plymouth Church in Brooklyn, a major stop on the Underground Railroad. At the height of his involvement with the antislavery movement, on separate occasions Ray sheltered fourteen fugitive slaves within his home and led an entire family to freedom, including a grandmother and toddler. By this time, the Underground Railroad was using new methods of transporting slaves. Steamboats, cargo-sloops, and canal boats (a majority operated by black men), were now being used as vessels by which escaped slaves gained their freedom.

In the early 1840s Ray become involved with the Vigilance Committee of the City of New York, which brought him in close company with Gerrit Smith who would later become president of the organization. Ray became a member of the executive board. During his years in the antislavery movement, Ray worked with many prominent abolitionists, including Reverend Theodore Wright, Henry Highland Garnet, Frederick Douglass and Samuel Cornish. Cornish along with John D. Russwurm began the *Freedman's Journal*, the nation's first African American newspaper. Although Ray was active in the antislavery movement prior to the involvement of Garnet and Douglass, he is often overlooked. At the time when Garnet joined the antislavery movement, Ray had been an active member for several years. Ray began his career as an abolitionist in 1833, five years before Douglass escaped from slavery.

Ray held prominent positions within antislavery organizations. He was a secretary with the Negroes of New York, a group that advocated the non-violent approach to the abolition of slavery. He was also instrumental in organizing the 1840 Negro National Convention in Buffalo, New York.

Works for *The Colored American*

In 1837, Ray joined *The Colored American* as a traveling reporter. Ray delivered speeches and sermons to audiences as a means of promoting his subscriptions to the publication. In his efforts to bring attention to the institution of slavery, Ray became a regular contributor to *The Colored American* and later he served as its co-editor. *The Colored American* was then the nation's sec-

ond-oldest African American newspaper: it began as *The Weekly Advocate* under the editorship of Reverend Samuel Cornish. Although Fredrick Douglass's *North Star* is widely credited as the most influential newspaper of its time, *The Colored American*, first published in February 1837 under the name *The Weekly Advocate* antedated the *North Star* by ten years and was funded by black leaders of New York. The *North Star* began publication in 1847 and was funded by white supporters.

As co-editor Ray wrote and edited articles on various subjects, including the importance of freedom and education, and the way in which freed slaves, particularly women, should present themselves to the public. In 1839, Cornish resigned as editor of *The Colored American*, which led Ray to become the owner and chief editor. By this time *The Colored American* was in financial straits. Ray wrote most of the articles himself as he continued to support the abolitionist cause. Following a long battle to keep the paper running, Ray finally suspended publication in April 1842.

Following the closing of *The Colored American*, Ray continued to support the antislavery cause. He worked to ensure that black children received a quality education. His dedication to and firm belief in education led in 1847 to his partnering with Charles L. Reason, an African American mathematician, to co-found the Society for the Promotion of Education Among Colored Children, an organization that oversaw black schools in New York City. President of the organization from 1861 to 1865, Ray was instrumental in founding two elementary schools, fighting for the desegregation of all white schools, and lobbying for adequate support for all black schools. While president of the organization, Ray was ordained as a pastor of New York's Bethesda Congregational Church, a position he held until his death. Ray died in New York on August 15, 1886, at the age of 79.

Ray's children followed their father's path. Henrietta Cordelia Ray, named in honor of Ray's first wife Henrietta Green Regulus, spoke four languages fluently: French, German, Greek, and Latin. She was a poet whose eighty-line ode, entitled "Lincoln," was read by William E. Matthews at the unveiling of the Freedman's Monument where Fredrick Douglass delivered the keynote address. Florence Ray, the second of three girls, and daughter of Ray's second wife Charlotte Augusta Burroughs, was college educated and trained as a teacher. Charlotte Ray, the youngest of the girls and also a daughter of Ray's second wife, was the first black woman to graduate from a law school in the United States, the first woman to graduate Howard University's School of Law in 1872, the first black woman to pass the bar exam, and the first woman to practice law in Washington, D.C. In 1887 Charlotte and Florence coauthored a biography of their father, *Sketches of the Life of Reverend Charles B. Ray.*

REFERENCES

Books

Mabee, Carleton. *Black Freedom: The Nonviolent Abolitionists from 1830 through the Civil War*. New York: Macmillan, 1970.

Quarles, Benjamin. *Black Abolitionists*. New York: Oxford University Press, 1969.

Swift, David. "Charles Bennett Ray." In *American National Biography*.. Eds. John A. Garraty and Mark C. Carnes. New York: Oxford, 1999.

Villard, Harold G. "Charles Bennett Ray." In *Dictionary of American Biography*. Ed. Dumas Malone. New York: Scribner's, 1963.

Periodicals

Work, M. N. "The Life of Charles B. Ray." *Journal of Negro History* 4 (October 1919): 361-71.

Online

"Beginnings: Charles B. Ray to Victor L. Butterfield." http://www.wesleyan.edu/admission/diversity/beginnings.html (Accessed 11 February 2006).

Davis, Ronald, Steve, et al. "The Black Press in Antebellum America." *Slavery in America* http://www.slaveryinamerica.org/history/hs_es_press.htm (Accessed 11 February 2006).

Williams, Scott, et al. *Mathematicians of the African Diaspora*. 1 July 2001. http://www.math.buffalo.edu/mad/special/reason_charles_1.html (Accessed 11 February 2006).

Felicia A. Chenier

J. Paul Reason

J. Paul Reason
1941–

Military leader

In 1996, J. Paul Reason's outstanding naval career peaked when he became the Commander in Chief of the Atlantic Fleet in the United States Navy. He concentrated on using computers and technology to update ships and enhancing his sailors' and staff's quality of life. His success was based in part on pursing excellence with honesty and integrity, and having a supportive family, especially his parents and his wife Dianne. He was always striving to learn more, and willingly helping others as he progressed. He also credits those pioneering African Americans whose accomplishments paved the way for his success and those individuals, such as ADM Hyman Rickover and Chief of Naval Operations Mike Boorda, who gave him opportunities to excel.

Reason urges America's youth to seek an education because having knowledge provides increased opportunities and life can be much more difficult without it. He also explains to them the importance of having a confident and positive attitude and a reputation as a good performer who has values. He works with minority recruiting programs at the Naval Academy and presents military service as an outstanding career option because promotion is based on job performance and test scores and how they rank you among your peers. Reason believes that one should not walk through obstacles but find a means of working around them.

Background, Upbringing, and Education

Joseph Paul was born to Joseph and Bernice Reason on March 22, 1941, in the nation's capital. He had a sister Barbara who succumbed to multiple sclerosis at the age of 50 after a career as an analyst and writer in international studies. With a doctoral degree in the romantic languages, his father taught at various schools including Florida Agricultural and Mechanical University in Tallahassee, Florida where he met fellow faculty member Bernice. After they were married, she taught in the District of Columbia school system, while he worked as the director of libraries at Howard University. Joseph Paul's middle class upbringing in the Brookland section of northeast Washington emphasized intellectual development, education, and being culturally well rounded. Seeing ships on the Chesapeake Bay in Maryland and his fascination with how they operated influenced his decision to consider joining the Navy. He also enjoyed playing sports and the Boy Scouts, shared with life long friend Fred Gregory, who became the first black space pilot.

Reason attended Benjamin Banneker Junior High School and McKinley High School where he applied for the Naval Reserve Officer Training Corps (NROTC), a military sponsored college program. His application, he later learned, was denied even though he scored the third highest exam score out of three hundred persons. The southern ROTC officials reviewing applications did not believe that an African American would be accepted at the southern schools. He attended Swarthmore College, Lincoln University, and Howard University studying mathematics and engineering prior to attending the Naval Academy. Democratic Congressman Charles Diggs of Michigan discussed the low number of black midshipmen at the military service academies with a dean at Howard University who recommended Joseph Paul Reason for an appointment.

Reason was over six feet tall, older, and more educated than the average first-year student and one of four blacks in the class of 1965. Like him, many of the persons he studied with went on to have tremendous success and to become his lifelong friends, such as former Secretary of the Navy John Dalton; Floyd Grayson, who started Grayson Homes of Ellicott City; Pete Tzomes, the first black officer to command a nuclear submarine; and Stanley Carter, a professor of naval science at Florida State University. While Reason admits that racism prevailed at the Academy, he prefers to focus on those individuals who helped him succeed. His extracurricular activities included the public relations club which involved announcing sporting events, the antiphonal choir, and intramural volleyball and field ball.

Three days after graduating from the Naval Academy, he married Dianne Fowler whom he had known since childhood, at the Academy chapel. He became a father with the birth of his daughter Rebecca in 1967. His wife had some familiarity with the military lifestyle as her father was a retired Army colonel and a professor of military science at Morgan State University in Baltimore, Maryland. Their son, Joseph was born April 22, 1968.

Becomes Nuclear Surface Warfare Officer

In 1965, Vice Admiral Hyman Rickover, the "Father of the Nuclear Navy" and later the first Jewish person to become a four-star admiral, personally screened hundreds of applicants for nuclear propulsion school. When Rickover interviewed Reason he commented that his class standing should be better and challenged him to improve it by twenty points before graduating. Reason responded that he could not do so within the next six months but promised to work as hard as he could to rank higher. Rickover asked him to leave his office and had him sit in a small office to reconsider his reply. Some twelve hours later, one of the admiral's aides asked Reason to sign a statement committing to the admiral's initial request. Reason amended it to read that he would endeavor to increase his class standing by trying to achieve all A's and signed it. At that point, he returned to the Naval Academy. The next morning he discovered that his name was third on the list of those persons entering the nuclear propulsion program. Long after Reason completed his training Rickover continued to follow his career. For instance, when Reason's commanding officer gave him an adverse fitness report following outstanding ones, Rickover inquired about the justification. His reports improved shortly afterwards. Reason was not aware of Rickover's intervention at the time.

The U.S. Navy assigned Reason to the USS *J. D. Blackwood*, a destroyer escort, before sending him to the Naval Nuclear Power School, Naval Training Center in Bainbridge, Maryland and the Naval Nuclear Power Training Unit in Schenectady, New York. Reason spent three years on the USS *Truxtun*, a nuclear-powered guided missile cruiser, and participated in its first deployment to Southeast Asia in 1967. While en route, the *Truxtun* responded to the North Korean seizure of the USS *Pueblo*.

Reason was a reactor training officer when he left the *Truxtun* in 1969. He reported to the Naval Postgraduate School in Monterey, California where he earned an M.S. in computer systems management. In 1970, he became the electrical officer on the USS *Enterprise*, a nuclear-powered carrier that completed two tours in the Southeast Asia and Indian Ocean areas.

His next two jobs during the 1970s returned Reason to the nation's capital as the detailer for the Surface Nuclear Junior Officer Assignment and Placement Branch in the Bureau of Naval Personnel and as the naval aide to President Jimmy Carter. His duties included carrying the "football," a case containing the codes for activating the country's nuclear weapons. This job gave him a chance to meet with ADM Rickover again.

During the 1980s, Reason served as the executive officer on the USS *Mississippi*, a nuclear-powered guided missile cruiser, and as the commanding officer of the USS *Coontz*, a guided-missile destroyer, and the USS *Bainbridge*, a nuclear-powered guided missile cruiser. He earned the nickname "Go Fast" on the *Coontz* because he seldom traveled under twenty-five to thirty knots.

When the navy designated Reason a rear admiral in 1986, he became the first member of his 1965 Naval Academy graduating class to achieve that rank and was assigned as commander of the naval base in Seattle, Washington. He managed all naval activities in Washington, Oregon, and Alaska. The navy acknowledged his skills and abilities by assigning him to command Cruiser-Destroyer Group One in 1988. He simultaneously led Battle Group Romeo through operations in the Pacific and the Indian Ocean regions and the Persian Gulf. His son Joseph graduated from the Naval Academy in 1990.

In 1991, the navy selected him for the commander of the naval surface force of the U.S. Atlantic Fleet following his promotion to three stars. Three years later, he became the deputy chief of Naval Operations for Plans, Policy and Operations (N3/5). President Bill Clinton nominated him for promotion to four stars in 1996 and the job as commander in chief of the Atlantic fleet. Reason's responsibilities included managing a significant portion of the navy's operational forces, a $5 billion budget, and over 140,000 civilian and military personnel. Reason's arsenal included 195 ships and submarines and 1,300 aircrafts that he used every five months or so to send a carrier battle group and an amphibious ready group in response to the various war fighting needs of the Atlantic, Europe, and Southwest Asia commanders in chief. Taking this position of four-star admiral made Reason the first African American to attain this rank.

Reason's military awards and medals are extensive; of special note, he received the Distinguished Service Medal, the Legion of Merit, and the National Defense Service Medal. He retired in 1999.

Becomes Successful Entrepreneur

After he retired, corporate America recruited Reason because of his exemplary leadership and management skills. In addition to consultant work and sitting on corporate boards such as Wal-Mart Stores Incorporated, he served as vice president for Ship Systems at Syntek Technologies, Inc., a technical and engineering services firm in Arlington, Virginia and the president and chief operating officer of the Metro Machine Corporation, an employee-owned ship repair and conversion business in Norfolk, Virginia, and Philadelphia, Pennsylvania. Reason also served as the director of Amgen Inc. and Norfolk Southern Corporation. He also presents at the Naval Academy's Admissions Outreach conferences.

REFERENCES

Books

1965 Lucky Bag. U.S. Naval Academy Year Book.

Periodicals

"DE Admiral Moving Up," *DESA News*, July-August 1996, 1.

Massaquoi, Hans J., "J. Paul Reason, The Navy's First Black Four-Star Admiral." *Ebony*, April 1998, 116-22.

Mintz, John, "Clinton Nominates First Black Admiral," *Washington Post*, May 14, 1996, A-13.

"Navy Pins 4th Star on D.C. Native, First Black Officer to Achieve Rank." *Washington Times*, May 14, 1996, A-6.

Simpson, Ann, "DC Native Sails to the Top in the Navy; Move Makes Joseph Reason 9th Black Admiral in Service's History." *Washington Post*, September 22, 1996.

Online

Williams, Rudi, "Reason is Navy's First Black Four-Star Admiral" American Forces Information Service News Articles, http://www.dod.gov/news/Feb1998 (Accessed 13 December 2005).

Regina T. Akers

Patrick Henry Reason
1817–1898

Engraver, lithographer

Engraver, lithographer, abolitionist, and fraternal order leader were roles Patrick Henry Reason filled during the 1800s. His artistic pieces often depicted the brutality of slavery. As an African American, he expressed his frustration regarding the oppression of slaves through his art. He became well known to the public and was listed within several documents for his creative designs.

Chronology

1817	Born in New York City; baptized on April 17 in the Church of St. Peter
1818	Sister Policarpe dies at age four
1830	First engraving is published, the frontispiece to Charles Andrews's *The History of the New York African Free-Schools*
1833-37	Apprenticed for four years to Stephen Henry
1835	Gains interest in portraiture
1837	Delivers a speech, "Philosophy of the Fine Arts," to the Phoenixonian Literary Society in New York on July 4
1838	Wins first premium (prize) for his India ink drawing exhibited at the Mechanics Institute Fairs
1846-66	Appears in the New York City directories as a "col'd" engraver
1862	Marries Esther Cunningham of Leeds, England on June 22
1869	Leaves New York with wife and young son Charles; moves to Cleveland, Ohio
1869-84	Works for the Sylvester Hogan jewelry firm
1898	Dies in Cleveland on August 12

Reason was born in April 1817 in New York City to Michael and Elizabeth Reason. His father was a native of Saint Anne Island, Guadeloupe, and his mother was from Saint-Dominique. Reason was one of four children; he had two brothers and one sister. Sadly, his sister Policarpe died in 1818 at age four.

Reason was recognized as an artist at an early age. His first engraving was made at the African Free School in New York where he was a student. He was only thirteen years old, but people were fascinated with his design. However, he was apprenticed to a white printmaker, Stephen Henry Gimber, shortly after his frontispiece and the death of his father. Reason soon established his own studio at 148 Church Street in New York, where he offered a wide variety of engraving services. His career was successful, and he was one of the earliest African American printmakers.

Along with being an artist, Reason often gave talks on fine arts. On July 4, 1837, Reason delivered a speech on the philosophy of fine arts to the Phoenixonian Literary Society in New York. A newspaper article described the speech as ably written, well delivered, and well researched. A year later, Reason won first prize for his India ink drawing exhibited at the Mechanics Institute Fair. He then began to offer his services to the public community. His engraving services included address, visiting, and business cards, certificates, and jewelry. He gave close attention to his neatness. His advertisements classified him as a historical, portrait and landscape engraver, a draughtsman, and lithographer. In addition, he offered evening instruction based upon scientific methods of drawing. He also worked for Harpers Publishers preparing map plates along with government

engraving. From 1846 to 1866, Reason was listed as a "col'd" (colored) engraver in New York City directories.

Artistic Value

Reason conveyed his beliefs through his art. He is considered an abolitionist because he objected to the unfair treatment and injustice of African Americans. He used his artistic gift to reveal his feelings about slavery. For instance, he often carved copper engravings of chained slaves. Reason also displayed his spirituality through his works such as engravings of men kneeling down with hands poised in prayer. His work was admired by many which led him to produce portraits and designs for periodicals and frontispieces in slave narratives in the mid-nineteenth century. Unfortunately, white engravers refused to work with him, and firms often refused to hire him.

On June 22, 1862, Reason married Esther Cunningham of Leeds, England. They had one son, Charles. Shortly after the marriage, the couple left New York with their young son and moved to Cleveland, Ohio. Several firms had invited Reason to work as an engraver with them in Cleveland. Reason spent more than fifteen years working with the jewelry firm of Sylvester Hogan. Hogan was a wholesale and retail dealer in fine jewelry and silver plate. Unlike the New York directories, the Cleveland directories until 1899 listed Reason as an engraver.

Reason belonged to the New York Philomathean Society; it was organized in 1830 for literary improvement and social pleasure. Along with others, Reason organized an Odd Fellows Lodge, an organization committed to assist its members in cases of sickness and death. Unfortunately, the Philomathean Society refused their application for a dispensation. However, they were granted a dispensation from another lodge number. His membership gave him the opportunity to design and engrave the first certificate of membership for the Odd Fellows. He was also active in the New York Masons.

Reason was diagnosed with carcinoma of the rectum. He suffered from the disease for a long time and eventually died at home in Cleveland on August 12, 1898, when he was eighty-two years old. He was survived by his wife Esther and son Charles.

REFERENCES

Books

Gates, Henry Louis Jr., and Evelyn Brooks Higginbotham, eds. *African American Lives*. Oxford: Oxford University Press, 2004.

Lewis, Samella. *African American Art and Artists*. Berkeley: Star Type, 2003.

Logan, Rayford W., and Michael R. Winston, eds. *Dictionary of American Negro Biography*. New York: Norton, 1982.

Clarence Toomer

Louis L. Redding
1901–1998

Lawyer

Louis L. Redding

The first African American lawyer in Delaware, Louis L. Redding seized the opportunity to change the legal principles that embraced racial segregation in his state and beyond. Through his efforts, in 1950 the University of Delaware broke down its racial barriers and admitted black students. Two years later he was successful in desegregating the public schools of Delaware. The case had national significance; it became a part of *Brown v. Board of Education* which in 1954 resulted in the U.S. Supreme Court's declaration that the separate-but-equal doctrine was unconstitutional. Redding also fought for passage of open legislation in Delaware. Redding spent his life fighting for the rights of African Americans, particularly in Delaware.

The oldest of Lewis Alfred and Mary Ann Holmes Redding's five children, Louis Lorenzo Redding was born on October 25, 1901, at the Holmes family homestead in Alexandria, Virginia. Both parents studied at Howard University in Washington, D.C. Mary Redding stayed for only two semesters and although she never graduated, she was an intellect who loved books and reading. Lewis Alfred Redding interrupted his education due to family and financial pressures, taught school in Maryland for a while, and returned to school and graduated from the Normal Department, or teacher's school, in 1897, when he was nearly thirty years old. The Reddings met while at Howard. Their backgrounds were vastly different, however: he was the son of a former slave while she was from the mulatto elite, free black artisans. The Holmes family disapproved of Lewis and the couple's interest in marriage.

After their marriage in 1900, the Reddings moved to Wilmington, Delaware, where Lewis set up a small grocery store that lasted only three years. They moved from one dilapidated neighborhood to another. Before the store closed, however, Lewis had landed a job as a postal worker, becoming one of four black postmen. The job carried prestige in the black community and brought him instant respectability. He took part-time jobs as well, and a few years later the family moved to a neighborhood of middle-class blacks.

The Reddings had seven children, although two died in infancy: the surviving children were Louis Lorenzo, Cora Gwendolyn, James Saunders, Lillian Mae Holmes, and Jennetta Mayson. They grew up with middle-class values and were known for their elegance and refinement, and according to the family biographer Annette Woolard-Provine, they were recognized as "the scholarly family of black Wilmington." Throughout their lives, they spoke English with precision and elegance, absent any trace of regional dialect. They were home-tutored for the first few grades and attended summer classes when they were very young. A college education for all of the Reddings was a given. One of the children, James "Jay" Saunders Redding, also known as Saunders Redding, became a highly recognized college professor who wrote and published works about the black experience.

Graduates from Brown University

Louis Redding studied at Wilmington's racially segregated Howard High School, where Edwina Kruse, a well-known black principal, was a dominating force. English teacher and Harlem Renaissance writer Alice Dunbar-Nelson, who brought prestige to the school, helped to lure Wilmington's best and brightest to Howard. Louis Redding continued to cross paths with Dunbar-Nelson through their work with the NAACP. During the Kruse era, Howard endured the racial caste system, where light-skinned students were traditionally favored and privileged while dark-skinned blacks were generally in disfavor. The Reddings, however, though dark-skinned, were Wilmington's privileged and received encouragement at the school. Redding became the school's first graduate accepted to Brown University and his sister Gwendolyn the first to enroll in Pembroke, a women's affiliate of Brown.

Chronology

1901	Born in Alexandria, Virginia on October 25
1923	Receives A.B. degree from Brown University
1923-24	Becomes vice principal of Fessenden Academy, Ocala, Florida
1924-25	Teaches at Morehouse College, Atlanta, Georgia
1928	Receives J.D. degree from Harvard Law School
1929	Becomes first black admitted to the Delaware bar; begins law practice
1944	Marries Ruth Albert Cook
1950	Wins lawsuit forcing University of Delaware to accept black students
1954	Joins other lawyers and NAACP, successfully arguing *Brown v. Board of Education* before U.S. Supreme Court
1965	Becomes public defender, State of Delaware
1972	Marries Gwendolyn Carmen Kiah
1973	Receives honorary LLD degree from Brown University
1984	Retires after practicing law for 55 years
1989	Receives NEA's Martin Luther King Jr. Memorial Award
1998	Dies in Lima, Pennsylvania on September 29
2000	University of Delaware establishes professorship in his name

Redding enjoyed the Ivy League tradition at Brown, breathed in the intellectual and urban sophistication of the campus, and developed a taste for fine clothes. In 1921, Redding and seven other black men established a chapter of Alpha Phi Alpha fraternity in Providence. At that time such fraternities provided a much-needed social life for blacks. On entering Brown, Louis Redding planned to become a doctor, due in part to his father's wishes for his son to live well and be shielded from racism. But Louis recognized early on his dislike for biology and was attracted by the lifestyles of several black lawyers in Providence and Boston. Thus, he decided to become a lawyer.

Fulfills Dream to Achieve His Law Degree

After graduating from Brown in 1923, however, Redding had to find employment because his family was unable to pay for a law school education. He moved to Ocala, Florida, where for one year, from 1923 to 1924, he was assistant principal in the racially segregated Fessenden Academy, one of the black schools supported by the American Missionary Association. Much later he told his brother Saunders that he had been disturbed by the aftermath of a race lynching that occurred while he was in Florida, an experience that he refused to discuss with others but one that obviously had an impact on the professional life that he was to lead. In 1924 and 1925 he taught English at Morehouse College in Atlanta. Atlanta was more protest-oriented than Ocala. Redding became seriously concerned about racial protest while there.

By now, Redding decided it was time to pursue a legal career. He knew that his choices were limited because white law schools accepted a token number of blacks and Howard University in Washington, D.C., where Charles Hamilton Houston was dean, was the only black school that provided quality legal education. He took a temporary post with the Chicago postal service and investigated the law school at the University of Chicago where blacks had been well accepted. Instead, he enrolled in the law school at Harvard University and graduated in 1928, the only black in a class of 250 and the second black to earn a J.D. from the program. While at Harvard he met the young Benjamin Davis, later a well-known Communist activist.

Redding hoped to become a big-city New England lawyer, but he yielded to his father's wishes for him to return to Wilmington and work for racial justice within the state. He returned to Wilmington in 1928. There he served a clerkship—in name only—with municipal court judge and later U.S. senator Daniel O. Hastings, who kept secret his sponsorship of the young black attorney. All law candidates for the state bar were required to serve a clerkship. Redding discussed with his friend and former teacher Alice Dunbar-Nelson his misgivings about Hastings and his belief that the man was corrupt. He completed his clerkship in February 1929, passed the state bar that year, and became the first black lawyer in Delaware. He was the state's only black lawyer for twenty-six years.

Louis Redding took aim at segregation in Wilmington's courtrooms, where whites and blacks sat on opposite sides. While at home visiting from law school, in 1926 he was ejected from the municipal court because he sat on the gallery's "white side." Now as a lawyer, he challenged the practice, asserting that he could find no law mandating it and there was no code supporting the tradition. The practice was discontinued. As a lawyer, however, he was professionally lonely. Mediocre white lawyers displayed contempt for his competence; generally, white lawyers were cool toward him; and in the courtroom some judges refused to make eye contact with him. His practice was small and provided little distinction among the large, corporate firms. Still he persevered and as clients found their way to him during the Great Depression and as he remained determined to take on controversial clients, his practice grew. He traveled the state to attract clients and practiced in three counties.

Becomes Desegregation Lawyer

Louis Redding became best known for his work as a desegregation lawyer. In 1950, black students in Delaware's segregated college system became restive about the conditions in the black, unaccredited Delaware State College where they studied. Over thirty students applied for admission to the University of Delaware and were rejected, and nine of these students sought relief in the courts. Redding and Jack Greenberg, lawyer for the NAACP Legal Defense and Educational Fund, took the case. In *Parker v. University of Delaware*, the Court of Chancery of Delaware on August 9, 1950, held for the plaintiffs and other similarly situated. Thus, the University of Delaware became the first public university, by court order, to admit black students. This victory became part of the monumental *Brown v. Board of Education*.

Redding argued successfully again in 1952 in behalf of eight black students who had been prevented from enrolling in the white public schools in Delaware. This was the nation's first case of court-ordered desegregation of public schools. The state appealed the victory. In *Brown v. Board of Education* the Supreme Court ruled against the separate-but-equal doctrine relating to public schools, desegregating them. Afterward, Redding practically stood alone among Delaware's power system in the general assembly, education, and elsewhere. As result of his desegregation work, he received threats against his life, hate mail, and frightening telephone calls, yet he continued his fight against racism.

Professional Memberships and Awards

Redding became public defender for the state of Delaware in 1965 and continued his support of poor clients. He held this post for twenty years until he retired in 1985. During his professional life he joined the National Bar Association, the National Lawyers Guild, the Emergency Civil Liberties Committee (sometimes called a left-wing organization), and NAACP. He became president of the Delaware Bar Association—the same organization that excluded him from membership early on. For most of his career he was legal counsel for the Wilmington NAACP.

Late in life Redding was highly publicized in the local media and sought out for interviews and speaking engagements. He received a number of recognitions after his death. The University of Delaware—the school that he legally forced to accept black students in 1950—honored him in 2000 by establishing the highly honored Louis L. Redding Chair in the School of Education. Redding Middle School in Middletown, Delaware, was named in his honor.

Redding had faith in the legal system; he firmly believed that grievances could be resolved through the system. At times his task was lonely, especially in his efforts to desegregate public accommodations in Delaware and in his maneuvers to establish an open housing law. He found relief in 1968 when the federal housing bill was passed and in 1969 when Delaware outlawed race-restricted housing sales and rent covenants. Although he worked primarily through legal protest and felt most comfortable when he did, at times Redding worked outside the system. He helped to devise a number of boycotts and sit-in strategies but seldom attended the events. To increase economic opportunities for blacks, he worked privately with local businessmen and political leaders. He participated in the March on Washington in 1963 and met with national civil rights leaders. He was discomforted by the grass-roots activism of the late 1960s, especially the work of Black Nationalism and its sometimes violent overtones. All protest, he thought, should be united, and he believed what he saw as competition between various civil rights groups would discourage mainstream empathy. Soon younger members of protest groups thought Redding was out-of-step with the times. Ultimately, however, civil rights efforts became mainstream, and he began to enjoy the positive attention that he attracted through his work.

Redding married Ruth Cook in 1944 and they had three daughters: Ann Holmes, Rupa Cook, and Judith Boardman. After he and his first wife divorced in the early 1970s, he married Gwendolyn Carmen Kiah in 1972. She died in June 1998. Redding experienced health problems as early as the mid-1980s, including the onset of Alzheimer's disease. He died on September 29, 1998, in a hospital in Lima, Pennsylvania, near his home in Glen Mills at the age of ninety-six. He is remembered as one who figured prominently in the struggle for desegregation in Delaware and as a lawyer who never lost a desegregation case.

REFERENCES

Books

Who's Who among African Americans. 12th ed. Detroit: Gale Research, 1999.

Woolard-Provine, Annette. *Integrating Delaware: The Reddings of Wilmington.* Newark: University of Delaware Press, 2003.

Periodicals

Pace, Eric. "L. L. Redding, 96, Desegregation Lawyer, Dies." *New York Times Archive* (2 October 1998).

Redding, Louis L. "Desegregation in Higher Education in Delaware." *Journal of Negro Education* 27 (1958): 254-57.

Online

"The Conscience of Desegregation: Louis L. Redding '23." *Brown Alumni Magazine* 99 (January-February 1999). http://www/brown.edu/Administration/Brown_Alumni_Magazine/99/1(Accessed 28 September 2004).

"Louis Redding '23." *Brown Alumni Magazine.* http://www/brown.edu/Administration/Brown_Alumni_Magazine/01/1 (Accessed 28 September 2004).

Morris, Irving. "Louis L. Redding 1901-1998." Delaware State Bar Association. http://www.dsba.org/novmem98.htm (Accessed 28 September 2004).

Jessie Carney Smith

Scovel Richardson
1912–1982

Judge, lawyer, educator

In an outstanding and diverse legal career, Scovel Richardson made a huge impact through his pioneering role as one of the first African Americans to serve in the federal judiciary system and his work in and on behalf of historically black colleges and universities (HBCUs) and the larger African American community. He was one of many African American professionals in the legal system who led by example and action during the transition from segregation to integration of blacks into the mainstream of U.S. society, and expanded his influence to national and international levels.

Scovel Richardson was born on February 4, 1912 in Nashville, Tennessee, to M. Scovel and Capitola W. Hawkins Richardson. His family eventually relocated to Chicago, where he attended and graduated from Wendell Phillips High School. Remaining in the state, Richardson attended the University of Illinois, where he received a B.A. in 1934 and an M.A. in 1936. The title of his master's thesis was "Denial of Justice in International Law."

In addition to his early intellectual achievements, Richardson was also noted for his athletic ability in boxing during his college years. He decided to pursue a career in law and was admitted to the Howard University law school in Washington, D.C., where he completed studies for his law degree in 1937.

Begins Legal Career in Midwest

Richardson returned to Chicago, where he worked for a time as a salesman at Michelson's, a retail establishment in the city, until he could develop a base of clients as a lawyer. He also married the former Inez Williston of Washington, D.C. on July 3, 1937. In 1938, Richardson entered the private practice of law with the firm of Lawrence and Richardson, where he remained for the next two years.

In the neighboring state of Missouri, events were taking place which would affect Richardson and the future direction of his legal career. Lloyd L. Gaines, a 1935 graduate of Lincoln University, the HBCU established in 1866, applied for and was refused admission to the law school at the University of Missouri. A lawsuit was filed against the state and the university (*Gaines v. Missouri*), and the state supreme court ruled that, since provision had been made for Gaines and other African Americans to attend law schools in other states, their rights to pursue a legal education had not been denied.

The court's decision was appealed to the U.S. Supreme Court, which outlawed tuition aid for out-of-state study by African American citizens of states practic-

Scovel Richardson

ing segregation in its 1938 ruling on the case and required the state of Missouri to provide access to equal in-state facilities. The University of Missouri had to admit Gaines, or the state had to establish a law school at Lincoln. The state chose the second option, and Richardson was recruited for a position on the law faculty of the new school, which opened in St. Louis with thirty students in September 1939.

Richardson was uniquely qualified to assist in the development of the Lincoln law school, as he had experienced both the dynamics of segregation and the HBCU setting while in Washington at Howard. In addition, W. E. Taylor, the former acting dean at Howard, was the dean of the Lincoln law school, so Richardson, who had been hired as an associate professor, and the five other faculty members could build the law school based on the Howard model.

While living in St. Louis, Richardson joined the St. Louis Negro Bar Association but made headlines when he moved his family into a white neighborhood in the city and challenged the city's leading bar association for not allowing black lawyers to join the organization. He remained in his home despite attempts at intimidation from white homeowners and real estate groups and won a lawsuit affirming his right to live where he chose.

In 1943, during World War II, Richardson made the decision to leave his professorship to accept his first government position, as a senior attorney in the Office of Price Administration (Stabilization). He relocated to Washington and worked in this capacity until 1947, returning to Missouri and Lincoln to become a full professor and dean of the law school. By this time the Richardson family includes four daughters: Frances Elaine, Alice Inez, and twins Mary Louise and Marjorie Linda.

Despite the significance of leading one of the few law schools at HBCUs, Richardson continued to challenge the legal segregation in the state that led to its existence. African Americans were still being denied admission to traditionally white institutions in southern and border states enforcing these laws, yet Richardson pressed forward, knowing that success in changing the established order could have negative implications for Lincoln and other HBCUs. At the same time, according to the *Washington Post*, he stressed in public forums such as the 1947 Young Republican National Federation convention in Milwaukee, Wisconsin, that "Negroes are a people unshaken in their devotion to their country" who would not be divided by "the merchants of hate."

Richardson and his African American colleagues in the legal profession were encouraged by Executive Order 9981 of President (and Missouri native) Harry S. Truman, which desegregated the military services/armed forces on July 26, 1948. His Howard mentors and peers such as Charles Hamilton Houston, Thurgood Marshall, James M. Nabrit, and others were involved in additional cases through the NAACP Legal Defense Fund that continued to attack legal segregation, culminating with the landmark *Brown v. Board of Education* case and decision in 1954.

Even though Richardson was a Republican, he, along with most African Americans, was supportive of the progressive policies of the Democratic administration led by Truman. As a result, African American voters may very

well have given Truman the margin of victory in the 1948 election. Richardson remained at his post as dean of the Lincoln law school during the presidency of his fellow Missourian, while also serving in various capacities with the National Bar Association (NBA), an alliance of blacks in the legal profession. He was elected as national president of the NBA in 1951 and served the organization in that role for a year.

Receives Presidential Appointments

With the election of Republican Dwight D. Eisenhower as president in the 1952 election, Richardson's national profile increased. The new president appointed him to the U.S. Board of Parole on August 3, 1953. He was the first African American to receive this distinction and made history again when he became the first African American member of the Bar Association of St. Louis in late 1953. Richardson also was the first African American from Missouri to be admitted into the American Bar Association and the American Law Institute, to serve as president of the Urban League of St. Louis, and to belong to the St. Louis Chamber of Commerce.

After resigning from his deanship at Lincoln, Richardson relocated to Washington with his family to assume his new responsibilities. The board had recently been enlarged from five to seven members and given additional jurisdiction over cases involving juvenile as well as adult offenders. One of the most celebrated cases heard by Richardson during his first year on the board involved denying the second parole application of Alger Hiss, a former government official convicted of perjury regarding his relationship with known Communists during the McCarthy era.

On September 28, 1954, Richardson became the chair of the parole board upon the recommendation of Attorney General Herbert Brownell Jr. During his years of service, he developed a reputation for being stern, yet kindly and fair to the thousands of prisoners and numerous cases that came before the board. In 1955 Richardson served on an advisory council on corrections organized by Brownell to examine treatment and correction of federal offenders and methods to prevent crime and delinquency. The 1956 report issued by Richardson indicated that the successful parole rate of federal prisoners had remained at 80 percent for the previous seven years, evidence that the system was working well in rehabilitation of offenders.

The success of Richardson in this role prompted speculation in late 1956 that he was under consideration for a higher level appointment, possibly a judgeship on the U.S. District Court for the Eastern District of Missouri. This would have made him the first African American to serve at that level in the continental United States, but he did not receive that particular appointment.

Richardson retained his position as chair of the parole board until March 4, 1957, when Eisenhower, upon another recommendation from Brownell, nominated him to fill a vacancy on the U.S. Customs Court in New York City after the death of Judge William A. Ekwall in October 1956. When his presidential nomination was confirmed by the U.S. Senate, Richardson became the first Howard University law graduate and second African American to serve on the court, joining Judge Irvin C. Mollison, a Truman appointee. This made him the third African American with the status of Article III federal judge (lifetime appointment based on Article III of the Constitution), and the only African American appointed by Eisenhower to the federal judiciary.

Federal Judge and Influential Role Model

In connection with his new position, Richardson and his family relocated again, this time to New Rochelle, New York, a suburb of New York City. His four daughters were all in their teens, with the eldest, Frances, already following in her father's footsteps at age sixteen as a pre-law student at American University in Washington. Richardson was an honored alumni guest at events celebrating the ninety-first anniversary of Howard University in March 1958, during which he received a citation from the university in recognition of his career and achievements.

Richardson also became a part of elite Washington and New York social circles, with invitations to such events as a 1959 state dinner at the White House hosted by President and Mrs. Eisenhower, in honor of President and Mrs. Sekou Toure of the newly independent African republic of Guinea. He and his family were often profiled in the society pages of the *New York Times* and the *Washington Post*, as well as prominent African American newspapers such as the New York *Amsterdam News*, the *Afro-American* (Baltimore), and the *Pittsburgh Courier*.

Richardson's work as one of nine judges on the U.S. Customs Court involved ruling on a wide variety of cases related to tariffs and other taxes on products, goods, and other items imported to the United States. One of the most celebrated cases during his early years on the court involved a work by Pablo Picasso, one of the most famous artists of the twentieth century.

In 1960 a three-judge panel from the court, including Richardson, overruled U.S. customs inspectors, who called the Picasso artwork "an article of glass" and levied a duty of 30 percent of its value instead of the 20 percent fee designated for pieces of art. This ruling was consistent with their earlier decision regarding a collage by another artist, Alberto Burri, in November 1958, which inspectors had called a "manufacture of vegetable matter," according to the *New York Times*. As a result of that case, New York Senator Jacob K. Javits introduced legislation to amend the Tariff Act of 1930 regarding art

objects. This became law in 1959 and further influenced the ruling of Richardson and his colleagues.

Richardson and his wife remained involved in the African American community through organizations such as the Howard University Alumni Club of New York; New York alumni chapter of Kappa Alpha Psi, his college fraternity; and the Northside Center for Child Development in Harlem. In 1961 Richardson was involved in the alumni celebration for his former legal colleague and fellow law school dean, James M. Nabrit Jr., who had become the president of Howard during the previous year. The Richardsons were also involved in a New York reception for the United Nations delegate from Tanganyika, Dr. V. Kyaruzi, and his wife on December 31, 1961.

In 1966 Richardson became the presiding judge of the Third Division of the U.S. Customs Court and continued in this capacity through 1970. In 1968 he was honored again when Howard elected him as chair of the university board of trustees and led the board in the selection process for a new president upon the retirement of Dr. Nabrit. During these years he also was active in the Bar Association of New York City, a trustee of Colgate University, a board member for the National Council on Crime and Delinquency and the National Judicial Commission of the Presbyterian Church, and a director of the New Rochelle Hospital.

Richardson worked to ensure a smooth transition of leadership at Howard, which experienced its fair share of controversy and student unrest in the late 1960s. He supported the interests of the older generation of faculty, alumni, and administrative leadership, who respected and supported Nabrit for his involvement with the NAACP Legal Defense Fund team that won the landmark *Brown v. Board of Education* case and his leadership of the law school and university.

Nabrit was rightfully lauded for his many achievements and contributions, yet Richardson and the selection committee made a bold choice for his successor in Dr. James E. Cheek, who had experienced great success at Shaw University, an HBCU in Raleigh, North Carolina, after becoming its president at age 31 in 1963. Cheek was viewed as being more attuned to the interests of both younger and older alumni, faculty, and current students interested in seeing the university become even more relevant to the larger African American community. The wisdom of Richardson and the Howard board became evident, as Cheek went on to successful leadership and presidency of the university.

In his primary responsibility as judge on the Customs Court, Richardson continued to issue key rulings on tariff and trade related cases that came before the judicial panels and the court as a whole. As technology imports increased in the 1970s, Richardson and his colleagues came in conflict with the U.S. Treasury Department when the court ruled that tariffs had to be paid by Japanese manufacturers of electronic goods. Their decision had major implications for U.S. trade relationships with Japan, and U.S. pricing practices for Japanese electronic products, while supporting the position that American manufacturers were hurt by the existing trade agreements.

The judicial panel, including Richardson, indicated that not requiring Japanese exporters to pay duties on their products was beyond the scope and intent of the 1930 Tariff Act and ordered the U.S. Treasury Department to estimate percentages of import taxes to be assessed on Japanese products by customs officers. Richardson personally noted, according to the *New York Times*, that the Treasury Department policy was "in conflict with the decisions of the Supreme Court of the United States construing the countervailing statute, and must yield", and that the Treasury Secretary "must discharge his responsibilities in accord with the Congressional intent in that statute as interpreted by the Supreme Court."

On October 31, 1980 the name of the U.S. Customs Court was officially changed to the U.S. Court of International Trade, and Richardson was formally reassigned to his same position on November 1. Despite the name change, his duties were unchanged, and he continued until his death after suffering a heart attack on March 30, 1982 in New Rochelle.

Judge Scovel Richardson was survived by his wife, four daughters, four grandchildren, a brother, Dr. Reuben Richardson, and a sister, Mary Walker. He left a legacy with the federal judiciary and with the HBCUs and other universities where he studied and served, in the African American community, and the nation at large.

Among the many awards and recognitions he received during and after his life, Richardson may very well have been most proud of the Scovel Richardson scholarship, awarded to African American law students by the Mound City Bar Association of St. Louis. Within his family, some of his children followed him into the legal profession and a grandson, John Lawrence Harrisingh, became a Howard graduate, Fordham University law school graduate, and practicing attorney in New York City by the end of the 1980s.

REFERENCES

Books

Chase, Harold W., Samuel Krislov, Keith O. Boyum, and Jerry N. Clark. *Biographical Dictionary of the Federal Judiciary.* Detroit, Mich.: Gale Research, 1976.

Matney, William C., ed. *Who's Who among Black Americans.* 3rd ed. Northbrook, Ill.: Who's Who Among Black Americans, Inc. Publishing Co., 1981.

Sanders, Charles L., ed. *1,000 Successful Blacks.* Chicago, Ill.: Johnson Publishing Co., 1973.

Periodicals

"Appointment ad Valorem: Scovel Richardson." *New York Times*, 5 March 1957.

Brooks, Charles. "Why the Judiciary Matters to Black America." *New York Amsterdam News*, 27 February 2003.

"Court Orders Duties on Electronic Goods Coming from Japan." *New York Times*, 13 April 1977.

"Forum Talks Mark Young GOP Sessions." *Washington Post*, 7 June 1947.

"Judge Heads Trustees at Howard U." *Washington Post*, 1 May 1968.

"Mosaic by Picasso is Art, Court Says." *New York Times*, 6 May 1960.

"President Names 7 to Parole Board." *New York Times*, 24 July 1953.

"Richardson Chosen for Judgeship." *Washington Post*, 5 March 1957.

"Richardson to Head U.S. Parole Board." *Washington Post*, 29 September 1954.

"Scovel Richardson, U.S. Judge." *New York Times*, 31 March 1982.

Online

Just the Beginning Foundation. "Scovel Richardson." http://www.jtbf.org/article_iii_judges/richardson_s. htm (Accessed 3 May 2005).

Lincoln University of Missouri. "The Question of Separate but Equal." http://www.lincolnu.edu/ ~library/darch/soldiersdream1/page21.html (Accessed 3 May 2005).

Mound City Bar Association. "Scovel Richardson Scholarship Award." http://www.mobar.org/ local_bars/scoville_cover.pdf (Accessed 2 May 2005).

United States Parole Commission, U.S. Department of Justice. "History of the Federal Parole System." http://www.usdoj.gov/uspc/historytxt.htm (Accessed 2 May 2005).

Fletcher F. Moon

Hilyard Robinson
1899–1986

Architect

One of the most successful and productive African American architects in Washington, D.C. during the first half of the twentieth century, Hilyard Robinson helped to address the housing needs of black Americans—from the poor to the affluent—and became the leading designer of public housing. His work helped to spur the passage of the first national housing act. He also supervised the construction of the Tuskegee Army Airfield in Alabama, where the famed Tuskegee Airmen trained.

Born in Washington, D.C., in 1899, Hilyard Robert Robinson graduated from the later historic M Street High School in the district and for one year, 1917, studied at the Pennsylvania Museum and School of Industrial Arts in Philadelphia. World War I was then in progress; Robinson left school and joined the U.S. Army Field Artillery Corps, 167th Brigade. He served in France as a second lieutenant. Back in the states after that, in 1919 he studied architecture at the University of Pennsylvania, under the tutelage of Paule Philippe Cret, who trained at École des Beaux Arts.

Robinson spent the summers of 1921 and 1922 in Harlem, where he was a draftsman for the noted black architect Vertner Woodson Tandy. There he was persuaded to transfer to Columbia University in 1922. From 1922 to 1924 Robinson worked as an architectural draftsman for Paul B. LaVelle, who also trained at École des Beaux Arts and was a friend of his former employer, Tandy. He taught part-time at Howard University in his home town, at the time when the university was developing its School of Architecture. Thus Robinson's relationship to Howard began before he received his bachelor's degree in architecture from Columbia in 1924. As instructor and later department chair at Howard until 1937, Robinson designed eleven buildings for the school and also played a part in establishing a distinct modernistic design on the hilltop campus. There he established contacts for personal residences that he designed or remodeled in the city.

Toward the end of the 1920s Robinson studied the slums that housed Washington's poorest blacks and then embarked on an exploration of congregated housing needs that would facilitate his work later on. On leave of absence from Howard, he completed his master's degree at Columbia University in 1931 and spent eighteen months on a subsidized tour of Europe. He examined and photographed government-sponsored housing solutions. Techniques for reconstruction of Rotterdam as well as Scandinavian contemporary style of architecture impressed him. When he returned to Howard in 1932, Robinson had a solid understanding of architectural trends in other countries.

In 1935 Robinson took a second leave of absence from Howard to pursue his interest in housing needs for the black poor and to apply low-cost techniques to new construction. The Public Works Administration, just established, was empowered to provide housing for the poor. Having studied the subject, Robinson was well suited to help the WPA pursue its mission; moreover, blacks had to be included in any plans that were advanced. Robinson began a partnership with two local white architects—Irwin Porter and Alexander Trowbridge—as well as the prominent and well-connected black architects Paul Revere Williams and his former boss Vertner Tandy. Robinson was the group's chief architect. Their charge was clear: design the first federally sponsored public housing development in the city and in the nation. Thus, Langston Terrace was born.

Because Langston Terrace was located near the U.S. capitol, it was highly visible to the general public and, in the words of Glen Leiner in *African American Architects*, "the most conspicuous of the fifty-one federal housing projects sponsored by the Public Works Administration." David Augustus Williston, a prominent black landscape architect also involved in the plan, developed a central common that served the modest dwellings. So attractive and functional was the development that it catapulted Robinson into the role of leading designer of public housing. It also remained his prized achievement. Because of its overall appeal and functionality, Langston Terrace and Robinson's work with it helped lead to the passage in 1937 of the first national Housing Act. Robinson moved on to other projects, including Aberdeen Gardens in Newport News, Virginia, in 1935 as well as housing for black defense workers.

Robinson contributed to the beauty of the upscale Brooklyn neighborhood located in Washington, D.C. near Catholic University of America. In 1941 he designed the home of Ralph J. Bunche, who went on to become the first black secretary of the United Nations. His home, located at 1510 Jackson Street, NE, had a distinctive hip-roof and was designed with a subtle international style. Robinson employed John Dennis Sulton to complete the house, for he was headed to another important assignment in Tuskegee, Alabama.

The segregated armed forces had kept blacks out of the U.S. Army Air Force—the "dream team" of the military. After agitation from blacks, particularly threat of a law suit from the NAACP and Howard University student Yancey Williams, blacks were accepted into the segregated 99th Pursuit Squadron, the legendary Tuskegee Airmen. This group was relegated to a new base developed about six miles from Tuskegee Institute (now University) in Alabama. The air base consisted of hangars, shops, classrooms, and other facilities, and needed an air field for flight training. Robinson moved to the Tuskegee campus in June 1941 to be near the project that he was to design and supervise in construction—the Tuskegee Army Airfield in Chehaw, Alabama. He had a staff of twenty-one architects, engineers, and administrative personnel. The architectural firm Alexander & Repass constructed the air base. Robinson had held and completed the first defense contract given to an African American.

Robinson was well-connected in Washington. He was a member of the Washington Housing Association from 1950 to 1955. He also headed the Washington Housing Authority. After the war, he was planning consultant to the Republic of Liberia from 1946 to 1949 and developed the plans for Liberia's 1947 Centennial Exposition. He designed buildings for Howard University, such as the School of Engineering and Architecture in 1952.

He fared well during the Great Depression, as projects or commissions continued to come to him. Robinson designed the small office building that housed his business, at 1927 11th Street, N.W. Through 1962, when he went into semi-retirement, he had a staff of six or seven people but never elevated any of them to a partnership. He hired numerous architects as well but held only nominal partnerships with those politically well-connected architects who helped him to secure commissions. In private life, he was married to Helena Rooks Robinson and had one daughter who died before her teen years. Robinson died on July 2, 1986, in Howard University Hospital. His most compelling legacy was seen in his design and construction of public housing.

REFERENCES

Books

Leiner, Glen B. "Hilyard Robert Robinson," In *African American Architects: A Biographical Dictionary 1865-1945*. Ed. Dreck Spurlock Wilson. New York: Routledge, 2004.

Jessie Carney Smith

Moses Roper
c. 1815 –?

Slave, abolitionist

Biographers and historians agree that there is little information on the life of the fugitive slave and abolitionist Moses Roper. Most of the available information comes from his slave narrative. Moses Roper is recognized for recording details of the horror of American slavery in his biographical account *A Narrative of the Adventures and Escape of Moses Roper, from American Slavery* (1838). The narrative challenges the romantic mythology of slavery. Roper painstakingly details his escape attempts and his punishments. Unlike many of his contemporaries who avoided disclosing the real names of their slave masters, Roper names his masters, overseers, and all persons responsible for his exploitation and abuse. Although his narrative in many ways is like a quest or adventure tale, his story has the unapologetic political mission of most slave narratives written after 1830.

Although Moses Roper indicates in his narrative that he is unsure of the exact date of his birth, most historians guess he was born in 1815 or 1816. He was born in Caswell County, North Carolina. He describes his father, John Roper, as a white man. John Roper was married to the daughter of Moses Roper's slave master. According to Roper his mother, Nancy, was part African, part Indian, and part white. Moses Roper's white skin and his resemblance to his father were not in his favor. In his narrative, he explains that when his father's wife, Mrs. Roper, discovered his birth and similar appearance to John Roper, she was determined to kill him. Fortunately, Roper's mother prevented her from harming him. Moses Roper was resented because of his white appearance. When his master died, he was separated from his mother. He was six years old and sent to live with Mr. Fowler. Fowler, not pleased with Roper, decided to sell him. However, because of Roper's color, he had difficulty selling him. He finally sold Roper to a trader whose name was Michael.

This trade was the beginning of an exhausting journey in which Roper was sold at least a dozen times and endured countless beatings and torture. During this time, he was sold and relocated to various parts of the South, including North Carolina, South Carolina, Georgia, and Florida. He did not remain long with any master, except for a Mr. Gooch. Roper was sold to Gooch around the year 1829 and lived with him at Liberty Hill in Kershaw County, South Carolina. A good portion of his narrative is devoted to recounting his experiences as Gooch's slave. He also tells of the horrifying experiences of other slaves owned by Gooch. Under Gooch, Roper attempted to escape a number of times. His perceived obstinacy resulted from Gooch's cruelty. According to Roper, Gooch demanded Roper do work that at times was

Chronology

1815?	Born into slavery in Caswell County, North Carolina
1821	Separated from his mother and sold to trader Mr. Michael
1829	Sold to Mr. Gooch (one of his cruelest masters); makes first attempt to escape
1832	Sold to Mr. Britton
1834	Sold a number of times and finally sold to Mr. Beveridge; escapes to Savannah; sails to New York City; travels throughout the northeastern part of the United States
1835	Sails for England, arriving in Liverpool
1837	Publishes in England *A Narrative of the Adventures and Escape of Moses Roper, from American Slavery*
1838	Publishes *Narrative* in the United States
1839	Marries Ann Stephen Price of Bristol, England
1844	Moves with wife and child to Ontario, Canada
1846	Returns to England on business matter
1854	Travels to England to give speech
??	Dies (date unknown), possibly in Ontario

impossible. Gooch did not provide adequate food. He often forced Roper to take off his clothes and then he would beat Roper naked. When Roper worked for a Mr. Hammans, Gooch's son-in-law, he was frightened when the overseer, a man named Condell, threatened him. Roper made the mistake of leaving the fodder out at night, and it rained. Condell promised to flog him severely for this "crime." Roper explains that he was about thirteen years old and decided to escape rather than be beaten. This attempted escape was the beginning of half a dozen efforts Roper made to escape slavery.

On one of his attempts, he managed to reunite with his mother, Nancy, and one of his sisters Maria. However, he was soon apprehended. Roper was severely beaten as punishment for his attempted escapes and was forced to wear various restrictive and torture devices. He was often made to wear heavy leg irons and chained to a woman slave who had also attempted to escape. These irons, coupled with the pairing with another slave, made doing daily work difficult. Consequently, he and the woman to whom he was attached were beaten more often. As a punishment after one of his escapes, he was made to wear a device he called "iron horns with bells." This heavy and cumbersome device was attached to the back of his neck. It was used both to deter escape and as a punishment. According to Roper, this instrument was used frequently by slave holders in South Carolina. After another escape attempt, Roper was suspended on a contraption called a cotton screw. He was strung up by the hands for long periods while being whipped. Pictures of both of these devices appear in his narrative. Gooch decided to sell Roper in 1832. Roper was bought and sold a few times before being purchased by a Mr. Louis, who is describe as more tolerable, but when he went aboard, Roper was left in the care of a lawyer, Mr. Kemp. Louis suddenly died, and Mr. Kemp "illegally" sold Roper to Mr. Beveridge, another tolerable master. Beveridge took Roper to Florida. But Beveridge died shortly after purchasing Roper, and Roper was purchased by the unmerciful, perverse, and depraved Mr. Register in 1834.

While the drunken Mr. Register slept, Roper made his escape. This time he was successful. He crossed the Chapoli River and the Chattahoochee River into Georgia. The whiteness of his skin assisted him in obtaining papers that stated he was free. He used the name John Roper. He tried to divert anyone pursuing him but asked directions to Augusta, Georgia. Instead of going to Augusta, he went to Savannah, Georgia. He sailed to New York on the schooner *Fox*, where he worked for his passage and was harassed by the sailors. When he arrived in New York, he feared he was being sought after so he traveled throughout the northeast. He stayed briefly in Vermont, Maine, New Hampshire, and Massachusetts. Since his hair seemed to identify him as black, Roper decided to shave his hair and wear wigs. Eventually, he decided that he could only be free if he left the United Sates.

On November 11, 1835, he sailed for England. He was assisted in his travels by abolitionists who gave him letters of reference. In England, Dr. Raffles, an abolitionist, helped him. Roper went to school at Hackney, and he became an active member of Dr. F. A. Cox's church. In 1837, the story of Roper's enslavement and escape, *A Narrative of the Adventures and Escape of Moses Roper from American Slavery*, was published in England. The narrative was published in 1838 in the United States. In addition to writing his slave narrative, during this period in England, Roper gave a number of antislavery speeches. Although he did attend the University College in London, he did not complete his degree. He married an English woman, Anne Stephen Price of Bristol, in 1839. Roper and his wife had one child. Although Roper talked and wrote about the possibility of moving to Africa or the West Indies, in 1844 he and his wife and child moved to Ontario, Canada. He returned to England on two occasions, once in 1846 and again in 1854 to give a speech. There is little information on Moses Roper's death. Sources suggest he may have died in Ontario.

Moses Roper's determination, perseverance, and courage allowed him to make important contributions to the abolitionist cause and to African American literature. His narrative provides valuable information about his life and about the nature of American slavery.

REFERENCES

Books

Starling, Marion. *The Slave Narrative*. Washington, DC: Howard University Press, 1988.

Online

"A Chronology of Moses Roper's Life." http://www.roperld.com/ropermoses.html(Accessed 14 March 2006).

"Speeches by Moses Roper." *Documenting the American South.* University of North Carolina at Chapel Hill. http://docsouth.unc.edu/roper/bio.html (Accessed 14 March 2006).

Rebecca Dixon

Louis C. Roudanez
1823–1890

Editor, physician

Louis Charles Roudanez started the first black daily newspaper in the United States in which he championed slavery's abolition, universal suffrage, desegregation, and ownership of plantations by ex-slaves. A successful physician, Roudanez was revered for his education, gentility, and wealth by both whites and blacks in New Orleans, Louisiana.

In the 1800s, the political and cultural climate of New Orleans differed from the rest of the United States. New Orleans had a population of free black Creoles, or free people of color, who enjoyed privileges that were not afforded to slaves or most freed blacks. Most of the black Creoles were of French descent and spoke French as their first language. Some were of Spanish and Portuguese descent. They comprised about 10 percent of Louisiana's black population and were, for the most part, affluent and educated and owned an estimated $20 million of New Orleans' wealth. Some were radical activists inspired by the French Revolution whom *New Orleans Tribune* editor Jean-Charles Houzeau called, "the vanguard of the African population of the United States."

Louis Charles Roudanez was born in Jefferson Parish, Louisiana, to Louis Roudanez, a French merchant, and Aimee Potens, a free woman of color. Listed as white on his baptismal registry, Roudanez was baptized as Catholic by the president of the College of New Orleans. The registry also lists Roudanez's birth year as 1823. For reasons unknown, Roudanez and his family always stated that 1826 was the year of his birth, and on the 1870 Federal Census form for New Orleans, Roudanez's age is listed as forty-four.

As a child, Roudanez was schooled in New Orleans and worked in Hill and Cooley's notion store. He later made a small fortune in his municipal bond investments then went on to earn a medical degree in 1853 at the Uni-

Chronology	
1823	Born in Jefferson Parish, Louisiana on June 12
1853	Earns M.D. at the University of Paris
1857	Earns a second medical degree at Dartmouth College; returns to New Orleans and establishes medical practice; marries Celie Saulay
1862	Helps launch *L'Union*
1864	*L'Union* ceases publication; launches the *New Orleans Tribune*
1868	Refuses to endorse Republican ticket; runs independent slate of candidates; *Tribune* ceases publication
1871	Becomes involved with unification movement
1879	Meets with leaders of Republican Party after a decade of not speaking to them
1890	Dies in New Orleans on March 11

versity of Paris, which was then considered to be the world's best medical school.

After the French Revolution of 1789, physicians became one of the most politically progressive professional groups in France. Living in France during the Revolution of 1848 and having French revolutionaries as professors instilled in Roudanez an idealism that he would be both praised and vilified for in later years. Many foreign students of color who studied there often stayed since France was a much friendlier place to people of color, but Roudanez returned to the United States. His friends encouraged him to live in the North first, so he moved to New Hampshire and earned his second medical degree at Dartmouth College in 1857.

Begins Medical Career and *L'Union* Newspaper

Roudanez returned to New Orleans, where he would live for the rest of his life, and began a successful medical practice in which he treated both black and white patients. Roudanez married Celie Saulay on September 15, 1857. They had eight children. Two of his sons became doctors and a third became a dentist. Another one of Roudanez's sons attended Louis le Grand College and lived in New Orleans his entire life. Three of his daughters lived in Paris; one of them was the head of a girls' school.

In April 1862 when south Louisiana came under Union occupation, the rights of the free black population were rolled back. Among other restrictions, the Union army required all blacks, even free people of color, to carry passes when in public. Roudanez and a group that was comprised mostly of black Creoles began *L'Union*, a bi-weekly French-language publication, aimed at the black Creole population, to campaign against slavery and for their own voting rights. On December 23, 1862, *L'Union* became a tri-weekly.

The paper was run by a board of directors that was elected by shareholders every six months. Those working on the paper received death threats. Often quoted in the paper was the French revolutionary philosopher, Lamartine, whom *L'Union* called "the Bard of liberty." *L'Union* promoted the literary heritage of black Creoles, but the exclusivity of a French-language paper widened the chasm between this small, elite group of Catholics and the much larger English-speaking group of black American Protestants, whose lives were more greatly affected by slavery and racism.

L'Union also called for suffrage for free black men, but stopped short of calling for voting rights for ex-slaves until near the end of the paper's run. The paper was printed in both French and English starting on July 9, 1863, and a year later, *L'Union*, realizing that the struggle for voting rights must include ex-slaves, publicly called for their suffrage. Five days afterwards on July 19, 1864, *L'Union* folded.

Launches *New Orleans Tribune*

Roudanez bought the paper's printing equipment and started the *New Orleans Tribune* two days after *L'Union*'s demise. The paper was published twice a week until October 4, 1864, when it was published every day except Monday. The *Tribune* was the first black daily paper in the United States and was a stronger publication than *L'Union*, with a more radical vision. Historian David C. Rankin said the *Tribune* was "perhaps the most brilliant newspaper to appear in the entire South during Reconstruction." One year after it debuted, the Republican Party adopted the *Tribune* as its own official publication.

Paul Trévigne was the original editor of the *Tribune*, but in November 1864, Roudanez brought on board Belgian astronomer Jean Charles Houzeau, who was the northern correspondent for *L'Union*, as editor-in-chief. Under Houzeau, the paper shed much of the perceived elitism on the pages of *L'Union* and the early issues of the *Tribune*. Gone were the literary sections and international news. But Houzeau was still paternalistic: Houzeau nicknamed himself "Cham" after the biblical father of slaves and blacks. Roudanez knew the asset that Houzeau was, despite his ego and arrogance, to the paper and increased his salary in order to keep him at the *Tribune*.

Those who ran the *Tribune* championed a bold agenda during a time when even the most radical abolitionists were hesitant to call for suffrage. The *Tribune* not only demanded voting rights for both free and freed blacks, but the paper demanded that blacks be allowed to serve on juries and called for integration of schools, restaurants, and theatres. The *Tribune* also called for the ownership of plantations to be transferred to ex-slaves and low wage workers who toiled in their fields. In their May 1, 1866 issue, the editors of the *Tribune* even called for women's suffrage, but this was the only time that the paper did so. Most of the pieces in these two newspapers had no bylines, but it is widely believed that Roudanez wrote at least

some of the articles as the white, conservative press praised Roudanez in some of his obituaries for his writing.

Joins Unification Movement

Unlike the other Republican newspapers, the *New Orleans Tribune* refused to endorse Abraham Lincoln in the 1864 presidential election for his timidity on suffrage, and the publication was also quite critical of the Republican Party on both the state and federal levels because of its lack of commitment to the rights of blacks.

During the 1868 State Republican Convention, the Union Republicans packed the Central Committee with their own people, and Illinois carpetbagger Henry Clay Warmoth won the Republican nomination by two votes. Warmoth chose Oscar Dunn, a former barber whose father was an ex-slave, as his running mate. Roudanez was incensed as he felt that carpetbaggers were political opportunists. Houzeau pleaded with Roudanez to support the Warmoth candidacy so that the Republican Party would not split and lose the election. Roudanez ran an independent ticket of candidates for governor (James Taliaferro), lieutenant governor (Francis Dumas) and other various offices. Both candidates for lieutenant governor, Dunn and Dumas had served on the board of *L'Union*. Houzeau soon resigned from the *Tribune*.

The Central Committee denounced Roudanez for running an independent slate and expelled all of its members who were loyal to him. The Republican press, both black and white, hotly rebuked Roudanez. Knowing that the Warmoth ticket would win, Roudanez withdrew the independent candidates right before election day.

One week after the votes were tabulated, the *New Orleans Tribune* stopped publication. Roudanez's prediction about Warmoth was accurate: Warmoth fought integration of schools and public services, and his administration was one known for corruption. Warmoth was impeached, and P. B. S. Pinchback, a black carpetbagger who had replaced Oscar Dunn as lieutenant governor when Dunn died in office, became acting governor.

The *Tribune* briefly returned in light of the corruption in the governor's office, but the paper was unsuccessful, and Louis Charles Roudanez, who over the years had sunk over $30,000 into the *Tribune*, left politics until he became involved with the short-lived Unification Movement of 1873. This movement was independent of the two existing parties, and it attracted many free blacks, including Roudanez. It promised integrated schools, transportation, and other public services. Equal division of elected offices between blacks and whites and the removal of the carpetbaggers from office were also goals. The movement failed as the white population did not like the concessions made to blacks and the freedmen did not trust the organizers.

In January of 1879, Roudanez met with leaders of the Republican Party for dinner in the French Quarter to patch up differences. Roudanez was cordial to both Warmoth and Pinchback, who had years before publicly castigated Roudanez for not supporting the Warmoth ticket, but did not return any of Pinchback's praise. The civility did not last long; the fight between the free black men and the careerist compromisers like Pinchback and Warmoth was reignited, though not by Roudanez, but by those loyal to him.

Louis Charles Roudanez donated money to charities and was known for accepting any patient, whether or not the patient was able to afford his services. He died on March 11, 1890. In *The Daily Crusader*, Paul Trévigne eulogized the compassionate doctor: "His name will be added to the galaxy of that brilliant constellation of Louisianans who have, here and abroad, honored their state and their race by their talents and their worth."

REFERENCES

Books

Foner, Eric. *Reconstruction: America's Unfinished Revolution, 1863-1877*. New York: Harper and Row, 1988.

Logsdon, Joseph, and Caryn Cossé Bell. "The Americanization of Black New Orleans." In *Creole New Americans: Race and Americanization*. Eds. Arnold R. Hirsh and Joseph Logsdon. Baton Rouge: Louisiana State University Press, 1992.

Periodicals

Connor, William P. "Reconstruction Rebels: The New Orleans *Tribune* in Post-War Louisiana." *Louisiana History* 21 (Spring 1980): 159-81

Nelson, Larry E. "Black Leaders and the Presidential Election." *Journal of Negro History* 63 (January 1978): 42-58.

Rankin, David C. "The Politics of Caste: Free Colored Leadership in New Orleans During the Civil War." *Louisiana's Black Heritage* (1979): 107-46.

Trévigne, Paul. "Obituary: Louis Charles Roudanez." *The Daily Crusader*, 11 March 1890. Reprinted in Charles Barthelemy Rousséve, *The Negro in New Orleans: Aspects of His History and His Literature*. New York: Johnson Reprint Corporation, 1970.

Online

Battle, Karen. "New Orleans Creoles of Color: Shattered Dreams and Broken Promises." *Loyola University Student Historical Journal* 23 (1991-1992). http://www.loyno.edu/history/journal/1991-2/battle.htm (Accessed 11 February 2006).

"Dr. Roudanez: Founder First Non-White (Creole) Daily Newspaper." frenchcreoles.com. http://www.frenchcreoles.com/CreoleCulture/famouscreoles/dr.%20roudanez/dr%20roudanez.htm (Accessed 11 February 2006).

"New Orleans Newspaper Marriage Index *Daily Picayune*, 1837-1857." New Orleans Public Library. http://nutrias.org/info/louinfo/nmarrrz.htm (Accessed 11 February 2006).

Dissertations

Rankin, David C. "The Forgotten People: Free People of Color in New Orleans, 1850-1870." Ph.D. dissertation, Johns Hopkins University, 1976.

Rouzan, Laura Velina. "A Rhetorical Analysis of Editorials in *L'Union* and the *New Orleans Tribune*." Ph.D. dissertation, Florida State University, 1989.

Collections

Roudanez's 1853 M.D. dissertation is housed at the Amistad Research Center, Tulane University.

Brandy Baker

George Lewis Ruffin
1834–1886

Lawyer, judge

George Lewis Ruffin graduated Harvard Law School just four years after Abraham Lincoln signed the Emancipation Proclamation. As the first African American graduate of Harvard Law School, Ruffin surmounted the same academic challenges as every student. Unlike the average student, however, he also had to face the racism of his classmates. Ruffin became the first African American on the Boston city council and the first African American elected to the Massachusetts legislature. He also served as a municipal judge in Charlestown, Massachusetts.

Ruffin was born in Richmond, Virginia, on December 16, 1834. He was the eldest of eight children of free blacks who had received some education. Ruffin's parents abandoned their small property in Richmond and moved their family to Boston in 1853, soon after the state of Virginia passed a law prohibiting blacks from learning to read. Ruffin, who was about nineteen years old at the time, entered public schools along with his brothers and sisters. He excelled in school and became active with the Republican Party, beginning a lifelong commitment to politics, social activism, and the judicial system.

Boycotts Dred Scott

When he graduated in 1858, Ruffin married Josephine St. Pierre, an African American woman from a prominent Boston family. Her father was an activist who objected to segregated schools. She was sixteen when she and Ruffin married, and the couple would have five children, but Josephine Ruffin was just as active as her husband in the fight for justice and equality. During the Civil War, the couple helped recruit soldiers for the Union army. Ruffin attempted to enlist himself in the 55th Massachusetts Colored Regiment but was unable to because he was nearsighted. Soon after they wed, the Ruffins moved to Liverpool, England, to protest the U.S. Supreme Court's Dred Scott decision of 1857, which essentially confirmed the legality of slavery. When they returned to Boston six months later, Ruffin worked as a barber, an occupation that left his mind restless.

When he was not cutting hair, Ruffin studied law with partners of a Boston law firm. In 1868, Ruffin enrolled in Harvard University's law school. It did not take long for him to feel the prejudice of his classmates. According to the *New Crisis*, at his first meeting of the student assembly, a group of students proposed a resolution that "every member of the school is by right a member of the assembly, except for colored students." Ruffin held his own with the group, however, and after a spirited debate convinced them to rescind the resolution. He was not at Harvard very long; Ruffin completed the three-year program in one year.

Ruffin was admitted to the bar of the Supreme Judicial Court of Massachusetts in September 1869. He then joined the law firm of Harvey Jewell, where he specialized in criminal law and represented both African American and white clients. He was elected to the Boston city council and ran for the state legislature and won seats in 1869 and 1870.

Ruffin's reputation increased with his involvement with the state legislature. He moved in abolitionist circles and became recognized for his leadership in organizations that sought to advance the causes of African Americans. He was close to several leading abolitionists of the era.

Makes Memorable Speech to Republicans

Ruffin was a delegate to the Massachusetts Republican convention in 1871. There, he made a memorable nomination speech for gubernatorial candidate and former Union General Benjamin F. Butler. Butler lost his bid for governor that year but was elected to the statehouse in 1882. The next year, Butler appointed Ruffin the first black judge in Massachusetts, in the Charlestown municipal court. It would be seventy-five years before another African American became a judge in Massachusetts. The same year Ruffin was appointed judge, he was named to the position of consul resident in Boston for the Dominican Republic.

By most accounts, Ruffin donated so much of his income to social causes and charities that he died poor. He died November 20, 1886, of Bright's disease after several weeks of illness. Ruffin's legacy was honored in 1984, the year the Justice George Lewis Ruffin Society was founded. The group studies and promotes the advancement of minorities in criminal justice professions and within the Massachusetts criminal justice system. The society is affiliated with the College of Criminal Justice at Northeastern University in Massachusetts and works with the college in planning its criminal justice classes and programs. The society also holds an annual criminal justice meeting and maintains the Ruffin Fellows program, which sponsors outstanding minority students pursuing a graduate degree from Northeastern's criminal justice program.

REFERENCES

Periodicals

Brown, C. Stone. "Harvard Law School Celebrates a Rich Tradition of Black History." *New Crisis*, 108 (March-April 2001): 44-47.

Online

"George Lewis Ruffin." Discover Richmond. http://www.discoverrichmond.com/servlet/Satellite?pagename=RTD/MGArticle/RTD_BasicArticle&c=MGArticle&cidamp;=1031780316820&path=%21news%21black history&s=1058750353270 (Accessed 14 March 2006).

"George Lewis Ruffin Society." Northeastern University's College of Criminal Justice. http://www.cj.neu.edu/george_lewis_ruffin_society/ (Accessed 14 March 2006).

Brenna Sanchez

Peter Salem
c. 1750–1816

Soldier, slave

The American Revolution, like all of the wars engaged in by the United States, included African Americans, enslaved and free. It has been estimated that between 5,000 and 7,000 African Americans were a part of the revolutionary fight for independence. Many of these individuals are unknown. However, one of the first known African Americans to take part fought along side Crispus Attucks, the first African American martyr, and Salem Poor at the Battle of Bunker Hill on June 17, 1775. He was Peter Salem, a former slave, Minuteman, and patriot. Salem's performance served as a catalyst in routing the British for a long enough period of time to give the Americans time to regain their confidence, rearm, and continue fighting. As a result of this heroic action, Salem was honored and gained a place in recorded American history. He remained with the Continental Army until the end of the war. Salem spent a total of seven years fighting on behalf of the country.

Peter Salem was born a slave in Framingham, Massachusetts about 1750. Little is known about his early life. He was originally owned by Captain Jeremiah Belknap. It is believed that Salem was named by Belknap for his own hometown of Salem, Massachusetts. Later, Belknap sold Salem to Major Lawson Buckminster. It was illegal for African Americans to serve in the military. However, as the need for soldiers grew, free blacks were recruited to join the militia. Salem's owner freed him in order that he might join Captain Simon Edgell's company of Minutemen. These were volunteers who were ready to fight at a moment's notice.

Salem served in the Continental Army until the close of the war. He received his discharge in 1870. Following the discharge, he took up residency in a cabin he built outside Leicester, Massachusetts, where he worked as a weaver. He made a living by weaving and making baskets and by making and weaving cane bottoms for chairs. In 1783, he married Katy Benson. Salem died in the

Chronology

1750?	Born in Framingham, Massachusetts
1775	Fights at Concord, Massachusetts on April 19; fights at Bunker Hill and gains fame
1776	Reenlists and fights at Saratoga and Stony Point
1780	Receives his discharge
1783	Marries Katy Benson
1816	Dies in Framingham, Massachusetts
1882	Framingham erects a monument in his honor

poorhouse in Framingham, Massachusetts in 1816. He is buried in the Old Burying Ground.

Battles of Lexington and Concord

Salem took part in the Battles of Lexington and Concord. On April 19, 1775, when British soldiers arrived in Lexington, Massachusetts, to seize and destroy the weapons and ammunition, they were confronted by the local Minutemen. The Minutemen fired on the British who continued on to Concord. However, they were again met by these intrepid Minutemen who were firing from behind walls, trees, and whatever gave them cover while the British were in the open. Additionally, the numbers of these local volunteers continued to grow, rather than diminish. The British retreated toward Lexington where they were met by other British soldiers. They joined forces and marched toward Boston.

The Battle of Bunker Hill

The British Army occupied Boston for several months but realized that their position would be greatly strengthened by capturing the heights which surrounded Boston: Dorchester Heights and Charlestown peninsula. The peninsula would strengthen the British Army's position in the face of growing ant-British sentiment. However, the Americans learned that the British planned to occupy one of the hills. Under cover of night, they attempted to fortify the area. However, rather than fortifying Bunker Hill, the high point of the Charlestown peninsula, they actually fortified Breed's Hill, a short distance away. In the light of day, the British saw the efforts made by the Americans and attacked. The battle actually took place at Breed's Hill. The Americans with troops from Massachusetts, Connecticut, Rhode Island, and New Hampshire were outnumbered, ill-equipped, and untrained, but courageous. The American troops fought valiantly. It is reported that as the American troops appeared to be on the verge of defeat, Major John Pitcairn, who had earlier led the British forces against the Americans at Lexington, came to the front and indicated the British had won. At this point, Salem distinguished himself by firing his musket and delivering a shot that ultimately led to the death of Pitcairn. This gave the British pause for a brief period. However, they eventually took the hill. At the time of this action, Salem had enlisted in Colonel Nixon's Fifth Massachusetts Regiment and was serving in the company of Captain Drury. The Battle of Bunker Hill was the first major battle of the American Revolution.

Battles of Stony Point and Saratoga

Salem also took part in battles at both Stony Point and Saratoga, New York. At the Battle of Saratoga in 1777 and following much maneuvering, marching, and shooting, the Americans routed and defeated the British Army. The British Major General Burgoyne surrendered on October 17, 1777 by leaving the British camp and piling British arms on the side of the Hudson River. This battle is considered by historians as a major victory and the turning point in the American Revolution.

Salem's fellow soldiers took up a collection for him following his action at Bunker Hill, and he was honored by a visit to meet General George Washington. Salem was honored by the citizens of Framingham when they buried him at the Old Burying Ground. Even though his gravesite is isolated from the others, it was a true recognition for it was unusual to bury an African American and former slave there. Additionally, years after his death, the townspeople provided Salem's grave with a gravestone.

In spite of the fact that there is still discussion over the veracity of the stories about Peter Salem, he has been recognized in several ways. In 1882, the town of Framingham, Massachusetts honored him by erecting a grave monument. John Trumbull's painting entitled "The Death of General Warren at the Battle of Bunker Hill" contains an unidentified African American at the far right. This individual has not been identified conclusively as Peter Salem, but it is accepted by many as his picture. On October 18, 1968, in New Haven, Connecticut, a stamp was issued honoring John Trumbull which depicts Peter Salem, and it is recognized in the Black Heritage Stamp Issues.

REFERENCES

Books

Kelley, Robin D. G., and Earl Lewis, eds. *To Make Our World Anew. Volume One: A History of African Americans to 1880*. New York: Oxford University Press, 2000.

Painter, Nell Irvin. *Creating Black Americans: African-American History and Its Meaning, 1619 to Present*. New York: Oxford University Press, 2006.

Online

The African American Registry. "Peter Salem, an original patriot!" http:www//aaregistry.com/African_american_history/1937/peter_salem_an_original_patriot (Accessed 14 March 2006).

Barton, David. "Black Patriots of the American Revolution." *Resources* Black History Issue, 2004. http://www.wallbuilders.com/resources/search/detail.php?ResourceID=107 (Accessed 14 March 2006).

"The Decisive Day Is Come: The Battle of Bunker Hill/Introduction." Massachusetts Historical Society. http://www.masshist.org/bh/ (Accessed 14 March 2006).

Hansen, Joyce. "A Brave and Gallant Soldier." *American Review*. http://www.amrevonline.org/museum2/index.cgi2?a=pageview&page_id=13 (Accessed 14 March 2006).

"Major John Pitcairn: Battle of Bunker Hill." *The Henderson Island Website*. http://www.winthrop.dk/majpitcairn.html (Accessed 14 March 2006).

"Peter Salem." http://www.framingham.k12.ma.us/dunning/salem.htm (Accessed 14 March 2006).

Helen R. Houston

John Patterson Sampson
1837–1928

Abolitionist, journalist, lawyer, judge, minister

John Patterson Sampson was born free in Wilmington, North Carolina on August 13, 1837. His parents, James Drawhorn Sampson and Fannie Kellogg, were of Scottish, Indian, and African extraction. His father, a clergyman and carpenter, was financially able to send his children north for their education. Sampson was educated in Massachusetts, graduating with his B.A. from Comer's College in Boston in 1856.

After college, Sampson traveled around New England for about two years lecturing on various topics and particularly against slavery. In 1859, he joined the New York Public School system and was assigned to teach in Jamaica, Long Island.

Chronology

1837	Born in Wilmington, North Carolina on August 13
1856	Receives B.A. from Comer's College, Boston
1859	Teaches for New York Public Schools system in Jamaica, Long Island
1860	Joins Adams Express Company in Cincinnati; begins *Colored Citizen*
1865	Commissioned as superintendent of the Freedmen's Schools, Wilmington, North Carolina
1867-82	Serves as head clerk in the mailing bureau of the U.S. Treasury Department
1868	Attends National University Law School in D.C.; pursues theological studies at Western Theological Seminary, Allegheny, Pennsylvania
1873	Admitted to bar in D.C.; appointed to D.C. district court as judge, where he remains for five years
1882	Retires from law practice; enters ministry of AME Church
1883	Ordained a minister
1888	Receives D.D. from Wilberforce University
1889	Marries Marianne Cole on September 10
1903-10	Serves as presiding elder and superintendent, Boston District, New England Conference
1917	Retires from ministry
1928	Dies

After a year of teaching, Sampson began publishing a paper advocating an end to slavery. He left New York for Cincinnati, Ohio, where he found employment with the Adams Express Company. During the evening hours, he worked on his paper which he titled the *Colored Citizen*. Sampson wrote editorials supporting emancipation and eventually recommended black enlistment in Union military. Initially he wrote under an assumed name to protect his job, as his employer at the express company was sympathetic to the South. The paper, formatted in the style of a daily journal, became known as the *National Negro War*; it disseminated war policy. Sampson officiated as the Washington war correspondent and reported the latest war news and stories of interest to colored soldiers. Thousands of copies were circulated to black soldiers by the Sanitary Commission in Washington and with the assistance of northern sympathizers. As the only black paper published during the war, it brought notoriety to its editor since many of its editorials were referred to in the local newspapers.

It seems that Sampson initially opposed the entry of black troops in the Civil War. In a letter written in 1862 to the *Cincinnati Enquirer*, the leading Democratic paper, Sampson argued that black enlistment in the Union Army would not be advantageous for the country. In his view, it would engender more sympathy from the Europeans for the confederate cause and would also sway the surrounding states to support the South. Many blacks disagreed with Sampson; in any event, Sampson apparently changed his opinion. Subsequently, his paper recommended black enlistment in the Union forces to fight alongside whites.

Instructor and Political Activist

Leaving Ohio and the publishing business behind, Sampson returned to Wilmington, North Carolina, after the Civil War. He engaged in reconstruction efforts on behalf of the newly manumitted colored citizens. He held several posts in Wilmington aimed at providing educational assistance for blacks. Beginning in 1865, he was commissioned as superintendent of the Freedmen's schools in the third district. He was also elected treasurer and assessor of. Wilmington.

In 1867, he made his official entry into the political arena when he was nominated by the Republicans to run for Congress. After several unsuccessful bids for a seat in Congress and as a representative in the state legislature, he moved on to other pursuits. His political associations proved beneficial in securing him a post as head clerk in the mailing bureau of the Treasury Department. He was one of the first blacks to hold such an appointment. He held this position for fifteen years. During this time he was also appointed as a member of the North Carolina Constitutional Convention.

At the time he was working in Washington, D.C., Sampson became interested in studying law. In 1868 he attended National University Law School in D.C. He also felt a calling to gospel ministry, and sometime between 1868 and 1870 he pursued theological studies at the Western Theological Seminary in Allegheny, Pennsylvania. Sources indicate that he was admitted to the D.C. bar in 1873 and thereafter entered into private law practice. That same year, President Rutherford Hayes appointed him to the D.C. District Court. He served as a magistrate in the civil courts for five years. He was the first African American lawyer to hold such a post.

Ministerial Career

The appeal that politics and law held for Sampson was soon lost. He retired from law practice around 1882 to enter the ministry of the African Methodist Episcopal Church. He was ordained as a minister in 1883. Sampson was forty-six years old when he was assigned to his first church in Bordertown, New Jersey. The church appointment required that Sampson also teach in a colored public school. Sampson pastured several AME congregations in New Jersey, Pennsylvania, and Massachusetts. In 1888 during his residence in Trenton, he was made a presiding elder over Bordertown and officiated as chaplain of the New Jersey state senate. In Bordertown, he met Marianna Cole who became his wife on September 10, 1889. John Patterson Jr., their only child, trained for medicine at Howard University.

Sampson was awarded the doctor of divinity degree from Wilberforce University in Ohio in 1888. He was regarded with high esteem in AME church circles and served in several key positions. He was appointed as a delegate to the 1888 General Assembly and to the Committee of Preachers at the New Brunswick Preachers' Meeting. From 1903 through 1910, he was presiding elder and superintendent of the Boston District, New England Conference. Sampson retired from active ministry in 1917.

Sampson was a prolific writer and thinker, one of a small number of black authors to have had works published and distributed in the United States. He wrote and lectured on a variety of religious, social, and scientific topics. His books, plays, and other works were published in the 1880s after he became a clergyman. His best-known work was a comprehensive study on the history, psychology, and phrenology of the black race. It was the first such study published by a black man. Awarded a gold medal prize at the Mount Holly Fair in 1885, it was highly praised by venerable black leaders of the day. Frederick Douglass declared the book a careful study and scholarly contribution to mental science and philosophy.

Sampson was a popular speaker. His views as a clergyman were moderate and, therefore, quite widely accepted. His lecture topics pertained to the unity of the races and on the integration of blacks into white society. He was an organizer of the Ironside Industrial School in New Jersey and one of the founders of the Frederick Douglass Hospital in Philadelphia in 1895. He served as president of the board of managers of the hospital and training school until 1900. Sampson was a black pioneer in journalism, law, and politics. His writings include a piece on how to live to be a hundred, but he died in 1928 nine years short of the century mark.

REFERENCES

Books

Johnson, Rossiter, ed. *The Twentieth Century Biographical Dictionary of Notable Americans.* Vol. 9. Boston: The Biographical Society, 1904.

Ripley, C. Peter, and Jeffrey S. Rossbach, eds. *The Black Abolitionist Papers.* Vol. 5. *The United States.* Chapel Hill: University of North Carolina Press, 1985.

Weinstein, Randy F. *Against the Tide: Commentaries on a Collection of African Americans, 1711-1987.* New York: Glenn Horowitz Bookseller, 1996.

———. "John Patterson Sampson." In *Encyclopedia of African-American Culture and History.* Supplement. Ed. Jack Saltzman. New York: Macmillan, 1996.

Wilson, James Grant, and John Fiske, eds *Appleton's Cyclopedia of American Biography.* Vol. 5. New York: D. Appleton & Co., 1888-1889.

Collections

Papers of John Patterson Sampson are housed in the Schomburg Center, General Research Collection, of the New York Public Library.

Janette Prescod

William Sanders Scarborough
1852–1926

Classical scholar, college president

While U.S. laws denied African Americans the right to education, William Sanders Scarborough learned to read and write and developed an interest in classical languages. When allowed to further his education, he pursued that interest, becoming the nation's first prominent African American classical scholar. During his career in higher education, Scarborough served as president of Wilberforce University, took active roles in politics and religion, and steadily worked toward the betterment of his race.

On February 16, 1852, Jeremiah and Frances Gwynn Scarborough welcomed son William Sanders Scarborough into their Macon, Georgia home. Scarborough's father, freed by his master in 1846, worked for Georgia's Central Railroad as a trainer for new employees and sometimes as a conductor. Scarborough's mother remained the slave of Colonel William DeGraffenreid, a lawyer. He allowed the family to live in their own home. Scarborough's older brother, John Henry, died at the age of four; his younger sister, Mary Louisa, at the age of two.

William Scarborough's parents belonged to different churches, his father to the African Methodist Episcopal Church, his mother to the Presbyterian Church. They taught their son about God and also taught him the alphabet. J. C. Thomas, a white man who had given the family land for their home, chose to ignore potential legal consequences and taught Scarborough to read and write. A free black family helped him study arithmetic, history, and geography. John Hall, his mother's half-brother, taught him carpentry.

When the Civil War broke out, Scarborough's father realized that his son needed to learn a trade. He apprenticed the boy to a local shoemaker named Gibson. Later, Scarborough worked in Mr. J. Burke's bookstore. He also served as a clerk in the Freedman's Bureau. But none of these occupations attracted his full interest. Michele Ronnick notes in *The Autobiography of William Sanders*

Chronology

1852	Born in Macon, Georgia on February 16
1871	Becomes first graduate of Atlanta University
1875	Graduates with honors from Oberlin College
1878	Appointed as chair of Latin and Greek at Wilberforce University
1881	Marries Sarah Cordelia Bierce; publishes Greek language textbook
1882	Becomes member of American Philological Association
1892	Becomes professor of Hellenistic Greek at Payne Theological Seminary
1897	Rejoins Wilberforce faculty as vice president
1908	Elected president of Wilberforce University, a position he holds for twelve years
1911	Serves as delegate to First Universal Races Congress in London
1920	Takes job with U.S. Department of Agriculture
1926	Dies in Wilberforce, Ohio on September 9

Scarborough: An American Journey from Slavery to Scholarship that early in life, Scarborough developed "affection for arts and letters." He wanted to become an orator like Frederick Douglass and a lawyer like John Langston.

When the war ended and he no longer needed to keep his education secret, Scarborough briefly attended Macon's Triangular Block Elementary School. Then the American Missionary Association opened Lewis High School, allowing him to study Latin, algebra, and geometry. In 1869, he went to Atlanta University, another enterprise of the missionary association. Ronnick states that Scarborough studied "Greek and Latin prose composition as well as Caesar, Livy, Cicero, Virgil, Tacitus, Xenophon, Homer, Demosthenes, Lysias and the New Testament." In 1871, Scarborough became the department's first graduate.

Professor and Scholar

Instead of attending at Yale as he had planned, Scarborough enrolled in Oberlin College, focusing on Latin and Greek. He often tutored classmates in mathematics as well as in languages. After graduating with honors from Oberlin in 1875, his search for a suitable teaching job took him to Macon, Georgia, then to Cokesbury, South Carolina, as principal of the Payne Institute for Blacks (1875-77). After various other teaching positions, he returned to Oberlin for an M.A. degree. Soon after completing his study, he learned of his election to the chair of Latin and Greek at Ohio's Wilberforce University.

On August 2, 1881, Scarborough married Sarah Cordelia Bierce, a white divorcee from Danby, New York. They met at Macon's Lewis High School where he taught and she served as principal. Later, they reunited at Wilberforce University, where they both served on the faculty. Despite the racial climate of the time, the marriage thrived. The Scarboroughs had no children.

In conjunction with his teaching, Scarborough wrote a textbook, *First Lessons in Greek* (1881), thus becoming the first African American to write a university-level textbook for study of the Greek language. The work received high praise from the scholarly community for its clarity and conciseness.

Scarborough actively sought involvement in the scholarly community. He joined the American Philological Association (APA) in 1882, becoming the third African American to receive this distinction. In 1884, he joined the Modern Language Association. His professional memberships grew to include such organizations as the American Social Science Association, the American Academy of Political and Social Science, the Archaeological Institute of America, the American Negro Academy, the American Dialect Society, the American Folklore Society, the American Spelling Reform Association, the Egyptian Exploration Fund, and even the Japan Society. As part of the North American Reading Program, he served as an unofficial reader for the *Oxford English Dictionary.*

The *Transactions of American Philological Association* published more than twenty articles by Scarborough, many of them summaries of his presentations at their conferences. His scholarly inquiry covered a wide range of topics, from "The Theory and Function of the Thematic Vowel in the Greek Verb" (1884) to "Notes on the Function of Modern Languages in Africa" (1896) to "The Greeks and Suicide" (1907). Scarborough represented the APA at England's Cambridge University for its Classical Association meeting in 1921.

Even though Scarborough's colleagues treated him with respect, his experiences at APA conferences sometimes proved unpleasant. During an 1894 meeting at Williams College in Massachusetts, he spent the night in a tool shed after a hotel refused to admit him. He chose not to attend a 1909 meeting in Baltimore because the conference hotel refused to serve blacks. The paper he had prepared, however, was mentioned at the conference.

Scarborough's writing interests extended beyond classical studies. Ronnick describes him as "a well-published and well-known polyglot interested in issues involving classical studies, modern languages, racial progress and education in general." He wrote articles for *The Arena, Education, The Manchester Guardian, The American Negro Academy, The African Times and Orient Review, Southern Workman, The New York Times, The London Times,* and many other publications.

In 1892, Scarborough temporarily lost his position at Wilberforce as the college moved toward a more industrial-oriented curriculum. He became professor of Hellenistic Greek at Payne Theological Seminary, a school associated with Wilberforce but with its own governing body. At Payne, Scarborough had to raise his own salary. He received some income from his writing, but necessarily depended partially on his wife's income as a Wilberforce professor. In 1897, the university reappointed him and named him vice president.

Elected President of Wilberforce University

In 1908, Wilberforce elected Scarborough president, a position he held until 1920. Under his leadership, the curriculum expanded and academic standards reached a higher level. The university instituted new methods of accounting. Indebtedness dwindled as financial stability increased due to additional state funding, private endowments, and alumni giving. A new building, Emery Hall, graced the campus. A new tradition of holding an annual Founder's Day celebration began.

Along with his university duties, Scarborough took an active role in the community. In 1879, he received appointment as Wilberforce's first postmaster. During the First World War, he served on the governor's Ohio Council of National Defense. As a member of the Committee of One Hundred, he helped garner public support for war efforts. He served on the staff of Ohio's federal food administrator, promoted food conservation, and represented blacks as a labor advisor for the state.

Scarborough devoted much of his energy toward advancing educational opportunities for blacks. He desired more for his race than the technical training advocated by his friend Booker T. Washington. Although not discounting Washington's ideas, he believed that blacks deserved a well-rounded education. His own experience proved that they could achieve respect and honor in higher education. His articles on race and education include "Future of the Negro" in the March 1889 *Forum,* "The Negro Farmer's Progress in Virginia" in the December 1926 *Current History,* and "The Educated Negro and his Mission" in *The American Negro Academy Occasional Papers,* No. 8 in 1903.

Active in politics, Scarborough gained respect as an outstanding advocate for black Republicans in Ohio. On the local level, he worked to abolish segregation in Ohio's schools. On a national level, he supported the candidacies of such men as Theodore Roosevelt and William Howard Taft and developed a strong friendship with Warren G. Harding.

Throughout Scarborough's presidency, he remained active in the African Methodist Episcopal Church. He edited church publications and wrote articles for the *AME Church Review* and the *Methodist Review.* He represented his church as a delegate to its 1901 conference in London. In 1911, he went to the University of London for the First Universal Races Congress. In 1919, he attended the Interchurch World Movement of North America conference in New York City.

Amid all these interests, Scarborough continued his work as a classicist. Harold Villard notes in *Dictionary of American Biography* that Scarborough's love of languages led him to study not only Latin and Greek but also "Sanskrit, Zend, Gothic, Lithuanian, and Old Slavonic." In recognition of his scholarly work and his contributions to higher education, a number of colleges granted him honorary degrees. In 1892, the State University at Louisville, or what he called Kentucky State University, granted him a Ph.D. He received honorary degrees also from West Africa's Liberia College in 1882, Morris Brown College in 1908, and England's St. Columbia's College in 1909.

Takes Job with Federal Government

Following his presidency at Wilberforce, Scarborough sought a job with the federal government. As part of his work with the Department of Agriculture, he spent time in Virginia studying the progress of black farmers. The resulting work, "Tenancy and Ownership among Negro Farmers in Southampton County, Virginia" became *U. S. Department of Agriculture Department Bulletin,* No. 1404 (1916).

After months of battling ill health, Scarborough died on September 9, 1926, in Wilberforce, Ohio. His body lay in state at the university he had served so faithfully. The autobiography that his wife began editing did not reach publication until 2005. Editor Michele Ronnick describes Scarborough as "an engaged intellectual, public citizen, and a concerned educator," concluding, "In terms of his classical studies he accomplished as much as some of the better-known figures from this era, and in fact more than many. Scarborough was in the widest sense of the word, a pioneer. He not only broke through barriers of race and class but stayed the course."

REFERENCES

Books

Ronnick, Michele Valerie, ed. *The Autobiography of William Sanders Scarborough: An American Journey from Slavery to Scholarship.* Detroit, Mich.: Wayne State University Press, 2005.

Villard, Harold G. "Scarborough, William Sanders." In *Dictionary of American Biography,* Vol. 16 Ed. Dumas Malone. New York: Charles Scribner's Sons, 1935. pp. 409-10.

Weisenburger, Francis P. "Scarborough, William Sanders." In *Dictionary of American Negro Biography.* Eds. Rayford W. Logan and Michael R. Winston. New York: Norton, 1982.

Periodicals

Ronnick, Michele Valerie. "Essay: Concerning Pap Finn's 'Mulatter' College Professor and William

Sanders Scarborough (1852-1926)." *Negro Educational Review* (January-April 1998): 89-92.

———. "William Sanders Scarborough: The First Professional Classicist of African-American Descent." *Negro Educational Review* (July-October 1996): 162-68.

Weisenburger, Francis P. "William Sanders Scarborough: Early Life and Years at Wilberforce." *Ohio History* 71 (October 1962): 203-292.

———. "William Sanders Scarborough: Scholarship, the Negro, Religion, and Politics." *Ohio History* 72 (January 1963): 25-50.

Collections

Some Scarborough papers are housed in the Wilberforce University Library.

Marie Garrett

Chronology	
1909	Born in Houston, Texas on April 18
1934	Graduates from Howard University Medical School
1935	Marries Sarah Rosetta Weaver
1936	Completes pediatric residency
1939	Passes examination of American Board of Pediatrics; returns to Howard
1945	Becomes acting director of pediatrics
1948	Produces first sickle cell article
1949	Becomes chairman of pediatrics
1969	Sarah Scott dies
1971	Lobbies Congress and gains passage of the Sickle Cell Anemia Control Act
1972	Starts the Center for Sickle Cell Disease
1990	Retires as director of the center
1995	*Ebony* names Scott "preeminent authority" on sickle cell
2002	Dies in Washington, D.C. on December 10

Roland B. Scott
1909–2002

Physician, medical researcher

Roland Boyd Scott, a major researcher into the causes and treatment of sickle cell anemia, devoted his life to advocacy for victims of this disease. An allergist by training, Scott became an advocate for children with sickle cell disease after seeing many children with symptoms of the disease admitted to the Howard University Hospital. Scott started the Center for Sickle Cell Disease in 1972 funded by a grant from the National Institutes of Health. Among the first black physicians accepted into the American Pediatric Society, he was internationally known as an expert on sickle cell anemia.

Roland Scott was born in Houston, Texas on April 18, 1909. He graduated from high school in Kansas City, Missouri in 1927. He chose to study at predominately black Howard University. His mother felt that even though he was also accepted at the University of Chicago, Howard would provide a more comfortable social environment. In 1935, he married Sarah Rosetta Weaver. They had three children: a son, Roland Scott Jr., and two daughters, Venice and Irene.

At Howard, Scott studied chemistry through his junior year then applied to medical school and was accepted. Alonzo DeGrate Smith, professor of pediatrics in the medical school, influenced Scott's decision to focus on diseases of children. Smith's earliest research was in nutritional diseases, including a study of the use of vita-min D to treat rickets. Scott completed his study of medicine at Howard in 1934.

Scott completed an internship in Kansas City, Missouri, and then decided to focus on a residency in pediatrics, though at the time there was very little interest in specializing in pediatrics. Scott spent four years as a pediatric resident and fellow in Chicago. He served as resident at Provident Hospital, Cook County Hospital, and the Municipal Hospital for Contagious Diseases.

While at the University of Chicago, Scott was interested in the work of Katsuji Kato, a pediatric hematologist from Japan, who published detailed drawings of normal and abnormal blood cells and bone marrow cells. After the Pearl Harbor bombing by Japan, Kato was considered an undesirable alien and forced into relocation. He later returned to Japan.

Returns to Howard University

In 1939, Scott passed the examination of the American Board of Pediatrics. He returned to Howard as a faculty member after he completed postgraduate pediatric training in Chicago. Smith and Scott were the first two black physicians in the United States to gain membership in the American Academy of Pediatrics. According to Carl Pochedly, their applications were first rejected because of race, but they both reapplied and were accepted. Scott was the first black physician to become a member of the American Pediatric Society and the Society for Pediatric Research.

In 1939, a full-time assistant professor of pediatrics at Howard University was paid $3,000 per year. Since Scott was married and had a child, the salary did not meet the family's needs. Through a special arrangement, the university allowed Scott to work part-time as a pediatric consultant. In his work at Freedmen's Hospital, he learned that most parents of children admitted with sickle cell anemia lacked knowledge of the disease. Many children died from complications. Scott began writing about the condition in 1948.

Scott published a number of articles that described clinical findings due to sickle cell disease in infants and children. With a group from his clinic, he prepared exhibits on the disease that were shown at medical meetings throughout the country and sometimes abroad. At first there was little outside financial support for sickle cell studies, due to the fact that the disease was perceived as only affecting blacks. Scott's research showed that blacks are not the only people who have sickle cell anemia. People in Mediterranean, South American, and Arabian countries also suffer from the disease. In 1971, the National Institutes of Health (NIH) awarded a grant to establish the Howard University Center for Sickle Cell Disease.

The NIH grant came about due to the Sickle Cell Control Act of 1971. Because of this act, ten centers (in Augusta, Boston, Cincinnati, Chicago, Indianapolis, Los Angeles, Memphis, New York, Pittsburgh, and Washington, D.C.) were established. The NIH grants were for more productive research and to provide more actual benefit to patients.

In 1945, Scott became acting director of pediatrics, when it was still a division of the Department of Medicine. In 1949, Scott was instrumental in changing the pediatric division to a full department, and he became chairman of the Department of Pediatrics. He remained as head of pediatrics for twenty-eight years. He was director of the Howard University Center for Sickle Cell Disease from its inception in 1971 until his retirement in 1990.

While on sabbatical in 1950, Scott studied allergic diseases at Roosevelt Hospital in New York City. When he returned to Howard, he started allergy clinics for children at D.C. General and Freedmen's Hospitals. Scott became board certified in both allergy and clinical immunology.

A prolific writer, Scott wrote or co-wrote more than three hundred scientific reports. His former students, residents, and other trainees have made significant contributions in medical care and education in the United States and in other countries. His pioneer work in sickle cell research resulted in the government developing a national program for research and clinical care.

In an interview with Carl Pochedly of the *American Journal of Pediatric Hematology/Oncology*, Scott listed coping with conventional racism in the United States as one of his biggest lifelong problems. He also expressed gratitude and admiration for the support of many friends and organizations and for the encouragement of his mentors, which included Dr. Frederic W. Schlutz, Chairman of the Department of Pediatrics at University of Chicago;

Joseph Brennemann at Children's Memorial Hospital; and Dr. Archibald Hoyne, an expert in infectious diseases at Municipal Hospital for Contagious Diseases. This support allowed him to persevere in his efforts to gain interest and funding in sickle cell research.

Scott traveled widely and received honors for his work in the United States and elsewhere. His honors include the Jacobi Award of the American Medical Association Academy of Pediatrics, pioneer in sickle cell research award from the Advisory Board of the Comprehensive Center for Sickle Cell Disease of the Columbia University College of Physicians and Surgeons, as well as a special award, according to Pochedly, from the National Sickle Cell Disease Program for "leadership and pioneering efforts in directing national and international attention to sickle cell disease."

Scott died on December 10, 2002, at Washington Adventist Hospital. His memorial service was held at Howard University on December 17, 2002.

REFERENCES

Periodicals

Bernstein, Adam. "Roland B. Scott Dies: Sickle Cell Researcher." *Washington Post*, 12 December 2002.

Jones, Marvin T. "Roland B. Scott, M.D.: A Portrait of Dedication." *Perspectives: Howard University College of Medicine* 7 (Winter 1985/86): 1, 8-9.

Pochedly, Carl. "Dr. Roland B. Scott: Crusader for Sickle Cell Disease and Children." *American Journal of Pediatric Hematology/Oncology* 7 (Fall 1985): 265-69.

Virginia D. Bailey

Samuel R. Scottron
1843–1905

Inventor, entrepreneur

A prominent entrepreneur and inventor, Samuel R. Scottron was an important member of Brooklyn's elite black community. From the 1870s through 1894, he concentrated on inventions and secured a number of patents for items that led to his becoming a wealthy man. A Republican, Scottron was prominent in political circles in the borough. He became the first African American member of Brooklyn's board of education and held the prestigious post for eight years. His work as an activist was seen in the articles on race that he published widely, and in his work as co-founder of the Cuban Anti-Slavery Society.

Chronology

1843	Born in New England or Philadelphia
1849	Family relocates to New York City
1852	Family relocates to Brooklyn, New York
1863	Travels to South Carolina with the firm Statia, Caffil, and Scottron
1864	Assists freedmen in voting in first general election, Fernandina, Florida
1865	Attends National Colored Convention in Syracuse, New York; opens grocery stores in Jacksonville, Gainesville, Lakeville, Tallahassee, and Palatka, Florida around this time
1872	With Henry Highland Garnett, founds Cuban Anti-Slavery Society and serves as secretary
1875	Graduates from Cooper Union
1879	Elected grand secretary general of the Masons
1880	Obtains patent for adjustable window cornice on February 17
1883	Obtains patent for a cornice on January 16
1884	Co-founds the Society of the Sons of New York
1886	Obtains patent for pole top on September 30
1892	Obtains patent for curtain rod on August 30
1893	Obtains patent for supporting bracket on September 12
1894	Perfects "porcelain onyx"; becomes first black member of Brooklyn board of education
1905	Dies

While some sources claim that he was born in Philadelphia sometime in 1843, Samuel Raymond Scottron, according to Gail Lumet Buckley in *The Hornes*, was born free in New England. He and his parents, whose names are not known, came from Springfield, Massachusetts. Buckley says that "his antecedents were probably West Indian-born Gold Coast Africans and the poorest of the British emigrants." They may have been "indentured servants, seamen, small farmers, and artisans," writes Buckley. Their lineage also included Native American, of the original inhabitants of eastern Massachusetts, from the Pequot tribe of the Algonquian nation. The Scottrons moved to New York in 1849 and then relocated to Brooklyn in 1852. Young Samuel enrolled in the public schools in New York City and later in Brooklyn; when he was fourteen years old, he graduated from grammar school in Brooklyn. His ambition was to continue his education, as many of his schoolmates had done, but much to Samuel's disappointment, his father had other plans for the course his son's life would take. He would not continue his education until later, when with great determination he entered night school on his own.

The elder Scottron was a barber, barkeeper, and baggage master on a boat plying the Hudson River between New York City and Albany. While on the New York to Albany journey, he often took Samuel with him to serve as his helper. Now with the possibility of additional education behind him, his son would gain practical experience instead. Soon after the Civil War began, the elder Scottron entered a partnership with a man whose name is known simply as Mr. Statia to form Statia, McCaffil, and Scottron. The firm already had a commission as a sutler for a black regiment, the Third U. S. Colored Infantry that had begun in Pennsylvania. In 1863 young Samuel went South with the regiment as his father's representative in the partnership. The regiment was stationed at Morris Island, South Carolina, in what was called the Department of the South. The small schooner on which they traveled was loaded with barrels of apples and other perishables, canned goods, and other items. The perishable items decayed as bad weather extended to six weeks what should have been a one-week trip to Hilton Head, South Carolina. Following that, they lost their deck load while traveling up the St. John's River to Jacksonville, Florida. The two-year ordeal was unprofitable for the firm.

While in Fernandina, Florida in 1864, Scottron assisted in the first general election that allowed the new freedmen to vote. He endeared himself to the black residents and won the right to represent them in the National Colored Convention held in Syracuse, New York in 1865. Scottron also sought out other ways to make money. He opened grocery stores in Jacksonville, Gainesville, Lakeville, Tallahassee, and Palatka, but he soon left the profitless ventures and returned north.

Inventions

Following one of his father's trades, Scottron opened a barbershop in Springfield, Massachusetts. His customers used hand mirrors to examine their haircuts. As Scottron observed the difficulty his customers experienced in trying to get a full view of the sides, rear, and top of the head, he decided to invent a mirror to provide the view desired. Thus, he invented what was known as Scottron's adjustable mirrors. In a 1904 article in the *Colored American Magazine*, he described his first invention as "mirrors so arranged opposite each other as to give the view of every side at once." This was, in his opinion, new, useful, and simple. So successful were the mirrors that Scottron soon took on a white partner and the new firm began at 658 Broadway in New York City, operating under the name Pitkin and Scottron. Thomas Richmond bought Pitkin's interest in the business and almost immediately lost all of his property in the Great Chicago Fire; this was disastrous to the mirror business as well.

Scottron traded his services as bookkeeper for looking-glass manufacturer W. A. Willard for space in his store located at 177 Canal Street in New York City. This arrangement gave him an opportunity to reestablish himself. After four years and a brief and unsuccessful business partnership with a man named Ellis to form Scottron and Ellis, Scottron decided to work alone. He opened his new firm at 211 Canal Street, where he invented several household objects, including an extension cornice. These items were so popular that he gave up the looking-glass business and concentrated on cornices. By then he had an agreement with the firm H. L. Judd & Co., located in New York City. That business employed forty men who worked constantly to manufacture Scottron's cornices. The business prospered, but as curtain poles became fashionable the cornices were no longer in demand. Then he diversified and began to manufacture curtain poles.

In 1882 Scottron became a traveling salesman and general manager for John Kroder, a German American whose export-import business was located at 13 Baxter Street in New York City. During his twelve years with Kroder, Scottron invented and patented an extension curtain rod. He bought and sold carloads of goods, which made both men prosperous. Scottron traveled throughout Canada, from Halifax, Nova Scotia, to Victoria, British Columbia. In the states he avoided the South due to segregated housing accommodations, but his work took him as far away as San Francisco.

Fortunately, Scottron patented at least some of his inventions and gained royalties from them. He obtained patents for an adjustable window cornice (February 17, 1880), a cornice (January 16, 1883), a pole tip (September 30, 1886), a curtain rod (August 30, 1892), and supporting bracket (September 12, 1893). Some of his inventions were never patented. One of these might have been what Gail Lumet Buckley in *The Hornes* called a "leather hand strap device" that trolley car passengers used for support when standing. It was this device that made him rich, according to Buckley.

In 1894 Scottron perfected a way to make glass look like onyx and other attractive stones; he called his product "porcelain onyx." By now his daughters were mature young ladies who, along with his wife, helped him in the production. Together the Scottrons manufactured several thousand tubes to be mounted into brass lamps and candlesticks. Four large firms in Connecticut manufactured the items. Scottron never sought a patent for this process. He envisioned making the porcelain onyx into pedestals. "We shall not stop at pedestals and tables," he wrote in *Colored American Magazine*, "but in a short time, hope to have the porcelain onyx tubes used inside architectural decorations, such as are made for church ornamentation, bar room and barbershop mirrors, mantle mirrors, pier mirror front and many ways too numerous to mention." In time, onyx went out of fashion and he stopped the process.

Still in business after the turn of the century, Scottron continued to promote his company and his products. An advertisement for Scottron Manufacturing Company in the *Colored American Magazine* for October 7, 1904, noted that the company made pedestals, tabourettes, lamp columns, and lamp and vase bodies. For these items they used imitation onyx, agate, fossil wood, and various pottery finishes from the United States and abroad. This prosperous business was located at 98 Monroe Street in Brooklyn and, of course, carried items he had patented.

Education Called Key to Success

Reflecting on his life, Scottron noted in the *Colored American Magazine*: "I did not begin business life as a manufacturer, but as a merchant and trader." He cautioned that "whatever line, professional or business, a man enters upon, he should have such education as befits that line, if he wishes to succeed." When he recognized that he had "inventive genius" and used it to make adjustable mirrors, which he says he patented, he acquired the education he needed by studying mechanics under a master mechanic. He became skilled in work with brass, iron, and glass by working in various foundries in Springfield, Massachusetts. That set the foundation for his prosperous future. He continued his studies for seven years at Cooper Union, a free school that Peter Cooper established in New York to provide public education, and graduated in May 1875, with a degree that Gail Lumet Buckley called "Superior Ability in Algebra." Some sources claim that he graduated in 1878. He was awarded one of the four medals given at graduation.

His interest in education caught the eye of Mayor Charles A. Schieren, who in 1894 appointed Scottron to the Brooklyn board of education. He was reappointed by Mayor F. W. Wurster and again by Mayor Van Wyck, of the consolidated city of Greater New York. Altogether he held the post for eight years, serving as the board's only black member; he never missed any regular or special meetings. He also attended all committee meetings and served on several of the board's most important committees. Although his duties remain unidentified in published sources, Scottron was actually placed in charge of many schools. Five black schools were in the system at the time of his appointment, and by the end of his term all except one was closed and the black teachers distributed to racially mixed schools and classes. When his term ended, New York City mayor Seth Low refused to renew his appointment, which some viewed as a result of pressure from the predominantly white district in which Scottron lived. The fact that only one black school remained in the district by then may also have had some influence on the mayor's decision. Fellow inventor Lewis Latimer (1848-1928) of electric light fame came to his defense in 1902, according to Rayvon Fouché in *Black Inventors in the Age of Segregation*, to "defend a gentleman of his social, intellectual, and professional class." As an advocate for Scottron, Latimer facilitated the submission of a petition appealing to the mayor's "sense of humor" stressing that, due to his "good and faithful service" he should be given "a position equally honorable." He should retain the prestige that the school board post provided, the petitioners believed. Although they were unsuccessful in their attempt, the petitioners and others held a tribute to honor Scottron on May 9, 1902. Clearly, Scottron and Latimer had a common bond and deep respect for each other.

Scottron consistently fought for better educational facilities for blacks. In doing so, he joined local African Americans of prominence, including Edward Valentine Clark Eato, Peter Guignon, Peter W. Ray, Charles Lewis Reason, and Philip A. White. These men and their families were school administrators, teachers, druggists, and members of various professional groups. While New York, especially Harlem, was pro-Booker T. Washington and supported at least some of his views and strategies, Brooklyn, where the city's black aristocrats lived, opposed him, the exception being Samuel Scottron. In fact, the *Booker T. Washington Papers*, Volume 7, shows that about fifteen people, including philanthropist George Foster Peabody, W. E. B. Du Bois, Scottron, and others, attended a private conference to discuss the welfare of blacks in New York City. Out of this and similar meetings grew the Committee for Improving the Industrial Condition of Negroes in New York City—an organization in which Booker T. Washington had an interest.

Becomes Activist and Writer

By 1872 Scottron demonstrated an interest in the Cuban war and worked with the abolitionist Reverend Henry Highland Garnet (1815-1882) to form the Cuban Anti-Slavery Society. Garnet was founding president and Scottron founding secretary. Two years later, after extending the society's scope to include labor, they renamed it the American Foreign Anti-Slavery Society and kept in close touch with the British Foreign Anti-Slavery Society. Quoted in Booker T. Washington's *The Negro in Business*, Scottron said, "To the moral force of these societies we ascribe the extinction of slavery in Cuba and Brazil, and the slave trade in . . . Africa." Scottron also traveled and lectured widely during this period, as he promoted the work of the organization. At some point in his life he was secretary of the National Liberal Republican Committee.

Scottron spent thirty-five years as an occasional writer for newspaper and magazines, often writing on race matters. He lashed out at the displacement of blacks by whites in such occupations as barbering and catering. His articles were published in a number of periodicals, including the *New York Age*, the *Boston Herald*, and the *Colored American Magazine*. At some point he was editor of the latter publication.

Samuel Scottron believed that black forefathers in New York were far superior to those of the early twentieth century; thus, he spent his last years gathering a library on the history of African Americans in New York, chronicling their past and extolling their values. His work in this area may be seen in the article "New York African Society for Mutual Relief—Ninety-Seventh Anniversary," published in the *Colored American Magazine* for December 1905.

Scottron belonged to the Cooper Union Alumni Society and the Brooklyn Academy of Sciences; both memberships confirmed his reputation as a scientist. Other memberships may have included the Society of the Sons of New York, comprised solely of blacks who were born in New York and/or those who were highly respected. The Scottrons were among those active in the founding in 1884 and early development of the society. The society was most active each April, when it hired an orchestra for its annual ball and had the food catered. He held membership in an elite temple founded in pre-Revolutionary Boston, the Ancient and Accepted Scottish Rite (33rd degree Mason). In 1879 he was elected grand secretary general of its supreme council of the United States and held the post for several years.

Scottron married Anna Maria Willet, a Native American who was born in Peekskill, New York, in 1844. The date of their marriage is uncertain, however; some claim that he married when he was nineteen years old, which would have been around 1862, while Gail Lumet Buckley claims that Scottron met Willet when he traveled as a glass salesman, which would have been later. Whatever the case, Anna Willet shared with the Scottrons her heritage—the Algonquian nation. They married and settled down in New York City and by 1888 bought their tall, narrow, brownstone home located at the corner of Stuyvesant Avenue and Monroe Street in Brooklyn. They had three daughters and three sons. Cyrus, the youngest son, married Brooklyn schoolteacher Louise Ashton; their daughter—Samuel Scottron's granddaughter—was actress and singer Lena Horne. Historically, the Scottrons were staunch Episcopalians. Samuel worshipped at St. Philips in Manhattan as well as St. Augustine's in Brooklyn, which Gail Buckley referred to as "two bastions of elite Episcopalianism." Willard B. Gatewood in *Aristocrats of Color* described New York's black upper crust of the late nineteenth century as those who were free born, West Indian émigrés, Northern-born, were connected by marriage, and so on, who included the Rays (the educators), the Guignons (including Peter the chemist), the Philip A. Whites (wealthy druggists), and the Scottrons. They were close-knit and socially exclusive, forming New York's best society. Inasmuch as they belonged to the same clubs, social organizations, and other groups, and even vacationed together, it follows that they would also worship together; hence, the select churches that they attended were known for their "conservative respectability."

Samuel Scottron was a very entertaining, refined, and courteous man. According to the *Cleveland Gazette*, he was a fine lecturer and "a splendid conversationalist." He also had great executive abilities which he put to good use in his business ventures. He became prosperous, and at one time had real estate and other properties valued at about $60,000, a handsome sum for that period. He died in 1905. Published works have yet to give this inventor and shrewd and prosperous businessman the highly visible place in biographical works that he deserved.

REFERENCES

Books

Baldwin, William Henry Jr. "Letter to Booker T. Washington, January 23, 1903." *The Booker T. Washington Papers.* Vol. 7, 1903-4. Eds. Louis R. Harlan and Raymond W. Smock. Urbana: University of Illinois Press, 1977.

Buckley, Gail Lumet. *The Hornes: An American Family.* New York: Alfred A. Knopf, 1986.

"Charles William Anderson to Booker T. Washington, July 28, 1904." *The Booker T. Washington Papers.* Vol. 8, 1904-6. Eds. Louis R. Harland and Raymond M. Smock. Urbana: University of Illinois Press, 1979.

Fouché, Rayvon. *Black Inventors in the Age of Segregation.* Baltimore: Johns Hopkins University Press, 2003.

Scottron, Samuel R. "Manufacturing Household Articles." *Colored American Magazine* 7 (October 1904): 620-24.

———. "New York Society for Mutual Relief—Ninety-Seventh Anniversary." *Colored American Magazine* 9 (December 1905): 685-90.

Sluby, Patricia Carter. *The Inventive Spirit of African Americans: Patented Ingenuity.* Westport, Conn.: Praeger, 2004.

Washington, Booker T. *The Negro in Business.* Boston: Hertel, Jenkins & Co., 1907.

Online

"Samuel Scottron." The African American Experience in Ohio, 1850-1920. *Cleveland Gazette,* 4 September 1887. http://dbs.ohiohistory.org/africanam/page.cfm?ID=15395 (Accessed 14 February 2005).

Jessie Carney Smith

Al Sharpton
1954–

Activist, minister

As an outspoken activist in the fight against racism, Al Sharpton has been as widely loved as he has been reviled. Unveiling the injustices of the American justice system, opposing police brutality, and criticizing the staggering disparity between the poor and the rich was not easy. In addition to having his activism characterized as disingenuous, Sharpton's finances as well as

Al Sharpton

his business and fraternal affiliations came under fire. Even so, among the New York community that he calls home, Sharpton is heralded as the champion of the underserved and the causes that matter to them. As an ordained minister, Sharpton has been making public appearances at age four. While his civic activism began when he was a teenager, Sharpton's political activism significantly enlarged after an attempt on his life in the early 1990s.

Albert Charles Sharpton Jr. was born on October 3, 1954 in Brooklyn, New York to Albert Sr., a contractor and landlord, and Ada Sharpton, a seamstress. As religious parents, the Sharptons regularly took young Sharpton to church from his infancy on. Even so, it was undoubtedly exceptional that the four-year-old was already addressing the congregation of the family's church. Ministering before Washington Temple Church of God in Christ's congregation of several thousand, the "Wonderboy," as he was nicknamed, was ordained as a minister at age ten in the Pentecostal Church by the Bishop F. D. Washington. As such a young minister, Sharpton made famous his evangelical appearances across the New York area throughout his childhood and even was included on a tour with renown gospel singer Mahalia Jackson.

However, the stability of the middle class enjoyed in their comfortable Queens home abruptly ended in 1963 when his father walked out on the family to marry Tina,

Chronology

1954	Born in Brooklyn, New York on October 3
1964	Ordained as a minister in the Washington Temple Church of God in Christ at age ten
1966	Meets the Reverend Adam Clayton Powell Jr., who becomes a lifelong mentor
1969	Nominated by the Reverend Jesse Jackson as the youth director of the New York branch of Operation Breadbasket
1971	Founds the National Youth Movement (NYM)
1972	Graduates from Tipton High School
1973-75	Attends Brooklyn College
1978	Runs as a candidate for State Senate
1985	Thrust to spotlight following two racial deaths in New York City
1986	Answers the call of a family seeking assistance in the racial killing of Michael Griffith
1987	Reputation suffers after he maintains his support to Tawana Brawley and her family despite a jury's conclusion
1989	Helps to bring attention to the murder of Yusuf Hawkins
1991	Attacked and stabbed by Michael Riccardi on January 12 during a protest rally in a Bensonhurst schoolyard; founds National Action Network (NAN) in Harlem, New York
1992	Runs as a candidate for the U.S. Senate
1994	Runs as a candidate for the U.S. Senate
2003-04	Vies for the Democratic nomination for president

who was his stepdaughter from Ada Sharpton's prior marriage. The shocking courtship as well as the subsequent separation of the family that it caused forced his mother, another sister, and young Al to move from their middle class home in Queens to the Crown Heights projects in Brownsville. Taking a job as a domestic, Ada Sharpton earned so little that the family qualified for welfare.

Shaping His Signature Personality

At age twelve, young Sharpton initiated a meeting with the Reverend Adam Clayton Powell Jr. after reading one of his books. As the first African American congressman from New York, the famous pastor of Harlem's Abyssinian Baptist Church had been elected to the House of Representatives in 1945 (a position that he maintained until 1970). By the time Sharpton met with Powell, the politician was already beloved by black communities for his flamboyant charm but was despised by his opponents for his outspokenness. Long after the meeting, Powell exercised considerable influence on Sharpton. Many whites viewed Powell as a troublemaker, but Sharpton liked his mentor's independent, self-assured and even arrogant carriage. As if a precursor for his own troubled political career, Sharpton witnessed Powell's suffering through innumerable personal and professional attacks by government agencies throughout his career.

Sharpton also joined the Southern Christian Leadership Conference (SCLC) as a teenager. After meeting the Reverend Jesse Jackson at a rally to attract young people as recruits for his Operation Breadbasket program, the teen joined in protests and demonstrations for civil rights. In 1969, Jackson nominated fifteen-year-old Sharpton as the youth director of the New York branch of Operation Breadbasket, an activist organization that directed boycotts against unfair business practices in predominately black American neighborhoods. His weekly preaching appearances, his activist leanings, and his probable political ambition led Sharpton to intern in the New York City Human Resources Administration as a high school student.

Flamboyance Raises Questions over Controversial Alliances

Encouraged by the success of his early activism (including a substantial protest against the A&P, the country's largest grocery store chain), Sharpton founded the National Youth Movement (NYM) in 1971. Designed as an extension of his battle against discriminatory hiring and business practices, NYM also worked to combat police brutality and deter substance abuse. Through NYM's activities, he met the soul artist James Brown who agreed to perform a benefit concert for the organization. The meeting offered Sharpton the opportunity to tour as a bodyguard of the performer and provided useful contacts between Sharpton and important African American personalities such as Don King, with whom he worked to promote boxing events, and Michael Jackson, whom he worked with to increase job opportunities for African Americans in the entertainment industry.

Years later, when Brown and King went through a series of legal troubles, Sharpton found himself at the center of a Federal Bureau of Investigation (FBI) attack on King. Although the FBI was convinced that the infamous fight promoter was linked to organized crime from which he profited, by the end of its investigation the bureau could only allege that Sharpton provided information about the Genoveses, New York's infamous crime family.

After his 1972 graduation from Tipton High School, Sharpton attended Brooklyn College from 1973 to 1975. Despite his not serving his own church as pastor throughout the 1970s and 1980s, the Reverend Al Sharpton remained a visible figure in New York City well into the 1990s. Regarded in some African American circles as a defender of black power traditions, Sharpton continued to appeal because of his speaking ability. His NYM activities and regular preaching appearances attracted considerable audiences who enjoyed his black preacher style. In the tradition of Afro-folk religion, his loud and sometimes raspy voice would methodically crescendo until its climax electrified audiences.

Successes and Challenges of the Grassroots Leader

Sharpton's attempt to win a seat in the New York legislature in 1978 was foiled when a judge ruled that he did not meet the Brooklyn district's residency requirements. In the mid-1980s Sharpton was suddenly on the chaotic stage of New York's racial politics. In 1985, Bernhard Goetz, a white subway rider, shot several young black men on a city subway. However, despite permanently paralyzing one of them, he was not even charged with having a firearm. The widely publicized incident and the lack of criminal action in its aftermath caused outrage in the black community. Assuming the role as its unofficial spokesman, Sharpton organized demonstrations and prayer vigils at Goetz's apartment as well as hosting interviews and attending the court proceedings. Sharpton's sustained protest almost certainly helped to see that Goetz was indicted, convicted of carrying a concealed weapon, and sentenced on the weapons charge.

Al Sharpton led other protests in high-profiled cases concerning the black community.. In 1986, Sharpton answered the call of a family seeking assistance in the racial killing of Michael Griffith, a black teen who was chased by whites onto a highway when his car broke down in Brooklyn's still-segregated Howard Beach. Again, Sharpton pushed to keep the incident in the press, holding rallies, offering a cash reward for information, and leading a march of thousands of supporters. While other black political leaders and even mayor Ed Koch joined in the condemnation of the murder, Sharpton's leadership identified him as a leader of black causes in New York City.

Sharpton was pulled into the 1987 case of Tawana Brawley. Sensationalized in the press over several months, the controversial case was dismissed within a year after being investigated by a grand jury which concluded that Brawley had made-up the entire incident to explain her four-day disappearance from home. Al Sharpton continued to support Brawley and her family and continued to assert that district attorney Steven Pagones was somehow implicated in wrong doing. Finally, Pagones sued him for $395 million for defamation of character. After dragging on for ten additional years, the case ended with an eight-month trial in which Sharpton and his cohorts were found guilty of slander, and Sharpton was fined $65,000. Vilified in the press, Sharpton was soon accused of being an FBI informant and became the subject of state and federal tax inquiries. Also accused of tax evasion and embezzlement, Sharpton was acquitted of these charges and others that included established contacts with wanted felons and wiretapping his associates.

In the years that followed, Sharpton continued to be attacked in the media as a shady figure whose stout physical appearance, combined with his signature hair and jogging suits, made him the regular source of jokes.

Despite his waning popularity, Sharpton maintained his NYM activities and interest in racial cases. The 1989 case of Yusuf Hawkins, a black sixteen-year-old, and three of his friends who were chased by a mob of white boys after getting off at the wrong subway stop, drew Sharpton in. The family of murdered Hawkins sought out Sharpton, who helped coordinate a series of marches to keep pressure on the justice system. A jury finally sentenced one of the boys to thirty-two years to life for the murder.

The Hawkins case illuminated existing racial tensions between African Americans and the predominately Italian American neighborhood where the attack took place. Similar tensions were building between blacks and Hasidic Jews in the Crown Heights community where the grand rebbe of the Lubavitcher accidentally killed Gavin Cato, a black teen, while swerving to avoid an oncoming car. Despite having peacefully lived together for decades, blacks and Jews were suddenly opposed. The incident caused outrage in Cato's neighborhood, and Yankel Rosenbaum, a young rabbinical student, was allegedly stabbed to death by a black teenager. Led again by Sharpton, protest marches helped to urge the return of the car driver who fled to Israel, and in the end, a jury acquitted the black youth. Sharpton continued to labor with other black leaders to bridge the gap between the black and Jewish community left by the ordeal.

An Attempt on His Life Changes Sharpton

On January 12, 1991, Sharpton was stabbed by Michael Riccardi, a drunken white male, during a protest rally in a Bensonhurst schoolyard. While Riccardi attempted to flee on foot, Sharpton removed the five-inch knife from his chest before collapsing. Public figures such as New York City's first black mayor David Dinkins, who had long sought to distance themselves from his controversial reputation, publicly denounced the attack and pledged their support to Sharpton. The truce was only one benefit of the attack. While on his hospital bed, Sharpton was reunited with both his long-estranged father Albert Sharpton Sr. and his young mentor, the Reverend Jesse Jackson.

Despite Sharpton's plea for leniency during the case, Riccardi was sentenced to five to fifteen years in prison. However, Sharpton was not as forgiving of the New York City Police Department (NYPD), whom he claimed had promised him protection before the protest and subsequent stabbing. Over a decade later, in December 2003, Sharpton filed a civil suit against the department in which he alleged that the police did not protect him during the protest, nor did they make any real attempt to apprehend Riccardi after the attack. Although the city's spokesman maintained that the NYPD acted appropriately, the city paid Sharpton a $200,000 out-of-court settlement.

Sharpton declared the attack changed his life. In 1991, he founded his National Action Network (NAN) in

Harlem. Dubbed the House of Justice, NAN's Harlem base served as the organization's national headquarters in the fight against racism in the business world, political arena, and criminal justice system. The activist organization prides itself on offering a cross-section of initiatives that empower the politically and economically underserved.

In 1992, Sharpton finished third in the Democratic primary for a U.S. Senate seat. When Mayor Dinkins was succeeded by Rudolph Giuliani, Sharpton's support base broadened to include other African American New Yorkers. Despite losing in a 1994 bid as well, Sharpton remained active in civil rights activities, including organizing a march against poverty in 1995 and a vigil outside U.S. Supreme Court Justice Clarence Thomas' home to protest the judge's opposition to affirmative action. In 1993 Sharpton served forty-five days in jail as a result of a 1987 protest march that shut down the Brooklyn Bridge.

In 1997, Sharpton ran in New York's Democratic mayoral primary, winning 32 percent of the vote and almost forcing a runoff. Despite some political success, Sharpton remained a grassroots organizer, who championed the causes of the underserved. He rallied politicians, entertainers, and members of the wider black community to pursue the police officer responsible for the 1999 arrest and sodomy of Abner Louima, a Haitian immigrant. In another case of police brutality, Sharpton helped to press the justice system to prosecute the officers responsible for shooting Amadou Diallo, a Guinean immigrant.

Sharpton vied for the Democratic nomination for U.S. president in the 2004 general election. While his August 2001 announcement was initially received with indifference by some, it was received with welcomed excitement by others. Arguing that the Democrats and Republicans had become too similar on issues such as war, health care, business deregulation and taxes, Sharpton insisted that he was running a broad-based campaign. Using the line, "Keep the Dream Alive: Don't Waste Your Vote," Sharpton's 10-point platform emphasized four goals: the right to vote, the right to public education of equally high quality, the right to healthcare of equally high quality and women's equal rights. One of ten candidates vying for the Democratic nomination, Sharpton did not have the financial backing that his competitors enjoyed. However, monetary restraints were not Sharpton's only challenges. Even so, Sharpton's public showing helped to keep the issues of the underserved in the forefront of the race well beyond his March 2004 concession of defeat to Senator John Kerry.

In 1996 Al Sharpton wrote his autobiography *Go and Tell Pharaoh*, and in 2002 he published *Al on America*. Married to former James Brown back-up singer Kathy Jordan since the mid-1980s, the couple has two daughters Dominique and Ashley.

REFERENCES

Books

Brennan, Carol. "Al Sharpton," In *Contemporary Black Biography*. Vol. 13. Ed. Shirelle Phelps. Detroit: Gale Research, 1997.

Formicola, Jo Renee. "The Reverend Al Sharpton: Pentecostal for Racial Justice," In *Religious Leaders and Faith-Based Politics: Ten Profiles*. Eds. Jo Renee Formicola and Hubert Morken. Lanham, MD: Rowman & Littlefield Publishers, Inc., 2002.

Klein, Michael. *The Man Behind the Sound Bite : The Real Story of the Rev. Al Sharpton*. New York: Castillo International, 1991.

Taylor, Clarence. "A Natural-Born Leader: The Politics of the Reverend Al Sharpton," In *Black Religious Intellectuals: The Fight For Equality from Jim Crow to the Twenty-First Century*. New York: Routledge, 2002.

Periodicals

Chappell, Kevin. "The 'New' Al Sharpton Talks about the 'Old' Al Sharpton and The New Threats to Black Americans." *Ebony* 56 (July 2001).

"The Reverend Al Sharpton Delivers Remarks at Democratic National Convention," *Political/Congressional Transcript Wire*, 28 July 2004.

Sherman, Scott. "He Has a Dream: The Grand Ambition of the Rev. Al Sharpton." *The Nation* 272 (16 April 2001).

Crystal A. deGregory

Arthur Davis Shores
1904–1996

Lawyer

Although Arthur Davis Shores began his career as an educator, it was his talent as a lawyer that skyrocketed him to fame. His significant achievements included his appointment as the first African American elected to the Birmingham, Alabama city council, providing legal assistance to Vivian Malone and James Hood in their efforts to integrate the University of Alabama, and numerous other cases during the civil rights movement and afterward.

Arthur Davis Shores was born September 25, 1904 (some sources say 1905) in Bessemer, Alabama to Richard H. and Pauline McGhee Shores. He grew up in Wenonah,

Arthur Davis Shores

Chronology

1904	Born in Bessemer, Alabama on September 25
1927	Graduates with B.S. from Talladega College in Alabama
1927-34	Teaches at Dunbar High School in Bessemer, Alabama
1935	Graduates with law degree from Chicago's LaSalle Extension University
1935-39	Serves as principal at Dunbar High School in Bessemer, Alabama
1937	Passes the Alabama Bar exam
1940	Begins to practice law and prosecutes brutality case
1954	Seeks state legislature seat
1963	Assists James Hood and Vivian Malone in integrating the University of Alabama
1968	Receives appointment to Birmingham City Council
1971	Receives honorary LL.D. from Miles College
1996	Dies in Birmingham, Alabama on December 15

Alabama (home of the Tennessee Coal and Oil Mining camp called Fossil). Shores graduated from Cameron Elementary and walked five miles each day to attend Industrial High (later Parker High) in Birmingham. Parker High was the only predominantly black school at that time. Shores attended Talladega College on a scholarship and graduated in 1927 with a bachelor of science degree. The University of Kansas awarded him a degree in 1934. In 1935 Shores graduated from Chicago's LaSalle Extension University with a law degree. He was awarded honorary degrees of doctor of law from Daniel Payne College in 1956 and Miles College in 1971 (both in Birmingham, Alabama). He received the honorary degree doctor of humane letters from the University of Alabama at Birmingham in 1975.

Shores taught at Dunbar High School from 1927 to 1934 and served as principal of the same school from 1935 to 1939. While at Dunbar, Shores studied nightly to become a lawyer. In 1937 Shores passed the bar, becoming the third black person of the twentieth century to be certified by the Alabama Bar Association. Shores began to practice three years later. Shores served as the only African American attorney until 1940 when Mahala Ashley Dickerson and Clarence Moses began their practices in Montgomery and Mobile.

In 1938 his first two cases involved voter registration and police brutality. Seven teachers filed complaints against the Jefferson County board of registrars. Like other prospective voters, these teachers had to name government agencies, members of Congress, and interpret parts of the Constitution. The case never went to trial because the registrars mailed the teachers their certificates.

Shores drew attention in 1940 when the Birmingham chapter of the NAACP asked him to prosecute a brutality case involving a white defendant and a black plaintiff. Shores was being paid only $50. He reported being bribed to give up the case, and the Ku Klux Klan threatened him if he continued with the case. Shores won the case in an appearance before the Jefferson County personnel board which gave the white officer a thirty day suspension. Shores won both cases (registration and brutality) since whites were fearful of an appeal.

Shores the Politician

Shores resigned from the NAACP in February 1952 to become involved in politics. If elected, Shores promised to alter the Right to Work Bill or abolish it altogether. He also promised to alleviate conditions that led to juvenile delinquency, increase public benefits and aid to hospitals, improve highways and education, push for compulsory inspection of automobiles at periodic intervals, and strengthen health laws to include compulsory testing for tuberculosis.

During his efforts to acquire a legislative seat, Shores was also involved in community affairs. He was vice chairperson of the interracial committee of the coordinating council, trustee at the First Congregational Church, president of the Jones Valley Finance Company, chair of the Eighteenth Street branch of the YMCA board of management, member of the national legal committee of the NAACP, and a thirty-third degree Mason. He was also a member of the Shriners, Elks, and Knights of Pythias.

History-Making Events

In 1954 Shores worked with Thurgood Marshall to desegregate southern schools, the same year as the significant *Brown v. Board of Education* case. In 1952, Autherine Lucy applied to the University of Alabama. The University denied Lucy admittance. However, she persisted and won admission in 1955 after the session had begun. She came to the University of Alabama in 1956, a riot occurred, and she was dismissed a few days later because of something she said about the school's board of trustees. In 1963 two other students, Vivian Malone and James Hood, applied for admission and walked into history despite the decision by Governor George C. Wallace to stand in the doorway. Shores served as legal counsel and assisted Malone and Hood in this endeavor, paving the way for African Americans to attend and graduate from a previously predominantly white institution.

In 1963 someone bombed the Shores home on Center Street in Birmingham twice. No one was injured in the first bombings that were heard over ten miles away. In the second bombing, Shores' wife was hospitalized.

In 1968 Shores served on the credential committee at the Democratic National Convention. He was the first of his race to speak at a national political convention. His role in organizing the Alabama Progressive Democratic Conference paved the way for his participation at the Democratic Convention. He was a delegate to the National Democratic Convention in 1968, 1972, and 1976 and served as a member of the Judicial Commission for the U.S. Fifth Circuit of Appeals, the appointment of President Carter.

Shores achieved another milestone in December 1968. He was the first African American appointed to the previously all white Birmingham city council, filling the vacancy caused by the death of R.W. "Red" Douglass. The *Birmingham News* had recommended former mayor Albert Boutwell because of his experience in municipal affairs. Boutwell declined for personal reasons, and the *Birmingham News* considered Arthur Shores.

Many African Americans in Birmingham praised the appointment of Shores to the Birmingham city council. Among these were Clarence Wood of the Urban League; Rev. Calvin Woods, a vigorous civil rights advocate; Dr. John Nixon, former head of the Alabama NAACP; Jessie Lewis, publisher of the *Birmingham Times*; Rev. Edward Garner of the Alabama Christian Movement for Human Rights; and numerous other friends.

Civic and Religious Memberships

Shores' memberships in professional organizations included the American Bar Association, Alabama Bar Association, Birmingham Bar Association, and the United States Supreme Court Bar Association. General memberships included the Presidents Club of Alabama, Alpha Phi Alpha Fraternity, and Delta Phi Theta Legal Fraternity.

Religious affiliations included membership in the First Congregational Church where he served as a Sunday School teacher and moderator. He did extensive work on the Board of Homeland Ministries, United Church of Christ. He attended the International Conference on Religion, Art, and Architecture in Jerusalem in 1973.

After retiring from the council in 1977, Shores spent more time at his law firm. He directed the Holy Family Hospital and served as chair of the Birmingham Housing Authority, president of the Urban League, vice president and general counsel for Citizens Federal Savings and Loan Association, and a board member for the Salvation Army. He was also a board member for the A.G. Gaston Boys Club, National Council of Christians and Jews, and other organizations.

Shores was married to the former Theodora Helen Warren; together they had two daughters. Shores died December 15, 1996 in Birmingham, Alabama after a long illness.

REFERENCES

Books

Baily, Richard. "Arthur Davis Shores." In *They Too Call Alabama Home: African American Profiles 1880-1999*. Montgomery: Pyramid Publishing, Inc. 1999.

Smith, Jessie Carney, ed. *Black Firsts*. Farmington Hills, Mich.: Thomson Gale, 2003.

Online

Alabama Academy of Honor: Arthur Davis Shores. http://www.archives.state.al.us/famous/academy/A_Shores.html (Accessed 2 March 2006).

University of Alabama Libraries, Gorgas Library Portraits and Plaques. http://www.lib.ua.edu/libraries/gorgas/about/Gorgas_portraits_plaques.htm (Accessed 2 March 2006).

Prudence White Bryant

Benjamin Singleton
1809–1892

Entrepreneur

The so-called father of the black exodus, as Benjamin "Pap" Singleton called himself, was a former slave and grassroots leader who facilitated the migration of

Benjamin Singleton

other former slaves to Kansas and other homesteading sites in the West where they hoped to be free from the racial and economic oppression that they had known in the South. He worked through what he believed was God's plan for him to help his race by moving westward, later encouraging African American owned businesses in order to strengthen the economic conditions of the race.

Little is known about Benjamin "Pap" Singleton's early life, from his birth on August 15, 1809 to the mid 1870s. Records show that during early adulthood he worked as a cabinetmaker in Nashville, Tennessee, where he was born a slave and spent his early years. To avoid being sold, he escaped to New Orleans but was later returned to Nashville. He was sold to owners who lived in Alabama and Mississippi but apparently escaped repeatedly and was captured and returned to his hometown. During one of his escapes, he went on to Windsor, Ontario, for a brief period and then lived in Detroit for a time. There he worked as a scavenger and also managed a boarding house where fugitive slaves were often sheltered. When the Civil War ended, he returned to Nashville.

Singleton was determined to ensure the safety of black people in Tennessee and beyond. In fact, he considered that he had a God-given mission to relocate these oppressed people from former slave states to states that offered them a friendlier environment than they had

known. When he returned to Nashville, he saw continuing evidence that many whites were hostile, even cruel toward blacks. In the late 1860s and 1870s he lived in a section called East Nashville, on Edgefield, across the Cumberland River that separated that section from the main part of town. He worked as a cabinet and coffin maker (possibly as a carpenter) in Nashville as well as in the surrounding counties. In fact, many of the coffins that he made were for blacks who were killed by white vigilantes. Some of the coffins were for the freedmen who lived in contraband camps near his Edgefield residence, who died from crowded and unsanitary conditions. Singleton envisioned a better life for the people of his race; he wanted them to be independent of whites and own their own land. Land in Tennessee was too costly for blacks; therefore, he looked elsewhere for land where they might settle.

Meanwhile, Singleton claimed that he was a Ulysses S. Grant Republican, but he was more interested in economics than in politics. In 1875, he was elected to the Tennessee Convention of Colored Men. Around this time, Singleton and two other craftsmen—W. A. Sizemore and Columbus M. Johnson—were active in the convention as well. So was another Singleton associate, A. W. McConnell, who in 1874 was elected to the Davidson County Republican Convention and was a Davidson County delegate to the State Convention of Colored Men. In *Exodusters*, Nell Painter asserts that the National Convention of Colored Men that met in Nashville around this time overshadowed Singleton's work as well as that of the Nashville convention's circle of Sizemore-Singleton-McConnell. All three men spoke at the 1875 State Convention of Colored Men and advocated migration out of the state.

In September 1874 Singleton and Sizemore, a carpenter and a member of the Davidson County (Tennessee) Republican Central Committee, founded the Edgefield Real Estate and Homestead Association located at No. 5 Front Street. Painter states that Sizemore "may have actually been more important in the migration movement in Tennessee than was Singleton." Columbus M. Johnson, a preacher, who recruited in nearby Sumner County's former contraband camps located in Hendersonville and Gallatin, also worked with Singleton and possibly did so longer than any other man. He went with Singleton to Kansas to explore the possibility of homesteading; Johnson also became the Kansas-based agent for Edgefield Real Estate and Homestead Association.

Migration was Singleton's central interest. Although he urged blacks to migrate to Kansas, he had tried to address the interests of those who wanted to remain in their old homes in Tennessee by seeking to buy farmlands. When that proved too expensive, he pursued what he thought was the only alternative—an exodus to Kansas. He visited Kansas in 1873 to survey homesteading possibilities. He and Columbus Johnson went to Kansas on an inspection tour in 1877 and returned to Nashville to promote his efforts in the local press. His real estate association held mass meetings during 1877 and 1878 and on July 31 and August 1, 1877, opened a mass meeting in Nashville to all residents of Tennessee. While some five hundred black laborers attended, many race leaders failed to attend. In 1879, Singleton made serious inquiries with government officials in Kansas regarding homesteading in that state.

Black Exodus Begins

The black exodus took off after Singleton and his association promoted their work through speeches and at festivals and picnics and distributed leaflets to blacks throughout the South. By some accounts, the migration really began in 1876; however, the lack of money and supplies prevented many African Americans from reaching their promised land. Association members led more blacks to Kansas in 1877 and 1878 and founded at least four all-black communities: in Cherokee, Graham, Lyons, and Morris counties. They incorporated Singleton colony in Dunlap, located in Morris County, Kansas, where Singleton lived temporarily between 1879 and 1880.

Some of his settlements survived into modern times, such as Nicodemus, which survives as a collection of buildings protected by the National Park Service. Some migrants settled in Topeka in a community known as Tennessee Town. The movement continued, and in 1879 some 20,000 destitute African Americans migrated to Kansas from Mississippi, Louisiana, and Texas. In 1880, some 2,407 African Americans from Nashville left for Kansas. Many "exodusters" suffered continuing hardships that they had known in their home states, such as difficulty in finding work, which resulted in economic problems. Others were successful and appreciated the move. Still others went to sites farther west.

The migrants' situation took on political meaning as Democrats accused Republicans of encouraging the move for political reasons. In 1880, Singleton was a witness before a U.S. Senate committee that investigated the exodus. The Republican Singleton was never shaken by the Democrats' cross-examination. He even gained fame for his claim that he was the whole cause of the Kansas migration. For his work, according to Stephen W. Angell, he became known as "the Moses of the Colored Exodus." By now, however, he was no longer an advocate of migration to Kansas.

From the late 1880s on, Singleton lived mostly in Tennessee Town, a neighborhood near Topeka named for the sizeable number of Tennesseans who settled there. He became politically active, founding and supporting many short-lived political associations. One of these was the United Colored Link that had as its mission race unity in order to establish African American-controlled businesses and to work through the Greenbacker Party to form a coalition with white workers. In 1885, Singleton organized the Trans-Atlantic Society, an outgrowth of his failed effort in 1883 to form a successful Chief League to support emigration to Cyprus, the island in the Mediterranean. The society also called for repatriation of African Americans to Ethiopia. By 1887, nothing more was heard about the group or its movement.

The dates of Singleton's activities, including his birth and death, vary in published sources. Whether he was married or had a family is thus far unknown. For a number of years he suffered poor health and, according to some sources, he died in St. Louis in 1892 and was buried in an unmarked grave.

Benjamin "Pap" Singleton achieved a part of his dream and had a long, established record of working to improve conditions for the people of his race. His mission was enormous but the financial support that he needed to achieve it was never forthcoming.

REFERENCES

Books

Angell, Stephen W. "Benjamin Singleton." *American National Biography.* Vol. 20. Eds. John A. Garraty and Mark C. Carnes. New York: Oxford University Press, 1999.

Bontemps, Arna, and Jack Conroy. *They Seek a City.* Garden City, N.Y.: Doubleday, Doran and Co., 1945.

Lovett, Bobby. "Benjamin 'Pap' Singleton." *Tennessee Encyclopedia of History and Culture.* Ed. Carroll Van West. Nashville: Tennessee Historical Society, 1998.

Painter, Nell Irvin. "Benjamin 'Pap' Singleton." *Dictionary of American Negro Biography.* Eds. Rayford W. Logan and Michael R. Winston. New York: Norton, 1982.

——. *Exodusters: Black Migration to Kansas after Reconstruction.* New York: Knopf, 1977.

Collections

The Kansas State Historical Society houses the scrapbook in which Singleton kept press clippings about his work.

Jessie Carney Smith

Rodney Slater
1955–

Secretary of transportation, lawyer

Overcoming the poverty and segregation of the Arkansas Mississippi Delta region, Rodney Slater gained national prominence as the chief administrator of the U.S. Federal Highway Administration and the secretary of transportation during President Clinton's second term. His rise to distinction resulted from his skillful understanding of the transportation industry and his ability to form coalitions in an environment of fierce competition and rivalry.

Rodney Earl Slater was born out of wedlock to Velma Slater on February 23, 1955 in Tutwyler, Mississippi. His mother soon moved with her newborn son to the town of Marianna in her home state of Arkansas. Shortly afterward, Velma married Earl Brewer, a mechanic and maintenance man, who fathered Slater's four half-siblings—two brothers and two sisters. Brewer instilled in Rodney Slater a strong work ethic. Slater remarked in an interview with *Ebony*: "[his father] was the person who was there. He was the person who worked five and six jobs to make it possible for my brothers and sisters to enjoy the things that were important." By age six, Slater had hired himself out to work in the cotton fields. He was strongly influenced by the elders of the neighborhood with whom he worked and lived. When Slater was in the third grade, his family moved into a public housing project where he remained throughout his childhood.

As a youngster growing up in Marianna, Slater showed a knack for public speaking. At age six, he read Bible passages on a radio program broadcasted from the church he attended. As a fourth grader, Slater was an accomplished public speaker, reading from the works of James Weldon Johnson, W. E. B. Du Bois, and others. Slater also became interested in government. Slater's former classmate, Carolyn Elliot, recalled in an *Arkansas Democrat-Gazette* interview, that "a sixth grade teacher named Willie Neal . . . challenged us to know about government, to know about ourselves. I think that probably was a turning point."

Rodney Slater

When Slater was in the tenth grade, the school district consolidated its white and black high schools. Racial tensions were high in Marianna at the time. When blacks boycotted white-owned businesses, Governor Dale Bumpers sent in state police to suppress the conflict. A dozen businesses in the city closed as a result of the boycott. On January 13, 1972, during Slater's junior year at Lee Senior High School, a sit-down strike by students to gain permission to hold an assembly in honor of Martin Luther King's birthday became disorderly when police used high-pressure water hoses to break up the strike. The incident led Slater and others to boycott the school. Slater and over two hundred other students were arrested and put on trial for inciting a riot. Through the efforts of African American civil rights attorney John Walker, the charges were dropped. Slater's great admiration for John Walker and the courtroom experience inspired him to pursue a career as a lawyer.

Slater enrolled at Eastern Michigan University in 1973 on a football scholarship. At Eastern Michigan, Slater excelled both athletically, as co-captain of the football team, and academically. Dennis Beagan, a college speech professor, was so impressed with Slater's performance in class that he offered him a spot on the school's nationally recognized forensics team. Slater made it to the national quarterfinals in the "interpretation

Chronology

1955	Born in Tutwyler, Mississippi on February 23
1972	Arrested with other students and put on trial in Marianna, Georgia on riot charges
1977	Graduates with B.A. from Eastern Michigan University
1979	Graduates with J.D. from University of Arkansas Law School
1980-82	Works in Arkansas State Attorney General's Office
1982-83	Serves as deputy campaign manager for Governor Bill Clinton
1983-87	Serves as special assistant to Governor Bill Clinton
1987-93	Serves as director of Government Relations, Arkansas State University
1993-97	Serves as administrator for the U.S. Federal Highway Administration
1997-2000	Serves as U.S. secretary of transportation
2001	Becomes partner in Patton Boggs law firm

of prose" category. At graduation in 1977, he was given the Eastern Michigan University Top Ten Student Award.

Slater returned to Arkansas and attended law school at the University of Arkansas at Fayetteville. He was mentored there by William Haley, the second black ever to graduate from the law school. Slater's knack for developing relationships with older, more experienced leaders helped him to excel professionally.

Immediately after graduation in 1979, he began working at the Arkansas State Attorney General's Office in Fayetteville. In 1980, Slater's future father-in-law, state representative Henry Wilkins of Pine Bluff, introduced him to Arkansas governor and future U.S. president Bill Clinton. Slater quickly gained a good rapport with the governor. Clinton was later quoted in the *Arkansas Democrat Gazette* as saying that he "put a lot of trust in him when he was young because I knew—when he was first working for me with the black community—that the older ministers, the older doctors, the older business people, the people that he dealt with, I knew they would trust him."

Becomes First Black on Highway Commission

In March 1982, Slater left his post in the attorney general's office to serve as deputy campaign manager for Clinton's second gubernatorial campaign. Following the successful campaign, Slater was named special assistant to Governor Clinton in 1983 and was promoted to executive assistant in 1985. In 1987, Slater was hired by Arkansas State University in Jonesboro to serve as the director of government relations and also appointed by Governor Clinton as the first black member of the Arkansas State Highway and Transportation Commission.

As a member of the state highway commission and an administrator at Arkansas State, Slater focused on the

economic development and transportation issues of the state's rural Mississippi Delta region. At Slater's U.S. Transportation Secretary Confirmation hearing, according to the *Arkansas Democrat-Gazette*, Arkansas republican Senator Tim Hutchinson praised Slater's role on the highway commission as "putting aside political differences to do what was best for the state." Hutchinson also said that "Rodney, without hesitation, tackled the great challenge of improving a poor rural state's infrastructure . . . He took on that challenge, not trying to please, but trying to do the right thing." Slater was also instrumental in initiating the "Mississippi Delta Symposium on Its People, Its Problems, Its Potential" at Arkansas State University. The symposium brought together a wide array of business leaders and local and state politicians to discuss current topics regarding economic development and job growth. As a result of his service, Slater gained the respect of legislators and business leaders throughout the state for his interpersonal skills and putting people first. He served as chairman of the commission from 1992 to 1993.

Following the 1992 election, President Bill Clinton named Slater the first African American administrator of the Federal Highway Administration in June 1993. As administrator, Slater successfully worked with Congress to pass the National Highway System Designation Act of 1995, which assigned 160,000 miles of roads in the United States as part of a national highway system. More importantly, the selected roads were eligible for $13 billion in additional federal funding. During Slater's term, the infrastructure investment in federal highway construction increased from $21 billion to $25 billion. Along with the increased funding, Slater and his staff worked to improve financing and contracting techniques to streamline the contracting process and improve quality.

Despite Slater's popularity and success on Capitol Hill, he was harshly criticized by consumer advocates led by Ralph Nader, who sent a letter to President Clinton and Vice President Al Gore calling for the firing of Slater because of his support of an amendment to the National Highway System Designation Act to abolish the national speed limit of fifty-five miles per hour. According to *Traffic World*, Nader also accused Slater of "currying industry's favor at the expense of motorists' safety" regarding the trucking industry's lobbying efforts to increase the maximum allowable weight limit for trucks from 80,000 pounds to 175,000 pounds. Slater's response to Nader's criticism was that he was only carrying out the implementation of policies that had already been put in motion by Congress.

Named U.S. Secretary of Transportation

In 1997, Slater was nominated by President Clinton and confirmed unanimously by the U.S. Senate to be the thirteenth U.S. secretary of transportation. He was the second federal highway administrator (John Volpe was the first), and the second African American (Bill Coleman was the first) to serve in the secretary post. Within the first eighteen months of his term, Congress passed the largest highway bill in U.S. history. The Transportation Equity Act guaranteed a record $200 billion in funds for surface transportation. Also, department negotiators led by Slater helped to avert a workers' strike against Amtrak and successfully lobbied for the Amtrak Reform and Accountability Act to improve the country's passenger rail system.

Another notable accomplishment of Slater's administration was increasing the number of open skies agreements with countries around the world to expand the aviation system and remove restrictions on commercial airline travel, including the first agreement with an African nation (Tanzania). Slater organized the first major international aviation conference in nearly fifty-five years to encourage countries to move beyond bilateral open skies agreements toward regional multilateral agreements. The first multilateral open skies agreement was signed shortly thereafter between the United States, Singapore, New Zealand, Chile, and Brunei.

On the domestic front, Slater worked to decrease the highway fatality rate and to expand safety regulations on motor vehicles. The Motor Carrier Safety Improvement Act of 1999 established the Federal Motor Carrier Safety Administration to enforce safety regulations and maximize public participation in motor safety. As a result, the National Safety Council's 1999 Injury Facts publication reported that seat belt use nationally rose to an all-time high of 70 percent.

After the 2000 presidential election, Slater left the Department of Transportation to join the law firm of Patton Boggs as head of its transportation practice group in Washington D.C. Although he was rumored to have political aspirations, he continued to stay focused on issues of transportation. In 2005, Slater agreed to serve as a representative for the ground workers union of Northwest Airlines on the company's board of directors.

Slater's rise from poverty has been an inspiration to many people. Thomas Donohue, president of the American Trucking Association, told the *New York Times* that "[Slater's] earned this by coming from very, very poor roots n Arkansas, working his way through college and law school, working on the campaign, and taking a real job in Washington. . . . He took a real job building highways in this country and he did a great job."

REFERENCES

Books

U.S. Department of Transportation. Bureau of Transportation Statistics. *The Changing Face of Transportation.* BTS00-007. Washington, D.C.: GPO, 2000.

U.S. Department of Transportation. *Transportation Decision Making: Policy Architecture for the 21st Century.* Washington, D.C.: GPO, 2000.

Periodicals

Fullerton, Jane. "Slater Wins Cabinet Post, Capping Climb From Poverty." *Arkansas Democrat-Gazette* (7 February 1997): A-8.

Holmes, Steven A. "Hard Work and Talent: Rodney Earl Slater." *New York Times* (21 December 1996): 10.

Kayal, Michele. "The Essence of Rodney Slater." *Journal of Commerce* (29 June 1998): A-11.

Kiely, Kathy, and Joe Stumpe. "Slater Takes the High Road All the Way to the Top." *Arkansas Democrat-Gazette* (9 February 1997): A-1.

O'Toole, Kevin. "Sky Opener". *Airline Business* 15 (December 1999): 36.

Randolph, Laura B. "Traveling in the Fast Lane." *Ebony* 53 (March 1998): 118-21.

Thurman, James N. "Man Who Keeps U.S. Moving." *Christian Science Monitor* (8 September 1998): 1.

Wilner, Frank N. "From DOT to the Stars." *Traffic World* (10 August 1998): 11.

Mark L. McCallon

Tavis Smiley
1964–

Journalist, broadcaster, writer, entrepreneur, philanthropist

In the early 2000s Tavis Smiley was recognized as an influential broadcast and print journalist, respected political commentator, noted author, highly sought-after speaker, entrepreneur, foundation executive, and philanthropist. He came from humble beginnings, overcame obstacles, and used his considerable influence to positively influence the lives of others through his work in multiple communications media.

The third oldest among ten children of Emory G. and Joyce M. Smiley, Tavis was born on September 13, 1964 in Gulfport, Mississippi, but spent nearly all of his early life in and around Kokomo, Indiana. The family relocated when his father, a master sergeant in the U.S. Air Force, was assigned to work at Grissom Air Force Base in Bunker Hill, Indiana. In addition to being a wife and mother, Joyce Smiley was a Pentecostal minister.

The large family lived in a mobile home for a period, in which the young Smiley had to share a bed with sev-

Tavis Smiley

eral brothers. Despite the family challenges, Smiley became an energetic and inquisitive youngster, with a particular interest in politics. He was elected class president in high school, a notable accomplishment in that the overwhelming majority of his classmates were not African Americans.

After graduating from Kokomo High School in 1982, Smiley attended Indiana University in Bloomington, Indiana, where he became increasingly interested in politics and activism along with classroom studies. While in the city as a student, he served as an assistant to the mayor, Tomilea Allison. When an African American classmate died after an altercation with the police, Smiley was sensitized to issues facing the larger national African American community and felt that pursuing a political career would enable him to make a difference. As a result, he left Indiana to spend a semester as an intern for Tom Bradley, the first African American mayor of Los Angeles, California.

Smiley then made the decision to remain in Los Angeles, where he worked for a time as a special assistant to the executive director of the city's branch office of the Southern Christian Leadership Council (SCLC) and networked with other young African American professionals. He eventually became an adviser to the city council president, administrative aide to Bradley, and campaigned unsuccessfully for a seat on the council.

Begins Media Career

Shortly after losing the election in 1990, Smiley started doing a short radio news commentary, *The Smiley Report*, which was favorably received by the local listening audience and eventually was syndicated to stations in other parts of the country. In 1994, Smiley was profiled by *Time* magazine as one of America's 50 most promising young leaders, which also attracted attention and recognition beyond his base of operations in Los Angeles.

Black Entertainment Television (BET), which had become a major success in the cable television industry since its founding by African American executive Robert L. (Bob) Johnson in 1980, approached Smiley about taking his talents to television and hired him to host a talk show, *BET Talk*, which began airing in 1996. During the same year Smiley published his book, *Hard Left: Straight Talk about the Wrongs of the Right*, and was introduced to Tom Joyner, the nationally syndicated radio host, by President Bill Clinton, who had been interviewed by both men. Shortly afterwards Joyner began to incorporate Smiley's commentaries into his *Tom Joyner Morning Show* (TJMS) broadcasts. As a result of this professional involvement, Smiley became a household name among the millions of TJMS listeners in various regions of the United States. Many of these listeners were also subscribers to cable television services, which included BET among their program offerings, and became viewers of Smiley's appearances on the cable channel.

The Smiley program filled a void in public affairs programming at BET, and *BET Talk* evolved into *BET Tonight with Tavis Smiley* as the program and its host became increasingly popular with its viewing audience. Like TJMS, it had tremendous access and influence, particularly in the African American community. The success of

BET Tonight with Tavis Smiley helped to deflect some of the criticism from detractors of the cable channel, especially after Smiley landed exclusive interviews with world figures such as Clinton, Pope John Paul II, and Fidel Castro, along with numerous African American leaders, celebrities, and other personalities. In the opinion of media observers, Smiley's access to national radio (through TJMS) and television (through BET) enabled him to speak to more African Americans on a daily basis than any other person. Media research at the time indicated that Joyner's radio program reached seven million listeners, while BET reached sixty-five million households.

From Advocacy to Controversy

Smiley used his radio and television broadcasts, celebrity status, and considerable influence to advocate positions regarding a variety of issues facing the African American community. As a result, he became involved in controversy for not always assuming the neutral stance traditionally expected of journalists. While Smiley sought to maintain the proper balance of perspective in his role as a television host, as a commentator and author he exercised the right to express his personal viewpoint. Smiley also became an in-demand public speaker, and in 1999 established the Tavis Smiley Foundation with the stated purpose "to encourage, empower, and enlighten youth through education and by developing leadership skills that will promote and enhance the quality of life for themselves, their communities, and the world," according to his web site.

In September 1999, Smiley and Joyner initiated a boycott of CompUSA, a national retailer of technology products, based on a letter Joyner received after he commented that the company was unwilling to advertise on radio and television outlets that attracted African American audiences. Listeners were asked to send receipts of their CompUSA purchases for totaling and forwarding to the company as proof of the consumer power of the African American community. Minority businesses and individuals were then encouraged to stop buying products from CompUSA, another way to illustrate their impact on the company's profits.

Smiley noted the poor grammar and spelling in the letter during his comments, and days later, the letter was proven to be a hoax. Smiley and Joyner were obliged to admit mistakes in rushing to judgment and called off the boycott. While an on-air apology was made to CompUSA, Smiley and Joyner received considerable criticism for their actions.

In 2000, Smiley continued to balance his multiple roles as broadcaster, author, activist, and advocate through a variety of platforms. He collaborated with Joyner, the NAACP, and its executive director, Kweisi Mfume, to develop the *Live Radio Town Hall* broadcast to encourage voter registration and participation in the 2000 elections and sponsored conferences through his foundation to encourage and develop young leaders. In the same year Johnson sold BET to Viacom, a media conglomerate, for $3 billion yet retained the position of chief executive officer for the network. The change in BET ownership was noted as a milestone for African American business and for Johnson personally, yet Smiley and others expressed concerns regarding the future of the network in terms of programming, staffing, and other areas of operation.

Loses One Platform and Gains Others

On March 21, 2001 Smiley was informed by his agent that his contract with BET would not be renewed when the agreement ended on September 6 of the same year. He had just arrived in Warren, Ohio for the beginning of his foundation's Youth 2 Leaders nine-city tour and had already scheduled a trip the next day to Midway, Georgia for the funeral of his grandmother, Adel Smiley.

Smiley addressed his situation during his TJMS commentary on March 22, also expressing concern for the future of the program at BET, the viewing audience, his production staff, and others, as close to 50 BET employees were also laid off around the same time. The program had retained its popularity and high ratings, with Smiley receiving several honors and recognitions, including the NAACP Image Award for three consecutive years. He also expressed dismay that he was given no detailed explanation by BET, only a fax message that he referred to as "five years, four sentences." In support, Joyner asked his radio audience to boycott BET, and to call, write, fax, and e-mail Mel Karmazin, Viacom's chief executive officer, to express their displeasure at the network's treatment of Smiley.

BET responded by firing Smiley immediately, instead of at the end of his contract. Johnson indicated in his press release that "recent actions by Mr. Smiley left us little recourse but to make this move," and also made a rare on-air appearance on March 26 during the regular time slot of the former Smiley program to explain his position to the viewing audience. Johnson indicated that the decision "was his, and his alone" to fire Smiley.

Smiley had produced and conducted an exclusive interview with Sara Jane Olson, a radical fugitive and former member of the Symbionese Liberation Army (SLA), which gained notoriety with the group's kidnapping of heiress Patricia (Patty) Hearst in the 1970s. He opted not to air the interview on BET (which he had the right to do under the terms of his contract) and sold the broadcast rights to ABC News after CBS (also owned by Viacom) showed no interest in the production. Smiley's interview aired on ABC's *Prime Time Live* program and received higher ratings than the CBS program scheduled at the same time. Johnson indicated that Smiley's actions demonstrated "a lack of mutual business respect" which led to the termination of his BET contract.

Smiley made a final statement regarding his situation on the March 27 broadcast of TJMS in an effort to set the record straight. He said it was time for all the persons involved to move on with their lives and work. Joyner agreed and asked listeners who had been honoring the boycott of BET to end the protest.

By the end of 2001 Smiley had received an unprecedented multimedia deal, in which he would work as a broadcaster for ABC News, ABC Radio Network, Cable News Network (CNN), and National Public Radio (NPR). He became the first African American ever to host a broadcast on NPR. Smiley had already become a contributing editor to *USA Weekend Magazine*, was contracted to write books for Doubleday and for his own imprint, Smiley Books, and he continued his other activities.

Smiley made additional history in 2004 when he became host of *Tavis Smiley*, his talk show on the Public Broadcasting System (PBS). When he chose to base the program in Los Angeles, it became the first national PBS program to originate from the West Coast. Smiley was also invited back to his hometown to receive an honorary doctorate from Indiana University-Kokomo.

In September 2004 Smiley celebrated his fortieth birthday and was honored by Texas Southern University in Houston, Texas, when it established the Tavis Smiley School of Communications and the Tavis Smiley Center for Professional Media Studies. This made him the youngest African American ever to have a professional school and center named for him on a college or university campus. Smiley expressed his appreciation by presenting a $1 million gift to the center.

Smiley resigned from the NPR position in December 2004, stating his view that the public radio network was not fully committed to diversity and multiple viewpoints in its programming. He continued his other obligations, with the assistance of The Smiley Group, his organization of associates based in Los Angeles.

Tavis Smiley has accepted challenges, overcome setbacks and obstacles, and created numerous opportunities to, in his words, "encourage, empower, and enlighten" others through his gifts as a communicator. He is considered one of the important political voices of his generation, a person who maintains faith and hope regarding the possibilities for positive change in the African American community, in the United States, and in the world.

REFERENCES

Books

French, Ellen Dennis. "Tavis Smiley." *Contemporary Black Biography*. Vol. 20. Ed. Shirelle Phelps. Farmington Hills, Mich.: Gale Group, 1999.

York, Jennifer M., ed. *Who's Who among African Americans*. 17th ed. Farmington Hills, Mich.: Thomson Gale, 2004.

Online

The HistoryMakers. "Tavis Smiley Biography." http://www.thehistorymakers.com/biography/biography.asp?bioindex=78&category=media... (Accessed 9 February 2005).

National Association for the Advancement of Colored People. "NAACP 2000." http://www.naacp.org/news/2000/2000-09-09.html (Accessed 14 February 2005).

National Newspaper Publishers Association. "Tavis Smiley Responds to BET." http://www.nnpa.org/nnpanewsite/newswire/3-26-01/TavisResponds.txt (Accessed 14 February 2005).

Public Broadcasting Service. "About the Show: All about Tavis Smiley." http://www.pbs.org/kcet/tavissmiley/about/ (Accessed 29 November 2004).

Smiley, Tavis. "How a Pink Slip Can Fire You Up." *USA Weekend Magazine*, 2 September 2001. http://www.usaweekend.com/01_issues/010902/010902smiley.html (Accessed 29 November 2004).

Tavis Smiley web site. http://www.tavistalks.com (Accessed 29 November 2004).

The Smiley Group, Incorporated. "About Tavis Smiley—Complete Biography." http://www.tavsitalks.com/TTcom/about_02.html (Accessed 29 November 2004).

TV Barn. "Black Entertainment Television Terminates Contract with BET Tonight Host Tavis Smiley; Will Use Guest Hosts Until Next Fall." http://www.tvbarn.com/2001/03/23.shtml (Accessed 14 February 2005).

Fletcher F. Moon

Robert Lloyd Smith
1861–1942

Organization executive, politician

Robert Lloyd Smith is responsible for the socio-economic uplift of thousands of African Americans living in Texas, Oklahoma, and Arkansas at the onset of the twentieth century. A man who championed hard work and education, Smith sought the betterment of African Americans through a host of professional vehicles. Evolving from an educator to a politician to a highly successful businessman, Smith epitomized the African American's industrious nature.

Born free in Charleston, South Carolina on January 8, 1861 to parents Francis Arthur and Mary Hamilton (Talbot) Smith, Smith was groomed at elite schools with those who eventually increased the black bourgeois as doctors, lawyers, businessmen, and teachers. At Avery Normal Institute in Charleston, Smith received an education that was modeled by missionaries in the classical tradition: students studied history, government, economics, languages and literature, methods of teaching, natural philosophy, and physiology, as well as applied subjects such as farming methods and sewing and cooking. Smith later enrolled in the University of South Carolina in 1875, but when the institution began denying African American applicants in 1877, he transferred to Atlanta University, later known as Clark Atlanta University, earning his bachelor of science degree in English and mathematics in 1880.

Becomes an Educator

After graduating from Atlanta University, Smith gravitated towards the teaching profession, a path that many alumni of Avery Normal Institute embarked upon. Unfortunately, in the 1870s, African American teachers were hired primarily in the rural areas of the South where schools floundered due to a lack of funding, poor attendance, dilapidated buildings, and scarce materials. The only recourse for aspiring teachers was to either travel north or west. Smith decided to venture west to Texas.

In Oakland, Texas, a small town midway between Houston and San Antonio, Smith began teaching at Oakland Normal School in Freedsmantown, the area of town predominately populated by African Americans. Founded in 1882, the mission of the Oakland Normal School was to prepare African Americans for the teaching profession. In 1885, when the city consisted of approximately two hundred residents, Smith became the principal of the school and continued to work for racial

progress. During this time, Smith also became an aide to Booker T. Washington, who also believed in the liberating effect of a standard education. The two men developed a close connection which is evident in their written correspondence.

Serves in Texas Legislature

In 1894 Smith was elected to the twenty-fourth legislature in Texas as a Republican. Ironically, his election to the state legislature was the result of overwhelming support from a predominately white Colorado County at a time when few African Americans and Republicans were elected to public office in Texas. In 1896, he was reelected. Never wavering from his commitment to his race, he consistently introduced legislation pertaining to increasing educational opportunities for African American Texans, particularly those opportunities resulting from the advancement of Prairie View Normal School, a historically black college founded in 1879 now known as Prairie View Agricultural & Mechanical University.

Smith later returned to Prairie View to teach when his political life ended. From 1902 to 1909, Smith was appointed deputy U.S. marshal for the Eastern District of Texas by President Theodore Roosevelt. However, after the election of William Taft, Smith was removed from his post. He never held a public office again, and seventy years passed before another African American was elected to the Texas state legislature.

Excels in Business

While Smith lived in Oakland, he noticed an unsettling trend in the business affairs of the city's farmers. Not only were the majority of farmers steeped in debt, but also their homes and farms were in disrepair. To combat this problem, Smith founded the Farmers' Home Improvement Society in 1890, which was aimed at eradicating the oppressive sharecropper system while generating wealth through savings, implementing more efficient farming practices, and emphasizing the importance of creating cooperative-business networks.

In eight years, the membership of the society rose to approximately 1,800 members, and by 1909 the society could boast of approximately 21,000 members from Texas, Oklahoma, and Arkansas. The success of the society catapulted many African Americans to the middle, and even upper, class, as the total assets of its members swelled to well over $1 million. As a result of the society's success, Smith founded several other cooperative institutions. They include a truck growers' union; an agricultural college at Wolfe City founded in 1906; the Farmers' Improvement Bank in Waco, founded in 1911; and the Woman's Barnyard Auxiliaries.

In 1907, due to his savvy business acumen, Smith was elected the first president of the Texas branch of the National Negro Business League. Founded by Booker T.

Washington in 1900, the National Negro Business League sought to manifest Washington's ideologies of self-reliance and racial solidarity through all means of African American commerce. Its membership consisted of upwardly mobile African Americans engaged in business across the country. During this time, Smith continued to create businesses, such as a factory for manufacturing overalls, while still maintaining an active role in a host of black fraternal orders. In 1915, he organized the state's Cooperative Extension Program for Negroes and became its first director while he was teaching at Prairie View. As director of the organization, Smith taught African American farmers improved agricultural methods.

Although Smith's businesses and the Farmers' Home Improvement Society flourished for nearly twenty years, after the Great Depression they gradually declined. For the remainder of his life, however, he was steadfast in his commitment to advancing the business practices of African Americans. When he died in 1942, Smith was survived by his second wife, Ruby Cobb, whom he married in 1919, and their two adopted children, Roscoe Smith, who worked as a cashier of the Farmers' Improvement Bank at Waco, and Olive Bell, who taught at the Farmers' Improvement Agricultural College.

REFERENCES

Books

Brewer, John M. *Negro Legislators of Texas and Their Descendants.*Austin, TX: Jenkins, 1970.

Rice, Lawrence D. *The Negro in Texas,1874-1900: A History of the Negro in Texas Politics from Reconstruction to Disfranchisement.* Baton Rouge, La.: Louisiana State University, 1971.

Online

Rice, Lawrence D. "Robert L. Smith 1861-1942." Handbook of Texas Online. www.tsha.utexas.edu/handbook/online/articles/SS/fsm37.html (Accessed 15 January 2006).

Irvin Weathersby, Jr.

Stephen Smith
c. 1795–1873

Entrepreneur, abolitionist

The colorful, rags-to-riches saga of Stephen Smith traces his rise from slavery and poverty to wealth. Smith learned the lumber business while still a slave and,

---

Chronology	
1795?	Born near Harrisburg, Pennsylvania
1801	Indentured to General Thomas Boude
1816	Purchases his freedom; opens lumber business in Columbia, Pennsylvania; purchases release from indenture; marries Harriet Lee
1830s	Moves to Philadelphia and expands his enterprises
1834	Becomes one of the first black agents for *Freedom's Journal*; attends national convention of free people of color in New York; white mob attacks his office and spurs race riot
1835	Attends national convention of free people of color in Philadelphia
1836	Joins general Conference of the African Methodist Episcopal church
1837	Attends first meeting of the Pennsylvania Anti-Slavery Society
1838	Ordained to preach in the AME church
1853	Attends national meeting of Pennsylvania Convention of Colored Citizens
1873	Dies in Philadelphia on November 4

---

when free, owned a thriving lumber enterprise. Smith found a way to manage his various business ventures and at the same time become immersed in antislavery and religious activities. Called the richest antebellum black, he shared his wealth generously with a number of institutions.

Born near Harrisburg, Pennsylvania, in Dauphin County around 1795, Stephen Smith was the son of a slave woman, Nancy Smith; his father was unknown. Young Stephen was indentured to General Thomas Boude on July 10, 1801, when he was four or five years old. Boude was a former Revolutionary War officer from Lancaster County, Pennsylvania who allowed Smith to manage his entire lumber business as Smith approached manhood. Smith borrowed $50 on January 3, 1816 for the purpose of purchasing his freedom, and in that same year he purchased release from his indenture. On November 17, 1816 Smith married Harriet Lee, who worked as a servant in the Jonathan Mifflin home. Already equipped with entrepreneurial skills, Smith opened a lumber business and became involved in lucrative real estate operations while his wife operated an oyster and refreshment house.

Stephen Smith became involved in civil rights activities early on. He opposed the policies of the American Colonization Society and demonstrated his opposition in 1831, when he led free blacks in Columbia in a public meeting. In 1834, Smith joined such men as David Ruggles, John Peck, Abraham Shadd, and John B. Vashon who were the first black agents for *Freedom's Journal* and later for *The Emancipator*. They were asked to secure subscriptions to the papers and collect what were called arrearages.

The astute businessman opened a lumber business in Columbia, Pennsylvania, and soon prospered. The risky work on the Underground Railroad did not intimidate such abolitionists as Smith and William Whipper. These two abolitionists and businessmen of Columbus, Pennsylvania escaped bodily harm and jail sentences for secreting slaves. Smith's success in real estate ventures and work as an abolitionist disturbed whites who led a mob in an attack on his office in August 1834, spurring a race riot, followed by a second one in October. They wanted to frighten Smith and force him and other black real-estate owners to sell their property below market value and leave town. They also accused Smith of inflating the value of his property. William F. Worner's account of the Columbia riots noted the letter that Smith received in 1835: "You must know that your presence is not agreeable, and the less you appear in the assembly of the whites the better it will be for your black hide, as there are great many in this place that would think your absence from it a benefit, as you are considered an injury to the real value of property in Columbia. You have [sic] better take the hint." In the 1830s, Smith and several antebellum blacks were members of various boards; for Smith, it was the Columbia Bank. He may have been the bank's largest stockholder, yet he could not become president due to bank rules preventing blacks from holding that post. His status, however, allowed him to name the white man who would be president.

Becomes Successful in Real Estate

When Smith moved to Philadelphia in the late 1830s, he continued to hold extensive real estate and a lumber enterprise in Columbia. He maintained his business in Columbia with William Whipper in charge. In Philadelphia, Smith lived at 921 Lombard Street, the home that his friend, Robert Purvis, sold to him. Later, Stephen and Harriet Smith also had a summer home in Cape May, New Jersey.

There Smith increased his real estate investment and became more successful. Entering a partnership with Ulysses B. Vidal, his wife's nephew, the men owned a large coal and lumber yard. The wealthy Smith owned $18,000 worth of stock in the Columbia Railroad while his stock in the Columbia Bridge Company was valued at $9,000.

Smith was also involved extensively in land speculation and development. In addition to the real estate that he owned in Columbia and in Lancaster, he owned fifty-two brick homes in Philadelphia. "Black Steve," as he came to be known, made wise choices and was held in high regard as a real estate dealer. He sought out bargains when property changed hands and was around to bid on property to be sold. In time, his properties in Philadelphia were valued at $50,000. Smith became the wealthiest American black in the North prior to the Civil War.

Urban land transportation was an important enterprise in the antebellum period, and several blacks had their own conveyances. Among these, the development of the

railroad marked the onset of industrial revolution. Both Stephen Smith and William Goodrich, of York, Pennsylvania, seized the opportunity to benefit from the railroad by establishing their own railroad enterprises. By 1850, Smith's firm had twenty-two fine merchantmen cars that ran from Philadelphia to Baltimore. Goodrich had considerable interest in the Baltimore Railroad's branch in Lancaster, Pennsylvania, and in 1849 he owned ten first-rate merchandise railroad cars, thus operating a profitable business. Both Smith and Goodrich aided fugitive slaves who had escaped the South by hiding them in a false end of a boxcar. The men lived in Pennsylvania—Smith in Lancaster County and Goodrich in York County—and Maryland, a slave state, touched its border.

According to Quarles in *Black Abolitionists*, Smith was listed in Wilbur H. Siebert's monumental "Directory of the Names of Underground Railroad Operators," which Siebert said contained 143 blacks. The list included Frederick Douglass, George T. Downing, Robert Purvis, Charles B. Ray, and William Whipper. In 1851, John Brown, who had an all-consuming passion for the abolition of slavery, sought to recruit both black leaders and the black rank-and-file to assist him in his various efforts toward that cause. He was especially interested in the support of such men as Frederick Douglass, Martin R. Delany, Henry Highland Garnet, Jermain W. Loguen, William Still, and Smith. In 1858, Smith hosted Brown in his residence for one week, apparently to discuss abolitionist activities.

Smith attended national conventions of the free people of color held in New York in 1834 and in Philadelphia in 1835. He helped to organize the American Reform Society and was one of seven blacks who attended the first meeting of the Pennsylvania Anti-Slavery Society in 1837. He also attended national meetings of the Pennsylvania State Convention of Colored Citizens, of which he was a member, in Rochester (1853) and in Philadelphia (1855). Smith supported the temperance movement. He held offices in such organizations as the Odd Fellows; Social, Civic, and Statistical Association; Grand Tabernacle of the Independent Order of Brothers and Sisters of Love and Charity; and the Union League Association.

As a philanthropist, Smith contributed much to the Institute of Colored Youth in Pennsylvania, the Home for Destitute Colored Children, and the House of Refuge. He joined white Quakers in establishing the House for Aged and Infirm Colored Persons, which was renamed the Stephen Smith Home for the Aged. A religious man as well, in 1832 Smith bought a church building for the Mount Zion African Methodist Episcopal congregation, and in 1836 he joined the general Conference of the African Methodist Episcopal church, becoming ordained to preach in 1838. He built several other churches, including one each in Chester and Cape May, New Jersey. Smith was a member of Philadelphia's historic Bethel African Methodist Church, known as Mother

Bethel. Having been ordained early on, he preached at Bethel's sister churches in Philadelphia.

Smith was a mulatto of medium size and a strong build and had pronounced features. He was described as quiet, stubborn man with principles who lived by his Christian creed. He remained courageous and patient even as he survived occasional white persecution. Smith died in Philadelphia on November 4, 1873, and was buried in one of the sites that he had supported financially, Olive Cemetery. His death brought public recognition for his efforts in race reform and his success as a wealthy black entrepreneur.

REFERENCES

Books

Fishel, Leslie H., Jr. "Stephen Smith." In *American National Biography*. Eds. John A. Garraty and Mark C. Carnes. Vol. 29. New York: Oxford University Press, 1999.

Ingham, John N. and Lynne B. Feldman. *African-American Business Leaders: A Biographical Dictionary*. Westport, Conn.: Greenwood Press, 1994.

Kranz, Rachel. *African-American Business Leaders and Entrepreneurs*. New York: Facts on File, 2004.

McCormick, Richard P. "Stephen Smith." In *Dictionary of American Negro Biography*. Eds. Rayford W. Logan and Michael R. Winston. New York: Norton, 1982.

Quarles, Benjamin. *Black Abolitionists*. New York: Oxford University Press, 1969.

Walker, Juliet E. K. *The History of Black Business in America: Capitalism, Race, Entrepreneurship*. New York: Macmillan Library Reference USA, 1998.

Worner, William F. "The Columbia Race Riots." Lancaster County Historical Society Papers 26, No. 8 (October 1922): 175-87. Cited in Juliet E. K. Walker. *The History of Black Business in America: Capitalism, Race, Entrepreneurship*. New York: Macmillan Library Reference USA, 1998, p. 124.

Jessie Carney Smith

Tubby Smith
1951–

Basketball coach

Tubby Smith is one of just six coaches to have led three different programs into the NCAA tournament's sweet sixteen, capped by the 1997-98 University of Kentucky squad that won a national title. In thirteen

Tubby Smith

seasons, he has never posted a losing record, and his teams have qualified for the NCAA tournament eleven straight times. He became one of the highest paid collegiate coaches in the profession, as well as one of the most generous.

Orlando Henry Smith was born in Scotland, Maryland on June 30, 1951 to Guffrie and Parthenia Smith. The sixth of seventeen children, Orlando grew up on a farm on the tip of the southwestern peninsula. Orlando acquired his nickname "Tubby" early on, owing to his delight in bathing in an old utility tub. Guffrie Smith, who had been awarded a Purple Heart during World War II while serving in Italy, was a farmer who worked several other jobs in order to support his large, but close-knit brood, including barber, school bus driver, construction worker, and maintenance man. Though the children were expected to complete their fair share of farm chores, the elder Smiths were keen on seeing their offspring attend school. Tubby attended segregated schools, including George Carver High School, until transferring to the newly consolidated and integrated Great Mills High School in tenth grade. At Great Mills, Smith played football, basketball, and track, earning all-state honors on the court in 1969, his senior season.

Although Smith was recruited by and signed to play basketball at the University of Maryland, a coaching change in 1969 resulted in the scholarship being

Chronology

1951	Born in Scotland, Maryland on June 30
1973	Accepts first coaching job at Great Mills High School as head coach
1979	Joins the staff of head coach J. D. Barnett at Virginia Commonwealth University
1991	Accepts first head coaching job at the University of Tulsa
1995	Becomes first black head basketball coach at the University of Georgia
1997	Becomes the University of Kentucky's first black head basketball coach
1998	Coaches Kentucky to an NCAA championship and a 35-4 record
2003	Wins 10 national coach of the year honors after leading Kentucky to a 32-4 record

rescinded. Fortunately, Smith was offered a scholarship by High Point College, a small, Methodist-affiliated school in High Point, North Carolina. Having grown up in a Methodist church, Smith found the college to be a good fit. He excelled in basketball at High Point, where he was a four-year letter winner (from 1970 to 1973) and All-Carolina Conference selection as a senior. This despite the fact that he played under three different head coaches, including J. D. Barnett, who would later play a vital role in Smith's coaching career. Additionally, Smith was honored by being named a team co-captain for his junior season and team captain his senior season. Smith graduated from High Point in 1973 with a B.S. degree in health and physical education.

After graduation, Smith headed home, hoping to be drafted by the NBA or at least get a chance to try out with the league's Baltimore Bullets. Neither of those opportunities, however, came to pass. Instead, a slightly different opportunity arose when the superintendent of Great Mills High School approached Smith when the head-coaching job opened. Rather than following through with his fall-back plan to pursue a master's degree before moving into coaching, Smith jumped at the chance to immediately become a head coach. At Great Mills, with the added difficulties of learning on the job and having to coach some of his own brothers and other relatives, Smith compiled a 46-36 record in four years. From there, he returned to North Carolina, where he led Hoke County High School, located in Raeford, to a two-year record of 28-18.

In 1979, Smith was able to make the leap to college coaching when he was chosen to become an assistant coach at Virginia Commonwealth University by J. D. Barnett, Smith's former coach at High Point College. It was under Barnett that Smith began formulating his long-term coaching philosophy. Smith would later say in a news release for Hawaii Pacific University: "I learned the game of basketball from J.D., and still use defensive and offensive plays at Kentucky that he taught me. He has a

brilliant mind, is a great motivator, and is someone I still consult with." In all, Smith spent seven years at VCU, the first six under Barnett. VCU enjoyed a 144-64 record while Smith was on the staff, winning three Sun Belt Conference championships and making the NCAA tournament field five times.

Smith's next stop was the University of South Carolina, where for three seasons he was an assistant coach under head coach George Felton. The Gamecocks posted a 53-35 record during Smith's stay. A decade later, Smith would reverse the roles by hiring Felton as an assistant at the University of Kentucky from 1998 to 2000. When Rick Pitino was building his staff at the University of Kentucky in 1989, he took the advice of athletic director C. M. Newton and brought Smith in as an assistant. Newton had been impressed with Smith while the former was the head basketball coach at Vanderbilt University and the latter was an assistant at South Carolina. Smith worked for Pitino from 1989 through 1991, during the time that Pitino laid the foundation for reversing the fortunes of Kentucky basketball, returning it to the lofty heights of previous eras. At each stop, Smith added to, and developed, his coaching strategies. He also learned to network in the profession. In a 1999 interview with *Scholastic Coach & Athletic Director*, Smith is quoted as saying: "It always goes back to the people you meet. The relationships you develop mean so much down the road. Good people don't burn bridges behind them. They build bridges. I know that concept has helped me every step of the way."

Collegiate Head Coach at Last

When Smith was offered the head-coaching job at the University of Tulsa in 1991, he felt he was ready to take the next step in coaching. However, he did have some misgivings due to the circumstances leading to the vacancy. The firing of one of his mentors, J. D. Barnett, had led to the creation of the opening. Smith accepted the position but faced the difficult task of taking over a team with just five returnees. His first two seasons with the Golden Hurricanes were sometimes trying, but he still managed to guide them to winning records, a 17-13 team was followed by a 15-14 team. Smith's final two Tulsa squads were a different story. Those teams had identical 15-3 conference records, both taking first place in the MVC and qualifying for the NCAA tournament. In addition, Smith was named MVC coach of the year both seasons. The 1993-94 team finished with a 23-8 mark with their NCAA run ending in the sweet sixteen. Similarly, the 1994-95 team advanced to the sweet sixteen, finishing with a 24-8 record that resulted in the third best win-total in school history. That final Smith-coached Tulsa squad finished with an impressive fifteenth ranking in the final *CNN/USA Today* poll. In four years, Smith compiled a 73-49 record at the Oklahoma school.

The University of Georgia came calling after witnessing Smith's quick turnaround of the Tulsa program. Smith signed on as the first black head coach in school history and immediately produced results. In Smith's first season, 1995-96, he coached the Bulldogs to a 21-10 record in the Southeastern Conference and took the team to the NCAA tournament, where it made it to the sweet sixteen. The next season, Georgia improved its record despite losing eight seniors, including the starting five. Their 24-9 record equaled the school record for wins in a season. Also, those back-to-back 20-win seasons were the first in Bulldog basketball annals. Making those two years even sweeter for Smith was the fact that his son, Orlando Guffrie Gibson Smith, or G.G., was a point guard and a key member of the team. The Bulldogs were ranked seventeenth in the final AP poll heading into the 1996-97 NCAA Tournament with a number three seed but were upset in the first round. That 45-19 two-year record, however, achieved with different starting line-ups, drew attention from the University of Kentucky (UK).

C. M. Newton, UK's athletic director, who had been instrumental in bringing Smith to Kentucky as an assistant under Rick Pitino, was now determined to steal Smith away from Georgia to head one of the most successful programs in collegiate history. Pitino, who was headed to Boston to coach the NBA's Celtics, initially supported the hiring of former assistant Billy Donovan, who had since become head coach at the University of Florida. Eventually, Newton's overwhelming support for Smith caused Pitino to endorse Smith's courting, even calling Smith himself to convince him to take the job. However, Kentucky had once been the home of legendary coach Adolph Rupp, who had had a reputation for racism. Even in the late-1990s, the possible hiring of Smith fueled controversy across the Bluegrass. Nevertheless, Newton interviewed only Smith and offered him the position. After a certain amount of soul-searching, Smith agreed to jump SEC institutions to take over the helm of the storied program. The University of Kentucky's athletic association unanimously approved the hiring in a mere seven minutes. Thus, Smith became the first black head coach in the program's history.

If winning will silence one's harshest critics, then Smith quickly closed the mouths of any Kentuckians doubting his abilities prior to his first season. In spite of a major loss of talent from Pitino's 1995-96 NCAA champions and 1996-97 NCAA runners-up (those teams lost six players to the NBA alone), Smith coached his young charges to take the regular season SEC title, as well as the SEC tournament title. Kentucky entered the NCAA tournament as a No. 2 seed and rolled through the first three games before colliding with top-seeded Duke University in the NCAA's South Region final. Down by 18 points in the first half and still trailing by 17 points midway through the second, the Wildcats rallied for an improbable two-point victory. The final four semi-final was similarly dramatic, as Kentucky came back from a five-point halftime deficit to beat Stanford University by one point in overtime. When the University of Utah led Kentucky by 10 points at halftime of the title game, it

looked dire; no team had ever recovered from more than eight points down in a final. The "Comeback Cats," however, once again proved their resiliency, fighting back to post a nine-point win and grab a national title at the Alamodome in San Antonio. Plus, Smith was able to share it with his second son, Saul, a freshman point guard on the 35-4 team. After the season several individual honors rolled in for Smith, including National Coach of the Year by *Basketball Weekly.*

In the six seasons completed after winning the NCAA title, Smith guided the Wildcats to SEC championships in 2000, 2001 and 2003, as well as SEC tournament championships in 1999, 2001, 2003 and 2004. Through 2004, all seven of his Kentucky squads qualified for the NCAA tournament and none has ever bowed out in the first round, while two have reached the elite eight. None of his Wildcat teams has won fewer than twenty-two games in a season and his cumulative record at the Lexington-based institution is 191-52, for a 78.6 winning percentage. The 2002-03 squad spent much of the year at number one, finishing 32-4, with a number one seed in the NCAA tournament. Though that team came up short in the NCAA regional final, Smith's coaching was universally lauded that season. He won coach of the year honors from AP, USBWA, Naismith, *Basketball Times, The Sporting News*, NABC, ESPN, Foxsports.com, the Black Coaches Association and College Sports Television in what may have been the biggest ever sweep of national coaching awards. Following the season, Smith signed a new eight-year contract running through 2011 that would be worth upwards of $2 million per year.

In addition to sons G. G. and Saul, Tubby and Donna Smith have a daughter, Shannon, and a third son, Brian, who like his father and brothers before him, has pursued basketball, specifically point guard. After a notable career at Lexington Catholic High School, where he graduated in 2003, Brian received interest from several collegiate programs and chose the University of Mississippi. At Ole Miss, Brian faced his father twice a season playing at the rival SEC school.

Smith's involvement with the community has been exemplary. He established the Tubby Smith Foundation to assist underprivileged children and between 2000 and 2005 raised more than $1.5 million. Given his and his wife's generosity, the United Way created in the summer of 2001 an award in their honor: The Donna and Tubby Smith Community Spirit Award. Not surprisingly, the Smiths were the inaugural recipients, in part for their $125,000 contribution to the organization that year, which was the highest of any individual contributor across the state. Now given annually, the award honors anyone whose outstanding service positively affects central Kentucky.

Tubby Smith is clearly much more than a record of scores. He is a devoted husband and father, a dedicated coach, and a committed community leader. Nevertheless, the numbers do speak volumes. Through the 2003-04 season, Smith compiled a 315-114 record, for a dazzling 73.4 winning percentage in thirteen seasons as a head at three Division I basketball programs. With the exception of his first two teams at Tulsa, he has taken all his teams to the NCAA tournament field. Eight of those eleven squads made it as far as the sweet sixteen, highlighted by the 1997-98 team, which cut down the nets as NCAA tournament champions.

REFERENCES

Books

"Tubby Smith." *Contemporary Black Biography*. Vol. 18. Detroit, Mich.: Gale Research, 1998.

Periodicals

DeCourcy, Mike. "Ungodly Pressure." *The Sporting News* 98:10 (3 January 2000): 10-11.

Evans, Howie. "Smith's Hiring at Kentucky Sets Off a Storm of Controversy." *New York Amsterdam News*, 17 May 1997.

Mazzola, Gregg. "Still Up-Tempo." *Scholastic Coach & Athletic Director* 68 (April 1999): 46-55.

Wahl, Grant. "Tubby's Terrors." *Sports Illustrated* 98:10 (10 March 2003): 34-37.

Wolff, Alexander. "State of Anxiety." *Sports Illustrated* 96:1 (7 January 2002): 54-57.

Online

"Coach Bio: Tubby Smith: Men's Basketball." Kentucky Wildcats / The Official Site of University of Kentucky Athletics. http://www.ukathletics.com/index.php?s=&change_well_id=2&url_article_id=10276 (Accessed 4 December 2004).

"J.D. Barnett Named Athletics Director and Men's Basketball Coach at Hawaii Pacific (24 July 2004)." Hawaii Pacific University. http://web1.hpu.edu/index.cfm?section=seawarriorsports4220 (Accessed 5 January 2005).

Kevin C. Kretschmer

Will Smith
1968–

Actor, rap musician

Fun-loving and funny, Will Smith captivates audiences in a variety of media: music, television, and film. By his twelfth birthday, Smith was known as a rap musician. He and Jeffrey Townes, as D.J. Jazzy Jeff and the Fresh Prince, recorded several platinum albums and won the first Grammy ever presented for the Best Rap Performance. Smith also starred in the television series *The Fresh Prince of Bel Air*. Then he moved into film, taking lead roles in such movies as *Independence Day*, *Men in Black*, and *Ali*.

Born September 25, 1968, Smith remembers his home as a supportive and solid environment and credits his parents with teaching him right from wrong. His father, Willard Christopher Smith, owned a refrigeration business, and his mother, Caroline Smith, served on the Philadelphia board of education. In Wynnefield, Pennsylvania, a suburb of West Philadelphia, the couple raised four children: Pam, Will Jr., and twins Ellen and Harry. Smith's parents created a loving environment for their children. Even when they divorced in Smith's thirteenth year, the entire family remained close.

Smith's parents played major roles in his life. He described them to Lynn Norment as "the only people [he had] ever idolized." His father, a veteran Air Force drill sergeant, focused on discipline. Smith recalls the routine of making tight hospital corners and bouncing coins off his bed. He told Janet Cawley that the question, "What do you think we could do to assist you in keeping your room clean?" sent him scrambling. But because of that discipline, he never tried drugs or became involved in some of the serious troubles many teens go through. One time, their father gave Will and Harry the time-consuming and challenging task of taking apart and rebuilding a crumbling brick wall. After they had completed the project, he pointed out that they had accomplished something that they had not thought possible. This memorable experience helped Smith find his self-confidence.

Caroline Smith helped her children learn to value education. The Smiths sent their children to a Catholic school, Our Lady of Lourdes, because it offered the best education available in their community. His mother encouraged Will's love of reading. He found himself especially drawn to Dr. Seuss books, which he later noted carried a hip-hop sound.

Music also played a strong role in the Smith household. Will played piano, his father played guitar, and the family often engaged in jam sessions. In 1979, Smith heard the Sugar Hill Gang's song "Rapper's Delight." He began to write and perform rap music for local parties and church programs. In 1981, he met Jeffrey Townes, and they began recording in the Townes' basement.

Smith, who graduated from Overbrook High School in 1986, admits he had trouble paying attention in class. His winsome attitude in seeking pardon for late assignments gained him the title "Prince Charming" with his teachers. Going to school first among mostly whites and then among mostly blacks helped Smith develop interpersonal skills.

Will Smith

Massachusetts Institute of Technology (MIT) offered Smith a scholarship, and the Milwaukee School of Engineering accepted him into their program. But when decision time came along, Smith chose not to attend college. He soothed his mother's disappointment about this decision with a signed record contract and the reassurance that he had a workable plan.

DJ Jazzy Jeff and the Fresh Prince's first album, *Rock the House*, released in 1987, sold around 600,000 copies. Two singles became especially popular: "Girls Ain't Nothing but Trouble" and "Parents Just Don't Understand." In 1988, their album *He's the D.J., I'm the Rapper* sold three million copies and received the first Grammy ever given for Best Rap Performance.

The duo's early records contained some of the profanity expected of hip-hop music. But Smith told Nancy Collins, "My grandmother got ahold of my rap book, read it and wrote in the back: 'Dear Willard, truly intelligent people do not have to use these types of words to express themselves.'" Smith's recordings thereafter became known for their clean-cut lyrics, or what Dream Hampton called the "raised right" style of rap. When responding to criticism from rappers noted for their more violent content, Smith pointed out that his lyrics reflect his own experience, just as harsher lyrics reflect the reality of a different lifestyle.

And in This Corner, released in 1989, sold a million copies, and one of its songs, "I Think I Can Beat Mike Tyson," received a Grammy nomination. A 900-number set up for fans brought in about $10 million. Smith rapidly spent his millions on cars, expensive travel, jewelry, and shopping sprees. He explained to Janet Cawley, "'Being able to buy anything you want makes you a little crazy.'" Deeply in debt, he needed to tighten his spending habits and find a more dependable source of income.

Launches Television Career

In December 1989, Smith flew to Los Angeles to sing in NBC's *Disneyland's 35th Anniversary Celebration*. While there, he attended an *Arsenio Hall Show* and met producer Benny Medina, who oversaw the black music division of Warner Brothers Records. Medina had spent much of his early life in foster homes and juvenile detention centers and then found himself adopted by white parents and living in Beverly Hills. He approached Quincy Jones about making a television series around a similar theme. They found their star in Will Smith, and NBC gained a sitcom popular with both hip-hop and mainstream audiences.

The Fresh Prince of Bel Air ran for six seasons (1990-96). In the show, the character Will Smith moves from an East Coast ghetto to live with his rich aunt and uncle in Los Angeles. Smith's friend Jazzy Jeff appeared frequently in the series. New to acting and nervous, young Smith overcompensated by memorizing the entire script. But even in those first seasons, audiences responded to Smith's wit and charm. A *TV Guide* poll named Smith the "hippest teen on TV." In its second and third seasons, the show placed among Nielson's Top Twenty ratings.

Smith spent the first years of the show observing set dynamics, studying the genre, and building his acting skills. By the fourth season, he began producing the program, making significant changes to the scripts. In 1992, *Fresh Prince* won an NAACP Image Award for Best Situation Comedy. Smith's hilarious antics won him a Golden Globe Award nomination for best actor in a television series. By the show's sixth season, it had become one of the longest-running comedies on prime-time television. In 1996 and 1997, Smith received a nomination for an Image Award as outstanding lead actor in a comedy series.

During summer breaks, Smith had begun making movies and found that he liked the chance to become different characters in front of the camera. That experience made the television role seem confining. He decided to make the sixth season the final one, choosing to quit while the show maintained its broad popularity. Smith had also continued recording with Jeffrey Townes. One of Smith's favorite songs, "Summertime," from their album *Homebase* (1991), won a Grammy for Best Rap Performance. After releasing the album *Code Red* in 1993, Smith decided to quit recording—partially in protest to increasing violence in rap lyrics—and focus on his acting career.

In May 1992, Will married songwriter Sheree Zampino in Santa Barbara, California. They divorced in 1995 and share joint custody of son Trey-Will Smith III.

Early Movie Career

In one of his early films, *Where the Day Takes You* (1992), Smith played Manny, a homeless man wrestling with survival in Los Angeles. In 1993, he played Tea Cake Walters in *Made in America*, featuring Ted Dansen and Whoopi Goldberg. That same year, he prepared for his first dramatic role by working with an acting coach and a dialect coach. *Six Degrees of Separation* (1993), a film version of John Guare's Broadway play, starred Stockard Channing and Donald Sutherland. Playing the role of a hustler claiming status as Sidney Poitier's son Paul stretched Smith's acting skills. But he performed the part in a way that made critics note his versatility and depth as an actor.

In 1995's *Bad Boys*, Smith and Martin Lawrence played undercover cops. Their assignment involved recovering $100 million of heroin that had been stolen from the police department while also protecting a witness to a murder. Smith's portrayal of Mike Lowrey contributed to the film's box office success, bringing in $15.5 million the first weekend, and won him the ShoWest Award for Male Star of Tomorrow. The movie garnered $140 million worldwide and a nomination for an MTV Movie Award for the best on-screen duo. Smith and Lawrence formed a lifelong friendship.

In 1996, Smith took on the role of Marine Corps Captain Steven Heller in the science fiction film *Independence Day*. With stars Bill Pullman and Jeff Goldblum, Smith's character protected the earth from an alien invasion. The film became a number one hit at the box office, grossing $96 million during its first six days and $306.1 million by year's end. The year 1997 brought Smith an MTV Movie Award nomination for Best Male Performance and a Blockbuster Entertainment Award for favorite actor in a science fiction film.

Director Steven Spielberg sent a helicopter for Smith to talk about a new film, and Smith noted that an actor does not say no to Spielberg. As James Darrel Edwards III, or "Agent J," Smith joined Tommy Lee Jones in *Men in Black* to once again save the world. In 1998, Smith won a Blockbuster Entertainment Award for favorite actor in a science fiction film. He and Jones received nominations for best comedic performance and best on-screen duo in the MTV Movie Awards. Smith's performance of the title song on the movie soundtrack won another NAACP Image Award and his third Grammy.

Saddened by the murder of rap star Biggie Small, Smith returned to music and released a solo album in 1997, *Big Willie Style*, which sold eight million copies. The single "I Jiggy with It" reached top ten multi-platinum status. Smith wrote another song, "Just the Two of Us," for his son Trey. Smith considered it the best song he had written to date. He told Nancy Collins that he felt the emotions so strongly that he wrote the lyrics in five minutes. When he received a 1998 MTV Music Award for the song, he carried Trey to the podium with him.

Smith crowned a successful 1997 with a relatively secret wedding. On New Year's Eve, he and Jada Pinkett married. They housed their guests in Baltimore, Jada's hometown. On the morning of the wedding, the guests received envelopes containing directions to the location. They gave the envelopes to limousine drivers, who delivered them to The Cloisters, a sixty-five-year-old mansion featuring medieval architecture. When Smith arrived, he relaxed by playing chess before dressing for the ceremony. Jada had arrived earlier. The couple walked down the aisle together and gave each other away. They declared their love through letters they had written to each other. The family now includes son Jaden Christopher Syre and daughter Willow Camille Reign.

Continues Success

Smith released two more solo albums: *Willenium* in 1999 and *Born to Reign* in 2002. Dream Hampton observed that Smith "single-handedly created a space for 'fun' rap." Smith told Hampton, "Speaking proper English on a rap record, rhyming about being punched in the eye and taking it, not pulling out some giant gun—that's the hard part."

Smith appeared in a succession of hit movies. In the 1998 thriller *Enemy of the State*, he co-starred with Gene Hackman. Smith played Robert Clayton Dean, a labor lawyer targeted by mobsters, spies, and National Security agents. In 1999, he played James West in *Wild, Wild West*, prequel to the popular television series. The year 2000 brought *Men in Black: Alien Attack* and a starring role as a golf caddy in *The Legend of Bagger Vance*. Smith observed to Dream Hampton, "Golf is the ultimate sport. . . . It's the perfect blend of physical ability and mental prowess."

Awards kept coming. In 1997, Smith won the National Association of Theater Owners/ShoWest Award for International Box Office Achievement. In 1998, he received the Nickelodeon Kids' Choice Award for Best Male Actor. ShoWest presented him its 1999 Actor of the Year Award. That same year, he won three trophies at the American Music Awards: favorite male artist, favorite R&B album for *Big Willie Style*, and favorite pop-rock album for *Big Willie Style*. At the eleventh World Music Awards in Monte Carlo, Smith received four titles: world's best-selling pop male, R&B male, dance male, and rap male.

Stars in *Ali*

For seven years, Smith declined a role as Muhammad Ali. Smith feared this part, but director Michael Mann outlined a convincing plan to help him prepare for the role. Mann told Harry Haun: "I knew this is the only person who could do it. I knew the commitment." It took a telephone call from Ali himself to finally convince Smith to accept the challenge of playing the part.

Smith gained weight, trained in the boxing ring, and studied Ali's faith and his gestures and speech for over a year. No one doubled for him in the boxing ring. He specifically asked that Jada appear in the role of one of Ali's wives, Sonji Roi. Smith wanted to do the love scene with his own wife. In an interview with *People* magazine, Smith stated that when the movie premiered in 2001, Ali turned to him during the show and said, "'Man, you almost as pretty as I was.'" Smith won an Oscar nomination in 2002 and Best Male Performer at the MTV Movie Awards.

Smith wanted a role in John Grisham's *Runaway Jury*, but Grisham said no to Smith. Still, the movies, television shows, and music kept coming: *Men in Black II* in 2002, *Bad Boys II* in 2004. Also in 2004, Smith played Detective Del Spooner in *I, Robot*, a film based on Isaac Asimov's 1950s short stories. That same year, Smith lent his voice to a little fish named Oscar in the animated film *Shark Tale*. He and Jada created the sitcom *All of Us*, relating the adventures of a blended family. In 2005, Smith starred in *Hitch* as the dazzling date doctor who specialized in solving romantic woes. Smith also kept singing. He released a new album, *Lost and Found*, in March 2005.

Aware of his public responsibility, Will Smith has chosen to live his life in a way that honors the parents who gave him such a good start in life. Writers often note his solid confidence and his charm. He has focused his talents in music, television, and film, but Smith assured Nancy Collins: "'I'm headed for something greater. . . . Right now I make people laugh. It's an important service to make people feel good. But I want to be here for a bigger reason.'"

REFERENCES

Books

Johnson, Anne Janette, and Ashyia N. Henderson. "Will Smith." *Contemporary Black Biography*. Ed. Shirelle Phelps. Farmington Hills, Mich.: Gale Group, 1998.

Shelton, Sonya. "Will Smith." *Newsmakers: The People Behind Today's Headlines*. Ed. Sean R. Pollock. Farmington Hills, Mich.: Gale Group, 1998.

Periodicals

Cawley, Janet. "Topping the Charts and Saving the World." *Biography Magazine* 3 (July 1999): 34-39.

Collins, Nancy. "Will Smith." *Rolling Stone* 80 (1 December 1998): 62-67.

Giles, Jeff, and David Ansen. "Don't Mention the Oscars!" *Newsweek* 139 (4 February 2002): 54-61.

Norment, Lynn. "Will Smith." *Ebony* 51 (August 1996): 34-38.

Ritz, David. "Will Power." *Ebony* 23 (February 1993): 60-65.

Ting Yu, et al. "Pop Quiz with Will Smith." *People* 57 (1 April 2002): 24.

Tresniowski, Alex, et al. "Mr. Smith Takes a Bride." *People* 49 (19 January 1998): 52-56.

"Will Smith Explains Why He Decided to Play 'Ali' in a New Movie." *Jet* 101 (24 December 2001): 58-63.

Marie Garrett

John H. Smyth
1844–1908

Diplomat, lawyer, educator, editor

John Henry Smyth (Smythe in some sources) was an influential national and international figure during the late nineteenth and early twentieth centuries. Armed with excellent credentials in education, he taught school, was one of the nation's first African American civil service

Chronology

1844	Born in Richmond, Virginia on July 14
1862	Graduates from the Institute for Colored Youth
1870	Becomes a clerk in the Bureau of Refugees, Freedmen, and Abandoned Lands of the War Department; graduates from the Howard University Law School; works as a clerk in the Interior Department's Census Office; marries Fannie Shippen
1872	Works at the Treasury Department
1873	Works at the Freedmen's Savings and Trust Company in Washington and later at its Wilmington, North Carolina branch
1874	Passes law examination in Raleigh, North Carolina
1875	Member of North Carolina's Constitutional Convention
1876	Practices law in Washington
1877	Becomes a clerk in the Office of the Comptroller of the Treasury
1878	Appointed U.S. resident/consul general to Liberia
1882	Reappointed U.S. resident/consul general to Liberia
1892	Edits *The Reformer*
1897	Establishes the Manual Labor School
1908	Dies on September 5

employees, worked at Freedmen's Savings and Trust, practiced law, was a diplomat, edited an African American newspaper, and founded a reformatory school for African American youth.

On July 14, 1844, Smyth was born to Sully Smyth, a slave, and Ann Eliza Goode Smyth, a free woman, in Richmond, Virginia. Their son received reading lessons from an African American woman in Richmond, and subsequently his parents decided that he should continue his education in Philadelphia, a city where African American children attended private schools as early as 1770 and public schools as early as 1822. When Smyth was seven years old, he moved to Philadelphia and attended a Quaker school and then a public school prior to his father's death in 1857. Smyth, who had entered his teen years, then dropped out of school and worked as an errand boy at a dry goods store for one year.

In 1859, Smyth enrolled in the Institute for Colored Youth (ICY). Formerly known as the African Institute, the ICY was founded in 1837 by Quakers in order to provide post-secondary education to African Americans and was chartered in 1842. Subsequently the ICY was known as Cheyney University of Pennsylvania, which is the oldest historically black institution of higher learning in the United States. During Smyth's matriculation at ICY, Ebenezer D. Bassett was principal. Bassett later gained distinction as the first African American diplomat when President Ulysses S. Grant appointed him to be the U.S. minister resident/consul general to Haiti in 1869. Nine years later, Smyth followed in his former principal's footsteps when he was appointed U.S. minister resident/consul general to Liberia.

After Smyth graduated from the ICY on May 4, 1862, he enrolled at the Academy of Fine Arts in Philadelphia where he was the first African American student to be granted admission. Smyth, who had studied drawing and painting prior to his entrance to the academy, displayed talent as a landscape painter. Decades later, William J. Simmons, in the preface to his book, *Men of Mark* (1887), acknowledged his gratitude to Smyth, whose biography is included in Simmons' collection of 177 concise biographies of distinguished national and international men of African descent, "for assistance in sketches and pictures of E. W. Blyden and President W. W. Johnson."

In 1865, Smyth, who had worked in the china house of Tyndale and Mitchell, in Philadelphia, as well as for the army as a sutler's clerk, decided to pursue his thespian dream. He left Philadelphia for London, where armed with letters of introduction, he attempted to meet tragedians Ira Aldridge and Samuel Phelps. Whether Smyth met Phelps is not clear; however, Smyth's attempt to meet Aldridge proved futile. During Smyth's visit to London, Aldridge performed in St. Petersburg. Smyth, unable to afford to study acting, returned to the United States.

Takes Advantage of Various Career Opportunities

Upon his return to the United States, Smyth earned a living as a manual laborer until he obtained a teaching position in Wilkes-Barre, Pennsylvania. Smyth then enrolled in the Howard University Law School where John Mercer Langston was dean. (In 1877, Langston was appointed U.S. minister resident/consul general to Haiti one year before Smyth received his diplomatic assignment to Liberia.) In 1870, Smyth was appointed a clerk in the Bureau of Refugees, Freedmen, and Abandoned Lands of the War Department, and he graduated from the Howard University Law School. In August of the same year, Smyth resigned from the Bureau of Refugees in order to accept a position as clerk in the Interior Department's Census Office, and in 1872, he was employed by the Treasury Department.

One year later, Smyth began his employment with the Freedmen's Savings and Trust Company (FSTC), also known as the Freedmen's Bank, in Washington, D.C. The FSTC was the nation's first black bank, established by Congress in 1865 to help former slaves achieve financial independence. There were more than thirty bank branches in various states. Smyth, who was a clerk at Freedmen's, transferred to the Wilmington, North Carolina branch where he was a cashier. After the FSTC's demise in 1874, Smyth remained in Wilmington, passed a law examination administered by members of North Carolina's Supreme Court in Raleigh, and according to Simmons, "entered upon the practice of his profession." In 1875, he was a member of North Carolina's Constitutional Convention.

Smyth returned to Washington in 1876, practiced law for a year, and was appointed a clerk in the Office of the Comptroller of the Treasury. In 1878 President Rutherford B. Hayes, heeding the recommendations of Frederick Douglass (who was appointed U.S. resident/consul general to Haiti and chargé d'affaires to the Dominican Republic in 1889) and others, appointed Smyth U.S. minister resident/consul general to Liberia. Smyth held the diplomatic position until December 22, 1881, when Henry H. Garnet succeeded him. After Garnet's death in February 1882, President Chester Arthur reappointed Smyth minister resident/consul general to Liberia. Smyth then stayed in office until December 14, 1885. During his terms in office, the U.S. government allowed Smyth to lead the German Consulate at Monrovia for sixth months as well as the Belgian Consulate in Liberia. In honor of his contributions to Liberia, Smyth was awarded an honorary LL.D. degree from Liberia College, and on December 28, 1885, Liberian president Hilary R.W. Johnson appointed Smyth knight commander of the Liberian humane order of African redemption. Earlier that month, Smyth spoke at the Congress of Africa, held in Atlanta during December 13-15; the topic of Smyth's speech was "The African in Africa and the African in America."

Establishes the Manual Labor School

In 1892, Smyth became the editor of *The Reformer*, a Richmond-based African American newspaper. In 1897, he accepted another challenge after he and several other African American men, concerned with the plight of African American juvenile offenders in Virginia who were denied admittance to the reformatory for white boys and were being sent to jails and the penitentiary instead, formed the corporation known as the Negro Reformatory Association of Virginia (NRAV). After receiving contributions from people in Connecticut, Massachusetts, New York, Rhode Island, and Virginia, the corporation purchased the Broad Neck plantation in Hanover, Virginia. Also in 1897 Smyth, as head of the NRAV, founded the Manual Labor School which was one of the first African American reformatory schools in the South. The school admitted minors of both sexes. Smyth remained in charge of the school until his death in 1908. Twelve years later, Virginia assumed control of the Manual Labor School and its 1,800 acres. The former farmland where Smyth's school was established later became the site of the Hanover Juvenile Correctional Center; its secondary school is named the John H. Smyth High School. An additional tribute is found in Hanover County; a highway marker on Route 301 near the intersection with VA 605 contains a brief biography of Smyth.

In 1870, Smyth married Fannie Ellen Shippen, who was the daughter of Rev. John Shippen from Washington, D.C. She was Smyth's former student in Howard University's first elocution class. The Smyths were the parents of at least one child. Although information about Smyth is scarce in contemporary sources, he remains an important forefather of African American educators, diplomats, government employees, and lawyers.

REFERENCES

Books

Culp, D. W., ed. *Twentieth Century Negro Literature or A Cyclopedia of Thought on the Vital Topics Relating to the American Negro by One Hundred of America's Greatest Negroes.* 1902. Miami, Fla.: Mnemosyne Publishing Co., Inc., 1969.

Du Bois, W. E. B. *The Philadelphia Negro.* 1899. Millwood, N.Y.: Kraus-Thomson Org. Ltd., 1973.

——, ed. *Some Efforts of Negro Americans for Their Own Social Betterment. Report of an Investigation under the Direction of Atlanta University; Together with the Proceedings of the Third Conference for the Study of the Negro Problems, Held at Atlanta University, May 25-26, 1898.* Atlanta: Atlanta University Press, 1898.

Jackson Coppin, Fanny. *Reminiscences on School Life and Hints on Teaching.* Philadelphia: AME Book Concern, 1913.

Simmons, William J. "Hon. John H. Smythe, LL.B., LL.D." In *Men of Mark: Eminent, Progressive and Rising.* Cleveland: Geo. M. Rowell and Co., 1887.

Online

"John Henry Smyth." Virginia Department of Historic Resources. http://www.highwaymarker.org/signtext.cfm?sm=1692 (Accessed 14 March 2006).

Leopold, Robert S. "Hon. John H. Smyth." In *A Guide to Early African Collections in the Smithsonian Institution.* http://voom.si.edu/leopold/early_african_collections.txt (Accessed 14 March 2006).

"Liberia." U.S. Department of State. http://www.state.gov/r/pa/ho/po/com/10906.htm (Accessed 14 March 2006).

Linda M. Carter

Jimmie Lee Solomon
1947–

Baseball executive

Jimmie Lee Solomon established himself as one of the most influential executives in professional sports in the United States. As the executive vice president for baseball operations for Major League Baseball (MLB), Solomon had administrative responsibilities ranging from organizing the All-Star game to negotiating legal agreements between the major league franchises and the minor league farming system. Solomon's stellar college athletic career, law degree from Harvard, and years of experience working in the major leagues assured his success in this position and allowed critics in 2006 to tout him as the next commissioner of MLB.

Jimmie Lee Solomon was born and raised in Thompson, Texas, a small rural community approximately thirty-five miles southwest of Houston, with a population of approximately two hundred people. He and his five siblings grew up under the watchful eye of his father, Jimmie Lee Solomon Sr., his mother, Josephine, and his grandfather, Jeremiah. Solomon's grandfather, his earliest and most influential role model, was college educated and continually encouraged Jimmie Solomon to excel academically. Solomon's mother, who worked in the K-Mart in Houston, forty miles away from the family home, also stressed the importance of education. Solomon's father, however, was a cattle rancher and believed a man's worth was in what he did with his hands. He expected his sons to follow in his footsteps and become field hands. Bound by the rules of his father's house, young Solomon and his siblings had to help with the farm. Waking as early as four o'clock in the morning, Solomon would have to put out the hay, pick cotton, and perform other chores. Solomon's father was a strict disciplinarian and instilled a strong work ethic in his children. However, his experiences in the rural South only made Solomon more determined not to comply with his father's wishes.

Athletics and Academics Pave the Way

Playing sports became an outlet for the young Solomon. Ironically, baseball was not one of the sports Solomon participated in much as a youngster, despite idolizing sporting legend Willie Mays. Solomon showed great promise as a track athlete and exploited his speed on the football field. By the seventh grade he was already making history in what was still the largely segregated South, becoming the first black to start for the Lamar Junior High School football team; Solomon was their star running back. His success as an athlete continued through high school where he captained both the track and football teams. His prowess on the field was equaled by his performance in the classroom, and these ultimately earned him a scholarship to Dartmouth College in Hanover, New Hampshire.

Solomon entered Dartmouth College in 1974 as a history major and graduated with honors, but not before setting a school record for the sixty-meter dash and becoming an All-Ivy sprinter. He also played wide receiver for the football team, catching thirty-seven passes for 420 yards over two seasons. In 1978 when he graduated, Solomon has his sights set on playing professionally in the National Football League (NFL). He was not drafted but got a tryout with the Houston Oilers. To his great disappointment, he was one of the first players cut. Head coach Bum Phillips made it clear that he would have little hope of ever making it to the big league, so Solomon took the coach's advice and accepted an offer from Harvard to go to law school.

From the Playing Field to the Boardroom

Solomon graduated from Harvard with honors in 1981 and immediately started working for the prestigious law firm Baker and Hostetler, in Washington, D.C. Solomon was the firm's first black attorney. After eight years at Baker and Hostetler, Solomon became a partner. However, he eventually felt burnt out, so he began looking for another career opportunity, which came in the form of Major League Baseball. At around the same time that Solomon was looking for a new venture, the league was looking to fill the new executive position. While practicing law, Solomon had represented a number of clients in the sporting industry, including the NFL Management Council and some professional athletes and coaches. Solomon's love of sports had not disappeared, and he even toyed with the idea of becoming a sports agent, so when the offer to interview for the position with the MLB arose, Solomon took it. He applied for the post, was hired as director of minor league operations in 1991, and moved to the MLB's main offices in New York.

Solomon was responsible for a huge operation, including seventeen minor leagues, with over 170 teams and better than 4,500 players. Upon his appointment, however, Solomon found himself at the center of hostile contract negotiations between the major league franchises and the minor league teams they owned. The minor league teams had traditionally functioned as a farm system for the major league teams, providing a forum where players could be developed and prepared for entry into the majors. Rookies were often brought up to the majors from tryouts with minor league teams.

Additionally, athletes recovering from injuries and older athletes who were seeing out the remainder of their contracts found a home in the minor leagues. Before Solomon came on board, there had been contract negotiations in 1990. However, the proceedings had been disastrous and the relationship between the two groups was highly antagonistic.

Solomon set about resolving the conflict and dispelling any concerns the MBL executives had about an African American being able to function effectively when confronted with prejudice in any sectors of the league. Solomon took to the road with the intent of ensuring that major players in baseball could put a face behind the corporate decision-making. He went across the country visiting minor league coaches and managers and their ballparks. With the majority of the key figures in the minor leagues coming from the South or Southwest, Solomon was able to use his own southern background to communicate effectively and engender smooth working relationships.

Back in the office, Solomon was busy scrutinizing the 1990 professional baseball agreement. Solomon's legal expertise enabled him to iron out the flaws in the agreement that were causing trouble between the groups. Solomon was largely responsible for the successful completion of negotiations in 1997. Issues regarding player contracts, financing, and the renovation of minor league facilities were addressed, and the negotiations were heralded as a groundbreaking event in baseball. Forcing the majors to invest in more state-of-the-art facilities and better-kept arenas attracted an increased number of fans around the country. Indeed, during Solomon's tenure, attendance at minor league baseball games rose dramatically as did the value of teams and the players' salaries.

Personal Life Takes New Direction

Solomon never married. His father died of a heart attack in 1997 and his mother was placed in a nursing home in Virginia. However, an unexpected addition to Solomon's family came to him during a visit back to his former high school in the late 1980s to receive an alumni award. While there, Solomon was introduced to a teenage girl, his daughter. Tricia, who was being raised by her maternal grandmother, was the result of a brief union Solomon had before he left for college. Subsequently, Tricia began spending summer vacations with her father in Washington, D.C., and, in 1992 when she was seventeen, she moved to live with Solomon permanently.

Solomon's contribution to the MLB continued unfalteringly, and his accomplishments were rewarded. Solomon was promoted to senior vice president of baseball operations in 1995. Essentially every important decision in baseball passed across his desk. He was responsible for major and minor leagues, international baseball operations, the major league scouting bureau, the Arizona Fall League, and other special projects. One of those projects was the rejuvenation of minority participation in baseball, particularly blacks and Latinos. With the number of black players in the major leagues on par with those during the times of the earlier Negro Leagues, the MLB was looking for ways to bring baseball to the inner cities. Solomon oversaw the project, negotiating deals for the major league franchises to invest in their local communities and providing financial support for new facilities and equipment. The Rookie league, for kids twelve and under, and the Reviving Baseball in Inner Cities (RBI) league, for thirteen to eighteen year olds, were launched in cities across the country. However, Solomon's vision was larger than just new venues. The new developments are designed to provide educational and vocational opportunities, promoting academic success as well as an appreciation for baseball. Launching the Major League Baseball Youth Academy at Compton College in Compton, California in 2005 was a major landmark in Solomon's efforts.

Solomon continued to demonstrate his business savvy and leadership ability and was promoted again in 2001, this time to executive vice president of baseball operations; in 2006 he became the highest-ranking minority official in MLB. In addition to his other responsibilities he oversees on-field discipline, security, and facilities management. In the early 2000s, Solomon's accomplishments continued to mount, and many believed he would be the next commissioner of Major League Baseball.

REFERENCES

Periodicals

Davis, Kimberly. "Making a big-league pitch off the field: Jimmie Lee Solomon." *Ebony* (August 2005): 162.

Geffner, Michael P. "Major Minor." *Texas Monthly* (August 1997): 68.

"Jimmie Lee Solomon." *Black Enterprise* (February 1995): 68.

Lee, Stanly M., Sr. "Jimmie Lee Solomon, Mr. Robinson Would be Proud." *New York Beacon*, 16 September 1994.

"Most Influential Blacks in Sports List: Jimmie Lee Solomon." *Black Enterprise* (March 2005): 88.

Online

DeGange, Jack. "Jimmie Lee Solomon." ivyleaguesports.com http://www.ivyleaguesports. com/documents/bh04-dartmouth-solomon.asp (Accessed 12 February 2006).

MLB Executives: Jimmie Lee Solomon, Executive Vice President, Baseball Operations. http://mlb.mlb.com/ NASApp/mlb/mlb/official_info/about_mlb/executives. jsp?bio=solomon_jimmie (Accessed 12 February 2006).

Gabriella Beckles

Maurice Sorrell
c. 1914–1998

Photographer

Maurice Sorrell captured the story of the civil rights movement in the Deep South from its earliest days; using his camera, he preserved in pictures such historic events as the march from Montgomery to Selma, Alabama, and other events. In his photographic career that spanned more than three decades, he also was eyewitness to urban riots of the 1950s and 1960s and captured the images of nine U.S. presidents and many members of Congress. His work regularly appeared in *Ebony* and *Jet* magazines, products of his employer, Johnson Publications.

Sorrell was born about 1914 in Washington, D.C. He became fascinated with the camera at an early age, capturing family gatherings and neighborhood events. He graduated from Armstrong High School, where he took full responsibility for class photographs. Sorrell worked as a laborer at the Bureau of Printing and Engraving but sought unsuccessfully to become a photographer's apprentice. In 1955, Sorrell accepted a photography position at the Pentagon, but because of his race he was restricted to work in the darkroom and forbidden to go out on assignments. He remained there for two years and then, though inexperienced professionally, left to become a freelance photographer.

As early as 1946 Sorrell had purchased a 4x4 Speed Graphic camera and shot local weddings and anniversary celebrations. He received some formal training in a photography program that the U.S. Department of Agriculture offered, and then, after he left the Pentagon, he launched his career as a freelance photographer. From this time on, he contributed regularly to the popular weekly newspaper the *Afro-American*. Now the public saw photographs of Washington's black events that were published in that newspaper.

In 1961, Sorrell joined the White House Photographers Association, becoming the first black to gain admission to that prestigious organization. His membership, however, came only after a dispute that reached national proportions. While attending a press conference, President John F. Kennedy was criticized for planning to participate in an awards banquet for the all-white photographers' group. After overcoming his embarrassment, Kennedy uncharacteristically stumbled through words as he implied that he would investigate the racial discrimination. A *Jet* magazine reporter had questioned Kennedy and in so doing created a situation that left Sorrell, the photographer for *Afro-American*, as the sole candidate for the diversity assignment. Sorrell's career suddenly improved. He took full advantage of the obvious opportunity, and a few weeks later joined Johnson Publishing Company's Washington team at the awards banquet.

Chronology	
1914?	Born in Washington, D.C.
1946	Begins photographing local weddings and celebrations
1955-57	Works in photography position at the Pentagon
1961	Becomes first black member of the White House Photographers Association
1962	Joins staff of Johnson Publishing Company as photographer; photographs civil rights movement of the South
1994	Retires from Johnson Publishing Company
1998	Dies in Washington, D.C. on June 22

Sorrell met some difficulties with the elite White House Photographers' Association. Early in his days at the White House, other photographers had no difficulty boxing out the comparatively short Sorrel, who stood 5 feet 4 inches; he counteracted them by using his elbows to jostle for a better position. But blacks held him in high regard and, according to *Jet* magazine for July 13, 1998, when they visited the White House they looked for "the little guy with the curly locks from JPC." Sorrell responded by taking their photograph and recording what was clearly their special place in history.

Captures the Civil Rights Movement through the Lens

Johnson Publishing Company hired Sorrell in 1962 and then sent him south to cover the turbulent civil rights movement. The next year, he documented the historic March on Washington. Both *Ebony* and *Jet* magazines— products of that firm—published the historic images that Sorrell captured. It was not uncommon for Sorrell to be confronted by angry crowds and police dogs or to be exposed to tear gas as he photographed civil rights leaders, participants, and events. Among the movement's leaders, he photographed: Martin Luther King Jr., Benjamin Hooks, A. Philip Randolph, Roy Wilkins, and Whitney Young. While with the publishing company, Sorrell also visited more than twenty-four countries. He took seven official trips to Africa and accompanied such officials as Vice President Hubert H. Humphrey, Secretary of State Dean Rusk, and U.S. Supreme Court Justice Thurgood Marshall. He also photographed nine U.S. presidents and took the first portrait of the Congressional Black Caucus. He remained news photographer for Johnson Publishing Company in its Washington bureau from 1962 to 1993. A man with compassion, Sorrell accompanied back to Washington the body of Whitney Young, who died in 1971 while swimming near Lagos. Sorrell retired from Johnson Publishing Company in 1994, after spending thirty-four years as news photographer for the Washington bureau.

Sorrell died of a heart ailment in Washington, D.C.'s Providence Hospital, on June 22, 1998, at the age of eighty-four. His survivors included his wife Beatrice, a public health nurse to whom he was married for fifty-two years, and a sister. After his death, he was honored with the 2000 African American Photographers Association's Lifetime Achievement Award. Others honored him as well; for example, former U.S. Secretary of Transportation Rodney Slater displayed Sorrell's work in a photographic exhibit that honored the Selma to Montgomery march.

Sorrell knew how to relate to people. A gentle man and an expert with the camera, he was known for capturing "the essence of a moment in a single portrait," wrote Louie Estrada for the *Washington Post*. He knew how to put his subjects at ease and to direct them to the position that suited him best and which enabled him to get the best shot. Sorrell was a mentor to many young photographers. He also helped young photographers to have their work published. According to Estrada in the *Washington Post* article, Jason Miccolo Johnson of the Exposure Group, an African American photographers organization, said that Sorrell "was like a grandfather figure who was worthy of a lot of respect. He paved the way for many of us, and we know it wasn't easy."

REFERENCES

Periodicals

Estrada, Louie. "News Photographer Maurice Sorrell, 84, Dies." *Washington Post*, 25 June 1998.

"Maurice Sorrell, 84, *Ebony* Photographer." *Washington Times*, 28 June 1998.

"Pioneer Jet Photographer Maurice Sorrell Dies at 84 in Washington, D.C." *Jet* 94 (13 July 1998): 17-18.

Online

Campbell, Jo. "Reach Out, and Do It Now!" *Shore Journal*. Editorial. http://shorejournal.com (Accessed 10 July 2001).

Jessie Carney Smith

Emanuel Stance
1843–1887

Soldier

Emanuel Stance was considered not to have the qualities needed for a good soldier when he sought to enlist in the U.S. Army. He had a slight build, about five feet tall, and was only nineteen years old. However, he

---

Chronology

1843	Born in Carroll Parish, Louisiana
1866	Enlists in the U.S. Army in October, Company F, 9th Cavalry Unit
1870	Awarded the Congressional Medal of Honor for valor in the fight against the Kickapoo Indians at Kickapoo Springs, Texas on May 20; becomes first African American to win the Congressional Medal of Honor in the Indian Campaigns
1887	Body is found near Crawford, Nebraska on December 25

---

was accepted and became a member of the 9th U. S. Cavalry, Company F, one of the two regiments of African Americans. Many of the enlistees were recently freed slaves and veterans of the Civil War. Stance and his company saw action against the Kickapoo Indians in the Battle of Kickapoo Springs, Texas. As a result of his performance, Stance received the Congressional Medal of Honor. He was the first African American to receive this medal.

Little is known about Emanuel Stance's life before he enlisted in the army. However, some sources, including the records at Fort McPherson National Cemetery, indicate he was born in 1843 at Carroll Parish, Louisiana. A former slave and sharecropper, Stance enlisted in the U.S. Army in 1866 in Lake Providence, Louisiana. The Greater North Carolina Chapter of the Ninth and Tenth (Horse) Cavalry Association of the Buffalo Soldiers reports that Stance's recruiter, Lieutenant John Maroney, recorded that Stance's eyes, hair, and complexion were black. Maroney indicated that Stance had determination and the gleam in his eyes that suggested he would make an excellent soldier. Stance proved himself to be a good fighter, but he also showed himself to be argumentative. Serving in the army was one of the more lucrative jobs a post-Civil War black man could have. The soldiers earned $13 a month plus room, board, and clothing.

Stance was sent to Fort McKavett in Texas for a rigorous six month training period. In March 1867, the Ninth Cavalry was reassigned to San Antonio, Texas where they policed and protected American settlers and stage and mail routes from outlaws and Indians. In June, Company F and other regiments were transferred to Fort Davis, Texas. Stance was at Fort Davis from July 1867 to February 1869.

Wins Congressional Medal of Honor

Stance was able to read and write, which made it possible for him to advance in rank since he could handle the paperwork that was a part of a noncommissioned officer's duty. He advanced to corporal and ended his career as a first sergeant. Stance saw action in five Indian encounters in a period of two years.

In May 1870, Stance was in charge of a scouting party sent out to look for two captured children and some stolen horses. He came upon the Indians and the stolen horses and gave the order to charge, scattering the Indians and capturing the horses. They continued on to Kickapoo Springs and came upon a band of Indians about to attack a wagon train. Stance and the soldiers attacked them and routed the Indians. They gained horses and the captured youth. As a result of the success of the engagement, which took place in broad daylight, he earned the Congressional Medal of Honor, the country's highest military honor. He was the first Buffalo Soldier to earn it. Don Stivers, an artist, depicted Stance and his men at the Battle of Kickapoo Springs in his painting "The Redoubtable Sergeant."

In 1875, the Ninth Cavalry was transferred to the District of New Mexico. The soldiers spent the next six years fighting the Apache. Finally, in 1874, the government forced the Apaches onto reservations. The Ninth Cavalry was assigned to Fort Robinson, Nebraska, but there was little for the soldiers to do in this posting. Stance was a strict disciplinarian, which may have posed a problem for his bored command. When his body was found, it was assumed that his men had turned on him and murdered him. Emanuel Stance is buried at Fort McPherson National Cemetery in Maxwell, Nebraska.

REFERENCES

Books

Miller, Robert H. *Reflections of a Black Cowboy; Book Two: The Buffalo Soldiers.* Englewood Cliffs, N.J.: Silver Burdett Press, 1991.

Online

"The Buffalo Soldiers on the Western Frontier." http://www.imh.org/imh/buf/buf2.html (Accessed 14 March 2006).

Greater North Carolina Chapter; Ninth and Tenth (Horse) Cavalry Association of "The Buffalo Soldiers." "Buffalo Soldier Emmanuel [sic] Stance Received the Metal [sic] of Honor and Became a Legend." http://www.ncbuffalosoldiers.org/history. asp?u_action=display&u_log=11 (Accessed 14 March 2006).

The Handbook of Texas Online. "Ninth United States Cavalry." http://www.cr.nps.gov/history/resedu/ bib_africanamericanwest.htm (Accessed 14 March 2006).

"Photo of Grave Site of MOH Recipient Emanuel Stance." http://www.homeofheroes.com/gravesites/ states/pages_pz/stance_emanuel.html (Accessed 14 March 2006).

"We Can, We Will! Emanuel Stance." http://www. 9thcavalry.com/stance.htm (Accessed 14 March 2006).

Helen R. Houston

John Carruthers Stanly
1774–1846

Barber, plantation owner

John Carruthers Stanly, the largest free black slaveholder in the South, is a paradox of history. He purchased his own family members out of slavery and eventually became one of the largest slaveholders in Craven County, North Carolina.

Stanly, born a slave in 1774, was the son of an African Ibo woman and, many believe, the white prominent merchant-shipper John Wright Stanly. As a young boy, he received an education and was taught the trade of barbering with the help of his owners, Alexander and Lydia Stewart. Alexander Stewart had served as captain of the ship that brought Stanly's mother to North Carolina and both Alexander and Lydia were John W. Stanly's friends and neighbors.

After learning the barbering trade, Stanly was allowed as a bondsman to establish a barbershop in New Bern. Many of the town's farmers and planters frequented his barbershop for a shave or a trim. As a result, Stanly developed a successful business and he became known as Barber Jack. Realizing that Stanly, at the age of twenty-one, was literate and could economically provide for himself, his owners petitioned the Craven County court in 1795 for his emancipation. However, he was not satisfied with the ruling of the court and in 1798, through a special act, the state legislature confirmed the emancipation of John Carruthers Stanly, which entitled him to all rights and privileges of a free person.

Between 1800 and 1801, Stanly purchased his wife, Kitty, and two mulatto slave children. By March 1805, they were emancipated by the Craven County Superior Court. A few days later, Kitty and Stanly were legally married in New Bern and posted a legal marriage bond in Raleigh. Stanly's wife was the slave daughter of Richard and Mary Green and the paternal granddaughter of Amelia Green. Two year later, in 1807, Stanly was successful in getting the court to emancipate his wife's brother. After securing his own and his family's freedom, Stanly began to focus more on business matters. He obtained two slaves, Boston and Brister, who were taught the barbering trade. They became very skillful at the trade, which prompted Stanly to turn the operation of the business over to them. He used the money earned from his barbering business to invest in additional town property, farmland, and slaves. Other factors that assisted Stanly in his rise were his close ties with his former owner Lydia Stewart, his half-brother, John Stanly, and many prominent whites, along with his thrift and business acumen.

Starting out with small holdings and eventually accumulating large holdings, Stanly became one of the

Chronology

1774	Born in New Bern, North Carolina
1795	Initiates petition for emancipation
1798	State legislature confers Stanly's emancipation
1800	Purchases Kitty Green and two slave children
1805	Marries Kitty Green
1807	Petitions for emancipation of brother-in-law
1824	Buries wife
1830	Owns about 163 slaves
1843	Owns 160 acres of land
1846	Dies in New Bern, North Carolina

wealthiest men and the largest slave owner in Craven County. He purchased property at low prices and sold it at higher prices. He also profited from his rental properties and slave operated barbershop, not to mention monies earned from the sale of his plantation commodities such as cotton and turpentine.

Stanly's plantations and rental properties were operated by skilled slaves and free blacks. To improve his rental properties in New Bern, he used skilled slaves and hired free blacks to build cabins and other residences and to repair and renovate these properties. In fact, slave labor during the depression of the early 1820s kept Stanly economically stable.

Regarding how many slaves Stanly owned, the 1830 census suggests he owned 163 slaves. He has been described as a harsh, profit-minded task master whose treatment of his slaves was no different than the treatment slaves received from white owners. Stanly's goal, shared by white southern planters, was on expanding his operations and increasing his profits. Prior to a series of financial difficulties in the 1830s, his economic net worth exceeded $68,000.

During the 1820s, Stanly's wife, Kitty, died and he faced a series of economic difficulties. Kitty had been ill for several years, eventually becoming bedridden. Despite careful attention by two slave nurses, she died around 1824. His fortune began to plummet when the Bank of New Bern, due to the national bank tightening controls of some state and local banks, was forced to collect all outstanding debts. Unfortunately, Stanly had countersigned a security note for John Stanly, his white half-brother, in the amount of $14,962. Stanly assumed the debt. This action along with his own debts forced him to refinance his mortgages and sell large pieces of property, including slaves. When these options did not resolve his economic woes, he resorted to mortgaging his turpentine, cotton, and corn crops, as well as selling his barbershop, which had been operating continuously for forty years. Without the steady flow of income from his bar-

bershop, it became increasingly difficult for him to stabilize his finances. By the early 1840s, much of Stanly's holdings with the exception of a small rural tract of land had been liquidated. Finally in 1843, when Stanly was seventy-one, his last 160 acres of land were sold at public auction. Three years later, with only seven slaves remaining, John Stanly died.

REFERENCES

Books

Franklin, John Hope. *The Free Negro in North Carolina, 1790-1860.* Chapel Hill: University of North Carolina Press, 1943.

——, and Loren Schweninger. *Runaway Slaves: Rebels on the Plantation.* New York.: Oxford University Press, 1999.

Periodicals

Schweninger, Loren. "John Carruthers Stanly and the Anomaly of Black Slaveholding." *North Carolina Historical Review* 67 (April 1990): 159-92.

Patricia A. Pearson

Robert G. Stanton
1940–

Federal government official, conservationist

The first park Robert G. Stanton ever visited was Greenway Park in Fort Worth, Texas, which was also the only park in Fort Worth that allowed African Americans. In 1997, after thirty-one years of service with the National Park Service (NPS), Stanton became the first African American to head the National Park Service.

Stanton was born in 1940 and was raised in the Fort Worth community of Mosier Valley, an area that was settled by freed slaves in the late 1800s. By the time he was eight years old he was driving a tractor for his father, who baled hay for local farmers. He attended the segregated Mosier Valley elementary school. The parents of the school filed one of the many lawsuits filed by African Americans after World War II in order to challenge the so-called separate-but-equal law that allowed segregated schools in the United States. The fight to desegregate public education in the United States was led locally by parents and educators and nationally by a network of legal scholars and activists and was one of the most significant events in the modern civil rights movement.

Robert G. Stanton

In October 1949, a group of Mosier Valley parents filed a federal lawsuit for equal access to schools for their children within the Euless Independent school district, Stanton's school district near Fort Worth. Without consulting any parents, local school officials had proposed to close down the area's segregated Mosier Valley School, and bus the African American children to Fort Worth schools. When the parents heard of the school district's plans, they refused to have their children transferred to the Fort Worth schools and, with the assistance of the National Association for the Advancement of Colored People (NAACP), filed suit. Even though the facilities in Fort Worth were better than those at the local schools, the parents argued that their children must be allowed to attend school locally. The court found in favor of the parents, agreeing that transferring the students to a different school district while operating schools for white children violated the separate-but-equal convention that was the justification for segregated school systems. As a result of this suit, a new segregated brick school building was built in 1953 to replace the dilapidated wooden building that had served as the only local school open to African Americans.

Follows Call to National Parks

Stanton attended Huston-Tillotson College, a church-supported, private, historically black college in Austin,

Texas. A National Park System (NPS) representative came to Huston-Tillotson to promote careers in the park service. In 1962, Stanton borrowed $250 to buy a uniform and a train ticket to Grand Teton National Park in Wyoming, where he worked as a seasonal ranger during the summers of 1962 and 1963. It was his first visit to a national park; in fact, he had never been outside Texas. Stanton earned a bachelor of science degree from Huston-Tillotson and completed graduate work at Boston University in Boston. He later received three honorary doctorate degrees: doctor of science, Huston-Tillotson College, Austin, Texas; doctor of environmental stewardship; Unity College, Unity, Maine; and doctor of public policy, Southern University and Agricultural and Mechanical College, Baton Rouge, Louisiana.

In 1966, after two years as the director of public relations and alumni affairs at Huston-Tillotson College, Stanton joined the NPS full-time as a personnel management and public information specialist in the Washington, D.C. headquarters office. In 1969, he became a management assistant in the central region, and in 1970, became superintendent of the eastern region, which includes Washington, D.C. and Maryland. A year later he was appointed superintendent of Virgin Islands National Park in St. John, U.S. Virgin Islands, and in 1974, he became deputy regional director of the southeast region in Atlanta. In 1977, Stanton returned to the Washington, D.C. headquarters as assistant director of park operations and in 1978 was appointed deputy regional director of the national capital region. In 1987, he returned to headquarters as associate director for operations. In 1988, he was named regional director of the national capital region, which includes forty national parks and monuments in and around Washington, D.C., including the White House, the Washington Monument, and the Lincoln and Jefferson memorials.

Retires, Briefly

When Stanton informed Secretary of the Interior Bruce Babbitt in 1996 that he was retiring after thirty-one years of service, Babbitt suspected the retirement would be short-lived. "I was thinking this might be one of the shortest retirements," Babbitt told the *Washington Post*. As it turned out, he was right. The former director of the National Park Service, Roger Kennedy, left his post on March 31, 1997. Babbitt enticed Stanton out of retirement, and Stanton was nominated by President Bill Clinton as Kennedy's replacement.

Stanton was sworn into the post in August 1997, after being confirmed by the Senate. He was the first career NPS employee to head the department in twenty years. At his swearing-in, Stanton was introduced by first lady Hillary Rodham Clinton and sworn in by Secretary of the Interior Babbitt in the Indian Treaty Room of the Old Executive Office Building. An audience of about 150 people attended.

As the fifteenth director of the National Park Service, Stanton took on responsibility for policy and administration for 375 park sites in 49 states, five territories, and Washington, D.C. The 80 million-acre park system is managed by 20,000 permanent and seasonal employees with an annual budget of about $1.6 billion. The NPS is notoriously short on funds, which is a challenge for its director. Stanton's directorship came at a time when the park service was facing declining congressional support in budget appropriation that led to first-time fees at some parks and increased fees at the more popular parks.

In addition to overseeing the nation's grand natural parks, the NPS also maintains urban parks and national historic sites. A number of these "inspire me personally," Stanton said in an interview at TPL.org, because they relate to African American history. These include such sites as the home of noted abolitionist, orator, and writer Frederick Douglass and the memorial to the educator and human rights leader Dr. Mary McLeod Bethune, both in Washington, D.C. The NPS also maintains the Atlanta home of Dr. Martin Luther King Jr. The *Brown v. Board of Education* National Historic Site in Topeka, Kansas commemorates the groundbreaking U.S. Supreme Court decision that desegregated public schools. "Under our Constitution," Stanton continued at TPL.org, "we never should have been a segregated society, but we recognize that segregation did take place. In a real sense, such a park teaches how the nation has matured from one era to another. I think parks have a way of unifying us as one people and one nation."

For his work, Stanton has been cited in professional and technical publications and has served as a keynote speaker at university functions and major national and international conferences. He has represented the National Park Service and the U.S. Department of the Interior on the John F. Kennedy Center for the Performing Arts board of trustees, Wolf Trap Foundation for the Performing Arts board of directors, the U.S. Holocaust Memorial Council, the Committee for the Preservation of the White House, and the National Park Foundation.

Travels as Leader in Conservation

Stanton has traveled to more than twelve different countries to participate in major international conferences, including the World Protected Areas Leadership Forum in Virginia (2000); in Spain (2001); in Australia (2002); and the World Commission on Protected Areas and World Conservation Congress in Amman, Jordan. He is also active with such civic groups as the Student Conservation Association, Inc.; the National Audubon Society; Accokeek Foundation; and the Woods Hole Research Center. He was a fellow of the American Academy for Park and Recreation Administration, an associate of the Roundtable Associates, and chairman of the Trustees of the African American Experience Fund of the National Park Foundation.

He has been honored with countless awards and citations from professional, governmental, and civil organizations for outstanding public service, conservation leadership, youth development, and diversity in employment and public programs.

Stanton moved on from the NPS in 2001, with the end of the Clinton administration. He remained active in conservation activities and led a study on the role minorities play in environmental groups. Grand Teton remains Stanton's favorite national park.

REFERENCES

Periodicals

"Giving direction: Meet Robert G. Stanton, a 31-year career employee, who has become the 15th director of the Park Service." *National Parks*, November-December 1997.

Sarasohn, Judy. "Diversity Survey Causes Broadside." *Washington Post*, 18 March 2004.

"Stanton 1st black to head National Park Service." *Jet*, 21 July 1997.

Wheeler, Linda. "Former Regional Chief Sworn In as Head of National Park Service." *Washington Post*, 16 August 1997.

———. "Retired D.C. Regional Director Nominated to Head Park Service; He Would Inherit Agency Squeezed for Funds." *Washington Post*, 29 June 1997.

Online

"A Conversation with Robert G. Stanton." The Trust for Public Land. http://www.tpl.org/tier3_cd.cfm?content_item_id=1451&folder_id=966 (Accessed 23 March 2005).

"The History of Public School Desegregation: A NPS Perspective—Robert G. Stanton." Organization of American Historians. http://www.oah.org/pubs/magazine/deseg/stanton.html (Accessed 23 March 2005).

Brenna Sanchez

Austin Steward
1793–1865

Abolitionist, slave

Despite having the status of slave, Austin Steward took advantage of business practices that he learned in order to become a prosperous merchant. His disdain for slavery and its oppression of black people led him to join the antislavery movement as soon as he became free. Although Steward remained a marginal figure, his abolitionist work brought him in touch with other black abolitionists, including Henry Highland Garnett, J. W. Loguen, and Frederick Douglass, who worked fervently for full citizenship for black people.

Born in Prince William County, Virginia, sometime in 1793, Austin A. Steward was the son of slave parents Robert and Susan Steward. He had one sister. His grandfather had been stolen from Africa while his mother washed clothes near the sea coast; he was sold in slavery to a Virginia planter. The Steward family lived in conditions common to slaves—a small cabin built with rough boards, an earthen floor, and small openings on the sides to serve as windows. Their furniture consisted of those pieces the slaves could procure while occasionally hired out to earn a little money.

Around 1800 William Helm, a wealthy planter who held about one hundred slaves, purchased the Steward family. In his autobiography, *Twenty-two Years a Slave*, Austin Steward recalled being taken to the "great house" or Helm's family mansion where he served as errand boy. He was required to stand in the presence of the Helm family—the two parents and their seven children—all day and a part of the night, in readiness for any task that they put before him. He also slept on the floor without a pillow or blanket, in the same room with his master and mistress. Captain Helm was a kind, pleasant, and humorous man and not harsh as a master; nonetheless, the Steward family was still enslaved.

Helm was a powerful man who kept his family in luxury and elegance. He had a racecourse on his plantation and owned fine horses as well, but he was a poor businessman. After losing heavily on a horse race and making other poor management decisions, Helm was in debt and was forced to sell his plantation and stock; however, he kept his slaves. He left his family behind and took his slaves as he moved from Virginia to Sodus Bay on Lake Ontario in upstate New York. They traveled about twenty miles each day and camped at night, and arrived at their destination after about twenty days. In 1803 Helms returned to Virginia, gathered his family, and moved his family and his slaves to Bath, New York. Austin Steward and another slave named Simon were hired out for a while to Henry Tower, who was from an enterprising family in Lyons, New York. The Tower family ran a large

Chronology

1793	Born in Prince William County, Virginia
1800?	Will Helm purchases the Steward family
1801?	Moves with Helm to Sodus Bay, New York
1803	Moves with Helm to Bath, New York
1814	Escapes from his master and lives in Canandaigua
1817	Relocates to Rochester and opens meat market
1818	Teaches Sabbath school to black children; builds house and expands his business
1825	Marries a woman referred to as "Miss B"
1827	Joins in Emancipation Day celebration on July 4; becomes agent for Freedom's Journal and the Rights of All
1830	Attends first annual Convention for the Improvement of Colored People and serves as vice president
1831	Moves with his family to Wilberforce, Canada
1837	Relocates to Rochester
1839	Attends the meeting of the Association for the Political Improvement of the People of Color held in New York City
1840–41	Works with New York Convention of Colored Men and serves as its president
1842	Returns to Canandaigua; teaches school; resumes antislavery activities
1856	Publishes his autobiography, *Twenty-two Years a Slave, and Forty Years a Freeman*
1865	Dies in Rochester, New York

grist mill and a distillery. Sometime later, Steward managed to purchase a spelling book and, as best he could, taught himself to read. After his master's son-in-law caught him reading—slaves were forbidden to read—Steward received a severe flogging, which made him even more determined to read and write. Helm's business suffered again and he began to sell off his slaves.

Steward worked for Tower until about 1812, when he was hired out to another master. Then his thoughts turned toward freedom. He had seen his sister, who also lived in Bath, brutally beaten by her master; he had seen how the privileged people lived. He also questioned the legality of his slave status in New York state, for he knew about the 1785 law banning the sale of slaves brought into New York, and the gradual emancipation of slaves provided by the 1799 statue. The court decision of 1800, *Fisher v. Fisher*, further helped his case, for it outlawed hiring out slaves, as a violation of the 1785 law. Steward talked to a prominent lawyer who gave him instructions for pursuing his dream. After receiving Helm's permission to visit friends in Geneva and Canandaigua in winter 1814, Steward talked with Dennis Comstock, president of the Manumission Society, who agreed to help him. Then Steward, now about twenty-two years old, escaped his master and was taken in by Comstock's brother, Otis.

Comstock hired Steward and gave him what Steward called in his autobiography "the dignity of collecting my own earnings." He enjoyed his freedom: for the first time in his life he was allowed to sit at a table and take meals with others. About a year later, he thought that his freedom was ensured when Comstock refused to turn him over to Helm and reminded Helm that his actions violated state laws. When autumn came and the farm work was over, Steward went to a bookstore in Canandaigua and bought several old school books. With books in hand, he walked to Farmington to enroll in the local academy conducted by a man whom he identified simply as Mr. J. Comstock. About twenty-three years old when he entered, Steward stayed for three winters.

Between 1817 and 1820, Steward's father died in Palmyra, of injuries and severe illness. Austin Steward began a peddling business in the flourishing city of Rochester, promoting farm items such as poultry, meat, cheese, corn, oats, butter, and other items that Comstock wanted to sell. He continued the prosperous business for several months. The next year he relocated to Rochester and went into business for himself. By now he could read well and had a good command of writing and arithmetic. In September 1817, he opened a meat market business in Rochester, in a room that he rented from a man named A. Weakley. He reached out to the community in the summer of 1818 by teaching Sabbath school, or Sunday school, to black children. "I hoped to be able to benefit in some measure the poor and despised colored children," he wrote in his autobiography, but their parents suffered such degradation from whites and lacked courage and determination that they wanted very little for their children. At first their children attended the school well; they soon dropped out and the school ceased to operate.

In 1818 as well, Steward bough a lot on Main Street for $500. He built a two-story dwelling and store and expanded his business. Although he believed early on that he was free, Steward soon learned that his freedom was threatened. His old master, Helm, learned about his prosperity, and now, having been reduced to one slave woman and living on public charity himself, Helm hired a lawyer named Lewland who visited Steward at his business establishment and demanded that he pay Helm $200. He left a notice forbidding anyone to remove or destroy any of Steward's property. Helm filed suit in the Court of Equity, claiming right to Steward's property. Steward then hired a lawyer named A. Sampson, and they prepared for court. Meanwhile, Helm, who had lived a profligate life of excessive drinking and gambling, died, and so did the law suit.

Steward's business flourished, and Steward was able to pay for his house and two lots. He built a valuable brick building for his grocery store, which included all kinds of food and grain, and all of his products sold rapidly. He considered that he needed a partner in life "to share my joys and sorrows, and to assist me on through the tempestuous scenes of a life-long voyage," he wrote in his autobiography. On May 11, 1825, Steward married a local woman, whom he called in his autobiography "Miss B____," the youngest daughter of a close and well-traveled friend. The Stewards had eight children.

Former Slave Becomes Abolitionist

Meanwhile, as his business prospered, Steward became an activist. The vestiges of slavery still plagued him, and he reached out to blacks in the North who, though free, endured considerable racial prejudice. He was a key figure in Rochester's July 4 celebration. Previously blacks and abolitionists had celebrated West Indian Emancipation Day; by 1827, blacks in New York had celebrated July 4 for a few years. They considered the 1817 law that extended slave emancipation to cover those born before July 4, 1799, noting that blacks were to be free as of July 4, 1827. Rochester's blacks celebrated July 4 with booming cannons, and the procession moved though main streets to the public square, where seats and a stage were arranged. Governor Tompkins was the chief architect of blacks' emancipation, but the honored speaker was runaway slave and prosperous grocer Austin A. Seward, who told the audience, "Let us, my countrymen, henceforth remember that we are men," reported Benjamin Quarles who cited *Freedom's Journal* for July 27 and September 8, 1827. Some twenty-seven years later, the celebration was resurrected for a single time in Auburn's Sanford Hall, where the audience was predominantly white. By then, Steward was an elderly man, yet he was seated on the platform along with prominent black abolitionists J. W. Loguen, Henry Highland Garnet, Frederick Douglass, and longtime friend of blacks and women's righter Lucretia Mott.

For two years (1827-29), Steward worked as an agent for the black newspapers *Freedom's Journal* and the *Rights All*. He became active in black organizations as well. When the first annual Convention for the Improvement of Colored People was held in Philadelphia in 1830, Steward served as vice president.

As blacks remained concerned about their liberty, many hoped for relief from oppression. Some moved west to California, only to encounter the Fugitive Slave Law that was still in force there in 1855. Some left for Canada, which they considered a safe haven. As many as 40,000 had moved to Canada during the antebellum period. Some settled close to the Canadian border, so that they might move back and forth across the border for safety. In 1829, Canada saw its first significant migration of blacks, who fled the aftermath of a race riot in Cincinnati. They organized a commune called Wilberforce, and made it a self-supporting and self-governing community. In 1831, Steward and his family moved to the newly organized black community, and Steward invested his savings in the community venture. He dabbled in politics, serving one term as clerk of Biddulph Township. He replaced agent Israel Lewis as principal community leader, but six years later the venture collapsed. The success that Steward knew in Rochester was missing in Wilberforce. He and Lewis were at odds over the handing of local finances and other issues. In 1836, Lewis was removed as the principal agent. After that brothers Benjamin and Nathaniel Paul replaced Lewis, but they were equally unsuccessful. The community was so wracked by turmoil and dissension that it all but ceased to exist by 1837. Once the community had lost all of its appeal and effectiveness and he had lost all of his money, Steward and his family left for Rochester on January 19, 1837.

The family reached Rochester on January 23, 1837, and immediately Steward worked to resume his grocery business for a season. He opened a small variety store at the corner of Main and North streets, and one year later moved to a store on Buffalo Street, opposite the courthouse. He took as his partner John Lee, an industrious young man; with his help, the business prospered. Around this time he embraced the temperance movement and provided dinner for a local temperance celebration. Steward and his business endured the aftermath of the 1837 panic and a fire that destroyed his business. But tragedy followed: on April 15, 1837, his oldest daughter died.

Around 1842 he moved back to Canandaigua, taught school, and resumed his antislavery work. Although he was a Presbyterian, soon afterward, he visited New York City and joined the African Methodist Episcopal Conference, where he developed a friendship with Bishop Alexander Walters of Baltimore. Steward became an agent for the *National Antislavery Standard*. He was active in the political antislavery movement of this period. He worked with the New York Convention of Colored Men in 1840, 1841, and 1845, and served as president of that organization. Steward was a member of the Association for the Political Improvement of the People of Color, formed in July 1838 in New York City. The group met in New York City on August 1, 1939, and the next year held a statewide meeting in Albany to protest political disenfranchisement. Austin Steward was president of the group, and William H. Topp, Charles L. Reason, and Henry Highland Garnet were secretaries. Reported in the *Emancipator* for December 31, 1840, and cited by Benjamin Quarles, the men called on blacks of the commonwealth to insist on the ballot: "Let every man send in his remonstrance. Let petitions be scattered in every quarter." In his work, Steward lobbied on behalf of black male suffrage, insisting that it should be on equal terms as white suffrage.

Throughout his life Steward remained committed to the cause of freedom for blacks. Wherever he lived, his home was open to fugitive slaves, particularly in Rochester, where he saw the distresses of poor, frightened fugitives who escaped from Southern bondage. He told his own story in his slave narrative, *Twenty-two Years a Slave, and Forty Years a Freeman*, originally published by William Alling in 1856. An engraving of Steward is printed on the frontispiece. Austin Steward died in Rochester in 1865, having lived long enough to see his people freed by the 1863 Emancipation Proclamation.

REFERENCES

Books

Low, W. Augustus, and Virgil A. Clift, eds. *Encyclopedia of Black America*. New York: McGraw-Hill Book Co., 1981.

Pease, William H., and Jane H. Pease. "Austin Steward." In *American National Biography*. Vol. 20. Eds. John A. Garraty and Mark C. Carnes. New York: Oxford University Press, 1999.

Quarles, Benjamin. *Black Abolitionists*. London: Oxford University Press, 1969.

Jessie Carney Smith

H. Patrick Swygert
1943–

College president

By 2005 attorney H. Patrick Swygert had served as Howard University's president for over a decade but his relationship with the university was even longer, spanning over forty years. Born March 17, 1943, in Philadelphia, Swygert was the seventh of fourteen children born to Gustina Huzzy and Leroy Swygert. The south Philadelphia working-class community where he grew up was comprised of African Americans, Irish, Jews, and Italians. Young Swygert had to demonstrate great determination as a youth to make something of himself. He is quoted in a 1996 *Washington Post* profile as saying, "When you are the seventh son, it's difficult to be shy and retiring because you don't get anything done that way."

According to *Post* reporter Valerie Strauss in the 1996 profile, when Swygert entered Howard University as a freshman in the fall 1961, he knew what he wanted to achieve and was willing to work his way through school as a baker and waiter in order to attain his goal. His father had died a year before, and his mother had thirteen other children to raise. Swygert fell in love with Howard University in particular and with education in general. In Strauss's profile, Swygert explained his love affair with his alma mater: "the campus community gave me a home and to a large extent raised me." He added: "it is difficult for me to see my life without Howard." Swygert recollected being overwhelmed soon after he arrived as a

H. Patrick Swygert

Chronology

1943	Born in Philadelphia, Pennsylvania on March 17
1961	Enters Howard University
1965	Receives B.A. in history from Howard University; enters Howard University Law School
1968-69	Graduates cum laude from Howard University Law School; serves as law clerk to Chief Judge William H. Hastie, Federal Court of Appeals
1969-71	Serves as associate of New York-based corporate law firm Debevoise, Plimpton, Lyons & Gates
1971-72	Serves as administrative assistant to Congressman Charles B. Rangel
1972-77	Holds assistant professorship of law, Temple University School of Law
1977-79	Serves as general counsel, U.S. Civil Service Commission
1980	Becomes Temple University School of Law counsel and professor of law
1982	Executive vice president for administration, Temple University
1990	Becomes president of the State University of New York at Albany
1995	Becomes president of Howard University
1997	Forms partnership between Howard University and Fannie Mae to revitalize the LeDroit Park neighborhood around the campus
1999	Appointed by President Bill Clinton as chair of a branch of BusinessLINC (Learning, Information, Networking and Collaboration)
2002	Appointed to a two-year term as chair of the HBCU Capital Financing Board
2003	Invites the historic Association for the Study of Afro-American Life and History to move its offices to Howard's campus

freshman on campus as he witnessed a debate between nonviolent civil rights activist Bayard Rustin and black Muslim leader Malcolm X. The debaters were both brilliant and articulate. For Swygert this represented the beginning of an exciting and challenging educational experience. Howard provided him with knowledge and appreciation of African and African American culture hitherto unknown to him. After Swygert completed his first degree at Howard in 1965, a bachelor of arts in history, he immediately enrolled in the Howard University School of Law from which he graduated cum laude in 1968. During his years at Howard, Swygert took seriously the advice of Howard president James M. Nabrit to educate himself not just for personal gain but for the higher purpose of serving others. In a 1999 *Capstone* article, Swygert said that he was taught to "seek the truth" and "sow it in service."

Swygert held several professional jobs before he found himself drawn again into academia. He served from 1968 to 1969 as a law clerk to Chief Judge William H. Hastie, of the Third United States Circuit Court of Appeals. Hastie, a graduate of Harvard Law School, was a former dean of Howard University Law School. In 1970 Swygert married Sonja J. Branson. (The union lasted thirty-three years and produced two sons, Hayward Patrick Jr., and Michael Branson.) For the year 1970-71 Swygert was an associate of Debevoise, Plimpton, Lyons

& Gates, a New York-based corporate law firm. Next, he worked a year as an administrative assistant to New York Congressman Charles B. Rangel.

For five years (1972-77) Swygert returned to his first love—academia—as an assistant professor of law at Temple University School of Law in his hometown, Philadelphia. He served a short stint—1977 to 1979—as general counsel of the U.S. Civil Service Commission and Special Counsel to the Merit Systems Protection Board in 1979. Swygert was back at Temple from 1980 to 1982 as special counsel to the university president and professor of law. He served as vice president for university administration at Temple University from 1982 to 1987 and executive vice president from 1987 to 1990. Peter Liacouras, Temple University president, called Swygert an exceptional administrator who was able to accomplish his goals without sacrificing his ideals. Swygert intermittently spoke and taught abroad in Israel, Ghana, Egypt, Hungary, Greece and Italy. He is a member of the bars of the District of Columbia, Pennsylvania, and New York.

University Administration

In 1990 trustees of Howard University were recruiting a new president, as were the regents of the State University of New York (SUNY) at Albany. Since Swygert had not served as president of any other university, the Howard trustees passed over him, but he was selected as president of SUNY-Albany, a school with a student body of 17,000. Swygert served at SUNY-Albany for five years, 1990 to 1995. Students, faculty, and administrators lauded him for his fairness and accomplishments during this period. He spearheaded a $55 million capital campaign; increased minority enrollment from 14 to 25 percent; won funding for a new technology research center; and defused a campus hostage situation as well as a potentially volatile racial incident on campus with tact; moved the athletic program from Division 111 to Division 11; built a vast student recreation area; installed cable TV and voice mail in the dormitories; oversaw the construction of a child care center; and in general showed himself to be an extremely competent administrator. Both SUNY-Albany academics and oft-overlooked university staff members congratulated Swygert for treating all as equals and showing his appreciation for all members of the university community. Swygert proved himself to be an apt student in the development of corporate relations with the academic community. In 2002 Swygert received the Medallion of the University Award from SUNY-Albany, the highest honor awarded by that institution.

Howard University President

Meanwhile, things were not going well at Howard University. Financial shortfalls; racial tensions; enrollment reductions; and faculty, staff, and student morale problems plagued the campus. The university president resigned, and Howard trustees began to look for a new president in the spring of 1995. Out of a pool that began with three hundred applicants, the trustees unanimously approved H. Patrick Swygert as the fifteenth president of the university. Howard's Board of Trustees' chairman, Wayman F. Smith II, is quoted in the April 23, 1995 *Washington Post* article: "Patrick Swygert has a proven track record in the academic world, characterized by the highest level of personal integrity and ethical standards." Funding concerns, a hospital that was "hemorrhaging money," according to another *Washington Post* article, dated May 2, 1995, and a myriad of other problems faced the new president. Although Howard had a $500 million budget, Swygert faced a $7 million shortfall which could be addressed most effectively by a reduction in force. "I had no honeymoon when I got to Howard," Swygert said for the Strauss profile. "I didn't anticipate one, I didn't get one. But we'll have a great marriage."

The university itself has an interesting history. Named after Union general and founder Oliver Otis Howard, Howard University—dubbed in its early years as "the capstone of Negro education"—was founded in 1867.

Howard, who served as the director of the Freedmen's Bureau, considered education one of the key functions of his agency. Howard's mission was to provide teacher and ministerial education for all but especially for freeborn and emancipated African Americans. To help with the university's support, the U.S. Congress awarded Howard University a special appropriation in 1879 and amended Howard University's charter in 1928 to authorize a yearly federal appropriation for construction, development, improvement, and maintenance of the university. Fifty-five percent of Howard's budget continued in the early 2000s to be provided by federal government funding. Howard University has produced American greats such as jurist Thurgood Marshall, diplomat Ralph Bunche, philosopher Alaine Locke, actress Debbie Allen, opera singer Jessye Norman, and presidential cabinet member Patricia Roberts Harris.

Howard was one of over a hundred educational institutions founded in the decade just after the Civil War to benefit newly freed slaves. These institutions are collectively called historically black colleges and universities (HBCUs). For almost one hundred years HBCUs attracted the most academically proficient African American students because few other institutions of higher education would open their doors to them. The 1954 *Brown v. Board of Education* U.S. Supreme Court decision and subsequent civil rights legislation opened doors for African American students, many of which had never been open to them before. This change presented two types of challenges for HBCUs. The most obvious was that there was suddenly greater competition for the best African American students, and the best and brightest professors of color were slowly being lured away by majority-white institutions. This forced financially strapped HBCUs to be more competitive with scholarships, salaries, and programs. HBCUs had to find ways to increase their funding just to be competitive. In the book *I'll Find a Way or Make One: A Tribute to Historically Black Colleges and Universities*, authors Juan Williams and Dwayne Ashley provide a list of twenty African American colleges and junior colleges that simply had to close their doors due to "low enrollment and lack of financial support." Other HBCUs had to spend much more time to raise the resources their institutions needed. By the 1990s when Swygert became Howard president, the institution was the only HBCU listed among the nation's eighty-eight Research I universities. By 1996 Howard had awarded almost 84,000 degrees during its long and illustrious history. The university ranked first in the nation in the number of Ph.D.s conferred upon African American students.

When Swygert became president, university enrollment was just over 10,000 students in sixteen schools and colleges located on four campuses. In 1996 about 13 percent of the students were from the District of Columbia, 74 percent were from other states, 11 percent were international students representing 104 countries, and 5 percent were international students who were permanent U.S. residents. Just over 2,200 students were members of the graduating class of 1996. The endowment was almost $160 million, the operating budget was $505 million, and the university staff numbered almost 4,000. Howard administrators stated that the university's vision was to be a comprehensive research institution demonstrating excellence in instruction, research, and service, with an ongoing commitment to educating youth. The institution continued to focus on African Americans and other people of color, particularly for leadership and service to the nation and the world.

Swygert and his staff designed a five-year plan for the university. The president articulated several challenges for HBCUs in the March 1998 edition of *Black Issues in Higher Education*. He was aware that high-scoring African American students were actively recruited by majority-white universities—after all, that was something he did successfully at SUNY-Albany—but he did not agree that students got a better education at these institutions than they did at Howard. He emphasized that in order to provide the quality education good students desired, he had to recruit talented faculty members and be able to pay them competitive salaries. He promised the faculty that Howard would do its best to provide them with the tools of their trade, including personal computers for every faculty member. Swygert was particularly interested in supplying the university community with a "technologically rich" environment.

The 2000 Howard University Annual Report demonstrates that in Swygert's first few years as the university chief administrator Howard underwent substantive growth and development, including the creation of the Louis Stokes Heath Sciences Library, a new School of Law Library, and the University's iLab. The iLab is a technology learning center comprising more than 200 computer workstations, distance learning classrooms, and a Webcasting facility. The iLab station, open-twenty-four hours a day, has voice, data, and video capabilities. Students have the ability to connect with the Internet without using a telephone line. Additionally, Oracle Corp. donated four thousand workstations for computer centers in the residence halls. Rapid changes in technological capabilities also led to an increase in distance learning programs available at the university.

LeDroit Park

Swygert was also instrumental in forming a unique partnership in 1997 between Howard University and Fannie Mae to revitalize the LeDroit Park neighborhood around the campus. By the time Swygert became president the neighborhoods surrounding the university had numerous vacant and abandoned houses. In the LeDroit Park area ninety buildings comprising 18 percent of the residential properties were either vacant or abandoned. Earlier university administrators had hoped to expand the campus into the community because the university owned many of these buildings, most of which are on the National Register of Historic Places.

Swygert decided not to expand the campus in that direction and began to work with the residents of the surrounding community. The plan was to help revitalize the businesses on streets adjoining the campus and give the homes facelifts. With Fannie Mae, Howard began renovating the homes, most of which are narrow town houses, and offered them for purchase on easy terms to university faculty and staff members. Fannie Mae offered low-interest financing. Howard helped keep the housing prices low by writing off many of the renovation costs. One of the homes in the historic community belonged to Robert Heberton Terrell and his wife Mary Church Terrell. Robert Terrell was a Harvard-educated lawyer who taught in Howard's Law School and served as a municipal court judge. Mary Church, who had two degrees from Oberlin, was an educator, feminist, celebrated clubwoman, and indefatigable civil rights advocate. Howard and the community together transformed the Terrell house into a museum. Other African Americans of note who lived in the LeDroit Park community included Senator Edward Brooke, diplomat Ralph Bunche, U. S. Army General Benjamin O. Davis Sr., and Washington, D.C. mayor Walter Washington.

National and International Activities

Swygert's role as president of what many consider to the foremost HBCU in the United States caused him to be at the forefront of many initiatives relating to African Americans. President Bill Clinton appointed Swygert as chair of a branch of BusinessLINC (Learning, Information, Networking and Collaboration) in 1999. BusinessLINC was a partnership with the U.S. business community that encouraged large businesses to work with and mentor small business owners and entrepreneurs. The goal of BusinessLINC was to stimulate business-to-business relationships, including one-on-one technical advice and consulting, classroom and group training, peer group and consulting strategic alliances, and development of suppliers and new sales channels. In 2002, U. S. secretary of education Roderick R. Paige appointed Swygert to a two-year term as chair of the HBCU Capital Financing Board. A Department of Education press release dated April 22, 2002 explained that "the capital financing program provides financial insurance through a designated bonding authority to guarantee academic construction loans to qualified HBCUs." Swygert was later reappointed to the board, extending his term to 2007. During his first term the board accessed new loan amounts totaling close to $87 million, more than the five previous years combined. A Howard University press release stated that "the fiscal year, 2003 to 2004, was the most successful in the program's history, with five loans to five institutions, totaling nearly fifty-five million dollars."

In addition to the HBCU Capital Financing Board, Swygert is a member of a number of corporate boards and national committees, including Fannie Mae; United Technologies Corporation in Hartford; the Hartford Financial Services Group, Inc.; and the Federal Security Agency. He has been active in the development of literacy and reading programs in the community and in historical preservation programs. He has tirelessly worked to provide scholarship opportunities for students and to provide employment doors for graduates. Swygert invited the historic Association for the Study of Afro-American Life and History, founded by Carter G. Woodson, to move its offices to Howard's campus. The move took place in 2003 and, in addition to daily business, the association holds it annual African American History Month luncheon at Howard's Blackburn Student Center in February. The Swygert administration supported or spearheaded other historical initiatives, including a Freedman's Bureau papers project and a registry of African American Civil War soldiers and sailors. Swygert worked on a commission to commemorate the fiftieth anniversary of the *Brown* decision and helped the Smithsonian Institute to select a director for the proposed African American history museum. In the 2005-06 academic year the university established The Howard University Public Charter Middle School of Mathematics and Science. It is the first charter middle school in the city to be established by a university.

Swygert has received awards for being an outstanding educator, administrator, and freedom fighter from various groups, including the Congressional Black Caucus, the National Conference for Community and Justice, and the government of the District of Columbia. Swygert has also received several honorary degrees.

REFERENCES

Books

Donnelly, Rory. "H. Patrick Swygert." In *Contemporary Black Biography*. Vol. 22. Farmington Hills, Mich.: Gale Group, 1999.

Jackson, Cynthia L., and Eleanor F. Nunn. *Historically Black Colleges and Universities: A Reference Handbook*. Santa Barbara, Calif.: ABC-CLIO, 2003.

Who's Who among African Americans. 18th ed. Farmington Hills, Mich.: Thomson Gale, 2005.

Williams, Juan, and Dwayne Ashley. *I'll Find a Way or Make One: A Tribute to Historically Black Colleges and Universities*. New York: HarperCollins, 2004.

Periodicals

Hardcastle, James R. "Howard University Looks to Its Neighbors." *New York Times*, 4 April 1999.

Howard University Annual Report, 2000. Washington, D.C.: Howard University, 2001.

Strauss, Valerie. "The Education of Howard: The President Who Does It All for U. with Humor." *Washington Post*, 3 October 1996.

——. "Friends and Foes Alike Praise Howard U.'s New Leader." *Washington Post*, 2 May 1995.

Swygert, H. Patrick. "Howard 101: Learning to Lead." *Capstone*, 14 August 1999.

Thomas-Lester, Avis. "Alumnus Named President of Beleaguered Howard U." *Washington Post*, 23 April 1995.

Online

"Charting a Black Research Agenda: An Interview with H. Patrick Swygert, Esq., President of Howard University." *Black Issues in Higher Education*, March 1998. http://138.238.41.254./HPSBlackIssues Mar98.htm (Accessed 14 October 2005).

"H. Patrick Swygert: Fifteenth President of the University. www.howard.edu/president/biography.asp (Accessed 14 October 2005).

"Howard President Swygert Appointed HBCU Capital Financing Board Chairman," 22 April 2002 Press Release, Department of Education.www.ed.gov/ print/news/pressreleases/ 2002/04/04222002.html (Accessed 17 October 2005).

Howard University. "The Mission." 1999 http://138. 238.41.254/presidentReports/Mission.htm (Accessed 14 October 2005).

Howard University. "Strategic Framework for Action." 1996. www.howard.edu/president/Strategic Framework (Accessed 20 October 2005).

"President Clinton and Vice President Gore Announce BusinessLINC—A Major National Effort Building on the Administration's New Markets Initiative." The White House, Press Release, August 1999. http://clinton6.nara.gov/1999/08/1999-08-10-fact-sheet-on-businesslinc.html (Accessed 14 October 2005).

"President Swygert Reappointed Chair of HBCU Financing Board." Howard University Announcement, 2001. http:/howard.edu/ newsevents/anouncements/04-11-17swygert.htm (Accessed 19 October 2005).

Debra Newman Ham

Robert H. Terrell
1857–1925

Lawyer, judge

Robert Herenton Terrell broke barriers within the legal profession and helped establish a fraternity for African American men. Terrell was born on November 27, 1857, in Charlottesville, Virginia. His parents were Harris and Louisa Ann Terrell. As was the case for most African American youths born during this time, Terrell was educated in public schools. He attended schools in the District of Columbia and was a graduate of the Groton Academy in Groton, Massachusetts. In order to pursue his college education, Terrell worked in a dining hall at Harvard. He was one of seven magna cum laude scholars to graduate from Harvard in June 1884. After graduation, he found work in schools within the Washington D.C. area.

After teaching for a few years, Terrell decided to attend law school and chose the Howard University Law School. He earned his LL.B. in 1889 and his LL.M. in 1893. In 1889, Terrell resigned from his job as a teacher in order to accept a position as the chief clerk in the office of the auditor of the U.S. Treasury.

By 1892, Terrell had his own private practice of law in Washington D.C. He married Mary Church on October 28, 1891. Terrell's legal practice continued until 1898, when he left it to returning to teaching. He later became the principal of the M Street High School. During the late 1890s, he also was elected to the Board of Trade.

In 1901, Terrell accepted an appointment to serve as a justice of the peace in Washington D.C., making him the first African American justice of the peace. Terrell's time of service marked a difficult time for him and other African American leaders who were in service positions. Terrell was conflicted by his allegiance to a government that seemingly believed in him enough to appoint him to be a judge, but did not believe in granting basic civil rights to African Americans everywhere. In 1910, President William H. Taft appointed Terrell to be judge of the Municipal Court of the District of Columbia, despite complaints from the racially biased Senate. Terrell accepted this appointment and served in this capacity

Chronology	
1857	Born in Charlottesville, Virginia on November 27
1884	Graduates magna cum laude from Harvard
1889	Earns his LL.B.; works as chief clerk in the office of the auditor of the U.S. Treasury Department
1892	Practices law privately
1893	Marries Mary Church, an Oberlin College graduate; earns his LL.M.
1901	Receives appointment as a justice of the peace in Washington, D.C.
1910	Accepts nomination by President William Taft as judge of the Municipal Court of the District of Columbia
1911	Becomes a charter member of Sigma Pi Phi, Epsilon Boule in Washington
1925	Dies in Washington, D.C. on December 20

until his death. He continued to serve in this position, even after suffering with asthma and having two strokes.

Terrell also was a member of the faculty at the Howard University Law School from 1910 to 1925. In 1911, he became one of the charter members of Sigma Pi Phi, Epsilon Boule in Washington.

A law school was named for Terrell in 1931: the Robert H. Terrell Law School operated until 1950. An elementary school in Washington, D.C., was also named in honor of Terrell.

Approximately four years before his death, Terrell suffered from his first stroke. He had another stroke a year later. The second stroke left him paralyzed on one side of his body. Despite these health conditions, Terrell continued to work as a municipal court judge. In early December of 1925, Terrell's asthma worsened and contributed to his declining health. He died at his home on December 20, 1925.

REFERENCES

Books

"Robert H. Terrell." In *The African American Almanac.* Ed. Jeffrey Lehman. 9th ed. Farmington Hills, Mich.: Thomson Gale, 2003.

Robinson, Aubrey. "Robert Herenton Terrell." In *Dictionary of American Negro Biography.* Eds. Rayford W. Logan and Michael R. Winston. New York: Norton, 1982.

Connie Mack

Dempsey J. Travis

Dempsey J. Travis
1920–

Real estate executive, writer

As a young man, Dempsey J. Travis focused his dreams on a career in music. But he also recognized his talent for organization and promotion. Eventually, he decided to go into real estate, establishing Travis Realty, Sivart Mortgage Corporation, Freeway Mortgage and Investment, and Dempsey J. Travis Securities. *Black Enterprise* listed Travis Realty among the Largest 100 Black Businesses in the United States. For seven years, *Ebony* included this self-made millionaire among the 100 Most Influential Black Americans. Interested in preserving history, Travis wrote a number of books about music, his Chicago hometown, and people he came to know.

Born February 15, 1920, Dempsey Jerome Travis credits his parents, Louis Travis and Mittie Strickland Travis, for their positive influence in shaping his life. His father worked at the Chicago stockyards and set an example of hard work. Neither parent liked debt, so they taught their son strong money values. But Travis notes in his autobiography, *I Refuse to Learn to Fail*, that they taught him something more important: "Both my mother and father taught me that internalizing negative and grossly inaccurate self-images about our Blackness ensures failure." His parents also provided a role model for marriage. Travis chose Moselynne Hardwick of Cleveland, Tennessee, as his life's mate. They married On September 17, 1949.

During Travis's preschool years, the family became the first blacks to live in an otherwise all-white twenty-four-flat building. The white boys often taunted Travis. After one unpleasant encounter, his mother showed him a jacket made of the "best and most expensive" fabric, black velvet. She reassured her son, "You are my black velvet." Travis later told John Seder and Berkeley Burrell, "My mother really deserves the credit for a great deal of what I have accomplished. She is the warmest, most outgoing kind of person—she just loves people."

Travis attended private kindergarten and then Doolittle Elementary School. When the family moved in 1931, he attended Francis C. Willard Elementary. Disliking school, he began skipping classes. Soon his mother found out and enrolled him in a different teacher's classroom. Although not interested in education, young Travis entertained a couple of dreams for his future. He wanted to become a professional musician and he wanted to earn money. One morning, he announced, "I dreamed last night that I was going to be rich and Daddy wouldn't have to get up before daylight to go to work anymore."

Travis began earning money at age five. He asked Charles Murray, seller of Murray's Pomade, if he needed a barber for his business. In the conversation that followed, Travis agreed to give out business cards for a wage of fifty cents. Excited about his mission, Travis ran across the street colliding with a Model T. Although he woke in a hospital with a broken left leg, he found the venture profitable. Mr. Murray brought him a fruit basket and gave him an extra dollar for his trouble. Later business ventures included selling for the *Chicago Defender* and the white-owned *Chicago American* newspapers.

For Christmas 1925, Louis Travis surprised the family with a player piano. Although Mr. Travis could not read music, his boogie-woogie blues inspired his four-year-old son to ask for lessons. Elmer Simpson charged fifty cents for a half-hour lesson, plus there was the fourteen-cents for streetcar fare. Before Travis's sixth birthday, he performed "Violets Blue" in a recital at West Point Baptist Church. After that, his father always mentioned his son's name alongside those of Louis Armstrong, Earl Hines, and other great musicians. Travis's mother often took him to hear the black orchestras that came to town.

He and classmate Herbert Moore, who played clarinet, often practiced together. During Travis's eleventh year, they performed a duet at school. Guitarist Jesse Miller soon joined them, and the group enjoyed playing such songs as "Lazy Bones" and "Sophisticated Lady." Travis enjoyed performing and found that he also liked organizing music events. He finished elementary school in 1935, convinced he would become a professional musician.

Travis attended Wendell Phillips High School, the first school built for blacks within the Chicago black community. Bandleader Walter Dyett thought him too cocky to join his popular Booster Band. So at age fifteen, Travis formed his own band. Sometimes each performer earned as much as $2 a night. By the next year, he had become the youngest orchestra leader in the local musicians' union.

When Travis needed discipline, his father punished him by not letting him work—a strategy that proved effective since Travis loved to work. In his autobiography, he said of his father, "The positive approach to work he instilled has guided me successfully through several changes in vocations." Travis graduated from what had become known as Jean Baptiste Pointe Du-Sable High School in May 1936 in a suit handed down from his uncle to his father to him. His classmates included future publisher John Johnson, singer Nat King Cole, and actor Redd Foxx.

Job prospects looked bleak. Travis's father gave him streetcar fare and sent him job hunting. He also provided fifty cents for lunch money—with the instruction to spend it only if he found a job. Travis passed by the stockyard where his father worked, and he paid the Factory Employment Agency $10 to become a porter for Apex Box Company. During off-work hours, he formed a seven-member band and played at the West Side Dance Hall. Band members received $6 a night; as band leader, Travis received $10.

On September 9, 1942, the United States Army drafted Travis and sent him to Fort Custer in Battle Creek, Michigan. His sergeant asked him to put together an orchestra to play for U.S.O. dances on Friday and Saturday nights. But Travis soon found himself transferred to Camp Shenago in Pennsylvania, where life became tough. Black soldiers faced isolation, deprivation, and discrimination.

One evening outside the makeshift black theater—the base did not admit blacks to the main theater—he and his friend Kansas encountered a crowd of angry men. Whites had beaten a black man who tried to purchase beer at the white Post Exchange. Suddenly, white soldiers opened fire on the black soldiers. Kansas died, and Travis was shot. Doctors thought he might never walk again. After a series of surgeries, he walked with a limp, and eventually he walked normally again. Travis took a thirty-day leave to Chicago. When he returned to Camp Shenago, he noticed a new service center for blacks and learned that blacks could now attend the main theater.

Officers soon put Travis in charge of a troop going to Camp Lee, Virginia. They enrolled him in Quartermaster School for Noncommissioned Officers. Then new orders sent him to Aberdeen Proving Ground in Maryland. Major Sloan needed a clerk. He handed Travis a typewriter instruction manual, assigned him a desk, and within a month, Travis typed fifty-five words a minute. Assigned to the black Post Exchange as clerk, Travis soon became assistant manager and then manager. Before long, he became the first black to manage an integrated PX in Maryland. When Travis won top prize for the best-operated Post Exchange, Major Sloan arranged to have a picture taken for the newspaper. But the picture never appeared, for fear of causing increased racial tension. Sloan wanted Travis to attend Officers Training School, but Travis wanted out.

Education Follows Military Service

Following an honorable discharge from the Army on February 2, 1946, Travis returned to Chicago and attempted to start a new band and to enroll in college on the G.I. Bill. The band never materialized, and the path to college proved longer than expected. After failing the entrance exams for Roosevelt, DePaul, and Northwestern Universities, Travis took a job with Armour and Company at the stockyards where his father had worked. The foreman, seeing his capabilities, notified Travis he would fire him within a couple of weeks and suggested he consider preparing income taxes. So for a while, although Travis had never filled out a tax form, he figured income taxes for other people.

Travis then took a job with the Veterans Administration. When he learned that Englewood Evening Junior College required no entrance exam, he signed up for accounting and sociology. Eventually, he passed the entrance exam for Wilson Junior College, with the requirement that he take remedial reading and English. He quit his job and studied long hours, attempting to understand what he laboriously read. Finally, one day in his late twenties, he discovered that he could make sense of what he was reading. In his autobiography, he recalls, "The words rolled together into sentences, and the sentences rolled into paragraphs and the paragraphs uncoiled into pages of thoughts and ideas."

Travis had also enrolled in an American literature course. He wrote his first essay on *Silas Marner.* Years later, he still remembered the teacher's angry response. Dr. Earnest Ernst made him write and rewrite paper after paper, but he also took the time to help him improve his writing. Finally, he could both read and write—an accomplishment he considers a turning point in his life. With renewed confidence, he reapplied to Roosevelt. On the strength of his credits from Wilson, he completed the remainder of his B.A. within a year, graduating in August 1949.

Enters Real Estate

Travis enrolled in Chicago's Kent College of Law but soon decided not to become an attorney. A course on real estate principles, however, caught his attention. The prospect of a $5,000 commission refueled his dream of becoming rich. His mother gave him part of the $50 fee for a real estate license. He founded Travis Realty Company in 1949 and made his first sale in May 1950. In borrowed office space, he conducted business with an orange crate for a desk and a bucket for a chair. His wife quit her job to answer the phone, type letters, and help match people and homes. He enlisted as a census taker to make ends meet.

In his autobiography, Travis comments: "In the 1950s when many Blacks sought solutions to racism through integration, I believed a mobile housing market for minorities would pave the way for a color blind society." But black men found it nearly impossible to acquire a home mortgage in Chicago. In 1953, Travis founded Sivart Mortgage Company, a reverse spelling of his name. He needed to learn more about real estate than he could glean from trade publications and newspapers. But Northwestern University opened its courses only to Mortgage Bankers Association members, which excluded blacks. He attempted to learn from successful white mortgage bankers, but they excluded him, too.

Meanwhile, he continued to take on other roles. From 1957 through 1959, Travis presided over the Deerborn Real Estate Board. He served as president again during 1970 and 1971. Fulfilling three terms, Travis became the only person other than the first president to have held the position for more than two years. During 1959-60, he served as the first vice president of the National Association of Real Estate Brokers, a black organization advocating democracy in housing.

In 1959, friends encouraged Travis to run for president of the Chicago chapter of the NAACP. Elected that December, he became an able spokesperson for the group, talking often with mayor Richard Daley and speaking out in state Senate hearings. He coordinated the first march of Martin Luther King Jr. in Chicago on July 24, 1960. Travis chose not to run for reelection because he needed to refocus his attention on his businesses.

In 1961, Travis started Freeway Mortgage and Investment Company and Dempsey J. Travis Security and Investment Company. That same year, he also organized the United Mortgage Bankers of America, a mortgage banking association for blacks. In 1962, President John F. Kennedy spoke out against racial discrimination in home mortgaging and appointed Robert C. Weaver, an African American, to head the Department of Housing and Urban Development. Travis served as president of the mortgage banking association until 1974. But he still wanted to join the white Mortgage Bankers Association so he could take courses. He wrote to President Lyndon Johnson seeking help.

In the summer of 1966, Northwestern University's School of Mortgage Banking finally admitted Travis. His graduation in 1969 represented a first for the school. Travis continued to expand his education throughout his career. He told Carlyle C. Douglas, "In addition to monthly trade journals, I read 11 newspapers a day, five newsmagazines a week and a half-dozen books a month."

Becomes a Writer

Through the years, Travis took a personal interest in preserving Chicago's history. After reading some books on publishing, he self-financed, distributed, and publicized his work *An Autobiography of Black Chicago.* The book appeared in stores at Thanksgiving 1981. By Christmas Eve, Travis became the first black author to see his book on the *Chicago Tribune*'s non-fiction bestseller list. He published many of his books through the Urban Research Institute, later called Urban Research Press, which he founded in 1969.

Travis wrote *An Autobiography of Black Jazz* (1983), *Racism, American Style, A Corporate Gift* (1991), *J. Edgar Hoover's FBI Wired the Nation* (2000), and more than a dozen other books. He wrote biographies of his childhood classmate Redd Foxx, his friend and Chicago mayor Harold Washington, and musicians Louis Armstrong and Duke Ellington. Travis reviewed books for the *Chicago Sun-Times*, served as financial editor for *Dollars and Sense* magazine, and as a contributing writer for *Ebony* and *Black Scholar*. He was the president of the Society of Midland Authors from 1988 to 1990.

Travis achieved his dream of becoming rich one business venture at a time. In his autobiography, he observed: "Academic training, combined with experience, taught me to look at an almost devastated piece of real estate and see a gold mine instead of a disaster." He then turned those disasters into valuable properties and followed through with good management and maintenance. A 1976 *Ebony* article reported: "To this day, most of the property Travis owns—and he still owns every building he ever bought—is mortgage-free. 'I'm just more comfortable out of debt than in,' he confesses. 'Because of that I probably will never be a multi-multi-millionaire.'"

Although noting in his autobiography, "The price I paid for vigorous involvement with civil rights came within a hairline of destroying my career," he remained active politically. In 1966, President Lyndon Johnson asked him to participate in a White House conference, To Fulfill These Rights. On a Housing Task Force appointed by President Richard Nixon, he helped draft the 1970 Housing Bill. President Gerald Ford appointed him to presidential task forces on urban renewal and on inflation. President Jimmy Carter invited him to the White House in 1979 for a briefing and luncheon.

Travis served as trustee for the Chicago Historical Society, Northwestern Memorial Hospital, and the Chicago World's Fair Committee, and on the boards of Roosevelt University, Columbia College, and Garrett Evangelical Seminary in Evanston. He chaired the Chicago mayor's real estate review committee and his Commission for the Preservation of Chicago's Historic Buildings. He held membership on the Cosmopolitan Chamber of Commerce and the Board of Governors of the Chicago Assembly. He held directorships with Unibanc Trust, Seaway National Bank, Sears Bank and Trust, and the Museum of Broadcast Communications.

In 1982, Travis received the Society of Midland Authors Award and, in 1985, the Chicago Art Deco Society award. The *Chicago Sun-Times* Sesquicentennial Celebration issue named him among People Who Have Made a Difference. In 1990, Travis received the Mary Herrick Award, named for one of DuSable High School's respected teachers. Other honors include: The Living African American Heritage Award in 1992, the Myers Center Award for the Study of Human Rights in North America in 1995, the First America Award in 1996, and Kennedy-King College's Humanitarian Award in 1997. In 2000, Chicago State University inducted Travis into its Literary Hall of Fame.

A number of business awards recognized Travis's pioneering efforts. On December 3, 1970, he received the first Black Businessman of the Year Award. On February 21, 1975, he traveled to the White House where then vice-president Nelson Rockefeller presented him the first *Black Enterprise* Magazine Finance Achievement Award. In 1995, Ameritech presented Travis Realty its Small Business Community Service Award and Junior Achievement inducted Travis into the Chicago Business Community Hall of Fame.

Travis often rode his bicycle early in the morning, before work, along Chicago's lakeshore. He told John Seder and Berkeley Burrell: "While I'm looking at the grass and the lake, my thinking clears up. I can get a lot of work done while my competitors are still asleep. When I get back to the house, I can fill out a whole notebook of things to be done." The city has now made him a part of itself by imbedding his name in the sidewalk of the Bronzeville Walk of Fame.

In fulfilling his own dreams, Dempsey J. Travis made other people's dreams come true. Blacks who otherwise could not have owned real estate established homes of their own. Blacks who wanted to enter the fields of real estate and mortgage banking have found the path smoother because Travis led the way. He ably fulfilled one of the ideas he espoused in his autobiography, that when a person honestly does his best, his "personal success will become important to thousands of people."

REFERENCES

Books

"Dempsey J. Travis: Astute Chicagoan Negotiates Millions in Mortgages for Blacks." *Famous Blacks Give Secrets of Success*. Chicago: Johnson Publishing Company, 1973.

Haskins, James. "Dempsey J. Travis." In his *African American Entrepreneurs*. New York: John Wiley and Sons, 1998.

Seder, John, and Berkeley G. Burrell. "Dempsey J. Travis: Mortgage Banker." *Getting It Together*. New York: Harcourt Brace Jovanovich, 1971.

Periodicals

"Chicago Businessman Pens, Publishes Historic Work." *Jet* 61 (8 March 1982): 22.

"Dempsey Travis." *Atlantic Monthly* 253 (July 1984): 58-63.

Douglas, Carlyle C. "Never Buy Other People's Paint (How to Become a Millionaire)." *Ebony*, 31 (February 1976): 132-34.

Online

Dempsey Travis website. http://www.dempseytravis.com/ (Accessed 19 December 2005).

Marie Garrett

James Monroe Trotter
1842–1892

Soldier, music historian, writer

Chronology

1842	Born in Grand Gulf, Mississippi on February 7
1856	Family moves from Cincinnati to Hamilton, Ohio
1863	Joins all-black 55th Massachusetts Regiment in Boston; rapidly moves up in rank
1864	Wounded in battle in Honey Hill, South Carolina
1865	Musters out of service and settles in Boston
1866-73	Serves in Boston post office
1868	Marries Virginia Isaacs
1878	Publishes survey of American music, *Music and Some Highly Musical People*
1883	Joins William Dupree in managing recitals for Henrietta Vinson Davis; publishes article on Marie Selika in the *New York Globe*
1883	Serves in Benjamin F. Butler's campaign for governor of Massachusetts
1887	Appointed recorder of deeds in Washington, D.C. on March 3
1892	Dies in Boston on February 26

James Monroe Trotter promoted racial advancement in the 55th Massachusetts Regiment in which he served, in his seminal and pioneer work *Music and Some Highly Musical People*, and in his protests against racial intolerance that he experienced in his position in Boston's postal service. He believed that African Americans should promote themselves, and he used the press to encourage them to do so. He followed abolitionist and orator Frederick Douglass as recorder of deeds in Washington, D.C., becoming the second African American to hold that post.

The son of Richard S. Trotter, a white man, and his black slave Letitia, James Monroe Trotter was born on February 7, 1842, in the hamlet of Grand Gulf, Mississippi, located twenty-five miles south of Vicksburg on the Mississippi River. (Some sources give Trotter's date of birth as November 8, 1842.) After Richard Trotter married in 1854, he sent Letitia and the children of their union—James and two younger daughters—to Cincinnati, where they lived free. Young James attended the Gilmore School, a famous institution for freed slaves founded by Methodist clergyman Hiram S. Gilmore. There he studied music with William F. Colburn. His musical training served him well later on. In Cincinnati, James helped to support the family by working as a hotel bellboy and a riverboat cabin boy on a Cincinnati-to-New Orleans run. About 1856 the family moved on to nearby Hamilton. Trotter attended Albany Manual Labor University, located near Athens. He may have been mostly self-educated. Whatever the case, he taught school for a short time in Muskingum and Pike counties located in southwestern Ohio.

Civil War Soldier

During the Civil War, Secretary of War Edwin Stanton urged Massachusetts governor John Andrew, who favored the use of black troops in the segregated Union Army, to find volunteer regiments that would include African Americans. Andrew sent recruiters throughout the North to look for such volunteers. John Mercer Langston, then a recruiter, urged Trotter to sign on. He headed for Boston and in 1863 joined the 55th Massachusetts Regiment, an all-black unit with practically all-white officers, one of them George Garrison, a son of abolitionist William Lloyd Garrison. It was through his connection to George Garrison that Trotter met other Garrison family members.

As he demonstrated unusual ability, Trotter moved through the ranks from private to first sergeant, sergeant major (November 1863), and second lieutenant (April

1864). Stephen Fox, in *Dictionary of American Negro Biography*, described Trotter as a "genteel militant". Beginning with his commission to second lieutenant and continuing throughout his life, Trotter demonstrated such behavior. When his commission was delayed for several months due to an effort to appease some white officers, Trotter found the action "discouraging" and "maddening, almost." There were only four African American commissioned officers in the regiment, and Trotter was one of them. As a result of racial bias, the War Department for fifteen months refused to commission the men; the department claimed that there was no law requiring or authorizing them to be commissioned. Genteel militant or not, Trotter definitely spoke out, calling racism exactly what it was. He felt the coldness of white officers, who had claimed to be friendly to the black officers; the discouraging consequences of the War Department's inaction; and the fact that the white officers as well as the War Department in effect insulted black officers. They blamed the black officers for the color of their skin, Trotter thought.

The pay scale for military officers was another area of concern. Before the two black regiments were formed—the 54th and Trotter's 55th—the War Department knew that blacks would serve the army as common laborers; thus, the 1862 militia act was the only legal basis upon which blacks could be paid. The two regiments, however, refused to accept laborer's wages, prompting Andrews to urge the Massachusetts legislature to bring parity into the pay scale, giving black troops the same pay as white soldiers. For the Massachusetts regiments, the wheels of justice turned slowly. The men served an entire year without pay, causing family hardships, poor morale, and a decline in discipline. Although Representative Thaddeus Stevens introduced a bill to equalize pay, the matter dragged. It was not until June 15, 1864, that Congress authorized equal pay, and most of the men received their overdue wages in full by that October. All the while, Trotter supported the agitation for equal pay.

In November 1864, Trotter was slightly wounded in a battle near Honey Hill, South Carolina, where he served as leader. Back at camp, he put his education to work as he taught classes in reading and writing. He also drew upon his musical skills and organized a regimental band. He completed his military assignment with South Carolina's Commission on Labor and was mustered out in Boston in August 1865.

Works in Boston Post Office

Trotter settled in Boston, which was regarded as a friendly and thriving environment for blacks to live in. The growing African American community was appealing, as were the racially integrated schools. African Americans had voting rights; they were eligible to hold public office, to serve on juries, and to give testimony in court. By state law, racial discrimination was prohibited on public conveyances and at inns and public places. Clearly, Boston was an area of enlightenment, and it attracted Trotter's attention as a place in which to live, work, and advance. Rewarding blacks for their military service, the Republicans gave Trotter and some other African American officers appointments to clerkships in the Boston Post Office.

While teaching school in Ohio early on, Trotter had met Virginia Isaacs, of Chillicothe, Ohio. He returned there in 1868, when the two married. Anne Elizabeth Fawcett (or Fossett), who was the mother of Virginia Isaacs, was born a slave at Monticello plantation, where Thomas Jefferson lived. Oral tradition, recorded in Stephen R. Fox's *The Guardian of Boston*, claims that Fawcett was the daughter of Thomas Jefferson's mulatto son. Fawcett was said to have descended from the Jefferson-Sally Hemings relationship, thus making James Trotter's children—William Monroe, Maude, and Bessie—related to Jefferson. Fawcett married Tucker Isaacs, of free black and Jewish extraction, who bought her freedom; they relocated to Chillicothe, where Virginia Isaacs grew up.

James Trotter brought his bride to Boston where they lived at South End. Trotter took his clerkship in the post office. But tragedy struck, when their first two children died as infants; the cause of their deaths, the Trotters believed, was the rigor of city life. When Virginia Trotter began her third pregnancy, she returned to Ohio and on April 7, 1872, gave birth to William Monroe Trotter. Seven months later the Trotters considered Virginia Trotter well enough to return to Boston, where they lived at their next residence, 105 Kendall Street. Two years later the Trotters moved again, this time to suburban Hyde Park, as they anticipated a shift in the black population to

the suburbs that came in the 1890s. They increased their family with two daughters, Maude (1874) and Bessie (1883). Of the three Trotter children, William Monroe, popularly known as Monroe, was the most widely recognized. He distinguished himself as a publisher, editor, civil rights activist, elite integrationist, and one of the nation's most important African American spokesmen of the early twentieth century. He was a bitter opponent of educator Booker T. Washington, his views, and his followers.

Publishes Work on Music

James Trotter never lost his racial consciousness. His work on music allowed him to express his admiration for blacks and their musical achievement and to draw upon the musical training that he had received early on. Though by no means an accomplished musician or music scholar, in 1878 Trotter published the 508-page work, *Music and Some Highly Musical People*, an important historical work. This was the first survey of American music that, according to Eileen Southern in *The Music of Black Americans*, explored "a body of American music that cut across genres and styles." The book was well received and reprinted in 1880, 1881, and again in 1969, when its popularity resurfaced. Some writers claim that the book was important to the musical development of poet James Weldon Johnson.

In the preface, Trotter wrote that his intent was to provide a service to "some of its noblest devotees and the race to which the latter belong," and not so much to "the cause of music itself." His work includes biographical sketches and images of many remarkable musicians of that era, including over forty individuals and groups, such as singer Elizabeth Taylor Greenfield (the "Black Swan"), pianist Thomas Greene Bethune ("Blind Tom"), vocalists the Hyers Sisters (Anna Madah and Emma Louise), bandleader Frank Johnson, the Georgia Minstrels, and the Fisk Jubilee Singers. Trotter praised the slave spirituals that these singers from Fisk University sang, noting that they "have been sung by the American bondmen in the cruel days of the past." These had "originated with the slave," he added. The songs were spontaneous "from souls naturally musical." Quoting an unnamed but eminent writer, he said that the songs formed "the only native American Music," or the spiritual. Added to this is a section with brief sketches of obscure musicians. An appendix containing thirteen vocal and instrumental pieces by black composers concludes the work. There are in the book press notices, reproductions of recital programs, essays on topics such as symphony orchestras in New Orleans, and The Colored American Opera company.

Trotter continued his work at the post office until racial injustice raised its ugly head—a white employee was promoted over him to a chief clerkship post. Although he felt secure in his post and considered the salary adequate, this was a racial insult that he found intolerable. In protest, he resigned. The next few years he engaged in a number of enterprises, such as musical promoter, real estate agent, and local agent for a telephone company that competed with the Bell system. In his musical promotions, in 1883 he and friend William Dupree managed Henrietta Vinton Davis' dramatic recitals. Musicians and assisting artists were involved in the recitals. Trotter and Dupree also managed the musical career of concert singer Marie Selika and others. He had become highly respected in the white Hyde Park section where he lived. On July 4, 1884, Trotter was called on to give a Fourth of July speech to white residents of Hyde Park.

Around this time as well, Trotter switched from the Republican to the Democratic Party. His interest in the political arena was great. In the fall of 1883 he served in the Benjamin F. Butler Democratic campaign for Massachusetts governor. When Butler won, Trotter celebrated openly by letting his views become known in the press—*The New York Globe*, then black America's most influential newspaper. The black Democrats of New England preferred to call themselves Independents. They held a conference in Boston in 1886 and Trotter served as temporary chair. When Rhode Island's black abolitionist George Downing declined the post, Trotter was elected permanent chair. From his position he stressed the importance of the black ballot and of political independence. He urged blacks to resist white oppression; he said the condition of blacks resulted from the manner in which they allowed themselves to be treated. Yet, according to Fox in *The Guardian of Boston*, Trotter was a race leader, "militant but a trifle distant, speaking down to the race from the comfortable life in Hyde Park." Although he was genuine in his concern for his race, he was fortunate enough to have elevated himself through his accomplishments and "he expected others to do the same through protest and work."

Goes to Washington

Trotter had endeared himself to black Democrats and rose to prominence among them as he moved on to a lucrative political job. President James A. Garfield appointed abolitionist and orator Frederick Douglass to the post recorder of deeds for the District of Columbia in March 1881 and he held that post for five years. He was the first African American in that position—a post that was the nation's highest office that an African American could hold and came to be customarily reserved for them. When Democratic President Grover Cleveland took office, Douglass resigned and another African American, New Yorker James C. Matthews, was nominated as his replacement. When the Senate twice refused to confirm him, in late February 1887 Cleveland nominated Trotter. But Democrats and Republicans resisted, their reasons being the Democrats' dissatisfaction with his race and the Republicans' objection to his politics. The nomination

seemed headed to failure, but Trotter's friends in Boston found the impasse unacceptable. On March 3, two Republican senators from Boston surprised those in session by endorsing Trotter on the Senate floor. He was confirmed that night by a mostly Republican 32-10 vote.

This was a prime time for Trotter, who held the post from 1887 to 1889. Real estate in the District of Columbia was booming; his salary was based on a percentage of the transactions, which meant that his post was financially rewarding. Although many people tried to induce him to join various protest efforts, he avoided protest activities of any kind. When the Republicans returned to office in 1889, Trotter left the lucrative post and returned to Boston and to his family, who had not joined him in Washington.

To support his family, Trotter established a real estate business. He could also devote more time to his family, for now his only son, Monroe, was doing well in high school. A demanding father, he set high standards for his son and daughters. Prominent in Hyde Park and in Boston, the family had among its friends the Archibald Grimkés, who also lived in Hyde Park. Archibald Grimké was a nephew of Angelina Grimké Weld and her sister Sarah Grimké, prominent abolitionists and suffragists, who became his surrogate parents while he was in college. By marriage, Archibald Grimké was related to abolitionist Theodore Weld. Other black luminaries of Boston visited the Trotters as well, but they had to accept his views of racial militancy. For a while, Trotter rejected William H. Duprees because the two men were in conflict over race and politics. Dupree had served with Trotter in the 55th Massachusetts regiment, but that did not matter then. He had also worked with Trotter at the post office and had married Virginia Isaac Trotter's sister. The Duprees were no longer allowed to visit the Trotters. In time, however, the men reconciled, much to the benefit of Virginia Trotter and her daughters. After Trotter's death, they lived with the Duprees on Northampton Street in Boston, while Monroe Trotter was enrolled at Harvard University.

Toward the end of 1899, Trotter's health was failing and political pressures began to take their toll on him. He died of tuberculosis on February 26, 1892 and was survived by his wife, son, and two daughters. Though labeled a genteel militant, he was an ardent supporter of the black race. He promoted racial pride and accomplishments in the press and in his enduring work on the history of music.

REFERENCES

Books

Fox, Stephen R. *The Guardian of Boston: William Monroe Trotter*. New York: Athenaeum, 1970.

———. "James Monroe Trotter." In *Dictionary of American Negro Biography*. Eds. Rayford W. Logan and Michael R. Winston. New York: Norton, 1982.

Simmons, William J. *Men of Mark: Eminent, Progressive, and Rising*. Cleveland: Geo. M. Rewell & Co., 1887.

Southern, Eileen. *Biographical Dictionary of Afro-American and African Musicians*. Westport, Conn.: Greenwood Press, 1982.

———. *The Music of Black Americans*. 2nd ed. New York: Norton, 1983.

Stevenson, Robert. "James Monroe Trotter." In *The New Grove Dictionary of Music and Musicians*. 2nd ed. Vol. 25. Ed. Stanley Sadie. New York: Macmillan, 2001.

Collections

Trotter's Civil War letters are in the Edward W. Kingsley Papers at Duke University, Durham, North Carolina. There is a manuscript sketch of him in the George W. Forbes Papers, Boston Public Library.

Jessie Carney Smith

Benjamin S. Turner

Benjamin S. Turner
1825–1894

Politician

While still a slave, Benjamin S. Turner acquired considerable wealth as a livery stable owner and merchant. After the Emancipation, he served Selma, Alabama, as tax collector then as city councilman. A short time thereafter, he became the first African American to represent Alabama in the United States House of Representatives.

Born March 17, 1825, in Halifax County, North Carolina, near Weldon, Benjamin Sterling Turner entered life as the slave of widow Elizabeth Turner. History does not record his parents' names. When Mrs. Turner moved to Dallas County, Alabama, in 1830, she took her five-year-old slave with her. Thus, Turner grew up in the heart of cotton country.

In 1845, Mrs. Turner sold Benjamin to Major W. H. Gee, her stepdaughter's husband, to pay off some debts. Despite laws against educating slaves, Gee's children taught Turner to read and write, a skill he practiced by reading newspapers. Even when one of Gee's overseers caught Turner reading a spelling book and threatened punishment, Turner persisted in his efforts to learn. Even-

tually, Turner's master put him in charge of the Gee House Hotel, a new family business in Selma, Alabama.

When Gee died, Turner became the property of Dr. James T. Gee, his former master's brother. Aware of Turner's previous work experience, Dr. Gee gave his new slave responsibility for the St. James Hotel, one of the largest in Selma. Unlike many slaveholders, Gee allowed Turner to earn extra cash by running a livery stable and a wood yard. Through his business dealings, Turner earned the respect of both blacks and whites. In *Neither Carpetbaggers nor Scalawags: Black Officeholders During the Reconstruction of Alabama, 1867-1878*, Richard Bailey comments that Turner's "perseverance, inquisitiveness, diligence, loyalty, and attentiveness" contributed to his success. The contacts he made with influential citizens of both races during this time eventually proved politically valuable.

Endures Civil War

Probably sometime in the 1850s, Turner married a young black slave named Independence. Some records indicate that the couple had a son named Osceola. But the marriage came to a heartbreaking end when a white man purchased Turner's wife for his mistress. Turner never married again.

Charles Carey notes in *African-American Political Leaders: A-Z of African Americans*, "When the Civil War broke out, Selma became a manufacturing center and supply base for the Confederacy." Turner invested in the war effort by purchasing $200 in Confederate bonds. Throughout the war, he cared for his own business and for that of his absent owner, who served with the Confederate Army.

On April 2, 1865, Union general James H. Wilson's cavalry captured Selma, took prisoners, and confiscated horses, equipment, and supplies. Worse yet, they burned a significant portion of the city. Turner lost most of his property and later filed a claim for an $8,000 reimbursement with the Southern Claims Commission. With or without the fulfillment of that claim, he began rebuilding his wealth.

In 1865, at the end of the Civil War and the beginning of Turner's freedom, he chose to settle in Selma and to open a mercantile business. Valuing the education he had earned despite adverse circumstances, he used his own money to finance the establishment of a school for Selma's black children. Some sources state that for a while he became a teacher.

Becomes Leader after War

Turner definitely became involved in efforts to reestablish order after the war. With a white doctor, John H. Henry, Turner urged fellow freedmen to make contracts with their former owners, or with other employers, and return to work. The white community noticed and appreciated Turner's peaceful efforts to bring order to a chaotic situation.

Seeing Turner's influence, officials appointed him Dallas County tax collector in 1867, after implementation of the Reconstruction Acts. Turner resigned after a year to run for Selma city councilman, running as an Independent. In 1869, he and another former slave became the city's first black city councilmen. When the city began paying its councilmen a salary, Turner resigned, prompted by his conviction that public servants should fulfill their roles without pay during such troubled times.

By 1870, Turner held property worth $10,000 and had gained a reputation as an honest, reasonable man. Holding the respect of the community and having experienced a taste of leadership, he sought further involvement in politics. Concerned about the racism he saw in the Democratic Party, he chose to affiliate with the Republican Party instead. He immediately used his influence to encourage many other blacks to join the Republicans.

Both blacks and whites supported Turner's nomination as a congressman that year. But Republicans from the North chose not to support him financially because of his moderate political views. Forced to resort to raising his own money for the campaign, Turner sold a horse. His platform of "Universal Suffrage and Universal Amnesty" helped him win the right to represent Alabama's First Congressional District at the 42nd Congress.

Represents Alabama in Congress

Turner became the first African American from Alabama to serve in the United States House of Representatives. Forty-five years old, he took office on March 4, 1871. Recently freed, he did not have years of background experience in politics. But this mild-mannered man took his new responsibility seriously and spoke well for the people he represented, even though Congress chose not to enact the bills he introduced. The man whom Carey called "a moderate with a vision," spoke for his state and his people nonetheless.

Turner's assignment involved serving on the Committee on Invalid Pensions. Three of the bills he introduced provided pensions for one black and two white veterans of the Union Army. According to William Rogers in *American National Biography*, Turner unsuccessfully "introduced five bills to remove the Fourteenth Amendment's political disabilities from eight white Alabamians." His attempt to obtain federal funding for repairs to an Episcopal church damaged during the war also proved unsuccessful.

Opposes Cotton Tax and Advocates for Federal Funding

Turner spoke eloquently for the repeal of the cotton tax imposed after the war. Calling the tax unconstitutional, he emphasized the extreme hardship imposed on the state and especially on the blacks who worked the fields. Although congressional colleagues recognized his political expertise, good judgment, and excellent understanding of congressional procedure, they ignored Turner's pleas.

Turner spoke in favor of appropriating $200,000 in federal funds for a public building in Selma that would serve as a custom house, post office, and revenue office. He argued the government's pressing need for this space, the work the project would create for suffering yet deserving people, and the commercial growth that would result from the investment.

Not given the opportunity to present his arguments verbally before Congress, Turner did at least see his two speeches concerning these matters printed in the appendix of the *Congressional Globe*. The cotton tax still stood and the Committee on Public Buildings and Grounds failed to introduce the bill for appropriation of funds before the full Congress.

Yet Turner continued his efforts toward influencing Congress to help revitalize the southern economy. He introduced a bill asking the government to sell land in small sections at greatly reduced rates to needy southern people, both black and white. His proposal involved selling tracts of 160 acres or less, according to the need. Buyers would pay 10 percent at the time of purchase and 10 percent each year until they completely paid for the land. The Committee on Public Lands never introduced this bill into Congress.

According to Rayford Logan in *Dictionary of American Negro Biography*, in Turner's last few months in Congress, he "introduced no bills, but out of party loyalty supported the test oath, mixed schools, civil rights, and the franking privilege, while opposing civil service and the removal of names of battles on war flags."

Returns to Private Life

In 1872, Turner returned to Selma to seek another term in Congress, supported by the Republican Party. He had a good chance to win the nomination until Philip Joseph, a black Independent and editor of the Mobile *Watchman*, decided to oppose him. Contrary to his quiet nature, Turner spoke out strongly against his opponent, attacking Joseph's actions during the Civil War. The rivalry between the two black men insured the victory of Frederick G. Bromberg, a white candidate supported by the Democrats and the new Liberal Republican Party.

With this defeat, Turner ended his participation in national politics, but he remained active in local politics. According to Rogers, by 1880 Turner had served on the Alabama Republican executive committee three times. During that year, he attended the Republican National Convention as a delegate at large and also served as a Republican presidential elector.

At the end of his term in Congress, Turner returned to Selma. With his congressional retirement fund, he purchased a three-hundred-acre farm. In the nation's extreme financial crisis during 1873 and the years thereafter, Turner went bankrupt. One source states that he became paralyzed following a stroke. For whatever reason, Turner was unable to overcome yet another financial setback. Creditors sold his farm to pay his debts. Turner died a few months later, on March 21, 1894, on his farm outside Selma. He is buried in Selma's Live Oak Cemetery.

In 1985, blacks and whites joined together to honor Benjamin S. Turner, noting his accomplishments and the manner in which he represented his people and state. They established a monument at his gravesite. Organizers chose Jeremiah Denton, a white man and Alabama's first Republican to serve as a United States senator since the Reconstruction, to speak at the dedication ceremony.

REFERENCES

Books

Bailey, Richard. *Neither Carpetbaggers nor Scalawags: Black Officeholders During the Reconstruction of Alabama, 1867-1878*. 3rd ed. Montgomery, Ala.: Richard Bailey Publishers, 1995.

Carey, Charles W., Jr. *African-American Political Leaders: A-Z of African Americans*. New York: Facts on File, 2004.

Christopher, Maurine. *America's Black Congressmen*. New York: Thomas Y. Crowell, 1971.

Foner, Eric. *Freedom's Lawmakers: A Directory of Black Officeholders During Reconstruction*. New York: Oxford University Press, 1993.

Haskins, James. *Distinguished African American Political and Governmental Leaders*. Phoenix, Ariz.: Oryx Press, 1999.

Logan, Rayford, W. "Turner, Benjamin S." In *Dictionary of American Negro Biography*. Eds. Rayford W. Logan and Michael R. Winston. New York: Norton, 1982.

McFarlin, Annjennette Sophie. *Black Congressional Reconstruction Orators and their Orations, 1869-1879*. Metuchen, N.J.: Scarecrow Press, 1976.

Rogers, William W. "Turner Benjamin Sterling." In *American National Biography*. Eds. John A. Garraty and Mark C. Carnes. Vol. 22. New York: Oxford University Press, 1999.

Marie Garrett

Charles H. Turner
1867–1923

Scientist, zoologist, researcher, educator

Charles Henry Turner, who lived during the late nineteenth and early twentieth centuries, was a scientist. He earned a Ph.D. from the University of Chicago in the biological sciences, conducted research on animal behavior, published in scientific journals, became a member of scientific organizations, and was elected to office in a scientific organization. In addition, Turner taught and/or served as an educational administrator during the more than three decades he conducted scientific research.

Turner was born in Cincinnati, Ohio on February 3, 1867. He was the son of Thomas Turner, a church custodian from Alberta, Canada, and Addie Campbell Turner, a practical nurse from Lexington, Kentucky. According to several sources, Addie Turner was a former slave. Her husband was a well-read man who owned several hundred books, and the couple displayed a love of learning that proved inspirational to their son. In Cincinnati, Charles Turner attended the Walnut Hills District School and Gaines High School, which opened one year before Turner's birth and was one of the first high schools for African Americans in Ohio. Turner graduated from Gaines as class valedictorian.

In 1886, Turner began attending the University of Cincinnati. He majored in biology, and Professor Clarence L. Herrick, a pioneer in psychobiology, was Turner's mentor. In 1891, Turner received his B.S. One year later, he was a volunteer at the Cincinnati Observatory. Also in 1892, Turner received his M.S. from the University of Cincinnati and became the first African American to earn a graduate degree from the university. Turner was awarded the Ph.D. degree in zoology from the University of Chicago in 1907. The title of his dissertation was "The Homing of Ants: An Experimental Study of Ant Behavior."

Becomes an Educator

Prior to receiving his undergraduate degree, Turner taught at the Governor Street School in Evansville, Indiana from 1888 to 1889. Also in 1889, Turner was briefly employed as a Cincinnati public school substitute teacher. In 1891, he began a two-year assistantship in biology at the University of Cincinnati. Turner's goal was to obtain employment at an African American educational institution. In April 1893 he wrote to Booker T. Washington, who was the principal of Tuskegee Normal and Industrial Institute (now known as Tuskegee University), for information about openings at African American colleges. Later that year, Turner was appointed professor of biology and chair of the Department of Science and Agriculture at Clark University (now known as Clark Atlanta University). Turner's years at Clark marked the early stages of the fulfillment of his goal to work at black institutions, and all of his subsequent full-time employment was at African American schools. Turner, who also served as dean of the Georgia Summer School in 1901, remained at Clark until 1905. In 1906, Turner was principal of the College Hill School in Cleveland, Tennessee. From 1907 to 1908, he was employed as a professor of biology and chemistry at Haines Normal and Industrial Institute in Atlanta, Georgia. In 1908, Turner moved to St. Louis, Missouri, where he taught at Sumner High School. Sumner, founded in 1875, was the first African American high school west of the Mississippi River and was known for its prestigious faculty, which included Edward A. Bouchet, who earned a Ph.D. in physics from Yale University in 1876 and consequently was the first African American to receive a Ph.D. from an American university. Bouchet taught mathematics and physics at Sumner from 1902 to 1903.

Although most sources state that Turner taught at Sumner High, the *African-American Heritage of St. Louis: A Guide* asserts that Turner taught at Sumner Normal School, which was established at Sumner High in 1890 in order to provide an additional year of education beyond high school as a means of training African American teachers. In 1925, two years after Turner's death, Sumner Normal School became Sumner Teachers' College and today is known as Harris-Stowe State University. Whether Turner taught at the high school or the normal school, he remained at Sumner until illness forced him to retire in 1922.

Sumner High School is located in the Ville, the historic district of St. Louis that was originally known as Elleardsville. In the late nineteenth century, the Ville was home to Irish and German immigrants as well as African Americans. Between 1920 and 1930, the neighborhood's African American population increased from 8 percent to 86 percent. Turner and his family moved into the middle class community in 1912. On October 24, 2005, in recognition of Turner's contributions to St. Louis and to the field of science, a proposal was submitted to the City of

St. Louis Preservation Board to nominate Turner's house for listing in the National Register of Historic Places. Also located in the Ville is the Turner Middle School, a National Registry property that was formerly known as the Charles Henry Turner Open Air School for Crippled Children. The St. Louis Board of Education had the school built in 1925 to honor Turner's memory. Many of the school's students had tuberculosis, and in the 1920s, fresh air was considered therapeutic for the children; thus the school was designated open air.

During his career as an educator, Turner authored articles such as "Reason for Teaching Biology in Negro Schools," published in *The Southwestern Christian Advocate* (1897), and "Will the Education of the Negro Solve the Race Problem?", published in *Twentieth Century Negro Literature* (1902), edited by D.W. Culp. In the second article, Turner advocates a college education rather than industrial training for African Americans. He also wrote nature stories for children and more than thirty poems that apparently remained unpublished.

Gains International Prominence as Researcher

Turner pursued his research interests for more than three decades. He was a prolific researcher who published between fifty to seventy articles. Turner's research was first published in 1891 when his undergraduate thesis, "Morphology of the Avian Brain," appeared in the first volume of the *Journal of Comparative Neurology*, a publication founded by Clarence L. Herrick in 1891 that was known from 1904 to 1910 as the *Journal of Comparative Neurology and Psychology* before it reverted to its original name in 1911. In addition to Herrick's journal, to which Turner contributed additional articles, Turner's work appeared in periodicals such as the *American Naturalist, Biological Bulletin, Journal of Animal Behavior, Psychological Bulletin, Science, Transactions of the Academy of Science at St. Louis,* and *Zoological Bulletin..* In 2003, which marked the eightieth anniversary of Turner's death, *Selected Papers and Biography of Charles Henry Turner (1867-1923), Pioneer of Comparative Animal Behavior Studies* was published.

Among Turner's most impressive works are "The Homing of Ants: An Experimental Study of Ant Behavior," which was based on his doctoral dissertation and was published in the September 1907 issue of the *Journal of Comparative Neurology and Psychology*, and the five hundred page treatise that Turner wrote with Clarence Herrick, *Synopsis of the Entomostraca of Minnesota; With Descriptions of Related Species Comparing All Known Forms from the United States, Included in the Orders Copepoda, Cladocera, Ostrocada* (1895).

Turner is best known as an expert on insect behavior. While investigating how ants find their way back to ant colonies, he found that ants use light and landmarks as factors to direct them to their nests. Turner was the first to describe a gyrating movement made by certain species of ants upon returning to their nests. Since 1910, when French scientists named the pattern of movement in honor of Turner's findings, it has been known as "Turner's circling." Among Turner's other findings were that certain insects can hear and distinguish pitch; that cockroaches can learn by trial and error; that bees respond to color, patterns, and odors; and that burrowing bees remember landmarks near their nests.

Turner was active in professional organizations. He became a member of the Academy of Science of St. Louis and was elected secretary of the entomology section and council member. Turner was also a member of the Academy of Science of Illinois and the Entomological Society of America. In 1907, he was a delegate to the Seventh International Zoological Congress.

In addition to his demanding work as an educator and researcher, Turner was active in civic affairs. In St. Louis, he improved social services for African Americans, served as the director of the Colored Branch, YMCA, and was involved in civil rights activities.

In 1887, Turner married Leontine Troy, who was from Cincinnati, during his undergraduate days at the University of Cincinnati. They were the parents of at least three children: Henry Owen Turner, Darwin Romanes Turner, and Louisa Mae Turner. Leontine Turner died in 1895 while her husband was employed at Clark. In 1907 Turner, who was then working at Haines, married Lillian Porter, who was from Augusta, Georgia. When Turner became ill in 1922 and retired from Sumner, he moved to Chicago, Illinois, and lived in Darwin's home. Henry Turner died on February 14, 1923, at the age of fifty-six. He was survived by his second wife and at least two children, Henry and Darwin, who were pharmacists. (Birth and date dates for Louisa, a teacher, are missing.)

REFERENCES

Books

Abramson, Charles I., Natasha D. Jackson, and Camille L. Fuller, eds. *Selected Papers and Biography of Charles Henry Turner (1867-1923), Pioneer of Comparative Animal Behavior Studies.* Lewiston, N.Y.: Edwin Mellen Press, 2003.

Culp, D.W., ed. *Twentieth Century Negro Literature: or, A Cyclopedia of Thought on the Vital Topics Relating to the American Negro by One Hundred of America's Greatest Negroes.* Naperville, Ill.: J. L. Nichols and Co., 1902.

Hayden, Robert C. "Charles H. Turner." In *Dictionary of American Negro Biography.* Eds. Rayford W. Logan and Michael R. Winston. New York: Norton, 1982.

Manning, Kenneth R. "Charles Henry Turner." In *African American Lives.* Eds. Henry Louis Gates, Jr. and Evelyn Brooks Higginbotham. New York: Oxford University Press, 2004.

St. Louis Public Library. *African-American Heritage of St. Louis: A Guide*. St. Louis: St. Louis Public Library, 1992.

Online

Abramson, Charles I., et al. "Charles Henry Turner: Contributions of a Forgotten African American to Scientific Research." Oklahoma State University. http://psychology.okstate.edu/museum/turner/turnermain.html (Accessed 21 January 2006).

Linda M. Carter

Chronology

1840	Born a slave in St. Louis, Missouri on May 16
1845	Freed from slavery at four years of age
1855	Attends Oberlin College, Ohio
1859	Works as a porter
1861	Body servant to Col. Madison Miller, a member of the Union Army
1868	Works with the Freemen's Bureau
1871	Arrives in Liberia as U.S. minister resident consul general
1877	Returns to United States from Liberia at the end of his tenure
1879	Organizes the Colored Emigration Aid Association
1886	Teaches in Kansas City
1915	Dies near St. Louis on November 1

J. Milton Turner
1840–1915

Consul, politician

Despite his humble beginning as a slave, James Milton Turner became a prominent African American politician during the Reconstruction period in the United States, serving in Liberia. He was an ardent advocate for black rights from 1865 to 1866 and after his return from Liberia in 1878. Turner's main focus was equality for all African Americans. He worked for voting rights, equal educational opportunities, and fair treatment for southern immigrants. He also fought for former slaves of the Cherokee nation to secure their equal tribal rights. Although Turner was recognized while he was active, he was never given the recognition that he deserved at his death.

James Milton Turner was born to slave parents on or about May 16, 1840, supposedly on the same day as James Milton Loring, his master's son, in St. Louis, Missouri. His father, John Turner, a literate black man, may have been born in Virginia. John Turner learned some veterinary skills from his master, and he was referred to as Black John the Horse Doctor; however, official records indicate he was a horse ferrier. He was also referred to as John Coburn, and he migrated with his master Frederick Coburn to St. Louis, Missouri where he met his wife, Hannah. There are conflicting stories about how she gained her freedom. One story is that Hannah's master, Loring, took her from Kentucky to Missouri, and after John Turner gained his freedom, he bought the freedom of his wife and son when the child was about four years old. Another story suggests that Theodosia Young, who had received Hannah as a wedding gift, freed her and her son.

Though James Turner was free, he had limited educational opportunities. Missouri State laws restricted blacks from learning to read. Despite these restrictions, Turner attended a school developed by a former slave, Reverend John Berry Meachum, which provided general education for slave children under the guise of religious instructions. Turner also attended St. Louis Catholic Cathedral where nuns taught black children. His outstanding reading skills are also attributed to an unconventional religious white man who believed that everyone should be able to read the Bible. At fourteen, Turner entered the Christian, integrated Oberlin College in Ohio. Oberlin's annual catalogue records his name in its 1855-1856 issue. His stint at Oberlin was brief, but he returned to his hometown an educated black man.

He married Ella De Burton from Cincinnati who was then living in Missouri. She died on March 2, 1908, in St. Louis, leaving her daughter from a previous marriage. Turner was a father to his stepchild and niece who was orphaned. These two girls attended Oberlin College.

Interest in Education for Blacks

Turner became a spokesman for black education. He became involved in the American Missionary Association (AMA) that established free schools for blacks. The AMA started these schools in St. Louis, but they were adopted in all the states. After he married, beginning in April 1886, Turner taught in Kansas City. The AMA enlisted the help of the Freedmen's Bureau that, in turn, asked Turner to assist with a program to evaluate black schools. Turner established and taught in schools for blacks in many locations. He also investigated the health of black schools and education in Missouri. He asserted the need for trained teachers, especially black teachers in black schools. When he visited Lincoln Institute, the first public black institution or normal school in Missouri, he became particularly committed to equal education. Turner believed that the same laws that governed and maintained white schools should govern black schools. He campaigned for black education all over the state.

Turner worked several jobs, but he was interested in politics. Returning to Missouri as an educated black man, he had worked as a porter from 1859 to 1860. During the Civil War, he worked as a body servant to Colonel Madison Miller, a member of the Union Army. He thought that he witnessed Colonel Miller's death, so he turned over Miller's money in his keeping to Miller's wife. On Miller's safe return from the war, Turner was rewarded. His official introduction to politics resulted from his honesty. He met Mrs. Miller's brother, Thomas H. Fletcher, who was involved in the Radical Republican Party. Turner believed that the Radical Republicans would serve the interest of the black people by extending civil liberties to them.

Turner was involved in the Underground Railroad, helping slaves escape from the South to the North. His interest in civil rights continued when he became involved in the Missouri Equal Rights League in 1865. He became secretary for the association in 1871. He was known for his promotion of political equality for blacks and equal educational opportunities. As an active member of the Equal Rights League, Turner worked to convince whites to vote for an amendment to the voting law that prevented black suffrage. He lobbied through the media. However, black suffrage did not occur until the ratification of the Fifteenth Amendment was accepted. Blacks were able to vote freely for the first time in 1870. Turner helped mobilize blacks to vote although they were fearful because of racism, and there was also widespread illiteracy. In addition, he fought for blacks to be able to sit on juries. His absolute goal was the elimination of white biases and the establishment of racial equality.

Turner was drawn to the Radical Republicans whom he believed had genuine interest in the plight of the blacks. He helped to mobilize blacks to vote for Republicans because he was convinced that federal power would strengthen the position of the blacks. The Republicans depended on the black vote. Because he was closely affiliated with the Republicans, educated, and had interest in black civil liberties, Turner was chosen by President Grant to be the U.S. minister resident consul general to Liberia, where African Americans were being colonized.

When he entered Liberia in 1871, Turner was not prepared for his job. The United States wanted friendly relations with Liberia. But native Africans were opposed to the emigration of African Americans because the newcomers were given lands by the American-led Liberian government that belonged to natives. Issuing these lands to colonists caused tension that led to open revolt by the Grebo people. Turner criticized the United States for colonizing people who were virtually displaced without any provision for self-reliance. Turner encouraged integration with natives. He also suggested education as a means of nation building. After returning from a stay in the United States, where he went to recuperate from malaria, he was more convinced that the United States was neglecting its colonized people just as it neglected African Americans in the States. Turner returned to the United States in 1887

disillusioned with the federal government but still committed to fighting for black civil liberties.

Continues Civil Rights Struggles

Two years after his return from his duties in Liberia, Turner organized the Colored Emigration Aid Association in 1879 to assist colored immigrants who were leaving the South. This organization was not successful, but at least the plight of emigrants was made public. Turner's last major act was to ensure that former slaves who belonged to the Cherokee nation gained full tribal rights. In these fights, Turner's position as a legal representative allowed him to perform the duties of a lawyer. He argued extensively that the tribal legislation, that gave the freedmen a share of land, was violated because these men did not receive their lands from the government. He also involved himself in similar problems faced by the Choctaw and Chickasaw nations.

Turner established schools for blacks throughout Missouri. He used his political power to oppose segregation and helped obtain education and voting rights. He was the first black U.S. ambassador. Mostly his allegiance was for the Republican Party. He preached self-sufficiency to blacks as he believed that they could uplift themselves. Turner's last days were active; however, he died on November 1, 1915 unexpectedly from an injury that he received a few days before from a car explosion accident.

REFERENCES

Books

Kremer, Gary R. *James Milton Turner and the Promise of America*. Columbia: University of Missouri Press, 1991.

Periodicals

Dilliard, Irving. "James Milton Turner: A Little Known Benefactor of His People." *Journal of Negro History* 19 (October 1934): 372-411.

Denise Jarrett

Waters E. Turpin
1910–1968
Writer

Waters Edward Turpin was a groundbreaking author who became prominent during the Harlem Renaissance. Driven by the need to write but full of self-

Chronology

1910	Born in Oxford, Maryland on April 9
1913	Father Simon dies
1922	Mother accepts job with Edna Ferber; moves with Turpin to New Jersey
1931	Receives B.A. in English from Morgan State College; begins work as a welfare fraud investigator for the Works Progress Administration
1932	Completes M.A. in English from Columbia University
1935	Begins teaching English at Storer College in Harpers Ferry, West Virginia
1936	Marries Jean Fisher
1937	Publishes first novel *These Low Grounds*
1938	Leaves Storer College to work on doctorate at Columbia University
1939	Publishes second novel *O Canaan!*
1940	Begins teaching English at Lincoln University
1941	Named Julius Rosenwald Fellow in Creative Writing
1949	Begins teaching English at Morgan State College
1957	Self-publishes third novel *The Rootless*
1960	Receives Ed.D. from Columbia University
1968	Dies of abdominal cancer in Baltimore, Maryland on November 19

doubt and uncertainty throughout much of his writing career, Turpin juggled the role of being the family bread-winner with his desire for independence. One catalyst for Turpin in his pursuit of a writing career may have been the racial discrimination he saw everyday as well as their uneven representation in literature. Turpin used his writing to protest the socio-economic and political plight of African Americans and to portray the courageous black men and women who helped to shape their race, culture, and the United States. Turpin's promise as a writer was never completely fulfilled; however, Turpin began the process which may have motivated African American authors such as Alex Haley who went on to write the saga of his own family.

Turpin was born April 9, 1910 in Oxford, Maryland, the only child of Mary Rebecca Henry and Simon Turpin. Turpin's father died when he was three years old, and thus Turpin's maternal grandfather played a large role in Turpin's life. Turpin's grandfather's stories about the struggles of black people on the eastern shore of Maryland were to remain as vivid memories throughout Turpin's life and helped to shape Turpin as a writer.

Turpin's dream since childhood was to become an educator and in that way to advance the lot of African Americans. In 1922 Turpin moved to New Jersey when his mother was hired by Edna Ferber as a cook and household manager. Mrs. Turpin ultimately ran the Ferber household and was Ferber's confidante. Turpin was sent to Morgan Preparatory Academy during his high school years. This school was a stepping-stone into Morgan College, now Morgan State University. During time off from school, Turpin stayed with his mother in New York. Ferber was quite impressed with Turpin's intelligence and encouraged Turpin to write; she acted as mentor and advisor sometimes assisting Turpin's entrance into literary circles.

Turpin began pursuing a B.A. in English at Morgan College in 1927. During his final years at Morgan, Turpin and some of his fellow students, including his future wife Jean Fisher, began a school newspaper, the *Morgan Newsletter* of which Turpin served as editor.

Turpin became a welfare investigator in the early 1930s for the Works Progress Administration (WPA), which provided work for millions of people during the depression. Finally in 1935, Turpin, with the help of Edna Ferber, obtained a job at Storer College in Harpers Ferry, West Virginia as an English professor, counselor, and football coach. Now defunct, Storer was the first college for African Americans in West Virginia.

While still at Storer, Turpin began writing his first novel, *These Low Grounds*, and began working on his M.A. in English at Columbia. *These Low Grounds* tells the story of the lives and struggles of four generations of an African American family beginning with Martha, a freed slave who becomes a housemaid, through her great grandson Jimmy who is an athlete with dreams of becoming a teacher and returning to his hometown in Maryland to improve the lives of his fellow men. *These Low Grounds*, published in 1937 by Harper and republished by McGrath in 1969, was the forerunner of family history legacies such as Alex Haley's *Roots*.

In 1937, Turpin married Jean Fisher. Turpin's marriage was unconventional in that for most of their married life, Turpin did not live with Fisher. Despite this arrangement, Turpin's wife was one of his biggest supporters.

Repeatedly throughout his writing career, Turpin struggled with the development of characters past the physical aspects (i.e. who they were as people, their thoughts, feelings, and motivation for their actions). Turpin also struggled with the conflict between his need to write and his need to provide for his family. Attempting to resolve this conflict, Turpin applied for a Guggenheim Foundation grant to support his writing a five-novel series which would trace one family back to its roots in Africa. The proposal included extensive research in the United States and Africa. While Turpin's wife and mother were supportive, Turpin sometimes felt emasculated by them. In fact, Turpin felt that African American women, in general, caused the men in their lives to be less than men. This theme was dealt with in Turpin's *Long Way Home*.

Turpin completed his M.A. in English at Columbia and began working on a doctorate in education in 1939. Turpin's second novel *O Canaan!*, published by Doubleday and reprinted by AMS Press in 1975, was the second novel in Turpin's five-part series. This book explores the efforts of blacks to survive in the northern U.S. cities. Rather than focusing on the negatives, Turpin wrote about hope and the importance of family values. Turpin addresses such themes as inter-racial tension and bigotry and the clashing of different values within a family. Turpin called the novel *O Canaan!* because of the parallel between blacks in the United States and the ancient Hebrews who traveled in search of a homeland where they could live happily in freedom and peace. The novel is divided into four parts with each part focusing on a different family member. In a February 1949 speech about the novel, Turpin stated that his purpose was not to portray what happened just to blacks, but to all people regardless of race who have persevered despite hard times.

Despite his literary successes, Turpin continued to be plagued by the need to be independent. In hopes of lessening his stress, Turpin's wife, mother, and Edna Ferber put in motion a series of events which ultimately led to Turpin landing a job at Lincoln University. Despite his misgivings about the help he received in getting the job at Lincoln, Turpin quickly proved himself and became a valued faculty member and a favorite among Lincoln University students.

Education Career

In March 1941 Turpin was named the Julius Rosenwald Fellow in Creative writing. Turpin took a leave of absence from Lincoln University to go to Baltimore to conduct the research necessary to fulfill the terms of the grant that would lead to the writing of *But the Earth Remains*, which was to explore the life of a free Maryland black man prior to the Emancipation Proclamation. Instead Turpin worked full-time on the *The Rootless* from the summer 1941 until spring 1942. The third novel in Turpin's series, *The Rootless*, looks at slavery from the slaves' point of view. This novel is by far Turpin's most controversial, so much so that his wife and mother urged him not to publish it, stating the American public was not ready for his debunking of the myth of the white woman's sexual purity during slavery. This novel was finished sometime between 1945 and 1950. Turpin acquiesced and put the book aside. *The Rootless* was not published until 1957. By this time Turpin had fallen from literary favor and was unable to find a publisher. The book was self-published by Turpin, and only one thousand copies were printed. In the end, Turpin gave away more copies than were sold, so the book received little if any acclaim and it did not incite the anticipated criticism.

In July 1948 Turpin took another leave of absence from Lincoln University, initially to return to Columbia to finish his doctorate. Instead he went to Baltimore and began teaching at Morgan State College in 1949. It was the first time in his marriage that he and his wife lived together on a full-time basis. Turpin continued to teach at Morgan until his death on November 19, 1968. The years at Morgan State were bittersweet. Turpin was a gifted professor much sought after by his students. He assisted with drama productions at Morgan State. However, the more he invested as an educator the less he invested in his life as a writer. Turpin mentored and advised students who like him were interested in creative writing. In the late 1950s, Morgan State began putting pressure on its faculty to obtain terminal degrees and to obtain membership and become active in professional organizations that accepted people of all races. Turpin became a member of the executive board of the National Council of Teachers of English, and he completed his doctorate in education, receiving his Ed.D. from Columbia University in 1960.

Turpin completed only two books of the five-novel series he had originally intended. While he never enjoyed the fame of Langston Hughes or Richard Wright, his literary and professional life was multifaceted. He coauthored five English textbooks and published in journals such as the *Negro History Bulletin*, *Phylon*, and the *CLA Journal*. He also wrote short stories, poetry, and five plays. Turpin gave numerous speeches, lectures, and made a forty-lecture television course. Turpin's final and unfinished novel, tentatively titled *Long Way Home*, was to deal with the role of black women as matriarchs' of their families. It was a subject on which Turpin and his wife Jean disagreed: he believed that black women often emasculated their men, Jean Turpin asserted that black women were forced into the role of family head by circumstances beyond their control.

Turpin was diagnosed with abdominal cancer in 1968. He underwent surgery for the cancer but died on the operating table on November 19, 1968 in Baltimore, Maryland. Turpin never reached the heights he might have as a writer, but he contributed to many students' development at Storer College, Lincoln University, and Morgan State.

REFERENCES

Books

Thomas, Elizabeth. "Turpin, Waters Edward." *Black Writers: A Selection of Sketches from Contemporary Authors*. Ed. Linda Metzger. Detroit, Mich.: Gale Research, 1989.

Periodicals

Fleming, Robert E. "Overshadows by Richard Wright: Three Black Chicago Novelists." *Negro American Literature Forum* 37 (Autumn 1973): 75-79.

Ford, Nick A. "Waters Turpin: I Knew Him Well." *CLA Journal* 21 (September 1977): 1-18.

Collections

Waters Edward Turpin Collection (1949-68) is located at Morgan State University in Baltimore, Maryland.

Anne K. Driscoll

Neil de Grasse Tyson
1958–

Astrophysicist, writer

Neil de Grasse Tyson

Neil de Grasse Tyson, an astrophysicist and writer, is the Frederick P. Rose director of the Hayden Planetarium at the American Museum of Natural History in New York City. He is also a research associate in the Department of Astrophysics in the museum. Tyson's position brings him full circle in a career which can be argued to have begun with his childhood visits to the Hayden Planetarium. His commitments to academic inquiry and public service in the field of astrophysics have brought him national recognition. In fact, his contributions to the general public's understanding of astrophysical phenomena have elevated his profile in the media. His publications include both works devoted to general understandings of astrophysics, especially for young adults, and scholarly works. He has commented on scientific issues on national news programs and twice has been appointed to presidential commissions.

Neil de Grasse Tyson was born on October 5, 1958 in New York City, and was raised in the Bronx. His mother, Sunchita Feliciano Tyson, is a gerontologist, a specialist in aging, for the Department of Health and Human Services. His father, Cyril de Grasse Tyson, is a retired sociologist. In his 2004 memoir *The Sky Is Not the Limit: Adventures of an Urban Astrophysicist*, Tyson explains that his elementary school teachers said that young Tyson showed more interests in social interaction with his classmates than in his lessons. His visits to Hayden Planetarium and his participation in classes for young adults at the planetarium helped to ground him. These experiences drew the young Tyson to astronomy and physics. He became more focused in his studies and determined to be an astrophysicist.

During the 1970s, Tyson traveled to Africa and Europe on scholarship. He attended the Bronx High School of Science where he emphasized astrophysics. In high school, he began wrestling and served as captain of the varsity wrestling team. He graduated from the high school in 1976. He attended Harvard University where he majored in physics. He continued to wrestle and was a member of Harvard's varsity wrestling team. He graduated with a B.A. in physics in 1980. In 1983, he earned his M.A. degree in astrophysics from the University of Texas in Austin, Texas. His area of research was star formation models for dwarf galaxies. In 1988, Tyson married Alice Young, a mathematical physicist. They have two children. In 1991, Tyson earned his Ph.D. in astrophysics from Columbia University in New York. His area of research was galactic bulge-chemical evolution, abundances, and structure.

While in Texas, Tyson began doing radio commentary on phenomena in outer space. He also began writing a column for *Star Date* magazine in which he responded to questions on space and science. In 1987, he accepted a position as lecturer for the Department of Astronomy at the University of Maryland at College Park. After completing his doctoral studies, he accepted a postdoctoral position as research associate in the Department of Astrophysics at Princeton University in Princeton, New Jersey. From 1994 through 2003, he worked at Princeton University, initially as a visiting research scientist and lecturer and later as an associate professor in the Department of Astrophysics. He also began working for the American Museum at the Hayden Planetarium in 1994. Initially employed as a staff scientist, he later became acting director. From 1996 through 1997, he chaired the Department of Astrophysics at the museum. In 1996, he became the Frederick P. Rose

Chronology

1958	Born in New York, New York on October 5
1976	Graduates from the Bronx High School of Science in Bronx, New York
1980	Receives B.A. in physics from Harvard University
1983	Receives M.A. in astronomy from University of Texas in Austin, Texas
1987	Serves as lecturer in the Department of Astronomy, University of Maryland
1988	Marries Alice Young, a mathematical physicist
1991	Receives Ph.D. in astrophysics from Columbia University, New York; appointed postdoctoral research associate in the Department of Astrophysics, Princeton University
1994	Serves as visiting research scientist and lecturer in the Department of Astrophysics, Princeton University
1995	Serves as Frederick P. Rose director and astrophysicist for the Hayden Planetarium of the American Museum of Natural History in New York
2001	Wins the American Institute of Physics, 2001 Science Writing Award for *One Universe at Home in the Cosmos*; appointed by President George W. Bush to a twelve-member commission to study the future of the United States Aerospace Industry
2003	Continues as director of the Hayden Planetarium and also accepts position as research associate, Department of Astrophysics, American Museum of Natural History in New York
2004	Appointed by President George W. Bush to nine-member commission on the Implementation of the United States Exploration Policy

director of the museum and planetarium; in addition, he is a research associate in the Department of Astrophysics at the museum.

Scholarship for Narrow and Broad Audiences

Tyson's research shows his commitment to scholarship and public awareness. His studies in astrophysics have included dwarf galaxies, the nucleus of the galaxy, star formations, star evolution, supernovae (explosions of massive stars), and the structure of the Milky Way galaxy. His research uses observations made with large telescopes located in Arizona, California, New Mexico, and the Andes Mountains in Chile. The Hubble Space Telescope has also been a source of data for his work. He has written books for the general public that explain complex phenomenon for a broad, non-academic audience. Books written for a general audience include *Merlin's Tour of the Universe* (1989), *Universe Down to Earth* (1994), and *Just Visiting This Planet* (1998). *Merlin's Tour of the Universe* was published while Tyson was still in graduate school. The book consists of articles written by Tyson for *Star Date* magazine. He won the American Institute of Physics 2001 Science Writing Award for the book he wrote with Charles Lui and Robert Irion, *One Universe at Home in the Cosmos* (2000). Tyson and Lui also prepared an online version of the book with links and review questions. In 2004, Tyson co-authored *Ori-*

gins: Fourteen Billion Years of Cosmic Evolution, with Donald Goldsmith. This book is a supplement to the PBS Nova series on cosmic origins. The book discusses different subjects related to science and astronomy, including the origins of life and the universe. His book, *Death by Black Hole and Other Cosmic Quandaries*, was anticipated to appear in 2006.

Tyson's academic papers and articles have appeared in the *Astronomical Journal*. From 1983 to 1998, he wrote a monthly response column for *Stardate* magazine. Since 1995, Tyson has written a column for *Natural History* magazine entitled "Universe." He has conducted colloquia on various topics related to astronomy and physics at major universities and colleges, including Yale University, Duke University, Penn State University, and Stanford University.

Tyson is a member of the National Society of Black Physicists, the American Astronomical Society, and the American Physical Society, and he is a Fellow of the New York Academy of Sciences. His contributions to the sciences have brought him appointments to national commissions, committees, councils, and boards, some of which are relevant to the national space program and to scientific studies in education. In 1997, he was appointed to NASA's Space Science Advisory Committee in Washington, D.C. From 1997 to 2002, he was a member of the Astronomy Education Board of the American Astronomical Society in Washington, D.C. From 2000 through 2003, he served on the National Science Foundation's Math and Physical Science Directorate Advisory Committee in Arlington, Virginia. He has been appointed by President George W. Bush to serve on two commissions and one committee. Tyson was a part of a twelve-member commission on the Future of the United States Aerospace Industry. He served on this commission from September 2001 to November 2002; the commission provided recommendations for Congress and other government agencies. From 2003 to 2005, he served on a committee for the Selection of the Presidential Medal of Science. In 2004, he was a part of a nine-member presidential commission on the Implementation of the United States Space Exploration Policy.

Tyson has provided expert commentary on national news programs. Since 1995, he has made several appearances on national news programs, including CNN's *American Morning*, ABC's *Good Morning America*, NBC's *Today Show*, ABC's *World News*, and CBS's *Evening News*. He has provided insight into topics such as the research for other life and planets in the universe, NASA's budget, and missions to the moon and Mars. In 2004, Tyson hosted and provided commentary for *Origins*, the PBS *Nova* four-part mini series.

At the Hayden Planetarium, Tyson acts as director, research, and teacher. He teaches classes such as the ones that inspired him as a child. As director of the planetarium, he has contributed to the facility's growth. In 2000, the planetarium was enlarged. The new 300,000 square-foot facility was designed to attract more visitors. Tyson has been awarded numerous grants to fund scientific programs, especially educational programs. He has also received an honorary doctor of science degree from several universities and colleges in recognition of his valuable contributions to academe. He was recognized by *Crain Magazine* in 2001 as being among the top one hundred most influential technology leaders in New York. He also was recognized by *Crain Magazine* in 2003 as one of one hundred most powerful minority business leaders in New York. Tyson's commitment to research and to education is evidenced by his continued research, teaching, service, and publications.

REFERENCES

Books

Heckert, Paul. "Neil de Grasse Tyson, Astronomer and Astrophysicist." In *Notable Black American Scientists.*. Detroit, Mich.: Gale Research, 1997.

Periodicals

Johnson, Constance. "New Star Rising." *Black Issues in Higher Education* 16 (17 February 2000): 18.

Wagner, Cynthia. "Learning to Look Up: A Scientist Is Teaching the World to See the Universe." *The Futurist* 38 (November-December 2004): 68.

Rebecca Dixon

Mahlon Van Horne
1840–1910

Diplomat, consul

One of only about twenty African Americans appointed to diplomatic posts abroad during the Progressive Era, Mahlon Van Horne served as the U.S. consul to St. Thomas, Danish West Indies from December 1896 to July 1903. He was appointed early in the administration of President William McKinley, winning that coveted position after a distinguished career as a prominent minister, civic leader, and first black state representative from Newport, Rhode Island. Though Van Horne earned praise for his nearly six years in the U.S. Foreign Service, a shift in the political climate during the administration of President Theodore Roosevelt resulted in his being ousted from his post under a cloud of suspicion. He devoted the last years of his life to missionary work in Antigua.

Van Horne was born on March 5, 1840, in Princeton, New Jersey, the eldest of the three surviving children of Mathias Van Horne and Diana Oakham Van Horne. At nineteen, he began his studies at the Ashmun Collegiate Institute for Colored Youth, established in Pennsylvania in 1854 to train African American youths for missionary work. In 1862, while still a student, he married Rachel Ann Huston. The couple had four children during their thirty-five-year marriage. Van Horne continued his education as Ashmun evolved into Lincoln University in 1866, known as the first institution in the world to provide higher education in the arts and sciences for African American men and women. He studied theology, education, Latin, Greek, and Hebrew, and became an ordained minister.

Educator and Minister

In 1867 during Reconstruction, as schools for newly freed African Americans sprang up throughout the South, Van Horne accepted an appointment as principal of the Zion School for Colored Children in Charleston, South Carolina. There he served as the administrator of eighteen faculty members and 900 students.

Chronology

1840	Born in Princeton, New Jersey on March 5
1841	Enrolls in the Ashmun Collegiate Institute for Colored Youth
1862	Marries Rachel Ann Huston on April 8 in Princeton, New Jersey; over the years, the couple has four children
1866	Becomes an ordained minister
1867	Accepts appointment as principal of the Zion School for Colored Children in Charleston, South Carolina
1868	Graduates from Lincoln University; moves to Newport, Rhode Island to accept a pastorate at the city's historic Union Congregational Church
1871	Builds a new church edifice after the original building is demolished; church membership includes both blacks and whites; becomes the first African American member elected to the Newport School Committee
1885	Becomes first African American representative in the Rhode Island General Assembly
1886	Elected as state representative for two more terms
1891	Named the "Most Popular Minister of Newport"
1896	Resigns as pastor of Union Congregational Church after serving for 28 years; on December 1 begins service as U.S. consul to St. Thomas, Danish West Indies after his appointment by President William McKinley
1902	In March American Protective League Congress petitions President Theodore Roosevelt to appoint Van Horne governor of the West Indies in the event of U.S. purchase of the island
1903	On July 31 Van Horne is removed from his diplomatic post as Consul to St. Thomas by President Theodore Roosevelt
1907	Wife Rachel dies
1910	Dies from heart trouble in Graceland, Antigua, on May 25 while serving as a missionary

A year later he earned his A.B. degree from Lincoln University and then accepted a pastorate in Newport, Rhode Island at the historic Union Congregational Church, which had been established for blacks in the eighteenth century. The struggling church had been without a regular pastor for three years before Van Horne's appointment. Van Horne served as pastor of the church until his consular appointment twenty-eight years later.

Called "The City by the Sea," Newport was a thriving summer resort for the black elite and the Gilded Age's wealthiest, most aristocratic white families, such as the Astors and Vanderbilts. During Van Horne's tenure as pastor of Union, he drew a number of prominent families from both communities into his interracial congregation. The charismatic minister earned accolades for his eloquent sermons. He also orchestrated the construction of a new church building in 1871 after the demolition of the original church. Such accomplishments led to his being named "Most Popular Minister of Newport" in 1891.

Emerges As Civic and Political Leader

Van Horne's popularity went beyond the boundaries of Union Congregational Church. His concern about the welfare of African Americans propelled him to become one of the leading citizens of Newport and of the state of Rhode Island. He served through the "Colored Masons," African American mutual aid societies, and the local and state branches of the Republican Party.

In 1871 Newport voters elected Van Horne the first African American member on the Newport School Board. Fourteen years later in 1885, the stalwart Republican became the first African American elected as a representative in the Rhode Island General Assembly. He served for three consecutive one-year terms.

Soon after the election of President McKinley, a Republican, Van Horne applied for an appointment to one of the limited number of U.S. consular positions. Van Horne faced stiff competition from black and whites vying for the coveted posts, yet he persisted, garnering endorsements from a number of influential Rhode Islanders, including the chairman of the Republican State Central Committee, former and current members of the Rhode Island state legislature, the attorney general and five justices of the state supreme court.

President McKinley appointed Van Horne as consul to St. Thomas in December 1896 at a pivotal juncture in history. The United States had begun its campaign to gain control of the western hemisphere and emerge as a world power. The federal government viewed its protracted efforts to purchase St. Thomas and neighboring islands from Denmark as crucial to this objective. The United States would then be one step closer to eliminating European colonial rule and spheres of influence in Central and South America as well as the islands of the Caribbean. Since the Civil War era, agents of the federal government had repeatedly botched attempts to purchase St. Thomas. These negotiations failed, in large measure, because of deception on both sides and U.S. attempts to bribe Danish officials. The United States would not succeed in purchasing St. Thomas from the Danish until 1917, fourteen years after the termination of Van Horne's consular appointment.

Loses Diplomatic Post Despite Praise

Supporters of Van Horne in the United States and St. Thomas praised the diplomat's record of service on St. Thomas even as the federal government charged him with incompetence in January 1903. Allegedly, a lack of communication and neglect of duties led to the mishandling of small sums of money during his administration. Ironically, just before the accusations, the American Protective League petitioned Congress to appoint Van Horne governor of St. Thomas in the event that the U.S. purchased it.

In June 1903, several months after the charges, a group of seventy merchants, officials, and other inhabitants of St. Thomas petitioned for the reappointment of Van Horne as the U.S. Consul, praising Van Horne for having done a worthy job over the previous five and a half years. Despite the petitions, President Theodore Roosevelt dismissed Van Horne from his post on July 31, 1903.

Stripped of his position in the U.S. Foreign Service, Van Horne returned to his religious roots and training by becoming a missionary in Antigua. Van Horne died of heart trouble in Graceland, Antigua on May 25, 1910. His wife had died three years before. Three of his children—Dr. M. Alonzo Van Horne, Mrs. Louise Miller, and Mrs. Florence Miller, all prominent members of the Newport, Rhode Island black community—survived him.

REFERENCES

Books

Jeter, Henry. *Pastor Henry N. Jeter's Twenty-five Years Experience with the Shiloh Baptist Church and Her History, Corner School and Mary Streets, Newport Rhode Island.* Providence, R.I.: Remington Printing Company, 1901.

Periodicals

Berdichevsky, Norman. "The Fate of Denmark's Caribbean Colony." *Scandinavian Review*, Summer 2003.

Justesen, Benjamin R. "African-American Consuls Abroad, 1897-1909." *Foreign Service Journal* (September 2004): 72-76.

Online

Effinger, Heidi. "Many Helped Shape Newport's Rich Heritage." *East Bay Newspapers*, 15 February 2003. http://www.eastbayri.com/story/317123424377375.php (Accessed 14 September 2005).

Watson, Vaughn. "Pastor's Leadership Marked a Golden Era." *Providence Journal*, 25 January 1999. http://www.projo.com/specials/century/month1/125eb1a.htm (Accessed 10 October 2005).

Collections

A small collection of contemporary articles and primary documents about the life of Mahlon Van Horne is located in the Newport Historical Society, 82 Touro Street, Newport, Rhode Island.

Clarissa Myrick-Harris

C. T. Vivian
1924–

Minister, civil rights activist

The Reverend Cordy Tindell Vivian, better known as the Reverend C. T. Vivian, was not a product of the South, but nevertheless had those normative experiences that made him realize that civil wrongs must become civil rights. Reared in a devout Christian home environment, he found racism intellectually and spiritually indefensible. Dedicated to the eradication of America's system of racial apartheid, he used direct nonviolent techniques to confront U.S. racial segregation policies.

Cordy Tindell Vivian, the only child of Robert and Euzetta Tindell Vivian, was born on July 28, 1924 in Boonville, Illinois. His mother and maternal grandmother, Annie Woods Tindell, reared him in McComb, Illinois, where they moved six years after his birth. At the apex of the Great Depression, his mother and grandmother lost everything, including their marriages, their agricultural holdings, and their house in the city. Because they wanted Vivian, nicknamed C. T., to have access to the best education possible, they moved to McComb because of its desegregated educational system and because it was the home of Western Illinois University. Consequently, Vivian grew up with the idea that college was in his future. Attending the public schools of McComb, he received his primary education at Lincoln Grade School. He refused to let the school's bullies beat up the weaker students. Said Vivian in an article in the *Peoria Journal Star*, "Those incidents meant nobody was going to mess with me and I could be free, in fact, [I]. . .could use [my]. . .position to free other people." Here he experienced for the first time the power of nonviolence. Upon completing his primary education, Vivian attended Edison Junior High School and McComb High School. He was an active youth member of the Allen Chapel African Methodist Episcopal Church, where he taught in the Sunday school and served as president of the youth group. He graduated from McComb High School in 1942. Upon graduating from high school, Vivian entered Western Illinois University in McComb.

During his tenure at Western Illinois University, Vivian was disturbed by a number of issues, including racism. Beginning at Western Illinois as a social science major, Vivian experienced intellectual clashes with the head of the department. Additionally, with the country in the midst of World War II, there were very few white men attending the university, as most entered the war. White male students tried to protect white females from black men on campus. These covert racial issues proved difficult for Vivian. Thinking that the behavior of the social science department's head was the exception rather than the rule, Vivian changed his major to English, only to find the department's chair was no better. He refused to

C. T. Vivian

let Vivian join the English Club and threatened those students who were his friends. These experiences demonstrated to Vivian how racism permeated the culture. Just as he had become aware of the power of nonviolence earlier, now he began to recognize that the beliefs entrenched at the upper echelons of a social order were not the same as those held by the people at the opposite end of the social strata. Notwithstanding the difficulties he experienced with faculty, Vivian worked for the university's school newspaper as its sports editor. In the mid-1940s, he left Western Illinois University and moved to Peoria, Illinois, where he worked for the Carver Community Center as assistant boys' director.

Becomes an Active Participant for Equality and Justice

Two years after arriving in Peoria, Vivian participated in his first sit-in demonstrations. Unlike the South, the country's northern region practiced de facto segregation, as opposed to the South's de jurie segregation. To Vivian, the morés of the North were only a little better than those in the South. Although the region's businesses posted no racially-specific signs, its customs and traditions were well known by its residents. In an attempt to alter the customs and traditions of Peoria, Vivian became an active participant in an integrated group to open restaurants and lunch counters to all people, regardless of race.

Chronology

1924	Born in Boonville, Missouri on July 28
1942-45	Attends Western Illinois University
1947-48	Participates in his first sit-ins, which leads to the racial integration of Barton's Cafeteria in Peoria, Illinois, among other restaurants and hotels
1953	Marries Octavia Geans of Pontiac, Michigan; elected vice president of Peoria's NAACP Chapter
1954	Receives his call to the ministry; preaches first sermon at Mount Zion Baptist Church in Peoria
1955	Moves to Nashville, Tennessee to attend American Baptist Theological Seminary
1962	Appointed by Dr. King to the executive staff of SCLC as National Director of Affiliates
1969	Publishes *Black Power and the American Myth*
1972	Becomes dean, alternative education and director of Seminary Without Walls, Shaw University Divinity School, Raleigh, North Carolina
1977	Establishes Black Action Strategies and Information Center
1978	Assists in organizing and serves as board chairman for National Anti-Klan Network, now known as Center for Democratic Renewal
1984	Serves as the national deputy director for clergy, during Rev. Jesse Jackson's presidential campaign
1985	Receives honorary doctorate from the New School for Social Research for his work in the civil rights movement
1994	Becomes founder and board member of the Capital City Bank and Trust Company, a black-owned bank in Atlanta
2006	Receives the Trumpet Award for civil rights work

Vivian, along with the Reverend Barton Hunter, a minister at West Bluff Christian Church, and Ben Alexander, a chemist, began efforts to desegregate the area's restaurants. Employing the methods used by the Congress of Racial Equality (CORE), they demanded service, not by the spoken word, but by non-threatening action. They simply stood in line and raised the issue in the consciences of those involved.

The integrated group employed other tactics by sending in a group of whites, whom the eating establishments seated. Then blacks entered, and the whites—in voices loud enough for everyone to hear—questioned why the blacks were not being served. Because of the efforts of Vivian and others, Barton's Cafeteria was desegregated in 1947. Between 1947 and 1948, he and the small group of protesters worked to desegregate other eateries in Peoria.

While working in Peoria, Vivian met and later married Octavia Geans, a native of Pontiac, Michigan, on February 23, 1953. The couple was married fifty-three years. They became the parents of six children:Denise, Cordy Jr., Kira, Mark, Charissa, and Albert. The same year that he married, the Peoria National Association for the Advancement of Colored People (NAACP) chapter elected Vivian as vice president. A year later, while working at Foster and Gallagher Mail Order Company, he

accepted his call to the ministry. Later that year, he gave his first sermon at Mount Zion Baptist Church. With financial assistance from his church and Helen Gallagher, he made plans to attend the American Baptist Theological Seminary in Nashville, Tennessee. Unknown to him, Vivian was about to embark upon one of the most important social movements of the twentieth century.

Becomes Part of America's Second Reconstruction

Arriving in Nashville the same year that the actions of Rosa Parks sparked the Montgomery Bus Boycott, which catapulted a young minister named Martin Luther King Jr. into the national spotlight, Vivian entered the American Theological Seminary in 1955. In addition to attending the seminary, he pastored the congregants of the First Community Church and worked as an editor at the National Baptist Sunday School Publishing Board of the National Baptist Convention. When the civil rights movement's line of demarcation was drawn between the litigious efforts of the NAACP and those of the grass-roots, which ushered in direct nonviolent protest, Vivian found himself in a constant struggle with the more conservative editors of the publishing board. The other editors wanted limited coverage on the new racial protest and the rise of King. When the editors rejected a twenty-four-page article that Vivian wrote after an interview with King, Vivian left the employment of the Sunday School Publishing Board and with his own money privately published and sold the booklet.

In the late fall 1956, Vivian boarded a Nashville Transit Authority bus and seated himself near the front of the half-filled vehicle. The driver of the bus, adhering to the city's customs, ordered him to the rear. A heated debate ensued and Vivian refused to acquiesce to the driver's orders. Subsequently, the driver ordered other passengers to vacate the bus and drove Vivian downtown to police headquarters. Earlier the United States Supreme Court's decision in the *Browder v. Gayle* case had ruled in favor of the Montgomery plaintiffs with regard to the desegregation of intrastate transportation. Nashville's law enforcement officials did not know the city's position or policy. After making phone calls to city hall, they learned that the city was in the process of ending segregated seating on public conveyances.

Joins Nashville's Civil Rights Movement

Four years after arriving in Nashville, Vivian joined with other ministers under the leadership of Kelly Miller Smith Sr. and established the Nashville Christian Leadership Conference (NCLC), a local affiliate of King's SCLC. During NCLC's organizational meeting, Vivian was elected vice president. At this time he met the Reverend James Lawson and others, who ultimately brought about the end of Nashville's racial segregation. In addition to other ministers and in his capacity as an NCLC official, Vivian affiliated himself with students such as Diane Nash, John Lewis, Bernard Lafayette, Marion Berry, and James Bevel, who became the student marshals of the Nashville movement.

As vice president, Vivian was in charge of the organization's direct action component. Lawson became a member of and served as chair of NCLC's Action Committee. After formulating a plan to conduct workshops on Gandhi's method of protest, NCLC leaders and students tested Nashville's racially exclusive policy of segregation in November and December of 1959. Because of the lack of media coverage, Nashville's sit-in movement of 1959 was eclipsed by the four Greensboro, North Carolina male students who held a sit-in on February 1, 1960. Within twelve days of the Greensboro sit-in, Nashville students moved into full action. Two months later, NCLC and the Student Committee, with the assistance of Fisk University's economic professor, Vivian Henderson, launched an economic boycott of Nashville's retail district.

With the economic boycott in full swing, on April 19, a would-be assassin hurled sticks of dynamite into the home of known civil rights attorney Z. Alexander Looby. Although the Loobys escaped, leaders in Nashville's black community called for a mass protest march to the office of mayor Ben West. Familiar with New York's silent march against lynching in the early 1900s, Vivian insisted that the silent strategy be the march's protocol. At the head of some 4,000 persons, once they started and until they reached the courthouse square, bystanders only heard the thump of walking feet. When West came out to meet with them, Vivian read a prepared speech denouncing the mayor's leadership. His defensive response angered West, and the two men, in caustic fashion, verbally retaliated against each other. According to the *Tennessee Historical Quarterly*, when Vivian asked West "if he thought segregation was moral," the mayor answered, "No." At that point, Nash picked up the questioning and asked the mayor to use the standing of his office to stop racial segregation. Immediately, he appealed to all citizens to end discrimination, to have no bigotry, no bias, and no hatred. Taking his answer the next level, Nash asked the question of the day, "Mayor, do you recommend that lunch counters be desegregated?" The mayor answered in the affirmative. Because Vivian's razor sharp questioning paved the way for Nash's questions, Nashville lunch counters began the desegregation process on May 10, 1960, two months before Greensboro, North Carolina, which captured national attention.

Leaves Nashville; Joins King's SCLC Staff

After the first wave of the Nashville sit-ins, Vivian and his family moved to Chattanooga, Tennessee, where he served as pastor of the Cosmopolitan Community Church. While there, his wife gave birth to their youngest son in a segregated hospital. Vivian used this occasion to end segregation in that city's healthcare facilities. In 1961, he participated in the Freedom Rides and became involved in several major campaigns, including Albany, Georgia (1961); Birmingham, Alabama (1962); St. Augustine, Florida (1964); and Selma, Alabama (1965).

In 1963, King appointed Vivian to SCLC's executive staff and named him national director of affiliates. In this position, he became the consultant to all SCLC organizations on voter registration, consumer actions, nonviolent training, direct action, human relations, and community development projects. Two years later, in Selma, Alabama, on the courthouse steps he challenged Sheriff Jim Clark during a voter registration drive. Because of Clark's reaction to Vivian's passionate discourse, Clark smacked the impassioned orator and thereby exposed himself to the world as a racist. After the Selma movement, he directed Vision (later known as Upward Bound), an educational program that put more than seven hundred Alabama students in college with scholarships.

Leaves SCLC

Three years after joining the staff of SCLC, Vivian left the organization to direct the Urban Training Center for Christian Mission in Chicago. There he trained clergy, community leaders, and others in ways to organize. In 1968, while residing in Chicago, Vivian served as the coordinator for the Coalition for United Community Action. The group of sixty-one became Chicago's Black Front. Leading a direct-action campaign against racism in building trades unions, Vivian and the community action group mediated a truce among Chicago gangs. Gaining 20,000 openings for both African American and Latino youth in the sixteen building trade unions, the Chicago Plan became the model for other cities.

The following year, Vivian published *Black Power and the American Myth*, the first book on the modern civil rights movement. Later, it became an Ebony Book Club selection. Three years after writing his book, Vivian became dean of Chapel at Shaw University. While at Shaw, he established and found funding for a national program, Seminary Without Walls. Between 1977 and 1979, Vivian established the Black Action Strategies and Information Center (BASIC), of which he served as chair of the board. The primary focus of BASIC was to teach the principle of managing a multiethnic force. He also established the Anti-Klan Network that later became known as the Center for Democratic Renewal. During Jesse Jackson's 1984 presidential campaign, Vivian worked earnestly as the National Director for Clergy. A year later, the New School for Social Research conferred upon him an honorary doctorate of humane letters. Vivian was among those who, in 1992, organized the National Voting Rights Museum in Selma, Alabama, of which he was a board member. Two years later, he served as a board member of the Capitol City Bank & Trust Company, a black-owned bank in Atlanta, Georgia.

In 1999, Vivian turned day-to-day operations of BASIC over to his son. Although he retired, he continued to lecture and be involved in numerous national and international boards and groups that promoted nonviolent tactics for social change. A year later, Vivian was the inaugural speaker in Stetson University's Howard Thurman Lecture Series. In 2001, he served as speaker for the United Nations International Conference Against Racism, Xenophobia, and Related Intolerances held in South Africa; speaker for the Fourth World Conference on Nonviolence at the University of Rhode Island; consultant to the United Nations World Conference of Religious and Spiritual Leaders in New York; and was the speaker for Jamaican Independence Day.

Because of his spirited commitment to the civil rights movement, Vivian has been placed in the Civil Rights Institute (Birmingham, Alabama); the National Civil Rights Museum (Memphis, Tennessee); the National Voting Rights Museum (Selma, Alabama); and the Portrait Hall of Fame, M. L. King Chapel, Morehouse College (Atlanta, Georgia.) Several television documentaries highlighting the civil rights era spotlighted Vivian as activist, analyst, and strategist. They include *Eyes on the Prize* and *The Healing Ministry of Dr. C. T. Vivian*, both of which aired on the Public Broadcast System (PBS).

The 2006 recipient of the Trumpet Award, Vivian lived in Atlanta, Georgia with his wife. There he continued to serve as a spiritual leader in the Providence Missionary Baptist Church and remained an active member of numerous civic groups and organizations. The ever-vigilante righter of wrongs, Vivian was a steadfast supporter of human causes that brought his dream of an equitable and just world closer to fruition.

REFERENCES

Books

Arsenault, Raymond. *Freedom Riders: 1961 and the Struggle for Racial Justice*. New York: Oxford University Press, 2006.

Conkin, Paul K. *Gone with the Ivy: A Biography of Vanderbilt University*. Knoxville: University of Tennessee Press, 1985.

Halberstam, David. *The Children*. New York: Random House, 1998.

Walker, Lydia. *Challenge and Change: The Story of C. T. Vivian*. Alpharetta, Ga.: W. H. Wolfe Associates, 1993.

Periodicals

Adams, Pam. "Changing the Nation: C. T. Vivian Reflects on the Days in Central Illinois that Forged His Soul." *Peoria Journal Star*, 24 October 1999.

Wynn, Linda T. "The Dawning of a New Day: The Nashville Sit-Ins, February 13, 1960-May 10, 1960." *Tennessee Historical Quarterly* L (Spring 1991): 42-54.

Interviews

Bennett, Kathy. Interviewer. "The Reverend C. T. and Octavia Vivian," Nashville Room, Nashville Public Library, Recorded 12 May 2003. Transcribed by Carolyn James, 28-31 July 2003.

Interview with author, 18 January 2006.

Linda T. Wynn

George Walker
1922–

Composer

When the 1996 Pulitzer Prize recipients were announced at Columbia University in New York, George Walker became the first African American to receive the prestigious distinction for music. It was a triumphant moment for Walker, whom the *New York Times* described as "a not-quite-overnight sensation," as he was more than sixty years into his career. In the Pulitzer's eighty-year history, Walker was the first black composer to win the award for music. The Pulitzer committee's selection "served to recognize an often overlooked minority group within a minority group: black musicians who compose classical music," according to the *Times*.

George Walker was born on June 27, 1922, in Washington D.C. His father was a Jamaican immigrant who came to the United States with no money but was determined to become a doctor. He put himself through medical school but was barred entry to the American Medical Association, which did not accept African Americans. Undeterred, he formed his own medical groups to conduct research with colleagues. George's mother, who tutored neighborhood children in math and writing, was known for her beautiful singing voice.

Walker began playing the piano when he was five years old. He gave his first concert at age fourteen at Howard University, and the next year he started at Oberlin College as a music major. He then attended the Curtis Institute in Philadelphia, where he studied piano under famed pianist Rudolph Serkin. Serkin, like many others, seemed surprised that his student was a purely classical musician. "Imagine my puzzlement," Walker recalled in an article he wrote for the *New York Times* in 1991, when Serkin told him to play part of a Beethoven sonata "like jazz." Serkin was just as surprised to hear his protégé tell him he did not play jazz and had never even listened to jazz until college.

Gets Late Start Composing

Primarily interested in a career as a concert pianist, Walker did not start composing until he was eighteen. He

George Walker

made his debut at Town Hall in New York City in 1945, followed by a performance with the Philadelphia Orchestra under Eugene Ormandy. Despite receiving "wonderful notices," as he recalled, it took Walker five years to find a management agency that would handle a black pianist. If not for the roadblocks facing a black performer in the 1950s, he might have made a career as a concert pianist, he told the *Times*: "I never got the opportunities that would have allowed me to concertize like a white pianist." But he added: "I never felt bitter. I strongly felt if I continued to press for what I hoped to achieve, I would achieve it."

In 1953, National Concert Artists booked him on his first European tour, which took him to Sweden, Denmark, Holland, Italy, and England. While on tour, he

Chronology

1922	Born in Washington D.C. on June 27
1927	Begins studying piano
1940	Begins composing
1945	Makes debut at Town Hall in New York City
1946	Composes his first orchestral work, "Lyric for Strings (Lament)"
1953	Makes first European tour
1956	Earns a doctorate from the Eastman School of Music in Rochester, New York
1961	Accepts teaching appointments at Smith College in Massachusetts and the University of Colorado
1969	Joins the faculty of Rutgers University
1992	Retires from Rutgers University
1995	Receives commission from Boston Symphony Orchestra; composes "Lilacs"
1996	Wins Pulitzer Prize for music

became seriously ill with ulcers and was in agony most of the time. When he came back to the United States, he realized that, if he continued to perform when he was sick, he risked seriously affecting his health. Walker's father encouraged him to teach, so in 1956 he earned a doctorate from the Eastman School of Music in Rochester, New York. He then went to Paris to study with Nadia Bulenje, who he claims was the first person to acknowledge his talent as a composer. When Walker's grandmother died in 1946, he composed the "Lyric for Strings (Lament)," his first orchestral work.

In 1961, he accepted teaching appointments at Smith College in Massachusetts and the University of Colorado, and in 1969 he joined the faculty of Rutgers University, where he became the chairman of the music department. He retired in 1992 during a dispute with the university over back pay and benefits that was resolved in March 1993.

Refers to Poet for Orchestral Piece

In 1995, Walker was commissioned by the Boston Symphony Orchestra to write a work for tenor and orchestra to commemorate Roland Hayes, the famous black tenor, whose career began in Boston with the symphony. Walker referred to Walt Whitman's "While Lilacs Last in the Door Yard Bloom," about the funeral train of assassinated President Abraham Lincoln. Walker said he had drawn inspiration from folk sources, spirituals, popular music and jazz "in small snippets so they're not recognizable," according to the *New York Times*. He composed the piece in his dining room at his Steinway concert grand piano.

In "Lilacs," he said, he used Whitman's piece because Lincoln represented freedom and emancipation to blacks.

Lilacs, Walker has said, also have a personal tie for him, as his family used to visit relatives who lived amid lilacs in Virginia.

Walker's body of work, including overtures, symphonies, concertos, sonatas, string quartets, cantatas and a Mass, consists mostly of compositions for full orchestra, for chamber orchestra, and for instrumental combinations. "Lilacs" was performed by the Boston Symphony Orchestra in February 1996. *Boston Globe* critic Richard Dyer wrote: "There is wonderful music in this cycle, which is profoundly responsive to the images in the text—you can hear the sway of lilacs in the rhythm, smell their fragrance in the harmony," according to the *Washington Post*.

Pulitzer Piece One of Many

"Lilacs" was Walker's seventieth published work. His commissions include works for the New York Philharmonic, the Cleveland Orchestra, and the John F. Kennedy Center for the Performing Arts, among many others. His works and piano interpretations have also been recorded on three CDs: *George Walker: A Portrait*, *George Walker in Recital*, and *George Walker*.

"Lilacs" came to the attention of the Pulitzer Prize Committee when one of Walker's two sons, a violinist in Colorado, submitted it. A rash of crank calls had been interrupting Walker at his music for the previous year, so when the telephone rang on a Tuesday afternoon in April 1996, as he worked over an organ piece, he picked it up expecting to hear the familiar click of a hang-up. Instead, he was told that he had just won the 1996 Pulitzer Prize for music.

"It's something one can never expect or take for granted; it's a kind of gift," Walker told the *New York Times*. Members of the Pulitzer nominating jury praised the piece as "masterly and rigorous," according to the *Times*, "one that deepens with successive hearings yet grips an audience from the first." Richard Wernick, chairman of the five-member music panel that recommended Walker to the Pulitzer Prize board, described "Lilacs" as "an American piece," adding, "don't ask me to define that."

As television vans, photographers, and reporters flooded Walker's quiet suburban street, Walker maintained his perspective. "It's always nice to be known as the first doing anything, but what's more important is the recognition that this work has quality," Walker told *USA Today*.

REFERENCES

Periodicals

Blumenthal, Ralph. "A Pulitzer Winner's Overnight Success of 60 Years." *New York Times*, 11 April 1996.

Kandell, Leslie. "A Hometown Tribute to a Composer's Life." *New York Times*, 6 October 1996.

McLellan, Joseph. "Hometown Homage to a D.C. Composer; Trailblazer Returns for His Day in the District." *Washington Post*, 8 June 1997.

Weeks, Linton. "A Bittersweet Pulitzer Prize; Young Playwright Honored Posthumously; Music Award Goes to Black for First Time." *Washington Post*, 10 April 1996.

Online

"Looking Past the Pulitzer: Do African American composers have a place in the classical music world?" Oberlin Alumni Magazine. http://www.oberlin.edu/alummag/oamcurrent/oam_summer2002/feat_looking.htm (Accessed 23 March 2005).

"The Online News Hour." PBS.org. http://www.pbs.org/newshour/bb/entertainment/pulitzer_music_4-11.html (Accessed 23 March 2005).

Brenna Sanchez

Hal Walker
c. 1934–2003

Television journalist

When Harold "Hal" Walker appeared on the CBS television network in 1969, his was the first African American face Americans had ever seen delivering the news. Walker was the first black news correspondent, and he remained in the television news business at CBS and ABC until his retirement in 1995. The award-winning television news journalist died November 25, 2003.

Harold William Walker was born about 1934 in Darlington, South Carolina, but he was raised in New York City by his mother, a domestic worker. He studied theater and English at Denison University in Granville, Ohio, graduating in 1954. He then served four years in the Army. After his service, he dabbled in acting. He was doing public relations work for the New York state mental health department in Albany, New York, when a friend told him that television stations were looking to hire minority journalists.

Walker began his television career in 1963 at CBS-TV's Washington D.C. affiliate, WTOP-TV, which was later called WUSA. While there, he became a mentor to a production trainee named Max Robinson who, in 1978, became the first black national news anchor when he was named co-anchor of ABC-TV's *World News Tonight*.

Chronology

1934?	Born in Darlington, South Carolina
1954	Graduates from Denison University in Granville, Ohio
1963	Begins work at WTOP-TV in Washington, D.C.
1968	Anchors civil rights documentary *A Dialogue with Whitey*
1969	Hired as first black television journalist at *CBS News*
1977	Promoted to CBS foreign correspondent in Bonn, Germany
1981	Begins work for *ABC News* as correspondent in Bonn
1995	Retires from *ABC News*
2003	Dies at home in Reston, Virginia on November 25

Walker got his break covering the civil rights movement. In 1968, he covered the rioting that took place in Washington after the assassination of Rev. Martin Luther King Jr. He anchored an hour-long documentary about the riots called *A Dialogue with Whitey*. The show earned Walker a local Emmy and the Ted Yates Award for outstanding professionalism from the Washington chapter of the National Academy of Television Arts & Sciences. Also in 1968, Walker was named Journalist of the Year by the Capitol Press Club. *CBS News* took notice of Walker and hired him to its Washington bureau the month after *A Dialogue with Whitey* aired.

CBS wasted no time assigning Walker to some of the nation's most important stories. One of his first assignments was the assassination of Sen. Robert F. Kennedy. He reported from Capitol Hill on campus unrest and on riot-torn areas of Washington for *CBS Evening News with Walter Cronkite*. During his career with CBS, Walker covered the inaugurations of presidents Richard M. Nixon, Jimmy Carter, and Ronald Reagan. He also contributed to the flurry of reporting that surrounded the Watergate scandal. In 1977, he was assigned to the CBS bureau in Bonn, Germany as a foreign correspondent for the network. Not everyone was supportive of Walker's breaking the race barrier of television news. Though he received bigoted hate mail, he never talked about it with his colleagues.

After eight years with CBS, Walker took a position with ABC and served as a foreign correspondent for that network, remaining in Bonn. He later was promoted to Frankfurt bureau chief. While in Europe, Walker covered several history-making stories for ABC. He covered the 1988 Pan Am Flight 103 disaster over Lockerbie, Scotland, and reported the fall of the Berlin Wall and communism in Eastern Europe in 1989.

Walker was known in the business as a "skilled beat reporter who did not rely on others to do his legwork," according the *Washington Post*. He was also "uncharacteristically polite" in an ordinarily "cutthroat" business.

Above All Else, a Professional

Jerry King, a retired ABC White House reporter, recalled in the *Washington Post* an incident in 1981 that gave example to Walker's professionalism. The Iranian hostage crisis, during which fifty-two American hostages were held in Iran more than fourteen months, had just come to an end. Both King and Walker were covering the story. The American hostages had just been released and were sequestered at a military hospital in Germany. Walker got a tip that one of the hostages had sneaked out of the hospital to visit his family near Frankfurt. Walker tracked the man down and interviewed him one-on-one in his doorway, away from the throng of military handlers with which other reporters were dealing. Walker apologized to King when his report earned more prominent airplay than King's that night. He later moved to ABC's London bureau. Walker remained with ABC for fifteen years, until his retirement in 1995.

Bernie Seabrooks, the first black producer at *CBS News*, was Walker's longtime friend and colleague. Seabrooks recalled Walker's easy temperament in an interview with *Television Week*. Seabrooks said Walker was the one to calm things down. Seabrooks also noted that, during an era at ABC when other reporters' expense accounts were lavish, Walker kept his spending to a minimum. Walker avoided the spotlight, preferring to keep his private life private. During the last few years of his life, Walker and Seabrooks conversed daily. Though Walker was battling prostate cancer, he always turned the conversation to Seabrooks' problematic knees. At his memorial in Washington, he was remembered by friends and colleagues as a "good and disarming" person, and a "jack-of-all-trades" reporter, according to *Television Week*.

Walker was married three times. His first two marriages ended in divorce. He kept a home in Washington D.C. for years and spent his retirement playing tennis and golf. He died November 25, 2003, at his home in Reston, Virginia from prostate cancer. His survivors included his wife of a year, Diane Blust Walker of Reston; three children from his first marriage, Harold Stephen Walker of Denver, Alison Schlatter of Charlottesville, and Sarah Walker of Jersey City; a sister; and four grandchildren.

After Walker's death, his colleagues remembered him with great fondness and respect. According to the Hampton Roads, Virginia *Daily Press*, a CBS news release stated that *CBS News* anchor Dan Rather, who worked with Walker when both were assigned to the White House, described his colleague as an "exceptionally alert reporter" who "could do it all." Rather said Walker rarely talked about race and merely "wanted to be judged as a pro." *Television Week* quoted *ABC World News Tonight* anchor Peter Jennings saying on air: "He loved his job. He loved being overseas. In the best tradition of a foreign correspondent, he was always ready to go somewhere. And he was very good company to boot."

REFERENCES

Periodicals

Bernstein, Adam. "Television Journalist Hal Walker Dies at 70." *Washington Post*, 28 November 2003.

Greppi, Michele. "Broadcaster Remembered; Hal Walker, CBS and ABC Foreign Correspondent, Broke Down Barriers." *Television Week*, 8 December 2003.

"Hal Walker, 70, Television Correspondent." *New York Times*, November 27, 2003.

Online

"TV newsman Hal Walker dies." CNN.com. http://www.cnn.com/2003/SHOWBIZ/TV/11/27/obit.walker.ap/ (Accessed 20 December 2005).

Brenna Sanchez

Matthew Walker
1906–1978

Physician, surgeon

Matthew Walker rose from humble beginnings to become an internationally recognized pioneer in medicine and surgery. He was also a teacher of doctors and surgeons, a medical college and health care administrator, and an advocate for community-based healthcare to poor, disadvantaged, and underserved populations. His varied achievements affected areas far beyond medicine and healthcare, shaping community development in urban and rural areas of the southern United States and providing models for services to communities in underdeveloped nations.

Matthew Walker was born on December 7, 1906 in the small community of Waterproof, Louisiana, bordering the Mississippi River in the northeastern part of the state. His father, Phillip Walker, was a Pullman porter, and his mother, Rosa Ware Walker, worked as a domestic. The family moved to New Orleans during Matthew's early childhood years, where he received his early educational training in the city's grammar schools.

Walker continued his studies at Gilbert Academy, where he completed high school in 1925. Remaining in the city he attended New Orleans University, where he received his B.A. with honors in 1929. The following year the university merged with Straight College to form Dillard University, making Walker a part of its last graduating class.

Chronology

1906	Born in Waterproof, Louisiana on December 7
1929	Receives B.A. from New Orleans University
1934	Receives M.D. from Meharry Medical College
1935	Joins teaching faculty at Meharry
1937	Marries Alice Johnson in Baldwin, Louisiana on August 5
1944	Becomes professor and chair of Meharry surgery department
1947	Launches rural health initiative in Mound Bayou, Mississippi
1952	Becomes assistant dean of Meharry school of medicine
1954	Serves as president of National Medical Association
1955	Integrates local, state, and national American Medical Association
1966	Secures funding for Mound Bayou and Nashville health centers
1970	Dedicates Nashville health center named for him on March 7
1973	Becomes provost for external affairs at Meharry
1978	Dies in Nashville, Tennessee on July 15

New Orleans University had discontinued its medical college in 1911, but it continued to operate the Flint-Goodridge Hospital and nursing school after the merger which created Dillard. Walker was forced to consider other options in order to study for a medical degree, which were limited due to segregation, finances, and other factors, including the Great Depression of the 1930s.

Two historically black colleges/universities (HBCUs) were the primary locations for blacks seeking medical training in the 1930s: Meharry Medical College in Nashville, Tennessee, and Howard University School of Medicine in Washington, D.C. Walker chose to attend Meharry, a decision which would not only change his life, but also greatly affect the future of the institution.

Walker completed his M.D. with high honors from Meharry in 1934, then he was a resident in surgery and gynecology at the college's George W. Hubbard Hospital from 1935 to 1938 after receiving diplomate status from the National Board of Medical Examiners. His abilities were such that he almost immediately went from being a student to a faculty member, serving as an instructor in anatomy, surgery, gynecology, orthopedics, anesthesia, and EENT (eye, ear, nose, and throat) during the same period.

Despite his scientific background, Walker was a member of the Methodist church, which was another important influence in his life. Both New Orleans University and Meharry were HBCUs that had been supported by the church, and Walker was active in the fellowship at Clark Memorial (United) Methodist Church from his student days at Meharry. He served the church in many capacities and, years later, would become chairman of the church board of trustees. Walker was also known to ask for God's guidance before performing surgery and

acknowledged the importance of prayer and faith in the healing process.

Even though he progressed through his medical training in Tennessee at a rapid pace, Walker still found time to return to Louisiana where he married the former Alice Johnson in her hometown of Baldwin, St. Mary Parish, on August 5, 1937. Children soon followed: Charlotte Rose (August 25, 1938), Maxine June (April 2, 1940), Matthew Jr. (June 1, 1941), and Daniel Phillip (August 17, 1942). Charlotte was born in Baldwin, while the other three children were born in Nashville at Hubbard Hospital on the Meharry campus.

During 1938 and 1939, Walker left Meharry to become a General Education Board fellow in surgery at Howard, then he returned to become an instructor in physiology and pathology until 1941. By 1942 he had resumed teaching in the areas of surgery and gynecology and was promoted to the rank of associate professor. In 1944 Walker was promoted to full professor and acting chair of the Meharry surgery department. He was named permanent chairman the following year.

Becomes Leader in Profession and Community Service

After receiving diplomate status from the American Board of Surgery in 1946 and having been admitted to fellowship in the International College of Surgeons in 1947, Walker was recognized as one of the outstanding medical practitioners in the nation, regardless of race. He had also become skilled in the development of physicians and surgeons through the resident training program he established at Meharry and was credited with training more African American surgeons than anyone else in the world.

Many out of the hundreds of men who came through his program would break the color barrier in hospitals and medical organizations throughout the South, in other regions of the country, and in international settings. Walker also took the bold step of admitting Dorothy Brown as a resident in surgery in 1949, against the advice of many colleagues. Brown, who graduated from Meharry in 1948, had interned at Harlem Hospital but had been rejected when she chose surgery for her specialty.

Walker did not agree with the belief that a woman could not handle the rigors of surgery and supported his student. Brown successfully completed five years of surgical residency under Walker at Meharry and became the first African American woman surgeon in the southern United States. She went on to serve as an assistant professor of surgery at the college, chief surgeon at Riverside Hospital (also in Nashville), and followed Walker's own footsteps in later years by also becoming a fellow in the American College of Surgeons. Brown became the second black woman to achieve this distinction. Brown was also the first single adoptive parent in Tennessee and had a political career as a state legislator.

Walker's abilities did not go unnoticed, as he was presented with numerous offers to take his talents elsewhere. While he never left Meharry, Walker became involved in local, regional, and national collaborations with other colleagues through research and public health initiatives. Most notable was the work with the Taborian Hospital in Mound Bayou, Mississippi, a rural, all-black community, and the development of neighborhood community health centers for poor and underserved communities in the city of Nashville.

Walker began his relationship with the Mound Bayou community in 1942, when he was recruited by representatives of Taborian to serve as chief surgeon. He declined at that time but suggested other capable surgeons for the position. In 1947 the hospital approached Walker again, but by that time he had already become chair of the Meharry surgery department and had launched his resident training program.

Demonstrating his commitment to both Meharry and the Mound Bayou project, Walker came up with the creative solution to provide medical and surgical services through rotation of students in his training program. He made frequent trips to Mississippi to supervise and consult at Taborian, while balancing his other responsibilities in Nashville. The project also had personal significance for Walker, in that Mississippi represented a symbolic as well as geographical link between his beginnings in Louisiana and his successful life and career in Tennessee.

Walker's plan of action was adopted, and a formal agreement was signed, with the option that other Meharry departments could be included as necessary. Fees for services were paid by Taborian to Meharry, which paid its doctors and students from the allotted funds. Persons in the Mound Bayou community paid small membership fees for outpatient care and up to thirty days of hospitalization if needed, supplemented by community fund drives and county payments. This arrangement became a pioneering example of what would later come to be called health maintenance and managed care organizations (HMOs and MCOs).

In 1948 Walker established the cancer teaching program at Meharry, which led to his becoming an in-demand speaker at public health forums and conferences related to the disease. In 1952 he was promoted to assistant dean of the school of medicine, with administrative responsibilities added to an already demanding professional schedule, work with numerous community organizations, church commitments, and family life with his wife and four children.

Despite his many personal, professional, and community involvements, Walker was also an active member and respected leader of the National Medical Association (NMA). The organization was formed by black doctors attending the 1895 Cotton States Exposition in Atlanta,

Georgia, the same event which catapulted Booker T. Washington to national prominence. It was fitting that after serving the association in several capacities, Walker was elected national president during its 1953 convention in Nashville, with Meharry as the host institution. The organization's founding president was Robert F. Boyd, a doctor from Nashville and Meharry, and its immediate past president was another Meharry alumnus, A. Porter Davis of Kansas City, Kansas. Walker served in the position from 1954 to 1955, presiding at NMA conventions in Washington, D.C. and Los Angeles, California.

In 1955 Walker and two Meharry colleagues, E. Perry Crump and Axel E. Hansen, made history when they became the first African American members of the Nashville Academy of Medicine. The local organization, along with other city and county medical societies in Tennessee, had lifted policies of segregation during the previous year. Memberships in these organizations automatically made Walker and other black doctors members of the Tennessee State Medical Association (TSMA) and the American Medical Association (AMA). While historic, it was also ironic in that this recognition came when Walker was president of the NMA, which came into existence because black doctors could not join the AMA.

Walker also focused on the healthcare needs of poor, underserved, and minority communities in the urban setting. Wisely, he used his home city of Nashville as the base for this project, establishing a storefront medical clinic on Jefferson Street in the heart of the black community and close to the Meharry campus. The ease of access to both college and community resources enabled Walker and his colleagues to apply successful strategies used in Mound Bayou and modify as necessary due to the differences of the city environment.

Walker was highly respected and appreciated by his students and colleagues, who were inspired to form the Matthew Walker Surgical Society in 1958. Over seventy physicians who had worked with or been trained by Walker came together to honor their mentor and friend when the society was established and presented him with a silver tray as a token of appreciation.

Through his many relationships and contacts from the local to the national level, Walker and his colleagues were able to secure significant funding from federal agencies in the 1960s to support both the Mound Bayou and Nashville public health projects. In the case of Mound Bayou, a 1966 grant from the U.S. Office of Economic Opportunity (OEO) facilitated the merger of Taborian and Sarah Brown hospitals, creating the Mound Bayou Community Hospital which served portions of five Mississippi counties. A second grant brought Walker and Meharry into collaboration with Tufts University Medical Center in Boston to extend medical services to an even wider region of Mississippi and to include another facility, the Delta Community Hospital.

Even with these successes and additional responsibilities, Walker continued projects and activities on behalf of the primary teaching mission of Meharry. He identified scholarships, fellowships, and other financial assistance for the continued development of medical students and faculty, as well as other research and service projects connected with the medical school.

With the success of the civil rights movement and new access and opportunities in formerly segregated institutions, Walker explored new avenues while remaining committed to his work at Meharry. His expertise led to his appointment to the Board of Hospital Commissioners by the mayor of Nashville in 1961, with oversight of all the city's medical institutions. Walker also gained professional access as a surgeon to all major hospitals in the Nashville area and served as a consultant in surgery at the Veterans Administration Hospital in Tuskegee, Alabama.

Walker served on the boards of numerous other organizations and institutions. These included the Citizens Savings Bank of Nashville, the oldest continuously operating black-owned bank in the United States; Universal Life Insurance Company of Memphis; the Nashville Area Chamber of Commerce; Scarritt College; and local chapters of the American Cancer Society, National Federation of Settlements and Neighborhood Centers, American National Red Cross, the National Council on Alcoholism, and United Givers Fund, among others.

By the end of the 1960s Walker had been promoted again by Meharry, to associate dean of the school of medicine, and in 1970 he received an additional appointment as clinical professor of surgery at the Vanderbilt University School of Medicine. Walker received yet another promotion at Meharry in 1973, when he became provost for external affairs at the college.

Walker's outstanding work was recognized on numerous occasions and by a variety of organizations during his life and career, including the NMA, which presented him with its distinguished service award in 1959. Some of his many other honors and awards are a commendation from President Richard Nixon, election to Alpha Omega Alpha honorary medical society, and honoree of the Meharry Alumni Association (1970); senior fellowship in the American Surgical Association (1972); participant in the Cine Clinic of the American College of Surgeons and national Man of the Year from Omega Psi Phi, his college fraternity (1973); inclusion in a video-recorded autobiographical interview series, "Leaders in American Medicine" (1974); and recipient of the Community Service Award from the Congressional Black Caucus (1975).

Walker was most proud when the Meharry Neighborhood Health Center, also established in 1966 with assistance from the OEO, opened for service in 1969. He was deeply touched when it was renamed the Matthew Walker Community Health Center (MWCHC) of Meharry Medical College in his honor when the $1.5 million facility was formally dedicated on March 7, 1970.

The community residents who served on the board of the center insisted to Meharry officials that Walker's vision and hard work in making the facility a reality be permanently acknowledged, with full agreement from his colleagues. Its location in north Nashville was a short distance from Meharry and Fisk University, and accessible from all parts of the city by public transportation and vehicles assigned to the center from the federal government motor pool. The residents also honored Walker by naming the community board the Matthew Walker Health Council.

Final Years and Legacy

Matthew Walker died on July 15, 1978 in Nashville. He had lived to see many changes in his profession and professional community, and he had seen changes in his family as well, including five grandchildren. His first-born daughter, Charlotte Rose, followed him into the medical profession, and one granddaughter, Candace Koney-Laryea, became an anesthesiologist practicing in New Port Richey, Florida. Students he had trained were practicing medicine in leading medical institutions all over the world, as well as following his lead in providing medical and health services to poor and underserved populations.

After more than thirty years of community service, the MWCHC broke ground on a new $5 million structure in 2003, returning to the Jefferson Street area where Walker and others began the center from the storefront location in the 1950s. Charlotte Rose Walker, a speaker for the groundbreaking ceremonies, commented that her father would have been pleased to see the continued progress of the center.

The new MWCHC building was completed during the same year, bringing the center into the new millennium with state of the art technology as an ongoing testament to the vision and commitment of Dr. Walker. He would have also been pleased to know that the former MWCHC location was purchased by Fisk University in 2005 with plans to renovate the building for use as a community leadership institute, yet another tribute to the life and legacy of Matthew Walker.

REFERENCES

Books

Morais, Herbert M. *International Library of Afro-American Life and History, Vol. 9: History of the Afro-American in Medicine*. Cornwells Heights, Pa.: Publishers Agency, Inc., 1978.

Summerville, James. *Educating Black Doctors: A History of Meharry Medical College*. University, Ala.: University of Alabama Press, 1983.

Periodicals

Carty, James. "Surgeon Asks God for 'Extra Hunch'." *Nashville Tennessean*, 6 March 1959.

Churchwell, Robert. "Health Center to Honor Meharry's Dr. Walker." *Nashville Banner*, 6 March 1970.

"Dr. Walker to Head NMA for 1954-55." *Nashville Tennessean*, 15 August 1953.

Finch, Cassandra. "Matthew Walker Breaks Ground on New $5 Million Facility." *Tennessee Tribune*, 23 July 2003.

Reed, W. A. "Dr. Matthew Walker 'Left Much More Than Memories'." *Nashville Tennessean*, 20 July 1978.

Thomison, John B. "Matthew Walker, M.D., R.I.P." *Journal of the Tennessee Medical Association* (September 1978): 692-93.

Walker, Matthew. "Mound Bayou: Meharry's Neighbor." *Journal of the National Medical Association* 65 (July 1973): 309-12.

Online

Meharry Medical College. "Maupin Challenges all Meharrians to Reach for Greatness." http://news. mmc.edu/page.asp?SID=4&Page=100 (Accessed 20 December 2005).

National Medical Association. http://www.nmanet.org/ History.htm (Accessed 31 May 2005).

Interviews

Walker, Charlotte Rose. Telephone conversation with Fletcher Moon, July 11, 2005.

Collections

Walker's papers are housed in the archives of Meharry Medical College in Nashville, Tennessee.

Fletcher F. Moon

Wyatt T. Walker
1929–

Minister, civil rights activist

Wyatt T. Walker

As a Baptist minister with multiple gifts, Wyatt Tee Walker has championed civil and human rights for oppressed peoples around the world. Walker has traveled to over ninety countries and preached on every continent with the exception of Australia. He has held numerous humanitarian leadership positions in the United States and abroad. As a southern minister and as the executive director of the Southern Christian Leadership Conference, Walker was a leader in the fight against segregation and racial discrimination in the South.

Walker was born on August 16, 1929 in Brockton, Massachusetts, but grew up in New Jersey. As a young man, he lived some years in the South where he earned his B.S. (magna cum laude) in 1950 and his M.Div (summa cum laude) in 1953 from Virginia Union University. Walker earned his D.Min. in 1975 from Colgate-Rochester Divinity School. He married Theresa Ann Edwards in 1951 and together they had four children.

During Walker's growing up years, racial discrimination and segregation against African Americans were prevalent. But Walker rejected the premise of Jim Crow and was a well-seasoned radical by the time he reached adulthood. Walker's father left the South because of Jim Crow only to find the same institution in the North. When he was nine years, young Walker and his siblings challenged the system by sitting in a movie theater, knowing very well that it was a whites-only establishment. His public involvement in resistance to segregation and discrimination began long before 1957 when he joined the Southern Christian Leadership Conference as a director of the board.

Becomes Minister and Civil Rights Leader

Walker was one of the founding directors of the Southern Christian Leadership Conference (SCLC) that was created in 1957 at the Ebenezer Baptist Church in Atlanta, Georgia, by a group of black men, most of whom were southern ministers. While the National Association of Colored People (NAACP) had worked for integration, namely in education with a favorable federal ruling in the *Brown v. Board of Education in Topeka, Kansas* case in 1955, the SCLC founders felt that the NAACP approach only addressed the legalistic aspect of the problems and was only a first step toward equal treatment for blacks. By contrast, the SCLC intended to use the power of the black church and direct, nonviolent action to bring about integration and civil rights for African Americans.

Directly after receiving his master's degree in divinity, Walker became the pastor of Gillfield Baptist Church in Petersburg, Virginia, and served that congregation for the next eight years. As a pastor and a director of the SCLC board, he also served as state director of the Congress for Racial Equality (CORE), of which he was a founding member in 1958, and was branch president of the NAACP in Petersburg, Virginia for five years. Walker also founded and headed the Petersburg Improvement Association (PIA), a protest organization, while serving as pastor of Gillfield. Several SCLC affiliates were set up in Virginia

under his leadership, and Walker coordinated many mass demonstrations to combat segregation. Two outstanding efforts made by Walker were the 1958 sit-ins in protest of segregation at the Petersburg Public library and the 1958 march on Richmond to protest the closing of public schools to avoid segregation set for January 1959. By virtue of the favorable ruling in federal court, the PIA successfully sued. In addition, the Prayer Pilgrimage in the Virginia State Capitol was successful. Walker's PIA became the model for direct action by the SCLC, whereby movement centers were set up across the state.

From the pulpit Walker, like other black southern ministers, preached about the injustice in segregation and discrimination, persuaded his congregation to contribute financially, and incited the congregation into action for change. By 1958, Gillfield Baptist Church represented the core of massive organizing efforts, the center of the SCLC networks, and the organizing headquarters for demonstrations in Virginia. According to Walker, the successes of the Virginia movement could be attributed to strong church leadership dependent on spiritual direction and a commitment to nonviolence that functioned under the leadership of Martin Luther King and the SCLC. Besides acknowledging his own outstanding administrative, organizing, and leadership abilities, according to Aldon Morris, Walker also claimed his abrasiveness as a gift from above that enabled him to get done the jobs he set out to do, despite unfavorable responses from colleagues, subordinates, and others. In 1958, Walker coordinated SCLC workshops held in Norfolk, Virginia, to teach techniques in resisting violence to black demonstrators. At the same time, the SCLC held a mass meeting which over 11,000 people attended and which raised $2,500. Between 1960 and 1963, he was the executive director of SCLC, and he developed Project C, the confrontation that dismantled the federal government's support of segregation in Birmingham, Alabama, the largest and most segregated city in the South.

Heads Civil Rights Organization

In 1960 Walker accepted the first full-time executive director position of the SCLC, headquartered in Atlanta, Georgia, foregoing his pastorate at Gillfield Baptist Church. By virtue of his performance in Petersburg, Walker gained respect among SCLC leaders as well as the respect of King. Walker had the privilege of administrative authority. In step with SCLC philosophy, Walker constantly reminded black church members and clergy of their unique social positions and urged their participation in the movement for civil rights for blacks.

One of Walker's first tasks as executive director was to add structure to the organization. For example, he implemented monthly budget control sheets to track spending. He introduced the organization to projected income on a fiscal basis. He hired assistants who, in turn, hired secretarial assistants to stabilize the clerical area of the organization. He developed and instituted personnel policies and procedures and a systematic policy for press releases. He also kept meticulous financial records to comply with the stringent and complicated tax laws for the 501-C4 status the SCLC had acquired as a protest organization. Next, Walker took control of King's travel and speaking schedule and often accompanied him on the road. With the help of a booking agency, Walker managed to arrange King's engagements so as to maximize his earnings in the least amount of time. With new arrangements and donations, the SCLC's income more than doubled within Walker's first year as the executive director. Besides a significant increase in income, the SCLC also increased the number of protest marches and demonstrations throughout the South. Walker participated in several protest marches in the South, but he played a significant role in helping to dismantle the economic well-being of the business community of Birmingham, Alabama.

Directs Project C in Birmingham

The 1960 sit-ins staged by southern college students brought international attention to the cause of blacks in the South and can be viewed as the basic paradigm for the nonviolent protests that followed. The SCLC adopted the students' principle along with many other forms of protest, but with an added dimension: the black church. The organization relied heavily on the participation of ministers and their congregations to carry out mass demonstrations throughout the South. In 1960 and 1961, Walker was active in the Freedom Rides in the South. More important, he was the mastermind of the mass demonstrations in Birmingham, Alabama, in 1963 that ultimately disrupted the economic construct there and crushed the federally supported segregation and discrimination against blacks. The goals of the SCLC in Birmingham were to confront segregation on a mass, nonviolent, and economic scale during the Easter season in 1963 and to attract big headline stories across the country that dramatized the mass jailing of blacks for seeking their civil rights. Walker documented three phases of strategy for the confrontation in eight pages and named it Project C (for confrontation). Phase one called for a few blacks to stage sit-ins at the lunch counters of three department stores; phase two called for protest marches by blacks on a limited scale through downtown; and phase three called for massive protests and demonstrations by thousands of school children. Well in advance of the day of confrontation, Walker made several trips to Birmingham to survey the downtown, which was the target of Project C. He documented logistics in detail, including the names of the department stores and their locations, the number of seats in the eating areas, and approximately how long it would take a young, middle-aged, or older person to walk from one point to another. While the first two phases of Project C did not generate the media attention needed to command

public outcry for police brutality and the jailing of blacks, phase three did. Over several days, thousands of school-aged children filled the Birmingham jails beyond capacity. This scenario generated the media attention Walker anticipated. Stories were published all over the country of police dogs and fire hoses used to attack and injure children and demonstrators. Such scenes and reports created more than enough national demonstration of police brutality and inhumanity to give the SCLC the needed leverage to engage in serious negotiations with the white power structures. Walker continued to assist the SCLC in the South through financial contributions. In June 1963, he sponsored a jazz concert that was held in the backyard of baseball legend Jackie Robinson. Jazz vocalists and musicians came from all over. The concert yielded over $14,000, which Walker turned over to the SCLC to continue its work.

Walker resigned his post as executive director of the SCLC in July 1964 to become vice president at Educational Heritage, Inc., a publishing firm in Yonkers, New York. The next year, he became an assistant pastor at the community-oriented Abyssinian Baptist Church in Harlem. In 1967, he was made senior pastor of the Canaan Baptist Church of Christ in Harlem. Walker had a loud voice in the South on behalf of African Americans, and his voice carried in the North as well. He served as urban affairs specialist to governor Nelson Rockefeller for ten years. During that period, Walker quieted racial tensions relative to desegregation of schools and labor union disputes. In addition, he is credited with the proposal and building of Harlem's state office building. It was a controversial project, but Walker succeeded as advisory board chairperson in advising the governor on which agencies should be housed in the new state building. Another project launched by Walker during his tenure in the Rockefeller administration was the Consortium for Central Harlem Development. Walker is responsible for $100 million in housing construction, whereby senior citizens and low to moderate-income families found affordable places to live. In 1975, Walker joined the Board of Directors of Freedom National Bank. He served three terms as chairman of the board during his decade of service. Freedom National was one of the nation's largest and most profitable minority-owned banks.

Gains Fame as Preacher and Humanitarian

Walker is a well-known international civil rights activist. In fact, Nelson Mandela's first stop in the United States as president of South Africa was to attend a service at Walker's church. As an antiapartheid activist and advocate for Palestinians, Walker was the first African American to meet with Yasir Arafat after the demilitarization of the Gaza Strip and Jericho. Walker was chairman of the board of the American Committee on Africa (ACOA), which was subsequently named Africa Action. In 2001, he became president of the Religious Action

Network (RAN), a project of ACOA. The project is a network of two hundred congregations working for peace and freedom in Africa. The focus of the organization is to challenge U.S. and international policies towards Africa that affect justice issues economically, politically and socially. This international effort on Walker's part constitutes only one of his many humanitarian efforts.

Walker is considered the foremost authority on the music of the African American religious experience, in addition to its influence on the freedom movement. He has written many books about the music of the African American church. Walker authored several books between 1965 and 2005, dealing with music, grace, faith, and love. One particularly outstanding effort in 1985 was Walker's appearance on a public broadcasting network, whereby he revealed his music tree in a two-part series. Walker's construct of the music tree may be found in videotape format.

Walker has received various awards for his outstanding efforts toward civil and human rights. In addition he has received honorary doctorate degrees from his alma mater and Princeton University. He was named in a 1993 *Ebony* magazine poll as one of the fifteen greatest African preachers in the United States. At the request of Coretta Scott King, Walker made the arrangements for Martin Luther King's funeral services, which were held at Ebenezer Baptist Church and Morehouse College in Atlanta, Georgia, on April 10, 1968, a daunting responsibility. Walker retired from the pastorate of Canaan Baptist Church in Christ in Harlem in 2004.

REFERENCES

Books

Branham, Charles R. *Profiles of Great African Americans*. Lincolnwood, Ill.: Publications International, Ltd., 1998.

Franklin, John Hope, and Alfred A. Moss Jr. *From Slavery to Freedom: A History of African Americans*. 7th ed. New York: McGraw-Hill, Inc, 1994.

Hampton, Henry, and Steve Fayer. *Voices of Freedom: An Oral History of the Civil Rights Movement from the 1960s to the 1980s*. New York: Bantam Books, 1991.

Morris, Aldon D. *The Origins of the Civil Rights Movement: Black Communities Organizing for Change*. New York: The Free Press, 1984.

Patterson, Lillie. *Martin Luther King Jr. and the Freedom Movement*. New York: Facts on File, Inc., 1993.

Powledge, Fred. *Free at Last? The Civil Rights Movement and the People Who Made It*. New York: Harper Perennial, 1992.

Weisbrot, Robert. *Freedom Bound: A History of America's Civil Rights Movement*. New York: Norton, 1990.

Woodward, C. Vann. *Strange Career of Jim Crow*. New York: Oxford Press, 1974.

Periodicals

Moorer, Talise D. "Faith Notes: News from the pulpit & pew: Rev. Dr. Wyatt Tee Walker to be honored during weekend celebration." *Amsterdam News*, 14 October 2004.

Online

"Africa Action Is Born." 21 March 2001.http://www. africa.upenn.edu/Urgent_Action/apic-032101.html (Accessed 15 February 2006).

Brown, Tony. *Tony Brown's Journal No. 1: Roots of Music*. Tony Brown Productions, [VHS1804] 1985. http://northonline.sccd.ctc.edu/pwebpaz/Media/ MediaT.html (Accessed 15 February 2006).

Shelhea C. Owens

Josiah Walls
1842–1905

Congressman

Josiah Thomas Walls became a major political figure during the post-Civil War period of Reconstruction. He often placed party interest and the national welfare above strict racial allegiance. As an early black political figure in the state of Florida, he had the distinction of participating in many political campaigns and elections. In 1870, he became the first African American from Florida to be elected to the United States Congress and served as the state's only representative. He also served one term in the Florida House and two terms in the Senate. He was twice elected to the House and twice unseated by challenges to his elections by his opponents.

Walls was born a slave near Winchester, Virginia (Frederick County) on December 30, 1842. When he was a child, his mother moved to Darkesville in what later became West Virginia. He briefly attended the county normal school in Harrisburg, Pennsylvania, and may have received additional education. He was forced into service in the Confederate Army, serving in an artillery battery, only to be captured by Union troops in 1862 at Yorktown.

He attended school for a year in Harrisburg, Pennsylvania, and in 1863 he joined the Third Infantry Regiment of the United States Colored Troops, organized at Camp Penn, near Philadelphia, obtaining the rank of corporal.

Josiah Walls

Chronology

1842	Born in Winchester, Virginia on December 30
1862	Captured at Yorktown, Virginia by Union troops
1863	Enters the Third Infantry Regiment, United States Colored Troops of Philadelphia
1864	Moves with regiment to Florida
1865	Discharged; works at a sawmill on Suwannee
1868	Delegate to the Florida State constitutional convention
1868	Elected to the state senate from the Thirteenth District
1870	Nominated for the state's lone seat in the House of Representatives
1871-73	Presents credentials as a member-elect to the Forty-second Congress
1875-76	Reelected and presents credentials as a member-elect to the Forty-fourth Congress
1876	Elected to the state senate
1879	Takes indefinite leave from the state senate
1884	Beaten by Horatio Bisbee for the Republican nomination to the House
1890	Defeated in another bid for the state senate
1895	Slips into ill health and loses his fortune due to weather conditions
1905	Dies in Tallahassee, Florida on May 15

The unit took part in the assault on Fort Wagner, South Carolina (July 1863), and in the Florida campaign (February and March 1864). Walls also had assignments at Baldwin, Jacksonville, and Picalata. He was appointed heavy and light artillery instructor to the troops, defending Jacksonville and the St. John's River.

Walls married Helen Fergueson in Newnansville, when she was only sixteen, on December 9, 1864. She was the daughter of Armstrong Fergueson, who was originally from South Carolina. Walls and his wife had only one child, a daughter Nettie Walls.

Walls was discharged from the Union Army in Florida in October 1865 and settled in Alachua County where he began working at a sawmill on the Suwannee River. He later taught school at Archer in Alachua County.

Launches Political Career

Like many blacks, Walls joined the Republican Party and became politically active with the politics of Reconstruction, and in 1867 he was elected to represent Alachua County at the upcoming Florida Constitutional Convention. In 1868, he attended the convention held in Tallahassee. He was one of only eighteen black delegates who attended the convention. The county convention of March 1868 also nominated Walls for the state assembly; he was elected and took his seat in June. Later that same year he was elected to the state senate from the Thirteenth District and took his seat the following January.

Walls participated in several national conventions, which were held to discuss problems facing blacks. At the Southern States Convention of Colored Men in 1871, he proposed an amendment to a resolution of support for President Ulysses S. Grant, which called on the Republicans to nominate John Mercer Langston for vice president in 1872.

Before the legislative reapportionment that was based on the census of 1870, Walls, who was under the age of thirty, became the first African American from Florida to be elected to the United States Congress where he appeared to win a narrow victory. This was Florida's only seat in Congress at that time. He took his seat, as a Republican member of the House of Representatives (March 4, 1871), accepting assignments on the Militia, the Committee on Mileage, and the Committee on Expenditures in the Navy Department. However, he was unseated following a protest by his defeated opponent, Silas L. Niblack, of Lake City. Niblack disputed the election five days after Walls won, charging that officials had unfairly rejected some of his votes while accepting Walls' illegal ballots. Though it was Walls who protested that voters were intimidated at the polls, the House Committee on Elections unseated Walls by declaring Niblack the winner on January 29, 1873. Still Walls had the last laugh because Niblack held office for less than two months before it was time for the next election. Walls had served almost twenty-three months in the 42nd Congress before being ousted.

When the state was divided into two districts in 1872, Walls ran for Congress and again won election, but this time to a full term. This election posed Walls against Niblack, and Walls beat him by a majority of seventeen hundred votes. So Niblack replaced Walls and served for two months before Walls was once again back in office.

Walls was a strong proponent of a national public education system that could be funded by the sales of public lands as well as mandatory schooling for all children and put forth bills that supported a federal education system for all children. He realized that education was the key for resolving many of the social problems, injustices, and oppressions that existed in the United States. He also introduced bills for relief of private pensioners and Seminole War veterans. One of his most significant bills was aimed at granting military support to the Cubans in their revolt against the colonial oppression of Spain. Spain had brought African slaves to Cuba to work the sugar and tobacco plantations and had wiped out the Indian inhabitants by treating them inhumanely. None of his bills was successful; however, Walls lived to see his dream realized when Cuba became independent in 1898, and the United States obtained a protectorate over Cuba in 1902.

The fifty-one bills Walls introduced during his five years in Congress covered such issues as private pensions, internal improvements of waterways and harbors, establishing mail routes, relief for men who had served in the Seminole Wars and for Florida citizens who had lost property during the Civil War, and general amnesty. He abstained from the final vote on the Civil Rights Bill (February 5, 1875) because it omitted reference to public schools.

Walls was re-elected in 1874, but the results were challenged by his opponent—former Confederate general Jesse Johnson Finley of Jacksonville, Florida. Walls served from March 4, 1875 to April 19, 1876. The subsequent recount gave the election to Finley. A majority of six Democrats and one Independent Republican of the Committee on Elections reported that Walls' votes in one Columbia county precinct had been tampered with by the Republican state senate candidate who had been mysteriously murdered in August 1875 and should be deleted from Walls' total, thereby making Finley the winner. The committee's three Republicans maintained that the disputed ballots, which had been burned in a suspicious courthouse fire, were not cast illegally and that Walls was entitled to his seat. The Democratic controlled House adopted the majority report, and Walls' congressional career ended.

In August 1876 Walls, without party support, was defeated by Horatio Bisbee for re-nomination to the House. In November, he was elected to the state senate, where be became a champion of mandatory public education.

Frustrated by his political isolation and overwhelmed with feelings of futility, Walls took an indefinite leave of absence in February 1879 and left the state senate. Upon his return to Alachua County, Walls owned and operated a successful tomato and lettuce farm, sawmill, and orange grove. He also remained interested in political developments. In 1884, after again being beaten by Bisbee for the Republican nomination to the House, he ran as an independent candidate but was unsuccessful. In the fall of 1890 he was defeated in another bid for the state senate.

In addition to his federal and state service, Walls was also mayor of Gainesville and a member of the Alachua County commission. His passion, and later his livelihood, was farming. He earned enough from his large farm, in what later became Paynes Prairie, to establish a newspaper, titled *Special attention to the wants and interests of People of Color.*

During the last years of his life, Walls faced personal tragedy, financial misfortune, and illness. On New Year's Day in 1885, Helen Fergueson Walls died, after nineteen years of marriage. Then he married Ella Angeline Gass, the first cousin of his deceased wife, on July 5, 1885, who was only fourteen, in Gainesville, Florida.

He slipped into ill health, and a hard freeze killed his orange grove and wiped him out financially in 1895. He moved his family to Tallahassee where he was director of the farm at the state's agricultural college that later became Florida Agricultural and Mechanical (A&M) University. Walls did not mention his past political career after moving to Tallahassee. He did not become involved with the political or social climate in Tallahassee. He spent most of his leisure time at home with his second wife and daughter. His home was a small white house that he purchased from J. F. Montgomery in 1900 for $350.

In 1900, Walls' daughter Nettie succumbed to a behavior problem and became a recluse, shutting herself in the house for long periods of time. Eventually Nettie killed a little girl, Maggie Gibbs, the daughter of a minister. The child was found stabbed and shot and stuffed in a closet at the Walls' home.

Apparently Nettie was involved with the minister who was a widower. They had broken off the relationship, and she sought revenge. Because of her mental condition she was sent to the state psychiatric institution at Chattahoochee, where she died after some months. Walls never recovered from these events.

Walls died in Tallahassee on May 15, 1905 and was buried in a black cemetery in Tallahassee, Florida. To commemorate his life, in Gainesville a plaque was placed on the site of his home on the northeast corner of West University Avenue and Northwest First Street.

REFERENCES

Books

Christopher, Maurine. *Black Americans in Congress.* New York: Thomas Y. Crowell Company, 1976.

Clay, William L. *Just Permanent Interests: Black Americans in Congress, 1870-1991.* New York: Amistad Press, 1992.

Klingman, Peter D. *Josiah Walls, Florida's Black Congressman of Reconstruction.* Gainesville: University of Florida Press, 1976.

Lindenmeyer, Otto J. "Josiah T. Walls: U.S. Congressman." In *Negroes in Public Affairs and Government.* Vol. 1. Ed. Walter Christmas. New York: Educational Heritage, Inc., 1966.

Ragsdale, Bruce A., and Joel D. Treese. *Black Americans in Congress, 1870-1989.* Washington, D.C.: U.S. Government Printing Office, 1990.

"Walls, Josiah T." In *Afro-American Encyclopedia.* Vol. 9. North Miami, Fla.: Educational Book Publishers, Inc., 1974.

Mattie McHollin

Lester A. Walton

Lester A. Walton
1882–1965

Diplomat, journalist

Lester Aglar Walton was mainly known for his diplomatic activity and his journalism, but he was also active in the entertainment arena in the early twentieth century. Although he claimed no direct personal hardship based on color in pursuit of his careers, he participated in obtaining employment for African Americans in a variety of theater roles and supported extending their opportunities in the theater.

Walton was born on April 20, 1882, in St. Louis, Missouri, where he attended the public schools. He graduated from Sumner High School in St. Louis. Later he received three honorary degrees: an M.A. from Lincoln University in Chester, Pennsylvania (1927); an LL.D., from Wilberforce University (1945); and an LL.D. from the University of Liberia (1958). He married Gladys Moore in 1912, the daughter of Fred A. Moore, who was the publisher of the *New York Age.* They had two daughters.

Career as Journalist

Walton's journalism career began at the *St. Louis Star* where he was a golf writer. He became the first African American to write for a daily paper in St. Louis when he accepted a fulltime job working on general assignment and as court reporter for the *St. Louis Star*, from 1902 to 1906. In 1906, Walton moved to New York City, and later he became the manager and theatrical editor for the *New York Age* from 1908 to1914. He returned to the *New York Age*, an African American paper, from 1917 to 1919. During this period in his career he also wrote for a white paper, the *St. Louis Glove-Democrat.* Walton continued his journalism career by becoming a special writer for the *New York World* from 1922 to 1931. In 1931, when the *World* collapsed, he became a feature writer for the *New York Herald Tribune*, but soon quit when he learned the paper would not be giving him a byline. In 1932, Walton returned to the *New York Age* in the position of associate editor.

His journalism career fed his interest in world affairs, and in 1919 he attended the Versailles Peace Conference as a correspondent. Liberia was one of his special interests and in 1933, he visited the country and wrote articles for the *Age* and the *New York Herald Tribune* during the International Liberian Committee. During this period, diplomatic relations between the Liberian government, the United States, and Great Britain were suspended because of problems between Liberian labor and foreign industrialists.

Walton served as an arbitrator in a labor relations dispute between the Newspaper Guild of New York and the

Chronology

1882	Born in St. Louis, Missouri on April 20
1908	Becomes managing editor and theatrical editor for the *New York Age*
1917-19	Directs Harlem's famed Lafayette Theater
1919	Attends the Versailles Peace Conference as a correspondent
1924	Appointed publicity director for the Colored Division of the Democratic National Committee; serves again in this role in 1928 and 1932
1927	Receives honorary M.A. from Lincoln University, Pennsylvania
1932-35	Returns to serve as associate editor of the *New York Age*
1933	Visits Liberia and sends back articles to the *Age* and *New York Herald Tribune*
1935	Appointed envoy extraordinary and minister penipotentiary to Liberia
1948-49	Serves as advisor to the Liberian delegation to the United Nations
1965	Dies in New York City on October 16

New York Amsterdam News, from 1957 to 1959. He also became an active member of the Society of the Silurians, an association of journalists.

Begins Political Career

Walton's interest in politics began around 1913, when be started a movement with the assistance of the Associated Press, for the spelling of the word "Negro" with a capital "N." His efforts were rewarded when newspapers and magazines took up the debate within their pages.

Walton was asked by the United Colored Democracy to write some political literature during a mayoralty campaign. He was later appointed publicity director for the Colored Division of the Democratic National Committee and served in 1924, 1928, and 1932.

Walton was referred to as the "Dean of the Diplomatic Corps." On July 2, 1935, he was appointed envoy extraordinary and minister plenipotentiary to Liberia, by President Franklin D. Roosevelt. Walton was appointed United States minister (ambassador) in July 1935, in what was then called the "Negro post," because Liberia and Haiti were the only places where black people held such positions.

Walton was ambassador to Liberia at a time when Liberia faced a major political crisis. Around 1930, President Charles D. B. King and his vice president resigned, after the League of Nations' investigation of slavery and forced labor implicated key Liberian leaders. When Edwin J. Barclay, the new president of Liberia, refused to implement measures recommended by the League of Nations (measures that could have compromised the independence of Liberia), the Roosevelt administration refused to recognize the new Liberian government.

When Walton arrived in Liberia, he helped to push for U.S. recognition of the Barclay administration. A few years later, during World War II, when Liberia had strategic importance for the United States, he helped Liberia to get much needed resources from the United States government. He concluded significant treaties between the United States and Liberia, including the terms under which the U.S. government established an army base in the country. He also negotiated with the Liberian government for the construction of a port in Monrovia (the first port constructed in Liberia) and concluded commerce, navigation, and aviation treaties. In the area of aviation, he presided over the Liberia-Pan Am deal, which established Liberia's first international airport (Roberts Field).

Yet, Walton was not uncritical of Liberia. Its government was ripe with corruption, and Walton was especially appalled by the human rights violations imposed by the government against its own people. According to the African Within website, he wrote to Harry Mcbride, who had served in Liberia as financial advisor to the Liberian government under the Loan Agreement, that "Forced labor, vicious exploitation of the natives by Frontier Force, unjust and excessive fines are some of the contributory factors to occasion resentment and dissatisfaction, impelling many natives to reluctantly settle in Sierra Leone."

Still, with World War II at hand and the Japanese army controlling the countries that manufactured rubber, the United States needed Liberia and her natural rubber reserves. In fact, Liberia was the only country where the United States and its allies could readily obtain natural rubber. Walton was instrumental in improving Liberian and U.S. relations. The U.S. and Britain also needed to use the country as a base for transporting American soldiers, military hardware, and supplies to North Africa. Roosevelt convinced Liberia to declare war against Germany, and Liberia's natural rubber supplied to the Allies helped seal Nazi Germany's fate.

Walton, after serving as ambassador to Liberia for ten years, resigned from the position. Still, from 1948 to 1949, he served as advisor to the Liberian delegation to the United Nations.

Explores the Entertainment Sphere

In about 1900, Walton had begun a long friendship with Ernest Hogan, taking minor roles in Hogan's productions so that he could learn more about the theater. Walton was active in the entertainment field during the late 1910s and the early 1920s. Working as manager of Harlem's Lafayette Theater from 1914 to 1916 and again from 1919 to 1921, he also served as the dramatic lyricist for the theater. He wrote concert reviews and editorials on black music, stressing the importance of musical knowledge and culture for African Americans.

Walton's entertainment experience was sought during World War I; he was a member of the Military Entertainment Service, where he supervised theatrical productions among the African American soldiers. He was later vice president of the Negro Actor's Guild and in the 1950s became chairman of the Coordinating Council for Negro Performers. Walton was dedicated to the council's mission of increasing and promoting greater integration of African Americans in the media, both television and radio. He was musically active in other ways as well: he wrote lyrics for and helped to direct such musicals as Joe Jordan's *Rufus Rastus* (1905-06), which starred Ernest Hogan; *The Oyster Man* (1909) also a Hogan musical; Alex Rogers and Will Marion Cook's *Black Bohemia* (1911); and Cook's *Darkeydom* (1914-15). In 1922, Walton was touring manager for Harry Pace's Black Swan Troubadours. He was a song writer during his career, from 1905 through 1956. Two of his best known songs are "Welcome to New York," which was dedicated to the mayor of New York, Robert F. Wagner, and "Jim Crow Has Got to Go," a rallying song for civil rights workers in the 1950s. Pursuing his interest in black writers and musicians, he set up the Walton Publishing Company to publish instrumental music.

Community Interests

Walton made New York his home and was a long-standing member of the Harlem community. He sought to make local improvements for African Americans, becoming one of the original volunteer members of the Commission on Intergroup Relations, a New York City agency founded in 1955, which in 1961 became known as the Commission on Human Rights. Under Mayor Wagner, the commission worked in the fields of civil rights and civil liberties, especially fair housing practices. He retired from the commission in 1964. On October 16, 1965, Walton died in New York City. His wife Gladys died in 1977.

REFERENCES

Books

Bradshaw, Clifford A. "Lester A. Walton: Minister to Liberia." In *Negroes in Public Affairs and Government*. Vol. 1. Ed. Walter Christmas. New York: Educational Heritage, Inc., 1966.

Southern, Eileen. "Walton, Lester Aglar." In *Biographical Dictionary of Afro-American and African Musicians*. Westport, Conn.: Greenwood Press, 1982.

"Walton, Lester A." In *Afro-American Encyclopedia*. Vol. 9. Ed. Martin Rywell. North Miami, Fla.: Educational Book Publishers, Inc., 1974.

Online

"American Liberia Relations During World War II." http://www.africawithin.com/tour/Liberia/relations. htm (Accessed 3 March 2006).

"Walton, Lester A. Papers, 1905-1977." New York Public Library Digital Library Collections. http:// digilib.nypl.org/dynaweb/ead/scm/scwalton/ @Generic__BookTextView/144 (Accessed 3 March 2006).

Mattie McHollin

Augustus Washington
1820–1875

Daguerreotypist, politician, educator

Augustus Washington was born September 21, 1820 in Trenton, New Jersey to a former slave and an Asian mother. Washington's mother died when he was very young. He was raised by his stepmother who was also a former slave. Washington received a solid elementary education, but lack of money stymied his attempts at further education for much of his life. In 1836, when Washington was only sixteen, he organized and taught at a school for African American children in Trenton. Washington eventually received money to continue his education through abolitionist friends. He attended the Oneida Institute and Kimball Union Academy before beginning his studies at Dartmouth in 1843. Washington was one of the earliest African Americans accepted at Dartmouth.

Becomes Daguerreotypist

In order to help finance his education, Washington learned how to take daguerreotypes. Since he was only able to attend Dartmouth for a year due to lack of money, photography eventually became his forte. Upon leaving Dartmouth in 1844, Washington traveled to Hartford, Connecticut where he taught at the North African School on Talcott Street. It was one of only two black schools in Dartmouth at that time. Washington continued to supplement his income by taking daguerreotypes. In 1846 Washington left education and opened one of the first daguerreotype studios in Hartford. By 1850, it was considered one of the best daguerreotype studios in Hartford. His success was due to his skill taking daguerreotypes and the service he provided for his clients. Everyone received the same high level of service regardless of whether they were rich or poor or black or white. Washington stamped his name and address on his work and their cases, thus assuring his work would always be rec-

Chronology

1820	Born in Trenton, New Jersey on September 21
1836	Organizes a school for black children in Trenton, New Jersey
1843-44	Attends Dartmouth College
1844-46	Teaches school in Hartford, Connecticut
1846	Opens daguerreotype studio in Hartford, Connecticut
1851	Writes letter to *New York Tribune* about the prospects of blacks in the United States
1853	Moves with family to Liberia
1854	Begins teaching Greek and Latin at Alexander High School
1865	Becomes Speaker of the Liberian House of Representatives
1871	Elected to the Liberian Senate
1873	Founds the newspaper *New Era*
1875	Dies in Monrovia, Liberia on June 7

ognized. If people came in to his studio in unsuitable clothing, he provided suitable garments or draperies to ensure that each person took the best possible picture. He also provided a dressing room for his female patrons. In addition to the daguerreotypes he offered a large selection of cases, frames, bracelets, lockets, and rings in which to put them. Many of Washington's portraits reflected his sentiments about slavery. Washington was so successful that by 1851 he was the only daguerreotypist still in business in Hartford. Washington worked as a daguerreotypist for much of his life. The last known reference to Washington working in the field was in 1858.

Washington was very concerned about the future of blacks in the United States. Initially, he was against the colonization of Liberia by the American Colonization Society. Washington felt that as Americans they should be able to live in peace and freedom in the United States. However, as the slavery controversy heated up, new laws were enacted, and old ones revamped, his concerns grew. In 1850 the Compromise of 1850 passed. It revised the Fugitive Slave Law of 1793, and allowed any slave owner to walk up to a black man, woman, or child, and claim them as a runaway slave and send them to the South. Whether a free person or a runaway, blacks had no legal right to plead their cases.

Before the annexation of Mexico by Texas, Washington along with several friends had been trying to purchase land in Mexico. Washington had hoped to live there in freedom and peace as a separate state of the United States. In 1851, fueled by his concerns for the safety and well-being of his family and all blacks, Washington wrote a controversial letter to the *New York Tribune* in which he discussed the prospects of blacks in the United States.

Washington was concerned that Africa may not be the best place for blacks to live. He had hoped to emigrate to Canada, the West Indies, British Guinea, the part of Mexico which had been annexed by Texas, or even to South America. However given the passing of the Compromise of 1850, he felt that blacks should settle Africa. Washington argued that black leaders in the United States had not done enough to secure opportunities or rights for blacks. He went on to state that white Americans would never believe in the rights of blacks to be free, and whites would never want blacks to have equal rights and opportunities. In fact, the constitutions of the existing states and of those attempting to enter the Union strengthened the rights of whites at the expense of blacks. Washington pointed out the irony that the United States was originally colonized by people who hoped to escape persecution and to be free and yet these people went on to enslave Africans.

Washington also faulted those black ancestors who had not fought harder to escape being pressed into slavery. Washington pointed a finger at abolitionists and those in favor of colonization because they wasted so much time and effort belittling and undermining each other instead of working together. Washington mentioned that as long as blacks were not allowed to pursue political office and to train for any but the most menial jobs, so long as they were denied an education, they would have little chance of advancing in American society. Finally, Washington stated his belief that if whites encouraged the education of blacks, they would leave the United States and do much to improve life for Africans as well as for those who emigrated from this country to Africa. Washington's letter pointed out the responsibility shared by everyone for the tragedy that was slavery.

Emigration to Liberia

In November 1853, Washington moved with his family to Liberia. Washington knew that life in Liberia would not be easy. Many blacks died from disease. The natives of Liberia and the colonists often did not get along. Nevertheless, Washington eventually prospered and became one of Liberia's leading citizens.

Upon his arrival in Liberia, Washington worked as a school teacher at Alexander High School in Monrovia where he taught Greek and Latin. In addition, Washington fulfilled his obligation to the American Colonization Society to photograph the colonization of Liberia by black emigrants. As quoted by Carol Johnson, in 1854 Washington wrote of his happiness in Liberia: "I love Africa because I can see no other spot on earth where we can enjoy so much freedom . . . I believe that I shall do a thousand times more good for Africa, and add to our force of intelligent men." Washington eventually left teaching, bought several hundred acres, and spent half the year growing sugar cane and the other half making daguerreotypes. The daguerreotype business was so successful that he eventually expanded his business into Sierra Leone, Gambia, and Senegal. By 1855, Washington had built and was renting out two houses in Monrovia. He became increasingly prominent in Liberia. By the end of the 1850s Washington had been appointed as a judge. In 1865, he became speaker of the Liberian House of Representatives. In 1871, Washington was elected to the Liberian Senate. Finally in 1873, Washington founded and became editor of the newspaper *New Era*. Washington died in Monrovia, Liberia on June 7, 1875. His death was mourned as signifying a great loss to western Africa.

REFERENCES

Books

Moses, Wilson J. *Liberian Dreams: Back-to-Africa Narratives from the 1850s*. University Park, Pa.: Pennsylvania State University Press, 1998.

Shumard, Ann M. *A Durable Memento: Portraits by Augustus Washington African American Daguerreotypist*. Washington, D.C.: The National Portrait Gallery, Smithsonian Institution, 1999.

Periodicals

Johnson, Carol. "Faces of Freedom: Portraits from the American Colonization Society Collection." *Daguerreian Annual Collection* (1996): 264-78.

Online

Connecticut Historical Society. *Augustus Washington: Hartford's Black Daguerreotypist*, 1999- 2002. http://www.chs.org/graphcoll/augwash.htm (Accessed 9 February 2005).

Washington, Augustus. *African Colonization—By a Man of Color*, July 3, 1851. http://teachingamerican history.org/library/index.asp?document=621. (Accessed 21 December 2005).

Anne K. Driscoll

Paul M. Washington
1921–2002

Religious reformer, minister

A man of righteous discontent, Paul M. Washington was the head of the Church of the Advocacy, which gained national attention in 1968 when it hosted the first national Black Power Convention. Washington was a controversial figure and social crusader who agitated for the acceptance of women in the ministry, civil rights,

Paul M. Washington

reparations for the descendants of slaves, prison reform, and later, partnership benefits for gay city workers. He rose from meager beginnings in Charleston, South Carolina to become known as a compassionate minister with a passion for helping the oppressed and the disaffected.

Paul Matthews Washington was born in Charleston, South Carolina on May 26, 1921, to Tom Washington, a blacksmith, and Mayme Washington, a school librarian. His only sibling was a sister. He was named Paul because Mayme Washington "so admired the courage and the eloquence of the Apostle Paul," Washington wrote in *Other Sheep I Have*. His father was a hardworking man, who gave his weekly paycheck to Mayme Washington, and she issued out the money, including his car fare.

Washington's mother was determined that he would be a minister. He was expected to join the church and work at a part-time job by the time he was ten years old. Before he reached that age, Washington's mother obtained a job for her son with a family friend, a printer named Saxton Wilson. She took him to Memorial Baptist Church where they attended a revival meeting. Deeply moved, he asked to be baptized and to join the church.

In high school, Washington saw black Charleston's real class structure. Since the public high schools offered classes through the eleventh grade only, college-bound blacks had a choice of enrolling at the Roman Catholic high school or at historic Avery Institute, a combined

Chronology

1921	Born in Charleston, South Carolina on May 26
1943	Enters Lincoln University in Pennsylvania
1946	Graduates from Philadelphia Divinity School
1947	Ordained as priest in the Episcopal Church; marries Christine Jackson on August 23; begins six-year stay as teacher at Cuttington College and local pastor in Liberia
1954	Becomes vicar of St. Cyprians-in-the-Meadows in Philadelphia
1962	Becomes rector of the Church of the Advocate in Philadelphia
1964	Begins service on Philadelphia's Human Relations Commission
1966	Hosts Black Unity Rally
1968	Hosts first national Black Power Convention at Church of the Advocate
1969	Begins support to agitate for black reparations
1970	Opens church to Black Panther Party's National Convention; receives Doctor of Divinity degree from Philadelphia Divinity School
1974	Hosts Philadelphia ordination of eleven women to priesthood
1980	Serves as delegate to conference on U.S. intervention in Iran
1985	Appointed to Philadelphia Special Investigating Committee (MOVE Commission); over 1,000 supporters gather to honor his work
1987	Retires from Church of the Advocate; takes on title of rector emeritus
1990	Attends American Institute for International Relations in Moscow
1994	Publishes *Other Sheep I Have: The Autobiography of Father Paul M. Washington*
1995	Participates in the Million Man March in Washington, D.C.
2002	Dies of heart failure in Philadelphia, Pennsylvania on October 7

high school and teacher's college. At Avery, the principal discouraged Washington, suggesting he lacked the appropriate background for Charleston's black elite, and they lived in the wrong section of town—a racially-mixed section with poor whites who lived alongside working class blacks. Washington grew up with knowledge of class and race in the South.

Washington left Charleston when he was seventeen years old and headed for the historically black institution, Lincoln University, in Pennsylvania. Instead of following his mother's prescribed course, initially Washington wanted to become a doctor. Eventually, though, he came back to the idea of the ministry. Lincoln's Episcopal chaplain, Reverend Matthew Davis, visited Washington and persuaded him to join St. Mark's. To the Washingtons, this was a radical change: historically, St. Mark's accommodated light skinned, upper-class blacks, and the Washingtons were neither. Also, Washington was raised a Baptist. Washington remained under Davis's wing, and on June 14, 1943, he was confirmed in the chapel of the Episcopal Church on Rittenhouse Square in downtown Philadelphia. Afterward, Bishop Hart, who confirmed him, sent Washington to Philadelphia Divinity School

where he was the first black seminarian to live in the residence halls (other blacks had lived with black families). As a part of the school's requirement, Washington took pastoral training at Bellevue Hospital in New York City.

In 1947, Washington was ordained a priest. He had met Christine Jackson, a recent high school graduate, whom he married on August 23. The couple went to Liberia, where their first two sons were born. Washington spent six years at Cuttington College in Liberia, where he also served as the school's business manager. With the skills he learned from his father, Washington helped to construct college buildings in the bush. In time, he became a full-time teacher and pastor of two congregations. One was English-speaking while Kru people comprised the second congregation, which he addressed through an interpreter. When the couple returned to Philadelphia in 1954, Washington was named vicar of St. Cyprian's-in-the-Meadows, a church in Eastwick with a black congregation. Located in Philadelphia's extreme southwestern corner, the area was thoroughly integrated both by race and by economic status. While there, Washington began a prison ministry that became an important part of his work for some time.

On June 15, 1962, Washington became rector of the Church of the Advocate. His vision was for the church to be known for its compassion and love—one that responded to human need, such as ministering to the poor, the hungry, the incarcerated, and all who were socially marginalized. This church was located in north Philadelphia which was, in those days, an area referred to by some as "the jungle." Many interpreted the nickname as a reflection of racial prejudice and fear. Poverty, broken homes, joblessness, overcrowding, landlord neglect, and an abundance of social problems were in evidence there. There were positive aspects as well, however; proud blacks lived in well-tended row houses and loved the community. Washington began his work by taking stock of the community and its relationship to the church. With the rectory next door to the church, he put in place immediately an open-door policy. He gave himself fully to everyone, with special concern for the needy who were usually treated poorly by social agencies and others who were in position to help. In his autobiography, Washington said: "I did not come to the Advocate with an agenda for social change. I came to be a pastor." His congregation remained small, compared to those of other Protestant churches, but the church was a focal point for many of Philadelphia's pressing needs during the turbulent 1960s.

Persuaded by Black Power Movement

By 1964, Washington was involved in civil and human rights. For seven years he served on Philadelphia's Human Relations Commission. While at first he supported Martin Luther King's passive resistance, by the end of the decade he was attracted to the black power movement and the militant stance of some blacks. His church became known for opening its doors to radical groups. One historical event that his church hosted was the first national Black Power Convention of 1968 that brought in leading black activists, such as Stokely Carmichael (later self-renamed Kwame Ture) and H. Rap Brown. It also brought national attention from the media and FBI probes. His church was known nationwide as the center of the Black Power movement in Philadelphia. Although previous conferences had created racial tensions and fears of disruptions in the cities where they were held, Washington believed deeply in the purpose of the 1968 conference and agreed to serve as host. He wrote in his autobiography that those who gathered at the conference were "sheep that I as a shepherd knew. They knew my voice and I knew theirs." He admitted, however, that at times he felt uneasy because "Black Power meant different things to different people." Although he participated in the conference, in fact, Washington lacked certain credentials for one associated with extremists.

The conference had as its theme "Black Self-Determination and Black Unity through Direct Action." Washington helped to alleviate the fears of many who thought that the thousands of activists might cause disruption within the church or the city. As local police officers raided the local Black Panthers' office and stripped some of its members to their underwear, Washington became even more anxious about blacks' reaction. In the end, Washington was credited with helping to keep peace and promote goodwill, and for helping to maintain an overall positive mood.

Washington and his church called a Black Unity Rally on February 4, 1966, hosting over two hundred people at the parish hall. Those who attended included Julian Bond and white and black members of CORE, SNCC, and other activist groups. The next day, the local media called the rally reverse discrimination, while a fellow Episcopalian minister called it "segregation in the House of the Lord." Still, Washington remained adamant that the conference was needed.

The Black Power movement entered another phase in 1969, when James Forman of the SNCC began to agitate for reparations for black Americans. He began his demand at Riverside Church in New York City, as he walked down the aisle during a Sunday service. "The Black Manifesto" that the National Black Economic Development Conference (BEDC) prepared at its Detroit conference in April 1969 made the case for reparations. The demand was for $500 million from Christian churches and Jewish synagogues. Foreman's presentation was dramatic, and the manifesto's demands frightened many religious whites. Washington became involved when he initiated a meeting with Muhammad "Mo" Kenyatta, a young Baptist preacher who had worked with Forman in civil rights struggles in the South and was a Philadelphia-area organizer for BEDC. In July 1969, Kenyatta demanded reparations from the Diocese

of Pennsylvania. Washington served on the Diocesan Council, and as the council debated the issue, he suggested that the word "restitution" replace "reparations." Thus, the Diocese of Pennsylvania responded to the demand by setting up the Restitution Fund, which was to be administered through the Restitution Fund Commission. None of the funds ever went to BEDC, however. After continuing debate in various conventions, church conferences, and committees, with Washington supporting the cause, nothing was done; instead, there was a backlash in the church against the idea of reparations. By September, the FBI probed the contents of Kenyatta's speech and considered grand jury proceedings.

Washington was controversial because of his activities and because he had caught the eye of federal officials. For example, in 1970, as Philadelphia was caught up in racial tension, Washington opened his church to the Black Panther Party's National Convention. In 1980 he and eight others defied a federal travel ban that Attorney General Ramsey Clark issued and attended a conference on U.S. intervention in Iran, at the same time that the country held fifty-three Americans hostage.

Washington's controversial views were brought to national and international attention in 1974. This time the defiance was in favor of the ordination of women to the Episcopal priesthood. Washington bucked church rules, shocked the Episcopal Church, and permitted three retired bishops to ordain eleven women. Although black Bishop Barbara Harris, a protégé of Washington's, was not among that group, in September 1988 she was elected suffragan bishop of the 110,000-member diocese of Massachusetts and became the first woman consecrated bishop in the Episcopal Church. By 1977, the church sanctioned such ordination, the stage having been set three years earlier. Church liberals and conservatives, however, remain at odds in their view on the issue.

Mayor W. Wilson Goode appointed Washington to the Philadelphia Special Investigating Committee (also known as the MOVE Commission) that reviewed the city's bombing of the compound for the organization MOVE on May 13, 1985. That tragedy ended with eleven people burned to death and sixty-one homes destroyed in West Philadelphia. John Africa founded the organization in the late 1960s.

In 1990, Washington traveled to Moscow where he attended a meeting of the American Institute for International Relations. Continuing his activism, Washington was attracted to the Million Man March in Washington, D.C., held in 1995, and he joined the group as a passionate supporter. However, Washington had contempt for the evangelical Promise Keepers, a conservative men's movement. He became a member of a group of clergy that challenged the fundamentalist organization. His opposition to the group placed him at odds with some black religious leaders who believed that a stronger male leadership was needed in the home. Taking another unpopular stance, Washington opposed Philadelphia's black clergy who denounced domestic partnership protection for homosexual city workers. As controversial as he remained throughout his religious practice, his church never censured him.

In 1970, the Philadelphia Divinity School awarded Washington the Doctor of Divinity degree. In all, Washington received five honorary doctorates and over seventy awards for his dedication to peace and justice. These included the National Urban League's Whitney M. Young Award for Community Service; the Golden Anniversary Award from the National Association of Christians and Jews; and the Philadelphia Award. In 1985 over one thousand civic, political, and religious people gathered to honor him and to celebrate his work. According to Macklin and Wagenveld in the *Philadelphia Inquirer*, at that gathering, William H. Gray III, then a U. S. representative, called him "the high priest of the progressive movement in Philadelphia." In 1994, Washington published *Other Sheep I Have: The Autobiography of Father Paul M. Washington*, which he wrote with the assistance of David M Gracie. According to the Philadelphia Folklore Project, Washington kept a personal planner—a leather-bound calendar in which he wrote words of inspiration. He wrote messages from the scripture, kept names of civil rights martyrs, and other information, and whenever he was asked to speak he could easily consult his planner as needed. He also kept dates and appointments—all reminders of the race struggle and the hard work that he did to help create a just society.

Father Washington, as he was often called, was a lean, bespectacled man. He had a commanding yet approachable appearance. William R. Machlin and Mark Wagenveld for the *Philadelphia Inquirer* called him "a compelling preacher with a deep, sonorous voice, whose highly refined speaking style encompassed both the thunderous expressions of the best African American preachers and the cool restraint of the Episcopal liturgical tradition." When he retired in 1987, Washington was named rector emeritus and moved from the Church of the Advocate rectory. He lived in the Strawberry Mansion neighborhood of Philadelphia and had a vacation home in Cape May, New Jersey. In the late years of his life, Washington endured repeated bouts of ill health. He suffered chronic muscle pain and his retirement was not restful. After a long illness, Washington died on October 7, 2002, of heart failure, at Lankenau Hospital. His survivors included his wife Christine, to whom he was married for fifty-four years; three sons (Marc, Keman, and Michael); a daughter (Donyor); and seven grandchildren. A memorial service was held at the Church of the Advocate, with Philadelphia native Bishop Barbara Harris officiating. She was one of several speakers who testified to his life and dedication to helping the oppressed.

REFERENCES

Books

Who's Who among African Americans. "Obituaries." 16th ed. Farmington Hills, Mich.: Thomson Gale, 2003.

Online

Corsaletti, Louis T. "Paul M. Washington." *Obituaries in the News*. http://www.nytimes.com/aponline/ national/AP-Deaths.html (Accessed 9 October 2002).

Moore, Acel. "How Great Was His Faithfulness: Recalling Father Washington." *Philadelphia Inquirer*. http://www.philly.com/mid/philly/news/columnists/ accl_moore/4249140.htm (Accessed 10 October 2002).

Jessie Carney Smith

J. C. Watts
1957–

Congressman

Self-described "conservative, faith-based minister congressman" J. C. Watts Jr. was the first African American to serve in the House Republican leadership. He gleaned his work ethic and conservatism from years of football training, the Baptist church, and his parents who, ironically, were staunch Democrats. He counted "Mr. Conservative" himself, Newt Gingrich, among his friends, and the *New York Times* once ran an editorial titled "The Trouble with J. C. Watts—He Thinks for Himself." Watts follows traditional Republican party lines on most issues: he is pro-life; believes in gun-safety reform, not gun control; and supports Social Security and welfare reform, tax relief, parental choice in education and reduction in government influence in the lives of Americans. But he does not follow his party blindly, often taking an independent stand on issues such as affirmative action and civil rights.

"Mine wasn't a Norman Rockwell childhood," Watts wrote in his autobiography *What Color Is a Conservative?* "There were too many black faces, too much poverty, and too little opportunity." Watts' father was J. C. "Buddy" Watts, whose family of sharecroppers and dairy farmers emigrated to Eufaula, Oklahoma from Canada and "did pretty well for a black family in that place and time," Watts wrote in his autobiography. Like families across the United States, black or white, the Watts clan was shaken by the Great Depression.

J. C. Watts

Buddy Watts, whom his son described in *What Color Is a Conservative?* as a "firecracker," was called out as a boy for his name, J. C. J. C. had to stand for something, a teacher insisted in front of his class. "And in an instant that would later determine my name, and that of my son," Buddy explained; he "proudly said, 'Julius Caesar!'"

Buddy quit school to work and married Helen Pierce in 1940, when he was 17. They had six children and were married until her death in 1993. J. C. Watts Jr. was the second youngest of the brood, born November 18, 1957. Buddy had an entrepreneurial spirit. He did odd jobs and sold illegal cholk beer to support his family. According to Watts in his autobiography, there was more love than money in his family. His parents, however, understood that saving and investment were their "ticket out of poverty," Watts wrote. Though money was tight, they managed to save enough to buy a second home and rent it out. Buddy bought "fixer-uppers," renovated them, and ultimately owned more than twenty rental houses in Eufaula. Watts counts his father, Martin Luther King Jr., and his uncle Wade, an activist, among his role models. His parents also taught him to turn the other cheek.

Buddy and Helen Watts were always willing to go where the work was. They packed up the family and picked cotton in Arizona and worked construction in California. They worked in Wichita, Kansas, and Milwaukee, Wisconsin. In the spring and summer, the family returned to Eufaula in their old GMC farm truck. Buddy and Helen rode up front, and the kids held down the furniture in the back. By the 1960s, with the children all in school, Buddy went off on his own looking for work in the winters. Always involved in the community, Buddy Watts became the town's first black policeman in 1969 and later became a preacher. Public policy was always a topic at the dinner table, and everyone in the Watts family was assumed to be a lifelong Democrat.

Watts credits his fiscal conservatism to his mother, who made the most of what little the family had. As a boy, she would send him to the grocery store with a list and $20. He longed to leave the store with a Hershey bar or soda bought with the change from the purchases, but his mother had the list figured to within 20 cents. As a teenager, Watts followed in his father's footsteps, earning money as a jack-of-all-trades, mowing lawns, hauling hay, and delivering newspapers.

Like his peers, Watts grew up without health insurance. As he recalled in *What Color Is a Conservative?*, "Nobody saw the doctor unless they were in childbirth or at death's door." His mother kept the family healthy with her own home remedies.

Watts and his family attended Sulphur Springs Baptist Church, where he and his siblings sang in the choir. Looking back on his youth in the church, Watts wrote in his autobiography that he remembers singing in front of the congregation and hearing people say: "Look at that little boy. He's going to be a preacher." Though he left behind his dreams of becoming the next Marvin Gaye or Al Green, Watts did sing onstage with the Temptations at the 2000 Republican convention in Philadelphia.

Watts' parents had grown up in the age of Jim Crow, and Eufaula was not immune to the second-class citizenship the bigoted system reinforced. By the time Watts was young, though, things were changing. The last black man lynched in Eufaula was of his grandparents' generation, but young Watts and a friend were the first black children to attend Eufaula's all-white Jefferson Davis Elementary.

Watts watched three local boys earn college football scholarships and go on to some achievement in the sport. His own brothers played, too. So Watts followed their lead and joined the football team at Eufaula High. As a sophomore, the coach promoted Watts to quarterback. Some people on the team and around town objected to a black quarterback. "If Eufaula was home to a few bigots," he wrote in *What Color Is a Conservative?*, "it was also home to a lot of people who didn't care what color I was if I could get the ball across the line." He also excelled on the basketball team and in the school chorus. Upon graduation, he was an All-State and All-American football star, showered with scholarship offers.

Watts' dreams of a college football career nearly came crashing down in 1976, his senior year. Watts fathered two daughters with two different women. He married one of the women, Frankie Jones, and raised their daughter, and an aunt and uncle raised the other child. With the support of his family, Watts went ahead with his college plans and took a scholarship with Oklahoma University, where he played for legendary coach Barry Switzer. Watts and his wife ultimately had five children together.

His years at Oklahoma University were tough. The culture shock of leaving tiny Eufaula and having to hold his own academically and in sports, among 23,000 other students, almost got the best of him. But by 1979 he was named starting quarterback for the Oklahoma University Sooners. The achievement drew criticism from some fans who wanted to see a white player in the position. Also that year, he and Frankie had their second child, son Jerrell. Watts worked summers on road crews. The Sooners won two Orange Bowls with Watts as quarterback, and Watts was named MVP both times.

Becomes Canadian Football Star

When the 1981 NFL draft came around, Watts was picked for the New York Jets. He quickly found that he would be unable to start in his position, quarterback, and that he likely never would. He was told there was simply too much quarterback talent in the NFL. But Watts acknowledged in his autobiography that black NFL quarterbacks were few and far between at that time. So he joined the Ottawa Roughriders, a Canadian Football League (CFL), where five of the nine league teams already had black quarterbacks.

After several games with the Roughriders, Watts made an impression on his teammates, coaches, and the fans. He earned an MVP award. According to *What Color Is a Conservative?*, one teammate told a reporter, "You know, there's something about J. C. He always has a way of getting it done."

A contract argument kept the quarterback off the field during the 1982 season. He looked to the CFL Players' Association for help, but the union refused to back him. It was his first experience in the complex arena of labor-management relations. But he was back in 1983 with a four-year contract. In 1986, he played his last season in pro football with the Toronto Argonauts.

Watts returned to Oklahoma and his family and took a position as youth minister of Sunnylane Baptist Church, on the outskirts of Oklahoma City. To his surprise, he found he did not miss football at all. Watts called on the leadership skills he had learned as a quarterback to teach and guide teenagers at Sunnyvale. His job there was to get to know the kids and help them learn how to be productive.

Switches Political Parties

As a journalism student in college, Watts covered a U.S. Senate campaign debate between a young Republican candidate named Don Nickles and Andy Coats, the Democratic mayor of Oklahoma City. "I left the hall that afternoon one confused African American," he wrote in *What Color Is a Conservative?*, "because I found myself agreeing more with what the Republican had to say than the Democrat." Watts had been raised in a 100-percent Democratic environment. He continued: "Every black I knew was a Democrat. It never crossed my mind that a black person could actually be a Republican." Nickles values appealed to Watts; his views on issues from agriculture to government spending made sense to him. Watts voted Democratic in the 1988 presidential election, but it was the last time. "I switched my party registration to Republican, " he wrote, "and to my surprise discovered that I didn't grow horns and a tail. . . ." His father took the news of his son's "defection" fairly well. Watts directs anyone trying to understand how he came by his political views to look to his childhood in Eufaula. "Rural America . . . raises children with dreams and the values to reach them," he wrote in his autobiography.

Watts and his growing family were having a hard time getting by on his modest salary, so Watts tapped into his entrepreneurial spirit. While still with the ministry, he took paid speaking engagements and, with his college experience on road crews, started Ironhead Construction, a highway construction company. He also formed Watts Energy, a company that sold fuel to military bases.

The fledgling businessman came face to face with "how overregulation stifles the entrepreneurial spirit in America today," he wrote in his autobiography. Though government regulations are established in the interests of safety and fairness, he wrote, small businesses often face as much regulation as Fortune 500 companies. He was frustrated with all the red tape he and other small business people faced. Sharing his complaints with a friend over lunch one day, Watts said offhandedly, "Maybe I ought to run for office," and then he began to seriously consider the idea.

Elected to First Office

After many miles on the campaign trail, Watts became the first African American elected to the Oklahoma Corporation Commission. In his autobiography, Watts described the experience as challenging and rewarding, but also frustrating and difficult. As he was sworn in January 1991, he wrote, "I approached my new commission responsibilities with the green enthusiasm of a novice politician."

Watts found politics a messy business, even at the state level. The commission was the focus of an FBI corruption scandal. Even though he was new on the scene, Watts stood out as a black Republican and found himself in the national spotlight almost immediately when President George H. Bush called on Watts for a photo opportunity.

The new politician discovered that being in the spotlight also made him a target, both personally and politically. Though the FBI investigation focused on the commission for events that took place long before Watts joined, his political foes tried to associate him with the mess. It was a trying time for Watts and his family, but he had some successes during his tenure as commissioner, among them an audit of utility companies that resulted in lower rates and better service for consumers. After four years on the state commission, Watts set his sights on Washington.

Sworn into Congress

Watts ran for the Fourth Congressional District of Oklahoma, a moderate to conservative area. The contest focused on several issues: defense, term limits, gun control, abortion, taxes, and Bush's Contract with America. The issues soon took a back seat to politics. Watts wrote in *What Color Is a Conservative?* that he believed "the last person who would use race to win an election would be my Democrat opponent. I was never more wrong in my life." Democrat David Perryman ran ads featuring photos of Watts in the seventies, when he sported a full-blown Afro, yet voters saw through the questionable ads. On election night 1994, Watts won 52 percent of the vote, becoming the first black Republican elected to Congress from a southern state since Reconstruction. He was also part of the first Republican majority in the House of Representatives in forty years. Watts was sworn into the 104th Congress in January 1995, staying in Washington, D.C. during the week, flying back home to his family and his district on weekends.

The black Republican was an anomaly to lobbyists and everyone else in Washington. Reporters and his fellow Congress members were stunned when he did not join the Congressional Black Caucus. The freshman Congressman did not want to be aligned with a single group. Watts joined the Congressional Banking Committee and facilitated 80 percent of the Republican "Contract with America" being passed into law in the first one hundred days of the session. Watts' exuberance with the pace the Republican majority was making in Washington ended, however, with the April 1995 bombing of the Murrah Federal Building on Oklahoma City. In *What Color Is a Conservative?*, Watts recounts that 1996 was the year in which he found his confidence as a congressman. He voted on crucial welfare reform and called the passage of the legislation "one of the proudest moments of my congressional career."

Watts was honored to be asked to speak at the Republican national convention. In his speech, he espoused three key actions Republicans intended to take in 1998. First, they wanted to increase the influence of "traditional and spiritual values" in solving problems in education, poverty, crime, and health care. Second, Republicans were solidly set on balancing the budget. Finally, Republicans wanted to decrease the U.S. racial divide.

Riding high with the Republican majority made Watts an even bigger political target. Because of his views to limit welfare and pare down what he called "intrusive" government, some African Americans called him an "Uncle Tom," a sellout to his race. Instead of dismissing the jibes as partisan nonsense, Watts shot back. As he recalled in his autobiography, he told a reporter that black leaders who felt that way were just people "whose careers are based on keeping black people dependent on government handouts. What scares them the most is that black people might . . . start thinking for themselves." Watts referred to these politicians as "race-hustling poverty pimps," a phrase that came back to haunt him as a *Washington Post* reporter linked it to Jesse Jackson and Washington mayor Marion Barry, though Watts never referred to either of these African American politicians.

After taking control of Congress by a great majority in 1994, the Republicans came out of the 1998 election with a thinner margin. Newt Gingrich and Bob Livingston resigned, and the party was looking for new leadership. Watts won the Republican conference chairmanship, which made him the fourth most-powerful office holder in Congress. Watts considered the position an opportunity to reach out to Americans who distrusted the Republican Party, minorities among them. When the Clinton impeachment hearing took place, led by Washington Republicans, Watts called his vote to impeach "the most heart-wrenching vote I've had to cast. . . . I prayed I had chosen the right course along with my colleagues." September 11, 2001 stalled the vicious partisan feuding for a time and shifted the course of first-year President George W. Bush and the Republican Party. The war on terrorism, which eventually led to military action in Afghanistan and Iraq, became the main focus of the administration.

"Being called 'Congressman' is a real honor," Watts wrote in *What Color Is a Conservative?*, "but it doesn't hold a candle to being called 'Dad.'" With this in mind in 2002, after eight years serving the Fourth District of Oklahoma, Watts decided not to run for reelection. President George W. Bush, African American Democrats, even civil rights icon Rosa Parks urged Watts to stay, according to *Time*. Some pundits suggested Watts had hit a "glass ceiling" and that there was no room for Watts in the Republican leadership. Upon Watts' departure from Congress, the Republican Party lost its sole African American congressman.

Back in the private sector, Watts returned to his business interests, started a consulting firm, J. C. Watts Cos., and wrote his autobiography. He also became a regular contributor to news, politics, and sports-based publications, including the *Sporting News*. In 2003, Watts was named chairman of FM Policy Focus, a group lobbying Washington to reinforce regulations on lending agencies Fannie Mae and Freddy Mac.

REFERENCES

Periodicals

Beston, Paul. "From the Orange Bowl to Washington." *American Spectator* (June/July 2003): 74.

Coates, Ta-Nehisi. "House Negro." *Washington Monthly* (December 2003): 49-50.

Hocker, Cliff. "And Then There Were None." *Black Enterprise*, November 2002.

"J. C. Watts Returns to the Offense." *Institutional Investor* (June 2003): 1.

"United States: Ave Atque Vale; The Retirement of J. C. Watts." *Economist* (6 July 2002): 46.

Wallas, Douglas. "10 Questions for J. C. Watts." *Time* (15 July 2002): 8.

Williams, Juan. "Profile: Decision by Representative J. C. Watts to not Seek Re-election." *Morning Edition*, 22 July 2002.

Online

"Watts: The GOP's American Dream Come True." CNN online, http://www.cnn.com/ALLPOLITICS/1997/02/04/watts.profile (Accessed 28 January 2005).

Brenna Sanchez

Milton P. Webster
1887–1965

Labor leader

Aconsummate union organizer, Milton P. Webster worked through the Chicago Division of the Brotherhood of Sleeping Car Porters (BSCP) in the interest of

---

Chronology

1887	Born (exact date unknown)
1924	Becomes assistant bailiff in Chicago's municipal court
1925	Becomes ward leader for the Republican party in Chicago
1926	Begins relationship with A. Philip Randolph and the Brotherhood of Sleeping Car Porters (BSCP)
1929	Elected first vice-president of the BSCP; announces forthcoming national labor conference in Chicago
1935	Pullman Company recognizes BSCP as bargaining unit for porters and maids
1941	President Franklin D. Roosevelt issues Executive Order No. 882, in the interest of jobs and for blacks; represents BSCP on the first Fair Employment Practices Commission (FEPC)
1965	Dies in Bal Harbor, Florida on February 24

---

its members and their right to fair treatment. He protested the Pullman Company's long practice of low pay, long work hours, and harsh treatment of its porters, most of whom were African American. Later, he handled BSCP cases before the Railroad Adjustment Board and was chief negotiator of contracts with the railroad. His work with the BSCP leadership resulted in the American Federation of Labor's acceptance of that group as its bargaining agency. This was the first African American union to win a national contract as well as the first bargaining agreement won against Pullman. The charter with AFL also led to Webster's position as office holder on its international board.

Virtually nothing is known about the circumstances of Milton Webster's birth or about his early life. It is known that he was the son of a Tennessee barber. While still a young man, Webster left Clarksville, Tennessee and moved to Chicago where for eighteen years he worked as a Pullman porter. Although the number of his siblings is unknown, he had an older brother, D. P. Webster, who may have founded the black postal workers' protest group, the Phalanx Forum Club. With less than a ninth-grade education, Milton Webster had limited employment options. But Webster was determined to provide for his wife Elizabeth and their three children so that she could devote all of her energy to raising their son and daughters. In time he became frustrated with the Pullman Company and resigned from service. He also became interested in the work of political figures. At some point Webster's political patron, Bernard Snow, who was chief bailiff of the municipal court, helped Webster to study law privately. In 1924 and in need of employment to support himself and his family, he became assistant bailiff under Snow. In this patronage position, he became a successful political operative in Republican politics. He held the position until 1930 and also managed at least two large apartment buildings in Chicago. Although this was during the Great Depression, Webster was still able to separate himself from the Pullman Company and to earn enough money and have sufficient time for union opportunities that came to him. He also gave the union financial support. Webster was influential in Republican politics as early as 1925, when he became a ward leader among the party's black membership. In time, he was transformed from ward "heeler" to labor leader.

The Pullman Company Develops

Between 1868 and 1968, an African American attendant in service on the railroads was a common site. A peak decade for the American railroad system was the 1920s, when there were some 20,224 African Americans working as porters for the Pullman Company and as railroad personnel elsewhere. The history of the Pullman Company, however, provides fertile ground for the developments that would occur involving its black workers.

George Mortimer Pullman founded the Pullman Palace Car Company shortly after the Civil War. The manufacturing and operating firm built luxury railroad cars, equipped with service personnel for the affluent passengers traveling long distances. The company flourished, and by 1925 there were Pullman cars on practically all railroads in the country. Race conditions at the time dictated that blacks were placed in service jobs; for the most part, black men, who were right out of slavery or descendants of slaves, would be hired for the menial tasks, thus becoming the workers on these cars. Their role, however, became stereotypical, as they were often seen, and portrayed, as servants with a ready smile and open hand, and displaying a readiness for duty. They were treated as slaves who, according to A. Philip Randolph, gave long, devoted, patient and heroic service. They were the "fabric of the company." The company was callous and heartless; in its view, black porters had no manhood. Even one young white man who Randolph referred to as "some sixteen-year-old whipper snapper messenger boy" insulted these men, some of whom had been with the company for thirty to forty years. He was simply a porter with a hapless lot. And all of the porters came to be known simply as "George," in so-called "honor" of the company's founder, George Mortimer Pullman.

By 1925, the company was in its heyday and was also the nation's largest single employer of blacks. Several forward-thinking black men, however, took issue with the ill treatment of the race, particularly the Pullman porters.

The Brotherhood of Sleeping Car Porters Emerges

In summer 1925, New York's black porters were persuaded that they needed a union. Something had to be done about the Pullman Company's treatment of its black porters, and leaders were needed to take them into arenas beyond the reach of the company's reprisals. Then a small group of porters held a number of secret meetings and worked out plans for founding a union. Their plans were formalized and the Brotherhood of Sleeping Car Porters was organized in the Elks Hall in the Harlem section of New York City on August 25, 1925. Later, A. Phillip Randolph was named general organizer of the union. Other officers were W. H. Des Verney, vice-president and assistant organizer; Roy Lancaster, secretary-treasurer; and Ashley Totten, assistant organizer. Their motto or password was "solidarity," which they called the key to freedom of the oppressed and exploited races and classes, and the group's sign was a clinched left fist with arm extended downward, denoting that justice and freedom will come only through a fight.

Randolph and Totten had difficulty persuading union men to work publicly for the union—as they would do as organizers—for the men feared retaliation from the Pullman Company if they did so. Some were apathetic, skeptical, and simply afraid. Soon they concluded that the company was trying to frighten them away, first by bringing in more blacks from the South who might be their replacement. This was warning enough for Randolph and Totten to find a strong leader whom the Pullman officials could not intimidate; hence, they located Milton P. Webster, who became the most notable of the district organizers. The Chicago area was the Pullman Company's most important district, its headquarters were there, and it employed more black porters than any other district. It ran cars in and out of the city to places throughout the country. Likewise, the Chicago area was important to the BSCP. For twelve years it would house the brotherhood's most militant local who agitated against the company's anti-union stance. The persuasive Randolph was successful in getting Webster to take the job. In time, union leaders found organizers—all Pullman Porters—for its other divisions in such cities as St. Louis, Detroit, and Pittsburgh.

Webster's writing skills were poor at that time; in fact, when the union needed to communicate with its members in the Chicago district, A. Philip Randolph often composed messages on circulars and attributed the work to Webster. Apparently Webster worked on his shortcomings and by 1926 Randolph had what William Harris in *Keeping the Faith* called "justifiable confidence in his ability to communicate both orally and in writing." Webster had a close friendship with Oscar De Priest, one of Chicago's leading black politicians. His important political connections as well as the strong, personal friendships that he had among the porters with whom he had worked led to his becoming the second most important person in the BSCP. Despite his importance to the BSCP's success, Milton Webster was barely mentioned in published sources until 1977, when William H. Harris published *Keeping the Faith* and included good details of Webster's union career. Webster had been content to remain in Randolph's shadow, which may have helped him to remain relatively obscure.

Despite his shortcomings early on, Webster immediately had the porter's respect. When he headed the local membership drive, the response that he received was overwhelmingly positive. Even so, most local black leaders were unenthusiastic because they lacked confidence that the porters could, or should, challenge the Pullman Company. Then too, they saw the company's long record of hiring blacks and felt that the men should not "bite the hand that feeds you." The Pullman Company had endeared itself to religious leaders and black organizations as well. Neither the NAACP, the Urban League black religious hierarchy, nor the African American press supported the BSCP. They were impressed when the Pullman Company donated $10,000 to the black YMCA, rented dormitories and meeting spaces in its facilities, and rented black churches as meeting sites for its Pullman Porters Benefit Association of America, a fraternal and death benefit society for blacks. Pullman accepted recommendations for employment from local black ministers and deposited at least $10,000 in the black-owed Binga State Bank. Some blacks held porters in high regard, especially since their salaries, as poor as they were, were a vast improvement over those that other blacks received. By now some of the porters were college graduates who were unable to find employment elsewhere. In all likelihood, however, these Pullman supporters were either unaware of, or unresponsive to, the poor treatment that their fathers, brothers, and sons received from their employer.

Since Webster had worked as a porter in his younger years, he knew well what was involved in a porter's work. He still had friends who were porters. This meant that he could enter certain circles with ease, where Randolph could not, or dare nor, tread. Because Webster had access to Chicago's political figures, he could perhaps use the friendships and connections to benefit the union. Oscar De Priest was one of these figures; and Webster was able to involve De Priest's friend, Robert L. Mays, in the union's efforts to organize Chicago's porters. By the end of 1925, however, Mays argued that the union should go before the Railroad Labor Board to have its cases heard (such as a demand for increased pay). Later he quit the union because he was at odds with Randolph and other leaders over this issue. He also condemned BSCP leadership and claimed the union's New York officials—including Randolph—exercised undue control over the union. Webster went on to become the BSCP's second most important leader due to his political connections as well as his ability to organize workers.

Division leaders faced mounting disgruntlement, some of the top division leaders threatened to quit, and the BSCP faced problems in recruiting members as well as sustaining itself. By 1926, however, BSCP's general office changed its attitude. On August 20, 1926, the New York office polled several district leaders for their attitude on wage-scale demands from members and the leaders themselves. After that, Randolph announced that a National Advisory Committee comprised of organizing committees from several districts would be the policy-making body and the New York crew would take a hands-off approach.

When this occurred, Randolph and other BSCP leaders around the country developed mutual respect as well as a friendship. This was especially important for the Webster-Randolph relationship that existed during mid-1926. The men were vastly different in personality and approach to issues, yet they complemented each other: Randolph was skilled in bringing in outside support, while Webster was an astute organizer, and was especially good for the Chicago district. Because they spent so much time together, some called the men "the gold dust twins." Thus, the union's progress lay squarely on the shoulders of these two leaders. Randolph was haughty and aloof, and left BSCP men feeling ill at ease around him. To the contrary, Webster was "down to earth" and approachable, unpretentious, direct, and gruff. Although at times they clashed, there was no doubt, however, that both thought that the porters must have a union and they worked diligently to accomplish their mutual goal and to set an example for black workers everywhere to follow. As they went about their work, Randolph took the porter's message to the public and functioned as moral leader for men in all ranks. Webster handled all day-to-day operations and strengthened union membership in Chicago's hostile environment.

Webster and Randolph became a dynamic speaking duo that American labor had never seen. According to Greg LeRoy, Randolph encouraged Webster to perfect his manner: he was "abrasive and booming, alternately abrupt and then flowing, tirades followed by asides." He was Randolph's "emcee" for forty years. When appearing before union members, Webster deliberately agitated the crowd and made them uneasy. After that, the eloquent Randolph appeared with his fine oratorical style that he had developed when he was a Shakespearean actor. According to Ely, he was "soothing" and "otherworldly," and like "a hell-fire Baptist preacher bringing on the Pope."

Webster became disillusioned with local Republicans and by 1927 spent less time in new political work and more in union activities. He knew also that there were "big shots" in the party who were racists as well as anti-BSCP, and he sought to interview Herbert Hoover, who was then Secretary of Commerce, to express his discontent over the Coolidge administration's anti-union stance. According to Greg LeRoy, when his attempts failed, Webster reasoned "that neither party is interested in the Negro. They are just interested in getting all the votes they can."

The BSCP and the Pullman Company remained at odds over a number of benefits for the porters. By 1928, Webster, Randolph, and other leaders met and decided to do whatever was needed to assist the union, including calling a strike against Pullman. On March 15, 1928, Randolph announced that the BSCP would ask its members to strike; it would occur on June 28, 1928. While Randolph actually wanted to avoid it, Webster wanted it to occur. Webster continued to support the strike and worked through the Citizens Committee that he had organized in Chicago in the interest of union workers. In his letter to Randolph dated March 27, 1928 and published in the *The Black Worker,* he noted: "I haven't been able to do much with this Citizens Committee. They seem to have all gotten cold feet since we commenced to talk strike. However, I plan to stage a big mass meeting on the 15th of April . . . . I am going to try to get the hardest boiled labor leaders in Chicago to speak in an effort to get the strike votes and raise funds for the strike."

He also wrote to Morris "Dad" Moore, who retired from the Chicago Division and founded the Oakland (California) Division. In his letter dated June 11, 1928 and published in *The Black Worker,* Webster explained why the strike was postponed: "It was done as a matter of strategy in the interest of all the men in the organization. The United States Mediation Board turned us down cold and their decision was so abrupt that it convinced us that we could expect no further cooperation from that body. Due to various legal actions, the strike never occurred, but the threat of it had caused the union some embarrassment and erroneously suggested some weaknesses in its leadership.

The brotherhood continued and called its first national convention in Chicago on September 9-15, 1929, adopted a constitution, and elected its first officers: Randolph, president; Webster, first vice-president; and Roy Lancaster, treasurer. The union barely existed now, for membership had declined after the Pullman Company suspended or fired all of those who voted for a strike. Much of the union's work went underground, both to protect union member's jobs and to avoid falling prey to "stool pigeons" who spied on meetings. To collect dues, agents visited barbershops, pool halls, cigar stores, and elsewhere, including member's private residences.

Now president of the Chicago Division of the BSCP, in December 1929 Webster announced the forthcoming national labor conference for Chicago, that would be held beginning January 26, 1930, extending for five days. It was under the auspices of the BSCP. At the time, critical problems existed in the employment industry for blacks; for example, there was industrial discrimination, wages were poor, employees worked long hours, and so on. To address these issues, BSCP invited all labor unions, religious organizations, Greek letter organizations, women's clubs, and other black groups that might have had an interest in race life to send one delegate to the conference. Quoted in the *Chicago Defender* for December 21, 1929, Webster said: "Race workers are the backbone of the Race, and upon their welfare and the advancement of labor depends the progress of all phases of life, whether religious, social, fraternal, civic or commercial. Hence the problems of the workers are of vital importance to all elements of the group and merit their cooperation and assistance in the efforts toward solution."

The NAACP finally became involved with the BSCP, and in the 1930s formally protested the AFL's policies on exclusion and discrimination. Representing the NAACP, noted attorney Charles Hamilton Houston protested at the 1934 AFL convention, for example. Webster and Randolph continued to introduce resolutions rejecting these policies to no avail.

The Walls Came Tumbling Down

The BSCP led a hard fight. As it fought to increase membership, it never attracted large numbers. In an effort to protect the porters from Pullman backlash, membership rolls were kept secret. Since the BSCP was established, it had fought long and vigorously for the most effective way to deal with the Pullman and its virtual monopoly on sleeping-car facilities across the county. The NAACP joined the BSCP in fighting the AFL's exclusionary and discriminatory practices during the 1930s and 1940s. Charles Hamilton Houston, who represented the NAACP, attended AFL's 1934 convention and protested its various forms of racial discrimination. As both groups sought a national charter from the AFL, the BSCP was refused in 1928 and again in 1934. Webster, Randolph, and other BSCP leaders continued their fight and struggled to keep the brotherhood alive. It was not until 1935, when the Franklin D. Roosevelt Administration insisted on protecting the rights of organized labor, that relief came. The administration outlawed company unions, and the Pullman Company finally recognized the BSCP as the bargaining unit for porters and maids. The victory may have actually been in making other black workers realize the value of solidarity and the importance of labor organizations. After the brotherhood received its international charter in 1937, Webster was elected a vice-president. He also was chief negotiator of contracts for the railroads.

When he was seven years old and lived next to an Illinois Central Railroad line, Webster saw firsthand a Pullman strike. Now he could feel a personal victory over his lifelong enemy. In a speech at the Chicago Historical Society taped around 1956, Webster commented on the white men that blacks envied on trains, men who had met the same success as the BSCP's victory: "They've had to organize and die and fight and sacrifice in order to get justice from other white men." Despite the BSCP's victory, it was not until after World War II that the barriers were penetrated in some of Pullman's operations; still some of the affiliates continued their old practices.

Between 1929 and 1935, several federal labor unions within the BSCP sent delegates to the American Federation of Labor conventions. Brotherhood delegates became representatives of an international union, beginning 1936. Webster had become vice-president of the organization and after 1936 collaborated with Randolph on introducing resolutions at AFL conventions. The two men knew the trade-union movement and acquitted themselves well when they spoke at the conventions, making their fellow delegates proud. Webster belonged to the Short Work Day Committee and was available to meet with members of the first international union of black workers. Notwithstanding the progress the BSCP had made, there was still work to be done. Randolph built on the union's platform and sought redress for a number of other racial issues. As a result of Randolph's call for a March on Washington on July1, 1941, in the interest of jobs in the National Defense, integration of the armed forces, abolition of Jim-Crow practices in government employment, and jobs in factories, on June 25, 1941, President Franklin D. Roosevelt issued Executive Order No. 8802 and on July 19, 1941 appointed the first Fair Employment Practices Commission (FEPC). Now that Randolph and the black masses had what they demanded, Randolph called off the strike. In addition to Webster as a representative of the BSCP, Roosevelt added to the committee the Louisville Courier's publisher Mark Ethridge as chair. Also added were Earl B. Dickerson, William Green, Philip Murray, and David Sarnoff. Webster held membership until the commission ceased to exist after World War II.

Webster, who lived at 8454 Vernon Street in Chicago, was involved in community life, having served as a Sunday school teacher. He held membership in the Phalanx Forum Club, the Labor Advisory Committee of the President's Committee on Equal Opportunity, and the Civil Rights Commission of the AFL-CIO. He was a lifelong Republican as well.

While attending the winter meeting of the AFL-CIO in Bal Harbor, Florida, Webster dined with A. Philip Randolph in the Americana Hotel. He collapsed shortly afterwards in the hotel corridor and was pronounced dead on arrival at St. Francis Hospital in Miami Beach, on February 24, 1965. According to his obituaries, he was survived only by his son Milton and two daughters, Jean and Rebecca; however, his wife Elizabeth was still living at that time. In *Labor's Heritage,* Greg LeRoy described Webster as "a stocky, profane, cigar chomping, bourbon sipping South Side Republican." His legacy, however, was his success as the "consummate organization man."

REFERENCES

Books

The Black Worker: A History from Colonial Times to the Present. Vol. V, *The Era of Post-War Prosperity and the Great Depression, 1920-1936*. Ed. Philip S. Foner and Ronald L. Lewis. Philadelphia: Temple University Press, 1981.

Brazeal, Brailsford R. *The Brotherhood of Sleeping Car Porters: Its Origin and Development*. New York: Harper & Brothers, 1946.

Foner, Philip S. *Organized Labor and the Black Worker, 1619-1981*. 2nd ed. New York: International Publishers, 1982.

Harris, William H. *Keeping the Faith: A. Philip Randolph, Milton P. Webster, and the Brotherhood of Sleeping Car Porters, 1925-37*. Urbana, Ill.: University of Illinois Press, 1977.

Randolph, A. Philip. "The Pullman Company and the Pullman Porter." In *The Black Worker: A History from Colonial Times to the Present*. Vol. V, *The Era of Post-War Prosperity and the Great Depression, 1920-1936*. Ed. Philip S. Foner and Ronald L. Lewis. Philadelphia: Temple University Press, 1981.

Periodicals

LeRoy, Greg. "The Founding Heart of A. Philip Randolph's Union: Milton P. Webster and Chicago's Pullman Porters Organize, 1925-1937." *Labor's Heritage* 3 (July 1991): 22-43.

"M. P. Webster, Rail Porters Official, Dies." *Chicago Tribune* (February 25, 1965).

"Sleeping Car Porters to Hold Labor Confab." *Chicago Defender* (December 21, 1929).

Online

"Records of the Brotherhood of Sleeping Car Porters. Series A: Holdings of the Chicago Historical Society and the Newberry Library, 1925-1969." University Publications of America. http://www.lexisnexis.com/academic/guides/african_american/bscp/bscp1.asp (Accessed September 8, 2005).

Collections

Records of the Chicago Division of the Brotherhood of Sleeping Car Porters (1925-1969) are in the Newberry Library in Chicago and the Chicago Historical Society. Numerous photographs of the BSCP are also in the Chicago Historical Society Records. The BSCP records include letters between A. Philip Randolph and Milton Webster and cover the period before 1940, verbatim minutes of BSCP conventions, and speeches by Webster and others on the philosophy of African American trade unionism, problems with other unions, and other issues. Other materials (technically not BSCP records) include the Milton P. Webster FEPC Files, 1941-1946. They shed light on racial discrimination in the railroad industry and segregation in the workforce during the early 1940s. Records of the larger Brotherhood of Sleeping Car Porters are in the Manuscript Division of the Library of Congress.

Jessie Carney Smith

Clifton R. Wharton
1926–

College president, business executive

Clifton Wharton Jr. decided not to follow his father's footsteps into foreign service but rather to pursue careers in foreign economic development, higher education, and business. Wharton worked with philanthropic organizations focused on economic and human resource development in Latin America and Asia. Later, he served as president of Michigan State University and then as chancellor of the State University of New York. He directed the largest U.S. pension system, the Teachers Insurance and Annuity Association and the College Retirement Equities Fund, and served briefly as United States deputy secretary of state. Writers often note his impressive list of "firsts" for African Americans.

Clifton Reginald Wharton, Jr., born September 13, 1926, in Boston, Massachusetts, spent most of his first six years in Spain's Canary Islands, where his father served as U. S. consul. The elder Wharton, a lawyer and the first African American to pass the U. S. foreign service exam, became the country's first black career ambassador. Based in Romania and Norway, he retired in 1964 after serving forty years. His wife, Harriet Banks Wharton, gave birth to four children; Clifton Jr. and a brother were born in the United States, and a sister and another brother were born in Spain. A chemistry professor and social worker, she served as teacher for her children.

In 1950, Wharton Jr. married Dolores Duncan of New York City. They met during his sophomore year at Harvard University on a blind date arranged by one of Dolores's cousins. Dolores Wharton founded and presided over the Fund for Corporate Initiatives, Inc., a nonprofit organization created to enhance the situation of women and minorities in corporate America. Among many other positions, she served on the boards of Phillips Petroleum, Kellogg, and Gannett companies. The Whartons had two sons, Clifton III and Bruce.

The early experience of Wharton Jr. in the Canary Islands prepared him for learning cultures and languages. In the absence of U.S. schools, his mother used books from a Baltimore correspondence school to begin his education. Wharton learned Spanish along with English, and his mother frequently took him to a local French school run by white Russians, where he learned French, as well.

When he was old enough, his parents took him to Massachusetts to attend the prestigious Boston Latin School, the first U.S. public school noted for its excellence in education. He lived with his maternal grandmother and worked at the local spool factory. During his free time, he trained for the track team.

Clifton R. Wharton

At sixteen, Wharton enrolled in Harvard University. He became the college radio station's first African American voice and founded the National Student Association, a lobbying group for college students. A strong performer on the track team, he abandoned the sport during his junior year because of an injury. In later years, a classmate described Wharton to David Bird as "well-heeled, well-bred, well-educated—a very bright guy, a very classy guy, and self-assured always." Wharton briefly trained as an Air Force pilot in Tuskegee, Alabama. He soloed in single engine planes, but before he earned his wings, the war ended.

In an interview years later with *Black Issues in Higher Education*, Wharton offered the following advice to college students: "This is one of the few times in your life when you have available to you this incredible range of extracurricular activities. Sample the ones that you think you might be interested in, because you may discover a hidden talent or hidden interest that you didn't realize you had." Wharton's college experience sparked his own interests.

Wharton received his B.A. in history, cum laude, from Harvard in 1947. In the commencement address, Secretary of State George C. Marshall emphasized the U.S. commitment to European recovery. He outlined a plan for achieving that goal that became known as the European Recovery Plan—or, more widely, the Marshall Plan.

The address impressed young Wharton, inspiring him to focus his career on international economic development. He had considered following his father's distinguished record in foreign service but chose now to establish his own path.

In 1948, Wharton earned an M.A. in international affairs from the School of Advanced International Studies at Johns Hopkins University, setting another first for blacks. Realizing his position as a role model, he worked extremely hard, foregoing many extracurricular activities. He finished second in his class despite his status as the youngest student.

Enters Foreign Economic Development

Between 1948 and 1953, Wharton worked with the American International Association for Economic and Social Development, established by Nelson Rockefeller. The organization helped Latin Americans develop higher standards of living by providing information about farming, nutrition, and homemaking. Wharton's experience as an executive trainee allowed him to gain a good overall perspective of the program. He spent time in a variety of areas, including public relations, accounting, and programming. As he progressed in the job, he became program analyst and then head of reports and analysis.

Wharton realized that to advance in his career, he would need a doctorate. In 1953, he enrolled in graduate school at the University of Chicago to study economics. He served as research assistant to noted economist Theodore W. Schultz, who would eventually win a Nobel Prize. Wharton's work involved evaluating technical assistance in Latin America. He earned his M.A. in 1956

and his Ph.D. in economics in 1958. His doctorate represented yet another first for blacks. Wharton would recall his work in Chicago as the most rigorous and intellectually demanding time of his academic career.

Even before Wharton completed his studies, he received a job offer from Arthur T. Mosher, executive director of the American Development Council (ADC). John D. Rockefeller III had founded the ADC as a non-profit organization to develop human resources and to improve agricultural and economic development in rural Asia. The council provided many Asians the opportunity to train in the United States and then return to their own countries. Making advances in human development and high-yield crops, the organization became known for its "Green Revolution" during the 1950s and 1960s.

Serves in Asia

Wharton served first as associate, then as director of operations for the ADC in Southeast Asia. Based in Malaysia, he directed operations in Cambodia, Laos, Thailand, and Vietnam as well. He spent time with the Asians in the rice fields and worked to help them develop their potential for expertise and leadership. Wharton told W. Hubert Keen: "We wanted Asians to work on the agrarian problems, not experts from the outside who would help for a couple of years and then leave."

Wharton advocated for less military emphasis in foreign policy and more focus on encouraging Asian leadership potential. In working among the Asian people, Wharton learned from them as well. The gentility and courtesy he experienced became a part of his own nature. His wife, Dolores, became interested also in the region's people and art, later publishing a book titled *Contemporary Artists of Malaysia: A Biographical Survey* (1972).

While in Asia, Wharton taught as a visiting professor at the University of Singapore (1958-60) and then taught economics at the University of Malaysia (1960-64). Many of the region's future economists benefited from Wharton's teaching. In 1964, he took a sabbatical year to teach economic development at Stanford University, bringing experienced insight into the differences and similarities between Eastern and Western cultures.

That same year, Wharton moved to New York to direct the ADC's American University Research Program. The AURP provided opportunities for scientists and scholars to focus on agricultural problems in the Third World. Wharton worked both within the United States and abroad, recruiting fifty to sixty Asians each year for fellowships in the United States. He oversaw research grants for universities studying Third World problems and held numerous workshops for professionals. From 1967 through 1969, he served as vice president of the program.

In the spring of 1969, Wharton organized a conference at Michigan State University in East Lansing. Nicholas

Luyks, an MSU professor of agricultural economics, submitted Wharton's name to a search committee appointed to select a new president for the university. The committee sent a couple of delegations to New York to interview Wharton, and after much deliberation, it chose him from around three hundred candidates.

Becomes President at Michigan State

In this new role in higher education, Wharton became the first African American president of a major research institution. On the evening of the Whartons' arrival on campus, students honored them with a huge welcome sign and a medley of Michigan State songs. In his first campus address as president, Wharton stressed the importance of the human element in education, the rights of all students to equal opportunity, the importance of scholarly creativity, and the university's responsibility to initiate positive change.

Wharton took office during turbulent times in academe, and the job demanded all the tact and diplomacy he had developed. The 1960s became characterized by demonstrations, sit-ins, strikes, riots, and financial difficulties on college campuses, and Michigan State proved no exception. About the time Wharton assumed presidency, Ohio National guardsmen killed four students and wounded others in a Kent State University protest over the U.S. invasion of Cambodia during the Vietnam War.

Wharton moved quickly, using closed-circuit television to reassure students of his own concern for Asian people. Five days later, he suspended classes for teachins that provided background on Indochina and information about effective protest measures and other relevant issues. He offered personally to take student and faculty concerns to Michigan congressmen in Washington. Wharton dealt with other campus disturbances with similar equanimity and respect.

Wharton soon gained a reputation for being a capable, tactful administrator and an encourager, sympathetic to both blacks and whites. Clif and Dolores Wharton made a special effort to get to know people, welcoming students and faculty into their home and making scores of visits to student dormitories and sororities and fraternities in the course of the semester. Dolores Wharton hosted in their home an art show featuring paintings and sculptures by MSU faculty.

Halfway through his career at MSU, Wharton told George Bullard, "This is one of the few jobs I know that demands every scrap of your experience and knowledge." As president, he advocated for universal access to higher education, led the university to growth, increased student involvement on advisory councils, and developed a new urban affairs college. He had initiated a Presidential Fellows program, giving selected students and junior faculty the opportunity to work in top administrative offices for six months. After eight strong years, Wharton

resigned in 1978. MSU later named a new building the Clifton and Dolores Wharton Center for Performing Arts (1982).

Becomes Chancellor at SUNY

In 1978, Wharton moved to Albany to become chancellor of the State University of New York (SUNY) system. While achieving yet another first for blacks, he emphasized to David Bird that "he had always tried to make it on his own merits. 'I am a man first, an American second and black man third.'" At SUNY he faced the challenge of bringing cohesiveness to a system of sixty-four diverse campuses serving thousands of students and requiring thousands of employees. He immediately toured the various campuses, reassuring faculty and students that he would move the university forward. John LoDico reported that in national survey of college leaders, Wharton attained status as "one of the top five most influential leaders in higher education."

In 1984, Wharton appointed an independent commission to study two of SUNY's most important problems: a layer of red tape that unnecessarily slowed basic expenditures and a need to increase the national standing of SUNY graduate and professional schools. Wharton followed up on advice from the commission's educators, politicians, and businessmen by pursuing legislation that would grant campus administrators more flexibility in funding decisions. He considered that legislation one of his major contributions to the university. Wharton announced his resignation on October 16, 1986. He had advanced SUNY's reputation and funding and had appointed a greater number of women to leadership roles. In 1987, SUNY established the Clifton and Dolores Wharton Economics Research Center.

Heads TIAA-CREF

On February 1, 1987, Wharton became chairman and chief executive officer of the nation's huge private pension system, the Teachers Insurance and Annuity Association and College Retirement Equities Fund (TIAA-CREF). The first university president to fill this position and the first African American to head a Fortune 100 company, Wharton doubled the fund's assets to $113 billion. He exercised his well-honed managerial abilities, paying particular attention to staff at the lower levels and increasing the number of women and minorities on the boards. He provided participants with increased options and greater control over their investments. In 1996, TIAA-CREF honored his leadership by naming the Clifton R. Wharton Auditorium.

Through the years, Wharton had served on several national fronts. In 1966, he joined President Lyndon Johnson's Task Force on Agriculture in Vietnam. From 1966 through 1969, he held membership on the U.S. Department of State's Advisory Panel on East Asia. In 1969, he served on Governor Nelson Rockefeller's Presidential Mission to Latin America. From 1976 through 1983, he chaired the State Department's Board for International Food and Agricultural Development, a position appointed by President Gerald Ford and reappointed by President Jimmy Carter. From 1978 through 1980, Wharton chaired President Carter's Commission on World Hunger. In 1983, Secretary of State George P. Shultz appointed Wharton co-chair of the Commission on Security and Economic Assistance. In 1991, President George H. W. Bush appointed him to the Advisory Commission on Trade Policy and Negotiations.

In January 1993, President Bill Clinton named Wharton deputy secretary of state to serve with Secretary Warren Christopher. Wharton had previously declined invitations to such positions, but now he felt he owed his county the benefit of his experience and expertise. Rather than participating in foreign policy decision-making as anticipated, however, he found himself engaged in administrative restructuring. Wharton became frustrated by not being able to use his expertise and by political rumors, including false assertions that he had no foreign policy experience. He resigned after eight months.

In 1993, although retired, Wharton returned to TIAA-CREF as an overseer and also became director of the New York Stock Exchange and Harcourt General. Later, he again served Agricultural Development Council as economist and vice president. Along the way, he had found time to write and publish on both international and academic matters. His books include: *Subsistence Agriculture and Economic Development* (editor, 1969), *Continuity and Change: Academic Greatness Under Stress* (with Theodore M. Hesburgh and Paul A. Miller, 1971), and *Patterns for Lifelong Learning* (1973).

Throughout his career, Wharton served on the boards of a variety of corporations. On February 26, 1969, the Equitable Life Assurance Society of the United States, one of the nation's largest companies, elected him director, another first for blacks. He served on the boards of Ford Motor Company, Time, Federated Department Stores, Burrough's, and other companies. He has also served on the boards of the Federal Reserve Bank of New York and the Public Broadcasting Service (PBS). He actively participated in such organizations as the Carnegie Foundation and the Museum of Modern Art.

Wharton fulfilled the responsibilities of chairman of the Rockefeller Foundation from 1982-87, the first African American to serve in that capacity. He contributed his expertise to the Aspen Institute for Humanities Studies, the Council on Foreign Relations, the Overseas Development Council, the Foreign Policy Association, and the Council for Financial Aid to Education. He served as chairman of the National Association of State Universities and Land-Grant Colleges.

Numerous awards reflect the quality of Wharton's accomplishments. In 1970, Boston Latin School named

him "Man of the Year" and the American Missionary Association presented him its Amistad Award. In 1971, he received the University of Chicago's Alumni Professional Achievement Award and, in 1977, the Joseph C. Wilson Award for achievement and promise in international affairs. In 1983, The President's Award on World Hunger included Wharton among its first recipients.

In 1985, the National Economic Association conferred its Westerfield Award. The Boston Black Achievers of the YMCA presented its 1986 Benjamin E. Mays Award. In 1987, the New York Associated Black Charities named him among its first Black History Makers. Wharton became a Fellow of the American Association of Agricultural Economics in 1988. The New York Urban League presented him the Frederick Douglass Medallion in 1989. Wharton received the Rockefeller Public Service Award in 1993 and the American Council on Education's Distinguished Service Award for Lifetime Achievement in 1994. Africare bestowed its Legacy Award in 2005.

More than sixty colleges and universities have granted Wharton honorary degrees, including Johns Hopkins (1970) and Harvard (1992). The Harvard citation read, "One of the commanding leaders of our time, yours is the great talent to transform organizations into communities of purpose working devotedly together to serve the common good of all people from all backgrounds."

By choosing to follow his own path, Clifton R. Wharton Jr. has touched the lives of thousands of people, helping improve quality of life and education both at home and abroad. He achieved many firsts for African Americans. But in the *Black Issues in Higher Education* interview, he observed, "It's great to be one, but I'd like to see more twos, threes, fours, and fives."

REFERENCES

Books

Keen, W. Hubert. "Wharton, Clifton Reginald Jr." *The Scribner Encyclopedia of American Lives*. Ed. William L. O'Neill. New York: Scribner, 2003.

LoDico, John. "Clifton R. Wharton Jr." *Contemporary Black Biography*. Ed. Barbara Carlisle Bigelow. Detroit, Mich.: Gale, 1994.

Metcalf, George R. "Clifton Reginald Wharton Jr." *Up from Within*. New York: McGraw-Hill, 1971.

Periodicals

Bird, David. "An Identity with Achievement: Clifton Reginald Wharton Jr." *New York Times Biographical Service*, 10 October 1977.

Bullard, George. "MSU President Wharton's 4 Years: The Velvet Touch." *Biography News* 1 (January 1974): 117.

"Reflections of a Trailblazer." *Black Issues in Higher Education* 15 (14 May 1998): 14-17.

Collections

Michigan State University libraries hold many of Wharton's papers and audiotapes of speeches.

Marie Garrett

Prince Whipple
c. 1750–1797

Slave

African Americans are rarely depicted in nineteenth-century paintings, unless they were shown as servants. Emanuel Leutze's familiar and dramatic *Washington Crossing the Delaware* (1851) is no exception. Many viewers of the work would focus on General Washington standing at the bow without noticing the leaning, straining boatman pictured behind the general's right leg. Legend has it that that African American man depicted rowing at Washington's knee is an actual figure from history, the slave named Prince Whipple. Scholarship and documentation tell another story, but the debate has continued for more than 150 years. His place in Revolutionary artwork may be dubious, but Prince was indeed a Revolutionary War veteran and abolitionist.

Accurate records for slaves are scarce. Mostly, they show up in their owner's wills, as property being left to heirs. But historical accounts place Whipple's birthplace in a village in Amabou, Africa, which was probably Anomabu in present-day Ghana, known as the Gold Coast when Prince Whipple was born, in the mid-1700s. His parents' names are unknown, but oral history suggests Whipple was born free and affluent and was sent abroad with a brother (or cousin) named Cuff (or Cuffee), two years his junior, to study in America. Instead, the youths were sold into slavery in North America. First sold in Baltimore, the boys were then purchased and renamed. Prince was purchased by William Whipple and Cuff by William's brother Joseph. The two were white merchants in Portsmouth, New Hampshire. Prince Whipple maintained that his name reflected the actual status he had left behind in Africa, which could very well be true. But many slaves were dubbed "Prince" mockingly by their owners.

Accompanies Master to War

An account of Whipple's experience exists in the form of a collective document Whipple and twenty other slaves signed in 1779 that describes being "torn by the cruel hand of violence" from their mothers' "aching bosom," and "seized, imprisoned and transported" to the United States and deprived of "the nurturing care of [their] bereaved parent," according to Mark J. Sammons and Valerie Cunningham in *Black Portsmouth*.

As with his name and origins, time and dubious reporting have left almost everything about Whipple's life open to question. It is known that William Whipple was a prominent member of Portsmouth society who would later represent New Hampshire by signing the Declaration of Independence. It is also known that William Whipple was a colonel in the First New Hampshire Regiment, who later became a brigadier general in the Revolutionary War. Some accounts suggest that he took his slave with him into battle. "During the American Revolution some of the most ardent Patriots could be found among the colonies' African-American residents," writer Jon Swan noted in *MHQ: The Quarterly Journal Of Military History*. However, historians overlooked the African Americans who participated in the American Revolution "until it was popular to include them."

Legend Results from Confusing Records

Prince Whipple's legend may have been part of this trend to include African Americans in later versions of Revolutionary history. History written decades after the war tell of Prince's participation in the American Revolution, but no documentation from the war substantiates the claim that Prince accompanied William Whipple on early revolutionary campaigns or to the Continental Congress in Philadelphia in 1776.

According to Sammons and Cunningham, the documentation argues against Prince's place in the boat with George Washington at the crossing of the Delaware River in December 1776. On that date, William Whipple was attending Congress, first in Philadelphia and then in Baltimore. Were Prince with him, it seems unlikely that William would have sent his slave unaccompanied 130 miles to a war zone. Prince's place in the Delaware River story first appears in William C. Nell's 1855 *Colored Patriots of the Revolution*, written at the height of the abolitionist movement. This volume was taken as factual for 150 years. Even in the early 2000s, such reference sources as PBS's *Africans in America*, various encyclopedias, and dozens of printed and electronic sites present Nell's information as historical truth.

Sammons and Cunningham suggest that Nell could have recorded an undocumented but accurate family tradition from Prince's heirs, a confused family tale, or attached Prince to the story to make up for previously overlooked black participation in the revolution. Leutze's painting (1851) does indeed include a black man, but New England traditions place other black men in Washington's boat, for example, Prince Estabrook of Lexington, Massachusetts. Moreover, enough time and geography were between the historical events and Leutze's painting to put accuracy at risk.

Leutze Paints *Crossing* with License

Leutze was born in Germany, and though he came to America with his parents at an early age, he spent half his life abroad. In fact, not only was *Washington Crossing the Delaware* painted seventy-five years after Washington's actual crossing of the river, but it was painted in Germany, where Leutze used live models. The work now hangs at the Metropolitan Museum of Art in New York City, where art historian Natalie Spasskey accepts the theory that the African American depicted is Prince Whipple.

Evidence bears out that Prince Whipple was involved in the revolution. He accompanied William Whipple, by then a brigadier general, on military campaigns to Saratoga, New York, in 1777 and to Rhode Island in 1778. There is also proof that Prince Whipple was steeped in revolutionary thinking. Prince was among twenty enslaved men, including Windsor Moffat, who signed a 1779 petition for the abolition of slavery in New Hampshire. Prince, Moffat, and the other signatories were slaves in prominent and politically active white patriot families and were thus privy to the revolutionary rhetoric coming from their owners' dining tables and parlors. Their petition was shelved, however, and slavery was not abolished in New Hampshire until 1857.

Gains Emancipation Years after War

Colored Patriots of the Revolution states that William Whipple emancipated Prince as a reward for his war service. The fact is Prince did not actually gain his freedom until seven years after the war. Prince married Dinah Chase of New Castle and Hampton, New Hampshire, on February 22, 1781. For the event, William Whipple prepared a special document that allowed Prince the rights of a freeman, but Prince was not formally emancipated until three years later. The document may have been drawn up at the behest of Chase's owner, a clergyman who emancipated Chase on her wedding day. Sammons and Cunningham suggest the tale of Prince being freed for his war service was told "as an increasingly abolitionist local white society preferred to remember it."

Free life was daunting for the Whipples. Though slavery had been formally abolished, there was little room in white society for recently freed slaves. Prince served as master of ceremonies at Assembly House balls for white socialites. Given recollections about his fine manners and general deportment, Prince was suited for the role. These events occasionally included other blacks as caterers and musicians, and it seems that Prince also acted as a liaison and manager of the black help for the white hosts.

William Whipple died one year after Prince's emancipation, and Whipple's widow allowed Prince and Dinah to live in a house on a lot behind her mansion. Prince, Dinah, their daughters, Esther and Elizabeth, Cuff, and Cuff's wife Rebecca Daverson, and their children crowded in to the house and lived there for forty years. Dinah also operated the Ladies Charitable African School for black children out of the house and worked for the North Church.

Mourned by Portsmouth Blacks and Whites

Documents show that Prince was not involved with Portsmouth's Negro Court, but his signature on the abolition petition alongside those of Portsmouth's black king, viceroy, sheriff, and deputy confirms Prince's active participation in the local black community. Prince's age was never known, but Sammons and Cunningham suggest he was probably at least a decade older when he died in 1797 than the age of forty-six sometimes supposed.

Prince was not buried in Portsmouth's segregated Negro Burial Ground, which may have been closed by the time he died. His grave in the North Burial Ground was marked with two rough stones until a grandson, John Smith, installed a more impressive stone. It is marked as that of a Revolutionary War veteran.

REFERENCES

Books

Kaplan, Sidney. *The Black Presence in the Era of the American Revolution 1770-1800*. Washington D.C.: National Portrait Gallery, 1975.

Melish, Joanne Pope. *Disowning Slavery: Gradual Emancipation and "Race" in New England, 1780-1860*. Ithaca, N.Y.: Cornell University Press, 1998.

Nell, William C. *The Colored Patriots of the American Revolution*. New York: Arno Press, c. 1968.

Piersen, William D. *Black Yankees: The Development of an Afro-American Subculture in Eighteenth-Century*

New England. Amherst, Mass.: University of Massachusetts Press, 1988.

Sammons, Mark J., and Valerie Cunningham. *Black Portsmouth*. Hanover, N.H.: University Press of New England, 2004.

Periodicals

McQuaid, Cate. "Was N.H. Slave Depicted in This Painting?" *Boston Globe*, 7 April 2002.

Swan, Jon. "America's Forgotten Patriots." *MHQ: The Quarterly Journal of Military History*, Autumn 2000.

Online

"Images in Action." Tolerance.org.http://www.tolerance. org/images_action/answer.jsp?p=0&id=16 (Accessed 4 March 2006).

"Prince Whipple." http://www.whipple.org/prince/ princewhipple.html (Accessed 4 March 2006).

"Prince Whipple: Symbol of African Americans at the Battle of Trenton." New Hampshire Individuals of Note. http://www.johnjhenderson.com/Notables/ Biographies/prince_whipple.htm (Accessed 4 March 2006).

"Prince Whipple's Story." Seacoast, New Hampshire. http://www.seacoastnh.com/blackhistory/prince.html (Accessed 4 March 2006).

Brenna Sanchez

Lenny Wilkens

Lenny Wilkens
1937–

Basketball coach, basketball player

As coach of the Seattle SuperSonics, Portland Trail-Blazers, Atlanta Hawks, Cleveland Cavaliers, and Toronto Raptors, Lenny Wilkens has scored more wins (1,332) and losses (1,155) than any other coach in the NBA. Wilkens is known for his quiet, sensible, and optimistic coaching style. His career was marked by consistent records rather than by championship cups. It was also fraught with NBA politics but, after more than forty years in the NBA, Wilkens wrote in his autobiography, *Unguarded*, "I still want to win."

Early Life

Leonard Randolph Wilkens Jr. was born October 28, 1937 in Brooklyn, New York to Leonard R. Wilkens, an African American chauffer, and Henrietta (Cross) Wilkens, an Irish Catholic woman. He was the second of four children. Wilkens' father was rushed to the hospital in 1943, treated for a "locked bowel," and died from a bleeding ulcer. In *Unguarded*, Wilkens described recollections of a man he barely knew, a sense of injustice over his father's death, and a yearning for his father to have shared in his successes. Wilkens' mother was left to raise four children on her own. At his father's wake, Wilkens' aunt took him aside and told him, "You're going to have to be the man of the family now." He was five years old.

At home, both his father and mother's family loved Wilkens. Outside, the kids called him "half-breed." People glared at the single white mother and her darker children. Understandably, race has always been a complicated issue for Wilkens. Though he is equal parts Irish and African American, he identifies himself as black. He is proud of his roots, especially because his heritage is all he ever had of his father. Still, he questions a system that defines a person by the color of his skin. "There is a racist theory in this country, that if you have a drop of black blood in you, then you're African American," Wilkens wrote in *Unguarded*. "The truth is that I'm as much Irish as I'm black, but I've never heard anyone say 'Lenny is Irish.'"

Left with no reliable income, the Wilkens' family struggled to get along between welfare and Henrietta's low-paying jobs. Each child was afforded one pair of ten-

Chronology

1937	Born in Brooklyn, New York on October 28
1943	Father dies from undiagnosed bleeding ulcer
1960	Drafted to play for the St. Louis Hawks
1962	Marries Marilyn Reed
1968	Becomes point guard for the Seattle SuperSonics
1969	First season as player/coach
1973	Traded to the Cleveland Cavaliers
1974	Signs four-year player/coach contract with Portland TrailBlazers
1975	Takes a job with CBS Sports
1977	Becomes general manager of Seattle SuperSonics, then coach
1979	Coaches SuperSonics to NBA championship; receives honors from CBS Sports and Congressional Black Congress
1984	Returns to sole position as general manager of SuperSonics
1985	Takes coaching position with the Cleveland Cavaliers
1992	Travels to Spain as assistant coach of U.S. Olympic basketball team; undergoes Achilles' tendon surgery, and nearly dies from blood clots
1993	Begins coaching Atlanta Hawks
1995	Beats Red Auerbach's record number of career coaching wins
1996	Wins gold medal as head coach of U.S. Olympic team
2004	Takes coaching position with New York Knicks
2005	Resigns from Knicks under questionable circumstances

nis shoes per year. Within a month Wilkens wore his out playing basketball, and covered the holes with pieces of linoleum. The Wilkens moved often, each apartment more dismal than the last. Still, Henrietta was a fastidious housekeeper and the children worked to keep the house, and themselves, tidy. Wilkens started working at age nine.

Basketball, the Church, and a Father Figure

Wilkens found a father figure in Father Thomas Mannion. Wilkens attended Holy Rosary School and was an altar boy. Wilkens learned Latin, the language of the Mass, and enjoyed church life. He especially enjoyed eating breakfast with the nuns after Mass, as they served bacon, eggs, pancakes, and waffles—a real departure from the breakfast he was accustomed to at home, which was "Oatmeal. Oatmeal. And more oatmeal," he wrote in *Unguarded*.

Despite his rough neighborhood, Wilkens kept out of trouble. He knew better, because his mother would hold him accountable. Involvement in the Catholic Youth Organization and Police Athletic League basketball teams helped. Father Mannion was always around and, like Wilkens' mother, tolerated no foolishness.

Wilkens was not a team player on the basketball court. It was clear to Father Mannion that Wilkens had no understanding of basketball as a team sport. The priest bought the boy his own basketball to practice with. Wilkens spent countless hours with Mannion, dribbling

and running drills. Wilkens also played baseball, stickball, and softball. He did not start playing high-school basketball until his senior year at Boys High in Brooklyn.

Wilkens balked at Father Mannion's talk of college. With his economic and social background, going to college, he wrote in his autobiography, "sounded about as realistic as going to the moon." But he followed Mannion's suggestion to keep his grades up, just in case. After graduation, he worked at Montgomery Ward and hoped to save money to attend City College of New York. A basketball scholarship was the furthest thing from his mind.

Wilkens remained amazed by the series of events that led him to college. Father Mannion wrote a letter to the athletic director at Providence College, in Rhode Island, recommending Wilkens for a basketball scholarship. Wilkens tried out for the team but heard nothing. Later, he was voted tournament MVP at the Flushing YMCA Tournament. The father of Providence's coach happened to be in the stands and noticed Wilkens, and mentioned him to his son. The coach remembered Mannion's letter and meeting Wilkens at the tryouts. In a matter of days, Wilkens was accepted to Providence with a full basketball scholarship. He had no designs on the NBA; Wilkens just wanted to keep his grades up at Providence, where there were just two black faces in the freshman class. Wilkens rose to the challenge, working hard and excelling in the classroom, on the court, and with the ROTC.

Wilkens was allowed to develop his game at a reasonable pace at Providence, and this atmosphere helped him shine. He averaged 21 points per game, and his freshman team scored a record 23 wins and no losses. The next year, he led his team in scoring and was the only sophomore selected to the Eastern Conference Athletic Conference All-Conference team.

Wilkens found the national spotlight at the National Invitational Tournament at Madison Square Garden in New York City. He shone in a game against a top-seeded St. Louis team. "The most credit for cutting the Missouri Valley down to size must go to Leonard Wilkens," sportswriter Louis Effrat wrote in the *New York Times*. "Aside from his 30 points, Wilkens' alertness, his ball handling and his steadying influence paid off in the end." Gene Roswell wrote in the *New York Post*, "Wilkens, a defensive genius, has a simple basketball strategy, 'Never let the other fellow's right hand know what your left hand is doing.'" In his senior year, the team lost only four games, and Wilkens was being hailed as a "defensive specialist." Still, he entertained no thoughts of the NBA. He had never even watched an NBA game.

Wilkens played in the East/West All-Star Game with his sights set on trying out for the 1960 Olympic team. Wilkens did not make the Olympic team but a number of lesser players, who were white, did. It was the first time Wilkens felt he had been held back by the color of his skin. The *New York Times* printed a scathing story about the slight and a number of national coaches came out in support of Wilkens, but it was in vain.

Wilkens was in an accounting class when the St. Louis Hawks drafted him as a point guard. After class, he had no idea why people were congratulating him. He planned to turn down the offer, get his M.A., and teach economics. He changed his mind when he compared the average economist's salary, $6,000 at the time, to the $8,000 a year the Hawks were offering him. Wilkens went to St. Louis, but was unprepared for what he found there.

First Taste of Intolerance

When Wilkens went to St. Louis in 1960, he suffered repeated bouts of discrimination; he had trouble finding an apartment to rent, and was denied service in certain restaurants. Wilkens was shocked by the new world he had entered. He and his young wife, Marilyn Reed, bought a house in a St. Louis neighborhood only to watch their neighbors put up "for sale" signs; someone even poisoned the couple's dog.

After watching the first part of the season from the bench, Wilkens finished the year in the starting lineup, setting a team record for the highest shooting percentage by a guard. Wilkens began to hear two incredible words from veteran players: "Nice game."

Life in the modern NBA is very different from Wilkens' early days as a pro player. There were no private jets, no decadent parties, none of the luxuries today's NBA stars take for granted. There were often no lockers in the locker rooms, just a nail to hang clothes on. Locker rooms and showers were always too hot or too cold, Wilkens remembered. They had to wash their uniforms in tiny hotel sinks. They ate coffee and doughnuts for breakfast. Wilkens had to work a desk job during the summer breaks to earn money. Still, he wrote in *Unguarded*, "That was all part of the almost blue-collar world of the NBA back then."

The year 1968 was a low point in Wilkens' career. With seven years in the NBA and four All-Star games under his belt, he left the Hawks. His final season was plagued by politics and infighting. The team won fifty-six games and Wilkens finished second to Wilt Chamberlain in the MVP voting, but management refused to offer him a salary competitive with that of his fellow players. The fledgling Seattle SuperSonics, headed into its second season, offered him $75,000 a year for two years. So Wilkens and his wife got a fresh start in Seattle.

From Player to Coach

Wilkens had no designs on coaching, but within a year of starting with the SuperSonics, he became the second black player/coach in the NBA. Dick Vertlieb, the team's general manager, hand-picked Wilkens for the job, citing his maturity, talent, judgment, the respect other players had for him, and his knowledge of the league. In

Unguarded, Wilkens looked back on the change, saying, "No matter . . . how ready you think you are for your first coaching job, I have news for you: You're never ready." Wilkens started as player/coach in August 1969, his second season with the SuperSonics.

The new coach had a rough start. He struggled to balance his two roles and found himself yelling at the players, though he had always detested coaches who yelled at their players. It took Wilkens until the midpoint of the season to get comfortable in his dual role. The team started winning games and finished the season with 36 wins and 46 losses, slightly ahead of the previous year. In his second season as coach, he did better still, with a 38-44 record. At the end of Wilkens' third coaching season, the SuperSonics enjoyed its first winning season, with a 47-35 record. Instead of launching into the next season as player/coach of the SuperSonics, Wilkens found himself inexplicably traded to the Cleveland Cavaliers.

Despite his increasing success with Seattle, Wilkens was traded solely as a player for the Cavaliers, which was then the worst team in the NBA. No one in the league could make sense of the trade, least of all Wilkens. The SuperSonics had dumped him into "the black hole of the NBA," according to Cleveland radio announcer Joe Tait in *Unguarded*. During his year with the team, its record improved slightly. When Wilkens returned to Seattle with the Cavaliers to play against the SuperSonics, fans chanted and raised signs: "This is Lenny's country," "We love you, Lenny," and "Come home, Lenny." He was gone, but not forgotten.

At age 37, knowing he was approaching the end of his playing career, Wilkens wanted another shot at coaching. He signed a four-year player/coach contract with the Portland TrailBlazers, a team that needed "all the help it could get," according to Wilkens in *Unguarded*. The 1974-75 year was Wilkens' final season as a player, and he brought the team's record from 27-55 to 38-44, despite a disjointed team fraught with injuries. When the team's record failed to improve the next year, with Wilkens working solely as a coach, the TrailBlazers let him go. Freed from his contract, the Wilkens family moved back to Seattle, where they were happiest. Wilkens took a job with CBS, working on their pro-basketball telecasts. After a year, he was hungry to coach again.

In another unexpected turn, Wilkens was approached to return to the SuperSonics as general manager. The team had failed to beat his 47-35 season since he left. Wilkens jumped into his new "front office" position, trying to build the best team, picking and trading players. But Wilkens' 1977-78 SuperSonics were a disaster. In a desperate attempt to save the team mid-season, Wilkens added "coach" to his job title. He coached his discouraged team with the confidence he had earned from nearly twenty years in the NBA, and ended up matching his own record season with the SuperSonics, 47-35. To everyone's surprise, the team made it through the playoffs and into the finals against Washington.

After a seven-game finals series in 1978, the Super-Sonics and their fans were primed for the 1978-79 season. The pressure was on Wilkens, who had never coached a team that was expected to win big. Though the team had no stand-out, superstar players, Wilkens noted in *Unguarded*: "Our team was special. Our team had its own blend of a balanced attack." The Sonics faced Washington again in the finals, but this time came away with the championship title. Wilkens was snubbed by the NBA for its Coach of the Year award, but received honors from CBS Sports and the Congressional Black Congress.

Wilkens' formula heading into the next season was simple: "We've found the secret. Let's not change it," he wrote in *Unguarded*. Instead, the team was hit with what he called "Championship Fallout." Players wanted more money, more recognition, or were just getting old. They won fifty-six games that season and made it to the finals but were stopped in their tracks by Magic Johnson and the Los Angeles Lakers, a team on its way to becoming a dynasty. In the next three seasons, the team slipped to 48 wins, then 42, then 31. They did not even make it to the playoffs in 1983-84, Wilkens' last season as coach. Wilkens spent the 1984-85 season working strictly as general manager.

Wilkens was eager to coach again and needed a change of scenery, so he took an offer to coach the Cleveland Cavaliers. In his seven years coaching the Cavaliers, Wilkens turned their dismal record into a respectable one. Unfortunately, few teams had a chance against then-rookie Michael Jordan and his Chicago Bulls. "We won a lot of games," Wilkens wrote in *Unguarded*: "We played for fans who appreciated our players and our style of play. Yet I still think about what could have been."

Another Shot at the Olympics

"I wanted to be the head coach of the first Dream Team," Wilkens wrote in *Unguarded*, mainly because of his missed chance at the 1960 Olympics as a player. Instead, head coach Chuck Daly named Wilkens assistant coach of the 1992 Olympic basketball team. Wilkens felt slighted, but sucked up his ego and took the job. The team was made up of NBA pros, including Magic Johnson, Michael Jordan, and Larry Bird. It was "the greatest basketball team the world has ever seen," Wilkens wrote, and they took home the gold medal. After the Olympics, Wilkens underwent surgery to mend a torn Achilles' tendon and suffered blood clots that nearly killed him. He later admitted it was a bad idea to return to coaching for the 1992-93 season. The team won fifty-four games that season and lost to the Bulls in the playoffs. But Wilkens was exhausted and needed a fresh start.

After a bidding war between the Los Angeles Clippers, Indiana Pacers, and Atlanta Hawks, Wilkens signed a five-year $1.5 million-per-year deal with the Hawks. They won fifty-seven games during the 1993-94 season, which was respectable. It meant the most to Wilkens, because he broke legendary Boston Celtic's coach Red Auerbach's record of 938 career-coaching victories. He was voted NBA Coach of the Year, and was in a position to clinch his dream of coaching the 1996 U.S. Olympic team.

Wilkens had won more games than any coach in history and by many counts was underappreciated for it. When he was asked to coach the 1996 Olympic team, he was awash with emotion; he was proud and knew he had earned it, but he wished his father could be there to see it. He also felt pressure to win.

The 1992 Dream Team's Johnson, Jordan, and Bird had retired. The 1996 team leaders were John Stockton, Scottie Pippen, Karl Malone, Charles Barkley, and Shaquille O'Neal. "Not exactly a bad team," according to Wilkens, but a team that faced bigger challenges: they had little time playing together, were "flat" during exhibition games, and were mobbed by fans during the Games in Atlanta. Wilkens held the team together, and was relieved to win the gold.

In his seven years with the Atlanta Hawks, the team remained stuck in a "rut," which consisted of a respectable fifty wins per season, and a run at the playoffs each year. Unable to clinch a championship, Wilkens was forced to resign. "When you're a coach," Hawks' general manager Pete Babcock said at a press conference (as quoted in *Unguarded*), "you become a lightning rod for what happens in an organization. It doesn't mean it's fair or right, but it's the reality of the situation."

In early 2004, at age 66, Wilkens was hired by New York Knicks' president Isaiah Thomas. After several seasons in what the *New York Times* called a "downward spiral," Thomas was thankful to have someone with Wilkens' experience on his team. Thomas told *Jet*, "I thought it was the perfect fit." A year later, Thomas had different thoughts, and Wilkens resigned from the Knicks. Many believe Wilkens' lackluster performance with the Knicks was a symptom of family problems: His mother was seriously ill in a Brooklyn nursing home and his wife, Marilyn, remained in Seattle when he took the job in New York. Team management insisted that Wilkens was not forced out, despite rumors to the contrary. Some suggested the move would point to Wilkens' retirement.

REFERENCES

Books

Wilker, Josh. *The Head Coaches*. Philadelphia: Chelsea House Publishers, 1998.

Periodicals

Beck, Howard. "Wilkens Resigns, Taken Down by Knicks' Downward Spiral." *New York Times* (23 January 2005): 8.1.

"Thomas Revamps Knicks, Hires Wilkens as Coach." *Jet* (2 February 2004): 51.

Brenna Sanchez

A. Wilberforce Williams
1865–1940

Physician, surgeon

Albert Wilberforce Williams was a prominent Chicago physician who practiced on Chicago's south side for forty-six years. He specialized in internal medicine, the treatment of tuberculosis, and heart and lung disease. He was the first African American physician to write a newspaper column on health and the first physician to focus attention on social diseases. He worked at Provident Hospital with Daniel Hale Williams, the renowned physician and surgeon who in 1893 performed the first successful operation on the human heart.

Williams served as health editor of the *Chicago Defender* from 1911 to 1929. The only other newspaper in the country to have a health editor at that time was the *Chicago Tribune*. Both papers were in the forefront of educating readers on health and hygiene issues, and both dared to refer specifically to sexually transmitted diseases such as syphilis, gonorrhea, and chancroid in their medical advice columns. Some of Williams's peers objected to his frank writings. When his topics began appearing, he received criticism and resistance; some readers did not like seeing what were considered private subjects discussed openly in a newspaper. Because of his persistence in writing and lecturing on these subjects, he lost his membership in one of the medical societies to which he belonged.

Urges Sensible Preventive Medicine

Williams's lectures and weekly columns covered tuberculosis, quacks and quackery, voodoo, and the effects of diet on health. Following a lecture in 1913, Williams was quoted in the *Chicago Daily Tribune* as saying that consumption was curable and preventable with good hygiene. In both his writings and lectures he asserted that the spread of disease could be prevented by people seeking medical advice and by early visits to medical dispensaries. To an audience at Quinn Chapel AME Church located at 2400 South Wabash in Chicago, he rec-

Chronology	
1865	Born in Monroe, Louisiana on January 31
1887	Graduates from Lincoln Institute, Jefferson City, Missouri
1894	Graduates from Northwestern University Medical School of Chicago
1894	Begins medical practice at Provident Hospital, Chicago
1902	Marries Mary Elizabeth Tibbs on June 25
1907-16	Serves as attending physician at Southside Municipal Tuberculosis Dispensary
1911-29	Serves as health editor for the *Chicago Defender*
1915	Writes article, "Tuberculosis and the Negro" for Mississippi Conference on Tuberculosis
1915-16	Serves as supervisor of the Chicago Municipal Tuberculosis Sanitarium Survey
1918-19	Serves in the American Expeditionary Force (AEF) in France during World War I, lecturing soldiers on health issues
1925	Becomes managing director, European Travel Educational Tours
1940	Dies in Chicago on February 26

ommended that people avoid "darkness, dirt, dampness, spitting, poor ventilation, and the use of whisky, beer, and patent medicines," according to the *Chicago Daily Defender*. In March 1922 he suggested that for people of color, moving to the south was not necessarily a cure for tuberculosis. He recommended instead that patients seek medical attention at hospitals and dispensaries in Chicago. He also wrote about and taught the value of ventilation, frequent baths, fresh air, and drinking cool water.

His column was named "Dr. A. Wilberforce Williams Talks on Preventive Measures, First Aid Remedies, Hygienics and Sanitation." No subject was taboo. He announced in each article that "no cures are diagnosed and no prescriptions given" in these weekly articles. He wrote and lectured on venereal disease, on constipation, and on healthy eating habits for people of African descent. Throughout his medical career, he pointed out the negative health impacts of eating heavy meats, excessive carbohydrates, hot sauces, and condiments because of their effect on the liver and the digestive system. He recommended that condiments were unnecessary if foods were properly prepared. He said men over forty need exercise, sufficient sleep, and a well-balanced diet. He even attacked the subject of voodoo medicine and the use of potions and powders sold by peddlers with no medical credentials. "Tie-them-Down" and "Bring-Back" powders were advertised and sold to women to keep wandering husbands at home. Williams warned against using these medical self-help devices that were not prescribed by qualified physicians.

William A. Evans, Chicago's first commissioner of health, was also the first health editor of the *Chicago Tribune*. He and A. Wilberforce Williams wrote health columns on disease prevention techniques. They encouraged people to have their blood, urine, and teeth examined before problems occurred. Some of Williams's articles were: "What Everyone Should Know about Cancer," "Disease and High Death Rates among Our Race," "Know Your Heart," and "The Leaky Heart." He never wavered from his efforts to educate the public. Eventually his views became accepted and set standards for medical and nutritional practices. In addition to writing for the *Defender*, he wrote an article on "Tuberculosis and the Negro" for the Mississippi Conference on Tuberculosis. It was published in the February 19, 1915 issue of the *Journal of Outdoor Life*, a magazine that supported an anti-tuberculosis campaign.

Williams was born in Monroe, Louisiana to Baptice and Flora Millsaps Williams. He grew up in Springfield, Missouri, where he attended grammar and high school. In 1887, he received a degree from Lincoln Institute (later Lincoln University) in Jefferson City, Missouri, and his first job was as a schoolteacher in Pierce City, Missouri. He was accepted at Northwestern University Medical School of Chicago and graduated in 1894. He also received a fellowship from the University of Chicago to study internal medicine at Harvard University. Williams served his two-year residency at Provident Hospital and Training School for Nurses, which was established in 1891. Initially this hospital was intended for black people only but later other races were treated there. Williams became professor of internal medicine and head of the postgraduate school medical department at this, the nation's first interracial hospital.

Williams practiced medicine at Provident Hospital from 1894 until his death in 1940. He joined the staff three years after the establishment of the hospital and remained after its founder, Daniel Hale Williams resigned in 1912. He also served as an attending physician of the south side Municipal Tuberculosis Dispensary from 1907 to1916 and as supervisor of the Chicago Municipal Tuberculosis Sanitarium Survey of 1915-16. Williams served as a second lieutenant in the American Expeditionary Force in France (AEF) for five months during World War I. The U.S. government sent him to France to lecture on hygiene, tuberculosis, venereal disease, and personal conduct of soldiers. He was a member of the advisory board of the Chicago Local Exemption Board and chairman of the Committee of Physicians of the Red Cross Home Service Medical Section.

Williams was a fundraiser and spokesperson for the economic survival of the often-struggling Provident Hospital. In an article in the *Chicago Daily Tribune* of October 16, 1917 he was listed among Chicago's Negro physicians who were starting a fund to open a free dispensary at Provident. Churches in the community were encouraged to donate to the cause. Williams was an active lifetime member of the Chicago branch of the NAACP, which allowed him to work with local and national civic leaders.

Financially successful, Williams decided to become an investor and entrepreneur. To aid his business knowledge, he attended and graduated from the Sheldon Business College of Chicago in 1907. Since he and his wife loved to travel abroad, he turned that into an opportunity to become managing director of the European Travel Education Tours. He invested freely in ventures such as the Black Diamond Oil Company and the Binga State Bank. The bank seemed to be a sound investment. In an April 1921 advertisement in the *Defender*, the bank purported to have assets totaling $400 million. Board members included businessman Oscar DePriest who became the first black Chicago alderman and the first African American of the twentieth century to win a seat in the House of Representatives. However, Williams lost large sums of money by investing in companies that were in truth not financially sound.

A civic-minded man, Williams was affiliated with many organizations. He held several positions in the National Medical Association, including executive board member, treasurer, and state vice president. He was president of the Physicians, Dentists, and Pharmacists Association of Chicago and a delegate to its national convention. He was a lecturer for the War Work Council. He was a member of the American Medical Association., the Illinois State and Chicago Medical Societies, the National Association for the Study and Prevention of Tuberculosis, the Chicago Tuberculosis Society, the American Social Hygiene Association, the Robert Koch Society for the Study of Tuberculosis, the Inter-State Postgraduate Assembly of America, and the Chicago Heart Association. He was also a member of the Chicago Fine Arts Association, the Field Museum of National History Association, Kappa Alpha Phi fraternity, the YMCA, the U.S. Civic Legion, the Frederick Douglass Center, and the fraternal Order of the Knights of Pythias, the Appomattox Social Club, and the Odd Fellows Club.

Williams was a member of the Episcopalian Church, and he was a Republican. He was listed in *Who's Who of the Colored Race* (1915), *Who's Who in Chicago* (1931), and *Who's Who in Colored America* (1938-40). He was an early member of the Association for the Study of Negro Life and History and agreed with Carter G. Woodson that the records of the Negro needed to be preserved and published. When he died his obituary listed only one survivor, his wife, Mary Elizabeth Tibbs of Danville, Kentucky whom he married June 25, 1902. He died in his Chicago home on February 26, 1940. *The Journal of Negro History* described him as an honored physician and "a force for social uplift."

REFERENCES

Books

Who's Who in Chicago. Chicago: Marquis Co., 1931.

Who's Who in Colored America, a Biographic Dictionary of Notable Living Persons of Africans Descent in America. 5th ed. Brooklyn: Thomas Yenser, 1938-40.

Who's Who of the Colored Race; a General Biographical Dictionary of Men and Women of African Descent. Vol. 1. Chicago: Frank Lincoln Mather, 1915.

Periodicals

"A. Wilberforce Williams." *The Journal of Negro History* 25 (April 1940): 262-63.

"Calls Consumption Curable." *Chicago Daily Defender* (3 September 1913). Chicago, Ill.: Defender Co., microforms.

Chicago Daily Defender (31 July 1909-August 1927). Chicago, Ill.: Defender Co., microforms.

City of Chicago. Municipal Tuberculosis Sanatorium Research Laboratory. "Collected Obituaries: A. Wilberforce Williams" *Chicago Daily Tribune* (1872-1963) 27 February 1940, p. 8.

"The Origins of Soul Food in Black Identity: Chicago, 1915-1947." *American Studies International* 37, February 1999. *Studies from City of Chicago Municipal Tuberculosis Sanitarium*, 1925.

Gloria Hamilton

Peter Williams, Jr.
c. 1780–1840

Minister, orator, writer, abolitionist

Peter Williams Jr. eschewed his upbringing in the African Methodist Episcopal Zion Church founded by his father, Peter Williams Sr., to join the Episcopal Church. He earned his own place in history as the first African American ordained as an Episcopal priest in the diocese of New York and as an influential clergyman, orator, writer, and abolitionist. He was the first rector of St. Philip's Church, the earliest African American Episcopal parish in New York City.

Born a slave in New Brunswick, New Jersey, about 1780, Williams was the son of a slave, Peter Williams Sr., and Mary Durham, an indentured servant from St. Kitts. After Williams Sr. purchased his freedom in 1785, Peter

---

Chronology

1780?	Born in New Brunswick, New Jersey
1808	Delivers "An Oration on the Abolition of the Slave Trade"
1812	Licensed as lay reader in the Free African Church of St. Philip
1820	Ordained to the Holy Orders of Deacons
1826	Ordained as first black Episcopal priest in the diocese of New York
1827	Co-founds *Freedman's Journal*, the first African American newspaper in the United States
1830	Helps organize the first session of the National Negro Convention in Philadelphia, Pennsylvania
1833	Founds the Phoenix Society
1840	Dies in New York, New York on October 17

Jr. lived, from age five, as a free black. A precocious youngster, he attended school at the New York African Free School run by the Manumission Society. Williams also received private tutoring from his pastor, Reverend Thomas Lyell, of the John Street Methodist Church. Lyell, originally an Episcopalian, became associated with the Methodist Church when he moved to New York. When Lyell returned to his Episcopal roots to become a priest, Williams began worshiping with a congregation of blacks who gathered at Trinity Episcopal Church. An Episcopal bishop, John Henry Hobart, confirmed Williams when he was about eighteen years old. In addition to working in his father's tobacco business and keeping his father's books, the young man began to take an active part in crusades against slavery. Though New York had passed a gradual emancipation act by 1799, white abolitionists refused to admit Williams to the Convention of Abolitionist Societies in Philadelphia in 1806. In spite of the rebuff, the black community acknowledged Williams as an important activist in the abolition movement.

Organizes African American Episcopalians

For a number of years, Williams assisted Thomas McCombs, an elderly white man, in giving religious instruction to children who attended Trinity Church on Wall Street on Sunday afternoons, the time when blacks were allowed to use the church. Weary of separate worship services, Williams organized the black Episcopalians into a separate group. Moving services from Trinity, the black parishioners established their own congregation, the Free African Church of St. Philip.

In 1812, following the death of McCombs, Bishop Hobart licensed Williams when the black congregation elected him lay reader, a position in which he served for several years. In 1818, the members of the parish erected a church at a cost of $8,000. Donations from Trinity Church and wealthy benefactors aided the parishioners in funding the project. Church members performed much of the construction of the new building. St. Philip's African Church was consecrated on July 3, 1819. In October 1819, the Right Reverend Bishop Hobart approved Williams as a candidate for Holy Orders and in 1820 ordained him to the Holy Orders of Deacons, the first step toward becoming a minister. Following his approval as a candidate, the *Commercial Advertiser* reported the event and described Williams as a person of color who was intelligent, studious, and zealous. The newspaper anticipated his success in spreading the Gospel to his fellow African brethren. St. Philip's was incorporated in 1820. Regrettably, a fire cut short the elation that followed the completion of the church; the wooden building burned down in December 1821. The building, however, was fully insured, allowing construction to begin soon after of a sturdy and more attractive brick structure. In December 1822, Bishop Hobart consecrated the new edifice.

The congregation, which consisted primarily of black middle-class tradesmen and female domestics, continued to grow. Williams' flock included several future abolitionists, such as James McCune Smith, George Thomas Downing, Alexander Crummell, and Charles L. Reason. When ordained on July 10, 1826, Williams became the first black Episcopal priest in the diocese of New York and the second black Episcopal priest in the United States following Absalom Jones. In spite of this achievement, Williams was subjected to discrimination within the Episcopal Church. His mentor, Bishop Hobart, advised Williams that St. Philip's congregation would not be admitted to the diocesan convention, although that right was granted to other ministers and churches. Similarly, colleagues in the Episcopal Church called Williams by his first name while white clergy were addressed by their appropriate title.

Assumes Leadership Role in Abolitionist and Community Activities

As a young man, Williams was active in black New York politics. A talented speaker and writer, he was selected to deliver a speech on January 1, 1808, celebrating the elimination of the slave trade. Also published as a pamphlet, the address, "An Oration on the Abolition of the Slave Trade," expressed the thoughts of other blacks. To dispel reservations regarding its authorship, the pamphlet included statements attesting that the text was Williams's work. "A Discourse, Delivered on the Death of Capt. Paul Cuffe" was a speech given to the New York African Institution in the African Methodist Episcopal Church in 1817.

While Williams' first priority was his parish, during the late 1820s and 1830s he was a leading community activist among the black population in New York City. He was a member of a benefit and burial organization, the African Society for Mutual Relief. Along with Samuel Cornish and John Russworm, in 1827, he co-founded *Freedman's Journal*, the first African American newspaper in the United States. A strong supporter of

education, the clergyman initiated the African Female Dorcas Association that provided clothes to needy school children. A believer in education as a means to elevate blacks, he helped found Canal Street High School, which provided classical studies for African Americans.

On July 4, 1830, Williams delivered a speech, "Discourse Delivered in St. Philip's Church for the Benefit of the Colored Community in Wilberforce in Upper Canada." In this speech, the rector protested racially motivated maltreatment of blacks and implored all Americans to accord equal privileges to blacks who had suffered and worked for its prosperity. In addition, Williams blamed the colonization movement, which advocated resettlement of freed slaves in other countries, for the decrease in the rights African Americans in the North had enjoyed. However, some judged his speech as too mild concerning the colonizationists. As a result, the cleric began to lose support in the community. Later in 1830, Williams joined with Richard Allen in convening the first session of the National Negro Convention in Philadelphia, Pennsylvania. Following the convention, as chair of the executive committee, Williams attempted unsuccessfully to establish a manual training college in New Haven, Connecticut. He and James Forten wrote, at the request of the 1833 National Colored Convention, to European liberals explaining that American Negroes favored abolition and opposed colonization in Liberia. Williams, however, personally supported those who chose to emigrate.

In 1833, Williams helped found the Phoenix Society, a self-help group that engaged in social assistance activities such as establishing a job bank, starting a lending library, supplying clothing, and promoting church attendance. During the same year, he was a member of the first executive committee when the American Anti-Slavery Society was founded. The abolition question, competition between blacks and whites for jobs, and a rumor that Williams had performed an interracial marriage erupted into a violent, anti-abolitionist riot by white workers in July 1834. During the melee, a white throng severely damaged St. Philip's church and rectory.

Williams' candor on issues of slavery and colonization intimidated his superior, Bishop Benjamin Onderdonk, who threatened the priest with closing his church and with defrocking. The bishop insisted that Williams leave the abolition society and keep away from political controversies. In an effort to ensure that his parish would eventually earn full standing in the Episcopal diocese, Williams reluctantly complied with the demands of his bishop. As a result, despite his commitment to African American causes, the priest lost respect among younger, more militant black activists.

Williams maintained his position as rector from 1820 until his death on October 17, 1840. His wife and daughter survived him. Reverend William Douglas preached a sermon in Philadelphia in memory of Williams, describing Williams as a modest, kind, and benevolent man who was a friend to all, in spite of their religious affiliations. In addition, Douglas noted that the priest was involved in myriad societies committed to improving the condition and character of blacks.

Enduring evidence of Williams' importance to the black community is the continued existence of St. Philip's. The parish, which sustains its tradition of outreach, resides in its fourth home, a New York City designated landmark, built in 1910 in the Harlem area.

REFERENCES

Books

Bragg, George F. *History of the Afro-American Group of the Episcopal Church*. Baltimore: Church Advocate Press, 1922.

———. *Men of Maryland*. Baltimore: Church Advocate Press, 1914.

Hayden, J. Carleton. "Peter Williams, Jr." In *Dictionary of American Negro Biography*. Eds. Rayford W. Logan and Michael R. Winston. New York: Norton, 1982.

Hewitt, John H. *Protest and Progress: New York's First Black Episcopal Church Fights Racism*. New York: Garland Publishing, Inc., 2000.

Hodges, Graham. "Peter Williams." In *African American Lives*. Eds. Henry Louis Gates and Evelyn Brooks Higginbotham. New York: Oxford University Press, 2004.

McMickle, Marvin A. *An Encyclopedia of African American Christian Heritage*. Valley Forge, Pa.: Judson Press, 2002.

Murphy, Larry G., Gordon J. Melton, and Gary L. Ward, eds. *Encyclopedia of African American Religions*. New York: Garland Publishing, Inc., 1993.

Online

"Our Glorious Beginnings." Saint Philip's Church. http://stphilipsharlem.dioceseny.org/history.html (Accessed 14 March 2006).

Cheryl Jones Hamberg

Peter Williams, Sr.
c. 1755–1823

Religious leader

Under Dutch rule, black slaves in New Amsterdam, the present site of New York City, had the right to own property and other legal protections. Similarly, there were no restrictions on free blacks based on race. However, after the British captured the colony, the atmosphere deteriorated for all African Americans. New York began to subject slaves to the cruel and repressive conditions present in the South. After the Revolutionary War, American groups organized religious denominations that were completely separate from their European counterparts. In the South many churches did not allow slaves to assemble for religious services, but many of those in the North created segregated worship facilities. Given this situation, Peter Williams Sr. founded the first African American church in New York.

Williams was one of ten children born to George and Diana Williams. His parents were slaves of James Aymar, a prominent tobacconist who lived on Beekman Street in New York City. Since he took his first breath in his slave owner's barn, Williams often remarked that he was born in a place as lowly as that of Jesus. Aymar encouraged the youth to attend religious services at Wesley Chapel on John Street in New York City, the first Methodist Episcopal Church in the city. From his place in the slave gallery, Williams listened to white clergy preach and developed into a devout and pious Methodist. While still a slave, the young man worked as sexton of the church. Church records from 1778 note that Williams received payment for his labor. It was in that same chapel that he met and married Mary Durham, an indentured servant from St. Kitts in the West Indies.

Buys Freedom

Taking the young couple with him, Aymar, a British loyalist, left New York to avoid the American revolutionaries. Their only child Peter Jr. was born around 1780 in New Brunswick, New Jersey. Three years later Aymar decided to move to England. Unlike his master, Williams was a devoted nationalist. The young father contacted the officials at John Street Church, and in 1783, at Williams' request, Aymar sold the Williams family to the John Street Methodist Church, the successor to Wesley Chapel, for £40. The arrangement required him to repay the money to the church. The Williams family moved in the basement of the parsonage. While the young man worked as the church sexton and undertaker, his wife Mary, affectionately known as Molly, worked as cook and maid for the single ministers in the area. Williams' hard work and gentility earned the respect of the white Methodists. From his experiences working in his former master's shop, he had learned the tobacco business. When not occupied with church duties, the young man made and sold cigars. Using the money he earned, Williams paid installments on his debt to the church. His first payment was a gold watch, probably earned through a special service he rendered. Church records affirm that on November 4, 1785, Williams completed that last of his promised payments and as a result, he became a free man. Although the arrangement seems curious, black

Peter Williams, Sr.

men and women in New York had a tradition of purchasing their freedom and then buying the liberty of relatives. For reasons unknown, despite the fact that Williams paid for his freedom in 1785, it was not until October 20, 1796 that he received his formal certificate of freedom. The paper symbolized his enduring stance as an abolitionist and as a patriot. Until his death, Williams considered that event as one of the most joyful days of his life.

With entrepreneurial spirit, Williams opened a tobacco business. The success of his venture enabled him to buy a house in 1808. There the tobacconist traded tobacco and made cigars in a shed behind his home. Although he could not read or write, Williams was a stanch supporter of education. He provided his son, Peter Williams Jr., the opportunity to attend the New York African Free School run by the Manumission Society. Later, his son became the first rector of St. Philip's Church, the earliest African American Episcopal parish in New York City.

In the early days, John Street Methodist Episcopal Church seemed devoted to saving the souls of its black worshipers. However, as black members of the church became more numerous, better educated and more sophisticated, they became more dissatisfied with their treatment. Blacks had to wait until whites received communion before they were served. There were pews set aside in the back for black members. The church did not permit blacks to be ordained as ministers. Frustration grew as the contradiction between post-revolution discussions of civil liberties and the demeaning, inequitable practices inflicted on black worshipers became more evident. Led by Peter Williams, a number of African American members decided in 1795 to break away from John Street Church.

Founds African Methodist Episcopal Zion Church

In August 1796, the dissidents petitioned Bishop Francis Asbury for authorization to hold separate services. After Asbury granted permission in August 1796, the group rented a house on Cross Street between Mulberry and Orange Streets. Under the leadership of Williams, James Varick, Francis Jacobs and others, the dissidents established the African Methodist Episcopal Church in October 1796. The first church, called Zion, was built in 1800 on the corner of Church and Leonard Streets. To avoid confusion with a similar African Methodist Episcopal (AME) group, the name of the church was added to the denominational name, resulting in the African Methodist Episcopal Zion (AME Zion) designation. In 1800 or 1801, the congregation gave Williams the honor of laying the cornerstone. The church charter, which bore Williams' signature, noted that he was a duly elected trustee.

The schism developed into a movement. Eventually, virtually every white denomination had a corresponding black sect. More than merely freeing blacks from the indignities they encountered in white churches, the establishment of black churches played a critical and comprehensive role in the lives of its members. Black churches furnished a center for anti-slavery efforts, social interaction, and charitable support. They provided a safe haven for slaves traveling along the Underground Railroad. Most importantly perhaps, black churches provided opportunity to develop black leaders with necessary organizational skills.

Williams died in February 1823, presumably in New York City. The original African Methodist Episcopal Zion was later known as Mother AME Zion Church. The present structure, built in 1923-25, is located at 146 W 137th Street in New York City. George W. Foster Jr., one of the first registered black architects, designed the Neo-Gothic structure. Continuing Peter Williams' legacy, the parishioners are politically active and committed to caring for less fortunate members of the community. Today, the African Methodist Episcopal Zion denomination claims about 1,200,000 national and international members.

REFERENCES

Books

Franklin, John Hope. *From Freedom to Slavery: A History of Negro Americans*. New York: Alfred A. Knopf, 1980.

Hewitt, John H. *Protest and Progress: New York's First Black Episcopal Church Fights Racism*. New York: Garland Publishing, Inc., 2000.

Murphy, Larry G., Gordon J. Melton, and Gary L. Ward, eds. *Encyclopedia of African American Religions*. New York: Garland Publishing, Inc., 1993.

Ottley, Roi, and William J. Weatherby. *The Negro in New York: An Informal Social History 1626-1940*. New York: Praeger Publishers, 1967.

Cheryl Jones Hamberg

William Taylor Burwell Williams
1869–1941

Educator

William Taylor Burwell Williams gained distinction as an educator. For many African Americans in the late nineteenth and early twentieth centuries, education served as a way to find professional success. Williams dedicated his life to academia and helped establish schools that educated and thus improved the lives of many African Americans.

Williams was born on July 3, 1869 in Stonebridge, Virginia. He was born to Edmund and Louise Williams, who ensured that Williams would get a sound education. He was educated in the local schools in Millwood, a small town in Clarke County, Virginia. After graduating at the age of seventeen, Williams became a teacher in the public schools in Clarke County. He enrolled in the Nor-

Chronology

1869	Born in Stonebridge, Virginia on July 3
1888	Graduates from the Normal Course at the Hampton Institute
1893	Graduates from Phillips Academy in Andover, Massachusetts
1897	Receives his B.A. from Harvard University
1902	Resigns as principal of School No. 24 to become field agent for Hampton Institute and the General Education Board
1906	Works as a field agent for the John F. Slater Fund
1910	Works as a field agent for the Anna T. Jeanes Fund
1918	Accepts appointment as an assistant supervisor of vocational training in the colored schools for the Committee on Education and Special Training of the U.S. War Department
1919	Becomes a consultant for the Tuskegee Institute
1922	Visits Haiti as a member of the United States commissions on higher learning
1927	Becomes the first dean of the College Department at the Tuskegee Institute
1930	Travels to Haiti again
1936	Becomes vice president of Tuskegee Institute
1941	Dies in Tuskegee, Alabama on March 26

mal Course of Hampton Institute in Hampton, Virginia in 1886. After two years, Williams went on to teach at Whittier School, an elementary teaching department of the Normal Course of Hampton Institute. In 1893, he graduated from Phillips Academy in Andover, Massachusetts. Williams attended Harvard University and graduated in 1897 with a B.A. During the next five years, he continued to work as a schoolteacher in Indiana. There he was eventually appointed to be the principal of School No. 24, later named the McCoy School in Indianapolis.

In 1902, Williams returned to the South to work as a field agent for the Hampton Institute and the Southern Education Board, a true calling for Williams. His primary role in this position was to study the educational conditions of Virginia and other southern states and present his findings. His expertise in this field of work was rewarded with his receiving more responsibility in his job duties. On June 29, 1904, he married Emily A. Harper.

Williams became a field agent for the General Education Board in 1904 also, which allowed him to work among the southern African American population where he promoted local activities that encouraged them to pursue education. He also used his expertise in education to assist communities that were working to improve the conditions of their schools.

In 1906, Williams became an agent for the John F. Slater Fund, an organization that worked to help implement county training schools for African Americans. These training schools extended elementary education and eventually would extend to the high school level. Training schools provided an education for African American youth who were often neglected by the state boards, which offered almost no real educational opportunities. Williams worked diligently for the Slater Fund and helped to establish some 384 training schools in thirteen southern states. The Slater Fund was the idea of James Hardy Dillard, who was its director and the president of the Jeanes Fund.

Williams also worked as a field agent for the Anna T. Jeanes Fund in 1910, which was established to provide a structured plan of monitoring the progress of rural schools by setting aside enough money for southern counties to ensure the employment of teachers who were responsible for this supervision. These teachers, commonly known as Jeanes teachers, supervised elementary instruction for the African American schools of the poor South, developed classes that were focused on industry, and promoted the establishment of community clubs. Williams directed the Jeanes teachers in their supervision and, when necessary, assessed the need for more supervisory instructors. He worked closely with leading educators and advocates of education, including whites and African Americans who sought to improve the educational system throughout the south. His meticulous observations of school provisions and recommendations did not go unnoticed. Williams was soon regarded as one of the premier authorities of the southern educational system. He was frequently requested to work for the state as well as agencies in the private sector.

Williams was the only African American to contribute to a report published in 1917 by the Department of Labor on the migration of African Americans to the North. The Department of Labor was interested in studying the increasing migration of African Americans to northern cities after World War I. Williams aided the War Department in formulating a way that the educational policies of technical training could be designed to aid the war needs. The result of this study was a report entitled, "Negro Migration in 1916-1917." In 1918, he became an assistant supervisor of vocational training in colored schools for the Committee on Education and Special Training of the War Department of the United States. Williams helped to initiate vocational units of the Student Army Training Corps.

In addition to studying the educational system in the South, Williams traveled abroad and assessed educational systems in other countries. In 1922 and 1930, he traveled to Haiti as a member of the United States commission on education, which was established to research the concerns recorded by many Haitians against the educational system supervised by American occupation personnel. Here, the situation mirrored the Jim Crow laws of the South. A vocational education system was maintained that was separate from the national system. The national school system received much less financial support than the vocational schools, contributing to substandard conditions. When Williams presented the results of his findings about the educational system in Haiti, he encouraged the provision of additional vocational and agricultural training for Haitian youth. It was Williams who observed that this increase would do much to promote self-reliant yeomanry there.

Further Successes

In 1919, Williams moved to Tuskegee, Alabama, to serve as a consultant in the educational training department of the Tuskegee Institute (now University). This position was offered by Robert R. Moton, who in 1916 became principal of Tuskegee Institute after Booker T. Washington. Even while working at the Tuskegee Institute, Williams continued to act as a consultant to the U.S. government. Williams became the first dean of the College Department of the Institute in 1927, when the Tuskegee Institute began offering its first B.S. degrees in agriculture and education. Under his direction, the College Department focused on ensuring that the agricultural and education programs were held up to college standards. By 1936, the Tuskegee Institute offered B.S. degrees in agriculture, teacher training, technical arts, and domestic science. Williams was elected to be vice president of Tuskegee Institute in 1941 and served in that capacity until his death.

In addition to being an advocate and proponent of education, Williams also wrote several articles on the education of African Americans. The majority of these articles appeared in a publication called the *Southern Workman*, and Williams held the distinction of being one of its editorial staff members. He also assisted Moton in establishing the Negro Organization Society of Virginia, which was charged with promoting better schools, homes, farms, and health for African Americans. Williams was also active in establishing the National Association of Teachers in Colored Schools, serving as its president for two terms.

Morehouse College in Atlanta, Georgia conferred an honorary L.L.D degree upon Williams in 1923. He was awarded the twentieth Spingarn Medal by the NAACP for his outstanding service to the education of African Americans. Williams died March 26, 1941, in Tuskegee, Alabama. His tireless crusade for education helped the educational pursuits of many who came after him.

REFERENCES

Books

Pryce, Joellyn and El Bashir. "William Taylor Burwell Williams." In *Dictionary of American Negro Biography*. Eds. Rayford W. Logan and Michael R. Winston. New York: Norton, 1982.

Stoner, John C. "William Taylor Burwell Williams." In *The Encyclopedia of African American Culture and History*. Eds. Jack Salzman, David Lionel Smith, and Cornel West. New York: Simon and Schuster Macmillan, 1996.

Connie Mack

William Julius Wilson
1935–

Sociologist, educator, writer

William Julius Wilson is a distinguished sociologist, teacher, and researcher; as well as a popular speaker and a prolific writer. Wilson's research and published works have caused controversy and stirred strong emotions. He has been labeled a neoconservative; he has been called an ultra-liberal. He has received high praise and vitriolic criticism. His peers have honored him, and he has been on the short list to communicate with well-known politicians. Wilson's views have been debated and used by both the political right and the left to promote some government programs and eliminate others. He has challenged liberal views about root causes of a permanent underclass in U.S. society and conservative views that attribute the state of poverty to a dependency on welfare, on cultural deficiencies, and to people who simply do not want to work. He has been criticized for de-emphasizing the lingering impacts of discrimination and segregation and for pushing for programs that are race neutral. He was disappointed with and strongly criticized welfare reforms put in place during President Clinton's first term because they provided no job training programs and cut social services. He recommends that government provide support for low-income women who want to go to college and create jobs programs comparable to that of the Works Progress Administration (WPA) during the FDR era.

Wilson turned down an invitation to the White House to meet President Reagan, after being labeled a neoconservative. In 1989, *Ebony* magazine identified Wilson as a pathfinder in a report on "Blacks as Leaders of Professional Organizations."

Early Years and Education

Wilson was born on December 20, 1935 and spent his early childhood in Derry Township, Pennsylvania. He attended primary and secondary school with children from Irish, Swiss, German, Hungarian, and Italian families. Even though he and his siblings grew up in a predominately white environment, they had a strong support system of blacks throughout the community. During his childhood, his parents, Pauline and Esco Wilson, placed high priority on family, hard work, and educational attainment even though neither of them had completed high school. His father was employed as a steel worker and a coal miner. After his father's death from black lung disease, his mother worked cleaning houses while raising six children.

Despite the family's economic hardships, all the Wilson children graduated from college because of the expectations set by their parents. In 1958, Wilson

William Julius Wilson

received his B.A. from Wilberforce University in Ohio, an institution where sociologist and historian W. E. B. Du Bois taught. Wilson entered the university with the intent of studying business administration but discovered sociology and went on to obtain his degree in that field. Following graduation, he served in the armed forces from 1958 to 1960. Prior to leaving Wilberforce he developed an interest in urban sociology and a desire to continue studying at the graduate level. In 1961, he earned his M.A. in sociology from Bowling Green State University (Ohio) and five years later received his Ph.D. in sociology and anthropology from Washington State University. Neither his master's thesis nor his doctoral dissertation dealt with race or racism. He was hired as an assistant professor of sociology at the University of Massachusetts (Amherst) in its nationally recognized department of sociology before he completed his doctorate degree. When he left University of Massachusetts in 1971 he was associate professor of sociology and had become interested in racial politics.

Influenced by Roles Models and Mentors

Wilson's most important influences were his parents and his father's sister, Janice Wardlaw, a psychiatric social worker from New York. They encouraged him to achieve academically and to always work hard. His aunt provided him with cultural experiences and with financial support when he entered Wilberforce. His research methods and teaching styles were influenced by Maxwell Brooks, his sociology professor at Wilberforce; Richard Ogles, professor of sociology at Washington State University; Robert Park (one of the founders of the Chicago School of Sociology); sociologist E. Franklin Frazier; W. E. B. Du Bois; and John Hope Franklin. Wilson was invited to the University of Chicago in 2003 to participate in a symposium, "Race in the Making of American History: Perspectives at the Onset of a New Century," that honored Franklin.

For nearly twenty-five years, Wilson was a professor of sociology at the University of Chicago. He arrived at the university in 1971 as a visiting professor and advanced to associate professor in 1972. Three years later he became professor of sociology. Twice he served as chair of the sociology department between the years 1975 and 1996. He became the Lucy Flower Distinguished Service professor of sociology and before he left the university was the Lucy Flower University professor of sociology and public policy and was director of the Center for the Study of Urban Inequality from 1990 to 1996. During his years at Chicago, he gained a reputation as a dedicated teacher and scholar. He focused his research on race, class, and the study of the urban poor. From his published articles and books on racial politics, he gained recognition beyond academia.

His first book *Power, Racism, and Privilege: Race Relations in Theoretical and Sociohistorical Perspectives*, published two years after his arrival at Chicago, compares race relations in the United States and South Africa. In it, according to a review by Thomas F. Pettigrew in *Michigan Law Review*, he "advances sociological thinking about race." In 1973 he joined Peter I. Rose and Stanley Rothman in publishing *Through Different Eyes: Black and White Perspectives on American Race Relations*. One of his most controversial works, *The Declining Significance of Race: Blacks and Changing American Institutions*, was published in 1978. This book of slightly over 50,000 words is described by Pettigrew as a "brief overview of American racial history that is provocative and engaging, if not novel and definitive." The book received the American Sociological Association's Sydney Spivack Award. *The Truly Disadvantaged: The Inner City, the Underclass and Public Policy*, published in 1987, deals with the plight of the urban poor. In it Wilson suggests that government needs to develop a plan for economic reconstruction for U.S. cities. From 1987 to 1988, Wilson and his students gathered research data for a study called the *Urban Poverty and Family Life Study*.

In 1989 Wilson served as editor of *The Ghetto Underclass: Social Science Perspectives* for the Annals of the American Academy of Political and Social Science. This book challenges the political views of neoconservatives who had sought to claim Wilson as one of their own. In 1995 he published a comparative study of inequality in Europe and the United States.

Joins the "Dream Team" at Harvard

Wilson joined Harvard in 1996 following twenty-four years at the University of Chicago. When he arrived it was announced in major news publications that the professor who was heralded for his explorations of the study of inner cities was joining two other African American scholars, Henry Louis Gates and Cornell West. The first title Wilson held was the Malcolm Wiener professor of social policy. Wilson is the Lewis P. and Linda L. Geyser university professor at Harvard University's John F. Kennedy School of Government. He is a member of the Department of Afro-American Studies and director of the Joblessness and Urban Poverty Research Program at the Kennedy School. He is also professor of social policy and the Andrew D. White professor-at-large at Cornell.

During his first year at Harvard, *When Work Disappears: The World of the New Urban Poor* was published. This book was selected by the *New York Times Book Review* as a notable book of 1996, and it was selected for the Sidney Hillman Foundation Award. It deals with unemployment of African Americans in inner cities and was read by many public figures, including President Clinton. It was described in *Time* magazine as a "profound and disturbing book." In 1999, Wilson wrote *The Bridge Over the Racial Divide*, an analysis of the socioeconomics of race. In 2001, he joined Neil J. Smelser in editing *America Becoming: Racial Trends and Their Consequences*, a two-volume study of evidence of racial disparities prepared for President Bill Clinton's Advisory Board on Race. For the Jacobs Foundation series on adolescence, he co-edited *Youth in Cities: A Cross-National Perspective* in 2002.

Awards and Honors

Wilson has received many honorary degrees and prestigious awards. One of his first awards was a Distinguished Teaching Award at the University of Massachusetts in 1970. While at the University of Chicago he was a MacArthur Prize Fellow from 1987 to 1992. In 1991 he was elected to the National Academy of Sciences, one of the highest honors granted to American academics, an award that is usually bestowed on natural scientists. In 1994, Wilson was the first recipient not in economics to receive the Seidman Award. When he was elected president of the 12,000-member American Sociology Association, he announced that sociology had not received the kind of nationwide attention it deserves. At the time of his election, he was only the second African American to hold that position. (The first was E. Franklin Frazier who was elected to the office in 1948.) Wilson was awarded the National Medal of Science Award in 1998, which has been described as the U.S. equivalent of the Nobel Prize. Wilson was only the second sociologist so honored. In 2002, Bowling Green State named him the President's First Visiting Scholar in Ethnic Studies. In 2003 he was the recipient of the Talcott Parsons Prize in Social Sciences.

Wilson is widely read and quoted, appears frequently on television, and testifies before Congressional committees. His books have been translated into many different languages, and he has taught at prestigious institutions of higher learning in the United States and the École des Hautes Études in Sciences Sociales in Paris. He was listed by *Time* magazine as one of twenty-five most influential persons of 1996 in the United States.

Wilson's scholarship has shaped the focus of articles by scholars, including Sandra Smith at the University of California/Berkeley and social scientist Alford Young. At a symposium held in 2003, participants, who were his former students of color, presented essays and discussed race and racism, urban poverty, and social inequality. In 2004, Frank Harold Wilson (no relation) wrote a biography entitled *Race, Class, and the Postindustrial City: William Julius Wilson and the Promise of Sociology*. This book discusses Wilson's political theories on race relations.

Wilson has spent much of his career studying and lecturing about crime, poverty, the unemployed, and the underemployed in urban environments. He has studied conditions that lead to the spread of concentrated poverty. He is respected for taking the study of sociology out of the classroom and introducing its concepts to the public and political arena.

Wilson is one of eighteen Harvard professors to hold a university professorship, Harvard's highest professorial distinction. He has conducted seminars for members of the Congressional Black Caucus, advised Mayor Harold Washington, and consulted with Mayor Richard M. Daley, senators Bill Bradley and Paul Simon, governor Mario Cuomo, and former President Bill Clinton. He serves on many boards, including the board of trustees of Wilberforce. He is married to Beverly Ann Huebner and is the father of Colleen, Lisa, Carter, and Paula.

REFERENCES

Books

"William Julius Wilson, 1935—Sociologist, educator." *Contemporary Black Biography*. Vol. 22. Detroit: Gale Group, 1999.

"Wilson, William Julius." *The Declining Significance of Race: Blacks and Changing American Institutions*. Chicago: University of Chicago Press, 1978.

Periodicals

FitzGerald, Marian. "Comment and Analysis, Letters: Segregation Won't Work." *Guardian Leader* (6 June 2005): 21.

"Harvard's Wilson Awarded National Medal of Science." *Black Issues in Higher Education* 15 (7 January 1999): 8.

Lyons, Douglas C. "Pathfinders of the '80s—Blacks as Leaders of Professional Organizations—Special Report: 25 Years after the Civil Rights Act of 1964. What's Changed? What Hasn't?" *Ebony* (August 1989): 60.

May, Reuben. "The William Julius Wilson Effect on a Young African American Scholar's Sociological Investigation of Race." *Ethics and Racial Studies* 26 (November 2003): 1088-95.

Pettigrew, Thomas F. *Power, Racism, and Privilege: Race Relations in Theoretical and Sociohistorical Perspectives* (Book Review). *Social Forces* 54 (September 1975): 291-92.

———. "Review: The Changing But Not Declining Significance of Race." *Michigan Law Review* 77 (January-March 1979): 918.

White, Jack E. "Let Them Eat Birthday Cake." *Time* 148 (2 September 1996): 45.

Online

"Harvard Professor and BGSU Graduate William Julius Wilson Is Visiting Scholar."http://www.bgsu.edu/offices/pr/news/2002/Jan02/scholar.html (Accessed 15 February 2006).

Sidney Hillman Foundation. Prize Awards Program. http://www.hillmanfoundation.org/about.html (Accessed 15 February 2006).

University of Chicago Chronicle. Vol. 13, no. 14., 31 March 1994. http://chronicle.uchicago.edu/ 940331/wilson.shtml (Accessed 15 February 2006).

William Julius Wilson Lewis P. and Linda L. Geyser University Professor full bio. http://ksghome. harvard.edu/~WWilson/FullBio.html (Accessed 15 February 2006).

Other

Wilson, William Julius. "The Political Economy and Urban Racial Tensions," acceptance paper for the Frank E. Seidman Distinguished Award in Political Economy. Memphis: P. K. Seidman Foundation, 1994.

Gloria Hamilton

BeBe Winans

BeBe Winans
1962–

Singer, songwriter, music producer

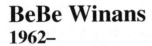rom a family of greats, vocalist, songwriter, and producer BeBe Winans has played a key role in the music industry. As a first-rate singer, he has performed alone and with groups. He is listed in the credits of over fifty albums, including those with his renowned brothers, the Winans, and his younger sister, CeCe. His talents as a songwriter land him in the credits of artists such as Gladys Knight, Yolanda Adams, Brandy, Bobby Brown, Eternal, Chante Moore, Dave Koz, Nancy Wilson, and Stephanie Mills. Not limited to producing gospel music or associated projects, Winans has become a celebrated radio show host and an actor in major films.

BeBe Winans' father, David Winans Sr., was a minister, gospel choir member, and a barber. Winans' mother, Delores Ransom, was a quiet and easygoing medical transcriptionist. As members of the Lemon Gospel Chorus, founded by Louise Lemon, David Winans, the saxophone player, and Ransom, the piano player, had an instant friendship while traveling locally and nationally.

Ransom had played for small storefront churches since she was a girl. As the grandson of a Church of God in Christ pastor, David Winans had always been exposed to music. The Lemon Gospel Chorus was an ideal match for both of them. The choir rehearsals, captivating music, and public performances contributed to their growing relationship. Their 1953 marriage produced ten children:

David II, Ronald, Carvin, Marvin, Michael, Daniel, Benjamin (BeBe), Priscilla (CeCe), Angelique, and Debbie.

David Winans was a barber by trade, but it was not uncommon for him to assume various working roles to insure food and shelter for his family. In the loving and nurturing home, the parents had strict rules that forbade dancing, parties, and movie going. Not having the option of listening to secular music, the family grew up listening to gospel greats such as Andrae Crouch and the Hawkins family.

Most of the rules left little time for outside entertainment, so the Winans household was always filled with singing and music. Routine tasks such as cooking, eating, or grooming were not complete without singing. Singing became a constant source of interaction amongst the siblings, and when financial times were tough singing was the sole source of entertainment.

The elder brothers seemed to have special gifts for improvising and harmonizing. Each child was unique and had his or her own style and distinctive sound. These voices often led songs at church or family gatherings. Their harmonies and powerful lyrics combined to make them a highly popular teenage quartet known in the early and mid-1970s as the Testimonials.

As a youngster, BeBe watched his five older brothers perform and years later, he got a chance to perform as

Chronology

1962	Born in Detroit, Michigan on September 17
1982	Appears with sister on PTL Club as PTL singer
1984	Records "Lord Lift Us Up" for PTL
1987	Records first album *BeBe and CeCe* with sister CeCe
1988	Takes home first Grammy
1997	Records first solo album *BeBe Winans*
2003	Opens company Movement Group
2004	Hosts weekly syndicated radio show, *The BeBe Winans Radio Show*
2005	Records fifth solo album

background in the group known as the Winans. The Winans were the five oldest brothers who had a heavy rhythm and blues style, yet they maintained a strong gospel presence. BeBe learned at any early age the importance of family and the healing power of music.

The Bright Lights

Early in 1980, BeBe and his sister CeCe received an opportunity to sing as a member of Jim and Tammy Faye Bakker's PTL Club Singers. The PTL Club, for Praise the Lord or People that Love aired daily and weekly. In between the talk show format and the easygoing preaching style of Jim Bakker, the PTL singers would appear on cue with various gospel renditions.

The most popular of the gospel melodies was performed by BeBe and CeCe.Tammy Faye asked them to sing a duet based on the song, "Up Where We Belong," popularized by Joe Cocker. Tammy Faye suggested changing the lyrics from "love lifts us up where we belong" to "Lord lift us up where we belong." The song was extremely popular and they were often asked to sing it. "Lord Lift Us Up" became a wonderful stepping stone for Winans. These early televised appearances provided the motivation and confidence he needed to appear onstage locally and abroad. PTL eventually released an album featuring BeBe and CeCe, and they soon had record deals with Sparrow and Capital Records.

As a teenager on PTL, BeBe had never meant to be part of a recording pair with his sister, but their national exposure as a team led to repeated requests across the world for the two of them. By most accounts, they were indeed breaking racial boundaries. Very rarely had black singers been invited to appear in all white evangelical Christian churches.

BeBe released a debut album with his sister in 1987 entitled *BeBe and CeCe Winans*. A departure from the heavily gospel sound, this album soared on the rhythm and blues charts and the gospel charts. This first album earned three Grammy nominations and a gospel award

for excellence. Together with his sister, Winans produced five albums, all of which helped them to reach platinum heights and numerous Grammy awards and nominations.

Going Solo

Winans had long imagined participating in solo projects. For years he had worked as a duet act with his sister, and he had worked as a background on the releases for his older brothers. In 1997, the time finally came for him to release his first solo album. The release of the self-titled album did very well on the gospel charts and the secular charts. Winans followed it with 2000's *Love & Freedom*, the concert album *Live and Up Close* in 2002, the holiday collection *My Christmas Prayer* in 2003, and *Dream* in 2005. Winans' exceptional voice allowed him the flexibility to honor his gospel root foundation, and it gave him opportunities to cross boundaries and formats.

With four Grammy awards, ten Dove awards, six Stellar awards, two NAACP awards and a Soul Train Award, Winans changed directions: he formed his own company, the Movement Group, which includes TMG Records as well as management and publishing divisions. His 2005 release *Dream* was produced under TMG Records.

In 2004, Winans began hosting a weekly syndicated radio show, *The BeBe Winans Radio Show*. He combined his knowledge of the gospel industry with unique content. The star-studded two-hour radio program is complete with exclusive interviews, gospel hits, contests, and superstar guest hosts each week. By 2006 the radio show was heard in fifty-seven of the top sixty markets.

Winans added the role of actor to his resume, making his feature film debut in Jonathan Demme's *The Manchurian Candidate*. He also starred on Broadway in the shows *Civil War* and *Don't Get God Started* and the national tour of *What's on the Hearts of Men*.

While Winans was expected to create a few more albums, his goal was to devote more time to acting and running his company, The Movement Group. Unbothered by criticism, he enjoys much success as a vocalist, songwriter, producer, talk show host, and actor, all while still loving his gospel music.

REFERENCES

Periodicals

Evans Price, Deborah. "Winans Woos Listeners in Many Formats." *Billboard* 117 (February 2005): 29.

Garrison, Greg. "Jim and Tammy Faye Bakker Propelled This Popular Duet." *Religion News Service, Birmingham Alabama News*, 15 June 2005.

Waldron, Clarence. "BeBe and CeCe Winans Talk about Their Gospel Sound and Famous Family." *Jet* 25 (January 1993): 24-28.

Janet Walsh

George C. Wolfe
1954–

Playwright, director, producer

George C. Wolfe is a premier writer, director, and producer who brings an inclusive, creative voice to the American theater. His openness and handling of political, social, and cultural topics have directed needed attention to the myths and truths of American society. Wolfe's talents have earned him two Tony Awards and numerous other accolades. As artistic director of the New York Shakespeare Festival and the Joseph Papp Public Theater for over ten years, he gave a platform to many plays which later became Broadway hits. Wolfe's talents also led him into the film industry. His director debut with HBO Films opened a new venue for Wolfe.

Born September 23, 1954 in Frankfort, Kentucky, Wolfe knew the nurturing benefits of an all-black community and the harsh realities of this segregated town. Wolfe was the third of four children born to Costello and Ana Lindsey Wolfe. Wolfe's father worked for the Kentucky Department of Corrections, and his mother was a teacher. Wolfe attended the private all-black academy where his mother taught and later was a principal. As a child Wolfe was encouraged to excel and told he was blessed with extraordinary gifts. The concept of racial inferiority was not allowed to infiltrate this protective world in which Wolfe grew up and thrived. At the age of seven he came to understand racism: Wolfe was not allowed to enter the Frankfort Capital Theater to see the animated Disney film *101 Dalmatians* because he was black. This experience made him determined to gain access to any place. It also reinforced his awareness that once having gained access, he should help others to do likewise.

Wolfe was interested in theater and wrote plays from an early age. At the age of twelve Wolfe travel to New York and saw his first Broadway play, Jerry Herman's *Hello, Dolly!* starring Pearl Bailey. Viewing this production was a most memorable experience. Back in Kentucky Wolfe joined theater workshops and pursued acting.

Eventually the family moved and Wolfe attended an integrated school. It was difficult for him at first, but through his involvement in directing plays he found a way to bridge his sense of isolation. After completing high school Wolfe enrolled in Kentucky State University, a historically black university, and his parents' alma mater. After a year he transferred to Pomona College in Claremont, California to study theater arts. In 1975 Wolfe's play *Up for Grabs* was performed at Pomona College and subsequently won the American College Theater Festival (ACTF) for playwriting in the Pacific Southern Region. Wolfe received his second ACTF award for playwriting in 1976 with *Block Party*. After receiving his B.A. in directing from Pomona College,

George C. Wolfe

Wolfe remained in California and continued writing. He took a teaching position at the City Cultural Center in Los Angeles and staged his plays *Tribal Rites* in 1978 and *Back Alley Tales* in 1979. While Wolfe's talents had earned him an almost cult following, he learned a great deal from the diverse communities in Los Angeles that were new to the Kentucky native. Wolfe came in contact with different communities, such as Asians and Hispanics, as well as the gay community. Wolfe himself began to come out more publicly. He also learned the use of theater as a social and political tool. Although enamored by this culturally enriching environment, Wolfe came to realize that Los Angeles was geared more toward television and movies than to the theater.

In 1979 Wolfe moved to New York City and enrolled in the M.F.A. program at New York University. He taught at City College and the Richard Allen Center for Cultural Arts while pursuing his studies. In 1983 he completed his master's degree in dramatic writing/musical theatre. His first musical *Paradise*, which was produced off-off Broadway in 1985 at the Playwrights Horizons, was not well received by the critics. His next play *The Colored Museum* was better received but controversial for some. It premiered at the Crossroads Theater in New Jersey in 1986. The play consists of eleven vignettes and offers an outrageous, satirical, and comical look at individuals in the black community who challenge some of black

Chronology

1954	Born in Frankfort, Kentucky on September 23
1966	Sees first Broadway play, *Hello Dolly* starring Pearl Bailey
1975-76	Becomes regional winner twice for original plays at the American College Theatre Festival
1976	Receives B.A. in directing from Pomona College, Claremont, California
1983	Receives M.F.A. in dramatic writing/musical theatre from New York University
1986	Wins Dramatics' Guild Elizabeth Hull-Kate Warriner Award for critically acclaimed play *The Colored Museum*
1991	Receives eleven Tony nominations for musical *Jelly's Last Jam*
1993	Receives Tony Award for *Angels in America* (first half); named director of the New York Shakespeare Festival and Public Theater
1996	Receives second Tony Award for *Bring in 'Da Noise, Bring in 'Da Funk*
2004	Announces plans to leaves New York Shakespeare Festival and Public Theater; directs first film project *Lackawanna Blues* for HBO

America's most cherished icons, such as Lorraine Hansberry's play *A Raisin in the Sun* and Eldridge Cleaver's *Soul on Ice*. Both black and white America are spoofed. The vignettes are driven by characters including a black woman who must choose between a Euro and an Afro hairpiece, a black transvestite, and a flight attendant who takes her passenger through a history lesson. Critics proclaimed Wolfe as a fresh new voice in the theater community, but others drew charges of reverse racism, and some blacks saw the work as anti-black. Wolfe stated his intent was the exorcism of black cultural myths. Amid the divergent responses, the theater community awarded Wolfe the Dramatists' Guild's Elizabeth Hull-Kate Warriner Award for the best play addressing a controversial political, social, or religious topic. Wolfe's talent also garnered admiration from Joseph Papp, the director of the New York Shakespeare Festival and Public Theater. Within a year the play was performed at the New York Public Theater and broadcast on public television as part of the *Great Performances* series.

The acclaim that Wolfe received for *The Colored Museum* opened new opportunities. Selected by Joseph Papp, Wolfe became resident director at the Public Theater in 1990. His most successful projects were *Spunk* (1990), which was a series of three vignettes adapted from short stories by Zora Neale Hurston, and *The Caucasian Chalk Circle*, an adaptation of a Brecht play done by Thulani Davis. Both works were well received. *Spunk* was praised as a powerful production full of irony and wit, and *The Caucasian Chalk Circle* was declared uplifting and exhilarating. Wolfe directed other works at the Public Theater and the Shakespeare Festival, but after the 1990s he set his sights on producing a musical for Broadway.

Based on the life of Ferdinand Joseph LeMenthe "Jelly Roll" Morton, a 1920s New Orleans jazz musician, Wolfe wrote a musical and also directed the play as well. The musical *Jelly's Last Jam* features songs and tap dancing and addresses uncomfortable racial topics. The musical opened in Los Angeles in 1991 and moved to Broadway in 1992 with Gregory Hines in the lead role. The musical received six Drama Desk Awards and eleven Tony nominations. E. R. Shipp of *Emerge* magazine stated in 1993 that Wolfe is "the hope for the future of American theater . . . he [shows] theatergoers that so much that is referred to as black culture is really about being human." Wolfe earned national acclaim for this work.

Two years after his success with *Jelly's Last Jam*, Wolfe directed the first part of Pulitzer Prize winner Tony Kushner's two-part epic drama *Angels in America: Millennium Approaches*. The drama looks at gay Americans, AIDS, and politics. This three-and-a-half hour play opened in May 1993 and earned Wolfe a Tony Award for directing. All of Wolfe's previous works had involved African Americans, so not only was this Wolfe's first award directing a white play, but also the first time an African American received a Tony Award for directing a white play. *Newsweek* described Wolfe as "the perfect director for the play's ricochet rhythm between realism and fantasy." The second part of the drama, *Perestroika*, opened in December 1993. Wolfe's other awards include the Hull-Warriner Award, the George Oppenheimer/Newsday Award, the CBS/FDG New Play Award, the New York University Distinguished Alumni Award, the HBO/USA Playwrights Award, and the Callaway Award.

In 1993, before *Angels in America* opened, Wolfe was named by the board of directors of the New York Shakespeare Festival as the new artistic head of the festival and the Public Theater. With waning corporate support and declining revenues, Wolfe was viewed as an energetic, fresh voice for the festival. As well as managing the organization of the theater, Wolfe was responsible for the budget. In order to reach clientele and theatergoers beyond the traditional "uptown whites," Wolfe created a community affairs department. Its goal was to reach out to other communities and promote diversity in the performances and the audiences. In 1996 Wolfe created the musical *Bring in 'Da Noise, Bring in 'Da Funk*, which was presented at the Public Theater and then moved to Broadway. The play was an ensemble of tap and music, starring Savion Glover. Wolfe earned his second Tony and the Public Theater sponsored a national tour of the play. This was a new step for the organization, but the play was well received around the country and was ultimately a success.

In the late 1990s Wolfe suffered a serious illness caused by kidney failure. After a year on dialysis, Wolfe had an organ transplant which was donated by his older brother. He continued to work during his illness and directed plays such as Kushner's *Caroline, or Change* and Suszan-Lori Parks' Pulitzer Prize winning play *Top-dog/Underdog*. After more than ten years as artistic director, Wolfe decided in 2004 to leave the Public Theater and move in the direction of film. His first undertaking was *Lackawanna Blues*, a screen adaptation of Ruben Santiago-Hudson's semi-autobiographical play which was produced on HBO. The film received excellent reviews at the Sundance Film Festival in January 2005.

REFERENCES

Books

Johnson, Anne Janette. "George C. Wolfe." In *Contemporary Black Biography*.Vol. 6. Detroit, Mich.: Gale Research, 1994.

Periodicals

Andreeva, Nellie. "Wolfe staging 'Blues' for HBO." *Hollywood Reporter* 380 (30 September 2003): 3.

Keene, John. "George C. Wolfe: A Brief Biography." *Callaloo* 16 (Summer 1993): 593.

Kroll, Jack. "Angels in America: Millennium Approaches." *Newsweek* 121 (17 May 1993): 70.

Shipp, E. R. "George C. Wolfe." *Emerge* (November 1993): 63-66.

Online

"George C. Wolfe." http://provost.syr.edu/lectures/wolfe.asp (Accessed 16 February 2006).

"George C. Wolfe." http://www.bridgesweb.com/blacktheatre/wolfe.html (Accessed 16 February 2006)

HBO Films. "Lackawannablues." http://www.hbo.com/films/lackawannablues/cast/george_c_wolfe.html (Accessed 16 February 2006).

Wolfe, George C. (b. 1954) http://www.glbtq.com/arts/wolfe_gc.html (Accessed 16 February 2006).

Lean'tin L. Bracks

James Wormley
1819–1884

Entrepreneur

James Wormley, a pioneering black nineteenth-century businessman and owner of the Wormley Hotel in Washington, D.C., opened the capital's first integrated hotel. He was also known for his business acumen and

Chronology

1819	Born in Washington, D.C. on January 16
1841	Marries Anna Thompson of Norfolk, Virginia
1849	Goes to California during the gold rush
1868	Accompanies Reverdy Johnson, minister, to England, as his personal caterer
1871	Opens the Wormley Hotel; sponsors legislation for the creation of public schools for blacks in Washington, D.C.
1877	Owns hotel famous as the site of the Wormley Conference
1884	Dies in Boston, Massachusetts on October 18

lobbying efforts to secure adequate funding for the first Washington, D.C. public schools for black Americans.

Wormley was born in Washington, D.C. to Pere Leigh and Mary Wormley. Both parents had lived as free people with a wealthy Virginia family prior to moving to Washington, D.C. in 1814. On January 16, 1819, while living in a small, two-room, brick building located on E Street, near Fourteenth Street, northwest, James was born. His father owned and managed a hackney carriage business, which he purchased for $175. Being located in the hotel section of Washington on Pennsylvania Avenue allowed his business to flourish. James, the eldest of five children, acquired his first job there. At the family business James began driving his own hack, learned skills and values, and won the confidence and trust of his patrons, which allowed him to monopolize the trade of the capital's two leading hotels, the National and Willard. Many of his patrons, some of the most wealthy and influential citizens of Washington, became lifelong friends and benefactors.

In 1841, Wormley married Anna Thompson of Norfolk, Virginia. From this union three sons and a daughter were born: William H. A., James Thompson, Garret Smith, and Anna M. Cole. His second son, James Thompson, became the first graduate of the School of Pharmacy at Howard University. In 1849, at the age of 30, Wormley went to California to prospect gold and subsequently served as a steward on a Mississippi River steamboat and various naval vessels. After returning to Washington, Wormley contacted some of his friends and used his new skills to become a steward at the elite Metropolitan Club in Washington, D.C. Unlike his father, he had acquired the rudiments of an education at the community Sabbath schools and had become confident about his business talents and contacts. As a result, shortly before the outbreak of the Civil War, he accumulated enough capital and support to open a catering business on I Street near Fifteenth, next door to his wife's candy store. Among his patrons were some of the most prominent public men.

Opens Elegant Hotel

In 1868, Maryland senator Reverdy Johnson was appointed minister to England. He had heard of Wormley's reputation as a caterer and decided to offer him a position as his personal caterer. Even though he had a wife and four children, he accepted the offer. It is said that his culinary skills contributed to Johnson's diplomatic success and Wormley's reputation as a caterer was that much improved. While abroad he visited the cuisine kitchens in Paris. Excited about the additional culinary skills learned in Paris, in 1871, he moved to a more spacious location on the corner of Fifteenth and H Streets near the White House. At this location, with the aid of U.S. Representative Samuel J. Hooper, the silent partner and nominal owner, Wormley opened an elegant hotel which became known as the Wormley Hotel. The older property on I Street was used as an annex to the hotel. The five-story building boasted 150 rooms, including a bar, a barbershop, and a world-renowned dining room noted for its cuisine (turtle soup and Chesapeake Bay seafood). It was also renowned for its well-managed rooms and became the first hotel in Washington, D.C. to have an elevator and a telephone connected to the city's first switchboard. For more than two decades the hotel was the meeting place for black and white elites as well as distinguished foreigners.

There are those who have said that Wormley's hotel was primarily for the wealthy and powerful white males in the capital. Wormley's granddaughter, Imogene, however, indicated that people of color were guests at the hotel. One person in particular was the Haitian minister and noted African scholar, Edward Wilmot Blyden. Other distinguished guests, friends, and allies included George Riggs, a banker; William Wilson Corcoran, philanthropist and financier; and Senator Charles Sumner, a frequent visitor to the Wormley Hotel.

Another milestone for Wormley on July 21, 1871, according to the Agribusiness Council in Washington, D.C., was a resolution he authored with the aid of Senator Charles Sumner. He and Sumner, a Massachusetts Republican and an abolitionist, persuaded Congress to provide legislation for funding the first public schools in Washington, D.C. for black Americans. As a result of his efforts, in 1885, a school known as the Wormley Elementary School for the Colored was built in Georgetown at Thirty-fourth and Prospect Streets. The school, the last physical monument attesting to Wormley's life and time, remained an all black school until 1952. Subsequently, it was used as a vocational training center for special needs students. The building was condemned in 1994 and was purchased in 1997 by Georgetown University with the intent of housing its graduate policy program. Unfortunately, the university later decided to sell the property.

The hotel was the site of the Wormley Conference of 1877, where representatives of the future president Rutherford B. Hayes and opponent Samuel Tilden resolved the disputed election of 1876. A "secret deal" later known as the "Compromise of 1877, or the Wormley Agreement," ended the dispute of the twenty electoral votes. Nineteen of the votes were from Florida, Louisiana, and South Carolina, and one from Oregon. The result of the agreement on February 26, 1877, was that Hayes received all twenty votes. There is no evidence that Wormley participated in this agreement, which signaled the end of the Reconstruction era and the fate of black Americans left to the southern state governments.

Never looking back, Wormley continued to operate his hotel and expanded his properties. In the 1870s and 1880s, Wormley and his eldest son, William, owned two country houses on what was then called Peirce Mill Road near Fort Reno in upper northwest Washington, D.C. In addition to being known for his hotel, Wormley was also recognized for his patent on a boat safety-device.

At the age of sixty-five on October 18, 1884, Wormley died after a kidney stone operation at Massachusetts General Hospital in Boston. Members of his family were present at the time of his death. His body was returned to Washington and "lay in state" in the Sumner room because the furniture in this room was purchased from Sumner's estate after his death. Because Wormley was held in high esteem, all of the hotels in the city flew their flags at half-mast. His funeral was attended by men prominent in public and private life. Many men of high ranking positions in the civil, military, and naval services of the United States were in attendance.

After his death, Wormley's estate was estimated to be over $100,000. His second son, James Thompson Wormley, managed the hotel into the 1890s. By 1893 it came under new management but retained the Wormley name until 1897 when the name was changed to the Colonial Hotel. The hotel was later torn down and replaced by the Union Trust building in 1906.

REFERENCES

Books

Logan, Rayford W., and Michael R. Winston, eds. "James Wormley." *Dictionary of American Negro Biography*. New York: Norton, 1982.

Malone, Dumas, ed. "James Wormley." *Dictionary of American Biography*. New York: Scribner, 1936.

Periodicals

"Charles Sumner Wormley." *Journal of Negro History* 20 (April 1935): 267-68.

Woodson, Carter G. "The Wormley Family." *The Negro History Bulletin* 11 (January 1948): 75-84.

Online

African American Heritage Trail Database. "Wormley Family Estate Site." Cultural Tourism DC.

http://www.culturaltourismdc.org/info-url3948/info-url_show.htm (Accessed 23 May 2005).

——. "Wormley's Hotel Site." Cultural Tourism DC. http://www.culturaltourismdc.org/info-url3948/info-url_show.htm (Accessed 23 May 2005).

"James Wormley Recognition Project." Agribusiness Council. http://www.agribusinesscouncil.org/jameswormley.htm (Accessed 12 March 2005).

Moscovitch, Ben. "James Wormley, Entrepreneur." West End Guide, vol. 4, no.3. http://www.westendguide.us/Weg0305/wormside.htm (Accessed 19 April 2005).

——. Georgetown's Wormley School for Sale." West End Guide, vol. 4, no. 3. http://www.westendguide.us/Weg0305/wormley.htm (Accessed 3 June 2005).

Shribman, David. "Friendship Shone in Reconstruction Washington." *Boston Globe*.http://www.uexpress.com/printable/print.html (Accessed 19 April 2005).

Patricia A. Pearson

Chronology

1863	Born in New York on September 28
1881	Graduates from the College of the City of New York
1884	Moves to Chicago
1890	Appointed to clerical position in state government
1895	Wins election as south town clerk
1896	Admitted to the bar; serves as county commissioner of Cook County
1915	Appointed by the mayor as assistant corporation counsel of the city of Chicago
1919	Appointed special attorney for the Traction Commission
1920	Elected first African American ward committeeman, Second Ward, Republican
1927	Ends political career
1930	Dies in Rochester, Minnesota on August 6

Edward Herbert Wright
1863–1930

Politician

Unlike many African American politicians who were stifled by segregation and unequal access, Edward Herbert Wright was able to use his sharp legal and political abilities and his influence in the Republican Party to become the first African American committeeman in the Second Ward of Chicago Illinois. As complex and layered as the Chicago political machine was, Wright was able to effectively work with white politicians to secure opportunities and appointments for qualified persons in the African American community. He was firm in his resolve and steadfast in championing a cause or appointment. As an able and respected lawyer Wright saw his political role as crucial to the successful of his people. He used this philosophy as the basis for his activities with all of his political activities. Although he served for only six years as a committeeman, his political know-how, his conscious goals of aiding the African American community, and his reputation as a man of his word allowed Edward H. Wright to bring much needed change in the white landscape of Chicago politics.

Though his parents have not been identified, historians know that Edward Herbert Wright was born on September 28, 1863 in New York City, New York. The desire to learn was for him a motivating factor from the beginning. He graduated from public school and went on to the College of the City of New York. After graduating in 1881 at seventeen years of age Wright taught in New Jersey for three years. Chicago became Wright's next stop as he arrived in the city in 1884, penniless and looking for opportunities. An industrious person, he earned his way to Chicago by assisting a Pullman porter, working in a real estate office, and working in the registry department of the post office. His energy and forcefulness attracted the attention of others, including Republican politicians. Wright was later hired in the county clerk's office. Wright was six feet tall, dark-skinned, heavy, and slow-spoken.

When the Republican National Convention came to Chicago in 1888, Wright was an active participant. He was rewarded for his commitment in 1890 with the position of bookkeeper and railroad incorporation clerk in the secretary of state's office in Springfield, Illinois. This position was the first clerical position to be held by an African American in state government. When the term of the person who appointed Wright ended, Wright returned to the city clerk's office for two years. He was then elected in 1895 for a one-year term as South Town clerk. Over the years Wright continued his activities in the Republican Party and helped Theodore W. Jones secure the nomination for county commissioner. This activity gave Wright the insight and connections that made possible his nomination for county commissioner in 1896.Wright was successful in being elected to the position as county commissioner for the city, the third African American to do so. He also was admitted to the bar the same year.

As county commissioner Wright was not reluctant to capitalize on and create opportunities that brought African Americans into the political system. On one occasion he held up the appropriation for the office of the state's attorney Charles S. Deneen to secure an assistant's position for an African American. His maneuver resulted in the placement of Ferdinand L. Barnett as the first African American assistant state's attorney for Cook County. Deneen's appropriation was subsequently passed after the appointment was made. Wright was re-elected as county commissioner in 1898. On another occasion when the president of the commission was away for a short time, Wright secured his own place as president pro-tem by seeking support from the thirteen members. He advised each that he did not expect to be elected but wanted one or two votes to show as a sign of recognition. He received all the votes except two and secured the position. At the end of his second term as county commissioner, however, Wright failed to receive a nomination and floundered in the political system for fifteen years.

Wright had some difficult times once his position as county commissioner ended. He attempted to capitalize on other Republican opportunities but without success. For example, he attempted in vain in 1910 to be elected to the city council. In spite of these difficulties, Wright continued to agitate for race recognition on the various political bodies and stirred up discussion in regular Republican ward meetings. Finally in 1915 he had the opportunity to be active in politics with the campaign and election of William Hale Thompson for mayor of Chicago. Wright assisted in getting pledge cards for Thompson. Once Thompson was elected Wright was appointed as an assistant corporation counsel at a salary well above any other African American appointee. With the indictment and trial of Alderman Oscar DePriest in 1917, Wright took over the role as the outstanding African American organization leader for Thompson's campaigns for senator in 1918 and mayor in 1919. Wright was rewarded again in 1919 as one of the attorneys for the Traction Commission.

Political Power Broker

When the primary for the 1920 Republican committeeman of the Second Ward was announced, Wright was nominated for the position. He was supported by Thompson and the Republican Party, which assured his election. Wright easily won the seat and became the first African American to hold this influential position. Committeemen had the power to nominate certain judges and to send representatives to conventions. Wright, who had clearly shown himself as race conscious, forceful, and shrewd, took this as an opportunity to advance the African American community just as he had done as county commissioner. Even though the law that allowed his election was later declared unconstitutional, Wright remained the recognized leader of the Second Ward committeemen and head of the Thompson forces. Over the six years that Wright was in office he successfully negotiated jobs and legislative favors from white politicians. With the voting block of the so-called black belt firmly behind him, Wright had the influence to request and support appointments. Under Wright's leadership Chicago saw blacks appointed as state senator, municipal judge,

and state representative. Thompson as mayor was well aware of this tide, having campaigned for African Americans. After Thompson's retirement in 1923, Wright was still able to secure other important appointments. In 1924, he accomplished one of his greatest political feats by getting Albert George elected as municipal judge.

When Thompson decided to seek re-election in 1926 as mayor, he and Wright had a disagreement over the nomination for a committeeman seat in First Ward. Wright lost out and his political slide began. Well aware of the consequences, Wright determined not to support Thompson in his campaign and stated that he was not a political slave. He reiterated that he had been elected by his people and had no intentions of selling them out. Wright's candidate lost and he left the political scene by choice.

Wright as a politician was aggressive in race matters, strict in discipline, and loyal to his word at all costs. Many saw Wright as a race hero because he did not bow and scrape and give in to white politicians. He had no inferiority complex even though the segregated times assumed he should. Wright won the respect of both his white and black colleagues. Although the exact cause of his death is not known, Edward Herbert Wright died August 6, 1930 at Colonial Hospital in Rochester, Minnesota.

REFERENCES

Books

Boris, Joseph J., ed. *Who's Who in Colored America*. 2nd ed. New York: Who's Who in Colored America Corp. Publishers, 1929.

Gosnell, Harold F. *Negro Politicians: The Rise of Negro Politics in Chicago*. Chicago: University of Chicago Press, 1935.

Online

"The Political Graveyard: Index to Politicians." http://politicalgraveyard.com/bio/wright3.html (Accessed 24 January 2006).

Lean'tin L. Bracks

Jonathan Jasper Wright
1840–1885

Lawyer, judge, politician

Jonathan Jasper Wright was an educator, lawyer, senator, and state supreme court justice during the era of Reconstruction in South Carolina. He distinguished himself as

Chronology

1840	Born in Luzerne County, Pennsylvania on February 11
1860	Graduates from Lancasterian Academy
1864	Serves as delegate to the National Convention of Colored Men, Syracuse, New York
1865	Organizes schools for newly freed slaves in Beaufort, South Carolina
1866	Admitted as first black to the Pennsylvania state bar
1868	Admitted as one of three blacks to the South Carolina bar; elected state senator in Beaufort, South Carolina
1870	Elected first black justice on a state supreme court
1877	Resigns from the state supreme court
1885	Dies in Charleston, South Carolina on February 18

the first black admitted to the Pennsylvania state bar, one of three blacks admitted to the South Carolina bar, and the first black justice elected to a state supreme court.

Jonathan Jasper Wright was born on February 11, 1840 in Luzerne County, Pennsylvania. Even though slavery was still in existence he is believed to have been born to free parents. There is no knowledge of his mother, but his father was a Pennsylvania farmer who relocated the family to Susquehanna County, Pennsylvania. After his matriculation from Lancasterian Academy at Ithaca, New York in 1860, Wright studied law and taught school in Pennsylvania.

In 1864 Wright was a delegate to the National Convention of Colored Men in Syracuse, New York. The convention's platform was to refute slavery, support every man's right to vote, and sanction racial equality for all people. The convention was chaired by former slave and present orator and reformer Frederick Douglass.

In 1865 the American Missionary Society sent Wright to Beaufort, South Carolina to organize schools for colored people. While there he taught newly freed slaves and soldiers of the 128th U.S. Colored Troops basic academic subjects, lectured on religion and self-control, and became a legal advisor. A year later Wright returned to Pennsylvania and became the first black admitted to the bar in that state. Soon after that achievement, he returned to South Carolina to work for the Freedman's Bureau. In that position he served as a legal advisor to former slaves and to the bureau's commanding officer. He resigned from the position in 1868. Within the same year Wright, Robert Brown Elliot, and William Whipper became the first three black men admitted to the South Carolina bar.

With an interest in politics, Wright joined the Republican Party and remained a moderate in his political views throughout his career. In 1868 he was elected a member of the South Carolina state constitutional convention. The convention's purpose was to assemble and renew constitutional and public government to the state. During this time Wright implored the Republican Party to nominate a black man for vice president of the United States.

Wright did not believe in lifetime appointments for judges nor was he in favor of public school integration. He favored fixed terms or no more than ten years for an elected judge. As for public school integration, he was concerned about education but was convinced that black and white children would not want to attend school with each other. Also in 1868, Wright was elected state senator from Beaufort, South Carolina. He was respected by fellow senators, who found him intelligent and articulate.

Career as Associate Justice

In 1870, at age thirty, Wright was named a justice of the South Carolina state supreme court by the legislature. He was elected to fulfill an unexpired term of Solomon L. Hoge who had been elected to serve in Congress. He was then re-elected for a full term of six years thus serving seven years as a justice. That same year other blacks rose to prominent positions in the state. The positions of lieutenant governor, treasurer, speaker of the house, and three congressional seats were all held by black men. Soon after his election to the state supreme court, Avery College in Pittsburgh, Pennsylvania, bestowed upon Wright an honorary LL.D. While on the court bench, Wright participated in 425 cases, wrote 87, and dissented in only one case.

In 1876 Wright faced a major career crisis when two rival candidates, Democrat Wade Hampton and Republican Daniel Chamberlain, each claimed the governor's election. Hampton's supporters were identified as white supremacists and Chamberlain was supported by blacks and moderate whites. In a case that involved the release of a prisoner, Hampton established himself as the official governor by issuing the pardon. The case was brought before the supreme court for associate justices Wright and A. J. Willard to decide because at that time Chief Justice Moses was gravely ill. Each justice ruled in favor of the pardon, thus recognizing Hampton as the legal governor.

Two days after the court decision, Wright attempted to revoke his opinion and the prisoner's pardon. His request was not honored, the order was upheld by the court, and Hampton was affirmed as the governor. Wright's actions became questionable and numerous rumors began to circulate. It was believed that he received threats from both political parties. Accusations of bribery and intoxication by Wright also surfaced. Wright's judicial career was tainted and ended abruptly. A Democratic investigating committee appointed by the legislature brought impeachment charges of corruption against Wright. Those charges were unfounded and after the Democratic Party regained control of the state government, Wright resigned from the state supreme court as an associate judge in 1877.

After his resignation, Wright relocated to Charleston, South Carolina, and resumed his law practice. A law department at Claflin University in Orangeburg, South Carolina was established under his leadership by the authorization of the board of trustees. He taught law classes and served as a trustee at the university. Wright was never married; he died of tuberculosis at his Charleston home on February 18, 1885.

REFERENCES

Books

Dykes, De Witt S., Jr. "Jonathan Jasper Wright." In *The Encyclopedia of Southern History*. Eds. David C. Roller and Robert W. Twyman. Baton Rouge: Louisiana State University Press, 1979.

Hine, William C. "Jonathan Jasper Wright." In *American National Biography*. Eds. John A. Garraty and Mark C. Carnes. New York: Oxford University Press, 1999.

Wienefeld, Robert H. "Jonathan Jasper Wright." In *Dictionary of American Biography*. Ed. Dumas Malone. New York: Charles Scribner's Sons, 1936.

Periodicals

Schwarz, Frederick D. "The Reluctant Judge." *American Legacy* (Fall 2004): 16-18.

Woody, R. H. "Jonathan Jasper Wright, Associate Justice of the Supreme Court of South Carolina, 1876-77." *Journal of Negro History* 18 (April 1933): 114-31.

Sharon D. Brooks

Frank Yerby
1916–1991

Novelist, poet

Poet, short story writer, and novelist Frank Yerby is the creator of the costume novel (which has been described by some as historical romance). Between 1946, when he published his first novel (*The Foxes of Harrow*), and 1985, when he published his last (*McKenzie's Hundred*), he published a novel almost yearly, which resulted in over thirty books. These novels were translated into several languages and sold in hardback and paperback, over 55 million copies worldwide. Of his first eight books, seven became Doubleday's Dollar Book Club selections, and his books were included in the list of ten given by the Literary Guild as incentives for membership.

Yerby's books were published in hardback, released the same year in paperback, and were frequently reprinted, attesting to his popularity and reception. Adding to this reception and recognition is the fact that Hollywood purchased the rights to several of his works: *The Foxes of Harrow*, *The Golden Hawk*, and *The Saracen Blade*. In spite of the public response, his popularity, and achievements, he was frequently criticized by scholars and reviewers for failing to address the racial problems of African Americans and writing what was seen as pulp fiction. However, late in his writing career, some critics began to recognize his fiction, which did not have an African American protagonist until 1969, as being a literature of protest, one that dealt with the oppressed and the disenfranchised. His protagonists are outcast who achieve success. However, his poetry and his short stories are more candid about the racial problems in the United States.

Frank Garvin Yerby was born in Augusta, Georgia on September 5, 1916, to Wilhelmina Smythe Yerby, who was Scots-Irish, and Rufus Garvin Yerby, an African American. He attended Haines Institute, a private school for African Americans, for both elementary and high school, graduating in 1933. He matriculated at Paine College in Augusta where he earned a B.A. degree in 1937, and he furthered his education at Fisk University

Frank Yerby

in Nashville, Tennessee, earning an M.A. in 1938. In 1939, he briefly entered a doctoral program at the University of Chicago. He worked with the Federal Writers Project of the WPA and came in contact with such writers as Margaret Walker and Richard Wright. Yerby later taught English at two southern institutions: Florida A&M College (now University) in Tallahassee and Southern University in Baton Rouge, Louisiana. Finding the work both demanding and unrewarding, he moved north and began working in Dearborn, Michigan as a technician at Ford Motor Company and later as an inspector at Ranger Aircraft in Jamaica, New York. Like many of his peers, he found the discrimination and restrictive racial nature of the United States stifling. He moved to Europe, spent some time in Paris, and finally in 1951 settled in Madrid, Spain where he lived until his death of congestive heart failure on November 29, 1991. Yerby was married twice: his first marriage in 1941, which resulted in four children, was to Flora Helen Clare Williams; they were later divorced. His second marriage occurred in 1956 after the move to Spain; his wife Blanca Calle-Perez was his secretary, translator, researcher, and general manager.

Literary Career

Yerby began publishing poems and short stories while at Paine College and continued with more publications at Fisk University. One of his most anthologized poems, "The Fishes and the Poet's Hand," was first published in *The Fisk Herald*; this poem and his short story, "A Date with Vera" (1937), demonstrate his ambivalence about handling racial content. This ambivalence about race was expressed by his refusal to identify his race; thus, his readers often did not know he was African American. His early works were published in small magazines, including *Challenge* and *New Challenge*. Following college, he continued to write and seek publication. He wrote a protest novel and submitted it to *Redbook*, but it was not accepted. However, the editor encouraged him to submit another piece. Yerby submitted a short story which again was not acceptable to the magazine, but it was forwarded to *Harper's* where it was published. This story, "Health Card," about the degrading of an African American soldier and his wife, won the O'Henry Memorial Award for best first short story (1944). Yerby's short stories also include "Homecoming" and "My Brother Went to College."

The Costume Novel

Realizing that he would not be published as long as he wrote protest fiction openly addressing the issue of race, he researched canonical fiction and the popular fiction of his day. One of the most marketable forms of the day was the historical novel. Given his research, he began to write what he called the costume novel. In a 1959 *Harper's* article, he explains the rules for the novel which include a use of picaresque characters, lean plots and conflict, and themes such as evil and man's relationship to others, to nature, and to God. In a 1966 conversation with Hoyt Fuller of *Ebony*, Yerby said the costume novel is to entertain, not to address serious issues. He later indicated that he believed the writer has no right to inflict his ideas and politics on the reader and that he had some doubts about his ability to write serious fiction. In spite of what he said, though, a close reading of Yerby's novels indicates that he is historically accurate, deals with the oppressed and disenfranchised (the outsider), and he sets out in many instances, especially the novels of the South, to correct historical stereotypes.

Once he began to use this genre, his fame and popularity were established; he became the first African American to have twelve bestsellers, books translated, and novels bought by Hollywood and turned into movies (*The Golden Hawk* [1948] and *The Saracen Blade* [1952]), and one televised. His first novel, *The Foxes of Harrow* (1946), which was set in New Orleans and has white protagonists, was a bestseller. It sold over two million copies, was translated into more than ten languages, and was made into a movie starring Maureen O'Hara and Rex Harrison.

Following this were several novels which deal with the South, including *Floodtide* (1950); *A Woman Called Fancy* (1951), the first of his books to have a female protagonist; and *Benton's Row* (1954). Other novels that followed include *An Odor of Sanctity: A Novel of Medieval Moorish Spain* (1965), *Goat Song: A Novel of Ancient Greece* (1967), *Judas, My Brother: The Story of the Thirteenth Disciple* (1968), *The Girl from Storyville: A Victorian Novel* (1972), and *Western: Saga of the Great Plains* (1982).

Yerby attempted to publish *The Tents of Shem* (1963), a protest novel, and like his first attempt it was not accepted. It was not until 1969, with *Speak Now*, that Yerby introduced a black protagonist. The novel, which is set in Paris, concerns an interracial relationship. This novel was followed in 1970 with *The Dahomean: An Historical Novel*, about an African whose story is chronicled from being stolen and sold at a slave auction in Virginia, to becoming a leader of men. As in Yerby's other works, this novel offers a new way of looking at history. It presents a complex, thriving, and dignified Dahomean culture. Here Yerby seemed to return to his beginning and a more overt exploration of racial injustice.

Yerby was criticized for not addressing the issues of race and for his use of a popular form of fiction. Clearly, he was successful at meeting the demands of a popular reading audience while masking his protest.

REFERENCES

Books

Pratt, Louis Hill. "Frank Garvin Yerby." In *Contemporary African American Novelists: A Bio-Bibliographical Critical Sourcebook*. Ed. Emmanuel S. Nelson. Westport, Conn.: Greenwood Press, 1999.

Periodicals

Fuller, Hoyt W. "Famous Writer Faces Challenge." *Ebony* (June 1966): 188-96.

Hill, James L. "Between Philosophy and Race: Images of Blacks in the Fiction of Frank Yerby." *Umoja* (Summer 1981): 569-77.

Moore, Jack B. "The Guilt of the Victim: Racial Themes in Some Frank Yerby Novels." *Journal of Popular Culture* 8 (Spring 1975): 747-56.

Turner, Darwin T. "Frank Yerby as a Debunker." *Massachusetts Review* 20 (Summer 1968): 569-77.

———."The Negro Novelist and the South." *Southern Humanities Review* 1 (1967): 21-9.

Yerby, Frank. "How and Why I Wrote the Costume Novel." *Harper's* 219 (October 1959): 145-50.

Dissertations

Crawford, Valerie Matthews. "Middle Ground: Frank Yerby's Novels in the African American Tradition." Ph.D. dissertation. University of North Carolina at Chapel Hill, 1999.

Hill, James L. "Anti-Heroic Perspectives: The Life and Works of Frank Yerby." Ph.D. dissertation, University of Iowa, 1976.

Helen R. Houston

York
c. 1772–?

Explorer, slave

York, the slave and body servant of William Clark, was an important part of the Lewis and Clark expedition which took place from 1804 to 1806. Although York was a slave, his opinion and his vote were considered when the explorers made decisions. Many historians have characterized York as a buffoon and embraced myth and stereotypes to define York's place in the expedition, but it has since been recognized that York's presence had a direct impact on making the expedition a success. York often affected the outcome

Chronology	
1772?	Born a slave in Caroline County, Virginia
1784	Becomes William Clark's slave/body servant
1804	Accompanies Lewis and Clark on expedition
1805	Actions support the opportunity for trade with the Shoshones
1806	Expedition returns
1811	Granted freedom
??	Death unknown

regarding negotiations with the Native Americans on the expedition because he was thought to be magical and even god-like. Recognizing the influence and contributions of York adds another dimension to the Lewis and Clark expedition and it acknowledges one who at the time received some recognition but who did not share in the reward of this exploration.

York was born a slave in about 1772 on the Clark family plantation. Most of what is known about York's early years is taken from the Clark family records. John Clark, the father of William Clark, lived with his wife Ann, in Caroline County, Virginia, on their plantation. William Clark was born August 1, 1770, and historians agree that York was also born around this time. One family member, William Clark Keenerly, wrote in his memoir *Persimmon Hill* about William Clark when he was a child. He noted that Clark was accompanied by "his little Negro boy York" as he rode about the countryside. When John Clark, William's father, died in 1799, listed among his slaves was "old York" and his wife Rose along with two children, Nancy and Jube. York was not listed but his parents and siblings were still on the Clark plantation. By this time York was an adult and in service to Clark.

Joins in Expedition

York may have become Clark's body servant when the Clark family moved to Kentucky in 1784. Young slaves were forced to leave their childhood behind between the ages of ten and twelve. They were sent to the field or did domestic work. Clark would have been fourteen, and York was a few years younger, about twelve. York remained Clark's body servant from childhood into adulthood. When Clark and his friend Meriwether Lewis were choosing men to go on an expedition as outlined by President Thomas Jefferson, numerous men were considered but only a select few were accepted. President Thomas Jefferson had given specific instructions. The men who were strong, steady, and reliable in a crisis were chosen, and York was among them. The expedition was believed to support the U.S. claim to the vast land of the Louisiana Purchase.

York was mentioned several times in Clark's diary which chronicled their travels. Clark notes that York, unlike many of the explorers, could swim. He was able to swim to various areas and collect greens for their dinner. York also took care of Sergeant Floyd, a member of the expedition, who became seriously ill and died. In 1804 when the expedition reached South Dakota and contact was made with the Native American tribe, the Arikaras, the natives were astonished to see a black man. York was said to be a large man with curly hair. The Native Americans would crowd around him touching his skin and hair. They found it difficult to believe that his color did not come off. The women of the tribes were said to offer themselves to York. Native women were also available to the other explorers, but this was not mentioned in detail. The Mandans in North Dakota reacted to York with similar amazement because of his dark skin. They referred to York as the "great medicine." In 1805 during the expedition's stay in North Dakota for the winter, Clark used York to keep the natives entertained. Lewis also found York useful. He had him dance for the Shoshones in Montana to keep them occupied until Clark arrived. The explorers had merchandise to bargain with the Shoshones for horses, but were unsure if the trade would happen. With the presence of York the Indians were won over and the horses were acquired. York enjoyed many freedoms while on the expedition; he was one of the hunters for the group and carried a firearm. York's contributions were such that he was given a vote when a decision was being made about where to build a fort for the winter on the Oregon coast.

When the expedition returned to St. Louis, York was admired and appreciated by all, but he did not receive any rewards. The other explorers received double pay and land for their services. York asked for his freedom after the expedition ended in 1806, but his request was not granted. In the years after the expedition ended, York's status with Clark declined. He went from a body servant to one of the lowest of jobs for a slave, a hired slave. While hired out to various masters and sent from one location to another, York met and married a slave woman. Shortly after that her master took her to Missis-sippi, and York knew he would never see her again. York is said to have been freed in 1811 by Clark, but his life after that is unclear. Washington Irving, who visited William Clark, recorded Clark's statements that York was so lazy and unsuccessful as a freeman and as a businessman that he had decided to return to Clark. Along the way, York was stricken with cholera and died in Tennessee. Another account of York was reported by a trapper in the Rocky Mountains who met an old black man living among the Crow Indians. The old black man said he had traveled the Pacific with Lewis and Clark. Because York's status as a slave provided no motivation to record further events in his life, his later years and his death remain unknown.

As a slave York had a difficult life, but while on expedition with Lewis and Clark he came to know on many levels what it was like to be treated in some ways as an equal. His contributions to the expedition in making the journey successful were important and assure that his name is counted among those who explored the American frontier.

REFERENCES

Books

Betts, Robert. *In Search of York*. Boulder Co.: Colorado Associated University Press 1985.

Periodicals

Hall, Brian. "The Slave Who Went with Them." *Time* 160 (8 July 2002): 58.

King, Wilma. "Robert B. Betts. *In Search of York*: The Slave Who Went to the Pacific with Lewis and Clark" *African American Review* 38 (Spring 2004): 165.

Online

"York." LewisAndClarkTrail.com. http://lewisandclark trail.com/york.htm (Accessed 14 March 2006).

Lean'tin L. Bracks

Cumulative Geographic Index

York, 2:721

Charles City County

Cary, Lott, 1:180

Charlottesville

Terrell, Robert H., 2:633

Clifton Forge

Reid, Ira De A., 1:1002

Danville

Scott, Wendell, 1:1054

Eastville

Blackwell, Robert, Sr., 2:47

Fairfax

Gray, William H., III, 1:478

Farmville

Blue, Thomas Fountain, 1:84

Bruce, Blanche Kelso, 1:143

Fluvanna County

Jasper, John, 2:372

Fredericksburg

DeBaptiste, Richard, 2:183

Hale's Ford

Washington, Booker T., 1:1181

Halifax County

Day, Thomas, 1:275

Hampton

Dett, R. Nathaniel, 1:297

Harvey, William R., 1:516

Holland, Jerome "Brud", 1:558

Moton, Robert Russa, 1:847

Harpers Ferry

Leary, Lewis Sheridan, 2:420

Henrico County

Prosser, Gabriel, 1:973

Jerusalem

Turner, Nat, 1:1137

Louisa County

Brown, Henry "Box", 2:74

Langston, John Mercer, 1:693

Lynchburg

Dean, William H., 2:182

Penn, I. Garland, 1:803

New Canton

Woodson, Carter G., 1:1256

New Glasgow

Penn, I. Garland, 1:803

Newport News

Granger, Lester B., 1:472

Michaux, Solomon Lightfoot, 2:473

Norfolk

Augusta, Alexander T., 2:21

Carney, William H., 1:176

Hunton, William Alphaeus, 1:584

Josey, E.J., 1:670

Proctor, Samuel D., 1:971

Petersburg

Mitchell, Arthur W., 2:477

Pocahontas

Branson, Herman R., 1:110

Prince Edward County

Farley, James Conway, 2:223

Prince William County

Steward, Austin, 2:626

Pungoteague

Bivins, Horace W., 2:46

Reston

Walker, Hal, 2:661

Richmond

Alexander, Archer, 2:6

Ashe, Arthur, 1:36

Brooks, Walter H., 2:72

Dabney, Wendell P., 2:157

Davis, Daniel Webster, 2:170

Farley, James Conway, 2:223

Fisher, Miles Mark, 2:230

Gilpin, Charles S., 1:460

Gravely, Samuel L., Jr., 1:473

Harris, Wesley L., 2:307

Jackson, Isaiah, 2:353

Jones, Eugene Kinckle, 1:645

Langston, John Mercer, 1:693

Logan, Rayford W., 1:732

Proctor, Samuel D., 1:971

Prosser, Gabriel, 1:973

Robinson, Bill "Bojangles", 1:1016

Robinson, Randall, 1:1025

Ruffin, George Lewis, 2:578

Smyth, John H., 2:615

Wilder, L. Douglas, 1:1217

Roanoke

Davis, Richard L., 2:178

Dudley, Edward R., 1:341

Rosslyn

Parker, Barrington D., 2:512

Saltville

Caliver, Ambrose, 1:160

South Boston

Dudley, Edward R., 1:341

Southampton County

Scott, Dred, 1:1049

Turner, Nat, 1:1137

Stonebridge

Williams, William Taylor Burwell, 2:704

Tidewater

Turner, Nat, 1:1137

White Plains

Goode, Mal, 1:466

Widewater

Hayden, Palmer, 2:312

Williamsburg

Smith, James McCune, 1:1073

Winchester

Walls, Josiah, 2:669

WASHINGTON

Bremerton

Miller, Dorie, 1:814

Seattle

Cayton, Horace R., 1:182

Charles, Ray, 1:186

Haley, Alex, 1:496

Hendrix, Jimi, 2:318

Lawrence, Jacob, 1:702

Raines, Franklin, 2:551

Wilkens, Lenny, 2:694

Wilson, August, 1:1241

Vancouver

Barnes, Steven, 1:55

WEST VIRGINIA

Charles Town

Delany, Martin R., 1:282

Charleston

Brown, Tony, 1:136

Jakes, T.D., 2:371

Johnson, Mordecai W., 1:635

Sullivan, Leon H., 1:1089

Huntington

Woodson, Carter G., 1:1256

Keyser

Gates, Henry Louis, Jr., 1:448

Lewisburg

Holmes, Dwight Oliver Wendell, 2:339

Malden

Washington, Booker T., 1:1181

Martinsburg

Myers, Walter Dean, 2:493

AFRICA

Gardner, Newport, 1:436

Amabou

Whipple, Prince, 2:692

THE BAHAMAS

Nassau

Williams, Bert, 1:1227

BERMUDA

Somerset

Anderson, Vinton Randolph, 2:16

St. Georges

Burch, Charles Eaton, 2:88

CANADA

Duncanson, Robert S., 1:347

Chatham, Ontario

Bell, James Madison, 1:73

Day, William Howard, 1:276

Delany, Martin R., 1:282

Hunton, William Alphaeus, 1:584

Colchester, Ontario

McCoy, Elijah, 1:787

Dresden, Ontario

Henson, Josiah, 2:325

Cumulative Occupation Index

Abolitionist

Bell, James Madison, 1:73
Brown, Henry "Box", 2:74
Brown, William Wells, 1:138
Coker, Daniel, 1:214
Craft, William, 1:234
Day, William Howard, 1:276
Delany, Martin R., 1:282
Douglass, Frederick, 1:326
Easton, Hosea, 2:220
Forten, James, 1:408
Garnet, Henry Highland, 1:437
Gibbs, Mifflin Wistar, 1:450
Hall, Prince, 1:502
Henson, Josiah, 2:325
Leary, Lewis Sheridan, 2:420
Loguen, J.W., 2:428
Martin, John Sella, 1:767
Nell, William C., 1:871
Pennington, James W.C., 1:923
Purvis, Robert, 1:976
Ray, Charles B., 2:560
Reason, Charles Lewis, 1:998
Remond, Charles Lenox, 1:1003
Roper, Moses, 2:574
Ruggles, David, 1:1034
Russworm, John Brown, 1:1038
Sampson, John Patterson, 2:582
Smith, James McCune, 1:1073
Smith, Stephen, 2:607
Steward, Austin, 2:626
Still, William, 1:1080
Walker, David, 1:1165
Ward, Samuel Ringgold, 1:1177
Williams, Peter, Jr., 2:700

Activist

Ali, Muhammad, 1:17
Ashe, Arthur, 1:36
Baraka, Amiri, 1:52
Belafonte, Harry, 1:68
Brown, Tony, 1:136
Browne, Hugh M., 2:84
Bush, John E., 2:94
Butts, Calvin O., 2:97
Carey, Archibald J., Sr., 2:109

Chambliss, Alvin O., 2:122
Clement, George Clinton, 1:207
Dancy, John C., 2:159
Davis, Benjamin Jefferson, 1:253
Denby, Charles, 1:291
Downing, George T., 2:196
Dymally, Mervyn M., 2:212
Eagleson, William Lewis, 2:219
Fletcher, Arthur A., 2:232
Garvey, Marcus, 1:441
Gomillion, Charles G., 2:281
Gregory, Dick, 1:484
Grimké, Francis J., 1:490
Hamilton, Thomas, 2:301
Holly, James T., 1:560
Hood, James Walker, 2:344
Jackson, Jesse L., 1:598
Johnson, Charles S., 1:616
Jones, Edward Perry, 2:390
Jones, John, 2:391
Josey, E.J., 1:670
Lomax, Louis E., 2:431
Macarty, Victor-Eugene, 2:447
Meredith, James H., 1:801
Meyzeek, Albert E., 1:806
Mitchell, Arthur W., 2:477
Mitchell, Parren J., 1:824
Phillips, Channing E., 2:538
Powell, Adam Clayton, Jr., 1:954
Ransom, Reverdy C., 1:990
Robeson, Paul, 1:1013
Robinson, Randall, 1:1025
Sharpton, Al, 2:592
Sullivan, Leon H., 1:1089
Trotter, Monroe, 1:1130
Vann, Robert L., 1:1149
Williams, Avon Nyanza, Jr., 1:1224
Young, Coleman A., 1:1285

Activist—Black Panther Party

Cleaver, Eldridge, 1:203
Newton, Huey P., 1:874
Washington, Paul M., 2:676

Activist—Congress of Racial Equality (CORE)

Carey, Archibald J., Jr., 2:106
Farmer, James L., Jr., 1:389
McKissick, Floyd, 1:795
Rustin, Bayard, 1:1039
Walker, Wyatt T., 2:666

Activist—Nation of Islam

Farrakhan, Louis, 1:393
Muhammad, Elijah, 1:853
X, Malcolm, 1:1276

Activist—National Association for the Advancement of Colored People (NAACP)

Bell, Derrick A., Jr., 1:71
Bond, Julian, 1:91
Branton, Wiley A., 2:64
Chase, William Calvin, 2:126
Du Bois, W.E.B., 1:336
Evers, Medgar, 1:386
Goodlett, Carlton B., 2:284
Grimké, Archibald Henry, 1:487
Hastie, William Henry, 1:519
Henry, Aaron, 2:322
Johnson, James Weldon, 1:626
Jones, Scipio Africanus, 1:660
Jordan, Vernon, 1:667
Lawson, James M., Jr., 2:416
Lee, J. Kenneth, 2:421
Looby, Z. Alexander, 1:737
Mfume, Kweisi, 1:808
Mitchell, Clarence M., Jr., 1:822
Moon, Henry Lee, 2:481
Murphy, Carl J., 2:490
Nixon, E.D., Sr., 1:878
Parrish, Charles H., Sr., 1:911
Pickens, William, 1:931
Steward, William Henry, 1:1078
Underwood, Edward Ellsworth, 1:1145
White, Walter, 1:1209
Wright, Louis Tompkins, 1:1266

Athlete—Olympics
Boston, Ralph, 2:55
Davenport, Willie, 2:166
Gourdin, Edward O., 2:290
Hubbard, William DeHart, 1:579
Johnson, Rafer, 1:638
Metcalfe, Ralph H., 1:803
Owens, Jesse, 1:893
Walker, Leroy T., 1:1166

Athlete—Rodeo
Pickett, Bill, 1:935

Athlete—Tennis
Ashe, Arthur, 1:36

Author. *See* **Writer.**

Banker
Binga, Jesse, 1:75
Church, Robert Reed, Sr., 1:200
Gaston, Arthur G., 1:445
Overton, Anthony, 1:890

Baseball Player. *See* **Athlete— Baseball.**

Basketball Player. *See* **Athlete— Basketball.**

Bibliophile
Arnett, Benjamin W., 1:34
Blockson, Charles L., 1:82
Brawley, Benjamin G., 1:112
Burch, Charles Eaton, 2:88
Jackman, Harold, 1:596
Murray, Daniel, 1:860
Schomburg, Arthur Alfonso, 1:1046
Slaughter, Henry Proctor, 1:1067

Boxer. *See* **Athlete—Boxing.**

Boxing Promoter
Gibson, Truman K., Jr., 1:456

Businessman (*see also*** Banker** *or* **Publisher)**
Binga, Jesse, 1:75
Blackwell, Robert, Sr., 2:47
Boston, Ralph, 2:55
Bousfield, Midian O., 2:59
Brimmer, Andrew F., 1:116
Chenault, Kenneth I., 1:191

Cuffe, Paul, 1:241
Dancy, John C., 2:159
Dash, Darien, 2:163
Davis, Gordon J., 2:175
Day, Thomas, 1:275
Dorsey, Thomas J., 2:194
Downing, George T., 2:196
Dudley, Joe, 2:202
Du Sable, Jean Baptiste Pointe, 1:349
Ellison, William, 1:373
Erving, Julius, 1:375
Farr, Mel, 2:224
Ford, Barney Launcelot, 2:240
Forten, James, 1:408
Fraunces, Samuel, 1:427
Free Frank, 2:249
Fuller, S.B., 1:433
Fuller, Thomas O., 2:256
Fuqua, Harvey, 2:259
Garvey, Marcus, 1:441
Gaston, Arthur G., 1:445
Gordy, Berry, 1:468
Graves, Earl G., 1:475
Herndon, Alonzo F., 1:544
Hightower, Dennis Fowler, 2:331
Hill, Jesse, Jr., 1:549
Hill, Peter, 2:333
Holland, Jerome "Brud", 1:558
Holsey, Albon L., 2:340
Holstein, Casper A., 1:563
Jackson, Daniel M., 2:351
Jackson, Robert R., 2:365
Johnson, John V., 2:381
Johnson, Robert L., 1:640
Johnson, William, 2:382
Jones, John, 2:391
Jones, Quincy, 1:656
Lafon, Thomy, 1:692
Lane, Lunsford, 2:413
Leidesdorff, William A., 1:711
Lewis, Reginald F., 1:720
McGirt, James E., 2:463
McKissick, Floyd, 1:795
Merrick, John Henry, 2:471
Montgomery, Isaiah T., 2:479
Morgan, Garrett A., 1:829
Myers, Isaac, 1:865
Overton, Anthony, 1:890
Pace, Harry H., 1:897
Parks, H.G., 2:515
Parsons, Richard, 2:522
Patrick, Deval, 2:524
Payton, Philip A., 2:529
Plinton, James O., Jr., 1:943
Scottron, Samuel R., 2:588
Singleton, Benjamin, 2:597
Smiley, Tavis, 2:602
Smith, Robert Lloyd, 2:605
Smith, Stephen, 2:607
Solomon, Jimmie Lee, 2:617

Spaulding, Charles C., 1:1075
Stanly, John Carruthers, 2:622
Sullivan, Leon H., 1:1089
Sutton, Percy E., 1:1094
Travis, Dempsey J., 2:634
Wharton, Clifton R., 2:688
Wormley, James, 2:713

Choreographer
Brown, James "Buster", 2:76

Coach
Davenport, Willie, 2:166
Gaines, Clarence E., 2:261
Metcalfe, Ralph H., 1:803
Robinson, Frank, 1:1020
Russell, Bill, 1:1035
Smith, Tubby, 2:609
Temple, Edward S., 1:1105
Walker, Leroy T., 1:1166
Wilkens, Lenny, 2:694

College President
Atkins, Simon Green, 2:18
Bond, Horace Mann, 1:88
Branson, Herman R., 1:110
Brawley, Edward M., 2:68
Brown, Roscoe C., Jr., 2:80
Butts, Calvin O., 2:97
Carter, Lisle C., 2:114
Clement, Rufus E., 1:208
Crogman, William H., 2:147
Dudley, James B., 2:198
Francis, Norman C., 1:420
Gilbert, John Wesley, 2:272
Gloster, Hugh, 2:275
Harvey, William R., 1:516
Holland, Jerome "Brud", 1:558
Holmes, Dwight Oliver Wendell, 2:339
Hope, John, 1:568
Johnson, Charles S., 1:616
Johnson, Mordecai W., 1:635
Lomax, Michael L., 2:432
Massey, Walter E., 1:773
Massie, Samuel Proctor, Jr., 1:775
Maupin, John E., Jr., 2:457
Mays, Benjamin E., 1:780
Moron, Alonzo G., 2:484
Nabrit, Samuel, 2:497
Patterson, Frederick D., 1:914
Payne, Daniel A., 1:917
Price, J.C., 1:963
Proctor, Samuel D., 1:971
Revels, Hiram Rhoades, 1:1005
Satcher, David, 1:1044
Scarborough, William Sanders, 2:584
Simmons, William J., 1:1066
Swygert, H. Patrick, 2:628

Washington, Booker T., 1:1181
Wesley, Charles H., 1:1200
Wharton, Clifton R., 2:688
Wright, Stephen J., 1:1272

Colonizationist
Cary, Lott, 1:180
Coker, Daniel, 1:214
Crummell, Alexander, 1:238
Cuffe, Paul, 1:241
Russworm, John Brown, 1:1038
Turner, Henry McNeal, 1:1133

Comedian
Cosby, Bill, 1:230
Gregory, Dick, 1:484
Mac, Bernie, 2:445
Murphy, Eddie, 1:856
Pryor, Richard, 2:542
Williams, Bert, 1:1227

Composer, Songwriter, Arranger
Bailey, DeFord, 1:43
Blake, Eubie, 1:77
Bledsoe, Jules, 1:79
Brown, James, 1:125
Burleigh, Harry T., 2:90
Calloway, Cab, 1:162
Charles, Ray, 1:186
Cleveland, James, 1:211
Cole, Nat "King", 1:215
Coltrane, John, 1:220
Cook, Will Marion, 2:141
Crouch, Andrae, 2:151
Davis, Gussie Lord, 2:177
Davis, Miles, 1:262
Dawson, William Levi, 1:272
Dett, R. Nathaniel, 1:297
Dorsey, Thomas Andrew, 1:319
Ellington, Duke, 1:364
Gardner, Newport, 1:436
Gillespie, Dizzy, 1:458
Hampton, Lionel, 1:506
Handy, W.C., 1:508
Hendrix, Jimi, 2:318
Jackson, Michael, 1:605
Jefferson, Blind Lemon, 1:614
Johnson, Frank, 1:619
Johnson, J. Rosamond, 1:621
Johnson, James Weldon, 1:626
Jones, Quincy, 1:656
Joplin, Scott, 1:661
Kay, Ulysses S., 1:679
Macarty, Victor-Eugene, 2:447
Marsalis, Wynton, 1:758
Morton, "Jelly Roll", 1:834
Parks, Gordon, 1:907
Still, William Grant, 1:1082

Tindley, Charles Albert, 1:1121
Van Peebles, Melvin, 1:1152
Walker, George, 2:659
Waller, Fats, 1:1171
White, Clarence Cameron, 1:1206
Winans, BeBe, 2:709
Work, John Wesley, III, 1:1259

Conductor
Cook, Will Marion, 2:141
DePreist, James, 2:190
Dixon, Dean, 1:310
Jackson, Isaiah, 2:353
Lewis, Henry, 1:716
McGruder, Robert G., 2:465

Cowboy
McJunkin, George, 2:467

Critic
Baraka, Amiri, 1:52
Bontemps, Arna W., 1:93
Braithwaite, William Stanley, 1:108
Brown, Sterling A., 1:133
Burch, Charles Eaton, 2:88
Delany, Samuel R., 1:286
Gates, Henry Louis, Jr., 1:448
Hall, George Cleveland, 1:499
Johnson, James Weldon, 1:626
Lewis, Theophilus, 2:427
Maynard, Robert C., 1:778
Moss, Carlton, 1:841
Redding, J. Saunders, 1:1000
Wideman, John Edgar, 1:1214

Dancer
Ailey, Alvin, 1:8
Baker, Houston A., Jr., 2:25
Brown, James "Buster", 2:76
Davis, Sammy, Jr., 1:266
Hines, Gregory, 2:334
Jackson, Michael, 1:605
Lane, William Henry, 2:414
Mitchell, Arthur, 1:819
Robinson, Bill "Bojangles", 1:1016

Diplomat
Ali, Muhammad, 1:17
Bunche, Ralph J., 1:152
Douglass, Frederick, 1:326
Dudley, Edward R., 1:341
Holland, Jerome "Brud", 1:558
Johnson, James Weldon, 1:626
Langston, John Mercer, 1:693
Perkins, Edward J., 1:925
Powell, William, 2:541

Smyth, John H., 2:615
Turner, J. Milton, 2:646
Van Horne, Mahlon, 2:653
Walton, Lester A., 2:672
Young, Andrew, 1:1280

Doctor. *See* **Medical/Health Care Professional.**

Dramatist. *See* **Writer—Playwriting, Screenwriting.**

Economist
Brimmer, Andrew F., 1:116
Brazeal, Brailsford R., 1:113
Dean, William H., 2:182
Loury, Glen C., 2:438

Editor
Baker, Houston A., Jr., 2:25
Baquet, Dean P., 2:29
Benjamin, Robert, 2:32
Brown, Sterling A., 1:133
Chase, William Calvin, 2:126
Coppin, Levi Jenkins, 1:227
Cornish, Samuel, 1:229
Culp, Daniel Wallace, 2:154
Dabney, Wendell P., 2:157
Davis, Frank Marshall, 2:173
Day, William Howard, 1:276
Delany, Martin R., 1:282
Denby, Charles, 1:291
Douglass, Frederick, 1:326
Du Bois, W.E.B., 1:336
Eagleson, William Lewis, 2:219
Elliott, Robert Brown, 1:367
Grimké, Archibald Henry, 1:487
Hayden, Robert E., 1:523
Herndon, Angelo, 2:328
Hughes, Langston, 1:580
Jackman, Harold, 1:596
Jackson, James A., 2:355
Johnson, James Weldon, 1:626
Jones, Robert Elijah, 2:395
Lacy, Sam, 2:411
Majors, Monroe A., 1:753
Maynard, Robert C., 1:778
McGruder, Robert G., 2:465
McKay, Claude, 1:791
Moon, Henry Lee, 2:481
Murphy, Carl J., 2:490
Pinchback, P.B.S., 1:938
Ray, Charles B., 2:560
Roudanez, Louis C., 2:576
Ruggles, David, 1:1034
Russworm, John Brown, 1:1038
Scott, Emmett Jay, 1:1051

Henson, Matthew A., 1:541
York, 2:721

Farmer
Bush, George Washington, 2:93
Craft, William, 1:234
Ellison, William, 1:373
Rapier, James T., 1:994

Filmmaker
Brown, Tony, 1:136
Greaves, William "Bill" G., 1:481
Lee, Spike, 1:705
Micheaux, Oscar, 1:810
Moss, Carlton, 1:841
Nelson, Stanley, 2:501
Parks, Gordon, 1: 907
Van Peebles, Melvin, 1:1152

Folklorist
Brewer, J. Mason, 1:114

Golfer. *See* **Athlete—Golf.**

Government Official (elected)
Alexander, Archie Alphonso, 2:7
Anderson, Charles W., Jr., 1:24
Arnett, Benjamin W., 1:34
Bond, Julian, 1:91
Bradley, Thomas, 1:104
Brooke, Edward W., 1:121
Brown, Willie L., Jr., 1:141
Bruce, Blanche Kelso, 1:143
Burris, Roland, 1:158
Cardozo, Francis L., 1:171
Conyers, John, Jr., 1:225
Crockett, George W., Jr., 1:236
Cuney, Norris Wright, 1:246
Davis, Benjamin Jefferson, 1:253
Dawson, William L., 1:269
DeLarge, Robert, 2:186
Dellums, Ronald W., 1:289
DePriest, Oscar S., 1:294
Diggs, Charles C., Jr., 1:301
Dinkins, David N., 1:304
Dymally, Mervyn M., 2:212
Elliott, Robert Brown, 1:367
Espy, Mike, 1:378
Fauntroy, Walter E., 1:396
Ford, Harold, Jr., 2:242
Ford, Harold, Sr., 2:244
Fuller, Thomas O., 2:256
Gibbs, Mifflin Wistar, 1:450
Gray, William H., III, 1:478
Green, John Patterson, 2:293
Hawkins, Augustus F., 1:522

Henry, Aaron, 2:322
Holder, Eric H., Jr., 1:556
Holland, William H., 2:338
Jack, Hulan, 1:594
Jackson, Jesse L., Jr., 2:359
Jackson, Robert R., 2:365
Jones, John, 2:391
Langston, John Mercer, 1:693
Lewis, John R., 1:718
Looby, Z. Alexander, 1:737
Lynch, John Roy, 1:748
Menard, John Willis, 2:469
Metcalfe, Ralph H., 1:803
Mfume, Kweisi, 1:808
Mitchell, Arthur W., 2:477
Mitchell, Parren J., 1:824
Montgomery, Isaiah T., 2:479
Morial, Ernest, 1:831
Napier, James C., 1:868
Nix, Robert N.C., Sr., 1:876
Obama, Barack, 2:505
Perkins, James, Jr., 2:537
Pinchback, P.B.S., 1:938
Powell, Adam Clayton, Jr., 1:954
Rainey, Joseph, 2:555
Ransier, Alonzo J., 2:557
Rangel, Charles B., 1:987
Rapier, James T., 1:994
Revels, Hiram Rhoades, 1:1005
Smalls, Robert, 1:1071
Smith, Robert Lloyd, 2:605
Stokes, Carl B., 1:1086
Turner, Benjamin S., 2:641
Underwood, Edward Ellsworth, 1:1145
Walls, Josiah, 2:669
Washington, Augustus, 2:674
Washington, Harold, 1:1189
Washington, Walter E., 1:1191
Watts, J.C., 2:679
Wilder, L. Douglas, 1:1217
Williams, Avon Nyanza, Jr., 1:1224
Williams, George Washington, 1:1233
Wright, Edward Herbert, 2:715
Wright, Jonathan Jasper, 2:716
Young, Andrew, 1:1280
Young, Coleman A., 1:1285

Government Official (non-elected)
Alexander, Clifford L., Jr., 1:15
Brown, Lee, 2:78
Brown, Ron, 1:131
Bunche, Ralph J., 1:152
Bush, John E., 2:94
Caliver, Ambrose, 1:160
Carter, Lisle C., 2:114
Chester, Thomas Morris, 1:197
Coleman, William T., Jr., 1:217
Cook, John Jr., 2:138
Cuney, Norris Wright, 1:246

Days, Drew Saunders, 2:180
Espy, Mike, 1:378
Gibbs, Jonathan Clarkson, 2:270
Gibbs, Mifflin Winstar, 1:450
Greener, Richard T., 1:483
Grimké, Archibald Henry, 1:487
Hastie, William Henry, 1:519
Hatcher, Andrew T., 2:309
Hubbard, William DeHart, 1:579
Jackson, Jesse L., 1:598
Jones, Eugene Kinckle, 1:645
Marshall, Thurgood, 1:762
McCree, Wade H., Jr., 1:789
Morrow, E. Frederic, 1:833
Morton, Ferdinand Q., 2:486
Paige, Rod, 2:509
Pelham, Benjamin, 2:532
Pendleton, Clarence M., Jr., 2:534
Pickens, William, 1:931
Pierce, Samuel R., Jr., 1:936
Raines, Franklin, 2:551
Rapier, James T., 1:994
Rowan, Carl, 1:1031
Satcher, David, 1:1044
Slater, Rodney, 2:600
Stanton, Robert G., 2:623
Sullivan, Louis, 1:1092
Turner, J. Milton, 2:646
Tyler, Ralph, 1:1142
Underwood, Edward Ellsworth, 1:1145
Vann, Robert L., 1:1149
Washington, Walter E., 1:1191
Weaver, Robert C., 1:1195
Wilkins, J. Ernest, 1:1220
Young, Andrew, 1:1280

Health Care Professional. *See* **Medical/Health Care Professional.**

Historian
Bennett, Lerone, 2:34
Bruce, John Edward, 2:86
Clarke, John Henrik, 2:132
Fisher, Miles Mark, 2:230
Marable, Manning, 2:448
Trotter, James Monroe, 2:638

Humanitarian, Philanthropist
Alexander, Clifford L., Jr., 1:15
Belafonte, Harry, 1:68
Binga, Jesse, 1:75
Cosby, Bill, 1:230
Davis, Sammy, Jr., 1:266
Douglass, Frederick, 1:326
Herndon, Alonzo F., 1:544
Jackson, Michael, 1:605
Jones, Quincy, 1:656
Lafon, Thomy, 1:692

Lane, Lunsford, 2:413
Prosser, Gabriel, 1:973
Roper, Moses, 2:574
Salem, Peter, 2:581
Scott, Dred, 1:1049
Steward, Austin, 2:626
Turner, Nat, 1:1137
Vesey, Denmark, 1:1158
Whipple, Prince, 2:692
York, 2:721

Sports Figure. *See* **Athlete.**

Television Executive
Brown, Tony, 1:136
Johnson, Robert L., 1:640
Sutton, Percy E., 1:1094

Tennis Player. *See* **Athlete—Tennis.**

Theater Director, Founder
Bullins, Ed, 1:150
Dodson, Owen, 1:315
Ward, Douglas Turner, 1:1176
Wolfe, George C., 2:711

Track and Field Athlete. *See*
Athlete—Olympics.

Writer—Fiction
Baldwin, James, 1:46
Barnes, Steven, 1:55
Bontemps, Arna W., 1:93
Brewer, J. Mason, 1:114
Brown, William Wells, 1:138
Chestnut, Charles Waddell, 1:193
Cullen, Countee, 1:243
Delany, Samuel R., 1:286
Dodson, Owen, 1:315
Dunbar, Paul Lawrence, 1:344
Ellison, Ralph, 1:369
Fisher, Rudolph, 1:400
Gaines, Ernest, 2:263
Haley, Alex, 1:496
Harris, E. Lynn, 2:304
Himes, Chester, 1:553
Hughes, Langston, 1:580
Johnson, Charles, 2:374
Jones, Edward P., 2:388
Kelley, William Melvin, 1:681
King, Preston, 2:405
McClellan, George Marion, 2:462
McGirt, James E., 2:463
McKay, Claude, 1:791
Micheaux, Oscar, 1:810
Mitchell, Loften, 1:823

Mosley, Walter, 1:839
Motley, Willard, 1:845
Myers, Walter Dean, 2:493
Nugent, Richard Bruce, 2:502
Ottley, Roi, 1:888
Parks, Gordon, 1:907
Thurman, Wallace, 1:1118
Toomer, Jean, 1:1125
Turpin, Waters E., 2:647
Walrond, Eric, 1:1173
Wideman, John Edgar, 1:1214
Williams, John A., 1:1236
Wright, Richard, 1:1268
Yerby, Frank, 2:719

Writer—Non-fiction
Arnett, Benjamin W., 1:34
Baldwin, James, 1:46
Bell, Derick A., Jr., 1:71
Bennett, Lerone, 2:34
Blockson, Charles L., 1:82
Bontemps, Arna W., 1:93
Brawley, Benjamin G., 1:112
Brewer, J. Mason, 1:114
Brown, William Wells, 1:138
Caliver, Ambrose, 1:160
Carson, Benjamin, 2:110
Carter, Stephen L., 2:116
Cayton, Horace R., 1:182
Clarke, John Henrik, 2:132
Cleaver, Eldridge, 1:203
Cullen, Countee, 1:243
Darlington, Roy Clifford, 1:251
Driskell, David C., 1:333
Du Bois, W.E.B., 1:336
Dyson, Michael Eric, 2:215
Fisher, Miles Mark, 2:230
Franklin, John Hope, 1:421
Frazier, E. Franklin, 1:428
Gates, Henry Louis, Jr., 1:448
Haley, Alex, 1:496
Henson, Josiah, 2:325
Higginbotham, A. Leon, Jr., 1:548
Holsey, Albon L., 2:340
Johnson, James Weldon, 1:626
Johnson, William, 2:382
Lewis, David Levering, 1:713
Locke, Alain Leroy, 1:728
Logan, Rayford W., 1:732
Long, Richard A., 1:734
Madhubuti, Haki, 1:750
Marrant, John, 2:450
Miller, Kelly, 1:815
Mitchell, Loften, 1:823
Myers, Walter Dean, 2:493
Ottley, Roi, 1:888
Parks, Gordon, 1:907
Quarles, Benjamin A., 1:979
Redding, J. Saunders, 1:1000

Rogers, J.A., 1:1029
Rowan, Carl, 1:1031
Smiley, Tavis, 2:602
Still, William, 1:1080
Travis, Dempsey J., 2:634
Trotter, James Monroe, 2:638
Tyson, Neil de Grasse, 2:650
Walker, David, 1:1165
Washington, Booker T., 1:1181
West, Cornel, 1:1202
Williams, George Washington, 1:1233
Wilson, William Julius, 2:706

Writer—Playwriting, Screenwriting
Baldwin, James, 1:46
Baraka, Amiri, 1:52
Barnes, Steven, 1:55
Bullins, Ed, 1:150
Cullin, Countee, 1:243
Davis, Ossie, 1:264
Dodson, Owen, 1:315
Fuller, Charles, 2:251
Gordone, Charles, 2:286
Hughes, Langston, 1:580
Jackman, Harold, 1:596
Johnson, Charles, 2:374
Lee, Spike, 1:705
Micheaux, Oscar, 1:810
Mitchell, Loften, 1:823
O'Neal, Frederick D., 1:885
Pryor, Richard, 2:542
Richardson, Willis, 1:1010
Thurman, Wallace, 1:1118
Van Peebles, Melvin, 1:1152
Ward, Douglas Turner, 1:1176
Wilson, August, 1:1241
Wolfe, George C., 2:711
Wright, Richard, 1:1268

Writer—Poetry
Baker, Houston A., Jr., 2:25
Baraka, Amiri, 1:52
Bell, James Madison, 1:73
Braithwaite, William Stanley, 1:108
Brewer, J. Mason, 1:114
Brooks, Walter H., 2:72
Brown, Solomon G., 2:82
Brown, Sterling A., 1:133
Burch, Charles Eaton, 2:88
Cotter, Joseph S., 2:144
Cullin, Countee, 1:243
Davis, Daniel Webster, 2:170
Davis, Frank Marshall, 2:173
Dodson, Owen, 1:315
Dunbar, Paul Lawrence, 1:344
Fortune, T. Thomas, 1:411
Hammon, Jupiter, 1:504
Hayden, Robert E., 1:523
Horton, George Moses, 1:571

Cumulative Subject Index

Page references to main entries for individuals appear in boldface. Page references to illustrations appear in italic.

Royal Opera, 1:1062

Ruby, George T., 1:247

Rudolph, Eric, 2:58

Rudolph, Wilma, 1:1106, 1187, 2:57, 58

Ruffin, George Lewis, 1:201, 2:28, **578–579**

Ruggles, David, **1:1034–1035**
    Cornish, Samuel, and, 1:230
    Douglass, Frederick, and, 1:327
    Smith, Stephen, and, 2:607

Rupp, Adolph, 2:262, 611

Rush, Benjamin, 2:207–208

Rush, Bobby, 2:506

Rush, Christopher, 2:346

Rusk, Dean, 2:620

Russell, Bill, 1:1020, **1035–1037**, *1036,* 2:454

Russell, Elizabeth, 2:90

Russell, Jim, 2:327

Russell, Kurt, 1:1020

Russell, Tom, 1:1160

Russworm, John D., 1:230, **1038–1039**, *1039,* 2:561, 701

Rust College (University), 1:921, 2:193, 390

Rustin, Bayard, **1:1039–1043**, *1040*
    Democratic National Convention, 2:325
    Farmer, James L., Jr., and, 1:391
    King, Martin Luther, Jr., and, 1:688
    Lawson, James J., Jr., and, 2:417
    Lowery, Joseph E., and, 1:744
    Nixon, E. D., Sr., and, 1:881
    Randolph, A. Philip, and, 1:985–986
    X, Malcolm, debate with, 2:629

Rutgers University
    Baraka, Amiri, 1:52
    Robeson, Paul, 1:1013
    Walker, George, 2:660
    Wedgeworth, Robert, Jr., 1:1198

Ruth, Babe, 2:363

Ryan, Kathleen, 2:523

Ryder, Don, 2:52

Ryder, Earl, 2:518

Sacramento Kings, 1:1037

Sager Gear Company, 1:1104

St. Augustine Seminary, 1:927

St. Bonaventure College, 1:889

St. Elsewhere (television program), 1:1187

St. John's University, School of Law
    Brown, Ron, 1:132
    Dudley, Edward R., 1:341
    Ottley, Roi, 1:889
    Rangel, Charles B., 1:987

St. Joseph's Major Seminary, 1:756

St. Jude Hospital, 1:1240

St. Louis Blues (film), 1:217

"St. Louis Blues" (Handy composition), 1:509, 1083

St. Louis Browns, 1:903

St. Louis Negro Businessman's League, 1:886

St. Marks Playhouse, 1:1177

St. Mary's Seminary (Techny, IL), 1:927

St. Paul Appeal (newspaper), 1:1222

St. Paul Normal and Industrial School, 1:357

St. Peter's AMEZ Church, 1:964

St. Thomas Episcopal Church, 1:22, 409, 644

St. Louis Hawks, 2:696

St. Phillips Church, 2:500

Salem, Peter, 1:948, **2:581–582**

Salinger, Pierre, 2:31, 310

Sam, Simon, 2:542

Sammy and His Friends (television program), 1:268

The Sammy Davis Jr. Show (television program), 1:268

Samper, Christian T., 2:83

Sampson, Frederick G., II, 2:216

Sampson, John Patterson, **2:582–584**

Sampson, Susan Wright, 2:199

Samuel Coleridge-Taylor Choral Association, 2:139

San Diego Conquistadors, 1:186

San Diego Open, 1:1064

San Diego Urban League, 2:534–535

San Francisco Giants, 1:786, 1021

San Francisco Law School, 1:874

San Francisco Museum of Art, 1:361

San Francisco Opera, 1:381

San Francisco Sentinel (newspaper), 2:34

San Francisco State College
    Ailey, Alvin, 1:9
    Brown, Willie L., Jr., 1:141
    Bullins, Ed, 1:151
    Dellums, Ronald V., 1:289
    Gaines, Ernest, 2:265
    Mathis, Johnny, 2:454–455

San Jose City College, 1:1008

San Jose State College (University), 2:78, 457

Sanchez, Sonia, 1:151

Sands, Laura, 2:42

Sands Against the Wind (Dancy), 2:160

Sanford, Scott v., 1:977, 1049–1050

Sanhedrin, 1:818

Santana, Carlos, 2:349, 350

Saperstein, Abe, 1:163, 185

Sarnoff, David, 2:687

Sasser, James, 2:242

Satcher, David, 1:416, *1:1044,* **1044–1046**

Satchmo. *See* Armstrong, Louis "Satchmo"

Satton, Lon, 2:162

Saturday Night Live (television program), 1:856, 2:545

Savage, Gus, 2:360

Savoy Ballroom, 1:164

Savoy Records, 1:211

Say Hey (Mays), 1:786

Shakur, Tupac, 2:217, 218

Shalala, Donna, 2:189

Shantytown (mural), 1:1249

Sharp, Granville, 1:409

Sharp, John, 2:511

Sharp Street Church, 1:214

Sharpton, Al, 2:399, *592*, **592–595**

Shaw, Bernard, *1:1059*, **1059–1060**

Shaw, Robert Gould, 1:176

Shaw University
Brawley, Benjamin G., 1:112
Dudley, James B., 2:199
Eckstine, Billy, 1:357
Fisher, Miles Mark, 2:231
Fuller, Thomas O., 2:257
Gary, Willie, 2:267, 269
Price, J. C., 1:963
Quarles, Benjamin A., 1:979
Vincent, U. Conrad, 1:1163
Vivian, C. T., 2:657

Shelby, Thelma K., 2:23

Shelby County Public Library, Sarah
Roberta Church Papers, 1:203

Shepard, Geoffrey, 2:523

Shepard, James, 1:315, 1076, 2:472

She's Gotta Have It (film), 1:706

Shiloh Church (New York City), 1:440

Shine, Ted, 1:315

"The Ship Outward Bound" (painting),
2:28

Shirley, George I., *1:1061*, **1061–1063**

Shlegel Hans W., 2:303

The Shoo-Fly Regiment (musical),
1:383, 622

Shook, Karel, 1:819–820

Shores, Arthur Davis, **2:595–597**, *596*

A Short Overture (Kay composition),
1:679

Shorter College, 1:223, 660

Show Girl (musical), 1:365

Showboat (musical)
Bledsoe, Jules, 1:79, 81
Robeson, Paul, 1:1014–1015
Warfield, William, 1:1180

Shreve, Israel, 2:150

Shriners, 2:596

Shuffle Along (musical), 1:77–79

Shultz, George, 2:235, 690

Shuttleworth, Fred, 1:689

Sickle cell anemia, 2:587, 588

Sidat-Singh, Wilmeth, 2:412

Siefert, Charles, 1:703

Sifford, Charlie, 1:363, **1063–1066**

Sigma Delta Chi Fraternity, 2:36, 55,
130

Sigma Pi Phi (the Boulé) Fraternity
Birch, Adolpho A., Jr., 2:45
Burgess, John M., 1:158
Holmes, Dwight Oliver Wendell,
2:340
Moron, Alonzo G., 2:486
Nabrit, Samuel M., 2:498
Parsons, James A., Jr., 2:518
Parsons, James Benton, 2:519
Terrell, Robert H., 2:633

Sigma Xi, 2:461

The Signifying Monkey (Gates), 1:450

Silkworm cultivation, 2:444

Sills, Beverly, 2:176

Simmons, Don Pearl, 2:440

Simmons, Michael, 2:93, 94

Simmons, William J., 1:912, *1066*,
1066–1067, 2:444

Simmons College, 2:379

Simmons University, 1:757–758,
912–913

Simms, Carroll, 2:42, 43

Simon, Paul, 2:151, 708

"Simple" character, 1:582–583

Simpson, Abraham, 2:145

Simpson, O. J., 1:213

Simpson, William H., 2:28

Simpson College, 1:178

Sims, Sandman, 2:335, 336

Sinatra, Frank, 1:267, 1240

Singleton, Benjamin, **2:597–600**, *598*

Singleton, John, 2:547

Siqueiros, David, 2:42

Sissie (Williams), 1:1237

Sissle, Noble, 1:78, 385

Sister, Sister (television movie), 2:387

Sit-in movement
Churchwell, Robert, reporting of,
2:129
King, Martin Luther, Jr., 1:689
Lee, J. Kenneth, 2:423–424
Nashville, 2:418
Vivian, C. T., 2:655–656
Walker, Wyatt T., 2:668
Wright, Stephen J., 1:1273

Sivart Mortgage Company, 2:636

Sizemore, W. A., 2:598

Skowhegan School of Painting and
Sculpture, 1:333

"The Sky Is Gray" (Gaines), 2:266

*The Sky Is Not the Limit: Adventures of
an Urban Astrophysicist* (Tyson),
2:650

Slater, John F., 2:19

Slater, Rodney, *2:600*, **600–602**

Slater Fund, 2:704–705

Slater Industrial Academy. *See*
Winston-Salem State University

Slaughter, Henry Proctor, **1:1067–1069**

The Slave (Baraka), 1:54

Slave narratives
Lane, Lunsford, 2:413
Loguen, J. W., 2:430–431
Roper, Moses, 2:574–575
Steward, Austin, 2:626

Sleet, Moneta J., Jr., 1:633,
1:1069–1070

The Slender Thread (film), 1:658

Sloyd Trianing School, 2:146

Slyde, Jimmy, 2:77, 336

Small, Len, 2:353

The Small Homes of Tomorrow
(Williams), 1:1240

Smalls, Biggie. *See* Wallace,
Christopher